A Treasury of
Southern Folklore

BOOKS BY B. A. BOTKIN

THE AMERICAN PLAY-PARTY SONG (*Out of print*)

Edited:

FOLK-SAY: A REGIONAL MISCELLANY, 1929, 1930,
1931, 1932 (*University of Oklahoma Press*)

LAY MY BURDEN DOWN: A FOLK HISTORY
OF SLAVERY (*University of Chicago Press*)

A TREASURY OF AMERICAN FOLKLORE

A TREASURY OF NEW ENGLAND FOLKLORE

A TREASURY OF SOUTHERN FOLKLORE

In Preparation:

A TREASURY OF WESTERN FOLKLORE

A Treasury of
Southern Folklore

*Stories, Ballads, Traditions, and Folkways
of the People of the South*

Edited with an Introduction by
B. A. BOTKIN

With a Foreword by DOUGLAS SOUTHALL FREEMAN

*Thus, the way of the South, as the way of culture,
has also been the way of history and the way
of America.*—HOWARD W. ODUM

BONANZA BOOKS NEW YORK

Copyright MCMXLIX by B. A. Botkin, copyright © MCMLXXVII
by Gertrude Botkin

This edition is published by Bonanza Books,
a division of Crown Publishers, Inc.,
by arrangement with Gertrude F. Botkin.
a b c d e f g h
BONANZA 1980 EDITION

Manufactured in the United States of America

Library of Congress Cataloging in Publication Data

Botkin, Benjamin Albert, 1901-   ed.
    A treasury of Southern folklore.

    Reprint of the ed. published by Crown Publishers,
New York.
    Includes index.
    1. Folk-lore—Southern States. 2. Southern States
—Social life and customs. I. Title.
GR108.B6 1980   390′.00975   80-26516
ISBN 0-517-33647-2

Foreword

Many a book is a table d' hôte affair. You are expected to eat the whole of it and, in doing so, to suspend judgment until you have finished. Then only, you will be told by an ambitious cook, will you be sure you have both your money's worth and an appreciation of the resourceful art of the kitchen. Somewhat skeptically, perhaps, you acquiesce and, in the end, may conclude that the meal is too meager to be satisfying, or that it is too abundant, or that good material has been marred by unskilled hands. Less frequently than you could wish, do you push back the plate of the last page and say, "Just right!"

This, in contrast, is an à la carte book. Confidently, on this first page, it may be said that you will come back to it, again and again, as you would go before the war to one of those incomparable "regional" restaurants of old Paris that offered a different and incredibly delicious entrée each day of the month. From Howard Odum's sage words that head "With a Southern Accent" to the last exhibit of "The Singing South," you ultimately will proceed, or else you will be cheating yourself; but you do not have to try to devour all of it at once. Today, on the menu, "Caste and Class" may fit your appetite; tomorrow it may be "Southern Story-Tellers." Every guest may pick as he pleases and pay with as much or as little of his time as he wishes to spend. The wine goes with the meal and it varies from the oldest Madeira in a Virginia cellar to the best Bordeaux in the French quarter of New Orleans, from grandmother's blackberry cordial to the mysterious, long-lost Norton Seedling vintage that even experts took to be a ripe Burgundy. There is savor, too, to this *Southern Folklore*—the smell of the cider mill in the lower Shenandoah Valley, of the hickory smoke in the Smithfield packinghouse, of the coffee and fried ham in the Carolina farmhouse, of the Georgia Elberta peach, of the Florida Valencia orange, of the Mississippi barbecue, and of the sauces of Louisiana. At least this early reader, tasting and drinking, had to telegraph his thanks to the publishers before he finished reading the galley proofs. He felt he was, so to say, at a literary Voisin's, back on the Rue St. Honoré, in the days when men's noses were not so bloody that they had lost the sense of smell.

v

Such a book as this probably could be compiled, with like diligence and discrimination, for half-a-dozen sections of this country. Diversity in union and a regionalism that no longer transcends nationalism are among the exhaustless delights of America. If surveys of the folklore of New England and of the Old South differed from similar books about other parts of the United States it would be, of course, in the depth of the background. Among Southern states, for example, some of the distinctive qualities that have shaped folklore have been the British stock, the presence of the Negro almost everywhere, the persistence of the Confederate tradition, the dominance of staple agriculture, and a climate that supplies outdoor themes for stories more appropriately told under a shade tree than from a chimney corner.

British blood has given homogeneity to the white population and has assured the same outlook on life, within the bracket of the variations of individual peculiarities. A story-teller may have a feeble charge in his gun but he may be sure that, such as it is, it will not miss fire. So certain is this that one hears the echo of the same laugh to an ancestral yarn that has been carried from one state to another and has been given local dress wherever migration has halted. Some salty observations that were old in England when brought to Jamestown in the 1600's are heard with a chuckle even now and are credited to some Texan whose grandfather carried them with him from Virginia via Tennessee. In contrast, German, Jewish, and even Irish jests seldom are heard in the South.

The pervasive presence of the Negro has sharpened the humor of men of British stock precisely as it has softened their speech. This has been a process of long continuance and of large influence. A British visitor complained in 1746 that Virginia parents would "suffer" their children, when young, "to prowl among the young Negroes, which insensibly causes them to imbibe their manners and broken speech." Any traveler of two centuries later could say the same thing, with the added observation that Southerners cherish so much affection for a language with no terminal g's that they have ceased to care whether the elisions were originally theirs or the Negroes'. If the dark people are grateful for their advancement in the South, they may assert that they have recompensed their teachers; and if the Negroes wished to avenge themselves for their bondage, they could say they had made their masters their captives in music, in mimicry, in humor, and in laughter. There was a period—it has not yet ended in some parts of the South—when certain of the Negro leaders regarded their people's music as an echo of slavery and their happy nature as reconciliation to inferiority. May they never prevail on the Negro to abandon his spirituals or to stifle his innate humor! A nation that has had the curse of two world wars in a single generation needs the solace of song and the tonic of laughter. As concerns this particular survey of folklore, it will interest any reader to observe how much of the wisdom as well as the wit of the South is credited to the Negro either as author or as subject.

For close to two generations the war of 1861-65 was the great fact in Southern life. Conversation of the elders gravitated to the heroes and the horrors of that conflict. The inexhaustible theme of argument was responsibility for the Confederate failure—it never was called the Confederate defeat—at Gettysburg. Second only to this was the question, Would Sherman ever have succeeded in marching to the Sea if Joe Johnston had not been relieved of command in front of Atlanta? It was much more a matter of parental duty to see that a son knew the Southern estimates of casualties in the principal battles than that he remembered with precision the provoking difference between seven times eight and nine times six. All constitutional questions were relatively unimportant in comparison with that of the right of secession. The thump of the wooden leg of a Confederate office-seeker on the wooden platform erected for "speaking on court day" was more eloquent than any speech a rival could spin out to the inevitable peroration on Southern womanhood. The four gradations of assured damnation were those of atheist, "nigger-lover," Republican and, in the very pit, Confederate deserter. Privately, individual Confederates might admit that such and such a veteran had told the same lie so often that he believed it, but if any Yankee disputed it, then a comrade most certainly had to be defended. All this of course, became the very web and woof of folklore. The first surprise in analyzing the effect of the glorification of the Confederacy is that so much sound historical writing was done almost from 1865, in complete independence of fanciful tales fervently retold and generally credited. Second among the surprises is the fact that out of so convulsing, so overwhelming a tragedy there came so little good poetry. No satisfactory explanation of this ever has been given. Thomas Nelson Page and Mary Johnston and Margaret Mitchell wrung dry the romance of the Confederacy as a theme of fiction. Until the appearance of "John Brown's Body" in 1928, even the most ardent Confederate would have been hard hit to pick out any single poem on battles or leaders or death or victory and to have said, "This is first class."

The cotton and the corn, the marshes of Glynn and the red hills of Georgia are the natural, indeed the ideal, setting for the development of a folklore in which the planter, the preacher, the politician, the "poor white," and the Negro are the central figures. A kindly climate did the rest. Uncle Remus never would have understood what "Brer Fox" was saying if the old man lived where he had to wear ear muffs. All this doubtless is true, *mutatis mutandis,* of the folklore and of the music of every country. The cold severity of Sibelius fitted and reflected Finland; Verdi never could have written *Aïda* in that icy land. As concerns the South, the implications are set forth with so much logic and intelligent citation in the various introductions to the different sections of this book that the student of environment will find color and action in many changing scenes.

On the stage thus set, heroes hold first place. Perhaps every land that has the tradition of a Lost Cause builds its monuments in a certain sentimental determination and seeks through its memorials both to exemplify and to perpetuate its ideal. There is much truth in the dictum, Show me a people's monuments and I will tell you what manner of men they are. The South was in the 1870's "a land of tombs"; by 1900, obelisks rose above the graves, and Confederate monuments stood in many a rural courthouse village. Sons and daughters may not retain their parents' belief that certain of these figures are as fine as Michelangelo's David and that every bronze rider deserves as much aesthetic reverence as the Colleoni, because the sculptors were Confederate veterans or, at the least, men of local origin. If today a certain reticence is observable when the pose of the county's marble Confederate defender is questioned, there is no wane whatsoever in the devotion of Southerners to their heroes. Exact knowledge of Confederate campaigns and commanders has yielded to the vagueness that covers nearly the whole of American history, but Lee and Jackson and Forrest and Beauregard have become the symbols of what Southern men ought to revere. This holds true even if some of these demigods have been portrayed as so flawless that a youngster despairs of emulating them.

In sharpest contrast is an older form of hero worship in Southern folklore. This is not regional. Perhaps one would not be stretching a thesis if one said the hero of the fireside and of the shade tree is not American, or even Aryan, but primal. Specialists may dispute origins, precisely as Mark Twain explored what he termed the geology of jokes. When all the variants of the "golden bough" have been classified, and when even Sir James George Frazer's resourcefulness has been worn to the last title of the final reissue of his books, are there more than two elemental qualities in the basic folklore of man? Are not those two strength and cunning? Say what you will, Jack is the great-grandfather of all the folk heroes; his beanstalk is the symbol of his prowess, the antecedent of David's sling and Arthur's Excalibur and all the weapons of all the great warriors. George Washington may be, after a thousand years, the legendary hero of America. At least, no man yet born on this continent seems to have so good a prospect of that form of immortality. If it should so eventuate, the Washington of folklore will not be the patient General who held together a demoralized Army, but the young man who breasted the ice-laden Alleghany, not the bold designer of the campaign of Trenton and Princeton, but the boy who was credited with throwing a dollar across the Rappahannock. It will matter not the least that no silver dollar circulated widely among the American Colonials in Washington's youth, and that if it had, he was so acquisitive that he probably would have been the last young resident of the Rappahannock Valley to throw a coin away. This story is the ideal raw material of folklore and, as such, has its place in this volume. Probably the tale of the dollar will outlive that of the cherry tree because, it is submitted, strength was admired before moral

virtue was. As for cunning, the other primal quality that found its way
into the stories the sire told the grandson in the cave, the adjective con-
notes Ulysses, but that Ithacan, son of Laërtes, was of an ancestry lost
in the earliest tales of China and of India. In Joel Chandler Harris's
delightsome tales and in all the other folk yarns about foxes, have we a
transference to the animal of the admired cunning of man; or was man
first likened to the fox because the exceptional human learned the way
of Reynard?

What may be said of the style of story-telling in the South? Was it as
good as the raw materials from which it was made? Did it have the rich
colors of the background? Few will give an unqualified, affirmative answer.
There were artists in narration but art no more was universal in this than
in any other form of human endeavor. Herein is disappointment because
in the rural South there was time enough for perfecting any embellishment the narrator devised. Some men who loved tall tales made the most
of clocks that ticked slowly. It was suspected of at least one famous
Southern raconteur, for example, that he set down on paper the best of
his stories, word by word, and that what appeared to be unconscious
adornment and a happy, instant fashioning of metaphor was actually
studied declamation from a much-revised manuscript. That may have
been slander of a gentleman whose verbal bait seldom failed of takers,
but the regrettable fact stands: story-telling was not as artful as it should
have been. It was too long-winded, and it had too much of the echo of
the political platform. Spontaneity was lost in the polishing of paragraphs.

Southern oratory drew heavily on folklore and perhaps contributed to
it but, in general, speech-making had much the same faults as story-telling.
Whether in the pulpit, striving for the souls of men or in the courtyard,
seeking votes, the orator of the early nineteenth century echoed the style
of a romantic age of literature. He was apt to be verbose and over-
ornate—to walk around a subject just as, on occasion, he wound his way
around the platform, lest the auditors on the left conclude that they were
not receiving as much attention as their brethren on the speaker's right.
If out of this there have come legends of audiences swept into the deep
seas of emotional storm by the eloquence of some "forest-born Demos-
thenes," some frontier John the Baptist, it is entirely probable that the
man most responsible is one now almost forgotten—William Wirt of Virginia. He was Attorney General of the United States for twelve years,
was himself a speaker of much charm, and was the author, among other
works, of "The Letters of the British Spy" (1803) and of the first detailed
biography of Patrick Henry (1817). The supposed experiences of the spy
included a halt at a church where a blind preacher, an authentic person
of standing, James Waddel, was describing the crucifixion. Wirt's account
of the minister's sermon was itself a remarkable piece of writing. As it
appeared in a book quite widely circulated, it inspired many to imitate
James Waddel. If students catch now and again the echo of stories of

some great, unappreciated orator of the backwoods, it is quite likely that the tale originated in the pages of William Wirt. He certainly was responsible not only for the supposed form of Patrick Henry's speech on the arming of Virginia in 1775 but also—and chiefly through that utterance—Wirt influenced for two generations the approved style of rotund Southern oratory.

Henry's peroration on "Give me liberty or give me death" probably has some title to authenticity. As much may be said of a few other sentences in the speech that schoolboys still "learn by heart." For the remainder of the deliverance, there is no authority beyond hearsay and old men's remembrance of youthful impressions. The speech, in the judgment of some, is one-tenth Henry and nine-tenths Wirt, but it was accepted as one hundred per cent the model of what an oration ought to be, and it was imitated endlessly and stylistically. The politician who aspired to be heir to Henry's eloquence was supposed to take off somewhere in the vicinity of the bottom C of the bass clef, to soar at least as high as F of the treble, to drop then abruptly a full octave and to twist to finality at any elevation he chose. This was known among fledgling orators as "curling" and it was all in all a most extraordinary, not to say a perplexing, device. Wirt assuredly ought not to be held responsible for this style of delivery, but insofar as he shaped a tradition, it is to be noted that he did not issue his life of Henry until almost the time of the Missouri Compromise.

Thus have we Americans, in Henry's supposed speech, a bit of developing folklore of an age not yet much more than a century and a third. That is by no means the latest example. What could be more completely in the mode of folktale than the familiar remark that it "was worth traveling all the way across the State just to hear William L. Yancey pronounce the word 'Alabama' "? Still again, witness the manner in which "The Wreck of Old Ninety-Seven" already has become a regional possession. Recent or remote, African or Aryan, the existing general pattern of Southern folklore probably was set in late "slave days" and during the Reconstruction. This is understandable. Behind the songs and the stories often were inextinguishable humor, zeal, faith and acceptation, in a spirit almost Hellenic, of the adversity man could not escape—a state of mind the South needed when her cities were ashes and her sons were slain. There is some dark laughter in Southern folklore; there is superstition, too; but there is manhood and mirth and cheer for dark nights.

DOUGLAS SOUTHALL FREEMAN

Richmond, Virginia

ACKNOWLEDGMENTS

The editor and publishers wish to thank the following authors or their representatives, folklore societies, publishers, and publications for their kind permission to use material in this book. Full copyright notices are given on the pages on which the material appears.

Mrs. E. C. L. Adams; American Folklore Society, Inc.; *The American Mercury;* American Music, Inc.; Geneva Anderson; Appleton-Century-Crofts, Inc.; Archive of American Folk Song, Library of Congress; Ellen M. Bagby; The Bobbs-Merrill Co., Inc.; Albert & Charles Boni, Inc.; Mrs. Roark Bradford; The British Broadcasting Corp.; Sterling A. Brown; Carl Carmer; Laura Baker Cobb; Stuart Covington; Curtis Brown, Ltd.; *The Dallas Morning News;* Carl Dann, Jr.; Decca Records, Inc.; J. Frank Dobie; Dodd, Mead & Co.; Edward Arthur Dolph; Doubleday & Co., Inc.; Louise Jones DuBose; Duell, Sloan & Pearce, Inc.; Duke University; E. P. Dutton & Co., Inc.; Garnett L. Eskew; Paul Flowers; Funk & Wagnalls Co.; Carl Goerch; *Greensboro Daily News;* The Grolier Society, Inc.; Harper & Bros.; Lucien Harris; Harvard University Press; Hastings House; Houghton Mifflin Co.; Arthur Palmer Hudson; International Mark Twain Society; Chas. Jacobson; The John Day Co.; Mrs. Clifton Johnson; Alfred A. Knopf, Inc.; Lewis Historical Publishing Co.; J. B. Lippincott Co.; Estate of John A. Lomax; Senator Russell B. Long; Mary Robertson Longley; Louisiana State University Press; Bascom Lamar Lunsford; The Macmillan Co.; Harold Matson; Julian Messner, Inc.; Chapman J. Milling; William Morrow & Co., Inc.; Marmaduke B. Morton; Artus M. Moser; The Naylor Co.; Oxford University Press; *The Paris News;* John Parris; People's Songs, Inc.; Julia Peterkin; Harold Preece; G. P. Putnam's Sons; Random House, Inc.; Quentin Reynolds; Rinehart & Co., Inc.; Sydney A. Sanders; Charles Scribner's Sons; George E. Shankle; William Sloane Associates, Inc.; Beverly Smith; Society for the Preservation of Spirituals; *Southern Folklore Quarterly;* Texas Folklore Society; Texas Tech Press; Jean Thomas; Allan M. Trout; University of Alabama Press; University of Chicago Press; University of North Carolina Press; University of Oklahoma Press; University of Pennsylvania Press; Vanguard Press, Inc.; *Virginia and the Virginia County Magazine;* Mrs. Charles H. Walsh; Benjamin West; Whittlesey House; The Williams & Wilkins Company; C. Vann Woodward; Young Men's Progress Club, Benton, Kentucky.

An exhaustive effort has been made to locate all persons having any rights or interests in material, and to clear reprint permissions. If any required acknowledgments have been omitted or any rights overlooked, it is by acci dent and forgiveness is desired.

Contents

Part One: With a Southern Accent

I. SOUTHERN LOYALTIES

III. Caste and Class

IV. Brethren and Sistern

Part Two: Southern Saga

I. ON THE SIDE OF THE ANGELS

II. Buccaneers, Bandits, and Bullies

III. The People's Choice

IV. Memorabilia

Part Three: Southern Story-Tellers

I. Yarns and Tall Tales

SWAPPING LIES

II. FOLK TALES

FABLES AND MYTHS

II. SOUTHERN LIGHTS AND SHADOWS

PECULIAR WAYS

PRIVATE JUSTICE

Sports, Pastimes, and Festivals

Ways That Are Dark

III. Rhythms, Rituals, and Folk-Say

Part Five: The Singing South

Lullabies and Game Songs

Dance, Instrumental, and Ministrel Songs

NEGRO WORK SONGS AND BALLADS

RELIGIOUS SONGS

xxxii

Introduction

Even on the printed page Southern folklore and Southern folk-say
succeed in catching the color, flavor, and excitement of a culture in the
making and in communicating something of the same glow of discovery
that the first settlers felt on going into a new country. Indeed, part of
the eternally fresh appeal and true meaning of folklore in the South
derives from its backwoods heritage—the pioneer saga of planting
colonies, fields, and cities and creating names, legends, and ballads in
that wild and wonderful country that the first Englishmen found in Virginia, the first Virginians in Kentucky, and the first Kentuckians and
Virginians in Texas. Somewhere between a Lost Paradise and a paradise
regained, the South of folklore is still an eden-land of the imagination,
where Old Adam and Miss Eve play the "shout" game of "pickin' up"
and "pinnin' up leave'" and the Lord and the Devil walk the earth like
natural men, the former bearing a close resemblance to Old Massa and
the latter to Brer Fox.

Never were land and lore more perfectly suited and wedded to each
other. For in the South folklore is truly a way of life, and the way
of life naturally breeds lore. The rural South is a land of the out-of-
doors come up to the door and even indoors, where the "gallery," the
store-porch, the kitchen, the parlor, and the nursery are made for story-
telling and for ballad-singing; where the climate and the open sky
make a man expansive and enduring of lung and tongue when it is his
"night to howl" or when he is haranguing his "friends and feller-citizens"
or "sistern and brethren."

In the story-telling belt of the South barnyard fowl and animals not
only come up to the door but enter into the stories themselves, to talk
and jest, while in the fields and forests, the hollers and ridges, are the
heroes of yarns and tales as tall as the timber—the mighty Nimrods and
"gamecocks" of the wilderness and their animal friends and prey: the
self-sufficient razorback, the Paul Bunyanesque mountain or piney-woods
rooter, the rabbit, the possum, the raccoon, the fox, and the bear.

This is the land of the sky, where fantasy and dread follow the winding
creek trails and penetrate the hidden ways of mountain fastnesses. It is

a land of many waters, including the father of them all, of "going fishing," of mysterious caverns, buried treasure, and spelunking. It is a land of big talk and big eating, of home, homefolks, and homeward thoughts, where people "stand and take it," "where they stand on their rights, they stand on faith in the Lord, and they stand on the justice of jury and court; they stand in self-reliance, and they stand ready to help a neighbor in distress." It is also a "dark and bloody ground," where the invaders were bidden to go into the land and "possess it and to smite the inhabitants thereof 'hip and thigh' "; where blood flows thicker than water and calls for blood when tempers flare; where the codes of personal and family honor, the duello, and the blood-feud make for strong loves and hates, violence, and a "stern and selfish conception of justice."

In this land of fighters and three wars against the invader, including the disastrous and unforgettable conflict in which brother sometimes fought against brother, men put daring above discipline and etiquette to give us heroes like the "Swamp Fox," "Old Hickory," Stonewall Jackson, and Jeb Stuart (not to mention the later Sergeant York), partisan rangers and raiders like Morgan and Mosby, and guerrillas like Quantrell. In this land of "our contemporary ancestors," one hears the English of Chaucer and Shakespeare, stories that might have been told by the Canterbury pilgrims, and ballads of seventeenth- and eighteenth-century England and Scotland, handed down and kept alive by people of the "purest Anglo-Saxon blood in America," by people "who do not like books so well, but . . . like to remember and memorize many things that [they] do love." Theirs is a land of "make it yourself or do without," with the accent sometimes on the second alternative; of "don't take no orders from nobody nohow," "I'm agin it," and "don't care a damn," where folks "down creek" or "yan side" are "furriners," where the "fotched-on" or "newfangled" is resented or distrusted.

It is a land where the word "old"—the Old South, the old folks, Old Man So-and-So, little old this-and-that—are terms of affection and pride rather than of reproach. It is a land of sectional-unity-in-regional-variety, where Southerners wear the name "Southern" as a badge of difference and a chip on the shoulder; where people like to stay put or move about and come back home as they please and live their own lives in their own way, without outside interference or criticism; where every man is caught in the giant web of his family inheritance and recollectiveness, his limited solidarities, class loyalties, and local rivalries; where people still live under the shadow of the plantation economy that created a unique folk culture and made the South the nation's No. 1 folklore region as well as its "No. 1 economic problem."

In a land where folklore, like history (in Voltaire's phrase) "does not *always* lie," it was natural for both to overlap considerably and both to partake of folk-say, a kind of individual folklore in which the people are allowed to tell their own story in their own way. And because folklore is closer to the way of life and more on the surface in the South, as compared with regions where, in the confusion of cities and babel of tongues, it is buried under a complicated overlay of artificial civilization, it was inevitable that a book of Southern folklore should shape itself around Southern life and character. And, finally, since certain ways of life and looking at life have proved common to the Southern people as a whole throughout their history, these provided a more logical and dramatic framework than divers regions, epochs, or groups.

Such ways and folkways were, of course, first of all American and universal before they were Southern, but because they have persisted longest in the South, in combination with one another, they have come to be considered characteristically, if not exclusively, "Southern." As the dominant Southern pattern is divided between the backwoods and the plantation heritages, these are the leitmotifs of the book. The twofold pattern includes strong family and clan loyalties, rooted in the land and the old farm folk culture; local pride and prejudice; a biracial caste system and racial etiquette based on slavery; religious fundamentalism, sectarianism, revivalism, and argumentativeness; "irrepressible cussedness," an indomitable fighting spirit, and the "pattern of violence"; the heroic spirit and hero-worship closely bound up with ancestor-worship, feudal virtues, and popular leaders; and politics viewed as a "family affair," a "family fight," and a game whose rule is "Enjoy yourself, but take it easy," and if you "get hot under the collar," "try to keep your shirt on." Above all, Southern folklore is very much alive and kicking. Here and there one comes across a few dry bones and dusty relics of an old race "gone and forgotten out of the earth"; but for the most part it is flesh and blood covered with the living integument and wearing the lively lineaments of a people living a legend, as most of them have lived on the land, through the might and magic of the fiddle, the rifle, the ax, and the Bible.

Also basic to the book is the view of folklore as a part of folk culture, which is broader and deeper than the straight folklore forms of song, story, custom, belief, speech, proverb, and saying, and includes the folkways of institutions that serve as a focus of folk attitudes as well as media of folklore creation and transmission. In the South, outside the home, folk culture centers in religion and politics. Thus the campaign and the camp meeting or revival have been basic to Southern folkways and folklore, combining folk ritual with folk improvisation, folk festival with folk drama, and providing an outlet and an incentive for mass-excitement and -incitement in an emotionally expansive (if intellectually exclusive), spontaneous, contentious, and gregarious society.

Traditionally, folklore in the South has been associated with three relatively uneducated groups: the mountaineer, the poor white, and the Negro. In line with the view that the educated classes also have their folklore, the present book adds a fourth group; the "quality," which has its own folkways and legends, rooted in the feudal, chivalrous past of the South, the plantation tradition in life and literature (with its white stereotypes of the black mammy, the faithful old darky retainer, the contented slave, etc.) and the Confederate myths of the Lost Cause and Reconstruction. To-day the plantation heritage survives chiefly in the Delta, "cotton obsessed, [according to Rupert B. Vance] Negro obsessed, and flood ridden . . . the deepest South, the heart of Dixie."

The first break with the aristocratic plantation tradition came before the War in the split between the Lowcountry idea of large slave-holding estates and the Upcountry idea of small non-slave-holding farms. After the War (traditionally said to have been won by the poor whites rather than the Negroes) another break came with the industrial invasion of the Piedmont, where the cotton mill, the cotton baron, and the cotton mill worker have supplanted the agrarian tradition as well as threatened the isolation of the mountaineer and where labor conflicts have created a new folklore-in-the-making, as in the songs of Ella Mae Wiggins.

Also faintly "aristocratic" in his notions of his Anglo-Saxon heritage and self-sufficient subsistence economy, the much-romanticized, much-caricatured patriarchal mountaineer of Virginia, West Virginia, North Carolina, Kentucky, and Tennessee represents perhaps the best example in America of the "cultural lag" and the purest survival of a static folk-culture of handskills and mindskills amidst conditions of comparative isolation and stability. He is the "mountainy singer" of whom Cecil Sharp wrote in 1917: "I found myself for the first time in my life in a community in which singing was as common and almost as universal a practice as speaking."

Among Southern folk groups the "poor white" (to be distinguished from the common lowland and mountain whites), like the Negro, has been penalized by the inherited myth of inferiority. Cast by the plantation system into the outer darkness of poor land and poor living, he represents the ebb and backwash of the frontier, especially in the "garden escapes" of the hillbilly and the swamp angel, with their reversion to the hunting and fishing culture of the backwoods. For the rest his folk culture fosters superstition and prejudice, chiefly directed at his traditional competitor, the Negro farm laborer, although both alike are victims of the evils of farm tenancy and the crop lien.

In the "state of perpetual war" existing during slavery, the Negro developed a defensive technique of physical resistance and evasion—the "dissatisfied look, and reluctant air and unwilling movement; the constrained strokes of labor, the drawling tones, the slow hearing, the feigned stupidity, the sham pains and sickness, the short memory," and, as their imaginative and verbal counterpart, the powerful secret weapon of the "Negro laugh," which appeased with its cleverness or disarmed with its dumbness. With the change from caste to minority status, the same wit, irony, and double meaning, now aggressive as well as defensive, have remained the chief assets and attributes of Negro folklore and literature, with their sharpened sense of struggle and protest inherent in the Negro's anomalous position as the least alien yet the most separate of American minorities.

In turning his laughter on himself as well as the whites, the Negro has taken over the objectionable word "nigger" (though not "darky") and made it a term of praise or blame, depending on the context, as other minority groups have taken over similar words and by frequent repetition made them terms of endearment. Hortense Powdermaker quotes the Negro saying: "You're not a nigger when another Negro calls you it." Still, "nigger" (inseparable from first-person narratives and dialogues in this book), like "poor white," can be a killing word as well as a fighting word in the South.

On a recent recording trip that took me from Washington, D. C. to Charleston, S. C., I was newly and duly impressed by the amount of good story-telling and singing that I heard (on various levels of naïvete and sophistication) and the camaraderie therein exhibited or thereby established between the native and the visitor as well as among natives of various groups and social levels. Far from being lost or even dying arts, the traditional folk expressions and techniques survive, like superstition, as an alternative mode of procedure to the literary and scientific modes because they combine individual with group expressiveness, with a plasticity and a sense of craftsmanship not afforded by standardized and ready-made forms.

Besides its rich folk heritage, the South is fortunate in having its share of culturally aware and folk- as well as regionally-conscious leaders who are doing their utmost to see that the folk resources are not dried up at the source. Chief among these are the "folk-sayers," the more articulate members of the folk—singers, story-tellers, musicians, teachers —who, sooner or later, have all had the same experience of growing up to discover (perhaps on going off to college) that what they have been talking and singing, playing and dancing all their lives is folklore. They have taken the lead in the revival of the folk arts, through such media as folk festivals, handicraft guilds, "playmakers," and community productions combining several arts like *The Lost Colony*. Even bureaus devoted to making the people of the state love it by knowing it recognize and utilize local tradition, folk humor, and folk-say, at the inevitable risk of diluting and exploiting them. For the folks "Down Home" not only are, as Carl Goerch would say, "Characters . . . Always Characters," but they give character to and determine the character of a culture.

Many and all sorts of folk down South and up North have been helpful and generous, in one way or another, in making this book representative of the folk expression and interpretation of the South, though the final responsibility for the over-all picture and particular emphases is mine.

Throughout, in the spirit of folk-say, I have preferred as far as possible to let Southerners speak for themselves in their own way, even in the introductions, so that the whole becomes a self-portrait. As always, I have had to leave out more than I could put in, at the risk of slighting particular states, localities, groups, and individuals, though, not I hope, at the expense of a comprehensive selection. I am particularly sorry that space did not permit the inclusion of Cajun and Creole songs, blues, sermons, and children's rhymes. For certain missing favorites the reader is referred to *A Treasury of American Folklore,* none of the considerable body of Southern material in which has been duplicated here. All I can say for my sins of omission and commission is that in trying to make a book of the South, of the people, and of America, I have often had to sacrifice the part to the whole.

Though it is impossible to list everyone, I want to thank personally all those who contributed to the book in one way or another, including Marc and Gypsy Appleton, Ruth Bass, Sterling Brown, Edward Dreyer, Louise Jones DuBose, Paul Flowers, E. Y. Harburg, Charles Hofmann, Arthur Palmer Hudson, Francis Marion Hutson, Dr. M. Jagendorf, Ed and Lydia Jervis, Guy B. Johnson, Leo Leggette, Bascom Lamar Lunsford, Ruby Lovingood Lunsford, Dr. Sol Brown McLendon, Mr. and Mrs. Artus Moser and their daughter Joan, Ruth Ann Musick, Lee Myer, Harold Preece, D. Hiden Ramsey, Mrs. Alice K. Rondthaler, Mr. and Mrs. Edward Rondthaler, Alexander S. Salley, Jr., George F. and Genevieve Scheer, Bill Sharpe, George Stephens, Samuel G. Stoney, John W. Thomason, Fant Thornley, Allan M. Trout, Rupert B. Vance, Ben West, Jim White, and Dr. George P. Wilson.

For many favors and services I want to thank the following libraries and archives and their staffs: the Library of Congress and its Archive of American Folk Song (especially Mrs. Rae Korson), the New York Public Library (especially Sylvester Vigilante and his colleagues in the American History and Local History and Genealogy Rooms as well as the staff of the Music Division), the Columbia University Libraries, the University of North Carolina Libraries (especially the Library of the Woman's College), the Sondley Reference Library of Asheville, the University of South Carolina Library, and the Historical Commission of South Carolina; also the Pageant Book Company.

Finally, to my publishers, for their incalculable help in making countless big and little decisions; to Bertha Krantz, for her unstinting energy and zeal in shaping the copy and seeing the book through the press; and to my wife and partner in this as in previous ventures, Gertrude F. Botkin, for her heroic labor in preparing the manuscript and reading proof, all gratitude and praise are due.

B. A. BOTKIN

Croton-on-Hudson, N. Y.
October 10, 1949

PART ONE

WITH A SOUTHERN ACCENT

Inherent in the glory that was the traditional South were qualities often estimated to be the most distinctive and glamorous in the American picture: . . . a certain heritage abounding in the concepts and experience of good living, strong loyalties, spiritual energy, personal distinctions, and strong individuality. . . .

—HOWARD W. ODUM

The South did in fact assume a unity in the face of Northern hostility. But in reality the situation was not so simple. The South was a vast congeries in which geographic variations, cultural deviations, and conflicting currents of historical development rested in yet imperfect adjustment.

—PAUL H. BUCK

If the Southern people are characterized as Protestant, Sabbath-observing, family-loving, patriarchal, of religious intensity, "quarreling" with government, individualists taking their politics, their honor, and their liquor "hard," was not all the nation so a century ago? Their attitudes toward work and play, toward women, children, and property, toward the dominant leader, are still very much of the early vintage.

—RUPERT B. VANCE

The romantic South of the professional Southerner with its soft sweet speech of Dixie is false and to some of us distasteful. The romantic South was a literary convention. . . . [But] the speech of our South . . . is oh, so sweet to the ears of a Southerner. . . . Let us preserve it.

—WILLIAM CABELL GREET

I. SOUTHERN LOYALTIES

You can get a Southerner out of the South, but you can't get the South out of a Southerner.—OLD SAYING

The South is still, to some extent, a family affair; every criticism of the South is taken as personal, and conversely, every Southerner is held responsible for the entire South. . . . Who ever heard of a book interpreting the North; who ever held a Western author responsible for Western character?
—HENRY STEELE COMMAGER

1. A FAMILY AFFAIR

THE notion of the South as a "family affair" is the key to Southern loyalties. Both the Southernism and the Southernness of the South reflect the "clan-virtues" (and their defects) of the old frontier and rural folkways—folkways that were first of all American and then Southern. But in so far as these folkways have had a longer and stronger hold on them, Southerners are prone to look upon themselves first as Southerners and then as citizens of the United States.

In 1837 Harriet Martineau noted in the slave states a "natural relation between the independence of property and occupation enjoyed by the agriculturist, and his watchfulness over State Rights and the political importance of individuals."[1] Again, Thomas Jefferson Wertenbaker sees in the Old South, in spite of wide diversities and conflicting groups and interests, a common bond and a "sense of brotherhood" based on agriculture and slavery[2]—the "Solid South" of history and folklore.

2. FOLKS AND KINFOLKS

In a society which measured wealth in terms of land, primary emphasis was placed on personal qualities and personal relationships. These, together with family connections, continue to dominate Southern business and politics. Hence, too, personal religion and the ethical code of honor.

We are primary people. We believe in tangible things—in abstract thought but in tangible things. In faith, in love, in cotton bales, in acres of lands, in mules. We do not understand shares and stocks, the use of money to make money. We want to own our own jobs, to work for a man whom we know personally, to live in our own house or in the house of a person with whom we are acquainted. . . . Again and again we come back to the central focus of all our economic fear—to the impersonal life, to the mechanical that kills you.[3]

---

[1] *Society in America* (New York and London, 1837), Vol. I, p. 292.
[2] *The Old South* (New York, 1942), pp. 348–352.
[3] Ben Robertson, *Red Hills and Cotton* (New York, 1942), p. 106.

2

Of all personal ties family ties are the strongest. The Southerner looking back on his childhood sees it as all "entangled with the past," [4] with the "loves, the loyalties, the heartaches, and the simple good times of a big family." [5] Typically, these values are part of the "complete experience," the "settled family enterprise" of what M. L. Wilson calls the "older type of self-sufficient, folklore farm culture." Although this culture was identified most closely with the freehold frontier and back-country farm, the plantation preserved and extended the old pattern of self-sustaining economy and community life; and some of its traits survive in the Southern hinterland and the Southern heritage today.

As the children of the Old South scattered over the region, the home place and home folks still served as a symbol if not a bond of unity. "Some one is always keeping the home place, some one always is there, and no matter how seldom or unexpectedly we may come in, we know some one will rise to give us our welcome." [6] This feeling of homewardness and at-homeness gives a comforting sense of security and stability in time as well as place, a "living sense of the long continuity of human life," an awareness of the past as living in the present and almost as real as the present. And the identification of the individual with a long line of kinfolks and their achievements gives a sense of personal participation in history and tradition.

Our folks are old and settled in our country; we have a sense of continuity, of the infinite age of time—the history of the United States has been told to us in our valley by kinfolks who have been told it by their kinfolks, and it is a personal epic, a personal saga, and in it from the beginning we have been taking our part. [7]

Along with the satisfaction of personal participation goes the responsibility of *noblesse oblige,* the obligation of carrying on a tradition of techniques and attitudes handed down from the fathers to the sons.

Time and again the old folks and relations have told us during the talk of the night to stand together, to remember what we are, to remember that blood flows thicker than water, that blood will tell, that we are obligated to our kinfolks, that we must amount to something, we must be somebody, we must never bring disgrace upon the kinfolks. Time and again they have told us we are obligated, we have our duty, we must be willing to fight against whatever it is that threatens. We have been told to ask about everything: Will it leave us free? [8]

3. LARES AND PENATES

In the closely-knit, homogeneous society of the home place, home folks, and homeland, the present is haunted by ghosts of the past inhabiting the "living record, the . . . mute witnesses of a family life."

<hr>

[4] Rebecca Yancey Williams, *The Vanishing Virginian* (New York, 1940), p. 45.

[5] Viola Goode Liddell, *With a Southern Accent* (Norman, Oklahoma, 1948), Foreword.

[6] Ben Robertson, *op. cit.,* p. 20.

[7] *Ibid.,* p. 19.

[8] *Ibid.,* pp. 19–20.

A home must reflect the personality of a family for many generations. It is a repository of treasure, not necessarily of any intrinsic value. A Morris chair is not a thing of beauty in itself, but, when a Morris chair has been the favorite chair of a beloved grandfather, it may be quite a suitable part of the library furniture. A clock which has been wound day in and day out for a life-time is treasured beyond a better model in a museum.[9]

What saves these relics of the past from being mere museum-pieces is their symbolic and often living relation to the culture of the region. Such a symbol is the rice-spoon of Charleston.

Of massive silver, about fifteen inches long and broad in proportions, it is laid on the cloth with something of the reverential distinction that surrounds the mace in the House of Commons at Westminster. And their functions are not dissimilar, for if you take away the bauble, as did Cromwell, the Commons of England are a mob without authority, and if you take away the rice-spoon from the Charleston dinner table, the meal that follows is not really dinner. In fact, it's hardly worth calling a meal; so little worthy of notice that one family, who, though only Low-Country Episcopalians, were noted for their piety, would never ask a grace before a meal without rice, even when their parson was at the table, thinking it hardly worth thanking the Lord for.[10]

4. THE LAND

As the type and symbol of the "unreconstructed Southerner," Donald Davidson selects "Cousin Roderick," an idealized Middle Georgia country gentleman, who combines the "bearing of an English squire" with the "frontier heartiness" of A. B. Longstreet's *Georgia Scenes*.[11] What prin-cipally distinguishes Cousin Roderick from "Brother Jonathan" (the Ver-mont "unreconstructed Yankee" who resembles the Georgian in so many ways), as well as from his "Southern brothers of Upcountry and Bluegrass" is the fact that he does not work with his own hands, though "in the past he has worked a-plenty with his hands and knows how it should be done." On his "several tracts of land," worked by some one hundred and fifty Negroes (who, though "no longer his slaves, . . . do not allow him to forget that he has the obligations of a master"), he plants anything that will grow, especially cotton, which "is money," but also enough of other things to feed his family, his hands, and his stock.

Cousin Roderick's idea of "all that matters" is not so very different from that of George W. Bagby's "native Virginian" or of Ben Robertson in Up-country South Carolina. All shared the simple, hearty country pleasures of good friends and neighbors centering in field, garden, porch, store, and

---

[9] Elizabeth O'Neill Verner, *Mellowed by Time* (Columbia, South Carolina, 1941) pp. 59–60.

[10] Samuel Gaillard Stoney, *Charleston: Azaleas and Old Bricks* (Boston, 1937), pp. 11–12.

[11] *The Attack on Leviathan*, Regionalism and Nationalism in the United States (Chapel Hill, 1938), pp. 131–154.

church, with their good eating, hunting, talking, joking, story-telling, singing, and visiting. In this culture, land—"more land, not less"—is the "only abiding thing, the only assurance of happiness and comfort," as illustrated by the following story:

Like most of his kin, Cousin Roderick has simply retreated into the old plantation economy. He tells how, when he was a young fellow, just beginning to take charge, his father came out to the plantation one day and asked for a ham. Cousin Roderick explained that hogs were up to a good price; he had sold the entire lot, on the hoof, and had good money in the bank. "Sir," said the old man, "let me never again catch you without hams in your smokehouse and corn in your crib. You've got to make this land take care of itself." "And that," says Cousin Roderick, "is what I aim to do."

B. A. B.

The South to the North

A SOUTHERNER never sells what he can eat, and a Northerner never eats what he can sell.[1]

The difference between a Yankee and a durnyankee is that the Yankee has sense enough to stay where he belongs.[2]

Comparative Salutations to Strangers

. . . IN NEW ENGLAND, the first question to a traveler is sometimes this:— "Mister, if I may be so bold, which way are you traveling and what is your name?" In Kentucky, the salutation is, "Stranger, sit down;—what will you take?" . . .

---

[1] From "Traditional Proverbs and Sayings from California," by Owen S. Adams, *Western Folklore,* Vol. VI (January, 1947), No. 1, p. 63. Copyright, 1947, by the California Folklore Society. Berkeley and Los Angeles: Published for the California Folklore Society by the University of California Press.

Cf. J. Russell Smith and M. Ogden Phillips (*North America,* 1940, p. 318): "Many Southerners declare that they have no desire to duplicate the 'Yankee' rate of speed and hustle and Yankee thrift. A delightful friend in the South once said: 'The Yankees eat what they can't sell. We sell what we can't eat.' There is a savor of truth in this. It is an admirable description of two points of view, and it is true that the Southern fried chicken and hot corn pone have a better reputation as delicacies than the fried potatoes and cold wheat bread of the North. A great gulf separates these two points of view—the gulf that separates debtor and creditor."

[2] From *Texas—Proud and Loud,* by Boyce House, p. 5. Copyright, 1945, by the Naylor Company. San Antonio, Texas.

From "Kentucky," by J. M., *The New-England Magazine,* Vol. 2 (March, 1832), p. 237.

John Sharp Williams and the Yankee Clock

. . . THE young representative [John Sharp Williams] had dined late and well one evening, and stumbled loudly into his apartment just as a mantel clock struck two. His wife, awakened, protested about his state. He denied the state. "What time is it?" she asked. "Ten o'clock, my dear," said the unrepentant John, thinking he had got away with it, and lay down to sleep. Presently the bed was shaken with sobs. "What's the matter, honey?" asked John. "What are you crying about?" Silence for a while, except for the sobs. "Do tell me what you're crying about, honey." "I'm crying," sobbed the wife, "because after these ten years you have lied to me, for the first time. I heard that clock." Silence for a while, and then the bed began to shake with sobs on John's side. "What's the matter with *you*, honey?" Silence for a while. "Please tell me what you're crying about." After an impressive interval: "I'm crying because after ten years you'd rather believe that damned little Yankee clock than your own husband."

The Same Old Gun

A TRAVELER lost his way in the backwoods country. While wondering which path to take, he heard the breaking of twigs in the underbrush, and presently there emerged an overgrown boy with a rifle on his arm. By way of opening conversation, the traveler remarked, "That's a good-looking gun you have."

"Yes," replied the youth, "this was grandpap's gun. He carried it through the Revolutionary War."

Surprised by this statement, the traveler looked at the gun more closely. "Why, the barrel," he said, "seems shorter than those of the Revolutionary period."

"Yes," said the boy, "Pap had a new barrel put on."

The traveler continued his examination of the gun. "That looks like a new stock," he observed.

"Yes," said the boy, "Pap had that put on."

"The lock can't be very old either," observed the traveler.

From *Humor of the Old Deep South*, edited by Arthur Palmer Hudson, p. 208. Copyright, 1936, by the Macmillan Company. New York.

A story which I have heard orally from a source that I have forgotten.—A. P. H.

From "Comic Exempla of the Pioneer Pulpit," by Mody C. Boatright, in *Coyote Wisdom*, Texas Folk-Lore Society Publications, Number XIV, J. Frank Dobie, Mody C. Boatright, Harry H. Ransom, editors, pp. 166–167. Copyright, 1938, by the Texas Folk-Lore Society. Austin.

My father once heard a Methodist preacher make the following refutation of the doctrine of apostolic succession.—M. C. B.

"Pap had that put on too," said the boy.

"Then you must have a new gun."

"No," said the boy, "it's the same old gun grandpap carried through the Revolutionary War."

A Student of Economics

A FEW weeks ago I was in a rather remote section of the Carolina low-country. Vast fields, once white with cotton, now offer safe shelter for deer and turkeys. Fire-blackened chimneys stand as silent reminders of great plantation houses. Poverty, stark and gaunt, peers from behind hingeless doors of tumbled-down cabins.

I saw an old darky plowing with an ox. Two frayed and knotted ropes weathered by the years were his trace chains. A plow, blunted and nicked, with home-made handles of hickory, made unavailing efforts to dig a straight furrow. I stopped alongside the road and called to him.

"Uncle, what are you planting?"

"Mekking up dis lan fuh plant corn, suh," he said.

"You're about the last person around here, aren't you?" I asked.

"Yes, suh, me an fo head ob gran [grandchildren] is all what dey bout hyuh. De res bin gone to de city fuh scape de depresshun."

"Aren't you afraid of the depression, too?" I inquired.

This old man straightened his shoulders, bent by years of toil, threw his head back proudly and said:

"Young Massa, dat depresshun new-come; ah bin hyuh. *New-come* can't beat *bin-hyuh*."

The Agricultural South

FROM the standpoint of being invaded, it was fortunate that the South was more agricultural than industrial, more rural than urban. . . . A planter in answer to a politician who had told him that Congress was about to pass a dreadful law against the South, asked, "Will it keep cotton from growing?" "No," said the politician. "Will it kill the corn?" asked the planter. "No," was the reply. "Then d—n the law," exclaimed the planter.

From *Cryin' in de Wilderness,* Sermons and Adventures of Reb'ren Nichodemus Ezra Malachi Lee of Maxfield on Santee, by Alfred Holmes von Kolnitz, pp. 58–59. (n.d.) Charleston, South Carolina: Walker Evans and Cogswell Company.

From the Augusta (Georgia) *Daily Chronicle and Sentinel,* May 18, 1871. Cited in *The South during Reconstruction, 1865–1877,* by E. Merton Coulter, p. 19. Copyright, 1947, by the Louisiana State University Press. Baton Rouge.

In Bourbon County

. . . IN BOURBON COUNTY [,Kentucky,] they tell of an old lady of ancient stock who was confined by illness several years ago when her niece, a Bluegrass belle, came to her with news of her engagement.

"Aunt Julia, I'm going to be married," she said.

"Oh, Lordy!" sighed Aunt Julia.

"He is a Presbyterian," was the next revelation.

"Oh, Lordy, Lordy!" groaned Aunt Julia, who was a devout follower of Alexander Campbell.

"He is a Northerner."

"Oh, Lordy, Lordy, Lordy!" cried Aunt Julia in anguish.

"He's a Republican."

"Oh, Lordy, Lordy, Lordy, Lordy!" moaned Aunt Julia from the depths of a broken heart.

The Best Carver

. . . IN RALEIGH [,North Carolina,] they told a story about a Baptist lady, whose family had grown rich after that war, and Captain Billy Boylan, whose family was much older though his wealth had not grown.

"Oh, Captain Boylan," she said, "you're just the man I wanted to see. We're going to entertain the Baptist State Convention and I understand you're the best carver in Raleigh. I wanted to get you to carve the turkeys."

The Captain, who was an Episcopalian, was not flattered by the invitation.

"I'll be delighted, madam," he said. "It is true that I have some skill as a carver. You see it takes ten generations to make a carver and only one to make a Baptist."

Family Pride

I[1]

IN VIRGINIA an eminent Biblical scholar visited the church and delivered a lecture on the Medes and the Persians. Afterwards a delicate little old

---

From *"Weep No More, My Lady,"* by Alvin F. Harlow, p. 103. Copyright, 1942, by Alvin F. Harlow. New York and London: Whittlesey House, McGraw-Hill Book Company, Inc.

From *Tar Heels, A Portrait of North Carolina,* by Jonathan Daniels, pp. 249–250. Sovereign States Series. Copyright, 1941, by Jonathan Daniels. New York: Dodd, Mead & Company.

[1] By Edmund Fuller, Hand's Cove, Vermont, March 5, 1949.

lady came forward and said, clasping his hand, "Doctuh, ah just *had* to come up an' speak to you—you know, mah mothuh was a Mead."

II [2]

. . . The irritating trick of bragging about one's lineage and aristocratic background was made fun of in a story of a Virginia lady and an old colored man. The lady, who was visiting in Louisville, Kentucky, sought to cover up her personal shortcomings by boasting about her home county and her maiden name. She told an ancient and dignified Negro of the Uncle Remus type that her maiden name was Morson. The old man replied, "I b'longed to Mars' Hugh Morson. I knowed we was related!"

The Ancestral Criterion

I suppose nothing seems so ridiculous to other people as our peculiar form of Virginia ancestor worship. But the thing has its uses. We must all have some kind of standard by which to judge people. Virginians are essentially lazy, and their ancestor worship prevents much unnecessary mental exertion. If one recognizes from a person's name, for instance, that he comes from a family which for generations has stood for the best traditions, then one can safely make a friend of that person without bothering any further. If he turns out to be a thief and a blackguard, it will be the exception, not the rule. And one won't make many mistakes.

Kinfolk

THE EVIL consequences of inbreeding of persons closely akin are well known to the mountaineers; but here knowledge is no deterrent, since whole districts are interrelated to start with. Owing to the isolation of the clans, and their extremely limited travels, there are abundant cases like those caustically mentioned in *King Spruce:* "All Skeets and Bushees are married back and forth and crossways and upside down till ev'ry man is his own grandmother, if he only knew enough to figger relationship."

[2] From *The Southern Country Editor*, by Thomas D. Clark, p. 129. Copyright, 1948, by the Bobbs-Merrill Company. Indianapolis and New York.

From *The Vanishing Virginian*, by Rebecca Yancey Williams, p. 169. Copyright, 1940, by Rebecca Yancey Williams. New York: E. P. Dutton & Company, Inc.

From *Our Southern Highlanders*, by Horace Kephart, p. 223. Copyright, 1913, by Outing Publishing Company. New York.

Why I Am a Democrat

[THEODORE] Roosevelt . . . was very popular in Birmingham, and no-where was his famous joke about "Why I'm a Democrat" more enjoyed. The joke, as told here, ran something like this:

A Northerner and a Southerner were discussing matters political in the smoking compartment of a Pullman, when the Northerner asked:

"Why is it that you men of the South are practically all Democrats? In the North we divide; there you will find Republicans, Democrats, Progressives, Independents, and so forth, while you of the South stick together in the Democratic party. Why is this? Why, for instance, are you a Democrat?"

"Well," drawled the Southerner, "my father was a Democrat, my grandfather was a Democrat and my great-grandfather was a Democrat, so, of course, I'm a Democrat."

"Ah," said the Northerner, "suppose your father had been a horse-thief and your grandfather had been a horse-thief and your great-grandfather had been a horse-thief, what would you have been then?"

"Oh, I guess in that case I'd have been a Republican," was the reply of the Southerner, according to the widely smiling Colonel.

Kissing and Politics

IN THE campaign of 1900, [Lieutenant Governor Bill] Thorne told the following story in a political speech:

It was just after W. O. Bradley was elected Governor of Kentucky, and the Republicans in my county were holding a big ratification meeting. Brass bands, all kinds of floats and banners, and hundreds of men, women and boys paraded the streets. A young girl claimed that while standing on her front porch, which was almost covered with vines and foliage of different kinds, she was repeatedly hugged and kissed by a young man she hardly knew. A warrant was sworn out for her assailant. He was arrested and it was my duty as Commonwealth's Attorney to prosecute him. John D. Carroll, now Judge of the Kentucky Court of Appeals, had been employed to defend him. I soon finished my examination of the witness and turned her over to Carroll for cross examination.

"What night was this?" thundered Carroll.

From *The Book of Birmingham,* by John R. Hornady, pp. 27–28. Copyright, 1921, by Dodd, Mead and Company, Inc. New York.

From *Stories and Speeches of William O. Bradley,* with Biographical Sketch by M. H. Thatcher, pp. 17–18. Copyright, 1916, by Transylvania Printing Co. Lexington, Kentucky.

"Thursday night," answered the witness.

"Thursday night, you say? What time of night?"

"About eight o'clock."

"That was about the time the parade was passing your house?"

"Yes."

"Did you ever cry out or scream?"

"No, sir, I did not."

"Will you tell this jury," asked Carroll with rising voice, "with the streets thronged with people, and this man hugging and kissing you against your will, as you claim, why you never uttered a single cry for help or assistance?"

"Yes, sir. I will tell the jury, and everybody else, that you'll never ketch me hollerin' at no Republican gatherin'."

Why the *Natchez* Lost the Race with the *Robt. E. Lee*

PEER of all races on the river was the race between the *Natchez* and the *Robt. E. Lee*. There has long been a legend that the crew of the *Natchez* took all the fanciest hams that hung in the cook's galley for the passengers, and burnt them in the fireboxes to make more steam for the engines. Wrinkled old Negroes, all along the course of the vessel, smacked their lips as a rich fragrance drifted out on the water and they murmured: "Ain't that wonderful frying ham? Ain't that sure wonderful ham?"

The crew of the *Natchez* did burn ham. But the meat did not come from the boat's stores. It was a supply of condemned hams donated for the purpose by the merchants of Natchez.

There is another colorful legend: the reason why the *Natchez* lost the race. The *Natchez*, an old riverman once told me, was steaming far ahead, and the prize seemed hers to a certainty; the exultant crew began to celebrate their victory. Suddenly, at the height of their jollity, a dismal thought occurred to one of the pilots, and continued to haunt him like a ghost at the feast: if the *Natchez* won, the name of the beloved *Robt. E. Lee* would be associated with defeat. He kept silence for a while, then communicated his fears to his companions. Instantly the merriment ceased. A council was held, and the matter gravely debated. The decision was made at last: for the sake of the great general, they must lose the race. The plan was quickly carried into execution. The boat swung to the shore, and hid deep in a cove. For hours she lay there, lost to the sight of any river travelers, waiting patiently, stoically, until the *Robt. E. Lee* roared past and went steaming into glory.

From *Big River to Cross*, Mississippi Life Today, by Ben Lucien Burman, pp. 31–32. Copyright, 1938, 1939, 1940, by Ben Lucien Burman. New York: The John Day Company.

Stonewall Jackson and the Farmer

THERE lived, in the summer of 1862, on the Mechanicsville turnpike, near Richmond, a generous, hospitable, whole-souled Virginia gentleman, who, however, was very passionate and excitable, and who, when flurried, was apt to mix up the reverential and the profane, the sublime and the ridiculous, in a very odd kind of way. He had given up all his crop, pasture-fields, and everything he could spare, to the Confederate States Government; but he had reserved one ten-acre lot of corn for his own use, and this he guarded with unceasing vigilance. One day, while on watch, he discovered a group of horsemen approaching, and, instead of going round his fence, they took the most direct road right through. His wrath was instantly aroused, and supposing that they belonged to that class of individuals whom a well-known French officer in our services used to call "de damn cavelree," he rushed out in great rage. "How dare you go through my field? Damn you, I'll report you to President Davis."

"We are on urgent business, and took the shortest cut," mildly replied the leading horseman, in an old faded-gray suit.

Gentleman.—"Do you command this company?"

Horseman.—"Yes, sir."

Gentleman.—"I'll teach you not to ride through my field, damn you! What's your name?"

Horseman.—"My name is Jackson."

Gentleman.—"What Jackson?"

Horseman.—"T. J. Jackson."

Gentleman.—"What is your rank?"

Horseman.—"I am a Major-General in the Provisional army!"

Gentleman (raising his hat).—"Bless my soul! you ain't *Stonewall* Jackson?"

Horseman.—"I am sometimes called by that name."

Gentleman (rushing eagerly up to him and shaking his hand).—"God bless you, General Jackson! I am so glad to see you! Go back and ride all over my field, damn you, ride all over my field! Get down, and come into my house. I am so glad to see you. Ride all over my field, all over it—all over it! Bless your soul, I'm so glad to see you."

From *The Grayjackets: and How They Lived, Fought and Died, for Dixie,* with Incidents & Sketches of Life in the Confederacy, Comprising Narratives of Personal Adventure, Army Life, Naval Adventure, Home Life, Partisan Daring, Life in the Camp, Field and Hospital: together with the Songs, Ballads, Anecdotes and Humorous Incidents of the War for Southern Independence, by a Confederate, pp. 139–140. Richmond, Atlanta, Philadelphia, Cincinnati, St. Louis, Chicago: Jones Brothers & Co. [1867].

The Origin of Dixie

IT WAS a day of wildcat currency. There being no stable system of issuing government paper, each state, each county, each bank issued its own notes, and naturally many were worthless or, if worth their face value in truth, were not trusted a stone's throw from the bank of their issuance. But one bank of the Mississippi Valley, along in the 'Thirties and 'Forties, had established a record for integrity and soundness that resulted in its notes being accepted as exchange in all the marts of the country. Louisville and Cincinnati and Pittsburgh and New York and Philadelphia knew and honored the ten dollar notes issued by the Banque des Citoyens de la Louisianne of New Orleans. The Creole has frequently been pictured, particularly by one George W. Cable, as having little or no business stamina. But it is on record that the notes of this Creole citizens bank of the Crescent City stood out pleasantly in contrast with the notes of other banking houses of that day.

Up the river on the steamboats came the ten dollar notes. For all the steamboatmen when in New Orleans did their banking at the Banque des Citoyens. They were printed, these ten dollar notes, in English on one side and in French on the other for the convenience of both the Creoles and Anglo-Saxons. In large letters on the back of each note was engraved "DIX," the French word for ten. You could see the dix before you saw the note, it was said.

"A dix note is always good," remarked a steamboat mate in Cincinnati, counting his pay money.

"You're right," responded the clerk. "A 'dixie' is bon-bon, as these French fellows say down South."

Unlettered as they were, they pronounced the dix as it was spelled. The town where the "dixies" came from they called "dixie's land."

"I'm going down the river after dixies," said the flatboatmen, of whom there were still a goodly number on the rivers as late as 1850.

"I bought this horse down in the dixie country," remarked a traveler on the wharf at Louisville.

As time went on and the sectional homogeneity of the southern people became more manifest, what with the darkening of the war clouds, the term "Dixie's land" came gradually to be applied to the whole section in which the dixies had the largest circulation. From there on, a step only was needed to extend the borders until it embraced all the United States territory south of the Mason-Dixon line.

Daniel Decatur Emmett, an Ohioan by birth, a traveling minstrel and showman by persuasion, made a song about "Dixie, the Land of Cotton."

From *The Pageant of the Packets*, A Book of American Steamboating, by Garnett Laidlaw Eskew, pp. 100–102. Copyright, 1929, by Henry Holt and Company, Inc. New York.

It was said that in his travels under a tent in the North in winter, he longed for the warm southern climate of Dixie land (for which few of us would blame him!) and expressed it in his "walk-around" song beginning:

> I wish I was in de land ob cotton,
> 'Simmon seed and sandy bottom, look away! etc.

and set to a rollicking tune in Bryant's minstrel house in New York. Instantly it made a hit and when Emmett took it South in '59, the Southerners seized upon it as their own property—especially those in and around New Orleans. It became the *chanson de guerre* of the gray armies of a few years later. . . .

The Origin of the Confederate Flag and Uniform

LOCATED in Louisville, in a well known business building, is a time-stained yet time-honored room. Its walls are darkened with the finger marks of the passing years, and the whole demeanor of the place is unobtrusive and unpretentious. Yet is this place rich in its treasured holdings of art, its clustered memories and traditions of the Old South or the southland of ante-bellum days.

It is the art studio of Nicola Marschall, musician, portrait painter and designer of both uniform and flag of the Confederate States of America. From his Prussian homeland, where he was made skillful musically and trained to the painter's art, this man, then in his youth, came over land and sea to America at one of the most rugged and picturesque periods of

---

From *The Florida Times-Union*, May 17, 1905. Reprinted from *Southern Treasury of Life and Literature*, selected by Stark Young, pp. 215–217. Copyright, 1937, by Charles Scribner's Sons. New York.

There have in the course of time arisen various disputes as to the origin of the Confederate flag. The most persistent claim, outside of Marschall's, has been that of Orren R. Smith of North Carolina. In this case, the pressure brought to bear on the United Confederate Veterans was such as to lead to a thorough investigation of a matter that, up to that time, had been taken for granted. The affidavits of many witnesses in Alabama who had direct knowledge of the case were taken. The evidence is such as to dispose of all claims except Marschall's. . . .

* * * * *

At Manassas it was discovered that the Confederate flag was often mistaken for the United States flag. General Beauregard, therefore, designed a battleflag that was adopted by the Confederate Congress and afterward used in battles. It is the flag most seen now in parades of Confederate veterans. The flag of the Confederacy was used on ships, public buildings, et cetera.—S. Y., *ibid.*, pp. 214, 217.

For Major Orren R. Smith's own story of his rival claim to the design of the Confederate flag, together with other testimonials and tributes, see *History of the Stars and Bars, Designed by Orren Randolph Smith, February 7, 1861, at Louisburg, North Carolina, Adopted by Congress of Confederate States of America at Montgomery, Alabama, March 4, 1861* (Raleigh, North Carolina, 1913), pp. 6–30.

this country's history, the memorable gold fever days of '49. It was in Alabama that he found the home for which he sought. With no other compensation than the pride it caused him to serve the South, and the pleasure it gave him to honor a woman's request, these designs were made by Nicola Marschall in 1861, and adopted by the Southern Confederacy. Mr. Marschall's studio is in the building on the southwest corner of Green and Fourth Streets. It is a veritable curiosity shop, a place wealthy in historical recollections, its souvenirs of bygone days and the works of this artist. There are many portraits about the place, portraits that show upon canvas the mental pictures still dear to the people of the South. Portraits of Robert E. Lee, Joseph E. Johnston, J. C. Breckenridge, William Preston and Bragg are among those in the studio. These are but a few of the Confederate leaders whose portraits he has painted. Among the best pictures he has ever painted were two of General N. B. Forrest, the "Wizard of the Saddle," who was a personal friend of Mr. Marschall.

The story of how Mr. Marschall came to design the uniform and flag of the confederacy is best told in his own words.

"I came to this country," he began, "when I was eighteen years of age. My home was in St. Windel, Prussia, and I left there that I might continue professionally with music and art, instead of having to serve in the army. I left with the permission of my government, something more easily obtained then than now. I landed in New Orleans and from there made my way to Mobile, where lived a relative of mine, who had preceded me here. I met him on the eve of his departure for California. It was in 1849 that I landed in America, when the tide of humanity was flowing towards the gold fields of the Pacific Coast.

"My kinsman tried to persuade me to join his mining party and go to California in search of wealth. But I was then as far away from home as I cared to be, and so declined to go. I became acquainted with one of the teachers in the female seminary at Marion, Ala., and learned that it was one of the garden spots of the South. Wealthy planters lived there; it was a seat of learning and claimed as citizens many of the oldest and most aristocratic Southern families. I decided to go to Marion and go I did. I became a teacher at the seminary there, where I taught painting, violin, piano, guitar and the French and German languages.

"My studies in Europe of drawing and painting now served me well. I came over here on an old sailing vessel, and well do I remember to this day how I had to draw the picture of every member of the crew from captain to humblest sailor. I had been in this country one year when my brother arrived from Prussia.

"In 1857 I returned to Prussia and remained in Prussia for two years continuing my studies of art. I studied both in Munich and Italy. It was while returning from Italy and passing through Verona, which then belonged to Austria, that I saw the uniform which some years later was to furnish me with a design for the Southern Confederate uniform.

"In Verona one day the notes of martial music came to me. On searching I found that a party of sharpshooters belonging to the Austrian army were passing.

" 'What splendid soldiers and what noble uniforms,' was my involuntary comment as I saw them. Well might this be said. They were all great manly soldiers and were dressed in the striking uniform of gray with green trimmings. The green denoted their branch of the army—the sharpshooters—and their rank was indicated by marks on the collars of their coats, bars for lieutenants and captains, stars for the higher officers.

"I returned to America in 1859 and again located in Marion. There I painted many portraits of the wealthy planters and members of their families, as well as of other prominent people of the South. Andrew Moore was then a judge at Marion. He afterward became War Governor of Alabama and was one of the most important men in those days in our part of the country.

"Mrs. Napoleon Lockett, a beautiful Southern woman of an old Virginia family and the wife of a wealthy planter, lived at Marion. Her eldest son married the eldest daughter of Governor Moore and one of her younger sons married one of the younger daughters of Governor Moore.

"Soon came the first notes of war. Mrs. Lockett was as loyal a daughter as the South had, and was much interested in its affairs. Then she came to me one day and said, 'Mr. Marschall, we have seceded and the Confederate Government wants a flag. Will you make us a design? It must not be too unlike the U. S. Flag, but different enough to be distinguished at a distance.' At once I took pencil and paper and made three different designs. The first was of two red stripes and one of white, with a blue field bearing seven white stars—indicating the number of States that had then seceded—in the upper left hand corner. The second design was the same, except that the blue field with stars was at the extreme left of the white stripe instead of the top red stripe. The third design had the two full red stripes at top and bottom, the white stripe in the middle—with the blue field and white stars in the center."

It is a matter of historical fact that this first design made by Mr. Marschall was the flag adopted by the Confederate Government. It is also well known to those familiar with Southern history, that this flag—the Stars and Bars—was placed on the staff above the Capitol at Montgomery, Alabama, on March 4, 1861, by Miss L. C. Tyler of Virginia. She was the granddaughter of John Tyler, ex-President of the United States.

Continuing his interesting narrative, Mr. Marschall said, "Mrs. Lockett thanked me for the flag designs. Then she came back, adding, 'We also want a design for a uniform, Mr. Marschall—can't you suggest one?' The thought occurred to me of the gray uniforms I had seen worn by the Austrian sharpshooters. I took a piece of paper and made several rough sketches, indicating the gray color, and also the colors on the collars to denote the branch of the service—buff for officers, yellow for cavalry, blue for infantry, red for artillery, etc.

"It did not occur to me then that I had done anything worthy of note. I simply made the sketches at the request of Mrs. Lockett. I knew no more about them from then, until I found that the uniform and one of the flags had been adopted by the Confederacy."

This is the story of how the gray of the Confederate army and the banner under which they fought were made—a story told by one who conceived the plans. Not boastfully, but with a measure of pride, does Mr. Marschall, when sought out, tell the story. He considers that he had done little in making the designs, but he is to this day proud that his were the ideas adopted for both the uniform and the flag of the South.

When war was declared Mr. Marschall enlisted as a private of volunteers, going with his command from Marion to garrison Forts Morgan and Gaines, at the mouth of Mobile Bay. There he served for a time, then returned to Marion on a furlough. While at home, on the advice of a friend, an officer, he employed a substitute for a year and three months. Then came the call for more volunteers, and again Mr. Marschall enlisted, this time in the Second Alabama Regiment of Engineers. He served with Colonel Lockett, a son of Mrs. Napoleon Lockett, under General Polk, just preceding the fall of Vicksburg. Mr. Marschall served then in the Confederate army until the curtain was finally drawn at Appomattox.

The Rebel Yell

PRESENTLY the rattle of musketry is heard in front. Skirmishers must have made contact with enemy pickets. All are alert. A signal gun is fired and the artillery joins in with accumulating fury. At last the command— "Forward!"—and an overpowering urge to make contact with the enemy. Soon lines of blue are discernible. Comrades begin to fall in increasing numbers. Now the shout, lost perhaps in the din of battle—"Charge!"—accompanied by a forward wave of officer's saber and the line leaps forward with the famous "Rebel yell."

This yell itself is an interesting thing. It was heard at First Manassas and was repeated in hundreds of charges throughout the war. It came to be as much a part of a Rebel's fighting equipment as his musket. Once, indeed, more so. Toward the end of an engagement near Richmond in May, 1864, General Early rode up to a group of soldiers and said, "Well, men, we must charge them once more and then we'll be through." The response came back, "General, we are all out of ammunition." Early's ready retort was, "Damn it, holler them across." And, according to the narrator, the order was literally executed.

The Confederate yell is hard to describe. An attempt to reproduce it

From *The Life of Johnny Reb*, the Common Soldier of the Confederacy, by Bell Irvin Wiley, pp. 71–72. Copyright, 1943, by the Bobbs-Merrill Company. Indianapolis and New York.

was made a few years ago when Confederate veterans re-enacted battle scenes in Virginia. But this, by the very nature of things, was an inadequate representation. Old voices were too weak and incentive too feeble to create again the true battle cry. As it flourished on the field of combat, the Rebel yell was an unpremeditated, unrestrained and utterly informal "hollering." It had in it a mixture of fright, pent-up nervousness, exultation, hatred and a pinch of pure deviltry. Yelling in attack was not peculiar to Confederates, for Yanks went at Rebels more than once with "furious" shouts on their lips. But the battle cry of Southerners was admittedly different. General "Jube" Early, who well understood the spirit of his soldiers, made a comparison of Federal and Confederate shouting as a sort of aside to his official report of the battle of Fredericksburg. "Lawton's Brigade, without hesitating, at once dashed upon the enemy," he said, "with the cheering peculiar to the Confederate soldier, and which is never mistaken for the studied hurrahs of the Yankees, and drove the column opposed to it down the hill." Though obviously invidious, the general's observation is not wholly inaccurate.

The primary function of the rousing yell was the relief of the shouter. As one Reb observed after a fight in 1864, "I always said if I ever went into a charge, I wouldn't holler! But the very first time I fired off my gun I hollered as loud as I could, and I hollered every breath till we stopped." At first there was no intention of inspiring terror in the enemy, but the practice soon attained such a reputation as a demoralizing agent that men were encouraged by their officers to shout as they assaulted Yankee positions. In the battle of Lovejoy's Station, for instance, Colonel Clark cried out to his Mississippians, "Fire and charge with a yell." Yankees may not have been scared by this Rebel throat-splitting, but they were enough impressed to set down in their official reports that the enemy advanced "yelling like fiends," or other words to the same effect.

Naturally a thing of such informal character as the Rebel yell varied considerably with the time and circumstance. Mississippians had a note quite different from that of Virginians. Rebs attacking Negro troops injected so much hatred into their cry as to modify its tonal qualities. A most interesting variant was that of the trans-Mississippi Indians organized by the Confederacy. Colonel Tandy Walker, commander of the Second Indian Brigade, reporting an action of his troops in Arkansas, said that when the Federals retreated Private Dickson Wallace was the first man to reach their artillery, "and mounting astride one of the guns gave a whoop, which was followed by such a succession of whoops from his comrades as made the woods reverberate for miles around."

Cotton Is King

I[1]

THE expression, *Cotton is King,** was the slogan commonly used by the people through the southern part of the United States, particularly from 1855 until 1865. This phrase was originated by David Christy, an anti-slavery writer, who lived from 1802 until about 1870. The slogan originated in the following manner:

In 1848 Christy was chosen as an agent of the American Colonization Society in Ohio, in which capacity he induced several persons to buy an area of land in Africa, located between Sierra Leone and Liberia, to which freed slaves might be transported and colonized. In January, 1849, the repeal of the Black Laws in Ohio, which had prevented colored men from immigrating into this state, provoked a heated controversy about the slavery issue in the State of Ohio. Christy, thereupon, redoubling his efforts to promulgate the idea of African colonization, delivered lectures and published a number of pamphlets and essays dealing with slavery.

Chiefly because of the nation-wide dissension over the Kansas-Nebraska Act of 1854 and because of the increasing radicalism of the Abolitionists, Christy was prompted to publish, in 1855, his most outstanding work, entitled *Cotton is King: or the Economic Relations of Slavery.* In this publication he set forth the argument that slavery was subject to control only by political economies and that the Abolitionists would fail in their method of attack on slavery so long as they made it a moral issue or hoped to eradicate it by means of physical force; in other words, as long as people kept buying the cotton products, made plentiful and cheap only by slave labor, they were encouraging the useless and superficial attempts to solve the slavery problem. The demand for cotton which increased annually explained why "cotton is king"; † that is, why it was the most important raw material that Southerners produced and that the Northerners and the other industrial nations bought to manufacture into finished goods. This work of Christy's evoked wide discussion while the phrase, *Cotton is King,* holding particular appeal for the Southerners, was adopted by them in championing the importance of cotton to the American people.

---

[1] From *American Mottoes and Slogans,* by George Earlie Shankle, pp. 32–33. Copyright, 1941, by George Earlie Shankle. New York: The H. W. Wilson Company.

* *The Fight for the Republic: a Narrative of the More Noteworthy Events in the War of Secession, Presenting the Great Contest in Its Dramatic Aspects,* Rossiter Johnson (G. P. Putnam's Sons, New York and London, 1917), p. 6.—G. E. S.

† *Cotton is King or the Culture of Cotton, and Its Relation to Agriculture, Manufacturers, and Commerce, and Also to the Free Colored People of the United States, and to Those Who Hold that Slavery Is in Itself Sinful,* David Christy (Derby and Jackson, New York, 1856), p. 27.—G. E. S.

The slogan, *Cotton is King,* was again publicized by James Henry Hammond of South Carolina when he used the expression in a speech, delivered before the United States Senate on March 4, 1858, on the admission of the State of Kansas into the Union. In this speech Senator Hammond declared that he would compare the North and the South politically, socially, and economically to show that, if either section should secede from the Union, the people of the South had ample resources to progress as a separate, independent, and powerful republic.

He elaborated upon this statement by giving statistics of the raw materials produced in and exported from the South, and avowed that if all commercial restrictions were removed from the South, the entire world would go to the Southerners to trade for cotton, their leading crop. Defiantly he asserted that the South could rely upon its cotton for strength and for protection, for he said, "You dare not make war on cotton. No power on earth dares make war on it. Cotton is King." ‡

II [2]

"King Cotton" was a popular personification of the cotton-plant. Its supremacy in commerce and politics was strongly asserted by the politicians of the cotton-growing States§ when civil war was ripening. "You dare not make war upon cotton; no power on earth dare make war upon it. Cotton is *King!*" said Senator James Hammond, of South Carolina. "Cotton is King!" shouted back the submissive spindles of the North. A Northern poet sang:

> "Old Cotton will pleasantly reign
> When other kings painfully fall,
> And ever and ever remain
> The mightiest monarch of all."

A Senator from Texas exclaimed on the floor of Congress, "I say, Cotton is King, and he waves his sceptre not only over these thirty-three States, but over the island of Great Britain and over Continental Europe; and there is no crowned head there that does not bend the knee in fealty, and acknowledge allegiance to the monarch." This boasting was caused by the erroneous estimate by the politicians of the money value of the cotton crop compared with the other agricultural products of the United States. It was asserted that it was greater than all the latter combined. The census of

---

‡ *Speech of the Honorable James Henry Hammond of South Carolina on the Admission of Kansas under the Lecompton Constitution, Delivered in the Senate of the United States, March 4, 1858* (Printed by Lemuel Towers, Washington, D. C., 1858), p. 12.—G. E. S.

§ Commonly known as the "Cotton Kingdom."

[2] From *Harper's Encyclopaedia of United States History,* from 458 A.D. to 1909, based upon the plan of Benson John Lossing . . . , Vol. II, p. 405. Copyright 1901, 1905, by Harper & Brothers. New York and London.

1860 showed that the wheat crop alone exceeded in value the cotton crop by $57,000,000; and the value of the combined crops of hay and cereals exceeded that of cotton over $900,000,000. The sovereignty of cotton was tested by the Civil War. At its close a poet wrote:

> "*Cotton* and *Corn* were mighty kings,
> Who differed, at times, on certain things,
>   To the country's dire confusion;
> *Corn* was peaceable, mild, and just,
> But *Cotton* was fond of saying, 'You must!'
> So after he'd boasted, bullied, and cussed,
>   He got up a revolution.
> But in course of time the bubble is bursted,
> And *Corn* is King and *Cotton*—is worsted."

A Long Time between Drinks

I. Its Origin [1]

"As THE Governor of North Carolina said to the Governor of South Carolina, it's a long time between drinks"—a favorite convivial apothegm in America, suggesting that it is time for some one "to set 'em up again for the boys," or, in other words, to order a fresh round of drinks. An historical origin has been found for the phrase, but, unfortunately with no apparent historical foundation. The story runs that early in the century a native North Carolinian who had moved across the border into South Carolina was forced to fly back again to escape arrest. The Governor of South Carolina straightway issued a requisition on the Governor of North Carolina for the fugitive criminal. But the latter Governor hesitated. The criminal had many and influential friends. Finally the South Carolina executive, with a large retinue, waited on his official brother at Raleigh, the capital of North Carolina. The visitors were received with all due honors. A banquet was given them; wine and brandy were served. When, at last, the decanters and glasses were removed, the Governor of South Carolina rose to state his errand. A long and acrimonious debate followed. The Governor of South Carolina lost his temper. Rising once more to his feet, he said, "Sir, you have refused my just demand and offended the dignity of my office and my State. Unless you at once surrender the prisoner, I will return to my capital, call out the militia of the State, and take the fugitive by force of arms. Governor, what do you say?"

All eyes were turned on the Governor of North Carolina. The latter rose slowly to his feet, and beckoned to a servant who stood some distance away. His beckoning was firm and dignified, as became his position. He was

---

[1] From *Handy-Book of Literary Curiosities,* by William S. Walsh, p. 426. Copyright, 1892, 1925, by J. B. Lippincott Company. Philadelphia.

slow about answering, and again the Governor of South Carolina demanded, "What do you say?"

"I say, Governor, that it is a long time between drinks."

The reply restored good humor. Decanters and glasses were brought out again, and while the visitors remained, if any one attempted to refer to the diplomatic object of the visit he was cut short by the remark that it was a long time between drinks. When the visiting Governor was ready to return home he was escorted to the State line by the Governor of North Carolina, and they parted the best of friends.

The fugitive was never surrendered.

II. Its Currency [2]

. . . In one of the many simple dignified apartments of this building my companion and I were introduced to the gentleman who was governor of the State at the time of our visit. It seemed to me that he had a look both worn and apprehensive, and that, while we talked, he was waiting for something. I don't know how I gathered this impression, but it came to me definitely. After we had departed from the executive chamber I asked the gentleman who had taken us there if the governor was ill.

"No," he replied. "All our governors look like that after they have been in office for a while."

"From overwork?"

"No, from an overworked jest—the jest about 'what the Governor of North Carolina said to the Governor of South Carolina.' Every one who meets the governor thinks of that joke and believes confidently that no one has ever before thought of this application of it. So they all pull it on him. For the first few months our governors stand it pretty well, but after that they begin to break down. They feel they ought to smile, but they can't. They begin to dread meeting strangers, and to show it in their bearing. When in private life our governor had a very pleasant expression, but like all the others, he has acquired, in office, the expression of an iron dog."

Some Southern Politicalisms

Bourbon.—A Democrat of the straitest sect, a "fire-eater" (*q. v.*). Applied for the most part to Southern Democrats of the old school. This use of the word probably antedates the Civil War, but no instance of such

---

[2] From *American Adventures,* A Second Trip "Abroad at Home," by Julian Street, pp. 276–277. Copyright, 1917, by the Century Co. New York.

From *Political Americanisms,* A Glossary of Terms and Phrases Current at Different Periods, by Charles Ledyard Norton, pp. 20–21, 23–24, 27, 29, 43, 45, 62–63, 70, 86, 93, 104. Copyright, 1890, by Charles Ledyard Norton. New York and London: Longmans, Green & Co.

use has been found in print. Bourbon County, Ky., is popularly associated with this kind of Democrat, but we must look to the old Bourbon party in France—uncompromising adherents of political tradition—for its true paternity. "They learned nothing and forgot nothing." The *Nation* (New York) defines the term as properly applicable to any one who adheres to tradition of any kind.

Buncombe, Bunkum, etc.—Talking merely for talk's sake. The original employment of the word in this sense is ascribed to a member of Congress from Buncombe County, N. C., who explained that he was merely "talking for Buncombe," when his fellow-members could not comprehend why he was making a speech. The use of the term is now universal among English-speaking people.

Burgoo.—A Southern and Southwestern term akin in meaning to barbecue. . . . The feast, however, was furnished by hunters and fishermen: everything—fish, flesh, and fowl—being compounded into a vast stew. After this was disposed of, speeches were made, if the meeting was to have a political character. Dr. Edward Eggleston believes it to be peculiarly the property of the Blue Grass region in Kentucky. It is in current use among English-speaking sailors as a common name for thick oatmeal porridge (Clarke Russell's "Sailor's Language"). An Irish comic song of the last century runs:

> They put me to mess with some of the crew,
> They called it "ban-yan-day" and gave me burgoo.

A well-informed Irish scholar of New York claims it as Irish, derived possibly from *boirce,* an ox, a word now obsolete.

Carpet-Bagger.—After the Civil War, numbers of Northerners went South, some with honest intent, others with the hope of profit from irregular means. They were for the most part looked upon with suspicion by Southerners, and as they were generally Republican in politics and affiliated with the freedmen at the polls, the term came to have and still retains a political significance. It was unjustly applied in an opprobrious sense to many well-meaning men, but at the same time it admirably fitted the great horde of corrupt adventurers who at that time infested the South. Originally, however, a carpet-bagger was a "Wild-cat banker" in the West—a banker, that is, who had no local abiding place, and could not be found when wanted.

Chivalry.—"The Southern Chivalry" was a common phrase before and during the Civil War. It was claimed as a proud title by Southerners and their friends, but has always been heard and used at the North with a shade of derisive contempt.

F. F. Vs.—A satirical abbreviation of "First Families of Virginia," applied generally to what was known as the Southern aristocracy. The abbreviation was of Northern origin, and was in common use prior to the Civil War.

Fire-Eater.—A bitter Southern partisan. It came into use during the early anti-slavery days, and is of frequent occurrence in the journals of that time. It is equivalent to Bourbon (*q. v.*), but probably of earlier origin.

Ku Klux Klan.—A secret association of Southerners formed shortly after the war. It was otherwise known as "The Invisible Empire," as "The Knights of the White Camellia," "Of the Golden Circle," and a score of other names. It is said on good authority (see *Century Magazine,* July, 1884) to have been originally organized by a few young men for amusement during the period of stagnation after the close of hostilities. It soon, however, outgrew the design of its founders, branches being established all over the South, and its political influence became almost absolute. That it was directly and indirectly chargeable with outrages against settlers from the North, and against Negroes, is not to be denied, but it is also believed that it was largely instrumental in preserving order during a period when lawlessness was rife at the South. The name is an alliterative corruption of the Greek κυκλος (a circle), the "Klan" being added to enhance the strange jingle of consonants. The Southern Negroes, who lived in mortal terror of the "Klan," believed that the name was associated with certain audible "clucks," by means of which signals were supposed to be interchanged during midnight raids. The Ku Klux Klan was founded in June, 1866, and it was nominally disbanded by its presiding "Grand Wizard" in February, 1869. Ku Klux raids were common, however, for several years after that date [and the Klan was reincarnated in 1915].

Mason and Dixon's Line.—A boundary line surveyed in 1766 by two English surveyors, named Charles Mason and Jeremiah Dixon, to settle a dispute as to territory between Pennsylvania and Maryland. It follows the fortieth parallel of latitude, and was originally marked by milestones having on one side the armorial bearings of Penn, and on the other those of Lord Baltimore. "Hang your clothes to dry on Mason and Dixon's line" was a saying current with variations in the early days of the anti-slavery agitation.

Peculiar Institution.—In full, "the *peculiar* domestic *institution* of the South"—meaning Negro slavery. It is believed to have been first used in the South Carolina *Gazette,* which advised that all strangers from the North should be kept under surveillance because of "the dangers which at present threaten the peculiar domestic institutions of the South" (*circa* 1852). The phrase is found in the New York *Tribune* of October 19, 1854, and soon became part of the current speech of the time.

Reconstruction.—After the Civil War the question of restoring the lately seceded States to their former places in the Union became the leading civil problem of the time. The measures introduced into Congress were popularly known as Reconstruction Bills, and it was common at the time to hear or read such phrases as "a reconstructed rebel," "the reconstructed States," etc. The "reconstruction period" may be said to cover the decade immediately succeeding the war (1865–1875). At that time a late rebel was "reconstructed" or "unreconstructed" according as he had or had not taken the "Amnesty Oath," and the term in all possible combinations was of frequent occurrence in the journals of the day.

Solid South.—The unbroken political bond of the Southern States; the united white vote (Democratic) as opposed to the solid Republican vote of the Negroes. The phrase has been traced back only to the reconstruction period succeeding the Civil War (*circa* 1868). It is alleged, however, that it was in use prior to that time. Its popular modern usage is believed to have originated in the lobbies at Washington, whence it soon found its way into print.

The Southern Mammy

I [1]

THERE are certain other characters without mention of which no picture of the social life of the South would be complete: the old mammies and family servants about the house. These were important, and helped to make the life. The Mammy was the zealous, faithful, and efficient assistant of the mistress in all that pertained to the care and training of the children. Her authority was recognized in all that related to them directly or indirectly, second only to that of the Mistress and Master. She tended them, regulated them, disciplined them: having authority indeed in cases to administer correction; for her affection was undoubted. Her *régime* extended frequently through two generations, occasionally through three. From their infancy she was the careful and faithful nurse, the affection between her and the children she nursed being often more marked than that between her and her own offspring. She may have been harsh to the latter; she was never anything but tender with the others. Her authority was, in a measure, recognized through life, for her devotion was unquestionable. The young masters and mistresses were her "children" long after they had children of their own. When they parted from her or met with her again after separation, they embraced her with the same affection as when in childhood she "led them smiling into sleep." She was worthy of their affection. At all times she was their faithful ally and champion, excusing them, shielding them, petting them, aiding them, yet holding them up too to a certain high accountability. Her influence was always for good. She received, as she gave, an unqualified affection. If she was a slave, she at least was not a servant, but was an honored member of the family, universally beloved, universally cared for—"the Mammy."

---

[1] From *Social Life in Old Virginia before the War,* by Thomas Nelson Page, pp. 56–58. Copyright, 1897, by Charles Scribner's Sons. New York.

II [2]

VOICE: Wuh is a ole mammy?

SCIP: Ole mammy ain' nothin' but a ole ooman wid a han'k'ch'ef tied round she head. Dere's all kind er ole 'ceitful niggers gittin' dey self called ole mammy—more'n you can shake a stick at. Dere's all kind er white folks runnin' round lookin' for ole mammys wuh been in dey fam'ly an' tooken care on 'em ever since dey was born—an' afore. An' Lord! some on 'em carries on at sech a rate 'bout "my ole mammy" till it jes natu'ally makes a respectable nigger sick on he stomach.

TAD: Dat nigger say a ole mammy is a respected, lousy ole ooman dat knows her place.

SCIP: All dese white folks dat got ole mammys from 'way down south! Oh, Jesus!

TAD: Scip, you oughter hush you' mout'. Them de white folks—the ole istockacy from 'way down south. Oh, Lord!

SCIP: Cash money is de istockacy. It gees de right to a ole mammy. Let a cracker git a little money an' he edecate he chillun, an' dey always has ole mammys, ef dey git far enough from home.

Bacon and Greens and the Native Virginian

. . . WE APPROACH that strange variety of mankind which is compounded of bacon on the one hand and cabbage or greens on the other hand. In the wildest flight of the imagination, who would ever have supposed that the savage boar of the German forests and the ugly pot-herb of the sea-cliffs of England would come together in the same dish to produce the Virginian? So true it is that truth is stranger than fiction. I say, the Virginian; for while other people eat bacon and greens (and thereby become very decent people indeed), the only perfect bacon and the only perfect greens are found in Virginia; and hence it follows, as the night the day, not that the Virginians are the only perfect people, but that they are a peculiar and a very remarkable people.

In point of fact, the native Virginian is different from all other folks whatsoever, and the difference between him and other folks is precisely the difference between his bacon and greens and other folks' bacon and greens. How great this difference is, you are by no means aware. There is a theory in the books that the superiority of the Westphalia and Virginia

---

[2] From *Nigger to Nigger*, by E. C. L. Adams, pp. 116–117. Copyright, 1928, by Charles Scribner's Sons. New York and London.

From *The Old Virginia Gentleman and Other Sketches*, by George W. Bagby, edited and arranged by his daughter, Ellen M. Bagby, pp. 179–187. Copyright, 1943, by Ellen M. Bagby. Richmond, Virginia: The Dietz Press, Inc.

bacon over all other bacon is due to the fact that our hogs are not penned up, but are allowed the free range of the fields and forests.

Nevertheless, you are not to infer that the Virginian is composed of equal parts of bacon and greens, and that he is, in point of fact, a saphead and a glutton. Such a conclusion would not only be unkind, but illogical. Drinking train-oil does not necessarily turn a man into an Eskimo, nor does the eating of curry compel one to become a coolie and worship Vishnu or Confucius. Still, there *is* a connection between diet and the ethnological characteristics of the human races; and I take it for granted, first, that a Virginian could not be a Virginian without bacon and greens; and, second, that in every Virginian traces of bacon and traces of greens are distinctly perceptible. How else are you to account for the Virginia love of good eating, the Virginia indifference to dress and household economy, and the incurable simplicity of the Virginia head? It has been affirmed by certain speculative philosophers that the Virginian persists in exhausting his soil with tobacco, because the cabbage he eats is itself an exhauster of the soil, and that, because the hog is fond of wallowing in mud-puddles, therefore the Virginian takes naturally to politics.

I am not prepared to dispute these points, but I am tolerably certain that a few other things besides bacon and greens are required to make a true Virginian. He must, of course, begin on pot-liquor, and keep it up until he sheds his milk-teeth. He must have fried chicken, stewed chicken, broiled chicken, and chicken pie; old hare, butter-beans, new potatoes, squirrel, cymlings, snaps, barbecued shoat, roas'n ears, buttermilk, hoe-cake, ash-cake, pancake, fritters, pot-pie, tomatoes, sweet-potatoes, June apples, waffles, sweet milk, parsnips, artichokes, carrots, cracklin bread, hominy, bonny-clabber, scrambled eggs, gooba-peas, fried apples, pop-corn, persimmon beer, apple-bread, milk and peaches, mutton stew, dewberries, batter-cakes, mushmelons, hickory nuts, partridges, honey in the honey-comb, snappin'-turtle eggs, damson tarts, catfish, cider, hot light-bread, and cornfield peas all the time; but he must not intermit his bacon and greens.

He must butt heads with little Negroes, get the worst of it, and run crying to tell his ma about it. Wear white yarn socks with green toes and yarn gallowses. Get the cow-itch and live on milk and brimstone for a time. Make frog-houses over his feet in the wet sand, and find woodpecker nests. Meddle with the Negro men at hog-killing time, and be in every-body's way generally. Upset beehives, bring big wasp-nests into the house, and get stung over the eye by a yellow-jacket. Watch setting turkeys, and own a bench-leg fice and a speckled shoat. Wade in the branch, eat too many black-heart cherries, try to tame a catbird, call doodlebugs out of their holes—and keep on eating bacon and greens.

He must make partridge traps out of tobacco-sticks; set gums for "mollie-cotton-tails," mash-traps and deadfalls for minks; fish for minnows with a pin-hook, and carry his worms in a cymling; tie Juney-bugs to strings, and swing 'em under people's noses; stump his toe and have it tied up in a rag; wear patched breeches, stick thorns in his heel, and split his thumb open slicing "hoss-cakes" with a dog-knife sharpened, contrary to orders, on the grindstone.

At eight years old he must know how to spell *b a* ba, *b e* be, and so on; and be abused for not learning his multiplication table, for riding the sorrel mare at a strain to the horse-pound, and for snoring regularly at family prayers. Still he must continue to eat bacon and greens. About this time of life, or a little later, he must get his first suit of store clothes, and be sorely afflicted with freckles, stone-bruises, hang-nails, mumps, and warts, which last he delights in trimming with a Barlow-knife, obtained by dint of hard swapping. He must now go to old-field school, and carry his snack in a tin bucket, with a little bottle of molasses, stopped with a corn-cob stopper, and learn how to play marbles for good, and to tell stories about getting late to school—because he fell in the branch. Also to steal June apples and bury them, that they may ripen the sooner for his big sweetheart, who sits next to him. He must have a pop-gun, made of elder, with plenty of tow to "chaw" for wads; also plenty of india-rubber, and cut up his father's gum shoes, to make trap-balls, composed of equal parts of yarn and india-rubber. At the same time he must keep steadily eating bacon and greens. He must now learn to cut jackets, play hard-ball, choose partners for cat and chermany, be kept in, fight every other day, and be turned out for painting his face with pokeberry juice and grinning at the school-master.

After a good whipping from his father, who threatens to apprentice him to a carpenter, he enjoys his holiday by breaking colts and shooting field-larks in the daytime and by possum-hunting or listening to ghost-stories from the Negroes in the night.

Returning to school, he studies pretty well for a time; but the love of mischief is so strong within him that, for his life, he can't refrain from putting crooked pins on the benches where the little boys sit, and even in the school-master's chair. The result is a severe battle with the school-master and his permanent dismissal.

Thrown upon the world, he consoles himself with bacon and greens, makes love to a number of pretty girls, and pretends to play overseer. Failing at that, he tries to keep somebody's country store, but will close the doors whenever the weather is fine to "ketch chub" or play knucks.

Tired of store-keeping, he makes a trip, sometimes all the way on horse-back, to the Far South, to look after his father's lands. Plays "poker" on the Mississippi, gets cheated, gets "strapped"; returns home, eats bacon and greens, and determines to be a better man. But the first thing he knows he is off on a frolic in Richmond, where he loses all his money at faro, borrows enough to carry him home and buy a suit to go courting in.

He next gets religion at a camp-meeting, and loses it at a barbecue or fish-fry. Then he thinks he will teach school, or ride deputy sheriff, or write in the clerk's office, and actually begins to study law; on the strength of which he becomes engaged to be married and runs for the legislature. Gets beaten, gets drunk; reforms, all of a sudden; eats plenty of bacon and greens; marries—much to the satisfaction of his own, and greatly to the horror of his wife's family—and thus becomes a thorough-going Virginian.

His name, for the most part, is Jeems—Jeems Jimmison. Sometimes it is rather a homely name, as, for example, Larkin Peasley. Occasionally it is a pretty and even romantic name, as for instance, Conrad, or, to speak properly, Coonrod—Coonrod Higginbottom.

Being a married man, it is incumbent on Coonrod to settle down in life; and to this end he selects, with unerring accuracy, a piece of the poorest "hennest" grass-land in his native county. The traveler enters this domain through a rickety "big-gate," partly upheld by mighty posts, which remind him of the druidical remains of Stonehenge. The road leads apparently nowhere, through thickets of old-field pine and scrub-oak. Here and there is an opening in the woods, with a lonely, crank-sided tobacco-house in the midst, looking as if it were waiting resignedly for the end of the world to come. He hears the crows cawing, the woodpeckers tapping, and the log-cocks drumming, but sees no human being. Far away the roosters are crowing, and perhaps the scream of the peacock is heard. Slowly sailing, white-billed buzzards eye him from on high and make him nervous. Over the trees, he can't tell where exactly, come the voices of the ploughers— "Gee," "Wo-haw," "Git up." . . .

. . . The native Virginian, with a Powhatan pipe in his mouth and a silver spectacle-case in his hand, awaits you, and asks you to "light" and "come in" in the same breath. While a Negro boy is running up from the "new ground" to take your horse, a mulatto girl is flying, with a pail on her head, to the spring for fresh water and a jug of milk. Two or three little Negroes are chasing the chickens whose necks are soon to be twisted or chopped off with an axe at the wood-pile; ham is being sliced, eggs are frying in the frying-pan, a hoe-cake is on the fire, another head of cabbage is thrown into the pot, somebody is sheeting the bed upstairs, and (before your leggings are off) the case-bottle is at your elbow, and the native Virginian has taken possession of you, as if you were the Prodigal Son or the last number of the Richmond *Enquirer*.

*   *   *   *   *

We will not stop to describe his old weather-boarded, often wainscoted, house, with its queer old furniture and its old family portraits, which indicate for Jeems Jimmison or his wife a better origin than his name would lead you to expect. One peculiarity, though, must not go unmentioned. No matter how small this house is, it is never full. There is always room for one more in it; and, on special occasions, such as a wedding or a Christmas frolic, the number of feather beds, straw beds, shuck beds, pallets, and shakedowns which this old house produces is literally incredible. To feed and lodge, if need be, the entire state is not a point of honor with Coonrod, but a matter of course—no other idea ever entered his head. What is called "hospitality" by other folks is with him so much a part of his nature that he has no name for it (unless he keeps an "Entertainment"), and he never uses the word. How he managed, on a worn-out estate, to repeat, as it were, the miracle of the loaves and the fishes is a mystery which must be charged, I fear, to the "barbarism of slavery," for the art of feeding and lodging everybody seems already to be passing away.

Nor can we stop to describe the good wife of the native Virginian, with her check apron, key-basket, and knitting sheath—the pattern of domestic virtue; a matron, compared with whom the Roman matron, so famed, is as inferior as paganism is to the religion of our Savior; the hardest-worked slave on the estate—toiling, as she does, from year to year and year after year, for every human being, black and white, male and female, young and old, on the plantation, and yet a Christian gentlewoman, refined, tender, pure—almost too good and pure for earth. Think what she has done for Virginia! Think, too, that, under the new order of things, she also may be passing away. Of all the sad things which press upon us, in these troubled days, there is none so sad as this; no, not one. For without the Virginia matron there is no longer any Virginia; and without Virginia, what, to Virginians, is this world? Let us hasten away from the thought.

In like manner, we must hasten away from Larkin's sons and daughters; the former brave and wild—destined to run much their father's course; the latter unaccountably pretty, spirited, and cultivated. If it be a matter of wonder how Mrs. Coonrod manages to get up such marvelous breakfasts and dinners out of her dingy, dirt-floored kitchen, still more wonderful are the girls whom she raises in her "shakledy" old house, ten miles from anywhere, and entirely out of the world. We cannot spare the time to praise the boys and girls—the noble products of a social system which mankind has united to put down—for the native Virginian, as we now find him, is almost entirely alone, his family being scattered far and wide—all married and thriving, except one "black sheep," who has taken to drink, to fiddling, and to shrouding everybody in the neighborhood who dies.

In person, the old man is above the medium height, "dark-complected," spare built and generally long and lean in the lower limbs—and that's the reason he rides a horse so well. His voice is loud, owing to a habit he has of conversing familiarly with the hands in the field about a mile and a half off. His vision is wonderfully acute—partly from long practice with the rifle, and partly from the custom of inspecting his neighbors' vehicles at incredible distances. If he live on the side of the road, you will see him on Sunday eyeing a cloud of dust on the remote horizon. "Jeems," he will say to his son; "Jeems, ain't that old Peter Foster's carry-all?" "Yes," says Jeems, without a moment's hesitation; "and I'll be dad-shim'd if that off mule has been shod yit." . . . He says "thar" and "whar," "upstars" and "down in the parster," talks about "keepin' a appintment," not next year, but "another year," when he expects to raise "a fine chance uv curcumbers" in the "gearden," and a "tollibly far crap o' tubbarker." If he is a Tidewater man, he does not say "chance," but "charnce," and instead of saying the "har" of the head, he says "heyar." If he eats cornfield peas much, he becomes a virulent Virginian, and caps the climax of bad English by some such expression as "me and him was a-gwine a-fishin'." This he does, not for the lack of knowledge, but partly because he loves to talk as unlike a Yankee as possible, partly because he "don' keer" particularly about his language or anything else, except his political and religious opinions, and mainly because he is entirely satisfied (as, indeed, all Virginians are) that the English is spoken in its purity nowhere on this earth but in Virginia. "Tharfo' " he "kin affode" to talk "jest" as he "blame chooses."

His individuality, his independence and indifference to matters on which other people set great store, is shown, not only in his pronunciation, but in his dress—you see it in the tie of his cravat, the cut of his coat, the fit of his waistcoat, the set of his pantaloons, the roaching of his hair, and the color of his pocket-handkerchief—a red bandanna with yellow spots. But the whole character of the man is fully told only when you come to open his "secretary." There you will find his bonds, accounts, receipts, and even his will, jabbed into pigeon-holes or lying about loose in the midst of a museum of powder-horns, shot-gourds, turkey-yelpers, flints, screws, popcorn, old horseshoes and watermelon seed.

* * * * *

How such a man, with such a "secretary," can succeed in life, and how, above all, he and the like of him contrived to play the part which they have played in the history of this country, is something to be accounted for only on the bacon-and-greens principle.

II. LOCAL PRIDE AND PREJUDICE

There are many Souths. Somewhere within the vast region almost, every race and almost every type of civilization is represented.
—GERALD W. JOHNSON

No one should ever ask a man whether he was born in Virginia because, if he was, he certainly will tell you himself, and if he was not, he will be ashamed to admit it.—WILLIAM CABELL BRUCE

Cotton is more than a crop in the Delta. It is a form of mysticism. It is a religion and a way of life. Cotton is omnipresent here as a god is omnipresent. It is omnipotent as a god is omnipotent, giving life and taking life away.—DAVID L. COHN

1. LIMITED SOLIDARITIES

IN THE loose federation of states that make up the "Solid" and yet not-so-solid South, every Southerner looks upon himself first as a Virginian,

Carolinian, Kentuckian, Texan, and the rest. Moreover, since the South is a congeries of regions and regional lines cut across state lines, within his state the Southerner thinks in terms of Eastern Shore or Tobacco Country, Tidewater or Valley, Low Country or Up Country, Piedmont or Smokies, Bluegrass or Blue Ridge, Bluffs or Gulf Coast, Delta or Bayou Country, etc. Thus, however solidly aligned the agrarian South as a whole may have been against the industrial North, an inevitable clash developed between the Lowcountry idea of large slaveholding estates and the Upcountry idea of non-slaveholding farms. The difference between the two ideas was, to be sure, partly a class difference, as between planter aristocracy and upper middle class yeomanry. But regional differences also involve adjustments of people to a place, through a particular type of land use, resulting in a community of interest and a homogeneous society, as in the sea-island cotton and rice culture of the Low Country.

> . . . From the original site at Charleston, settlement extended up the Santee, Congaree, and Edisto rivers, and through the winding channels onto the coastal islands of South Carolina, until plantation and crossroad settlements merged into a region bound together by a community of interest among a homogeneous people. This represented an adjustment to fertile moist soil and warm climate favoring production of sea island cotton and rice along channels where ships of that time could enter to load these cargoes for outside markets. Upon such a base, a distinct set of cultural and economic interests arose, interests which later spread over the entire southeastern portion of the country.[1]

Limited solidarities also grew up about the capitals, seaports, and culture centers of the Old South, whose history, architecture, society, commerce, etc., both reflected and enriched the life of their regions.

In the rapid expansion of many Southern cities, especially in connection with the tourist trade, the local boosters have had a field day. Thus in Virginia during the 1920's automobile license plates flaunted such slogans as "Richmond and Proud of It," "Norfolk Where Prosperity Is a Habit," "Boost Bumpass."[2] Regional culture also joins hands with utility in the "annual festivals in honor of the chief agricultural products, flowers, or animals of various Southern communities."[3]

For one week each year during the Cotton Carnival Memphis takes on some of the aspects of New Orleans during Mardi Gras, as Mardi Gras itself has undergone the Chamber of Commerce influence. Back of the Cotton Capital's Cotton Carnival is the "Chamber of Commerce's determination to fight the bustling Texas towns and her other Southern rivals for any new business that might be headed South."[4]

---

[1] National Resources Committee, *Regional Factors in National Planning and Development* (Washington, 1935), p. 140.

[2] Virginius Dabney, "Virginia," *The American Mercury,* Vol. IX (November, 1926), No. 35, p. 351.

[3] See p. 43 below.

[4] Harold R. Martin, "The Cities of America: Memphis," *The Saturday Evening Post,* Vol. 219 (November 16, 1946), No. 20, p. 56.

2. Local Color and Flavor

Even after the center of rice production moved westward, to Louisiana, Arkansas, and Texas, the rice culture of the Low Country left behind it unmistakable traces in the banks, canals, and irrigation systems along the tidal rivers; in the "homes, the histories, the manners and the morals of the Rice Planter [which] have filled Charleston with much of her character, her romance, and her beauty"; and, above all, in the ritual of rice on the tables and the palates of Charlestonians. Although other Southern staples —cotton, tobacco, sugar, oranges, lumber, naval stores—have given rise to their own folkways and, in some cases, folklore, "there was nothing in the other North American colonies," according to Samuel G. Stoney, "that quite approached the status of rice in and around Charleston." [5]

Of all regional and ethnic influences in the South none is more subtly effective and pervasive than those of food and diet. Harnett Kane tells of the Yankee husband who was watching his Delta wife in the kitchen, as she tried to prepare a New England boiled dinner which he dimly remembered from his boyhood. "She cut the vegetables, she washed them, she put them in the pot; and then she added tomatoes, bayleaf, thyme, onions, and five or six other items without which she was sure no dish was complete. The husband, grinning, told her: 'Bébé, no matter what you put on that stove, it's going to come out French—your own kind of French.'" [6]

3. Local Brags and Jests

Perhaps the supreme example of the occult effect of food on the "ethnological characteristics" of the Southerner is George W. Bagby's Virginian, who "could not be a Virginian without bacon and greens" and whose incomparable perfection follows from the perfection of Virginia bacon and greens as the night follows the day. At this point (in some imaginary bragging contest) the Kentuckian rises to proclaim the superiority of Kentucky over Virginia ham, and the Texan to challenge all comers to surpass the quantity, if not the quality, of Texas hogs and Texas steers. Thereupon the Kentuckian counters with some wild tale of the Bunyanesque rooting prowess of the mountain hog. Or if the Kentuckian should give his recipe for mint juleps, the Virginian is moved to tell how an old Tidewater Virginian went to Kentucky to pay a visit to his son, and on the way, in return for a night's lodging "mixed a mint julep for his host, and showed him how to drink it by burying his face in the fragrant mint." On the way back home from Kentucky several months later, stopping to inquire of the old Negro servant as to his master's health he was grieved to learn of the latter's death. It seems that some young city Virginian had told him that in town they drink juleps with straws, and the folks all say that's what killed him—drinking with straws.[7]

---

[5] Samuel G. Stoney, *Charleston: Azaleas and Old Bricks* (Boston, 1937), p. 12.
[6] *Deep Delta Country* (New York, 1944), p. 77.
[7] James J. McDonald, *Life in Old Virginia* (Norfolk, 1907), pp. 303–304.

Finally, travel reminds the Virginian of the dirt roads of Southside Virginia "washed to pieces by every thunder-shower" so that one man, "after trying in vain to keep those on his farm in a permanently good condition . . . concluded that the best plan was to make a road for himself as often as he required one." And yet it was with these "unsightly gullies" in the eroded hillsides that Governor Henry A. Wise, "in his extravagant State pride, said he would no more quarrel than he would with the wrinkles on his old mother's brow."[8]

B. A. B.

Local Cracks and Slams

NORTH CAROLINA is a valley of humility between two mountains of conceit.[1]

South Carolina is a mountain of conceit between two vales of depression.[2]

In Charleston they say: "The Ashley and the Cooper Rivers run together to form the Atlantic Ocean."[3]

"Atlanta," they say down in Savannah, "has the nerve of a government mule. If it could suck as hard as it can blow, it could bring the ocean to it and become a seaport."[4]

"If a man's from Texas, he'll tell you. If he's not, why embarrass him by asking?"[5]

They have a saying in Arkansas that the little frogs in the swamps pipe in their shrill voices: "Quinine, quinine, quinine!" while the big bullfrog with his deep bass voice chimes in, "Double the dose! Double the dose!"[6]

---

[8] William Cabell Bruce, *Below the James* (Boston and New York, 1918), p. 12.

---

[1] From *I Came Out of the Eighteenth Century,* by John Andrew Rice, p. 178. Copyright, 1942, by Harper & Brothers. New York and London.

[2] Louise Jones DuBose and Chapman J. Milling, Columbia, South Carolina.

[3] *Ibid.*

[4] From *Georgia: Unfinished State,* by Hal Steed, p. 165. Copyright, 1942, by Hal Steed. New York: Alfred A. Knopf.

[5] From *Inside U. S. A.,* by John Gunther, p. 817. Copyright, 1946, 1947, by the Curtis Publishing Co. New York and London: Harper & Brothers.

[6] From *North America:* Its People and the Resources, Development, and Prospects of the Continent as the Home of Man, by J. Russell Smith and M. Ogden Phillips, p. 300. Copyright, 1925, 1940, by Harcourt, Brace & Company, Inc. New York.

Maryland Free State

MARYLAND has had half a dozen or more nicknames since colonial times, but only *Old Line State* and *Terrapin State* have any remaining vitality today. Both are under formidable competition from *Maryland Free State,* which was invented in 1923 by Hamilton Owens, then editor of the Baltimore *Evening Sun.* The story is thus told in *"The Sunpapers* of Baltimore": [1]

Some time in 1923, at the height of the debate over Prohibition, Congressman William D. Upshaw, of Georgia, a fierce dry, denounced Maryland as a traitor to the Union because it had refused (largely through the urgings of the *Evening Sun*) to pass a State enforcement act. Mr. Owens thereupon wrote a mock-serious editorial headed *"The Maryland Free State,"* arguing that Maryland should really secede from the Union and go it alone. The irony in this editorial was somewhat finely spun, and on second thought Mr. Owens decided not to print it, but the idea embodied in the title stuck in his mind, and in a little while he began to use it in other editorials. It caught on quickly, and the *Maryland Free State* is now heard of almost as often as Maryland.

It was first used in the *Evening Sun* on April 4, 1923, in the headline over a brief extract from a "Geographical Compilation for the Use of Schools," published in Baltimore in 1806. The late Albert C. Ritchie, then Governor of Maryland, adopted it with delight, and it spread over the country during his campaign for the Democratic presidential nomination in 1924. It appealed greatly to Marylanders, for it was a convenient crystallization of a body of ideas that had been traditional in their State since colonial days, and had been revived and revivified by the *Evening Sun* after its establishment in 1910. These ideas were all favorable to personal liberty, and had been exemplified in a radical and even somewhat scandalous manner in Articles 6 and 44 of the State Declaration of Rights, adopted September 18, 1867, as follows:

That . . . whenever the ends of government are perverted, and public liberty manifestly endangered, and all other means of redress are ineffectual, the people may, and of right ought reform the old or establish a new government; the doctrine of non-resistance against arbitrary power and oppression is absurd, slavish and destructive of the good and happiness of mankind.

That the provision of the Constitution of the United States and of this State apply as well in time of war as in time of peace, and any departure therefrom, or violation thereof, under the plea of necessity, or any other plea, is subversive of good government, and tends to anarchy and despotism.

From *Supplement II: The American Language,* An Inquiry into the Development of English in the United States, by H. L. Mencken, pp. 602–603. Copyright, 1948, by Alfred A. Knopf, Inc. New York.

[1] By Gerald W. Johnson, Frank R. Kent, H. L. Mencken and Hamilton Owens: New York, 1937, p. 389.—H. L. M.

Once he had launched the *Maryland Free State* Mr. Owens used it assiduously and it was taken up by other editors throughout the nation, and soon spread the idea that Maryland was a sanctuary from the oppressive legislation and official usurpation that beset the country in general and most of the other States in particular. This idea was given powerful reinforcement in 1938, when President Franklin D. Roosevelt came into the State in an effort to purge the United States Senate of one of the Maryland Senators, Millard E. Tydings, then an active opponent of the New Deal. In a speech made at Denton, Md., on September 5 Roosevelt sought to disarm the Marylanders by describing "the *Free State of Maryland*" as "proud of itself and conscious of itself," but then proceeded to argue for submission to "the flag, the Constitution and the President." The result was that Tydings was reelected by an overwhelming majority.

A Virginian

THERE was once upon a time a lady who was a Virginian. I know about her because she was an ancestor of mine. She was born in Virginia, but when she was a small child—a child of only seven or eight—her parents moved across the mountains to Kentucky, and for the rest of her life she lived in Kentucky. She married there and raised crops of children and grandchildren. She never went back to Virginia, excepting for short visits; but to the day of her death she always referred to Virginia as "home," and if some stranger, meeting her on her travels, asked her where she hailed from the invariable reply was: "I'm a Virginian—at present stopping out in Kentucky."

'Ginia

FAMILY pride followed the Negro wherever he went and even now in the Southern States the Negroes boast their Virginia descent and brag so much about Virginia and Virginians that their own children get tired and rebuke them. Witness the following anecdote furnished me by a lady of Mississippi. "Uncle" Isaac bragged about his Virginia origin so often and so loudly that his disgusted grandson could stand it no longer.

"Grandpar, I sick o' hearing 'bout 'Ginia. 'Ginia family, 'Ginia dis and 'Ginia dat, day and night, nuthin' but 'Ginia, 'Ginia. Dey tell me lan' so po'

From *Some United States,* A Series of Stops in Various Parts of This Nation with One Excursion across the Line, by Irvin S. Cobb, pp. 256–257. Copyright, 1926, by George H. Doran Company. New York.

From "The Old Virginia Negro," in *The Old Virginia Gentleman and Other Sketches,* by George W. Bagby, edited and arranged by his daughter, Ellen M. Bagby, pp. 275–276. Copyright, 1943, by Ellen M. Bagby. Richmond, Virginia: The Dietz Press, Inc.

in 'Ginia dat dey feed nigger on 'simmon seed. I don' wan' live in no sich country, 'mong no sich people. I wouldn' give dis piece o' cane [sugar cane that he was munching] for all de 'Ginians dat ever fotch breath from Gin'l Washintun and Wharas down to Gin'l Lee and Amen."

Virginia Mountaineer Traits

. . . WE SAW a solitary log-cabin, for example, standing upon the summit of a mountain, whereupon he exclaimed, "That man has a passion for dogs." "Why so?" I inquired. "Because he owns no less than nine, three to keep off the wolves, three to keep off the bears, and three to pump up water by a patent pump." We saw another cabin situated in a hollow, between two very steep but partly cultivated mountains, and this called forth the following remark: "That's a very fortunate man; for, when his pumpkins are ripe and his potatoes dug, all he has to do is to start them and they roll right down into his kitchen." I questioned him with regard to the occupant of a particularly dilapidated cabin, and he replied, "That man is the victim of mountain wine." "What kind of a beverage is that?" I continued. "It's made of Jamestown-weed and *Fish-berries,* and is the fashionable liquor of this region, when people haven't any money and can't get trusted." We met a pedestrian on the road, whose clothes were very much worn and torn, and my friend informed me that he was a fair specimen of the mountaineers of Hampshire county. "But why don't they dress more comfortably?" "Oh, they can't help it," he replied; "they live upon persimmons, and damage their clothes by climbing."

A Kentucky Breakfast

THIS potation, to be thoroughly enjoyed, should be prepared in the following manner:

Supply each guest with a glass containing about one-half inch of water and one-quarter teaspoonful of sugar, and a spoon.

All should sit comfortably and stir the sugar until it is thoroughly dis-

---

From *Adventures in The Wilds of The United States and British Provinces,* by Charles Lanman, Vol. I, p. 478. Philadelphia: John W. Moore. 1856.

By Senator Millard Tydings. From *Eat, Drink & Be Merry in Maryland,* An Anthology from a Great Tradition, compiled by Frederick Philip Stieff, pp. 299–300. Copyright, 1932, by Frederick Philip Stieff. New York: G. P. Putnam's Sons.

Senator Tydings of Maryland has represented his state in a truly masterful manner. Although one of the younger members of the Senate, he has made his presence felt on all matters of importance. That he has ever been able to keep an even balance in times of turbulence probably is due to a large extent to a well defined sense of humor appropriately applied.—F. P. S.

solved. The host should tell the following story in a low voice while the sugar is being stirred:

"Have you gentlemen ever participated at a Kentucky breakfast?"

The answer is likely to be in the negative. Then some guest will probably ask:

"What is a Kentucky breakfast?"

At this point the sugar is completely dissolved. The host passes around a bottle of Bourbon and each person pours into his glass, containing the dissolved sugar, such amount as suits his inclination. This is stirred for a while, during which time the host replies:

"A Kentucky breakfast is a big beefsteak, a quart of Bourbon and a houn' dawg."

One of the guests will then ask:

"What is the dog for?"

The host then replies:

"He eats the beefsteak."

Ice water is then passed around in a silver pitcher to dilute the drink to meet the requirements of the discriminating taste of each. A part of the Kentucky breakfast is then consumed.

(In order to extract the nth power of enjoyment from this receipt, when stirring the sugar and water, each should sit on the very edge of his chair or sofa, rest his arms on his knees with a slightly forward posture. Unless this is done the drink will taste just a little less good.)

Kentucky vs. Tennessee

AT THE battle of New Orleans, in the War of 1812, bands of these rugged [Kentucky] frontiersmen, wearing coonskin caps, poured into General Jackson's ranks, without guns. "Old Hickory" said to them, "Boys, where are your guns?" "Got none," came the response. "Then what are you going to do?" There was a pause, and finally one of them answered: "I'll tell you what we'll do, Gin'ral, we'll foller them there Tennesseeans into battle, and ever' time one falls we'll jist inherit his gun."

Tennessee—"The Heart of the Western Hemisphere"

TENNESSEE lies on the happiest lines of latitude and longitude which girdle the globe; she lies on the dividing line between the two great agricultural

From *The Kentucky Highlander from a Native Mountaineer's Viewpoint*, by Josiah Henry Combs, p. 21. Lexington, Kentucky: J. L. Richardson & Co. 1913.

Extract from "Speech of Governor Taylor at St. Louis, Missouri, on January 8, 1898, before 'The St. Louis Tennessee Society.'"
From *Echoes, Centennial and other Notable Speeches, Lectures, and Stories*, by

regions of the world. On the south are the tropical fruits and flowers and cotton-fields, where labor toils and sings and tosses the snowy bales by the million into the lap of commerce. On the north are the fruits and cereals of the north temperate zone, where industry smiles and pours its streams of amber and gold into the garners of nations. But Tennessee combines them both. The pecans of the South fall among the hickorynuts of the North on her soil. The magnolia blooms in the same grove where the Northern apple ripens, and the Georgia plum woos the blushing peach of Delaware. Corn and cotton, blue-grass and wheat, all grow in adjoining fields, while the mockingbird and the snowbird sing and chatter together on bough and bush away down in Tennessee.

I sometimes think that when the Lord God had banished the first guilty pair from Paradise, and when the flaming sword of his angel had mounted guard over the barred portal, loath to destroy its glories and its beauties, he transferred them all to Tennessee. And when civilization first peeped over the Alleghanies and looked down upon the gorgeous landscape below, I think she shouted back to the advancing hosts, Lo, this is Paradise regained! Is it any wonder, then, that this beauty-spot on the face of the earth long ago became the shrine of heroes and statesmen? Is it any wonder that the star of destiny guided the peerless Jackson here to live and die?

In the Mountains

. . . IF THE pedestrian tries a short-cut he will learn what the natives mean when they say: "Goin' up, you can might' nigh stand up straight and bite the ground; goin' down, a man wants hobnails in the seat of his pants."

*   *   *   *   *

As our territory was sparsely occupied, there were none of those "perpendicular farms" so noticeable in older settlements near the river valleys, where men plow fields as steep as their own house roofs and till with the hoe many an acre that is steeper still. John Fox tells of a Kentucky farmer who fell out of his own cornfield and broke his neck. I have seen fields in Carolina where this might occur, as where a forty-five degree slope is tilled to the brink of a precipice. A woman told me: "I've hoed corn many a time on my knees—yes, I have"; and another: "Many's the hill o' corn I've propped up with a rock to keep it from fallin' down-hill."

*   *   *   *   *

Governor Robt. L. Taylor, pp. 103–104. Copyright, 1889, by S. B. Williamson & Co. Nashville, Tennessee.

From *Our Southern Highlanders*, by Horace Kephart, pp. 21, 35, 36. Copyright, 1913, by Outing Publishing Company. New York.

. . . Another neighbor would say, "This is good, strong land, or it wouldn't hold up all the rocks there is around hyur."

The Origin of "Tar Heels"

. . . SOME years ago I made an investigation as to the origin of the term "Tar Heels" as applied to North Carolinians, and I found that the term had been in general use long prior to the Civil War. My investigation convinced me that the expression was applied to North Carolinians because of the fact that tar, pitch, and turpentine in the early days of the state were among the chief articles of export from North Carolina. It will be found upon examination of the old geographies published prior to the Civil War that nearly all of them in listing the exports of the various states mentioned "tar, pitch, and turpentine" as being the chief export from this state. These articles were in great demand during the days of wooden sailing ships and were known and still are known as "naval stores."

Prior to and during the first part of the Civil War the term Tar Heel was used in a rather derogatory sense somewhat as the term "cracker" is applied to certain citizens of Georgia and Florida, and "hillbillies" is applied to some of the residents of our southern mountains.

Any one who has ever seen a tar kiln in operation or been around a turpentine distillery will realize what a sticky and dirty work it is. Many of the workers were accustomed to go barefooted so as to protect their shoes from accumulation of tar and pitch; they did not seem to mind so much the accumulation on their bare feet.

It is an interesting fact, however, that this term which was originally considered uncomplimentary and somewhat derogatory has become one of pride, and the origin of this change is of real historic interest. While making my investigation I had an occasion to consult my good friend, Will Graham, of Lincoln County, then State Commissioner of Agriculture. He called my attention to a speech which his father, the late Major W. A. Graham, had made in Oklahoma many years previous when addressing a meeting of the State Commissioners of Agriculture, he at the time being the Commissioner of Agriculture for North Carolina. After alluding to certain backward conditions in North Carolina in this speech, Major W. A. Graham, who had himself been a Confederate soldier, said:

"While the illiteracy is to be regretted, what good is accomplished by the insistent publication to the world? Illiteracy is generally considered ignorance; this is a great mistake. Few stop to consider the matter, but adopt the common verdict. The characters of our people are injured by this course now as was the case in former times. The North Carolina Con-

By Haywood Parker, Asheville, North Carolina.

From *Down Home,* by Carl Goerch, pp. 97–100. Raleigh, North Carolina: Edwards & Broughton Company. 1943.

federate soldier, on account of this publicity, at the beginning of the war did not have the respect of his fellows, but was the object of much ridicule, and all kinds of ignorant expressions were attributed to him, as 'the seventh regiment spider wagon'; 'the sixth regimint hoss-pital'; 'you got any tobacco?' 'No, but I've got some of the best rosam [rosin] you ever chawed.' Such conduct and expressions could be greatly multiplied if desired. In 1862 'tar-heel' was introduced as a term of ridicule. The boys replied in different styles, 'Got any tar?' 'No, Jeff Davis has bought it all.' 'What for?' 'To put on you fellows' heels to make you stick.' The fourth Texas had lost its flag at Sharpsburg. Passing the sixth North Carolina a few days afterwards they called out, 'Tar heel,' and the reply was, 'If you had had some tar on your heels, you would have brought your flag back from Sharpsburg.'

"It was recognized as a term of affront until 1864. Governor Vance, when he visited the army of Northern Virginia, in opening his speech, said: 'I do not know what to call you fellows. I cannot say fellow soldiers, because I am not a soldier, nor fellow citizens, because we do not live in this state; so I have concluded to call you fellows Tar-heels.' There was a slight pause before the applause came and from that time 'Tar-heel' has been honored as an epithet worthy to be offered to a gallant North Carolina soldier."

Confederate Nicknames for Southerners

THE WAR originated a great many new phrases in the imaginative South— far more, if they were all recorded, than in the North. "Cousin Sal" is pretty generally lamented throughout the South as the deceased and only daughter of our very worthy and revered "Uncle Sam"—the same having been begotten by him in the bonds of lawful wedlock with "Aunty Extension." You may hear the word "Confederate" singularly used. For instance, when a Texan wishes to express the strongest possible approval of some sentiment, he will exclaim, "You're mighty Confederate!" The Rebels had their "bluebacks" for money; but in Texas, where they have always clung tenaciously to their silver, they made slow progress, and were received with much reluctance. $100 bills were there called "Williams," and $50 bills "Blue Williams." Nevertheless, a Texan once told me, with a fierce glitter of satisfaction in his eye, that "he had $100,000 in 'Williams' laid up against that day, which was certain to come, when he could exchange it, dollar with dollar, for greenbacks." The poor fellow! I should much prefer a draft for ten cents on the Old Lady of California

From "South-Western Slang," by Socrates Hyacinth, *The Overland Monthly*, Vol. III (August, 1869), No. 2, pp. 125–131. Entered . . . 1869, by John H. Carmany. San Francisco: A. Roman & Company.

street. Neither did greenbacks succeed well at first in invading the State. In March, 1868, they had gotten no farther west than Marshall, and everywhere west of that, when a man named a price, he meant "spizerinctums" (corrupted from specie).

The fierce military spirit of the South is shown in the scorn and contempt which they heaped on men who refused to go out to battle. In Texas they were called, with a play on the word *women* (in the South often pronounced *weemen*), and a hint at their former gasconade as to what "we" could do—"we-men." Some boasted that one Southerner could "whale" ten Yankees. Lieutenant J. W. Boothe, of the Seventh Texas Battalion, I am told, first applied to this sort of phrase "ten-strikers," which became immensely popular in that State. In the cis-Mississippi States they were generally dubbed "bomb-proofs."

A story is related of a brigade of North Carolinians, who, in one of the great battles (Chancellorsville, if I remember correctly) failed to hold a certain hill, and were laughed at by the Mississippians for having forgotten to tar their heels that morning. Hence originated their cant name, "Tar-heels."

For a very obvious reason, the South Carolinians are called "Rice-birds." Wherever in the South you see a man take boiled rice on his plate and eat it heartily without condiments, you may know he is a South Carolinian as infallibly as you may that a man is plebian-bred when he picks his teeth in the horse-car without holding his hand before his mouth. On the other hand, when you see a man, at the traditional hour sacred in New England to mince-pie, get a cold, boiled sweet potato a little smaller than his calf, quarter it length-ways, take a quarter in one hand, and a piece of cane-brake cheese in the other, and eat them by the light of a pine fire, you may be certain he is a North Carolinian.

A Georgian is popularly known in the South as a "Gouber-grabbler" ["gouber" for *gopher*, pea-nut—a nut which is exceedingly abundant in that State].

For no particular reason that I am aware of, a Virginian is styled a "Clover-eater."

The cant designation in the Rebel army for a man of Arkansas was "Josh." This is said to have originated in a jocular attempt to compare Arkansas, Texas, and part of Louisiana to the two tribes and a half who had their possessions beyond Jordan, but went over with Joshua to assist the remaining tribes. Just before the battle of Murfreesboro' (the story hath it) the Tennesseans, seeing a regiment from Arkansas approach, cried out, a little confused in their Biblical recollections: "Here come the tribes of Joshua, to fight with their brethren!"

For the Texan soubriquet "Chub" I know of no explanation, unless it be found in the size of the Eastern Texans. It is related of the Fifteenth Texas Infantry, for instance, that at the mustering-in no member was of a lighter weight than a hundred and eighty pounds, while the large number made the scale-beam kick at two hundred.

On account of the great number of gophers in that State, and the former use of their skins for money, a Floridian is called a "Gopher."

Names in the Red Hills

FROM generation to generation we have had favorite names among our kinfolks. We have had Washingtons and Lafayettes (we put the accent on the *fay*) and there have been many with such Southern combinations as Jim Ed and Stephen John. We have had many with Carter for a Christian name, for like thousands of Southerners we were related originally to those Carters who settled in early Virginia. Sometimes I have wondered about those Carters—they must have married everyone in sight. We have liked the good sassafras sound of our Southern names—their American sound; names like ours have never been heard of beyond the United States. We have called boys Reece and Forrest and Boone, and girls Narcissa and Clarissa and Temperance and Unity and Jude. Of late we have been naming ourselves after one another, and nowadays only Southerners could understand the maze—such combinations as Willis O'Dell Bowen, Willis Bowen, Willis Chapman, Otis Chapman, Otis Bowen, Otis O'Dell Bowen, William Clayton Bowen, Katie Taylor Clayton, Taylor O'Dell, O'Dell Clayton, Alfred Taylor O'Dell, Wade Taylor O'Dell, Arie Parsons O'Dell, Bowen Parsons, Boone Bowen, Boone Moss, Hattie Boone Robertson, Arretha Robertson Bowen, Genie Moss Bowen, Mary Bowen Robertson, Artemissa Clayton Robertson, Frances Robertson O'Dell. On and on— the wheels in the wheel. . . .

Local Festivals and Totems

OF TWENTIETH-CENTURY origin were the annual festivals in honor of the chief agricultural products, flowers, or animals of various Southern communities. Virginia had its Apple Blossom Festival at Winchester, its Tobacco Festival at South Boston, and a Dogwood Festival at Bristol. North Carolina held the Tulip Festival at Washington, Dahlia Show at Durham, Cotton Festival at Gastonia, and a Rhododendron Festival at Asheville. Charleston gave an Azalea Festival. Kentucky had its Strawberry Producers Revel at Paducah, Strawberry Carnival at Beaver Dam and a Tobacco Festival at Lexington. Tennessee promoted the Dogwood Festival at Knoxville, Strawberry Festival at Humboldt, Rhododendron Festival at Gatlinburg, and a Cotton Carnival at Memphis. Not to be

From *Red Hills and Cotton,* An Upcountry Memory, by Ben Robertson, pp. 53–54. Copyright, 1942, by Ben Robertson. New York: Alfred A. Knopf.

From *The South Old and New,* A History, 1820–1947, by Francis Butler Simkins, p. 301. Copyright, 1947, by Alfred A. Knopf, Inc. New York.

outdone, Alabama featured an Azalea Trail at Mobile, a Flower Show at Tuscaloosa, a Dogwood Trail at Birmingham, and a Strawberry Festival at Cullman. In Louisiana and Texas, a background of French-Catholic and Mexican-Catholic culture gave the flower and crop festivals a variety not possible in states of purely Anglo-Saxon and Protestant background. Louisiana presented a Spring Fiesta at New Orleans, an Azalea Tour at Lafayette, a Strawberry Festival at Hammond, a Cotton Carnival at Tallulah, a Rice Carnival at Crowley, and a Sugar Festival and Carnival of Flowers at New Iberia. Texas gave a Citrus Fiesta at Mission, an Oleander Fete at Galveston, a Rose Festival at Tyler, and a Forest Festival at Lufkin.

The utilitarian triumphed over the esthetic in the Potato Tour at Robertsdale, Alabama; in the Blessing of the Berries at Parksville, Kentucky; in the Onion Festival at Raymondville in the Rio Grande Valley. There was even a Turkey Trot at Cuero, Texas, and an appropriately named "Yamboree" in honor of the sweet potato of Gilmer in the same state; also there was Mule Day at Columbia, Tennessee, an all-day affair for the "orneriest and workingest work-critter living." [1]

Henry W. Grady's Parable of the Pickens County Funeral

I ATTENDED a funeral once in Pickens county in my State. A funeral is not usually a cheerful object to me unless I could select the subject. I think I could, perhaps, without going a hundred miles from here, find the material for one or two cheerful funerals. Still, this funeral was peculiarly sad. It was a poor "one gallus" fellow, whose breeches struck him under the armpits and hit him at the other end about the knee. . . . They buried him in the midst of a marble quarry: they cut through solid marble to make his grave: and yet a little tombstone they put above him was from Vermont. They buried him in the heart of a pine forest, and yet the pine coffin was imported from Cincinnati. They buried him within the touch of an iron mine, and yet the nails in his coffin and the iron in the shovel that dug his grave were imported from Pittsburgh. They buried him by the side of the best sheep-grazing country on the earth, and yet the wool in the coffin bands and the coffin bands themselves were brought from the North.

---

[1] American Guide Series, *Tennessee,* p. 133.—F. B. S.

From *Henry W. Grady,* Spokesman of the New South, by Raymond B. Nixon, p. 10. Copyright, 1943, by Alfred A. Knopf, Inc. New York.

His famous story of the "Pickens County Funeral," for example, probably did more to call attention to the potential wealth of the South than any set of cold facts he could have produced. Grady used the story in numerous speeches and articles, the best version in print being that taken down by a shorthand reporter at Boston in 1889.—R. B. N.

The South didn't furnish a thing on earth for that funeral but the corpse and the hole in the ground. There they put him away and the clods rattled down on his coffin, and they buried him in a New York coat and a Boston pair of shoes and a pair of breeches from Chicago and a shirt from Cincinnati, leaving him nothing to carry into the next world with him to remind him of the country in which he lived, and for which he fought for four years, but the chill of blood in his veins and the marrow in his bones.

Georgia Marriage Ceremony

BY THE authority vested in me as an officer of the State of Georgia, which is sometimes called the Empire State of the South; by the fields of cotton that spread out in snowy whiteness around us; by the howl of coon dogs, and the gourd vine, whose clinging tendrils will shade the entrance to your humble dwelling place; by the red and luscious heart of the watermelon, whose sweetness fills the heart with joy; by the heavens and earth, in the presence of these witnesses, I pronounce you man and wife.

Florida Hurricane Lore

. . . THE oral tradition of the [Florida] region is filled with tales of the hurricanes' fabulous feats of destruction. As the Negro bean-pickers in the 'Glades say about the big blow of '28, "It blowed so hard it blowed a well up out of the ground, blowed a crooked road straight, and scattered the days of the week so bad that Sunday didn't get around till late Tuesday mornin'." Another delightfully Negroid anecdote has it: "The hurricane met the storm in West Palm Beach, and they ate breakfast together. Then the hurricane said to the storm, 'Let's breeze on down to Miami and shake that thing!' "

There is scarcely a place in the whole region that does not have its true local legends about boats blown far inland and automobiles blown out to sea; boards driven through trees; railway tracks stood on edge like a picket

---

From *The Southern Country Editor*, by Thomas D. Clark, p. 131. Copyright, 1948, by the Bobbs-Merrill Company. Indianapolis and New York.

Bragging about the South often resulted in humorous bits. [Southern] Editors were always conscious that the South was their first love, and they often wrote of the region with the same glowing warmth they bragged about new brides and babies. Perhaps no Southerner put his feeling more eloquently in words than an effusive justice of the peace in Sandersville, Georgia. According to the Choctaw (Mississippi) *Plaindealer*, he concluded a marriage ceremony thus.—T. D. C.

From *Palmetto Country*, by Stetson Kennedy, pp. 34–35, 42. Copyright, 1942, by Stetson Kennedy. In *American Folkways*, edited by Erskine Caldwell. Duell, Sloan & Pearce, Inc. New York.

fence; two-ton bridges lifted from their moorings; cows, horses, and pigs carried away on the wings of the wind, never to be heard of again; and houses lifted from their foundations to be turned in mid-air and set down intact again on the same foundations, but facing the opposite way.

One story tells of an incident in the hurricane of 1906, when Miami was a frontier settlement. Judge Robert R. Taylor was reputedly playing pool in Hill's Place, when the sky suddenly took on a pinkish glow. The terrified Negro population thought Judgment Day was at hand. When the hurricane struck, Judge Taylor ran for his office in the Fussell Building. Across the hall he found Judge George A. Worley down on his knees praying. After listening apprehensively for a few minutes to Judge Worley's praying and the hurricane's howling, Judge Taylor cried, "Get up from there, George—you ain't doin' a damn bit of good! Let me try it!"

* * * * *

. . . It was the day before Christmas, and God was on his way to Palatka. It happened the Devil was travelin' the same road, and when he seen God comin' he jumped behind a stump.—He wanted to catch God "Christmas gift" so God would have to give him a present. God was sorta busy in his mind, countin' over how many new angels he had to buy presents for, so he wasn't payin' no attention to stumps. When God passed by, the Devil jumped out and hollered "Christmas gift!"

"You done caught me for once," God said, lookin' back over his shoulder. "Take the East Coast."—And that's why the Florida East Coast has so many hurricanes—it belongs to the Devil.

Florida Climate

RECENTLY the Rotary Club at Clearwater, Florida, and the Kiwanis Club, of Largo, were informed of a miracle of Florida climate. It was Edwin J. L. Page, of Clearwater, who made the report, which reads as follows:

REMARKABLE CURATIVE POWER OF FLORIDA SUNSHINE

In the North lived a young man sadly afflicted with tuberculosis. Doctors said his only help lay in sunshine treatment. Arrangements were at once made for his transportation to Florida. A male nurse was engaged, and the patient was carried aboard a de luxe train. The helpless invalid was given the most constant care. As the train slowed up for Clearwater station, a passenger carelessly raised a window curtain and a small ray of sunshine fell directly on the poor fellow. A second later, the horrified nurse heard a loud yell and saw his patient disappearing through the window. As the train stopped, they all rushed out, but there was no trace of the sick

From *Tall Stories*, The Rise and Triumph of the Great American Whopper, by Lowell Thomas, pp. 235–237. Copyright, 1931, by Funk & Wagnalls Company. New York.

man. Two days later he was located at Ringling's Circus, where he had been engaged as a lion tamer.

There are times when the life-giving sun of Florida is something of a handicap to the natives of the healthful State. B. A. Trussell, of Miami, tells of an embarrassing experience. Some years back Mr. Trussell was engaged in the sale of cemetery lots, and business was very bad; in fact, there was no business at all, because the Florida climate was so salubrious that nobody died. Finally, the enterprising business men decided that they would have a funeral at the cemetery just to show that it was in operation. The question was how to get a corpse. They finally had to import one from Chicago. They purchased the body of a gangster who had been taken for a ride. They gave him another ride, down to Florida.

A solemn and impressive funeral was arranged. Thousands of Floridians came from all parts of the country to witness such a novel spectacle as a mortuary ceremony. The coffin was taken to the graveside and the lid was opened to give the bystanders a glimpse of the beautiful way the corpse had been laid out, a masterpiece of the undertaker's art. As the Florida sunshine hit the body, there was an immediate stir. The gangster arose with a yell, feeling for his gun. The bystanders had to kill him again before they could go on with the funeral.

Alabama Leads Again

. . . An Alabama farm boy who came into the possession of some money decided to tour the old world and see if anywhere on the globe there was a spot half so favored as his native State, but while he traveled far and observed much, he saw nothing to compare with the wonders at home. No matter what he was shown, he always had something more remarkable to refer to in "Old Alabama." After seeing and discounting the marble quarries, the coal deposits and other natural resources of the Old World, he was carried to Birmingham, England, and permitted to view that great industrial city. Gazing upon it, he said, "There ain't none of you fellows ever been down to Birmingham, Alabama, has you?" When they replied "No," he said, "Then you don't know what an industrial town is. Why, there in Birmingham the smoke of industry is so thick that you can't recognize your best friend on the street."

Before the excursion of this Alabama booster was over, he was taken one night to the catacombs, this after he had been entertained at a function where flowed that which can't flow under the Eighteenth Amendment, and there he was left among the dead of bygone generations. The next

According to Judge William Brandon.

From *The Book of Birmingham*, by John R. Hornady, pp. 123–124. Copyright, 1921, by Dodd, Mead and Company, Inc. New York.

morning, as faint rays began to creep into the gloomy cells, the lad awoke. In front of him he saw a skeleton, and glancing backward he saw another. Looking to left and to right he saw others. Then leaping to his feet and yelling in a voice that made those dreary chambers ring, he exclaimed: "It's the resurrection morn; I'm the first man up; Old Alabama leads again!"

Mississippi Soil

IN COAHOMA COUNTY there's some pretty rich land, too. A few years ago a government man come down in Coahoma to see some of the big trees he had heard about. Well, he walked out in some woods he seen clost by, and passin' a likely lookin' tree he noticed that it was different from any tree he had ever seen, so he broke off a limb and took it up to a farmer's house and ast him what kind of a tree was that. The farmer ast him whereabouts he'd found that limb, and the man told him. "Well," the farmer answered, "you ain't never got to the woods yet. That there's a limb offen one of them old rag weeds that growed up this spring on a piece of land that I figgered was too pore to plant in cotton."

Wood-Yard Laconics

THE wood-yards on the Mississippi are sometimes of a size corresponding with the magnitude of their surroundings. We have seen twenty thousand cords of wood in one "pile," the value of which as it lay upon the ground was seventy thousand dollars. We can hardly comprehend what must be the aggregate amount of all the fuel consumed in one year upon the Western waters. These large yards, however, result from a combination of capital and enterprise, and are exceptions rather than characteristic.

It is quite a relief to the traveler, after many days' confinement, to get out at one of these temporary landing-places, and if the chief woodchopper be at leisure, much valuable information is often obtained. It is a singular fact that when a steamer hails a wood-yard no direct answer to any question is ever obtained. We believe there has been no exception to this rule even in the memory of the oldest steamboat captain on the river. The steamer is desirous of getting "ash wood," provided it is "seasoned." The captain, as his boat approaches the shore, places his hands to his mouth, and forming them into a tube, calls out,

"What kind of wood is that?" The reply comes back,

By Ruth Bass, Hazlehurst, Mississippi, November 30, 1938.

From "Remembrances of the Mississippi," by T. B. Thorpe, *Harper's New Monthly Magazine,* Vol. XII (December, 1855), No. LXVII, pp. 39–40. New York: Harper & Brothers, Publishers.

"Cord wood."

The captain, still in pursuit of information under difficulties, and desirous of learning if the fuel be dry and fit for his purpose, bawls out,

"How long has it been cut?"

"Four feet," is the prompt response.

The captain, exceedingly vexed, next inquires, "What do you sell it for?"

"Cash," returns the chopper, replacing the corn-cob pipe in his mouth, and smiling benignly "on his pile."

Wood-yards are apparently infested with mosquitoes—we say *apparently* infested. Such is the impression of all accidental sojourners; but it is a strange delusion, for though one may think that they fill the air, inflame the face and hands, and if of the Arkansas species, penetrate the flesh through the thickest boots, still upon inquiring of any permanent resident if mosquitoes are numerous, the inevitable answer is,

"Mosquitoes—no! not about here; but a little way down the river they are awful—*thar* they torment alligators to death, and sting mules right through their hoofs."

The Mississippi

WHEN God made the world, He had a large amount of surplus water which he turned loose and told to go where it pleased; it has been going where it pleased ever since and that is the Mississippi River.

A New Orleans Duel Vindicating the Honor of the Mississippi

THE Creoles of New Orleans were always very spirited and courageous, but sometimes fought on provocations which the Americans would not have resented in a manner so deadly.

The Creole element was impatient of dissent, and resorted to small arms on all occasions of differences even among themselves. One paper was especially provocative of such disputes. The writers were Americans, who expressed their opinions without much circumlocution, and so provoked the fiery native greatly. There was one article upon a performance at the

By S. S. Prentiss. Quoted in *Where I Was Born and Raised,* by David L. Cohn, p. 56. Copyright, 1935, 1947, and 1948 by David L. Cohn. Boston: Houghton Mifflin Company.

From *Historical Sketch Book and Guide to New Orleans and Environs,* with Map, Illustrated with Many Original Engravings; and Containing Exhaustive Accounts of the Traditions, Historical Legends, and Remarkable Localities of the Creole City, edited and compiled by several leading writers of the New Orleans Press, pp. 186–187. New York: Will H. Coleman. 1885.

opera. This critique occasioned three duels, and upon reading it carefully one will be at a loss to find material to have justified one, even conceding that rational people should peril life at all on a question of singing or dancing.

There appeared in New Orleans, some forty years ago, a very learned savant and academician, from whom there was no appeal on any question of science, known as the Chevalier Tomasi. Tomasi published a communication on the hydraulics of the Mississippi. He would either stop the river, or make it deeper, or restrict it within boundaries specified by science. The style of the article was dogmatic and dictatorial. The Academy of Sciences in Paris was declared as omnipotent in physics as the Sorbonne had been in ethics. Americans were an ignorant tribe expelled from Europe for stupidity or other crimes. To cite a Creole authority only provoked a grimace or a sarcasm. It is proper to say that there was a vehement feud between the Creoles and French. Men grew tired of the society of their superiors, and to have Paris eternally thrown in their teeth, with a word now and then about the *filles de cassette* and an assumption of general superiority, would disturb the equanimity of the most phlegmatic, much less of the most mercurial people.

So Tomasi was descanting to a Creole upon the perfection of the system, whatever it was, when a Creole associate ventured to remark that the Mississippi was a very headstrong stream, and that possibly the basis of calculation assumed for the smaller rivers of Europe would not be found applicable to so mighty a stream. At this Tomasi merely employed a gesture of contempt, and added with a sneer, "How little you Americans know of the world! Know that there are rivers in Europe so large that the Mississippi is a mere rill, figuratively speaking." To this the enraged Creole replied, "Sir, I will never allow the Mississippi to be insulted or disparaged in my presence by an arrogant pretender to knowledge." This he accompanied with the flirt of a glove in the face of the Chevalier. A challenge was the consequence, and Professor Tomasi was wounded, as is supposed, mortally. A day or two afterwards, however, the Chevalier appeared in the streets wearing what the surgeons call a T bandage, about his face and jaw. He wore quite a ghostly aspect, and when asked about it, remarked, "*C'est rien; une egratignure seulement,*" and stripped away the bandage, to show that the sword of his antagonist had duly vindicated the dignity of the Mississippi by passing entirely across the mouth of the defamer from one cheek to the other. "But," said the Chevalier, as he replaced his bandage, "I should have killed my antagonist but for the miserable character of your American steel. My sword, sir, doubled like lead. Had it been a genuine *colichemarde* he would have fared properly for having brutally outraged the sensibilities of a French gentleman." He here opened a lecture on the carbonization of iron, which could nowhere be effected properly except with wood cut in a certain forest of France. This lecture was delivered with pain and contortion of visage, but no doubt gave him great relief, as all his premises and deductions were accepted without dispute.

Arkansas and Heaven

. . . A YOUNG man on the road to Little Rock, Arkansas, . . . overtook an elderly traveler and asked him where he was going. "I am going to heaven, my son, I have been on my way eighteen years."

"Well, good-by, old fellow," replied the youngster, "if you have been traveling toward heaven eighteen years and got no nearer to it than Arkansas, I'll take another route."

Arkansassy and Illinoisy

IN CONWAY COUNTY there happened to be a neighborhood of old timers who came in 1819; near by was another band of immigrants from Illinois who came in 1830. The first set having lived on the soil eleven years were natives and held their heads high above the other set. They had to worship God in the same house, but they sat on different sides. Sometimes the women met but they did not mix. They always clashed. One day an old maid from the Illinois set got out of humor and said: "You sisters on that side of the house are the most cantankerous people I ever saw. I have seen sassy people, but of all sassy people in the world Arkansassy people are the worst." Amidst loud applause from her side she sat down. Then another old maid from the other side got up and said: "I hate noisy people, and of all the noisy people in the world the Illinoisy ones are the worst." Great was the applause on the other side. Here we have the genesis of the modern woman's clubs of the State and their motive. The idea is always to do the other fellow before he does you, and if he does get his oar in first, come back with remark called for brevity, "The Retort Courteous."

The humor of the old Conway Club was that the young people of these two factions had to intermarry, and the children were not only "sassy" but "noisy," which accounts for a great deal of our modern history.

Oklahoma Oil Jokes

PEOPLE told jokes:
Birds flew into town by the big long clouds, lasting two or three hours

---

From the Jackson (Tennessee) *Whig and Tribune*. Cited in *The Southern Country Editor*, by Thomas D. Clark, p. 126. Copyright, 1948, by the Bobbs-Merrill Company. Indianapolis and New York.

From *Pioneers and Makers of Arkansas*, by Josiah H. Shinn, p. 258. Copyright, 1908, by M. C. Shinn. Washington, D. C.: Genealogical and Historical Publishing Company.

From *Bound for Glory*, by Woody Guthrie, p. 115. Copyright, 1943, by E. P. Dutton & Co., Inc. New York.

at a time, because it was rumored around up in the sky that you could wallow in the dust of the oiled roads and it would kill all kinds of fleas and body lice.

Dogs cured their mange, or else got it worse. Oil on their hair made them hotter in hot weather and colder in cold weather.

Ants dug their holes deeper, but wouldn't talk any secrets about the oil formation under the ground.

Snakes and lizards complained that wiggling through so many oil pools made the hot sun blister their backs worse. But on the other hand they could slide on their belly through the grass a lot easier. So it come out about even.

Oil was more than gold ever was or ever will be, because you can't make any hair salve or perfume, TNT, or roofing material or drive a car with just gold. You can't pipe that gold back East and run them big factories, either.

The religion of the oil field, guys said, was to get all you can, and spend all you can as quick as you can, and then end up in the can.

Dry Texas

AN EL PASOAN, an Amarillan, and a Beaumontian met at the State Fair, the story goes.

"How do you like living in El Paso, John?" said Beaumont. "I understand it gets mighty hot out there."

"Yeah," replied the El Pasoan. "The thermometer goes to 110 in the shade and there isn't much shade. We have our thermometers made with rubber bulbs so's they won't blow off the top. It sure does get hot; but then it's a *dry* heat, and we don't mind it."

"Bill, I've heard Amarillo gets pretty cold in the winter," persisted Beaumont.

"Well," admitted the Amarillan, "there's nothing between us and the North Pole but some barb-wire fences with the gates open. So what would you expect but cold when one of them Dakota blizzards gets going good? It gets so cold sometimes that a poor cow will freeze standing up and not fall down till the thaw. But you see our cold is a *dry sort* of cold, and we enjoy it."

"By the way, I understand you have quite a lot of rain at Beaumont," said El Paso. "We don't have to put up with more'n ten or fifteen inches a year out our way. More sunshine days than Yuma!"

Beaumont did not hesitate. "Sure we have rain—fifty—sixty inches a

From *East Texas*, Its History and Its Makers, by Dabney White and T. C. Richardson, Vol. I, pp. 46–47. Copyright, 1940, by Lewis Historical Publishing Company. New York.

year. Furnishes fine muskrat range and irrigates our rice. Plenty of rain at Beaumont, yes sirree. But it's a kind of *dry rain,* and it doesn't bother us a-tall!"

Gone to Texas

UNTIL a few years ago, the outside world knew very little about Texas; and a great deal of that little was merely invented history and unsubstantial romance. Texas was formerly regarded as the home of the murderous Indian, and the refuge of the equally murderous criminal who had escaped from justice in the older States. Before the civil war, when a murder was committed in the older States, or when a Sunday-school superintendent appropriated funds from the bank of which he was cashier, newspaper accounts of such indiscretions invariably ended with the laconic announcement, "Gone to Texas."

They tell of a criminal in Eastern Texas, who, thirty years ago, was under arrest for horse-stealing. His lawyer told him that his case was a desperate one. "You will assuredly be convicted on the evidence," said he, "and then you will be hung. My advice to you is to try and make your escape."

"Escape! Where?" said the horse-thief. "For Heaven's sake, where can I escape to? Sure, *I'm in Texas now!*"

The Road to Texas

ON THE way to Texas, the roads divided, one leading to Arkansas, the other to this State. The latter route bore a sign: "This road to Texas."

All who could read came to Texas; the others settled in Arkansas.

The Texas Rangers

A CITY was threatened by mob violence, so a telegram was sent to the governor to rush a force of Texas Rangers to the scene.

When the train arrived, a delegation was on hand to welcome the

From *On a Mexican Mustang Through Texas from the Gulf to the Rio Grande,* by Alex E. Sweet and J. Armoy Knox, p. 66. Copyright, 1883, by Sweet and Knox. Hartford, Connecticut: S. S. Scranton & Company.

From *I Give You Texas,* 500 Jokes of the Lone Star State, by Boyce House, p. 4. Copyright, 1943, by the Naylor Company. San Antonio, Texas.

Ibid., p. 31.

Rangers. A lone, leathery-cheeked, big-hatted, high-booted, keen-eyed individual alighted. It was apparent that he was a Ranger but the citizens were disappointed, and the spokesman said:

"Did the governor send only one Ranger?"

"H——, there ain't but one mob, is there?" he asked.

Dallas vs. Fort Worth

. . . According to Tom Gooch, of the *Dallas Times Herald,* a Dallas coffin manufacturer once had to ship his wares for Fort Worth via St. Louis because people in Fort Worth wouldn't be caught dead in anything from Dallas.

* * * * *

The climax of the rivalry between Dallas and Fort Worth [came in 1936]. To reduce the focus, it was an all-out head butting between Amon Carter, of Fort Worth, and Banker Robert Thornton, of Dallas. In the early 30's, the Texas legislature was trying to decide where to hold the state's official Centennial Exposition in '36. Every city in Texas fought hard to get it. But Bob Thornton got it for Dallas when he told the legislative committee, "We've got the plant, we've got the money, and, to show our pride in Texas, we've got the guts to spend it." The plant to which Mr. Thornton referred was the group of fine buildings where Dallas holds the Texas State Fair, "Show Window of the Southwest." And when he promised that Dallas could get up $12,000,000 in public and private funds, he'd bought himself a centennial exposition.

Amon Carter was out of the state at the time, but when he heard Dallas would get the centennial, it threw him in a hard bind. Had Houston or San Antonio been the lucky city, he would not have felt so directly invited into the fight. But he couldn't stand by and see Dallas wallow in all that glory.

He rallied Fort Worth's business people and found them ready for the fray. Then he made a public pronunciamento. Fort Worth, he said, would stage a centennial celebration on its own, and one that would make Dallas look like a Sunday-school picnic.

Now that the fat was in the fire, the long-distance phone lines began crackling like a Chinese celebration. Mr. Carter got hold of Billy Rose and offered him $1,000 a day for 100 days if he would come to Fort Worth and put on a show that not only couldn't be beat but couldn't be tied.

Over in Dallas, Bob Thornton and his cohorts stood at the Rubicon. The question was whether to make their show cultural and dignified, there-

From "The Cities of America—Dallas and Fort Worth," by George Sessions Perry, *The Saturday Evening Post,* Vol. 218 (March 30, 1946), No. 39, pp. 22, 45–46. Copyright, 1946, by the Curtis Publishing Company. Philadelphia.

by inviting grave risks at the box office, or whether to seize onto the sure-fire old carnival maxim of "kewpies, curiosity and sex." Uplift won.

Also in the Dallas camp, crafty Bill Kittrell, famed in Texas political circles for his ability to turn water into wine, was waging a powerful and successful campaign to bring big-time industrial exhibitors to the Dallas exposition. At the same time he was busily organizing a five-alarm pageant to be called *Cavalcade of Texas*, which was to have a typically dashing Kittrellesque flair. He persuaded D. W. Griffith, who'd done all right with *The Birth of a Nation*, to come to Dallas and lend a hand.

Both cities began to stump the nation. Amon Carter plastered the state with billboards and posters saying: GO TO DALLAS FOR EDUCATION. COME TO FORT WORTH FOR ENTERTAINMENT.

Dallas, with the full weight of the state of Texas behind it, staged a smash exhibition and, knowing how Texans love their own state history, chinned itself on each bar of the Lone Star flag. The price of admission was only fifty cents and the Dallas show naturally sold more tickets than the Fort Worth Frontier Exposition which featured Billy Rose's show, a supper night club called Casa Mañana, which cost $2.20, with dinner included. Rose mounted his production on a 100-foot revolving stage. It was loaded with pretty girls in various conditions of deshabille. There were no kewpies at Casa Mañana, but Sally Rand fanned interest in the two other carnival musts. What's more, the customers left singing the brand-new hit tune, "The Night Is Young and You're So Beautiful." Even today it's hard to find a Texan who'll admit that he ever saw a better show.

Of course, both cities lost money on their spectacles, but that wasn't the point. The idea of each was to beat the rival show. Texas ruled that it was a draw. And both sides came out bloody but unbowed.

Bigness of Texas

TEXAS occupies all the Continent of North America except the small part set aside for the United States, Mexico and Canada. Texas owns everything north of the Rio Grande, the only dusty river in the world; also the only one with the possible exception of the Trinity which is navigable for mudcats and pedestrians.

From *Texas Almanac and State Industrial Guide*, (1945–1946), The Encyclopedia of Texas, p. 407. Copyright, 1945, by A. H. Belo Corporation. Dallas, Texas: The Dallas *News*.

The war which brought its influx of men from other states during the last few years has also brought it heightened discussion of Texans' pride in Texas. That the issue is not new is indicated by the following lines, supposedly by a visitor to Texas, which have been used occasionally for many years as an after-dinner speech, and have been printed at times in newspapers and magazines, usually signed "A Texas Visitor." Origin is unknown to the editor of the *Texas Almanac*. . . . Editor, *Texas Almanac*.

Texas is bounded on the north by twenty-five or thirty states, on the east by all the oceans in the world except the Pacific and on the south by the Gulf of South America, and on the west by the Pacific Ocean, the Milky Way and the Sidereal universe.

If Texas were chopped off loose from the rest of the United States and the Panhandle it would float out into the ocean, as it rests upon a vast sea of fresh water.

Texas is so big that the people in Brownsville call the Dallas people Yankees, and the citizens of El Paso sneer at the citizens of Texarkana as being snobs of the effete east.

It is one hundred and fifty miles farther from El Paso, Texas, to Texarkana than it is from Chicago to New York. Fort Worth is nearer St. Paul, Minn., than it is to Brownsville, Texas.

The chief occupation of the people of Texas is trying to keep from making all the money in the world. The chief pursuit of the people of Texas was formerly Mexicans, but now it is the land buyers, steers and Texas crop records.

The United States with Texas off would look like a three-legged Boston terrier.

Texans are so proud of Texas that they can not sleep at nights. If a Texan's head should be opened the map of Texas would be found photographed on the brain. This is also true of his heart. Unless your front gate is eighteen miles from your front door you do not belong to society as constituted in Texas. One Texan's gate is one hundred fifty miles from his front door and he is thinking of moving his house back so he will not be annoyed by the passing automobiles and peddlers.

Other Texas landlords have whole mountain ranges and rivers on their ranches. One Texan has forty miles of navigable river on his farm. If the proportion of cultivated land in Texas were the same as in Illinois, the value of Texas crops would equal that of forty-seven other states.

Texas has enough land to supply every man, woman and child in the world with a tract of five feet by twenty and have enough left over for the armies of the world to march around the border five abreast.

If the alfalfa grown in Texas were baled and built into a stairway it would reach the pearly gates.

If all the hogs in Texas were one big hog, he would be able to dig the Panama Canal in three roots.

If all the Texas steers were one big steer, he would stand with his front feet in the Gulf of Mexico, one hind foot in Hudson Bay and the other in the Arctic Ocean, and with a sweep of his tail brush the mist from the Aurora Borealis. Some State!

III. CASTE AND CLASS

The Southern folk society was a variegated fabric made from a fourfold pattern: the upper levels of the plantation aristocracy; the upper levels of the middle white South; the lower levels of the disadvantaged whites; and the Negro folk society itself reflecting three levels.

One of the three levels of the Negro folk society was that of the slave level distinguished in any story of universal culture and exerting a powerful influence upon the institutions and behavior of the white South. Another was the white-Negro folk society after freedom, a dual culture that distinguished the South from the rest of the country and symbolized folkways for which men were willing to die. The third was the new Negro folk society separate from and within the state society of the white South.

Whereas the common connotation of the folk in the South has been that of the white mountain or flatwood people who retain the remnants of the earlier societal unwritten culture or of the folklore and folksongs of the Southern Negroes, among the most powerful folk cultures were those of the aristocratic planter class and the conflicting ideologies of the upper brackets of the white South where always democracy and earned privileges have been the folk motif.—HOWARD W. ODUM.

1. TOP AND BOTTOM RAIL

AT THE head of the traditional class structure of the South was the aristocratic planter. Although his influence was out of proportion to his numbers and his importance has been exaggerated far beyond that of the great middle group of plain folk that constitute the bulk and norm of the Southern people, he has not quite been given his due place in the folk culture of the South. In Odum's concept of the folk as extra-technological and extra-organizational, plantation society before the Civil War was a folk society, homogeneous and communal, with master and slave classes co-existing in a state of equilibrium maintained by a rigid caste system.

Although the planter class was removed by slave labor from direct contact with the soil, its culture was transitional between frontier wilderness society and modern civilization. The legend and literature of the old South have stressed the social graces of plantation society (good breeding, mannerliness, hedonism, etc.); and tales of old plantation families (like those with which this section opens) preserve grateful memories of aristocratic honor, pride, and opulence. But the more humble and homely folklore of master-slave must not be overlooked.

In the folk-regional society and culture of the plantation, master and slave met halfway, through the partial contact and partial segregation or "social distance" inherent in the etiquette or social ritual of the caste system. In a society in which "The Negro is a Negro, and nothing more," the be-all and end-all of etiquette and other forms of social control were to keep the Negro in his place and to bring him into co-operative, if involuntary, participation in plantation labor and society. Thus the imaginative life of the "quality" or "squirearchy" like its fortunes was inseparably bound up with that of the slave, chiefly through the Negro servants, nurses, and childhood companions who have been traditionally the transmitters of folklore and fable to white children.

When two unequal and different cultures come together, the dominant, more advanced, or socially superior group imposes its culture on the minority, backward, or socially inferior group. But at certain points of contact there is an interchange or fusion of elements. As the Negro is the central theme and problem of the bi-racial civilization of the South, coloring "every phase of Southern life . . . every impression which outside observers had of the South," [1] so the Negro has colored the entire folk expression and folkloristic literature of the South, as well as made original contributions to Southern folk speech, folk belief, folk song, folk tale, and folk-say.

After freedom the roles of master and slave were assumed by landlord and tenant, with Negro and white tenant or cropper ranged both against the landlord and against each other. The traditional feuds between landlord and tenant, between Negro and poor white, are reflected in the following Negro folk rhymes and sayings:

> Aught's a aught,
> And a figger's a figger.
> All for the white man,
> None for the nigger.[2]

> Aught's a aught,
> And a four is a four.
> I'm gonna take all of this cotton this year
> And let you go work next year for some more.[3]

> My name's Ran, I wuks in de san';
> But I'd druther be a Nigger dan a po' white man.[4]

> Ev'y time I gits paid I don't git nothin'; deducks done got it all! [5]

2. OLD JOHN AND OLD MASSA

The chief protagonist and antagonist of master-slave folklore are Old Massa and Old John. Although Old Massa is the kind or cruel protector or oppressor and Old John is the faithful or rebellious servant or underdog,

---

[1] Howard W. Odum, *The Way of the South* (New York, 1947), p. 53.
[2] Recorded by B. A. Botkin, Asheville, North Carolina, January 20, 1949.
[3] *Ibid.*
[4] Thomas W. Talley, *Negro Folk Rhymes* (New York, 1922), pp. 42–43.
[5] *Alabama, A Guide to the Deep South* (New York, 1941), p. 70.

each seems to exist for the sole purpose of serving as a foil or scapegoat for the other's wit or cunning—like Brer Fox and Brer Rabbit.

Old John is the wizard and "hope-bringer" of slave days, an outlet for all the slave's repressed, unfulfilled yearnings for freedom, equality, and happiness. For conjure he has his wisdom and his laughter. As High John de Conquer (in Zora Neale Hurston's version [6]) he shares his name and magic power with the "king root of all the forest," high John-the-conqueror. This—the root of the marsh St. John's-wort—gives protection against rattlesnake bites, ghosts, witches, and nightmares. "It is a cure-all for any kind of wounds, and the dew that gathers upon its leaves is excellent for strengthening the eyesight." [7] A fitting symbol for a slave hero as the protector, healer, and prophetic eye of his people.

The humorous folk tales of John's "scrapes and tight squeezes" (turning the tables on Old Massa, winning freedom by wager, stratagem, etc.) reflect the restrictions, immunities, and evasions of plantation etiquette and at the same time hark back to the old tradition of trickster, trickster tricked, and noodle or simpleton stories. The New South has produced a whole cycle of related anecdotes and jests in which the "simple" Negro takes his place in the long line of persons of an out-group used as a scapegoat and butt of ridicule. Curiously, Negro folklore has made the Irishman the similar embodiment of absurd ignorance and stupidity, in such jokes as the one about the Irish hunter who refuses to shoot at a deer which he takes to be a man with a chair on his head.[8]

Over against the stereotype of the simple Negro folk as "quaint, artless, naïve children," Sterling Brown cites the following anecdote to illustrate the irony that is often mistaken for or disguised as simplicity.

A student of sociology visited an old woman's cabin in the Black Belt. The cabin was ramshackly; boards were off the sides and at night the stars could be seen through the openings in the roof. The student asked the old woman: "Does it leak in here?" The old woman looked long at the questioner, took her pipe out of her mouth and spat. "No, honey, it doan leak in here. When it rain, it rain in here, and it leak outside." [9]

B. A. B.

---

[6] "High John de Conquer," *The American Mercury,* Vol. LVII (October, 1943), No. 238, pp. 450–458.

[7] Ruth Bass, "Fern Seed—for Peace," *Folk-Say, A Regional Miscellany: 1930* (Norman, 1930), p. 150.

[8] Cf. "Irishman Stories," *Southern Workman and Hampton School Record,* Vol. 28 (May, 1899), No. 5, pp. 192–194.

[9] Paper read at Folk Literature Craft Session, Third American Writers' Congress, New York, June 4, 1939.

A Debt of Honor

IN MY childhood an old house called Colross stood on the outskirts of Alexandria, and was the home of Mr. William A. Smoot, whose daughter Betty was a schoolmate of my sister and myself. Mr. Smoot's wife was a lovely woman, of the great McGuire family, who have furnished generations of beloved physicians to the state of Virginia. Everybody was at home at Colross, but in the carelessness of youth none of us concerned ourselves as to the history of the great old house. There was the usual hall running through it, the slave quarters to each side, and the arched corridors from the outside kitchens and rooms where the heavy work was done. All of the best old brick, and the best type of Georgian architecture.

The section of Alexandria in the direction of Washington had not then been built up with lumber yards and coal yards and cheap tenements; the railroads had not hedged the house in on both sides; Colross was more than aristocratic, almost isolated, a fine suburban residence which we regarded with great respect.

Its history, as I acquainted myself with it long years after our childhood's familiarity, is interesting. In 1785, a gentleman from Massachusetts, answering to the famous name of Jonathan Swift, arrived in Alexandria, and soon became what is termed a "prominent citizen." In his official capacity as Consul for several counties, he was efficient during the war of 1812–14, in protecting property in the town during the occupancy of the British, for which the citizens held him in great esteem. His marriage with a daughter of General Robedeau further endeared him to the community, and after building Bel Air, as Colross was first called, and raising a large family, he was accounted a true son of the soil. The ground on which he built, however, belonged to the great Alexander estates, and when he died in 1824, considerably in debt on the ground rent, the Alexanders again took possession.

The joint owners were Gustavus Brown Alexander and his sister Mrs. Susan Pearson Chapman. Gustavus was addicted to looking upon the wine when it was red and he was also a notorious gambler. One night he got into a game with Thomas Mason, and they played till morning. After losing everything negotiable that he possessed, Gustavus in the spirit of a sportsman, staked, and lost, his mansion. Large sums of money had changed hands during the night, but the slave who served the drinks witnessed the secreting of the funds in a sideboard drawer, and when his masters were unobservant, being finally quite overcome with wine, this wily individual got away with the cash and was never heard of again.

Morning brought to Gustavus a painful realization of the predicament into which he had got himself, but all efforts to reason with or appeal to

From *George Washington's Country*, by Marietta Minnegerode Andrews, pp. 39–41. Copyright, 1930, by E. P. Dutton & Co., Inc. New York.

Mr. Mason were without effect. He would have his pound of flesh. Then a brother, Lee Massie Alexander, the family lawyer, advised Gustavus that a loophole might be found in the fact that his sister, Mrs. Chapman, was joint heir with him, and he could not hypothecate nor gamble away what belonged to her. Therefore Mr. Mason's claim was not valid.

But here enters the female of the species—not always reckoned with. It seems that the sister, Mrs. Chapman, was just at this inconvenient moment a convert to religion, having been recently confirmed at Christ Church, and taking the matter very seriously. She therefore in this financial crisis made a most edifying and unexpected example of faith, steadfastly refusing to assist her brother in evading his obligation, a debt of honor, as it was considered; no, Mrs. Chapman stood to lose her interest in this handsome inheritance, rather than take advantage of the law! And Thomas Mason took, and kept, Colross.

His superstitious neighbors saw, in many tragic happenings that overtook him and his, a vengeance of the Lord upon him. The wise ones shook their heads and quoted from Romans XII "Vengeance is mine: I will repay, saith the Lord." His children met with fatal accidents, his house fell into disrepair and neglect. Finally the unmarked graves of his family were plowed up and the bones removed. It was a melancholy tale, of which remains but a few vague memories in the minds of surviving octogenarians, and the fallen walls of the once noble house he won on a gamble.

Culpepper's Pride

SHE died under an umbrella. . . .

* * * * *

It was a large umbrella of yellow and white, and as I recall it had an Italian's name stamped on it. "Musso" I think. It was a most ordinary umbrella, but it served its purpose. . . .

Do you see that little mound over there by the summer house? Well, that is a pile of shingles. It has been lying there for twenty years, and I suppose they are all rotten now. It does not matter any more.

You see, that was a proud family, and after all the old people died, Bessie was left with her bachelor son. Bessie and I were the same age, and the son was old enough to be your father. They lived pretty much to themselves and they were very poor. They were sensitive too, for they had always held their heads so high. The old house began to go to pieces and a bad leak developed in Bessie's bedroom. Because she was sick that winter, she was in her room a great deal. I remember going to see her

From *The Friends of Joe Gilmore*, by Lyle Saxon, and *Some Friends of Lyle Saxon*, by Edward Dreyer, pp. 105–109. Copyright, 1948, by Hastings House, Publishers, Inc. New York.

and noticing that the rain had spotted the red silk on the tester of her big four-post bed. She laughed a little bit about it and said that all of the bedrooms were leaking, but that through great good luck they had found enough money to buy new shingles. The shingles had been ordered and would arrive any day. They had arranged that a Negro carpenter come and put them on. She was very pleased about it, and we joked a little bit about hard times.

Well, the shingles arrived and were unloaded and piled up right there by the summer house, and the son, Culpepper—that was a family name on her mother's side—was very pleased that the leaky roof was to be renewed at last. The work was to begin the following day.

But the most unfortunate thing happened. One of the neighbors, really he was a man without any tact whatever, rode by on his horse, and began to tease Culpepper. "Well, it is high time you had a new roof," he said. "I understand that the water drips right through onto your piano in the parlor."

Now I told you that family held their heads high, and Culpepper was furious. He said, "There is no hurry about repairing the roof. I shall do it when I get damn good and ready, but not before." And with that he turned to the Negro carpenter and said, "Don't come tomorrow. I've decided to delay the work until the comments of our impertinent neighbors have stopped."

Naturally, his neighbor was furious and never spoke to Culpepper again.

Well, time passed and the shingles lay there and the roof was not repaired. Culpepper would have none of it. I did not dare speak to him about it, but I felt sorry for Bessie up there in the damp. I don't know how she felt about it, but I think she agreed with him on general principles. It was not the business of anybody to comment on their domestic arrangements.

My, how it rained that summer! It was the wettest August I ever remember, and every time it rained I kept thinking about poor Bessie. Surely, I thought, Culpepper would have the roof fixed by Thanksgiving. But, All Saints' Day and Thanksgiving passed and the shingles lay there. We laughed a little bit about it at home and joked about it in a friendly fashion; but none of us said anything to Bessie or Culpepper. Christmas came, and I dropped over to take a fruit cake. Culpepper met me upstairs in the hall and said that his mother was really sick. And so I went up. There she was lying in that great bed with big stains on the pillow where the rain had dropped through that morning. The red satin on the top of the bed was soaking wet. I just didn't know what to do. I finally suggested that we get some Negroes in and move the bed, but Culpepper said that one part of the room leaked just as much as any other part. Bessie did not say anything. So I left the cake and went downstairs and talked to Culpepper. We sat in the parlor and I let him have a piece of my mind.

"Culpepper," I said, "it is none of my business whether you have the roof fixed or not, but Bessie is my girlhood friend, and I love her like a sister, and she is sick. I think you should get a trained nurse right away."

He agreed with me and he said that he would attend to it at once.

I went over that night and stayed with Bessie until the trained nurse could get there. None of us said anything about the roof, but it stopped raining about that time. The nurse came in the next morning, and I declare I never was so glad to see anybody in my life. It was really the most fortunate thing that ever happened, because as it turned out she was one of the Magee girls. They were another plantation family nearby."

* * * * *

. . . I never saw such spirit in my life. She talked right sassy to Culpepper. "This is perfectly ridiculous—you and your pride. My father is just as proud and just as silly as you are, but by the good Lord, sir, if I am to take care of Miss Bessie, I am to have full charge." Now, nobody had ever talked to Culpepper like that in his life, and he just stood there looking at her. I knew those Magee girls and I knew she would get her way, no matter what he did. To tell the truth, I think he was beginning to feel pretty uncomfortable just through that stiff neck of his.

Along about four that afternoon it began to rain again, and Sally Magee was furious when the drops began to fall on poor Bessie's bed. It was just at that time that a fruit peddler drove up to the house. And do you know what that girl did? She went right downstairs without a word to Culpepper or anybody and she took Musso's big white and yellow umbrella right off his wagon and carried it inside along with a small bunch of grapes she had bought. She just left Culpepper to settle with the Italian. I don't know what arrangements he made, but he probably paid a good price for that parasol. Well, anyway, Sally Magee carried it upstairs and fastened it up in the top of the four-post bed, changed all the linens, and made her patient as comfortable as she could.

It was not much use though, because pneumonia had set in; and a few days later the umbrella was not needed any more.

* * * * *

Well, there is one comfort; Bessie died dry.

Monsieur Durand's Grand Gesture

A few years before the outbreak of the Civil War, two of his [Charles Durand's] daughters simultaneously accepted the marriage proposals of members of native Louisiana families. Bayou Teche looked for something unusual from Monsieur Durand for the occasion. Few expected anything like the thing that they experienced.

From *The Bayous of Louisiana*, by Harnett T. Kane, pp. 254–256. Copyright, 1943, by Harnett T. Kane. New York: The Hampton Publishing Co., and William Morrow & Company. 1944.

The planter sat long at that desk, and concentrated, before he conceived his project. He chose spiders for the basis of the ornamentation. One source says that he imported a cargo of enormous creatures from Cathay. His granddaughter insists that he sent merely to the woods near Catahoula, Louisiana. In any event, they were large spiders, capable of large deeds.

Shortly before the marriage day, the spiders were set loose, while the slaves watched, big-eyed, among the trees in the long avenue. For days the spiders worked, lacing the spaces between the trees with yards of delicate webs. All wondered; would it rain between then and the wedding day, and his efforts melt away? Monsieur Durand was not one to fret over trifles. It would not rain.

It did not rain. On that morning, the planter called his slaves, gave them bellows and supplies of silver and gold dust. Over the long canopy of cobwebs, says the tradition, they spread this gossamer covering. ("It must have been superb," said Mrs. Madere, softly. "So many times have they told of it. . . .") Others worked beneath the canopy, laying a series of carpets to cover most of the three-mile passage under the trees. At one end of the avenue they placed an open-air altar; between the trees, at the sides, were tables covered with food, to be served by as many of the slaves, domestic and field, as could be fitted with aprons and drilled for the occasion. Bands played from strategic points. The wedding was open to all—French and Americans—up and down the Teche.

Thousands attended and watched. Toasts, dancing, songs, and the giving of gifts continued until dusk. Then up the bayou came a steamboat, to take the two couples on their honeymoon to New Orleans. The crowd accompanied them to the landing, shot off fireworks, and bade the young people good-by; and the four stood at the rail and waved until they were out of sight.

Charles Durand had made his last grand gesture. The war came, and he fought in it with sons and grandsons. His slaves were freed, his sugar mill was seized, his home was damaged; and the golden carriages also went. He did not survive the war by many years. In his last months he talked of money that he had hidden somewhere, perhaps under the oaks and pines, perhaps somewhere else. The children asked him many times: "Where is it? Where?" He never told. Later, one of them dug for months —and found nothing.

The house and the sugar mill fell away with the years. A barn and a few slave houses are all that can be found today of the former grandeur of the Durands, among the trees. These, too, have been reduced to about half their original number. The spiders? I tried for a time, but I failed to find more about them, whether they were truly imports from Cathay, or merely from Catahoula; and just how well they performed their assignment.

Many Servants

I [1]

ONE day, while I was at Morotoc, I asked a colored woman, whom I met on the colonnade, what her duties were.

"I picks de chickens," she replied, with an old-fashioned curtsy.

On another occasion, when I asked the same question of a small girl I saw moving about in the august wake of the Mistress, she answered: "I finds Mistis' keys for her when she loses dem."

I even heard an improbable story to the effect that, when some one, impelled by a motive I have forgotten, called out to a young girl, who had been a visitor for some time at Morotoc, to run, one of the house servants observed reproachfully: "Do'an yer know dat' Nervy Ann does all her runnin' for her?"

II [2]

. . . The following colloquy . . . took place when two young Negroes sought service away from their former master and mistress immediately

---

[1] From *Below the James,* A Plantation Sketch, by William Cabell Bruce, pp. 51–52. Copyright, 1918, by William Cabell Bruce. Boston and New York: Houghton Mifflin Company.

. . . Domestic service in that part of the world was so inefficient that the only satisfactory plan was to have two persons doing the work of one. On this principle, he employed even three cooks, one to cook breakfast and supper, one to cook dinner, and one to make desserts.

"Why not?" he said to me on one occasion. "What they cost me in house-rent and fuel is like the duty that your New England system of protection imposes upon my clothes. It is not sensibly felt; and the actual money that I pay the three, under the peculiar economic conditions of Southside Virginia, is, perhaps, not more than you would pay one in Boston. And each is the happier," he added, "for not having to toil in my hot kitchen all the day through."

* * * * *

The fundamental infirmity in the economic organization of the ante-bellum South was the fact that it was too easy for a white boy or girl to get some Negro man or woman to do something for him or her that it would have been well for him or her to have done for himself or herself.

Occasionally a merely nominal duty was imposed by Charles' kind heart upon some aged dependent as a pretended return for a small monthly pension. Such a dependent was an ancient woman whom I observed several times engaged about the task that he had set her of each day putting into and out of operation, with a stick, the hydraulic ram at Morotoc.—W. C. B., *ibid.,* pp. 49–50, 52–53.

[2] From *Life in Old Virginia,* A Description of Virginia, More Particularly the Tidewater Section, Narrating Many Incidents Relating to the Manners and Customs of Old Virginia So Fast Disappearing as a Result of the War between the States, together with Many Humorous Stories, by James J. McDonald, edited by J. A. C. Chandler, p. 245. Copyright, 1907, by the Old Virginia Publishing Company, Inc. Norfolk, Virginia.

after the Civil War. The lady to whom they applied for work asked: "Can you cook?"

"No'm, we ain't nevah been cook none. Polly cooked."

"Can you wash?" said the lady.

"No'm, we ain't been wash none neither. Aunt Sally she wash!"

"Can you clean house then?" was asked.

"No'm, least we nevah been cleanin' none."

The lady asked question after question with like negative results; finally she asked:

"What have you been accustomed to do?"

"Sukey, heah, she keep flies off Marster, an' I hunt fo' ol' Missus' specks."

III [3]

During the depression a Louisville college girl asked an eastern friend home to visit her but explained that there would be little gayety and that since the family was feeling the universal pinch of poverty, many erstwhile luxuries, including service, would have to be done without. The visitor took this literally and so when she arrived at breakfast time, was surprised to sit down to a spread of broiled old ham and waffles, bacon, eggs and hominy, plus the usual coffee, orange juice, etc., served by a not too stylish but affable and friendly colored woman. After breakfast her bags were carried to her room by a smiling servitor in a spotless white coat. A couple of hours afterwards she was asked if she would like for Mamie to shampoo her hair and upon accepting found that Mamie, whose status in the household she could not quite place, but whom she found to be a skilled and competent hairdresser, seemed equally at home. While the guest's hair was being dried in front of a snapping coal fire in the upstairs sitting room, in walked a little old man in an alpaca coat and a black silk skullcap who, with a word of greeting to the ladies, wound the Empire clock on the mantelpiece and then, with a good-by nod, took his departure.

The goggle-eyed guest managed to get her hostess off by herself before lunch and demanded: "Just what do you call 'service' in this part of the world? My mother, who is a very wealthy woman, has only a cleaning woman come in to help her once a week. Are you Southerners so languid that you can't even wind your own clocks?"

The hostess explained that the man who wound the clocks was the uncle of a half-brother of the nurse whom she and her sister had had when they were babies. He was old and poor and needed the weekly dollar which he made winding clocks, for tobacco money. Mamie for years had washed a certain number of ladies' hair, all up and down Third Street, as had her mother before her. Certainly, in hard times she could not be cut off the payroll. As for the baggage-carrier, he was the neighborhood furnace

---

[3] From Louisville, *The Gateway City*, by Isabel McLennan McMeekin, p. 162–163. Copyright, 1946, by Isabel McLennan McMeekin. New York: Julian Messner, Inc.

man, who "favored" each family on the block several times a day. Only the cook was a "permanent" and she had been one for thirty years. She couldn't be let go, because of hard times, any more than could a member of the family. The guest said, "Oh, I see," with proper humility and began to unpack her seventy-dollar coatsuit as the hostess, quite happily, got out her own twenty-dollar one which had been made by Miss Nellie, who had been the family seamstress since her mother was a girl— All of which is part of Louisville being a "museum piece" and not at all ashamed of that fact!

Captain Ridgely of Hampton

HAMPTON, during a century and a half, had been a center of a survival of the provincial life in all its most exhilarating features. Captain Ridgely had so many slaves that he did not even know them all by sight. In illustration of this fact one of the family tells the following anecdote:

"One day, while riding along the road, he met a ragged Negro, and asked him to whom he belonged. 'To Cap'n Ridgely, sar,' answered the darky, grinning from ear to ear, and pulling his forelock as if it were a bell-rope summoning his wits to the door of his brain. 'Tell the overseer that Captain Ridgely wishes to see him at once.' With another grin, another tug, and a 'Yes, Marsa,' the slave shot off on his errand. When the overseer arrived, he was severely berated for not keeping his slaves better clothed, as means were provided for him to do.

"Another story is told of the Captain in reference to his teamster, a white slave named Martin, who, for some misdemeanor, was made to wear an iron collar. Twice had he managed to get rid of it, when the Captain said he would not have it put on again, if Martin would tell how he accomplished the feat. This he agreed to do, saying, 'Well, I fastened one end of a chain to the back of the collar, and t'other end to the gate-post; then I fastened another chain to the front of the collar, and t'other end to my team. Then saying, 'Break neck or break collar,' I cracked my whip, and the mules pulled, and the collar broke."

But Hampton is rich in such tradition. It is said that when Captain Ridgely had completed his mansion and called in a company of congenial friends for a house-warming, he entertained some of them in one part of the house with whist and punch, while in another there were prayers led by his zealously pious wife. There is just a suggestion in that incident of the domestic state of the Custises at Arlington in Tidewater Virginia. Another Ridgely of Hampton cultivated a taste for horses, and he had a famous stable. It is still told how his racer Postboy broke his leg in a steeplechase, then "won on three legs, sir," and had to be shot where he lay, to relieve his hopeless agony.

From *Tidewater Maryland,* by Paul Wilstach, pp. 200–201. Copyright, 1931, by Paul Wilstach. Indianapolis: The Bobbs-Merrill Company.

Marster's Body and Soul

WHEN ole man Shiger come to die, Ole Miss were so worry 'bout de condition er he soul till she send for all de niggers to hold a prayer-meetin' over him. You know ole man Shiger been a wicked ole man. He have a heap er niggers an' he been a sportin' man. He love to fight game chickens an' play cards an' race horses an' gamble, an' he have hound dog an' run fox, an' dat wha' he mind run on—dat an' livin'.

When all dem niggers git dere, he had he niggers bring him out in a big armchair an' set him down wey he could look at 'em an' listen to dey prayer in he behalf. An' he pick out two ole niggers to lead in prayer. De fust one been ole man July, an' he say:

"Lord, dey ain't nothin' to all dis talk 'bout Ole Marster guh die. He guh be here. Luh him live, Lord, for de peace er dy servants. Luh him live to breed dat mare an' raise one more colt like de one he done raise, for he got de greatest race horse in all de land. Listen to my voice, Lord, an' luh him live to take he game chickens an' keep on whippin' all de other chickens like he been doin'.

"Luh him live, my Lord, so dat dis community kin keep de best hound. Ole Marster's hound kin outrun all de hound er all de other white folks in de world. Lord, you know dey ain't no nuse for you to worry an' debil Ole Marster 'bout dyin' now. He nothin' but a youth."

You know ole man July was a hundred an' fifteen year ole an' Ole Marster ain't been but eighty.

"Lord, hear my prayer. Put Ole Marster's mind at ease. Don't debil him no more. Put he mind at ease, Lord. Dey ain't nothin' de matter wid he body."

Ole Marster love to hear dat. He git 'side he self he so please.

"Lord, I done axe you—"

An' de sisters was hollerin':

"Hear him, Lord! Hear him! Amen!"

An' den Ole Miss call ole man Noae an' ole man Noae git up an' say:

"Lord, listen to my prayer. I ain't botherin' 'bout Ole Marster' body. I guh axe you 'bout he soul. Help him, Lord. Take him up an' turn him round in de palm er you' hand an' luh him git a glimpse into de life he been leadin'. Luh him see he self as all dese lyin' niggers sees him. Save he soul, Lord. Save he soul.

"Take him up, Lord, an' hold him over hell an' swinge he hind-part good. Make tenst like you guh drap him in. Lord, bring him to he senses. Lord, it ain't matter 'bout he body. Save he soul, Lord."

An' den all dem niggers got to hollerin' an' geein' answer:

From *Nigger to Nigger*, by E. C. L. Adams, pp. 206–208. Copyright, 1928, by Charles Scribner's Sons. New York and London.

‘'Save he soul, Lord! Save he soul! Swinge he hind-part, Lord! Swinge he hind-part good!"

An' Ole Marster call he overseer an' tell him to gee ole man July a quart er liquor an' a plug er tobacco, an' to take ole man Noae into de stable an' gee him twenty lashes.

An' he die next day.

The White Sign

THE complexions of various members of many slave families, from jet black to almost pure white, would have interested an ethnologist. Curious situations arose from this variety of appearance. The Reverend Ishrael Massie tells the story of black Jason, whose baby looked "too white to be his'n."

"You see de overseer been makin' up to Jason's wife. Purty soon Sarah got another baby, an' sho nuf, it was kinda light skinned. One day Jason was sittin' in de door holdin' de baby wid all his other chillun runnin' roun' in de yard. Jason looked at dem other chillun of his'n, den he looked at dat new baby's face.

"So he called to Sarah an' said, 'Ole lady, how come dis chile ain't like our other chillun?' 'Ole man, stop steddyin' yo' foolishness.' He rocked dat chile an' think a little mo'. Den he say, 'Dis chile's got blue eyes; dis chile got white finger nails. Dis chile got straight hair jus' like our overseer.' She say, 'Ole man, you know jus' as well as me how come dat chile look white.' He say, 'How come?' 'You know dat night I sent you over to Ant Minerva's arter dat buttermilk?' He answered, 'Yes, you sent me arter buttermilk, all right! Didn't git back till de next mornin'.' 'Yes, an' I drank it, didn't I?' 'Well, what dat got to do wid it?' 'Well, 'twas dat buttermilk put de white sign on dis chile.' He thought a while, den he says, 'Guess you right. You sho musta drank a lotta buttermilk, though.' But he was satisfied it was his chile. Never figured how dat ole overseer done put a white sign on his wife whilst he was gone."

The Difficulties of Collaboration

OLD Colonel B——, of Amherst County, Virginia, an indefatigable spinner of "hunting yarns," being one day in company of several of his friends, boasted that he had a few days before killed a large buck by shooting him

From *The Negro in Virginia*, Compiled by Workers of the Writers' Program of the Work Projects Administration in the State of Virginia, pp. 84–85. Copyright, 1940, by The Hampton Institute. New York: Hastings House.

From "Editor's Drawer," *Harper's New Monthly Magazine*, Vol. XIX (July, 1859), No. CX. p. 282. New York: Harper & Brothers, Publishers.

through the hoof of one of his hindfeet, the ball passing out at his forehead Of course some doubts as to the possibility of performing such a feat arose in the minds of his hearers; whereupon the Colonel called upon his old body-servant, "Bob," to verify his statement. This Bob did, by saying that, "as the deer raise he foot to scratch he head massa's bullet pass through bofe." A short time after, when the company had dispersed, Bob turned to the Colonel, and exclaimed, "For Hebben's sake, massa, when-eber you tell anuder sich a big lie prease to not scatter dem so; for I tell you what, Sir, I had mighty hard work to bring um togeder!"

The Humor of the Negro

THERE is a feeling among most Americans that the Negro is quite naturally and incurably humorous. One has only to see Africa to be cured of this. There is nothing more dignified or serious than the African in his natural tribal relations. I shall never forget the sight of a Mandingran Moham-medan striding along in his beautiful white cloak and embroidered boots, tall, black, and with perfect dignity; or the way in which Black West Africa went to its knees at sunset and bowed toward Mecca. Further down the coast the chiefs of the villages I visited, the porters, the children had nothing of what we associate with Negro humor.

On the other hand, in the United States and the West Indies, the Negroes are humorous; they are filled with laughter and delicious chuckling. They enjoy themselves; they enjoy jokes; they perpetrate them on each other and on white folk. In part that is a defense mechanism; reaction from tragedy; oppositions set out in the face of the hurt and insult. In part it supplies those inner pleasures and gratifications which are denied in broad outline to a caste-ridden and restricted people. Of course this is not universally so. There is an undercurrent of resentment, of anger and vengeance which lies not far beneath the surface and which sometimes exhibits itself at the most unexpected times and under unawaited circumstances.

In general it would be impossible to classify, without such careful study as has not been possible in my case, the variety of jokes which characterize the American Negro. I imagine that in the large they would fall in the same general categories with those of people the world over. Certain traits of humor have been exaggerated and emphasized among Negroes; for instance, the dry mockery of the pretensions of white folk. I remember when a celebrated Texas politician was shouting a fervent oration, two undistinguished Negroes listened to him from a distance. "Who is dat

By W. E. B. Du Bois, in *The Mark Twain Quarterly*, Vol. V (Fall-Winter, 1942–1943), No. 3, p. 12. Webster Groves, Missouri: The International Mark Twain Society.

man?" said one. The other looked on, without smiling: "I dunno, but he sutinly do recommen' hisself mos' high." Many is the time that a truculent white man has been wholly disarmed before the apparently innocent and really sophisticated joke of the Negro whom he meant to berate.

Then among themselves Negroes have developed a variety of their own humor. The use of the word "nigger," which no white man must use, is coupled with innuendo and suggestion which brings irresistible gales of laughter. They imitate the striver, the nouveau riche, the partially educated man of large words, and the entirely untrained. Williams and Walker in their celebrated team work brought this to a high and delicious point of efficiency. Probably the new anthropology will have something to tell us of Negro humor in the future, which will be illuminating and instructive. As it is, one can only say that to the oppressed and unfortunate, to those who suffer, God mercifully grants the divine gift of laughter. Those folk are not all black nor all white, but with inborn humor, men of all colors and races face the tragedy of life and make it endurable.

Swapping Dreams

MASTER Jim Turner, an unusually good-natured master, had a fondness for telling long stories woven out of what he claimed to be his dreams, and especially did he like to "swap" dreams with Ike, a witty slave who was a house servant. Every morning he would set Ike to telling about what he had dreamed the night before. It always seemed, however, that the master could tell the best dream tale, and Ike had to admit that he was beaten most of the time.

One morning, when Ike entered the master's room to clean it, he found the master just preparing to get out of bed. "Ike," he said, "I certainly did have a strange dream last night."

"Says you did, Massa, says you did?" answered Ike. "Lemme hear it."

"All right," replied the master. "It was like this: I dreamed I went to Nigger Heaven last night, and saw there a lot of garbage, some old torn-down houses, a few old broken-down, rotten fences, the muddiest, sloppiest streets I ever saw, and a big bunch of ragged, dirty niggers walking around."

"Umph, umph, Massa," said Ike, "you sho musta et de same t'ing I did las' night, 'case I dreamed I went up to de white man's paradise, an' de streets was all of gol' an' silver, and dey was lots o' milk an' honey dere, an' putty pearly gates, but dey wasn't a soul in de whole place."

From "Juneteenth," by J. Mason Brewer, in *Tone the Bell Easy*, Publications of the Texas Folk-Lore Society, Number X, 1932, edited by J. Frank Dobie, pp. 18–19. Copyright, 1932, by the Texas Folk-Lore Society. Austin, Texas.

Cussing Master

. . . WELL, all Master Ed Mobley's niggers like to stay with him after freedom. They just stay on without the whippings. Instead of whippings they just got cussings, good ones too. There was two old men, Joe Raines and Joe Murray, that he was particular fond of. Maybe he more love Joe Raines the bestest. One day Joe Murray let the cows get away in the corn field. At dinnertime Master Ed cuss him before the whole crowd of hands, laying around before dinner; and he cuss him powerful. After dinner Joe Murray grieve and complain much about it to the crowd. Joe Raines up and allow: "Next time he cuss you, do like I do, just cuss him back. This is a free country, yes sir. Just give him as good a cussing as he gives you."

Not long after that, the boar hog get out the lot gate, when Joe Murray was leading his mule out. Master Ed lit out on Joe Murray a-cussing, and Joe Murray lit out on Master Ed a-cussing, and then Master Ed catch Joe and give him a slavery-time whipping and turn him loose. Joe Murray take his mule on to the field, where he glum with Joe Raines. Joe Murray tell about the boar hog getting out and the cussings and the whippings. Joe Raines allow: "You didn't cuss him right. You never cuss him like I cuss him, or you'd-a never got a whipping." Joe Murray allow; "How you cuss him then, Joe?" Say Joe Raines very slow: "Well, when I cuss Master Ed, I goes 'way down in the bottoms where the corn grow high and got a black color. I looks east and west and north and south. I see no Master Ed. Then I pitches into him and gives him the worst cussing a man ever give another man. Then when I goes back to the house, my feelings is satisfied from the cussing I have give him, and he is sure to make up with me, for Master Ed don't bear anger in his bosom long. The next time cuss him, but be sure to go 'way off somewhere so he can't hear you, nigger."

Roast Pig

OLD John was working in Old Massa's house that time, serving around the eating table. Old Massa loved roasted young pigs, and had them often for dinner. Old John loved them too, but Massa never allowed the slaves to eat any at all. Even put aside the left-over and ate it next time. John de

As told by Ed McCrorey (Ed Mack), age 82, Winnsboro, South Carolina, to W. W. Dixon. From *Lay My Burden Down*, A Folk History of Slavery, edited by B. A. Botkin, pp. 8–9. Copyright, 1945, by the University of Chicago. Chicago: The University of Chicago Press.

From "High John de Conquer," by Zora Neale Hurston, *The American Mercury*, Vol. LVII (October, 1943), No. 238, pp. 454–455. Copyright, 1943, by the American Mercury, Inc. New York.

Conquer got tired of that. He took to stopping by the pig pen when he had a strong taste for pig-meat, and getting himself one, and taking it on down to his cabin and cooking it.

Massa began to miss his pigs, and made up his mind to squat for who was taking them and give whoever it was a good hiding. So John kept on taking pigs, and one night Massa walked him down. He stood out there in the dark and saw John kill the pig and went on back to the "big house" and waited till he figured John had it dressed and cooking. Then he went on down to the quarters and knocked on John's door.

"Who dat?" John called out big and bold, because he never dreamed that it was Massa rapping.

"It's me, John," Massa told him. "I want to come in."

"What you want, Massa? I'm coming right out."

"You needn't do that, John. I want to come in."

"Naw, naw, Massa. You don't want to come into no old slave cabin. Youse too fine a man for that. It would hurt my feelings to see you in a place like this here one."

"I tell you I want to come in, John."

So John had to open the door and let Massa in. John had seasoned that pig *down*, and it was stinking pretty! John knowed Old Massa couldn't help but smell it. Massa talked on about the crops and hound dogs and one thing and another, and the pot with the pig in it was hanging over the fire in the chimney and kicking up. The smell got better and better.

Way after while, when that pig had done simbled down to a low gravy, Massa said, "John, what's that you cooking in that pot?"

"Nothing but a little old weasly possum, Massa. Sickliest little old possum I ever did see. But I thought I'd cook him anyhow."

"Get a plate and give me some of it, John. I'm hungry."

"Aw, naw, Massa, you ain't hongry."

"Now, John, I don't mean to argue with you another minute. You give me some of that in the pot, or I mean to have the hide off of your back to-morrow morning. Give it to me!"

So John got up and went and got a plate and a fork and went to the pot. He lifted the lid and looked at Massa and told him, "Well, Massa, I put this thing in here a possum, but if it comes out a pig, it ain't no fault of mine."

Old Massa didn't want to laugh, but he did before he caught himself. He took the plate of brownded-down pig and ate it up. He never said nothing, but he gave John and all the other house servants roast pig at the big house after that.

Massa's Gone to Philly-Me-York

. . . Ole Massa said: "Well, John, . . . I goin' to Philly-Me-York and won't be back in three weeks. I leave everything in yo' charge."

So Ole Massa and his wife got on de train and John went to de depot with 'em and seen 'em off on de train bid 'em good-bye. Then he hurried on back to de plantation. Ole Massa and Ole Miss got off at de first station and made it on back to see whut John was doin'.

John went back and told de niggers, "Massa's gone to Philly-Me-York and left everything in my charge. Ah want one of you niggers to git on a mule and ride three miles north, and another one three miles west and another one three miles south and another one three miles east. Tell everybody to come here—there's gointer be a ball here to-night. The rest of you go into the lot and kill hogs until you can walk on 'em."

So they did. John goes in and dressed up in Ole Massa's swaller-tail clothes, put on his collar and tie; got a box of cigars and put under his arm, and one cigar in his mouth.

When the crowd come John said: "Y'all kin dance and Ah'm goin' to call figgers."

So he got Massa's biggest rockin' chair and put it up in Massa's bed and then he got up in the bed in the chair and begin to call figgers:

"Hands up!" "Four circle right." "Half back." "Two ladies change." He was puffing his cigar all de time.

'Bout this time John seen a white couple come in but they looked so trashy he figgered they was piney woods crackers, so he told 'em to g'wan out in de kitchen and git some barbecue and likker and to stay out there where they belong. So he went to callin' figgers agin. De git fiddles [1] was raisin' cain over in de corner and John was callin' for de new set:

"Choose yo' partners." "Couples to yo' places like horses to de traces." "Sashay all." "Sixteen hands up." "Swing Miss Sally round and round and bring her back to me!"

Just as he went to say, "Four hands up," he seen Ole Massa comin' out the kitchen wipin' the dirt off his face.

Ole Massa said: "John, just look whut you done done! I'm gointer take you to that persimmon tree and break yo' neck for this—killin' up all my hogs and havin' all these niggers in my house."

John ast, "Ole Massa, Ah know you gointer kill me, but can Ah have a word with my friend Jack before you kill me?"

"Yes, John, but have it quick."

So John called Jack and told him; says: "Ole Massa is gointer hang me under that persimmon tree. Now you get three matches and get in the

From *Mules and Men,* by Zora Neale Hurston, pp. 112–114. Copyright, 1935, by Zora Neale Hurston. Philadelphia and London: J. B. Lippincott Company.
[1] Guitars.—Z. N. H.

top of the tree. Ah'm gointer pray and when you hear me ast God to let it lightning Ah want you to strike matches."

Jack went on out to the tree. Ole Massa brought John on out with the rope around his neck and put it over a limb.

"Now, John," said Massa, "have you got any last words to say?"

"Yes sir, Ah want to pray."

"Pray, and pray damn quick. I'm clean out of patience with you, John."

So John knelt down. "O Lord, here Ah am at de foot of de persimmon tree. If you're gointer destroy Old Massa to-night, with his wife and chillun and everything he got, lemme see it lightnin'."

Jack up the tree struck a match. Ole Massa caught hold of John and said: "John, don't pray no more."

John said: "Oh yes, turn me loose so Ah can pray. O Lord, here Ah am to-night callin' on Thee and Thee alone. If you are gointer destroy Ole Massa to-night, his wife and chillun and all he got, Ah want to see it lightnin' again."

Jack struck another match and Ole Massa started to run. He give John his freedom and a heap of land and stock. He run so fast that it took a express train running at the rate of ninety miles an hour and six months to bring him back, and that's how come niggers got they freedom to-day.

Setting John Free

OLE John was a slave, you know. And there was Ole Massa and Ole Missy and de two li' children—a girl and a boy.

Well, John was workin' in de field and he seen de children out on de lake in a boat, just a-hollerin'. They had done lost they oars and was 'bout to turn over. So then he went and tole Ole Massa and Ole Missy.

Well, Ole Missy, she hollered and said: "It's so sad to lose these 'cause Ah ain't never goin' to have no more children." Ole Massa made her hush and they went down to de water and follered de shore on round till they found 'em. John pulled off his shoes and hopped in and swum out and got in de boat wid de children and brought 'em to shore.

Well, Massa and John take 'em to de house. So they was all so glad 'cause de children got saved. So Massa told 'im to make a good crop dat year and fill up de barn, and den when he lay by de crops nex' year, he was going to set him free.

So John raised so much crop dat year he filled de barn and had to put some of it in de house.

So Friday come, and Massa said, "Well, de day done come that I said I'd set you free. I hate to do it, but I don't like to make myself out a lie. I hate to git rid of a good nigger lak you."

So he went in de house and give John one of his old suits of clothes to put on. So John put it on and come in to shake hands and tell 'em good-bye. De children they cry, and Ole Missy she cry. Didn't want to see John go. So John took his bundle and put it on his stick and hung it crost his shoulder.

Well, Ole John started on down de road. Well, Ole Massa said, "John de children love yuh."

"Yassuh."

"John, I love yuh."

"Yassuh."

"And Missy *like* yuh!"

"Yassuh."

"But 'member, John, youse a nigger."

"Yassuh."

Fur as John could hear 'im down de road he wuz hollerin', "John, Oh John! De children loves you. And I love you. De Missy *like* you."

John would holler back, "Yassuh."

"But 'member, youse a nigger, tho!"

Ole Massa kept callin' 'im and his voice was pitiful. But John kept right on steppin' to Canada. He answered Old Massa every time he called 'im, but he consumed on wid his bag.

Mister White

". . . I KNEW a man (they call him Mister White) had a plantation about fifty or sixty miles square and he didn't even want a Negro to come through his place. The government highway ran *through* his land, you know? What they call a pike, a main highway where everybody had to go, but he built a special road, ran all around his place, and when you got there it was a sign said 'NEGRO TURN.' You had to turn off the highway and go all around his plantation."

"I knew him, knew him well," Leroy muttered.

"And this Mister White had all white fences around his place. The trees, he painted them white as high as he could reach. All his cattle, his sheeps, goats, hogs, cows, mules, hosses, and everything on his place was white. Anytime one of his animals have a black calf or a black goat—whatsonever it was—Mister White give it to the niggers. Even down to the chickens. He had all white chickens, too. And when a chicken would hatch off some black chickens, he'd say, 'Take those chickens out and find a nigger and give 'em to him. Get rid of 'em. I won't have no nigger chickens on this plantation!'"

"I've seed all that, too," said Leroy. "And you know the time a Negro and a white man was standin' by a railroad crossin'? They was talkin',

From "I Got the Blues," by Alan Lomax, *Common Ground,* Vol. VIII (Summer, 1948), No. 4, pp. 51–52. Copyright, 1948, by Alan Lomax. Reprinted by permission of Duell, Sloan, and Pearce, Inc. New York.

you know. The white man was tellin' the Negro what he wanted him to do. So along come another Negro drivin' a wagon with a white mule hitched to it. Well, the railin' was kinda high at this crossin' and the wheels got caught and the wagon stopped. This Negro who was drivin' begin to holler at that mule. 'Get up!' he says. 'Get along there.'

"So the white man holler up there and asked him, say 'Hey you, don't you know that's a *white* mule you talkin' to?'

" 'Yassuh, boss,' the Negro tell him. 'Get up, *Mister* Mule!' "

* * * * *

"And how about that Prince Albert tobacco?" gasped Natchez, when he could speak again.

"I've heard of that," said Leroy.

"You know you couldn't go into one of these here little country stores and say 'Gimme a can of Prince Albert'? Not with that white man on the can."

"What would you say?"

"Gimme a can of *Mister* Prince Albert!"

Booker T. Washington and Teddy Roosevelt

THE change in the status of the Negro from that of a caste to minority group has not come about without some interesting changes and quaint compromises in the racial ritual, growing out of the contradiction between present conditions and the traditional attitudes of both races as they have become enshrined in the traditional racial etiquette. An anecdote told me years ago by Booker Washington will illustrate better than any exposition the point I am seeking to make.

One of the methods adopted by Washington to spread his gospel of education was to organize from time to time statewide educational campaigns. On such occasions he and his party traveled sometimes for a week in a special car visiting and speaking in every city and center of Negro population. On these occasions he was frequently visited by delegations of white folk from remote villages along the way who, attracted by the legendary reputation he had achieved, wanted to see this extraordinary man. Southern white people have always been interested in Negro prodigies.

On one of these occasions a delegation, headed by a lanky and rustic but enterprising member of the village intelligentsia, waited upon Mr. Washington at the station and introduced himself and his fellow-villagers in good-natured, backwoods fashion:

"Y'u know, Booker, I been hear'n about you, I been hear'n for a long time now, and I sure did want to see you. I been a-tellin' my friends about

By Robert E. Park. From "Introduction" to *The Etiquette of Race Relations in the South*, A Study in Social Control, by Bertram Wilbur Doyle, pp. xxii–xxiii. Copyright, 1937, by the University of Chicago. Chicago: The University of Chicago Press.

y'u. I been tellin' them you was one of the biggest men in this country to-day. Yes, sir, one of the biggest men in the whole country."

At this time Theodore Roosevelt was at the height of his reputation, and Mr. Washington, somewhat at a loss for a reply, but thinking it well to discount the exuberance of his visitor replied, "Well, what do you think about President Roosevelt?"

"Oh! Hell, Roosevelt! Well, I used to be all for him until he let you eat dinner with him. That finished him as far as I'm concerned."

This retort was not perhaps as naïve as it may at first appear, but it illustrates, at any rate, the curious and incongruous association of ideas and attitudes that arise out of the necessity of maintaining the customary caste distinctions in a world which is gradually outgrowing them.

Racial Etiquette

I [1]

. . . HE AND his pardner were working on top of a high, tall building, when he got too close to the edge and he fell off. His pardner called out to him, "Stop, Jim, you'se falling." But he sang out, "I can't stop. I'se done fell."

His pardner leaned over the edge an' call to him an' say, "You, Jim! You'se gwine to fall on a white lady!" An' Jim stopped and come right on back up. . . .

II [2]

It seems that one day a Negro who lived in the upper part of Richland County came into the city of Columbia with his wife and children in an old dilapidated T-model Ford. As he reached the city limits and the first traffic light, a traffic officer on a motorcycle noticed that he would stop for the green light and when the red light came on he would move forward. After this occurred once or twice he stopped him and questioned him as to running through the red traffic signal. And the old Negro replied:

"Lord, white folks," he said. "I ain't mean to do no harm. When that there light come on, I seed all the white folks goin', so I just naturally thought that that red light was for us colored folks to go on."

---

[1] From *On the Trail of Negro Folk-Songs*, by Dorothy Scarborough, p. 30. Copyright, 1925, by Harvard University Press. Cambridge.

For the Negro audience the Negro story-teller may substitute "Miss Rope" or "Miss Hemp" for "white lady."

[2] As told by Dr. S. B. McLendon, South Carolina State Hospital, Columbia, South Carolina, January 25, 1949. Recorded by B. A. Botkin.

In the Negro version the old man would appear "smart" rather than "simple."

Getting into Heaven

NEGRO went to heaven by land. Went there an' knocked on the door. St. Peter come to the do', say, "Who is that?" Nigger say, "This is me." St. Peter say, "You ridin' or walkin'?" Nigger says, "I'm walkin'." St. Peter says, "Well, you can't get in here les'n you're ridin'." Nigger left; come on back down the road about five miles, meets up wid a white man. Say, "Mr. White Man, where you goin'?" White Man say, "I'm goin' to heaven." Nigger say, "You can't git in dere walkin'. I just left dere." Nigger say, "I'll tell you a way we'll get in dere." Nigger say, "Let me be your horse an' you get straddle me an' I'll go ridin' an' carry you up to heaven; an' you knock on de gate an' Salt Peter ask you who you is an' you tell him it's you, an' he gonna say, 'Bof you all come on in.'" White Man says, "All right, get down." White Man straddles the nigger, nigger goes runnin' back up to heaven wid him. Rode him right up to de door. White Man knocks on de do'. St. Peter say, "Who is dere?" White Man say, "Dis is me." St. Peter say, "You ridin' or walkin'?" White Man says, "Yes." St. Peter says, "Hitch your damn horse outside an' come on in."

Working on Shares

WHEN the Civil War ended and emancipation of the slave became a fact throughout the whole United States, both the former master and the former servant were met with new problems in the labor market. . . .

* * * * *

The problem of labor was finally solved in the majority of instances by the owner of the lands "sharing the crops" with the laborer. Under this method, a certain part of the crops were to be set aside for the hire of the lands, the team, and the implements, and the remainder was to be divided between the owner and the tenant. This plan was known as "working on shares," and under the conditions prevailing at that date, it probably was the better plan, as the owner of the lands was not at that period prepared with ready money to hire labor, and the Negro was in the same condition

From "Negro Folk Tales from the South (Alabama, Mississippi, Louisiana)," by Arthur Huff Fauset, *Journal of American Folklore*, Vol. 40 (July–September, 1927), No. 157, p. 274.

From *Life in Old Virginia*, A Description of Virginia, More Particularly the Tidewater Section, Narrating Many Incidents Relating to the Manners and Customs of Old Virginia So Fast Disappearing as a Result of the War between the States, together with Many Humorous Stories, by James J. McDonald, edited by J. A. C. Chandler, pp. 173, 176–177. Copyright, 1907, by the Old Virginia Publishing Company, Inc. Norfolk, Virginia.

as to the means to purchase teams, implements, and food to last until the crops were harvested.

This arrangement continued for many successive years, and is yet the plan followed in many instances.

It is related that there was a certain close-fisted farmer who persuaded a Negro away from his former master's service by making him the liberal offer of one-half of the crop, reserving the other half for the use of the land and team.

After the crop was harvested this old servant was met on the road by his former master, and inquiry was made as to how he succeeded in farming on such liberal sharing of the crop.

"Ise gittin' on mighty slow, Boss," said he. "I wucked Mistuh C——'s co'n crap on half shar's, an' kaze uv de drouf dar warn't mo' dan half a crap raise, an' Mistuh C—— he say to me dat dar's no use 'sputin' 'bout it, kaze de half crap dat wuz raise mus' sholy go fo' de lan' an' de mules. I done quit 'sputin' wid him, an' I done quit wuckin' on sich shars as dat."

Landlord and Tenant

I [1]

A TENANT offering five bales of cotton was told, after some owl-eyed figuring, that his cotton exactly balanced his debt. Delighted at the prospect of a profit this year, the tenant reported that he had one more bale which he hadn't yet brought in. "Shucks," shouted the boss, "why didn't you tell me before? Now I'll have to figure the account all over again to make it come out even."

II [2]

Store owners were dependent upon land to produce crops with which to pay accounts and to sustain trade. Because of this, storekeepers often branched out into landowning and farming. Too, they acquired other property to such an extent that they were generally the most enterprising men in the community. A story was told of a country merchant who died and went to hell, and immediately the devil had him imprisoned under an upturned washpot. Later a visitor to the lower region was being showed its

---

[1] From *The Collapse of Cotton Tenancy*, by Charles S. Johnson, Edwin R. Embree, and W. W. Alexander, p. 9. Copyright, 1935, by the University of North Carolina Press. Chapel Hill.

[2] From *Pills, Petticoats and Plows*, The Southern Country Store, by Thomas D. Clark, p. 330. Copyright, 1944, by the Bobbs-Merrill Company. Indianapolis and New York.

wonders, but when he undertook to look under the pot the devil became greatly agitated and shouted at him to keep hands off. "Don't lift that pot! We have Old Man George Cobb under there and if you let him out he'll foreclose a mortgage on all hell in the first crop season!"

Deducts

WHEN the crops were garnered, would come the settlement between the owner and tenant. The value of the products was ascertained, and fifty percent of the whole was credited to the landowner and fifty percent to the tenant. Then from the tenant's half was deducted the amount charged against him for supplies. This system, practiced with honesty as between the conscientious land owner and the ignorant black, worked in an equitable and satisfactory manner, but, as might have been expected, the time came when the land fell into the hands of some who had no scruples about dealing with the Negro, and out of this condition grew a long chain of abuses. The "advance merchant" came upon the scene, removing from the shoulders of the land owner the burden of providing the tenant with the things needful for producing the crop and maintaining his family between seasons.

Many of these merchants played a useful and constructive part in keeping the agriculture of the South moving, but as always under such circumstances, the man looking for a big profit, and having no compunctions as to how it was obtained, found this a lucrative field. The schemes to which he would resort in robbing the Negro of the fruit of his toil is the theme of many a story, and they illustrate a genius for wrongdoing, as well as a surprising indifference to the Golden Rule. One of the common practices of this element is said to have been to start a "charge column" with the year, then add the purchases from time to time, thus:

Bought: Sept. 1, 1868
1 sack of meal $2.40
1 pr. shoes 3.00
10 lbs. coffee 1.50

When the time of settlement came, the year went into the total charged against the farmer, along with such other extraordinary charges as might have suggested themselves during the twelve months, and he was a lucky individual who had anything left after the settlement.

The impression made upon the mind of the Negro tenant by practices of this kind was well illustrated on one occasion when a wealthy citizen from the North came into Alabama with a view to buying a large plantation which had been offered for sale. The deal was considered so impor-

From *The Book of Birmingham*, by John R. Hornady, pp. 206–211. Copyright, 1921, by Dodd, Mead and Company, Inc. New York.

tant that the real estate man handling the matter called upon the Agricultural Department of the State for the assistance of an expert in explaining the nature of the soil and the wide variety of products to which it was adapted. The visitor was much impressed and was about to close the deal when he fell into conversation with an aged darky, and then it looked for a few minutes as though the real estate man might lose a fat commission and the State a new citizen.

While the parties to the transaction were seated upon the broad veranda of the old mansion which adorned this plantation, the prospective buyer observed an aged Negro seated by an overflowing artesian well that bubbled up near the house, and he strolled over to the darky, whereupon the following conversation was overheard by the real estate dealer and the agent from the Agricultural Department:

"How long have you lived here?" asked the prospective buyer.

"All my life, Boss; I was borned on this here place befo' de wah, an' when de niggers was freed I stayed on here," was the reply of the darky.

"Then you know this plantation very well?"

"I does dat; I knows every foot of it, an' I knows it am de best place in dis whole country. I knows mo' cawn an' cotton is hauled off'n dis place ever year dan off'n nair uther place hereabout."

At this the prospective buyer smiled his appreciation, and the real estate man whispered "that ought to cinch matters," but the conversation at the well was not over, for the gentleman continued:

"Then I ought to make a lot of money off of this plantation, eh?"

"No, sah, Boss, you can't make no money. If you does it'll be the fust time anybody ever done it since de wah."

The jaw of the Northerner sagged and he gasped:

"If it's such fine land and produces such splendid crops, why is it money cannot be made here?"

"Well, Boss, to tell you de truf, de ducks eats it all up; yes sah, de ducks takes it all!"

"The ducks eat it up! What on earth do you mean by that?"

"Yes, sir, de ducks eats it up, just like I's tellin' you. We niggers raises heaps of cotton an' heaps of cawn, an' den we takes it to town to de sto'. Den de white folks dey figgers an' figgers, an' dey ducks dis and dey ducks dat, and 'fo de Lawd, by time dey's done, de ducks is et up ever' thing we's raised!"

*　*　*　*　*

Today the old-time advance merchant largely is a creature of the past, education and diversification having proved his undoing. Many farmers are able to finance their own operations, and those who cannot have the help of the banker or the legitimate merchant. So "de ducks" are not so destructive of farm values as they were in olden times.

Plow It Good and Deep, Boys

SOME fellers back in Georgia, in a little small country town, you know, back in the country, back there where they haul logs and things—they were just plowin and goin on. So one feller had been up in Detroit workin, you know. That was his home town down there. Well, he come back there to stay a while. He got into trouble up there, and he had to go home. He was back there on that farm.

The boss had about twelve mules. And he rode a great big red horse, you know. So this feller was plowin—you can't stay home and eat. You got to work down there. And he told the oldest feller that had been with the man thirty years: "This man just give us $3.00 a week and our dinner and buy us clothes. Them folks up the road make a dollar a hour." And he said, "When he come down here this evenin"—he told the oldest feller that had been there thirty years—"you tell him to give us more money or else just all of us gonna quit." And this old feller says, "Yes. Do you reckon he'll get to jump on us about it." "No," he said, "when he come you just tell him, because you're the oldest. You've been here the longest. You just tell him, and he'll realize it's you."

So the boss rode down on his horse, with a great big .45 over here and a great big black hat. He says, "Now you all just be quiet," the old man says, "let me do the talkin." The old boss got down there. All the fellers just stopped their mules out in the field. And the old boss said, "Well, boys, how you all gettin along?" He said, "Boss, we're gettin along fine. Yes. You're goin over some land, I see you is. Yes, we're all doin' fine," he said. "Plow it good and deep, boys." They says, "Yes, sir, we've plowed it good and deep." So the boys told this old feller, "Go ahead and tell him. Go ahead and tell him. Go ahead and tell him." He said, "Boss." "Ah-ha." He says, "These boys all says that if you don't give 'em a little bit more, they're all goin to quit." The boss snapped back real hard: "What did you say?" He says, "If you don't give 'em nothin, we're just gonna work over here fine like we've been doin."

Staying All Night at Buck Bradley's

I KEPT on going up and up the creek, and the homes got further apart and poorer looking, and it was getting near sundown, so I began to wonder where I could spend the night. Finally another cabin hove in sight around

As told by James White, Asheville, North Carolina, January 20, 1949. Recorded by B. A. Botkin.

By James Larkin Pearson, Boomer, North Carolina. Manuscripts of the Federal Writers' Project of the Works Progress Administration for the State of North Carolina.

the bend of the road and I made up my mind that I would have to stay all night in that house. It looked like a very small house, and there seemed to be several children around. Anyhow, I slapped old Mollie with the reins and drove up to the door.

"Howdy," I said to the man who came out smoking a strong pipe and looking at me over the top of his specks as if trying to size me up. "Who lives here?" I went on.

"Buck Bradley's the name, suh. How do you do, stranger? Light and come in."

He wore dirty overalls and had a two-weeks' growth of stubble on his face.

"Thank you, Mr. Bradley," says I. "If you don't object I will. I been traveling all day and it's purty late, so if you don't mind I'd like to spend the night with you."

There happened to be an empty cow-stall on the place, and we put the mare in it and fed her, and then went into the house. Mag Bradley and one or two of her oldest gals were bustling around inside to fix me some supper. Mag had about a pound of snuff in her lower lip, and every little while I could see the juice drip out, but I couldn't quite see where it fell.

Well, sir, supper was got through somehow, and the old folks set down to talk with me while the children sot around on the floor and looked on like scared things. I had been looking around in the cabin and I couldn't see but one bed anywhere, and there were at least eight children ranging in age from five to fifteen. I didn't have long to wait until I begun to see the light. Mag took the two youngest children and put them in the bed. In a few minutes they were sound asleep, and then she carefully took them up and stood them against the wall. Then she put the two next youngest into the bed. When they were safely asleep she took them up, stood them in line against the wall, and put in two more. After the children were all gotten to sleep and stood against the wall, they told me I might go to bed. I was very tired and gladly availed myself of the opportunity to sleep and rest. So I got into the bed and was soon asleep.

But next morning when I woke up I was standing up against the wall with the eight children, and Buck Bradley and his wife were in the bed sound asleep.

Moving House

A GROUP of men were talking about moving house and the trouble that it was, when one old cracker piped up, " 'Tain't no trouble for me to move. All I got to do is outen the fire and call the dogs."

As told by Alexander S. Salley, Jr., Columbia, South Carolina, January 28, 1949. Recorded by B. A. Botkin.

Brer Rabbit's Boy and the Devil

... BRER RABBIT .... had trouble with his low-down, sorry, trifling tramp of a wife. Brer Rabbit went to sunset prayer meeting to get himself freshened with the Lord, and when he got home, bless God, he found his wife had left him. She had slept with him in the same bed, had been the mother of his children, and she had left him.

* * * * *

... So he said, doggone her, if that was the sort of good-for-nothing trash she was, then she could just leave and stay left—damn her, she could shuffle for herself. All women were trouble, Brer Rabbit said, and he made up his mind he was going to save his youngest boy from having to go through what he had gone through. He wasn't going to let him know there were women even in existence. With that, Brer Rabbit built a high brick wall and put his boy in there and kept him in there until he was twenty-one years old. Then, when the boy was twenty-one, Brer Rabbit cranked up the T-model and took his son over to Pickens to show him the sights. He showed him the Courthouse and the square with the county officials fanning themselves under the cool shade trees. He showed him the drug store, and the ten-cent store, and the filling station, and the jail. And everything was fine, the boy thought it was great. And then the boy saw something with silk stockings on and a red dress and an umbrella.

"Pa," said the boy, "for God's sake, what's that?"

"That there," said Brer Rabbit, "is the devil, and you leave the devil alone. The devil is trouble."

Brer Rabbit then grabbed the boy, shoved him in the T-model, cranked up, and headed straight for home and the high brick wall. By and by, after they had crossed Golden Creek and were close to Twelve Mile, Brer Rabbit said to the boy: "Well, son, you've seen the sights. You've seen them all. Which one of them did you like the best?"

"Pa," said the boy, "I liked that devil."

The Hillbilly Caricatured

THE popular beliefs about, but not *of*, the mountain people in Arkansas and other Southern States contain many misconceptions. According to fic-

---

From *Red Hills and Cotton*, An Upcountry Memory, by Ben Robertson, pp. 188–190. Copyright, 1942, by Ben Robertson. New York: Alfred A. Knopf.

From *Arkansas*, A Guide to the State, compiled by Workers of the Writers' Program of the Work Projects Administration in the State of Arkansas, pp. 99–100. American Guide Series. Copyright, 1941, by C. G. Hall, Secretary of State, Arkansas. New York: Hastings House, Publishers.

tion, the hillman is a seven-foot combination of malnutrition and hookworm, asleep on his front porch with the dogs. His great bare feet, dangling off the porch, flap from time to time when the flies get too pesky, but nothing awakens him except a hound's salute to a stranger. Then he shoots up his astounding neck to its full length, ogles the visitor, and on his hunting horn blows a series of long and short blasts that means, "Hide yore stills and oil yore guns; they air a stranger h'yar." This feat of mountain Morse is all the more remarkable because he can neither read nor write, and, indeed, cannot count well enough to enumerate his hogs, but must identify them by name. Should one be missing for a day or two, he musters all his kin down to second cousins and step-uncles and goes across the "mounting" for a feud. While the menfolks shoot out one another's eyeballs at artillery distances, the "chillern" go down in the valley and throw rocks, it being considered unmanly to kill women and children except in a fit of anger.

At the height of the fighting, the hog in question reels in, red of eye, and the feudists deduce that he was not killed at all, but merely knocked over somebody's barrel of mash and subsequently went off down the valley, hunting wolves. The patriarchs and their relatives regretfully suspend the fighting and repair to a clan stronghold for a square dance. Between sets they hold spitting contests in the moonlight or mournfully intone Elizabethan ballads in purest Shakespearean idiom. When every keg of white lightning has been emptied, each man gathers up a rifle that saw service at Kings Mountain, and, followed by his twelve-year-old bride carrying a tub of clothes and two buckets of water, walks nine miles up the holler to his cabin.

Downing such an exaggeration is difficult, because there really is a rugged, homespun quality about the hill people. They appreciate a good pocketknife, a true rifle, and a cold-nosed coonhound. They look upon exceptional skill with an ax or a gun as an art. They take for granted an ability to "read sign" along creek banks, or to find a mule that has strayed in the woods.

A Mule and a Fool

PLOWLINES in reality were connecting links between men and mules. They were stout bonds which forced the two to move across hot sandy fields in unison. A philosopher who annually stood by a store stove and watched clerks reel off twenty-six feet of cheap Yankee manufactured cotton put his homely thoughts in writing. He spoke in profound sincerity for all those whose wrists were scarred by a continuous sawing of heart-

From *Pills, Petticoats, and Plows,* The Southern Country Store, by Thomas D. Clark, pp. 279–281. Copyright, 1944, by the Bobbs-Merrill Company. Indianapolis and New York.

less dust- and dew-laden cotton reins. "Over a hill," he philosophized, "trailed a man behind a mule drawing a plow. Unexpectedly the plow hit a root, the mule stopped, and the man began to grumble as he fixed the hames: 'Bill, you are just a mule, the son of a jackass, and I am a man made in the image of God. Yet here we work hitched up together year after year. I often wonder if you work for me or I work for you. Verily, I think it is a partnership between a mule and a fool, for surely I work as hard as you, if not harder. Plowing or cultivating we cover the same distance, but you do it on four legs and I on two, therefore I do twice as much as you.

" 'Soon we will be preparing for a corn crop. When the corn is harvested I give one-third to the landlord for being so kind as to let me use a small speck of God's earth. One-third goes to you, the rest is mine. You consume all your portion, while I divide mine among seven children, six hens, two ducks and a storekeeper. If we both need shoes, you get 'em. You are getting the best of me and I ask you, is it fair for a mule, the son of a jackass, to swindle a man, the lord of creation, out of his substance?

" 'Why, you only help to plow and cultivate the ground, and I alone must cut, shock, and husk the corn, while you look over the pasture fence and heehaw at me. All fall and most of the winter the whole family from baby up picks cotton to help raise enough money to pay taxes and buy a new set of harness and pay the mortgage on you. Not a thing, you ornery cuss, do you have to do. I even have to do the worrying about the mortgage on your tough, ungrateful hide.

" 'About the only time I am your better is on election day, for I can vote and you can't. After election I realize that I was fully as big a jackass as your papa. Verily, I am prone to wonder if politics were made for a man or a jackass, or to make jackasses out of men.

" 'And that ain't all, Bill, when you are dead, that's supposed to be the end of you. But me? The preacher tells me that when I die I may go to hell forever. That is, Bill, if I don't do just as they say. And most of what they say keeps me from getting any fun out of life.

" 'Tell me, William, considering these things, how can you keep a straight face and still look so dumb and solemn?' "

The Miller and the Devil

ONCE there was a miller who could "toll 'em heavy" or "toll 'em light" as he ground corn for rich farmers, ordinary farmers, and farmers who made

By George C. Taylor. From *Coyote Wisdom,* edited by J. Frank Dobie, Mody C. Boatright, and Harry H. Ransom, Texas Folk-Lore Society Publications, Number XIV, pp. 251–252. Copyright, 1938, by Texas Folk-Lore Society. Austin.

A story for use by any political party against any other political party.

The few folklore specialists whom I have consulted tell me they do not know the story of The Miller and the Devil. I am very sure no man, certainly not I, could barely enough to eat. As he ground the corn, the miller always carried on a conversation with the devil, who stood behind his shoulder, as to whether or not he should play fair with his customers.

One day, a little before noon, there drove up to the mill a very rich farmer with fifty wagon loads of corn. The miller began to grind.

And as he ground, he turned his head over his shoulder and said, "Devil, he's rich. Must I toll him heavy or toll him light?"

And the devil said to the miller, "He probably got rich being hard on the poor. Toll him heavy."

And the miller tolled him heavy.

Early that afternoon came to the mill just an ordinary farmer with ten wagon loads of corn. And the miller put the corn into the mill and began to grind.

And as he ground, he turned to the devil and said, "This fellow is not poor, he is not rich. How must I toll him, heavy or light?"

And the devil said, "Oh, he'll get along all right. Certainly he will not starve. He is contented with his lot. He is healthy. He is happy. Toll him heavy."

So the miller tolled him heavy.

A little before sundown came to the mill another farmer. He had one sack of corn on his back, about a bushel perhaps. He was tired from walking a long way. He was hungry. And the miller put his corn into the mill and began to grind it.

And as he ground, he turned once more to the devil and said, "Devil, this fellow certainly is poor. He's tired. He's hungry. What must I do with him, toll him heavy or toll him light?"

And the devil answered, "He's poor, damn him, keep him poor! Toll him heavy."

And the miller tolled him heavy.

The Hounds and the Law

. . . THE fox . . . had his eye on a turkey perched in a tree-top. "Hey, Brer Turkey," called Brer Fox, "is you heard about the new law?—Foxes can't eat no more turkeys, and hounds can't chase foxes. Come on down and we'll talk about it." "Nothin' doin'," said Brer Turkey, "we can talk about it right where we is." Just then some hounds were heard coming

---

make one up like this. It seems to me a fine example of folk accretion. After fifty years I remember it somewhat as follows as my uncle, Albert Rhett Taylor, of Columbia, South Carolina, told it to me, a bare-legged boy riding behind him on horseback down to the mill to grind corn, late one July afternoon.—G. C. T.

From *Palmetto Country*, by Stetson Kennedy, pp. 96–97. American Folkway Series, edited by Erskine Caldwell. Copyright, 1942, by Stetson Kennedy. New York: Duell, Sloan & Pearce.

over the hill. "Guess I'll be runnin' along," said Brer Fox. Brer Turkey said, "I thought you said the new law says no more fox hunts." And Brer Fox said, "Thas right—but them dogs will run right over that law."

A Deal in Dreams

. . . An amusing story is told of how McKnight acquired one of his plantations in Currituck. John Durant, the Chief of the Yeopims, had very astutely made it known to his own braves, as well as to his white neighbors, that the visions that visited him in his somnolent hours must somehow, somewhere, if within the range of possibility, materialize into visible, tangible realities, and that those who could, and did not help in their materialization, would incur the anger of the great chief. Now it was the habit of the wily red man, whenever he greatly desired to acquire a new possession, to dream that the owner of the coveted article had presented it to him. Having dwelt near the paleface for a number of years, the old chief adopted the white man's mode of dress to a certain extent. Needing, or coveting, a new coat, he very conveniently dreamed that McKnight, who had kept a trading store on Indian Ridge, gave him a bolt of bright cloth which appealed strongly to his innate love of bright colors. Presenting himself at the trader's store, he related his dream to the owner of the cloth; and McKnight not daring to incur the enmity of the Indian by refusing to let him have the coveted article, presented it to him forthwith; but McKnight, equally as shrewd as the chief, soon did some dreaming on his own account, and in his vision he saw himself the owner of some four hundred acres of land in Indian Ridge, the property of John Durant. So with due ceremony he approached the chief and solemnly related his dream; and the old Indian, realizing that in the Anglo-Saxon he had met his match—nay, his superior in cunning—made over to McKnight the land.

Why the Seminoles Would Not
Learn to Read and Write

When the Floridas were erected into a territory of the United States, one of the earliest cares of the Governor, William P. Duval, was directed

From *In Ancient Albemarle,* by Catherine Albertson, pp. 150–151. Copyright, 1914, by Catherine Albertson. Published by the North Carolina Society Daughters of the Revolution. Raleigh: Commercial Printing Company.

The most noted of these Tories was Thomas McKnight, . . . a prominent citizen of Indian Town.—C. A., p. 149.

From *Wolfert's Roost and Other Papers,* Now first Collected, by Washington Irving, Author's Revised Edition, pp. 330–333. New York: G. P. Putnam and Son. 1865.

to the instruction and civilization of the natives. For this purpose he called a meeting of the chiefs, in which he informed them of the wish of their Great Father at Washington that they should have schools and teachers among them, and that their children should be instructed like the children of white men. The chiefs listened with their customary silence and decorum to a long speech, setting forth the advantages that would accrue to them from this measure, and when he had concluded, begged the interval of a day to deliberate on it.

On the following day, a solemn convocation was held, at which one of the chiefs addressed the Governor in the name of all the rest. "My brother," said he, "we have been thinking over the proposition of our Great Father at Washington, to send teachers and set up schools among us. We are very thankful for the interest he takes in our welfare; but after much deliberation have concluded to decline his offer. What will do very well for white men, will not do for red men. I know you white men say we all come from the same father and mother, but you are mistaken. We have a tradition handed down from our forefathers, and we believe it, that the Great Spirit, when he undertook to make men, made the black man; it was his first attempt, and pretty well for a beginning; but he soon saw he had bungled; so he determined to try his hand again. He did so, and made the red man. He liked him much better than the black man, but still *he* was not exactly what he wanted. So he tried once more, and made the white man; and then he was satisfied. You see, therefore, that you were made last, and that is the reason I call you my youngest brother.

"When the Great Spirit had made the three men, he called them together and showed them three boxes. The first was filled with books, and maps, and papers; the second with bows and arrows, knives and tomahawks; the third with spades, axes, hoes, and hammers. 'These, my sons,' said he, 'are the means by which you are to live; choose among them according to your fancy.'

"The white man, being the favorite, had the first choice. He passed by the box of working-tools without notice; but when he came to the weapons for war and hunting, he stopped and looked hard at them. The red man trembled, for he had set his heart upon that box. The white man, however, after looking upon it for a moment, passed on, and chose the box of books and papers. The red man's turn came next, and you may be sure he seized with joy upon the bows and arrows and tomahawks. As to the black man, he had no choice left, but to put up with the box of tools.

"From this it is clear that the Great Spirit intended the white man should learn to read and write, to understand all about the moon and stars, and to make everything, even rum and whiskey. That the red man should be a first-rate hunter, and a mighty warrior, but he was not to learn anything from books, as the Great Spirit had not given him any; nor was he to make rum and whiskey, lest he should kill himself with drinking. As to the black man, as he had nothing but working tools, it

was clear he was to work for the white and red man, which he has continued to do.

"We must go according to the wishes of the Great Spirit, or we shall get
into trouble. To know how to read and write is very good for white men,
but very bad for red men. It makes white men better, but red men worse.
Some of the Creeks and Cherokees learnt to read and write, and they are
the greatest rascals among all the Indians. They went on to Washington,
and said they were going to see their Great Father, to talk about the good
of the nation. And when they got there, they all wrote upon a little piece
of paper, without the nation at home knowing anything about it. And the
first thing the nation at home knew of the matter, they were called together
by the Indian agent, who showed them a little piece of paper, which he
told them was a treaty which their brethren had made in their name with
their Great Father at Washington. And as they knew not what a treaty
was, he held up the little piece of paper, and they looked under it, and
lo! it covered a great extent of country, and they found that their brethren,
by knowing how to read and write, had sold their houses, and their lands,
and the graves of their fathers; and that the white man, by knowing how
to read and write, had gained them. Tell our Great Father at Washington,
therefore, that we are very sorry we cannot receive teachers among us; for
reading and writing, though very good for white men, is very bad for
Indians."

Indians and Oil

OKLAHOMA, an Indian word for "the land of the red man," was a state.
The red men were still an important influence in its eastern portion where
oil was producing an economic and social revolution. The Indians were
not always the honest, innocent children of Nature which sentimental writing has suggested. Some were as devious and unscrupulous as the whites
who sought to exploit them, although usually with more limited imagination.

For example, when the first land office was opened in the Chickasaw
Nation for enrollment of Indians for allotments under the Dawes Commission, the official in charge cautioned employees to be patient with the
"ignorant" Indians. When the doors were thrown open a long line of men
and women of all ages and conditions began to press toward the counter.
The official, noticing one feeble old woman tottering in the line, besought
the man who stood ahead of her to give her his place. The man refused.
The official thereupon led the old woman from the line to a rear door, took
her in and made out her registration certificate. Before he had finished

From *Then Came Oil,* The Story of the Last Frontier, by C. B. Glasscock, pp. 161–
164. Copyright, 1938, by C. B. Glasscock. Indianapolis and New York: The Bobbs-
Merrill Company.

a second squaw entered from the rear and asked similar service so that she could take the old woman home. Another and another found excuse for precedence bearing on the same case. Eighteen had thus gotten ahead of the line before the official realized that he was being tricked by the "ignorant" Indians. Hasty investigation revealed that two Indians outside were rounding up the squaws, providing each with a suitable story and moving them through the back door.

That was a petty fraud, interesting only as it indicated the fact that the Indians were as willing and eager to trick the white man as the white man had ever been to trick the Indian. But most of the latter lacked the imagination to carry their trickery to more profitable lengths. At times one appeared with a more effective plan of defrauding the white brother.

In the early days when independent oil operators and lease buyers were most active, some of the shrewder and less scrupulous Indians sold leases on their allotments for cash to every buyer who applied. It is recorded that one old Cherokee signed six leases, for cash each time, on the same allotment. That was made possible in part by the fact that Secretary Hitchcock's arbitrary restrictions upon actual drilling prevented each lessee from starting a well immediately, and none of the buyers was aware that the privilege of drilling had been sold. Then all the buyers rushed in with their drilling rigs only to find that the "ignorant" Indian had taken the cash, in effect multiplying his legitimate bonus by six, and left them to scramble over what they had purchased.

*   *   *   *   *

Oil prospectors and lease buyers did their best to make fools of them. Frequently it did not work. [An] item from the Muskogee *Times-Democrat* makes the point.

"Now you see," said one high-pressure lease buyer to an Indian whom he considered a prospect, "in thirty days [a lie] there will be oil wells dotted all over your land."

"Ugh!" was Lo's response.

"And your children can go to Yale."

"Ugh!"

"And your wife can have a new red silk dress every day."

"Ugh!"

"You see, it's like this: Oil's eight dollars a barrel [a lie] and out of every one hundred barrels you get ten—understand?"

"Ugh! Where hell get um barrel?"

IV. BRETHREN AND SISTERN

The difference between a Northern Methodist and a Southern Methodist is the difference between cold light bread and hot biscuit.—J. J. METHVIN

1. "THE COUNTRY OF THE WORD"

LIKE other "unifying" forces in the South, religion has served to divide as well as unite. For example, the dozen rival sects of a typical milltown in Western North Carolina, following the lines of caste and class, split the community sharply into tight little groups that visit and marry within themselves, making any sort of co-operation among them, and so any real progress, impossible. In this sense as well as in the sense of religious and moral fundamentalism, the church is one of the chief "bulwarks against change" in the South.

All through the South, of course, the church is an important social and cultural force, its sociability running the gamut of church-going, baptizings, funeralizings, brush-arbor revivals, all-day singings with dinner on the grounds, church suppers, singing schools and conventions. Moreover, the church not only serves as an outlet for traditionally gregarious or emotionally starved folk, but also continues the democratizing process of frontier religion that produced the Great Awakening. In a sense the small sects are the "only functioning democracies for millions of the disinherited, disfranchised and dispossessed."

This was particularly true in the South, where a poor man was barred by the tax on voting from becoming a judge or a senator. But he could be elected chief steward of the local Congregational Methodist Church, or moderator of his district association of the Duck River Baptists. A poor boy with talent couldn't go to college and become a lawyer or business man. But he could exercise his bent for leadership when the Lord "give him the call to preach" in one of the little sects. And that little sect was the one place where he might speak his mind, where every man stood equal with every other man before God. It was the place where Aunt Tut stood equal with her better-off cousin, Mr. Marion, the storekeeper.[1]

As the older and more conservative sects become identified with higher social and economic status, the common folk continue to express their "resentment against the prosperous world" by gathering against Babylon more and more "little armies waving calico flags of Jehovah." Thus over against the extremes of foot-washing and snake-handling cults must be set movements like the People's Institute of Applied Religion, founded by Claude Williams, the Western Tennessee hill Messiah who has sought to revive the socialism of primitive Christianity by "educating the Southern masses through organization and organizing them through education."[2]

In the frontier tradition of personal, practical religion, with a definite relation to social welfare as well as to crop culture and healing, the new sects continue the cultural process of religious pioneering—the South is still the "Country of the Word."

---

[1] Harold Preece and Celia Kraft, *Dew on Jordan* (New York, 1946), pp. 220–221.
[2] Cedric Belfrage, *South of God* (New York, 1941), p. 315.

For the promise of the Word is that some day the children of the Word will find a land of milk and honey where each man may eat of his own vine, sit under his own fig tree and whittle on his own sticks.[3]

2. ARGUING THE BIBLE AND COMIC EXEMPLA

In still another sense the religious South is the "Country of the Word." Among the favorite subjects of conversation and dispute, religion rivals politics in the talkative, argument-loving South.

In regions where Methodists, Presbyterians, Disciples of Christ and Baptists were predominant faiths, there were eternal arguments over church organization—deacons versus elders and stewards. But the hottest of all was over baptism. . . . One side believed in infant baptism and the other did not. Two of them sprinkled and the other two immersed, and their members argued back and forth on long summer afternoons. Perhaps no one was ever convinced, but at least he found the discussions delightfully infuriating.[4]

In good folk fashion Harold Preece thus sums up the doctrinal differences between sprinkling and immersion: "If you were a sprinkled devil, you were just a dried-up devil when the water dried up. But if you were ducked, you were really saved."

In all doctrinal disputes, including baptism, the Bible was the infallible authority and the court of last appeal. "When the Bible speaks we speak; when the Bible is silent, we are silent" was the motto of more than one church.

Allan M. Trout tells a good story on the Bible as a source of all wisdom:

Bill Bush, of Campton [in Wolfe County, Kentucky] used to live on the edge of the county, near the Lee County line. His post office, however, was Zachariah, in Lee County. Mr. Bush was on his front porch one day, reading his Bible, when Brother Peter R. Legg, an old-time Campbellite preacher, passed along the road out front.

"Good morning, Brother Bush," said the preacher. "I'm glad to see you reading the Scriptures this fine morning."

"Thank you, Brother Legg," replied Mr. Bush. "But I'm afraid appearances are deceiving. To tell you the truth, I've just ordered a gallon of whisky from Brown-Forman, and I'm looking in the Bible to see how to spell Zachariah.[5]

Anent the liquor question, a subject which has continually agitated and torn asunder the South, Carl Carmer relates the story of the fence-straddling Alabama candidate at a combination singing, rally, and barbecue who, when asked where he stood on the question, replied:

When I think of all the homes the demon rum has ruined, when I think of the hearts of pure women and little children—broken by a husband's accursed habit, when I think of the lives alcohol has snuffed out in their prime— then, ladies and gentlemen, I'm agin it. . . . But . . . *but*—when I rise on a chill mornin' and pull the window down an' hug the fire an' shiver an' I can't get warm nohow—an' my wife says to me, "Ol' man, how about a bit of toddy to warm your innards?" THEN, BOYS, I'M FOR IT.[6]

---

[3] Harold Preece and Celia Kraft, *op. cit.*, p. 12.

[4] Thomas B. Clark, *Pills, Petticoats and Plows* (Indianapolis and N. Y., 1944), p. 60.

[5] "My People Stand and Take It," paper on Kentucky Folklore read before the Filson Club, Louisville (October 4, 1948).

[6] *Stars Fell on Alabama* (New York, 1934), p. 88.

In an educationally and economically backward society, as Harold Preece points out, where the educational requirements for preaching have to be waived in favor of the mystical and miraculous "call to preach," the call to ministry is the subject of countless anecdotes involving the skepticism of deacons who believe that "Many are called but few are chosen." Perhaps the best known of these is the story of the young man to whom the Lord had appeared in a vision, showing him three flaming letters in the sky, "G.P.C.," which he interpreted as "Go Preach Christ." To this testimony the old deacon objected, saying, "But knowing this young man as I do, and appreciating to some degree the great wisdom of the Lord, I am sure that you all misinterpret what this vision meant. 'G.P.C.' in this case can only mean 'Go Pick Cotton.' " [7]

According to an East Texas version, another convert, who was considered too idiotic to preach, was cleverly disqualified on the basis of his size-thirteen shoes in the light of the Biblical injunction, "How beautiful are the feet of them that preach the Gospel of peace and bring glad tidings." [8]

As one more phase of the practicalness of Southern religion, the telling of such illustrative anecdotes or "comic exempla" has enabled the Southern preacher since pioneer days to hold his audience and expound his text. Especially when he is a lay preacher or recruited from other trades and professions he is able to draw upon his own experience—close to the experience of his congregation—for stories that soon pass into the "inherited repertoire," if they are not already a part of it. [9]

B. A. B.

The Episcopal Gentleman

THE Episcopal Church is decidedly the "social" church of the South. The Presbyterians are also acceptable, if less exalted. But the Baptists, Methodists, et al., are, in the old tradition, the churches of the plebeian elements.

I recall the midweek evening service, in Virginia, at which a parishioner rose and asked: "Pastor, is it possible for a man to achieve salvation outside the fold of the Episcopal Church?" The paster, struggling with his soul, replied: "It is conceivable that there *might* be such a possibility—but no gentleman would avail himself of it."

A Presbyterian Missionary in Texas

. . . THE following one was current in Texas twenty years ago:

---

[7] *A Treasury of American Folklore* (New York, 1944), p. 416.
[8] As told to Harold Preece by J. B. Upton, Austin, Texas.
[9] Cf. Mody C. Boatright, "Comic Exempla of the Pioneer Pulpit," *Coyote Wisdom,* Texas Folk-Lore Society Publications, No. XIV (Austin, 1938), pp. 155–168.

By Edmund Fuller, Hand's Cove, Vermont, March 5, 1949.

From "Comic Exempla of the Pioneer Pulpit," by Mody C. Boatright, in *Coyote*

A Presbyterian home missionary came to a cabin and engaged a woman in conversation.

"Are they any Presbyterians in this country?" he asked.

"Now, I jest couldn't say about that," replied the woman. "These woods is full of all kinds of varmints, but I ain't paid much attention to 'em. My husband, he's out with the dogs now. If he was here, he'd know. He keeps his hides on the south wall of the cabin. You might go around there and see if he's got any Presbyterian hides nailed up. I know he's got foxes and bars and painters, and I know if there's any Presbyterians in the country, he's caught some of 'em before now."

The Secret of Success in Preaching

AN O. S. P. divine, who had preached many years without any accessories to his church, met a Methodist preacher who had had many new converts every quarter, and said: "Brother, I want you to give me the secret of your success in preaching. You know that I have studied divinity for years before I went to preaching, while you did not know the A-B-C's. I write out my sermons and make them most perfect. I read them off to my congregation, which never increases. Now tell me how I may, as you have yours, increase my congregation?"

"I can tell you how it is," said the Methodist preacher. "You sit down and write out a good sermon, full of the true religion. The demon who sits on your right shoulder whispers in your ear, 'Now don't you know if you read that out from your pulpit that Miss Wilson, John Doe, Richard Doe, Bob Jones and Bill Smith will never come to hear you preach again?' Whereupon you scratch it all out and you commence again and you write out another good sentence and then it is that the devil pops up on the other side and says, 'How foolish it would be in you to read that out from your pulpit; why, all the business men in town would quit you and pay no more pew rent, and, besides that, they would be getting a new minister,' whereupon you write off a long sentence of platitudinous religious propositions and possibilities that nobody understands or cares for, for it has nothing in it understandable; and then it is that the devil pats you on top of your head and says, 'That's the sort of stuff to feed them on. That's sense. You need have no fear about holding your job.' Now, my dear Christian brother, when I get up to preach, the devil himself does not know what I am going to say."

Wisdom, Texas Folk-Lore Society Publications, Number XIV, J. Frank Dobie, Mody C. Boatright, Harry H. Ransom, editors, pp. 162–163. Copyright, 1938, by the Texas Folk-Lore Society. Austin.

From *Autobiography and Reminiscences of Theophilus Noel,* p. 76. Copyright, 1904, by Theophilus Noel. Chicago: Theo. Noel Company Print.

A Paying Business

AT THE close of a great meeting a Presbyterian minister gave notice that a collection would be taken up for Gospel purposes in the neighborhood. A Methodist preacher, also present, and who had just preached the sermon, it being his regular Sabbath at the place, then rose, and remarked that very little had been done toward the proper support of the Gospel or himself; that he had begun his circuit with two horses—one was used; he expected the other would soon go, and he would have to go afoot; Charity began at home; and "Besides, brethren, Christianity is a *paying* business —it pays a profit even in this world. Did you ever hear the story of the infidel in the Tennessee camp-meeting? Well, I'll tell you: Up in Tennessee once there was a camp-meeting held in a notorious bad neighborhood; and when, at the close of the exercises, the hat was sent round, a roll of notes, about fifty dollars, was found. The brethren in those parts, in those days, being rather poor, considerable speculation was had as to whar that fifty dollars come from; and next year it was decided to keep an eye on *that* hat, and see if it was done over agin. Sure enough, next year's meeting there was another fifty just as before, and it was traced to an infidel reviling country store-keeper near the camp, and who was never known to say or do a good thing for God's people. So the elders called the man aside, and says, "Did you put that 'ere fifty in that hat?" "Well, I did." "Mistake, ain't it?" "No, Sirs; I never makes mistakes. It's all right. Afore you chaps cum around these diggins preaching I couldn't keep ne'er a shoat, ne'er a yearling no whar, and I lost a powerful sight of truck; and now, gen-tle-men, I keeps the most of 'em! It's a *paying* business to keep you here, and I goes in for it!"

Prayer for Rain

SPEAKING of droughts in Texas reminds me of an occurrence of which I know well. In the country of the Wacos the drought had been long and continued and the ground around was parched and dry. The Brazos River was dry and there was a pool of water in the Tewa Kana Hills north of Waco and another at Robinsonville, a few miles south. It was decided that all of the people, regardless of creed, should congregate at the Robinsonville pool and there petition Divine power for rain, in a proper and befitting manner. They came from long distances and in great numbers and it was said that no one was left at home because there was nothing left at home

From "Editor's Drawer," *Harper's New Monthly Magazine,* Vol. XVIII (April, 1859), No. CVII, pp. 709–710. New York: Harper & Brothers, Publishers.

From *Autobiography and Reminiscences of Theophilus Noel,* pp. 45–47. Copyright, 1904, by Theophilus Noel. Chicago: Theo. Noel Company Print.

living that required attention. On the meeting ground there was no dissension; all was humiliation and contrition, even unto sackcloth and ashes. Prayers were started by first one and then another, and they were long and zealous and fervent and had been presented for many days, and yet the hot sun poured down on a famishing people its scorching rays and no relief seemed to develop in the way of clouds.

It seemed that one or two parties had taken control of matters and wrote the names of the prayer-makers on the bulletin board early in the morning. There was among the congregation an old-school Hard-shell Baptist preacher; a man well along in years and of powerful physique and a voice that might have been equaled but surely not surpassed. He was a man of indomitable will power. He was a man of considerable wealth, owned several Negroes on a fine plantation, and was the father of a very large family at home. Brother C—— was out of whack with the people for and by reason of what Brick Pomeroy termed "clerical indiscretions." He had not been called upon to pray and could no longer stand the strain. He procured a chunk of chalk—he was a good writer—rubbed out what was on the blackboard and wrote on it:

"This is Brother C——'s day to pray."

At which all of the camp took a squint, and tongues began to wag and some were against going under the arbor, but finally better judgment prevailed and soon after the old horn sounded the seats were filled and the ground was all covered Brother C—— commenced.

(I have always wished that I could tell such as this and use the party's actual words, but I cannot and I do not believe a man ever lived who could have used Brother C——'s words at this time. I propose to only give a synopsis.)

"Almighty God, Thou knowest the wants of us, Thy men-servants and Thy maid-servants, and we need not be telling you. We have come on this ground to show Thee our penitence and how badly whipped we feel and how willing we are to thank Thee for past blessings and prepare ourselves to thank Thee for the blessings Thou art going to give us in the future. Now, Almighty God, Thou knowest how we are suffering down here, and we want you to come to our relief. We want you to come with no little sprinkle or Pentecostal shower, but, Oh God in heaven, send down upon us an old-time, old-fashioned gully-washer and root-soaker, and be quick about it. Amen."

And so said all the people who arose and beheld in the northwest a black cloud which rose higher and higher and in a few hours the rain that was falling was something terrible to behold and in a very short time not only the cracks of the earth were filled, the ravines and the gullies were washed out and the Brazos came rushing down overflowing its banks and there was water in all the land. There was great rejoicing and the rain continued and continued, and it was suggested that Brother C—— be importuned to have another "heart-to-heart talk" with Deity lest a second flood come.

The Different Persuasions

I [1]

"A WHITE mule never dies," declares the farmer. "When he gets to be fifty years old he turns into a Methodist preacher." If the speaker is a Methodist, he substitutes "Baptist preacher."

II [2]

Master John had a big fine bird dog. She was a mammy dog, and one day she found six puppies out in the harness-house. They was 'most all girl puppies, so Master gwine drown 'em. I axed him to give 'em to me, and pretty soon the missus sent me to the postoffice, so I put the puppies in a basket and took 'em with me. Dr. Lyles come by where I was setting, and he say, "Want to sell them pups, Siney?" I tell him "Uh-huh." Then he say, "What 'nomination is they?" I tell him, "They's Methodist dogs." He didn't say no more. 'Bout a week after that Old Missus sent me to the postoffice again, so I took my basket of puppies. Sure 'nough, 'long come Dr. Lyles, and he say, "Siney, see you still ain't sold them pups." I say, "No, sir." Then he axed me again what 'nomination they belong to. I told him they was Baptist dogs. He say, "How come? You told me last week them was Methodist pups." Ha! Ha! Bless God! Look like he had me. But I say, "Yes, sir, but you see Doctor, they got their eyes open since then." He laugh and go on down to his newspaper office.

III [3]

. . . You know better'n dat. Baptis' and Methdis' always got a pick out at one 'nother. One time two preachers—one Methdis' and de other one Baptis'—wuz on uh train and de engine blowed up and bein' in de colored coach right back of de engine they got blowed up too. When they saw theyself startin' up in de air de Baptis' preacher hollered, "Ah bet Ah go higher than you!"

---

[1] From *South Carolina*, A Guide to the Palmetto State, compiled by Workers of the Writers' Program of the Work Projects Administration in the State of South Carolina, p. 396. American Guide Series. Copyright, 1941, by Burnet R. Maybank, Governor of South Carolina. New York: Oxford University Press.

[2] As told by Siney Bonner, age about 90, Birmingham, Alabama, to W. F. Jordan. From *Lay My Burden Down*, A Folk History of Slavery, edited by B. A. Botkin, p. 28. Copyright, 1945, by the University of Chicago. Chicago: University of Chicago Press.

[3] From *Mules and Men*, by Zora Neale Hurston, p. 47. Copyright, 1935, by Zora Neale Hurston. Philadelphia and London: J. B. Lippincott Company.

IV [4]

. . . In the first place, we have the 'Piscapalions, and they are a high sailin' and a highfalutin' set, and they may be likened unto a turkey-buzzard, that flies up in the air, and he goes up and up till he looks no bigger than your finger-nail, and the fust thing you know, he cums down and down, and is a fillin' hisself on the karkiss of a dead hoss by the side uv the road—and "He played on a harp uv a *thou*-sand strings—sperits of just men made perfeck."

And then, thar's the Methodis, and they may be likened unto the squirrel, runnin' up into a tree, for the Methodis believes in gwine on from one degree uv grace to another, and finally on to perfekshun; and the squirrel goes up and up, and he jumps from lim' to lim', and branch to branch, and the fust thing you knows, he falls, and down he comes kerflummux; and that's like the Methodis, for they is allers a fallin' from grace, ah! And "He played on a harp uv a *thou*-sand strings—sperits of just men made perfeck."

And then, my brethring, thar's the Baptist, ah! and they hev been likened unto a possum on a 'simmon tree, and the thunders may roll, and the earth may quake, but that possum clings thar still, ah! And you may shake one foot loose, and the other's thar; and you may shake all feet loose, and he laps his tail around the lim', and he clings fur-ever—for "He played on a harp uv a *thou*-sand strings—sperits of just men made perfeck."

Joining the Church

THERE was a hardened sinner who had determined to join the church, but his record for meanness was such that when he applied for admission, he was told to wait awhile and pray for spiritual aid to improve his manners and morals. At length he became tired of waiting for a call from the brethren, and made a new application. The preacher asked him if he prayed and communed with the Lord as to whether he should join the church.

"Yas indeed, I suttinly has prayed, an' I tol' de Lawd dat I don' quit all ma badness an' dat I wants to jine Shiloh Chu'ch."

"Well," said the preacher, "how'd de Lawd answer yo' pray'rs?"

"De Lawd he say to me, I wish yo' bettah luck dan I has Stephen, kase I'se be'n tryin' to jine dat chu'ch fo' mo' den fohty years mahse'f!"

---

[4] From "The Harp of a Thousand Strings," by Henry T. Lewis, *Spirit of the Times*, Vol. 25 (September 29, 1855), No. 33, p. 387. New York.

From *Life in Old Virginia*, A Description of Virginia, More Particularly the Tidewater Section . . . , by James J. McDonald, edited by J. A. C. Chandler, pp. 281–282. Copyright, 1907, by the old Virginia Publishing Company, Inc. Norfolk, Virginia.

The Winning Hand

I HAD an uncle . . . who late in life started to join the Baptist Church of which many of my family are members. On the day my uncle was to be baptized, his wife and small boy sat on the bank of the creek happy over his conversion. As my uncle was led out into the water by the preacher, there floated out of his pocket face up, the ace of spades, and a few moments later, the king of spades. As the preacher was just getting ready to take hold of him, there floated behind those cards the queen and jack of spades, and then out came the ten of spades. His wife saw the situation and screamed:

"Don't baptize him, parson, my husband is lost . . . my husband is lost!"

But the young boy on the bank yelled out excitedly:

"No he ain't, ma! If pa can't win with that hand, he can't win at all!"

Adjourning the Service

IT IS related by the Reverend Eli Lindsay—the noted "Get there, Eli," who preached at Strawberry, Arkansas, as early as 1814, that when the men used to go to meeting carrying their guns with them, he attended all the house-raisings, log-rollings, quilting bees, marriages, and frolics. He would encourage the young people to dance, and after the dance he would preach to them. In 1816, he visited the spot where Batesville now stands and found a man who had just finished building a little store. Lindsay asked and was granted permission to christen the house. He notified the people from Miller's Creek, Lafferty's Creek, Greenbrier and the surrounding country to attend. Many came, *and the men stacked their guns around the walls.*

Arms were necessary in those days. Men could shoot bears with deadly precision, and with equal skill bring down an Indian or a desperado. . . .

* * * * *

Well, old Eli began his sermon, but in a short while the dogs outside started a bear. Eli announced, "The service is adjourned, in order that the men may kill the bear." They rolled out of the house with alacrity, mounted their horses, pursued bruin and killed him. Then back they came to the new house, where Eli "thanked God for men who knew how to shoot and for women who knew how to pray," and finished his sermon.

Salvage and Salvation

How all-absorbing wrecking was in those days may be seen from the following incident. The county court house in Jackson Square was the common place of worship for all denominations. On one occasion Brother Eagan (Squire Eagan as he was called), a good old Methodist, was holding services there, and from his position on the rostrum, which served as a pulpit, he had a clear view of the ocean, whence he saw a brig beating down the gulf dangerously near the Sambos. He saw her miss stays, and drift towards the reef. With cautious eye he watched her until he was certain that she was fast ashore, and then began making his plans. Brother Eagan was the owner and master of a wrecking vessel. The rules of wrecking established by the United States court give the master of the first vessel to reach a ship in distress the right to have charge of the salvage operations, for which he receives extra compensation. He is called the wrecking master.

Brother Eagan knew if he announced from the pulpit that there was a "wreck ashore" his congregation would all get out of the church ahead of him, and the chances were that someone would reach the wreck before him.

His text was from the Ninth Chapter, I Corinthians, twenty-fourth verse: "Know ye not that they which run in a race run all, but one receiveth the prize? So run, that ye may obtain."

Warming to his subject he came down from the pulpit and exhorted his hearers to equip themselves for the great race for the prize of eternal salvation. Down the aisle he strode, hammering his text into the congregation, with forceful gesture and apt illustration. When he reached the door, he startled his hearers with the cry "Wreck ashore! Now we will all run a race and see who receiveth the prize," and dashed down the steps, and out into the street, with the entire male portion of the congregation at his heels. He had a good start on them, however, and soon got to his schooner, the Godspeed, and with a crew made up of members of his congregation who had overtaken him, set sail and reached the wreck first, and became the wrecking master.

This incident was typical. The cry of "Wreck a-s-h-o-r-e," taken up and repeated, with the last syllable drawn out in a long monotone, was a familiar sound in old Key West, and would empty a church as promptly as a cry of "fire!" It seemed to electrify the slow moving population, and soon the streets would be full of men running to their vessels, carrying small bundles of clothes—for they knew not whether they would be absent a day or a month— and from every quarter of the city, the cry "Wreck a-s-h-o-r-e" would echo and re-echo.

From *Key West, The Old and The New*, by Jefferson B. Browne, pp. 165–166. Copyright, 1912, by Jefferson B. Browne. St. Augustine: The Record Company, Printers and Publishers.

Cured of Hatred

AT THE camp meeting down in Christian County the preacher was holding forth against the sin of hatred. He begged the brethren and sistern to shun, abjure, cast out and renounce this hideous, unchristian emotion. Then pausing, he asked any members of his congregation who had succeeded in conquering hatred to stand up.

Only one man got to his feet, the 104-year-old Uncle Beauregard, the oldest man in the county.

"You don't hate anybody, Uncle Bo?"

"No, sir."

"That's wonderful, Uncle Bo. Tell us why that is."

"Well," piped Uncle Beauregard, "all them skunks who done me dirt, all them blankety-blanks I hated"—here he cackled triumphantly—"they're all dead."

A Call to Preach

I HAVE no doubts as to the call to the Christian ministry. I concede all that is claimed for it by intelligent orthodox Christians; but as to the "call" contained in the story below I shall not decide. My business is to detail facts. Somebody is always telling stories about the "Hard-shell Baptists." Wags have the run on them, and they may as well be content and bear it. Here follows a tale told of them not long since. My informant locates it in the mountains of North Carolina, where the Hard-shells are quite numerous, and where they believe pretty strongly in dreams and voices. In the important matter of a call to the ministry, a dream or a voice is a thing almost indispensable.

Now it came to pass that a man by the name of Walker felt himself considerably moved to "hold forth" and "kept spreading the fleece," Gideon-like, to ascertain his duty in the important premises. To assist him in his pious investigations, he called at a still-house one evening to get some of the "good critter." After *refreshments*, the story runs, he left for home, and on the way he felt "moved" to go into a thick grove a few hundred yards from the road, "thar to wrastle on to subjeck." While he was "wrastlin' " most earnestly, scarcely outdone by the patriarch, some

According to Vice-President Alben W. Barkley.

From "Washington's Greatest Storyteller," by Beverly Smith, *The Saturday Evening Post*, Vol. 222 (July 2, 1949), No. 1, p. 19. Copyright, 1949, by the Curtis Publishing Company. Philadelphia.

From *Fisher's River (North Carolina), Scenes and Characters*, by "Skitt," "Who Was Raised Thar" [H. E. Taliaferro], pp. 233–236. New York: Harper & Bros. 1859.

one passed the road with a long-eared animal, politely called a John Donkey, and John let off, as his race is wont to do sometimes, in a most moving and thrilling manner.

Walker's imagination, by his earnest "wrastlin'," was wrought up to great intensity, and he converted Major John's discordant music, which to most men resembles the filing of a saw-mill saw, into a call from heaven urging him to preach the Gospel. No time was to be lost. He rose from his knees duly commissioned, went to his church, and demanded a license, when the pastor interrogated him thus:

Pastor. Do you believe, Brother Walker, that you are called of God to preach, "as was Aaron?"

Walker. Most sartinly I does.

Pastor. Give the Church, that is, the bruthering, the proof.

Walker. I was mightly diffikilted and troubled on the subjeck, and I was detarmined to go inter the woods and wrastle it out.

Pastor. That's it, Brother Walker.

Walker. And while there wrastlin', Jacob-like, I hearn one ov the curiousest voices I uver hearn in all my borned days.

Pastor. You are on the right track, Brother Walker. Go on with your noration.

Walker. I couldn't tell for the life ov me whether the voice was up in the air ur down in the sky, it sounded so curious.

Pastor. Poor creetur! how he was diffikilted. Go on to norate, Brother Walker. How did it appear to sound unto you?

Walker. Why, this a-way: "Waw-waw-*ker—*waw-waw-*ker!* Go *preach,* go preach, go *preach,* go *preach-ee,* go *preach-ah,* go *preach-uh,* go *preach-ah-ee-uh-ah-ee.*"

Pastor. Bruthering and sisters, that's the right sort of a call. Enough said, Brother Walker. That's none ov yer college calls, nor money calls. No doctor ov divinity uver got sich a call as that. Brother Walker must have license, fur sartin and fur sure.

The license was granted, the story goes, and Walker is now, doubtless, making the mountains ring with his stentorian lungs.

The Value of Religious Instruction

A GENTLEMAN who was very attentive to the religious instruction of his slaves, was a good deal distressed at hearing one or two flagrant delinquencies "on his place." He called up one of his most faithful people, and expressed his mortification that, notwithstanding all his care, and the expense he went to in procuring them religious instruction, he had heard of

From "Cotton and Its Cultivation," by T. B. Thorpe, of Louisiana, *Harper's New Monthly Magazine,* Vol. VIII (March, 1854), No. XLVI, pp. 461–462. New York: Harper & Brothers, Publishers.

several cases of highly improper conduct, and concluded by remarking that he did not believe that the Negroes were better than before they had preaching. The old man answered as follows: "You see, massa, de thing is jest dis: a heap of things used to go on before dat you didn't know nothen about; *but now*, when any thing goes wrong, it gets to your hearin' 'mediately. We ain't badder, but we are more honest in tellin' you de truth."

Washpot Services

DR. BOYD told me incidents of the history of various songs. For example, he said of the familiar old spiritual, *Steal Away*, that it was sung in slavery times when the Negroes on a few plantations were forbidden to hold religious services. That was because the masters were afraid of gatherings which might lead to insurrections like some that had occurred. So the Negroes would gather in a cabin and hold their service by stealth. They would resort to a peculiar practice to prevent their singing from being heard at the big house. They would turn an iron washpot upside down on the dirt floor and put a stick under it, and would sing in such a way that they thought the sound would be muffled under the pot. Dr. Boyd says that he had often gone to such services with his mother in his childhood and seen this done. He said that, in fact, he believed the white people knew of the gatherings and allowed them, though the Negroes were fearful of being found out.

No Time for Children

THERE is a story told of an old colored woman, who had been walking on the streets in Charleston when the great earthquake came, many years ago.

Desperately and in terror she started to run. The rocking, quaking earth, trembling beneath her feet, made running an impossibility. She fell to her knees, and as a rescuing party reached her, she was praying with all the intensity of her race.

"Oh mah Gawd an mah Father, ain' Yuh see how dis ground do trimble same like Jedgement Day? Come down hyuh, Lawd, an help po people in dere trial and tribbilation, but, oh do, Mass Gawd, be sho an come Yoself an doan sen Yo Son, because dis ain' no time fuh chillun!"

From *On the Trail of Negro Folk-Songs*, by Dorothy Scarborough, pp. 22–23. Copyright, 1925, by Harvard University Press. Cambridge.

From *Cryin' in de Wilderness*, Sermons and Adventures of Reb'ren Nichodemus Ezra Malachi Lee of Maxfield on Santee, by Alfred Holmes von Kolnitz, pp. 30, 44–45. (n. d.) Charleston, South Carolina: Walker Evans and Cogswell Company.

The Logic of Faith

I[1]

A FEW years ago one of the house servants of my uncle, a planter on the Santee River, disappeared; a very fat and much prized goose disappeared mysteriously at the same time. My uncle was quite indignant and spent several hours each day trying to locate both servant and goose, believing that by finding one he would also find the other. He was entirely unsuccessful during the week, and strange to say, none of the darkies on the plantation had seen either cook or goose. One Sunday afternoon he drove to the little settlement church. Along came the missing woman, dropped a graceful curtsy, and inquired as to the health of the entire family.

"Well!" said my uncle, completely taken aback at the coolness of the culprit. "Are you going to church to worship God in the very same week you stole my goose?"

"Do, Mass Will," said the old woman. "Yuh nebber tink Ah was goan let one geese keep me frum mah Jedus, does yuh?"

II[2]

Uncle Bob Jordan was the out-prayingest Christian on the Green plantation. He had long been known for his prayers, but now he was praying more than he had ever prayed. He was seventy-two years old and, as he could no longer work much, his master had promised him his freedom for twenty dollars. So Uncle Bob would go down into the woods near the big house every night about seven o'clock and get down on his knees and pray, asking God to please send him twenty dollars for his freedom.

He had been praying for about a month, when the master passed near the tree where Uncle Bob was praying one night and overheard the prayer. The master decided that the next night he would have some fun out of Uncle Bob. So just before dark he went down to the prayer tree and climbed up in it.

At dark Uncle Bob came under the tree, got down on his knees, and started praying as usual, "Oh, Lawd, sen' me twenty dollers to buy my freedom. Oh, Lawd, sen' me twenty dollers to buy my freedom."

"All right, Uncle Bob," came the master's voice from overhead, "look down at the foot of the tree and you will find a ten-dollar bill."

---

[1] *Ibid.*, pp. 45–46.

---

[2] From "Juneteenth," by J. Mason Brewer, in *Tone the Bell Easy*, Publications of the Texas Folk-Lore Society, Number X, 1932, edited by J. Frank Dobie, pp. 28–29. Copyright, 1932, by the Texas Folk-Lore Society. Austin, Texas.

Sure enough, Uncle Bob looked and found a ten-dollar bill.

"Come back tomorrow night," said the voice, "and you will find a five-dollar bill."

"Sho, sho, Lawd," said Uncle Bob, taking the ten-dollar bill and sticking it in his pocket. "Thank you, thank you."

The next night the master beat Uncle Bob to the tree again and hid in its branches. At dark Uncle Bob came and prayed his accustomed prayer: "Oh Lawd, please sen' me ten mo' dollers to buy my freedom."

"Uncle Bob," responded the voice from overhead, "look at the foot of the tree and you will find another five-dollar bill. Take the ten-dollar bill I gave you last night, and the five-dollar bill I gave you tonight, and bring them back tomorrow night. Put them underneath the tree so that I can get them, and the next night I will bring you a twenty-dollar bill."

"No, sah, no sah, dat's aw right, Lawd," answered Uncle Bob. "I sho thanks you for de fifteen, but I'll git de udder five some place else."

III [3]

There was a slave named James Hay, who belonged to a neighbor of master's. He was punished a great many times because he could not get his task done. The other slaves pitied him because he seemed unable to perform his task. One evening he got a severe whipping. The next morning as the slaves were having their tasks assigned them an old lady by the name of Aunt Patience went by, and said, "never mind, Jim, my son, the Lord will help you with your task to-day"; he answered, "yes, ma'am." He began his work very faithfully and continued until it was half done, then he lay down under a tree; the others not understanding his motive, thought he was tired and was taking a rest, but he did not return to his task until the overseer called him and asked him why he did not have his work nearer done. He said, "Aunt Patience told me dis morning that the Lord would help me to-day, and I thought as I did half of the task, the Lord might have finished the other half if he intended to help me at all." The overseer said, "You see that the Lord did not come to help you and we shall not wait for him, but we will help you"; so Jim got a severe punishment. Sometime after this, Jim Hay was called upon by some professors of religion; they asked him if he was not tired of serving the devil, and told him that the Lord was good and had helped many of his people, and would help all who asked him and then take them home to heaven. Jim said that if the Lord would not do half an acre of his task for him when he depended on him, he did not think he could trust him, and Jim never became a Christian to my knowledge.

---

[3] From *My Life in the South,* by Jacob Stroyer, pp. 51–52. New and Enlarged Edition. Salem: Salem Observer Book and Job Print. 1885.

Measuring Eternity

A NEW preacher who was conducting a revival without much success, not-withstanding he pictured to his hearers in glowing language the great joys of heaven and the tortures of eternal fires, and the imprisonment therein for all eternity of the condemned souls, at last awakened his congregation to a sense of their danger by asking:

"Does yo' know w'at all etern'ty is? Well, I tell yo'. Ef one uv dem li'l sparrows w'at yo' see roun yo' gyarden bushes wuz to dip his bill in de 'Lantic Ocean an' taik one hop a day an' hop 'cross de country an' put dat drop uv watah into de 'Cific Ocean, an' den he hop back to de 'Lantic Ocean, jes one hop a day, an' ef he keep dat hoppin' up 'twell de 'Lantic Ocean wuz dry as a bone, it wouldn't be break o' day in etern'ty."

"Dar now," said one of the brethren, "yo' see for yo'se'f how long yo' suffer."

The Vision of Daddy Jupiter

LAS night, dis befo fus fowl crow, me bin er leddown een me bed. De moon done set. Caesar, him bin ter sleep by de fire een de tarruh room. Eberyting on de plantation gone bed. Me bin study bout de time wen old Jupiter hab ter meet him Lord and Master, and me berry happy een me bussum. Den me drap ter sleep. How long me bin ter sleep me dunno, but all ob er sutten pear like ebry shingle and boad hab er crack, and de light stream tru, an de room bin bright es day. Wile me duh wonder wudduh dat, four leely angel, wuh dress een wite an hab wing on eh back, fly een de room. Two topper de foot er de bed, and one on arur side er me. My! but dem bin pooty! Me see heap er pooty wite chillun een me time, but me nebber bin see nuttne teh come up ter dem, nur ter ketch nigh um. Dem look pon topper me so kind, and dey open and shet dem wing, an mek sich a cool breeze een de house. Bimeby me retch out ma han fuh tell de one huddy wuh bin an close me bed on de right side, but eh draw back, an eh say: "Jupiter, we come fuh leh you know de blessed Jesus duh commin fuh cahr you up ter Hebben and show you de seat wuh eh hab ready fur you." Me

From *Life in Old Virginia*, A Description of Virginia, More Particularly the Tidewater Section, Narrating Many Incidents Relating to the Manners and Customs of Old Virginia So Fast Disappearing as a Result of the War between the States, together with Many Humorous Stories, by James J. McDonald, edited by J. A. C. Chandler, pp. 280–281. Copyright, 1907, by the Old Virginia Publishing Company, Inc. Norfolk, Virginia.

From *Negro Myths from the Georgia Coast*, by Charles Colcock Jones, pp. 161–164. Copyright, 1888, by Charles C. Jones, Jr. Boston and New York: Houghton, Mifflin and Company.

dat glad me yent bref mek ansur. Me hard fuh bleebe me own yez. Me
harte rise up een me troat, and me yent duh say nuttne, but me duh watch
fur de Lord. Soon de blessed Jesus, wid de print er de nail een eh han an
eh foot, an wid de star on eh head, drap right down tru de top er de house
dout crack er shingle, an eh call me name an eh tell me fuh rise, an eh pit
eh han onder me shoulder, an eh liff me up light es er fedder. Me ole cloze
an me old body leff behine, an somehow narruh me sperit, him keep de
shape er de body. Den eh pit eh han onder me arm, an eh cahr me way
up eenter de element, beyant de sun an de moon an de star, an de
leely angel duh foller we. We gone an we gone way up tel we git ter er
big alabaster house, wid high piazza all roun an roun, wuh shine same
luk de sun, buil in de middle er a beautiful gaden wid flower, an fruit, an
humminbud, an butterfly, an angel wid harp duh sing and duh joy ehself
onder de tree. Dis es we git ter de big gate, wuh mek wid pearl, eh swing
open dout tetch um, and de blessed Jesus lead dis poor ole nigger up de
shinin paat to de big house way de Lord lib.

We gone up to step an enter de pahler, way de great God bin er set on
eh golden trone. Den de blessed Jesus mek de good Lord sensible dat dis
duh Jupter wuh him hab sabe, an dat eh fetch um fuh show um eh seat
wuh eh done prepare fur um. Wid dat de Lord, him call teh one angel,
an eh tell um fuh bring one chair an set um down befo eh trone. Soon es
dis bin done eh say: "Jupter, yuh you chair; set een um. Eh blants ter
you." Mossa, you nebber bin see sech chair een all you life. Eh hab gold
rocker ter um. Eh hab welwit cushin een eh bottom. Eh hab high back,
an eh arm stuff. Eh so soffe an easy. Eh look pootier den dat big rockin
chair wuh old Mossa bin gib Missy wen eh marry you farruh. Me shame
fuh set een de chair, but de blessed Jesus him courage me, an me tek me
seat, an me so tankful dat me hab one chair een de mansion een de sky.

Den de blessed Jesus tell anurruh angel fuh bring me some milk an
honey fuh drink. Eh bring um een a nice glass tumbler, an eh gen me fuh
drink. Me tase um, an eh sweet mone anyting me ebber drink een me life.
Eh tell me fuh drink um down, an wen me drink all outer de glass, an me
yeye ketch sight er de bottom er de tumbler, me see some speck. De ting
trouble me, fuh me dunno wuh mek speck day een de bottom er dat clean
tumbler. Den de blessed Master notus me, an eh say: "Don fret, Jupter;
dem speck duh you sin, but now dem all leff behine."

All dis time me bin er set wid me face tun way from de Lord an eh
trone, cause eh so great an bright me couldn't look pon topper um. Mossa,
me cant scribe wuh me see an yeddy een dat Hebben. Eh yent fuh tell.
De blessed Jesus tek me tru de gaden, down by de ribber, an een de orchud
way de bigges peach, an fig, an orange, an pomegranate, an watermillion,
an all kin der fruit der grow. Me see heap er good people wuh me bin
know befo eh dead. Ole Mossa, Cappne Maxwell, ole Mr. Ashmore, Buh
Jack, Sister Masha, me own Dinah, an mo bin day, an dem all hab harp,
an bin der sing, an walk bout, an der pledjur ehself. Dem glad fuh see me
too, an gen me de right han er fellership.

Arter me bin in Hebben good while, de blessed Master, him say: "Come, Jupter, I gwine show you way de bad people go." Den eh lead me down to one bottom wuh dark an kibber wid cloud. In de fur een me see smoke duh rise, an me yeddy people duh cry an duh holler so bad. Wen we git ter that spot, lo an behole! day was de mouf er Hell. Satan, him bin day wid eh pitchfork, an eh black head wid screech-owl yez, an eh red yeye, an eh claw-han, an eh forky tail. Eh tan right at de mouf er de big hole way de smoke an de fire duh bile out. Fas as de tarruh debble bring sinner ter um, eh push um wid eh pitchfork an eh trow um een de fire. Lord Amighty! Mossa, how dem sinner did kick an holler an try fuh pull way! But twant no use. De minnit ole Satan graff eh claw on um eh gone, an you could yeddy um duh fry een de fire same luk fat een me pan yuh. Me bin rale skade. De ting mek me sick. Me hole on ter me Jesus, an him tell me not teh fade, dat nuttne shill trouble me.

Dis at dat time me wake. Me hair bin a rise on me head, an wen me come fuh fine out me bin een me own bed, an fowl bin a crow fuh day. Oh, Mossa! dat ting wuh dem call Hell duh a bad place. Me no wan shum no mo, an me yent gwine day nurrer. Enty de blessed Jesus done show me de chair wuh eh done sabe fuh me een Hebben? Yes, Mossa, me seat eh fix, an ole Jupter ready fur go wenebber de Lord call.

Ain't No Corn-bread There

My BROTHERS an' sisters, we is here today to pray, to weep an' to moan over de earthly remains of our beloved brother. His life has been full of trouble an' hardship an' he last days was spent in pain an' sorrow an' great sufferin', an' he's gone, gone at last to a restful place; done wid de people of dis world; done wid de doctors an' medicine an' pain an' pizen. De Great Master is his doctor now.

On dis earth his trial was great, his labors hard an' his misery many. He live on bacon an' corn-bread an' cabbage, but wey he's gone he picks he food from de tree er life; he drinks of Jordan's holy waters; he feeds on heavenly manna, for dey ain't no corn-bread dere. No, my brother, dey ain't no corn-bread dere. Dey don't eat no bacon and dey ain't eat no cabbage. Dat's de feed dey gee to hogs. Down here in dis world you see people buildin' fence round dey cabbage patch, sickin' dog on de hog when dey tryin' to bu's' in de garden, but in heaven you see our Heavenly Father directin' He angels to tear down de fence an' drive de hogs into de cabbage patch. Dey don't eat no cabbage. Dem angel wouldn't dare to set de dog on a hog in a cabbage patch in heaven, not when de hog' Master was lookin' on.

Yes, our brother is gone, gone to de Lord. He days er corn-bread an' cabbage is done.

From *Nigger to Nigger*, by E. C. L. Adams, pp. 242–243. Copyright, 1928, by Charles Scribner's Sons. New York and London.

Flying Fool

THERE wuz a cullud man en he died en went to hevven en the Lawd gevvum all wings, en he flew en he flew. . . . After he flew round there fur 'bout a week he looked down en saw a reel *good*-lookin' lady, a-settin' on a cloud. She wuz *reel* good-lookin'. En he dun the loop-the-loop.

The Lawd cum en sez: "Don' you know how to act? There ain't nuthin' but nice people here, en you beehavin' like that. Git out." But he told the Lawd he jest didn't know en he wuzzent never gonner do nuthin' like that no mo', en please let him stay. So the Lawd got kinder pacified en let him stay. En he flew en he flew. En after he had been flying round fur 'bout a week, he ups en sees that same good-lookin' lady a-settin' on a cloud en he jest couldn't hep it—he dun the loop-the-loop.

So the Lawd stepped up en he sez: "You jest don't know how to act, you ain't fitten fur to be with decent folks, you'se a scanlus misbeehavor. Git out." En he got.

He felt mighty bad en hung round the gate three or four days tryin' to ease up on St. Peter, but St. Peter 'lowed there wuzn't no way, he jest couldn't let him in en the onliest way he might git in wuz to have a *conference* with the Lawd. Then the man asked if he couldn't 'range fur a conference en they had a lot of back-and-forth. En finally St. Peter eased him in fur a conference. . . . But the Lawd wuz mad, he wuz mad sho-nuff, he wuz hoppin' mad en told him flat-footed to git out en stay out. Then the cullud man sez:

"Well, jest remember this, Lawd: while I wuz up here in yo' place I wuz the flyin'est fool you had."

Catch Hell Just the Same

Two fellows had a conversation about heaven and hell and they decided to take the trip. And one went to hell and one went to heaven. He had to put out the sun and take it in, and he had to put out the stars and take them in; and he had to seat the angels and watch the throne, and pour out the water for it to rain, and when it stopped raining he had to pick that water up. The other one went to hell. He just had to stand and watch the fire burn and eat brimstone. So when they come back they met each other. So the one went to heaven asked the man what did he do in hell. He said he had a easy job; all he had to do was ketch the heat, eat brimstone and

From *Lanterns on the Levee,* Recollections of a Planter's Son, by William Alexander Percy, pp. 292–293. Copyright, 1941, by Alfred A. Knopf, Inc. New York.

From "Negro Folk Tales from the South (Alabama, Mississippi, Louisiana)," by Arthur Huff Fauset, *Journal of American Folklore,* Vol. 40 (July–September, 1927), No. 157, p. 275. New York: The American Folklore Society.

burn. And he said to the other man, "What did you do?" He said, "Oh, I had a fine job, but I caught hell." The man said, "How was that?" He said, "Well, I had to put out the sun an' take it in; I had to put out the stars an' take them in; an' I had to seat the angels an' watch the throne, an' pour out water for it to rain, an' when it stopped rainin' I had to pick that water up, an' I had no rest for myself." The other man said, "I'd damn rather be in hell than in heaven because you ketch hell just the same."

Oil and Hell

"BRETHREN," he said, "the Lord made the world round like a ball."

"Amen!" agreed the congregation.

"And the Lord made two axles for the world to go round on, and He put one axle at the North Pole and one axle at the South Pole."

"Amen!" agreed the congregation.

"And the Lord put a lot of oil and grease in the center of the world so as to keep the axles well greased and oiled."

"Amen!" cried the congregation.

"And then a lot of sinners dig wells in Pennsylvania and steal the Lord's oil and grease. And they dig wells in Kentucky, Louisiana, Oklahoma, and Texas, and in Mexico and Russia, and steal the Lord's oil and grease. And some day they will have all the Lord's oil and grease, and them axles is gonna git hot. And then that will be hell, brethren, that will be hell!"

Where the Lion Roareth and the Wang-doodle Mourneth

MY BELOVED Brethering: I am a unlarnt Hard-Shell Baptist preacher, of whom you've no doubt hearn afore, and I now appear here to expound the scripters and pint out the narrow way which leads from a vain world to the streets of Jaroosalem; and my tex which I shall choose for the occasion is in the leds of the Bible, somewhar between the Second Chronik-ills and the last chapter of Timothytitus; and when you find it, you'll find it in

By Velma Sample, Little Rock, Arkansas, January 2, 1937. Manuscripts of the Federal Writers' Project of the Works Progress Administration for the State of Arkansas.

By William P. Brannan.

From *Tall Tales of the Southwest*, An Anthology of Southern and Southwestern Humor, 1830–1860, edited by Franklin J. Meine, pp. 253–255. Copyright, 1930, by Alfred A. Knopf, Inc.

This sermon is still found in oral tradition. Substantially the same version was recorded by B. A. Botkin from the recitation of Bascom Lamar Lunsford, Asheville, North Carolina, January 18, 1949.

these words: "And they shall gnaw a file, and flee unto the mountains of Hepsidam, whar the lion roareth and the wang-doodle mourneth for his first-born."

Now, my brethering, as I have before told you, I am an oneddicated man, and I know nothing about grammar talk and collidge highfalutin, but I am a plane unlarnt preacher of the Gospil, what's been foreordaned and called to prepare a pervarse generashun for the day of wrath—ah! "For they shall gnaw a file, and flee unto the mountains of Hepsidam, whar the lion roareth and the wang-doodle mourneth for his first-born"—ah!

My beloved brethering, the tex says they shall gnaw a file. It does not say they *may*, but shall. Now, there is more than one kind of file. There's the hand-saw file, the rat-tail file, the single file, the double file, and profile; but the kind spoken of here isn't one of them kind nayther, bekaws it's a figger of speech, and means going it alone and getting ukered; "for they shall gnaw a file, and flee unto the mountains of Hepsidam, whar the lion roareth and the wang-doodle mourneth for his first-born"—ah!

And now there be some here with fine close on thar backs, brass rings on thar fingers, and lard on thar har, what goes it while they're yung; and thar be others here what, as long as thar constitooshins and forty-cent whiskey last, goes it blind. Thar be sisters here what, when they gets six-teen years old, cut thar tiller-ropes and goes it with a rush. But I say, my dear brethering, take care you don't find, when Gabriel blows his last trump, your hand's played out, and you've got ukered—ah! "For they shall gnaw a file, and flee unto the mountains of Hepsidam, whar the lion roareth and the wang-doodle mourneth for his first-born."

Now, my brethering, "they shall flee unto the mountains of Hepsidam"; but thar's more dams than Hepsidam. Thar's Rotter-dam, Had-dam, Amster-dam, and "Don't-care-a-dam"—the last of which, my brethering, is the worst of all, and reminds me of a sirkumstans I onst knowed in the state of Illenoy. There was a man what built him a mill on the north fork of Ager Crick, and it was a good mill and ground a sight of grain; but the man what built it was a miserable sinner, and never give anything to the church; and, my dear brethering, one night there came a dreadful storm of wind and rain, and the mountains of the great deep was broke up, and the waters rushed down and swept that man's milldam to kingdom cum, and when he woke up he found that he wasn't worth a dam—ah! "For they shall gnaw a file, and flee unto the mountains of Hepsidam, whar the lion roareth and the wang-doodle mourneth for his first-born"—ah!

I hope I don't hear any body larfin; do I?

Now, "whar the lion roareth and the wang-doodle mourneth for his first-born"—ah! This part of my tex, my beseaching brethering, is not to be taken as it says. It don't mean the howling wilderness, whar John the Hard-Shell Baptist fed on locusts and wild asses, but it means, my brethering, the city of New Y'Orleans, the mother of harlots and hard lots, whar corn is wuth six bits a bushel one day and nary a red the nex; whar niggers are as thick as black bugs in spiled bacon ham, and gamblers, thieves, and pickpockets goes skiting about the streets like weasels in a barn-yard; whar honest men are scarcer than hen's teeth; and whar a strange woman once took in your beluved teacher, and bamboozled him out of two hundred and twenty-seven dollars in the twinkling of a sheep's-tail; but she *can't* do it again! Hallelujah—ah! "For they shall gnaw a file, and flee unto the mountains of Hepsidam, whar the lion roareth and the wang-doodle mourneth for his first-born"—ah!

My brethering, I am the captain of that flat-boat you see tied up thar, and have got aboard of her flour, bacon, taters, and as good Monongahela whiskey as ever was drunk, and am mighty apt to get a big price for them all; but what, my dear brethering, would it all be wuth if I hadn't got religion? Thar's nothing like religion, my brethering: it's better nor silver or gold gimcracks; and you can no more get to heaven without it than a jay-bird can fly without a tail—ah! Thank the Lord! I'm an oneddicated man, my brethering; but I've sarched the Scripters from Dan to Beersheba, and found Zion right side up, and hard-shell religion the best kind of re-ligion—ah! 'Tis not like the Methodists, what specks to get to heaven by hollerin' hell-fire; nor like the Univarsalists, that get on the broad gage and goes the hull hog—ah!; nor like the Yewnited Brethering, that takes each other by the slack of thar breeches and hists themselves in; nor like the Katherliks, that buys threw tickets from their priests; but it may be likened unto a man what has to cross the river—ah!—and the ferry-boat was gone; so he tucked up his breeches and waded acrost—ah! "For they shall gnaw a file, and flee unto the mountains of Hepsidam, whar the lion roareth and the wang-doodle mourneth for his first-born!"

Pass the hat, Brother Flint, and let every Hard-Shell Baptist shell out.

V. IRREPRESSIBLE CUSSEDNESS

A streak of inherent cussedness keeps most men from acknowl-edging defeat. The combination of adverse circumstances at last reaches the point where the only thing left to do is to grin and bear it. At the moment an overburdened man grins he in-variably says something that contains a trace of wisdom and truth. That is how my brand of folklore is born.

—ALLAN M. TROUT

And all the time, there was High John de Conquer playing his tricks of making a way out of no-way. Hitting a straight lick with a crooked stick. Winning the jack pot with no other stake but a laugh. Fighting a mighty battle without outside-showing force, and winning his war from within.

—ZORA NEALE HURSTON

1. "Don't-Care-a-Dam"

"Thar's more dams than Hepsidam," proclaimed the Hardshell Baptist preacher, and the "worst of all" is "Don't-care-a-dam." Besides the sinfulness of a "pervarse generashun" which the flatboat captain was called to prepare for the day of wrath, this phrase denotes a streak of "irrepressible cussedness" inherent in the Southern backwoods heritage.

Out of his original relation to the universe and the exigencies of depending upon his own resources, the backwoodsman developed a kind of toughness, wiliness, and intractability that, if it got him into as many tight places as it got him out of, enabled him to extract from difficult and trying circumstances the consolations of folklore.

We can say my brand of folklore relates to the fundamental reactions of plain people to the propositions they rub against—such propositions are life and death, religion and politics, railroads and jurisprudence.[1]

Southern folklore (including the writings of humorists and travelers concerned with the "oddities of Southern life and character") is full of the unexpected, grim, or preverse humor of robust, independent, stubborn, and often ignorant folk in so far as their actions and reactions proceed from the need of "making a way out of no-way" (or vice versa), of having their own way, or of insisting that their way is better than other ways.

If the "Don't-care-a-dam" philosophy sometimes stands in the way of progress, as in the sullen or cheerful apathy of the Arkansas squatter or the Tussie family, it is also the courageous stuff of which heroes and never-say-die, "unreconstructed" Southerners are made.

2. Coonskin Democracy

From the beginning the pages of Southern humor have been filled with the rough-and-tumble antics and tall talk of the half-man, half-horse, and half-alligator backwoodsman of Kentucky—"a third half," as Washington Irving put it, "being provided for their particular convenience." The eccentricities of Davy Crockett, the "original humorist and irrepressible backwoodsman" set the pattern for the coonskin democracy whose "irrepressible cussedness" consists in distrust of the high and mighty and a fondness for taking them down a peg.

One gentleman asked me to come and see him; but he gave me so many directions about getting to where he lived, that I asked him to write it down, and told him if ever he came to my part of the country, I hoped he would call and see me. "Well," said he, "how will I find where you live."—"Why, sir, run down the Mississippi till you come to the Obion river, run a small streak up that, jump ashore anywhere, and inquire for me.[2]

---

[1] Allan M. Trout, *Greetings from Old Kentucky* (Louisville, 1947), p. 106.
[2] *An Account of Colonel Crockett's Tour to the North and Down East in 1834* (Philadelphia, 1835), pp. 87–88.

Even more pointed is the reply of the eccentric Arkansas bear-hunter, Jack Smith, to the well-dressed gentleman from Memphis who asked him the secret of his success in hunting. He said

that formerly he dressed in customary buckskin trousers and other hunting apparel, but the animals, especially the deer, became so well acquainted with his appearance that they recognized him from afar, and were always on the lookout for him. Consequently, he could not get near enough to shoot them. It then occurred to him that he must change his garb and deceive the animals. So he dressed up like his visitors. Now, when he approached a herd of deer, the sentinel buck informed the rest of the herd that there was no danger— that he was only some finely dressed gentleman from Memphis who was perfectly harmless and couldn't hit a deer at ten paces. Thus he claimed he deluded the game, and succeeded in killing a great many animals.[3]

In his casual, easy-going way, Will Rogers also loved to prick the bubble of pretense and crack the shell of arrogance, as when he bragged of his Cherokee ancestry: "My ancestors didn't come over with the Mayflower but they met the boat"; or when he gently rebuked a friend who criticized his grammar: "Maybe ain't ain't so correct, but I notice that lots of folks who ain't usin' ain't ain't eatin'."

3. Man vs. the Machine

In his encounters with "damyankee" machinery (and mechanical civilization) the "Don't-care-a-dam" Southerner often gives vent to his "irrepressible cussedness" in the most surprising and violent manner. Bert Vincent tells a sadistic story of Uncle Andy Lewallen and the corn shredder. While Ray, one of the Babcock boys, was feeding the machine, he accidentally got his hand near the teeth and lost a finger. His brother Henry came up to see what was the matter, and similarly lost the end of one of his fingers. Finally Uncle Andy came up, and, while peering into the box, got his long beard caught. Archie Rose, while snipping Andy's beard off with the sheep shears, started to laugh, and got his own finger caught and torn off in the corn crib door. "Three fingers and a beard. 'Just too damned much trouble over a corn shredder,' said old Mr. Lewallen." [4]

One of Ben Robertson's cousins had a fight with a fertilizer-spreader, which he couldn't get to working properly. After struggling for two hours with the adjustments, he lost his temper and beat the thing into bits with a rock, yelling, as he threw the pieces over the pasture fence: " 'You dirty low-down evil contraption, stay there,' and going to the barn, he got out the old cow horn and from then on spread fertilizer as his father and grandfather had spread it." [5]

"I doubt if any other of the contraptions and inventions introduced into these mountains have left behind as much to laugh over as the automobile," says Bert Vincent. There was the time when Grandpa decided he was going

---

[3] Mrs. Bernie Babcock, *Folklore of Romantic Arkansas*, by Fred W. Allsopp, Vol. II (New York, 1931), p. 246.

[4] *Bert Vincent Strolling* (Knoxville, 1940), n.p.

[5] Ben Robertson, *Red Hills and Cotton* (New York, 1942), pp. 210–211.

to drive the pickup truck the boys had bought for the farm. He got it started someway or other but couldn't stop it, and ran through the barn, hitting the posts and knocking down all the sheds. Finally he managed to straighten the truck and head straight into a big oak tree.

I ran up just as it hit, and when all the pieces had stopped falling, Grandpa, still sitting stiffly behind the wheel, sort of grinned and said: "Guess, by gum, that stopped ye.". . .

Back when the Aluminum Company was buying up land for the Alcoa project an old fellow got enough for his few acres to buy a car.

"Um-God," the old fellow said next day when telling the neighbors about the car. "Um-God, hit's got a self starter, the blamed thing has, an' Um-God, I jis chain the blamed thing to the corn crib of nights. Um-God, I don't aim fer it to jis get goin' when I ain't round." [6]

4. DARK LAUGHTER

The humor of the Negro is rich in "irrepressible cussedness." This ranges all the way from the more "meretricious 'racial' humor of stage and fiction" to the razor-keen weapon of defense and protest. Of the former type is the story of Ananias, the coachman, who had the reputation of being the most exact wielder of the coachwhip in the county. Showing off his prowess one day while driving his master down a long lane to a neighboring plantation, he first split a horsefly into pieces, and then tore a bumblebee into shreds with the snapper on the end of his whip. But when his master pointed out a hornets' nest hanging from the limb of a tree by the side of the road, and asked him to try his skill on them, he replied: "No, sah, Massa, ah ain't gwine bothah dem hornets, 'case dey's auganized." [7]

More "cussed," if no less "irrepressible," is the Negro humor "concerned with fooling the white man." According to Arthur P. Davis, "A large part of the Negro's fun comes out of appearing stupid when in reality he has complete control of the situation and knows that he has." [8]

A case in point is that of the patriotic Louisiana sharecropper, who read in the town newspaper about gas rationing. Instructed by the gasoline-hoarding plantation owner to take a ten-gallon can of gasoline out back of the barn and bury it, he returned an hour later to report: "I buried that gasoline like you told me. What do you want me to do with the empty can?" [9]

B. A. B.

---

[6] Bert Vincent, *Here in Tennessee* (Knoxville, 1945), p. 49.

[7] J. Mason Brewer, "Juneteenth," *Tone the Bell Easy*, Publications of the Texas Folk-Lore Society, No. 10 (Austin, 1932), pp. 23–24.

[8] "Dark Laughter," *The Best of Negro Humor*, edited by John H. Johnson and Ben Burns (Chicago, 1945), p. 88. For the simulated "Negro Laugh" and humor of "bright sayings" and "dumbness," see Gunnar Myrdal, *An American Dilemma* (1944), Vol. II, pp. 960–961.

[9] *Ibid.*, p. 31.

The Unreconstructed South

IT WAS a veteran soldiery that repeopled the plantations and the home-steads of the South, and withstood the forces thrown against them during the period of Reconstruction. In addition to such racial traits as personal pride, self-reliance, and physical courage, they possessed also race pride, which is inestimable in a great popular struggle. This race pride the war had only increased. However beaten and broken they were, the people of the South came out of the war with their spirit unquenched, and a belief that they were unconquerable.

A story used to be told of an old Confederate soldier who was trudging home, after the war, broken and ragged and worn. He was asked what he would do if the Yankees got after him when he reached home.

"Oh, they ain't goin' to trouble me," he said. "If they do, I'll just whip 'em agin."

Confederate Battle Ruses

. . . IT WAS more pleasant to talk of how Jeb Stuart at Second Manassas beguiled the Yankees into exaggerated ideas of Rebel strength by having his men drag brush along the roads to stir up huge clouds of dust; or of how the Yankee General Banks was duped into abandoning several strong positions during his Red River campaign by such Confederate ruses as sending drummers out to beat calls, lighting superfluous campfires, blowing bugles, and "rolling empty wagons over fence rails"; or of how George Cagle, while lying on a ridge at Chickamauga, kept at work four or five muskets gathered from incapacitated comrades, and as Yankee bullets whistled overhead he simulated the activity of an artillery unit, giving such commands as "attention Cagle's Battery, make ready, load, take aim, fire"; of how Sergeant Nabors scared nervous Yankee prisoners who asked him at Atlanta if he were going to kill them by replying, "That's our calcula-tion; we came out for that purpose."

From *The Old Dominion*, Her Making and Her Manners, by Thomas Nelson Page, 247. Copyright, 1908, by Charles Scribner's Sons. New York.

From *The Life of Johnny Reb*, the Common Soldier of the Confederacy, by Bell Irvin Wiley, pp. 77–78. Copyright, 1943, by the Bobbs-Merrill Company. Indianapolis and New York.

Boone's Knife-Swallowing Trick

BOONE, according to James Hall, was once resting in the woods with a small number of his followers, when a large party of Indians came suddenly upon them and halted—neither party having discovered the other until they came in contact. The whites were eating, and the savages, with the ready tact for which they are famous, sat down with perfect composure, and also commenced eating. It was obvious they wished to lull the suspicions of the white men, and seize a favorable opportunity for rushing upon them. Boone affected a careless inattention, but, in an undertone, quietly admonished his men to keep their hands upon their rifles. He then strutted towards the reddies unarmed and leisurely picking the meat from a bone. The Indian leader, who was somewhat similarly employed, arose to meet him.

Boone saluted him, and then requested to look at the knife with which the Indian was cutting his meat. The chief handed it to him without hesitation, and our pioneer, who, with his other traits, possessed considerable expertness at sleight of hand, deliberately opened his mouth and affected to swallow the long knife, which, at the same instant, he threw adroitly into his sleeve. The Indians were astonished. Boone gulped, rubbed his throat, stroked his body, and then, with apparent satisfaction, pronounced the horrid mouthful to be *very good*.

Having enjoyed the surprise of the spectators for a few moments, he made another contortion, and drawing forth the knife, as they supposed, from his body, coolly returned it to the chief. The latter took the point cautiously between his thumb and finger, as if fearful of being contaminated by touching the weapon, and threw it from him into the bushes. The pioneer sauntered back to his party, and the Indians, instantly dispatching their meal, marched off, desiring no further intercourse with a man who could swallow a scalping knife.

The Last Word

. . . JOHN CUSTIS married Frances Parke, daughter of Daniel Parke, Governor of the Leeward Islands, and their son, Daniel Parke Custis, was the first husband of Martha Dandridge, afterwards Martha Washington. John Custis and Frances Parke lived at "Arlington" many years. The alliance

---

From *Our Western Border,* Its Life, Combats, Adventures, Forays, Massacres, Captivities, Scouts, Red Chiefs, Pioneer Women, One Hundred Years Ago, . . . carefully written and compiled by Charles McKnight, pp. 289–290. Philadelphia: J. C. McCurdy & Co. 1876.

From *Ye Kingdome of Accawmacke, or the Eastern Shore of Virginia in the Seventeenth Century,* by Jennings Cropper Wise, pp. 331–334. Copyright, 1911, by Jennings Cropper Wise. Richmond: The Bell Book and Stationery Co.

seems to have been a very unhappy one, and many stories of their contentious life have been handed down to us. Frances was a lady of much determination, which led to frequent conflicts with her eccentric husband. It
is said that for weeks at a time they lived together without speaking to each
other. During these long periods of silence, all communication was carried on between them by means of the servants. For instance, Mrs. Custis
would say to the butler: "Pompy, ask your master if he will have coffee
or tea, and sugar and cream," and to the servant's question, Mr. Custis
would reply: "Tell your mistress that I will have coffee as usual, with no
cream."

After one of these long spells of non-intercourse, Mr. Custis dressed himself with great care one day, ordered his best horse and gig to the door,
and in the most polite and dignified manner, invited Mrs. Custis to accompany him on a drive. "Certainly, Mr. Custis, certainly, sir, I will be delighted, but when were you ever so courteous before?" inquired the grand
lady.

Instead of taking the usual route along the bay beach, the gallant whip
headed his horse straight out into the bay, the water deepening very gradually near Arlington. "Where are you going, Mr. Custis?" asked his wife.
"To h—l, Madam," he replied. "Drive on," said she, "any place is prefer-
able to Arlington."

Presently the water began to enter the gig. "Again I ask, where are
you taking me to?" said Mrs. Custis. "To h—l, Madam, as I have already
told you," answered Mr. Custis. "And again, I say, drive on, Mr. Custis,
the prospect is far brighter than that of a return home," retorted the bold
lady.

After proceeding so far out from shore that the horse was all but forced
to swim, Mr. Custis turned his animal's head to the shore, saying to his
wife with much emphasis, "If I were to drive to h—l and the devil himself
came out to meet us, I do not believe, Madam, that you would be frightened." "Quite true, sir," she replied, "I know you so well that I would
not be afraid to go where you would go."

After this adventure, the couple seem to have lived more happily together, for a deed, to which they were both parties, was soon drawn up, in
which mutual concessions were made in the hope that domestic tranquillity
might ensue. . . .[1]

Mr. Custis survived his wife seven years. Whether her memory was held
in great affection by him may be determined by the reader from the in-

---

[1] Article 2 reads: "That Frances shall henceforth for bear to call him ye sd John
any vile names or give him any ill language, neither shall he give her any but to live
lovingly together and to behave themselves to each other as a good husband & good
wife ought to doe. And that she shall not intermeddle with his affairs but that all
business belonging to the husband's management shall be solely transacted by him,
neither shall he intermeddle in her domestique affairs but that all business properly
belonging to the management of the wife shall be solely transacted by her."—*Ibid.*,
p. 348.

scription which he ordered to be put on his tombstone. The deed of settlement seems to have been only partially successful at most.

> Beneath this marble tomb lies ye body
> of the Honorable John Custis, Esq.,
> of the City of Williamsburg and Parish of Bruton
> Formerly of Hungar's Parish on the Eastern Shore of
> Virginia and the County of Northampton the place
> of his nativity.
> Aged 71 years and yet lived but seven years
> Which was the space of time he kept
> a Bachelor's House at Arlington
> On the Eastern Shore of Virginia.
> This information put on this tomb was by his
> own positive order.
> Wm. Colley, Mason, in Fenchurch Street, London, Fecit.[2]

Moving the Dinner Out of a Burning House

SAVANNAH's plantation owners were actual potentates. The McAlpins out
at the Hermitage plantation manufactured the famous old Savannah gray
brick as a sideline. Legend has it that when the house caught fire during
a dinner party at the Tattnalls' Bonaventure plantation, the host, not
wishing to have his guests' dinner interrupted, had the table carried to
the lawn, where dinner was finished with at least every outward appearance
of tranquillity and aplomb.

The Old Lady and the Bacon

AN OLD lady in Cincinnati had a large quantity of bacon to ship to New
Orleans, where she herself was going for supplies. She stipulated with the

---

[2] The inscription of this old tombstone could easily be read until a year or so ago,
I am informed that the stone has been recently destroyed.—J. C. W.

From "Savannah," by George Sessions Perry, *The Saturday Evening Post,* Vol. 221
(July 17, 1948), No. 3, p. 57. Copyright, 1948, by the Curtis Publishing Company.
Philadelphia, Pa.

From "Editor's Drawer," *Harper's New Monthly Magazine,* Vol. VII (October,
1853) No. XLI, pp. 709–710. New York: Harper & Brothers, Publishers.
In another version of the story the old lady has her wish. Cf. Herbert and Edward
Quick, *Mississippi Steamboatin'* (New York, 1926), pp. 207–210. In the original
ending of the story given above, "The captain did not, as we gather, comply with the
generous suggestion, and the 'old boat' went puffing its way ahead, much to the
mortification and discomfort of the old lady." As a compromise between the two
versions, we have left the ending indeterminate.

/

captain of the steamer that he should have her freight, provided he would not race during the trip. The captain consented, and the old lady came on board.

After the second day out, another steamboat was seen close astern (with which, by-the-by, the captain had been racing all the time) and would every now and then come up to the old lady's boat and then fall back again. The highest excitement prevailed among the passengers as the two boats continued, for nearly a day, almost side by side. At length the old lady, partaking herself of the excitement, called the captain, and said:

"Captain, you *ain't* going to let that thar old boat pass us, are you?"

"Why, I shall have to madam, as I agreed not to race."

"Well, you can just *try* it a little; *that* won't hurt."

"But, madam, to tell you the truth, I *did*."

"Gracious! but do try a little more; see, the old boat is even with us."

A loud cheer now arose from the old boat, and the exultations of the passengers made the old lady more anxious than ever.

"I can't *raise* any more steam, madam," said the captain, in reply to the old lady's continued urgings, "all the tar and pine-knots are burned up."

"Good gracious!" she exclaimed, "what shall we do? The old boat is going by us! Isn't there any thing *else* on board that will make steam?"

"Nothing, madam," replied the captain, "except—except"—(as if a new idea had struck him)—"except your bacon! But of course you want to save your bacon."

"No," exclaimed the old lady, "throw in the bacon!—throw in the bacon, captain—and beat the old boat!"

Southern Travel

A VERY fair satire by a foreigner upon Southern travelling ran as follows: A gentleman walking near the verge of a swamp saw a man's hat on the ground. As the beaver appeared to be in good condition, he stooped to pick it up, when, to his great surprise, he heard a voice proceed from beneath, desiring him not to meddle with it. He lifted it, nevertheless, and perceived a man's head just above the surface of the earth. Alarmed at his situation, he proposed to call his slaves and have him dug out. "Don't trouble yourself, friend," replied he of the swamp, "I'm very well mounted." "Mounted? good heavens, sir! is it possible that you have a horse under you?" A capital one," was the answer, "for he has carried me some hundreds of miles." "But permit me," persisted the planter, "to send for assistance, or you

From *Retrospections of America, 1797–1811*, by John Bernard, p. 210. Edited from the Manuscript by Mrs. Bayle Bernard, with an Introduction, Notes, and Index by Laurence Hutton and Brander Matthews. Copyright, 1886, by Harper & Brothers. New York. 1887.

will lose him." "Lose him?" exclaimed the stranger; "my good sir, he has travelled fifty miles since daybreak, and this is the first firm footing he has come to."

The Toughest of the Tough

THIS story they tell about the people of Madison County. For a great many years they were considered to be the toughest of the tough, especially those mountaineers living in the vicinity they call Shelton Laurel. They tell a tale of an old feller coming to Asheville for an appendicitis operation. They put him in a hospital and operated on him. The following morning the physician went in to see how he was getting along, and instead of finding him in bed he found him sitting in a chair hovered over a radiator. The physician said to him, "Ah-*ah*! you ought not to be sitting up. You'll tear your stitches out." And the old feller looked up at the doctor and he says, "What's the matter, doc? Ain't your thread no good?"

Fine These Men

. . . JUDGE PATTON, whose district lay in the Big Sandy Valley, was one of the most famous as well as one of the most eccentric lawyers and judges Eastern Kentucky has ever produced. He once instructed his grand jury something like this: "Gentlemen, you have here a most beautiful piece of public property upon which rests this hall of Justice. Its verdant, rolling grass and majestic towering tree tops attest at once God's loving kindness and infinite great mercy. A lovely fence encircles this property and hall, where justice is wont to be meted out. But, gentlemen, our people are hitching their horses to this fence. There is a class of people in this world, gentlemen, who would ride right up to the Garden of Eden, push aside its Heavenly-commissioned guardian, fling the gate wide open, loiter down its Tempe-like vales, hitch their horses to the Tree of Life, and banter Moses for a horse-swap. Fine these men, gentlemen, fine them!" At another time he instructed them: "Gentlemen! whenever you see a great big overgrown buck sitting at the mouth of some holler, or at the forks of some road— with a big slouch hat on, a blue collar, a celluloid artificial rose on his coat lapel, and a banjo strung across his breast, and a-pickin' of Sourwood Mountain, fine that man, gentlemen, fine him! For if he hasn't already done something, he's a-goin' to!"

As told by Lewis Richel, Swannanoa, North Carolina, at Wilson's Cove, January 23, 1949. Recorded by B. A. Botkin.

From *The Kentucky Highlander from a Native Mountaineer's Viewpoint*, by Josiah Henry Combs, pp. 22–23. Lexington, Kentucky: J. L. Richardson & Co. 1913.

Getting the Corn Cut

COUSIN Stephen John dropped in, on his way up the river from the sawmill. He told about seeing a man in the mountains who had a corn patch in a field between a mountain and a swift river—a patch from which no road led. He said to the man: "Friend, how in the world do you get your corn out of that patch?" And the man answered: "I distil it into liquor and I fight my way out."

One Way Passage

A REVENUE officer called at a mountain cabin and found no one there but a boy. The following conversation ensued:
"Where's your father?"
"Pappy's at the still."
"Where's your mother?"
"Maw's at the still."
"Where's your brothers and sisters?"
"They're at the still."
"I'll give you a dollar to take me to the still."
"Gimme the dollar."
"I'll give it to you when I get back."
"Mister, you ain't comin' back."

The Sheriff and the Moonshiners

I WAS reminded of the story told us down in Newton County, Arkansas, where liquor-making in the good old days was considered just about as important as putting in a garden. Maybe more so, because a family could get along without garden sass. Once a well-known citizen who spent his lifetime in the county was elected sheriff. One of his first acts was to call into his office all the moonshiners of the county, and at the appointed time, they came. Men who were there say it was an assembly of astounding size and picturesqueness.

From *Red Hills and Cotton*, An Upcountry Memory, by Ben Robertson, p. 40. Copyright, 1942, by Ben Robertson. New York: Alfred A. Knopf.

From *I Give You Texas*, 500 Jokes of the Lone Star State, by Boyce House, p. 24. Copyright, 1943, by the Naylor Company. San Antonio, Texas.

From *Fresh from the Hills*, by Marguerite Lyon, pp. 46–47. Copyright. 1945, by the Bobbs-Merrill Company. Indianapolis and New York.

The sheriff stood behind his big desk, pushed his hat to the back of his head, hooked his thumbs in the armholes of his vest, so the shiny new star would show in all its glory, and gave forth with words of surpassing wisdom:

"Fellers," he said, "they elected me to be sheriff of this-here county and I've swore to do my duty. Now I know you boys make moonshine and that puts me in one helluva spot. I've knowed you fellers, man and boy, since we went fishin' and swimmin' together there in the Buffalo runnin' t'other side o' the grocery store. I know ever' one o' you by name and I know where yore stills are.

"Now I'm willin' to do my part if you'll do yores. If you jis keep on a-makin' wildcat for yoreselves and yore friends without infringin' on the life, liberty 'r pursuit o' happiness o' anyone else, you can keep on a-makin' wildcat till hell freezes over, fur's I'm concerned. That's all, boys!"

The peace and quiet of that regime are still the talk of the hills. If a moonshiner got out of line, he had to answer to his fellow moonshiners.

The Steamboat Captain and the Robbers

THAT eccentric creature, David Crockett, used to mention an odd affair, which happened at "Natchez-under-the-Hill," a sort of "Five-Points" in the "lower regions" of that flourishing town. A steamboat stopped at the landing, and one of the hands went ashore under the hill, and the thieves and "experts" in that "Scoundrel's Retreat" managed to rob him of every cent of his money. The captain of the boat, a most determined man, and full of the wild courage of the Southwest, went ashore and tried to persuade the thieves to return the money they had stolen from a poor hard-working laboring man. But he might as well have talked to the winds.

But he "fetched them at last," said Crockett's informant; "for, assisted by his crew and some three or four hundred passengers, he made fast an immense cable to the frame tenement, where the theft had been perpetrated, and then sung out:

" 'I allow you just fifteen minutes to have that money forthcoming! If at the end of that time it isn't handed over, I'll put steam to the boat and drag your house into the river!'

"The money was 'handed over' quicker than you could say 'Jack Robinson.' They knew the captain, and that he would do what he said he would do."

From "Editor's Drawer," Harper's New Monthly Magazine, Vol. VI (January, 1853), No. XXXII, p. 275. New York: Harper & Brothers, Publishers.

Canada Bill's Gambling Story

IT WAS Canada Bill who originated the story which has become the classic gambling anecdote. He and one of his partners were marooned for the night in a little Louisiana river town a few years before the Civil War, and after diligent search Canada Bill found a faro game and began to play. His partner urged him to stop.

"The game's crooked!" he declared.

"I know it," replied Bill, "but it's the only one in town!"

A Good Reputation

ONE day, during the last year of my residence in Arkansas, a white man, residing in the Indian Territory, was being tried for assault and battery. His attorney, a shrewd lawyer, was cross-examining a witness, brought by the government to testify to the reputation of the complaining witness as a law-abiding, peaceful citizen. The witness, on direct examination, had sworn to the angelic character and disposition of the complainant.

"Now," said the attorney for defense, "don't you know that this complainant frequently gets into trouble with his neighbors?"

"Yes," assented the witness.

"Don't you know, sir, that he gets drunks and whips his wife, and that he was arrested last spring for badly beating a boy, and that he gets into quarrels nearly every time he goes to town?"

"Yes," again admitted the witness.

"What, sir! You know all this, and yet you come here and state on your oath that his reputation is good in the neighborhood where he resides?"

"Oh!" replied the witness without the least sign of discomfiture, "*it takes more than that* to give a man a bad reputation *up where I live.*"

From *The French Quarter,* An Informal History of the New Orleans Underworld, by Herbert Asbury, p. 209. Copyright, 1936, by Alfred A. Knopf, Inc. New York and London.

From *Hell on the Border;* He Hanged Eighty-Eight Men, A History of the Great United States Criminal Court at Fort Smith, Arkansas, and of Crime and Criminals in the Indian Territory, and the Trial and Punishment thereof before His Honor Judge Isaac C. Parker, "the Terror of Law-Breakers," . . . by S. W. Harman, compiled by C. P. Sterns, pp. 104–105. Copyright, 1898, by the Phoenix Publishing Company. Fort Smith.

The Test

A STRANGER came once from Texas to a house of one of these kinfolks and announced to one of our great-uncles that he was a brother-in-law.

"You are?" asked our great-uncle.

"I am," said the Texan.

"Can your wife tell through a brick wall twenty feet thick if you have had a drink of liquor?" inquired our great-uncle.

"She can."

"Can she tell it two days later?"

"She can."

Our great-uncle shouted with wild laughter. "You're my brother-in-law all right," said he. Then reaching into a meal bin he pulled out a jug. "Help yourself, brother," he said. "Just help yourself."

A Flatboat Passenger Finds Excitement

THE story is familiar of the man who took passage in a flatboat from Pittsburg bound for New Orleans. He passed many dreary, listless days on his way down the Ohio and Mississippi, and seemed to be desponding for want of excitement. Superficially, he was quiet and inoffensive; practically, he was perfectly good-natured and kindly disposed. In course of time the craft upon which he was a passenger put into Napoleon, in the State of Arkansas, "for groceries." At the moment there was a general fight extending all along the "front of the town," which at that time consisted of a single house.

The unhappy passenger, after fidgeting about, and jerking his feet up and down, as if he were walking on hot bricks, turned to a "used-up spectator" and observed:

"Stranger, is this a free fight?"

The reply was prompt and to the point: "It ar; and if you wish to go in, don't stand on ceremony."

The wayfarer did "go in," and in less time than we can relate the circumstance he was literally "chawed up." Groping his way down to the flat, his hair gone, his eye closed, his lips swollen, and his face generally "mapped out," he sat himself down on a chicken coop, and soliloquized thus:

From *Red Hills and Cotton,* An Upcountry Memory, by Ben Robertson, pp. 125–126. Copyright, 1942, by Ben Robertson. New York: Alfred A. Knopf.

From "Remembrances of the Mississippi," by T. B. Thorpe, *Harper's New Monthly Magazine,* Vol. XII (December, 1855), No. LXVII, p. 37. New York: Harper & Brothers, Publishers.

"So this is Na-po-le-*on*, is it?—upon my word it's a lively place, and the only one at which I have had any fun since I left home."

Insensible as this man was to wounds and bruises, we think that we once met with a more striking example in a "half-horse, half-alligator" fellow, who by some accident was cut up with twenty dirk-knife wounds at least, some of which, according to his own statement, "reached into the hollow." On our sympathizing with his deplorable condition, he cut us short by remarking:

"Stranger, don't be alarmed about these *scratches*—I've mighty healing flesh."

Old Bolivar

. . . A BLIND man . . . went to the race track, bet on a horse named Bolivar, and then was compelled to rely upon a friend to keep him informed on Bolivar's progress during the race.

"How is Bolivar at the quarter?" asked the blind man.

"Going good," replied his friend.

"And how is Bolivar at the half?" inquired the blind man a few seconds later.

"Running strong," the friend replied.

A few more seconds passed. "How is Bolivar at the three-quarters?" anxiously asked the blind man.

"Holding his own," the friend responded.

"Now how is Bolivar in the stretch?" the blind man asked eagerly.

"In there running like hell," replied his friend. "He's heading for the line, driving all the other horses in front of him!"

Fox Story

. . . A FOX-HUNTING farmer had a favorite hound and was fond of boasting of his dog's speed. One morning, at break of day, he and his friends started a fox, and the dogs went yelling, the favorite in the lead. On they sped, over hills, and across creek and vale, the hunters at last outstripping all the pack, except the favorite dog. He was clear out of sight, but ever and anon, they heard the deep bark of the flying hound, and the excitement

After William O. Bradley.

From *Greetings from Old Kentucky*, by Allan M. Trout, p. 120. Copyright, 1947, by Allan M. Trout. Louisville, Kentucky: Published by the *Courier-Journal*.

After William T. Haskell.

From "The Old-Time Tennessee Orator," by Philip Lindsley, *The Taylor Trotwood Magazine*, Vol. VII (July, 1908) No. 4, pp. 359-360. Copyright, 1908, by the Taylor-Trotwood Publishing Co. Nashville, Tennessee.

was at fever pitch. Then they came upon a woodman, cutting down a tree. "Did you see anything of a dog and fox running by just now?" exclaimed the farmer.

"Yes," said the woodman.

"How were they making it?"

"Oh," said the woodman, "the dog was a lettle ahead!"

Robin and the Bitch

. . . ROBIN had a fine pack of fox hounds and on one occasion after turning his pack out for a race, it soon became apparent that the hounds were not interested in finding a fox but were following a certain bitch among them that happened to be in heat. Yell, cajole, and curse, by whistle and call and shout, Robin could not sufficiently distract the interest of the hounds from the bitch to get them to hunt. Nor could he catch the offender, who soon led the whole pack out of sight. Eventually Robin caught up with them, all gathered around the entrance to a little cave under a cliff. Since the bitch was nowhere to be seen, Robin decided that at last he had her cornered in the cave and would catch her and, once and for all, put an end to this tomfoolery. So he waded through the baying hounds and went in with a small stick, intending to bring out the disturbing element and teach her a thing or two. But, in no time flat, Robin tore out screeching, with a wildcat on his back, and the racket that ensued with him and the wildcat in the midst of a pack of frantic hounds left Robin nearer dead than alive. As soon as he could get what was left of himself extricated from the melee, he stormed and swore that he'd kill the bitch as soon as he laid hands on her. But she was nowhere to be found. Fortunately, by the time he reached home, Robin had cooled off and reconsidered, for what should he see sitting at his gate waiting for him and wagging her tail in welcome, as unconcerned and as noncommittal as you please, but the innocent bitch? "Wal, sister," he said to her at last and gently enough, "it jes goes ter show whut comes uv a man when he thinks he's got more sense than a dawg."

The Razorback and the Dynamite

No TYPE of community has been more distinctive of America than has the backwoods; and no American humor is better defined or more robust

---

From *With a Southern Accent*, by Viola Goode Liddell, pp. 156–157. Copyright, 1948, by the University of Oklahoma Press. Norman.

From "There's a Geography of Humorous Anecdotes," by Charles F. Arrowood, *In the Shadow of History* edited by J. Frank Dobie, Mody C. Boatright, and Harry H. Ransom, pp. 80–81. Texas Folklore Society Publications, Number XV. Copyright, 1939, by the Texas Folk-Lore Society. Austin.

than the humor of the backwoods. The device most employed by back-woods humor for its effect is exaggeration; but its quality is by no means wholly dependent upon this device. Exaggeration is employed with telling effect because it is used to caricature some distinctive trait or foible.

Take, for example, this story of an Arkansas razorback hog. The razor-back has been as distinctive of the Southern swamps and pine barrens as the long-horned steer has been of Texas. He was a principal support of life in the region of the Dismal Swamp when Byrd and his party ran the dividing line, and he has been an important economic and social factor in the region ever since. Nothing tougher ever ran on four legs. The razor-back may lack the speed of the wolf, the fighting equipment of a wildcat, the strength of a bear, but no wolf, cat or bear can exceed him in ability to absorb punishment and come back for more.

A farmer was clearing a new ground—grubbing up the stumps labori-ously, by hand. A county demonstration agent came by and showed him how easily and cheaply the stumps could be removed by the use of dyna-mite. The farmer was delighted. He went to the store, bought dynamite, fuse, and caps. Coming home, he dug a hole by a big white oak stump, set a charge of dynamite under it, lighted the fuse, and went to his house for supper. The fuse went out, but by that time the farmer was clear of the new ground; so he decided to wait until the next morning before lighting it again.

The next morning, early, the farmer's big razorback hog got up and went foraging. He found that stick of dynamite and ate it. Then he saw the farmer about the barn lot and hustled up to see if he could steal a little corn from the mule's breakfast. He broke into the mule's stall, and made for the feed trough. The mule, naturally, kicked at him, and, for the first and last time in his life, connected. The dynamite, at last, went off.

A neighbor heard the explosion and hurried over. He found the owner leaning over the fence of his barn lot, viewing the ruins.

The neighbor heaved a sympathetic sigh. "It looks pretty bad, friend," he said, "pretty bad."

"Yes," said the victim, "it is bad. Killed my mule, wrecked my barn, broke every window out of one side of my house, and, brother, I've got an awful sick hog."

The Durnedest Fellow for Hard Luck

"WELL, I have been lookin' for my luck to change, but I done give up. I ain't got a chancet. You see, I got this little ole place that use to bring in purty good stuff, but here lately somethin's always happenin'. I didn't git

As told by Lee Morris, Marion, North Carolina, to Dudley W. Crawford. Manu-scripts of the Federal Writers' Project of the Works Progress Administration for the State of North Carolina.

my corn worked at the right time and the crabgrass taken it. I always raises a lot o' beans but this year the beetles et 'em up. My wife she run off with one o' them sawmill fellers from over on North Fork and that fine fox dog o' mine up and died the other day. And there's that oldest gal o' mine. Durned if she ain't turned out to be a schoolteacher. Have a drink?"

I had one. I sorta begun to want to talk some myself. "Too bad about that grass takin' your crop," I said.

"Oh, that's all right. It'll give me the finest hay crop in the county."

"Well, it sure is too bad about your wife leavin' you thataway."

"Now, I don't know as that's so. I'll be a long time forgittin' the way she rung a skillet over my head and I had to go to the blacksmith to git the rim filed off my neck."

"Well, it's awful about the beetles gittin' your beans."

"Aw no, not a-tall. Them beetles is the finest feed in the world for guinea. My guinea hens is layin' mo' aigs than I know what to do with. I has a nice fat guinea ever' Sunday for dinner."

"Well, I know you hated to lose that fine fox dog, didn't you?"

"In a way, yes. But she had just dropped seven o' the finest pups you ever see. They're gonna be the finest pack o' fox dogs in this state."

"Is that so! Well, at least it must be nice to have a schoolteacher in the family."

"Nope. That gal has got the walls o' this cabin papered with the awfullest lookin' pictures I ever seen. Drawin's and photygraphs o' human chitlin's bein' devoured by alcohol. I can't hardly go inside, they's so ugly. Yep, I am the durnedest feller for hard luck that ever was."

The Man Yoked with an Ox

QUITE a number of places and people have laid claim to this story. I think I have written it up as supposed to have happened in Clay County [North Carolina]. But they say it did take place in Mitchell County, where there was a man who was out with his yoke of oxen and one of his oxen got sullen and lay down and wouldn't pull. And he was in a rough place in the ad, and it required a pretty good pull. And he didn't have but one ox to pull. So he just took the yoke off the ox's neck and got in himself— put his head through the yoke and he with the good ox pulled that wagon out.

And they pulled out of the hole and the ox kept going faster and faster, the ox did. He kept going faster and faster. After a while he struck a trot and then from a trot he put into a lope. And he kept going and finally ran in toward home. Ran over a bee bench, started the bees to flying all over, stinging chickens. Went on and hit the shed, knocked the shed down, and

As told by Bascom Lamar Lunsford, Leicester, North Carolina, January 19, 1949. Recorded by B. A. Botkin.

a lot of stuff in the shed loft dumped into the porch. And as he passed the porch of the house, he hollered to the folks on the porch, he says: "Here we come! Head us! Damn our fool souls! Head us!"

The Ungrateful Constituent

. . . His [Vice-President Alben W. Barkley's] story of the Ungrateful Constituent . . . has become a classic among politicians. Its moral is: never take your political support for granted.

It is the story of Farmer Jones. It opens with a long chronicle of the political favors done for Farmer Jones over the years, by County Attorney Barkley, Judge Barkley, Congressman Barkley, Senator Barkley. Back in World War I days, Barkley visited Jones in a hospital in France to console him; he interceded with Pershing to get him home sooner after the Armistice; he cut red tape to speed his disability compensation; he helped Jones get loans from the Farm Credit Administration. And so on, down to the mid-1930's, when Barkley got Jones a Disaster Loan to rebuild his farm after the floods washed it away, and an appointment for Mrs. Jones as the local postmistress.

In 1938, when Barkley had a hot fight on his hands with Happy Chandler for renomination to the Senate race in Kentucky, he was thunderstruck to hear that his old protégé, Farmer Jones, was supporting Chandler.

Barkley hastened around to see Jones, who admitted as how he guessed maybe he would vote for Chandler. Barkley, choking down his indignation, recited the long saga of his political labors in Jones' behalf.

"Surely," said Senator Barkley, "you remember all these things I have done for you?"

"Yeah," said Jones sullenly. "But what in hell have you done for me lately?"

Captain Quill and Si

FATHER could never mention his river-captain friends without being reminded of some of their yarns. The one he repeated most often was told to him by Captain Morrisette about his rival, Captain Quill, of the famous *Nettie Quill*.

It seems that Captain Quill had stationed out in the woods an old Negro named Si Samson, whom he furnished with gun and shells, traps and snares, hooks and seines, to get the fresh fish and game which he liked to serve on his little packet. Si always waited for the *Nettie Quill* around the mouth of Bear Creek with something for the Captain's larder, and if the boat came in at night, Si would flag her down with a lighted lantern.

One cold winter night when the *Nettie* was fighting her way upstream against a driving, freezing rain, Captain Quill saw on shore a light waving around in a circle, Si's sign that he had something to be taken aboard. Bad as Quill hated to stop, after the dickens of a time, he landed the *Nettie* and went out in the blinding rain and sleet to get what he expected to be a gunny sack full of squirrel and quail. When Si got close enough to hear through all the noise of the storm and gale, Quill yelled, "What in hell's creation have you got on a devilish night like this?"

"I got you a coon, Boss," answered Si hopefully.

"A coon! You damn-fool nigger," swore the captain, "don't you know a coon's not fit to eat?"

"They're fine, Cap'n," Si assured him. "You jes try this 'un an' see."

"Hell, no," the captain bawled back at him, "and I'll break your no-account neck if you ever make me stop on a night like this for any such varmint. Why, I'd sooner eat a dog."

"I's sorry," said Si mournfully, "but I guess it all depends on how a pusson wus fotch up. Now, myself, I'd ruther eat a coon."

A Monument to the Boll Weevil

THE town of Enterprise, Alabama, is the place that put up a monument to the boll weevil—the insect that destroys cotton. That's like putting up a monument to a hurricane, you'd think. The story was that when the weevil wiped out the only crop those parts had ever known, the townspeople woke up and turned to other things, and were better off than they had been with cotton.

But the monument was really a kind of accident. In 1919, when new street lights were installed at Enterprise and things were torn up, the town built a circular pool and fountain in the middle of the main street, with a statue of a woman something like "Liberty" in the center. So many passers-by stopped and asked the workmen what they were doing that finally one of them, just wise-cracking, said "We're putting up a monument to a boll weevil." A traveling salesman overheard it. He went on to Montgomery, called a newspaper office, and told them Enterprise was putting up a statue to the boll weevil. The paper came out with a big story the next day. Then the town had to live up to the story. It put a bronze plaque on the statue base which read: "In Profound Appreciation of the Boll Weevil and What It Has Done as the Herald of Prosperity, This Monument Is Erected by the Citizens of Enterprise—December 11, 1919."

Scientific Agriculture

. . . [THERE is] a revealing story about one of the combination farmer-merchant-bankers of Southeast Arkansas. A book agent came to sell him a set of books on scientific agriculture. The old man thumbed through them.

"No, I don't want 'em."

"You ought to buy these books, sir. If you had these books you could farm twice as good as you do."

The old fellow settled himself more comfortably in his chair.

"Hell, son," he said, "I don't farm half as good as I know how now."

The Potato Story

ILLUSTRATIVE of the generous hospitality of the Kentucky mountaineer, Col. John W. McCullough, of Owensboro, Kentucky, relates:

I was traveling through the Kentucky mountains and lost my way. The sun had gone down and darkness was rapidly approaching as I rode up to an humble cabin and stated my unfortunate plight, and asked if I could remain over night.

"Light, stranger, and come in if you can put up with our fare," was the ready response.

When supper time arrived, I was invited to partake, and was astonished to observe that the only food on the table was a plate of potatoes. My host passed the plate with the request:

"Stranger, take a 'tater," which I readily did.

In a short time he invited me to "take another 'tater." At length, seeing that I had eaten the second potato, he pushed the plate over to me and said,

"Stranger, take d——d nigh all the 'taters."

From *A Southerner Discovers the South,* by Jonathan Daniels, pp. 163–164. Copyright, 1938, by the Macmillan Company. New York.

From *Stories and Speeches of William O. Bradley,* with Biographical Sketch by M. H. Thatcher, pp. 159–160. Copyright, 1916, by Transylvania Printing Co. Lexington, Kentucky.

Get Up, Mule

OLD Mose had made the best crop of cotton he ever made, but still he came out even. The landlord told him he had done fine, and that he could start the next year out of debt. Old Mose didn't say nothing, just sat there looking. Old Cracker kept on making admiration over the crop and how fine it was to be out of debt. Mose didn't say nothing. Cracker kept throwing out chances for Mose to talk. Finally his curiosity got the best of him. "What you thinking about, Mose?" Mose just looked at him. Old Cracker banged his office desk and hollered, "What the hell you thinking about, Mose! If you don't tell me what you thinking, I'm gonna run you off my place." Mose said, "Oh, I was jes thinking, Mr. Landlord, jes thinking that the next time I ever say 'giddap' to a mule, he gonna be setting in my lap."

Previous Experience

ON ONE of the plantations in Beaufort County some time ago a gang of men were doing some ditch work. The man in charge reproached one of the men for doing shoddy work, and tried to shame him by comparing his work with that of one of the other men. The Negro promptly replied: "Boss, ain't you know John jus' git off de chain gang? How kin you spec me fo' do as good work as he when him is jus' hab two yeahs' trainin' in dis kind of work?"

Josh and the Corn

A MAN was engaged in stripping fodder and put some green ears of corn in the fire to roast for himself to eat, as the slaves generally do in fodder stripping time, although they were whipped when caught. Before they were roasted enough, the overseer approached, and Josh took the ears out with some live coals stuck to them and put them in his shirt bosom. In running away his clothes took fire and Josh jumped into a creek to put it out. The overseer said to him, "Josh, what are you doing here?" He answered, "It

---

From "Out of Their Mouths," by Sterling A. Brown, *Survey Graphic*, Vol. XXXI (November, 1942), No. 11, p. 480.

From "The Plantation Negro of To-day," by Francis Marion Hutson, Historical Commission of South Carolina, Columbia, South Carolina, January, 1949.

From *My Life in the South*, by Jacob Stroyer, p. 62. New and Enlarged Edition. Salem: Salem Observer Book and Job Print. 1885.

is so warm to-day I taut I would go in de creek to git cool off, sir." "Well, have you got cooled off, Josh?" "Oh! yes sir, very much cooler, sir."

Answer to Prayer

AND dat put me in de mind of a nigger dat useter do a lot of prayin' up under 'simmon tree, durin' slavery time. He'd go up dere and pray to God and beg Him to kill all de white folks. Ole Massa heard about it and so de next day he got hisself a armload of sizeable rocks and went up de 'simmon tree, before de nigger got dere, and when he begin to pray and beg de Lawd to kill all de white folks, Ole Massa let one of dese rocks fall on Ole Nigger's head. It was a heavy rock and knocked de nigger over. So when he got up he looked up and said: "Lawd, I ast you to kill all de white folks, can't you tell a white man from a nigger?"

Things Equal to the Same Thing

UNCLE Abraham invited Brother Gabriel to take tea with him Christmas Eve. Brother Gabriel was a colored minister and was considered the most pious man of his day. Uncle Abe set before him a roasted pig and a fine dish of potatoes, and several other good things. Knowing that these things must have been stolen, Brother Gabriel refused to eat until Uncle Abe had said grace and made a confession before him. He said his grace as follows: "A-Lord-er, dou art-er did-er taught dy sarvents dat it want no harm fur ter take de corn out er de barril and put it into de kag. De barrill 'longs to de marster and de kag longs ter de marster, dar-forth it aint no diffunce when de darkie take de marster's pig out er de pen and put it into de darkie, case de darkie longs ter de marster, an de pig pen longs ter de marster."

Hill Farm Hazards

HILLSIDE cultivation is no easy matter, and hilltop farming is not much better. The natural difficulties that beset the West Virginia hill farmer

From *Mules and Men*, by Zora Neale Hurston, pp. 120–121. Copyright, 1935, by Zora Neale Hurston. Philadelphia and London: J. B. Lippincott Company.

From *Southern Workman and Hampton School Record*, Vol. 26. (October, 1897) No. 10, p. 210. Hampton, Virginia: Hampton Normal & Agricultural Institute.

From *West Virginia, A Guide to the Mountain State*, compiled by Workers of the Writers' Program of the Work Projects Administration in the State of West Virginia, pp. 136–137. American Guide Series. Copyright, 1941, by the Conservation Commission of West Virginia. New York: Oxford University Press.

are the source of much humor and exaggeration; however, the story of the clifftop farm in Wayne County, where the fields are reached by ladders and the mule and plow are hoisted by block and tackle up the cliff, is no myth. Slightly exaggerated is the story of the motorist on a narrow valley road who, perceiving a great commotion and a cloud of dust ahead, pulled to one side and stopped his car. As the cloud settled and a gnarled figure emerged rubbing his elbow and beating the dust from his denim jeans with a tattered hat, the startled traveler inquired:

"What in the world happened?"

In a tone of plaintive disgust the dusty one replied:

"That's the third time I've fell outen that danged cornfield this mornin' and I've still got seven rows to grub."

The Last of the Arkansas Squatters

THE Squatter, once so famous in Arkansas, and who gave rise to the song and the dialogue of the Arkansas Traveler, has almost entirely disappeared. Where his cabin stood there is now a cotton factory, and at the forks of the road, where his daughter Sal saw "sperets," there is an academy for young women. The old man and the old woman are asleep away off somewhere beneath the trees, and Sal's son is the prosecuting attorney of his district, and next year he may go to Congress.

I am inclined to believe that I saw, or encountered would be the better expression, the very last of the genuine Arkansas Squatters. A newspaper had sent me up among the hills to stir a sensation out of an alleged discovery of gold, and I was returning, horseback, when one evening about "half an hour by sun" I came to the typical log house of the traditional Squatter. I had long since lost the road and was simply riding at large. The Squatter, with his wheat-straw beard, his hay hair and his autumn leaf complexion, was standing with his arms resting on the rail fence that made a pretense of surrounding his cabin, but I noticed that the fence was thrown down in several places and that a skinny hog and a hip-shot cow wandered in and out at will. The old fellow nodded at my approach and immediately withdrew his attention from me, and I believe that he would have suffered me to pass on without a word on his part, so careless was he and so unconcerned with regard to the children of the world. But I drew rein and spoke to him, and not ignorantly, for I knew his character—knew that to get directions from him I must indeed be adroit.

"How are you, sir?"

"About the same."

"Fine weather."

By Opie Read. From *Library of Southern Literature*, Edwin Anderson Alderman, Joel Chandler Harris, Editors in Chief, Vol. X, pp. 4374–4377. Copyright, 1907, 1909, by The Martin and Hoyt Co. Atlanta.

"So I hearn."

"You live here, I suppose."

"Ain't died here."

"I see! and I suppose you have been here long enough to give me instructions as to the best way to reach the Dardanelle road. I am lost."

"When do you expect to find yourself?"

"That's what I don't know. But as soon as I strike the Dardanelle road I'll know where I am."

"Don't you know where you are now?"

"I must confess that I don't."

"Well, I'll tell you."

"I'll be much obliged to you."

"You are right here talkin' to me."

"That's true, but where are you, that's the question."

"Why, I'm with you," he answered with a drawl.

"I don't suppose there's any disputing of that fact. But I'd like to go to the Dardanelle road."

"Then why don't you?"

"I will as soon as I can."

"There ain't nobody a-holdin' of you."

"That's a fact, but I don't know which way to go."

"Go as you please."

"But that might not be right."

"Then turn to the left."

I saw that this tact was useless, so I thought that I would try the effect of skilful flattery. Surely the old scoundrel had a weak place hidden somewhere. "By the way, didn't I see you in Little Rock last winter?"

"Don't know what you seed last winter nur summer befo' last."

"I didn't know but I saw you at the state house. Weren't you in the Legislature?"

"It must have 'a' been my brother you seen."

"Was he in the Legislature?"

"No, in the penitentiary."

That wouldn't do. I must try some other way. "You look as if you might be a pretty good sort of a man."

"I've had 'ligion four times."

"How did you lose it?"

"Cussin' that cow out yan; and I wanter tell you she would snatch the 'ligion outen the possul. Peter and the rest of them. She's a caution."

"I mean you must be a good man physically, boxing or wrestling."

"I used to be, but since I broke the neck of the county jedge an' crippled the sheriff for life rasslin', w'y I ain't prided myself much."

"I don't suppose you could be induced to show me how to get to that road."

"I'm afeerd not."

"But do you think you are showing a Christian spirit?"

"Don't reckon I am, but as I tell you I ain't a Christian since I lost my 'ligion a-cussin of the cow."

"Look here, the night is going to be fearfully dark. Are you going to see me sleep in the woods?"

"I won't be thar to see you."

"I am half inclined to get down and take a fall out of you." I believed that I might possibly have found his weak spot. His old eyes brightened.

"Pardner, git down and look at yo' saddle, won't you?"

I dismounted, tied my horse and told him that I was ready, and with many a capering, didoish for so old a fellow, he came toward me—he wrapped his long arms about me and told me to help myself; he laughed with a strange glee; he swore that he hadn't been so happy since he broke the neck of the county judge. I clutched him, and began to struggle, in the pretense of exerting my might to throw him down, but in reality looking out for a place to fall; and I did fall. "Got enough?" the old rascal asked, a yellowish grin spreading broadcast over his face.

"Yes, plenty," I answered. "I know when I have enough. I can tell a man as soon as I put my hands on him, and I want to say without shame, either, that you are the first man that has thrown me since I reached my prime. You talk of throwing the county judge—why, not long ago I threw a circuit judge."

"You don't tell me!" he cried, his eyes sparkling.

"Yes, I do tell you and it is a fact; and furthermore, I believe you can throw down the supreme judge of the state."

He put his head affectionately on my shoulder. "Podner," said he, lifting his head to wipe his eyes, "you ain't going to leave me to-night. It's goin' to rain, an' thar ain't a house over yonder on that road. I'll give you the best on the place, and tomorrow mornin' I'll take you to the road. Mother," he yelled at his wife who had just appeared in the doorway, "kill the finest chicken you've got, git out yo' Sunday stuff, for the Progician son is here."

Crockett and the Inquisitive Landlord

I MOUNTED my horse and pushed forward on my road to Fulton. When I reached Washington, a village a few miles from the Red river, I rode up to the Black Bear tavern, when the following conversation took place between me and the landlord, which is a pretty fair sample of the curiosity of some folks:-

"Good morning, mister—I don't exactly recollect your name now," said the landlord as I alighted.

"It's of no consequence," said I.

From *Life of David Crockett*, the Original Humorist and Irrepressible Backwoodsman . . . , pp. 286–290. Philadelphia: John E. Potter and Company. 1860.

"I'm pretty sure I've seen you somewhere."

"Very likely you may, I've been there frequently."

"I was sure 'twas so; but strange I should forget your name," says he.

"It is indeed somewhat strange that you should forget what you never knew," says I.

"It is unaccountable strange. It's what I'm not often in the habit of, I assure you. I have, for the most part, a remarkably detentive memory. In the power of people that pass along this way, I've scarce ever made, as the doctors say, a *slapsus slinkum* of this kind afore."

"Eh heh!" I shouted, while the critter continued.

"Traveling to the western country, I presume, mister?"

"Presume anything you please, sir," said I; "but don't trouble me with your presumptions."

"O Lord, no, sir—I won't do that, I've no ideer of that—not the least ideer in the world," says he; "I suppose you've been to the westward afore now?"

"Well, suppose I have?"

"Why, on that supposition, I was going to say you must be pretty well— that is to say, you must know something about the place."

"Eh heh!" I ejaculated, looking sort of mazed full in his face. The tarnal critter still went ahead.

"I take it you're a married man, mister?"

"Take it as you will, that is no affair of mine," says I.

"Well, after all, a married life is the most happiest way of living; don't you think so, mister?"

"Very possible," says I.

"I conclude you have a family of children, sir?"

"I don't know what reason you have to conclude so."

"Oh, no reason in the world, mister, not the least," says he; "but I thought I might just take the liberty to make the presumption, you know; that's all, sir. I take it, mister, you're a man about my age?"

"Eh heh!"

"How old do you call yourself, if I may be so bold?"

"You're bold enough, the devil knows," says I; and as I spoke rather sharp, the varment seemed rather staggered, but he soon recovered himself, and came up to the chalk again.

"No offence I hope — I — I — I — wouldn't be thought uncivil, by any means; I always calculate to treat everybody with civility."

"You have a very strange way of showing it."

"True, as you say, I ginerally take my own way in these ere matters. Do you practise law, mister, or farming, or mechanicals?"

"Perhaps so," says I.

"Ah, I judge so; I was pretty certain it must be the case. Well, it's as good business as any there is followed nowadays."

"Eh heh!" I shouted, and my lower jaw fell in amazement at his perseverance.

"I take it you've money at interest, mister?" continued the varment, without allowing himself time to take breath.

"Would it be of any particular interest to you to find out?" says I.

"Oh, not at all, not the least in the world, sir; I'm not at all inquisitive about other people's matters; I minds my own business—that's my way."

"And a very odd way you have of doing it, too."

"I've been thinking what persuasion you're of—whether you're a Unitarian or Baptist, or whether you belong to the Methodisses."

"Well, what's the conclusion?"

"Why, I have concluded that I'm pretty near right in my conjectures. Well, after all, I'm inclined to think they're the nearest right of any persuasion—though some folks think differently."

"Eh heh!" I shouted again.

"As to pollyticks, I take it, you—that is to say, I suppose you—"

"Very likely."

"Ah, I could have sworn it was so from the moment I saw you. I have a knack at finding out a man's sentiments. I dare say, mister, you're a justice in your own country?"

"And if I may return the compliment, I should say you're a just ass everywhere." By this time I began to get weary of his impertinence, and led my horse to the trough to water, but the darned critter followed me up.

"Why, yes," said he, "I'm in the commission of the peace, to be sure—and an officer in the militia, though, between you and I, I wouldn't wish to boast of it."

My horse having finished drinking, I put one foot in the stirrup, and was preparing to mount. "Any more inquiries to make?" said I.

"Why, no, nothing to speak on," said he. "When do you return, mister?"

"About the time I come back," said I; and leaping into the saddle, galloped off. The pestiferous varment bawled after me, at the top of his voice—

"Well, I shall look for ye, then. I hope you won't fail to call."

Now, who in all natur do you reckon the critter was, who afforded so fine a sample of the impertinent curiosity that some people have to pry into other people's affairs?

I knew him well enough at first sight, though he seemed to have forgotten me. It was no other than Job Snelling,[1] the manufacturer of cayenne pepper out of mahogany sawdust, and upon whom I played the trick with the coon skin. I pursued my journey to Fulton, and laughed heartily to think what a swither I had left poor Job in, at not gratifying his curiosity; for I knew he was one of those fellows who would peep down your throat just to ascertain what you had eaten for dinner.

---

[1] See "The Coon-Skin Trick," *A Treasury of American Folklore* (New York, 1944), pp. 20–23.

The Man Who Would Not Stay Dead

AARON Kelly dead, so dey berry 'im. Fay-ye-well, Aaron Kelly!

Dat night dem all set roun' de fiah, hopin' dat the dead deceased is gone whun dey berry well know Aaron Kelly ain't got one uthly chance o' goin'. De widder say: "Ah hopes 'e gone whuh ah spec's 'e ain't!" When in walk de co'pse, lookin' dusty. *Oh, my Lawdy!*

He pick 'im a seat twix' de widder an' de lead mounah; an' sezzee: "Wut disyuh all about. You-all ack lak somebuddy dead. Who dead?"

De widder look at 'im . . . she say: "Oh, my Gawd!"

Aaron say, kina fretful: "Dammit, 'oman! Ah ax you, who dead?"

"You is," sez de widder, shakin' lak a cold dog in a wet sack.

"Me dead?" say Aaron. "Huccum? Ah don't feel dead." He tell 'em 'e don't belieb 'em, 'cuz 'e don't feel dead.

Dem tell 'im dey yent duh cayeh how 'e feel . . . 'e dead.

"But," sezzee, "Ah don't feel dead a dam bit!"

"Orri," dem 'spond. "Oonah don't feel dead; but oonah look dead orri. Oonah bettah gone back tuh de grabe whuh oonah blongst."

"No," sezzee, "Ah ain't gwine back to no grabe twell ah feels dead. 'Top you-all oggyment. Ain't no use fuh oggyment. Ah ain't gwine back to no grabe twell ah feels dead fo' true."

"Oh, my Gawd!" sez de widder. "How long oonah spec' de co'pse gwine las'?"

"Not so long," say de lead. "Not in dis hot time. 'E cain't las' long."

Yut, spite de widder, de wedder, de hot, de rainy, an' all, Aaron las'. An' 'e ain't done one fo'm t'ing cep' set by de cookin' fiah wa'min' 'e han's an' 'e foots, an' chillin' off de room. 'E des set dey, sundown an' sunup, wa'min' 'e han's an' foots.

De 'surance 'sociation won't pay de 'surance cuz Aaron sway to Gawd 'e ain't dead. An' de fambly cain' pay de coffin, cuz dem ain't git de 'surance. An' de undehtakeh sez 'e gwine graff de coffin effen de dead deceased won't ockepy 'em; an' dey's de berry ol' debble to pay.

De widder 'puzent dese t'ing to Aaron; but Aaron des' say, sezzee: "Le' me be, 'oman! Ah ain't gwine back to no berr'in groun' twell ah dead. Don't oonah miss me?"

"My Gawd!" say de widder. "Miss oonah? How ah gwine miss oonah? Ah ain't tab no chance fuh miss oonah. Oonah ain't gone. Ah could miss oonah dat easy."

"Ain't oonah goin' in mou'nin' fuh me?" sezzee, fretful an' grumblesome.

"Wut de use o' me goin' in mou'nin, when ah ain't lost oonah yet?"

As told by Sarah Rutledge and Epsie Meggett.

From *The Doctor to the Dead*, Grotesque Legends & Folk Tales of Old Charleston, hy John Bennett, pp. 249–252. Copyright, 1943, 1946, by John Bennett. New York nd Toronto: Rinehart & Company, Inc.

"Oonah ain't pay no propah 'tention tuh me," sezzee.

"Ain't pay no propah 'tention? Oh, my Gawd! Ain't we took oonah out an' berrit oonah? Ain't de Reb'ren Rab'nel preach de funeral? Oonah t'ink us gwine berry oonah two time? Us ain't. Quit yo' complainin'."

Den Aaron des' set by de fiah, wa'min 'e han's an' 'e foots, an' lookin' peevish. 'E des set by de fiah, an' creak an' crack. 'E j'ints dry; 'e back stiff; an' ebry time 'e mobe 'eseff 'e crack an' creak lak dead tree in de wind.

One night de bes' fiddleh come a-cou'-tin' de widder. 'E sot on one side de fiah; Aaron sot tudder side, wa'min' 'e han's an' foots, an' stretchin' 'e laigs fuh wa'm . . . an' all de time creakin' an' crackin'.

De fiddleh him des' wore out hearin' 'im creak an' crack. 'E 'sid an' 'e 'cide sumpin otter be done. But 'sidderin' an 'ciderin' don' make Sal's baby a shirt. Bum-bye de widder say, "Hullong us gotter put up wid dis dead co'pse? Hullong us gotter wait twell 'e molder? Hullong us gotter set hyuh by us own fiah, oonah, an' me, an' *him*?"

De fiddleh 'sidder; but 'e yent 'cide. Bum-bye Aaron stretch 'eseff, an', sezzee: "Dis ain't berry jovy. Le's we be jovy. Le's we dance fuh limbeh us laigs."

So de fiddleh git out 'e fiddle an' 'chune 'um. De fiddle begin fuh sing. Aaron stretch 'eseff; 'e shuk 'eseff; 'e giddup; 'e tek a step or two; him begin fuh jig, wid 'e ol' bone a-crackin', an' 'e yallar teet' a-snappin', an' 'e bald bonehead a-wagglin' an' 'e ahms a-flip-floppin' . . . roun' an' roun' an' roun'.

De fiddle sing, an' Aaron dance. Up and down de flo' 'e dance, cuttin' de buck an' frowin' de wing; an' 'e bones go rattle-rattle.

'E skip an' 'e prance, hidder an' yander roun' de room, 'e long shanks clockin', an' 'e knee bones a-knockin' . . . landy Lawdy! How dat dead man dance! Pooty soon a piece fly loose, an' fall on de flo'.

"My golly! Look at dat!" say de fiddleh.

"Play mo' fasteh!" say de widder. De fiddleh play mo' fasteh. De co'pse 'e creak an' 'e crack. Ebry time 'e jump 'e crack. An' ebry time 'e crack a piece drap on de flo'.

"Play mo' loudeh!" say de widder.

De fiddleh play mo' loud. An' crickety-crack, down an' back, de dead man go hoppin', an de dry bone a droppin', disaway, dataway, dem pieces keep poppin'. Ebry hop a dry bone drap. Ebry jump 'e shuck a bone. "Oh, my Gawd!" say de fiddleh; an' 'e han' shake so's 'e cain't sca'cely fingeh de string. "Play, man, play!" say de widder.

De fiddleh fiddle fasteh; dead Aaron dance; an' all de time 'e dance de bone keep a-droppin' . . . twell all to once 'e crumble down . . . 'e rib bone roll like a barrel hoop roun' de flo' . . . an' dere dead Aaron lay, des' a heap o' dry bone on de flo' . . . an' all de time de bal' headbone dance by itseff midst er de flo', grinnin' at de fiddleh, an' crackin' it' teeth. Dat head go a-dancin' bop, bop, bop!

"Oh, my sweet Lawd! Lookat dat!" say de fiddleh.

"Play mo' loudeh yet!" say de widder.

"Ho, ho!" say de bonehead. "Ain't us des' a-cuttin' de buck!" But dat fiddleh 'e ain't int'res' in head wuh do like dat head do. Sezzee: "Widder, ah gotta go git me mo' rozzum fuh ma bow!" So 'e gone fum dat house . . . an' ah reckons 'e still gittin' dat rozzum . . . cauze 'e didn't come back.

Dem gadder de bone tugedder, an' put 'em back in de grabe. But dey ben keerful fuh lay 'em all cristy-cross an' unj'int; so's Aaron cain't 'cide wey dem bone go. An', after dat, dead Aaron didn't gie up no mo'.

But de widder stan' widder fum dat day till yet. Dat dancin' dead-head spile de match.

PART TWO

SOUTHERN SAGA

We have heard with our ears, and our fathers have declared unto us, the noble things that were done in their days and in the old time before them.
—THE BOOK OF COMMON PRAYER

Wasn't Washington the Father of his Country? Hasn't Virginia been the Mother of Presidents? Isn't it on Virginia earth that more good hot American blood has been spilt in defense of principle than on the earth of any other state, North or South, East or West? Whose aristocracy is the purest? Whose heritage of Colonial achievements is the richest? Whose record of outstanding leadership in statecraft and in the profession of arms is the longest? How came the name of Old Dominion to be won? Where did the Cavaliers settle thickest? Whence sprang the greatest captain of the Revolutionary cause and the greatest captain of the Confederacy? Well then, what have you to say to all that?
—IRVIN S. COBB

Keep your eye on the log cabin. It is the hallmark of distinction in Kentucky, for there it was our people learned to do the best they can with what they have got, according to their lights.
—ALLAN M. TROUT

They [Micajah Harpe and Mike Fink] are not typical; their deeds establish a high-water mark of brutality and rowdyism; others aped them, but none excelled.
—ARCHER BUTLER HULBERT

Thus the politics of the Old South was . . . an arena wherein one great champion confronted another or a dozen, and sought to outdo them in rhetoric and splendid gesturing. It swept back the loneliness of the land, it brought men together under torches, it filled them with the contagious power of the crowd, it unleashed emotion and set it to leaping and dancing, it caught the very meanest man up out of his own tiny legend into the gorgeous fabric of the legend of this or that great hero.
—W. J. CASH

I. ON THE SIDE OF THE ANGELS

It is from posterity we are to expect remuneration for the sac-
rifices we are making for their service, and I fear not the appeal.
— THOMAS JEFFERSON

In the South the heroes were nearly all soldiers. With the excep-
tion of Mr. Jefferson in Virginia, the Southern pantheon was a
soldiers' temple. No politician, not Patrick Henry nor Tom Wat-
son, could compete for popular reverence with Lee and Jackson
and even such politically ambiguous heroes as Longstreet. Even
in Louisiana the new fame of the martyred Huey Long has to
fight with the old fame of Pierre Toutant Beauregard.
— D. W. BROGAN

1. "OF, FOR, AND BY THE SOUTH"

IN THE South, as elsewhere, myth and legend have a way of rewriting history to conform to the people's notion of what is memorable, esti-mable, and especially worthy of admiration and emulation. What is his-tory's loss is folklore's gain. If at times, however, the immortals of South-ern history seem to lack folklore appeal, that is because the folk stories have died with the people that told them or because the biographers have been more interested in erecting a marble monument than in portraying a flesh-and-blood creature. In any case, enough anecdotes survive (some of them told interchangeably about different heroes) to make them an integral part of folk history if not of folk-say. And as surely as the heroes of myth and legend, the heroes of history have their own mythos and golden age.

First of the golden ages of the South's heroic saga is the epic period of English exploration and colonization, which flowered in the legends of Vir-ginia Dare and Pocahontas, the patron saints of the founding of the South's greatness. While the high and pristine birth of Virginia Dare satisfies the historical requirements of an ancestral deity, her disappearance with the "Lost Colony" of Roanoke is akin to the sacred myth of the sacrifice of the first-born child to purchase divine favor and insure the welfare of the tribe.[1] To fulfill the aesthetic and romantic demands of legend, there are the pretty fairy tale of "The White Doe" (in which her Indian lover kills her with a silver arrow whose magic is supposed to restore her to human form) and the poetic fable of the origin of the purple scuppernong grape in the seedling that sprouted on the edge of the pool stained with her blood from the silver arrow.[2]

---

[1] Cf. James Branch Cabell, *Let Me Lie* (New York, 1947), pp. 67–71.
[2] Cf. Sallie Southall Cotten, *The White Doe,* the Fate of Virginia Dare (Philadelphia, 1902), pp. xiv-xvii.

In Virginia the princess Pocahontas (who married the English gentleman John Rolfe) helped to found another noble line, from which Virginians like John Randolph of Roanoke proudly claimed descent. Her special legend (in the Captain John Smith story) is that of the compassionate maiden who saves a foreign captive from death at the hands of her cruel father.[3]

To carry on the noble tradition of this noble lineage, the South has inherited a noble company of warrior and statesman heroes who exemplify the blending of the Anglo-Saxon heritage (more purely preserved in the South than anywhere else, we are told) and the American spirit of liberty with the defensive and self-conscious Southern tradition.

. . . The defensive and self-conscious South did the nation a high service, by projecting into its body of energy a spirit of loyalty to ideas, of passion for principles, of romantic devotion to causes. . . . And, as we forge still further forward, I believe we shall hark back with benefit to that single-minded but romantic age, blotted out almost without warning as by the fury of a tempest, with its consciousness of self and personal values, such as dignity held second to honor; that gameness in the blood; that grand manner; that archaic pride of honorable descent; that steadfastness of ideas; that mingling of the simplicity of a shepherd with the pride of a king; that "moral elegance" in matters constituting a public trust.[4]

Here the heroic spirit and hero myth assume such proportions that Southern history becomes an epic and Southern biography a saga, full of high adventure and high tragedy.

In writing of Gen. R. E. Lee and of the Confederate States of America, one felt always the pervasion of tragedy and, after 1862, the faster approach of the trampling horsemen. For Lee and for most of his lieutenants it was a drama of ill-fortune nobly borne and, in that way, a triumph of character over catastrophe, but it was drama played in the twilight. With Washington, the atmosphere is that of dawn. Disaster is never without hope. Battles may be lost, but the war will be won.[5]

To the tragic "twilight of the gods" in which Lee wore "defeat like a laurel crown," Confederate memories and myths have added the elegiac mood noted by James Branch Cabell in the Richmond of his childhood, where Lee and his lieutenants were King Arthur and the Knights of the Round Table to the heirs of the "Lost Cause." The flawlessness assumed in Lee's character was akin to the flawlessness that the "integrity of the United States" (according to Douglas Southall Freeman [6]) presupposed in Wash-

---

[3] Cabell, *loc. cit.* For the story of Juan Ortiz and the Florida Pocahontas, the daughter of Hirriga, Chief of Ucita, see "The Narrative of the Expedition of Hernando de Soto," in *Spanish Explorers in the Southern United States, 1528–1543* (New York, 1925), pp. 149–153.

[4] Edwin Anderson Alderman, "The Growing South," *Library of Southern Literature,* Vol. XIV (Atlanta, 1910), pp. 6199–6200.

[5] Douglas Southall Freeman, *George Washington, A Biography,* Vol. I (New York, 1948), p. xxvi.

[6] *Ibid.,* p. xv.

ington's character. Personal perfection was also assumed in the aristocratic pattern of the ideal warrior and gentleman, with its "exaltation of personality and of the class feeling above general social progress."[7]

Finally, in the deification of Lee we have the Southern counterpart of the Northern myth of Lincoln as the "great father" and the "dying god."

2. "Of the People—"

The difference between the monumental heroes of history and the people's heroes is the difference between the florid, stilted tributes of Confederate Memorial Day addresses and the juicy anecdotes and racy tall talk of picturesque backwoodsmen like Davy Crockett.

In so far as popular heroes are chosen rather than inherited by the people, they are on the side of the people rather than of the angels and they speak (as we shall note under "The People's Choice") with the tongues of the people rather than of angels. Moreover, in conspicuous contrast to the assumed perfection of the patrician patriots, stands the assumed imperfection of the people's heroes. For the people like their heroes to be human; and a certain amount of human weakness is necessary to the myth of the self-made man, allowing room for self-improvement as well as for the editorial improvements of time and tradition.

As "heady" and spontaneous representatives of the "heroic tradition . . . making its last stand in the new West against efficiency and correctness and form,"[8] these people's heroes have, through their gesturing and posing, their quarrels and scandals, helped to create their own legend, with the ready collaboration of gossip and controversy.

Unlike the official hero, the popular hero finds his "remuneration" in, and makes his "appeal" to (in Jefferson's phrase), not so much posterity as popular tradition. In his confidence in the final verdict of the people and his faith in the soundness of their judgment, Andrew Jackson was most resolute. When his secretary, N. P. Trist, warned him that certain political enemies were trying to get hold of some of his private papers in order to "pin something" on him, he said bluntly:

"They are welcome, sir, to anything they can get out of my papers. They will find there, among other things, false grammar and bad spelling; but they are welcome to it all, grammar and spelling included. Let them make the most of it. Our government, sir, is founded upon the intelligence of the people —it has no other bases—upon their capacity to arrive at right conclusions in regard to measures and in regard to men; and I am not afraid of their failing to do so from any use that can be made of any thing that can be got out of my papers."[9]

B. A. B.

---

[7] Alderman, *op. cit.*, p. 6199.
[8] *Ibid.*
[9] Tom W. Campbell, *Two Fighters and Two Fines* (Little Rock, 1941), p. 533.

Virginia Dare

I. THE LOST COLONY [1]

SHORTLY after the arrival of the settlers (at Fort Raleigh, Roanoke, July, 1587) there occurred two events, or perhaps more properly three, of interest and importance not merely to the little community, but in their relation to the history of this country. These events are thus related in Hakluyt's Voyages, Volume III:

"The 13 of August our Savage Manteo * was christened in Roanoke, and called Lord thereof and of Dasamonguepeuk in reward of his faithfull service. The 18, Elenor, daughter to the Governour (John White), and wife to Ananias Dare, one of the Assistants, was delivered of a daughter in Roanoke, and the same was christened there the Sunday following, and because this child was the first Christian born in Virginia, she was named Virginia."

These baptisms were, so far as is known to this writer, the first celebrations of record of a Christian Sacrament within the territory of the thirteen original United States. The baptism of Manteo and his being made Lord of Roanoke were by order of Sir Walter Raleigh, and the latter, it is believed, is the only instance of the conferring of a title of nobility upon a native American. By the Indians, "Elenor Dare," the first mother of the white race known to them, is said to have been called, in their figurative and descriptive way, "The White Doe," and her baby, the little Virginia, the first white infant they had ever seen, "The White Fawn"; and there is a pretty tradition that after her death her spirit assumed that form—an elfin Fawn, which, clad in immortal beauty, would at times be seen haunting like a tender memory the place of her birth, or gazing wistfully over the sea, as with pathetic yearning for the far-away mother land. Another tradition is that in that sweet form she was slain by her lover, a young Indian Chief, who had been told that if he shot her from ambush with a certain enchanted arrow it would restore her to him in human form.

Soon after the birth of Virginia, her grandfather, Governor White, returned to England to obtain supplies for the colonists.

* * * * *

On the 16th of October he arrived on the Irish coast, and coming to England, straightway made efforts to carry succor to his people, but never again did he look upon the faces of his daughter, or his grand-daughter, or of any of their companions. England was in the midst of her bitter contest with Spain and the Invincible Armada, and had sore need at home for every man and ship. There was neither time nor means to be devoted to an

---

[1] From *Virginia Dare*, by Major Graham Daves, *North Carolina Booklet*, Vol. I (May 10, 1901), No. 1, pp. 11–16. Raleigh: Capital Printing Company.
* A friendly Indian chief.

obscure little company thousands of leagues away in an unknown land beyond the stormy Atlantic. Three years elapsed before White returned to
Roanoke, and when he came he found it deserted, and the settlers gone—
whither? No one was left to tell and their fate was enshrined, and will ever
remain, in mystery pathetic. The dead past will not give up its dead. . . .

*   *   *   *   *

The colonists had evidently gone to Croatan, as we now have the word,
the home of Manteo the friendly chief, the banks and islands of our coasts,
extending from Hatteras to Beaufort harbor, but none of them was ever
seen of white men again. They "died and made no sign"; though it is
believed by many, and with considerable reason, that their descendants
may still be found among the Croatan, or more properly, Hatteras Indians
of Robeson county. White does not explain satisfactorily why he did not
seek his daughter at Croatan, which was not very far away. . . .

*   *   *   *   *

And little Virginia Dare, what of her? Did she die in infancy, and does
her dust, mingled with the soil of her birthplace, blossom there into flowers
that blush unseen? Did her little feet join in the wanderings of the settlers
from Roanoke to Croatan? Did she grow to womanhood in their second
home, and did her life end in tragedy amid the darkness which enshrouds
the fate of the Colony? From the deep abysm of the past comes no answer.
Yet a faint echo, a possible trace of the lost White Fawn, comes to us
which may have reference to her, and with it the record closes forever:

In his first volume of "The History of Travaile," William Strachey, Secretary of the Jamestown Colony, writing in 1612 of events that occurred
in Virginia in 1608-10, says:

"At Peccarecemmek and Ochanahoen, by the relation of Machamps, the
people have howses built with stone walles, and one story above another,
so taught them by those English who escaped the slaughter at Roanok, at
what tyme this our Colony, in the conduct of Captain Newport, landed
within the Chesapeake Bay, where the people breed up tame turkies about
their howses and take apes in the mountains, and where, at Ritanoe, the
Weroance Eyanoco preserved seven of the English alive, *fower* men, two
boys and one *young mayde*, who escaped the massacre, and fled up the river
Chanoke" (Chowan).

This "young mayde" may well have been Virginia Dare, who, at the time
mentioned, would have been about twenty-one years of age. The extract
is of interest, also as showing that the existence, and even the location, of
certain of Raleigh's colonists were well known to the Jamestown settlers.
Indeed both John Smith and Strachey made mention of scattered parties
of those colonists several times, and the Virginia Company writes of some
of them as "yet alive, within fifty miles of our fort, * * * as is testified
by two of our colony sent out to search them who (though denied by the
savages speech with them) found crosses * * * and assured Testimonies
of Christians newly cut in the barks of trees." Here the veil of mystery falls
around the White Fawn and her companions probably never to be raised!

II. The Legend of the White Doe [2]

In the early part of the seventeenth century, that is, about the year 1615, or 1620, the Indian hunters who lived on Roanoke Island were greatly excited by seeing a milk-white doe among the herd of deer that were then commonly found on the island.

It attracted the attention of the hunters because it was the most beautiful one of all the herd, because it was the fleetest, and because the most skilful marksmen had never been able to kill it with an arrow. Okisco, a noted hunter, who lived among the Chawanooke tribe, was sent for, and he drew his bow upon the beautiful white doe, but he never could do her harm.

She came to be well known to the Indian hunters of Roanoke Island, and was often found on the situation of the old city of Raleigh, apart from the herd of deer, with her sad face toward the east. Again and again she was hunted, but all the arrows aimed at her life fell harmless beside her. She bounded over the sand-hills with the swiftness of the winds and always turned in the direction of Croatan.

Hunting parties of Indians were made up to entrap her by stationing themselves along the tracks of her flight, which had become known to the hunters by her always taking the same course. But all their efforts were without avail. The swift white doe seemed to have a charmed life, or to be under the protection of some Divine power. Everyone now talked of the white doe, and everyone had his own opinion about her. The braves, the squaws, and the papooses talked of the milk-white doe. Some had fears of evil from the strange apparition. Some thought she was the omen of good, and some thought it was the spirit of some sad departed.

Sometimes she would be seen on the high grounds of Croatan, sometimes in the swamps of Durant's Island, sometimes upon the cranberry bogs of East Lake, often on Roanoke Island near Raleigh City, and sometimes, though rarely, on the sands of Kill Devil Hills; sometimes alone, always sad and beautiful.

The news of the white doe spread far and wide, and old Wingina determined to call a council of chiefs to determine what to do.

Okisco, chief of the Chawanookes, Kuskatenew and Kilkokanwan, of the Yeopoms, and others attended the council. They all came with their attendants, all armed with their war weapons, the bow and arrow. They determined to have a grand hunt in the early Indian summer time, and without delay. In November, when the leaves had fallen and the earth was carpeted with its brown and russet covering of forest leaves, all the friendly chiefs came to Roanoke Island to join the fierce Wingina in his appointed hunt for the milk-white doe, and each with his chosen weapon of the chase.

The chiefs, after their feast, prepared by the wife of Wingina, agreed

[2] From *Grandfather's Tales of North Carolina History*, by Richard Benbury Creecy, pp. 15–18. Copyright, 1901, by R. B. Creecy. Raleigh, North Carolina.

that they should station themselves along the course of the white doe when pursued by the hunters, and either exhaust her in the chase, or slay her with their deadly arrows. Wingina, the most powerful of all, took his place at Raleigh City, where the doe always passed and always stopped.

Old Granganimeo, the brother of Wingina, took his stand at Croatan Sound, where she crossed to Roanoke Island.

Okisco took his stand upon the goodly land of Pomonik, in the low grounds of Durant's Island.

Kind old Manteo went up into the shaky land [of] Wocokon, among the prairies and cranberry bogs of East Lake.

Minatonon, the fierce chief who made his home at Sequaton, took his stand at Jockey's Ridge, by the sea, in the land of Coristooks.

Wanchese took his stand at Kill Devil, in the country of Secotan.

They had all brought with them their best bows and arrows, and also their chosen archers. But the bow of Wanchese differed from the others. When, long ago, he had gone over the sea to England, the great Queen had given him an arrow-head made of solid silver, like the stone arrow-head that Amadas carried to Sir Walter Raleigh with his other Indian curiosities. It was made by her most expert workers in silver, and she told him it would kill the bearer of a charmed life that no other arrow could wound. Wanchese carried this with his other weapons, and determined to test its power upon the swift white doe.

Manteo started the doe in the shaky land of Wocokon. She started unharmed at the twang of the bow-string. She sped with the swiftness of the north wind's breath. Through the tangle wood of Wocokon, through the bogs and morasses of Pomonik, across the highlands of Croatan, on, on, she went, and the twang of the bowstring was the harmless music of her flying bounds. She plunged into the billows of Croatan Sound. She reached the sand hills of Roanoke, leaving the Indian hunters far behind her. As she came to the Island, old Granganimeo drew his bow and sped his harmless arrow. She stood upon the top of the old fort at Raleigh City, sniffed the breeze and looked sadly over the sea. Wingina carefully and steadily drew upon her panting side the deadly arrow. All in vain. She bounded into Roanoke Sound and across to the sea. Menatonon was at Jockey's Ridge, but his arrow, too, was harmless. The panting white doe found time at the Fresh Ponds to slake her thirst, and then, turning to the sea that she seemed to love with an unnatural affection, sped onward, until she reached the steep hills of Kill Devil. There, alas! was her doom. Wanchese, taking aim with his silver arrow, aimed at her heart, let fly the fated bowstring, and the sad and beautiful milk-white doe sprang into the air with the fatal arrow in her heart, and fell to the ground.

Wanchese ran to the spot and found the victim writhing in the death agony. She lifted her dying, soft eyes to the red man and uttered her last sound, "Virginia Dare." Under her throat the words "Virginia Dare" were plainly pencilled in dark hair, and on her back was pencilled in brown hair the name "Croatan."

Pocahontas

AT LAST they brought him to *Meronocomoco* [5 *Jan.* 1608], where was *Powhatan* their Emperor. Here more than two hundred of those grim Courtiers stood wondering at him, as he had beene a monster; till *Powhatan* and his trayne had put themselues in their greatest braveries. Before a fire vpon a seat like a bedsted, he sat covered with a great robe, made of *Rarowcun* skinnes, and all the tayles hanging by. On either hand did sit a young wench of 16 or 18 yeares, and along on each side the house, two rowes of men, and behind them as many women, with all their heads and shoulders painted red: many of their heads bedecked with the white downe of Birds; but every one with something: and a great chayne of white beads about their necks.

At his entrance before the King, all the people gaue a great shout. The Queene of *Appamatuck* was appointed to bring him water to wash his hands, and another brought him a bunch of feathers, in stead of a Towell to dry them: having feasted him after their best barbarous manner they could, a long consultation was held, but the conclusion was, two great stones were brought before *Powhatan:* then as many as could layd hands on him, dragged him to them, and thereon laid his head, and being ready with their clubs, to beate out his braines, *Pocahontas* the Kings dearest daughter when no intreaty could prevaile, got his head in her arms, and laid her owne vpon his to saue him from death: whereat the Emperour was contented he should liue to make him hatchets, and her bells, beads, and copper; for they thought him as well of all occupations as themselues. For the King himselfe will make his owne robes, shooes, bowes, arrowes, pots; plant, hunt, or doe any thing so well as the rest.

> They say he bore a pleasant shew,
> But sure his heart was sad.
> For who can pleasant be, and rest,
> That liues in feare and dread:
> And having life suspected, doth
> It still suspected lead.

From *The Generall Historie of Virginia, New England and the Summer Isles, 1624,* The Third Book, in *Travels and Works of Captain John Smith, President of Virginia and Admiral of New England, 1580–1631,* edited by Edward Arber, a New Edition, with a Biographical and Critical Introduction, by A. G. Bradley, Volume II, pp. 399–400. Edinburgh: John Grant. 1910.

Captain John Smith, Disciplinarian

I. A Cure for Swearing [1]

Soon after the settlement of Virginia, the celebrated Captain John Smith, during the time he was president of the council, conducted a party of men a short distance from Jamestown to cut timber. Among them were two gentlemen, who had been unused to labor. While they were at work, their hands blistered, and the pain of holding their axes was such as to extort an oath at almost every second or third stroke. To put a stop to it, Captain Smith directed the oaths each day to be numbered, and at night sentenced each man to have a mug of water, for every oath, poured into his sleeve. These ablutions had the desired effect; and it was afterwards a rare thing to hear an oath.

II. Work or Starve [2]

The martial figure of the soldier-ruler will not intrude much longer on the narrative. He is going away from Virginia, and the fainéants are coming back. Let us see what he accomplished before their arrival. He forced the idle to go to work—the hardest of tasks. There was a pressing necessity for that. A swarm of rats, brought in Newport's ship, had nearly devoured the remnant of food, and unless corn were planted in the spring days the colony would starve. All must go to work, and the soldier made it plain to the sluggards that they now had a master. He assembled the whole "company" and made them a public address. There was little circumlocution about it. A few sentences will serve as examples of his persuasive eloquence to the murmuring crowd:—

"Countrymen," said Smith, "you see now that power resteth wholly in myself. You must obey this, now, for a law—that *he that will not work shall not eat*. And though you presume that authority here is but a shadow, and that I dare not touch the lives of any, but my own must answer [for] it, yet he that offendeth, let him assuredly expect his due punishment."

This was plain, but the soldier made his meaning still plainer. "Dream no longer," he said sternly, "of this vain hope from Powhatan, or that I will longer forbear to force you from your idleness, or punish you if you rail. I protest by that God that made me, since necessity hath no power to force you to gather for yourselves, you shall not only gather for yourselves, but for those that are sick. They shall not starve!"

The idlers "murmured" but obeyed. The corn was planted, and the

---

[1] From *American Anecdotes, Characters and Incidents;* Revolutionary and Miscellaneous, Original and Selected, p. 83. Philadelphia: Published by John Conrad. 1823.

[2] From *Virginia*, A History of the People, by John Esten Cooke, pp. 53–54. Copyright, 1883, by John Esten Cooke. Boston: Houghton, Mifflin & Company. 1884.

drones in the hive were forced to aid the working bees in another enterprise. This was to build a fort as "a retreat" in case of an Indian war. Smith took nothing on trust. The friendly relations with Powhatan might end at any moment, and the result was the erection of a rude fortification, of which this is the account: "We built also a fort, for a retreat, near a convenient river, upon a high commanding hill, very hard to be assaulted and easy to be defended, but ere it was finished this defect caused a stay—the want of corn occasioned the end of all our works."

Washingtoniana

I. THROWING A DOLLAR ACROSS THE RAPPAHANNOCK [1]

WHILE he was perfecting his penmanship, he was developing his great body to heroic power and skill; schooling his extraordinarily big feet to dance, to leap with the long pole, and to outrun all the other boys; training freakishly huge hands to pitch quoits, toss bars, and hurl weights. Tradition has hallowed a spot near the lower ferry of old Fredericksburg where his playmate and kinsman, Lewis Willis, often said that he had often seen him throw a stone (some say a dollar) to the incredibly distant opposite bank of the Rappahannock. It was probably a stone, for while certain coins had long been called dollars, it was not characteristic of George Washington to throw money away. He had always some poor dependent to give it to, if no other use for it.

II. RETURNING A NEGRO'S COURTESY [2]

. . . George Washington, . . . meeting a colored man in the road once, who politely lifted his hat, lifted his own in return. Some of his white friends who saw the incident criticized Washington for his action. In reply to their criticism George Washington said: "Do you suppose that I am going to permit a poor, ignorant colored man to be more polite than I am?"

III. AT THE SIEGE OF YORKTOWN [3]

Small incidents of the time were afterwards recalled and recorded. Washington was in one of his batteries, awaiting the result with great anxiety.

---

[1] From *George Washington, the Human Being and the Hero, 1732–1762*, by Rupert Hughes, Vol. I, p. 31. Copyright, 1926, by William Morrow and Company, Inc. New York.

[2] From *Up from Slavery*, An Autobiography, by Booker T. Washington, pp. 101–102. Copyright, 1900, 1901, by Booker T. Washington. Garden City, New York: Doubleday, Doran & Company, Inc. 1928.

This anecdote has also been related of Sir William Gooch, Governor of Virginia (*American Anecdotes, Characters and Incidents; Revolutionary and Miscellaneous*, Philadelphia, 1823, p. 15) and of Robert E. Lee.

[3] From *Virginia, A History of the People*, by John Esten Cooke, p. 469. Copyright, 1883, by John Esten Cooke. Boston: Houghton, Mifflin & Co. 1884.

The position was exposed, and an aide-de-camp ventured to suggest the fact, when he said in his grave voice:—

"If you think so, you are at liberty to step back, sir."

A bullet struck a cannon at his side, when General Knox suddenly grasped his arm, exclaiming:—

"My dear General, we can't spare you yet."

"It is a spent ball, no harm is done," Washington replied. When the works were carried on the right and left, and the long shout of the French and Americans was heard, he turned to Knox and said:—

"The work is done, and well done."

Jeffersoniana

I. Jefferson and the Connecticut Farmer [1]

Perhaps I cannot conclude these recollections more pleasantly than by relating an anecdote of himself, which he [Jefferson] told with great humor as having occurred shortly after his election to the presidency. He was riding one day in the neighborhood of Washington, in his usual plain attire —a black suit verging on brown—when, from a cross-road, a Connecticut farmer trotted up to him, and immediately displayed his provincial spirit of barter by surveying the president's superior steed, and asking him to "swap." Jefferson, however, asked too much money in exchange, so, after a fruitless attempt to draw him into a commercial transaction in respect to the saddle and bridle, the stranger began to favor the president with his history. He had lately quitted "Down East," and was coming South to "explore" a brother, hid away somewhere among the "niggers in Virginny." He was anxious, therefore, to obtain all the knowledge he could of the country and the state of politics in parts "contagious" to the seat of government.

This wish led directly to the topic of the new president, Thomas Jefferson, who had been elected to that dignity in direct opposition to the said stranger's advice. "I," said he, "support John Adams, a real old New Englander, after the manner of our forefathers, the Pilgrims of Plymouth Rock. I have smallish faith in these chaps from the nigger states, upon principle. Doesn't it stand to reason, mister, that they must be a largish bit tyrannical?" Jefferson attempted some refutation of the charge, but the farmer scarcely listened to ten words before he rejoined, "Come, come, mister, I guess you don't see the moral sin of niggery; but it ain't only

1 From *Retrospections of America, 1797–1811*, by John Bernard, edited from the Manuscript by Mrs. Bayle Bernard, with an Introduction, Notes, and Index by Laurence Hutton and Brander Matthews, pp. 240–242. Copyright, 1886, by Harper & Brothers. New York. 1887

that. This Thomas Jefferson—did you ever see him?" The president nodded. "Well, that's more luck than I've had; but that doesn't matter. Now I hear that this Thomas Jefferson is a very wasteful chap with our hard-earned money" (Jefferson stared), "and you'll allow mister, that that's unpatriotic upon principle. They tell me he never goes out but he's got clothes on his back that would sell for a plantation, or kiver a wagon-load of immigrants; he's a couple of watches or more, that he never thinks of swapping; rings on all his fingers; and a frill to his shirt big enough to turn a windmill. Now, if you've seen him, mister, you can tell me if that's about right." Jefferson laughed, and replied that, on the contrary, the president was seldom better dressed than himself at that moment. The farmer had his prejudices, and shook his head knowingly as he continued, "Come, come, squire; I see you are a small measure biased. I guess now this Jefferson's a friend of your'n?" The president confessed it. "I dare say a man you speak to when you please?" Another nod. "Perhaps the smallest eend of a relation?" Nod and laugh. "There, now! I guessed it. I knew you could not speak the truth on principle."

At this moment they came in view of the president's house, and the farmer inquired whom it belonged to. As soon as he received the intelligence he burst into one of those conventional substitutes for oaths which emphasize the language of the Northern lower orders. "Well, now, may I be 'tarnally starved down for mutton broth, if that sight doesn't come over a man like a suspension of the works of natur'. Now, mister, doesn't that prove my words, awfully strong? There's a house as big as Noah's ark! At the smallest count, there's thirty rooms in it. What can any careful chap, 'pon principle, want with more than *six*? I ha'n't got more than *four*. I say this Jefferson's wasting the people's money, and Congress is winking at it, and I guess it's all naked truth about the frill and watches; and I ain't afraid to affirm that it's my guess the inside of that house shows just as much wastefulness as Jefferson a-horse-back."

To this charge the president could make but one reply—an offer to introduce the farmer to the mansion and give him ocular conviction. The latter readily consented, and they rode on, Jefferson planning an elaborate lesson of reproof to his calumniator. But, as they approached the gate, some gentlemen, who were engaged to dine with him, stepped forward and exclaimed, "Good-morning, president; you have had a fine day." At the word "president" the farmer, who was trotting on briskly, drew up so short he was near flying over his steed's ears. He turned and stared at Jefferson with a mixture of curiosity and alarm, which drew from the latter a quiet smile of enjoyment. In another instant he had struck his spurs into his horse and was flying away like a whirlwind, fully convinced that he should in some way pay for his temerity. "Hallo, friend!" shouted Jefferson, "won't you go over the house?" "No, thank ye, president," was the reply; "I'll look in when I come back."

II. THOMAS JEFFERSON'S OWN EPITAPH [2]

Could the dead feel any interest in monuments or other remembrances of them, when as Anacreon says,

> A scanty dust to feed the wind,
> Is all the trace 'twill leave behind.

the following would be to my manes the most gratifying: on the grave a plain die or cube of three feet without any mouldings, surmounted by an obelisk of six feet height, each of a single stone; on the faces of the obelisk the following inscription, and not a word more:

> HERE WAS BURIED
> THOMAS JEFFERSON
> AUTHOR OF THE DECLARATION OF AMERICAN
> INDEPENDENCE,
> OF THE STATUTE OF VIRGINIA FOR RELIGIOUS FREEDOM,
> AND FATHER OF THE UNIVERSITY OF VIRGINIA:

because by these, as testimonials that I have lived, I wish most to be remembered. [It] to be of the coarse stone of which my columns are made, that no one might be tempted hereafter to destroy it for the value of the materials. My bust, by Ceracchi, with the pedestal and truncated column on which it stands, might be given to the University, if they would place it in the dome room of the Rotunda.

> On the die of the obelisk might be engraved:
> Born Apr. 2, 1743, O. S.
> Died ——— ——— ———

Marion, the "Swamp Fox"

I. A BROKEN ANKLE [1]

IN THE gallant and heroic defence of Fort Moultrie, he [Marion] took an honorable part, and the last gun fired on that day was directed by him.

---

[2] From *The Wisdom of Thomas Jefferson,* Including The Jefferson Bible, "The Life and Morals of Jesus of Nazareth," selected and edited by Edward Boykin, pp. 212–213. Copyright, 1941, by Doubleday, Doran & Company, Inc.
This was Thomas Jefferson's own epitaph found among his papers after his death. Strangely enough, he omitted the fact that he had twice been President of the United States.—E. B.

---

[1] From *The Romance of the Revolution,* Being a History of the Personal Adventures,

In the surrender of Charleston, he was saved from captivity by an accident which occurred to him during the siege. He was dining with some friends, when the host, after the manner of the mistaken hospitality of the time, locked the door upon his guests until they should be gorged with wine. Marion, who was a man of abstemious habits, and not willing to offend his host by raising a disturbance with his half-tipsy companions, coolly threw up the window and flung himself to the street below. The room was on the second story, the height considerable, and the result was a broken ankle. This severe injury totally unfitted him for action, and he was removed from the city in accordance with the orders for the departure of our officers unfit for duty.

II. Marion's Brigade [2]

Somewhere near the twelfth of August, 1780, he received a summons from a brave band of patriots near Williamsburg to join them and become their leader. Accepting the invitation he went to Linch's Creek, where the force was encamped. Governor Rutledge, of South Carolina, conferred on him a general's commission, and placed him in command of that part of the State. The band numbered not more than thirty men at first, but after Marion's arrival it increased, and soon became famous as Marion's Brigade. The force was mounted, and was soon put in excellent shape for service. They became renowned for their skill in the use of the rifle, and their daring deeds were the admiration of the patriots and the dread of the Tories. Sawmills were plundered of their saws to furnish sabres for these bold troopers, and blacksmiths were employed to convert them from their original uses into rude swords. The men were good riders, were active and hardy, and well adapted to the life they led. "To join Marion, to be one of Marion's men, was esteemed the highest privilege to which a young man could aspire who wished to serve his country." Thus "Marion commenced the forest warfare which was his only hope." His refuge was the swamp fastness, from whose gloomy depths he would sally forth at the head of his troopers and strike the enemy a blow which never failed of success, and retreating to his swamp remain secure until ready for another attack. "No vigilance could guard against his attacks; no persevering efforts could force him to a conflict when the chances of war were against him. At one time he would appear at one point, and after sweeping a troop of Tories before him and securing their munitions, in an incredibly short period he would strike another point far distant from them."

Heroic Exploits, and Romantic Incidents, as Enacted in the War of Independence, edited by Oliver B. Bunce, p. 47. New York: Published by Bunce & Brother. 1852.

---

[2] From *Heroes of Three Wars*, by Captain Willard Glazier, pp. 110–111. Philadelphia: Hubbard Brothers, Publishers. 1882.

III. Leaping a Fence [3]

Marion, who was of diminutive stature, and his person uncommonly light, placed little dependence on his personal prowess. It is related of him that, on one occasion, when he went to draw his sword, he could not because of the rust. Certainly a rich incident in the life of one whose career was so active, but it proves to us that his successes were obtained by the strong power of intellect, and that he ruled his rough, undisciplined men, many of whom were giants in strength and confirmed in obstinacy, by the mere exercise of moral force. He always rode a high-spirited horse, one of the most powerful chargers the South could produce. When pursuing, nothing could escape, and when retreating, nothing could overtake him.

"Being once nearly surrounded by a party of British dragoons, he was compelled, for safety, to pass into a corn-field, by leaping the fence. This field, marked with a considerable descent of surface, had been, in fact, a marsh. Marion entered it at the upper side. The dragoons in chase leapt the fence also, and were but a short distance behind him. So completely was he now in their power that his only mode of escape was to pass over the fence at the lower side. But here lay a difficulty which, to all but himself, appeared insurmountable. To drain the ground of its superfluous waters, a trench had been cut around this part of the field, four feet wide, and of the same depth. Of the mud and clay removed in cutting it, a bank had been formed, on its inner side, and on top of this was erected a fence. The elevation of the whole amounted to more than seven feet, a ditch four feet in width running parallel with it on the outside, and a foot or more of space intervening between the fence and the ditch. The dragoons, acquainted with the nature and extent of this obstacle, and considering it impossible for their enemy to pass it, pressed towards him, with shouts of exultation and insult, and summoned him to surrender, or perish by the sword. Regardless of their clamor, Marion spurred his horse to the charge. The noble animal, as if conscious that his master's life was in danger, and that on his exertion depended its safety, approached the barrier in his finest style, and with a bound that was almost supernatural, completely cleared the fence and ditch, and recovered himself without injury, on the other side. Marion, immediately, faced his pursuers, discharged his pistols at them, but without effect, and then bidding them 'good morning,' he dashed into an adjoining thicket, leaving the dragoons astonished at what they had seen, and almost doubting if their foe was mortal."

---

[3] From *The Romance of the Revolution,* Being a History of the Personal Adventures, Heroic Exploits, and Romantic Incidents, as Enacted in the War of Independence, edited by Oliver B. Bunce, pp. 49–50. New York: Published by Bunce & Brother. 1852.

IV. MARION AND THE BRITISH OFFICER [4]

While lying at Snow's Island, an exchange of prisoners having been agreed upon, a young British officer was sent from Georgetown to complete the arrangements with Marion. He was conducted into the camp blindfolded. When his eyes were unbandaged a forest scene greeted his gaze. Tall trees surrounded him. Groups of rudely-costumed soldiers were lying under their shadow, and horses stood near by ready to be mounted at a moment's notice. "Before him stood Marion himself, small in stature, slight in person, dark and swarthy in complexion, with a quiet manner, but a brilliant and searching eye." The young English officer was struck with astonishment. Was this the man whose name had become so famous, and were these the soldiers who had filled with terror the hearts of the Tories? After business was over, the officer was asked to remain to dinner. He did so. "Sweet potatoes smoking from the ashes were placed upon a piece of bark, and set before the general and his guest."

"Doubtless this is an accidental meal," said the bewildered officer; "you live better in general?"

"No," was the reply, "we often fare much worse."

"Then I hope at least you draw noble pay to compensate?"

"Not a cent, sir," replied Marion, "not a cent."

The officer reported at Georgetown that he had seen an American general and his officers, without pay and almost without clothes, living on roots, and drinking water—all for liberty. "What chance have we against such men?" said he. This officer resigned his commission, and never afterwards served during the war. . . .

How Sumter, the "Game Cock," Won His Sobriquet

THE *sobriquet* of "Game Cock" was applied to Sumter, the renowned partisan chief of South Carolina, which he received, it is said, under the follow-

---

[4] From *Heroes of Three Wars*, by Captain Willard Glazier, pp. 115–116. Philadelphia: Hubbard Brothers, Publishers. 1882.

From *The Romance of the Revolution*, Being a History of the Personal Adventures, Heroic Exploits, and Romantic Incidents, as enacted in the War of Independence, edited by Oliver B. Bunce, p. 361. New York: Published by Bunce & Brother. 1852.

Cf. the origin of the nickname for the people of Delaware, "Blue Hen's chickens": "In the revolutionary war, . . . Captain Caldwell [of Delaware] had a company . . . called by the rest 'Caldwell's game cocks,' and the regiment after a time in Carolina was nicknamed from this 'the blue hen's chickens' and the 'blue chickens.' . . . But after they had been distinguished in the south the name of the *Blue Hen* was applied to the state. . . . The whigs of the revolution never ceased to boast of the Blue Hen and her chickens."—*Niles' National Register*, May 9 (1840), p. 154. Cited by Richard H. Thornton, *An American Glossary* (1912), Vol. I, p. 77.

ing circumstance. While he was seeking recruits, he applied one day to several brothers, by name Gillespie, who were remarkably fond of cock-fighting. They had in their possession a blue hen, of the fighting species, whose progeny were celebrated for their courage. Among them was one named Puck, which had never been defeated in a conflict. Sumter suddenly appeared among the brothers, while they were engaged in their sport, and with ill-disguised contempt, he pronounced their employment childlike and cruel, and abruptly told them that if they would go with him, he would give them worthier game, "and teach them how to fight with men." Struck with his courageous and fiery bearing, they took him at his word, and cried out, "Puck for ever! He is one of the 'Blue Hen's chickens!'" The *sobriquet* stuck to him always, and afterwards, and he was known among his enemies, as well as among his men, by the *nom de guerre* of the "Game Cock."

Daniel Boone

I. How He Won Rebecca [1]

THE first woman who went to Kentucky was Rebecca Boone, and a most noble, heroic and excellent wife and mother she was in every respect. Here is the way Daniel Boone is said to have won her. It will be remembered Boone's father lived on the Yadkin, N. C.

Daniel was once, when a young man, out on a "fire hunt," with what might be called a "boone companion." They had got into a heavily-timbered piece of "bottom," skirted by a small stream which bordered the plantation of a Mr. Morgan Bryan, (a very respectable farmer and head of a family,) the hunter's friend preceding him with the "fire pan," when all at once Boone quietly gave the concerted signal to stop—an indication that he had "shined the eyes" of a deer. Dismounting and tying his horse, he then crept cautiously forward—his rifle at a present—behind a covert of hazel and plum bushes, and, sure enough! there again were the two blue, liquid orbs turned full upon him.

Boone now raised his fatal rifle, but a mysterious something—only tender lovers can say what—arrested his arm and caused his hand to tremble—when off sprang the startled game with a bound and a rustle, and the ardent young hunter in hot chase after it. On! on! they go; when, lo and behold! a fence appears, over which the nimble deer vaulted in a strangely human sort of a way, while Boone, burdened with his rifle and hunting gear, clambered after as best he could. Another kind and differently spelled

---

[1] From *Our Western Border*, Its Life, Combats, Adventures, Forays, Massacres, Captivities, Scouts, Red Chiefs, Pioneer Women, One Hundred Years Ago . . . , by Charles McKnight, p. 708. Philadelphia, Cincinnati, Chicago, and St. Louis: J. C. McCurdy & Company. 1876.

deer now takes possession of Boone's fancy, as he sees Bryan's house in the distance. "I will chase this pet deer to its covert," thinks he, and so, fighting his way through a score of snarling and scolding hounds, he knocked at the door, and was admitted and welcomed by farmer Bryan. The young hunter, panting from his recent exertions, had scarce time to throw his eyes about inquiringly, before a boy of ten, and a flushed and breathless girl of sixteen, with ruddy cheeks, flaxen hair and soft blue eyes, rushed into the room.

"Oh, father! father!" excitedly cried out young hopeful. "Sis was down to the creek to set my lines, and was chased by a 'painter' [panther] or something. She's too skeared to tell." The "painter" and "deer" were now engaged in exchanging glances, and apparently the eyes of *both* had been most effectually "shined," for, to make a long story short, that is how Rebecca Bryan became Rebecca Boone, and a most excellent wife she made.

II. HIS POWERS OF MEMORY [2]

[1815.] Daniel Boone, or, as he was usually called in the Western country, Colonel Boone, happened to spend a night with me under the same roof, more than twenty years ago. We had returned from a shooting excursion, in the course of which his extraordinary skill in the management of the rifle had been fully displayed. On retiring to the room appropriated to that remarkable individual and myself for the night, I felt anxious to know more of his exploits and adventures than I did, and accordingly took the liberty of proposing numerous questions to him. The stature and general appearance of this wanderer of the western forests approached the gigantic. His chest was broad and prominent; his muscular powers displayed themselves in every limb; his countenance gave indication of his great courage, enterprise, and perseverance; and when he spoke, the very motion of his lips brought the impression that whatever he uttered could not be otherwise than strictly true. I undressed, whilst he merely took off his hunting shirt, and arranged a few folds of blankets on the floor, choosing rather to lie there, as he observed, than on the softest bed. When we had both disposed of ourselves, each after his own fashion, he related to me the following account of his powers of memory, which I lay before you, kind reader, in his own words, hoping that the simplicity of his style may prove interesting to you.

"I was once," said he, "on a hunting expedition on the banks of the Green River, when the lower parts of this State [Kentucky] were still in the hands of nature, and none but the sons of the soil were looked upon as its lawful proprietors. We Virginians had for some time been waging a war of intrusion upon them, and I, amongst the rest, rambled through the

---

[2] From *Audubon and His Journals*, by Maria R. Audubon, with Zoological and Other Notes by Elliott Coues, Vol. II, pp. 241–246. Copyright, 1897, by Charles Scribner's Sons. New York.

woods in pursuit of their race, as I now would follow the tracks of any ravenous animal. The Indians outwitted me one dark night, and I was as unexpectedly as suddenly made a prisoner by them. The trick had been managed with great skill; for no sooner had I extinguished the fire of my camp, and laid me down to rest, in full security as I thought, than I felt myself seized by an indistinguishable number of hands, and was immediately pinioned, as if about to be led to the scaffold for execution. To have attempted to be refractory would have proved useless and dangerous to my life; and I suffered myself to be removed from my camp to theirs, a few miles distant, without uttering even a word of complaint. You are aware, I dare say, that to act in this manner was the best policy, as you understand that, by so doing, I proved to the Indians at once that I was born and bred as fearless of death as any of themselves.

"When we reached the camp, great rejoicings were exhibited. Two squaws and a few papooses appeared particularly delighted at the sight of me, and I was assured, by very unequivocal gestures and words, that, on the morrow, the mortal enemy of the Redskins would cease to live. I never opened my lips, but was busy contriving some scheme which might enable me to give the rascals the slip before dawn. The women immediately fell a-searching about my hunting-shirt for whatever they might think valuable, and, fortunately for me, soon found my flask filled with *monongahela* (that is, reader, strong whisky). A terrific grin was exhibited on their murderous countenances, while my heart throbbed with joy at the anticipation of their intoxication. The crew immediately began to beat their bellies and sing, as they passed the bottle from mouth to mouth. How often did I wish the flask ten times its size, and filled with aqua-fortis! I observed that the squaws drank more freely than the warriors, and again my spirits were about to be depressed, when the report of a gun was heard at a distance. The Indians all jumped on their feet. The singing and drinking were both brought to a stand, and I saw, with inexpressible joy, the men walk off to some distance and talk to the squaws. I knew that they were consulting about me, and I foresaw that in a few moments the warriors would go to discover the cause of the gun having been fired so near their camp. I expected that the squaws would be left to guard me. Well, sir, it was just so. They returned; the men took up their guns and walked away. The squaws sat down again, and in less than five minutes had my bottle up to their dirty mouths, gurgling down their throats the remains of the whisky.

"With what pleasure did I see them becoming more and more drunk, until the liquor took such hold of them that it was impossible for these women to be of any service. They tumbled down, rolled about, and began to snore; when I, having no other chance of freeing myself from the cords that fastened me, rolled over and over towards the fire, and, after a short time, burned them asunder. I rose on my feet, stretched my stiffened sinews, snatched up my rifle, and, for once in my life, spared the Indians. I now recollect how desirous I once or twice felt to lay open the skulls of the wretches with my tomahawk; but when I again thought upon killing beings unprepared and unable to defend themselves, it looked like murder without need, and I gave up the idea.

"But, sir, I felt determined to mark the spot, and walking to a thrifty ash sapling, I cut out of it three large chips, and ran off. I soon reached the river, soon crossed it, and threw myself deep into the canebrakes, imitating the tracks of an Indian with my feet, so that no chance might be left for those from whom I had escaped to overtake me.

"It is now nearly twenty years since this happened, and more than five since I left the Whites' settlements, which I might profitably never have visited again had I not been called on as a witness in a law-suit that was pending in Kentucky, and which I really believe would never have been settled had I not come forward and established the beginning of a certain boundary line. This is the story, sir.

"Mr. —— moved from Old Virginia into Kentucky, and having a large tract granted to him in the new State, laid claim to a certain parcel of land adjoining Green River, and, as chance would have it, took for one of his corners the very ash-tree on which I had made my mark, and finished his survey of some thousands of acres, beginning, as it is expressed in the deed, 'at an Ash marked by three distinct notches of the tomahawk of a white man.'

"The tree had grown much, and the bark had covered the marks; but, somehow or other, Mr. —— heard from some one all that I have already said to you, and thinking that I might remember the spot alluded to in the deed, but which was not longer discoverable, wrote for me to come and try at least to find the place or the tree. His letter mentioned that all my expenses should be paid, and not caring much about once more going back to Kentucky, I started and met Mr. ——. After some conversation, the affair with the Indians came to my recollection. I considered for a while, and began to think that after all I could find the very spot, as well as the tree, if it was yet standing.

"Mr. —— and I mounted our horses, and off we went to the Green River Bottoms. After some difficulties, for you must be aware, sir, that great changes have taken place in those woods, I found at last the spot where I had crossed the river, and, waiting for the moon to rise, made for the course in which I thought the ash-tree grew. On approaching the place, I felt as if the Indians were there still, as if I was still a prisoner among them. Mr. —— and I camped near what I conceived the spot, and waited until the return of day.

"At the rising of the sun I was on foot, and, after a good deal of musing, thought that an ash-tree then in sight must be the very one on which I had made my mark. I felt as if there could be no doubt of it, and mentioned my thought to Mr. ——. 'Well, Colonel Boone,' said he, 'if you think so, I hope it may prove true, but we must have some witnesses; do you stay here about, and I will go and bring some of the settlers whom I know.' I agreed. Mr. —— trotted off, and I, to pass the time, rambled about to see if a Deer was still living in the land. But ah! sir, what a wonderful difference thirty years makes in the country! Why, at the time when I was caught by the Indians, you would not have walked out in any direction for more than a mile without shooting a buck or a bear. There were then thousands of buffaloes on the hills in Kentucky; the land looked as if it never would become poor; and to hunt in those days was a pleasure indeed. But when I was left to myself on the banks of Green River, I dare say for the last time in my life, a few *signs* only of deer were to be seen, and as to a deer itself, I saw none.

"Mr. —— returned, accompanied by three gentlemen. They looked upon me as if I had been Washington himself, and walked to the ash-tree, which I now called my own, as if in quest of long-lost treasure. I took an axe from one of them, and cut a few chips off the bark. Still no signs were to be seen. I cut again until I thought it was time to be cautious, and I scraped and worked away with my butcher knife until I *did* come to where my tomahawk had left an impression in the wood. We now went regularly to work, and scraped at the tree with care, until three hacks as plain as any three notches ever were could be seen. Mr. —— and the other gentlemen were astonished, and, I must allow, I was as much surprised as pleased myself. I made affidavit of this remarkable occurrence in presence of these gentlemen. Mr. —— gained his cause. I left Green River forever, and came to where we now are; and, sir, I wish you a good night."

John Sevier and the Lost State of Franklin

JOHN SEVIER, one of the leading spirits in the King's mountain affair, and commander of the transmontane militia, was a brilliant, daring, dashing character; the idol and leader of bold frontiersmen, who nicknamed him "Nollichucky Jack." The whole of Tennessee then belonged to North Carolina, but the settlers on the Holston were so far removed from the seat of government that, practically, they were without government. Sevier and his friends conceived the idea of organizing a new state, which, being in the nature of a measure for self-protection, was unquestioned west of the mountains as a just and proper proceeding, but by the home government denounced as an insurrection. The new state was named Franklin, in honor of the Philadelphia philosopher and patriot. For four years there was civil contention, which, in one instance, resulted in contact of arms and bloodshed. After this the parent state adopted a radical policy for the restraint of her premature liberty-seeking child. "Nollichucky Jack," the

From *The Heart of the Alleghanies of Western North Carolina* comprising its Topography, History, Resources, People, Narratives, Incidents and Pictures of Travel, Adventures in Hunting and Fishing, and Legends of its Wilderness, by Wilbur G. Zeigler and Ben S. Grosscup, pp. 220–222. Copyright, 1883, by Wilbur G. Zeigler and Ben S. Grosscup. Raleigh, North Carolina: Alfred Williams & Co. Cleveland, Ohio: William W. Williams.

governor of the insurrectionary state, was arrested for "high treason against the state of North Carolina" and taken to Morganton for trial.

The prisoner's chivalric character and gallant military services, on the one hand, and the extraordinary nature of the indictment on the other, gave the trial momentous interest. The village streets were crowded with old soldiers and settlers from far and near, eager to catch a glimpse of the court. There were others there with different purposes. The chivalry of the infant settlement of Tennessee; the men who had suffered with the trials of frontier life and savage warfare, who had fought under him to establish their country's freedom, and who loved him as a brother, armed to the teeth, had followed the captive across the mountains, determined to "rescue him, or leave their bones." Their plan was to rescue him by stratagem, but if that failed, to fire the town, and in the excitement of the conflagration make their escape.

On the day of trial, two of the "Franks," as they were called, leaving their companions concealed near the town, and hiding reliable sidearms under their hunting shirts, rode up before the court-house, one of them on "Governor" Sevier's fine race mare. He dismounted, and with the rein carelessly thrown over her neck, stood with the manner of an indifferent spectator. The companion, having tied his horse, went into the court-room. Sevier's attention, by a slight gesture, was directed to the man outside. During a pause in the trial, the bold "Frank" stepped into the bar, and with decided manner and tone, addressed the judge: "Are you done with that there man?" The scene was so unusual, the manner and tone of the speaker so firm and dramatic, that both officers and audience were thrown into confusion. The "Governor" sprang like a fox from his cage, one leap took him to the door, and two more on his racer's back. The quick clash of hoofs gave notice of his escape. The silence of the bewildered court was broken by the exclamation of a waggish by-stander: "Yes, I'll be damned if you hain't done with him."

Sevier was joined by his neighbors with a wild shout, and they bore him safely to his home. No attempt was made to re-arrest him. The State of Franklin died from various causes, and a few years later the new State of Tennessee honored "Nollichucky Jack" with the first governorship, and later, by an election to the United States Senate.

Andrew Jackson

I. Jackson and Russell Bean

JUDGE JACKSON was holding court at a shanty at a little village in Tennessee, and dispensing justice in large and small doses, as seemed to him

From *Life of Andrew Jackson,* by James Parton, pp. 228–229, 380–382. Copyright, 188? by James Parton. Boston and New York: Houghton. Mifflin & Co.

to be required in the case before him. One day during court, a great hulking fellow, armed with pistol and bowie knife, took it upon himself to parade before the shanty court house, and cursed the judge, jury, and all there assembled, in set terms.

"Sheriff," sang out the judge, "arrest that man for contempt of court, and confine him."

Out went the sheriff, but soon returned with the word to the judge that he had found it impossible to take the offender.

"Summon a posse, then," said the judge, "and bring him before me."

The sheriff went out again, but the task was too difficult; he could not, or dared not, lay his hands on the man, nor did any of the posse like the job any better than he did, as the fellow threatened to shoot the first skunk that come within ten feet of him.

At this the judge waxed wroth, to have his authority put at defiance before all the good people of that vicinity; so he cried out, "Mr. Sheriff, since you can not obey my orders, summon me; yes, sir, summon me."

"Well, judge, if you say so, though I don't like to do it; but if you will try, why I suppose I must summon you."

"Very well," said Jackson, rising and walking toward the door, "I adjourn this court ten minutes."

The ruffian was standing a short distance from the shanty, in the center of a crowd of people, blaspheming at a terrible rate, and flourishing his weapons, and vowing death and destruction to all who should attempt to molest him.

Judge Jackson walked very calmly into the center of the group, with pistols in hand, and confronted him.

"Now," said he, looking him straight in the eye, "surrender, you infernal villain, this very instant, or I'll blow you through!"

The man eyed the speaker for a moment, without speaking, and then put up his weapons, with the words, "There, judge, it's no use, I give in," and suffered himself to be led by the sheriff without opposition. He was completely cowed.

A few days after the occurrence, when the man was asked why he knocked under to one person, when he had before refused to allow himself to be taken by a whole company, he replied:

"Why," said he, "when he came up, I looked him in the eye, and I

. . . When our lawyer of the wilderness held his first court at Jonesboro [, Tennessee, he] arrested the redoubtable rifle-maker, Russell Bean. . . . The Russell Bean ancedote, which, with variations, has been going the rounds of the papers for about forty years, is a good illustration of the gradual development of a popular story. The *truth* of it has already been related by Colonel Avery. [See page 167.] The *anecdote*, founded on that truth, is infinitely more amusing.

This story I have in several different versions, cut from newspapers of various dates, which show that, like the steam engine, it is a growth, rather than an invention, each period contributing some little addition to the delightful whole. It was reserved for this ingenious generation to add the crowning paragraph, which alludes to the vocalization of the noblest of quadrupeds.—J. P.

saw shoot, and there wasn't shoot in nary other eye in the crowd; and so I says to myself, says I, hoss, it's about time to sing small, and so I did."

II. The General Wins His Nickname

At the last moment came the orders of the government (which ought to have accompanied the order to disband), directing the force under General Jackson to be paid off, and allowed pay and rations for the journey home. It was too late. The General was resolved, whatever might betide, to conduct the men back to their homes, in person, as an organized body. "I shall commence the line of march," he wrote to Wilkinson, "on Thursday, the 25th. Should the contractor not feel himself justified in sending on provisions for my infantry, or the quarter-master wagons for the transportation of my sick, I shall dismount the cavalry, carry them on, and provide the means for their support out of my private funds. If that should fail, I thank my God we have plenty of horses to feed my troops to the Tennessee, where I know my country will meet me with ample supplies. These brave men, at the call of their country, voluntarily rallied round its insulted standard. They followed me to the field; I shall carefully march them back to their homes. It is for the agents of the government to account to the State of Tennessee and the whole world for their singular and unusual conduct to this detachment."

It was on this homeward march [from Natchez, begun April 25, 1813,] that the nickname of "Old Hickory" was bestowed on the General. From the time of leaving Nashville, General Jackson had constantly grown in the confidence and affection of the troops. The man was in his element at last, and his great qualities began to make themselves manifest. Many of the volunteers had heard so much of his violent and hasty temper that they had joined the corps with a certain dread and hesitation, fearing not the enemy, nor the march, nor the diseases of the lower country, so much as the swift wrath of their commander. Some, indeed, refused to go for that reason alone. How surprised were those who entered the service with such feelings to find in General Jackson a father as well as a chief. Jackson had the faculty, which all successful soldiers possess, of completely identifying himself with the men he commanded; investing every soldier, as it were, with a portion of his own personality, and feeling a wrong done to the least of them as done to himself. Soldiers are quick to perceive a trait of this kind. They saw, indeed, that there was a whole volcano of wrath in their General, but they observed that, to the men of his command, so long as they did their duty, and longer, he was the most gentle, patient, considerate and generous of friends.

This resolve of his to disobey his government for their sakes, and the manner in which he executed that resolve, raised his popularity to the highest point. When the little army set out from Natchez for a march of five hundred miles through the wilderness, there were a hundred and fifty men on the sick list, of whom fifty-six could not raise their heads from the pillow. There were but eleven wagons for the conveyance of these. The rest of the sick were mounted on the horses of the officers. The General had three excellent horses, and gave them all up to the sick men, himself trudging along on foot with the brisk pace that was usual with him. Day after day he tramped gayly along the miry forest roads, never tired, and always ready with a cheering word for others. They marched with extraordinary speed, averaging eighteen miles a day, and performing the whole journey in less than a month; and yet the sick men rapidly recovered under the reviving influences of a homeward march. "Where am I?" asked one young fellow who had been lifted to his place in a wagon when insensible and apparently dying. "On your way *home!*" cried the General, merrily; and the young soldier began to improve from that hour, and reached home in good health.

The name of "Old Hickory" was not an instantaneous inspiration, but a growth. First of all, the remark was made by some soldier, who was struck with his commander's pedestrian powers, that the General was "tough." Next it was observed of him that he was as "tough as hickory." Then he was *called* Hickory. Lastly, the affectionate adjective "old" was prefixed, and the General thenceforth rejoiced in the completed nickname, usually the first-won honor of a great commander.

Davy Crockett: "Gamecock of the Wilderness"

I. Obtaining a Cask of Powder

I GATHERED my corn, and then set out for my fall's hunt. This was in the last of October, 1822. I found bear very plenty, and, indeed, all sorts of game and wild varments, except buffalo. There was none of them. I hunted on till Christmas, having supplied my family very well all along with wild meat, at which time my powder gave out, and I had none either to fire Christmas guns, which is very common in that country, or to hunt with. I had a brother-in-law who had now moved out and settled about six miles west of me, on the opposite side of Rutherford's fork of the Obion river, and he had brought me a keg of powder, but I had never gotten it home. There had just been another of Noah's freshets, and the low grounds were flooded all over with water. I knowed the stream was at least a mile wide which I would have to cross, as the water was from hill to hill, and yet I determined to go on over in some way or other, so as to get my powder. I told this to my wife, and she immediately opposed it with all her might. I still insisted, telling her we had no powder for Christmas, and, worse than all, we were out of meat. She said, we had as well starve as for me to

From *Life of David Crockett*, the Original Humorist and Irrepressible Backwoodsman . . . , pp. 125–129, 154–155, 269–272. Philadelphia: John E. Potter and Company. 1860.

freeze to death or to get drowned, and one or the other was certain if I attempted to go.

But I didn't believe the half of this; and so I took my woolen wrappers, and a pair of moccasins, and put them on, and tied up some dry clothes, and a pair of shoes and stockings, and started. But I didn't before know how much anybody could suffer and not die. This, and some of my other experiments in water, learned me something about it, and I therefore relate them.

The snow was about four inches deep when I started; and when I got to the water, which was only about a quarter of a mile off, it looked like an ocean. I put in, and waded on till I come to the channel, where I crossed that on a high log. I then took water again, having my gun and all my hunting tools along, and waded till I came to a deep slough, that was wider than the river itself. I had crossed it often on a log; but behold, when I got there, no log was to be seen. I knowed of an island in the slough, and a sapling stood on it close to the side of that log, which was now entirely under water. I knowed further that the water was about eight or ten feet deep under the log, and I judged it to be about three feet deep over it. After studying a little what I should do, I determined to cut a forked sapling, which stood near me, so as to lodge it against the one that stood on the island, in which I succeeded very well. I then cut me a pole, and then crawled along on my sapling till I got to the one it was lodged against, which was about six feet above the water. I then felt about with my pole till I found the log, which was just about as deep under the water as I had judged. I then crawled back and got my gun, which I had left at the stump of the sapling I had cut, and again made my way to the place of lodgment, and then climbed down the other sapling so as to get on the log. I then felt my way along with my feet, in the water, about waist deep, but it was a mighty ticklish business. However, I got over, and by this time I had very little feeling in my feet and legs, as I had been all the time in the water, except what time I was crossing the high log over the river, and climbed my lodged sapling.

I went but a short distance before I came to another slough, over which there was a log, but it was floating on the water. I thought I could walk it, and so I mounted on it; but when I had got about the middle of the deep water, somehow or somehow else, it turned over, and in I went up to my head. I waded out of this deep water, and went ahead till I came to the highland, where I stopped to pull off my wet clothes, and put on the others, which I had held up with my gun, above the water, when I fell in. I got them on, but my flesh had no feeling in it, I was so cold. I tied up the wet ones, and hung them up in a bush. I now thought I would run, so as to warm myself a little, but I couldn't raise a trot for some time; indeed, I couldn't step more than half the length of my foot. After a while I got better, and went on five miles to the house of my brother-in-law, having not even smelt fire from the time I started. I got there late in the evening, and he was much astonished at seeing me at such a time. I staid all night, and the next morning was most piercing cold, and so they persuaded me not to go home that day. I agreed, and turned out and killed him two deer; but the weather still got worse and colder, instead of better. I staid that night, and in the morning they still insisted I couldn't get home. I knowed the water would be frozen over, but not hard enough to bear me, and so I agreed to stay that day. I went out hunting again, and pursued a big *he-bear* all day, but didn't kill him. The next morning was bitter cold, but I knowed my family was without meat, and I determined to get home to them, or die a-trying.

I took my keg of powder, and all my hunting tools, and cut out. When I got to the water, it was a sheet of ice as far as I could see. I put on to it, but hadn't got far before it broke through with me; and so I took out my tomahawk, and broke my way along before me for a considerable distance. At last I got to where the ice would bear me for a short distance, and I mounted on it, and went ahead; but it soon broke in again, and I had to wade on till I came to my floating log. I found it so tight this time that I knowed it couldn't give me another fall, as it was frozen in with the ice. I crossed over it without much difficulty, and worked along till I got to my lodged sapling, and my log under the water. The swiftness of the current prevented the water from freezing over it, and so I had to wade, just as I did when I crossed it before. When I got to my sapling, I left my gun, and climbed out with my powder keg first, and then went back and got my gun. By this time I was nearly frozen to death, but I saw all along before me, where the ice had been fresh broke, and I thought it must be a bear straggling about in the water. I, therefore, fresh primed my gun, and, cold as I was, I was determined to make war on him, if we met. But I followed the trail till it led me home, and I then found it had been made by my young man that lived with me, who had been sent by my distressed wife to see, if he could, what had become of me, for they all believed that I was dead. When I got home, I wasn't quite dead, but mighty nigh it; but had my powder, and that was what I went for.

II. How to Keep from Freezing to Death

I suffered very much that night with cold, as my leather breeches and everything else I had on was wet and frozen. But I managed to get my bear out of this crack after several hard trials, and so I butchered him and laid down to try to sleep. But my fire was very bad, and I couldn't find anything that would burn well to make it any better; and so I concluded I should freeze, if I didn't warm myself in some way by exercise. So I got up and hollered awhile, and then I would just jump up and down with all my might, and throw myself into all sorts of motions. But all this wouldn't do; for my blood was now getting cold, and the chills coming all over me. I was so tired, too, that I could hardly walk; but I thought I would do the best I could to save my life, and then, if I died, nobody would be to blame. So I went to a tree about two feet through, and not a limb on it for thirty

feet, and I would climb up the limbs, and then lock my arms together
around it, and slide down to the bottom again. This would make the in-
sides of my legs and arms feel mighty warm and good. I continued this
till daylight in the morning, and how often I clumb up my tree and slid
down I don't know, but I reckon at least a hundred times.

III. Target Shooting

As there was considerable time to be killed, or got rid of in some way,
before the dinner could be cooked, it was proposed that we should go beyond the village [of Little Rock], and shoot at a mark, for they had heard
I was a first-rate shot, and they wanted to see for themselves, whether
fame had not blown her trumpet a little too strong in my favor; for since
she had represented "the Government" as being a first-rate statesman, and
Colonel Benton as a first-rate orator, they could not receive such reports
without proper allowance, as Congress thought of the Post Office report.

Well, I shouldered my Betsey, and she is just about as beautiful a piece
as ever came out of Philadelphia, and I went out to the shooting ground,
followed by all the leading men in Little Rock, and that was a clear majority of the town, for it is remarkable, that there are always more leading
men in small villages than there are followers.

I was in prime order. My eye was as keen as a lizard, and my nerves
were as steady and unshaken as the political course of Henry Clay; so at
it we went, the distance, one hundred yards. The principal marksmen, and
such as had never been beat, led the way, and there was some pretty fair
shooting, I tell you. At length it came to my turn. I squared myself, raised
my beautiful Betsey to my shoulder, took deliberate aim, and smack I sent
the bullet right into the centre of the bull's eye. "There's no mistake in
Betsey," said I, in a sort of careless way, as they were all looking at the
target, sort of amazed, and not at all over pleased.

"That's a chance shot, Colonel," said one who had the reputation of
being the best marksman in those parts.

"Not as much chance as there was," said I, "when Dick Johnson took
his darkie for better for worse. I can do it fives times out of six any day
in the week." This I said in as confident a tone as "the Government" did,
when he protested that he forgave Colonel Benton for shooting him, and
he was now the best friend he had in the world. I knew it was not altogether as correct as it might be, but when a man sets about going the big
figure, halfway measures won't answer no how; and "the greatest and the
best" had set me the example, that swaggering will answer a good purpose
at times.

They now proposed that we should have a second trial; but knowing
that I had nothing to gain and everything to lose, I was for backing out
and fighting shy; but there was no let-off, for the cock of the village,
though whipped, determined not to stay whipped; so to it again we went.
They were now put upon their mettle, and they fired much better than the

first time; and it was what might be called pretty sharp shooting. When it came to my turn, I squared myself, and turning to the prime shot, I gave him a knowing nod, by way of showing my confidence; and says I, "Look out for the bull's eye, stranger." I blazed away, and I wish I may be shot if I didn't miss the target. They examined it all over, and could find neither hair nor hide of my bullet, and pronounced it a dead miss; when says I, "Stand aside and let me look, and I warrant you I get on the right trail of the critter." They stood aside, and I examined the bull's eye pretty particular, and at length cried out, "Here it is; there is no snakes if it ha'n't followed the very track of the other." They said it was utterly impossible, but I insisted on their searching the hole, and I agreed to be stuck up as a mark myself, if they did not find two bullets there. They searched for my satisfaction, and sure enough it all come out just as I had told them; for I had picked up a bullet that had been fired, and stuck it deep into the hole, without any one perceiving it. They were all perfectly satisfied, that fame had not made too great a flourish of trumpets when speaking of me as a marksman; and they all said they had enough of shooting for that day, and they moved, that we adjourn to the tavern and liquor.

Robert E. Lee

I. "Marse Robert" and His Men [1]

GENERAL LEE's affectionate regard for those under his charge and his tender solicitude for their welfare were equaled only by their admiration and love for him. Unlike some military chieftains who would sacrifice thousands of men without scruple, if their fame demanded it, he was willing at any time to allow his own reputation to suffer in order to preserve his men. His soldiers knew that he would not expose them when he could avoid it; that it was through no fault of his if their rations were scant and their hardships many; and that he regularly robbed his own poorly supplied mess-table of luxuries which friends would send him, in order that they might go to his ragged, suffering boys in the hospital.

They knew that their great chieftain cared for their welfare, and did all in his power to promote it, and their admiration for his splendid genius as a soldier was even excelled by their love for him as a man. Time and again have I seen these brave men—many of them the very *élite* of Southern society, who had been raised in luxury, and never knew what want was before—ragged, barefooted, and hungry, and almost ready to break out into open revolt at the idea that their sufferings were due to the inefficiency of the quartermaster and commissary departments. But a single word from General Lee, assuring the men that the supply department was doing all

---

[1] From *Personal Reminiscences, Anecdotes, and Letters of Gen. Robert E. Lee,* by Rev. William Jones, pp. 315–316, 319. New York: D. Appleton and Company. 1876.

that it could to relieve their wants, would act like a charm, and the magic words, "Marse Robert says so," would hush every murmur and complaint.

When he rode among his troops he was always greeted with enthusiastic cheers, or other manifestations of love and admiration. I one day saw a ragged private, whom he met on the road (while riding alone, as was his frequent custom), stand with uncovered head, as if in the presence of royalty, as he rode by. General Lee instantly took off his own hat, and treated the humble man with all possible courtesy and respect, and, as he rode on, the soldier enthusiastically said: "God bless 'Marse Robert'! I wish he was emperor of this country, and that I was his carriage-driver."

* * * * *

One day he met coming to the rear a gallant Georgian whose right arm was very badly shattered. "I grieve for you, my poor fellow," said the tender-hearted chief; "can I do any thing for you?" "Yes, sir!" replied the brave boy with a proud smile; "you can shake hands with me, general, if you will consent to take my *left* hand." General Lee cordially grasped the hand of the ragged hero, spoke a few kind words which he could never forget, and sent him on his way rejoicing that he had the privilege of suffering under such a leader.

One night some soldiers were overheard discussing the tenets of atheism around their camp-fire, when a rough, honest fellow cut short the discussion by saying: "Well, boys, the rest of us may have *developed* from monkeys; but I tell you *none less than a God could have made such a man as 'Marse Robert!'* "

II. LEE'S HUMOR [2]

While at winter quarters at Petersburg, a party of officers were one night busily engaged in discussing, at the same time, a mathematical problem and the contents of a stone jug which was garnished by two tin cups. In the midst of this General Lee came in to make some inquiry. He got the information he wanted, gave a solution of the problem, and went out, the officers expressing to each other the hope that the general had not noticed the jug and cups. The next day one of the officers, in the presence of the others, was relating to General Lee a very strange dream he had the night before. The general listened with apparent interest to the narrative, and quietly rejoined: "That is not at all remarkable. When young gentlemen discuss at midnight mathematical problems, the unknown quantities of which are a stone jug and two tin cups, they may expect to have strange dreams."

One day, at Petersburg, General Lee, who never suffered a day to pass without visiting some part of his lines, rode by the quarters of one of his major-generals, and requested him to ride with him. As they were going he asked General —— if a certain work which he had ordered to be

[2] *Ibid.,* pp. 242–244.

pushed was completed. He replied with some hesitation that it was, and General Lee then proposed that they should go and see it. Arriving at the spot it was found that little or no progress had been made since they were there a week before, and General —— was profuse in his apologies, saying that he had not seen the work since they were there together, but that he had ordered it to be completed at once, and that Major —— had informed him that it had been already finished. General Lee said nothing then, except to remark, quietly, "We must give our personal attention to the lines." But, riding on a little farther, he began to compliment General —— on the splendid charger he rode. "Yes, sir," said General ——, "he is a splendid animal, and I prize him the more highly because he belongs to my wife, and is her favorite riding-horse." "A magnificent horse," rejoined General Lee, "but I should not think him safe for Mrs. —— to ride. He is entirely too spirited for a lady, and I would urge you by all means to take some of the mettle out of him before you suffer Mrs. —— to ride him again. And, by-the-way, general, I would suggest to you that *these rough paths along these trenches would be very admirable ground over which to tame him.*" The face of the gallant soldier turned crimson; he felt most keenly the rebuke, and never afterward reported the condition of his lines upon information received from Major ——, or any one else. His spirited charger felt the effect of this hint from headquarters.

III. How He Spared Chatham [3]

It is one of the town legends that General Lee, standing on the heights behind Fredericksburg during the battle, looked across at Chatham which the Federal commander occupied as headquarters and was urged to turn his fire on it. But, the story continues, Lee remembered that he had courted his wife, old William Fitzhugh's granddaughter, there, and had not the heart to unloose his guns against it.

Who were then at Chatham? Abraham Lincoln, they say; and, nursing the blue-coated wounded and dying, was a young man named Walt Whitman, not yet the "good grey poet."

IV. A Portrait of Traveller [4]

. . . Amongst the soldiers this horse was as well known as his master. He was a handsome iron-gray with black points—mane and tail very dark— sixteen hands high, and five years old. He was born near the White

---

[3] From *Tidewater Virginia*, by Paul Wilstach, pp. 275–276. Copyright, 1929, by Paul Wilstach. Indianapolis: The Bobbs-Merrill Company.

[4] From *Recollections and Letters of General Robert E. Lee*, by his son, Captain Robert E. Lee, pp. 82–84. Copyright, 1904, by Doubleday, Page & Company. New York.

Sulphur Springs, West Virginia, and attracted the notice of my father when he was in that part of the State, in 1861. He was never known to tire, and, though quiet and sensible in general and afraid of nothing, yet if not regularly exercised, he fretted a good deal, especially in a crowd of horses. But there can be no better description of this famous horse than the one given by his master. It was dictated to his daughter Agnes at Lexington, Virginia, after the war, in response to some artist who had asked for a description, and was corrected in his own handwriting:

If I were an artist like you I would draw a true picture of Traveller—representing his fine proportions, muscular figure, deep chest and short back, strong haunches, flat legs, small head, broad forehead, delicate ears, quick eye, small feet, and black mane and tail. Such a picture would inspire a poet, whose genius could then depict his worth and describe his endurance of toil, hunger, thirst, heat, cold, and the dangers and suffering through which he passed. He could dilate upon his sagacity and affection, and his invariable response to every wish of his rider. He might even imagine his thoughts, through the long night marches and days of battle through which he has passed. But I am no artist; I can only say he is a Confederate gray. I purchased him in the mountains of Virginia in the autumn of 1861, and he has been my patient follower ever since—to Georgia, the Carolinas, and back to Virginia. He carried me through the Seven Days' battle around Richmond, the second Manassas, at Sharpsburg, Fredericksburg, the last days at Chancellorsville, to Pennsylvania, at Gettysburg, and back to the Rappahannock. From the commencement of the campaign in 1864 at Orange, till its close around Petersburg, the saddle was scarcely off his back, as he passed through the fire of the Wilderness, Spottsylvania, Cold Harbour, and across the James River. He was almost in daily requisition in the winter of 1864–65 on the long line of defenses from Chickahominy, north of Richmond, to Hatcher's Run, south of the Appomattox. In the campaign of 1865, he bore me from Petersburg to the final days at Appomattox Court House. You must know the comfort he is to me in my present retirement. He is well supplied with equipments. Two sets have been sent to him from England, one from the ladies of Baltimore, and one was made for him in Richmond; but I think his favorite is the American saddle from St. Louis. Of all his companions in toil, "Richmond," "Brown Roan," "Ajax," and quiet "Lucy Long," he is the only one that retained his vigor. The first two expired under their onerous burden and the last two failed. You can, I am sure, from what I have said, paint his portrait.

Stonewall Jackson

I. How He Won His Sobriquet

IT WAS on the field of Manassas, a bright Sunday afternoon, the 21st of July, 1861. The armies of McDowell and Beauregard had been grappling

From "Stonewall Jackson and His Men," by Major H. Kyd Douglas, in *The Annals of the War*, Written by Leading Participants North and South, Originally Pubwith each other since early morning, and, in their mutual slaughter, took no note of the sacredness of the day, nor its brightness. In Washington General Scott was anxiously awaiting the result of his skilful plan of battle, and General Johnston had come down from the Valley of Virginia, in response to Beauregard's appeal—"If you will help me, now is the time." Hotly had the field been contested, and the hours passed slowly to men who had never tasted of battle before. Wavering had been the fortunes of the day, but it was evident the advantage was with the Federal Army, and, before our brigade went into action, it seemed to us the day was lost. After changing position several times, without fighting, General Jackson learned that Bee was hard pressed, and he moved to his assistance, marching through the wounded and the stragglers, who were hurrying to the rear. It was then after two o'clock, and the General formed his brigade along the crest of the hill near the Henry House, the men lying down behind the brow of it, in support of the two pieces of artillery placed in position to play upon the advancing foe.

General Bee, his brigade being crushed and scattered, rode up to General Jackson, and, with the excitement and mortification of an untried but heroic soldier, reported that the enemy were beating him back.

"Very well, General, it can't be helped," replied Jackson.

"But how do you expect to stop them?"

"We'll give them the bayonet!" was the answer, briefly.

General Bee wheeled his horse, and galloped back to his command. As he did so, General Jackson said to Lieutenant Lee of his staff:

"Tell the colonel of this brigade that the enemy are advancing; that when their heads are seen above the hill, let the whole line rise, move forward with a shout, and trust to the bayonet. *I am tired of this long range work.*"

In the storm which followed Bee's return to his command, he was soon

---

lished in the Philadelphia *Weekly Times,* pp. 642–644, 645–647. Philadelphia: The Times Publishing Company. 1879.

And apropos of "Stonewall." A correspondent, over the signature of "Altamount," contributed to the *Tribune* a sketch of the vigorous rebel, in some respects fresher and fuller than any that had appeared before, and therein his soubriquet was traced back, not to the stone bridge at Bull Run, nor to the "There stands Jackson like a stone wall" of Gen. Bee, or to the stone fences of Winchester Heights; but to Jackson's original "Stonewall Brigade," so called because principally recruited in a stone-wall country—the valley counties of Jefferson, Clarke, Frederick, Page, and Warren; and the writer showed that the brigade had borne this name before the first battle of Bull Run, and of course before the affair of Winchester Heights, and that the brigade had lent its name to its stout leader, not derived it from him. Since his death this sketch has been reproduced in many papers, but the light it threw on the "Stonewall" question has been everywhere ignored; nevertheless, Stonewall Jackson, in his last hours, was careful to explain to some members of his staff who hung upon his parting words that the honorable title belonged to his men, not to him; it was not personal and figurative like "Old Hickory," as the newspapers persisted in making it—but the local designation of a corps.—Frank Moore, *Anecdotes, Poetry, and Incidents of the War: North and South, 1860–1865* (1866), p. 172.

on foot, his horse shot from under him. With the fury of despair he strode among his men, and tried to rally and to hold them against the torrent which beat upon them; and finally, in a voice which rivaled the roar of battle, he cried out: "Oh, men, there are Jackson and his Virginians standing behind you like a *stone wall!*" Uttering these words of martial baptism, Bee fell dead upon the field, and left behind him a fame which will follow that of Jackson as a shadow.

It would be but the repetition of history to mention, at length, the movements of Jackson's Brigade that day. It was Bee who gave him the name of "Stonewall," but it was his own Virginians who made that name immortal. This brigade checked the victorious tide of battle, but to turn it back was no easy labor. Around the Henry House and its plateau the contest raged with renewed violence and vacillating success for an hour; and then Jackson led his men in their last bayonet charge, and pierced the enemy's center. The timely arrival of Kirby Smith and Early upon their flank finished the work, and defeat was turned into a rout. General Jackson will be forgiven for this sentence in a letter to a friend: "You will find, when my report shall be published, that the First Brigade was to our army what the Imperial Guard was to Napoleon; through the blessings of God it met the victorious enemy, and turned the fortunes of the day."

And who was Stonewall Jackson, and of what stock? Although he was of sterling and respectable parentage, it matters little, for, in historic fame, "he was his own ancestor." And it is well enough that Virginia, who gave to the war Robert Edward Lee, of old and aristocratic lineage, should furnish Jackson as the representative of her people. On the 21st of January, 1824, in Clarksburg, among the mountains of Western Virginia, was born this boy, the youngest of four children; and, with no view to his future fame, he was named Thomas Jonathan Jackson. It was a rugged, honest name, but is no cause of regret that it is now merged in the more rugged and euphonious one he afterward made for himself. . . .

II. "OLD JACK"

In face and figure, Stonewall Jackson was not striking. Above the average height, with a frame angular, muscular, and fleshless, he was, in all his movements, from riding a horse to handling a pen, the most ungraceful man in the army. His expression was thoughtful, and generally clouded with an air of fatigue. His eye was small, blue, and in repose as gentle as a young girl's. With high, broad forehead, small, sharp nose, thin, pallid lips, deep set eyes, and dark, rusty beard, he was not a handsome man. His face in the drawing-room or tent, softened by his sweet smile, was as different from itself on the battle-field as a little lake in summer noon differs from the same lake when frozen. Walking or riding the General was ungainly; his main object was to go over the ground, without regard to the manner of his going. His favorite horse was as little like Pegasus as he was like Apollo; he rode boldly and well, but certainly not with grace and ease. He was not a man of style. General Lee, on horseback or off, was the handsomest man I ever saw. It was said of Wade Hampton that he looked as knightly when mounted as if he had stepped out from an old canvas, horse and all. Breckenridge was a model of manly beauty, and Joe Johnston looked every inch a soldier. None of these things can be said of Jackson.

Akin to his dyspepsia, and perhaps as a consequence, was his ignorance of music. One morning, at Ashland, he startled a young lady from her propriety by gravely asking her if she had ever heard a new piece of music called "Dixie," and as gravely listening to her while she sang it. He had heard it a thousand times from the army bands, and yet it seemed new to him. Judged by the Shakespearean standard, who could be more "fit for treasons, stratagems, and spoils?" And yet there was one kind of music which always interested and delighted him. It was the "rebel yell" of his troops. To this grand chorus he never failed to respond. The difference between the regular "hurrah" of the Federal army and the irregular, wild yell of the Confederates was as marked as the difference in their uniforms. The rebel yell was a peculiar mixture of sounds, a kind of weird shout. Jackson was greeted with it whenever he made his appearance to the troops, on the march or in battle; and just as invariably he would seize his old gray cap from his head in acknowledgment, and his "little sorrel," knowing his habit, would break into a gallop and never halt until the shout had ceased. I remember one night, at tattoo, this cry broke forth in the camp of the Stonewall Brigade, and was taken up by brigades and divisions, until it rolled over field and wood throughout the whole corps. The General came hastily and bareheaded from his tent, and going up to a fence near by, he leaned upon it and listened in quiet to the rise, climax, and conclusion of that strange serenade, raising his head to catch the last sound, as it grew fainter, and until it died away like an echo along the mountains. Then turning toward his tent he muttered, in half soliloquy, "That was the sweetest music I ever heard."

General Jackson's troops and his enemy's believed he never slept; the fact is, he slept a great deal. Whenever he had nothing else to do, he went to sleep, especially in church. I remember during the invasion of Maryland, on Sunday night he rode three miles in an ambulance to attend church in Frederick, and then fell asleep as soon as the minister began to preach; his head fell upon his breast, and he never awoke until aroused by the organ and choir. He could sleep anywhere and in any position, sitting in his chair, under fire, or on horseback. On a night march toward Richmond, after the battles with McClellan, he was riding along with his drowsy staff, nodding and sleeping as he went. We passed by groups of men sitting along the roadside, and engaged in roasting new corn by fires made of fence-rails. One group took us for cavalrymen with an inebriated captain, and one of the party, delighted at the sight of a man who had found whisky enough to be drunk, sprang up from the fire and, brandishing a roasting-ear in his hand, leaped down into the road, and seizing the General's horse, cried out: "I say, old fellow, where the devil did you get

ON THE SIDE OF THE ANGELS

your liquor?" In an instant, as the General awoke, the fellow saw his mistake; and then bounding from the road he took the fence at a single leap, exclaiming: "Good God, it's old Jack!" and disappeared in the darkness. Yes, General Jackson slept a great deal, but he was never caught napping.

Jeb Stuart: The Chevalier of the Lost Cause

I. A LESSON IN TACTICS

. . . IT WAS not until General Patterson began his feint against Winchester that our colonel had full opportunity to give us his field lectures. When the advance began, and our pickets were driven in, the most natural thing to do, in our view of the situation, was to fall back upon our infantry supports at Winchester, and I remember hearing various expressions of doubt as to the colonel's sanity when, instead of falling back, he marched his handful of men right up to the advancing lines, and ordered us to dismount. The Federal skirmish line was coming toward us at a double-quick, and we were set going toward it at a like rate of speed, leaving our horses hundreds of yards to the rear. We could see that the skirmishers alone outnumbered us three or four times, and it really seemed that our colonel meant to sacrifice his command deliberately. He waited until the infantry was within about two hundred yards of us, we being in the edge of a little grove, and they on the other side of an open field. Then Stuart cried out, "Backwards—march! steady, men—keep your faces to the enemy!" and we marched in that way through the timber, delivering our shot-gun fire slowly as we fell back toward our horses. Then mounting, with the skirmishers almost upon us, we retreated, not hurriedly, but at a slow trot, which the colonel would on no account permit us to change into a gallop. Taking us out into the main road he halted us in column, with our backs to the enemy.

"Attention!" he cried. "Now I want to talk to you men. You are brave fellows, and patriotic ones, too, but you are ignorant of this kind of work, and I am teaching you. I want you to observe that a good man on a good horse can never be caught. Another thing: cavalry can *trot* away from anything, and a gallop is a gait unbecoming a soldier, unless he is going toward the enemy. Remember that. We gallop toward the enemy, and trot away, always. Steady now! don't break ranks!"

And as the words left his lips a shell from a battery half a mile to the rear hissed over our heads.

"There," he resumed. "I've been waiting for that, and watching those

From *A Rebel's Recollections*, by George Cary Eggleston, pp. 114–117, 118–120, 121–123, 124–129. Second Edition. New York: G. P. Putnam's Sons. 1878.

fellows. I knew they'd shoot too high, and I wanted you to learn how shells sound."

We spent the next day or two literally within the Federal lines. We were shelled, skirmished with, charged, and surrounded scores of times, until we learned to hold in high regard our colonel's masterly skill in getting into and out of perilous positions. He seemed to blunder into them in sheer recklessness, but in getting out he showed us the quality of his genius; and before we reached Manassas, we had learned, among other things, to entertain a feeling closely akin to worship for our brilliant and daring leader. We had begun to understand, too, how much force he meant to give to his favorite dictum that the cavalry is the eye of the army.

II. Riding Past a Federal Picket

. . . Once I was his only follower on a scouting expedition, of which he, a brigadier-general at the time, was the commander. I had been detailed to do some clerical work at his headquarters, and, having finished the task assigned me, was waiting in the piazza of the house he occupied, for somebody to give me further orders, when Stuart came out.

"Is that your horse?" he asked, going up to the animal and examining him minutely.

I replied that he was and upon being questioned further informed him that I did not wish to sell my steed. Turning to me suddenly, he said—

"Let's slip off on a scout, then; I'll ride your horse and you can ride mine. I want to try your beast's paces"; and mounting, we galloped away. Where or how far he intended to go I did not know. He was enamored of my horse, and rode, I suppose, for the pleasure of riding an animal which pleased him. We passed outside our picket line, and then, keeping in the woods, rode within that of the Union Army. Wandering about in a purposeless way, we got a near view of some of the Federal camps, and finally finding ourselves objects of attention on the part of some well-mounted cavalry in blue uniforms, we rode rapidly down a road toward our own lines, our pursuers riding quite as rapidly immediately behind us.

"General," I cried presently, "there is a Federal picket post on the road just ahead of us. Had we not better oblique into the woods?"

"Oh, no. They won't expect us from this direction, and we can ride over them before they make up their minds who we are."

Three minutes later we rode at full speed through the corporal's guard on picket, and were a hundred yards or more away before they could level a gun at us. Then half a dozen bullets whistled about our ears, but the cavalier paid no attention to them.

"Did you ever time this horse for a half-mile?" was all he had to say.

III. The Wish That Was Granted

It was on the day of my ride with him that I heard him express his views of the war and his singular aspiration for himself. It was almost immediately after General McClellan assumed command of the Army of the Potomac, and while we were rather eagerly expecting him to attack our strongly fortified position at Centreville. Stuart was talking with some members of his staff, with whom he had been wrestling a minute before. He said something about what they could do by way of amusement when they should go into winter-quarters.

"That is to say," he continued, "if George B. McClellan ever allows us to go into winter-quarters at all."

"Why, general? Do you think he will advance before spring?" asked one of his officers.

"Not against Centreville," replied the general. "He has too much sense for that, and I think he knows the shortest road to Richmond, too. If I am not greatly mistaken, we shall hear of him presently on his way up the James River."

In this prediction, as the reader knows, he was right. The conversation then passed to the question of results.

"I regard it as a foregone conclusion," said Stuart, "that we shall ultimately whip the Yankees. We are bound to believe that, anyhow; but the war is going to be a long and terrible one, first. We've only just begun it, and very few of us will see the end. *All I ask of fate is that I may be killed leading a cavalry charge.*"

The remark was not a boastful or seemingly insincere one. It was made quietly, cheerfully, almost eagerly, and it impressed me at the time with the feeling that the man's idea of happiness was what the French call glory, and that in his eyes there was no glory like that of dying in one of the tremendous onsets which he knew so well how to make. His wish was granted, as we know. He received his death-wound at the head of his troopers.

IV. His Audacity

General Stuart was, without doubt, capable of handling an infantry command successfully, as he demonstrated at Chancellorsville, where he took Stonewall Jackson's place and led an army corps in a very severe engagement; but his special fitness was for cavalry service. His tastes were those of a horseman. Perpetual activity was a necessity of his existence, and he enjoyed nothing so much as danger. Audacity, his greatest virtue as a cavalry commander, would have been his besetting sin in any other position. Inasmuch as it is the business of the cavalry to live as constantly as possible within gunshot of the enemy, his recklessness stood him in excellent stead as a general of horse, but it is at least questionable whether his want of caution would not have led to disaster if his command had been of a less mobile sort. His critics say he was vain, and he was so, as a boy is. He liked to win the applause of his friends, and he liked still better to astonish the enemy, glorying in the thought that his foeman must admire his "impudence," as he called it, while they dreaded its manifestation. He was continually doing things of an extravagantly audacious sort, with no other purpose, seemingly, than that of making people stretch their eyes in wonder. He enjoyed the admiration of the enemy far more, I think, than he did that of his friends. This fact was evident in the care he took to make himself a conspicuous personage in every time of danger. He would ride at some distance from his men in a skirmish, and in every possible way attract a dangerous attention to himself. His slouch hat and long plume marked him in every battle, and made him a target for the riflemen to shoot at. In all this there was some vanity, if we choose to call it so, but it was an excellent sort of vanity for a cavalry chief to cultivate. I cannot learn that he ever boasted of any achievement, or that his vanity was ever satisfied with the things already done. His audacity was due, I think, to his sense of humor, not less than to his love of applause. He would laugh uproariously over the astonishment he imagined the Federal officers must feel after one of his peculiarly daring or sublimely impudent performances. When, after capturing a large number of horses and mules on one of his raids, he seized a telegraph station and sent a dispatch to General Meigs, then quartermaster-general of the United States Army, complaining that he could not afford to come after animals of so poor a quality, and urging that officer to provide better ones for capture in future, he enjoyed the joke quite as heartily as he did the success which made it possible.

The boyishness to which I have referred ran through every part of his character and every act of his life. His impetuosity in action, his love of military glory and of the military life, his occasional waywardness with his friends and his generous affection for them—all these were the traits of a great boy, full, to running over, of impulsive animal life. His audacity, too, which impressed strangers as the most marked feature of his character, was closely akin to that disposition which Dickens assures us is common to all boy-kind, to feel an insane delight in anything which specially imperils their necks. But the peculiarity showed itself most strongly in his love of uproarious fun. Almost at the beginning of the war he managed to surround himself with a number of persons whose principal qualification for membership of his military household was their ability to make fun. One of these was a noted banjo-player and ex-Negro minstrel. He played the banjo and sang comic songs to perfection and *therefore* Stuart wanted him. I have known him to ride with his banjo, playing and singing, even on a march which might be changed at any moment into a battle; and Stuart's laughter on such occasions was sure to be heard as an accompaniment as far as the minstrel's voice could reach. He had another queer character about him, whose chief recommendation was his grotesque fierceness of appearance. This was Corporal Hagan, a very giant in frame, with an abnormal tendency to develop hair. His face was heavily bearded almost to his eyes, and his voice was as hoarse as distant thunder, which indeed it closely resembled. Stuart, seeing him in the ranks, fell in love with his peculiarities of person at once, and had him detailed for duty at headquarters, where he made him a corporal, and gave him charge of the stables. Hagan, whose greatness was bodily only, was much elated by the attention shown him, and his person seemed to swell and his voice to grow deeper than ever under the influence of the newly acquired dignity of chevrons. All this was amusing, of course, and Stuart's delight was unbounded. The man remained with him till the time of his death, though not always as a corporal. In a mad freak of fun one day, the chief recommended his corporal for promotion, to see, he said, if the giant was capable of further swelling, and so the corporal became a lieutenant upon the staff.

"Fustest with the Mostest" Forrest

LEGEND has had its way the more with the story of Forrest because so much of his fame is folk-fame. Among the Southern people, or at least that portion of them to whom Shiloh and Chickamauga are more than vaguely familiar names of fields of battle, it rests quite as much upon the remembered talk of the veterans as it does upon the records. By most of the rest of the world he is remembered chiefly, especially in these latter days when the world's attention is focused on war of swift movement and sudden surprise, not so much by what he did as by what he is supposed to have said—"Git thar fustest with the mostest men."

Of course that wasn't just what he said. Forrest would have been totally incapable of so obvious and self-conscious a piece of literary carpentry. What he said, he said simply and directly—"Get there first with the most men," although doubtless his pronunciation was "git thar fust," that being the idiom of the time and place. Such a phrase, compacting about as much of the art of war as has ever been put into so few words, had no need of the artificial embellishment of double superlatives.

The first man who heard the phrase and wrote about it, though the writing was not until long afterwards, was Basil Duke, brother-in-law and second in command to General John Hunt Morgan. Both Morgan and Forrest were serving under General Bragg at the time. Both of them had recently carried out brilliant little operations, Morgan in Kentucky and Forrest in Middle Tennessee. The two were comparing notes at Murfreesborough, Tennessee, each more interested in finding out what the other had done and how he had done it than in telling his own exploits, when Forrest explained his success with the impatient exclamation, "I just . . . got there first with the most men." The phrase is given in the same form in perhaps the earliest printed reference to it, in Lieutenant General Dick Taylor's informative and delightful memoirs. To Federal officers whom Forrest met under flag of truce in Mississippi, in the dying days of the war, he "reflectively declared that he had not the advantage of a military educa-

From *"First with the Most" Forrest,* by Robert Selph Henry, pp. 18–19. Copyright, 1944, by the Bobbs-Merrill Company. Indianapolis and New York.

tion, and knew but little as to the art of war; but he always made it his rule 'to get there first with the most men.' "

And so Forrest's phrase gradually gained currency, but it was not until he himself had long been dead that its embellishers began to transmute his simple and direct words into the jargon of superlatives in which it is now most often quoted. The "mostest" seems to have appeared first, with the "fustest" as a natural corollary once some one started the thing.

Morgan and His Raiders

I. A Deal in Meal

A CORRESPONDENT of the *Memphis Appeal*, (April 3d, 1862) vouches for the truth of the following exploit of Captain Morgan:—

The heroic young Kentuckian is as full of stratagem as he is of daring. He disguised himself as a countryman and took a wagon load of meal to Nashville the other day. Driving straight to the St. Cloud Hotel, he left his wagon at the door in charge of a trusty follower, and went into the dining-room of the hotel about dinner, where he sat down opposite to General McCook.

"General McCook, I suppose," said the disguised partisan, bowing across the table.

"You are right, sir," said McCook, "that is my name."

"Well, gineral, if thar's no seceshers about, I've got something to tell you right here."

Looking around, the general requested his new acquaintance to proceed with what he had to say.

"Well, gineral, I live up here close by Burk's mills, right in the midst of a nest of red hot seceshers, and they swear your soldiers shan't have a peck of meal if they have to starve for it. But, gineral, I'm all right on the goose, though I don't have much to say about it, about home, and so I got a wagon load of meal ground, and I've brung it down here to-day, and it's now out thar in the street, and you can have it if you want."

General McCook was highly delighted—expressed his gratitude to the plain-looking countryman for his kindness, praised his loyalty to "the old flag," etc., etc., and at once ordered the meal to be taken to the commissary of his brigade and paid for in gold and silver. This transaction accomplished, the counterfeit wagoner again repaired to General McCook's head-

From *The Grayjackets: and How They Lived, Fought and Died, for Dixie;* with Incidents & Sketches of Life in the Confederacy, Comprising Narratives of Personal Adventure, Army Life, Naval Adventure, Home Life, Partisan Daring, Life in the Camp, Field and Hospital; together with the Songs, Ballads, Anecdotes, and Humorous Incidents of the War for Southern Independence, by a Confederate, pp. 317–321, 323–327, 331. Richmond, Atlanta, Philadelphia, Cincinnati, St. Louis, Chicago: Jones Brothers & Co. [1867.]

quarters, where, after requesting a strictly private interview, he told the "gineral" that if he would send out one hundred and fifty men to such a place, in such a neighborhood in Davidson county, he would guide them right into that "nest of seceshers and traitors," where they might "bag" a large quantity of meal and other "contraband of war," besides a number of the worst rebels that ever assisted in "bustin' up" this "glorious Union." General McCook fell into the snare "as easy as falling off a log," and all the preliminary arrangements were made, and time and place agreed upon, for the one hundred and fifty Federal soldiers to meet their trusty guide.

McCook's detachment of one hundred and fifty men kept the appointment faithfully, and, of course, Captain Morgan, no longer disguised, was there to meet them; but, unfortunately for them, he was not alone—he had a sufficient number of well-armed horsemen to capture the whole Yankee force without firing a gun. So he took them quietly, and sent them swiftly "to the rear," to be exchanged "in due course"—all but one, an officer, whom he released on parole, and bade him return to General McCook, with the compliments of his meal-selling acquaintance, who had the pleasure of meeting him at the St. Cloud a few days before.

II. He Wanted to see Morgan

The operator at Lebanon, Kentucky, sat in his office silent and grum (*sic*). He had just completed the forwarding of a dispatch from Louisville to Nashville, relative to Morgan's captured men, to the effect that they must be sent immediately to the former city by rail. The reason assigned was that Morgan could at any time enter Nashville, and, with the assistance he would there obtain from rebel sympathizers, could force the prison and liberate the prisoners.

"Confound Morgan and his men!" said the operator to himself, biting his lips in rage; "I wish the last one of them was at Old Nick this very minute! They are always doing some devilment to make trouble. Who knows but what they may pounce down on me some of these days, and take me off to some of their cursed prisons? Confound the whole batch of them, I say. I wish I had Morgan here; I'd soon put an end to his villainy —the cursed rebel!"

Just at this juncture of the soliloquy, a horseman alighted in front of the door, and, with whip in hand, walked carelessly in. The surly operator scarcely raised his head to speak to the intruder, as he caught a glimpse of his butternut suit, all bespattered with mud, and the old slouched hat with rim partly torn off. But the visitor was not to be repulsed by this very uncivil reception. Stepping forward toward a vacant chair, which stood beside the window in the further side of the room, he seated himself and asked for the news.

"No news!" was the curt reply.

There was a morning *Journal* on the desk. The stranger reached out his hand, and, with the most perfect *sang froid*, took the paper, and, opening it, commenced to read.

"John Morgan at work again!" he said, as he glanced down the first column; "a great pity that that man can't be caught—he plays the wild with everything!"

At the mention of Morgan's name, the operator, as if suddenly seized by his satanic majesty himself, sprang from his chair, doubled up his fist, and then with a sudden jerk withdrawing it again, as if practising the pugilistic art on some hapless victim, and then thrusting his arm out at full length, while his eyes darted vengeful fire, exclaimed:

"Yes, the scoundrel, villain—I wish I had him here; I'd blow his brains out this very moment! I'd show him. Just let him come in reach of me, and he'll soon get a ball put through his cursed body. No more pranks from him, the mighty John Morgan, I tell you!" And the infuriated man went through all the gestures of shooting his hated foe.

"You wouldn't kill him, would you?" asked the stranger, quietly looking up from his paper, and lifting the torn brim of his old white hat.

"Kill him? Aye, and I would, sooner than I'd shoot a mad dog. I just dare him, at any time, to cross that door, and if he isn't a dead man in less than five minutes there's no truth in me!"

The stranger rose, took off his hat, and stood before the bloodthirsty operator, and with a quiet mien, and voice gentle as a maiden's, said:

"I am John Morgan, sir; execute your threat! Here is a pistol—you are entirely welcome to use it!"

As he spoke, he fixed his large piercing eyes steadfastly on the operator. Every feature of that noble face bespoke daring and defiance.

"Here is a pistol, use it!"

"Oh! thank you; I—I—didn't know—I hadn't any idea—that you were—Colonel Morgan, sir—indeed I didn't—beg pardon, sir! So much annoyed to-day—every thing gone topsy-turvy. Man gets so fretted—excuse me!—really didn't mean what I said—wouldn't have any man's blood on my conscience—oh, no! Remember the commandment. Thousand pardons, sir; hope you'll forgive!" And the frightened man bowed himself quite back to the wall, where he stood pale and trembling.

"You have my pardon, sir," replied Morgan in a firm, gentlemanly tone. "Another time I advise you to be less boastful of your courage and veracity. I have but little time to stay. Seat yourself, and send the messages that I shall dictate, to Louisville. Make no mistake; if you do, your life is the forfeit!"

The bewildered man, but too glad to escape so easily, obeyed the order of the Colonel with alacrity.

"I understand this operation, sir; don't you attempt to give any information but what I instruct you to do."

Had the trembling man felt disposed to disobey the warning, the close proximity to his head of that formidable pistol would have forever lulled all such desire.

"Now," said Colonel Morgan, "show me all the dispatches that have passed through this office in the last twenty-four hours."

The man sprang from his seat and with a most obsequious air obeyed the bidding.

"That will do, sir," said Morgan, bowing politely, and bidding the pusillanimous wretch "good morning." Reaching his horse, he mounted and rode away, leaving the confused operator dumb with wonder and surprise at the strange and startling occurrence.

III. SELLING A FEDERAL GENERAL

DURING one of his expeditions, Morgan reached a point on the railroad near Mumfordsville, Kentucky. His operator at once attached his instrument to the telegraph, and sent a dispatch to the Federal General Boyle, commanding at Louisville, as if from General Granger, the Federal commander at Bowling Green. This stated that Morgan was in the vicinity of Bowling Green, threatening an attack, and asked for aid.

General Boyle made answer that he could not give him any.

General Granger (Morgan) then asked if there were no troops in Louisville which could be sent to his aid.

General Boyle sent word that there were no troops in Louisville at all.

General Granger asked Boyle what disposition had been made of the troops.

General Boyle told him the force and position of his troops, spoke of their efficiency, etc., and gave all the information in regard to them that Morgan wanted.

Morgan then sent in his own name a dispatch to General Boyle, calling him a "very smart boy," and thanking him politely for the important information he had given him.

II. BUCCANEERS, BANDITS, AND BULLIES

They know that pirates are wicked men, that, in fact, they are sea-robbers or maritime murderers, but their bold and adventurous method of life, their bravery, daring, and the exciting character of their expeditions, give them something of the same charm and interest which belong to the robber knights of the middle ages.—FRANK R. STOCKTON

[Jesse] James was a retail rascal; Murel, wholesale.
                                        —MARK TWAIN

You call yourselves half horse and half alligator, but I'll let you know that I'm whole alligator with a cross of the wildcat.
                                        —*Crockett Almanac*

There was a great deal of admiration for [bank robbers] because they were so brave and generous and because it was said that they took from the rich and gave to the poor.—ANGUS McDONALD

1. UNEASY LIES THE HEAD

EACH year, on February 9, the Florida West Coast metropolis of Tampa is the scene of a mimic invasion by a mock band of fully costumed pirates known as "Ye Mystic Krewe of Gasparilla" (organized in 1904), membership in which is a social distinction limited to three hundred and fifty of the city's "gayer blades." During the night before, the city is posted with King Gasparilla's proclamation to the Mayor and inhabitants: "Surrender, or be put to the torch and sword!"—to which the Mayor replies: "Our city will never surrender." And at noon a pirate-swarming three-masted sloop-of-war, flying the Jolly Roger, sails into Tampa harbor.[1]

Thus begins the Gasparilla carnival of February 9–14 in honor of the city's patron rogue. In addition to parades, open house aboard the pirate ship, and fireworks on the last night when it puts out to sea, the festivities include a coronation ball on the second night, at which a new King Gasparilla and his queen are crowned to reign for the coming year. By this elaborate mummery the memory of a "noted desperado of blackest dye" is kept alive in the way that time and tradition have of placing a halo of romance and mystery on the very head on which there was once a price.

Although José Gaspar or Gasparilla's fame has been eclipsed by that of another pirate of the Gulf, Jean Lafitte (who once mortified him by cheating him in a joint venture), he is eminently worth remembering here for his witty statement of the piratical creed. After raiding the ship *Orleans,* off Cape Antonio in September, 1821, he wrote (in French) to one of the ship's passengers, a United States naval officer:

AT SEA, AND IN GOOD LUCK

SIR:

Between buccaneers, no ceremony; I take your dry goods, and in return I send you pimento; therefore we are now even. I entertain no resentment. Bid good day to the officer of the United States, and tell him that I appreciate the energy with which he has spoke of me and my companions-in-arms. Nothing can intimidate us; we run the same fortune, and our maxim is that the goods of this world belong to the strong and valiant. The occupation of the Floridas is a pledge that the course I follow is comfortable to the policy pursued by the United States.

RICHARD COEUR DE LION [2]

Gasparilla was also distinguished by the fact that when he was finally overtaken and defeated, he saved his head by wrapping a heavy chain around his waist and neck and leaping overboard, brandishing his sword in a last defiant gesture. When, on the other hand, Blackbeard lost his head,

---

[1] Joseph R. Mickler, "Phantom of the Buccaneer," *Highway Traveler Magazine,* Vol. 20 (December, 1947), No. 6, pp. 18–19, 34.

[2] *Florida, A Guide to the Southernmost State* (New York, 1939), p. 397.

in gory single-handed combat, his headless body is reputed to have swum three times around the ship of his vanquishers; and his skull was later made into a silver-tipped drinking vessel. Even more macabre is the fate of "Big" Micajah Harpe's skull, which, after being nailed to a tree for many years, was taken down by an old woman to be pulverized and concocted into a cure for her nephew's fits.[3]

2. THE UNTAMABLE

Certain parallels may be drawn between the primitive, lawless conditions of new lands and new settlements that produced both a Blackbeard and a John A. Murrell. Between the outlaws of the Natchez Trace and the wilds of the Lower Mississippi valley, a paradise of "sudden bountifulness" and safe refuge, there existed a special bond. The threat and the promise of the wilderness called out the best and the worst in men.

> Its perfumed appeal, its dark menace particularized them: as if in a kind of intimate abandonment—as if, alone against the dark heart of the continent, their own hearts unfolded—they revealed by their violences, or by their heroisms, how different they were from other men. . . . Always the sinister suggestion, like the river at the bank, was sapping, prying: if it found the least flaw in a man's character it would enter and undermine all.[4]

In John A. Murrell, with his elaborate dreams of an empire of crime—the Mystic Confederacy—and his fantastic scheme of a monster slave revolt, the evil forces of the wilderness produced their master mind.

Besides madmen and devils the Mississippi River also bred giants—the keelboatmen whose acknowledged king was Mike Fink. The physical and mental exaggerations which made it possible for these "wild spirits" to endure and relax from the superhuman ordeal of propelling the keelboats over fifteen hundred miles of whirlpool-, snag-, and sawyer-infested waters were the supreme creations of the violence and monotony of the wilderness.

3. "NO ROBBER"

In Lafitte we see the transition from the old swashbuckling, throat-slitting, ship-scuttling pirate to the business-like and not unpatriotic privateer and smuggler. To the latter as to the mountain moonshiner or "blockader" the local environment and the people were both congenial. While the steamboat displaced the river giants and rowdies of the Mike Fink breed, it brought in a new crowd of adventurers, including the card sharpers and confidence men who preyed upon the passengers, finding in steamboat travel ideal conditions for their operations. The cosmopolitanism and diversity of the passengers of a typical Mississippi steamboat are illustrated by the strange incongruities of their baggage—

> a large box of playing-cards supports a very small package of Bibles; a bowie-knife is tied to a life-preserver; and a package of garden seeds rejoices

---

[3] Robert M. Coates, *The Outlaw Years* (New York, 1930), p. 67.
[4] *Ibid.*, pp. 26, 114.

in the same address as a neighboring keg of powder. There is an old black trunk, soiled with the mud of the Lower Nile, and a new carpet-bag direct from Upper California; a collapsed valise of new shirts and antique sermons is jostled by another plethoric with bilious pills and cholera medicine; an elaborate dress, direct from Paris, is in contact with a trapper's Rocky Mountain costume; a gun-case reposes upon a bandbox; and a well-preserved rifle is half-concealed by the folds of an umbrella. The volume of a strange, eventful, and ever-changing life is before you, on the pages of which are impressed phases of original character such as are nowhere else exhibited, nowhere seen, but on the Mississippi.[5]

In addition to fugitives from justice, this motley crew included refugees from work like George Devol. For several years he and his brother Paul earned $4.00 a day caulking steamboats in Cincinnati. Since he also became infatuated with the game of faro, which kept him broke, he "concluded to either quit work or quit gambling." One day, after having given the matter much thought, he pushed his tools into the river with his foot and said he was through. To his surprised brother he said that he "intended to live off of fools and suckers. I also said, 'I will make money rain'; and I did come near doing as I said." [6] But his weakness for faro pursued him to the end and prevented him from becoming the wealthy man he might have been. "My old head is hard and thick, and maybe that is the reason I never had sense enough to save my money." His thick skull was also responsible for his reputation as a "terrible rough and tumble fighter," who could "kill any man living, white or black, by butting him." Besides being a "tough citizen" and one of the most daring sporting men in the country, he was also something of a philosopher. "A gambler's word is as good as his bond, and that is more than I can say of many business men who stand very high in a community." [7]

When the Oklahoma bank-robber, Henry Starr, was killed by a banker while holding up the bank at Harrison, Arkansas, "it was a sad time in Sallisaw." One of the best-loved men in his community, he was mourned by the people who respected and admired "the nobility, the gentleness, the bravery, and the shooting skill of the great man." [8] And the perfect epitaph for him, as for all the other bank-robbers and train-robbers, all the buccaneers, bandits, and bullies who ever enlisted popular sympathy and captured the popular imagination, was what the people said of Henry Starr in Sallisaw, Oklahoma: "Henry Starr is no robber. . . . He's just getting back a little of the money that the bankers have stolen." [9]

B. A. B.

---

[5] T. B. Thorpe, "Remembrances of the Mississippi," *Harper's New Monthly Magazine*, Vol. XII (December, 1855), No. LXVII, p. 34.

[6] George H. Devol, *Forty Years a Gambler on the Mississippi* (New York, 1892), p. 14.

[7] *Ibid.*, p. 296.

[8] Angus McDonald, *Old McDonald Had a Farm* (Boston. 1942), p. 23.

[9] *Ibid.*, p. 242.

Captain Teach, alias Blackbeard

I. BLACKBEARD'S TREASURE [1]

As IT was impracticable in summer to explore these meandering rivers by boat (for a reason which will appear), I invited an old riverman who knew them well to visit them with me at such points as we could reach by car. We set out from Cambridge and, during the drive south, my companion entertained me with tall tales of rivers. We had been talking about the deep, unexpected holes that are to be found in all Eastern Shore rivers, due to some obscure action of the tide. My friend said, with a perfectly grave face:

"There is such a hole near the mouth of Watts' Creek that is ninety feet deep. It is called Jake's Hole. Its exact depth is known because it's been sounded often enough, and I'll tell you why. There was aplenty pirates round here in the old time. The one that mostly cruised in these waters was Blackbeard; Edward Teach was his right name. Well, Blackbeard picked Jake's Hole for one of his caches, and dropped an oaken chest bound round with copper bands in there. It's still there. God knows what's inside it!

"Many knew about this and aimed to recover the treasure, but Blackbeard had left a school of man-eating red herring to guard the place and none could come near. Well, there was an Englishman called Lord Longbow bought a fine place on the river and his cousin, Prince Fakir, came to spend the summer with him. Lord Longbow took him out in a boat to show him the river, and as they passed by Jake's Hole he was trying to teach Prince Fakir to sing 'Yankee Doodle.' This tickled the man-eating red herring so that they laughed theirselves to death.

"Those that knew about it thought it would be a cinch, then, to recover Blackbeard's treasure, so they proceeded to Jake's Hole with their ropes and grappling irons and so forth. But it turned out that Blackbeard had left another spell on the chest. It was easy enough to catch holt of it, but as soon as they histed it near the surface, the ropes bust into flames and burned through with an awful stink of sulphur, and the chest dropped to the bottom of the hole again. Many have tried it, but it was always the same. They only lost their grappling irons for their trouble. So the chest is there yet, if you want to have a try for it. . . .

"That famous beard of his," the storyteller continued, "started growing right under his eyes and would have hung down over his chest, only he used to plait it in many little tails which he tied with different colored ribbons and caught behind his ears. . . . I suppose you've heard how Blackbeard came to his end?"

---

[1] From *Rivers of the Eastern Shore,* Seventeen Maryland Rivers, by Hulbert Footner, pp. 156–158. Rivers of America. Copyright, 1944, by Hulbert Footner. New York and Toronto: Farrar & Rinehart, Inc.

I said I had not.

"Well, that was off Sharp's Island out in the bay. Blackbeard was lying in wait under the island at the edge of Dick's Hole for a richly laden East Indiaman that was expected down from Baltimore. He was so intent upon it, he failed to notice the tops'l schooner *Julia Harlow* lying inside the hook. Young Joshua Covey was her master. Covey was able to creep up on Blackbeard in a yawl boat, and to board him before he was discovered. Covey cut off Blackbeard's head with one mighty sweep of his saber.

"But a pirate, you know, prided himself on never losing his head. Blackbeard threw the copper plate that showed the location of all his caches into Dick's Hole and jumped in after it. He swam around the vessel three times without his head before he disappeared from sight." *

From the frequency with which one meets with his name on the Eastern Shore, one would think that Blackbeard must have sailed up here, but the facts of his brief piratical career are known, and he never sailed north of the Carolinas. The truth is, he laid a spell of horror on the whole Atlantic seaboard.

II. The Death of Blackbeard [2]

The sloops trading up and down this [Pamlico] river, being so frequently pillaged by Blackbeard, consulted with the traders and some of the best planters what course to take. They saw plainly it would be in vain to make an application to the governor of North Carolina, to whom it properly belonged to find some redress; so that if they could not be relieved from some other quarter, Blackbeard would be like to reign with impunity; therefore, with as much secrecy as possible, they sent a deputation to Virginia, to lay the affair before the governor of that colony, and to solicit an armed force from the men-of-war lying there to take or destroy this pirate.

This governor consulted with the captains of the two men-of-war, viz., the *Pearl* and *Lime,* who had lain in St. James's river about ten months. It was agreed that the governor should hire a couple of small sloops, and the

---

* The legend around Ocracoke is that Blackbeard's bad fortune on this occasion [of his slaying] came to him because of the unlucky number of his matrimonial adventures, the story being that he had thirteen wives. It is said also that his vanquishers cut off his head and hung it at the yard-arm of their ship, throwing his body into the sea, and that as soon as the body struck the water the head began to call, "Come on, Edward!" whereupon the headless body swam three times around the ship. Personally I think there may be some slight doubt about the authenticity of this part of the story. For, while from one point of view we might say that to swim about in such aimless fashion would be the very thing a man without a head might do, yet from another point of view the question arises: Would a man whose head had just been severed from his body feel like taking such a long swim?—Julian Street, *American Adventures* (1917), pp. 287–288.

[2] From *The Buccaneers and Marooners of America,* Being an Account of the Famous Adventures and Daring Deeds of Certain Notorious Freebooters of the Spanish Main, edited by Howard Pyle, pp. 246–247, 249–254. London: T. Fisher Unwin. 1897.

men-of-war would man them. This was accordingly done, and the command of them given to Mr. Robert Maynard, first lieutenant of the *Pearl*, an experienced officer, and a gentleman of great bravery and resolution, as will appear by his gallant behavior in this expedition. The sloops were well manned, and furnished with ammunition and small arms, but had no guns mounted.

About the time of their going out the governor called an assembly, in which it was resolved to publish a proclamation, offering certain rewards to any person or persons who, within a year after that time, should take or destroy any pirate. . . .

*   *   *   *   *

The 17th of November, 1718, the lieutenant sailed from Kicquetan, in James river in Virginia, and the 31st, in the evening, came to the mouth of Okerecock inlet, where he got sight of the pirate. This expedition was made with all imaginable secrecy, and the officer managed with all the prudence that was necessary, stopping all boats and vessels he met with in the river from going up, and thereby preventing any intelligence from reaching Blackbeard, and receiving at the same time an account from them all of the place where the pirate was lurking. But notwithstanding this caution, Blackbeard had information of the design from his Excellency of the province; and his secretary, Mr. Knight, wrote him a letter particularly concerning it, intimating "that he had sent him four of his men, which were all he could meet with in or about town, and so bid him be upon his guard." These men belonged to Blackbeard, and were sent from Bath Town to Okerecock inlet, where the sloop lay, which is about twenty leagues.

Blackbeard had heard several reports, which happened not to be true, and so gave the less credit to this advice; nor was he convinced till he saw the sloops. Then it was time to put his vessel in a posture of defense. He had no more than twenty-five men on board, though he gave out to all the vessels he spoke with that he had forty. When he had prepared for battle he sat down and spent the night in drinking with the master of a trading sloop, who, it was thought, had more business with Teach than he should have had.

Lieutenant Maynard came to an anchor, for the place being shoal, and the channel intricate, there was no getting in where Teach lay that night; but in the morning he weighed, and sent his boat ahead of the sloops to sound, and coming within gun-shot of the pirate, received his fire; whereupon Maynard hoisted the king's colors, and stood directly towards him with the best way that his sails and oars could make. Blackbeard cut his cable, and endeavored to make a running fight, keeping a continual fire at his enemies with his guns. Mr. Maynard, not having any, kept a constant fire with small arms, while some of his men labored at their oars. In a little time Teach's sloop ran aground, and Mr. Maynard's, drawing more water than that of the pirate, he could not come near him; so he anchored within half gun-shot of the enemy, and, in order to lighten his vessel, that he might run him aboard, the lieutenant ordered all his ballast to be thrown overboard, and all the water to be staved, and then weighed and stood for him; upon which Blackbeard hailed him in this rude manner: "Damn you for villains, who are you; and from whence came you?" The lieutenant made him answer, "You may see by our colors we are no pirates." Blackbeard bid him send his boat on board that he might see who he was; but Mr. Maynard replied thus: "I cannot spare my boat, but I will come aboard of you as soon as I can with my sloop." Upon this Blackbeard took a glass of liquor, and drank to him with these words: "Damnation seize my soul if I give you quarter, or take any from you." In answer to which Mr. Maynard told him "that he expected no quarter from him, nor should he give him any."

By this time Blackbeard's sloop fleeted as Mr. Maynard's sloops were rowing towards him, which being not above a foot high in the waist, and consequently the men all exposed, as they came near together (there being hitherto little or no execution done on either side), the pirate fired a broadside charged with all manner of small shot. A fatal stroke to them!—the sloop the lieutenant was in having twenty men killed and wounded, and the other sloop nine. This could not be helped, for there being no wind, they were obliged to keep to their oars, otherwise the pirate would have got away from him, which seems, the lieutenant was resolute to prevent.

After this unlucky blow Blackbeard's sloop fell broadside to the shore; Mr. Maynard's other sloop, which was called the *Ranger,* fell astern, being for the present disabled. So the lieutenant, finding his own sloop had way and would soon be on board of Teach, he ordered all his men down, for fear of another broadside, which must have been their destruction and the loss of their expedition. Mr. Maynard was the only person that kept the deck, except the man at the helm, whom he directed to lie down snug, and the men in the hold were ordered to get their pistols and their swords ready for close fighting, and to come up at his command; in order to which two ladders were placed in the hatchway for the more expedition. When the lieutenant's sloop boarded the other Captain Teach's men threw in several new-fashioned sort of grenades, viz., case-bottles filled with powder and small shot, slugs, and pieces of lead or iron, with quick-match in the mouth of it, which, being lighted without side, presently runs into the bottle to the powder, and, as it is instantly thrown on board, generally does great execution besides putting all the crew into a confusion. But, by good Providence, they had not that effect here, the men being in the hold. Blackbeard, seeing few or no hands aboard, told his men "that they were all knocked to head, except three or four; and therefore," says he, "let's jump on board and cut them to pieces."

Whereupon, under the smoke of one of the bottles just mentioned, Blackbeard enters with fourteen men over the bows of Maynard's sloop, and were not seen by him until the air cleared. However, he just then gave a signal to his men, who all rose in an instant, and attacked the pirates with as much bravery as ever was done upon such an occasion.

Blackbeard and the lieutenant fired the first shots at each other, by which the pirate received a wound, and then engaged with swords, till the lieutenant's unluckily broke, and stepping back to cock a pistol, Blackbeard, with his cutlass, was striking at that instant that one of Maynard's men gave him a terrible wound in the neck and throat, by which the lieutenant came off with only a small cut over his fingers.

They were now closely and warmly engaged, the lieutenant and twelve men against Blackbeard and fourteen, till the sea was tinctured with blood round the vessel. Blackbeard received a shot into his body from the pistol that Lieutenant Maynard discharged, yet he stood his ground, and fought with great fury till he received five-and-twenty wounds, and five of them by shot. At length, as he was cocking another pistol, having fired several before, he fell down dead; by which time eight more out of the fourteen dropped, and all the rest, much wounded, jumped overboard and called out for quarter, which was granted, though it was only prolonging their lives a few days. The sloop *Ranger* came up and attacked the men that remained in Blackbeard's sloop with equal bravery, till they likewise cried for quarter.

Here was an end of that courageous brute, who might have passed in the world for a hero had he been employed in a good cause.

The lieutenant caused Blackbeard's head to be severed from his body, and hung up at the boltsprit end; then he sailed to Bath Town, to get relief for his wounded men.

In rummaging the pirate's sloop, they found several letters and written papers, which discovered the correspondence between Governor Eden, the secretary and collector, and also some traders at New York, and Blackbeard. It is likely he had regard enough for his friends to have destroyed these papers before action, in order to hinder them from falling into such hands, where the discovery would be of no use either to the interest or reputation of these fine gentlemen, if it had not been his fixed resolution to have blown up together, when he found no possibility of escaping.

III. A FURY FROM HELL [3]

Now that we have given some account of Teach's life and actions, it will not be amiss that we speak of his beard, since it did not a little contribute towards making his name so terrible in those parts.

Plutarch and other grave historians have taken notice that several great men amongst the Romans took their surnames from certain odd marks in their countenances—as Cicero, from a mark, or vetch, on his nose—so our hero, Captain Teach, assumed the cognomen of Blackbeard, from that large quantity of hair which, like a frightful meteor, covered his whole face, and frightened America more than any comet that has appeared there a long time.

---

[3] *Ibid.*, pp. 255–258.

This beard was black, which he suffered to grow of an extravagant length; as to breadth, it came up to his eyes. He was accustomed to twist it with ribbons, in small tails, after the manner of our Ramilie wigs, and turn them about his ears. In time of action he wore a sling over his shoulders, with three brace of pistols hanging in holsters like bandaliers, and stuck lighted matches under his hat, which, appearing on each side of his face, his eyes naturally looking fierce and wild, made him altogether such a figure that imagination cannot form an idea of a fury from hell to look more frightful.

If he had the look of a fury, his humors and passions were suitable to it. In the commonwealth of pirates, he who goes the greatest length of wickedness is looked upon with a kind of envy amongst them as a person of a more extraordinary gallantry, and is thereby entitled to be distinguished by some post, and if such a one has but courage, he must certainly be a great man. The hero of whom we are writing was thoroughly accomplished this way, and some of his frolics of wickedness were so extravagant, as if he aimed at making his men believe he was a devil incarnate; for being one day at sea, and a little flushed with drink, "Come," says he, "let us make a hell of our own, and try how long we can bear it." Accordingly he, with two or three others, went down into the hold, and closing up all the hatches, filled several pots full of brimstone and other combustible matter, and set it on fire, and so continued till they were almost suffocated, when some of the men cried out for air. At length he opened the hatches, not a little pleased that he held out the longest.

The night before he was killed he sat up and drank till the morning with some of his own men and the master of a merchantman; and having had intelligence of the two sloops coming to attack him, as has been before observed, one of his men asked him, in case anything should happen to him in the engagement with the sloops, whether his wife knew where he had buried his money? He answered, "That nobody but himself and the devil knew where it was, and the longest liver should take all."

Those of his crew who were taken alive told a story which may appear a little incredible; however, we think it will not be fair to omit it since we had it from their own mouths. That once upon a cruise they found out that they had a man on board more than their crew; such a one was seen several days amongst them, sometimes below and sometimes upon deck, yet no man in the ship could give an account who he was, or from whence he came, but that he disappeared a little before they were cast away in their great ship; but it seems they verily believed it was the devil.

One would think these things should induce them to reform their lives, but so many reprobates together, encouraged and spirited one another up in their wickedness, to which a continual course of drinking did not a little contribute, for in Blackbeard's journal, which was taken, there were several memorandums of the following nature found writ with his own hand: Such a day rum all out; our company somewhat sober; a damned confusion amongst us; rogues a-plotting; great talk of separation; so I looked sharp for a prize; such a day took one with a great deal of liquor on board, so kept the company hot, damned hot, then all things went well again.

Thus it was these wretches passed their lives with very little pleasure or satisfaction in the possession of what they violently take away from others, and sure to pay for it at last by an ignominious death.

IV. The Legend of Blackbeard and Miss Eden [4]

. . . Though many of the streams and towns in the Albemarle region retain these traditions of Blackbeard, in little Bath, the oldest town in North Carolina, can the greatest number of these tales be heard; and with good reason, for here in this historic village, the freebooter made his home for a month or so after he had availed himself of the king's offer of pardon to the pirates who would surrender themselves and promise to give over their evil mode of life.

This ancient village, founded in 1705, is situated on Bath Creek, by which modest name the broad beautiful body of water, beside which those early settlers built their homes, is called. The banks of the creek are high and thickly wooded, rising boldly from the water, in striking contrast with the low, marshy shores of most of our eastern rivers.

Near the shores of the creek, just outside the town, there is still to be seen a round brick structure resembling a huge oven, called Teach's Kettle, in which the pirate is said to have boiled the tar with which to calk his vessels. Across the creek from the town are the ruins of "the Governor's Mansion," where, it is claimed, Governor Eden died. In an old field a short distance from the mansion is a deep depression filled with broken bricks, which was the governor's wine cellar. Nearly on a line with this, at the water's edge is shown the opening of a brick tunnel, through which the Pirate Teach is said to have conveyed his stolen goods into the governor's wine cellar for safe keeping. That Governor Eden, for reasons best known to himself, winked at the pirate's freebooting expeditions, and that there was undoubtedly some collusion between Blackbeard and the chief magistrate of the State, was generally believed; though Eden vehemently denied all partnership with the freebooter.

To the latter class of narrative the following thrilling tale, which combines very ingeniously the various points of historic interest in Bath, must, it is to be feared, belong. The story goes that Blackbeard, with the consent of her father, was suing for the hand of Governor Eden's daughter. The young lady, for the excellent reason that she preferred another and better man, declined absolutely to become the pirate's bride.

Finally, in a desperate attempt to elude his pursuit, Miss Eden bribed two of her father's slaves to row her across the creek in the dead of the night to Bath. Here she took refuge in the "Old Marsh House" with her

---

[4] From *In Ancient Albemarle*, by Catherine Albertson, pp. 57–60. Copyright, 1914, by Catherine Albertson. Published by the North Carolina Society Daughters of the Revolution. Raleigh: Commercial Printing Company.

friend, Mrs. Palmer, whose memorial tablet is now in St. Thomas Church at Bath, the oldest house of worship in the State.

Teach, infuriated at the lady's continued rejection of his suit, put out to sea on one of his piratical excursions. The prize he captured on this occasion was Miss Eden's lover, his hated rival. The story goes that Blackbeard cut off one of the hands of the unfortunate captive, threw his body into the sea, and enclosing the gruesome relic in a silver casket, as if it were some costly gift, sent it with many compliments to his lady love. When the unfortunate maiden opened the casket and saw the ghastly object she uttered a terrible shriek and swooned from horror; then, as was the fashion in the old romances, pined slowly away and died of a broken heart.

Now, at first blush, it seems that this interesting tale has enough corroborating evidences of its veracity to pass down to the coming ages as true history. A visitor to Bath can see for himself every one of the places mentioned in the story. The tablet in old St. Thomas Church testifies in many a high-sounding phrase [to] the many virtues of Miss Eden's friend, Mrs. Margaret Palmer; and the "Old Marsh House" is still standing, a well preserved and fascinating relic of the past, where the above lady is said to have sheltered her friend. We speak of facts as hard and stubborn things, but dates are as the nether millstone for hardness. And here are the rocks on which our lovely story shatters: Teach was captured and beheaded in 1718; Mrs. Palmer's tablet reports her to have been born in 1721, and the Marsh House was not built until 1744. The story is a beautiful instance of the way in which legends are made.

V. BLACKBEARD'S SKULL [5]

. . . [We] returned to Alexandria, where, until our duties called us away, we spent our time in fishing-excursions to the Potomac, frequently dining at a tavern on its banks. Here a drinking-vessel supposed to give a particular zest to punch was a skull tipped with silver, said to be a relic of the celebrated pirate Teach, or "Blackbeard." The tradition ran as follows:

One evening this scourge of the Southern coast moored his craft at the mouth of the river and went ashore with his crew in two parties, one to obtain provisions, the other to assist in secreting their treasures. He was busy at this work when an English sloop-of-war, which had quietly followed him, suddenly dropped anchor in a position to prevent his escape, and sent a well-manned barge to capture his ship. Teach and his companions sprang into their boat, and by violent exertion reached their ship nearly at the same moment. But the opposing force was too superior

[5] From *Retrospections of America, 1797–1811*, by John Bernard, edited from the Manuscript by Mrs. Bayle Bernard, with an Introduction, Notes, and Index by Laurence Hutton and Brander Matthews, pp. 174–175. Copyright, 1886, by Harper & Brothers. New York. 1887.

to give even more than their usual desperation any hope of success. The commander of the boarders was a brave Scotchman who, desiring the credit of subduing Teach in person, waved his Andrew Ferrara and challenged him to combat. The rover clinched his weapon in defiance, and hostilities were suspended fore-and-aft to witness the result. For some minutes the contest was dubious, but the coolness of the Scot enabled him to plant a severe blow upon the pirate's shoulder, which let out a stream of crimson. "Ha!" exclaimed the latter, still firm upon his legs, "well struck, brother seaman?" "Weel," replied the Scot, "gin ye like it ye sall hae more on't," and with the next stroke severed the pirate's black head from his shoulders. He then ordered it to be put in boiling water and thoroughly cleansed, when he took it on shore and made it a present to the progenitor of its present possessor.

Jean Lafitte, the Pirate of the Gulf

I. LAFITTE'S TREASURE [1]

. . . THE whole Louisiana coast is Lafitte treasure territory. The buccaneers were everywhere; modern men pry everywhere for their leavings. Owners in many places still threaten to shoot the next person whom they catch prospecting for gold near their good oyster beds. They plan to do some investigating there themselves some day, when the oysters play out! The pirate appears often in the daily conversation of the Gulf people. When a man sees a friend who has taken on some weight since they last met, he gibes at him, "What you got there, Estève?" He taps Estève's big belly. "Lafitte's treasure, ahn?"

II. THE MYSTERY OF LAFITTE [2]

For more than a hundred years Lafitte's treasure has been the El Dorado of the Gulf coast. The search for it today is as fresh and eager as it was when Jackson fought the British at New Orleans. Probably a majority of the people in New Orleans could give a more extensive account of Jean Lafitte than of Andrew Jackson. In Galveston school-boys cherish a bit of what is purported to have been Lafitte's jacket, and a fine new hotel—perhaps with unintended irony—bears his name. A recent dispatch from Yucatan said that his seal had there been dug up. His strange career, his

---

[1] From *The Bayous of Louisiana*, by Harnett T. Kane, pp. 79–80. Copyright, 1943, by Harnett T. Kane. New York: The Hampton Publishing Co., and William Morrow & Company. 1944.

[2] From *Coronado's Children*, Tales of Lost Mines and Buried Treasures of the Southwest, by J. Frank Dobie, pp. 306–317, 332. Copyright, 1930, by The Southwest Press. Dallas, Texas.

fabled hoard, and his uneasy ghost will not let his name die. Yet, despite a considerable body of undisputed facts about Lafitte's political machinations, the man himself remains veiled, enigmatical.

*   *   *   *   *

. . . Enough novels and pulp paper stories to fill a deep five-foot shelf have made Lafitte their theme. Folk whose only knowledge of history consists of inherited tradition tell of his daring adventures and look for his legendary millions all the way from the Keys of Florida to Point Isabel at the mouth of the Rio Grande. They call him "the Pirate of the Gulf."

Maybe he was not a pirate. Maybe, as he always claimed, he was a gentleman smuggler and privateer. His birthplace has been variously fixed as St. Malo, as a village on the Garonne, as Bayonne, as Marseilles. Mr. Stanley Faye, relying on documentary evidence not wholly satisfying, thinks he was born in Orduña, a valley in the Basque provinces of Spain. He could pass for either Spaniard or Frenchman. A Spanish agent in New Orleans reported that his friendship for Spaniards was equaled only by his detestation of English and Americans; indisputably he spent a good part of his life preying on Spain. Biographers with imaginary gift have said that his family were Bourbon aristocrats; also, that they were mere peasants. His very name has been in dispute; he signed it—two or three times at least—as Laffite, but traditionally it has been spelled Lafitte.

His whole life was a series of contradictions. . . . He was gallant to women, but whether he was ever in love is doubtful. Legend says that he married more than once; it also says that he had a low caste Creole mistress in Louisiana who gave birth to a son. At Galveston he was accompanied by a luscious quadroon. A journalist who saw this quadroon and asked Lafitte for "the story of his life," received—so he reported—the following account. At the opening of the nineteenth century Lafitte was a rich merchant in San Domingo, where he married a rich and beautiful wife. Soon after marrying, he sold out his business with the intention of going to Europe to live. He bought a ship and loaded it with goods and specie. At sea he was captured by a Spanish man-of-war. "They took everything—goods, specie, even his wife's jewels." Then they landed the Lafittes on a barren sand key with just enough provisions to keep them alive a few days. An American schooner rescued them and took them to New Orleans, where the wife contracted fever and died.

It is asserted that from boyhood Lafitte "loved to play with old ocean's locks" and that once he recklessly dared a West Indian hurricane by driving his fleet straight across water-covered Galveston Island. On the other hand, it is asserted that he was so subject to seasickness that he seldom boarded a vessel and that he "did not know enough of the art of navigation to manage a jolly boat." In truth, he was not so much a seaman as he was a boss of seamen. He was a brilliant conversationalist, but in conversing he was careful to avoid the secrets and duplicities that characterized nearly his whole existence. It seems safe to assert that he died quietly in a bed in Yucatan, in 1826; nevertheless, the story has come down that he died in a dare-devil engagement with a British war-sloop, his buccaneers cheering around him, his locks "matted with blood," the dagger in his swarthy hand streaming red.

* * * * *

There may have been three Lafitte brothers, but only two, Jean and Pierre, enter the story. One tradition has it that Jean was an adopted brother. Whether brothers by blood or adoption, never were two men more devoted to each other than Jean and Pierre. They appeared in New Orleans about the time of the Louisiana Purchase (1803). New Orleans in those days was French to the backbone, and—despite any Spanish blood that may have flowed in their veins—the Lafittes found themselves among their own kind. What they did upon arrival we know not. They apparently had money. Ere long they were the proprietors of a mighty blacksmith shop between Bourbon and Dauphine streets. It seems, however, that they never worked at the smithy themselves but had the work done by a corps of efficient slaves. Their real business was over on Barataria. Some old maps mark Barataria as "Smugglers' Retreat."

From New Orleans the Mississippi River sprangles out into the Gulf through a maze of bayous and interlocking lakes. To the west the great Bayou La Fourche sprawls gulfward through another maze of marsh and sluggish, twisting currents. Between the two is Barataria Bay. Curtaining off Barataria Bay from the Gulf is a sliver of an island called Grand Terre, sometimes Barataria. From Grand Terre to the coast the Bay is sprinkled with islands. A pass from the Gulf into the Bay gives entrance to a fine harbor on the main island.

* * * * *

The men who plied their piratical trade in this region, the Baratarians, as they were called, were a motley crew—Portuguese, French, Italian, Malay, adventurers from every nation. For a full and vivid picture of these highly interesting people there is only one place to go, though there are many places where one might go—a chapter upon them in *New Orleans, the Place and the People,* by Miss Grace King, who has, I think, blended literature and history more effectively than any other writer of the land where Lafitte's memory dwells. The Baratarians were not exactly pirates in the manner of the ship-scuttling and throat-slitting Blackbeard, Morgan, and L'Olonoise crews who more than a hundred years before had given to the Mexican waters their tradition of piracy. The days of the great pirates had waned. British warships had chased their successors into marshy holes of refuge. The Baratarians were privateers—licensed pirates.

The times were propitious to privateers. South America, Central America, Mexico were all seething with the yeast of revolt against Spain. The republic of Cartagena, a mere seaport of Colombia, was glad to issue letters of marque against Spanish shipping. France and, for a time, the United States were authorizing privateers to prey on English commerce. England, embroiled in the Napoleonic wars, had only limited forces to police the western seas. The naval power of America was a farce. Armed with their letters of marque and also with brass cannon and steel cutlasses, the Baratarians could sally forth from their snug refuge and thrive off Spanish merchantmen, with now and then a prize of some other nationality thrown in for lagniappe.

But the Baratarians needed a market for their plunder. Next door to them was New Orleans. Perhaps thirty thousand consuming human beings made up its population; it was the gateway to the commerce of the Mississippi valley. Most of the goods that the Baratarians had for sale could not be declared. It was not their manner to pay duty anyhow, and they sold cheap, as buyers from Memphis and Saint Louis as well as from New Orleans soon learned. The marshes and bayous afforded approaches that no revenue officer could ever follow. The citizens, almost without exception, were as friendly to the smugglers as was the secret land.

With plunder in hand and a market at their door, the Baratarians required an agent and banker. Jean Lafitte became that agent. He was an energetic and efficient business man. He spoke English, French, Spanish, and Italian fluently, if not correctly. He had a gift for making phrases. He had a conscience as elastic as any politician could wish for. Nature seemed to have designed him for agent to the Baratarians.

From agent to chieftain is only a step. Lafitte insisted upon two things: strict obedience and that word "privateer." He avoided the term "pirate" as a "mortician" avoids "undertaker." Once, according to an old story, a certain Grambo, who had known rougher days, hooted at the name, boldly declaring himself a pirate and calling upon his comrades to put down this genteel privateer who had come to rule over them. Lafitte pulled his pistol and shot Grambo through the heart. Thereafter his rule and his choice of diction were undisputed.

Early in 1813 certain American merchants and bankers of New Orleans became so alarmed over the loss of their legitimate business to the smugglers that they called on the naval authorities for help. The naval authorities sent out two minor expeditions that were successively put to flight. Then the merchants and bankers called on the state legislature. The legislature debated and declared that they had no funds. It was clear that Lafitte had friends. While the legislature was debating, he held at Barataria one public auction of 450 Negroes.

Meantime Governor Claiborne of Louisiana had proclaimed the Lafitte brothers to be "banditti and pirates," and had offered a reward of $500 for the arrest and delivery of Jean. Jean retaliated by offering a reward of $15,000 for the arrest and delivery of Claiborne to him! He continued to visit New Orleans when he pleased. He even dallied on the streets laughing and chatting with his friends while he leaned on a wall that placarded the governor's proclamation.

One day Claiborne's men captured Pierre and clapped him into jail. He soon escaped, but the federal grand jury brought an indictment. To fight the case Jean engaged the two best lawyers in Louisiana at a stipulated fee of $20,000 each. One of the lawyers was the district attorney, John R.

Grymes, who resigned his office to enter Lafitte's services. After the trial, which amounted to nothing, he was invited out to the "Pirates' Lair" to receive his fee. He stayed a week amid feast and revelry, and then "in a superb yawl laden with boxes of Spanish gold and silver" was returned to the mainland. "What a cruel misnomer it is," he declared upon returning, "to call the most honest and polished gentlemen the world ever produced bandits and pirates!" Only on the stage he had elected, at the time nature had destined him, could Lafitte have gestured so magnificently.

In 1812 the United States declared war on England. The British prepared to lay siege to New Orleans. In September, 1814, two English officers landed on Grand Terre and offered Jean Lafitte $30,000 in cash, a captaincy in the British navy, and a chance at enlistment for all his men provided he would aid in the proposed capture of New Orleans.

The British did not know Lafitte. He played for time. Then he informed the United States officials of what was brewing and offered his services in defense of the city. "Though proscribed by my adopted country," he wrote, "I never let slip any occasion of serving her or of proving that she has never ceased to be dear to me."

As a reply to such friendly advances Commodore Patterson of the United States Navy made an attack on the privateer stronghold and captured a large quantity of booty. Lafitte himself was away at the time; most of his men escaped and fortified themselves on Last Island.

Hickory-tough old Andrew Jackson was at Mobile when he heard of the British proposal and of Lafitte's offer. Forthwith he issued a thundering proclamation to the Louisianians in which he bitterly denounced the British for attempting to form an alliance with "hellish banditti." "The undersigned," he concluded with a flourish, "calls not upon pirates and robbers to join him in the glorious cause."

When he reached New Orleans, however, and saw the desperate need for more men, he came down off his high horse. These Baratarians were men of his own mettle. He placed Lafitte and his "hellish banditti" in charge of two important batteries. The battle was won, and in a general army order Old Hickory praised Lafitte and his captains as "gentlemen of courage and fidelity." President Madison issued a full pardon to all Baratarians who had taken part in the battle.

What Lafitte next did legend has been profuse in explaining. One story has him going to Washington and squandering $60,000 in gaudy living. A persistent story has him returning to Europe and in his own ship carrying Napoleon from Elba to France—and the Hundred Days' War that ended with Waterloo. The story goes on that Lafitte had even made arrangements to bring Napoleon to America and that he did bring a vast treasure belonging to the fallen emperor, which, of course, he properly buried. Impossible fictions!

Lafitte had become associated with Toledo, Herrera, Gutierrez, Peter Ellis Bean, Perry, and other adventurers who were seeking to overthrow Spanish rule in Mexico and establish an independent state in Texas. He now secretly engaged with Spanish agents to act as spy upon such filibusters and insurgents. Such an engagement, however, in nowise checked his privateering upon Spanish shipping. The record of his double-dealings from the time he landed on Galveston Island until he was driven away from it would make a steel windmill giddy.

It was along in 1816 when he began making a new Barataria at Galveston and, with Pierre to aid, resumed the old business of distributing "purchases"—goods and Negroes—to Louisiana buyers. To his American audience he announced that he had selected Galveston as headquarters, first, in order to be near the United States should that dear country again need his services; secondly, in order to further the cause of liberty in Mexico. To his Spanish masters he announced that he was going to collect in one place—Galveston—all the privateers infesting the Gulf so that they could be captured at one fell swoop. He seems to have collected them all right.

Galveston Island already had a history. At the time Lafitte arrived, Louis Aury, a Mexican "republican" soon to vacate, was using it as a base for smuggling slaves and pilfering ships. Here with a thousand men of mongrel breed under him, making and unmaking captains, Lafitte lived in his Maison Rouge like a lord in feudal splendor. An old French legend has it that the devil built Maison Rouge in a single night. In contracting with the devil for its erection, Lafitte agreed to give him the life and soul of the first creature he cast his eyes upon in the morning. Lafitte then contrived to have a dog pitched into his tent about daylight; so all the devil got out of the deal was a dog.

They called him "the Lord of Galveston island." He was at this time about forty years old, and is described as being exceedingly handsome, even noble in appearance. He had magnetism, charm, suavity, every quality necessary for one who would run innocently with the hare and at the same time bay lustily with the hounds. He seldom smiled, but he cultivated in a rare manner the art of being agreeable. He set an orderly table with abundance of plate, linen, and choice wines. Generally he went unarmed, but with a nose that sniffed the lightest wind of adversity he could be depended upon to appear at the right moment provided with a brace of pistols and a "boarding sword." When aroused, he was a desperate man indeed, and he was both an expert swordsman and an unerring shot.

On his lonely island, a wilderness of wild land behind it, a world of silent waters before it, "the Pirate of the Gulf" played host to a train of strange characters. Here—if report be true—came Peter Ellis Bean, who had mustanged in Texas with the filibuster Nolan, who had for six years somehow existed in a solitary cell of a Spanish prison, his only companion a pet lizard, and who had then secured his liberty in time to fight beside Lafitte at New Orleans. Here came "Old Ben" Milam, "war-born," who had also fought at New Orleans, who was to help Mexico throw off the Spanish yoke, and who was to meet his death leading the Texans into San Antonio. Doctor Long, who at the head of three hundred men had declared Texas a republic—this was years before Austin settled Texas with Americans—

came also, seeking Lafitte's aid in his enterprise. Lafitte was generous in giving "good wishes"—and at the same time reported him to Spanish authorities. Here, too, came half a thousand French refugees seeking an asylum, and Lafitte sent them up the Trinity River, where they established the short-lived and tragic Champ d'Asile—happily ignorant of their benefactor's plot to annihilate them. The savage Carankawas came to wonder and barter. Their visit ended in blood.

"Spanish doubloons," said a frontiersman whom Maison Rouge entertained, "were as plentiful as biscuits." Jim Campbell, one of Lafitte's lieutenants, who remained on to become a citizen of the Republic of Texas after his master had sailed away, used to tell how Galveston Bay, preceding any dangerous expedition, "was covered with boats seeking select places to bury treasures." Once from a rich haul, so the story goes, Lafitte took for his own share—though he usually received a "royal fifth"—only a delicate gold chain and seal that had been removed from the neck of a Spanish bishop on his way to Rome. He gave the chain to Rezin Bowie, brother of the famous James Bowie. The Bowies must have been visitors more than once, for we hear of their buying Negroes from Lafitte at a dollar a pound to smuggle into Louisiana. Another man who was to win a name in Texas, L. D. Lafferty, in his old age recalled clearly how in urging him to enlist as a buccaneer Lafitte "frankly confessed that he had enough silver and gold on the island to freight a ship."

* * * * *

In time an American warship put in to call on the Lord of Galveston. His letters of marque, furnished now by Mexican revolutionists, authorized him to prey, as usual, upon Spanish shipping; but his men frequently made no distinction in flags. To show his sentiment and patriotism, Lafitte had an offending pirate hanged on the seashore, and the warship departed. But the offense against American traders was soon repeated. Lieutenant Kearney, in command of a United States man-of-war, appeared one day in 1820 with polite orders that Lafitte abandon Galveston. Lafitte left forever. The rest is legend—mostly about pirate treasure.

Just before he sailed away, so one oft-told tale runs, some of Kearney's men saw him walking to and fro, apparently in great distress, and heard him muttering words about "my treasure" and "the three trees." The three trees were a well-known location on Galveston Island. The eavesdroppers stole thither and began digging in ground that had evidently been disturbed only a short time before. The earth was loose. They made fast time. Soon they struck a box. They dug it up. They tore it open. It contained the body of a beautiful girl, Lafitte's bride—his "treasure." Henry Ford was not the first man to regard history as "bunk."

For a thousand miles along the Gulf coast every inlet and island has its Lafitte treasure. Somebody is always searching for this treasure, and nearly always there is a legend of great detail and realistic circumstance to back up the search. Once or twice a year—of recent years more frequently perhaps than in the past—a newspaper item from some town in Texas or

Louisiana reports a hunt for Lafitte treasure; but the most ardent hunts are made in secret and the best tales never get into print. . . .

*　　*　　*　　*　　*

Like the man Lafitte, his treasures are uncertain, elusive, mysterious, Doubtless, too, most of the legends concerning them are, like many of those concerning Lafitte, without foundation. Yet there are few moments so potent to make a name remembered as its association with a great lost treasure. As long as Grand Terre and Galveston Island are above water, "Lafitte's Treasure" is likely to keep the name of Jean Lafitte green.

Mike Fink

I. THE HERO OF THE BOATMEN

. . . AMONG the most celebrated of these [boatmen] every reader of western history will at once remember Mike Fink, the hero of his class. So many and so marvellous are the stories told of this man that numbers of persons are inclined altogether to disbelieve his existence. That he did live, however, does not admit of a doubt. Many are yet living who knew him personally. As it is to him that all the more remarkable stories of western river adventure are attributed, his history will form the only example here given to illustrate the character of the western bargemen. It is, however, necessary to observe, that while Mike possessed all the characteristics of his class, a history of the various adventures attributed to him would present these characteristics in an exaggerated degree. Even the slight sketch here drawn cannot pretend to authenticity; for, aside from the fact that, like other heroes, Mike has suffered from the exuberant fancy of his historians, he has also had in his own person to atone to posterity for many acts which never came from under his hand and seal. As the representative, however, of an extinct class of men, his ashes will not rise in indignation even if he is again made the "hero of fields his valor never won."

Mike Fink was born in or near Pittsburg, where certain of his relatives still reside. In his earlier life he acted in the capacity of an Indian spy, and won great renown for himself by the wonderful facility with which, while yet a boy, he gained a knowledge of every act and movement of the foe. But while in the exercise of this calling, the free, wild and adventurous life of the boatmen attracted his youthful fancy, and the enchanting music of the boat-horn soon lured him away from Pittsburg to try his fortunes on the broad Ohio. He had learned to mimic all the tones of the boatman's horn, and he longed to go to New Orleans where he heard that the people spoke French and wore their Sunday clothes every day. He went,

From *The History of Louisville,* from Its Earliest Settlement till the Year 1852, by Ben Casseday, pp. 71–75, 77–79. Louisville, Kentucky: Hull & Brother. 1852.

and from an humble pupil in his profession soon became a glorious master. When the river was too low to be navigable, Mike spent his time in the practice of rifle-shooting, then so eminently useful and desirable an accomplishment; and in this, as in all his serious undertakings, he soon surpassed his compeers. His skill with the rifle was so universally acknowledged that whenever Mike was present at a Shooting-Match for Beef, such as were then of common occurrence all over the country, he was always allowed the fifth quarter, i.e., the hide and the tallow, without a shot. This was a perquisite of Mike's skill, and one which he always claimed, always obtained and always sold for whisky with which to "treat the crowd." His capacity as a drinker was enormous; he could drink a gallon in twenty-four hours without its effect being perceptible in his language or demeanor. Mike was a bit of a wag, too, and had a singular way of enforcing his jests. He used to say that he told his jokes on purpose to be laughed at, and no man should "make light" of them. The consequence was that whoever had the temerity to refuse a laugh where Mike intended to raise one, received a sound drubbing and an admonition for the future, which was seldom neglected.

II. Mike Fink and the Sheep

His practical jokes, for so he and his associates called their predations on the inhabitants of the shores along which they passed, were always characterized by a boldness of design and a sagacity of execution that showed no mean talent on Mike's part. One of the most ingenious of these tricks, and one which affords a fair idea of the spirit of them all, is told as follows: Passing slowly down the river, Mike observed a very large and beautiful flock of sheep grazing on the shore, and being in want of fresh provisions, but scorning to buy them, Mike hit upon the following expedient. He noticed that there was an eddy near to the shore, and, as it was about dusk, he landed his boat in the eddy and tied her fast. In his cargo there were some bladders of scotch-snuff. Mike opened one of these and taking out a handful of the contents, he went ashore and, catching five or six of the sheep, rubbed their faces very thoroughly with the snuff. He then returned to his boat and sent one of his men in a great hurry to the sheep-owner's house to tell him that he "had better come down and see what was the matter with his sheep." Upon coming down hastily in answer to Mike's summons, the gentleman saw a portion of his flock very singularly affected; leaping, bleating, rubbing their noses against the ground and against each other, and performing all manner of undignified and unsheeplike antics. The gentleman was sorely puzzled and demanded of Mike "if he knew what was the matter with the sheep."

"You don't know?" answered Mike very gravely.

"I do not," replied the gentleman.

"Did you ever hear of the black murrain?" asked Mike in a confidential whisper.

"Yes," said the sheep owner in a terrified reply.

"Well, that's it!" said Mike. "All the sheep up river's got it dreadful. Dyin' like rotten dogs—hundreds a day."

"You don't say so," answered the victim, "and is there no cure for it?"

"Only one as I knows on," was the reply. "You see the murrain's dreadful catchin', and ef you don't git them away as is got it, they'll kill the whole flock. Better shoot 'em right-off; they've got to die anyway."

"But no man could single out the infected sheep and shoot them from among the flock," said the gentleman.

"My name's Mike Fink!" was the curt reply.

And it was answer enough. The gentleman begged Mike to shoot the infected sheep and throw them into the river. This was exactly what Mike wanted, but he pretended to resist. "It mought be a mistake," he said; "they'll may be git well. He didn't like to shoot manny's sheep on his own say so. He'd better go an' ask some of the neighbors ef it was the murrain sure 'nuf." The gentleman insisted, and Mike modestly resisted, until finally he was promised a couple of gallons of old Peach Brandy if he would comply. His scruples thus finally overcome, Mike shot the sheep, threw them into the eddy and got the brandy. After dark, the men jumped into the water, hauled the sheep aboard, and by daylight had them neatly packed away and were gliding merrily down the stream.[1]

III. How Mike Fink Came to Court at Louisville

In all his little tricks, as Mike called them, he never displayed any very accurate respect to the laws either of propriety or property, but he was so ingenious in his predations that it is impossible not to laugh at his crimes. The stern vigor of Justice, however, did not feel disposed to laugh at Mike, but on the contrary offered a reward for his capture. For a long time Mike fought shy and could not be taken, until an old friend of his, who happened to be a constable, came to his boat when she was moored at Louisville and represented to Mike the poverty of his family; and, presuming on Mike's known kindness of disposition, urged him to allow himself to be taken, and so procure for his friend the promised reward. He showed Mike the many chances of escape from conviction, and withal plead so strongly that Mike's kind heart at last overcame him and he consented— *but upon one condition!* He felt at home nowhere but in his boat and among his men: let them take him and his men in the yawl and they will go.

It was the only hope of procuring his appearance at court and the constable consented. Accordingly a long-coupled wagon was procured, and with oxen attached it went down the hill at Third Street for Mike's yawl. The road, for it was not then a street, was very steep and very muddy at this point. Regardless of this, however, the boat was set upon the wagon, and Mike and his men, with their long poles ready, as if for an aquatic

---

[1] This incident is by some accredited to William Creasy, a bargeman of the James River.—B. C.

Cf. "Jim Girty's Beef Story," p. 213.

excursion, were put aboard, Mike in the stern. By dint of laborious dragging the wagon had attained half the height of the hill, when out shouted
the stentorian voice of Mike calling to his men—*Set Poles!* and the end
of every long pole was set firmly in the thick mud—*Back Her!* roared
Mike, and down the hill again went wagon, yawl, men, and oxen. Mike
had been revolving the matter in his mind and had concluded that it was
best not to go; and well knowing that each of his men was equal to a
moderately strong ox, he had at once conceived and executed this retro-
grade movement. Once at the bottom, another parley was held and Mike
was again overpowered. This time they had almost reached the top of the
hill, when *Set Poles—Back Her* was again ordered and executed. A third
attempt, however, was successful and Mike reached the court-house in
safety; and as his friend, the constable, had endeavored to induce him to
believe, he was acquitted for lack of sufficient evidence. Other indictments,
however, were found against him, but Mike preferred not to wait to hear
them tried; so, at a given signal, he and his men boarded their craft again
and stood ready to weigh anchor. The dread of the long poles in the hands
of Mike's men prevented the *posse* from urging any serious remonstrance
against his departure. And off they started with poles "tossed." As they
left the court-house yard Mike waved his red bandanna, which he had fixed
on one of the poles, and promising to *"call again"* was borne back to his
element and launched once more upon the waters.

Colonel Plug, the Wrecker

IN THIS little history, Mr. Audubon has said nothing of what was by far
the most "dangerous danger" to which the crews of these craft were exposed. This was the attack, open and fearless as well as sneaking and
treacherous, of the Boatwreckers. The country on both sides of the river
from Louisville to the mouth of the Ohio was an almost unpeopled wilderness. On the north side of the river from Fort Massac to the Mississippi,
there lived a gang of these desperadoes, whose exploits need only the
genius of a Schiller to render them the wonder of the world and the admiration of those who love to gloat over tales of blood. There was an impudence
and recklessness of life and of danger connected with these fellows, coupled
with a dash of spirit and humor, that would render them excellent *materiel*
in the hands of a skilful novelist; but they lacked that high sense of honor
and that gentlemanly bearing which made heroes of the robbers of the
Rhine, of Venice or of Mexico.

Their plan of action was to induce the crew of the passing "broad-horn"
to land, to play a game of cards (the favorite passion of the boatmen)
and to cheat them unmercifully. If this scheme failed, they would pilot the
boats into a difficult place, or, in pretended friendship, give them from

Ibid., pp. 67–71.

the shores such directions as would not fail to run them on a snag or dash them to pieces against some hidden obstruction. If they were outwitted in all this, they would creep into the boats as they were tied up at night, and bore holes in the bottom or dig out the caulking. When the boat was sinking, they would get out their skiffs and craft of all kinds, and in the most philanthropic manner come to save the goods from the wreck. And save them they did, for they would row them up the little creeks that led from swamps in the interior and no trace of them could afterwards be seen. Or if some hardy fellow dared to go in pursuit of his *saved* cargo, he was sure to find an unknown grave in the morasses.

One of the most famous of these boatwreckers was Col. Fluger of New Hampshire, who is better known in the West as Col. Plug. This worthy gentleman long held undisputed sway over the quiet boatwreckers about the mouth of Cash Creek. He was supposed to possess keys to every warehouse between that place and Louisville, and to have used them for his own private purposes on many occasions. He was a married man and became the father of a family. His wife's soubriquet was Pluggy and like many others of her sex, her charms were a sore affliction to the Colonel's peace of mind. Plug's lieutenant was by him suspected of undue familiarity with Mrs. Col. Plug. The Colonel's nice sense of honor was outraged, his family pride aroused—he called Lieutenant Nine-Eyes to the field.

"Dern your soul," said he, "do you think this sort of candlestick ammer [clandestine amour he meant] will pass. If you do, by gosh, I will put it to you or you shall put it to me."

They used rifles, the ground was measured, the affair settled in the most proper and approved style. And they did put it to each other. Each received a ball in some fleshy part, and each admitted that "he was satisfied."

"You are all grit!" said Col. Plug.

"And you waded in like a raal Kaintuck," rejoined Nine-Eyes.

Col. Plug's son and heir, who very possibly was the real subject-matter of dispute, and who was upon the ground, was ordered to place a bottle of whisky midway between the disputants. Up to this they limped and over it they embraced, swearing that "they were too well used to these things to be phazed by a little cold lead"; and Pluggy's virtue having been thus proved immaculate, the duel as well as the animosity of the parties ceased.

Col. Plug, man of honor as he was, sometimes met with very rough treatment from the boatmen, whose half savage natures could ill appreciate a gentleman of his birth and breeding. An instance of this is recorded by the same historian upon whom we have drawn for the greater part of the above account of the duel.[1] A broad-horn from Louisville had received rough usage from Plug's men the year before, and accordingly, on their next descent, they laid their scheme of revenge. Several of their crew left the boat before arriving at Plug's domain, and quietly stole down the river

---

[1] *Western Review* for January, 1830.—B. C.

bank to its place of landing. The boat with its small crew was quietly harbored, the men hospitably received and invited to sit down to a game of cards. They were scarcely seated and had placed their money before them, when Plug's signal whistle for an onset sounded in their ears. The reserve corps of boatmen also heard it, knew its import and rushed to the rescue. The battle was quickly over. Three of Plug's men were thrown into the river and the rest fled, leaving their brave commander on the field. Resistance did not avail him. Those ruthless boatmen stripped him to the skin, and forcing him to embrace a sapling about the size of his dear Pluggy's waist, they bound him immovably in this loving squeeze. Then seizing the cowhide each applied it till he was tired, and so they left him alone with his troublesome thoughts and with a yet more troublesome and sanguinary host of mosquitoes, which, lured by the ease with which they could now get a full meal of that blood which had before been effectually preserved from their attacks by a thick epidermis, sallied forth to the feast by myriads. Pluggy, finding her bower lonely without its lord, came forth to seek him. Closely embracing the tree and covered from any immodest exposure of his person by a gauzy cloud of mosquito wings, she found him. Clasping her hands, with a Siddons-like start and air, she cried, in her peculiarly elegant but somewhat un-English dialect: "Yasu Cree! O carissimo sposo, what for, like von dem fool, you hug zat tree and let ze marengoes eat up all your sweet brud?"

The historian is pained to record that all the answer she obtained to this tender solicitude was a curse. Plug cursed her, but Plug's evil spirit was aroused. Let the reader suppose himself in Plug's position and he will not blame that gentleman for the ungenerous reply that forced itself to his lips.

Not very long after this, Col. Plug came to his untimely end. Just as a squall was coming up, Col. Plug was in a boat whose crew had left it for an hour or so, engaged in the exercise of his profession; that is, he was digging the caulking out of the bottom, when the squall came on rather prematurely and broke the fastenings of the boat. It began to sink, and Col. Plug, after vain endeavors to reach the shore, sank with it and was seen no more. Whether Pluggy still bewails her lost lord or has followed him in sorrow to the other shore, history does not tell us.

Jim Girty

I. Jim Girty's Beef Story [1]

IT TOOK Jim Girty to show how to hook beef in flatboat times. On a trip up the Tennessee River, Jim and his crew got out of meat. They could

---

[1] From *The Spirit of the Times,* Vol. XVII (November 25, 1849), p. 473.

not think it fair play to be without meat in a cane country where there were so many fat cattle.

So, as usual, they selected the best and fattest beef they could find; they obtained one that weighed about seven hundred pounds. They dressed it neatly and took it on board. About three hours afterward, fourteen men came down to the boat with rifles, charging Jim with having stolen beef. Jim did not show fight. The crew paid no attention to what was going on; some were sitting on the running boards, with their feet dangling in the water; several were lying upon the deck on blankets—everyone seemed dull and stupefied. Jim was seated on the bow of the boat, his head resting on his hand, when again assailed.

"I say, your men have been stealing the best beef in all these parts."

"There must be some mistake," said Jim very quietly.

"You lie, your men were seen skinning it."

"There is strangers about there, maybe," said Jim.

"Yes, yes, we know there is strangers here, on this very boat—they have the beef on board, and we will have it off."

"The boat is open, go look for yourselves, gentlemen, but you will find a mistake, certain—but satisfy yourselves, gentlemen, on that head."

"That we will, and in an instant order have the beef."

So at it they went, first having placed three men as a guard, to see that the crew did not play some trick. The others made a search by rolling and rerolling everything in the boat, and still no beef was found. One fellow declared that they had left no place untouched where the fore-quarters of a cat could be hid, let alone a big ox.

The same gravity was preserved by Jim; he wished the gentlemen to be satisfied.

The fact was while the crew was skinning the beef one of them discovered a man watching him from behind a tree. They took no notice of it, but when they came to the boat, they told Jim that they were caught.

He scratched his head a while, and then prepared for just such a visit as he received.

He placed the four quarters of beef on the deck of the boat, and spread the hide over them; on this he spread all the blankets, and four men lay down on these blankets. Jim, as before stated, was on the bow of the boat, continually wishing "the gentlemen to be satisfied, but they would find a mistake, certain."

"Look about and be satisfied, gentlemen—look where you please and be satisfied, gentlemen; but there is one thing I must ask of you, not to disturb them-there sick men—we buried two yesterday, with smallpox, and them four are very sick—very sick indeed, gentlemen, and I must beg of you not to disturb them; it always is the worst thing you can do, to disturb a sick man, especially if he be near his last; it kind of makes the blood fly to the head, to be disturbed." But long before Jim closed his speech he had no listeners.

If ever there were pale faces, fallen jaws, and ghostly looks, among a set of men, it was about that time and place—they marched off without speaking a word. Jim got clear of his visitors, and kept the beef.

II. JIM GIRTY'S RIBS [2]

The spot [Natchez under the Hill] had its natural leaders. Best known was the bearded, immensely tough Jim Girty, who withstood fate and the knives through many years. Impressed citizens made folklore about him: He didn't have ribs like you and me, that you could shoot through or cut in. No, sir, he got thick bone like a man's head, only thicker. . . . So endowed, Jim ruled his roost. His woman, Marie Dufour, ran a bawdy house of good reputation. She kept it good; for Marie, a pink blond Amazon, could open a bottle with her teeth, and shoot off a man's nose at a hundred feet. Jim and Marie loved one another if only for their unchallenged strength and their cold scorn for the universe.

Eventually several individuals elected to test the belief about Jim's no-ribs. On a dark evening they ambushed him. Jim cursed and reached, but they had reached first. Guns exploded, girls screeched. Marie thrust forward, firing, and two of the men fell. But Big Jim was on the floor, and silent behind his beard. Marie turned him over, and his mouth sagged. He *had* had ribs, like anyone else. Moaning, Marie thrust her gun into her mouth and sent the bullet crashing through the top of her head. That evening, several places closed for the first time in years. There'd never be another Jim and Marie.

Harpe's Head

MICAJAH HARPE was the outlaw, par excellence, of the Ohio Valley, as Mike Fink was the rowdy. They are not typical; their deeds establish a high-water mark of brutality and rowdyism; others aped them, but none excelled. Harpe could hardly have borne a more fitting name, with all its revolting allusion to classic times. He was above medium stature, bony and muscular, powerful of limb, broad of chest—in short, of heroic mould. If he was extraordinary in physical strength, he was not less extraordinary in appearance; according to his biographers no man's face was more revolting. "Instead of the healthy hue which indicates the social emotions," writes Collins, "there was a livid unnatural redness, resembling that of a dried and lifeless skin. His face, which was larger than ordinary, exhibited the lines of ungovernable passion, and the complexion announced that the ordinary feelings of the human breast were in him extinguished."

When he entered the Ohio Basin, presumably from North Carolina, he was accompanied by his younger brother, Wiley Harpe, of less gigantic proportions but of hardly less revolting appearance. With them came three women, two of them the "wives" of the greater Harpe and one that of the lesser. At the opening of the story of their last and most desperate outrage the wives of the Harpes were living but a few miles from Henderson, Kentucky, on the Ohio River, and their husbands were journeying to them, preparatory to moving through Kentucky toward the South. Entering Hopkins County they passed through the wild region south of Green River in the guise of Methodist preachers, dressed in broadcloth coats, but well horsed and well armed. Stopping at the home of James Tompkins, near Steuben's Lick, they carried out their rôle to the end, one of them saying grace at the table with deliberation and at great length. Their host acknowledged that his powder-horn was nearly empty, whereupon the good Samaritans generously divided with him their supply. Proceeding on toward the Ohio River they passed the home of Moses Stigall, five miles on, and that of Peter Ruby, eleven miles from Stigall's. In a day or so they reached their wives and began the return journey with precipitation—undoubtedly planning deliberately to leave a broad trail of blood in their wake. Hon. Joseph R. Underwood leaves the following account of their journey, which he received in part from John B. Ruby, who saw the Harpes at the Ruby cabin on their way to the Ohio River:

They encamped for the night, a few miles from the residence of Stigall, who owed one of the women a dollar Stigall met the party in the flats of Deer Creek, as he was going to the Robinson Lick, north of the Ohio, for salt, and told the women to call on his wife, and tell her to pay the dollar. He said his wife did not know where he kept his money, and, accordingly, sent proper directions. One or all of the wives of the Harpes went to the house of Stigall, and told his wife what her husband had said. She found his purse, which contained about forty dollars in silver, out of which she paid the dollar due her. The wives told their husbands how much money seemed to be in the pile poured out of the purse. . . . Mrs. Stigall was a young woman with only one child. A man named Love was staying that night at the house. The two Harpes left their camp and went to the house . . . got the money, murdered the wife and child and Mr. Love; then set the house on fire, and burnt up the murdered bodies, and all that was in it. Two men named Hudgens and Gilmore were returning from the lick with their packs of salt, and had camped for the night not far from Stigall's. About daylight the Harpes went to their camp, and arrested them upon pretence that they had committed robbery, murder, and arson. . . . They shot Gilmore, who died on the spot. Hudgens broke and ran, but was overtaken . . . and put to death.

News of these murders spread . . . with rapidity. The conclusion was universal that these crimes were the deeds of the Harpes. Large rewards were offered by the Governors of Kentucky and Tennessee for their heads.

. . . The pioneers of the wilderness resolved to capture them. A company was formed, consisting of John Leeper, James Tompkins, Silas Magby, Nevil Lindsey, Mathew Christy, Robert Robertson, and the infuriated Moses Stigall. . . . These men, armed with rifles, got on the trail of the Harpes and overtook them at their camp, upon the waters of Pond River. . . . About a quarter of a mile from camp, the pursuing party saw Little Harpe, and a man named Smith . . . conversing near a a branch of water. Little Harpe charged Smith with being a horse-thief and blew in his charger —(a small implement with which the hunter measures his powder for loading his gun). The shrill sound, their usual signal for danger, soon brought Big Harpe to see what was the matter. . . . Big Harpe came mounted on a fine gray mare, the property of the murdered Love. . . . The pursuers, not doubting the guilt of those whom they had overtaken, without warning, fired upon them, badly wounding Smith, but not hitting either of the Harpes. Big Harpe was in the act of shooting Smith. . . . He had already cocked his gun and told Smith he must die. But surprised by the volley . . . he reserved his fire, whirled Love's mare and galloped off to his camp. Little Harpe ran off on foot into a thicket, and was not seen afterward.

The pursuers hastened toward the camp, and saw Big Harpe hastily saddling the horses and preparing to take the women with him. Seeing their rapid approach, he mounted Love's mare, armed with rifle and pistols, and darted off leaving the women and children to provide for themselves. They were made prisoners. . . . Love's mare was large and strong, and carried the two hundred pounds weight of her rider, Big Harpe, with much ease, and he seemed to call on her to expend all her strength in his behalf. Tompkins, rather a small man, rode a thoroughbred full-blooded bay mare of the best Virginian stock, and led in the pursuit. He had chased thieves before, and the only account he gave of *one* of them was, "that he would never steal another horse." Nance, his mare, exhibited both speed and bottom in this race for life or death. . . . In the first two or three miles Harpe kept far ahead, no one trailing in sight except Tompkins. There was no difficulty in following, through the rich mellow soil of the wilderness, the tracks made by the horses of Harpe and Tompkins. Leeper was second in the chase and the rest followed as rapidly as possible. As the race progressed, Big Harpe drove into a thick forest of large trees upon a creek bottom. As he approached the stream to cross it he encountered a large poplar tree . . . which had been blown down. . . . The bank was so high and perpendicular that it was impossible to descend and cross the creek with safety, and alike dangerous to attempt jumping over the tree. He retraced his steps to the head of the tree, and there met Tompkins face to face, with some thirty steps between them. Each reined up his steed and stopped. Neither attempted to fire. Tompkins told Harpe that escape was impossible, and he had better surrender. "Never" was the brief reply. Harpe dashed off at full speed, while Tompkins tarried for Leeper. As soon as he came up, he said: "Why didn't you shoot?" Tompkins replied that his mare was so fiery he could not make a safe shot upon her, and he would not fire unless he was sure of execution.

Leeper had fired upon the Harpes at the branch, and finding that his ramrod could not be drawn in consequence of its having got wet, told Tompkins he could not reload, that his horse was failing, and that Harpe would escape unless Nance should catch him. Tompkins replied: "She can run over him upon any part of the ground." Leeper said, "Let us exchange horses and give me your gun and shot-pouch, and I'll bring him down, if I can overtake him." They dismounted, exchanged horses and arms, and Leeper dashed forward after Big Harpe. The noble mare proved her ability to "run over him upon any part of the ground."

Leeper crossed the creek, and, after passing through the thick tall trees in the bottom, came in sight of the fleeing Harpe as he reached higher ground, with its prairie grass and scattered trees. Nance gradually gained. When Leeper came up within thirty yards, Harpe warned him "to stand off, or he would kill him." Leeper replied: "One of us has to die, and the hardest fend off." As the woods became more open and interposed fewer obstructions, Leeper thought he had "a good chance." Suddenly putting Nance to her full speed, he rushed up within ten steps of Harpe, threw his leg over the mane, and the bridle over Nance's head, jumped to the ground, took aim, and fired. Harpe reined up, turned, presented his gun, and it snapped—all without dismounting. Leeper afterwards said: "If Harpe's gun had not snapped, the ball would not have passed within twenty yards of me, so badly was it aimed." Harpe then threw his gun down, wheeled the gray mare, and pushed on his course. From these circumstances, Leeper knew he had hit him. He caught and remounted Nance, and soon overtook Harpe, who told him to keep off, or he would shoot him with a pistol. In a few seconds, Harpe ceased to urge the gray mare forward, and put both his hands to the pommel of the saddle to hold on. Leeper rushed alongside and threw him to the ground. Two balls had entered near his backbone; and come out near the breastbone. Harpe begged that he might be taken to justice and not be put to instant death. Leeper told him his request was useless; that his wound was fatal, and he must soon die. Tompkins and the other pursuers came up one by one. Stigall immediately presented his gun, with a view to blow his brains out; but Harpe moving his head backwards and forwards, so as to prevent it, Stigall placed the muzzle against his body as he lay on the ground, and shot him through the heart.

Thus perished the most brutal monster of the human race. His head was cut off by Stigall. . . . The party intended to use the head in getting the large rewards which had been offered . . . but the heat of summer rendered its preservation impracticable. A tall young tree, growing by the side of the trail or road, was selected, and trimmed of its lateral branches to its top, and then made sharp. On this point the head was fastened. The skull and jaw-bone remained there for many years. The place where this tree grew is in Webster County, and is known upon the map of Kentucky as "Harpe's Head" to this day.

This point is three miles from Dixon, Webster County, and some twenty miles back from the river at a point where the roads from Henderson, Morganfield, and Hopkinsville meet.

Samuel Mason

ONE of the most noted desperadoes of those early times was a man by the name of Mason. He first established himself at the "Cave in Rock"—a remarkable limestone formation about one hundred miles above the mouth of the Ohio—where, under the guise of keeping a store for the accommodation of boatmen and emigrants, he enticed them into his power. After murdering these victims of treachery, he would, by the hands of his confederates, send their boats to New Orleans for sale. He finally disappeared from his old quarters, and established himself on the great "trace" made through the wilderness of Mississippi and Tennessee by the flatboatmen and traders while returning, by land, from New Orleans to their homes in the West. Mason increased in power, and, with his organized band, became so celebrated for his robberies and murders that he was dreaded from the banks of the Mississippi to the high lands of Tennessee. Over all this vast extent of country, if the buzzards were seen high in the air, circling over any particular spot, the remark was made, "Another murder has been committed by Mason and his gang."

Numerous attempts were made to arrest him, but he always managed to escape. A romantic incident is related of one of these unsuccessful forays into his domain: A party of gentlemen, mostly wealthy planters from about the vicinity of Natchez, organized themselves into a party, and went in pursuit of the bold robber. Coming to the banks of Pearl River, "signs" were manifest that his camp was in the vicinity. Before attempting to make the proposed seizure, it was determined to rest the horses and partake of refreshments. These things having been accomplished, two of the party, seduced by the beauty and coolness of the stream, went in to bathe. In the course of their recreation they crossed to the opposite bank, and found themselves in the hands of Mason. The outlaw, aware that he was pursued, determined to effect by stratagem what he did not deem policy to effect by force. It was therefore that he rushed down and seized the two prisoners. The party on the opposite shore saw the manoeuvre, and instantly seized their arms. Mason, who had a commanding figure, admirably set off by a hunter's dress, presented a bold front, and announced that any further hostile demonstrations would result in instant death of his helpless captives. He then ordered his pursuers, if they desired to save the lives of their friends, to obey him implicitly and at once—that for the

From "Remembrances of the Mississippi," by T. B. Thorpe, *Harper's New Monthly Magazine*, Vol. XII (December, 1855), No. LXVII, p. 32. New York: Harper & Brothers, Publishers.

time being he was willing to negotiate for the safety of himself and men.
He then ordered the party to stack their arms and deposit their ammunition
on the beach, stating that he would send for them, but that [upon] any violence offered to his messenger or upon any visible hesitation to obey, he
should destroy his prisoners; if otherwise, they were to be set at liberty—
Mason pledging his *honor* that he would not take any advantage of his
victory.

There was no choice. The weapons were duly deposited as directed, and
two of Mason's gang, out of a number who had arrived, dashed into the
stream to take possession of them, the prisoners meanwhile standing in full
sight with rifles pointing at their heads. The desired property was finally
placed in the outlaw's possession, whereupon he released his prisoners, and
waving a good-humored farewell, he disappeared in the deep shadows of the
surrounding wilderness.

Treachery, however, at last effected what courage and enterprise could
not accomplish. A citizen of great respectability, passing with his two
sons through the forest, was plundered by the bandits; their lives, however, were spared. The public was aroused. Governor Claiborne, of the
Mississippi Territory, offered a large reward for the outlaw, dead or alive.
The proclamation was widely distributed—a copy reached Mason, and
was to him a source of intense merriment. Two of his band, however, were
determined to obtain the reward; and while they were engaged with Mason
in counting some money, one of them drove a tomahawk into his brain.
His head was severed from the body, and placed in a sack, borne in
triumph to Washington, then the seat of the Territorial Government.

The head of the robber was recognized by many of the citizens who saw
it. Large crowds from the surrounding country assembled to assure themselves that their enemy was really dead, and curious to see the individuals
whose daring prowess had relieved the country of a scourge. Among the
spectators were the two young men, who, unfortunately for the hero-
traitors, recognized them as the robbers of their father and themselves.
The wretches were seized, tried for their crimes, and hung. And thus ended
the last and most noted gang of robbers that infested the "Natchez and
Nashville trace." *

---

* One of these men was Wiley (Little) Harpe, who disappeared in 1799 (as related
in "Harpe's Head" above) and then became a member of Mason's gang under the
name of John Taylor or John Setton. " 'That's Harpe all right,' [several boatmen]
said. He denied it. But at last a man named John Bowman, from Knoxville, Tennessee, made identification absolute: 'If he's Little Harpe, he'll have a scar under the
left nipple of his breast, because I cut him there in a little difficulty we had, one night
at Knoxville.' Harpe, still bluffing, protested but they tore off his shirt: the scar was
there."—Robert M. Coates, *The Outlaw Years* (1930), pp. 162–163.

John A. Murrell's Own Story

I WAS born in middle Tennessee. My parents had not much property; but they were intelligent people; and my father was an honest man I expect, and tried to raise me honest; but I think none the better of him for that. My mother was of the pure grit: she learnt me and all her children to steal so soon as we could walk, and would hide for us whenever she could. At ten years old I was not a bad hand. The first good haul I made was from a pedlar who lodged at my father's house one night. I had several trunk keys, and in the night I unlocked one of his trunks and took a bolt of linen and several other things, and then locked the trunk. The pedlar went off before he discovered the trick; I thought that was not a bad figure I had made. About this time there was some pains taken with my education. At the age of sixteen I played a trick on a merchant in that country. I walked into his store one day, and he spoke to me very polite, and called me by the name of a young man who had a rich father, and invited me to trade with him. I thanked him, and requested him to put down a bolt of superfine cloth; I took a suit and had it charged to the rich man's son.

I began to look after larger spoils, and run several fine horses.—By the time I was twenty, I began to acquire considerable character as a villain, and I concluded to go off and do my speculation where I was not known, and go on a larger scale; so I began to see the value of having friends in this business. I made several associates; I had been acquainted with some old hands for a long time, who had gave me the names of some royal fellows between Nashville and Tuscaloosa, and between Nashville and Savannah, in the State of Georgia, and many other places. Myself and a fellow by the name of Crenshaw gathered four good horses, and started for Georgia. We got in company with a young South Carolinian just before we got to Cumberland mountain, and Crenshaw soon knew all about his business. He had been to Tennessee to buy a drove of hogs, but when he got there pork was dearer than he had calculated, and he declined purchasing. We concluded he was a prize. Crenshaw winked at me, I understood his idea. Crenshaw had travelled the road before, but I never had; we had travelled several miles on the mountain, when we passed near a great precipice; just before we passed it Crenshaw asked me for my whip, which had a pound of lead in the butt, I handed it to him and he rode up by the side of the South Carolinian, and gave him a blow on the side of the head and tumbled him from his horse; we lit from our horses and fingered his pockets; we got twelve hundred and sixty-two dollars. Crenshaw said he knew of a place to hide him, and gathered him under the arms and me by his feet,

From *A History of the Detection, Conviction, Life, and Designs of John A. Murel, The Great Western Land Pirate* [including his story as told to Virgil A. Stewart, alias Hues, who "detected" him], by Augustus Q. Walton, Esq., pp. 30–34, 41–46. Athens, Tenn.: Republished by G. White. 1835.

and conveyed him to a deep crevice in the brow of the precipice, and tumbled him into it, he went out of sight; we then tumbled in his saddle, and took his horse with us, which was worth two hundred dollars. We turned our course for South Alabama, and sold our horses for a good price. We frolicked for a week or more, and was the highest larks you ever saw. We commenced sporting and gambling, and lost every d——d cent of our money.

We was forced to resort to our profession for a second raise.—We stole a Negro man and pushed for Mississippi. We had promised him that we would conduct him to a free State, if he would let us sell him one time, as we went on the way; we agreed to give him part of the money. We sold him for six hundred dollars; but when we went to start, the Negro seemed to be very uneasy and appeared to doubt our coming back for him, as we had promised.—We lay in a creek bottom, not far from the place where we had sold the Negro all the next day, and after dark we went to the china tree, in the lane, where we were to meet Tom; he had been waiting for some time. He mounted his horse, and we pushed with him a second time. We rode twenty miles that night to the house of a friendly speculator. I had seen him in Tennessee, and had give him several lifts. He gave me his place of residence, so I might find him when I was passing. He is quite rich, and one of the best kind of fellows. Our horses were fed what they would eat, and two of them was foundered the next morning. We were detained a few days, and during that time our friend went to a little village in the neighborhood, and saw the Negro advertised, and a description of the two men, of whom he had been purchased; and giving his suspicions of the men. It was rather squally times, but any port in a storm; we took the Negro that night on the bank of a creek which runs by the farm of our friend, and Crenshaw shot him through the head. We took out his entrails, and sunk him in the creek; our friend furnished us with one fine horse, and we left him our foundered horses. We made our way through the Choctaw and Chickasaw nations, and then to Williamson county, in this State. We had made a d——d fine trip, if we had taken care of all we made.

* * * * *

My stock of cash was soon gone, and put to my shift for more. I commenced with horses, and run several from the adjoining counties; I had got associated with a young man who had got to be a circuit preacher among the Methodists, and a sharper he was; he was as slick on the tongue as goose grease. I took my first lessons in divinity from this young preacher. He was highly respected by all that knew him, and well calculated to please; he first put me in the notion of preaching to aid me in my speculation.

I got into difficulties about a mare that I had taken, and was imprisoned for near three years. I shifted it from court to court, but I was at last found guilty, and whipped. During my confinement I read the scriptures, and became a good judge of scripture. I had not neglected the criminal laws for many years before that time.—When they turned me loose I was prepared for any thing; I wanted to kill all but my own grit; and one of them I will die by his side before I will desert him.

My next speculation was in the Choctaw nation. Myself and brother stole two fine horses, and made our way into the Choctaw nation. We got in with an old Negro man and his wife and three sons to go with us to Texas, and promised them that if they would work for us one year after we got there, that we would let them go free, and told them many fine stories. We got into the Mississippi swamp, and was badly bothered to reach the bank of the river.—We had turned our horses loose at the edge of the swamp, and let them go to hell. After we reached the bank of the river we were in a bad condition, as we had no craft to convey us down the river, and our provisions gave out, and our only means for a support was killing varments and eating them. Eventually we found an Indian trail through the bottom, and we followed it to a bayou that made into the river, and we had the pleasure of finding a large canoe locked to the bank; we broke it loose and rowed into the main river, and were soon descending the river for New Orleans.

The old Negro man became suspicious that we were going to sell them, and became quite contrary. We saw it would not do to have him with us; so we landed one day by the side of an island, and I requested him to go with me around the point of the island to hunt a good place to catch some fish; after we were obscured from our company I shot him through the head, and then ripped open his belly and tumbled him into the river! I returned to my company and told them that the old Negro had fallen into the river, and that he never came up after he went under. We landed fifty miles above New Orleans, went into the country and sold our Negroes to a Frenchman for nineteen hundred dollars.

We went from where we sold the Negroes to New Orleans, and dressed ourselves like young lords. I mixed with the loose characters of the *swamp* every night. One night, as I was returning to the tavern where I boarded, I was stopped by two armed men, who demanded my money. I handed them my pocket book, and observed that I was very happy to meet with them, as we were all of the same profession. One of them observed, "d——d if I ever rob a brother-chip. We have had our eyes on you and the man that has generally come with you, for several nights: we saw so much rigging and glittering jewelry, that we concluded you must be some wealthy dandy, with surplus of cash, and had determined to rid you of the trouble of some of it; but if you are a robber, here is your pocket book, and you must go with us to-night, and we will give you an introduction to several fine fellows of the block—but stop, do you understand this motion?" I answered it, and thanked them for their kindness, and turned with them. We went to old mother Surgick's and had a real frolic with her girls. That night was the commencement of my greatness, in what the world calls villainy. The two fellows who robbed me, were named Haines and Phelps; they made me known to all the speculators that visited New Orleans; and gave me the name of every fellow who would speculate, that lived on the Mississippi river, and many of its tributary streams from New Orleans up to all the large western cities.

I had become acquainted with a Kentuckian, who boarded at the same tavern I did, and suspected he had a large sum of money; I felt an inclination to count it for him before I left the city; so I made my notions known to Phelps and my other new comrades, and concerted our plan. I was to get him off to the *swamp* with me on a spree, and when we were returning to our lodgings, my friends were to meet us and rob us both. I had got very intimate with the Kentuckian, and he thought me one of the best fellows in the world. He was very fond of wine; and I had him well fumed with good wine before I made the proposition for a frolic. When I invited him to walk with me, he readily accepted the invitation. We cut a few shines with the girls, and started to the tavern. We were met by a band of robbers, and robbed of all our money. The Kentuckian was so mad, that he cursed the whole city, and wished that it would all be deluged in a flood of water, so soon as he left the place. I went to my friends the next morning, and got my share of the spoil money, and my pocket book that I had been robbed of. We got seven hundred and five dollars from the bold Kentuckian, which was divided among thirteen of us.

I commenced travelling and making all the acquaintances among the speculators that I could. I went from New Orleans to Cincinnati, and from there I visited Lexington, in Kentucky. I found a speculator about four miles from Newport, who furnished me with a fine horse, the second night after I arrived at his house. I went from Lexington to Richmond, in Virginia, and from there I visited Charleston in the State of South Carolina; and from thence to Milledgville, by the way of Savannah and Augusta, in the State of Georgia. I made my way from Milledgville to Williamson county, the old stamping ground. In all the route I only robbed eleven men; but I preached some d——d fine sermons, and scattered some counterfeit United States' paper among my brethren.

*   *   *   *   *

After I returned home from the first grand circuit I made among the speculators, I remained at home a very short time, as I could not rest when my mind was not actively engaged in some speculation. I had commenced the foundation of this mystic clan on that tour, and suggested the plan of exciting a rebellion among the Negroes as the sure road to an inexhaustible fortune to all who would engage in the expedition. The first mystic sign which is used by this clan, was in use among robbers before I was born; and the second had its origin from myself, Phelps, Haines, Cooper, Doris, Bolton, Harris, Doddridge, Celly, Morris, Walter, Depont, and one of my brothers, on the second night after my acquaintance with them in New Orleans. We needed a higher order to carry on our designs, and we adopted the sign, and called it the sign of the grand council of the mystic clan; and practiced ourselves to give and receive the new sign to a fraction, before we parted: and in addition to this improvement, we invented and formed a mode of corresponding by means of ten characters, mixed with other matter, which has been very convenient on many occasions, and especially when any of us gets into difficulties. I was encouraged in my new undertaking, and my heart began to beat high with the hope of being able, one day, to visit the pomp of the southern and western people, in my vengeance; and of seeing their cities and towns one common scene of devastation, smoked walls and fragments.

I decoyed a Negro man from his master in Middle Tennessee, and sent him to Mills' Point by a young man, and I waited to see the movements of the owner.

He thought his Negro had run off. So I started to take possession of my prize. I got another friend at Mills' Point to take my Negro in a skiff and convey him to the mouth of Red River, and I took a passage on a steamboat. I then went through the country by land, and sold my Negro for nine hundred dollars, and the second night after I stole him again, and my friend run him to the Irish bayou in Texas; I followed on after him, and I sold my Negro in Texas for five hundred dollars. I then concluded to visit South America, and see if there was no opening in that country for a speculation; and I had concluded that I could get some strong friends in that country to aid me in my designs relative to a Negro rebellion. . . . I stopped in a village and passed as a doctor, and commenced practising medicine. I could ape the doctor first rate, having read Ewel, and several other works on primitive medicine. I became a great favorite of an old Catholic; he adopted me as his son in the faith, and introduced me to all the best families as a young doctor from North America. . . . I was soon on the road for home again; I stopped three weeks in New Orleans as I came on home, and had some high fun with old mother Surgick's girls.

I collected all my friends about New Orleans, at one of our friends' houses in that place, and we set in council three days, before we got all our plans to our notion; we then determined to undertake the rebellion at every hazard, and make as many friends as we could for that purpose. Every man's business being assigned him, I started to Natchez on foot; having sold my horse in New Orleans, with the intention of stealing another after I started; I walked four days, and no opportunity offered for me to get a horse. The fifth day, about twelve o'clock I had become very tired, and stopped at a creek to get some water, and rest a little. While I was sitting on a log, looking down the road the way I had come, a man come in sight riding a good looking horse. The very moment I saw him I was determined to have his horse, if he was in the garb of a traveller.—He rode up, and I saw from his equipage, that he was a traveller. I arose from my seat, and drew an elegant rifle pistol on him, and ordered him to dismount. He done so, and I took his horse by the bridle, and pointed down the creek, and ordered him to walk before me. We went a few hundred yards and stopped. I hitched his horse, then made him undress himself all to his shirt and drawers, and ordered him to turn his back to me; he asked me if I was going to shoot him. I ordered him the second time to turn his back to me.

He said, "If you are determined to kill me, let me have time to pray before I die." I told him I had no time to hear him pray. He turned round and dropped on his knees, and I shot him through the back of the head. I ripped open his belly and took out his entrails, and sunk him in the creek. I then searched his pockets, and found four hundred and one dollars and thirty-seven cents, and a number of papers that I did not take time to examine. I sunk the pocket book and papers, and hat in the creek. His boots were brand new, and fit me very genteel, and I put them on, and sunk my old shoes in the creek to atone for them. I rolled up his clothes and put them into his portmanteau, as they were brand new cloth, of the best quality. I mounted as fine a horse as ever I straddled, and directed my course for Natchez in much better style than I had been for the last five days.

I reached Natchez, and spent two days with my friends at that place, and the girls under the hill together. I then left Natchez for the Choctaw Nation, with the intention of giving some of them a chance for their property. As I was riding along, between Benton and Rankin, planning for my designs, I was overtaken by a tall and good looking young man, riding an elegant horse: which was splendidly rigged off; and the young gentleman's apparel was of the richest that could be had, and his watch chain and other jewelry were of the richest and best. I was anxious to know if he intended to travel through the Choctaw Nation, and soon managed to learn. He said he had been to the lower country with a drove of Negroes, and was returning home to Kentucky. We rode on, and soon got very intimate for strangers, and agreed to be company through the Indian Nation. We were two d——d fine looking men, and to hear us talk we were very rich. I felt of him on the subject of speculation, but d—n it, how he cursed the speculators, and said that he was in a bad condition to fall into the hands of such d——d villains, as he had the cash with him that twenty Negroes had sold for; and that he was very happy that he had happened to get in company with me through the nation. I concluded that he was a noble prize, and longed to be counting his cash. At length we came into one of those long stretches in the nation, where there was no house for twenty miles, on the third day after we had been in company with each other. The country was high, hilly, and broken, and no water; just about the time I reached the place where I intended to count my companion's cash, I became very thirsty, and insisted on turning down a deep hollow, or dale, that headed near the road, to hunt some water. We had followed down the dale for near four hundred yards, when I drew my pistol and shot him through. He fell dead. I commenced hunting for his cash, and opened his large pocket book that was stuffed very full, and when I began to open it, I thought it a treasure indeed; but, Oh! the contents of that book; it was filled with the copies of songs, the forms of love letters, and some of his own composition—but no cash. I began to cut off his clothing with my knife, and examine them for his money. I found four dollars and a half in change, in his pockets, and no more. And is this the amount for which twenty Negroes sold, thought I. I recollected his watch and jewelry, and I gathered them: his chain was rich and good, but it was swung to an old brass watch. He was a puff for true; and I thought all such d——d fools ought to die as soon as possible. I took his horse, and swapped him to an Indian native for four ponies, and sold them on the way home. I reached home, and spent a few weeks among the girls of my acquaintance, in all the enjoyments that money could afford.

My next trip was through Georgia, South Carolina, North Carolina, Virginia and Maryland, and then back to South Carolina, and from there round by Florida and Alabama. I began to conduct the progress of my operations, and establish my emissaries over the country in every direction. After I turned for home from Alabama, I was passing by where one of my friends lived, in company with three of my associates, who were going home with me; we stopped to see how our friend was doing; while we were sitting out in his portico, there was a large drove of sheep came up to his blocks. He went out and examined them, and found them to be the flock of an old Baptist, who lived about six miles up the road from his house, and they had been gone from their owner for three months, and he could hear nothing of them. The old Baptist had accused my friend of having his sheep drove off to market, and abused him for stealing his sheep very much. My friend acquainted me with the circumstance, and I concluded to play a trick on the old jockey for his suspicions, so we gathered up all the flock, and drove them on before us, and got to the old Baptist's just after dark; we called the old man out to the gate, and wanted to lodge with him all night; but he refused to take us in, and urged as a reason, that his old woman was sick, and he could not accommodate us as he would wish. To these objections I told him that we could wait on ourselves—that I had three active young men with me, who could do all that was wanting to be done. I told him that I had moved down below in the spring of the year, when my sheep was scattered, and I concluded to leave them until fall; and that I had been up to my old place after them, and was going home: and complained of the hard drive I had made that day, as an excuse to stop with the old Baptist. I then told him I had a very fine wether that I wished to kill, as he was very unruly, and hard to drive, and what we did not use that night he was welcome to. The old man shewed us a lot to pen our sheep, and the corn crib and stables, and told us that if we could wait on ourselves that we were welcome to stay. We soon fed our horses, and had the mutton dressed, and a large pot full cooking.—The old man told us where to find meal, milk and butter; and while my associates were cooking the sheep, I was conversing with the old Baptist on religion; I told him I was a Baptist preacher. When news came that the sheep was done, I went into the kitchen, and we had a real feast of mutton, at the expense of the old Baptist.

After supper we went in where the old lady was lying sick. The old man got his bible and hymn book, and invited me to go to duty. I used the books, and then prayed like hell for the recovery of the old lady. The next morning we were up before day-light, and had the sheep all on the road.

We drove them about one mile, and scattered them in the woods, and left them.

We left the head of the wether that we killed lying in the lot where the old man could see that it was his own mark. I arrived at home after a trip of six months.

I have been going ever since from one place to another, directing and managing, but I have others now as good as myself to manage. This fellow, Phelps, that I was telling you of before, he is a noble fellow among the Negroes, and he wants them all free; and he knows how to excite them as well as any person: but he will not do for a robber, as he cannot kill a man unless he has received an injury from him first; he is now in jail at Vicksburgh, and I fear will hang. I went to see him not long since: but he is so strictly watched, that nothing can be done. He has been in the habit of stopping men on the high-way and robbing them, and letting them go on; but that will never do for a robber: after I rob a man he will never give evidence against me; and there is but one safe plan in the business, and that is to kill.—If I could not afford to kill a man I would not rob. I have often told Phelps he would be caught before he knew it. I could raise men enough to go and tear down the jail, and take Phelps by force; but that would endanger all of our other plans. I have frequently had money enough to have settled myself rich; but I have spent it as free as water in carrying on my designs. The last five years of my life have been spent in the same way that I have been telling you, Hues: I have been from home the best part of the time; and I have let but few chances escape me, when I could rob, that I did not do it. It would take a week, Hues, to tell over all of my scrapes of that kind. You must come and stay at my house the week before I start with them Negroes to Irvin, and I will have time to tell over all my ups and downs for the last five years. I want you to go that trip with me. You can arrange your business in the nation in two weeks, and get to my house in Madison County. You will make more that trip than all your concerns are worth in the nation, so you had better give away what you have than to be confined to it.

Annie Christmas

ALONG the colorful water front of New Orleans, and up the river even as far as Natchez, Mississippi, folks talk a great deal about a strange woman. Though they say she's been dead for some time, rivermen still measure strength by her standards.

"He's almost as strong as Annie Christmas," they say about men who have done superhuman things.

From *The Hurricane's Children,* Tales from Your Neck o' the Woods, by Carl Carmer, pp. 103–109. Copyright, 1937, by Carl Carmer. New York and Toronto: Farrar & Rinehart, Inc.

For Annie Christmas weighed two hundred and fifty pounds, stood six-foot-eight barefooted, wore the largest and most beautifully curled mustache along the entire river, and was more powerful than any riverman who ever lived.

Annie Christmas could carry three barrels of flour at once, one balanced on her head and one under each arm. When the river got high one spring and was about to flood the country above New Orleans, Annie Christmas prevented the disaster by throwing up a new and higher levee all by herself in one day.

One time she wanted to get a loaded flatboat from New Orleans up the river to Natchez in a hurry—so she just grabbed the towline and set out on a dead run. They say the bottom of that flatboat scarcely touched the water on the entire trip. The captain just leaned back in his chair and tried to make his fiddle sound like a mockin' bird, and the crew amused themselves by making bets with the river gulls about who would get to the next bend the quickest.

Annie Christmas was a great fighter, too. When she knew she was going to have a fight, she dressed in men's clothes and trimmed her long curling mustache close, so that it wouldn't offer anybody a good hold. She licked the daylights out of every bully on the lower river and, they say, Mike Fink, the champion fighter of the Ohio Valley, never came to New Orleans again after she sent him word that if he showed up in Louisiana once more she would have him poled back up the river lashed to the keel of his keelboat.

Annie wore a bead necklace when she was all dressed up and looking pretty. It had a bead in it for every ear or nose she'd chawed off and every eye she'd gouged out in her fights. When she died it was thirty feet long.

Annie had just one weakness—a gamblin' man named Charlie. Charlie had a curvin' mustache that was even longer and shinier than Annie's, and he wore waistcoats that would put your eye out. Annie was in love with Charlie for a long time before he'd have anything to do with her, but he finally gave in and married her, and the next year she presented him with twelve sons all at once, and before they were six years old every one of them was over seven feet tall.

One night Charlie went to a gambling hall in New Orleans—on Tchoupitoulas Street—and began to play roulette. He put a quarter on red, leaned his head on his hand, and watched the little ball finally come to rest. Red won. Charlie never moved—just let his money ride. Red won again, and again. After it had won five times straight, Charlie's friends begged him to stop while he was so far ahead. He was bound to lose sooner or later, they said. But Charlie paid no attention—just sat there with his head on his hand and not moving a muscle. When red had won for the sixteenth time and Charlie was over eight thousand dollars ahead, the croupier announced that the house would not play with him any longer and ordered him to leave. Charlie didn't move. The croupier pushed him and Charlie fell out of his chair to the floor. He had been dead for some time. The house had been playing against a dead man—and the dead man had won. When Annie Christmas found out that Charlie was dead she was inconsolable. She gave him a very grand funeral and spent most of the eight thousand Charlie had won on it. Then she put on her thirty-foot necklace, her black silk dress, gave instructions to her twelve sons, and shot herself. The sons did what their mother told them to. They put their mother's body in a coal-black coffin and loaded it in a coal-black hearse drawn by sixteen coal-black horses. Then, six on each side, clothed in coal-black suits, they walked beside the hearse as the horses slowly rolled it down to the river. A coal-black barge waited there and they put the coffin on it. At midnight, in the dark of the moon, they cut the coal-black moorings and Annie Christmas with six seven-foot sons on either side of her drifted down the river and out to sea, never to be seen again. And as they floated downstream between the levees, folks living near the river heard a strange mournful tune rising in the air. The tallest of her sons was singing a last song for Annie Christmas.

George Devol: Mississippi River Gambler

I. A Woman with a Gun

I was on a boat coming from Memphis one night, when my partner beat a man out of $600, playing poker. After the game broke up, the man went into the ladies' cabin and told his wife. She ran into his room and got his pistol, and said, "I will have that money back, or kill the man." I saw her coming, pistol in hand, and stepped up to the bar and told the barkeeper to hand me that old gun he had in the drawer, which I knew had no loads in it. She came on, frothing at the mouth, with blood in her eyes. I saw she was very much excited, and I said to her: "Madame, you are perfectly right. You would do right in shooting that fellow, for he is nothing but a gambler. I don't believe your pistol will go off; you had better take my pistol, for I am a government detective, and have to keep the best of arms." So I handed her the pistol, and took hers. Just a moment later out stepped the man who had won the money, and she bolted up to him and said: "You won my husband's money, and I will just give you one minute to hand it to me, or I will blow your brains out in this cabin." Well, you ought to have seen the passengers getting out of the cabin when she pulled down

From *Forty Years a Gambler on the Mississippi*, A Cabin Boy in 1839; Could Steal Cards and Cheat the Boys at Eleven; Stock a Deck at Fourteen; Bested Soldiers on the Rio Grande during the Mexican War; Won Hundreds of Thousands from Paymasters, Cotton Buyers, Defaulters, and Thieves; Fought More Rough-and-Tumble Fights than Any Man in America, and Was the Most Daring Gambler in the World, by George H. Devol, pp. 27, 145–146, 267–269. Second Edition. Entered according to Act of Congress, the 6th Day of October, 1887, by George H. Devol, in the Office of the Librarian of Congress at Washington, D. C. New York: George H. Devol. 1892.

on him; but he knew the joke and stood pat, and showed what a game fellow he was. He told the woman her husband lost the money gambling, and he could not get a cent back. Then she let go; but the pistol failed to go off, and he got her to go back into the cabin, and pacified her by giving her $100. After taking the charges out of her pistol, I returned it to her. So, reader, you can see what a gay life there is in gambling.

II. THE PERSUADER

Bluff is a good game, and sometimes it will turn a trick when everything else fails. I boarded Morgan's Railroad, as it was called, upon one occasion at Algiers. Trains on that road were generally full of suckers, as the road connected with the Galveston steamers at Burwick's Bay. Tom Brown and Holly Chappell, my partners, were both along; and as game was plenty along the road, we carried our shotguns along, and in the event of no bigger game were accustomed to get off and shoot snipe, catching the return train to the city in the evening. Sure enough, there was a party of traders aboard, and Brown lost no time in making their acquaintance and opening out. One of them commenced to cut his clothes the minute he got a glimpse of the corner after Chappell made one cap. To make matters more binding, I came up and lost $1,200. Then the ball opened, and it was not more than half an hour before we had downed the party. Then the devil was to pay. One of the party said: "Look here; I must have my money back, or h——l will flop around here mighty quick." Then they all joined in and made a big kick; and as I saw fun brewing, I slipped into the baggage-car, changed hats and coats with the baggage-master, got his badge and my double-barrelled shotgun. Then I rushed into the car and drew the bead on the party who had collected around the boys, giving a war-whoop and demanding in stentorian tones, "Who has been playing cards in this car?"

"I have," said Brown.

"Get off this train mighty quick"; and I pulled the rope. My partners lost no time in getting off. Pulling the rope again, the train started; and when the conductor came back, I explained that somebody would have been hurt, had I not acted as I did. This was satisfactory, and going back he told the party that gambling on the road was against the rules, and that he could have them all arrested when the bay was reached, if he wished. This had the effect of quieting them down, especially as they knew that the man who had won their money was off the train. I was not long in reaching the baggage-car and returning the borrowed articles, and quietly slipping off at the first station, not forgetting my shotgun. Hunting was good that day, and I bagged ten snipe and thirteen robins, which the boys helped me eat at our old friend Cassidy's restaurant, on Gravier Street, opposite the St. Charles Hotel. The boys all agreed that my conduct was all that saved the boodle, which consisted of $3,300 and two gold watches. Thus it is that a little management, backed by a double-barrelled shotgun and an official badge, is oftentimes a powerful persuader.

III. George the Butter

In most all of the many fights that I have been engaged in, I made use of what I have called "that old head of mine." I don't know (and I guess I never will while I'm alive) just how thick my old skull is; but I do know it must be pretty thick, or it would have been cracked many years ago, for I have been struck some terrible blows on my head with iron dray-pins, pokers, clubs, stone-coal, and boulders, which would have split any man's skull wide open unless it was pretty thick. Doctors have often told me that my skull was nearly an inch in thickness over my forehead. They were only guessing at it then, of course, but if my dear old mother-in-law don't guard my grave, they will know after I am dead, sure enough, for I have heard them say so.

For ten or fifteen years during my early life, the sporting men of the South tried to find a man to whip me, but they couldn't do it, and finally gave it up as a bad job. After they gave up trying to have me whipped, and they knew more about my old head, they would all go broke that I could whip or kill any man living, white or black, by butting him. I have had to do some hard butting in my early days, on account of the reputation I had made for my head.

I am now nearly sixty years of age, and have quit fighting, but I can to-day batter down any ordinary door or stave in a liquor barrel with "that old head of mine"; and I don't believe there is a man living (of near my own age) who can whip me in a rough-and-tumble fight. I never have my hair clipped short, for if I did I would be ashamed to take my hat off, as the lines on my old scalp look about like the railroad map of the State in which I was born.

During the winter of '67 or '68, John Robinson's circus was showing in New Orleans, and they had with them a man by the name of William Carroll, whom they advertised as "The man with the thick skull, or the great butter." He could outbutt anything in the show, except the elephant. One night after the show, Al and Gill Robinson were up town, and their man Carroll was with them. We all met in a saloon and began drinking wine. While we were enjoying ourselves, something was said about butting, when Gill spoke up and said Carroll could kill any man in the world with his head. "Dutch Jake," one of the big sporting men of New Orleans, was in the party, and he was up in an instant, and said:

"What's that? I'll bet $1,000 or $10,000 that I can find a man he can't kill or whip either."

I knew what was up; and as we were all friends, I did not want to change the social to a butting match, so I said:

"Boys, don't bet, and Mr. Carroll and I will come together just once for fun."

The Robinson boys had great confidence in Carroll, and so did "Dutch Jake" have in me. I was at least fifty pounds heavier than Carroll, and I knew that was a great advantage, even if his head was as hard as my own. It was finally agreed that there would be no betting, so we came together. I did not strike my very best, for I was a little afraid of hurting the little fellow; but then he traveled on his head, so I thought I could give him a pretty good one. After we struck, Carroll walked up to me, laid his hand on my head, and said:

"Gentlemen, I have found my papa at last."

He had the hardest head I ever ran against; and if he had been as heavy as I was, I can't say what the result would have been if we had come together in earnest.

Poor fellow! He is dead now, and I know of no other man with as hard a head, except it is myself. My old head is hard and thick, and maybe that is the reason I never had sense enough to save my money. It is said of me that I have won more money than any sporting man in this country. I will say that I hadn't sense enough to keep it; but if I had never seen a faro bank, I would be a wealthy man to-day.

Quantrell, the Guerrilla

I. THE BLACK FLAG [1]

THE idea seems to obtain in many sections that Quantrell, the Youngers, the James boys and Kit Dalton were a gang of outlaws whose sole object in life was to prey indiscriminately on such corporations as were best prepared to furnish booty worthy of our enterprises and to kill all who opposed our undertakings.

Nothing could be more ridiculous. Quantrell was never an outlaw, but a soldier whose genius and energy in behalf of the Southern people made the world ring with his daring exploits. He fought under the black flag for a while, but not then till he had been driven to these desperate measures by a public proclamation issued by Major Blunt to the effect that all persons caught bearing arms against the United States of America would be summarily executed. This order is responsible for the birth of the black flag and though many weird tales have been told concerning the sable pennant, they are all fabrications, for after we had raised the black flag we paroled our captives just the same, and in this we were put at a great disadvantage, for whenever any of our men were captured they were executed as traitors. The object of the black flag in our ranks was more to intimidate the enemy than anything else, as it never carried out its

---

[1] From *Under the Black Flag*, by Captain Kit Dalton, A Confederate Soldier, a Guerrilla Captain under the fearless leader Quantrell, and a Border Outlaw for seventeen years following the surrender of the Confederacy. Associated with the most noted band of freebooters the world has ever known, pp. 70–71. [Copyright, 1914.] Memphis, Tennessee: Lockard Publishing Company.

threats, but it did let the enemy know we were not using war as a pastime and that when we met them it was our intention to fight to the death. This is about all there is to the black flag matter. It caused the enemy to stand up and fight like men or run like cowards.

That is the only kind of an outlaw Quantrell was.

Now, as to the rest of us, it's different. We were outlaws. There's no gainsaying that. Our living depended on our acts as lawless men. We had no other means of obtaining our meat and bread. But our lives as outlaws are wholly separate from our lives as soldiers, though there was no material difference in our conduct. We preyed on the enemy during the war, while the enemy preyed on us then, and have kept it up ever since with that iniquitous pension roll.

The government raised the black flag over us and by this act told us it did not think we would make model prisoners, and for this reason they preferred capturing our dead bodies to our living ones. They could bury the dead out of their sight, but our living bodies they would be compelled to feed until they could get the scaffold ready for our execution.

Now, I trust the reader will keep it well in mind that while we were fighting the innumerable battles of the West we fought them as patriotic soldiers —fighting for the Southern cause—for what we thought our duty to our country and our firesides. These are the battles I am relating and are wholly segregated from those acts of lawlessness which were enacted after Appomattox, and all who bore arms against the Federal government had been permitted to lay down their arms and return to the peaceful pursuits of life—all but us, who had fought the Western battles and fought them with a ferociousness not equalled in any warfare in the history of the world. These are the battles I am relating—the battles of the few against the many.

II. QUANTRELL'S BEGINNINGS [2]

Charles William Quantrell was a Marylander. . . . I do not know the date of his birth, but I judge he was about 30 years old when the war broke out. At this time he was a school teacher in Jackson or Clay County, Missouri. Don't know what sort of a teacher he was, but if his efforts were directed towards "Teaching the young how to shoot," I should judge from the sequence that he was eminently successful. He also taught school in Kansas at one time, and it may have been the results of a willow sprout in his strong right hand that created so many Kansas *Red Legs*.

Having become inoculated with the virus of western fever, Quantrell and his brother started out in a covered wagon for Colorado, but had not gotten out of the borders of Kansas when a horrible tragedy was enacted which changed the whole course of his life. The two wayfarers had pitched camp near a little rivulet and were spread out on their heavy blankets for

[2] *Ibid.*, 241–243.

rest and sleep when thirty Kansas Red Legs and highwaymen swooped down upon them with no other purpose in view than murder, pillage, and plunder. At the first onslaught the brother was instantly killed and William was thought by the assassins to have been in the same fix, for his body was riddled with bullets and he fell across the body of his dead brother. The robbers took possession of the team and the whole outfit of the murdered brothers, and leaving them for dead, took their loot and were preparing to move on when one of the number discovered that dead bodies needed no blanket on which to rest, wherefore he called to his comrades and taking hold of two corners of the blanket, rolled their victims off on the wet ground, folded up the couch of the dead and resumed their journey.

It was not until broad daylight the next morning when William regained consciousness, and for three days he lay there nearer dead than alive, using what small energy he had in an almost vain endeavor to keep the buzzards off of his dead brother.

It was late in the afternoon of the third day when William heard the voice of an Indian in the distance calling to his missing dog. By superhuman effort he raised his feeble voice in a wail of distress. The Indian heard him and came straight away to investigate. The awful sight which met the old savage's eye touched his tough heart with pity and without ceremony he bundled up the wounded man and bore him to his cabin on the distant prairie.

For four months Quantrell remained a welcome guest of the Indian, who had busied himself the while in trying to locate the assassins. He finally struck a warm trail and located them at last in Lawrence, Kansas. He knew them by the wagon and team they had taken from their victims. After several days' quiet investigation, the Indian succeeded in getting the names of the thirty murderers and brought them to Quantrell.

As soon as Quantrell was able to mount a horse he went in pursuit of the robbers and he never ceased in his efforts to wipe them off the face of the earth till his own unhappy career was brought to a tragic close on Wakefield Farm.

Quantrell told me a few days before his death that he had the grim satisfaction of knowing beyond the question of a doubt that he had killed twenty-seven of the thirty.

A more polished gentleman, a truer friend, a braver soldier nor a more daring scout never lived in any age of the world.

I have related the time and place of his death in the records. But to make it plainer to you, he was killed on Wakefield Farm in Prentiss county, Kentucky, in 1865.

III. SKIRMISHES IN MISSOURI [8]

A few months following the Lawrence "atrocity" we were in the vicinity of Fort Webster, when Quantrell got news that Adjutant General Curtis

---

[8] *Ibid.,* 107–110.

would pass that way the next day with a band of musicians, troubadours, cooks, flunkeys and other "Northern army accessories" on his way to Independence, and he forthwith made ready to take possession of the caravan. We came upon them about six miles from Fort Webster, and after a little skirmish, overpowered and captured them.

Curtis was literally scared out of his wits and piteously begged Quantrell to spare his life.

"Would you dare ask mercy of me?" asked Quantrell, as he took from his pocket a paper and, unfolding it, showed Curtis his own order to kill Quantrell's men wherever and whenever they could be found. "Is not that your order?" shrieked Quantrell.

"I was forced to issue the order," whined the craven hearted wretch. "It was an order from headquarters."

"It is no such thing," said Quantrell. "Had it been from the Federal government, it would have been so worded. This is your infamous work, Curtis, and you've got to answer to me for it right here and now. I am going to kill you, sir, and I advise you not to appear before your maker with a lie on your lips. Now, sir; is not this your original order?"

Curtis hung his head for a moment, as if in prayer, and seeing death was inevitable, he said, with a sigh: "Yes, it is my work."

"And you wanted it obeyed, of course?"

"Yes."

"Would you have practiced the doctrine you preached, had the opportunity offered?"

"Yes, such are the fortunes of war."

"And you expect mercy at my hands?"

"No, nothing but death."

He was not disappointed.

With Curtis and his band of merrymakers was a Mr. O'Neill, an artist on Leslie's Magazine. He had in his possession an unfinished picture of some hypothetical battle, in which were portrayed Rebels in full flight before the gallant boys in blue, who were mowing them down in merciless abundance with rifles, pistols, swords and bayonets. Oh, our boys in gray were certainly having a tough time in that "Battle Scene." Poor O'Neill. It was his own Waterloo he had so graphically portrayed for the edification of the foulest periodical of that day and generation.

But Leslie's was not cheated out of the picture. Quantrell sent it in with these memorable words written in his own bold hand:

"O'Neill's last contribution to Leslie's, sent in by Quantrell, with regrets that the artist's physical condition was such that he could not attend to the matter in person."

I have no doubt that the picture is now somewhere in the old junk heaps of this illustrious periodical, and I sincerely trust that Leslie's has, by this time, come to look on the South as a considerable part of the Federal government.

Poor troubadours, they had twanged the last cord for the merriment of Northern audiences. Poor cooks, they had baked their last pone of bread for camp or festal board. Poor soldiers, they had for the last time tented on the old camp ground. Poor Curtis, he had lost his head—one of his most valuable possessions—also a magnificent silk banner, presented him by the worthy ladies of Leavenworth, Kan.

In this engagement of the 150 men, including soldiers, minstrels, cooks and flunkies, they lost 150 men, while our losses, out of the 195 who went forth to battle, was two killed and about a dozen wounded.

For the rest of that year we preyed on the enemy's wagon trains and by this means kept ourselves well in food and raiment, but all along we were losing from one to half a dozen men in little skirmishes, as well as horses, and for this reason Quantrell called me in one bright spring morning to discuss the prospects of recruiting our commands in Kentucky.

I did not think well of the enterprise, and so advised my chieftain, but to all my negations he shut his ears and his reason, and announced his intention to start forthwith for the east. When I signified my willingness to go, he limbered up considerably and as nearly as I can recall his words, he harangued me about as follows:

"The jig is up, Kit. Federal troops in the South are as thick as fiddlers in purgatory. Fort Fisher has fallen and the South's gateway to the outside world is forever closed. Pemberton has surrendered Vicksburg, Banks has captured Fort Hudson and the trans-Mississippi department is cut off from the East. Farragut has the southern seaboard; Ben Butler is roosting like a buzzard in New Orleans, and it's only a matter of time, my boy, when Lee will have to hand over his blade to Lincoln's little bulldog, Grant, and all is over but the misery. To hold out longer is foolishness in the extreme. Lee is a great and a sensible man. He must realize that further resistance will be a cruel sacrifice of men. Had they only fought as we have fought the results would have been different and Lee's army would now be quartered in the Federal capitol. I foresee the end and it is a most pathetic one. In the terms of capitulation, the battling portion of the trans-Mississippi department will be left out of the reckoning and we guerrillas will be outlawed by the victors. We raised our oriflamme on the western plains and the banner presented me on that memorable night by Miss Anderson will never trail in dust while I live. We will have to keep up the fight to the bitter end. A price will be placed on those ringlets of yours and your scalp will be appraised at a greater value than your whole body would bring now at public auction. I raised the black flag in all seriousness, and I will die under it. There is no other way. Make up your mind to the same enviable fate. I will not cringe and with suppliant knee beg mercy of those whom I have defied. I know how dangerous it is to go back into Kentucky, my boy, and there in all likelihood, I will be buried in her sacred soil. So, cheer up, and let's make ready for the long journey."

IV. THE SURVIVAL LEGEND OF QUANTRELL [4]

It deals with the alleged survival of the Confederate guerrilla Quantrell after the Civil War. I don't vouch for its authenticity. I only present it as folklore, and to me it is akin to the survival stories of Jesse James and Billy the Kid and many others—even stories that are circulating to-day that Pretty Boy Floyd is still alive. Anyhow, according to the story, Quantrell was badly wounded during the Civil War, but not killed. He was taken incognito to East Texas by some of his followers, by Frank Dalton, who claims to be a cousin of the famous Daltons of Oklahoma. Quantrell is supposed to have set up in a house in East Texas and to have lived incognito as a country school teacher for many years. And this is of course akin to the survival legend of Marshal Ney in North Carolina, who is also supposed to have become a country school teacher. Well, that's not the only incident of it. According to the story, the James gang was in touch with Quantrell all this time. And there is even a legend that the James gang survives to-day through secret codes and passwords.

I know a man who claims to know where the Quantrell house is, who says that if we could get into a certain old trunk we would find many papers which would shed much light on a great many things. It is his theory that the James gang was only the outward expression with Quantrell as the master mind—Quantrell still surviving, of course—of an organized attempt to restore the Confederacy and that their raids were calculated to get capital for another Southern revolt. Quantrell is supposed to have died in the midst of an East Texas community that to this day is still populated by James descendants. Interestingly enough, one of them is named Cole James after the James boys' cousin, Cole Younger.

The man who was my informant tells me that his grandfather had a special liking for him because he was not like his city brothers and cousins. He called him aside and gave him certain secret passwords whereby he could identify a certain man who still stood high in the councils of the James gang after Jesse's alleged death—a point that still is not settled—and that finally after years of wandering he found this man in the East Texas oilfields by giving the password. And that this man knows where all of the secret treasure of the James gang is buried; that even during the Civil War Quantrell and the James boys saw that the Confederacy was licked, but that they buried treasure all over from Missouri to Texas so that they could locate it to finance another war. They buried a great deal of it in the Oklahoma hills.

Several years ago a man who answers to the description, the man who answered the passwords in East Texas, turned up in Oklahoma at the home of a man who had been close to the James gang and gave him a

---

[4] As told by Harold Preece, New York City, formerly of Austin, Texas, at Croton-on-Hudson, New York, March 6, 1949. Recorded by B. A. Botkin.

certain map whereby he could find certain treasures and by following certain marks on the rock—and I have seen this verified in the Dallas News and have the clippings—he uncovered a great many old coins and he uncovered a stone with the names of certain people who can be identified as members of the James gang.

This is all that I have on this at present. It's an interesting legend. It may be just legend. I think that certain exaggerated claims are made for the old man who showed up in Oklahoma. As I've said, I pass it on only as folklore and not as history.

Railroad Bill

WHITE folks say Railroad Bill's real name was Morris Slater. But black boys and girls who tell stories and sing songs about him have never known him by any other name than Railroad Bill. Whatever his name was, he lived and still lives, they say, in the Alabama woods near the roadbed of the Louisville and Nashville Railroad. Sometimes when a poor old black woman wakes up in the morning and opens the door of her cabin she finds a neat little pile of canned goods on the step. There may be a couple of cans of soup, a can of snap beans, perhaps some black-eyed peas.

"God bless Railroad Bill," says the old woman, and she hurries to put the cans out of sight. She knows that Railroad Bill has taken those cans from a freight car on the L. & N. tracks and she knows he shouldn't have done it, but she is happy because she is hungry and now she knows she will be fed.

For many years now Railroad Bill has been stealing cans of food from the freight cars and sharing them with the poor black folks he knows. The railroad men and the police have tried to catch him for a long time. All the black folks know why the chasers can't come up with him. Once the sheriff of Escambia County and all his men started out after him. They ran very fast and they were getting close to Railroad Bill. As they raced through a little clearing in the woods they saw a black sheep standing there watching them run. They didn't realize until long afterwards that the little clearing was a strange place for a black sheep to be. Some of them don't believe to this day that the black sheep was Railroad Bill, but it was.

Another time the sheriff was out after Railroad Bill all his officers took a train to a lonesome place where they thought he was hiding. But Bill was in the car behind them all the time and when they got off the train

From *The Hurricane's Children,* Tales from Your Neck o' the Woods, by Carl Carmer, pp. 115–121. Copyright, 1937, by Carl Carmer. New York and Toronto: Farrar & Rinehart, Inc.

Tune from *Negro Workaday Songs,* by Howard W. Odum and Guy B. Johnson, p. 247. Copyright, 1926, by the University of North Carolina Press. Chapel Hill.

and went looking for him he just stayed on and collected a lot of canned goods that he gave away all over Escambia County that night.

When that story got out all the people in the county laughed at the sheriff and that made him mighty mad. So he schemed as hard as he could to catch Railroad Bill. One day he was sure he had him. He followed Bill's tracks through the swamp and by and by he came to a little clearing, and no tracks left from there. So the sheriff decided Railroad Bill must be hiding under the low bushes in the clearing and he began looking around. Pretty soon he started a little red fox that lit out through the woods. The sheriff let go with both barrels of his shotgun, but he missed. After the second shot the little red fox turned about and laughed at him a high, wild, hearty laugh—and the sheriff recognized it. That little fox was Railroad Bill.

The time that made the sheriff the maddest, though, was when Railroad Bill chased himself to his best girl's house. The sheriff heard Bill had been courtin' a good-looking black girl over by Piney Grove. So he got some bloodhounds from Bob Gant over in Mississippi and he gave them a scent from one of Bill's old hats that he had dropped when he was running away, and sure enough the dogs started to follow a track right straight for Piney Grove.

By and by the sheriff said:

"Did we get three dogs from Bob Gant or four?"

Nobody seemed to be able to remember, but there were four dogs on the trail, and one of them was a black bloodhound.

When they got to the cabin of Bill's best girl the sheriff saw her on the porch and asked her if she'd seen Bill. She said, No, she hadn't for sure. The dogs seemed to want to go on, and so the sheriff and his men followed them. But now when the sheriff looked there were only three bloodhounds on the trail. The black one was gone. When the sheriff got home all tired out and took the dogs back to Mississippi, Bob Gant told him he had rented him just three dogs. The sheriff never *did* know that the black hound was really Railroad Bill who had chased himself all the way out to his girl's house and had stayed behind to do some courtin' when the sheriff left.

White folks say that the sheriff finally caught Railroad Bill. But the black folks in the woods cabins around Nymph and Volina and Astoreth and Elwy and Keego and Piney Grove just laugh when they hear that and tune up their banjoes and sing a song that goes like this:

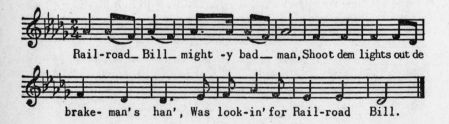

Rail-road— Bill— might -y bad— man, Shoot dem lights out de brake- man's han', Was look-in' for Rail-road Bill.

The old sheriff had a special train,
When he got there was a shower of rain,
Was lookin' for Railroad Bill.

Ten policemen all dressed in blue,
Comin' down the street two by two,
Lookin' for Railroad Bill.

Ever'body told them they better go back,
Policemen comin' down the railroad track,
A-lookin' for Railroad Bill.

Railroad Bill mighty big spo't,
Shot all buttons off the sheriff's coat,
Was lookin' for Railroad Bill.

The End of Rube Burrow

CHAPTER XIX

. . . HIS CAPTURE

. . . JESSE HILDRETH, a very worthy and reliable colored man, had discovered Rube in an abandoned cabin Tuesday morning [, October 7, 1890]. Hildreth had noticed smoke arising from the cabin chimney the night previous, and repairing thither early next morning found the outlaw asleep. He woke him and at once recognized the fugitive described to him the previous day. Rube said he was hunting work, and asked Jesse to get him some coffee. Jesse, pretending to be in search of his horse, told Rube he would go by home and order coffee sent him. Jesse kept watch on the cabin, and finding Rube about to depart, rejoined him at the cabin and endeavored to detain him by selling Rube his horse. Rube, however, did not want to buy a horse, and asked the way to Blue Lick. Jesse, determined to keep Rube in sight, offered to go and show him the way. Rube mounted Jesse's horse, while the latter walked.

About noon, while passing the house of a colored man, George Ford, Jesse suggested to Rube, as it had begun to rain very hard, to stop and get dinner, and wait till the rain should be over. To this Rube consented. While dinner was being prepared, Jesse, on the alert for "some of the bosses," as he expressed it, went out of the house. Frank Marshal, a colored man, who

From *Rube Burrow, King of the Outlaws, and His Band of Train Robbers, An Accurate and Faithful History of Their Exploits and Adventures,* by G. W. Agee, Supt., Western Division, Southern Express Company, pp. 160–170. Chicago: The Henneberry Company. [Preface dated 1890.]

was also looking for the stranger, at this moment rode up to the cabin. Jesse quickly explained that the man was in Ford's house, and while the colored men were in conference they discovered, to their great joy, two white men about a quarter of a mile distant, riding in their direction. Joining them at the foot of the hill the two men proved to be McDuffie and Carter.

Ford's cabin was in an open field, and McDuffie and Carter found they could not approach it within less than two hundred yards without being seen. It was agreed that Jesse and Frank should go ahead, enter the cabin, seize the outlaw, and give the signal to McDuffie and Carter, who would approach cautiously under cover.

Entering the cabin, the Negroes found Rube making ready for his departure, having eaten dinner. He was wholly unsuspicious of anything wrong in the movements of the colored men, however. Rube was in the act of wrapping his trusty Marlin rifle in an oil cloth, when Jesse said:

"Boss, let me wrap it for you."

Rube handed the rifle to Jesse, who carefully wrapped it, and feigning to hand it back, dropped it. Quick as thought Jesse gathered his great brawny arms about the outlaw, and with a grip like that of an octopus he struggled for the mastery. Frank Marshal threw himself upon the outlaw at the same time, but not being very robust, was not able to greatly assist Jesse. The latter was as strong as an ox. His weight was one hundred and eighty lbs., his height about five feet ten inches, and there was not an ounce of surplus flesh upon him. He wore no shoes, and his great, broad feet looked as big as a pair of Virginia hams.

"Where was Frank while you were struggling with Rube?" said someone afterwards to Jesse.

"'Fore de Lord, boss, he had his mouf full of Frank."

Rube had caught Frank's shoulder in his teeth, while Jesse grappled with him. Biting Frank and stamping Jesse's bare feet, the outlaw struggled with herculean strength for liberty. He dragged his captors across the floor of the little cabin, shaking it from bottom to top. The noise of the scuffle within was heard by McDuffie and Carter, who meanwhile had been quietly approaching. Just at the moment when Rube was falling to the floor, the colored men on top, they rushed in, and seizing Rube, disarmed him. He was searched and tied before being allowed to rise. A Colts revolver, forty-five caliber, and $175 were found on his person.

The capture was made about one o'clock P.M., eighteen miles from Demopolis. His captors concluded to avoid the risk of escape consequent upon a journey after dark to Demopolis, and, therefore, took him to Linden, the county seat, only nine miles distant.

Rube was made to mount McDuffie's horse, with his hands tied in front, his arms pinioned by tight cords to his body, and his feet tied underneath the animal. McDuffie mounted behind the prisoner, and, escorted by Carter and the two colored heroes, Hildreth and Marshal, the party set out for Linden, reaching there just at dark. The great desperado was in the toils of his pursuers at last. He was destined, however, in a short time, to outwit his captors, and to perform the last and most daring exploit of his career.

CHAPTER XX

RUBE'S LAST DESPERATE ACT—ESCAPE FROM JAIL—THE DEADLY DUEL, ON THE STREETS OF LINDEN—THE OUTLAW KILLED.

On arrival at Linden, the sheriff being absent with the keys, the prisoner was taken to a room of the jail. The ropes still bound his hands, heavy iron shackles were locked around his ankles, and the chain uniting them was securely fastened to the floor.

McDuffie repaired to the telephone office and reported the capture to the express officials at Demopolis. After obtaining a full description of the outlaw from McDuffie, and being satisfied the right man had been captured, McDuffie was asked:

"How many pistols had he?"

"Only one," said McDuffie.

"There must be some mistake," answered the express official; "he had three when he crossed the Alabama River."

"Rube says he has sold the other two," was the answer.

"Rube never sells pistols," replied the official, and knowing from the reports received that Rube always carried a sack, the inquiry was:

"What's in the sack?"

"Nothing but provisions," answered McDuffie.

The official then instructed McDuffie to handcuff and shackle the prisoner, put him in a cell of the jail and place half dozen men on guard.

McDuffie replied: "There are forty men on guard."

Indeed, the whole town of Linden surrounded the jail, and McDuffie's answer was not, perhaps, exaggerated.

When Rube's supper was brought his hands were untied that he might eat and they were not again manacled. Rube sat and joked with his guards and visitors, entertaining them with his droll humor, which seemed never to forsake him. His shoes were badly worn, and a visitor remarking it, said:

"Rube, your shoes are badly run down—you need a new pair."

"Yes," replied Rube, "some people always praise their shoes up, but I always run mine down."

One by one the visitors dropped out, and at midnight John McDuffie, Jesse Hildreth and Frank Marshall were left in charge of the prisoner. Carter, not feeling well, had retired to Glass' store, just across the street from the jail. He had possession of Rube's rifle and money.

George Ford, in whose cabin the capture occurred, found, after the departure of the prisoner, a greasy cloth sack, and knowing it to be the property of Rube, carried it to Linden, arriving some half hour after the prisoner. He deposited the sack on the steps of the court-house and reported the fact to the colored men, who informed McDuffie. It was said to contain provisions.

About four o'clock A. M. Rube complained that he was hungry. McDuffie said:

"You will have to await the usual hour for breakfast. I can not get anything to eat now."

"Where is my grub sack?" said Rube.

"George left it on the court-house steps," said Frank.

"Mr. McDuffie, please send Frank for it. I have some ginger snaps and some candy in it, and I will give the boys some; I reckon they are hungry, too," said Rube.

McDuffie consented, and when Frank returned he did not even look to see what was handed Rube. For full half an hour the wily prisoner sat eating ginger snaps and candy from the sack, which he occasionally shared with the colored men. Watching his chance, Rube suddenly pulled from the sack one of his trusty pistols, and covering McDuffie, who sat only about ten feet away, said:

"If you make a move I will kill you."

McDuffie's pistol was lying in a chair beside him. Rube, turning to Jesse, said:

"Hand me that pistol quick, or I will shoot your head off."

Jesse tremblingly obeyed, and Rube covered all three of the guards with the two pistols. He then bade Jesse unlock his shackles. This being done, he said:

"Now put them on McDuffie."

McDuffie protested and made a motion to approach Rube, but seeing he was powerless, said:

"All right, Rube; you have the drop, and can have your way."

Rube then made Jesse shackle McDuffie and Marshal together. Taking the key of the jail-yard door from the chair where McDuffie had placed it, Rube, jumping up about two feet from the floor, cracked his heels together and exclaimed:

"I have the big key to the jail. I am boss of the town, and as some people say I am not Rube Burrow, I will paint Linden red, and show them who I am."

He then ordered Jesse to go with him to find Carter. Carter's exact whereabouts were not known to either Rube or Jesse. To the hotel and thence to the sheriff's office they journeyed, and spending nearly an hour in a fruitless search for Carter, Rube thought Jesse was purposely delaying him.

"I will kill you," said Rube, "if I find you are fooling with me."

Jesse, however, was innocent. He did not know where Carter could be found. Further inquiry developed that he was in Glass' store. Rube knocked loudly on the door, and stepping aside, covered Jesse with his pistol, and in a stern whisper said:

"Tell him the express people have come, and McDuffie wants him at the jail quick."

A clerk answered the call to the door, and to him Jesse repeated the order in a voice loud enough to be heard by Carter, who was in the rear part of the store. Carter's footsteps could be distinctly heard as he came across the floor. Just as he appeared in the doorway Rube threw himself in front of him, and placing his pistol within a few inches of Carter's breast, commanded:

"Give me my rifle and my money, or I will shoot your head off."

Carter, instantly taking in the situation, replied, "All right," and placing his hand in his hip pocket pulled a thirty-two caliber Smith & Wesson pistol.

The hour was just at dawn of day. The two men stood face to face, the one gleaming with rage and thirsting for revenge, the other cool, fearless and determined, with law and justice on his side, not to accede to the outlaw's demand.

When the sheen of Carter's pistol flashed upon Rube's vision the outlaw fired, and Carter, anticipating the shot, threw his body to the right. The ball pierced the left shoulder, just above the collar bone, making a painful wound. Carter's intrepid courage was not dashed by his wound, and he instantly returned the fire.

Rube, for the first time in all his career of crime, was called to stand and fight. He had "held the drop" on many a field of rencontre, but here was an even gauge of battle, with the *qui vive* as the vantage ground for him.

Carter boldly advanced upon the outlaw, and, with steady nerve, pressed the trigger of his faithful revolver, but Rube backed away after the first shot from Carter's pistol, and continued backing and firing until he had retreated some thirty paces, and until he himself had fired five shots. Just as Carter fired his fourth round, Rube turned, and running some ten paces, leaped a few feet in the air and fell prostrate upon the earth, stone dead.

After falling upon his knees, from loss of blood, Carter managed to fire a fifth shot. The fourth shot from Carter's pistol, however, had entered the upper abdomen, and cutting the portal artery, caused instant death. This was the only shot that hit Rube.

McDuffie and Marshal, meantime, by means of a duplicate key, had liberated themselves, and had visited several places in the town in the endeavor to secure fire-arms with which to recapture Rube. Being unsuccessful, they reached the store just as the duel was ended.

Rube had given to Jesse the fateful sack as they started from the jail, and while the duel between Carter and Rube was in progress Jesse opened the sack, drew out a pistol, and rushing to Carter's assistance, commenced firing.

"Stand up to him, Mr. Carter; I'm gwine to be wid you," said the heroic Jesse. He fired two shots, without effect, however, and was the first man to reach the dead outlaw and take from his hand his smoking revolver. All honor to Jesse Hildreth. He has written his name in the annals of his race and times as a hero.

Kinnie Waggoner

I WAS about seventeen when I first went hog hunting in "de po' folks' lan'." I was a reporter then for the Hattiesburg (Mississippi) *American*.

Some strange things happened during my brief service there, including a few lynchings, a political campaign that almost was a lynching, a strike, and the story of Kinnie Waggoner. . . .

. . . Kinnie Waggoner, a white man, gave us enough news for months. Folks didn't know much about Kinnie. He was with a mangy circus that got stranded near the sawmill town of Garner. Garner was on a railroad between McClain and Piave. The line was twenty-eight miles long and had thirty-two stops. That's how thick sawmills were in those days after northern money had learned to rob the forests of "de po' folks' lan'" and crush the saplings.

Kinnie got a job at the Garner sawmill, but he was too lazy to work. A handsome fellow, with bushy hair and the grace of an eel, he was the best shot I ever saw. Kinnie could shoot a circle with a pistol and dot its middle with the last bullet. He used to shoot off moccasins' heads just for the fun of it.

Fired at the mill, Kinnie began to make himself a little liquor in the ridges. That was all right until he sold some of it to the Negroes. So a deputy sheriff went for him. Kinnie shot a circle in the deputy's chest and put a hole in the middle of the ring just for the practice.

When they found the deputy's body on a ridge, everybody knew Kinnie had done the killing. I went down to help hunt Kinnie. We got a pack of bloodhounds and set out. All day we "beat the brush" and that night we hunted until almost dawn. Then we camped by a tiny creek and cooked some fresh meat. I'll never forget that dawn. Our posse was resting by a fire, the guns across our laps. The dogs dozed near by. It was dark one minute, then light the next, or so it seemed. The dawn was a deep gray. Its birth sent the owls flapping to nooks in huge trees. A whippoorwill sounded a requiem to the night. The bird must have been just over us and he seemed to be whistling:

"These poor hills, these poor nills."

We found Kinnie that morning resting at a cabin. He was sitting on a porch, swinging his feet and talking with the hostess and host. He didn't even go for his pistol as we walked into the yard. He just sort of looked up and said:

"Hi dee, men. Pull up a chair and sit."

From *Look Away!* A Dixie Notebook, by James H. Street, pp. 62–66. Copyright, 1936, by James H. Street. New York: The Viking Press.

Our leader told him we had come to take him to jail. Kinnie rolled a cigarette and passed the makings to some of the posse-men. He stood and stretched and said: "All right, men." He joked with us all the way to town. I always liked Kinnie. We decided not to take him to the jail in Greene County where the killing was done for fear there might be a lynching bee, so we packed him down to the neighboring hamlet of Lucedale in George County.

Kinnie laughed as the sheriff locked him in the little red-brick jail. "Think I'm goin' to stay in here, sheriff?" he asked. "Well I ain't. I'm goin' to get out, kiss the prettiest girl in town, and high-tail no'f."

The report that he was going to kiss the prettiest girl in town caused some alarm among the fathers. But the village girls just tittered. Many took him sweets to jail and they would stand near the jail and shout to him as he poked that bushy head against the bars and kidded with them.

Sure enough, three days later Kinnie clouted the sheriff when he brought his only prisoner food. Then Kinnie took the sheriff's pistol, walked deliberately to the stable, took the sheriff's horse, rode three times around the jail, firing the pistol as his mount galloped. And with a whoop, he wheeled the stolen horse and went down the road toward a big house. He stopped there long enough to kiss a girl who was on the gallery. She tried to scream. Then she giggled. Kinnie had figured she was the prettiest girl in town. He next headed for the ridge.

Kinnie's escape caused a heap of excitement. It wasn't so much that he hit the high sheriff or stole the horse, but that he kissed that girl. All the other girls and their mothers were pretty mad about it.

It's something to be the prettiest girl in Lucedale, for there are a lot of pretty girls there. I always figured Kinnie's selection was perfect and I told the girl so. But I didn't tell anybody else. A fellow has to be cautious in "de po' folks' lan'."

The next time I heard of Kinnie he was reported in Bluefield, West Virginia. I had left Hattiesburg and gone to New Orleans, thence to Pensacola, Florida. Kinnie escaped capture in West Virginia and hurried to Kingsport, Tennessee. He was at an old water mill one day when three officers flushed him. Kinnie started shooting. He didn't blow a circle in their chests, because he didn't have that many bullets. But he shot the right eye out of each man and killed the trio without any apology. Kinnie went west then and got kind of tough. He played with the Kimes bandits and became downright orn'ry. He even sank to stealing and bank robbing.

I was working then for the *Arkansas Gazette* in Little Rock—a state editor myself—when a report came that the sheriff of Miller County had been shot near Texarkana. Texarkana is in two states. The main street separates Texas and Arkansas, so it's pretty easy at times to break the law in one state and jump into another. The sheriff had gone to a "barrel house" to stop a fight. A barrel house is a sort of roadhouse, a tourist-camp tenderloin.

The sheriff entered with his gun cocked and he got shot. Our correspondent told me all about it on the phone.

"And"—he spoke slowly as a good correspondent should—"there is a circle of holes in his body and a dot in the middle."

"That's Kinnie Waggoner's work," I shouted.

We drove all night to get to Texarkana. Meanwhile the sheriff's widow had been sworn to his job. She strapped a brace of guns about her buxom middle and vowed she was going after Kinnie.

She went out alone. And she came back with Kinnie.

I asked him why he surrendered and he told me:

"I saw her coming across the field. I could have blown her ear off. She saw me and said: 'All right, Kinnie Waggoner, you are under arrest.' I said 'Yes'm.' She brought me to town. You know I never could hurt a woman."

All the states in which Kinnie had killed started a scramble for his custody. Mississippi won. Each county in Mississippi always does its own hanging and maybe they figured Kinnie would get hanged at a public celebration. He was tried in Meridian and got life imprisonment.

"Pretty Boy" Floyd

THE caves and limestone ledges of the Ozark Mountains yield amazing crops—sightless cavern fish to please the evolutionary zoölogist, basketweaver Indian relics for the ethnologist, and living sagas which carry on and outdo the historic relics of Jesse James and Billy the Kid.

I wonder if the "authentic" histories of Billy the Kid and Jesse James which the new historians of the Old West are so busily building out of yellowed newspaper clippings and the even more discolored memories of swaggering old pioneers are any more authentic than the tales of "Pretty Boy" Floyd which are on the tongues of garage mechanics, hitch-hikers and restaurant waitresses throughout Arkansas, Oklahoma and Texas.

* * * * *

Sometimes we picked up farm boys on the way to the next town; sometimes we carried old "geologists" laden with incredible oil and mineral lore. The hikers were always full of local gossip; in Arkansas, Oklahoma and Texas we found them bubbling over with tall tales of Pretty Boy Floyd.

In Arkansas we were told that the boy bandit was a native Arkansawyer, at that very time known to be lurking in a near-by mountain cabin which he had rigged up as an arsenal. He was a bad man with his guns, but we need not fear; he shot none but police officers.

A son of Shamrock, Okla., whom we found pensively sitting on his suitcase at Stroud, had more detailed information. Everybody in Shamrock

From *Sweet Land,* by Lewis Gannett, pp. 37–41. Copyright, 1934, by Lewis Gannett. Garden City, New York: Doubleday, Doran & Company, Inc.

knew Charley ("Pretty Boy") Floyd, it seemed; he had lived there for years, coming with his family from Sallisaw, in the Bushy Horse range of the Ozark Mountains. A nice, soft-spoken boy, good to his mother. Indeed, he had been seen in Shamrock recently, though the police were reported searching for him in New York City and in Cheyenne, Chicago and Carson City. As a matter of fact, the son of Shamrock said, "everybody" knew that he had his hideout in a cave back of Pensacola—Pensacola, Okla.; not Florida.

No Oklahoma police officer was eager to go after Pretty Boy, however; the gentleman from Shamrock entertained us all the way to Oklahoma City with tales of young Floyd's harsh ways with sheriffs. It was his custom, we were assured, to inform the sheriffs ahead of time when he was about to rob a bank, and it was so well known that he would rather pot a sheriff any day than rob a bank that nowadays the sheriffs invariably locked themselves in and barred the doors or left town as the date approached. The lists of sheriffs and deputies whom "Pretty Boy" had shot in the head—he never shot except at the head and there was only one record of his missing—was desperately long.

Texas wayfarers contradicted Shamrock's local pride, but confirmed the rest of the epic. The Texans held that "Pretty Boy" was no Oklahoman at all. Some held that he was a genuine West Texan, others that he was in reality nothing but a Chicago gangster, probably a foreigner, travelling under an assumed name and reputation. But as to his ways with sheriffs there was no disagreement at all; it was accepted that the sheriff who courageously arrested "Pretty Boy's" wife and son had found good legal reasons to release them on bail on the day before that on which "Pretty Boy" had announced he would arrive to rescue her in person. One curious element in the epic was that "Pretty Boy" was generally held to be twenty-six years old; but he had a twelve-year-old son.

So epics grow; so doubtless, the stories of Tombstone, Arizona's glory, and the older Missouri sagas of the James brothers grew. When, twenty years hence, effete Easterners seeking to earn masters' degrees by digging into the byways of American history turn their attention to "Pretty Boy" Floyd, no one will any longer be able to distinguish in his memory what he read in the papers and what he heard on the road. Nor will one be any truer than the other. Some marvellous books will be written.

III. THE PEOPLE'S CHOICE

GENTLEMEN AND FELLER CITIZENS: *I come before you today as a candidate for Congress in Washington at the next session, and I know my friends will be willing and ready to support me in that campaign. Now I want to say that my opponent has charged that I am an oneddicated man, that he has been eddicated between college walls. I want to say that I got my schoolin a-plowin a bull in a medder, where the sun don't rise before ten o'clock in the mornin and it sets afore the shank of the evenin. But I want to say that when it comes to ridin a jackass into Washington I will be with him then.*

My platform you all want to know it. It is simply this: it's to be likened unto one of your hillside plows. You just plow out to the eend, turn the wing over, and plow back t'other way. Just a simple twist of the wrist, that's all.

Of course I want to be elected to Congress and I think it is right. They charge that they're goin to beat me in this campaign, but I beg of you—don't let 'em do it. I want to say to you that when it comes to Stony Point, I'll break even with them. When it comes to Busthead precinct, I'm neck and neck with 'em there. And when it comes to Lower Fork, you boys know that I've always stayed with 'em there.

Now we have the grandest dee-strict in the state o' North Carolina. It stretches from the Great Mt. Mitchell on the east to the Great Smoky Mountain Park on the west. It stretches from the dark corner close to South Carolina on the south to the mouth of South Turkey Creek—

(Voice: Let 'er stretch! Hoorah for the Democratic party!)
—BASCOM LAMAR LUNSFORD

1. THE VOICE OF THE PEOPLE

FOR the kind of bombastic political speaking recalled by Bascom Lamar Lunsford,[1] the name of his own county, Buncombe, in western North Carolina, has become proverbial. But "talking for talk's sake" or for any other purpose knows no county or state lines in the South. As the region is generally noted for its love of good talk (correlated with leisure, gregariousness, sociability, and outdoor living in a mild climate), so it is distinguished for its orators, spellbinders, and raconteurs.

In designating the South as a "story-telling belt," Irvin S. Cobb is of the opinion that speaking (especially stump speaking) rather than writing is the South's forte, thus agreeing (if for different reasons) with the friends of Southern letters who lamented, in the *Southern Literary Mes-*

---

[1] Recorded by B. A. Botkin, Asheville, North Carolina, January 18, 1949.

senger, that politics and oratory were absorbing some of the best literary talents of the South. After the Civil War, Cobb says:

> Some of the gifted sons . . . coined the poetry and the drama and the romance of their souls into oratory, and up sprang a race of silver-tongues whose descendants, bearing onward the same inheritance, still may be heard in county court-houses and on the stump in political campaigns. And yet others turned their talents to the anecdotal vein as a simpler and almost equally effective medium of expression.[2]

As statesmen degenerated into politicians and the silver-tongues became slightly tarnished, campaigning often descended to the level of what Bilbo called a "family fight," full of "cuss-fighting" and disputing. For, as the Southern demagogues like Pitchfork Ben Tillman arose as leaders of an "emerging Southern middle class in increasing successful revolt against the Bourbons," so they quite naturally broke with the classic tradition of Bourbon oratory and brought eloquence down to the level of two-fisted invective.

When it comes to knock-down-and-drag-out, no-holds-barred political bickering and out-jawing, out-cussing, out-ridiculing, and out-smarting one's opponent—well, as Donald Davidson's typical Middle Georgia country gentleman, "Cousin Roderick," puts it, "Politics is for lawyers." In the single-party system of the South politics is for lawyers because it is factional politics; and the candidates' joint debate (one of the basic folkways of Southern politics) calls for forensic skill if not "juristic technique." With the stump and the legislature taking the place of the bench and bar, the rival candidates appear as their own counsel before a jury of the voters, who are themselves also on trial, as it were. And if the people's case is often settled out of court, that is because politics in the South, as befits a "family fight," is also a "family affair."

> . . . In Rebelville political action is generally no more than a confirmation of what has been talked around among the clans. If you really want things done, you speak quietly to Cousin So-and-So and others that pass the word to everybody that counts. And then something is done.[3]

On the subject of talking the people's language (which is necessary to success in "family" politics) Huey Long was quite explicit when he said, "I do not talk one way back there in the hills of Louisiana and another way here in the Senate." The classic example of this vernacular appeal is the delightful discourse on "Potlikker and Corn Pone" which he introduced into his historic fifteen-and-one-half-hour filibuster in the Senate in June, 1935, sandwiched in among biographies of Frederick the Great and Judah P. Benjamin and recipes for frying oysters and Roquefort cheese salad dressing.[4]

2. Bread and Circuses

The spectacle of Huey Long "holding aloft a waste basket to represent a pot, [as] he told the Senate how turnip greens should be washed, seasoned

---

[2] *Some United States* (New York, 1926), pp. 266–267.

[3] *The Attack on Leviathan* (Chapel Hill, 1938), pp. 152–153.

[4] Franklin L. Burdette *Filibustering in the Senate* (Princeton, 1940), p. 4.

with side meat, and cooked," recalls his prototype Pitchfork Ben Tillman, who is generally credited with first making politics a circus. Before Tillman, however, S. S. Prentiss of Mississippi made the canvass "a sort of political and intellectual carnival"; and he is perhaps the only politician on record who ever campaigned with a menagerie and spoke from the top of a lion's cage. The like of the ensuing din of the frightened animals and the delighted audience was never heard; and Prentiss equaled his performance only on that other memorable occasion when he made a brilliant four-hour defense of a bedbug, following Judge Gohlson's two-hour prosecution.

In the political circus the successful demagogue is a master of the anecdotal art. As a backwoods raconteur Davy Crockett was one of the first to discover and exploit the vote-getting possibilities of the illustrative and entertaining anecdote. With Tom Heflin the formula reached new heights in the "raucous tale, with mimicry of Negro or rural characters, followed by an irrelevant interpretation in terms of . . . issues." Bob Taylor and Jeff Davis excelled not only in apt and amusing stories but also in striking metaphor and clever epigram. Bilbo further diverted his audiences with hymns sung at the melodeon. And with the coming of the radio, which supplemented the rally and barbecue with a variety show, folk music (including hillbilly songs and sacred songs) was added to the folk art of story-telling by such radio personalities as W. Lee O'Daniel and his Light Crust Doughboys.

The last touch of demagogic showmanship is dress. Both Bilbo and Gene Talmadge were famous for their red suspenders, which Talmadge loved to snap and to which the former added loud checked suit, flaming necktie, diamond stickpin, and rakish snapbrimmed felt hat. But it was the "Affectionate Candidate," Judge F. T. Fox, as recalled by William O. Bradley, that took the cake in the matter of dress. When he ran for County Attorney of Pulaski County, Kentucky, his opponent was a very plain man who "thought it would be a popular move to dress even more plainly than usual." Fox, on the other hand, appeared in spotless linen and broadcloth suit and was twitted by his opponent as an aristocrat who set himself up above the poor people and, if elected, would spend his time in display instead of looking after their interests. To which taunt the Judge replied:

"Now, fellow citizens, I am going out to see you. I love you, and for this reason I desire to dress in the very best clothes I can claim. I do this because I respect you and want your respect. My opponent thinks any old clothes are good enough for you, but when he goes to see his sweetheart or to church, he dresses far more handsomely than I. . . . He has no respect for you or himself and is doing this with the hope that he may arouse your prejudices against me and make a few votes. He is actually too dirty to make a County Attorney. I dress this way because I love you, and I wish I could take each one of you in my arms and hug you." The Judge was elected by a large majority.[5]

B. A. B.

---

[5] *Stories and Speeches of William O. Bradley* (Lexington, 1916), pp. 1–2.

Patrick Henry, Lawyer

I. THIEVING KNAVES [1]

MOST of the anecdotes about Henry's shrewdness in extricating clients from difficulties relate to this period of his practice. No doubt some of these stories, as told in Virginia to-day, are tinctured by the medium through which they have passed in coming down to us. If the tale be coarse, as it often is, it may have got its coarseness in franker times than ours, or it may have been vulgarized by tavern gossips, who put into it a coloring all their own. Many of the anecdotes have variants, according to the locality in which they are told. But humor usually runs through them; and Henry is invariably the hero.

There are several thieving knaves in the Henry anecdotes. He missed so much corn from one of his corn cribs that he decided to bring the culprit to book. Accordingly, a steel-trap was set inside the crib, near an opening through which the thief drew out the corn. Henry himself paid an early morning visit to the crib; and lo! alongside it, by the aperture, was a neighbor of good substance and repute. One arm was invisible, and the entrapped rogue stood as if leaning against the crib. "Good morning, sir," said Henry, with politeness and friendly warmth. He asked after the man's family; spoke volubly of the weather, the crops, politics; and, turning finally, cried out in the heartiest manner, "Come in to breakfast— come on in!" And with that he walked briskly away. One may imagine the grin and the glib observations of the black boy secretly sent by Henry to liberate the poacher.

Since Henry undoubtedly had "a tendency to grace," it is hard to believe the traditional shoat story heard in the Lynchburg region, where he is still spoken of as "the Governor." It is told in about this style: "A man stole a hog, dressed it, and went to the Governor to defend him. The Governor said: 'Did you walk away with that shoat?' 'I don't like to say.' 'Out with it!' 'Yessir.' 'Have you got the carcass?' 'Yessir.' 'You go home, you wretch; cut the pig lengthwise in half, and hang as much of it in my smokehouse as you keep in yours.' At court the Governor said: 'Your Honor, this man has no more of that stolen shoat than I have. If necessary, I'd kiss the Bible on this.' The man was cleared."

As Henry keenly enjoyed practical jokes at the expense of his friends on the bench, as he liked to do surprising things of a harmless sort, and as he was a privileged character in some degree, it is possible that the various petit larceny anecdotes were based on actual happenings. One Sunday evening, while on the way to a court in which he was to appear next morning, he fell in with a witness in a horse-stealing case. They talked it

---

[1] From *The True Patrick Henry,* by George Morgan, pp. 372–373. Copyright, 1907, by J. B. Lippincott Company. Philadelphia & London.

over. Said Henry, commenting on an assertion: "You wouldn't say *that* in open court if I'd give you every guinea I'm jingling here in my hand." Vowing that he would, the man took the money. When he stood up to testify next day, Henry, who was counsel for the defendant, also rose, and made short work of him and of the case, on the ground that a witness who would permit himself to be influenced by money was incompetent.

II. HENRY AND HOOK [2]

. . . Hook was a Scotchman, a man of wealth, and suspected of being unfriendly to the American cause. During the distresses of the American army, consequent upon the joint invasion of Cornwallis and Phillips in 1781, a Mr. Venable, an army commissary, had taken two of Hook's steers for the use of the troops. The act had not been strictly legal; and on the establishment of peace, Hook, under the advice of Mr. Cowan, a gentleman of some distinction in the law, thought proper to bring an action against Mr. Venable, in the district court of New London. Mr. Henry appeared for the defendant, and is said to have disported himself in this cause to the infinite enjoyment of his hearers, the unfortunate Hook always excepted.

After Mr. Henry became animated in the cause, says a correspondent [Judge Stuart], he appeared to have complete control over the passions of his audience. At one time he excited their indignation against Hook; vengeance was visible in every countenance. Again, when he chose to relax and ridicule him, the whole audience was in a roar of laughter. He painted the distresses of the American army, exposed almost naked to the rigor of a winter's sky, and marking the frozen ground over which they marched, with the blood of their unshod feet—"Where was the man," he said, "who had an American heart in his bosom, who would not have thrown open his fields, his barns, his cellar, the doors of his house, the portals of his breast, to have received with open arms, the meanest soldier in that little band of patriots? Where is the man? *There* he stands—but whether the heart of an American beats in his bosom, you, gentlemen, are to judge."

He then carried the jury, by the powers of his imagination, to the plains around Yorktown, the surrender of which had followed shortly after the act complained of. He depicted the surrender in the most glowing and noble colors of his eloquence—the audience saw before their eyes the humiliation and dejection of the British, as they marched out of their trenches—they saw the triumph which lighted up every patriot face, and heard the shouts of victory, and the cry of "Washington and Liberty!" as it rang and echoed through the American ranks, and was reverberated from the hills and shores of the neighboring river—"but, hark! what notes

---

[2] From "Anecdotes Concerning Noted Men," *Library of Southern Literature,* Edwin Anderson Alderman, Joel Chandler Harris, Editors in Chief, Vol. XIV, compiled by C. Alphonso Smith, pp. 6341–6343. Copyright, 1907, 1910, by The Martin and Hoyt Company. Atlanta.

)f discord are these which disturb the general joy, and silence the acclamations of victory? They are the notes of *John Hook*, hoarsely bawling through the American camp, *beef! beef! beef!*"

The whole audience was convulsed. A particular incident will give a better idea of the effect than any general description. The clerk of the court, unable to command himself, and unwilling to commit any breach of decorum in his place, rushed out of the court-house, and threw himself on the grass, in the most violent paroxysm of laughter, where he was rolling, when Hook, with very different feelings, came out for relief into the yard also.

"Jemmy Steptoe," said he to the clerk, "what the devil ails ye, mon?" Mr. Steptoe was only able to say, that *he could not help it.* "Never mind ye," said Hook, "wait till Billy Cowan gets up, *he'll show* him the la'."

Mr. Cowan, however, was so completely overwhelmed by the torrent which bore upon his client, that when he rose to reply to Mr. Henry, he was scarcely able to make an intelligible remark. The cause was decided almost by acclamation. The jury retired for form's sake, and instantly returned with a verdict for the defendant. Nor did the effect of Mr. Henry's speech stop here. The people were so highly excited by the Tory audacity of such a suit that Hook began to hear around him a cry more terrible than that of *beef;* it was the cry of *tar and feathers*—from the application of which, it is said, nothing saved him but a precipitate flight.

III. A BOB-TAIL POLITICIAN [3]

Governor Giles, of Virginia, once addressed a note to Patrick Henry, demanding satisfaction:

Sir, I understand that you have called me a "bob-tail" politician. I wish to know if it be true; and if true, your meaning.

WM. B. GILES

To which Mr. Henry replied in this wise:

Sir, I do not recollect having called you a bob-tail politician at any time, but think it probable I have. Not recollecting the time or occasion, I can't say what I did mean, but if you will tell me what you think I meant, I will say whether you are correct or not. Very respectfully,

PATRICK HENRY

IV. PATRICK HENRY AND THE LOVERS [4]

. . . Here is a more pleasing story, illustrative of Henry's ingenuity. It is a part of the folk-lore of Virginia. As told by a graybeard, sitting on the

---

[3] From *Bench and Bar: A Complete Digest of the Wit, Humor, Asperities, and Amenities of the Law,* by L. J. Bigelow, p. 155. New York: Harper & Brothers, Publishers. 1871.

[4] From *The True Patrick Henry,* by George Morgan, pp. 374–375. Copyright, 1907, by J. B. Lippincott Company. Philadelphia & London.

steps of St. John's Church, within a few feet of the spot where Henry stood while making his "Liberty or Death" speech, it had a charm and an effectiveness impossible to reconvey on this poor page, since no birds sing for us here as they sang in the beautiful grove, with its graves of great men, its trees, and its flowers.

"Did you ever know," said the graybeard, resting his hands on the knob of his hickory stick, "how Patrick Henry untwisted a little love-tangle? I'll tell you. A young fellow wanted to get married without being overtaken by the law. The girl, ditto; but her parents objected. She was not of age, and the law had it all fixed that if he ran away with her and was caught, he could be sent to jail. That's where the trouble was. But the young fellow took his trouble to Patrick Henry, and Patrick said: 'You really love her, do you? How much do you love her? Do you love her better than gold? How much would you give out of pocket if you could get your sweetheart and never cast a shadow in the doorway of a jail?' 'I'd give a hundred guineas,' said his client. 'Agreed! Now do as I tell you. Go see your ladylove; request her to take a horse out of her father's stable, mount, make off, and meet you at an appointed place. You are to be on foot. You are to get on behind her. Ride to the nearest preacher's and get married. You will be arrested; but never mind that, for I shall be there to see you through.' Now we come to the second chapter—with everybody in court from five miles round. The Commonwealth's attorney said it was so plain a case that he would simply state the law and the facts, and be done with it. He did so; after which Patrick got up, and admitted that the law was just as the prosecutor had urged. But he would be better satisfied, he said, if the young woman should take the stand and give an account of the elopement. So up she went, the pretty bride, and all the men shuffled and craned, and the judges sat straight. Then she said, said she: 'I told my lover to meet me at a certain spot. I got out a good horse from my father's stable, and rode to where he was. I took my lover up behind me, and ran away with him.' 'Did he run away with you?' said the sly old Pat. 'No, sir, I ran away with him.' 'Oh!' said Patrick, 'I see!' The court got into a side-splitting shake; the crowd roared; the Commonwealth attorney came down the persimmon-tree, and the happy chap marched off with the persimmon."

Anecdotes of Henry Clay

I. A CHANCE SHOT

MR. CLAY had been speaking for some time, when a company of riflemen, who had been performing military exercise, attracted by his attitude,

From "Henry Clay, Personal Anecdotes, Incidents, etc.," *Harper's New Monthly Magazine*, Vol. V (August, 1852), No. XXVII, pp. 394, 395, 396–397.

concluded to "go and hear what the fellow had to say," as they termed it, and accordingly drew near. They listened with respectful attention, and evidently with deep interest, until he closed, when one of their number, a man of about fifty years of age, who had seen much backwoods service, stood leaning on his rifle, regarding the young speaker with a fixed and sagacious look.

He was apparently the Nimrod of the company, for he exhibited every characteristic of a "mighty hunter." He had buckskin breeches, and hunting shirt, coonskin cap, black bushy beard, and a visage of the color and texture of his bullet pouch. At his belt hung the knife and hatchet, and the huge, indispensable powder-horn across a breast bare and brown as the hills he traversed in his forays, yet it covered a brave and noble heart.

He beckoned with his hand to Mr. Clay to approach him.

Mr. Clay immediately complied.

"Young man," said he, "you want to go to the Legislature, I see."

"Why, yes," replied Mr. Clay; "yes, I *should* like to go, since my friends have put me up as a candidate before the people. I don't wish to be defeated, of course; few people do."

"Are you a good shot, young man?" asked the hunter.

"I consider myself as good as any in the county."

"Then you shall go; but you must give us a specimen of your skill; we must see you shoot."

"I never shoot any rifle but my own, and that is at home," said the young orator.

"No matter," quickly responded the hunter, "here's 'Old Bess'; she never failed yet in the hands of a marksman. She has put a bullet through many a squirrel's head at a hundred yards, and daylight through many a redskin *twice* that distance. If you can shoot *any* gun, young man, you can shoot 'Old Bess'!"

"Very well, then," replied Mr. Clay, "put up your mark! put up your mark!"

The target was placed at about the distance of eighty yards, when, with all the coolness and steadiness of an old experienced marksman, he drew "Old Bess" to his shoulder, and fired. The bullet pierced the target near the center.

"Oh, that's a chance shot! a chance shot!" exclaimed several of his political opponents; "he might shoot all day, and not hit the mark again. Let him try it over!—let him try it over!"

"No, no," retorted Mr. Clay, "*Beat that,* and *then* I will!"

As no one seemed disposed to make the attempt, it was considered that he had given satisfactory proof of being, as he said, "the best shot in the county"; and this unimportant incident gained him the vote of every hunter and marksman in the assembly, which was composed principally of that class of persons, as well as the support of the same throughout the county. Mr. Clay was frequently heard to say: "I had never before fired a rifle, and have not since!"

It was in turning little things like these to account, that Mr. Clay, in the earlier period of his career, was so remarkable.

II. A Rifleman's Analogy

During an excited political canvass, Mr. Clay met an old hunter, who had previously been his devoted friend, but who now opposed him on the ground of "the Compensation bill."

"Have you a good rifle, my friend?" asked Mr. Clay.

"Yes," said the hunter.

"Does it ever flash in the pan?" continued Mr. Clay.

"It never did but once in the world," said the hunter, exultingly.

"Well, what did you do with it? You didn't throw it away, did you?"

"No; I picked the flint, tried it again, and brought down the game."

"Have *I* ever 'flashed,' " continued Mr. Clay, "except on the 'Compensation bill?' "

"No, I can't say that you ever did."

"Well, will you throw *me* away?" said Mr. Clay.

"No, no!" responded the huntsman, touched on the right point; "no; *I'll pick the flint, and try you again!*"

And ever afterward he was the unwavering friend of Mr. Clay.

III. The Randolph-Clay Duel

The particulars of the duel between Mr. Randolph and Mr. Clay may be unknown to some of our readers. The eccentric descendant of Pocahontas appeared on the ground in a huge morning gown. This garment constituted such a vast circumference that the "locality of the swarthy Senator" was at least a matter of very vague conjecture. The parties exchanged shots and the ball of Mr. Clay hit the centre of the visible object, but Mr. Randolph was not there! The latter had fired in the air, and immediately after the exchange of shots he walked up to Mr. Clay, parted the folds of his gown, pointed to the hole where the bullet of the former had pierced his coat, and, in the shrillest tones of his piercing voice, exclaimed, "Mr. Clay, you owe me a coat—you owe me a coat!" to which Mr. Clay replied, in a voice of slow and solemn emphasis, at the same time pointing directly at Mr. Randolph's heart, "Mr. Randolph, I thank God that I am no *deeper* in your debt!"

Calhoun's Fascination

I. Calhoun and "Uncle Jacob"[1]

Few anecdotes of the late Hon. John C. Calhoun are floating in the public mind. He was not a man *of the people,* but his genius and his habits placed

---

[1] From *Bench and Bar:* A Complete Digest of the Wit, Humor, Asperities, and Amenities of the Law, by L. J. Bigelow, pp. 188–190. New York: Harper & Brothers, Publishers. 1871.

him above the masses, whom he nevertheless held with a fascination as hard to explain as to resist. The following is remarkably characteristic of Mr. Calhoun, and well deserves to be preserved:

In the early days of his political career Mr. Calhoun had a powerful rival and opponent in the Abbeville District, South Carolina was at this time in a state of high excitement, and party feeling raged fiercely in a struggle to overthrow an aristocratic feature of the Constitution. The issue was upon topics that enlisted the interests and prejudices of parties and they waged the contest with the energy of a civil war. Mr. Calhoun and Mr. Yancey were on opposite sides, the leaders of hostile bands, and the idols of their respective hosts. There was, and is, for he still lives, a man named Marvin, one of the most violent of Mr. Yancey's party, warmly attached to him as a personal and political friend, and following him blindly as an infallible guide. He was a very eccentric man, and his peculiarities had perhaps led the people to call him "Uncle Jacob," by which name he was better known than that of Marvin. Bitter in his prejudices and strong in his attachments, he could see no right in an enemy, no wrong in a friend. On the other hand, Mr. Yancey was one of the most amiable and candid of men. The strength of his mind, combined with the tolerance of his feelings, raised him above the meanness of clinging to error when reason opposed it. In the discussion that ensued, Mr. Calhoun's arguments overpowered him, and he candidly confessed himself a convert to his great rival's opinions. Great was the rage of "Uncle Jacob" when he heard that Yancey had struck his colors to Calhoun. He swore a big oath that he would *thrash* Calhoun if the story was true. He soon found that it was so, and started at once to put his threat into execution.

He found Mr. Calhoun walking slowly and calmly back and forth, for exercise, on the piazza of the hotel where he was boarding. Mr. Calhoun had been informed of Marvin's intention, and, as soon as he saw him coming, prepared himself for a triumph, not of force, but of manner and address. Marvin took his stand where Mr. Calhoun was to pass, and awaited the trying moment. Mr. Calhoun approached, spoke kindly, and passed on with his blandest smile. Again he passed, and again, each time repeating his soothing salutation, and expecting the man to commence his attack. But a strange fascination had seized upon "Uncle Jacob." The spell which genius throws over those who approach it had unmanned him. At last he could stand it no longer, but, bursting into tears, he grasped the proffered hand of Mr. Calhoun, told him frankly the errand on which he had come, and begged his pardon. Mr. Calhoun then began to press his arguments cautiously, but forcibly, and in a few minutes Marvin was one of his converts, and a decided friend. From that day onward Mr. Calhoun had no more ardent follower than Marvin, and of all "rabid Nullifiers" Uncle Jacob was the rabidest, and to this day he believes there never was such a man in this world as that same John C. Calhoun whom he tried to whip, and who conquered him without raising a finger or saying a word.

II. EULOGY OF JOHN C. CALHOUN [2]

And how—how, sir, shall I speak of him—he who is justly esteemed the wonder of the world, the astonisher of mankind? Like the great Niagara, he goes dashing and sweeping on, bidding all created things give way, and bearing down, in his resistless course, all who have the temerity to oppose his onward career. He, sir, is indeed the cataract, the political Niagara of America; and like that noblest work of nature and of nature's God, he will stand through all after time no less the wonder than the admiration of the world. His was the bright star of genius that in early life shot madly forth, and left the lesser satellites that may have dazzled in its blaze to that impenetrable darkness to which nature's stern decree had destined them; his the mighty magazine of mind, from which his country clothed herself in the armor of defence; his the broad expansive wing of genius, under which his country sought political protection; his the giant mind, the elevated spotless mien, which nations might envy, but worlds could not emulate. Such an one needs no eulogium from me, no defence from human lips. He stands beneath a consecrated arch, defended by a lightning shut up in the hearts of his countrymen—by a lightning that will not slumber, but will leap forth to avenge even a word, a thought, a look, that threatens him with insult. The story of his virtuous fame is written in the highest vault of your political canopy, far above the reach of grovelling speculation, where it can alone be sought upon an eagle's pinions and gazed at by an eagle's eye. His defence may be found in the hearts of his countrymen; his eulogium will be heard in the deep toned murmurs of posterity, which, like the solemn artillery of heaven, shall go rolling along the shores of time until it is ingulfed in the mighty vortex of eternity. Little minds may affect to despise him; pigmy politicians may raise the war cry of proscription against him; be it so; insects buzz around the lion's mane, but do not arouse him from his lair. Imprecations will add but other links to the mighty chain that binds him to his countrymen; and each blast of your war trumpet will but awaken millions to his support.

---

[2] From *An American Glossary, Being an Attempt to Illustrate Certain Americanisms upon Historical Principles,* by Richard H. Thornton, Vol. II, p. 983. Philadelphia: J. B. Lippincott Company. 1912.

By Mr. Albert G. Brown of Mississippi, in the House of Representatives, April 17, 1840: *Cong. Globe,* p. 390. App.

If Mr. Calhoun ever read these remarks, which were not spoken, but written "for Buncombe," he must have ejaculated, "Save me from my friends."—R. H. T.

Davy Crockett: Coonskin Congressman

I. How Crockett Defeated Huntsman [1]

In his last two campaigns for Congress Davy Crockett was opposed by Adam Huntsman. Huntsman defeated Crockett the second time (1835) and it is thought that he would have triumphed the first time (1833) but for the following trick of Crockett's: They were campaigning together and stopped one night on their rounds at a well-to-do farmer's, who was a great Andrew Jackson man and hence for Huntsman. Crockett and "Peg-leg," as Huntsman was called because he had a wooden leg, were put in the same room to sleep. The house consisted of two log cabins with a passage between, and a porch extending the whole length in the rear, with shed-rooms at each end, in one of which the two candidates were placed, while the farmer's daughter occupied the other. After all had retired, Huntsman went to sleep and Crockett to planning. Then, getting up quietly, he opened the door, taking a chair, and walking stealthily across to the young lady's room, made an apparent effort to force her door, which awoke the girl, who uttered a scream, when Crockett, firmly catching the chair by the back and placing his foot on the lower round, using it as a "leg," hurried back to his room, dropped the chair, popped into bed, and went to hard snoring. The next moment the farmer rushed in and was about to kill Huntsman, to whose protestations of innocence he paid no attention. "Oh, you can't fool me," he exclaimed, "I know you too well, and heard that darned old peg leg of yourn too plain." The consequence was that the farmer, with numbers of others, changed their votes and Crockett was triumphantly elected. It is said that Huntsman would never have ventured to stand another canvass had not Crockett considered the joke too good to keep.

II. Crockett's Rules for the Guidance of Politicians [2]

"Attend all public meetings," says I, "and get some friends to move that you take the chair; if you fail in this attempt, make a push to be appointed secretary; the proceedings of course will be published, and your name is introduced to the public. But should you fail in both undertakings, get two or three acquaintances, over a bottle of whiskey, to pass some resolutions, no matter on what subject; publish them even if you pay the printer

---

[1] From *Early History of Memphis,* by James B. Davis, 1873, cited by A. B. Armstrong, in *Backwoods to Border,* edited by Mody C. Boatright and Donald Day, pp. 147–148. Texas Folk-Lore Society Publications, Number XVIII, J. Frank Dobie, General Editor. Copyright, 1943, by the Texas Folk-Lore Society. Austin and Dallas: Texas Folk-Lore Society and University Press in Dallas, Southern Methodist University.

[2] From *Life of David Crockett,* The Original Humorist and Irrepressible Backwoodsman . . . , pp. 274–276. Philadelphia: John E. Potter and Company. 1860.

—it will answer the purpose of breaking the ice, which is the main point in these matters. Intrigue until you are elected an officer of the militia; this is the second step towards promotion, and can be accomplished with ease, as I know an instance of an election being advertised, and no one attending, the innkeeper at whose house it was to be held, having a military turn, elected himself colonel of his regiment." Says I, "You may not accomplish your ends with as little difficulty, but do not be discouraged—Rome wasn't built in a day.

"If your ambition or circumstances compel you to serve your country, and earn three dollars a day, by becoming a member of the legislature, you must first publicly avow that the constitution of the state is a shackle upon free and liberal legislation; and is, therefore, of as little use in the present enlightened age, as an old almanac of the year in which the instrument was framed. There is policy in this measure, for by making the constitution a mere dead letter, your headlong proceedings will be attributed to a bold and unshackled mind, whereas, it might otherwise be thought they arose from sheer mulish ignorance. 'The Government' has set the example in his attack upon the constitution of the United States, and who should fear to follow where 'the Government' leads?

"When the day of election approaches, visit your constituents far and wide. Treat liberally, and drink freely, in order to rise in their estimation, though you fall in your own. True, you may be called a drunken dog by some of the clean shirt and silk stocking gentry, but the real rough necks will style you a jovial fellow, their votes are certain, and frequently count double. Do all you can to appear to advantage in the eyes of the women. That's easily done—you have but to kiss and slabber their children, wipe their noses, and pat them on the head; this cannot fail to please their mothers, and you may rely on your business being done in that quarter.

"Promise all that is asked," said I, "and more if you can think of anything. Offer to build a bridge or a church, to divide a county, create a batch of new offices, make a turnpike, or anything they like. Promises cost nothing, therefore deny nobody who has a vote or sufficient influence to obtain one.

"Get up on all occasions, and sometimes on no occasion at all, and make long-winded speeches, though composed of nothing else than wind— talk of your devotion to your country, your modesty and disinterestedness, or on any such fanciful subject. Rail against taxes of all kinds, office-holders, and bad harvest weather; and wind up with a flourish about the heroes who fought and bled for our liberties in the times that tried men's souls. To be sure you run the risk of being considered a bladder of wind or an empty barrel, but never mind that, you will find enough of the same fraternity to keep you in countenance.

"If any charity be going forward, be at the top of it, provided it is to be advertised publicly; if not, it isn't worth your while. None but a fool would place his candle under a bushel on such an occasion.

"These few directions," said I, "if properly attended to, will do you.

business; and when once elected, why a fig for the dirty children, the promises, the bridges, the churches, the taxes, the offices, and the subscriptions, for it is absolutely necessary to forget all these before you can become a thorough-going politician, and a patriot of the first water."

Sam Houston Gives Satisfaction

IT WAS during Houston's second term as a member of Congress that his first and only serious duel took place. The appointments of postmasters under the new Federal Administration were naturally not of the Jackson-Houston party. One Colonel Irwin had been appointed postmaster at Nashville, and Houston had expressed his opinion about him with that vigor which always characterized his animadversions upon his political opponents. Houston's words were carried to Colonel Irwin, and it was understood that he would hold him personally responsible for them on his return to Tennessee.

Colonel Irwin selected as the bearer of his challenge one Colonel John T. Smith, a noted desperado of Missouri; Houston's friend, Colonel McGregor, refused to accept the challenge from Smith's hands. The challenge was offered and refused in front of the Nashville Inn, McGregor dropping the paper to the ground as it was handed to him. No encounter followed between Smith and McGregor, as was expected, and the news of the action was taken to Houston, who was in a room of the inn with some of his friends. General William White, who was present, expressed himself to the effect that Smith had not been treated with proper courtesy. Houston overheard the remark, and said to White, "If you, sir, have any grievance, I will give you any satisfaction you may demand." White replied, "I have nothing to do with your difficulty, but I presume you know what is due from one gentleman to another."

Nothing farther followed at the time, and it was soon spread about the streets of Nashville that Houston had "backed down" General White. This attack upon his courage reached the ears of General White, and he sent a challenge to Houston, which was promptly accepted. An attempt was made by the sheriff to arrest them both for the preservation of the peace, but Houston escaped to the house of a friend in an adjoining county, and sent word to White, who had also evaded arrest, that he was ready to meet him across the state line in Kentucky.

The duel was fought at sunrise, September 23, 1826, at a noted dueling-ground in Simpson County known by the name of Linkumpinch, just across the Tennessee line, and on the road from Nashville to Bowling Green. White was severely, and it was supposed at first mortally, wounded, having

From *Sam Houston and the War of Independence in Texas*, by Alfred M. Williams, pp. 28–32. Copyright, 1893, by Alfred M. Williams. Boston and New York: Houghton, Mifflin and Company.

been shot through the body at the hip. Houston escaped untouched. As they took their places to fire, Houston was observed to slip something into his mouth which he afterward explained was a bullet, which he had placed between his teeth on the advice of Jackson, who said that it was good to have something in the mouth to bite on—"It will make you aim better."

On the evening of the day of the fight a large crowd was gathered at the Nashville Inn to hear the news, and among them General Jackson. Presently one John G. Anderson, "a noted character" and a friend of Houston's, who had witnessed the duel, came dashing over the bridge on horseback with the news that Houston was unharmed and White mortally wounded. The grand jury of Simpson County in June, 1827, brought in an indictment against Houston for felony in shooting at William White with intent to kill, and the Governor of Kentucky issued a requisition on the Governor of Tennessee for his surrender. It was not complied with on the ground that the facts showed that Houston had "acted in self-defense." In fact a prosecution for such an offense in those dueling days must have been understood as a farce, and the fight undoubtedly increased Houston's popularity as an evidence of his "game."

Houston's bitter and abusive tongue frequently got him into personal difficulties in which the "satisfaction of a gentleman" was demanded by his antagonists; but he never fought again, while sober, and was equally ready with a lofty assumption of dignity or a joke to avoid the necessity. To a challenge from a political inferior in Texas he replied that he "never fought down hill." On another occasion, when called to account by a gentleman whom he had been denouncing, he said, "Why, H., I thought you were a friend of mine." "So I was, but I do not propose to be abused by you or anybody else." "Well, I should like to know," said Houston, "if a man can't abuse his friends, who in h—— he can abuse," and the affair ended in a laugh.

Mr. John J. Linn in his *Reminiscences of Fifty Years in Texas* tells the story that Houston and ex-President Burnet had an acrimonious newspaper controversy in which they bandied abusive epithets until finally Houston accused Burnet of being a "hog-thief." There was no retort in Texan phraseology capable of over-matching this, and Burnet sent a challenge to Houston by Dr. Branch T. Archer. "What does he predicate the demand upon?" said Houston in his loftiest manner. Archer replied that it was for his abuse of Mr. Burnet. "Hasn't he abused me to an equal degree? He has done so publicly and privately until I am compelled to believe that the people are equally disgusted with both of us." Houston's dignity of manner overpowered Archer, and he took back the challenge.

Houston received challenges from President Lamar, General Albert Sidney Johnston and Commodore E. W. Moore of the Texas Navy, and a good many others, which he did not accept. On one occasion being visited by a gentleman with a warlike message, he took the challenge and handed it to his private secretary with instructions to indorse it "number fourteen," and file it away. He then informed the expectant gentleman that his affair must wait its turn until the previous thirteen had been disposed of.

It is perhaps a wonder that he preserved his reputation for courage in such a community as that of Texas, while persistently declining to fight, but it does not seem to have been seriously doubted. In a speech to his constituents at Tellico, after his duel with White, Houston said that he was opposed to dueling, but had been compelled to fight in defense of his honor. "Thank God," he said, "that my antagonist was injured no worse." There is no record of how his affair with the Nashville postmaster terminated, but it certainly led to no more fighting.

Antics of Sergeant S. Prentiss

I. Campaigning with a Menagerie

THE first election of Mr. Prentiss was contested, and he was refused his seat. He returned to Mississippi, and appealed to the people against what he pronounced an unjust decision of the House. It was in this great canvass that he displayed the unrivaled abilities that at the time attracted so much attention. According to Southwestern custom, he made his appointments to speak at designated times all over the state. Crowds followed him wherever he went. The canvass became a sort of political and intellectual carnival. After a while Prentiss discovered that whenever he entered a town a traveling menagerie was sure to accompany him. It was, on examination, discovered that the proprietor of the wild beasts had advertised his show on the same days that Prentiss had announced himself to make a speech. The "boys," after consultation, decided that as the showman had made himself a sort of interloping partner in the political campaign, Prentiss should speak under the menagerie-tent, and on top of the lion's cage. It is unnecessary to say that the show was crowded at the proper time. Prentiss was introduced, and mounted his singular rostrum. For a while the audience and animals were quiet—the former listening, the latter eying the speaker with grave intensity. The first wild burst of applause electrified the permanent inmates of the menagerie. The elephant threw his trunk into the air, and echoed back the noise, while the bears and tigers significantly growled. On went Prentiss, and as each particular animal vented its rage or approbation, he most ingeniously alluded to its habits and appearance as suggestive of some man or passion. In the mean time, the stately king of beasts, who had been quietly treading the mazes of his prison, became alarmed at the footsteps overhead, and, placing his mouth close to the floor of his cage, made everything tremble by a terrible roar. This, joined

From *Bench and Bar:* A Complete Digest of the Wit, Humor, Asperities, and Amenities of the Law, by L. J. Bigelow, pp. 207–208, 211–212. New York: Harper & Brothers, Publishers. 1871.

with the already excited feelings of the audience, caused the ladies to shriek, and a fearful commotion followed. For an instant it seemed as if some terrible catastrophe was impending, when Prentiss suddenly changed his tone and manner. He commenced a playful strain, and introduced the jackal and hyena, and capped the climax by likening some well-known political opponent to a grim baboon that presided over the cage with the monkeys. The resemblance was instantly recognized, and bursts of laughter followed that literally set many persons present into convulsions. The baboon, all unconscious of the attention he was attracting, suddenly assumed a grimace, and then a most serious face, when Prentiss exclaimed, "I see, my fine fellow, that your feelings are hurt by my unjust comparison, and I humbly beg your pardon." The effect of all this can not be even vaguely imagined.

II. Prentiss's Bedbug Trial

Many years ago, when Prentiss was engaged in his large practice in Mississippi, he and his friend, Judge Gohlson, were on the circuit in some of the eastern counties of the state, and stopped for the night at Hernando. Late at night Prentiss discovered that Judge Gohlson and himself were not the only claimants for possession of the bed, as he was vigorously beset by a description of vermin which do not make very comfortable bed-fellows. Accordingly he awoke Gohlson, and a consultation was had whether they should beat a retreat, or make an effort to exterminate their assailants. The latter course was, however, adopted, and for this purpose they took from their saddle-bags a brace of pistols, with caps, powder, and other munitions of warfare. With pistol in hand, they proceeded to raise the bed-clothing, and as one of the creeping "reptiles" started from his hiding-place, "bang! bang!" would go the pistols. This, of course, aroused and alarmed the worthy landlord, who came in hot haste to the room, and, when he learned the facts, was in great rage. Prentiss demanded he should leave the room, claiming that he was only "exercising the right of self-defense—the right which the law of God and the law of man had given him." Both the entreaty and the threats of the landlord proved unavailing. The firing continued until bed, bedstead, and bedding were completely riddled with balls. At last they succeeded in capturing one of the enemy, when a difference of opinion arose between Prentiss and Judge Gohlson as to what should be his fate. At length it was agreed that the offending vermin should be "fairly and impartially tried by a *jury of his countrymen.*" Three of the landlord's sons were brought in, and forced to sit as members of the jury, and a third lawyer who was present acted as judge. The prisoner was then pinned to the wall. Judge Gohlson (who was a very able lawyer) opened for the prosecution in a speech of two hours in length. Prentiss followed for the defense in a speech of four hours. There were those present who had known Prentiss intimately, and had heard him on great occasions of his life, and who now assert that this was perhaps the most brilliant speech he ever delivered.

Mark Hardin's Argument

MARK HARDIN, of Kentucky, was a soldier, lawyer, politician, and wag when Kentucky was young. He lived in the county (Hardin) named after his father, one of the pioneers of the state. A proposition arose while he was a candidate for the Legislature to cut off a new county from Hardin, to be called Larue. The county seat was not determined upon, but Hodgenville was the favorite in the race. Mark opposed the division bitterly, but, he soon found, uselessly. Both sections wanted it to go. The candidate, seeing farther resistance was useless, made an appointment to speak at Hodgenville, the very hot-bed of county secession, and duly appeared on the stump. He began his speech somehow in this way:

"Fellow-citizens, I hear everywhere that there is a decided wish to divide our county, and some, I regret to say, oppose it. Why? I ask, why? fellow-citizens. Look at this end of Hardin. It comes out of the way. It is detached naturally from Hardin. It projects like the toe of a boot; and, fellow-citizens, the toe of that boot ought to be applied to the blunt end of any candidate who opposes this just, proper, and natural division. [Cheers.] Having shown you that this end [Larue] is thus by nature, and should be divided by law from the other, my next consideration is the county seat. To gentlemen as intelligent as you, and as familiar with the section to be divided off, I need not point out that Hodgenville will be the center of the proposed county; and where, but at the center, should the county seat be? [Cheers.] Gentlemen, you have doubtless heard the removal of our state capital spoken of. As it is, it is tucked up in a north corner of the state, where it is about as convenient a situation for the capital of the whole state as Elizabethtown [the county seat of Hardin] is to be the county seat of Larue. The same reasons that induce us to separate this part of the county from the other should make us move the capital. We must move it, and to the center of the state. Now take a map. Kentucky is 420 miles long by about 140 (in the center) wide. Now Larue county is on a perpendicular line just 70 miles from the Ohio River, and 210 from each end of the state, and Hodgenville is the center of Larue county. I have thus mathematically demonstrated to you that the state capital should be removed to Hodgenville. [Enthusiastic cheering.] Fellow-citizens, I have been inadvertently led into these questions, but I will proceed farther. In the late war [the War of 1812] Washington City was burned by the British; and why? Because it was on our exposed border. The national capital should be removed from the Atlantic coast, and to the center of the Union. Kentucky is the great seal set in the center of our mighty republic, as you will see by enumerating the surrounding states, and, as I have already shown you that this is the center of Kentucky, the national capital should be removed to Hodgenville." As some had begun to smell a large

Ibid., pp. 179–181.

Norway by this time, the cheering was not quite so loud. "Nay," said the orator, in a burst of enthusiasm, "Hodgenville is the center of God's glorious and beautiful world!"

"How in the devil do you make that out?" said an irritated voice in the crowd.

The speaker, drawing himself up, and sweeping his forefinger in a grand circle about the horizon, said, "*Look how nice the sky fits down all around!*"

Hardin didn't go to the Legislature that time, though he had mathematically demonstrated every point he made.

Quitman Heckled

WHEN General [John A.] Quitman—glorious old hero!—was a candidate for the Governorship of Mississippi, in opposition to Foote, the present writer happened to see something of the canvass. At one point, in the interior of the State, General Q. was addressing a vast meeting, and arousing all that wild enthusiasm which he was so well calculated to inspire in the hearts of the masses. He began by saying that he had come into that section a poor, friendless youth; that he had met the hand of good-fellowship, and been lifted by it through the various grades of public position; he was deeply sensible that he owed to that people all that he was, all that he hoped to be; a lifetime devoted to their service could never repay them. About this period a fellow directly in front of the stand, whose coon-skin cap and patchwork coat of many colors proclaimed him to be a mountaineer, burst forth, with a loud yell:

"Gin'ral! you're punkins!"

Considerably enlivened, the General went on: "Gentlemen, when the tocsin of war sounded over the land I endeavored to prove, to the extent of my humble capacity, not unworthy of your confidence. It is always an invidious task to speak of self, but I think I may safely say that the flag of Mississippi, under my guidance, was ever among the foremost in danger and in victory!"

The fellow in the coon-skin cap again led the crowd in a shout of tremendous excitement:

"Gin'ral! you're *some* punkins!"

Quitman continued: "The rush of war is over; I return to you in the garb of peace. I find you torn by political agitation; and my friends are kind enough to think that I can be of service in this crisis. If so, I am willing and anxious to serve. I have toiled for you unremittingly; I am ready to toil for you still. You know the present issue, and you know my views.

From "Editor's Drawer," *Harper's New Monthly Magazine*, Vol. XIX (September, 1859), No. CXII, p. 569. New York: Harper & Brothers, Publishers.

Therefore it is that I come before you to-day, asking to be made Governor of this State!"

Coon-skin could contain his emotions no longer. With tears streaming from his eyes he dashed his cap upon the ground, and exclaimed:

"Gin'ral! I'm goll darned ef you ain't *all* punkins! an' we've kept you workin' fur us all yer life, an' it's a durn shame, so it is! I go in fur lettin' you rest a little bit now; an' so *I'll jest vote fur the other man!*"

The General's speech came to an abrupt termination; and several persons were heard to inquire how "that same old coon" had forced himself into the meeting.

The Left-Handed Candidate

PERHAPS in no place in the world are there greater extremes of society shown than in Kentucky; certainly none more elegant, intelligent, or refined, and perhaps none more crude and uncultivated—though through all there runs the same generous hospitality. And this difference seems to run coincident with the surface of the country. In those beautiful garden spots of Bourbon, Fayette, and Scott counties you may with certainty depend on the finest society in the world. But pass into the hilly white-oak regions of the rivers, and you equally know the people. It has been the custom, time out of mind, for opposing candidates for office to canvass their district in company, and discuss together their issues before the people. In the good regions the candidates discuss principles, but in the white-oak they take other means of convincing or persuading the people. On one occasion two very distinguished opposing candidates offered themselves for Congress from the same district—both since deceased—W. W. Southgate, Whig, and John W. Tibbatts, Democrat. Of course they canvassed together. Both were talented, accomplished, and witty, and both knew well how to please the people. Personally they were friends and relatives. In the intelligent districts they battled like intellectual giants. In the poor regions they fired wit at each other, and made the people laugh. In one of these places they had been peculiarly happy in their remarks, and the people greatly enjoyed it. When they left, sentiment was about equally divided, and the even cry of "Hurrah, Southgate!" "Hurrah, Tibbatts!" was shouted from the harmonious throats of even parties. Both candidates mounted their horses, and left together for their next appointment; but the people, determined to have a good time, remained to finish the enjoyment with a dance. As the opposing aspirants slowly left the scene of mirth each longed for the finishing touch in molding political sentiment, and each distrusted the other. When they had gone a mile, Tibbatts discovered he had left something at the meeting, and, asking Southgate to wait for him, rode back. Southgate, distrusting him, waited a while, and then also returned, where his suspicions

From "Editor's Drawer," *Harper's New Monthly Magazine*, Vol. XXV (June, 1862), No. CXLV, pp. 140–141. New York: Harper & Brothers, Publishers.

were verified; for there he found Tibbatts playing the fiddle, and the people dancing. Sentiment was all on one side; it was all "Hurrah for Tibbatts!" He had carried the day. (Both played with equal skill, but Tibbatts only left-handed.) Southgate, mortified at his loss, determined to regain his position. Making his acknowledgments, he told the people that with their leave he would play a second to his brother Tibbatts's delightful music, and with a bow he played his best, and soon divided again the people. Throwing aside his violin, he remarked, he hated fiddling, but by their leave he would join in the dance. In that he had no equal, and soon brought the unanimous "hurrahs" for Southgate. He had triumphed, and Tibbatts was vanquished.

Before filling their next appointment Southgate was taken sick, and Tibbatts, after waiting two weeks, continued his canvass alone. When recovered, Southgate followed. He found his rival had stolen the hearts of the people, and it was an up-hill business with poor Southgate. In one place, like that mentioned, Tibbatts had pleased them so well—telling stories and jokes, and playing for them—that they utterly refused to hear Southgate. They said Tibbatts was the man for them, that they wanted no better, and Southgate had better go home; they wouldn't vote for him, etc. He told them that Tibbatts was a dear friend and relative of his, and a noble fellow —no better man was to be found (Southgate seems like an honest fellow, said they; let us hear him). "And, fellow-citizens," said Southgate, "if I can't go to Congress without abusing my dear friend Tibbatts, I'll stay at home forever." (Hurrah for Southgate! Good! He ought to go to Congress too.) "Why, fellow-citizens! he is the most talented man in Kentucky; and for accomplishments, he hasn't his equal in the world!" (We know; we heard him; he played for us. Hurrah for Tibbatts!) "But here, my friends, is one thing I can not approve of in my dear brother: he plays better left-handed than most musicians with their right! But if you only heard him right-handed, he would bend the trees with his sweet tones. What I blame in him is, that when he is among nice people whom he likes he plays right-handed; but when he is among ignorant people for whom he has no regard, whom he thinks jackasses, he says any thing is good enough for them, and so he plays for them left-handed!" (What! Why he played left-handed here! Does he mean to insinuate we are ignorant jackasses? D——n Tibbatts; away with him! Southgate is my man! Hurrah for Southgate! etc.) When the election came Tibbatts got but sixteen votes in that precinct.

The Helpful Candidate

IN THE good old times before the war, . . . the candidates for office in this Southern country were accustomed to resort to strange dodges to con-

From "Editor's Drawer," *Harper's New Monthly Magazine*, Vol. XXVII (November, 1863), No. CLXII, p. 857. New York: Harper & Brothers, Publishers.

ciliate the people and get their votes. One of them, in the Old Dominion, while stumping the outskirts of his district, came early one morning upon a clearing where a solitary man was hoeing. Alighting from his horse, he took an extra hoe standing by, and commenced working very vigorously, at the same time delicately hinting who he was, and for what purpose he had come. The man, however, was obtuse, not seeming conscious of his visitor's design till just as the sun was sinking beneath the horizon, when he suddenly brightened up and said:

"Wa'al, I reckon you're mighty good at hoein', and if I was only over in Old Virginny I'd vote for you."

The dismayed politician did not let the grass grow under his horse's feet till he was safely out of North Carolina, where he had labored hard all day for naught.

* * * * *

Another candidate came upon a "poor white man," who had a vote to give, if he did have to do his own milking. The candidate, Jones, asked him if he should hold the cow, which seemed to be uneasy, and the old man consenting very readily, he took her by the horns and held fast till the operation was done.

"Have you had Robison [his rival] around here lately?" he asked.

"Oh, yes," said the old man; "he's behind the barn now, holding the calf!"

The Cautious Candidate

Soon after the War between the States an old Warren County, Kentucky, politician was canvassing the county in a race for a seat in the state legislature. He dealt in generalities and was careful as far as possible not to commit himself on any proposition. One of his constituents was a farmer whose sheep had been killed by dogs, and consequently he was much interested in the passage of a dog law then under discussion. The old politician knew how dangerous to his kind dog laws were, and had never mentioned the subject once. Finally the farmer in question began to follow him around, and ask him in a loud voice during his speeches: "How do you stand on the dog law?"

At last the candidate, being forced against his will to make a declaration, said:

"Yes, I am in favor of a dog law."

"What kind of dog law?" called out his tormentor. "That's what we want to know."

"Well, I'll tell you," said the orator, and then hesitated.

"Go on," yelled the farmer, "and tell us what kind of a dog law you are for."

From *Kentuckians Are Different*, by M. B. Morton, p. 88. Copyright, 1938, by M. B. Morton. Louisville, Kentucky: The Standard Press.

"Wait a minute," said the candidate, "and I will tell you. I am in favor of a good law that will protect the sheep and at the same time will not hurt the dogs."

Alexander Stephens' Gastronomical Humor

WHOLLY fictitious is the anecdote which represents some burly Georgian, first Mr. Toombs and then Judge Cone, as saying to Mr. Stephens that if his ears were pinned back and his head was greased he could swallow him whole, and which represents Mr. Stephens as retorting that if the swallower could actually do this he would have more brains in his stomach than he ever had in his head.¹ Perhaps the anecdote has been told around nearly every stove in Georgia. But neither General Toombs nor Judge Cone could have been so stupid as to make the boorish remark, which is supposed to have called forth the famous retort; and General Toombs and Mr. Stephens, it must be remembered, though sometimes at variance upon political issues, were devoted lifelong friends. Some of the graybeards have actually gone so far as to say that they heard Mr. Stephens make the reply in question; but Uncle Ephraim could also swear that "he seed Marse Henry's ghost." . . .

Within the limits of authentic tradition the nearest approach to this specimen of gastronomical humor dates back to the presidential contest of 1860, when Mr. Stephens, who supported the Douglas ticket, engaged in joint debate with Colonel Ranse Wright, afterward General A. R. Wright, who supported the American or Know-Nothing candidates.

Colonel Wright was one of the ablest campaigners in the State, and on this particular occasion he made one of his best efforts. But the effect of the speech was broken by the skillful manner in which Mr. Stephens was reported to have said that, metaphorically speaking, he could eat Ben Hill for breakfast, Ranse Wright for dinner, and Bob Trippe for supper; and of course this ridiculous yarn brought down the house. The laugh was long and continuous as the audience gazed upon the diminutive storage room of the invalid statesman and thought of the little man with the big appetite.

But it came Mr. Stephens' turn to speak; and, after denying that he had made such a statement, he added that if he had contemplated a feast of the character described, he would certainly have changed the order; he would have taken Ben Hill for breakfast, Bob Trippe for dinner, and

---

From "Anecdotes Concerning Noted Men," *Library of Southern Literature*, Edwin Anderson Alderman, Joel Chandler Harris, Editors in Chief, Vol. XIV, compiled by C. Alphonso Smith, pp. 6354–6355. Copyright, 1907, 1910, by The Martin and Hoyt Company. Atlanta.

¹ The same retort to the same threat was made by Judge William "F——d," of West Tennessee, to Davy Crockett, when the former beat the latter in a campaign for Congress, according to the "Editor's Drawer," *Harper's New Monthly Magazine*, Vol. XVIII (April, 1859), No. CVII, pp. 710–711.

remembering the advice of his mother, always to eat light suppers, he would have tipped off with his friend Colonel Wright. The building fairly shook with the mirth which followed this sally. Colonel Wright realized that he was worsted in the tilt, but he joined heartily in the laugh at his expense.

"Private" John Allen

THE dry-as-dusts solemnly asseverate that humor never did any good. They are cocksure of that. Now, let's see. How did Private John Allen of Mississippi get to Congress? He joked himself in. One "fetching" bit of humor sent him to Washington as a national lawmaker. The first time John ran for the congressional nomination his opponent was the Confederate General Tucker, who had fought gallantly during the Civil War and served with distinction two or three terms in Congress. They met on the stump. General Tucker closed one of his speeches as follows: "Seventeen years ago last night, my fellow citizens, after a hard-fought battle on yonder hill, I bivouacked under yonder clump of trees. Those of you who remember as I do the times that tried men's souls will not, I hope, forget their humble servant when the primaries shall be held."

That was a strong appeal in those days, but John raised the general at his own game in the following amazing manner: "My fellow citizens, what General Tucker says to you about the engagement seventeen years ago on yonder hill is true. What General Tucker says to you about having bivouacked in yon clump of trees on that night is true. It is also true, my fellow citizens, that I was vedette picket and stood guard over him while he slept. Now then, fellow citizens, all of you who were generals and had privates to stand guard over you while you slept, vote for General Tucker; and all of you who were privates and stood guard over the generals while they slept, vote for Private John Allen!" The people caught on, took John at his word, and sent him to Congress, where he stayed till the world was filled with his renown.

Pitchfork Ben Tillman

ONE day, during a hot political campaign, bets were laid that Gus [the livery-stable keeper] could not, as he said he could, tell a Tillmanite from

From "Wit, Humor, and Anecdote," by Champ Clark, *Library of Southern Literature*, Edwin Anderson Alderman, Joel Chandler Harris, Editors in Chief, Vol. XIV, compiled by C. Alphonso Smith, pp. 6235–6236. Copyright, 1907, 1910, by The Martin and Hoyt Company. Atlanta.

From *I Came Out of the Eighteenth Century*, by John Andrew Rice, pp. 66, 93–97. Copyright, 1942, by Harper & Brothers. New York and London.

an Anti-Tillmanite at sight. Presently a well-dressed stranger came down the street and Gus said, "He's a Anti." When the stranger reached the crowd of loafers and was asked, "Are you for Tillman?" he replied indignantly, "Certainly not," and Gus collected his dollar. Another of the same looks gave the same answer, and Gus collected another dollar. Then a broganed blue-jeaned unwashed customer came along; Gus put him down as a Tillmanite and won again. At last he grew so confident that when another man came in sight, unkempt and unshaven and dressed in a suit that had once been decent but was now spotted and caked with mud, Gus varied his question and said to him, "You're for Tillman, ain't you?" The man gave him a cur-dog look and said, "No, pardner, I ain't. The reason I look this way I bin drunk three days."

*   *   *   *   *

While Senator Hammond was making his last stand for the old order—Southerners are never so happy as when making a last stand—and charming his audience with Ciceronian periods, an eleven-year-old boy in Edgefield County was nursing a swollen eye and, when the ball fell from the socket and hung down on his cheek, enduring the pain without flinch or whimper. In his reading, Lincolnian in its breadth, he had run across the Spartan boy and he would be another. Years later he told this to Judge Hammond, grandson of the Senator, and laughed at himself. "Lord no," he said, "I ain't such a damn fool now. Even a little bellyache starts me howling like hell for the women folks to come and make a fuss over me." This was Ben Tillman, the villain of my childhood, lovingly and hatefully called "Pitchfork Ben," for he said, when running for the Senate, "Send me to Washington and I'll pitchfork the guts out of Grover Cleveland," and the name had stuck as a symbol of his native violence.

We were all, except the postmaster and mail carriers, Democrats, which meant that there was no party, only factions, and factional politics are personal politics. The aristocracy had kept this fact veiled in oratory, but Tillman knew, and in order to expose his opponents to public view and castigation, he invented a kind of circus: candidates for state offices traveled about the state together, speaking from the same platform and pommeling each other, often in the same words, every day at a new place. Sometimes the followers of a favorite made such a hubbub that his opponent's speech was drowned out; this was counted a great success. People came from long distances, as distance was counted then, to listen and laugh and eat and drink; white people, not Negroes—Negroes were excluded, but often some of them stood on the edge of the crowd and looked on and listened with quiet faces while they were being denounced by their white fellows, and sometimes laughed with appreciation at a flight of invective.

Small boys took politics as passionately as their elders and early learned the language. Tillmanites were the scum of the earth, consigned to Hell and cast into outer darkness. Justice, glory, honor, all the words that men use to drug and enslave their fellows, rolled off our tongues with the self-righteous assurance of invincible ignorance. Tillman's offense, in the light of the time, consisted in bringing injustice up to date. (Renewed truth is always in bad taste.) The enemy was no longer the Yankee, who was gone now, but the aristocrat, the planter and his social equals. Small farmers, who year round wore black felt hats grimed with sweat and dirt while they scraped a mean living from their worn-out land, were being driven into tenantry or worse by falling cotton prices. Economists would now say that the real enemy was overproduction, but who can hate an abstraction so abstract? South Carolinians liked their hatred to be personal, and the "Wool Hat Boys" whooped with delight when Tillman ripped the hide off the "Columbia Ring" and the Charlestonian gentlemen, whose dignified literary replies were unheard in the general din.

To a state inured to oratory, Tillman's was another language. Instead of transporting his hearers to a mythical past and dulling their souls with praise of what they never were, he used the words of cotton patch and cornfield, and waked men to their present. "I'm fits on facts," he said. "The war is over and we are whipped." Overwhelmed veterans struck back with a question as to his own war record, although they knew that his missing eye gave the answer. Wade Hampton's periods were forgotten, but Tillman's words stung and stuck. In Columbia, "the head center of devilment," members of the Ring, "rapscallions and scalawags who scramble for a place at the public crib," took country legislators to the Columbia Club and gave them a taste of high life. "No wonder," he said, "the corn-bread-and-bacon fellows like it." When he had been governor for two years, he ran for the United States Senate. "I went into the fight for the biggest plum, and I shook it down, and now I'm after another." No gentleman ever spoke that way, whatever his private thoughts might be. "The poor man is a farmer, the rich man a planter" put into simple words the economic foundation of social distinctions, and brought forth a reply that, with a change of a name, might be used to-day: "Tillman has built up class against class; there is but one name for it, Communism—Russia over and over."

My father, who was the only one of the family who had any sympathy for Tillman—Uncle Ellie strung along with the other side, while learning the language of Tillman—often told of the campaign of 1890, the year this charge of Communism was made; how the crowds, drunk with oratory and corn liquor, howled speakers down and broke up meetings, and how the gentleman, in the moment of defeat, uncovered his savage nature. At the meeting in Columbia Tillman pointed to his opponent, who had just finished speaking, and said, "When I touched him a moment ago on the stand, he stood back as though I was an adder and said, 'Don't touch me.'" My father sometimes said, after some social humiliation, "I have often wished I had been a gentleman," but when he told the story of Tillman and the gentleman he was the proud poor boy from Colleton County.

One flaw reserved Tillman to mediocrity—his hatred, which was fear, of the Negro; a hatred that, dripping from the tongues of his followers and successors, has poisoned the soul of South Carolina. And yet he, as they have not, put his prejudice in its only terms: "for the simple reason that God Almighty made him colored and did not make him white." Otherwise he saw as clearly as a politician can. . . . When he took over the running of the state, public education on the higher level—I do not use the words facetiously—was concerned with the making of scholars and gentlemen. (Ladies were presumably home-made.) Tillman established Clemson and Winthrop, colleges for farm boys and girls, not without opposition, particularly as to Clemson. Thomas Clemson had inherited the estate of John C. Calhoun from his wife, who was Calhoun's daughter; when he died childless he left it to the state for an agricultural college. The Charleston *News and Courier* objected to its acceptance, on the ground that it would mean robbing of her ancestral rights the only surviving granddaughter of the old statesman. . . . Tillman wiped out the saloon and set up in its stead a state dispensary, incurring alike the anger of the wicked and the pious. The W.C.T.U. raged in a manner that belied its middle initials, and the liquor interests tried to cut off all sources of supply. When it looked as if they would succeed, he went himself to Ohio and found a distiller who would sell, and forced his reform on the state. (The bottles, with a palmetto blown in the glass, are now collectors' items.) . . . He cowed his opponents with his single blazing eye and scornful jibing tongue. Editors and orators whipped at him with screaming anger; he loved it, and let no chance go by, as he said, "to grind the grit in 'em." In the days of his crusading nothing could buy him off, neither honors nor money, offered or withheld. By a paradox he was trying, through dictatorship, to make democracy a reality where before it had been only a name. He failed, and lived to see that, under leaders who were followers, an ignorant, mean, and prejudiced mob can be a dreadful thing. Here was the spiritual progenitor of Huey Long.

Stories and Sayings of Governor Bob Taylor of Tennessee

. . . I STOOD on the stump in Tennessee as elector for Grover Cleveland, and thus I turned my eagle loose:

"Fellow-citizens, we live in the grandest country in the world. It stretches

> From Maine's dark pines and crags of snow
> To where magnolia breezes blow;

it stretches from the Atlantic, on the east, to the Pacific, on the west."

An old fellow jumped up and threw his hat in the air and shouted:

From *Life Pictures,* by Senator Bob Taylor, Being a Collection of Senator Taylor's Lectures and Public Addresses; also, His Editorials in Bob Taylor's Magazine and Taylor-Trotwood Magazine, pp. 26–28, 41–42, 111, 140, 272–273. Copyright, 1907, by Taylor-Trotwood Publishing Co. Nashville, Tenn.

"Let 'er stretch, durn 'er! Hurrah for the Dimocrat party!"

* * * * *

An old Dutchman in my neck of the woods had a beautiful boy, of whom he was very proud, and he decided to find out the bent of the little fellow's mind. He adopted a very novel method. He slipped into the boy's room one morning and placed on his table a Bible, a bottle of whisky, and a silver dollar. "Now," said the old man, "ven dot boy comes in, ef he takes dot dollar, he iss going to be a beezniss man; ef he takes dot Bible, he vill a preacher be; ef he takes dot visky, he iss no good—he iss going to be a drunkard."

He hid himself behind the door to see which his son would choose. In came the boy whistling. He ran up to the table, picked up the dollar and put it in his pocket; he picked up the Bible and put it under his arm; then he snatched up the bottle of whisky and took two or three drinks, and went out smacking his lips; and the old Dutchman poked his head out from behind the door and exclaimed:

"Mein gracious! He iss going to be a politician!"

* * * * *

. . . I saw the school commissioners visit him [the "old field" school teacher], and heard them question him as to his system of teaching. They asked him whether, in geography, he taught that the world was round or that the world was flat. With great dignity he replied:

"That depends upon whar I'm teachin'. If my paytrons desire me to teach the round system, I teach it; and if they desire me to teach the flat system, I teach that."

* * * * *

. . . An old Texan once told me it [the Texas climate] was the quickest climate in the world. He said that an old farmer was driving along one day; his team was composed of oxen; and it was so hot that one of the oxen fell dead from sunstroke, and, while he was skinning him, the other one froze to death.

* * * * *

. . . There [on the rolling prairies of Texas] I have sailed and sailed and sailed across landscapes of gorgeous beauty, and through cross-timbers of gorgeous length, until I landed upon a typical Texas sand bank, where the fleas are so thick that the engineer pulls his train up and has the flat cars loaded with sand; and when he gets to the place where the sand has to be unloaded, he gives his engine a toot or two and the whole thing hops off.

* * * * *

. . . There is one branch of business in which we are as vigorous as our Northern brethren, and that is politics. Our annual crop of politicians is equal to the annual crop of cotton bales—not in weight, but in numbers. Now and then we are blessed with a statesman, for many are called and but few are chosen. We produce more majors and colonels in time of peace

than any other country in the world, and sometimes we raise a little of
that sulphurous article which begins with "h" and ends with an "ell."

* * * * *

An old politician once shouted from the stump, "Fellow-citizens, I know
no North, I know no South, I know no East, I know no West"; and a
barefooted boy yelled from the gallery: "You'd better go an' study jog-er-
fey!"

I think the boy was right. I believe in sectional lines so long as they
are not the demarcations of prejudice. I believe that the sectional lines of
peace and patriotism are the very safeguards of the republic.

I believe not in sectional hatred, but in sectional patriotism, which loves
home better than any other spot on earth. I would despise the Yankee who
does not love the rocks and rills of New England better than all the roses
and palms and dreamy landscapes of the whole South. I would loathe the
Westerner who does not believe that sixteen pounds of silver is as good as
one pound of gold—especially if he owns a silver mine.

But I love the land of Dixie best. There . . . the oranges and mag-
nolias bloom, except when blighted by a blizzard from the land of Yankee
Doodle.

Sayings and Speeches of Governor Jeff Davis of Arkansas

I[1]

EVERY woman is entitled to a baby and a bonnet.

If the boys in the hills will but touch hands with the boys in the valleys,
we will in this campaign gain a victory for good government and good
citizenship in Arkansas.

I'd rather talk to 300 sharecroppers than 3,000 bankers any day in
the week.

* * * * *

When Powell Clayton was ambassador to Mexico, Jeff Davis was serving
his first term as governor. Colonel Clayton, on his way from Washington City, to his post in Mexico City, stopped off in Little Rock for a brief
visit with old friends. While in Little Rock it was planned to tender him
a banquet in recognition of his appointment to Mexico. The committee on
arrangements called on Jeff Davis at his office and wanted to know if the
governor would like to have a plate at the banquet, the cost of which
was $5. Governor Davis said, "I won't give $5 to go to old Clayton's
banquet, but I'll make it ten to go to his funeral."

---

[1] From *What a Preacher Saw, Through a Key-Hole, in Arkansas*, by L. S. (Sharpe)
Dunaway, pp. 80–82 *passim*. Copyright, 1925, by L. S. Dunaway. Little Rock, Arkansas: From the Press of the Parke-Harper Publishing Company.

Jeff Davis declared that the ground on which the new state capitol was constructed was "too poor for two Irishmen to raise a row on!"

Are you a Democrat or a dog?

Politics was so rotten when I left Russelville, you could not get two Democrats to sleep together—they would steal the cover off of each other.

* * * * *

Lots of planters live in town and farm with their mouths on the edge of town.

Old John D. Rockefeller would give half the oil he's got, if he could eat half as many biscuits as I can.

If some of them high-collared, fly-weight dudes of the East had sense enough to set down to a big dish of turnip greens, poke sallet, and hog jowl, they might sweat enough of that talcum powder off to look a little like a man.

II [2]

I do not know that I will ever marry again, but if I do, I am coming out here in the country and marry one of these big, fat country girls, that can cook an oven of hot biscuits, throw them up in the chimney, and run around and catch them in her apron before I can get my boots on.

Some men want a woman to sing "Amazing Grace, How Sweet the Sound," and know how to tune a piano, but I want one that knows how to tune a hot stove and bake big hot biscuits with pimples on them.

I have got eight children and nine pointer dogs in Little Rock. If any of you farmers should come to the city, come to my house and make it your home. The fatted calf will be killed, and I will roll down a few big yellow yams, fry some country hams and cook about two dozen eggs and we will eat eggs until we have every old hen in Arkansas cackling. Just come down there and act like you had good sense.

I am a Hard Shell Baptist in religion. I believe in foot-washing, saving your seed potatoes, and paying your honest debts.

Old Armour and Cudahy never raised a sow and pigs in their life. Yet the prices of meat are so high that I can hardly buy breakfast bacon in Little Rock enough to support my family. I just buy one little slice, hang it up by a long string, and let each one of my kids jump up and grease their mouths and go to bed.

If you red-necks or hill-billies ever come to Little Rock be sure and come to see me—come to my house. Don't go to the hotels or wagon yards, but come to my house and make it your home. If I am not there tell my wife who you are, that you are my friend and belong to the sunburned sons of toil. Tell her to give you some hog jowl and turnip greens. She may be

---

[2] From *The Life Story of Jeff Davis*, the Stormy Petrel of Arkansas Politics, by Chas. Jacobson, His Private Secretary, pp. 231–239 *passim*. Little Rock, Arkansas: From the Press of Parke-Harper Publishing Co. 1925.

busy making soap, but that will be all right; you will be properly cared for, and it will save you a hotel bill. The word "Welcome" is written on the outside of the door for my friends.

When I licked that gang at Little Rock during the last campaign, they went around on the streets with their faces looking as long as a saddle blanket. The barbers actually charged them double price for a shave. Some of them call them Colonel, some Captain, some Judge, Judge of what? Judge of good-looking women and good whiskey? There's where the judge shines. The high-collared crowd haven't got sense enough to beat me for Governor, but they know whether it is Schlitz, Budweiser or Pabst.

I have been led many a time to a farm house on the hillside or valley by the smell of fried meat, as I can smell it further than I can hear a dinner horn or an old cow bell.

If there is any profession the American people can do without, it is the lawyer. Most of them want to go to the Legislature, become the proprietor of a railroad pass or be appointed beer inspector. Lawyers can't do anything but raise a row and get you farmers into a lawsuit. There are more little puny, half-starved lawyers around Little Rock than any town of its size in the United States. . . .

The other day an old hay-binder from Skipper's Gap attended our speaking. He took Judge Wood off, and I supposed they were behind the smokehouse to take a drink of booze. He asked Judge Wood who is his campaign manager. Judge Wood replied that it was a little lawyer at Little Rock. Yes, ladies and gentlemen, a little two-by-four upstart lawyer by the name of Wiley who hasn't sense enough to bound Pulaski county. The farmer also drug me to one side and I thought he was going to bum me for a chew of Hillside Navy. He asked me who is my campaign manager. I told him it was just the farmers of Arkansas.

I am getting tired of politics; politics will ruin anybody in the world. It has almost ruined me.

In the midst of one of his speeches an old farmer in the audience yelled, "Go on, Jeff, and speak as long as you want to, we are all for you." Laughter followed. Jeff replied: "Much obliged, Captain; but I wish you would sit down and let one fool talk at a time."

Ah! ladies and gentlemen, as I came through on the sun-kissed prairies of Arkansas county, the beautiful city of DeWitt recalled old times. It recalled the time when I was a barefoot boy with laughing eyes, chasing the winged butterfly up at Dover, away up there off the railroad in Pope county, where the moon, the sun and stars shine thirteen months in the year; recalled the time when I learned to play "naught is naught, figger is figger, multiply the white man and subtract the nigger"; when I learned to play the flute and fiddle, and of course to part my hair in the middle. [This sounded like Bob Taylor.] Many a moonlight October night, I have turned my hounds out o'er the hills and valleys of good old Pope county, and the most beautiful music that could come from the keys of an organ, would come from those long, flop-eared hounds of mine. I have picked cotton, possum hunted and raised great big old yaller yam potatoes and pumpkins. Mr. Chairman, isn't your mouth watering? . . .

Our fathers did not guarantee to us happiness itself. They guaranteed the right to pursue happiness. The door of opportunity is not today open to all alike.

Everything is in trust except acorns and persimmons; those are all that are left to the poor people of this country.

In the Holy Writ the Master says, "Go into the vineyard and work." He does not say, "Go into the vineyard and corner all the grapes."

It is time to disconnect God Almighty from the dollar when you have to go out and buy it.

I am for the under-dog in every fight. I do not care what kind of a fight it is. You can just pick out your kind of a dog and wherever you see a dog fight, I do not care where it is, you may just swear that Jeff Davis is for the under-dog of that fight.

Stories and Sayings of Henry W. Grady

AN ATLANTA woman called on him one day to inquire indignantly why he had printed a certain article.

"Did you read it?" Grady asked.

"Yes, I did," was the reply.

"Well," said the editor, "that's why I put it there."

* * * * *

An Atlantan who knew of Grady's ventures in the market called one day to present him with an array of statistics on the production, consumption, and export of cotton. Each time the visitor made a point he would ask: "Ain't that true?" Each time Grady would assent. Finally the interviewer asked: "If all these things are true, is it not clear that the price of cotton must go up, and I will make a killing if I buy futures on this set of facts?"

"Yes," replied Grady, "except for one thing."

"What is that?" inquired his visitor.

"Cotton is a damned fool!"

* * * * *

The American Senate is the baldest-headed body of men on earth—or in the heavens above or the waters beneath, for that matter. . . . I have heard that women have no beard because they keep their jaws wagging so perpetually that the whisker has no time to bloom; so I suppose the constant turmoil of the brains beneath the skulls of these seigniors have worn their hair off, just as volcanoes with any vim in their craters have no shrub-

From *Henry W. Grady*, Spokesman of the New South, by Raymond B. Nixon, pp. 14, 20–21, 121, 178, 329. Copyright, 1943, by Alfred A. Knopf, Inc. New York.

bery about their summit. The best explanation, however, that I ever had of bald-headedness, came from an old fellow that I once accosted with the question, "How come you bald-headed?" "My son," said he, leaning paternizingly [sic] over me, "I was born so."

* * * * *

. . . We have the best country in the world. The sun shines on us kindly, the soil yields us abundant crops, the earth gives us gold, iron and coal at every fissure. How grander a mission it is to develop this section into its full power and production than to win a share of public patronage. What we need is fewer stump-speakers and more stump-pullers—less talk and more work—fewer gin-mills and more gins—fewer men at the front and more men at the hoe. One plow is worth twenty politicians. In the old days of slavery it was a passion with us to lead in politics—in these days of close competition, he should be the best man who can lead in the corn row.

* * * * *

If I die, I die serving the South, the land I love so well. Father fell in battle for it. I am proud to die talking for it.

The Kentucky Candidate and the Voter

I. Campaigning in the Mountains of Kentucky

In some cases the self-importance of the individual voter amounts to absurdity. For instance, not long ago a present county Judge, who was a candidate for reëlection, was watering his horse in the ford of a creek, when a lank, loosely built fellow on a saddleless mule came down from the opposite mountain, and turning neither to the right nor the left, rode splashing and plunging straight through the stream, almost bumping into the gasping, struggling Judge as he passed.

"Hey, there, what you doing?" cried the man with the Judge who was getting his share of the sprinkling.

"Acrossin' this crick in the ford," drawled the mountaineer.

"But Lord," cried the other, "you needn't drown people."

"Hadn' a' been thar, ye wouldn't a' got splattered," returned the mountaineer, unmoved.

"But you could have ridden over a little," expostulated the other.

"Hain't never seed no call to git out of a straight road yit," remarked the mountaineer serenely.

"I suppose of course you know that this gentleman you have treated to a shower bath is the Judge of this county?"

From *Wit and Humor of American Politics*, A Collection from Various Sources Classified under Appropriate Subject Headings, pp. 8–12. Copyright, 1903, by George W. Jacobs & Co. Philadelphia.

"Knowed it all the time," admitted the mountaineer, indifferently. " 'Tain't so much, though. I 'low Jedges is made by votin'. Hain't they? I'm a voter—me," and a touch of arrogance came into his voice. "Got six boys and ten nephys and three o' my gals got husbands—all voters—we. That air somethin'. Gee-up, mewl."

And he disappeared through the low-growing laurel.

II. "PAP'S" INDIFFERENCE

Sometimes an old fellow will take it into his head not to commit himself with regard to his intentions on election day. With such a one the candidate always sees a time. One afternoon a candidate for sheriff rode up to a cabin built high upon the side of a mountain. In answer to the "Hello!" eight shock-headed children came rolling out of the only opening in the side of the house.

"Where's your father?" asked the candidate.

Several of the youngsters disappeared around the side of the house at the sound of the voice, but they gave no answer.

"Your father—where is he?" again demanded the candidate. Still he got no answer.

"Well, then, where is your pap?"

"Aw, pap?" A look of intelligence spread over their faces. "He's smokin'."

"Tell him to come out here, will you?"

The remainder of the brood scampered off. Presently a boy stuck his head around the corner of the house. "Pap 'lows he never meanders about when he's a-smokin'. He jest sets an' smokes."

"Well, is he in the house or out of it?" asked the candidate, politely.

"Out," was the laconic reply.

"Do you suppose he will object to our riding around where he is 'settin' ' and a-smokin'?"

The boy darted out of sight and soon came back again. "Pap 'lows he ain't holdin' yore horses?"

The candidate thought he would risk it, so he went around in the direction taken by the boy. "Pap" was sitting on a log taking long draws from a much-discolored cob pipe. Ordinarily, the mountaineer is the most hospitable fellow in the world, but "pap" paid no attention to the candidate.

"Fine afternoon," remarked the candidate for sheriff.

"Seed many a one as fine," returned "pap," listlessly.

"The warm, earthy smell makes a fellow feel like he wants to get hold of his hoe," again tried the would-be sheriff.

" 'Pears like you hain't got hold o' yourn yit," returned "pap."

The candidate made another effort to be agreeable. "You have a pretty clearing here. I presume you raise fine potatoes and corn."

"Pap" removed his pipe, spat deliberately, and returned the pipe to his mouth. " 'Tain't a good idee to presoom."

Seeing that the man disdained to pass the pleasantries of the day, the unlucky candidate plunged at once into politics. "You are interested in the coming primary, I suppose?" he began blandly.

"Hain't much more sense in supposin' than they is in presoomin'."

The candidate began to get exasperated.

"Well, then, leaving supposin' and presoomin' out of the question, how do you stand in the coming election?"

"Hev stood in water and snow, but never tried standin' in elections," snapped "pap."

"Well," cried the thoroughly flustered candidate, "I reckon you know I'm running for sheriff, and I'm here to ask you to vote for me."

"Pap" cocked his eye at him speculatively. "How do you know you hain't walkin' fer sheriff?"

This was too much for the candidate, so he got on his horse and rode away without another word.

More Money for Hooper

ALONG in the 80's a lawyer by the name of Hooper settled in one of the county-seat towns of East Texas. No one knew just where he came from or why he came to Texas, but it was rumored that he had come from Virginia. No one ever questioned Hooper about his personal history. He was dignified and aloof, and made no effort to cultivate intimacy—indeed, he kept to himself and made few friends.

But it was evident from the start that Hooper was a man of learning. He dressed in the fashion of his day, wore a Prince Albert coat, carried a gold-headed cane, and conducted himself with such decorum that he soon gained the respect, although not the friendship, of the people generally. He owned an excellent library and at times he quoted Latin and Greek authors. He rode in a fine carriage and was generally attended by a Negro footman. What with his aristocratic bearing and cool courtesy, it soon became apparent to the people that Hooper was haughty and that he disdained the common run of folks.

Without doubt Hooper's attainments were such that he could have been popular had he so desired, but he evidently did not want popularity. He had a passion for attending to his own business and leaving other people to theirs. He was in fact a stoic, if not a cynic. In a small county-seat town he did the unusual thing of confining his practice to civil matters. He simply would not take a criminal case. Neither would he take small civil cases; that is, he would not practise in the justice courts. But such was his

From "Anecdotes about Lawyers," by Lloyd E. Price, in *Backwoods to Border*, edited by Mody C. Boatright and Donald Day, pp. 208–212. Texas Folk-Lore Society Publications, Number XVIII, J. Frank Dobie, General Editor. Copyright, 1943, by the Texas Folk-Lore Society. Austin and Dallas: Texas Folk-Lore Society and University Press in Dallas, Southern Methodist University.

learning and skill as a technical civil lawyer that he soon enjoyed a large practice. It was he, you might say, that introduced in his section the custom of appealing to the higher courts. When he was defeated in the local courts, he nearly always appealed and in most instances he succeeded in reversing the judgments of the lower courts. Such was his success that it was not long until he represented almost all of the monied clients in his county.

As Hooper became more independent financially, he became more independent in his views and bolder in expressing them. For instance, one day in arguing a motion for rehearing before a judge who had held against him more from political than from legal reasons, Hooper said in the course of his argument, "It was plain to the honest and fearless statesmen who founded this nation, as it is plain to intelligent people of this day, that the greatest danger to the institutions of America lies in the uneducated masses of people when led by self-seeking politicians and demagogues." He also said that when America was destroyed it would be destroyed by some power-loving demagogue with the howling majority behind him. He said that unless officials, including judges, stood up to their oaths and obligations the country would eventually disintegrate.

It was only natural that Hooper should be unpopular.

One of Hooper's best clients was the largest bank in the town where he practised. One fall that bank was sued out in one of the rural Justice of the Peace Courts for $100 by a tenant farmer. Now Hooper decided that he wanted to represent his bank in all its business, and so he decided to make an exception to his rule. As the plaintiff was represented by a popular young orator who had political ambitions, Hooper expected hard sledding in the rural court out where the plaintiff lived.

But Hooper faced the music. On the day of the trial he dressed more immaculately than usual and drove out to the precinct court in his rubber-tired carriage. The Justice of the Peace convened court in the lower story of an old frame lodge building. There were an old pine table and a few chairs with cow-hide bottoms. The jury of six men were close neighbors and friends of the plaintiff and no doubt had prejudged the case in his favor before court convened. Hooper did not ask the jury a question, and made no objections whatever. Both the old Justice of the Peace and the members of the jury were dressed in their ordinary work clothes, and their appearance contrasted strongly with that of the spic and span Lawyer Hooper. As the young lawyer for plaintiff put on his evidence, the jury squirted long streams of tobacco juice on the floor. At times they glared ominously at Hooper who sat there in splendid isolation with not a single representative of his client present save himself, and without a single defendant witness.

When the plaintiff had made his case against the bank and rested, Hooper arose and curtly announced, "No evidence for defendant will be offered."

The plaintiff's lawyer then addressed the jury and you may be sure that he castigated the bank. Dramatically, he depicted the plaintiff as a hard-

working, honest man who made his living by the sweat of his brow working in the field from sun-up to sun-down, while the defendant was a
rich, greedy, soulless corporation that increased its wealth by feeding on
the meagre earnings of men like the plaintiff. He concluded by comparing
the defendant bank to the greedy money-changers whom Christ drove out
of the temple. By the time he had finished the jury were as mad as biting
sows and at times cast sullen glances at the cool and immaculate Hooper,
who sat there as the sinister representative of corporate wealth and
greed.

Hooper arose to speak but before saying a word he first flecked some
dust from his tailored coat and then addressed the jury, "Gentlemen of the
jury, if I may call you such, there never was a bigger lie ever told on earth
than by old Tom Jefferson when he said that all men are created equal.
Why, look at me and then look at you; here I stand, well-educated and
well-dressed—bathe every day while there you sit with snuff and tobacco
all over you. Some of you haven't bathed in weeks; there you sit with
your cheap breeches held up by one suspender prong fastened by a
shingle nail. Yes, I assert there never was a bigger lie ever told on earth
than that by Jefferson when he said that all men are created equal."

The Justice of the Peace was too astonished to remonstrate and the
jury from some cause seemed determined to listen to the end.

"I know," said Hooper, "exactly what you're going to do. You are
prejudiced against my bank and you are going to bring in a judgment in
favor of your friend, the plaintiff, and that is just what I want you to do.
The defendant bank has plenty of money, it has already paid me one good
fee to come down here; and it is able to pay me several more fees in this
case. When you decide against me here, I will appeal right away to the
county court and that will mean another good fee for me—more money for
Hooper. [At this point he tapped his breast significantly.] The county
court is some little better than this court, but even if I am defeated there I
shall appeal to the Supreme Court of Texas, which, for your information, is
a court composed of three scholars and gentlemen who know the law, and
incidentally, that appeal will mean another fee for me—more money for
Hooper. At last in the Supreme Court we will get justice and that court will
reverse the lower judgments and this plaintiff will get nothing except that
he will get all the costs of every court taxed against him. Now go ahead,
and do what you want to do."

One husky juror looked as if he were about to lunge at the offending
lawyer, and Hooper squared himself, but the bailiff interfered and commanded the jury to retire to make up their verdict, which they did.

In just a few minutes they returned and their foreman read their verdict
which went like this:

"We, the jury, find against the plaintiff and in favor of the defendant
bank."

Subsequently the plaintiff's lawyer asked the foreman just why they
had brought in such a verdict. The foreman said, "Why, that old devil

Hooper would do just what he threatened, and we did not want him to get another damned cent out of this case."

A Waste of Lightning

LIEUTENANT GOVERNOR BILL THORNE, noted for his wit and geniality, was employed in a suit against the Western Union Telegraph Company for damages. When the trial came on there was a great drouth prevailing, while the spring before there had been unprecedented floods.

"Gentlemen of the jury," Thorne exclaimed, with flashing eyes, "this soulless corporation is meaner than h——l itself. There is nothing it will not do. Not content with grinding the people by exorbitant charges, not content with failing to deliver dispatches informing people of the approaching death of their loved ones, so that they might be able to see them for the last time, it has actually appropriated the lightning from the clouds in order to send dispatches to fill its already bloated pocket-book. There is a certain amount of lightning necessary, as you all know, to purify the air and regulate the elements. Last spring they used so much lightning that everything was thrown out of gear and great floods swept over the land, devastating the crops and drowning thousands of good people. So much rain fell then that later there was none left to fall, and now you are wilting in heat, with a drouth that is parching and destroying your crops and drying up the water courses, so that there is not enough water for man and beast. Their entire business should be broken up and every mother's son of them confined in the penitentiary. I sometimes wonder why the Lord does not strike them dead for thus interfering with His business and bringing desolation on the people."

A good round verdict was the result of this impassioned appeal.

Tom Heflin's Stories

. . . A PERFECT example of a man who for a score of years ministered to the southerner's delight in the sport of politics may be descried in the career of J. Thomas Heflin.

* * * * *

. . . Heflin relied upon his unvarying formula with the Alabama voter:

From *Stories and Speeches of William O. Bradley,* with Biographical Sketch by M. H. Thatcher, pp. 16–17. Copyright, 1916, by Transylvania Printing Co. Lexington, Kentucky.

From *90° in the Shade,* by Clarence Cason, pp. 72, 75, 77–78, 81–82. Copyright, 1935, by the University of North Carolina Press. Chapel Hill.

the raucous tale, with mimicry of Negro or rural characters, followed by an irrelevant interpretation in terms of whatever issues might be pressing at the moment. The convulsed assemblage was never a stickler for precise logical progression.

*   *   *   *   *

In the speaking campaign, Heflin laid violent stress upon the issues of 1928, for he wished to capture the 120,000 anti-Smith votes in Alabama. Toward this end he interpreted the favorite old story of the early days of the telephone. "When these telephone people were first trying to buy up tracts of land so they could set up their rural lines, they couldn't persuade Uncle Johnny to listen to reason," Heflin began. "All Uncle Johnny would say was, 'I'm agin 'em.' They tried to explain just how the contraption worked. 'Do you mean to tell me yer words goes along of them thar little wires?' Uncle Johnny asked. 'Is them wires hollow? If they ain't hollow, why don't them words fall offen the wires? An' why don't the rain wash 'em off?'

"Finally they got the old man in town one day and made a connection with his wife in a little place about ten miles away. 'Come on now, Uncle Johnny,' they said, 'an' talk to yer old woman.' 'Is she in that 'ere little box?' Uncle Johnny wanted to know. They pushed him up to the telephone, in spite of his protests, and put the receiver to his ear. Just then there came a streak of lightning and a big thunder clap. Uncle Johnny was struck. As he fell back five feet and began to crawl under a table, he yelled out, 'That's her all right—that shore is my old woman!' "

As soon as his voice could be heard above the uproar, Heflin continued, "Now you can't blame old Uncle Johnny for being a little skeptical when he first heard about that mysterious telephone, and I can't blame you for wanting proof about some of the things I'm telling you. It takes a stroke of lightning to wake up some people. Well, . . ."

*   *   *   *   *

All the characters and episodes of Mr. Heflin's tales were close to the life experiences of his followers. . . .

Old Tom related that a stranger in a certain rural district was visiting an old man who lived by himself. Noticing a series of ten or twelve holes bored through the wall near the floor, the stranger inquired what they were. "Them's cat holes," the old man said. "Cat holes?" the stranger answered in surprise. "Why do you need ten or twelve of them? Ain't one hole enough? Don't all them make hit powerful drafty in here?" "Mebbe you don't understand, stranger," the old man explained, "but them cats do. They knows that when I says 'Scat!' I means *scat!*" Drawing himself up proudly and waving his arms belligerently in a sweeping gesture, Heflin declaimed, "And these Raskobites and traitorous hirelings know that when I say 'Scat!' I mean *scat!*"

Tom Watson Defends Jack Peavy

As AN example of his [Tom Watson's] juristic technique and forensic methods, there is the case of Jack Peavy.[1] This case came fairly early in his career; in itself it is relatively unimportant and little known; it is not selected to illustrate Watson's legal skill, but for what it may reveal about the lawyer himself, his methods, his clients, his juries.

Peavy, it seems, had boarded a train in an intoxicated condition and made himself such a nuisance that the conductor had ejected him from the train. Whereupon, it was charged, Peavy attempted to shoot the conductor, but instead was shot by the conductor. Peavy then escaped. Discovered later by a constable's posse he was again wounded, this time by an incredible number of buckshot, placed under arrest, and later tried for assault with intent to murder. Watson was appointed to defend him. It appears that Peavy did not enjoy an enviable reputation in Warrenton, where he was tried, and that public sentiment was strongly against him. It was, naturally, Watson's first concern to propitiate and if possible to convert this prejudicial atmosphere into one favorable to the defendant. He began with what appears to be an unconscious travesty upon Antony's oration on the fallen Caesar—baring the wounds of the victim. *Pianissimo.*

Why, gentlemen, Jack Peavy has been shot till his hide wouldn't hold shucks. If he was a cow his skin wouldn't be worth tanning. His coffin will be a lead mine. It's a wonder to me all the little boys who are learning to shoot don't practice on his carcass. The law certainly would not interfere. . . . No! Let the brave work go on! Barnett shot *him* and the law accuses Peavy. A constable's crowd shot him without warning till the wife of his bosom might have tracked him seventeen miles by the life blood as it drained his veins. And the law makes no complaint.

This having taken effect, he proceeds with another trend. *Crescendo.*

The further we go the more clearly will we see one of these cruel class differences that disgrace the justice of men.

Suppose Gen. Toombs passing on this Washington train had cursed. Is there a man on the jury who believes that this young conductor would have collared him and have spoken to him as he did Peavy? How absurd. Toombs, sacred by reason of his class, his cloth; powerful in the golden strength of his hundreds of thousands. . . .

But Peavy! That's another matter. Slouch hat and homespun dress

---

From *Tom Watson, Agrarian Rebel*, by C. Vann Woodward, pp. 49–51. Copyright, 1938, by the Macmillan Company. New York.

[1] MS. Journal 2, p. 305. The case was apparently tried in 1882.—C. V. W.

inspire the youth with no such awe. Hear how his conduct speaks: "I will collar him like I would a slave, speak to him as I would to a slave and if he dares resent either I'll shoot him like a dog. Such men have no rights that I am bound to respect."

And finally for the "grand spread eagle." *Fortissimo.*

Peavy answers the shaking of the pistol in his face by saying, "You—. You damned son of a ——," and is shot. At least he had endured all he could and his whole nature rose up in arms. "You have collared me as if I were a cur. You have talked to me like you would a servant. You have insulted me before all the passengers—put me off the train after I had bought my ticket and now you threaten me while I am down. I'll stand no more. Your rank and your riches give you no right to wipe your feet on me. God Almighty breathed into my nostrils as well as yours. My blood came from the dust and so did yours. I throw my defiance in your teeth and meet you face to face—

> "What tho on homely fare we dine,
>   Wear hodden gray and all that;
>   Give fools their silks and knaves their wine—
>   A man's a man for all that."

Jack Peavy was cleared. "By the time I had spoken half an hour," wrote Watson, at the end of the above account, "the popular tide was with us and many a manly eye was dim."

Out of such victories as this—and it was multiplied a hundredfold—was built the legend of his invincibility. It became a widely prevalent belief that there was a sort of rule, or at least an agreement of honor, that Tom Watson should not assist in the prosecution of one charged with murder, for if he did, it meant certain death for the defendant. His talent was reserved for the defense. He was a tribune of the people, and hundreds had found shelter within his voice.

And might not a whole people find shelter there likewise? Were not they all so many Jack Peavys in "slouch hat and homespun"? Were they not forever being collared and booted about by arrogant young conductors of the railroads who charged them such outrageous rates to carry their cotton? Or by some upstart millionaire of Wall Street, "sacred by reason of his class"? By city folk in general? And might they not, with the words Tom had put in Jack Peavy's mouth, some day rise in their wrath and say, "I'll stand no more"? And with such a voice and such a tribune for their leader, might they not become so many Jack Cades?

Huey Long

I. THE LANGUAGE OF THE PEOPLE [1]

I AM not undertaking to answer the charge that I am ignorant. It is true. I am an ignorant man. I have had no college education. I have not even had a high school education. But the thing that takes me far in politics is that I do not have to color what comes into my mind and into my heart. I say it unvarnished. I say it without veneer. I have not the learning to do otherwise, and therefore my ignorance is often not detected. I know the hearts of the people because I have not colored my own. I know when I am right in my own conscience. I do not talk one way in the cloakroom and another way out here. I do not talk one way back there in the hills of Louisiana and another way here in the Senate. I have one language. Ignorant as it is, it is the universal language within the sphere in which I operate. Its simplicity gains pardon for my lack of letters and education.

II. THE TEARS OF EVANGELINE [2]

And it is here under this oak where Evangeline waited for her lover, Gabriel, who never came. This oak is an immortal spot, made so by Longfellow's poem, but Evangeline is not the only one who has waited here in disappointment.

Where are the schools that you have waited for your children to have, that have never come? Where are the roads and the highways that you send your money to build, that are no nearer now than ever before? Where are the institutions to care for the sick and disabled? Evangeline wept bitter tears in disappointment, but it lasted through only one lifetime. Your tears in this country, around this oak, have lasted for generations. Give me the chance to dry the eyes of those who still weep here!

III. EVERY MAN A KING [3]

The slogan, *Every Man a King* *, was widely used by the late Huey

---

[1] From a speech in the United States Senate. Cited in *Southern Regions of the United States,* by Howard W. Odum, pp. 531–532. Copyright, 1936, by the University of North Carolina Press. Chapel Hill. 1943.

[2] Extract from speech "delivered under the historic oak where Evangeline waited for her lover Gabriel, as described by Longfellow."
From *Every Man a King,* The Autobiography of Huey P. Long, p. 99. Copyright, 1933, by Huey P. Long. New Orleans: National Book Co., Inc.

[3] From *American Mottoes and Slogans,* by George Earlie Shankle, pp. 55–56. Copyright, 1941, by George Earlie Shankle. New York: The H. W. Wilson Company.

* *The Story of Huey P. Long,* Carleton Beals (J. B. Lippincott Company, Philadelphia, 1935), p. 78.—G. E. S.

Pierce Long in his Share-the-Wealth program which he so extensively popularized during his political career from 1928 until his death in 1935.

He is reported to have taken this slogan from William Jennings Bryan's "Cross of Gold" speech,† which he delivered before the members of the Democratic National Convention in Chicago, in 1896.

In 1910, Huey Long was peddling books and other goods for a living; in 1928 he was elected Governor of Louisiana; in 1929 the members of the Louisiana Legislature threatened to impeach him on account of his high-handed methods of securing legislation favorable to his program; and in 1930 he began to build the new Louisiana State Capitol. His rise to power in Louisiana politics was largely due to his capacity to organize, his ability as a speaker, and to his tactics in ridiculing his opponents. He ridiculed the landed aristocracy and the Southern gentlemen business class by publicly calling them such names as *Whistle-Breeches,* which caused the common laboring men to shout with laughter. Long's rule in Louisiana has been designated an odd conglomeration of "Hitlerism, hokum, and Tammany Ring methods." ‡

Long's Share-the-Wealth program had its genesis in a booklet published by Senator S. J. Harper, entitled *Issues of the Day—Free Speech—Financial Slavery,* which he published in 1918 in an attempt to arouse the American people to the point of demanding that America keep out of the World War. Senator Harper was indicted under the Espionage Act. Long, then an attorney, defended Harper both in the courts and in the press. Long published his initial idea of his Share-the-Wealth program in *The Times Picayune,* New Orleans, on February 22, 1928. It was in this article that he brought out his doctrine that 10 per cent of the people of the United States own 70 per cent of the wealth of the country.

It has been stated that Senator Harper's booklet "contains all of the ideas, much of the wording and statistics" which Huey Long used in his Share-the-Wealth program. Long placarded the State of Louisiana with posters and banners bearing the slogan, *Every Man a King, but No Man Wears a Crown,* in August, 1927. He was virtually the Democratic Party in Louisiana from 1928 until he was shot to death by Dr. Carl A. Weiss in a corridor of the State Capitol on September 8, 1935.

IV. The Kingfish [4]

In the course of our several political battles we from time to time termed various of our political enemies the "Kingfish," most prominent of which was in our designation of a certain corporation lawyer as the generalissimo of the political policies of a newspaper.

---

† *Ibid.,* p. 11.—G. E. S.

‡ *Ibid.,* p. 24.—G. E. S.

[4] From *Every Man a King,* The Autobiography of Huey P. Long, pp. 277–278. Copyright, 1933, by Huey P. Long. New Orleans: National Book Co., Inc.

It so happened that in our writing the bond laws of the State I so worded the last road statute as to have the highway bonds sold by the Highway Commission instead of by the Governor, a change which I did not notice for some time, because the Governor was still required to sign the bonds.

On one occasion when we were considering bids submitted for bonds, one of the prospective bond purchasers made the point that under the statute the sale of the bonds had to be awarded by the Highway Commission and not by the Governor, although members of the Commission had always sat with me when such bids were opened. Upon glancing at the law I readily recognized that the official award must be made by the Commission instead of by the Governor.

"I am participating here anyway, gentlemen. For the present you can just call me the Kingfish," I said.

Having dubbed so many of my political opponents by such a title, the newspapers instantly took advantage of the incident and heralded my name far and wide as the self-styled Kingfish. It has persisted ever since. It has served to substitute gaiety for some of the tragedy of politics. I have made no effort to discourage it. The sound of the name and the word "Long" over the telephone for some reason is a bit difficult to understand. It has saved time and effort on many occasions to say, "This is the Kingfish."

V. Potlikker and Corn Pone [5]

When I saw hard times ahead in this country, I undertook to encourage the people of the South, and, for that matter, of the United States, to raise gardens and to feed themselves and their children food products which they might not have the money to buy in days of stress. I began the propaganda with regard to potlikker and corn pone, which can be fed to a family for a few cents per week and the whole family kept strong and healthy.

Potlikker is the juice that remains in a pot after greens or other vegetables are boiled with proper seasoning. The best seasoning is a piece of salt fat pork, commonly referred to as "dry salt meat" or "side meat." If a pot be partly filled with well-cleaned turnip greens and turnips (the turnips should be cut up), with a half-pound piece of the salt pork, and then with water, and boiled until the greens and turnips are cooked reasonably tender, then the juice remaining in the pot is the delicious, invigorating, soul-and-body-sustaining potlikker. The turnips and greens, or whatever other vegetable is used, should be separated from the juice; that is, the potlikker should be taken as any other soup and the greens eaten as any other food.

---

[5] *Ibid.*, pp. 263–265.

Corn pone is made simply of meal, mixed with a little salt and water, made into a pattie and baked until it is hard.

It has always been the custom to eat corn pone with potlikker. Most people crumble the corn pone into the potlikker. The blend is an even tasting food.

But, with the progress of education, the coming of "style," and the change of the times, I concluded that refinement necessitated that corn pone be "dunked" in the potlikker, rather than crumbled in the old-fashioned way. So I suggested that those sipping of potlikker should hold the corn pone in the left hand and the spoon in the right, sip of the soup one time, then dip the corn pone in the potlikker and bite the end of the bread. My experience showed this to be an improvement over the crumbling.

But upon my undertaking not only to advertise and to bring about a wider use and distribution of potlikker and corn pone, but also to introduce a more elegant method of eating this delectable concoction, I met with opposition, first State-wide, then nation-wide, later international.

When Franklin D. Roosevelt, the present President of the United States, sent his telegram to the Atlanta Constitution, lining up his forces with the crumblers, I compromised—I compromised with all foes on the basis that it would be a commendable pursuit to eat potlikker with corn pone, whether it be done by crumbling or by dunking.

But the serious strain here is that the health of the entire nation would be marvelously improved if people would boil their vegetables and eat the juice left after such vegetables are removed from the kettle, as there are in these foods properties such as iron, manganese, and others which are needed for health and complexion, sound bodies and minds, and "the perfect 36."

VI. "THE MARTYRED GOVERNOR" [6]

. . . The Cajuns of the bayous and the sharecroppers of the cane brakes swear by him to-day no less devotedly than they did a decade ago. Nobody ever caught him with his hands in the till, they say, and even though he did some highhanded and illegal things, even though he may have taken money which didn't belong to him, he distributed most of it to the poor, who needed it. After all, they point out, Huey left only $153,000 when he died, over $58,000 of it in life insurance, and $20,000 more in his law library. When one considers his almost unparalleled opportunities for graft, and the manner in which his successors seized those opportunities, it is arguable that the contrast between Long and those who came after him was considerable.

---

[6] From *Below the Potomac*, A Book about the New South, by Virginius Dabney, pp. 47–50. Copyright, 1942, by D. Appleton-Century Company, Inc. New York and London.

Even in New Orleans, for so many years the focus of anti-Long feeling, his memory is kept wrapped in bay leaves. Not that there is any less aversion for him on the part of his onetime enemies there—the upper crust of New Orleans society and the business, banking and industrial interest, which always had excellent reasons for despising him. But as late as 1941 one could go down to what once was called the Place d'Armes, the lovely square near the Mississippi, which is the heart of old New Orleans—where artists sun themselves beneath the palms, the dulcet accents of France are heard along the walkways, and the bells of St. Louis Cathedral summon the faithful to matins. One turned into the Cabildo, that fascinating repository adjoining the cathedral, where the story of the city is told in thousands of relics, from the time of 'Sieur de Bienville, the founder, down through the revolutionary and ante-bellum eras to the present day. And after one had lingered over the statue of mighty Bienville, who laid out Nouvelle Orléans in the name of the Sun King, and had looked into a hundred showcases with their rusty swords of long-dead warriors and their faded gowns of dark-eyed Creole belles who once roamed the streets of the Vieux Carré, one came suddenly upon a room on the topmost floor which was unlike anything which had gone before. It was the room dedicated to Huey Pierce Long, "the martyred governor."

There was the desk at which Governor Long worked, and the original manuscript of a law course which he outlined for a friend, several records of songs which he wrote or helped to write, including *Every Man a King*, and many photographs showing him leading cheers at L. S. U. football games, campaigning with Hattie Caraway in Arkansas, exchanging banter with Governor O. K. Allen, and in other characteristic poses. There was also a picture of his rather unpretentious home in Audubon Place, with the announcement that it was open to visitors daily, without charge.

It seemed rather incongruous that these relics should be housed in the Cabildo—as redolent otherwise of ante-bellum New Orleans as the Musée de Cluny in Paris is of pre-revolutionary France. When, therefore, the collection was removed to the former Long residence in Audubon Place, the change appeared salutary. It is visited there by a steady stream of admirers from many parts of the Union.

So the memory of Huey Long is not fading in the state which gave him birth. Some of his chief henchmen are wearing prison stripes, and the voters have smashed the remnants of his machine at the polls, but the thousands who poured into Baton Rouge for his funeral back in 1935, with mud on their shoes and a few coppers in their jeans, still look upon him as a Messiah, who would have provided them with a $5,000 homestead and $2,000 income, if fate had not intervened.

"There would be a revolution in Louisiana, if anybody tried to move Huey Long's grave from the capitol grounds at Baton Rouge," one of the state's best-known and best-informed newspapermen told the writer recently.

VII. Legends of Huey Long [7]

"Pierre," his younger brother suggested, "maybe they haven't heard the story that Huey did not die at all. But instead was taken back to the capitol and that somewhere between the observation tower and the ground he is kept in a prison by his 'friends.' Some say he is not a prisoner but a lunatic. The Cajuns say that when the wind is just right in Baton Rouge you can hear him. He seems to be making some kind of speech."

* * * * *

"And what about the cult of the Second Coming of Huey Long?" I asked.

"Well," Pierre said, smiling, "it is a waiting that will require a little more patience than that which went along with his sharing of the wealth. When Huey returns, riding on a golden cloud, the poor will be eased of their burdens, and, if every man is not a king, at least, those who wait are confident that they will have more than they have now. Most of them could not have less. Some of them have picked out the property of their expectation, I understand. 'Dat's goin' to be mine den.' "

The Rival Candidates

WHEN he [Vice-President Alben W. Barkley] ran for Congress in 1912 . . . there were three other contenders for the office, Judge Hendrick, Denny Smith, and Jake Corbett. The four rivals hired two buggies and went about together, according to Kentucky custom, engaging in joint debates.

"In sharing the buggies, we switched around," Barkley explained. "One day I would ride with Hendrick, the next with Smith, the next with Corbett."

"What would you talk about as you drove along?" I asked.

"We would talk about what terrible old demagogues those other two fellows were—the two in the other buggy. We could always agree on that."

Hendrick, an older man, centered his fire on Barkley. He pictured him to the voters as a young man of boundless, almost dangerous ambition. "First he is county attorney. Then he is county judge. Now he wants to go to Congress. Where will such ambition end?"

Soon Barkley was ready with his counterattack.

[7] From *A Southerner Discovers the South*, by Jonathan Daniels, pp. 232–233. Copyright, 1938, by the Macmillan Company. New York.

From "Washington's Greatest Storyteller," by Beverly Smith, *The Saturday Evening Post*, Vol. 222 (July 2, 1949), No. 1, p. 68. Copyright, 1949, by the Curtis Publishing Company. Philadelphia.

"This charge of political ambition comes strangely from my good friend, Judge Hendrick," said Barkley. "He has been running for one office or another all his life. He runs for everything that is not nailed down. Why, when the Pope of Rome died some years back, Mrs. Hendrick mentioned the news to her son. 'But for heaven's sake, don't tell your pa the Pope is dead,' she cautioned him, 'or your pa will be a candidate to succeed him.'"

This story not only spiked Hendrick's guns but so delighted the voters that it helped Barkley's election to Congress.

In Defense of Hanging

WHEN Pat M. Neff was governor of Texas and when the Nation, under President Harding, was doing its best to return to normalcy, there was introduced in the Texas Legislature by a member from Dallas a bill to abolish hanging at the various county seats and to centralize capital punishment in the penitentiary at Huntsville.

* * * * *

. . . A large, deep-voiced member from South Texas gained the floor.
. . . His speech was substantially as follows:

"Mr. Speaker and Gentlemen of the House:

"I had not thought that I would say anything with reference to this bill, but I feel that I would not be true to my own sentiments or to the wishes of the constituency whom I have the honor to represent, if I did not raise my voice against this iniquitous measure.

* * * * *

. . . "Mr. Speaker, and Gentlemen of the House, one of the great evils of this country to-day is that all the attractions in the country are gradually being moved and centralized in the cities, so that with nothing left to entertain them the country boys and girls are flocking in droves to the attractive cities, where, like moths, they are singeing their wings on the gay white lights. My friends, this measure is not progressive; on the contrary, it is unnatural and abnormal. I, for one, still believe that the people in this country have rights which ought not to be snatched from them by legislative enactment. Why, Mr. Speaker, one of the few attractions now left in the country is for the people to gather together at their own county seat and witness an occasional hanging, and now you want to take even that away from them. Mr. Speaker, I don't know what you think about it, but as for me, hanging was good enough for my fathers and it's good enough for me."

From "Anecdotes about Lawyers," by Lloyd E. Price, in *Backwoods to Border*, edited by Mody C. Boatright and Donald Day, pp. 214, 216–217. Texas Folklore Society Publications, Number XVIII, J. Frank Dobie, General Editor. Copyright, 1943, by the Texas Folk-Lore Society. Austin and Dallas: Texas Folk-Lore Society and University Press in Dallas, Southern Methodist University.

Sayings of Governor William H. ("Alfalfa Bill") Murray

I LEARNED my politics out there in the country.—Don't know as I'm much of a politician, but I do know people, and people make the government.

I am the most ignorant man in the world on subjects I never thought about—therefore I never talk about them.

We have a world of moonshiners in Oklahoma's hills. If oil plays out we can hook the stills to the pipe lines and satisfy Chicago. Who else wants to "get on the hook-up?"

Besides other specimens, we have two bugs—the humbug and the shambug. The latter imagines that, because a man gets rich quickly, he is a new generation and must control all things.

Unmistakably alcoholic liquor is a medicine, but it is not fit to drink as a beverage any more than quinine tea, although more palatable.

The Spartan mother reared a generation that gave Greece her glory. The Spartan mother of the western plain reclaimed a wilderness for civilization. But neither the Spartan mother of Greece nor of America ever gave birth to a jelly-bean laddie nor a lip-stick lassie.

A college boy cannot successfully go through life by graduating in football, baseball, or highballs, for the responsibilities of life are not ball-bearing.

Civilization begins and ends with the plow—when the plow turns at the end of the furrow with a profit, that preserves commerce and civilization; when the plow is junked at the end of the furrow, it destroys both. Any civilization can live on the plow alone. No civilization can live without the plow.

"Them Hillbillies Are Politicians Now"

THE next step in the development of the flour business in Texas was to go on the air for advertising. Like his start in the selection of a business field, O'Daniel thinks his connection with radio was purely accidental. A group of unemployed musicians called at his office and asked O'Daniel to sponsor them on a program for advertising flour. After trying them out he agreed to a thirty-day period by way of experiment. The programs were to be broadcast over KFJZ, then "just a home-made radio station in a

From *Murray Grams* Selected from Speeches of Governor Wm. H. Murray from 1906 to 1931. (No date, no publisher.)

From *W. Lee O'Daniel and Texas Politics, 1938–1942*, by Seth Shepard McKay, pp. 21–23, 31–33, 36, 49–50. Copyright, 1944, by Texas Tech Press. Lubbock, Texas.

little back room in Meacham's store." The transmitter was on the top of a telephone post at the edge of town, and the programs could be heard from ten to fifteen miles from Fort Worth. There was little tangible evidence that the public was impressed by the Light Crust Doughboys during their first thirty-day period, but the expense was very small and it was decided to continue their contract for another month. Soon afterwards the public became interested in their programs, and the flour mill management became convinced that the advertising was well worth while.

Lee O'Daniel had no part in the earlier programs. But he was interested in the music as well as the business side, and soon found himself in the studio at broadcasting time about as often as near a radio receiver. As the Light Crust Doughboys grew in popularity invitations began to come in for them to make personal appearances at various celebrations. A loud-speaker system was fitted up and put in an old rented bus, and the boys began to make short trips out of Fort Worth. On one occasion they were to go on a short good will tour with the Fort Worth Chamber of Commerce. At the last minute the regular announcer found he was unable to go and told O'Daniel that he would have to do the announcing. The first stop was at Weatherford, where the new announcer brought many laughs from the crowd and was received with enthusiasm. This reception at Weatherford made O'Daniel an announcer.

As their programs became more popular other radio stations sought contracts with the Light Crust Doughboys. WBAP already had a large station with 10,000-watt power, and its management finally made a proposition which the Burrus interests could afford to pay. The new series of programs started at 12:30 noon, which proved to be a very popular time. In addition to the WBAP programs the Doughboys were taken to Dublin every Wednesday night for a program over a small station there, and on Friday nights they put on a thirty-minute program at Waco. This was before there were any broadcasting networks in Texas. O'Daniel thinks that his first audiences over KFJZ in 1928 could not have numbered more than a thousand persons; but that early in 1938 the regular programs over the Texas Quality Network may have been heard by as many as a million people, and that during the campaign for governor the audiences must have been much larger.

After he began announcing O'Daniel wrote and directed almost all of the programs put on the air by his group. He says the radio brought out the poet and song writer in him, and that he has written more than one hundred fifty poems and songs. His habit of discussing religion and religious teachings and subjects caused many people of his radio audiences to think he was a minister. His own feeling is that his radio experience has served as a great lesson in human sympathy and human understanding.

When O'Daniel organized his own company in 1935 he adopted "Hill-billy" as his trade name and trademark. His band had become well known and was identified with the type of music known by that name, and its members were called the "Hillbilly Boys." By this time a definite radio following of fans had been built up, and O'Daniel had begun to broadcast a great variety of programs. In addition to hillbilly music, sacred songs, and religious talks, there were memorial programs of every sort, programs on the Constitution of the United States, and programs commemorating Texas heroes. Erring husbands were advised to correct their behavior, school children were given good advice on thrift and conduct, traffic safety was emphasized, childless couples were advised to adopt babies, and religious and humanitarian movements and organizations were supported.[1]

*   *   *   *   *

W. Lee O'Daniel was among the last few to enter the race for governor, and except for references to his campaign made on his regular commercial broadcasts his speaking campaign lasted only six weeks. In the early part of the campaign he and his family of four were in their thirteenth year as residents of Fort Worth.[2] The flour business was good, the combination advertising and entertaining radio broadcasts occupied his time, and his was a happy family. But his radio fans had begun to ask him "every two years" to make the race for governor. At first O'Daniel considered the idea ridiculous, but his fans kept writing their requests "in increasing numbers." Finally, on Palm Sunday of 1938 he asked the people of his radio audience if he should make the race, and within a few days had received messages from 54,499 persons asking him to enter the contest, while only four advised him not to do so.[3] In a later comment on the replies to his question, O'Daniel said: "If I had hesitated until then about making the race all doubt about the wisdom of doing same was wiped out in the flood of letters so overwhelming in their endorsement of the idea. . . ."

In his Sunday broadcast of May 1, 1938, O'Daniel made his announcement as a candidate for governor, and outlined his platform as the Ten Commandments, adjustment of taxes in Texas, opposition to a sales tax, abolition of the poll tax prerequisite for voting, and pensions of $30 a month for all persons over 65 years old. He said his motto would be the Golden Rule. A week later, again on the radio, O'Daniel spoke at length of the plan to increase old age pensions, and announced his slogan of "Less Johnson grass and politicians; more smokestacks and business men." On this broadcast also he announced the plan for financing his campaign:

The only thing that can prevent us from winning is lack of sufficient campaign funds. If you want me to run the race on a bicycle, while the other candidates have high-powered racing cars, that is up to you. . . . I say to you in all sincerity . . . you had better take that old rocking chair down and mortgage it

---

[1] In the sketch of the background of W. Lee O'Daniel I have followed generally his own life story as told to Sam Acheson and run in the *Dallas Morning News* for sixty days, beginning with August 14, 1938.—S. S. M.

[2] O'Daniel points out that all five members had different native states: he was born in Ohio, his wife in Colorado, Pat in Kansas, Mike in Missouri, and Molly in Louisiana.—S. S. M.

[3] O'Daniel's Own Life Story in *Dallas Morning News*, September 27, 1938.—S. S. M.

and spend the money in the manner you think best to get your pension. . . . We have not one dollar in our campaign fund." [4]

The Texas gubernatorial campaign of 1938 warmed up very slowly. Newspapers and public men predicted freely during the early weeks of the contest that the race would be between McCraw and Thompson, and occasionally someone would substitute for one of those two the name of Hunter. The press took almost no notice of the O'Daniel entry during the first few weeks while he was conducting his radio campaign. On May 8, the *Fort Worth Star-Telegram*, his home-town paper and owner of WBAP, the radio station he had long patronized, announced briefly that among the candidates for governor was "W. Lee O'Daniel, of Fort Worth, the radio entertainer, who has formerly announced." A week later the same paper again mentioned his name: "The O'Daniel combination again will feature the capable showmanship of O'Daniel, the vocal work of Leon and Texas Rose and lively instrumentation by the entire group." [5] But outside of his own home town the press did not seem to know that O'Daniel was in the race until he took to the road with his sound truck and hillbilly band.

* * * * *

A leading weekly magazine explained the new interest in the governor's race as follows: "The hottest political topic in Texas right now is an Ohio-born Irishman who is riding around over the state in a sound truck with his right arm in a sling, speaking to the largest crowds to greet a candidate for governor in many a year. . . ." The editor goes on to explain that O'Daniel was shaking hands with tens of thousands of citizens daily, "now with his left hand," and outlines the chief theories given to explain the big crowds. One was that he had "a free show that is really good." A second was that many of the people came to see a radio group they had been hearing on the air for ten years. A third theory was that the people were tired of the professional politicians and were interested in the O'Daniel promise of a business administration of the state government. It was then pointed out that Texans in Washington were trying to find out "who O'Daniel is and what the fuss is all about." After remarking that Molly was passing around the audiences a miniature flour barrel marked "Flour, not Pork" and getting more than enough to pay all campaign expenses, the editor followed up with the O'Daniel platform. [6]

* * * * *

More than 94 per cent of the people [who voted] lived in the counties in which O'Daniel led all other candidates. A study of the returns will show that the O'Daniel plurality counties are in all cases those which were served most efficiently by the radio stations over which the successful candidate had been broadcasting his programs regularly for ten years imme-

---

[4] *Ibid.*, October 4, 1938.—S. S. M.
[5] *Fort Worth Star-Telegram*, May 14, 1938.—S. S. M.
[6] *Texas Weekly* (Dallas), July 2, 1938.—S. S. M.

diately prior to the campaign. One may go even farther in this analysis. Most of the counties in which the O'Daniel pluralities were largest are in the immediate vicinity of Fort Worth, indicating the probability that many of their citizens had the advantages of the early broadcasting programs and personal appearances of the Light Crust Doughboys, at the time when radio receiving sets as well as broadcasting stations were much less efficient than they were in 1938. It seems evident that the O'Daniel following knew their candidate through his broadcasts.[7] He had no political organization of any kind, no campaign manager except Mrs. O'Daniel, no newspaper support in the earlier part of the contest, and was totally lacking in political experience. The only possible conclusion is that the O'Daniel victory of 1938 was due to the power of the radio, or perhaps to the skill of O'Daniel in the use of the radio.[8]

No explanation of this political contest could be full without additional reference to the entertainment features of the typical O'Daniel political rally. The first part of the program usually consisted of music by the hillbilly band, played while the crowd gathered or was increased by late arrivals. The featured soloists were Leon Huff and a young girl called "Texas Rose." The musical selections consisted of lively hillbilly tunes, sacred hymns, or any other kind of music that seemed to have appeal for the crowd. Some of the Texas music teachers have expressed their pleasure at the fact that the hillbilly boys did not feature the "cowboy's blues" type of song; yet we find that they were not unwilling to make use of one of the more optimistic Western songs. At Mineral Wells, late in the final week of the campaign, the rally ended with the hillbilly boys singing *Home on the Range*, in the rendition of which the crowd was invited to join in.

On occasion the rally program had songs and string music interspersed with parts of the O'Daniel speech, which always followed O'Daniel's self-introduction. One is led to wonder if the candidate introduced himself only because it was the custom of the "professional politicians" to be introduced and recommended by some local dignitary. The music at the rally was sometimes used to supplement or illustrate a point or argument made by the speaker, and sometimes was employed apparently to cover possible embarrassment of the candidate when he was asked how he stood on certain political issues. The song *Beautiful Texas*, written by O'Daniel several years before the campaign and known to most Texas public school children, was considered the "theme song" of the O'Daniel rally. Somewhat earlier the state legislature had passed a resolution of appreciation for that song, and in return O'Daniel had asked Leon to salute the legisla-

---

[7] See an excellent analysis of the returns by Peter Molyneaux in *Texas Weekly* (Dallas), March 18, 1939.—S. S. M.

[8] O'Daniel said in the Preface to his story as told to the *Dallas Morning News:* "I knew that we were no strangers in tens of thousands of Texas homes. . . ."— S. S. M.

ture over the radio with another of his songs, *My Million Dollar Smile.*
A third song, said to have been written by O'Daniel for the political campaign, ran as follows:

> They've come to town with their guitars
> And now they're smoking big cigars
> Them hillbillies are politicians now.
>
> They've chucked their boots and overalls,
> They've even dropped their "howze you alls,"
> Them hillbillies are politicians now.[9]

The Man Bilbo

BESIDES maintaining close touch with the masses, the "Poplarville
Prophet" exploits all the techniques of demagogic showmanship. Indeed,
so important does Bilbo consider this factor that he has been known to
say of politics, "Psychology, psychology—all is psychology." Ever mind-
ful of this concept, the "Pearl of Pearl River County" is careful to keep
always in the public eye. Even when not himself a candidate, he stumps
the state in all elections and he makes every effort to impress his audiences. Not only does he act the role of a flamboyant political leader, but
he dresses the part. To impress his hill-country followers, he wears a loud
check suit, red suspenders, a roaring red necktie with a diamond horseshoe
stickpin, and a rakish snapbrimmed felt hat.

In addition to feasting the eyes of the yokels, "The Man" also provides
entertainment and excitement. From the outset of his career Bilbo has
sought favorable consideration by singing hymns while accompanying himself on the melodeon. In another approach to the sympathies of his auditors, "The Man" exploits the scandals in his career by posing as a greatly
wronged martyr who needs vindication on election day. More generally,
however, Bilbo fills the ears of the "red necks" with anathemas against "the
interests" and with promises that give glimpses of the millennium. Bilbo's
dramatic rhetoric so sways his audiences that they weep when he weeps,
shout when he shouts, and for the most part vote as he urges them. So effective is Bilbo's demagogic showmanship that he has built a blindly loyal
following throughout Mississippi.

Senator Bilbo's rabble-rousing oratory is chiefly composed of personal

---

[9] *San Angelo Weekly Standard,* August 5, 1938.

From "Theodore G. Bilbo, 'Shibboleths for Statesmanship,'" by Roman J. Zorn,
in *Public Men In and Out of Office,* edited by J. T. Salter, pp. 283–285. Copyright,
1946, by the University of North Carolina Press. Chapel Hill.

invective. As he explains, "It is always a family fight down here, and a family fight is best of all. We're all Democrats and we have to deal in personalities because there are no issues—we're all in favor of the same things. So you don't show the other fellow is in favor of this or against that, you just show he's a low-down blankety blank."

Since backwoods folk are not interested in vague generalities, Theodore Bilbo has specialized in dispensing vitriolic and personalized oratory. In one of his earliest campaigns he denounced an opponent as a "cross between a hyena and a mongrel . . . begotten in a nigger graveyard at midnight, suckled by a sow, and educated by a fool." Eventually the target of this abuse caught up with Bilbo and battered him into unconsciousness for twenty-four hours. But this mishap did not deter the oratorical flights of "The Old Maestro of the Stump." Again in the 1915 gubernatorial election, he crushed his opponent under this barrage: "John Armstrong is a vicious, malicious, deliberate, cowardly, pusillanimous, cold-blooded, lop-eared, blue-nosed, premeditated, and self-made liar." And as late as the 1934 U. S. senatorial campaign, Bilbo branded the incumbent senator as a "tool of cannibalistic capitalism" and "more reactionary than Herbert Hoover," and after a choice selection of Billingsgate concluded, "Hubert Stephens is a . . . plain United States Senatorial liar."

Such rhetorical outbursts are usually leavened with assiduous courting of the sovereign electorate. A prime example of this mob-appealing tactic, taken from a 1934 campaign speech, runs:

Friends, fellow citizens, brothers and sisters—hallelujah.—My opponent—yea, this opponent of mine who has the dastardly, dew-lapped, brazen, sneering, in-sulting, and sinful effrontery to ask you for your votes without telling you the people of this almighty state of Mississippi what he is a-going to do with them if he gets them—this opponent of mine says he don't need a platform. Why does he ask you for your votes? He asks, my dear brethren and sisters, that you vote for him because he is standing by the President. Standing by the President, folks! So am I. But I'm doing better by you, folks, than that. I'm a-standing right smack on his corns, folks, lest he forget the great sovereign Magnolia state of Ole Miss. . . . I shall be the servant and senator of all the people of Mississippi, brothers and sisters. I shall know no North, no South, no East, no West. The appeal and petition of the humblest citizen, yea, whether he comes from the black prairie lands of the east or the alluvial lands of the fer-tile delta; whether he comes, yea, from the vermilion hills of north Mississippi or the sun-kissed shores of the Gulf of Mexico, yea, he will be heard by my heart and my feet shall be swift. But listen to fair warning, brethren and sisters: Don't you go a-sending me up there to Washington to be anything but your servant, your voice that will never cease to ring down the great, gray marble corridors of our Capitol, your Senator whose thoughts will not wander from the humble, God-fearing cabins of Vinegar Bend or the lowing sheep-folds of Honeysuckle Creek, your champion who will not lay his head upon his pillow at night before he has asked his Maker for more strength to do more for you in the morrow— don't go a-sending me to those mighty classic halls of government, if you don't want that kind of a man. Brethren and sisters, I pledge. . . .

Senator Claghorn

GREAT commotion came to the region recently when the Richmond *Times Dispatch* printed a brief editorial about that distinguished contemporary southerner Senator Claghorn:

CLAGHORN, THE DIXIE FOGHORN

For years, yes, decades, we've been battling to bring some measure of rationality into the fried-chicken-watermelon-mammy-magnolia-moonlight-mocking-bird-moon-June-croon school of thinking on Southern problems, and now we've run up against the toughest proposition yet. We refer, of course, to that bombastic bumbling, brou-ha-ha of the air waves, Senator Beauregard Claghorn, "from the deep South, that is." . . .

This amazing character on the Sunday evening Fred Allen program must have given millions in the North and West the notion that southern Senators spend their time in making frightful puns, and bellowing "That's a joke, son!" and in such professionally southern deliverances as: "When in New York ah only dance at the Cotton Club. The only dance ah do is the Virginia reel. The only train ah ride is the Chattanooga Choo-Choo. When ah pass Grant's tomb ah shut both eyes. Ah never go to the Yankee Stadium! Ah won't even go to the Polo Grounds unless a southpaw's pitchin'."

We "southrons" have been kept sufficiently busy asserting to our northern friends that we aren't all morons and degenerates a la Tobacco Road, or banjo-picking mammy-singers, a la Al Jolson, but now we have to go around protesting that we aren't all raucous nitwits and foghorns like Senator Claghorn, "from the South, that is." Gad!

I suspect that my friend Virginius Dabney wrote this skit, but I'm not sure. At any rate Mr. Dabney was obliged to report later in the New York *Times* that his paper had been swamped with protests, especially when a chauvinistic Southern congressman caused the offending editorial to be inserted in the *Congressional Record*. Mr. Dabney stuck to his point, but he did handsomely admit that Claghorn brought in plenty of laughs, for instance when he said, "In college ah was voted the member of the senior class most likely to secede and ah was graduated magnolia cum laude." (New York *Times*, May 4, 1946.)

Sayings of Will Rogers

You folks know I never mean anything by the cracks I make here on politics. I generally hit the fellow that's on top because it isn't fair to hit a

---

From *Inside U. S. A.*, by John Gunther, p. 657. Copyright, 1946, 1947, by the Curtis Publishing Co. New York and London: Harper & Brothers.

From *Will Rogers, Greatest Exponent of Simple Homely Truths That Will Endure Forever, World-Beloved Humorist and Philosopher, Memorial Issue*, pp. 3, 8, 10, 11, 13–14, 19, 20, 22, 23, 25. Copyright, 1935, by Union Associated Press. New York.

fellow that's down. If a big man laughs at jokes on him, he's all right.
Compared to them [Congress] I'm an amateur, and the thing about
my jokes is they don't hurt anybody. You know—you can say, well,
they're not funny, or they're terrible, or they're good, or whatever it is,
but they don't do no harm. But with Congress, everytime they make a
joke it's a law. And everytime they make a law it's a joke.

We won't really hear what was done at this [disarmament] conference
[of 1930] till we read one of the delegates' memoirs after the next war.

Yep. Spinnin' a rope's a lot of fun—providin' your neck ain't in it.

At that [Senator Long's all-night filibuster] he pulled the biggest and
most educational novelty ever introduced into the Senate. He read 'em
the Constitution of the United States. A lot of 'em thought he was reviewing a new book.

Let everybody put it [the South's surplus of cotton] in their ears to
keep from hearing Republican speeches.

The South is dry and will vote dry; that is, every one that is sober
enough to stagger to the polls will.

Then [in the good old horse and buggy days] you lived until you died
and not until you were just run over.

Congressional investigations are for the benefit of the photographers.

All I know is what I read in the newspapers. Sure [I read fiction], the
newspapers.

IV. MEMORABILIA

*You know we people in the mountains do not like books so well,
but we like to remember and memorize many things that we do
love.*—As told by Bascom Lamar Lunsford to B. A. Botkin

*In the history of any country it is often true that the stories that
are recorded of private individuals rather than those often in the
public eye afford us a deeper insight into the character and the
spirit of a people than the careers of the famous and the great.
Stories, when true, of the deeds of the humble, or at least of those
of whom proud History takes small note, should be preserved.*
—ARCHIBALD RUTLEDGE

*The torrential recollectiveness, derived out of my mother's stock
. . . became a living, million-fibered integument that bound me
to the past, not only of my own life, but of the very earth from
which I came, so that nothing in the end escaped from its in-
rooted and all-feeling explorativeness.*—THOMAS WOLFE

1. The People Remember

THE memorabilia of the South are made up not so much of the things that ought to be remembered as of the things that people like to remember. Here belong heroes who, because of local or temporal limitations, are not of the first order; public figures in their off-moments or little known aspects; private individuals who became public figures only after their lifetime; unacknowledged "heroes of endurance that was voluntary, and of action that was creative and not sanguinary"; and a variety of obscure and humble folk who, as the result of a single dominant trait or a single deed of heroic action or passion, have had greatness thrust upon them.

These out-of-the-way chapters in the Southern saga take on special importance because, in so far as they deal with crises or aberrations in the lives of what for the most part are ordinary people, they throw light on Southern character in relation to the Southern environment and give insight into the well-springs of human motives and the workings of popular tradition.

In their concern with problems and struggles that are closer to the everyday lives of Southern folk than are the affairs of war and politics, memorabilia are closer to historical fiction or fictionized biography than they are to myth or legend. Myth resembles the Bourbon oratory of the Old South, which lulled men into dreams of the glory that was the South and of the grandeur that is no more. Memorabilia resemble the cotton-patch and cornfield eloquence of the demagogues, which wakes men to the realities and problems of the present.

Like myth, popular tradition (as seen in memorabilia) has a way of rewriting history. It does so, however, not according to the pattern of the ideal warrior and gentleman but according to the love that people have of telling and listening to stories and their sense of what makes a good story. As a form of collective memory, popular tradition resembles the reminiscences of old people and old-timers, especially among the untutored and unlettered classes. Such folk retrospect has the faculty of recapturing the past more freshly and vividly, if less reliably, than written history, because it moves in the restricted world in which (according to Goldenweiser) "the past comes to the present as things or words; what is neither seen nor said nor remembered vanishes beyond recovery."

2. "Oddities of Southern Life and Character"

In the memorabilia of the patriotic South the women of the Revolution have been somewhat overshadowed by the men. But a place is reserved here for two who may be considered typical of the rest: Betsy Dowdy, the young "Banker" girl, who made her famous night ride on Black Bess to keep the British from stealing her ponies; and Mrs. Motte, of South Carolina, who facilitated the burning of her plantation house after it had been made the British headquarters, and thus assisted in the capture of the British fortifications. "Too much," she would say, when praised for her sacrifice, "has been made of a thing that any American woman would have done."

Passing to the industrial South—with a casual suggestion, a Georgia woman, Mrs. Miller, helped her house guest, Eli Whitney, solve the problem of the cotton gin.

In the building of the South the railroad and the steamboat are second to none in importance and romance. Alongside of Casey Jones, the folk hero of the rails, the people of Mississippi remember William Faulkner's grandfather, Colonel William C. Falkner, as one of the hero-sized founders of the Rebel Route. Among rivermen Billy King made steamboat history when he designed the far-famed *J. M. White,* unequaled for her speed, and he made legend when he destroyed its model in order to keep it from being duplicated. The people also remember the courageous ones, "the gallant hearts," who "took a chance" or defied fate—Bras Coupé, Hal, Eliza, Horatio Williams, Newt Knight, and Black Gold and his owners.

Among the heroes and heroines of passion, crime, and disaster, Naomi Wise, Frankie Silvers, Floyd Collins, Claude and Sidna Allen have inspired and (in the case of the second) composed ballads, testifying to the variety as well as the vitality of their legend and satisfying the demands of "poetic justice." On the scaffold Frankie Silvers read a rhymed confession, which, as it was in the approved tradition of contrite warnings, became a traditional song after her death.

> You all see me and on me gaze—
> Be careful how you spend your days
> And ne'er commit this awful crime,
> But try to serve your God in time.

And in "Floyd Collins' Fate" Adam Crisp, of Fletcher, North Carolina, points a gloomy moral:

> Young people, all take warning,   It may not be in a sand cave
> With this, for you and I,   In which we find our tomb,
> We may not be like Collins,   But at that mighty judgment
> But you and I must die.   We soon will find our doom.[1]

The pattern of violence also claims its victims in Steve Renfroe, who was a "better champion of rights than an administrator of them," and so fluctuated between upholding the law and defying it; Britt Bailey, who wanted to be buried standing up so that he could "have the last shot in hell with any s.o.b.'s that comes down there challengin'" him; and Floyd Allen, who shot up the court that convicted him, flinging down the challenge: "Gentlemen, I don't aim to go."

Then there are the queer ones, who are the central figures in a historical engima, like Marshal Ney, or in a legend of their own making, like Bernard Marigny or Temple Houston; the strong ones, like "Big Tom" Wilson,

---

[1] Jean Thomas, *Blue Ridge Country* (New York, 1942), pp. 238–239.

whose uncanny tracking powers led him infallibly to the body of Dr. Elisha Mitchell, in a saga that has all the suspense and clues of a mystery novel; and those with a mission, like Harriet Tubman, the Negro "Moses," who assisted in the liberation of her people by the Underground Railroad.

And there are the Southern writers, caught in the "giant web" of their inheritance and their legend, whose lives were literary masterpieces—O. Henry and Thomas Wolfe. Among the folk bards and minstrels of the mountains, a Kentucky coal miner's wife, Aunt Molly Jackson, became a militant symbol, with her songs that set the miners' troubles to traditional tunes and patterns:

> This minin' town I live in is a sad and lonely place,
> Where pity and starvation is pictured on every face.
>
> Ragged and hungry, no shoes nor slippers on our feet,
> We bum around from place to place to get a little bite to eat.
>
> Some coal operators may tell you the hungry blues are not bad;
> They are the worst blues this poor woman ever had.[2]

The South has many memorable "local characters" who fall short of greatness or even near-greatness and yet somehow deserve to be better known. One of the most colorful of these is Major Lamar Fontaine, soldier-of-fortune and knight-errant extraordinary, who took as his motto "I will find a way, or make one." Born in what is now Texas, in 1829, at the age of ten he was stolen by Comanches and lived among them for over four years. In 1846 he involuntarily accompanied Lieutenant M. E. Maury on an Arctic exploration. Thereafter he successively fought at Vera Cruz, was with Bolingbroke in China and with Perry in Japan, was made a Buddhist priest in the Himalayas, and fought at Sebastopol. He spent his last years as a surveyor in the Yazoo Valley, where he died in 1922, at ninety-four. Of all his Civil War exploits, which took him through many strenuous campaigns, daring raids, and hair-breadth escapes, he was most proud of having written (as he claimed) "All Quiet Along the Potomac," the Civil War favorite attributed to Ethel Lynn Beers. A fitting tribute to his memory is the comment written by a female admirer in her copy of *Immortal Songs of Camp and Field,* in which she had crossed out Mrs. Beers' name and written in his:

> Major Lamar Fontaine was a Confederate officer and a Christian Gentleman. If he said he wrote "All Quiet Along the Potomac," he did write it.[3]

B. A. B.

---

[2] "Miners' Wives' Ragged, Hungry Blues," cited by Alvin H. Harlow, *"Weep No More, My Lady"* (New York, 1942), p. 253.

[3] For my introduction to Major Fontaine, I am indebted to Paul Flowers. Cf. Fontaine's *My Life and My Lectures* (1908).

The Real Evangeline

NOT the least interesting feature in the story of Evangeline and her people is that of the original of the character. However much the exigencies of poetry may have caused a divergence from the facts in producing a harmonious whole, the tradition preserved in one of the exile families, of the wanderings and the peculiarly sad fate of a young Acadian girl, evidently forms the basis of Longfellow's poem.

The Mouton family of Louisiana, descended from the Acadian exiles, has long preserved as part of its family inheritance the sad story of Emmeline Labiche, the original Evangeline.

Senator Mouton, of Louisiana, who was a personal friend of Longfellow, gave to the poet the story of the young girl who was adopted into his family in the village of St. Gabriel in the old Acadian days, and after the dispersion, and in all their wanderings, found her home with the family in its exile. It is told in the words of an ancestor who was among those deported, and is substantially as follows:

"Emmeline Labiche was an orphan girl of Acadia, whose parents died when she was yet a child, and who was taken into our family and adopted.

"She was sweet-tempered and loving, and grew to womanhood with all the attractions of her sex. Although not a beauty in the sense usually given to the word, she was looked upon as the handsomest girl in St. Gabriel. . . . Emmeline had just completed her sixteenth year, and was on the eve of marrying a deserving, laborious, and well-to-do man of St. Gabriel, named Louis Arsenaux. Their mutual love dated back to their earliest years, and was concealed from no one. . . . Their banns had been published in the village church, the nuptial day was fixed . . . when the barbarous scatterment of our colony took place. Our oppressors had driven us toward the seashore where their ships rode at anchor, and Louis, resisting with rage and despair, was wounded by them.

"Emmeline witnessed the whole scene. . . . Tearless and speechless, she stood fixed to the spot. When the white sails vanished in the distance . . . she clasped me in her arms and in an agony of grief sobbed piteously. By degrees the violence of her grief subsided, but the sadness of her countenance betokened the sorrow that preyed upon her heart.

"Henceforward she lived a quiet and retired life, mingling no more with her companions, and taking no part in their amusements. The remembrance of her lost love remained enshrined in her heart.

"Thus she lived, in our midst, always sweet-tempered, with such sadness depicted on her countenance and with smiles so sorrowful that we had come

From *An Historical Sketch of the Acadians, Their Deportation and Wanderings,* together with a Consideration of the Historical Basis for Longfellow's Poem *Evangeline* . . . , by George P. Bible, pp. 138–140. Copyright, 1906, by Ferris & Leach. Philadelphia to look on her not as for this earth, but rather as our guardian angel. Thus it was that we called her no longer Emmeline, but 'Evangeline,' or 'God's little angel.' . . .

"Emmeline had been exiled to Maryland with us. She followed me in my long overland journey from Maryland to Louisiana.

"When we reached the Teche country at the Poste de Attakapas, we found the whole population congregated to welcome us. . . . Suddenly as if fascinated by a vision she stopped, and then, the silvery tones of her voice vibrating with joy, she cried: 'Mother! mother! it is he. It is Louis!' and she pointed to a tall figure of a man standing beneath an oak. It was Louis Arsenaux. . . . She flew to his side, crying out in an ecstasy of joy and love. He turned ashy pale, and hung his head without uttering a word. 'Louis,' she said, 'why do you turn your eyes away? I am still your Emmeline, your betrothed!'

"With quivering lips and trembling voice he answered: 'Emmeline, do not speak so kindly to me. I am unworthy of you. I can love you no longer. I have pledged my faith to another. Tear from your heart the remembrance of the past and forgive me.' Then he wheeled away and disappeared in the forest.

"A pallor overspread her countenance, and her eyes assumed a vacant stare. . . .

"She followed me like a child without resistance. I clasped her in my arms and wept bitterly. 'Emmeline, my dear, be comforted. There may yet be happiness in store for you.' 'Emmeline, Emmeline,' she muttered to herself, as if to recall that name, and then: 'Who are you?' She turned away, her mind unhinged. . . .

"Emmeline never recovered her reason, and a deep melancholy ever possessed her. Her beautiful countenance was lighted by a sad smile which made her all the fairer. She never recognized any one but me, and nestling in my arms . . . would bestow on me the most endearing names. She spoke of Acadia and Louis in such terms that one could not listen to her without shedding tears. She fancied herself still the sweet girl of sixteen on the eve of marrying her chosen one, whom she loved with so much devotion and constancy. . . . Sinking at last under the ravages of her mental disease, she expired in my arms."

Such is the story of Emmeline Labiche, as told to Longfellow by Governor, afterwards Senator, Alexander Mouton, of Louisiana, and as handed down in the records and traditions of the Mouton family, in which the young girl found home, shelter and loving-kindness.

John Randolph and John

I [1]

A RATHER cruel test of the affection of his servant John was tried on the occasion referred to. John had in some way offended his master that morning; and, as he was preparing the trunks, Mr. Randolph said to him:

"Finish that trunk at once, John, and take it down to the steamboat; and, on your return, take passage in the Philadelphia boat; and when you get to Philadelphia, call on Mr. ——, in Arch-street, and tell him that I have sailed; then go on to Baltimore, and call on Mr. ——, in Monument-place, and say that I shall write to him from London; thence proceed to Washington, pack up the trunks at my lodgings, take them with you to Roanoke, and report yourself to my overseer."

After a pause, he added, in a sarcastic tone:

"Now, John, you have heard my commands; but you need not obey them, unless you choose to do so. You can, if you prefer it, when you arrive in Philadelphia, call on the Manumission Society, and they will make you free; and I shall never look after you. Do you *hear*, sir?"

This unjust aspersion of John's love was too much for the faithful fellow; his cheek swelled, his lip quivered, his eyes filled—and he replied, in great agitation:

"Massa John, this is too hard! I don't deserve it! You know I love you better than any body else; and you *know* you will find me at Roanoke when you come back!"

"I felt my blood rising," says Mr. Randolph's friend, "and could not avoid saying:

"'Well, Mr. Randolph, I could not have believed this, if I had not seen it. I thought you had more compassion for your slaves. Surely, you are unjust in *this* case; you have punished him severely enough by leaving him behind you, without hurting his feelings. You have made the poor fellow *cry*, Mr. Randolph.'

"'What!' said he, with true emotion. 'Does he shed tears?'

"'He does,' I replied, 'and you may see them yourself.'

"'Then,' said Mr. Randolph, '*he shall go with me!* John, take down your baggage; and let us forget what has passed.'

"'I was irritated, sir,' he added, turning to me; 'and I thank you for the rebuke.'"

Thus ended this singular scene between Randolph and his servant. John instantly brightened up—soon forgot his master's anger—and in a very few moments was on his way to the boat, perfectly happy.

---

[1] From "John Randolph of Roanoke, Personal Characteristics, Anecdotes, etc., etc.," *Harper's New Monthly Magazine*, Vol. V (September, 1852), No. XXVIII, pp. 534–535.

II [2]

Next morning (the day on which he died), Dr. Parish received an early and an urgent message to visit him. Several persons were in the room, but soon left it, except his servant John, who was much affected at the sight of his dying master. The doctor remarked to him, "I have seen your master very low before, and he revived; and perhaps he will again." "John knows better than that, sir." He [Randolph] then looked at the doctor with great intensity, and said in an earnest and distinct manner, "I confirm every disposition in my will, especially that respecting my slaves, whom I have manumitted, and for whom I have made provision."

"I am rejoiced to hear such a declaration from you, sir," replied the doctor, and soon after proposed to leave him for a short time to attend to another patient. "You must not go," was the reply; "you can not, you shall not leave me. *John!* take care that the doctor does not leave the room." John soon locked the door, and reported, "Master, I have locked the door, and got the key in my pocket; the doctor can't go now."

He seemed excited, and said, "If you do go, you need not return." The doctor appealed to him as to the propriety of such an order, inasmuch as he was only desirous of discharging his duty to another patient. His manner instantly changed, and he said, "I retract that expression." Some time afterward, turning an expressive look, he said again, "I retract that expression."

The doctor now said that he understood the subject of his communication, and presumed the will would explain itself fully. He replied, in his peculiar way, "No, you don't understand it; I know you don't. Our laws are extremely particular on the subject of slaves—a will may manumit them, but provision for their subsequent support requires that a declaration be made in the presence of a white witness; and it is requisite that the witness, after hearing the declaration, should continue with the party, and never lose sight of him, until he is gone or dead. You are a good witness for John. You see the propriety and importance of your remaining with me; your patients must make allowance for your situation. John told me this morning, 'Master, you are dying.' "

*   *   *   *   *

The doctor now introduced the subject of calling in some additional witnesses to his declarations, and suggested sending downstairs for Edmund Badger. He replied, "I have already communicated that to him." The doctor then said, "With your concurrence, sir, I will send for two young physicians, who shall remain, and never lose sight of you until you are dead; to whom you can make your declarations—my son, Dr. Isaac Parish, and my young friend and late pupil, Dr. Francis West, a brother of Captain West."

---

[2] From "The Death of John Randolph of Roanoke," *Harper's New Monthly Magazine,* Vol. II (December, 1850), No. VII, pp. 82–83.

He quickly asked, "Captain West of the Packet?" "Yes, sir, the same." "Send for him—he is the man—I'll have him."

Before the door was unlocked, he pointed toward a bureau, and requested the doctor to take from it a remuneration for his services. To this the doctor promptly replied that he would feel as though he were acting indelicately, to comply. He then waived the subject, by saying, "In England it is always customary."

The witnesses were now sent for, and soon arrived. The dying man was propped up in bed, with pillows, nearly erect. Being extremely sensitive to cold, he had a blanket over his head and shoulders; and he directed John to place his hat on, over the blanket, which aided in keeping it close to his head. With a countenance full of sorrow, John stood close by the side of his dying master. The four witnesses—Edmund Badger, Francis West, Isaac Parish, and Joseph Parish—were placed in a semi-circle, in full view. He rallied all the expiring energies of mind and body, to this last effort. "His whole soul," says Dr. Parish, "seemed concentrated in the act. His eyes flashed feeling and intelligence. Pointing toward us, with his long index finger, he addressed us.

" 'I confirm all the directions in my will, respecting my slaves, and direct them to be enforced, particularly in regard to a provision for their support.' And then raising his arm as high as he could, he brought it down with his open hand, on the shoulder of his favorite John, and added these words, 'Especially for this man.' " He then asked each of the witnesses whether they understood him. Dr. Joseph Parish explained to them what Mr. Randolph had said in regard to the laws of Virginia, on the subject of manumission—and then appealed to the dying man to know whether he had stated it correctly. "Yes," said he, and gracefully waving his hand as a token of dismission, he added, "The young gentlemen will remain with me."

Betsy Dowdy's Ride

JOE DOWDY and old man Sammy Jarvis lived on the "banks" opposite to Knott's Island. They were near neighbors and intimate friends. Early in December, 1775, Jarvis went over to the "main" to hear the news of Colonel Howe's movement toward Great Bridge. When he returned home, late in the evening, he was greatly excited. He was impressed with the dangerous situation of the dwellers by the sea. He was constantly saying, "Dunmore and them blamed Britishers will come down the coast from Norfolk and steal all our 'banks' stock and burn our houses, ding 'em." After a short rest and a hasty bite of supper, old man Jarvis went over to Dowdy's to tell him the news.

Dowdy was a wrecker for the money that was in it, and a fisher for the

From *Grandfather's Tales of North Carolina History*, by Richard Benbury Creecy, pp. 90–95. Copyright, 1901, by R. B. Creecy. Raleigh: Edward & Broughton, Printers.

food that was in it. He was always watching the sea. He was a devout man, always prayed for the safety of the poor sailor who was exposed to the perils of the deep, and always closed with a silent supplication that if there should be a wreck, it might be on the Currituck beach. He had prospered in the business of a wrecker, had saved many lives and much wreckage and money. His visible store of chattels was beef cattle and banker ponies. He herded them by the hundreds.

Uncle Sammy came in without ceremony and was cordially received. "Well, Uncle Sammy," said Dowdy, "what are the news; tell us all." "Well, Joseph," said Jarvis, "things is fogerty. Gregory, Colonel Isaac, is hurrying up his Camden milish to join Howe, and Tom Benbury, of Chowan, is pushing on his wagons of commissaries. If they don't reach Great Bridge in time to bear a hand in the fight, they'll hurry on to Norfolk and drive Dunmore out of the old town. But if Dunmore beats our folks at Great Bridge then our goose is cooked, and our property is all gone, all the gold and goods saved in our hard life-work, and all our cattle and marsh ponies." "You don't tell me," said Dowdy. "Yes, it's so, just as sure as 'old Tom.' The only thing that can save us is General Skinner, of Perquimans, and the militia, and he is too far away. We can't get word to him in time." As Jarvis said these words slowly and with emphasis, Betsy Dowdy, Joe Dowdy's young and pretty daughter, who was present with the family, said: "Uncle Sammy, do you say the British will come and steal all our ponies?" "Yes," said he. She replied: "I'd knock 'em in the head with a conch shell first." Betsy soon left the room. She went to the herding pen, and Black Bess was not there. She then went to the marsh and called aloud, "Bess! Bessie! Black Beauty!" The pretty pony heard the old familiar voice and came to the call. Betsy took her by her silken mane, led her to the shelter, went into the house, brought out a blanket and also a small pouch of coin. She placed the blanket on the round back of the pony, sprang into the soft seat and galloped over the hills and far away on her perilous journey. Down the beach she went, Black Bess doing her accustomed work. She reached the point opposite Church's Island, dashed into the shallow ford of Currituck Sound and reached the shore of the island. On they sped, Black Bess gaining new impulse from every kind and gentle word of Betsy. The wonderful endurance of the banker pony never failed, and Black Bess needed no spur but the cheering word of her rider. "Bessie, pretty Bess; my black, sleek beauty, the British thieves shan't have you. We are going after General Skinner and his milish. They'll beat 'em off of you." She almost sang to the docile pony as they went on their journey. Through the divide, on through Camden, the twinkling stars her only light, over Gid Lamb's old ferry, into Pasquotank by the "Narrows" (now Elizabeth City), to Hartsford, up the highlands of Perquimans, on to Yeopim Creek, and General Skinner's hospitable home was reached. The morning sun was gilding the tree tops when she entered the gate. She was hospitably welcomed, and when she briefly told the story of her coming, cordial kindness followed. The

General's daughters, the toast of the Albemarle, Dolly, Penelope and Lavinia, made her at home. He listened to her tale of danger and promised assistance.

Midday came, and with it Betsy's kind farewell. Filial duty bade her, and she hied her home. As she neared her sea-girt shore the notes of victory were in the air. "They are beaten, beaten, beaten, they are beaten at Great Bridge." The reports materialized as she went. The battle at Great Bridge had been fought and won. Howe had assumed command of the Virginia and Carolina troops upon his arrival, and was in hot pursuit of Dunmore toward Norfolk, where, after a short resistance, Norfolk was evacuated by the British troops, who sought refuge on board their ships, and, after a few cannon shot into the town, they departed for parts unknown.

Then, and long after, by bivouac and camp fire and in patriotic homes was told the story of Betsy Dowdy's Ride.

Mrs. Motte's Sacrifice

IN THE history of any country it is often true that the stories that are recorded of private individuals rather than those often in the public eye afford us a deeper insight into the character and the spirit of a people than the careers of the famous and the great. Stories, when true, of the deeds of the humble, or at least of those of whom proud History takes small note, should be preserved. Surely few tales in American history better merit a place in our national annals than the story of the Revolutionary heroine, Rebecca Motte, for it was she who, for patriotic reasons, set fire to her own magnificent home.

During the Revolution there was much skilful skirmishing and a little hard fighting in my neighborhood in the Carolinas, between the famous partisan leader, General Francis Marion, and the British, especially the British cavalry led by the restless and gallant Colonel Tarleton. In the course of some of these maneuvers the beautiful Motte plantation home fell into the hands of the British; and it was made the headquarters for the enemy. Indeed, rude fortifications were built to prevent the recapture of the place by the patriots. The British made rather free use of whatever they found on the plantation, though it is said that they made some show of asking Mrs. Motte's permission to appropriate whatever they needed; their desire for fowls appeared insatiable. A letter from Colonel Tarleton, still extant, refers to the fact that some of the soldiers had carried off the horses of his hostess, but he expresses a willingness to return them. Long after, General Thomas Pinckney, when minister from our country to Eng-

From "Plantation Lights and Shadows," by Archibald Rutledge, in *The Carolina Low-Country*, by Augustine T. Smythe, and others, pp. 159–162. Copyright, 1931, by the Macmillan Company. New York. 1932.

land, happened to meet Tarleton, and was introduced to him as the son-in-law of Mrs. Motte, "whose horses, you know," added the introducer, "you stole when you were in Carolina."

After a considerable time, the American troops succeeded in capturing one of the outposts of what was called Ft. Motte. Major McPherson, the British officer in command, afraid, perhaps, longer to harbor so declared an enemy, desired Mrs. Motte to remain no more in the camp. She therefore betook herself to a small house within the generous limits of the plantation. . . . The American troops, under Marion and Lee, advanced rapidly to the siege of Ft. Motte, and were joyfully received and entertained by Mrs. Motte in her somewhat humble abode. Meanwhile a rumor came that the British were soon to be formidably reinforced; and, that object once effected, there would be no further thought of surrendering the fort. Close siege to the place was laid by the Americans; but the British held out. There apparently remained but one way of ending it speedily and successfully. It occurred to General Marion that, by firing the roof of the house, which served at once as headquarters and the very heart of the English fortification, this end might be attained; and with many misgivings at the military necessity of destroying so valuable a home, especially the home of one who was a devoted patriot, he talked the matter over with General Light-Horse Harry Lee. The latter told Mrs. Motte of the design of the patriot commander.

Strangely enough, on the day that the family was ordered out of Ft. Motte, one of them, as she left, picked up and carried off for safekeeping, a small quiver of arrows which had many years before been presented to Mrs. Motte by a captain who had brought them from the East Indies. He had declared that they would set on fire any wooden substance against which they struck. It was also said that their tips were poisoned; and a British officer handling one incautiously was warned of the danger. . . .

When Colonel Lee questioned Mrs. Motte concerning the burning of her own beautiful home for the purpose of military strategy, her reply was characteristic. "Do not," she said, "hesitate a single moment. And I will give you something to facilitate the destruction." Then she went in search of the three East Indian arrows. There was no bow for them; consequently they were shot from a rifle. With intense excitement and interest the flight of the first arrow was watched. It fell quietly and harmlessly. The second one had no more effect. Then some one suggested that they should wait until later in the day, when the roof had been well dried by the rays of the sun. At length, about midday, the third and last arrow was dispatched; and after a few moments a thin curling of smoke from the roof of the house told the watchers that the strange arrow had done its work well. The British garrison were soon aware of their new danger, and made vigorous efforts to extinguish the flames. The besiegers meanwhile attempted to prevent the extinguishing of the flames by directing their rifle-fire on the point where the staircase gave access to the roof. In a short time the white flag gave place to the English colors, and Ft. Motte fell into the hands of the wily patriots. It was not too late even then to save the house; and the American soldiers showed their appreciation of the patriotic spirit of their countrywoman by making the most strenuous exertions to save her property, so that only the roof was consumed. It is said that even the British, with a chivalry worthy of their highest traditions, joined their conquerors in an attempt to save Mrs. Motte's home.

The quiver, emptied of its fateful arrows, was ever kept with laudable sentiment hung in Mrs. Motte's parlor, holding knitting needles. Whenever, in after years, Mrs. Motte's part in the capture of the fort was alluded to in her presence, she would say simply, "Too much has been made of a thing that any American woman would have done."

Mrs. Miller, Eli Whitney, and the Cotton Gin

ELI WHITNEY, at the time of inventing the cotton gin, was a guest at Mulberry Grove, near Savannah, Georgia, the home of General Nathaniel Greene, of Revolutionary fame. After the death of the general, his widow married Phineas Miller, tutor to General Greene's children, and a friend and college mate of Whitney's. The ingenuity of the Yankee visitor, as exhibited in various amateur devices and tinkerings about the premises, inspired the family with such confidence in his skill that, on one occasion, when Mrs. Miller's watch was out of order, she gave it to Mr. Whitney for repair, no professional watchmaker being within reach. Not long thereafter, a gentleman called at the house to exhibit a fine sample of cotton wool, and incidentally remarked while displaying the sample: "There is a fortune in store for some one who will invent a machine for separating the lint from the seed." Mrs. Miller, who was present, turned to Whitney and said: "You're the very man, Mr. Whitney, for since you succeeded so well with my watch I am sure you have ingenuity enough to make such a machine."

After this conversation, Mr. Whitney confined himself closely to his room for several weeks. At the end of this time he invited the family to inspect his model for a cotton gin. It was constructed with wire teeth on a revolving cylinder. However there was no contrivance for throwing off the lint after it was separated from the seed and it wrapped around the cylinder, thereby greatly obstructing the operation. Mrs. Miller, seeing the difficulty, seized a common clothes brush, applied it to the teeth, and caught the lint. Whitney, with delight, exclaimed: "Madam, you have solved the problem. With this suggestion my model is complete!"

From *Georgia's Landmarks, Memorials, and Legends,* by Lucian Lamar Knight, Vol. I, pp. 126–127. Copyright, 1913, by Lucian Lamar Knight. Atlanta: Printed for the Author by the Byrd Printing Company, State Printers.

The story as recalled from memory by Miss [Eliza F.] Andrews, [daughter of Judge Garnett Andrews, of Washington, Georgia], was reduced to writing years later. It was also verified by a letter from Mrs. P. M. Nightingale, then an old lady

The Nags Head Picture of Theodosia Burr

IN THE winter of 1812 there drifted ashore at Kitty Hawk, a few miles below Nags Head, a small pilot boat with all sails set and the rudder lashed. There was no sign of violence or bloodshed; the boat was in perfect condition, but entirely deserted. The small table in the cabin had been spread for some repast, which remained undisturbed. There were several handsome silk dresses, a vase of wax flowers with a glass covering, a nautilus shell beautifully carved, and hanging on the wall of the cabin was the portrait of a young and beautiful woman. This picture was an oil painting on polished mahogany, twenty inches in length and enclosed in a frame richly gilded. The face was patrician and refined: the expression of the dark eyes, proud and haughty; the hair dark auburn, curling and abundant. A white bodice cut low in the neck and richly adorned with lace, revealed a glimpse of the drooping shoulders, and the snowy bust, unconfined by corset.

The wreckers who boarded the boat possessed themselves of everything of value on board. The picture, wax flowers, nautilus shell and silk dresses fell into the possession of an illiterate banker woman, who attached no especial value to them.

This picture, which has since attracted so much attention, hung on the wall of a rude cabin among the North Carolina hills for fifty-seven years. In the year 1869, it fell into the possession of the late Dr. William G. Pool, a prominent North Carolina physician. Dr. Pool was a man of marked individuality. He had the tastes of an antiquarian, was literary, cultured, and noted for his remarkable conversational gifts. While summering at Nags Head, he was called upon to visit professionally the old banker woman referred to above. He was successful in his treatment of the case, and knowing the circumstances of his patient, would accept no payment for his services. In her gratitude for his kindness, the old woman insisted upon his accepting "as a gift" the portrait hanging on the wall of her cabin. When questioned concerning its history, she related the facts above mentioned. This she did with apparent reluctance, possibly sup-

---

in her eighty-second year, but with her mental faculties unimpaired. . . . Miss Andrews, the author of the following account, is an eminent Southern educator, who has achieved wide note in the realm of letters. Her father, Judge Garnett Andrews, was one of Georgia's most distinguished jurists. [One of the original cotton gins invented by Eli Whitney was for years in his possession.] The author wrote her first account of the invention for the *Scientific American* some time in the early seventies, after which she published, in the Augusta *Chronicle*, on September 20, 1905, an article on the part played by Mrs. Miller in Whitney's great invention.—L. L. K., *ibid.*, pp. 125–126.

From *The Eyrie and Other Southern Stories*, by Bettie Freshwater Pool, pp. 1–25. Copyright, 1905, by Bettie Freshwater Pool. New York: Broadway Publishing Company.

pressing many interesting details that might have thrown more light upon the subject. Her husband had been one of the wreckers who boarded the pilot boat, and the picture and other articles referred to had been his share of the spoils. Her story was that the wreckers supposed the boat to have been boarded by pirates, and that passengers and crew had been made to "walk the plank." The picture and its strange history became a subject of much interest and conjecture to Dr. Pool. Artists pronounced it a masterpiece, and the unmistakable portrait of some woman of patrician birth.

Chancing one day to pick up an old magazine in which appeared a picture of Aaron Burr, Dr. Pool was forcibly struck by the strong resemblance between it and the portrait in question. Like a flash it occurred to him that this might be a likeness of Theodosia, the ill-fated daughter of Aaron Burr. Eagerly he compared dates and facts, until he became thoroughly convinced that he had found a clue to that mysterious disappearance, which is one of the most awful tragedies of history. A brief account of this discovery was published in the New York *Sun,* and immediately letters innumerable were received by him asking for more particulars.

Photographs of the portrait were sent to the numerous members of the Burr and Edwards families, and almost without exception the likeness was pronounced to be that of Theodosia Burr. Charles Burr Todd, the author, and Mrs. Stella Drake Knappin, descendants respectively of the Burr and Edwards families, visited Dr. Pool's residence on Pasquotank river for the purpose of examining the portrait. They were both convinced that it was a likeness of Theodosia Burr.

The wife of Col. Wheeler of Washington, D. C., who is a daughter of Sully, the famous portrait painter and is herself an artist, compared a photo of the Nags Head picture with a likeness of Theodosia Burr, in her possession. She at once perceived that both features and expression were identical.

There was probably no woman in America at the time of Theodosia Burr's death, more universally known and admired than she. Her high social rank, her beauty, her genius, her accomplishments, as well as her heroic devotion to her father in the dark days of his disgrace and banishment, had made her a prominent figure and had won for her the admiration of thousands.

When Aaron Burr upon his return from exile sent for his daughter to visit him in New York, she decided to make the voyage by sea. Her health had been almost completely wrecked by grief over her father's disgrace, and the recent death of her only child, young Aaron Burr Alston. It was thought that a sea voyage might prove beneficial. She accordingly set sail from Georgetown, S. C., in the *Patriot,* a small pilot boat, December 30th, 1812. Days and weeks passed, but Aaron Burr waited in vain for the arrival of his daughter. Months and years rolled away and still no tidings came. The *Patriot* and all on board had completely vanished from the face of the earth, and the mystery of its disappearance remained unsolved for more than half a century.

Governor Alston did not long survive the loss of his beloved wife, and

Aaron Burr, in speaking years afterwards of his daughter's mysterious fate, said that this event had separated him from the human race.

Let us now compare dates and facts: A pilot boat drifts ashore during the winter of 1812 at Kitty Hawk, a few miles below Nags Head. There are silk dresses in the cabin, and other indications that some lady of wealth and refinement has been on board. There is a portrait on the wall of the cabin that has been pronounced by artists and members of her family to be a likeness of Theodosia Burr.

The *Patriot* was lost during the winter of 1812. On the voyage from Georgetown, S. C., to New York, it would pass the North Carolina coast. The sea at this time was infested by pirates. A band of these bold buccaneers may have boarded the little vessel and compelled passengers and crew to "walk the plank." Becoming alarmed at the appearance of some Government cruiser, they may, from motives of prudence, have abandoned their prize.

This theory is not mere conjecture. Years ago two criminals executed in Norfolk, Va., are reported as having testified that they had belonged to a piratical crew who boarded the *Patriot*, and compelled every soul on board to "walk the plank." The same confession was made years subsequently by a mendicant dying in a Michigan almshouse. This man said he would never forget the beautiful face of Theodosia Burr, as it sank beneath the waves, nor how eloquently she pleaded for her life, promising the pirates pardon and a liberal reward if they would spare her. But they were relentless, and she went to her doom with so dauntless and calm a spirit, that even the most hardened pirates were touched.

I cannot vouch for the truth of these confessions which have appeared from time to time in print. I only introduce them as collateral evidence in support of the banker woman's story. The *Patriot* was supposed to have been wrecked off the coast of Hatteras during a terrific storm which occurred soon after it set sail. This, however, was mere conjecture which has never been substantiated by the slightest proof.

It is not improbable that the *Patriot* during a night of storm was lured ashore by the decoy light at Nags Head, and that passengers and crew fell into the hands of the land pirates in waiting, who possessed themselves of the boat and everything of value it contained.

This also, of course, is mere conjecture; but the all-important fact remains that a pilot boat went ashore at Kitty Hawk during the winter of 1812, and that in the cabin of this boat was a portrait of Theodosia Burr.

Naomi Wise

THE spirit of Naomi Wise is the tragic muse of Randolph county. This woman, who lived over 100 years ago in what was then almost a wilder-

By J. W. Cannon. From *Greensboro (N. C.) Daily News,* November 15, 1925. Clipping file, Library of the Woman's College of the University of North Carolina, Greensboro, North Carolina.

ness, who was drowned in Deep River at what is now Naomi Ford, has become the subject for many sketches and several ballads, some of them having been printed. There is not a person in miles of Randleman and New Salem that does not know at least one story about her death, all of them having a few essential details corresponding. Most of the people list her among the saints and let her stand for all that was pure and holy in womanhood sacrificed to the beast in man.

At New Salem, just off the old Greensboro-Asheboro road, there is a spring now covered with a cupola. This spring has come in a way to represent Naomi Wise and the events that led to her death. The community built the cover and laid concrete blocks around the bubbling water and it has become known as the Naomi Wise spring. No one drinks the water and it is said to be hallowed ground.

It was here that somewhere near 1808 Naomi Wise had a rendezvous with her lover. It was supposed to be on a spring night that she set out from the home of William Adams with pail in hand supposedly to draw water for household use. But as a matter of fact she went to meet the man whom she thought she was going to marry.

Naomi was an orphan and since childhood had lived at the Adams home at New Salem. She is now credited with having been very beautiful and a lovable woman with the weakness that is more or less common to her sex, the weakness of trusting a man.

It so happened that New Salem lay on the route from Old Centre Friends meeting house in Guilford county to Asheboro, the county seat of Randolph county. Jonathan Lewis, who lived near Centre, was a clerk in Elliott's store at Asheboro and passed by New Salem occasionally. Tradition says that he fell in love with Naomi Wise and that it was he who met her from time to time at the spring and courted her there. Tradition also has added that Lewis was not approved by the Adams family, that he was from a rough family that shot on sight.

At all events whether for this reason or for others Naomi Wise met him from time to time at the spring and it was whispered around the community that the two were to be married. The art of gossip was almost as perfect then as it is to-day and there was many a bit of scandal whispered about the name of Naomi Wise around ovens and fireplaces in that section of Randolph county.

Finally one night Naomi Wise left the home with her bucket in hand to go to the spring. She went there and met some man, who succeeding generations have declared to be her lover. The two left the spring on horseback, she riding behind him, toward Deep River. The stories have it that she thought she was to be married to him at Asheboro.

That wedding never took place. Witnessed only by the hills of Randolph county and the person who did the crime, the dress of Naomi was tied over her head and she was thrown into the middle of Deep River right below an old mill dam. The body was found next morning near the place where it was supposed to have been cast.

On this same day Jonathan Lewis spent the night at the home of Samuel Free just a few miles from the place of the drowning and had his horse shod there. That old log house is still standing but has been remodeled since that time. The next morning he left for the western part of the United States and lived out in Ohio many years. In records left by Braxton Craven it is found that two Randolph officers went out west for the purpose of finding Naomi Wise's slayer and Lewis was brought back to this section of North Carolina and tried in the Guilford court. He was acquitted for lack of evidence. At least one source of information leads to the fact that on his deathbed he confessed to having slain the young woman.

He is reported as having repeated her pleas for help and with his face drawn in contortions and the death rattle in his throat he described her action as she learned that she was going to her Maker instead of to her husband.

From this alleged confession and from other information some unknown author has composed the . . . ballad which has been sung in that community for many years.[1]

. . . Every little bit of material thing that had anything to do with the tragedy is cherished. There is a spot marked on a stone just below that old mill dam and also near the Naomi Ford that is said to be where the footprint of the young woman was found the next morning. There was an old stump which stood at the spring that up until a few years ago was said to be the thing on which Naomi stood to mount the horse behind her lover.

More than once Negroes have reported that they have seen the lovely figure of what they thought to be Naomi Wise, hovering over the old mill dam and near the place she was drowned.

An old woman, who died not so many years ago and who said that she has seen Naomi, told a certain Asheboro citizen that Naomi Wise was not pretty. But be that as it may, she might have been as ugly as an old hag; her sins might have been as scarlet, yet passing years and generations have decreed that all such was washed away when she was thrown into Deep River and if her ghost does not hover pure and white above the old mill dam, at least a lovely spirit hangs over Randolph county, and people have named it Naomi Wise.

Frankie Silvers

THE most sensational murder case in the history of the Toe River Valley was that of Frankie Silvers, accused of killing her husband, Charles Silvers.

---

[1] For texts and tune of "Little Oma Wise" or "Poor Omie," see Mellinger E. Henry, "Still More Ballads and Folk-Songs from the Southern Highlands," *The Journal of American Folk-Lore,* Vol. 45 (January–March, 1932), No. 175, pp. 135–141.

The defendant, who was tried in Morganton two years before county government was established in the Valley itself, was the first woman hanged in North Carolina. It is an old story of jealousy and revenge, played out in a cabin in the Deyton Bend of Toe River, a story that keeps turning over and over and adding to itself like a snowball. There are half a dozen versions. . . .

*   *   *   *   *

In her ninetieth year Aunt Cindy Norman, sister of the murdered man, gave W. W. Bailey, of Spruce Pine, the following account of the killing.

In the winter of 1831 Charles Silvers was living in the Deyton Bend with his wife, Frankie, and their baby daughter. Very early on the morning of December 23rd Frankie dropped in at her father-in-law's and found the family preparing to wash. "My washing is done and I've scoured too," she boasted, and her mother-in-law marvelled at her smartness to do a day's work before dawn. Frankie went on to tell the reason for her visit. Charlie had gone over the river on the ice the day before for his Christmas liquor, and had not returned. She was worried and begged his people to look at the crossings to see if he had fallen through. They searched the river for a considerable distance, but there was neither trail nor break in the ice. When he was still absent after several days, other families joined in the search. Frankie shook the valley with her lamentations. Word of the strange disappearance seeped into the country around Bear Creek and Art'ur's Knob.

An old man named Jakie Collis determined to go and walk over the ground himself to satisfy his curiosity on certain points. He went first to the father's house, where Cindy Silvers, the eight-year-old sister of the lost man, offered to take him to Charlie's empty cabin. Frankie had by now given up his return and refused to stay there alone with her grief. At the deserted cabin Jakie and Cindy and others who had joined them scrutinized closely the mantel and sides of the fireplace. There were fresh irregular chippings at intervals over the whole surface where someone had hewn lightly with an axe. It gave Jakie an idea.

"Help me lift the puncheons," he said to one of the men.

The upper surface of the slabs was neatly scoured, but the rounded sides underneath were streaked at the cracks with old blood stains. There was a fresh layer of ashes between the puncheons and the earth. Old Jakie thrust his hand into them and found them clotted with what appeared to be dried blood. Just then Frankie, who had watched from a distance, pushed her way among the men like a mad woman and ordered them off. The men stood still, looking at her with horror in their eyes that told her what they suspected. Then they went on with their work. In a frenzy of despair she wept and swore and made wild protestations while she saw the men sift the ashes in the fireplace and find human teeth and the remains of bones showing hack marks. Somebody realized that the big pile of hickory wood that had stood by the door was gone. When they looked at the axe, its edge was dulled with chopping something other than wood. The facts were plain enough without Frankie's extraordinary behavior. They sent for the sheriff to take charge of her.

More evidence came to light as the weather grew warmer. The investigation of a hollow sourwood where a dog sniffed suspiciously revealed the intestines and other parts of the body that did not burn readily. The horror of the tragedy shook the Valley from end to end.

Judge Donnell sentenced Frankie to death at the June term, 1832. She appealed, but Judge Ruffin sustained the conviction. When there was no hope through the regular channels of the law, her kinfolks took a hand in the affair. They spirited her out of jail and took her through the streets in a load of hay. As soon as they were out of town, Frankie climbed off the wagon. Dressed in a man's clothes and carrying a gun, she tramped behind the hay. The sheriff's posse overtook the suspicious load too quickly for her to crawl back out of sight. She tried to brazen it out.

"Want to buy some hay?" she asked in the deepest possible voice.

"No. We don't want hay," answered the sheriff, helping himself to the gun. "But we do want you, Frankie."

It was no use. She went back to jail. In the beginning she had protested her innocence. Now when there was no hope she made full confession.

According to her story she had been goaded by jealousy to kill her husband, and was awaiting the first opportunity to do it. On the night of December 22nd, he came into the house tired and cold from a day spent chopping wood to last over Christmas. He had a big pile of hickory chunks laid by to show for his labor. After supper he took the baby in his arms and lay down on a sheepskin in front of the fire to get the chill out of his bones. The axe lay handy, and in her anger she longed to seize the chance to kill him. In case she should find courage to go through with it, she gently slid the sleeping baby out of his arms. He did not waken.

At last, to end the torment of indecision, she seized the axe and tried to sever his head from his body in one mighty stroke. The blow glanced, and Charlie, horribly mutilated, sprang up and thrashed about making noises that frightened her half to death. She jumped into bed and covered her head to shut out the sound until he commenced to grow quieter from loss of blood. There was no way but to go on with it now. When she could muster courage, she got out of bed and struck the blows that quieted him forever. The rest of the night she spent dismembering and burning the body. It took a hot fire, and in a single night she used the whole of the Christmas hickory. Then in that blazing, suffocating cabin she carefully whittled away the spatters of blood and grease from the mantel and sides of the fireplace and scoured every stain from the floor that had been generously smirched as the body thrashed about. She washed the spattered bedding. That was the washing of which she boasted to her mother-in-law a few hours later.

Frankie Silvers must have had some feeling, because in the last days of

her imprisonment she contrived a long, gloomy poem which she recited
from the scaffold before her execution, July 12, 1833.[1]

On one dark and dreary night
I put his body out of sight.
To see his soul and body part
It strikes with terror to my heart.

I took his blooming days away,
Left him no time to God to pray,
And if sins fall on his head
Must I not bear them in his stead?

The jealous thought that first gave strife
To make me take my husband's life.
For days and months I spent my time
Thinking how to commit this crime.

And on a dark and doleful night
I put his body out of sight;
With flames I tried him to consume
But time would not admit it done.

You all see me and on me gaze—
Be careful how you spend your days
And ne'er commit this awful crime,
But try to serve your God in time.

Judge Daniel has my sentence passed
These prison walls I leave at last;
Nothing to cheer my drooping head
Until I'm numbered with the dead.

But O, that dreadful Judge I fear;
Shall I that awful sentence hear?
"Depart, ye cursed, down to Hell,
And forever there to dwell."

I know that frightful ghosts I'll see,
Gnawing their flesh in misery,
And taken and there attended be
For murder in the first degree.

Then shall I meet that mournful face
Whose blood I spilled upon this place,
With flaming eyes to me he'll say,
"Why did you take my life away?"

His feeble hands fell gently down,
His chattering tongue soon lost its sound.
[*Incomplete.*]

My mind on solemn subjects rolls
My little child—God bless its soul;
All you that are of Adam's race
Let not my faults this child disgrace.

Farewell, good people, you all now see
What my bad conduct brought on me;
To die of shame and disgrace
Before this world of human race.

Awful, indeed, to think of death,
In perfect health to lose my breath;
Farewell, my friends, I bid adieu,
Vengeance on me must now pursue.

Great God! How shall I be forgiven?
Not fit for earth, not fit for Heaven,
But little time to pray to God
For now I try that awful road.

Throughout her trial and imprisonment Frankie maintained a philo-
sophic indifference. People whispered that she had not told all she knew;
that some of her kinfolks helped her murder her husband and she was
shielding them; that even as she mounted the scaffold, she expected a pardon. Everyone looked forward to a spectacular last moment development.
At the top of the gallows steps Frankie indicated to the hangman that she
wanted to say something. Now it was coming.

"Die with it in you, Frankie!" called her father from the crowd.

But Frankie was not going to tell anything more than everyone knew
already. She wanted to read her poem. One story says that she had a
piece of cake in her hand as she ascended the gallows platform. When
the hangman asked if she were ready, she said that she would be when

---

[1] For the history and text of the song "Frances Silvers" (somewhat garbled in the
present version), see Mellinger E. Henry, *op. cit.*, pp. 62–65.

she finished eating her cake. Then Frankie Silvers pulled the black cap down over her face herself and shut out the daylight forever.

At that period it was the custom of the state to turn over a hanged man's body to medical students for dissection. There were many petitions for Frankie's body because a woman's corpse was hard to obtain. The father, harassed with the fear of such ignominy for his daughter, caused several graves to be dug before the execution, all of which were made into mounds by the following morning. Meanwhile he spirited the body away. The night after the execution it lay hidden under sacks in the barn of the Buck Horne Tavern ten miles from Morgantown. Then it was secretly buried in a private burying ground nearby.

The words of the poem were eagerly seized upon by a countryside familiar with the dramatic story. It became a song, but it could be sung only when no members of either family were present, lest they be reminded of the tragedy. This is not a feud country, and while neither family took up the grudge, everyone felt that it was better not to meddle with fresh wounds. The song survives today in an eerie, mournful tune whose urgent minor beat is the restless scurrying of unlaid ghosts in lonely places.

The Duels of Bernard Marigny

BERNARD MARIGNY, of the most illustrious family in Louisiana, was a great wag. Among his friends was a Monsieur Tissier, afterward a prominent judge, who was a confirmed beau, or dude we would call him in this generation. Marigny delighted in nothing more than to quiz his friend, and did so upon every occasion. Meeting him in the street or in the ball room, Marigny would throw up his hands, assume an attitude and expression of the most intense admiration, and exclaim, "What a beau you are! How I do admire you!" Monsieur Tissier bore it for a long time without remonstrance, but forbearance at last ceased to be a virtue, and he insisted that Monsieur Marigny should be more considerate of his feelings. Monsieur Marigny waited until he met his friend in a ball room among the ladies, and repeated the offensive exclamation, whereupon Monsieur Tissier challenged him. The challenge was accepted, pistols were chosen, and the whilom friends repaired to the Oaks [a favorite dueling ground]. They were placed in position, and the word was about to be given, when Monsieur Marigny threw up his hands, his face assumed the old expression and he said in tones of the deepest grief, "How I admire you! Is it possible that I am soon to make a corpse of Beau Tissier?" Monsieur Tissier's anger was not proof against this attack, and he burst into laughter, threw

From *Historical Sketch Book and Guide to New Orleans and Environs,* with Map, Illustrated with Many Original Engravings; and Containing Exhaustive Accounts of the Traditions, Historical Legends, and Remarkable Localities of the Creole City, edited and compiled by several leading writers of the New Orleans Press, pp. 17–18. New York: Will H. Coleman. 1885.

himself into his opponent's arms, and the duel was brought to a sudden and peaceful termination.

Another affair is recorded somewhat later, in which Monsieur Marigny was also one of the principals. Marigny was sent to the Legislature in 1817, at which time there was a very strong political antagonism between the Creoles and Americans, which provoked many warm debates in the House of Representatives and in the Senate. Catahoula parish was represented by a Georgian giant, an ex-blacksmith, named Humble, a man of plain ways, but possessed of many sterling qualities. He was remarkable as much for his immense stature as for his political diplomacy, standing, as he did, nearly seven feet in his stockings. It happened that an impassioned speech of Monsieur Marigny was replied to by the Georgian, and the latter was so extremely pointed in his allusions that his opponent felt himself aggrieved and sent a challenge to mortal combat. The Georgian was nonplussed. "I know nothing of this dueling business," said he; "I will not fight him."

"You must," said his friend; "no gentleman can refuse."

"I am not a gentleman," replied the honest son of Georgia; "I am only a blacksmith."

"But you will be ruined if you do not fight," urged his friends; "you have the choice of weapons, and you can choose in such a way as to give yourself an equal chance with your adversary."

The giant asked time to consider the proposition, and ended by accepting. He sent the following reply to Monsieur Marigny:

"I accept, and in the exercise of my privilege I stipulate that the duel shall take place in Lake Ponchartrain in six feet of water, sledge hammers to be used as weapons."

Monsieur Marigny was about five feet eight inches in height, and his adversary was almost seven, as has been stated. The conceit of the Georgian so pleased Monsieur Marigny, who could appreciate a joke as well as perpetrate one, that he declared himself satisfied, and the duel did not take place.

Bras Coupé

ONE of the famous Bamboula dancers of the early days, and also an expert wielder of the beef bones, was a gigantic Negro owned by General William de Buys, who is said to have been the first to attach little bells to his ankles instead of the customary bits of metal. He could leap higher and shout louder than any of the other slaves who stamped and cavorted in

From *The French Quarter,* An Informal History of the New Orleans Underworld, by Herbert Asbury, pp. 244–247. Copyright, 1936, by Alfred A. Knopf, Inc. New York and London.

For Bras Coupé's story, see also George W. Cable, *The Grandissimes* and *Strange True Stories of Louisiana.*

the dance; his stamping, indeed, shook the ground, and when he cried: "Badoum! Badoum!" the tops of the sycamore-trees trembled and swayed in the wind caused by his mighty bellowings. And in his ham-like fists the beef bones rattled upon the head of the Bamboula drum with a crashing roar that resembled nothing less than a salvo of artillery fire. His name during the period of his fame as a Bamboula artist was Squier; a few years later, as Bras Coupé and the Brigand of the Swamp, he acquired a different sort of renown.

General de Buys was well known in New Orleans as a remarkably kind and indulgent master; he petted, coddled, and spoiled the Negro Squier, taught him to shoot, and permitted him to go alone on hunting expeditions in the forests adjacent to the city. And Squier practiced assiduously with the General's rifle; premonition, he said afterwards, warned him that he would eventually lose an arm, and so he became an expert marksman with either hand alone. The taste of freedom which Squier experienced on his journeys into the woods after game was too much for him. He began running away, and received only slight punishment when he was captured and returned to General de Buys. Early in 1834 Squier was shot by a patrol of planters searching the swamps for runaway slaves, and his right arm was amputated, whence the sobriquet Bras Coupé, by which he was thereafter known. As soon as his injury had healed, Bras Coupé fled into the swamps and organized a gang of escaped blacks and a few renegade white men, whom he led on frequent robbing and murdering forays on the outskirts of the city, with an occasional venture into the thickly settled residential districts. He was New Orleans' most feared outlaw for nearly three years, and the successor of the *Kaintock* as the hobgoblin with which nurses and mothers frightened the Creole children. Reviewing his career, the *Picayune* after his death described him as "a semi-devil and a fiend in human shape," and said that his life had been "one of crime and depravity."

Among the slaves Bras Coupé soon became a legendary figure endowed with superhuman powers; in the folklore of the New Orleans Negroes he was installed alongside the redoubtable Annie Christmas and in many respects was accounted her superior. He was, of course, fireproof and invulnerable to wounds, for he was familiar with the miraculous herbs described by the French travelers Bossu, Perrin du Lac, and Baudry des Lozières, and with many others which these avid searchers after botanical wonders had not discovered. Hunters returned to New Orleans from the swamps and told how, having encountered Bras Coupé, they fired at him, only to see their bullets flatten against his chest; some even said that the missiles had bounced off the iron-like body of the outlaw and whizzed dangerously close to their own heads, while Bras Coupé laughed derisively and strode grandly into the farthest reaches of the swamps. And according to the slave tradition, detachments of soldiers sent after him vanished in a cloud of mist. Moreover, his very glance paralyzed, if he so wished, and he fed on human flesh.

The popular belief in Bras Coupé's invulnerability received a rude shock when, on April 6, 1837, he was wounded by two hunters who braved his magical powers and shot him near the Bayou St. John. And it was dissipated entirely on July 19 of the same year. On that day a Spanish fisherman named Francisco Garcia, who was known to the slaves as a friend of Bras Coupé's, drove slowly through the streets of New Orleans a cart drawn by a decrepit mule, and watched with tender solicitude an ungainly bundle, wrapped in old sacks, which jounced in the bed of the vehicle. Garcia stopped in front of the Cabildo and carried his bundle into the office of Mayor Dennis Prieur, where he unwrapped it and disclosed the body of Bras Coupé. The fisherman told the authorities that on the day before, the 18th, he was fishing in the Bayou St. John when Bras Coupé fired at him and missed, whereupon the indignant fisherman went ashore and beat out the brigand's brains with a club. The truth, however, appears to have been that Bras Coupé was slain as he slept in the fisherman's hut. Garcia demanded the immediate payment of the two-thousand-dollar reward which he had heard had been offered for Bras Coupé dead or alive, but he received only two hundred and fifty dollars. The body of the outlaw was exposed in the Place d'Armes for two days, and several thousand slaves were compelled to march past and look at it, as a warning.

The Mystery of Peter Ney

In 1874 a reporter for the Dayton, Ohio, Journal fell in with an old fellow named Philip Petrie and got from him an odd yarn.

This Petrie, obviously a Frenchman, said he had fought in Napoleon's army and, six months after Waterloo, had left France by shipping as a seaman on a vessel bound from Bordeaux to America. Some days after leaving the French port, he noticed among the passengers a man whose appearance seemed familiar. A closer view of this passenger left Petrie shaking, for only a short time before the ship sailed from Bordeaux, Marshal Ney had been executed in the Luxembourg Gardens, yet here was Marshal Ney walking the deck.

There was no doubt about it, Petrie told the Journal reporter, for in the army he had seen Red Peter scores of times and would know him anywhere. The ship finally reached Charleston, he said, and both he and this dead man who had been Marshal Ney landed there. The dead man then walked to a music store in Broad Street and bought a flute, and this lifted the hair on Petrie's nape, because in the old days in the army Red Peter had been a great flute player. Then in the manner of ghosts, he had vanished.

It was in the autumn of 1874 that Petrie, then a very old man, told his

From "The Mystery of Peter Ney," by Herbert Ravenel Sass, *The Saturday Evening Post*, Vol. 219 (November 16, 1946), No. 20, pp. 84, 86. Copyright, 1946, by the Curtis Publishing Company. Philadelphia.

story to the Ohio reporter, but he remembered perfectly the date of the vessel's arrival in America; it was January 29, 1816. Where the man whom Petrie believed to be Marshal Ney or his spirit spent the next few years is known only in part. There are traces or imagined traces of him in Indiana at about this time, and later he himself said that after reaching this country he passed several years in seclusion, preparing for the career of a schoolmaster by studying the classics and the higher mathematics. Then one day in the fall of 1819 three French refugees—the country was full of them just then—in the little village of Georgetown on the South Carolina coast stopped in their tracks, as though each at the same instant had seen a ghost.

So they thought for a moment as they stood transfixed, staring at the big man striding along under the live oaks on the opposite side of the wide street. Marshal Ney! But that was impossible. In a flash they remembered the rumors which had flown about Paris just after the execution. But those rumors had been refuted. The Bourbon government had published the most positive official accounts of the execution and the burial.

Meanwhile the big man across the street had turned a corner, and when the three excited Frenchmen reached the corner, he had disappeared.

"No, Maurice," one of them was saying, "it can't be he. I talked with a man who saw the blood; he said the marshal was red from head to waist, and the ground was soaked with it."

But the thoughts of the two other Parisians, reaching back across three years, were recovering from memory certain details which now suddenly seemed significant.

"Don't you recall," one of them said, "how Madame Ney was criticized because she didn't attend the burial in Père-Lachaise? Well, why should she, I ask you, if the coffin was empty or contained some criminal's body, while her husband at that very moment was on his way to the coast?"

"Gentlemen," the third man declared impatiently, "we've just seen Michael Ney or his ghost, and I don't believe in ghosts. Now, I have an excellent memory. I am sure it was no more than a month after the so-called execution of Ney that General La Valette, who also had been condemned to be shot, escaped. The thing became known so that it couldn't be concealed, and the French government, you recall, accused some of Wellington's officers. I recollect the name of one, a Captain Hutchinson, and I think another was named Brice or, rather, Bruce. There was a great stir about it, you remember, and the officers were reduced or reprimanded or something. Now if those English fellows rescued La Valette—and they admitted it—I think I understand how it is that we've seen Marshal Ney."

The one called Jacques still shook his head, but they turned the corner and walked slowly along the almost-deserted street. Though Georgetown was a small place and though they kept their eyes open throughout their stay, they had no luck. The big man whom they had seen striding along the street had vanished like the ghost they at first took him to be.

But it wasn't a ghost that stopped a fight and prevented a murder at

Mocksville. At that little crossroads town deep in the North Carolina backwoods a hot-tempered Irishman named Schools was the village doctor, and
one day when a group of men were talking politics in front of the tavern, a
farmer with too much Monongahela whisky aboard insulted Schools. The
doctor's temper flared; he drew his long knife, the favorite backwoods
weapon, and was about to carve the fellow when someone gripped his arm.
He whirled and saw a man he had never seen before—tall, powerful, with
massive chin, reddish hair and steel-blue eyes.

The stranger spoke quietly. "What, sir?" he said. "Kill a man unarmed,
with no chance to defend himself?"

Schools and the big man stood for a moment looking at each other; then
the doctor put away his knife. He had forgotten the matter of the insult
altogether. This stranger fascinated him; he'd never seen so compelling a
face. Without effort, the stranger dominated the crowd. "Gentlemen," he
said in perfect English, but with a slight accent, "let me introduce myself.
My name is Peter Stuart Ney, and I am a French refugee who would like
to establish a school here in your village."

"Why, sir," cried Doctor Schools, and somehow he knew that this was
the mightiest event that had ever happened at Mocksville, "that's the very
thing this town needs more than anything else."

So the man who called himself Peter Stuart Ney began his work in the
red-hill country around Third Creek in North Carolina where he was to become first a tower of strength, then a legend. He had slipped out of
Georgetown soon after the three Frenchmen had seen him. For three years
he had taught a small school in the village of Brownsville, South Carolina;
then suddenly he left, and some time later turned up in Mocksville.
Thenceforward, though he also taught for short periods in Virginia and
South Carolina and probably made at least one trip to Indiana, the Piedmont Region of North Carolina was his home.

Wherever he went—and he taught at different times in five counties—he
won instant respect. All knew at once that this was no country school-
master. They knew him to be the greatest man that had ever come into that
country, and this conviction they held despite his one serious weakness. He
was in this classroom at Brownsville when the news of Napoleon's death
at St. Helena reached him. He fell instantly in a dead faint on the floor
and that night tried to kill himself with a knife, which, fortunately,
broke.

He had recovered physically by the time he moved to the Third Creek
country, but his spirit never recovered. His hope had been that the Bona-
partist dynasty would be restored, so that he could return to his wife and
family—it was always his wife that he spoke of; never a woman who lived
in Babylon Street.[1] But now his hope of an early return was shattered.

---

[1] The adventuress Ida Saint Elme, who tells of her love for Michael Ney in her
Memoirs of a Contemporary (Paris, 1828). See Herbert Ravenel Sass, as cited, pp.
83–84.

And now, in his disappointment, he sometimes drank too much, and at such times he talked.

He said that he was Marshal Ney, of France. He said that after he had been condemned to death, a plan had been arranged to rescue him and that the Duke of Wellington had made its success possible. The soldiers detailed to kill him were veterans of his old command and were instructed to fire over his head. He had been given a small sack containing a liquid resembling blood, and this he hid under his shirt front. When he gave the command "Fire!" he struck his hand upon his breast, bursting the sack, so that the red stuff spurted all over his upper body and made a crimson spot on the ground when he threw himself down. He was taken up, removed to a near-by hospital and disguised. That night, after a farewell visit to his wife, he rode toward the coast, finally reaching Bordeaux, where he boarded a ship bound for America. Once during the voyage, he said, he was recognized by a seaman who had formerly served under him in the army.

At first he talked thus only on the infrequent occasions when he was a little drunk. Later he told the same story, when perfectly sober, to a number of men who had become his intimate friends, relating, too, many experiences in the field.

His body was scarred with old wounds, and apparently these corresponded to the wounds which Marshal Ney was known to have had. In every physical feature published descriptions of Marshal Ney described Peter Stuart Ney also. Marshal Ney had been one of the best swordsmen in Europe, and the schoolmaster of Third Creek was an expert fencer. So similar were the handwritings of Marshal Ney and Peter Stuart Ney that every handwriting expert who has examined them, including the celebrated David N. Carvalho, has declared them the work of the same man.

While he lived, the outside world knew nothing of him, but in the red hills of Rowan and its neighboring counties the legend of the mysterious schoolmaster grew as he grew older. Three North Carolinians—J. A. Weston, J. E. Smoot and, most recently, Le Gette Blythe—have gathered in as many books much impressive evidence, only a small part of which can be given here. In Statesville one day John Snyder, born near Prague and formerly a soldier in Napoleon's army, saw Peter Stuart Ney and flung up his hands exclaiming, "Lordy God, Marshal Ney!"

Col. J. J. Lehmanowski, a Polish follower of Napoleon, had been sentenced to be shot the day after Marshal Ney's execution, but had been helped to escape and had made his way to America.

He was living near Knightstown, Indiana, when, to his amazement, he was visited one day by a big man of military bearing whose identity he would not reveal even to his family. Years later, shortly before his death, he told his daughter that the mysterious visitor was Marshal Ney. After Peter Stuart Ney's death in 1846, a Dr. E. M. C. Neyman, of Indiana, claiming to be a son of Marshal Ney who had been sent by his mother, Aglae, to America in 1821, appeared at Third Creek with the intention of carrying his "father's" body to Indiana for final burial. But so strong was the affection of the people of Rowan for their old schoolmaster that Neyman agreed to let him rest where he lay.

Most impressive of all is the fact that the hundreds of pupils that Peter Stuart Ney taught and the scores of men and women who knew him well during the more than twenty-five years of his honorable and useful career as a teacher believed that he was Marshal Ney, not only because the evidence seemed to them overwhelming, but also because they had never known him tell anything but the truth. On his deathbed, when he was seventy-seven years old, his physician and devoted friend, Dr. Matthew Locke, told him that his end was at hand and asked him to say finally who he was. He looked Doctor Locke straight in the eyes and replied, "I am Marshal Ney, of France."

But History says that he was not. History says that this man, so justly beloved, was a supreme imposter, for it declares that Michael Ney died under the volley of the Royalist firing squad in the Luxembourg Gardens in Paris. . . .

The Bowie Knife

. . . Who made the first Bowie knife? How did it originate?

According to an unpublished letter, dated 1890 and preserved among the historical archives of the University of Texas, from John S. Moore, grandnephew of James Bowie, the original knife was modeled as a hunting knife by Rezin Bowie, Sr., and wrought by his own blacksmith, Jesse Cliffe. Some time later Jim Bowie had a "difficulty" with one Major Morris Wright, in which a bullet from Wright's pistol was checked by a silver dollar in Bowie's vest pocket. While Wright was in the act of shooting, Bowie "pulled down" on him, but his pistol snapped and the two foes parted expecting to meet another day. When Jim told his father of the trouble and of how his pistol had snapped, the old gentleman got out his prized hunting knife and presented it to his son with these laconic words: "This will never snap."

In the "Sandbar Duel," as it is called, that followed, the knife fully realized all expectations. This duel was in reality a free-for-all fight that took place among twelve men who met on a sandbar of the Mississippi River near Natchez, September 19, 1827. In it two men were killed and three badly wounded. Bowie was down, shot in four places and cut in five, when his mortal enemy, Major Wright, rushed upon him, exclaiming, "Damn you, you have killed me." Bowie raised himself up and stabbed Wright to the heart. At once Bowie's knife became famous and copies of it were widely disseminated.

From "Bowie and the Bowie Knife," by J. Frank Dobie, Southwest Review, Vol. 16 (April, 1931), No. 3, pp. 354–362. Copyright, 1931, by the Southwest Review. Dallas, Texas: Southern Methodist University.

According to notes kept by another scion of the Bowie family, Dr. J. Moore Soniat du Fosset, of New Orleans, now deceased, it was Rezin P. Bowie, the brother of James, who devised the knife. The occasion for it arose thus:

The Bowie brothers were very fond of riding wild cattle down—a sport popular among planters of Louisiana at the time. There were two ways of dealing with the maverick animals. One was to shoot them from horseback as sportsmen on the plains shot buffaloes; the other was to ride against them and stab them with a large *couteau de chasse.* Sometimes the cattle were lassoed and then stabbed. The chase with knife and lasso was wilder and more exciting than the chase with pistol or rifle. Hence the Bowies preferred it.

One day while Rezin P. was thrusting his knife into a ferocious bull, the animal lunged in such a way as to draw the blade through the hunter's hand, making a severe wound.

After having his hand dressed, Rezin called the plantation blacksmith, Jesse Cliffe, and told him that he must make a knife that would not slip from a man's grasp. Using a pencil in his left hand, he awkwardly traced on paper a blade some ten inches long and two inches broad at its widest part, the handle to be strong and well protected from the blade by guards. The model having been settled upon, Rezin gave the smith a large file of the best quality of steel and told him to make the knife out of that. With fire and hammer the smith wrought the weapon—just one. It proved to be so serviceable in hunting and Rezin came to prize it so highly that for a long time he kept it, when he was not wearing it, locked in his desk.

Then one day, Dr. Soniat du Fosset's account goes on, Jim Bowie told his brother how his life had been jeopardized by the snapping of a pistol while it was pointed at a man firing on him. After hearing the story and learning how the final reckoning between the enemies was yet to be made, Rezin unlocked the desk, took out his prized personal possession, and handed it to his brother with these words: "Here, Jim, take 'Old Bowie.' She never misses fire."

Another story has it that in preparation for the "Sandbar Duel" Jim Bowie himself took a fourteen-inch file to a cutler in New Orleans known as Pedro. Pedro had learned his trade in Toledo, where the finest swords in all Spain were forged; and all his skill went into the making of a blade which was to be, in Bowie's words, "fit to fight for a man's life with." Yet another story avers that while recovering from wounds sustained in the famous fight Jim Bowie whittled from soft wood a pattern of the knife that was to make his own name historic, and had a blacksmith named Lovel Snowden fashion the weapon.

*   *   *   *   *

But let us not be too rash in drawing conclusions. Arkansas has yet to be heard from, and Arkansas has better right to speak on the subject than any encyclopedia. The bowie knife used to be commonly known as the

"Arkansas toothpick," and Arkansas is sometimes yet referred to as "the Toothpick State." Arkansans certainly knew their toothpicks. . . .

*   *   *   *   *

. . . It has already been said that John J. Bowie established a plantation in that state. A former Arkansas judge, William F. Pope, maintains in his *Early Days in Arkansas* (1895) that Rezin P. Bowie once came to Washington, Arkansas, and engaged an expert smith named Black to make a hunting knife after a pattern that he, Bowie, had whittled out of the top of a cigar box. "He told the smith that he wanted a knife what would disjoint the bones of a bear or deer without gapping or turning the edge of the blade. Black undertook the job and turned out the implement afterwards known as the the Bowie knife. The hilt was elaborately ornamented with silver designs. Black's charge for the work was ten dollars, but Bowie was so pleased with it that he gave the maker ten dollars [more].

"I do not hesitate to make the statement," concludes Judge Pope, "that no *genuine* Bowie knives have ever been made outside the state of Arkansas. . . . Many imitations have been attempted, but they are not Bowie knives."

Despite such strong assertions, it would appear that Judge Pope based his judgment on a false premise. The classic Arkansas story comes from Dan W. Jones, governor of Arkansas from 1897 to 1901. The manuscript containing it lay long unpublished but finally saw the light in the *Arkansas Gazette,* November 20, 1919, and has since been several times reprinted.

According to Governor Jones, the James Black who alone made the only "genuine" Bowie knife also designed it. Black was born in New Jersey, May 1, 1800, and, after having served as apprentice to a Philadelphia silver-plate manufacturer, came south in 1818, settling that year at Washington, Hempstead County, Arkansas.

Here he found employment with Shaw, the village blacksmith. Shaw was an important man and he had ambitions for his daughters. Consequently, when Anne fell in love with the young smith, only a hired hand, Shaw objected. The young people married nevertheless, and James Black set up a smithy of his own.

He specialized in making knives, and very soon they had won a reputation. "It was his rule," to quote the Governor Jones narrative, "after shaping and tempering a knife, and before polishing it, to cut very hard wood with it, generally an old hickory axe-handle which had been used for a long time and had become quite tough and hard. This he would do for half an hour, and then if the knife would not easily shave the hair from his arm, he would throw it away. . . .

"About 1831 James Bowie came to Washington and gave Black an order for a knife, furnishing a pattern and desiring it to be made within the next sixty or ninety days, at the end of which time he would call for it. Black made the knife according to Bowie's pattern. He knew Bowie well and had a high regard for him as a man of good taste as well as of unflinching courage. He had never made a knife that suited his own taste in point of shape, and he concluded that this would be a good opportunity to make one. Consequently, after completing the knife ordered by Bowie, he made another. When Bowie returned, he showed both the knives to him, giving him his choice at the same price. Bowie promptly selected Black's pattern.

"Shortly after this Bowie became involved in a difficulty with three desperadoes, who assaulted him with knives. He killed them all with the knife Black had made. After this whenever anyone ordered a knife from Black, he ordered it made 'like Bowie's,' which finally was shortened into 'Make me a Bowie knife.' Thus this famous weapon acquired its name. . . .

"Other men made knives in those days, and they are still being made, but no one has ever made 'the Bowie knife' except James Black. Its chiefest value was in its temper. Black undoubtedly possessed the Damascus secret. It came to him mysteriously and it died with him in the same way. . . . He often told me that no one had taught him the secret and that it was impossible for him to tell how he acquired it. Large offers were made him for the secret, but he refused them all. He was stealthily watched, in order that his process might be discovered, but his reputation for courage was such that no one approached him too closely after having been warned to desist."

The death of the secret is a part of the story. About 1838 Black's wife died. Not long thereafter Black himself was confined to his bed by a fever. While he was down, his father-in-law, who had all along been jealous of Black's growing reputation, came into him and beat him over the head with a stick. Probably he would have killed him had not Black's dog seized Shaw by the throat. As it was, inflammation set up in Black's eyes and he was threatened with blindness. As soon as he had strength enough to travel, he set out for expert treatment. A quack doctor in Cincinnati made him stone blind. He returned to Arkansas to find his little property gone and himself an object of charity. A Doctor Jones, father of the future Governor Jones, gave him a home. When Doctor Jones died, the blind man went to live with the son.

"Time and again," recalls Governor Jones, "when I was a boy, he said to me that notwithstanding his great misfortune, God had blessed him in a rare manner by giving him such a good home and that he would repay it all by disclosing to me his secret of tempering steel when I should arrive at maturity and be able to utilize it to my own advantage.

"On the first day of May, 1870, his seventieth birthday, he said to me that he was getting old and could not in the ordinary course of nature expect to live a great while longer; that I was now thirty years old, with a wife and growing family, and sufficiently acquainted with the affairs of the world to utilize properly the secret which he had so often promised to give me; and that, if I would get pen, ink, and paper, he would communicate it to me and I could write it down.

"I brought the writing material and told him I was ready. He said, 'In the first place'—and then stopped suddenly and commenced rubbing his brow with the fingers of his right hand. He continued this for some minutes, and then said, 'Go away and come back again in an hour.'

"I went out of the room, but remained where I could see him, and not for one moment did he take his fingers from his brow or change his position. At the expiration of the hour I went into the room and spoke to him. Without changing his position or movement, he said, 'Go out again and come back in another hour.' I went out and watched for another hour, his conduct remaining the same.

"Upon my speaking to him at the expiration of the second hour, he again said, 'Go out once more and come back in another hour.' Again I went out and watched. The old man sat there, his frame sunken, immobile, his only movement the constant rubbing of his brow with the fingers of his right hand.

"When I came in and spoke to him at the expiration of the third hour, he burst into a flood of tears and said:

" 'My God, my God, it has all gone from me! All these years I have accepted the kindness of these good people in the belief that I could repay it all with this legacy, and now when I attempt to do it, I cannot. Daniel, there were ten or twelve processes through which I put the knives, but I cannot remember one of them. When I told you to get pen, ink, and paper, they were all fresh in my mind, but they are all gone now. My God, my God, I have put it off too long!'

"I looked at him in awe and wonder. The skin from his forehead had been completely rubbed away by his fingers. His sightless eyes were filled with tears, and his whole face was the very picture of grief and despair. . . .

"For a little more than two years longer he lived on, but he was ever after an imbecile. He lies buried in the old graveyard at Washington, and with him lies buried the wonderful secret" of the genuine Bowie-knife steel.

*   *   *   *   *

The exact proportions of the original Bowie knife will probably never be known, though the blade was undoubtedly about ten inches long. The *ideal* Bowie knife was forged from the best steel procurable. It was differentiated from other knives by having more curve to the blade, near the point, by having a heavier handle—often of horn—and by having handle, blade, and guards all so well balanced that the knife could be cast a maximum distance with the most deadly effect.

Britt Bailey

BRITT came to Texas a long time ago. Came like a great many men to Texas, about six jumps ahead of the sheriff. He had been a member of the Kentucky legislature at Frankfort. Everybody thought he'd get to be

As told by Harold Preece, of New York City, formerly of Austin, Texas, at Croton-on-Hudson, New York, March 6, 1949. Recorded by B. A. Botkin.

the governor. Like everybody else in Kentucky, he took his politics very seriously, and he got into a debate one day on the floor of the legislature. He and his political opponent, a member from another mountain county, started cuss-hollering at each other, right there on the floor. The speaker got them quieted down. No sooner had the house adjourned than each made for the other with a gun. Britt got the drop. And Britt cut his enemy right through the jugular with his gun, dashed out the capitol, got on his horse, and lit out for Texas. Because there's where you used to go when you got in trouble anywhere in the old South. You lit out for Texas.

Well, maybe all the things that happened to Britt might not have happened if he had just killed one man. Back there if you killed one man, that was kind of an accident. It might happen to anybody. But when you killed a dozen that was something else entirely. Everywhere Britt went on that long ride from Kentucky down into Texas he killed men. In New Orleans, he thought that he recognized a cousin of that legislator. He thought they was on his trail. He shot him—shot him dead. In Natchez he shot another man who was trying to be friendly and asking him if he wasn't a stranger in town. He thought he was a sheriff. The same thing happened everywhere. He had a round dozen notches on his gun when he got into Texas.

Texas was a faraway place. When he crossed the Sabine River, he headed right down for the main American colony, the old town of Brazoria. At that time, Texas was still a part of Mexico. American settlers were coming there mighty fast. He introduced himself as a gentleman planter to John Austin, the head of the Brazoria Colony. John Austin was a relative of Stephen F. Austin, who's the daddy of Texas. Well, John Austin wanted settlers and he wanted gentlemen; he didn't want no outlaws. And he thought this man was a gentleman. So he gave him a strip of land. It got to be known as Bailey's Prairie.

Then traveling under an assumed name, Britt's wife came down with her children and slaves. They set themselves up there on Bailey's Prairie. They gave big parties in the biggest Southern tradition. All the best of the Anglo-American settlers and the Mexican officials were mighty glad to come to Britt's big blowouts.

He had black slaves picking the cotton for him, and he had black cowboys tending his cattle. Everything might have been well if it hadn't been for the fact that Britt was still politically ambitious. John Austin was the alcalde or the judge of the Brazoria Colony under the Mexican government. Britt Bailey found out that John Austin's term was just about to run out and he put in for the job. This was the first time Stephen and John Austin thought of investigating this man who was making such a big splash in their colony. So they sent people back to Kentucky and they found out his record, that the man who wanted to be judge had twelve notches in his gun, not counting the great big notch for his mortal enemy that he had killed there on the floor of the Kentucky legislature. Then of

course that meant that he got blackballed because John Austin passed an
edict that Britt was a gun man and had to leave.

Britt Bailey had a mighty fine property there on Bailey's Prairie with
all them black slaves and black cowboys, and he was no mind to get out of
Texas. He said he'd shot his way into Texas and if anybody wanted him
out they'd have to shoot him out. So he armed his slaves and he enlisted
every bad man he could find, and he recruited them into a force called
Bailey's Army. He dared the Mexican government and all of Stephen F.
Austin's colonists to root him out. Time after time they organized volunteer regiments to take Bailey's Army. But always they lost their nerve
when they got to the border and saw that army of white and black men.

Of course, he had no visitors then; he was ostracized. Then the Texas
Revolution come along, and Bailey's Army went through the battle of
Velasco. They acquitted themselves so well that Sam Houston, who was
commander-in-chief of the army, sent them a citation. Then the Revolution ended. Texas became a republic. Britt Bailey thought that this
citation, the record of Bailey's Army, would restore him to respectability.
First he disbanded Bailey's Army as such. Then he announced himself
as a candidate for President of the Texas Republic, the other two candidates being Sam Houston and his old enemy, Stephen F. Austin. He went
around over the country making speeches, calling himself the hero of the
Velasco. When the election came, Sam Houston won, and Britt Bailey got
one vote—his own. Then he knew he was washed up there. He took to
drinking again. He started seeing by the fireplace this man he had killed in
Kentucky. Then right about that time he had a falling out with his foreman, a man named Smith. Smith said, "I'm getting out, Britt Bailey, but
I'm comin' back to blast you to hell." Night after night he would sit there
staring into the fireplace and seeing the face of this man in Kentucky.
Some times there would be two men—the Kentuckian, on the one hand,
and Smith, on the other. And he remembered what that man in Kentucky
had said to him when he shot him down: "I didn't have the last shot with
you on the floor of the legislature, but I'll have the last shot with you in
hell."

That went on for several years. And Britt said that he would never die
fallen down, that he would die standing up. One day he met Smith in the
road. They shot it out. A posse from Brazoria County was looking for
Smith, and they found Smith crawling along in the road like a dog. He
said: "You'll find Britt Bailey up the road a piece." And Britt Bailey was
shattered with bullets when they found him. But he was holding his hands
so tight to the tree—so that he wouldn't fall down—that the bark and the
leaves were bloody, and they had to pry him loose. His last words were:
"Bury me a-standin' up with my gun on my shoulder and the whisky at my
feet. Bury me standin' up so I can have the last shot in hell with any
s.o.b.'s who comes down there challengin' me."

They held the funeral. And I got the story of the funeral from an old
Negro preacher down there who said that his daddy had helped dig the

grave. It was a great big grave and they had to put lean-tos on each side
to hold him up. But for his burial they had to find the black broadcloth
suit that he'd worn when he was a member of the Kentucky legislature.
They got out the finest bond whisky that he had brought from Louisville,
and they put it at his feet. They loaded his gun well and good. And then
before they started shoveling in the dirt, somebody said awkwardly:
"Shouldn't somebody say a prayer?" Nobody knew what to say. But
then one of the Austins stepped forward and led the crowd in the Lord's
Prayer. After that they filled in the grave, and the last they saw of Britt
were those two glaring, staring eyes.

Well, after he died his wife took the family back to Kentucky, and a
mysterious green light began shining from the grave. You can still see it
there. Sometimes, too, you can hear rumblings under the ground. A
geologist has told me that the green light is associated with some kind of
mineral deposit, that the rumblings may be hidden oil reserves. But until
they can prove otherwise, I'll believe what the old timers say down there in
Brazoria County—that the rumbling underground is Britt Bailey target-
practising for a million years of shooting in hell.

Harriet Tubman

HARRIET TUBMAN, known at various times, and in various places, by many
different names, such as "Moses," in allusion to her being the leader and
guide to so many of her people in their exodus from the Land of Bondage;
"the Conductor of the Underground Railroad"; and "Moll Pitcher," for the
energy and daring by which she delivered a fugitive slave who was about
to be dragged back to the South; was for the first twenty-five years of her
life a slave on the eastern shore of Maryland. Her own master she represents as never unnecessarily cruel; but as was common among slaveholders,
he often hired out his slaves to others, some of whom proved to be tyrannical and brutal to the utmost limit of their power.

She had worked only as a field-hand for many years, following the oxen,
loading and unloading wood, and carrying heavy burdens, by which her
naturally remarkable power of muscle was so developed that her feats
of strength often called forth the wonder of strong laboring men. Thus was
she preparing for the life of hardship and endurance which lay before her,
for the deeds of daring she was to do, and of which her ignorant and darkened mind at that time never dreamed.

The first person by whom she was hired was a woman who, though
married and the mother of a family, was still "Miss Susan" to her slaves,
as is customary at the South. This woman was possessed of the good things
of this life, and provided liberally for her slaves—so far as food and cloth-

From *Scenes in the Life of Harriet Tubman*, by Sarah H. Bradford, pp. 9–27.
Auburn, New York: W. J. Moses, Printer. 1869.

ing went. But she had been brought up to believe, and to act upon the belief, that a slave could be taught to do nothing, and *would* do nothing but under the sting of the whip. . . .

*   *   *   *   *

While with this woman, after working from early morning till late at night, she was obliged to sit up all night to rock a cross, sick child. Her mistress laid upon her bed with a whip under her pillow, and slept; but if the tired nurse forgot herself for a moment, if her weary head dropped, and her hand ceased to rock the cradle, the child would cry out, and then down would come the whip upon the neck and face of the poor weary creature. The scars are still plainly visible where the whip cut into the flesh. Perhaps her mistress was preparing her, though she did not know it then, by this enforced habit of wakefulness, for the many long nights of travel, when she was the leader and guide of the weary and hunted ones who were escaping from bondage.

"Miss Susan" got tired of Harriet, as Harriet was determined she should do, and so abandoned her intention of buying her, and sent her back to her master. She was next hired out to the man who inflicted upon her the life-long injury from which she is suffering now, by breaking her skull with a weight from the scales. The injury thus inflicted causes her often to fall into a state of somnolency from which it is almost impossible to rouse her. Disabled and sick, her flesh all wasted away, she was returned to her *owner*. He tried to sell her, but no one would buy her. "Dey said dey wouldn't give a sixpence for me," she said.

"And so," she said, "from Christmas till March I worked as I could, and I *prayed* through all the long nights—I groaned and prayed for ole master: 'Oh Lord, convert master!' 'Oh Lord, change dat man's heart!' 'Pears like I prayed all de time," said Harriet; " 'bout my work, everywhere, I prayed an' I groaned to de Lord. When I went to de horse-trough to wash my face, I took up de water in my han' an' I said, 'Oh Lord, wash me, make me clean!' Den I take up something to wipe my face, an' I say, 'Oh Lord, wipe away all my sin!' When I took de broom and began to sweep, I groaned, 'Oh Lord, wha'soebber sin dere be in my heart, sweep it out, Lord, clar an' clean!' " No words can describe the pathos of her tones, as she broke out into these words of prayer, after the manner of her people. "An' so," said she, "I prayed all night long for master, till the first of March; an' all the time he was bringing people to look at me, an' trying to sell me. Den we heard dat some of us was gwine to be sole to go wid de chain-gang down to de cotton an' rice fields, and dey said I was gwine, an' my brudders, an' sisters. Den I changed my prayer. Fust of March I began to pray, 'Oh Lord, if you ant nebber gwine to change dat man's heart, kill him, Lord, an' take him out ob de way.'

"Nex' ting I heard old master was dead, an' he died jus' as he libed. Oh, then, it 'peared like I'd give all de world full ob gold, if I had it, to bring dat poor soul back. But I couldn't pray for him no longer."

The slaves were told that their master's will provided that none of them should be sold out of the State. This satisfied most of them, and they were very happy. But Harriet was not satisfied; she never closed her eyes that she did not imagine she saw the horsemen coming, and heard the screams of women and children, as they were being dragged away to a far worse slavery than that they were enduring there. Harriet was married at this time to a free Negro, who not only did not trouble himself about her fears, but did his best to betray her, and bring her back after she escaped. She would start up at night with the cry, "Oh, dey're comin', dey're comin', I mus' go!"

Her husband called her a fool, and said she was like old Cudjo, who when a joke went round, never laughed till half an hour after everybody else got through, and so just as all danger was past she began to be frightened. But still Harriet in fancy saw the horsemen coming, and heard the screams of terrified women and children. "And all that time, in my dreams and visions," she said, "I seemed to see a line, and on the other side of that line were green fields, and lovely flowers, and beautiful white ladies, who stretched out their arms to me over the line, but I couldn't reach them nohow. I always fell before I got to the line."

One Saturday it was whispered in the quarters that two of Harriet's sisters had been sent off with the chain-gang. That morning she started, having persuaded three of her brothers to accompany her, but they had not gone far when the brothers, appalled by the dangers before and behind them, determined to go back, and in spite of her remonstrances dragged her with them. In fear and terror, she remained over Sunday, and on Monday night a Negro from another part of the plantation came privately to tell Harriet that herself and brothers were to be carried off that night. The poor old mother, who belonged to the same mistress, was just going to milk. Harriet wanted to get away without letting her know, because she knew that she would raise an uproar and prevent her going, or insist upon going with her, and the time for this was not yet. But she must give some intimation to those she was going to leave of her intention, and send such a farewell as she might to the friends and relations on the plantation. These communications were generally made by singing. They sang as they walked along the country roads, and the chorus was taken up by others, and the uninitiated knew not the hidden meaning of the words—

> When dat ar ole chariot comes,
> I'm gwine to lebe you;
> I'm boun' for de promised land,
> I'm gwine to lebe you.

These words meant something more than a journey to the Heavenly Canaan. Harriet said, "Here, mother, go 'long; I'll do the milkin' to-night and bring it in." The old woman went to her cabin. Harriet took down her sun-bonnet, and went on to the "big house," where some of her relatives lived as house servants. She thought she could trust Mary, but there were others in the kitchen, and she could say nothing. Mary began to frolic with her. She threw her across the kitchen, and ran out, knowing that Mary would follow her. But just as they turned the corner of the house, the master to whom Harriet was now hired, came riding up on his horse. Mary darted back, and Harriet thought there was no way now but to sing. But "the Doctor," as the master was called, was regarded with special awe by his slaves; if they were singing or talking together in the field, or on the road, and "the Doctor" appeared, all was hushed till he passed. But Harriet had no time for ceremony; her friends must have a warning; and whether the Doctor thought her *"imperent"* or not, she must sing him farewell. So on she went to meet him, singing:

> I'm sorry I'm gwine to lebe you,
> Farewell, oh farewell;
> But I'll meet you in the mornin',
> Farewell, oh farewell.

The Doctor passed, and she bowed as she went on, still singing:

> I'll meet you in the mornin',
> I'm boun' for de promised land,
> On the oder side of Jordan,
> Boun' for de promised land.

She reached the gate and looked round; the Doctor had stopped his horse, and had turned around in the saddle, and was looking at her as if there might be more in this than "met the ear." Harriet closed the gate, went on a little way, came back, the Doctor still gazing at her. She lifted up the gate as if she had not latched it properly, waved her hand to him, and burst out again:

> I'll meet you in the mornin',
> Safe in de promised land,
> On the oder side of Jordan,
> Boun' for de promised land.

And she started on her journey, "not knowing whither she went," except that she was going to follow the north star, till it led her to liberty. Cautiously and by night she traveled, cunningly feeling her way, and finding out who were friends; till after a long and painful journey she found, in answer to careful inquiries, that she had at last crossed that magic "line" which then separated the land of bondage from the land of freedom; for this was before *we* were commanded by law to take part in the iniquity of slavery, and aid in taking and sending back those poor hunted fugitives who had manhood and intelligence enough to enable them to make their way thus far towards freedom.

"When I found I had crossed dat *line*," she said, "I looked at my hands to see if I was de same pusson. There was such a glory ober every ting; de sun came like gold through the trees, and ober the fields, and I felt like I was in Heaben."

But then came the bitter drop in the cup of joy. She said she felt like a man who was put in State Prison for twenty-five years. All these twenty-five years he was thinking of his home, and longing for the time when he would see it again. At last the day comes—he leaves the prison gates—he makes his way to his old home, but his old home is not there. The house has been pulled down, and a new one has been put up in its place; his family and friends are gone nobody knows where; there is no one to take him by the hand, no one to welcome him.

"So it was with me," she said. "I had crossed the line. I was *free;* but there was no one to welcome me to the land of freedom. I was a stranger in a strange land; and my home, after all, was down in Maryland; because my father, my mother, my brothers, and sisters, and friends were there. But I was free, and *they* should be free. I would make a home in the North and bring them there, God helping me. Oh, how I prayed then," she said; "I said to de Lord, 'I'm gwine to hole stiddy on to *you*, an' I *know* you'll see me through.' "

She came to Philadelphia, and worked in hotels, in club houses, and afterwards at Cape May. Whenever she had raised money enough to pay expenses, she would make her way back, hide herself, and in various ways give notice to those who were ready to strike for freedom. When her party was made up, they would start always on Saturday night, because advertisements could not be sent out on Sunday, which gave them one day in advance.

Then the pursuers would start after them. Advertisements would be posted everywhere. There was one reward of $12,000 offered for the head of the woman who was constantly appearing and enticing away parties of slaves from their master. She had traveled in the cars when these posters were put up over her head, and she heard them read by those about her— for she could not read herself. Fearlessly she went on, trusting in the Lord. She said, "I started with this idea in my head, 'Dere's *two* things I've got a *right* to, and dese are, Death or Liberty—one or tother I mean to have. No one will take me back alive; I shall fight for my liberty, and when de time has come for me to go, de Lord will let dem kill me." And acting upon this simple creed, and firm in this trusting faith, she went back and forth *nineteen times*, according to the reckoning of her friends. She remembers that she went eleven times from Canada, but of the other journeys she kept no reckoning.

* * * * *

It will be impossible to give any connected account of the different journeys taken by Harriet for the rescue of her people, as she herself has no idea of the dates connected with them, or of the order in which they were made. She thinks she was about 25 when she made her own escape, and this was in the last year of James K. Polk's administration. From that time till the beginning of the war, her years were spent in these journeyings back and forth, with intervals between, in which she worked only to spend the avails of her labor in providing for the wants of her next party of fugitives. By night she traveled, many times on foot, over mountains, through forests, across rivers, mid perils by land, perils by water, perils from enemies, "perils among false brethren." Sometimes members of her party would become exhausted, foot-sore, and bleeding, and declare they could not go on, they must stay where they dropped down, and die; others would think a voluntary return to slavery better than being overtaken and carried back, and would insist upon returning; then there was no remedy but force; the revolver carried by this bold and daring pioneer would be pointed at their heads. "Dead niggers tell no tales," said Harriet; "Go on or die"; and so she compelled them to drag their weary limbs on their northward journey.

At one time she collected and sent on a gang of thirty-nine fugitives in the care of others, as from some cause she was prevented from accompanying them. Sometimes, when she and her party were concealed in the woods, they saw their pursuers pass, on their horses, down the high road, tacking up the advertisements for them on the fences and trees.

"And den how we laughed," said she. "*We* was de fools, and *dey* was de wise men; but we wasn't fools enough to go down de high road in de broad daylight." At one time she left her party in the woods, and went by a long and roundabout way to one of the "stations of the Underground Railway," as she called them. Here she procured food for her famished party, often paying out of her hardly-gained earnings, five dollars a day for food for them. But she dared not go back to them till night, for fear of being watched, and thus revealing their hiding-place. After nightfall, the sound of a hymn sung at a distance comes upon the ears of the concealed and famished fugitives in the woods, and they know that their deliverer is at hand. They listen eagerly for the words she sings, for by them they are to be warned of danger, or informed of safety. Nearer and nearer comes the unseen singer, and the words are wafted to their ears:

> Hail, oh hail ye happy spirits,
>   Death no more shall make you fear,
> No grief nor sorrow, pain nor anger (anguish)
>   Shall no more distress you there.
>
> Around him are ten thousan' angels,
>   Always ready to 'bey comman'.
> Dey are always hobring round you,
>   Till you reach the hebbenly lan'.
>
> Jesus, Jesus will go wid you;
>   He will lead you to his throne;
> He who died has gone before you,
>   Trod de wine-press all alone.
>
> He whose thunders shake creation;
>   He who bids the planets roll;
> He who rides upon the temple (tempest),
>   An' his scepter sways de whole.

> Dark and thorny is de desert,
> Through de pilgrim makes his ways,
> Yet beyon' dis vale of sorrow,
> Lies de fiel's of endless days.

I give these words exactly as Harriet sang them to me to a sweet and simple Methodist air. "De first time I go by singing dis hymn, dey don't come out to me," she said, "till I listen if de coast is clar; den when I go back and sing it again, dey come out. But if I sing:

> Moses go down in Egypt,
> Till ole Pharo' let me go;
> Hadn't been for Adam's fall,
> Shouldn't hab to died at all,

den dey don't come out, for dere's danger in de way."

And so by night travel, by hiding, by signals, by threatening, she brought the people safely to the land of liberty. But after the passage of the Fugitive Slave law, she said, "I wouldn't trust Uncle Sam wid my people no longer; I brought 'em all clar off to Canada."

Hal's Lake

IN THE fork of the Alabama and Tombigbee Rivers, about fifty miles above Mobile, is said to be a lake, beautiful and clear, which is called Hal's Lake. The name is derived from an incident that occurred in the days of slavery. A runaway slave from a Mississippi plantation found refuge and secretion in this dismal resort, and hither he lured other slaves, all of whom lived in the region of the lake for an unknown time.

Having run away from a plantation in Mississippi, Hal, a stalwart slave, made his way across the Tombigbee, and on reaching the swamp of big cane, tangled underbrush and large trees, he found his way into it with great difficulty, where he discovered that the bears of the swamp had regular paths, the tall canes on the sides of which being worn smooth by their fur. For a day or two the runaway subsisted on the wild fruits of the swamp; but on exploring further toward the north, he found that there were plantations on the opposite side of the Alabama River, and by means of the use of a piece of wood to support him in swimming across, he made his way, a hungry man, to a plantation at night, where he told his story and procured food.

Hal soon became an expert forager, as was indicated by the loss of an

From *Makers and Romance of Alabama History*, Embracing Sketches of the Men Who Have Been Largely Instrumental in Shaping the Policies and in Molding the Conditions in the Rapid Growth of Alabama—together with the Thrilling and Romantic Scenes with which Our History is Resplendent, by B. F. Riley, pp. 615–618. [No publisher, place, or date.]

occasional pig, lamb, goat, or turkey from the plantation. Not content with his own freedom, he determined to bring his family to this swampy retreat. Making his way back to his distant home, he succeeded at night in mounting his family on two or three choice horses, and being familiar with the country in that region, he chose to travel during the first night along plantation paths, and the next morning, after leaving the home, he and his were fully thirty miles away. The horses were turned loose, and the remainder of the journey was pursued at night, while the fleeing slaves would sleep during the day. When the Tombigbee was reached, he succeeded in conveying his family over by lashing some logs together. After a perilous passage, they finally reached the swamp, and set about providing a temporary home on the lake, by constructing a booth of canes and saplings, covering it with bark.

In his trips to the neighboring plantations across the river for necessaries, Hal induced other slaves to join him in his safe retreat. After a time, he had a colony in a quarter where white men had never gone, and on the shores of the lake chickens crew, turkeys gobbled, with the mingled notes of the squealing of pigs and the bleating of goats.

Hal was the sovereign of the tiny commonwealth, and in due course of time he found it unnecessary himself to go on foraging expeditions and would send others. Still the population of the colony grew, as an occasional runaway slave would be induced to join it. In those days of "underground railroads," the continued absence of a slave from a plantation would be taken to mean that he had fled by some of the numerous means of escape, and after a period, search for the missing would be given up. Not only was there a mysterious disappearance of slaves, but that of pigs, chickens, sheep and other domestic animals as well. The secret of this slave haunt was well preserved, and the news of its security became an inducement to a large number of slaves, some from a considerable distance, to join Hal's colony beside the lake.

Not only was Hal autocratic in his immured fastness between the rivers and in the jungle of cane, but he became tyrannical, which in turn provoked revolt. A burly slave refused to obey his dictation, and Hal straightway expelled him from the colony, exiled him. Bent on revenge, the exile made his way back to his master, surrendered and told the story fatal to Hal's colony. The mysteries of several years were thus cleared up to planters along the rivers. The exile became the guide to the retreat where was ensconced the slave colony, and with packs of dogs and guns, the stronghold was surrounded and the slaves captured. But slight resistance to the dogs was offered, and the submissive black men and their families were conveyed across the river, the ownership of each ascertained and each was sent, under guard, to his owner. As for Hal and his family, the sheriff notified the owner on the distant Mississippi plantation of their capture, and he came, in due time, proved his chattels, and they were taken back to their original home.

How long they might have remained in this secure retreat, but for the intolerance of the original leader, it is impossible to say. Hal was not unlike many another with advantages vastly above his—power made him top-heavy, and soft seductions were turned into tyranny, all of which reminds us of the comment of Artemus Ward on the conduct of the Puritans of New England. Artemus said: "They came to this country to worship God according to their own consciences and to keep people from worshippin' Him accordin' to theirn."

The capture of Hal and his party led to the discovery of this phenomenal body of clear water in that interior retreat not only, but to the discovery of bears, which in fact made it the hunting ground for big game for many years. It is said that much big game is still to be found in that region between the two great rivers.

How much of truth there is in the details of this story which comes to us from the old slave days none can tell, but it reveals to us one of the features of slave life. That the story has its foundations in fact, there seems to be no doubt, and it still lingers as a tradition in that quarter of the state.

Eliza Crossing the Ice

ELIZA HARRIS, of "Uncle Tom's Cabin" notoriety, the slave woman who crossed the Ohio River, near Ripley, on the drifting ice with her child in her arms, was sheltered under our roof and fed at our table for several days. This was while we lived at Newport, Indiana, which is six miles west of the State line of Ohio. To elude the pursuers who were following closely on her track, she was sent across to our line of the Underground Railroad.

The story of this slave woman, so graphically told by Harriet Beecher Stowe in "Uncle Tom's Cabin," will, no doubt, be remembered by every reader of that deeply interesting book. The cruelties of slavery depicted in that remarkable work are not overdrawn. The stories are founded on facts that really occurred, real names being wisely withheld, and fictitious names and imaginary conversations often inserted. From the fact that Eliza Harris was sheltered at our house several days, it was generally believed among those acquainted with the circumstances that I and my wife were the veritable Simeon and Rachel Halliday, the Quaker couple alluded to in "Uncle Tom's Cabin." I will give a short sketch of the fugitive's story, as she related it.

She said she was a slave from Kentucky, the property of a man who

From *Reminiscences of Levi Coffin,* Being a Brief History of the Labors of a Lifetime in behalf of the Slave, with the Stories of Numerous Fugitives who Gained Their Freedom through His Instrumentality and Many Other Incidents, pp. 147–150. London: Sampson Low, Marston, Searle, & Rivington; Cincinnati, Ohio: Western Tract Society. 1876.

lived a few miles back from the Ohio River, below Ripley, Ohio. Her master and mistress were kind to her, and she had a comfortable home, but her master got into some pecuniary difficulty, and she found that she and her only child were to be separated. She had buried two children, and was doubly attached to the one she had left, a bright, promising child, over two years old. When she found that it was to be taken from her, she was filled with grief and dismay, and resolved to make her escape that night if possible. She watched her opportunity, and when darkness had settled down and all the family had retired to sleep, she started with her child in her arms and walked straight toward the Ohio River. She knew that it was frozen over, at that season of the year, and hoped to cross without difficulty on the ice, but when she reached its banks at daylight, she found that the ice had broken up and was slowly drifting in large cakes. She ventured to go to a house near by, where she was kindly received and permitted to remain through the day. She hoped to find some way to cross the river the next night, but there seemed little prospect of any one being able to cross in safety, for during the day the ice became more broken and dangerous to cross. In the evening she discovered pursuers nearing the house, and with desperate courage she determined to cross the river, or perish in the attempt. Clasping her child in her arms she darted out of the back door and ran toward the river, followed by her pursuers, who had just dismounted from their horses when they caught sight of her. No fear or thought of personal danger entered Eliza's mind, for she felt that she had rather be drowned than to be captured and separated from her child. Clasping her babe to her bosom with her left arm, she sprang on to the first cake of ice, then from that to another and another. Some times the cake she was on would sink beneath her weight, then she would slide her child on to the next cake, pull herself on with her hands, and so continue her hazardous journey. She became wet to the waist with ice water and her hands were benumbed with cold, but as she made her way from one cake of ice to another, she felt that surely the Lord was preserving and upholding her, and that nothing could harm her.

When she reached the Ohio side, near Ripley, she was completely exhausted and almost breathless. A man, who had been standing on the bank watching her progress with amazement and expecting every moment to see her go down, assisted her up the bank. After she had recovered her strength a little he directed her to a house on the hill, in the outskirts of town. She made her way to the place, and was kindly received and cared for. It was not considered safe for her to remain there during the night, so, after resting a while and being provided with food and dry clothing, she was conducted to a station on the Underground Railroad, a few miles farther from the river. The next night she was forwarded on from station to station to our house in Newport, where she arrived safely and remained several days.

Other fugitives arrived in the meantime, and Eliza and her child were sent with them, by the Greenville branch of the Underground Railroad, to Sandusky, Ohio. They reached that place in safety, and crossed the lake to Canada, locating finally at Chatham, Canada West.

Slave Legends of Lincoln

I[1]

I THINK Abe Lincoln was next to the Lord. He done all he could for the slaves; he set 'em free. People in the South knowed they'd lose their slaves when he was elected president. 'Fore the election he traveled all over the South, and he come to our house and slept in Old Mistress' bed. Didn't nobody know who he was. It was a custom to take strangers in and put them up for one night or longer, so he come to our house and he watched close. He seen how the niggers come in on Saturday and drawed four pounds of meat and a peck of meal for a week's rations. He also saw 'em whipped and sold. When he got back up North he writ Old Master a letter and told him he was going to have to free his slaves, that everybody was going to have to, that the North was going to see to it. He also told him that he had visited at his house and if he doubted it to go in the room he slept in and look on the bedstead at the head and he'd see where he'd writ his name. Sure enough, there was his name: A. Lincoln.

II[2]

Abraham Lincoln gits too much praise. I say, shucks, give God the praise. Lincoln come through Gallatin, Tennessee, and stopped at Hotel Tavern with his wife. They was dressed just like tramps, and nobody knowed it was him and his wife till he got to the White House and writ back and told 'em to look 'twixt the leaves in the table where he had set and they sure enough found out it was him.

III[3]

Oooh, child, you ought to been there when Mr. Linktum come down to free us. Policemen ain't in it. You ought to seen them big black bucks. Their suits were so fine trimmed with them eagle buttons and they was gold too. And their shoes shined so they hurt your eyes. I tell you I can't remember my age but it's been a long time ago.

---

[1] As told by Bob Maynard, 79, Weleetka, Okla.; born Falls County, Texas, slave in Texas and Mississippi. From *Lay My Burden Down: A Folk History of Slavery*, edited by B. A. Botkin, p. 16. Copyright, 1945, by the University of Chicago. Chicago: University of Chicago Press.

[2] As told by Alice Douglass, 77, Oklahoma City, Oklahoma; born December 22, 1860, Sumner County, Tennessee; slave in Tennessee. *Ibid.*, p. 16.

[3] As told to Mrs. Mildred Thompson and Mrs. Carol Graham by Aunt Pinkey Howard, about 85, El Dorado District, Arkansas. *Ibid.*, pp. 16–17.

I wouldn't take $100 for living in slavery days, and I 'member when they all parted out. Mr. Linktum come down. Yes'm, Mr. Abe Linktum and his partner, Horace Greeley, comed down. Lieutenants and Sarges all come. And some big yellow buck niggers all dressed up fine. I served Mr. Linktum myself with my own hands. Yes'm, I did. I fotched cold water from the spring on a waiter, and I stood straight and held it out just like this in front of me. Yes'm, and his partner, Mr. Horace Greeley, too. And them big yellow buck niggers went in the kitchen where my mammy was cooking and told her: "Git outa here, nigger. You don't have to wait on these white folks no more." Yes'm, they did. And they done said: "You ain't got no more master and no more missus. You don't have to work here no more." But my mother said: "I's putting Old Master's victuals on to cook. Wait till I gets 'em on." And they told her again that she didn't have no more master and no more missus. I told my mammy to kick him down the step, but she said she was afeared he would shoot her. All I hates about them Sarges and Lieutenants is they never did shave. Them days all wore whiskers. . . .

IV [4]

I knowed the time when Abram Linkum come to the plantation. He come through there on the train and stopped over night oncet. He was known by Dr. Jameson, and he came to Perry to see about the food for the soldiers.

We all had part in entertaining him. Some shined his shoes, some cooked for him, and I waited on the table, I can't forget that. We had chicken hash and batter cakes and dried venison that day. You be sure we knowed he was our friend, and we catched what he had to say. Now, he said this (I never forget that so long as I live): "If you free the people, I'll bring you back into the Union. [To Dr. Jameson.] If you don't free your slaves, I'll whip you back into the Union. Before I'd allow my wife and children to be sold as slaves, I'll wade in blood and water up to my neck."

Now he said all that. If my mother and father were living, they'd tell you the same thing. That's what Linkum said.

He came through after freedom and went to the Shed's first. I couldn't 'magine what was going on, but they came running to tell me, and what a time we had.

Linkum went to the smokehouse and opened the door and said, "Help yourselves; take what you need; cook yourselves a good meal!" and we sure had a celebration.

V [5]

In them days they was peddlers gwine round the country selling things. They toted big packs on they backs filled with everything from needles

---

[4] As told by Salena Taswell, Miami, Florida; slave in Georgia. *Ibid.*, p. 17.
[5] As told to Travis Jordan by Mary Wallace Bowe, 81, Durham, North Carolina. *Ibid.*, pp. 18–19.

and thimbles to bedspreads and frying pans. One day a peddler stopped at Miss Fanny's house. He was the ugliest man I ever seed. He was tall and bony with black whiskers and black bushy hair and curious eyes that set 'way back in his head. They was dark and look like a dog's eyes after you done hit him. He set down on the porch and opened his pack, and it was so hot and he looked so tired that Miss Fanny give him a cool drink of milk that had done been setting in the springhouse. All the time Miss Fanny was looking at the things in the pack and buying, the man kept up a running talk. He ask her how many niggers they had; how many men they had fighting on the 'Federate side, and what was she gwine do if the niggers was set free. Then he ask her if she knowed Mr. Abraham Lincoln.

'Bout that time Miss Virginia come to the door and heard what he said. She blaze up like a lightwood fire and told that peddler that they didn't want to know nothing 'bout Mr. Lincoln, that they knowed too much already, and that his name wasn't 'lowed called in her house. Then she say he wasn't nothing but a black devil messing in other folks' business, and that she'd shoot him on sight if she had half a chance.

The man laughed. "Maybe Mr. Lincoln ain't so bad," he told her. Then he packed his pack and went off down the road, and Miss Virginia watched him till he went out of sight round the bend.

Two or three weeks later Miss Fanny got a letter. The letter was from that peddler. He told her that he was Abraham Lincoln heself; that he was peddling over the country as a spy; and he thanked her for the rest on her shady porch and the cool glass of milk she give him.

When that letter come, Miss Virginia got so hopping mad that she took all the stuff Miss Fanny done bought from Mr. Lincoln and made us niggers burn it on the ash pile. Then she made Pappy rake up the ashes and throw them in the creek.

"The Not Uncivil War"

OF COURSE some of the most beautiful episodes were supplied by the gentle son of Kentucky who sat through four years of soul-agony in the White House, and whose finest trait was his humanity, his love for his fellow men. Enemies made much of the fact that the wives of two Kentucky Rebels, Mrs. Ben Hardin Helm and Mrs. Clement White, were guests in the White House, although they were both sisters of Mrs. Lincoln. The former, the beautiful Emilie Todd, was a favorite of the President, and after her husband, General Helm, had been killed at Chickamauga (the third commander of Kentucky's "Orphan Brigade" to fall, Hanson dying at Murfreesboro and Albert Sidney Johnston at Shiloh), Lincoln invited

From *"Weep No More, My Lady,"* by Alvin F. Harlow, pp. 164–165. Copyright, 1942, by Alvin F. Harlow. New York and London: Whittlesey House, McGraw-Hill Book Company, Inc.

her to visit her sister. He sent her passes, and she reached Baltimore without trouble. But there, Federal officers insisted that she must take the oath of allegiance to the United States before she could proceed to Washington. Much distressed, she refused; it would be treason to the South, to her husband's memory. The officers insisted; it was a general order which they could not disobey; but she was equally firm in her refusal. At last, one said, "We will telegraph the President." Back came a curt order, "Send her to me. A. Lincoln"; and so she went without taking the oath.

J. Stoddard Johnston, the future historian of Louisville, and his wife were young married folks with a new baby when he, after long and painful deliberation as to his course, went away to join the Confederate army. Two and a half years passed without his coming home, and the parting was insufferably long. Finally one winter when he was in camp in the Shenandoah Valley and the armies were inactive, his wife took the baby and reached Washington at a time when the oath was not required. She went to Secretary of War Stanton for permission to cross the lines, and as might be expected was barked at; he wasn't extending any favors to rebels. "Why waste time on that ruffian," said a friend to her. "Go to the President." She went and was received, of course; Lincoln saw everybody. He rose and seated her courteously.

"It is a most unusual request," he said gently, when she had told her story, "coming from the wife of one who is at war against the Nation. But I can understand the circumstances—" a faint smile touched the sad, rugged countenance—"and I'm going to grant it." He leaned forward and wrote a pass—not only sending her as far as the railroad could carry her, but giving her an army ambulance to take her the rest of the way to the Confederate lines. Nobody thereafter could utter unchallenged in the presence of the Johnston family any derogatory thing about Abraham Lincoln.

The Legend of Barbara Frietchie

I [1]

THAT Barbara Frietchie lived is not denied. That she died at the advanced age of ninety-six years and is buried in the burial-ground of the German Reformed Church in Frederick is also true.

There is only one account of Stonewall Jackson's entry into Frederick,

---

[1] From "The Historical Basis of Whittier's 'Barbara Frietchie,'" by George O. Seilheimer, condensed from a contribution to the *Philadelphia Times* for July 21st, 1886, in *Battles and Leaders of the Civil War*, Being for the Most Part Contributions by Union and Confederate Officers Based upon "The Century War Series," edited by Robert Underwood Johnson and Clarence Clough Buel, of the Editorial Staff of *The Century Magazine*, Vol. II, pp. 618–619. Copyright, 1884, 1887, 1888, by the Century Co. New York.

and that was written by a Union army surgeon who was in charge of the hospital there at the time. "Jackson I did not get a look at to recognize him," the doctor wrote on the 21st of September, "though I must have seen him, as I witnessed the passage of all the troops through the town." Not a word about Barbara Frietchie and this incident. Dr. Oliver Wendell Holmes, too, was in Frederick soon afterward, on his way to find his son, reported mortally wounded at Antietam. Such a story, had it been true, could scarcely have failed to reach his ears, and he would undoubtedly have told it in his delightful chapter of war reminiscences, "My Hunt for the Captain," had he heard it. Barbara Frietchie had a flag, and it is now in the possession of Mrs. Handschue and her daughter, Mrs. Abbott, of Frederick. Mrs. Handschue was the niece and adopted daughter of Mrs. Frietchie, and the flag came to her as part of her inheritance, a cup out of which General Washington drank tea when he spent a night in Frederick in 1791 being among the Frietchie heirlooms. This flag which Mrs. Handschue and her daughter so religiously preserve is torn, but the banner was not rent with seam and gash from a rifle-blast; it is torn— only this and nothing more. That Mrs. Frietchie did not wave the flag at Jackson's men Mrs. Handschue positively affirms. The flag-waving act was done, however, by Mrs. Mary S. Quantrell, another Frederick woman; but Jackson took no notice of it, and as Mrs. Quantrell was not fortunate enough to find a poet to celebrate her deed she never became famous.

Colonel Henry Kyd Douglas, who was with General Jackson every minute of his stay in Frederick, declares in an article in *The Century* for June, 1886, that Jackson never saw Barbara Frietchie, and that Barbara never saw Jackson. This story is borne out by Mrs. Frietchie's relatives.

As already said, Barbara Frietchie had a flag and she waved it, not on the 6th to Jackson's men, but on the 12th to Burnside's. Here is the story as told by Mrs. Abbott, Mrs. Handschue's daughter:

"Jackson and his men had been in Frederick and had left a short time before. We were glad that the rebels had gone and that our troops came. My mother and I lived almost opposite aunt's place. She and my mother's cousin, Harriet Yoner, lived together. Mother said I should go and see aunt and tell her not to be frightened. You know that aunt was then almost ninety-six years old. When I reached aunt's place she knew as much as I did about matters, and cousin Harriet was with her. They were on the front porch, and aunt was leaning on the cane she always carried. When the troops marched along aunt waved her hand, and cheer after cheer went up from the men as they saw her. Some even ran into the yard. 'God bless you, old lady,' 'Let me take you by the hand,' 'May you live long, you dear old soul,' cried one after the other, as they rushed into the yard. Aunt being rather feeble, and in order to save her as much as we could, cousin Harriet Yoner said, 'Aunt ought to have a flag to wave.' The flag was hidden in the family Bible, and cousin Harriet got it and gave it to aunt. Then she waved the flag to the men and they cheered her as they went by.

She was very patriotic and the troops all knew of her. The day before General Reno was killed he came to see aunt and had a talk with her."

The manner in which the Frietchie legend originated was very simple. A Frederick lady visited Washington some time after the invasion of 1862 and spoke of the open sympathy and valor of Barbara Frietchie. The story was told again and again, and it was never lost in the telling. Mr. Whittier received his first knowledge of it from Mrs. E. D. E. N. Southworth, the novelist, who is a resident of Washington. When Mrs. Southworth wrote to Mr. Whittier concerning Barbara, she inclosed a newspaper slip reciting the circumstances of Barbara Frietchie's action when Lee entered Frederick.

When Mr. Whittier wrote the poem * he followed as closely as possible the account sent him at the time. He had a cane made from the timber of Barbara's house,—a present from Dr. Stiener, a member of the Senate of Maryland. The flag with which Barbara Frietchie gave a hearty welcome to Burnside's troops has but thirty-four stars, is small, of silk, and attached to a staff probably a yard in length.

Barbara Frietchie was born at Lancaster, Pennsylvania. Her maiden name was Hauer. She was born December 3d, 1766, her parents being Nicholas and Catharine Hauer. She went to Frederick in early life, where she married John C. Frietchie, a glover, in 1806. She died December 18th, 1862, Mr. Frietchie having died in 1849. In 1868 the waters of Carroll Creek rose to such a height that they nearly wrecked the old home of the heroine of Whittier's poem.

II [2]

When General Jackson was in Maryland, in September, 1862, he rode out into the Middletown Valley, north of Frederick City. As he and his aide, Major Kyd Douglas, approached Middletown, two young girls ran into the roadside, and each waved the Stars and Stripes in the face of the twain. General Jackson's only notice of the incident was to observe to his escort: "It is evident that we have no friends in this place." Apropos of that remarkable "historic lie" regarding Barbara Fritchie, and Jackson,

---

* Writing to the editor of *The Century* on the 10th of June, 1886, Mr. Whittier said: "The poem 'Barbara Frietchie' was written in good faith. The story was no invention of mine. It came to me from sources which I regarded as entirely reliable; it had been published in newspapers, and had gained public credence in Washington and Maryland before my poem was written. I had no reason to doubt its accuracy then, and I am still constrained to believe that it had foundation in fact. If I thought otherwise, I should not hesitate to express it. I have no pride of authorship to interfere with my allegiance to truth." Mr. Whittier, writing March 7th, 1888, informs us further that he "also received letters from several other responsible persons wholly or partially confirming the story, among whom was the late Dorothea L. Dix."—Editors.

[2] From *"Stonewall Jackson."* A Thesaurus of Anecdotes and Incidents in the Life of Lieutenant General Thomas Jonathan Jackson, C.S.A., by Elihu S. Riley, p. 108. Annapolis, Maryland. 1920.

Major Douglas says he was with General Jackson every minute that he was in Frederick City, Maryland, and that no such incident as has been alleged about Jackson and Barbara Fritchie occurred, and furthermore, General Jackson did not go on the street where Barbara lived. Barbara's nephew joins the witnesses against the truth of the report and adds to the proof that this slanderous allegation never had a form or being in fact. This relative, in a written statement early after the report was put forth, stated that at the time of the alleged occurrence of the flag waving and Jackson's action in regard to it, his venerable aunt was a palsied invalid in bed.

The Free State of Jones

TRADITION has it that during the war Jones County seceded from the Confederacy. In the last year of the war the story of the "Republic of Jones" gained wide circulation. In 1886 J. Norton Galloway, "Historian of the Sixth Army Corps," told the story in its most exaggerated form in the *Magazine of American History*. According to Galloway the citizens of Jones County, infuriated at the Conscription Act, assembled in convention late in 1862, passed an ordinance of secession from the Confederacy and, declining to join the old Union, set up a republic of their own with one "Nate Knight" as its president. These ingenious makers of governments were then supposed to have established a bicameral assembly and proceeded to draft a code of laws. There were dissenters, of course; but Knight, with "an army of 10,000 people," plagued them under a veritable reign of terror until his activities were brought to an end by the Confederate cavalry.

The earliest versions of the story of Jones County's "secession" appeared in 1863. In the spring of that year Jackson papers were reporting the arrival of "prisoners" who exhibited paroles written on birch bark by the counter-revolutionists. In 1864, the news of the Republic of Jones worked its way into Natchez, New Orleans, and New York newspapers, where the story was embellished with the fanciful details of a victory won by Knight's army under a Major Robinson, who on January 26, 1864, reputedly defeated Colonel Henry Maury's Confederate troops.

* * * * *

From *Confederate Mississippi*, The People and Policies of a Cotton State in Wartime, by John K. Bettersworth. Copyright, 1943, by Louisiana State University Press. Baton Rouge.

Among the sources cited by the author are *The War of the Rebellion*, Official Records of the Union and Confederate Armies (Washington, D. C., 1880–1901); W. A. Duckworth, "A Republic within the Confederacy and Other Recollections of 1864," *Annals of Iowa*, Ser. III, Vol. XI, pp. 324–351; J. Norton Galloway, "A Confederacy within a Confederacy," *Magazine of American History*, Vol. XVI, pp. 387–390; and Thomas J. Knight, *The Life and Activities of Captain Newton Knight* (Ellisville, 1934).

It is not strange that tales grew up about Jones County in the war, for the disloyalty of the region is the stuff of which legends are made. Newton Knight, the "Nate Knight" of Galloway, was no figment of the imagination. As the leader of a gang of deserters in his county, a fearless and generous soul who set himself up as defender of the rights of the people against the hated Confederate cavalry, Newt Knight was a Robin Hood of the Piney Woods.

Newt was a peace-loving farmer, a housebuilder, and a shoemaker who would work far into the night making shoes for his neighbors. He was "strictly business and did not believe in any kind of foolishness." An unlettered "Hardshell" Baptist, who was never heard to "sweer an oath," he had married Serena Turner, who taught him to read and write and helped him make a new home in Jasper County. About the time the war began Newt's home in Jasper County burned, and he returned to Jones County. Being a Unionist, he refused to join the army until he was conscripted. Even then he swore he would not fight, and to pacify him the officers allowed him to serve as a hospital orderly. Eventually, what he regarded as the injustice of the "Twenty Negro Law" and the unfairness of the cavalry, who had crowned their atrocities by taking his old mother's horse, moved Newt to secure a furlough and set out for home. Arriving in Jones County, Newt found the people infuriated over the depredations of the cavalry. Then and there he decided to desert and form a military company "to fight for our rights, for which to live, and to protect our families and also our property." The members of the organization swore never to surrender to the Confederates, and their officers took an oath before Vince Collins, a justice of the peace. At its organization in October, 1863, the company numbered six officers and seventy-three privates, but Knight obtained additional recruits later on.

There were secret passwords like "I am for the Red, White and Blue"; and to assemble the men there were signal horns, one of which, because of its peculiar sound, was used to warn of the approach of the cavalry. When not engaged in defending themselves and pillaging the countryside, the outlaws posted watchmen and worked one another's cornfields. On one occasion, when their supplies were low, a detachment of them went to Paulding, in Jasper County, and seized government stores, distributing part to the Irish families of the town, who had not been fed because they would not fight, and carrying the remainder off to Jones County.

The company obtained its arms by raiding Confederate ammunition trains as they passed through the vicinity. Rumor even had it that the men were in league with Federals who supplied them by way of the Gulf Coast. Knight did take steps to get his company accepted by the Federal commanders, first at Memphis, and later at Vicksburg and New Orleans; but a detachment sent out from Vicksburg to join Knight was captured on the way, and recruiting officers promised from New Orleans never arrived. That Knight's men were essentially outlaws who were not particularly eager to serve under either flag is suggested by the fact that they threatened to go to Enterprise and murder paroled Union prisoners stationed there. So alarmed was the town by the threat that both Northerners and Confederates joined to defend themselves, two Federals and one Confederate going out to patrol each road leading into the town, a detachment keeping watch on the bridge to tear it to pieces should the outlaws approach, and prisoners stationing themselves along the streets to give the signal for the bell ringer to sound the tocsin.

The raids of Knight's men and other deserter bands upon the loyal in Jones and near-by counties created great terror. At Enterprise trains were kept fired night and day to carry away the frightened people in case of an attack. Wild rumors spread about these "Southern Yankees." On one occasion, for example, they were reported to have hoisted the Federal flag above the courthouse in Ellisville. At another time the story got abroad that the deserters were going to stop the repairing of the Mobile and Ohio railroad. Soon, estimates of their numbers became greatly magnified; and in March, 1864, they were said to be around six hundred strong.

* * * * *

In March, 1864, General D. H. Maury sent his son, Colonel Henry Maury, to put down the rebellion. Young Maury took with him a clergyman, one of the few members of the Collins family who were not in Knight's company, to "use his personal influence to induce the men to return to their colors." Although Maury was convinced when he returned that he had so frightened the women that they no longer encouraged the men to "take to the woods," the deserters themselves were by no means subdued; and in May, Polk sent Robert Lowrey to finish the work.

Lowrey proceeded vigorously, shooting and hanging a number of the rebels, and tracking with bloodhounds those who escaped into the swamps. When the people retaliated by gorging the dogs with food containing red pepper, Lowrey shut the old men and boys of the countryside in pens and threatened to hang them if they did not reveal the whereabouts of the deserters. While the cavalry were in Jones County, news of an amnesty declared by Polk arrived, whereupon some of the deserters delivered themselves up. Many of the others, however, fled southward down Pearl River or northwestward toward the Yazoo-Mississippi Delta.

* * * * *

The evidence that Jones County seceded is rather scant. Anarchy rather than government prevailed in this "free state" during the war; and one must look in vain for anything like an organized movement of counter-secession, even though the fact that the majority of the people were in one way or another disloyal to the Confederacy is fairly well established. At the end of the war the loyal and contrite got together and sent a petition to the legislature, asserting that, since Jones County had within the last two years "become notorious if not infamous, at least to sensitive ears and the public spirited," they desired that "its past history and name . . . be obliterated and buried so deep that the hand of time may never resurrect it." The obliging legislature forthwith named the state's most disloyal county after the president of the Confederacy and changed the name of Ellisville, the county seat, to Leesburg.

Captain Horatio Williams and the Schooner *Paragon*

CAPT. HORATIO WILLIAMS of Ocracoke Island, master of the schooner *Paragon,* was a long way from home and he was worried.

He was in danger of losing his ship.

He loved that ship, loved her almost as much as he did his wife, whose way to his heart was by having a mess of chitterlings waiting for him when he came home from the sea.

Horatio wasn't ordinarily a cussin' man, arguing that cussin' was only biting a naked hook, but he cussed now. He spit a few salty words into the night, aimed them at both the Yankees and the Confederates.

But his cussin' didn't make him feel any better. It didn't ease his mind a smidgin.

The port authorities had told him in no uncertain terms the afternoon before that the *Paragon* couldn't leave Charleston harbor just then. A Yankee fleet was on its way to Charleston, they told him, and they might need the *Paragon.*

"You'll get her sunk," he had shouted, "or captured by them damn-yankees! That's what you'll do. Let me get her out of here before it's too late."

The port commander smiled. "You wouldn't stand a chance of making a run for it," he said. "The Yankee fleet would be on top of you before your sails got filled. And then where would you be? Sunk or captured."

Horatio stalked off, fuming.

Now he stood on the Battery, looking out toward Fort Sumter. People jammed the wharves and the ships tied up alongside. They were waiting for the bombardment to begin, the bombardment that would plunge the South into war against the Union.

A little group of men hurrying past jostled Horatio. He heard one say: "Those Yankees won't dare try to hold out. They'll haul down their flag and up will go ours."

Above the clamor of mass-filled streets came a shout: "Blast 'em out! Lincoln can't insult us!"

Somewhere on the battlements along the Battery stood old Edmund Ruffin, a frail little man with white hair hanging uncut below his shoulders, a violent advocate of Southern independence. He stood beside a cannon waiting for the word that would open up the bombardment. To him had

By John Parris. From *The News and Observer,* Raleigh, North Carolina, February 13, 1949, p. 8–IV.
Based on an interview with Horatio Williams II.

been given the honor of firing the first shot into Sumter if the Yankee commander refused to evacuate the fort.

It was long after midnight when Edmund Ruffin yanked the lanyard of the first gun in Charleston harbor sending the roundshot screaming upon Sumter.

Other guns picked up the signal.

Horatio stood there for a long time watching the flashes, listening to the boom of many guns, the pound of running feet, the rumble of wagons on the cobblestones, the shouts of jubilant men. His own tongue was stilled and there was no joy in his heart.

Edmund Ruffin had yanked a lanyard of a gun and Horatio knew that the old man's effortless gesture was destined to send the master of the *Paragon* into retirement for—well, he didn't want to think for how long.

Finally, Horatio turned from the Battery, shuffling off toward his room above the waterfront tavern where he could think things out. What with the worry that pricked at his heart and mind and the beat of the guns in his ears, a gray dawn was breaking over Charleston when he finally got to sleep.

He slept most of the day. It was late afternoon when he came awake. Heavy rain clouds were forming. He dressed, not bothering to shave, and went below to seek food and drink, and to think.

When he had finished his meal his mind was made up.

He would take the *Paragon* out during the night, he would make a run for it up the coast. To hell with the port authorities! To hell with the Yankee fleet! He was going home to Ocracoke—or die trying.

Horatio figured that maybe in the confusion of the cannonading that had been going on now for almost 18 hours he might have a chance of sneaking out of the harbor without being noticed.

He began searching the crowded room for his two crew members. He knew they were there some place. This was their favorite haunt, and when they hit Charleston they holed in here until he was ready to sail.

Unable to spot either of them from his corner table, Horatio got up and began moving between the tables, looking here and there. Finally, he spotted Tom, who was just about to order a drink.

Horatio moved over to the table, leaned down. "I say, Tom. . . ." A bearded face looked up. "Why, hello, captain, sit down and join me."

The skipper of the *Paragon* slipped into a chair across from Tom. "There isn't time," he whispered. "Now keep quiet and listen. Don't raise your voice. I've decided we'll make a run for it. Where's Jeb?"

"Why, he was here a minute ago. He's not gone far. He'll be back." Tom looked across the room, then paused. "There he is, over there at the fire."

"Get him and meet me outside." Horatio got up and made his way toward the door.

A few minutes later the three had slipped aboard the *Paragon*. Sails were run up, the tow lines drawn in, and the anchor hauled up.

Holding in close to shore, the *Paragon* slipped through the harbor, seeming barely to move. Now and then there was a "b-o-o-m" from the Battery, an answer from Sumter.

The night was dark. There was a drizzle of rain. Fog swirled over the harbor. Horatio stood at the wheel, nursing the *Paragon* through the roadstead until the shoreline was no longer visible.

Dawn came, gray and murky. The land had fallen away. He scanned the sea north and south, east and west. The *Paragon* was alone.

"Tom!" he yelled. "Tom!" The bearded seaman, a good ten years Horatio's senior, stuck his head out of the galley.

"Take over," Horatio commanded. "The worst is behind, I'm thinking. Coffee's what I crave."

Tom came up and took over the wheel. "Where's we headin'?"

"Keep her running north. Past Ocracoke and Hatteras. Right to the Roanoke. We'll go into Pamlico Sound at Ocracoke Inlet. Then up to Albemarle Sound."

"But why the Albemarle? Why not run her in home at Ocracoke?"

Horatio grinned. "You'll see, in time. We're taking the *Paragon* where nobody's going to lay hands on her. The damnyankees will never get the *Paragon*." He turned and strode off toward the galley.

Tom shook his head. He was puzzled. He wondered just what the captain had in mind. You never could tell about these young fellows.

A week later Horatio ran the *Paragon* into Albemarle Sound. It was midmorning when he edged her past Bull Bay, keeping her headed due west toward the mouth of the Roanoke River.

He was grinning. His gray eyes were sparkling. Jeb and Tom were puzzled. They talked among themselves. They didn't have much to say to Horatio. When midafternoon came the *Paragon* was well up the Roanoke.

"You can ease up on the sails," Horatio told them. "We're just about at the end of our trip." The *Paragon* slowed down. On either side of the river there were oaks and cedar, thick underbrush.

"We'll sink her here," Horatio told them. "Let the anchor go. Down with the sails." Tom and Jeb looked at him.

Horatio laughed. "Sure we're sinking her. Nobody'll use the *Paragon* till the war's over. Now step to it."

The sails were taken down, folded and placed in a dinghy. Horatio went below, into the hold that so recently had carried corn and rice and fertilizer. When he again appeared on deck, water was rushing into the hold of the *Paragon*.

He and Tom and Jeb got into the dinghy. Tom and Jeb at the oars. When they reached the river bank Horatio said: "We'll bury the sails. They'll come in handy when we raise her."

By the time the canvas had been buried in the woods the *Paragon* had settled until only the tops of her masts were above water.

"I reckon," said Horatio, "the *Paragon* couldn't be in a safer place. She'll be waiting there when it's safe for her to sail again."

* * * * *

Horatio the Second [who told me this story] leaned back in his chair. ". . . It was 18 months after the war was over that they raised her. It was quite a job, too. They had to pontoon her with barrels until her decks were above water. They pumped the water out of her with hand pumps. She wasn't damaged in the least. She had been in fresh water. You know, in the old days when they built ships they docked them before they was finished, that is, they let them lie in fresh water for a while. So the *Paragon* wasn't hurt none. And the heart of red cedar, of which she was built, won't rot. So she was just about as good as ever, and that canvas my father buried was still in good condition, too.

"They sailed the *Paragon* right down the Roanoke to Ocracoke and put her in the trade again."

The Story of the *J. M. White*

WE HAVE compared the old-time steamer to the race-horse, and the comparison was altogether fitting. Only a slight knowledge of the traveling public of that day is necessary to realize how much the quality of speed would be prized; it was the one great desideratum. The records of arrivals and departures of boats were the study of owners and rivals and the public at large. New devices for generating great heat in the shortest space of time absorbed the attention of engineers, who soaked their coal in rosin and opened so many draughts that the fires all but dropped out. And it is interesting that during the middle decades of the century records were made that have never again been equalled. The story of the building of the farfamed *J. M. White* and her record run from New Orleans to St. Louis is of sufficient interest and value to repeat in detail.

This boat was built at the home of the renowned *Monongahela Farmer*, Elizabeth, Pennsylvania, in the summer of 1844 in what was known as the "upper yard," owned and operated by Samuel Walker, Sr. Her builder was J. M. Converse of St. Louis, the funds being furnished by Robert Chauteau of the same city.[1] It was William King, familiarly known as

---

From *The Ohio River*, A Course of Empire, by Archer Butler Hulbert, pp. 338–342. Copyright, 1906, by G. P. Putnam's Sons. New York and London: The Knickerbocker Press.

[1] Our facts are largely taken from the "Boat Building Centennial Edition" of the Elizabeth, Pa., *Herald* (June 7, 1900), a most valuable compilation prepared by Editor Wylie. The story of the *J. M. White* had previously been written by John A. Lambert, of the Somerset *Standard*.—A. B. H.

"Billy" King to a whole generation of rivermen, however, who drafted the boat and made a lasting reputation. He designed the boat so that she would get added speed from her draft; his calculation was to make the boat pro- duce but two swells under way, one midway under the boilers and one under the wheels. The master-thought of the scheme was to set the wheels just where they would catch the forward swell and make the most of it.

King drew his plans and submitted them to Converse, who at once noted the variation from the time-tried pattern and opposed it. King was a man of few words; to the criticism of Converse, who frankly said the boat would be ruined by such a radical departure as placing the wheel beams twenty feet farther aft than usual, King made almost no reply except that he should build the boat on those lines or not at all.

"Converse went to Walker [writes Mr. Lambert] and told him where King wanted to place the beams, and what he had said to King.

" 'And what did King say?' asked Walker. 'He didn't say anything.' 'Well,' said Walker, 'if he has made up his mind to put them there he'll do it or he won't finish the boat. You had better write Chauteau and ask his advice.' Converse wrote to Chauteau at once, explaining the matter fully, saying that if the wheels were placed where King wanted to put them, the boat would be spoiled. The reply came in due time, and it was brief enough: 'Let King put beams where he pleases.'

"That settled it, and Converse did not interfere further with King's plans. The keenness of King's judgment was eloquently told by his masterpiece, when she made her famous run from New Orleans to St. Louis in three days, twenty-three hours, and nine minutes.

"That run of the *J. M. White* made 'Billy' King famous, and the steam- boat owners of St. Louis besought him with princely offers to draft a steamboat that would beat her time, but he refused to do so. He simply said: 'If any man drafts a boat that shall beat her time, I will then draft one to beat that.'

"After the *J. M. White* had been worn out it dawned upon steamboatmen that there had never been a boat that equalled her in speed, and they then tried to secure her draft. This King refused to surrender, and no other man had a copy of it or could duplicate it.

"It was not known that King had made a model of the *White,* but he had. After building the *White* he went to St. Louis in the employ of a boat-building company. His wife remained at Elizabeth for some time. About four months after he had gone to St. Louis, King wrote to a friend at Elizabeth—John Lambert, Sr., father of the writer—and this is briefly the substance of what he said in the letter: 'Bring my wife to St. Louis as soon as she can get ready. Go into the attic of my house, and close under the comb of the roof you will find a model in a box; bring that box with you, and don't open it or allow any one to see it. Lock it in a stateroom on the boat, and leave it there until you reach St. Louis. I will pay all ex- penses.' When this gentleman went to Mrs. King with the letter she knew nothing of the model. 'If there is one in the attic,' she said, 'I don't know when he put it there.' The box was found, however, where King said it was, and was taken to St. Louis as requested.

"King met his wife and the gentleman on their arrival, and his first inquiry after greeting them was concerning the model. Being told that it was locked up on the boat, he went for it and carried it to his home, where he at once opened the box in the presence of the gentleman who had taken it to St. Louis. It was probably never seen by any other person than King, his wife, and the gentleman referred to. It was a beautiful model made of pine and black walnut. It was ten feet two inches long, and otherwise in beautiful proportion. Without saying a word King went to his tool-chest, took therefrom a saw, and cut the model into several pieces, then with a hatchet completed its destruction by cutting it into kindling wood. The gentleman present said, 'Say, Billy, I could have done that at home just as well as you have, and saved you the expense of bringing it here.' 'That may all be,' replied King, 'but I never would have been satisfied that it had been done.'

"King said at the time that he still had a draft of the *White* on paper, but, although it was sought for time and again by men who would have given a fortune for it, it has never been found, and the equal of the famous *J. M. White* has never been built."

It is believed that an "exhibition" model of the great racer was a prized ornament of Secretary Stanton's office at the War Department during Lincoln's administration.

The Race between the *Natchez* and the *Robert E. Lee*

No STEAMBOAT race ever excited so much interest throughout the civilized world as that which took place between the *Robert E. Lee* and *Natchez* in June, 1870, from New Orleans to St. Louis. On the 24th of that month Capt. T. P. Leathers telegraphed Capt. Perry Tharp of this city, that the *Natchez* had arrived at St. Louis, having overcome the distance from New Orleans, 1,278 miles, in 3 days, 21 hours and 58 minutes. From the time that she was built at Cincinnati much rivalry in regard to speed had been exhibited between her and the *Robert E. Lee,* which was built at New Albany during the war, and was towed across the river to the Kentucky side to have her name painted on the wheelhouse, a measure of safety that was deemed prudent at that exciting time. Capt. John W. Cannon

From *Historical Sketch Book and Guide to New Orleans and Environs*, with Map, Illustrated with Many Original Engravings; and Containing Exhaustive Accounts of the Traditions, Historical Legends, and Remarkable Localities of the Creole City, edited and compiled by several leading writers of the New Orleans Press, pp. 239–240. New York: Will H. Coleman. 1885.

commanded the *Lee,* and Capt. Thomas P. Leathers, owner of the present *Natchez* and her half-dozen or more predecessors of the same name, commanded the *Natchez* of that time. Both were experienced steamboatmen, but, as the sequel proved, Capt. Cannon was the better strategist. While each boat had its special corps of friends, the name of the *Robert E. Lee* was the most honored and most popular along the Mississippi River.

Before the return of the *Natchez* to New Orleans, Capt. Cannon had determined that the *Lee* should beat the record of her rival, the fastest that had ever been made over the course. He stripped the *Lee* for the race; and removed all parts of her upper works that were calculated to catch the wind, removed all rigging and outfit that could be dispensed with to lighten her, as the river was low in some places; engaged the steamer *Frank Pargoud* to precede her a hundred miles up the river to supply coal; arranged with coalyards to have fuel-flats awaiting her in the middle of the river at given points to be taken in tow under way until the coal could be transferred to the deck of the *Lee,* and then to be cut loose and float back. He refused all business of every kind, and would receive no passengers.

The *Natchez* returned to New Orleans and received a few hundred tons of freight and also a few passengers, and was advertised to leave again for St. Louis, June 30. At 5 o'clock in the afternoon the *Robert E. Lee* backed out from the levee, and five minutes later the *Natchez* followed her, but without such elaborate preparation for a race as had been made on the *Lee,* Capt. Leathers feeling confident that he could pass the latter within the first 100 miles.

A steamer had preceded the racing boats up the river many miles to witness all that could be seen of the great race that was to be. The telegraph informed the people along both banks of the river and the world at large of the coming great struggle for supremacy in point of speed, and the world looked on with as much interest as it would had it been an event local to every part of it. Wherever there was human habitation the people collected on the bank of the mighty river to observe the passage of the two steamers. The *Lee* gained slightly every hundred miles as the race progressed, which gain at Natchez, three hundred miles from the starting point, amounted to ten minutes, attributable more to landings that had been made by the *Natchez* for fuel than anything else. The people of the whole city of Natchez viewed the race. At the bend at Vicksburg, although the two steamers were ten miles apart by the course of the river, the smoke of each was plainly discernible from the other. Thousands of people were congregated on the bluffs. At Helena and other points it seemed that the population for miles back from the river had turned out to witness the greatest race of this or any other age.

At Memphis ten thousand people looked at the passing steamers, neither of which landed, the *Natchez* by this time having adopted the *Lee's* method of receiving fuel. At every point where there was a telegraph instrument the hour and the minute of the passing steamers were ticked to all points of America that could be reached, and newspapers throughout the country displayed bulletins denoting the progress of the boats.

The time of passing Memphis, Vicksburg, and Cairo was cabled to Europe. When Cairo was reached the race was virtually ended, but the *Lee* proceeded to St. Louis, arriving there in three days, eighteen hours and fourteen minutes from the time she left New Orleans, beating by thirty-three minutes the previous time of the *Natchez*. The latter steamer had grounded and run into a fog between Memphis and Cairo, which detained her more than six hours.

When the *Lee* arrived at St. Louis, thirty thousand people crowded the wharf, the windows and the housetops to receive her. No similar event had ever created so much excitement. Capt. Cannon was tendered a banquet by the business men of the city, and was generally lionized while he remained there. It was estimated that more than $1,000,000 had been wagered on the race by the friends of the two steamers. Many of the bets were drawn, on the ground that the *Lee* had been assisted the first one hundred miles by the power of the *Frank Pargoud* added to her own; and men of the coolest judgment have ever since regarded the *Natchez* as the faster boat, but out-generaled by the commander of the other.

How "Mark Twain" was Born

WE HAD some talk about Captain Isaiah Sellers, now many years dead. He was a fine man, a high-minded man, and greatly respected both ashore and on the river. He was very tall, well built, and handsome; and in his old age—as I remember him—his hair was as black as an Indian's, and his eye and hand were as strong and steady and his nerve and judgment as firm and clear as anybody's, young or old, among the fraternity of pilots. He was the patriarch of the craft; he had been a keelboat pilot before the day of steamboats; and a steamboat pilot before any other steamboat pilot, still surviving at the time I speak of, had ever turned a wheel. Consequently, his brethren held him in the sort of awe in which illustrious survivors of a bygone age are always held by their associates. He knew how he was regarded, and perhaps this fact added some trifle of stiffening to his natural dignity, which had been sufficiently stiff in its original state.

* * * * *

The old gentleman was not of literary turn or capacity, but he used to jot down brief paragraphs of plain, practical information about the river,

From *Life on the Mississippi*, by Mark Twain (Samuel L. Clemens) pp. 367, 370–371. Copyright, 1874 and 1875, by H. O. Houghton & Company; 1883, by Samuel L. Clemens. Boston: James R. Osgood & Company. 1883.

For evidence and discussion disproving Mark Twain's account, see George Hiram Brownell, "A Question as to Origin of the Name 'Mark Twain,'" *The Twainian*, New Series, Vol. I (February, 1942), No. 2, p. 6; also Thomas Ewing Dabney, *ibid.*, No. 4, pp. 7–8, and E. E. Leisy, *ibid.*, No. 5, pp. 3–4.

and sign them "MARK TWAIN," and give them to the New Orleans *Picayune*. They related to the stage and condition of the river, and were accurate and valuable; and thus far they contained no poison. But in speaking of the stage of the river to-day at a given point, the captain was pretty apt to drop in a little remark about this being the first time he had seen the water so high or so low at that particular point in forty-nine years; and now and then he would mention Island so and so, and follow it, in parentheses, with some such observation as "disappeared in 1807, if I remember rightly." In these antique interjections lay poison and bitterness for the other old pilots, and they used to chaff the "Mark Twain" paragraphs with unsparing mockery.

It so chanced that one of these paragraphs became the text for my first newspaper article. I burlesqued it broadly, very broadly, stringing my fantastics out to the extent of eight hundred or a thousand words. I was a "cub" at the time. I showed my performance to some pilots, and they eagerly rushed it into print in the New Orleans *True Delta*. It was a great pity; for it did nobody any worthy service, and it sent a pang deep into a good man's heart. There was no malice in my rubbish: but it laughed at the captain. It laughed at a man to whom such a thing was new and strange and dreadful. I did not know then, though I do now, that there is no suffering comparable with that which a private person feels when he is for the first time pilloried in print.

Captain Sellers did me the honor to profoundly detest me from that day forth. When I say he did me the honor, I am not using empty words. It was a very real honor to be in the thoughts of so great a man as Captain Sellers, and I had wit enough to appreciate it and be proud of it. It was distinction to be loved by such a man; but it was a much greater distinction to be hated by him, because he loved scores of people; but he didn't sit up nights to hate anybody but me.

He never printed another paragraph while he lived, and he never again signed "Mark Twain" to anything. At the time that the telegraph brought the news of his death, I was on the Pacific Coast. I was a fresh, new journalist, and needed a *nom de guerre;* so I confiscated the ancient mariner's discarded one, and have done my best to make it remain what it was in his hands—a sign and symbol and warrant that whatever is found in its company may be gambled on as being the petrified truth. How I've succeeded, it would not be modest in me to say.

Steve Renfroe, the Outlaw Sheriff of Sumter County

STEVE RENFROE rode a milk-white horse into Livingston. The Black Belt town felt his presence, tall and blue-eyed and handsome, when he swung

From *Stars Fall on Alabama*, by Carl Carmer, pp. 126–133. Copyright, 1934, by Carl Carmer. New York: Farrar & Rinehart, Inc.

into Main Street, the horse dancing along beside the bored well and the courthouse in the square. Straight to the undertaker's he rode, and bought a coffin for his dead wife.

Some said he came from Virginia; others that they knew his people up in North Alabama, near Anniston. Folks from the south of the county reported he had bought a big cotton plantation down there.

Steve Renfroe had a way with women. They liked him because he was beautiful and reckless and courtly. He soon had another wife from one of the finest families in the Belt. Men liked him because he liked them—and hated the Yankees.

Sumter had been having a hard time before Steve came. The Republicans and the Negroes had been raising hell. Black congressmen were sitting in the state house at Montgomery. Carpetbaggers were sitting in judgment at the Livingston courthouse. The Ku Klux had tried to help matters but only made them worse, for after they had ridden a few times a detail of Yankee soldiers had been sent to Livington—to prevent further "outrages." Then things began to happen. Steve took a hand.

Over in Greene County conditions were just as bad. Yankee soldiers were in Eutaw, too. But one night when all the Harwoods and the McQueens and the Jemisons and the rest were having a friendly game with the Yanks down at the court-house, a Republican judge disappeared. A trembling Negro told the soldiers on the next day of seeing a little group of ghosts gallop up to the judge's house. He said a tall ghost on a white horse rode ahead.

A week or so later, while Steve and a few friends and the Livingston Yankee soldiers were putting aside all hard feelings, the bodyguard of a certain Livingston magistrate was shot down. The magistrate left town the next day at three o'clock, bound for Boston.

Then there was that business about Mr. Byrd. He's still alive and his sons are grown men but I think none of them knows how near he came to death about a half century ago. He was going to make a Republican speech in Eutaw and the Livingston Ku Klux fixed it up to kill him while he was making it. The hall had a center aisle and the Klan arranged to have one of their men at the end of each row on the aisle. The man who sat in the front row was to shoot Mr. Byrd and toss the gun to the man behind him. It would then be passed from hand to hand to the back of the hall and thrown in the fountain outside. But just as the appointed killer was taking aim, another objector to Republicanism could stand heresies no longer and let go at the speaker with a quart whisky bottle. It knocked Mr. Byrd off the platform and out. And it saved his life.

But secret methods seemed roundabout to a man who was never very good at deception. The next time a carpetbagger overstepped himself Steve Renfroe met up with him on Main Street and ordered him to get to hell out of town on the next train or take the consequences. The man went. The soldiers and the scalawags and the carpetbaggers decided that this was too much. So they had Steve arrested on the charge of being a Ku Klux raider. They did their best to fake some evidence but Steve was acquitted —the most popular man in town. When the election for sheriff came around he rode into office as jauntily as ever he rode down Main Street.

God help the carpetbaggers and the scalawags then! Sumter County was saved and the damn Yanks were licked and Steve Renfroe did it. Men warmed to the sight of the white horse and its rider. They went out of their way to receive a wave of the hand from their champion who was a prince of good fellows. And hearts fluttered, a little panic-stricken, when he swept his hat from that curly head, and a smile came to that firm mouth and crept into those blue eyes. Children loved him. Negroes worshiped him.

But like many another pretender to power Steve Renfroe proved a better champion of rights than an administrator of them. The good-fellowship of politicians, the admiration of his fellow townsmen and a few bad cotton crops were contributing causes. On one sad day in Livingston the civil authorities were forced to arrest Sheriff Renfroe for embezzlement of county funds and to confine him in the same jail to which he had committed many an offender.

Imprisonment was not for Steve's free spirit, though. One night he broke down the jail door and set all the prisoners free (save one Negro who chose to stay and be hanged). Then followed a day of anxiety in the town. Steve's indictment papers were in the circuit clerk's office and that officer feared for their safety. Being a brave man, he watched over them all day and all the following night. When the little town square grew light again, however, he thought all danger past and walked home. Standing at his own doorway he turned to see the flames from his office licking up into the gray morning sky.

No man had more loyal friends than Steve Renfroe. Despite the case against him, the men of Livingston raised a large sum of money and gave it to him. Take this, they said, go somewhere else and get a new start. He took the money, but he came back, hiding near Livingston. Then his friends said, come back and stand your trial, we will sign your bond and defend you. And so he rode around the square again, as straight and tall and arrogant as ever. A few days before his trial he was rearrested and put in jail. His friends had discovered his plan to run away. The next morning the jailer found the bars of Renfroe's window all but sawed through. Then they bound him and took him north—all the way to Tuscaloosa where there was a stronger jail. And another dawn saw a great hole burned in the eighteen-inch floor of the Tuscaloosa jail and Steve Renfroe, the outlaw Sheriff of Sumter County, free again.

More money from friends, more promises. Then James Little's best mule and Nathan Weisenburg's beautiful saddle disappeared at the same time. They and Steve were found together in Slidell, Louisiana, a few days later.

"Well, Frank," said Steve to an interviewer from the Livingston *Journal* as the two sat together in the (improved) county jail, "when I left here the first time I tried to do right. I struck some good jobs but just as I'd get to doing well, along would come some man and say: 'That's Steve Renfroe. He used to be sheriff of Sumter County,' and that would almost kill me and I would go to drinking. I haven't been any account since I left here just because of that."

While he was in jail this time Steve sent the following letter to the editor of the Livingston *Journal*. It tells its own story:

It would be better for me perhaps to say nothing, for I feel that I cannot gain, nor do I expect to get any sympathy from the citizens of this county, but inasmuch as the *Journal* has of late made pretty free use of my name, I have concluded to drop you a line in regard to the note written by me to one J. C. Giles. I did write the note and the following is a copy:

DEAR JAKE:

Please go to Meridian and get me four ounces of nitricmuriatic acid and a bunch of pure yarn thread. Dip the string in the acid and pull it across a piece of iron and see if it will cut it. Get the acid put up in two ounce bottles so I can get them through these bars. Come at night, at the back of the jail, and fasten them to the end of a fishing pole about eight feet long and poke them to me. I am in the second story a little to the right of the window. You can't miss it; since it is the only window in the back of the jail. You can come in sometime in the day light to speak to me. Then you can take in the whole thing. If the acid will not do the work, try and find out what will cut these bars. It will be no trouble to get out of this place. Try and get everything ready before the August term of court. You can get the acid at any drug store, and it is not very costly.

Truly your friend,

STEVE

I am informed that he objected to the note being published because he did not wish the public to know that he had received such a friendly note from me. This is strange, for he has always, when I was at large, professed the greatest friendship for me. When I have been in the neighborhood he has endeavored to impress upon the community the fact that he knew where I was, and could see me whenever he liked. Professing such friendship, I had the right to believe that he would not betray me, at least. I find, however, that I was mistaken and that he is a traitor. I would not have censured him if he had burned the note up, and said nothing about it, but I suppose he thought he could safely betray me, now as I am in jail with no hope of escape. Does anyone believe he would have done it if I had been at large? Why did he not tell the sheriff where I was when I was in the county, not in jail?

I am accused of some bad things, but none so mean as being a traitor.

Yours truly,

S. S. RENFROE

Indictments charged embezzlement, grand larceny, burglary, assault with intent to murder, and a number of lesser offenses. The prisoner pleaded guilty to embezzlement and burglary and was sentenced to the penitentiary for five years. Livingston felt a relief it had not enjoyed in a long time. But the men were a little shamefaced. After all, Steve was their friend and they had not forgotten carpetbag days. They did not like it much when they heard that he had been set at hard work in the mines of the Pratt Coal and Iron Company. Neither, apparently, did Steve, for in less than sixty days the Pratt Coal and Iron Company was spreading the alarm for an escaped convict. A posse tried hard to find Steve. They worked with bloodhounds, but their prey escaped them by walking backward for miles down a small creek to his favorite resort and, from then on, to his head-quarters—the "Flat Woods." This was a belt of uninhabited and mostly sterile timber lands about ninety miles in length and from five to fifteen in width. Here he lived desperately, making quick forays into the surrounding country to rob plantation homes, even daring to plunder houses in the small towns. At last he came to be known, even to his despairing friends, as the "outlaw."

Negroes living about the Flat Woods worshiped and feared Steve. They served him faithfully and they kept watch against the officers of the law. He had them cut him a special road through the woods to Mississippi, and whenever a posse was on his trail, he made for that and galloped madly to the state line and safety.

By this time he made no discrimination between former friend and foe. None were secure from pillage or violence. The little, widely separated communities of the Black Belt were thrown into a panic at the report that Renfroe had been seen near by. Almost every day a new and more reckless crime was laid to him.

Still he could not stay away from Livingston. The scene of his former triumphs always drew him back. Never, even, did he give up the idea of returning there to live as he had once lived, proud among his friends.

On the day before Steve Renfroe's final capture a Negro slunk across the fields behind the Pickens plantation home. He came to the back door with a message for Mr. Pickens. The master of the house received him and was informed that "someone" wished to see him behind the house and across the railroad track. Mr. Pickens said: "It's Steve." Despite the entreaties of his wife and daughter (who are my authority for this anecdote) he went with the Negro—answering their protestations simply: "He will not hurt me. He is my friend."

When Mr. Pickens came back from that interview he told little of what had transpired. His wife gathered that Steve wanted to know what would happen if he gave himself up—hoping that his friends would again rally to his defense. Perhaps, too, he told Mr. Pickens, what several of his contemporaries have alleged he told others—that if his old Ku Klux friends would not raise a large sum of money for him he would furnish the Federal Government with a list of their names and evidence of their affiliation. There is still much dispute on this point in Livingston. Many insist he never descended to this form of blackmail. But there are others who are not quite sure.

What Mr. Pickens told Steve is not known, but it must have been discouraging, for on the same night a mule belonging to the outlaw's brother-in-law disappeared. So did the silverware of a kindly lady with whom he had boarded and who had befriended him many times in former years.

Some days later three Mississippians who had read the story of the crime saw a man riding a mule like the one described therein. Surrounding the man, they called on him to surrender. He drew a pistol and one of his captors fired. A load of small shot in the back and side considerably facilitated his arrest.

Then began the long journey to the nearest town, Enterprise, sixty miles south. It was only when they arrived there and Steve was recognized that the three men learned how important a capture they had made. They brought him back once more to the Livingston jail. And once more his old friends came to see him there. But the jaunty air, the spirit in the blue eyes were gone.

About eighty-thirty on the second night after his capture a silent group of twenty men appeared before the jail. Two of them entered and seized the jailer's keys. Then they got Renfroe and moved off. As soon as they had gone the jailer gave the alarm and a posse started in pursuit. They did not go far. At the old "Tan Yard" about a mile south of town they found the body of Renfroe, hanged to a chinaberry tree.

There are people in Livingston who know who the members of that group of twenty were. Although the executioners were bitterly condemned by many of their own friends, it is still impolitic to ask about them. But a little has seeped out about that journey of a mile and its tragic end. Renfroe rode as he had always ridden, fearless. When they came to the tree and he saw their purpose, he struggled, called them cowards and challenged any one of them to single combat. No one accepted. One of the men said: "We're doing this for your own good, Steve, and the good of the community."

He was quiet while they put the rope about his neck. He looked about him at the stern faces of these men who had for so long been his friends. Perhaps he was thinking of the days when he wore a silver star and the milk-white horse danced down Main Street, for he said at last: "Will no one say a word for me?"

There was a grim silence. Again Steve said: "Won't someone say a prayer for me?"

Then the leader of the company, his boon companion in another time, said in one and the same breath:

"God rest your soul—string him up, boys!"

The chinaberry tree still stands. And the story of Steve Renfroe is so well remembered that to this day whenever Livingston children play about it they stop for a moment while the bravest of them says in a quavering voice: "Renfroe, Renfroe, what did you do?"

And the chinaberry tree says: "Nothing." [1]

---

[1] For another instance of the same tradition, related of Captain Kidd, see *A Treasury of New England Folklore* (New York, 1947), p. 535.

How Big Tom Wilson Tracked the Body of Elisha Mitchell

. . . DR MITCHELL had come to the Black Mountain to identify the peak which he had ascended some years before and to assert his claim to its discovery and measurement. He and his son had ascended the mountain from the south or Swannanoa side to the Patton House, and the son not being able to proceed further, the doctor made his way to the summit alone, and left word with his son that he would descend the mountain on the north side by a trail he was directed to take to Big Tom Wilson's, who knew all the peaks and who had had a conversation with the doctor's former guide and could certainly identify the spot to which the guide had taken him when he measured the height. This was the last ever seen of Dr. Mitchell alive; it was on Saturday the 27th of June, 1857.

From an account, based on an interview with Big Tom, Sept. 26, 1877, by Judge David Schenck, a copy of which was loaned to me by Bill Sharpe, of Raleigh, with the note that it was "copied, I believe, from an old issue of an Asheville paper," which I am unable to identify. According to D. Hiden Ramsey, of The Asheville Citizen-Times Company, "This copy was transcribed from a framed copy which apparently hangs in Ewart Wilson's cabin on the slopes of Mt. Mitchell. I can find no references to the Schenck article in any of the other accounts of the finding of Dr. Mitchell's body. This leads me to believe that the story had very limited circulation."

For the history of "Mount Mitchell and Dr. Elisha Mitchell," including Zebulon Baird Vance's account of the search, see the pamphlet by Chas. A. Webb, published by The Asheville Citizen-Times Company, Asheville, North Carolina, June, 1946.

Big Tom's own story, preserving his quaint spelling, appeared in the *Asheville Daily Citizen,* November 20, 1889.

There are some skilled woodsmen left in the rugged Black Mountains range, and it is understood that out in the west some pretty good trail followers are still practising. But ninety-one years after Big Tom Wilson found the body of Explorer Elisha Mitchell, following for miles a ten-day old trail, the people in this country doubt that his equal as a tracker has lived since.

Tracking of that kind, they say, is simply a lost art. Dogs, yes; but humans no longer have the kind of eyesight which was co-ordinated with the wilderness savvy of Big Tom.

Big Tom has been dead for many years, but he already was a legend while still in his prime; a legendary woodsman and hunter even before his notable tracking feat in 1857. . . .

Before that he was known as the best bear-hunter in the Appalachians, and his descendants—son Adolph, now dead; grandson Ewart and great-grandson Ned—all followed in his footsteps. The last two still hunt over the 17,000 acres of Wilson bearlands.

*   *   *   *   *

[In 1946] the neighboring peak, which had heretofore been known on maps merely as "the north folk of the Black Brothers," was named for Big Tom, but it was merely a governmental recognition of local usage. For nearly one hundred years the somber, balsam-draped mountain, lying closest to Mitchell, had been Big Tom to the Yancey boys.—Bill Sharpe, "Big Tom Is Still Champion Tracker," State News Bureau, Raleigh, North Carolina, September, 1948.

The Friday following, persons in search of the doctor had been at Big Tom's and not finding him, it was agreed to make search for him in the mountain. So on Saturday, in company with some half dozen others, they ascended the mountain on the north side some three miles, where they met a party from Buncombe, who had searched the trail the doctor was directed to take and had found no trace of him, and as it was now growing late, they returned with sad hearts to Big Tom's to rest for the night and agree upon a plan of operation for the morrow.

Sunday, July 5th, the two parties ascended the mountain again, one going to the east fork and one to the west fork of Caney River, "Big Tom" taking the east fork leading directly towards the peak, then through the Beech Nursery Gap, and on the south side of the mountain to the top of the Black Mountain, then over to the Buncombe road which leads to the Patton House, where they arrived hungry, weary and without rations, at 3 o'clock in the evening. No trace of the doctor was yet found.

Governor Vance, who was one of another party hunting on the southern side, soon came into the Patton House, and taking in the situation, at once directed the men to drive up a fat heifer that was grazing on the mountain and gave command to slay and eat. The skill of Ephraim Glass soon sent a bullet through the heifer's brain and she lay a sacrifice to the heroic men who had been toiling in fruitless search all day. So great was the hunger of the men that many did not wait to cook the meat, which they ate without bread or salt. In the meantime the Governor had started another party down the Swannanoa side for flour, salt and a little "extract of corn" as Big Tom called it. This party returned during the night, winding their way up by the dim light of torches, and the whole crowd partook of provisions and were refreshed.

On Monday, it having been reported that Eldridge and Frederick Burnett, old mountain bear hunters, had seen the sign of broken balsam twigs near a shelving rock on the west prong of the Caney River, the party resolved to search in this region again. Big Tom protested, as he wished to go to the peak and search for signs from that point, but he was overruled. The west prong, which led rather to the south side of the mountain instead of the north side where the doctor started to go, was searched all day but without success, and the searchers returned again to the Patton House almost hopeless and concluded to give up the search for the present and renew it again in three or four days, when the assembling of birds of prey over the dead body might indicate its locality.

Dr. Mitchell's son, who was present, became much affected with emotion and expressed great horror of leaving his father's body to become the prey of birds or food for the beasts of the forest, and entreated that more effort should be made. Big Tom at once assented and expressed his opinion again that the doctor was on the east prong of Caney, which led down to his house where the doctor started, and those who agreed to assist him next day prepared scanty rations from what was left of the flour and beef and ascended to the peak to spend the night at the Stepp cabin. This party was composed of Big Tom, Adoniram D. Allen, James Allen, Burton Austin and Bryson McMahan. All mountaineers and well acquainted with every path and road around the Black Mountain.

On Tuesday, the 7th of July, 1857, this little band of persevering heroes rough and rugged in appearance, but whose generous, noble hearts glowed with enthusiasm and swelled with emotions of compassion for the living and pity for the dead, began their laborious and tiresome search amidst the gloom of this rugged solitude. They first examined the area of ground on Mitchell's peak where the doctor went, and then going to the trail he was directed to take, and finding no sign, then commenced the descent toward the south side by the easy prong. They had not gone more than a quarter of a mile until Adoniram D. Allen found an impression in the moss, which covers the whole surface of the ground like a green velvet carpet at this great altitude.

Soon the scattering party gathered around the "sign" to give their opinion as to its origin. As it was a mere depression scarcely describable, three of the party expressed their belief that it was a bear "sign" but Big Tom said no, and argued that the instinct of a bear always led him to follow rocky ledges, where he could not be trailed or followed, and that a man would naturally walk where it was the easiest to his foot. The cause was argued for some time, with all the sagacious logic of the crafty mountaineers, looking earnestly into each other's faces; and, finding that they were not agreed, they began to search again in silence and moved on. Twenty steps from this impression they found a broken balsam tree about the size of one's arm, which had fallen down the mountain and lodged on a log below, raising the trunk about four feet high. The trunk was rotten and freshly broken as if a weight had been put on it which it could not support. Another council convened, and Big Tom said that this little tree was broken by a man, for he said, "only men and bears ever get up here, and if a bear had passed he would have gone under the trunk, whereas it being rotten, a man would naturally break it down in front of him and go on." Then looking down at the broken ends where they rested on the moss he discovered depressions on each side. "Now," said he, "look at this; a bear's foot is too short to go across the trunk, but a man's would show the toe of his shoe on one side and the heel on the other."

Adoniram D. and James Allen seemed convinced and the others became hopeful, and they quickened their pace, now taking the direction from the impression to the broken balsam. Impressions like the first were discovered and soon led them to an open spot two hundred yards distant, from which could be seen a farm belonging to Big Tom about six miles off. Here were impressions of a footstep, as if the person was walking from side to side to catch a glimpse of the distant farm, which, no doubt, was the first awakening of hope in the doctor's bewildered brain. Examining the sign more closely, Big Tom at last raised up with a smile of triumph on his face, and pointing to a small root of a balsam tree said, "See the print of the shoe tacks which his heel scraped off that root. There is no doubt that this is his track. Did you ever see a bear's heel with tacks in it?"

All were now agreed and became intensely interested in the further progress of the search. Old man Allen slapped Big Tom on the shoulder and said, "We'll stick together as long as there is a button on our coats," and met the response from Big Tom, "Bully for you."

After consultation it was now agreed that they would go back first and report what they had found and examine where the track left the peak. This was soon done and they found that the doctor had taken a horse trail by mistake, for the trail which led to Big Tom's. McMahan and Austin now left for home and Wilson and the Allens soon met Robert Patton, Calvin Patton, Thomas Wistall and a Mr. Burgin, who were on the other side toward the Patton House. These seven men now returned and renewed the search. They soon came to a pine log which was rotten, and on it could plainly be seen the doctor's track. This track was exactly in the trail which the doctor had traveled with Allen and Wilson some years before the ascent to the peak. The position of the foot indicated that the doctor was now turning directly toward the clearing which was visible in the distance and which no doubt he hoped to reach by following a straight line to it. The tracks were now easily traced for half a mile toward the clearing. Here the party stopped to take their scanty rations for dinner and sent back two of their number for more help.

After dinner they continued the search, and in a short distance found impressions again where the doctor would move from side to side as if taking observation across a small creek in front of him, which was making its way down a gorge in the mountain.

The footsteps now left the bear trail and turned immediately down the rocky bluff to the creek below. No doubt his purpose now was to take the water course and follow it to the settlement below. His track was now invisible, yet Big Tom passed on, calling out, "Here he went! Here he went!" Mr. Robert Patton now demanded how he could trace the way. "By the broken laurels," said Big Tom. "Don't you see the white side of the laurel leaf turned toward you there in front? That is where he broke a twig as he passed through the thicket and you can follow it by this sign all along."

Big Tom and the Allens passed on, the others following and soon cried out, "Here night overtook the doctor." "And how do you know that?" said the followers. "In this way," replied Tom. "Don't you see that back there among the laurels the doctor picked the best ways and crept through the open places, but here he ran up against a bush and there he fell over a rock. Don't you see where he slid down and this shows he could not see his way longer."

The signs now led them down to the creek about two hundred yards above the falls, where there were evidences of the doctor's having slipped and fallen several times as far as four or five feet until finally he got into the creek, at the mouth of the branch where the water was waist deep. No sign could now be seen, and it was evident that the doctor had waded down the creek. So the party divided, one taking one side and one the other, to find where he came out. A short distance below Wilson discovered broken sticks in a drift, which indicated that the doctor had climbed over the drift and displaced some rubbish. Here Big Tom heard the falls and said, "I hear a fall roaring that must be fifty feet high, and I fear the poor man has met his death there."

No human being, so far as these mountaineers knew, had ever been along this dreadful chasm before. Big Tom says he now literally climbed along from rock to rock and tree to tree by the overhanging sides of the creek below until he came to the head of the falls. Here he secured himself and looked over. A large spruce pine had washed over the falls from above and was standing erect with one end resting in the pool below. As it obstructed his vision he clambered about twenty feet further on and descended the rocky bluff, and here he saw where the doctor had slipped on the shelving rock. He had evidently tried to work his way around the falls in the darkness and had gotten this far and was trying to get into the creek again. Big Tom says after the creek poured over the falls it ran to the right under this shelving rock and deadened the sound so that the doctor was deceived as to the distance it was from him, and ventured too soon to turn towards the channel, which he was seeking. From this point where the doctor slipped Big Tom gazed down into the pool under the falls and discovered the doctor's soft fur hat washed up on a log. No one was present and he could not hear his call made for the noise of the many waters.

As this tenderhearted old man came to this point of the story, his voice choked with emotion and the big bright tears rolled down his rugged cheeks and he said, "Wait a while, I can't go on now."

After a while the other members of the party came up and he pointed out the hat. Big Tom now worked his way down to the pool and looking into its crystal waters said, "Poor old man, here he is."

The sun was shining directly down in the water and the body was distinctly visible. The pool was fifteen feet deep and the body had risen up about halfway and was prevented from coming to the surface by a log on which the rigid arm had lodged below. Its position indicated that the doctor had fallen to the bottom of the pool and had died there on his all fours face downwards, and when the gases formed in the body it rose until it came in contact with the log, where it rested about seven feet from the surface.

The doctor's watch had stopped at sixteen minutes before nine o'clock, which was no doubt the hour he fell and came to his death, and Big Tom's guess as to where night overtook him was correct. The body looked natural and was not disfigured. Further examination showed that the doctor had slipped down forty-five feet and then fallen over the precipice fifteen feet into the pool below. The body was left as found until a coroner was procured and an inquest held.

Big Tom Wilson was born December 1, 1823, and lives now nine miles south of Burnsville, near the Green ponds. He is known as the Black Mountain Guide and helps to support his wife and ten children by conducting visitors to Mitchell's Peak. His name deserves to be respected wherever the memory of Dr. Mitchell is honored. Porte Crayon, he says, drew a good picture of him in his sketches of North Carolina.

These men of the mountains carried the body of Dr. Mitchell to the top of the mountain which now bears his name, where an excited debate ensued. The men of Buncombe County wanted the body buried in Asheville. Big Tom Wilson and the men of Yancey County wanted the body buried on the peak whose height Dr. Mitchell had measured. A dispute had arisen between Dr. Mitchell and the then Congressman from this district, General Thomas Clingman, as to the respective heights of this particular mountain and that of Mt. Clingman, and it was in the attempt to remeasure the height of this mountain that Dr. Mitchell lost his life.

The Buncombe men outnumbered the Yancey men and accordingly the body was taken to Asheville for interment, but in the next year at the request of the members of Dr. Mitchell's family, the body was disinterred and carried by gentle hands to the highest spot in Eastern America, the top of Mount Mitchell, 6,711 feet above the roaring sea, and buried to await the resurrection morning.

A beautiful tower has been erected in honor of this great man on this peak and donated to the State of North Carolina by the Hon. Charles J. Harris of Dillsboro, N. C.

Colonel Falkner and the Rebel Route

MOST colorful among the founders of the Rebel Route, as it is now called, was Col. William C. Falkner, a dreamy-eyed lawyer and novelist who looked like Charles Dickens and was slain by a rival on the very day of his election to the Mississippi State Legislature [, builder of an arm of the future Gulf, Mobile & Ohio Railroad]. . . .

* * * * *

. . . Born in Knox County, Tennessee, on July 6th, 1825, William C. Falkner studied law and served through the War with Mexico and the Civil War. After laying aside the sword, he turned to railroad construction. The first road he built bore the bewildering title of Ripley, Ship Island & Kentucky. It was completed in 1872, connecting Ripley, Miss.,

From "Rebel Route," by Stuart Covington, *Railroad Magazine*, Vol. 37 (January, 1945), No. 2, pp. 6, 13–16. Copyright, 1944, by Popular Publications, Inc. Chicago, Illinois.

The Rebel Route (the Gulf, Mobile & Ohio Railroad), between East St. Louis, Memphis, Birmingham, Montgomery, Mobile, and New Orleans, is so called because it "serves a section of the Mississippi Basin rich in Civil War traditions, [including] Montgomery, Ala., one-time capital city of the old Confederacy, . . . the home of Jeff Davis, [and] Corinth, Miss., [where] General Albert Sydney Johnson lost his life in the bloody battle of Shiloh."

with the Memphis & Charleston line at Middletown, Tenn., and was one of the first narrow-gages in the country to provide both freight and passenger service.

The financing of this little pike was an epic in itself. Falkner tossed in all of his own slender capital and all he could borrow on credit. Besides that, people along the route were so eager to see the rails laid that they donated labor and the use of horses and wagons, also lumber, tools, land for the right-of-way—anything usable they could spare.

Falkner's original intention was to build clear through to Chicago, an ambitious project indeed! Under various names—the Gulf & Ship Island and the Gulf & Chicago—this venture was pushed. Falkner applied to the State for financial aid. At that time Mississippi had a standing offer of $4000 per mile for railroad construction within its borders. However, this applied only to broad- or standard-gage roads. The Colonel, who was also a lawyer, presented his case so effectively that legislation was passed including narrow-gages in the grant. Falkner then continued his efforts to extend his line both north and south, and it got as far as Pontotoc, Miss.

In those dark days the State of Mississippi resorted to the practice of leasing convicts to private industrial concerns for enforced labor. Those taking advantage of this system were mostly railroad and highway contractors, among them the outfit which built the narrow-gage G & C from Ripley to Pontotoc. Nearly all that stretch was the work of convicts. Prisoners who performed this drudgery were closely guarded by men armed with whips and rifles. Punishment of barbaric cruelty is said to have been meted out for small offenses, and many a poor devil would make a break for freedom when opportunity offered. Under bond for returning inmates to the penitentiary, the contractors often found it easier to shoot a felon trying to escape rather than attempt to capture him.

* * * * *

Colonel Falkner was not only a soldier, lawyer, and railroad builder; he was also a novelist. His best known literary work, *The White Rose of Memphis,* was rather widely read in its day. This book was first published serially in a local newspaper, *The Ripley Advertiser,* in Falkner's home town. The owner of that paper, R. F. Ford, sleeps today in a modest grave adjoining Colonel Falkner's.

The Colonel's first literary work is said to have been a little pamphlet telling the life story of a criminal named McCammon, who was hanged at Ripley. The condemned man turned over this story to the Colonel, who as a young attorney had defended him in court, with permission to publish it. Falkner, doubtless after making the manuscript more readable, had it printed as soon as he received it; and on the very day of the execution he sold out the entire edition.

Another incident of note in Falkner's stormy career was his peaceful meeting with the senior of the two train-robbing James brothers. This meeting occurred on a Memphis race-track not long after Jesse had been shot dead by one of his own men and Frank, clearing himself in court, had foresworn banditry and taken to the "strait and narrow path." The former gunman said in his Missouri drawl:

"Colonel, it's a real pleasure to know you, sir. I've enjoyed reading some of your books."

Falkner was equally gracious. "Mr. James," he replied, "there are some things I admire in the record of you two brothers. But," he added with a sly grin, "I hope that if you ever decide to resume the outlaw business you won't molest my railroad."

The railroad builder's career, always dramatic, ended with a sensational tragedy. One of Falkner's backers, R. J. Thurmond, presented a financial ultimatum to the Colonel, at a time when money was needed to tide the railroad over a crisis; but Falkner turned it down and, instead, borrowed from a Memphis commission house. Thurmond regarded this as a deadly insult to his honor. When the Colonel became a candidate for the Mississippi State Legislature with the avowed object of promoting legislation to put the railroad on its feet, Thurmond ran against him. The campaign was a knock-down-and-drag-out affair. Falkner won. On election day, November 6th, 1889, he had just verified the returns and was walking quietly along the streets of Ripley when the embittered Thurmond shot and killed him.

Falkner lies buried in the local cemetery, very near to rails that flash the glint of Mississippi sunlight onto the white marble monument over his grave. Surmounting this shaft is an heroic-sized statue of the Colonel himself, dignified with whiskers and frock coat, extending one hand toward the railroad as if to guard and bless his handiwork. A friend of his commented: "Every time the roar of a passing train resounds in the Tippah hills beyond; every time the shrill blast of its whistle echoes over the intervening vales; always, as these vehicles of progress pass northward or southward, they perpetuate the memory of the man whose genius and hard work made their existence in these hills possible."

Jay Gould's Curse

THE tremendous power of the railroads to destroy as well as to build can be seen clearly in the case of such a town as Jefferson, once a thriving community of thirty thousand or more inhabitants, in Northeast Texas. In 1860, Jefferson was known over what was then the new frontier, as the "Queen of the West." Packet boats, piled high with bales of cotton, steamed down Big Cypress Bayou, carrying planters, gamblers, cattlemen, ladies and gentlemen of the Old South. There were times when twelve or fifteen big river steamboats were docked at the same time along the three-mile wharf where today there is only a shallow pond.

From *Saddle in the Sky,* The Lone Star State, by J. H. Plenn, pp. 140–141. Copyright, 1940, by the Bobbs-Merrill Company. Indianapolis and New York.

It was "Jay Gould's curse" that sent Jefferson on the down-grade. When he came to Texas, demanding concessions for his line, the citizens, content with what they regarded as an assured future, spurned his proposition. They refused to disturb the tranquil streets, lined with large frame buildings. They did not desire the clang and smoke of iron horses. About the same time, the federal government undertook some dredging work below Shreveport, Louisiana. The net result, as far as Jefferson was concerned, was to deprive the Big Cypress of its water, and it was no longer navigable. No water route, no railroad.

The hotel register, on which Jay Gould signed the pictograph of his name—a line drawing of a jaybird—is still preserved, and on it is the curse which Gould pronounced. He wrote, on the same page: "end of Jefferson, Texas."

> Grass will grow in your streets and bats
> will roost in your belfries if you do not
> let me run my railroad through your town.

Jay Gould took his railroad three miles away. Jefferson sank into a period of quiet decay. Only recently has it begun to show signs of life—oil.

That story of Jefferson is pretty much the story of scores of towns throughout Texas, passed up by the railroads; sometimes because they preferred to go elsewhere; other times because they could not get what they wanted from the town in the way of land grants and other gifts.

Casey Jones

I. How He Got His Name

"When J. L. came to Jackson to work," she [Mrs. Jones] says, "he ate breakfast at a boardinghouse [at Jackson, Tenn.] which my mother kept for railroad men. There he introduced himself to a young engineer named Bose Lashley. 'Your name won't do,' said Mr. Lashley. 'There are too many Joneses on this division. Where did you hail from?' J. L. mentioned the town of Cayce [pronounced "Casey"] and his new friend said: 'That's fine! We'll call you Cayce.' So that is how my husband got his name."

The prevalence of Joneses in railroading, as elsewhere, is shown by the fact that in 1944 there were 1,078 Joneses on the Canadian National pay roll, of which 118 were John Jones and 4 John L. Jones.

Anyhow, it seems that J. L. liked his new nickname very much. Letters are extant showing that he used it in writing to his correspondents, sign-

From *Railroad Avenue,* Great Stories and Legends of American Railroading, by Freeman H. Hubbard, pp. 7, 8–11, 12–14, 18–20, 22–23. Copyright, 1945, by Freeman H. Hubbard. New York: Whittlesey House, McGraw-Hill Book Company, Inc.

ing himself "Cayce." Many folks, among them newspaper reporters, preferred the Irish spelling; so the headlines in local papers that told of his death spelled the name "Casey" and that form was adopted when the song was written.

II. BUILDING THE LEGEND

In the 1890's engineers had locomotives assigned to them more or less permanently. Every man considered that he owned his iron horse, took a personal pride and interest in her condition, and had many of her fittings adjusted to his individual liking. There was no standard whistle on the Illinois Central then as there is now; the engineman put on a whistle of his own with a tone that suited him and then practised a technique of blowing it that would be distinctive. This was called "quilling" and was a highly developed art. Many people who lived along the railroad could tell the engineer's name the moment his whistle was heard.

Casey soon "went on the air" with a long, plaintive wail that advertised to the world that "the man at the throttle was Casey Jones." This business of quilling was especially dear to the Negroes and seemed to induce in every colored boy within earshot a peculiar hero worship for the engineers, often expressed in ballad form. The untold number of primitive chants that were improvised and sung and forgotten would have made a rich addition to American folk music. Engineer Jones had a six-chime whistle, formed by six slender tubes banded together, the shortest being exactly half the length of the tallest. With its interpretive tone the ballest scorcher could make that quill say its prayers or scream like a banshee.

Even during his lifetime Casey built up a sort of legendary reputation for himself. Dispatchers regarded him as a "fast roller," a runner who could be depended upon to get his train over the road "on the card," to take advantage of every break they could give him at passing points. They knew he never dawdled at coal chutes, water cranes, or cinder-pit tracks or wasted time along the pike.

*   *   *   *   *

Consolidation engines have enormous tenders, but the water stops on Casey's division were far apart, and the water in his tank often would drop rather low if the engine were hauling a heavy train. Nearly all the engineers could be counted on to use up their water somewhere and be obliged to put the train away on a passing track and "run for water" to the next point. This practice caused annoying delays. But not so with Casey. That tall fellow could get more mileage out of a tankful of water, according to tradition, than anyone else on the road. Seldom did he cut off and run for water. According to Tony Hayes, one of his fellow engineers, "when Jones ran for water he took his train right with him."

In those days many runners considered it smart to keep round-house work on an engine down to a minimum—the fewer the defects they reported, the better standing they had at the round-house. Consequently,

flues would be leaking and cylinder packing worn through, but if the locomotive could move at all she was taken out day after day and reported "in
good condition." Naturally, fuel consumption would get out of proportion, and the pulling power of an engine would often be much less than was
expected. Casey Jones did not follow this general custom, however. Casey
turned in his engine for every slight defect, so that she was always kept in
prime condition. And Casey's fuel-consumption record was among the best
on the Illinois Central. He understood his "old girl" as a cowboy knows
his horse; he knew just how much she could perform and how to treat her
to get the best results.

During his ten years at the throttle, from 1890 till his death in 1900,
Casey was never involved in a serious accident or in the death of a passenger or fellow worker, although he was disciplined nine times for various
infractions of rules, with suspensions of from five to thirty days levied
against him on such occasions. Some of these lapses, such as running
through switches or leaving them open behind him or negligence in handling
train orders, could have led to serious consequences. Casey was never
the type known as a "rule-book engineer." On two occasions he was concerned in a minor way in smashups, for which he drew suspensions of
thirty days for contributory negligence in one form or another. Casey's
record showed no stain of blood, however, save, eventually, his own. He
was impetuous and daring, not deliberately reckless. He wanted to get
there and would take a reasonable chance if he thought circumstances
called for it. He never used liquor or frequented saloons, and there is not
a whisper of loose moral conduct in the numerous anecdotes concerning him
that abound in the South.

III. Sim Webb's Account of the Wreck [1]

"We were called in Memphis at 10 P.M. That was Sunday, April 29,
1900. Number 1 was reported to be thirty minutes late. We had doubled
over on Mr. Sam Tate's run on No. 3 and No. 2, on account of Mr. Tate
being ill, and had come into Memphis that morning at 6:25. But that
gave us time to have a good rest and get ready for our regular run; and
we were both feeling good when we answered the call that night. We reported at the McLemore Avenue roundhouse and found old 382 hot and
ready to go. We looked her over to see we had tools, plenty of oil, and
everything.

"The regular time for us to leave Poplar Street depot, the main station
in those days, was 11:35 P.M. Thirty minutes late would have put us out
at twelve five. But it finally happened that No. 1 was an hour and thirty
minutes late. Well, we got going. We ran down the track along the Beale
Street trestle and on to the Central Station, where we had to stop five

---

[1] For the complete interview with Sim Webb, Casey's last fireman (at the age of 62),
see "Casey Jones's Fireman," by Eldon Roark, *Railroad Magazine*, Vol. XIX (March,
1936), No. 4, pp. 36–38.

minutes. We held a late order saying that we were running thirty minutes late from Memphis to Sardis. There was a freight train coming north, and that was the only thing in front of us.

"We'd been having rainy, foggy weather for two weeks. That night the clouds were mighty dark and low. But Mr. Casey seemed to be in an extra good mood. As we pulled out of Central Station he opened her up and said: 'We're going to have a pretty tough time getting into Canton on the dot, but I believe we can do it, barring accidents.' And I replied: 'You can depend on me, Mr. Casey, I'll sure keep her hot.'

"Sardis was our first stop. That's about fifty miles. It took us one hour and two minutes from Poplar Street Station in Memphis to Sardis, which included the stop at Central Station, Memphis. Our actual running time was between forty-five and forty-seven minutes. On south we roared, with everything working just fine. At some places we got to clipping a mile off every fifty seconds. Old 382 was steaming mighty well that night —and using very little fuel. I hadn't even taken down the top coal gate on the tender.

"We made Grenada, fifty miles from Sardis, in what seemed like no time at all. Then came Winona, twenty-three miles further on, and the next stop, Durant, thirty-three miles from Winona. Everything was still going fine. We were whittling that lost time away to nothing, and Mr. Casey was still in high spirits. As we left Durant, he stood up and hollered to me over the boiler head: 'Oh, Sim! The old girl's got her high-heeled slippers on tonight! We ought to pass Way on time.'

"Way was just six miles north of Canton, and he had it figured out that we'd be back on time when we hit there, and we would coast on it. We hadn't received any more orders. Down the track we went, approaching Vaughan, which is twelve miles above Canton. Vaughan was at the lower end of a double S curve. The north switch was just about the middle of the first S, and as we roared down on it we saw two big red lights. They appeared to me as big as houses. I knew it was a train not in the clear. I could see the lights, but Mr. Casey couldn't, because there was a deep curve to the fireman's side. I yelled to Mr. Casey: 'Look out! We're gonna hit something!'

" 'Jump, Sim!' he shouted, and these were his last words. He was sitting down at the time. I heard him kick the seat out from under him and apply the brakes. About that time I swung down as low off the engine as I could, and hit the dirt. When I came to, half an hour later, Mr. Casey was dead. Our engine had plowed through the caboose of the freight and two other cars—a car of shelled corn and a car of hay!"

According to Mr. Lee's biography,[2] when Casey's body was found in the wreckage, an iron bolt was driven through his neck and a bale of hay rested on his chest, while corn lay scattered about. *Life* magazine stated:

---

[2] Fred J. Lee, *Casey Jones,* Epic of the American Railroad (Kingsport, Tennessee, 1939).

"For a number of years a stand of wild corn, from kernels scattered in the wreck, marked the scene for railroaders."

IV. The Song

Casey's loss was mourned by the whole countryside. Among his many friends was a simple-minded Negro named Wallace Saunders, who worked in the Canton roundhouse. Wallace had a gift for improvising ballads as he labored at wiping engines or shoveling coal. He would sing in rhythm with his muscular activity; and one of his creations, as innumerable witnesses agreed, was the original version of "Casey Jones."

The lines were rendered in a singsong, pretty much like a Negro spiritual and with the same mournful undertone. They were not meant to be printed and read. The way Wallace Saunders crooned them, you wouldn't have noticed the poor rhyming, the faulty sentence structure, the many inaccuracies. Instead, you would have recognized the ditty for what it was, the sincere attempt of an illiterate black to voice what must have been a supreme tragedy of the world in which he lived. Wallace Saunders, no less than Casey Jones, was a railroader. They spoke the same language. Casey could not have desired a better tribute.

There is some doubt as to the exact process by which this folklore was transmuted into a national song hit. We do know that there were several adaptations of the original lament. One was sung on the vaudeville stage by Bert and Frank Leighton, brothers of an Illinois Central engineer named Bill Leighton. In 1902 it was finally published, and in 1903 it was listed among the ten best sellers in sheet music. In that year, three years after the Vaughan collision, the Southern Music Company of Los Angeles put out a song sheet entitled "Casey Jones, the Brave Engineer." In one corner was reproduced in miniature the cover of an earlier issue of the same ballad, and in another a hogger waving from an engine numbered 5, with the information: "Words by T. Lawrence Siebert. Music by Eddie Newton." . . .

* * * * *

Neither Mr. Saunders nor Mrs. Jones received a cent of royalty from the "Casey Jones" sheet music, phonograph records, or movie or radio renditions, although one governor of Mississippi wrote the widow that she was entitled to collect.

V. In Memoriam

Casey lies buried in Mt. Calvary Cemetery at Jackson. The grave is unmarked except by a small wooden cross.[3] But at Cayce, Ky., the town

---

[3] Forty-seven years after his death at Vaughan, Mississippi, in the most celebrated wreck in the history of American railroading, a bronze and granite memorial was erected over the grave of John Luther ("Casey") Jones. Until this time the spot where the hero lay in Mt. Calvary Cemetery at Jackson, Tennessee, bore no marker but an unpainted wooden cross.

The memorial was the gift of Lucius Beebe and Charles M. Clegg, railroad historians for which he was nicknamed, you can see an impressive bronze plaque, about three feet high by two feet wide, set just outside the schoolhouse facing the crossroads. A bas-relief of engine 382 is engraved on this plaque, together with the words:

"In this community the famous locomotive engineer, John Luther Jones (alias Casey Jones) spent his boyhood days. Casey's many record feats as a locomotive engineer engrossed him deeply in the hearts of his fellow workers. On the morning of April 30th, 1900, while running the Illinois Central fast mail train No. 1, 'The Cannonball,' and by no fault of his, his engine bolted through three freight cars at Vaughan, Miss. Casey died with his hand clenched to the brake helve and his was the only life lost. Famous for bravery and courage, the name of Casey Jones lives deeply set into the hearts of American people in both tradition and song. It can be truthfully said of him, 'Greater love hath no man than this that a man lay down his life for his friends.' Erected by admirers of Casey Jones, July 9th, 1938."

The tablet was dedicated by Kentucky's senior senator, Alben W. Barkley, assisted by local talent and two of Casey's old firemen, Sid A. Law, white, and Sim Webb, colored. Senator Barkley, who had recently returned from a foreign trip, used his impressions of Europe as a text for his address. He said he beheld the scene at Cayce with unbridled satisfaction because, unlike most of the monuments he had seen abroad, this one was erected to the memory of a man of peace, "just a human being, respected by all who knew him." That was Casey Jones.

Temple Houston

TEMPLE HOUSTON was one of the most picturesque characters I have ever met. He was a son of General Sam Houston, the only man who ever

---

and frequent contributors to *Railroad Magazine* and authors of *Mixed Train Daily, A Book of Short Line Railroads.* Through a recent issue of *Railroad* they learned of the neglect of Jones' grave, and determined upon the rectification of what Beebe, in his dedicatory speech, called "a reproach to the good heart of railroading."—*Railroad Magazine,* Vol. 44 (November, 1947), No. 2, p. 116.

The inscription on the memorial reads:

John Luther
Jones
1864 —— 1900

To the memory of the locomotive engineer whose name as "Casey Jones" became a part of folklore and the American language. "For I'm going to run her till she leaves the rail, Or make it on time with the southbound mail."

This memorial erected 1947 to perpetuate the legend of American railroading and the man whose name became its symbol of daring and romance—Casey Jones.

From *Oklahombres,* Particularly the Wilder Ones, by Evett Dumas Nix, as told to Gordon Hines, pp. 241–245. Copyright, 1929, by E. D. Nix. St. Louis-Chicago: Eden Publishing House.

For a portrait of Temple Houston, see Edna Ferber's *Cimarron.*

served as governor of two separate states, as United States Senator from two different states, as commander-in-chief of an army and president of a republic.

With the impressive background of his father's career, and with an inheritance of his father's mental brilliance, Temple Houston became one of early Oklahoma's best known characters. Oklahoma has produced no other orator who could approach the beauty and eloquence of Temple Houston's speeches.

The man allowed his hair to grow so long that it fell about his shoulders and he dressed most eccentrically. He was an admirable horseman and few men ever equaled his marksmanship with a pistol or rifle. I don't believe a more fearless man ever lived. Perhaps Houston's principal fault was in his bull-dog stubbornness. When he had considered any given proposition or circumstance and had formed his opinion, no power on earth could induce him to change. His manner was quiet and unassuming.

I remember an incident that occurred in Judge Burford's court that amused me a great deal. Judge Burford, who was trying special cases for Judge Dale at Guthrie, seemed to share my own aversion to snakes. There are a good many things in this world that I am not afraid of, but I wouldn't touch a snake alive for five hundred dollars! I was sitting near the judge's bench one morning when Temple Houston walked into the court-room, sporting a very conspicuous necktie made of rattlesnake skin. The idea of that snake-skin being tied around a man's neck worried me, as the thought was very repulsive. I didn't notice Judge Burford's nervousness until about an hour later, when I observed that the judge was not able to keep his eyes off that rattlesnake tie.

I watched Judge Burford and became convinced that he was very much worried about that snake-skin tie. Just as the court was adjourning for the noon-hour, the judge turned to Temple Houston and said: "Colonel Houston, I wish you would change that tie at noon. I have been deathly afraid of snakes since I was a kid and that thing gives me the willies." Houston laughed, and when he returned to the court-room that afternoon he wore a more conservative necktie.

I remember that day particularly because of the eloquent speech Houston made on behalf of a prostitute who was brought before the court. Houston had been sitting, unoccupied, in the court-room listening to the procedure. When the judge learned that the woman had no counsel, he appointed Temple Houston to defend her. Houston's extemporaneous speech in her defense was so powerful and appealing that he won an acquittal. The court's stenographer was besieged for copies of the oration and later many thousands of copies of it were circulated. It had a true classic quality.

Houston often resorted to very unique methods of impressing the jury. I remember an occasion when he was defending a man on a murder charge. The accused man had killed a cowpuncher and his plea was self-defense. Witnesses testified the cowpuncher had not drawn his gun. Houston attempted to show that his client had been impressed by the cow man's reputation as a quick-drawing gunman, and that his fear had caused him to shoot before the other man had time to draw. The prosecution had attempted to blast this defense. Houston was making his argument before the jury and stressing that the dead cowpuncher might have drawn his guns and killed his client if he had been given the slightest advantage.

"Gentlemen of the jury," Houston was saying, "this cow man had a reputation as a gunman. My client is a peaceful citizen with little experience in such matters. There are gunmen in Oklahoma so adept at drawing and shooting that they can place a gun in the hands of an inexperienced man, then draw and shoot their own weapons before he can pull a trigger. Like this—!" he shouted, and, with a lightning movement, Houston drew his forty-five, pointed it at the jury box and shot six times so quickly that the men had barely time to dodge. The jury scattered like frightened quail. Houston turned toward Judge McAtee, whipped out his other gun and emptied it at the judge's rostrum. Judge McAtee jumped off his chair and crouched behind the bench.

When the shooting had ended and Houston stood grinning with the smoking guns in his hands, Judge McAtee peeped out to see if all was clear.

"Your Honor," Houston chuckled, "you need not be afraid . . . my cartridges were all blanks."

Judge McAtee was very much peeved when he mounted his seat but without discussing the matter he ordered the bailiff to call the jury back to the court-room. He then turned to Houston and said: "Sir, you seem to have very little respect for the dignity and person of this court."

Houston bowed low and said: "Your Honor, I apologize. I only wanted to impress the jury with the speed with which guns may be drawn and fired by an accomplished two-gun man."

The gesture was perhaps an unwise one, for the jury decided against Houston's client. However, he was able to obtain a new trial because the jury had been allowed to separate and leave the court-room during the hearing of the case.

Temple Houston had attained a great deal of notoriety because of such eccentric acts as this, although he had also attained a wide reputation as a successful criminal lawyer. His reputation as a fighter had made it easy for him to intimidate opposing counsel with well-directed sarcastic remarks, and Houston often took advantage of this fact, precipitating many bitter clashes in the Territory's court-rooms.

The Physic and the Corpus: A Story of Solomon's Island, Maryland

HERE is a story that perfectly depicts the place [Solomon's Island] before it began to be modernized. This happened when my friend, Mr. Ed Sollers,

From *Maryland Main and the Eastern Shore*, by Hulbert Footner, pp. 280–283. Copyright, 1942, by D. Appleton-Century Company, Inc. New York and London.

who told me the story, was a young man, say fifty years ago. The story concerns a Dr. Carsley, member of a county family who was domiciled on the island for the convenience of his practice. He preferred to be known as "Physic" and was always so called. In Mr. Ed's words, "Physic" was "a little fellow and a mighty ranter and a tanter, with baldhead and big mustachios." To continue, in Mr. Ed's own words:

He was too free a man for the liking of the churchgoers. When folks got mad at him they said he hadn't the proper education for a doctor. I don't know. There was a sheepskin framed on the wall of his office all in order. Howsoever, it rankled in Physic's mind, and many's the time I hear him say "Jehu Kingdom Come! If I had a skeleton hanging in the corner my office 'twould stop all this talk." Physic, he reckoned a skeleton would impress our people more'n any God's amount of sheepskins.

Well, one day in summertime a deckhand fall overboard from the steamboat down at Solomon's Island and drown before they could fish him out. He was a kinless man and old Mr. Button Billings, the magistrate, he call a jury together and they sat on him in the shed alongside Virgil Longcope's store. The shed is still there. He was a big buck nigger with an ugly blue scar from eye to chin, right side. Verdict was death by accidental drowning.

Physic, being County Medical Officer, was present, and he up and make little speech. He say: "Mr. Magistrate and Gentlemen of the Jury," he say, "in all the large cities of this great country of ours it is the usage and custom for the bodies of paupers to be handed over to medical men for the investigation of science. Being as I am cut off from the meetings and gatherings of my fellow medical profession," he say, "I ask, Mr. Magistrate and Gentlemen o. Jury, that this here body be handed over to me for the proper investigation of science."

Now, Mr. Button Billings, he was a churchwarden along with ev'thing else, and there wa'nt no manner of love lost between him and Physic. He up with his gray beard sticking straight out and trem'ling, and he say: "As to the ungodly customs and usages of our large cities we hear too much," he say. "Please God, while I am at the hellum," he say, "such hideous practices shall gain no hold in this God-fearing community!"

He call in Jimmy Kemp, the odd-job man, and give him a dollar. "Mr. Kemp," he say, "take the body of this unfortunate man and bury him decently on Moll Legg Island. Let all be done in a proper Christian manner," he say, looking at Physic. "Set up a wooden cross at head of the grave and letter it: Unknown Negro, drown such and such date."

Moll Legg Island is that little lump like a vessel at anchor out in the harbor at Solomon's. Don't belong to nobody. Nameless and kinless men been buried there since time out of mind.

So Physic was sent home with a flea in's ear, as they thought. They hadn't taken the measure of the man. He had a Negro working for him call' John Stagg, a fellow of similar kidney. And the two of them fix to row out to Moll Legg Island that night and fetch the body.

It was a right dark night, I mind, suitable for the work in hand. They put out with a couple of spades, a lantern and a jug of corn to keep their spirits up. Out on the island Physic hang his coat over a bush, and put the lantern behind it so light wouldn't show on the village side. Well, they get the corpus up all right, and fix the grave like 'twas before. 'Twas right gruesome work by lantern light, and first Physic take a pull at the jug, then John Stagg. So when they come to row home, the jug was empty and the men was full.

Midway across the creek, John Stagg drap an oar ov'board, and in reaching for the oar, he pitch in hisself. When Physic scram'le to pull him out, the skiff capsize, and all were thrown in the water together, the living and the dead. John Stagg holp his master ashore and fetch in the skiff and the oars after. As for the corpus, it float away quiet in the dark.

Now Miss Molly Carsley, Physic's wife, she was en'taining the Rector's Aid that night with husbands. That's how I come in on this. Physic, he despise card parties, so nothing was made of him not being there. We was having refreshments, and a wench who was handing round cake sort of nudge me in passing, and then look towards the door. So I santer out, feeling for my pipe, and out in the yard I find Physic and John Stagg all wet and chattering. John couldn't get Physic in the house 'thout running foul of the Rector's Aid. They wa'nt no back stair in that house.

So John, he plant a ladder against the front porch, and together we drug Physic up and over the porch roof and through a window. Made unholy noise. My wife tell me after, that the guests make out to take no notice of it, but only talk louder to drown us out. That was their politeness. All knew 'twas old Marster coming home drunk again.

Upstairs Physic was in a way. "Jehu Kingdom Come!" he was crying; "that so-and-so of a black corpus is floating out in the harbor, and when he's found, the whole story will come out! Stand by me, Ed," he say real pitiful. "Take my skiff out before sun-up; take the fifty pound anchor out of my shed, and go look for him. It won't rouse no suspicion if they see you rowing around. And when you find him, tie the anchor to him good and let go."

I say I would. Come morning, when I got down to Solomon's there was two, three men on Longcope's wharf. They say Bill Hanson done bring in a dead body before light. Bill been out to fish his net. Nobody reco'nize it for the same body in the dark. It was locked in the shed there, and word sent over to Mr. Button Billings. Inquest was called for eight o'clock. Same jury.

That was the news I had to take back to Physic. He was like a crazy man. Want to jump in his old buggy and light right out for California. I had to wrastle with him right smart. "Sure, there'll be a stink," I say, "but you got to see it through now. It'll be an all-hell stink, certain, but it'll blow over. Think of all the stinks been raised this county past ten, fifteen years. Where are they now?" So I get him quiet down some.

I take a bite breakfast Physic's house, and him and I walk down to the inquest. He muttering and cussing the whole way. "Grave robber!" he say, "that's a fatal word to put on a man! A man could never live that down! I'll see my wife and children starve by the roadside, Ed!" Then he come to stand in the road and rip out a string of cuss words. "I wouldn't mind it if anybody but that condemned old Heaven-pointer wasn't magistrate! Jehu! Jehu! it burn me up to give Button Billings the chance to exhort me!"

We was the last to get there. Magistrate and jury was standing outside the shed discussing the price fish. So we go in. Body was lying under a sheet on a door across a pair of trussles. Old Button Billings, he make a speech while Physic trem'le and cuss under his breath beside me. About myster'ous ways of Providence and the sea giving up its dead on our fair shores and all that. Button Billings was never one to scamp a period. Tournament or inquest, 'twas all one to him when he speechifying.

He say: "It's a very remarkable thing," he say; "we ain't had an inquest in three year come August and now we got two two days running! Very remarkable!" Then he say: "Let us view the remains, gentlemen," and Physic catch holt me, and whisper: "Now it's coming! now it's coming!" Mr. Button Billings take edge of the sheet and pull it down. . . .

At this point in the story Mr. Ed paused to knock the dottle out of his pipe and I was forced to ask: "Well, what happened?"

"Corpus's face was et away by crabs," Mr. Ed said casually. "It wa'nt reco'nized for the same nigger."

The body was buried on Moll Legg Island beside the other grave and a cross put at its head. However, a skeleton did eventually appear in the corner of Dr. Physic's office. "He give out he order it from a surgeons' supply house in Baltimore," said Mr. Ed, "but when I look real close I seen a suspicious nick right side his jaw bone and I remember that scar."

The Allens of Virginia

I. THE ALLENS SHOOT UP THE COURT [1]

THIRTY-SIX years have veiled and confused the story of the Allens and how the court was "shot up" on the morning of March 14, 1912, in Hills-

---

[1] From "The Fatal Doom of the Allens of Carroll County, Virginia," Part II, by Louise Jones DuBose, *Virginia and the Virginia County*, Vol. II (November–December, 1948), No. 6, pp. 15, 17, 18, 30–31. Petersburg, Virginia: Central Printing Company.

For the events leading up to and following this scene, see Louise Jones DuBose, *op. cit.*, pp. 15–18, 30–36; also, Part I, "The Fatal Doom of the Allens of Carroll County, Virginia," *Virginia and the Virginia County* (September–October, 1948), pp. 11–15, 38–46, and Part III, *ibid.* (January, 1949), pp. 23, 26–27, 34–44.

Floyd Allen survived the shooting, was tried and, with Claude, was condemned to die in the electric chair. Victor Allen was acquitted. Sidna Allen was sentenced to fifteen years in prison. In *My Oklahoma*, Vol. I (September, 1927), No. 6, pp. 30, 56, Ruby Eleanora Cummins published "An Interview with an Outlaw?" relating the Oklahoma experiences of "Sidney" Allen.

ville, seat of Carroll County. The Judge, the Commonwealth's Attorney, the Sheriff, two jurors, and a witness were killed instantly or died from their wounds.

The Allens, around whom the circumstances largely centered, had lived in the isolated mountains ever since a forefather had returned from the Revolutionary War and settled there. Through hard work and intelligence they had become probably the most prominent family in the community, with large possessions and prestige. Floyd Allen, the head of the family in 1912, had held public office and was a Democrat. Stories were told of bouts between the Allens and officials, many of whom were Republicans. There was the affair in 1904 when Floyd, refusing to go to jail for one hour, secured a pardon from the governor. Most important, however, was the "noted schoolhouse row" when Floyd's nephews, the fatherless Edwards boys, had a fight with other youths and were arrested in North Carolina by Virginia officers with no authority to cross the state line for that purpose. Floyd met the company on their way from North Carolina to the Carroll County courthouse and after a fracas on the road, several Allens with relatives and friends were indicted under twenty-odd charges. On the night of March 13, 1912, Floyd and his party waited for the jury's verdict in the third case against himself.

*   *   *   *   *

Judge Massie called for the verdict.

Floyd Allen leaned forward to listen and Judge Bolen turned his head to hear better with his good right ear.

"Guilty as charged in the indictment—one year in the penitentiary." It was signed by C. L. Howell, foreman.

The blank stillness of the next few seconds was portent, tense. Spectators waited with sudden indrawn breath.

*   *   *   *   *

"Take it easy, Floyd, there are better days ahead." Judge Bolen put out a hand toward his client's arm.

"I'm a-going to take it calm, I just hate it account of my two boys," came the reply from Floyd in even tones as he continued to stare at the clerk.

"The sheriff will take charge of the prisoner," Judge Massie announced, leaning forward on his right elbow.

Floyd caught the "arms of his chair and riz up," and his right hand began fumbling with the buttons of his sweater. His sharp eyes turned from Goad to the sheriff. Men around him began to hedge him in.

As he stood up, he paused briefly.

"Gentlemen," he said slowly, "I don't aim to go."

And the shooting began.

"It sounded like the crackling of laurel leaves somebody throwed in the fire," a man said later.

In less than a minute the horror-stricken people were fighting each other to get to the doors and windows. Black smoke from the guns filled the courtroom, threaded by spurts of flame from the mouths of the pistols. The dark day became night and a person could hardly tell friend from foe. Shrieks of terror, curses, wails from children and prayers from women intermingled with the shots. Chairs and tables and benches slammed over the floor, blocking the flight of the crowd.

The jurors, "expecting trouble," scattered like a covey of quail. One fell to his knees, crawled between the rushing stumbling bodies, and found refuge in the fire-proof vault of Clerk Goad's office. Juror Cain fell wounded in the back and leg. Faddis, fearing he would be shot into a frazzle, escaped down the stairs and ran all the way home. Another sought safety in the judge's office and found the door locked against him.

Young Attorney Floyd Landreth, attending court to observe the older members of the bar, slumped over in his chair, unaware of what was happening.

"Help me take care of my baby." A woman held the child above her head and a man stepped between her and the crowd.

At the doors leading to the outside steps, men, women and children swarmed and fell over one another.

"Let me out of here," shrieked little Bettie Ayers, who had been called as an Allen witness.

"Lord, have mercy on us," cried another.

A bit of fluff bounced from Bettie's back as she fell and was almost trampled. Somebody pulled her to her feet and she stumbled down the steps.

A. T. Howlett, witness for another case, jumped in front of his wife and baby and was shot in the back. Stout Tom Hall, proprietor of the Elliott House, was knocked down in the rush and the meat man, William Hodge, equally hefty, fell on top of him. H. K. Lindsay felt a bullet part his hair as he ran. From the offices in front and back, men rushed out, guns in hand. Deputy Quesenberry from the clerk's room pulled the trigger of his .25.

Floyd fell against Judge Bolen, knocking him down, as the bullets spat around his head, shattering the bannisters of the railing just beyond.

"Get off me, for God's sake, before they kill me shooting at you," panted the corpulent attorney.

Floyd got up, jumped over the railing and made for the door. His bullets spent, he grabbed another gun from the hands of Sidna Edwards, and shouting, "I'm shot bad," ran down the steps to the ground.

The sheriff had whirled once and slumped to the floor, a spurt from his gun pointing to the ceiling as he fell. Commonwealth Foster, his big book in one hand and a gun in the other, staggered out of the enclosure, on around the rail to the jury room, blood pouring out of the right side of his head. Judge Massie fell forward on his desk.

The shooting continued. Jurors and spectators were falling. Goad fired as he ran from his desk toward the door of his office. A bullet had hit him through his open mouth, nicked off a tooth, and passed out the back of his neck, breaking the collar button. Blood ran out of his mouth and down the back of his neck. Ten other shots struck him but without serious effect. He threw his gun down, pulled another from his pocket. It caught briefly before he jerked it loose.

Claude Allen was aiming at Goad. His uncle Sidna had paused, dropped on one knee and reloaded his revolver. They raced toward the door firing as they ran, and dodging the fire of others. They reached the ground and Sidna took refuge behind one of the white columns while he and Goad cracked at each other. Then Sidna rushed behind the monument, still firing.

Floyd had reached the street, bullets still whizzing around him. He stepped on a stone as he was about to mount his horse and his leg gave way. Sidna and another helped him in the saddle and he collapsed.

"Get a buggy," he called as the stains around his hip and knee began to cover his trousers.

He fainted again when the buggy arrived and they put him in it. They took him out and laid him on the ground near Burnett's stable, thinking he was dying.

Up in the courtroom, the smoke was clearing away as cold fresh air poured in from the open windows and doors. Daniel Thomas who had managed to escape both bullets and stampede, gazed about the blood shottened shambles. Judge Bolen lumbered to his feet. Deputy Quesenberry pocketed his .25. Only the three were left in the courtroom besides the dead and wounded.

Sheriff Webb lay flat on his back, a tooth pick protruding from half opened lips. Thomas and Bolen picked him up, stretched him out on a table. They felt for a heartbeat. But the sheriff was gone. No use trying to do anything for him.

Above them Judge Massie, slumped over, stirred feebly. Thomas mounted the platform, caught hold of the judge's shoulders, and tried to raise him.

"I'm dying—I'm dying—Sidna Allen shot me—give me a drink," he moaned, gasping.

By that time Judge Bolen had reached him.

"Go get a doctor," he ordered and Thomas ran out for a physician.

Other men had begun to filter into the courtroom, from the offices and from the street.

The judge cried out again in agony, "My wife—my wife—"

Somebody put a pillow under his head, snatched from the hands of a frightened girl who had come running from the Thornton House next door. The doctor arrived and administered a hypodermic.

"Tell my brother to take care of my wife and children," Judge Massie panted as he went limp.

"He's dead," the doctor said. A bullet had passed through his lungs, in addition to other wounds.

They turned to the other injured, two jurors and three spectators. They lifted them from the floor and made their way down to the street.

Back in the jury room behind the clerk's desk, Commonwealth Foster lay on a couch, his head resting on his big book. His clothing was beginning to stiffen with the blood that dripped from his head. His automatic had fallen to the floor. Mrs. Foster rushed in, surrounded by others, and just as she reached the attorney, he breathed his last, never regaining consciousness nor knowing she was there. They picked him up and a handful of bullets fell from his pockets. Somebody took charge of the gun, passed it to another, and they examined it.

The Judge and the Commonwealth Attorney were dead. The sheriff was dead, Bettie Ayers was to die the next day, and Juror Fowler, the day after that.

Out in the rain Floyd Allen still lay prostrate on the ground. Victor Allen, Mrs. Edwards, and Byrd Marion stood over him, not knowing whether the next breath would be his last. One bullet had entered the upper part of his leg and another, from a .25 like Quesenberry had used, had pierced his shin bone. The bone had held together until he had turned his ankle on a stone as he tried to mount his horse. Then it had broken and he had fainted the first time.

"This thing hurts me—I've always tried to do right." Victor spoke slowly and shook his head as he gazed down at his father and began to realize the enormity of the day's tragedy.

Floyd rousing briefly, said, "I made peace with my God about seven years gone—methinks I see him now," and a voice from the crowd that had gathered around him came back, "No—it's the devil that you see."

II. CLAUDE ALLEN [2]

Claude Al-len, he— and his dear old pap-py—— Have met their fat - al doom— at— last. Their friends are— glad— their trou-ble's end-ed—— And hope their souls— are now at rest.—

---

[2] From *Folk Music of the United States,* Album 7, "Anglo-American Ballads," edited

Claude Allen was that tall and handsome,
  He still had hopes until the end
That he'll some way or other
  Escape his death from the Richmond
  pen.

The governor being so hard-hearted,
  Not caring what his friends might say,
He finally took his sweet life from him.
  In the cold, cold ground his body lay.

Claude Allen had a pretty sweetheart,
  She mourned the loss of the one she
  loved.
She hoped to meet beyond the river,
  Her fair young face in heaven above.

Claude's mother's tears was gently flowing,
All for the one she loved so dear.

It seemed no one could tell her troubles,
  It seemed no one could tell but her.

How sad, how sad, to think of killin'
  A man all in his youthful years,
A-leaving his old mother weepin'
  And all his friends in bitter tears.

Look up on yonder lonely mountain,
  Claude Allen sleeps beneath the
  clay.
No more you'll hear his words of mercy
  Or see his face till Judgment Day.

Come all young boys, you may take
  warning.
  Be careful how you go astray,
Or you may be like poor Claude Allen
  And have this awful debt to pay.

Floyd Collins

. . . A young man named Floyd Collins, a native of the hills a few miles north of the Mammoth [Cave], had long been a confirmed "spelunker," or cave bug. Near his home a man named Edwards had discovered in 1915 the beautiful Great Onyx Cave. In December, 1917, Collins, crawling into a hole near his home, unearthed a network of passages with some fine formations and at least one large hall or dome, which, after much mental travail, he named Great Crystal Cavern. He explored five or six miles in it, and from that time forward, he was an addict. The present writer knows the feeling.

His cave at the time was so far off any traveled road that he couldn't lure visitors to it. So he continued in his spare time to prowl into sinks and lateral holes in the glen to southward, hoping either to find a great new

by B. A. Botkin. Record No. AAFS 35B. Washington, D. C.: Archive of American Folk Song, Library of Congress, 1943.
  Sung with guitar by Hobart Smith, Saltville, Virginia. Recorded by Alan Lomax.
  For texts and notes, including the ballad of "Sidney Allen," see *Folk-Songs from the Southern Highlands,* collected and edited by Mellinger Edward Henry (New York, 1938), pp. 316–320. For a historical note on the "courthouse massacre," see *Folksongs of Mississippi and Their Background,* by Arthur Palmer Hudson (Chapel Hill, North Carolina, 1936), p. 242.—B. A. B.

From *"Weep No More, My Lady,"* by Alvin F. Harlow, pp. 407–411. Copyright, 1942, by Alvin F. Harlow. New York and London: Whittlesey House, McGraw-Hill Book Company, Inc.

cave or another entrance to the Mammoth. (L. J. Procter, manager of the Mammoth Cave during the Civil War, after he lost that position, bought a cave three or four miles south of the Mammoth entrance, named it Procter's Cave, and spent the rest of his life in exploring it, trying to find a connection with the Mammoth, but in vain. This cave contains some fine formations, a subterranean river and one of the largest underground rooms, yet to the present-day public it is wholly unknown.)

Eight years after Collins had located his Crystal Cavern, he found along-side the Cave City-Mammoth Cave road an intriguing hole in a glen but little more than a mile, air-line distance, from Morrison's New Entrance to the Mammoth. Another curious fact is that only a mile or so east of this glen prospectors were finding oil at no great depth, though no signs of oil are seen in any of the big caves.

The low cliffs horseshoeing around this glen are sandstone, which of course is not cave rock. A deep, dry grotto extends several feet back into the sandstone, and at the left, in its floor, is an orifice from which a small passage twists downward; a strange phenomenon—a mere wormhole through a brittle rock. But Collins hoped that through it he might reach a cave in the limestone below it. He followed the passage downward in a rough spiral for 287 feet, as was determined afterward by measurement. It became so small that he could barely slide through it, feet first, and slimy with dripping water. He had almost completed a corkscrew circle and was 69 feet below the surface of the earth in front of the grotto when a loose rock shaped like a huge, fifty-pound cashew nut, jarred by his feet, slipped down over one of his ankles, locking that foot immovably. He could not reach it with his hands.

It was not unusual for him to take a lunch and stay over-night on one of these expeditions, so nobody worried about him save a crippled neighbor boy who was particularly fond of Floyd. When he did not return in twenty-four hours, this youth went to the hole, descended a little way, shouting, and presently heard an answering call from the explorer. Learning of his terrible predicament, the boy climbed out and hurried for help. Collins's brothers and neighbors rushed to the spot and tried to extricate Floyd, but found it impossible. His body filled the passage as a cork does a bottle-neck, and neither he nor anyone else could reach the rock which was locking his ankle fast. Food and drink were taken to him, though it was difficult for him to eat; and with gunnysacks they tried to protect his face from the torture of the dripping water.

His plight was discovered on Saturday morning. On Sunday the Kentucky newspapers carried items on the subject, but not until that evening did it begin to look like a big story, though the Associated Press was telling it throughout the country. On Monday even New York was reading about it. Sunday night the Louisville papers rushed reporters and photographers to the scene, and the great build-up began. It was a classic example of the power of the press to create heroes and martyrs out of obscure and unimportant material.

The Governor decided that troops were needed at the spot, and sent a detachment of militia. An oil operator, who had wells near by, suggested drilling a shaft from the surface down to Collins, offering the use of a rig for the purpose. A quarryman wanted to widen the passageway down to Collins. Meanwhile the brothers conceived the desperate expedient of fastening a rope to a harness around Floyd's upper body and dragging him out of the trap by main force. But when it was tried, he screamed with pain and cried that he would rather die than have his foot torn off. Another idea was to slip a crowbar alongside his body until it touched the rock that was holding his foot, and then try to move it with a jack set against the other end. This, too, failed.

Five days after he was trapped, there was a small cave-in in the hole—luckily no other person was down there with Collins at the moment—which thereafter blocked access to him. And then drilling was begun, after a hasty survey, just in front of the grotto. Collins had for the most part remained cheerful and hopeful up to that time, but now, although his voice could still be heard past the obstruction in the hole, he gradually relapsed into gloomy silence. The diggers at first had nothing to encounter but earth washed into the glen from the adjacent slopes. Then they struck rock. Electric wires had been strung and lights placed for night work. Sixteen men worked at high pressure, an hour on and an hour off. Meanwhile, great city newspapers were running long articles every day, with photographs, and the crowds daily grew larger. People were coming from other States to slog and slither through mud down into the ravine, often in cold rain or snow flurries, to stare morbidly at the gloomy hole, enchanted for them by the thought of a human enduring hideous and probably fatal torture in its depths. Refreshment stands and peddlers sprang up to minister to their wants. A fake Collins appeared in Kansas, sold his story to a writer, and was jailed.

Hard Shell and Holy Roller preachers ranted and prayed. Persons went through the crowd, making collections, "to buy food and supplies for the volunteer workers trying to rescue Floyd," and it is charged that some of them were unauthorized and that no little of the money garnered stuck to their fingers. Adjutant General Denhardt of the State militia was charged with "running it into politics," trying to further his gubernatorial aspirations. On the second Sunday it was estimated that there were 10,000 cars and 50,000 people as near as they could get to the spot. The road from there back to Cave City was immovably blocked with automobiles. People left them and walked for miles, trying, often vainly, to get near enough to peer into the gulch.

Soon after that, Collins ceased to answer his rescuers. It took the drillers eleven days to get down to him, and long before that time elapsed, he was dead. When they broke into the cavity near him, a coroner's jury went down, one by one, thrusting a candle through a crevice to peer at his head, some putting a hand through to touch it. A doctor on the jury thought he had been dead four or five days. It was then seventeen days after his accident. There had been much wrangling towards the end. Some said they should have continued trying to pull him out the way he went in. One man was even accused of killing Floyd. And now, after they had reached him, what were they to do? There seemed nothing else but to leave him where he was; and so the shaft was filled up.

Meanwhile, vaudeville offers had been pouring in on Floyd's father and his two brothers, and they signed up, to shamble on the stage and tell to packed houses in their backwoods dialect the story of Floyd's life and death. Homer, one of the brothers, made the worst deal. His contract called for $500 a week, but of this he received only $50 and his expenses; the slick promoter who put him over got the rest. Old man Collins did better; he had a larger stipend, and after each of his talks, he was permitted to take a collection from the audience, "to pay the expenses of the effort to save Floyd."

Now earning undreamed-of money, the Collins family yearned to recover Floyd's body. There might even be commercial possibilities in it. They employed some coal miners from western Kentucky for a fee of $3,000 to dig out the rubble thrown into the shaft, cut the rocks around the body, and bring it forth. But in what condition! It had been nine weeks since he died. Rats had eaten off the ears and a part of the face, and decay had set in. When the poor remnant was brought to an undertaker's shop in Cave City, the odor almost drove the population out of town. After three days the morticians got it into some sort of preserved condition, and in a glass-windowed coffin, it was placed in the great room—the "Floyd Collins Memorial Hall"—of Crystal Cavern, where you may shock yourself with a glance at it, if you wish. This deponent denied himself the pleasure, having been told that it looks like nothing human. Even today, sixteen years after the tragedy, people frequently come into the post office at Cave City and ask, "Where can we see Floyd Collins?" The cave and its wonders do not matter greatly to them.

Black Gold

IF IT's a story of courage you want, glorious unreasoning courage, the kind that almost transcends human understanding—then listen to the tale of Black Gold, the one they called the little black horse. It's the story of a gallant heart. It's been written before and it'll be written again and it'll be told and retold wherever horsemen gather, for it forms one of the most glamorous pages in the saga of the horse world. It begins . . .

Useeit was a wispy mare; she wasn't very big and she didn't look like much of a horse at all. Her father, Bonnie Joe, had been a good horse, but

"The Little Black Horse," by Quentin Reynolds. From *Collier's*, The National Weekly, Vol. 94 (August 11, 1934), No. 6, pp. 9, 47–48. Copyright, 1934, by the Crowell Publishing Co. New York.

somewhere back of him there had been a break in the thoroughbred chain, so Useeit had a streak of "cold blood" in her. It may have been that cold blood which gave Useeit and later her son Black Gold a certain toughness and hardiness not usually given to thoroughbreds.

Al Hoots owned Useeit and Al used to ride the mare through the canyons and across the mesas of Oklahoma. Al was a true son of the plains. He was at home when he led Useeit over the sandstone ledges north of the Okmulgee River. He was at home trotting Useeit over the big salt plain of the Cimarron, and the trackless prairies north of the Arkansas were open books to Al.

But most of all he was at home in the country of the Osage, the Pawnee and the Choctaw, and it may have been because, as many claimed, Al was part Indian himself. Certainly he and Useeit were adopted children of the Osage tribe, for the Indians love a fast horse and a good rider—and Useeit and Al were that.

Now in the Indian country of Oklahoma they have horse races that are unlike any other horse races in the world. Usually they are short races and held on the flatness of the nearest plain. They throw a blanket on the ground and that is the starting post. They throw another blanket on the ground perhaps a half a mile away and the horse that reaches there first wins the race. The braves always ride their own horses and there is no such thing as a handicap of weight. Al Hoots was not very heavy and he could ride like the devil. Many a time in his travels Al and Useeit would come to an Indian settlement and always they'd a new horse there which they thought would beat Useeit. Al would grin, lead Useeit to the starting blanket and then ride the eyeballs out of those mustangs. This was back in 1916.

They couldn't beat Useeit—so they adopted the little mare with the sleepy eyes and the twinkling hoofs. So it was that Useeit became known as an Osage horse and to this day the tribe claims her and her son as its own.

Then Al would take Useeit from county fair to county fair; from small race track to small race track and Al and the mare became known all over Oklahoma. Useeit was Al's one-horse stable, his meal ticket and his life. One day he entered Useeit in a claiming race, but when the race was over and a bidder appeared Al couldn't part with the mare. He led Useeit away from the track and according to the tenets of the horse world Al was in disgrace and he and the mare were ruled off the Oklahoma turf. You see, in a claiming race if a bidder appears you are forced to sell. The Osage tribe still insists that Al was framed in that race. In any case, he couldn't part with Useeit.

There was a great bond between these two, for each was everything to the other. They had bunked together in the tall grass of the prairies and had watched the miracle of a cool dark night extinguish the mad redness of a late afternoon sun. Oh, but these two were friends indeed—the solemn-eyed wisp of a pony and the laughing-eyed Al Hoots.

And that's why he couldn't give up Useeit to the bidder who had appeared. That's why he led Useeit home to the small house and bit of property which he and his wife Rosa owned. That's why Al Hoots ceased to be a wanderer, ceased to be a laughing caballero of the plains. Useeit grew older and suddenly the thought came to Al that some day the mare would die. She should not die, he decided, without leaving some tangible monument to her greatness. A son or daughter should carry on after her.

He took the mare to Colonel Bradley's farm over in Kentucky and bred the mare to a great stallion—Black Tony.

Now Al had a new interest in life. He talked of nothing but the foal that was to be born to Useeit. Things weren't going very well with the Hoots family, and then to make it worse Al fell ill. That strange intuition given to the dying told him that he would never rise from his bed. But he did want to live until the foal was born.

"If I die before it comes," he'd whisper to Rosa, "never sell it. That foal will bring you luck."

"Hush, Al," Rosa would soothe, "you're not going to die."

Al would smile weakly and then murmur, "The foal will bring you luck, Rosa." Then one day his smile became fixed and Rosa knew that he was dead.

Despair gripped her and the future looked black. All she had was the aging Useeit and her expected foal. Then the youngster was born, a tiny black mite of horseflesh with spindly legs, and the heart of Rosa must have been heavy. This looked to be a sorry luck piece. But still it was a lovable thing which lacked the shyness of most foals and it seemed sturdy enough despite the thin stems on which it stood. Rosa wondered what to name it.

Then a kindly fate, thinking perhaps that Rosa Hoots had known enough poverty, enough heartaches, enough misfortune, decided to take a hand in the game. An oil prospector appeared from nowhere, did mysterious things with mysterious instruments to the land which was owned by Rosa Hoots, and then stepped back as a roaring black cascade gushed forth from the dark red loam of the Oklahoma earth.

They call oil black gold in Oklahoma. As Rosa Hoots watched the gusher springing forth, she wasn't seeing oil, she was seeing gold. This was in 1920 and it was easy to translate oil into gold. There was so little of the former and so much of the latter. Rosa Hoots watched them harness this stream of oil, tame it so that it flowed more gently into tanks, and she remembered the dying words of her husband, "The foal will bring you luck."

She named it Black Gold.

Mrs. Hoots was wealthy now and she bedecked herself with jewels and she sent to Paris for her frocks. Mrs. Hoots was wealthy now and she could have hired the best-known horse trainers in the land to care for the spindly foal. But she was the wife of Al Hoots and she hired, instead, Harry Webb, an old friend of Al's, who, like him, was part Indian. Now Harry knew horses as only Indians and gypsies and the Irish know horses. Harry didn't believe in coddling a horse. A horse, Harry thought, was like a child. First you've got to make a horse (or a child) obey you. Then it respects you and if you have been wise in its rearing it finally gets to love you.

Black Gold grew up in the Oklahoma pastures just as the Indian horses did. Black Gold shuddered in the cold and the rain of winter nights and Black Gold thrived under the burning sun of summer days. Even as a youngster the little black horse galloped long miles over rough pasture land and over uneven country roads.

In 1923 Black Gold was two years old and it was time for him to enter the lists. His first start in fast company was the Bashford Manor Stakes at Churchill Downs and it was fitting that he win that one, for later he was to write his name indelibly in the history of that lovely old Louisville track. Yes, he won that one all right and the experts were a bit surprised. You see, Black Gold then didn't look so much. He was so small and he didn't have that well-groomed, sleek appearance which characterized the youngsters which ran for the Whitneys, for Colonel Bradley, for Widener or the Vanderbilts. But they pay off on speed once that barrier is sprung— not on looks.

Black Gold did all right as a two-year-old but of course the test didn't come until a year later. Then Webb shipped him to the Louisiana Derby. It was a rainy day and the mud was fetlock deep as the horses went to the post. The rain slanted into the eyes of the horses and the high-strung thoroughbreds were jittery. The wind was cold and it sent sharp chills up their legs and the chills made them the more nervous. Black Gold just stood there. This sort of weather was an old story to him. He'd slept in open pastures many a night when the weather was worse than this. He stood there— and then the barrier was sprung and he was a black phantom. He won as a great horse should win—going away.

Harry Webb was now satisfied that he had a great race horse in his care. The greatness of the little black horse began to be bruited about the land. Wherever horsemen gathered they discussed Black Gold and his chances of winning the Kentucky Derby, but most of all they discussed the little black horse in the Osage country.

Now in many respects the Kentucky Derby is the world's greatest horse race. There are others which pay the winner more but none has the color, the tradition and the carnival air of America's greatest classic. The race is as American as the bourbon whisky they put in the mint juleps which Colonel Matt Winn and Colonel Phil Chinn serve to favored visitors at a Derby breakfast. There are those who say that it is only an imitation of the English Derby, but that is nonsense. It isn't even pronounced "Darby," as is the English classic, except by a few teacup-balancing, racing dilettantes who attend just because they know that the photographers from the Sunday papers will be on hand. To your Kentuckian it's the Derby and it's called Derby, and two years ago when Lord Derby, sponsor of the English event, attended they taught him to call it Derby—just like that, just as it's spelled. But it doesn't matter—we're talking of a little black horse and of a bright sunny day—May 15, 1924.

White clouds hang lazily in a deep blue sky. Hardly a wisp of breeze ruffles the big American flag that hangs atop the gabled tower over the grandstand at Churchill Downs. Ninety-five thousand people have come to pay homage to the thoroughbreds and to help Kentucky celebrate the golden anniversary of its great race.

Mrs. Rosa Hoots, bedecked with jewels and with orchids on her shoulder, sits in her box and not a sign of emotion shows on her face.

Nineteen beautiful bundles of nerves and sinews prance out to the track and the crowd roars a welcome. Garner, Fator, Sande, A. Johnson, Pony McAtee, McDermott, Mooney—the best jockeys in the land—are crouching over the necks of their horses, whispering into the ears of their horses, calming the nerves of their horses.

The crowd has been roaring but now a band leader lifts his baton and an overpowering silence settles over the stands. Then the almost unbearably sweet strains of My Old Kentucky Home hang in the still air and you find that your hands are trembling and you feel a lump in your throat. This lovely lament should never be played anywhere but in Kentucky, and it should be borne to you only on a blue-grass-scented Kentucky breeze. It is more than a song—it is a prayer and an expression of pride by Kentuckians who love their native soil.

The horses prance a bit nervously. The crowd hums, then softly sings the song. Many a tear is trembling on quivering eyelids. It's a song that creeps into your blood; that twists your heart but that withal makes you feel proud somehow. You can only understand when you've seen a Derby and heard the Derby crowd sing the song with soft voices.

Black Gold is on the rail and, strange to say, he's nervous. Jockey Mooney growls, "Easy, easy, boy." Altawood, Klondike, Baffling, Mr. Mutt, Transmute, Bracadale, Thorndale, the light-footed Chilhowee, the well-thought-of Beau Butler, and nine others are finally ready.

Then, "Now—come on," Starter Billy Snyder roars and his cry is echoed by a mighty "They're off" from the packed stands and the infield crowd. As though by prearrangement a brisk wind springs out of the east and whips the flag over the grandstand into a dancing frenzy. It is a good start but the astute Sande has Bracadale of the Rancocas Stable out in front. We know his strategy. He wants to kill off the field so that Mad Play, the No. 1 Rancocas entry, can breeze in. They pass the stand and Albert Johnson on Chilhowee goes after Bracadale. Black Gold is fifth, well placed inside, ready for anything but not making his bid yet.

They're around the turn now and running in the far stretch opposite the stands. Through your glasses you see Sande going to his whip. Bracadale is feeling the pace. Through your glasses you see the old rose silks which Useeit once raced under moving up as Jockey Mooney gives Black Gold his head. He's outside where he won't be interfered with but Mooney isn't making his real bid even yet.

They reach the far turn and Sande looks back for a moment out of

desperate eyes hoping to see the brown nose of Mad Play. Instead he sees
Chilhowee and Beau Butler. Now they're halfway around the turn and
through your glasses you see Jockey Mooney raise his whip, then bring
it down smartly. That's no ordinary whip. Black Gold wouldn't feel the
lash of an ordinary whip. This is a leather thong weighted heavily with
buckshot—an Indian whip which calls to the blood of the Indian horse
Useeit, and that blood is coursing through the veins of this little black
horse.

Mrs. Rosa Hoots, bedecked with jewels and with orchids on her shoulder, sits in her box—and now her face is white.

They're in the stretch and again Mooney raises his whip. That whip
sends the little black horse a message. It's a message from the dead Al
Hoots and from Useeit. It says to Black Gold: "This is the destiny toward
which you have been advancing. This is the moment for which you were
born. Are you equal to your destiny?"

Does Black Gold answer the question?

Good Lord, how he answers it! He surges past Chilhowee and now you
could put a blanket over the first four horses. He lunges in front of Altawood and he's even with Bracadale and destiny is just one furlong away.
He must be tired but you'd never know it—he's running truly, steadily,
as a great horse should run. His heart is pounding, for the pace has been
fast, but it's a heart that can stand plenty of pounding. "Black Gold!"
the roar comes from ninety-five thousand throats and it tempers the thunder of the pounding hoofs.

Mrs. Rosa Hoots, bedecked with jewels and with orchids on her shoulder,
sits in her box. She sits in her box and her right hand is clenched and perhaps she's clasping the ghostly hand of Al Hoots. And tears are rolling
unashamed down the white face of Rosa Hoots and perhaps it's because she
and she alone is hearing a celestial murmur, faint but proud, calling "Black
Gold," and the voice is the voice of the man in whose mind this little black
horse was conceived nearly four years before.

Then the black phantom flashes across the line with the other horses
chasing him. Al's baby has pounded home in front. He trots back to the
stewards' stand; Mooney twirls his whip and tosses it to Harry Weber;
the crowd is still roaring its adulation of the little horse. They lead the
little black horse into that sacred green-blanketed enclosure in front of
the stands—the enclosure that is entered only by Derby winners.

Maybe Black Gold is thinking: "So you ruled my mother off the track,
hey? You stewards, with your high and mighty airs. She was an Indian
pony, was she? Well, what's wrong with being an Indian pony? There's
cold blood in me, is there? Well, I've licked all your hot-blooded horses.
I've . . ."

Rosa Hoots has her right arm around the neck of the little black horse.
Rosa Hoots kisses the soft sheen of the neck of the little horse. Black
Gold turns his head and rests it on her shoulder. Is he whispering,
"Wouldn't Al be proud of us if he were here now?"

But Rosa Hoots is weeping and something is clutching at the hearts of those who watch. You feel as though you have lived through a perfect moment—that one matchless note has emerged from the usually discordant symphony of life. Then they lead Black Gold away. They lead him away still wearing that horseshoe of roses around his neck.

Shortly after the Kentucky race Black Gold went on further to establish his greatness by winning both the Ohio and Chicago Derbies. Then Mrs. Hoots retired him and again he roamed in the open pastures of Oklahoma. It was as though his retirement was a signal for fate to withdraw the kindly hand which had guided the Hoots destinies since the death of Al. The roses of that horseshoe had hardly turned to dust when the blow fell. The details are unimportant. Perhaps the magic spring of black gold that had been gushing forth from the red loam in a seemingly inexhaustible stream spent itself. Bad investments, bad luck, helped and Mrs. Hoots no longer wore orchids on her shoulder. With the same miraculous swiftness that her fortune had come it was swept away. Black Gold and Rosa Hoots were alone now and the friends of the glorious days were nowhere to be found.

It was 1927 and Black Gold was almost seven years old. He was still sturdy, steel-sinewed. Rosa Hoots looked at him prancing in the pasture, looked at the sturdiness of him and looked into the honest eyes of him. She made her decision. Black Gold had brought her luck once. Perhaps he would do it again.

Faithful Harry Webb was again called for. He shipped the little horse to New Orleans, scene of his first great triumph. There was great interest in the comeback of Black Gold. Webb, pointing for the rich Coffroth Handicap, intended starting Black Gold in a few tune-up races. The public was dubious. It was shown when Black Gold was quoted at 200 to 1 for the Coffroth event in the winter books.

Black Gold was to open his campaign in the fifth race at the New Orleans Fair Grounds on January 18, 1928. There was much shaking of heads among the horsemen at the track. "Black Gold doesn't work right. . . . The black horse limps a bit. . . . Seems to have a sore left foreleg. . . ."

Nine horses were at the barrier that day ready to race for the Salome Purse. Black Gold would have run this field dizzy four years before—but now? He was seven years old, middle age on the track.

Then they were off. The crowd arose instinctively as Black Gold flung himself from the barrier a stride ahead of the field. He still had his early speed, anyway. But they had to go a mile. Jockey Emory steadied him. Around the track they went, closely bunched, with Black Gold running easily. They rounded the far turn and then they were at the post which told the jockeys they had one more furlong to go.

Jockey Emory went to his whip. A single lash of that same heavily weighted whip and Black Gold trembled. He was being asked the question again just as he had been asked before, in the Kentucky Derby. Polygamia was leading and the little black horse was in sixth place only a length behind the leader.

He plunged forward as the field passed the grandstand. Every nerve and sinew and muscle of him was being urged ahead by the heart of him. More speed. Another lash of that whip. Then—there was a shocked cry from the crowd. Black Gold had stumbled, had almost gone down, had recovered himself. His left foreleg had seemed to buckle for a moment. It had thrown him off stride, but now he was after the leaders again.

From the grandstand you only saw that his stride was uncertain. You couldn't see the agonized look in his eyes, nor could you hear the mighty beat of the greatest heart they ever put in the body of a horse. You couldn't see him quiver under Jockey Emory—you couldn't see him surge forward, stumbling a bit now, swaying a bit now, but surging forward none the less. He would finish. That was his destiny, to finish as best he could. The crowd, sensing tragedy, was silent. Black Gold faltered across the line and for the moment no one knew that he had gained immortality.

Then he swayed. His left foreleg slowly gave way. He fell and then as the heart of him screamed to his nerves and his muscles to rise he tried to struggle to his feet. Harry Webb rushed to him, looked at the left foreleg and his face went white and in his eyes there was a look of disbelief. Black Gold had run that last furlong with a broken leg. The crowd realized it now. It knew it had seen such courage as it is the privilege of few to see.

Harry Webb looked into the eyes of the little black horse. There was a faint bewilderment in them. They were asking Harry, "I tried but I failed you. Why? What has happened to me?"

Webb had to steel himself. Webb couldn't break down now. He had a duty toward this horse which he had seen as a foal, had raised as a yearling, had trained to greatness. A single shot rang out.

The racing papers carry the results of the races in simple, terse language. The racing papers of May 18, 1928, told the story of the fifth race at New Orleans. The last paragraph read, "Black Gold showed early speed. Was in fifth place when broke left foreleg in final furlong. Was destroyed."

That was his epitaph. They buried Black Gold there in the infield of the track at the Fair Grounds. That's a long way from Oklahoma.

Well, that's the story of the little black horse.

Aunt Molly Jackson's First Song

YES, I'm fifty-nine, goin' on sixty now, and I've had a turrible sight of trouble in my life. First thing, my paw sold his farm to my grandpaw,

From *"Weep No More, My Lady,"* by Alvin F. Harlow, pp. 243–247. Copyright, 1942, by Alvin F. Harlow. New York and London: Whittlesey House, McGraw-Hill Book Company, Inc.

Anything that touched my heart, I liked to compose a poem or song about it, and since then I have composed quite a few more songs. I composed one one morning in Harlan County when fifteen children went to a soup kitchen in the field. I recognized the voice of Flossie, my sister's child. Blood was coming down through their toes in

and went down into a coal minin' camp and started a store; trusted
ever'body hither and yon, and lost ever'thing he had.

That was when I was about twelve or thirteen, and in the fall of the
ye'r, I went up to stay with my grandpaw and grandmaw a while. Hit was
sorter lonesome up thar for a young-un, and come Christmas, hit seemed a
heap worse. I'd allus been used to bein' around with chillern at Christmas
time, a-frolickin' and havin' fun. We never had no money to spend, but
we had a good time; and up at Grandpaw's with Christmas comin' on and
no young folks in the house, I was lonesome enough to die. Hit seemed
turrible to have Christmas go by, and no pleasurin'. I thought, What kin I
do? and finally, I says, I'll dress up comical and go over to Bill Lewis's
house and have some fun with the young-uns over thar. Bill Lewis—
Straight-Back Bill, we called him—lived a couple o' miles away and had a
whole passel o' chillern.

They was a pair of old Eastern jeans pants of Grandpaw's—

(Query: Eastern jeans? Aunt Molly explains that is was home-made
jeans; the kind they wove on the old home-built looms in some mountain
cabins. But why "Eastern"? Aunt Molly ponders this, but can't think
of any explanation, unless it was because it was made in Eastern Kentucky.
Ef that ain't right, she can't say no more.)

Well, I tuck them old jeans pants and cut 'em off so they was short
enough fur me; and I put on an old coat of Grandpaw's with the sleeves
turnt up and a sorter derby plug felt hat of his'n, and I smeared bacon
grease and sut out o' the chimbly on my face, so I was black like a nigger;
and then I tuck a pig-rifle that was hangin' on the wall—

(A pig-rifle? Yes, they called it that because they shot wild hogs with
it sometimes, she reckons.)

—I tuck that rifle and went over to Bill Lewis's, and got up on a stump
in front of the house and danced around, p'intin' the gun this way and that
and hollerin', "Kin you tell me how to git to Manchester?" and some other
foolishness. Now, them chillern o' Bill Lewis's hadn't never seen no
niggers, and hit skeered 'em to death. They run ever' which way, and
some of 'em, even growed-up gals, run and hid behind corn-shocks in the
field; and one little six-ye'r-old boy was so skeert, he fell down in a faint.

I put out fur home, and old Bill Lewis follered me till he was shore who
I was. That was a Sat'day evenin' and he couldn't do nothin' then; but
a Monday mornin' he went to town and got out a writ again me fur
dis-guise.

the rain. Why are these children so naked in the cold rain? Some of these children
haven't had anything to eat since day before yesterday. My stepson said to me, "Ma,
they are very low in the soup kitchen. Could you make me gravy and corn pone instead of going to the soup kitchen?" I sang of the exact situation and surroundings
and how I felt at that time, in "Miners' Wives' Ragged, Hungry Blues." I mobilized
women and children. I led the way into the mines singing the "Hungry Blues" and
said I would stay in the mines. Today conditions are better than when I composed
the song.—Aunt Molly Jackson, at Folk Literature Craft Session, Third American
Writers' Congress, New York, June 4, 1939.

Now, *dis*-guise was a turrible thing down thar in them days; the law was plumb down on it. A man that lived near my grandpaw come ridin' up in a hurry that day and told us about the writ. So my grandpaw started right away, without losin' a minute, and tuck me away over on Big Sexton, in the next county, where some of our kin lived, me ridin' behind him on a horse. Hit tuck us nigh a day and a half, and I remember 'twas a cold rain part of the time, and I got wet to the skin and mighty nigh froze. I stayed thar with my kinfolks fur three weeks. The courts found out I was gone, and didn't even send out fur me. But my grandpaw didn't know what was goin' on in town, and in three weeks he come fur me.

"I think it's all blowed over," he says, "so you can come on home with me. Your grandmaw needs you," he says, "fur getherin' up the eggs and he'pin' around the house," he says. "I don't believe you'll have no trouble."

But he was wrong. The very next day atter I got home, Alphus Cotton, a deputy, rid up with the writ and tuck me down to Manchester—that was the county seat—and tuck me before Judge Wright.

Now, Judge Wright had married a cousin of my paw's. He ast me, he says, "Molly, did you do what they say you done?" and I says, "Yes," I says, "but I didn't mean no harm by it. Hit was Christmas and I was lonesome, and I jest wanted to have a little fun. I think Mr. Lewis done a mighty sorry thing," I says, "when he had a girl like me arrested fur a little thing like that."

"I think so, too," he says. "But now that he's done it and you've confessed," he says, "I gotta do my duty. *Dis*-guise is a ser's crime," he says. "The least sentence I kin give you is twenty-five dollars fine and ten days in jail."

I says, "Judge, do you mean to tell me you're goin' to disgrace my whole gineration?[1] You know good and well," I says, "they hain't none o' my gineration ever been inside a jail-house, and I don't want to be the first one."

"Hit's either that," he says, "or if you have a reg'lar trial before a jury, they'll send you to reform school till you're twenty-one."

Now, the jailer, Bill Cundiff, he'd married another cousin of my paw's, and he come around and says to me, kinder quiet, "Never mind, Molly," he says. "You jest come on around and stay with your Cousin Bem and me, and we'll purtend like you was in jail," he says. "You kinder keep out o' sight when folks come in, and nobody'll know the difference." You see, the co't house and the jail and the jailer's livin' rooms was all in the same buildin'. And he says, "Maybe we can take up a collection and raise that twenty-five dollars."

Well, finally I give up and went with Cundiff, but I didn't like it. I tuck a notion that if I acted crazy, maybe they'd let me off sooner. So I mussed up my ha'r and talked foolish, and Miss Cundiff says to her

---

[1] Family or breed.—A. F. H.

husband, s'she, "They hain't never been no idjits in the Garland gin-eration," she says, "but ef this gal hain't a plumb fool, then I never seen one."

That made me sorter mad in spite of myse'f, and I says, "You gimme a pencil and paper, ef ther is sech a thing, and I'll show you how much of a idjit I am," I says. "I'm goin' to write a song about this." And so I wrote out the words and I composed the music, and when I sung it to Cundiff, he was so tickled that he says, "I'm goin' to git the judge and a passel of other men here to hear ye sing that song," he says, "and I bet we'll raise that money fur ye."

So on a Sunday mornin, hyer was the judge and the shur'ff and the county clerk and all the officials thar in Cundiff's kitchen. There was a cell right next to the kitchen and a door with a bar acrost it, and Cundiff says to me, "You git inside that cell before they come, and shet the door, but I won't lock it," he says. "We've got to make like you was in jail, you know," he says. "And you sing through the bars, and after they're gone, you kin jest open the door and walk out agin."

Now, in them days, I was like many another gal in the mountain—I chewed tobacker. I've quit it long since, though I do take a few draws on an old pipe once in a while. But when I stood thar, lookin' through the bar, I says, "I hain't goin' to sing nare word unless every man gives me a dime and a plug o' Cup-Greenville tobacker." We called it Cup-Greenville because ther' was a tincup-like on every plug. Hit was black tobacker, strong and sweet—lot's o' licuish in it. I seen the men begin takin' out ther' knives and ther' tobacker plugs; and this hyer is the song I sung to 'em:

> The day before Christmas I had some fun;
> I blacked my face and took my gun.
> I went up to Bill Lewis's and made 'em run.
> Mr. Cundiff, I wisht you'd turn me loose.
>
> The next Monday mornin' Bill Lewis got out a writ.
> When I found it out, the wind I split.
> Jest three weeks more till I come back to Clay;
> Alphus Cotton arrested me the very next day.
>
> Then I thought my case would be light.
> Cotton tuck me before Judge Wright.
> Judge Wright told me I had done wrong
> Fur blackin' my face and puttin' britches on.
>
> He listened to me till I told my tale,
> And give me ten days in Cundiff's jail.
> When I went in jail, they thought I was a fool;
> They did not offer me as much as a stool.
>
> But old Miss Cundiff treated me kind
> Because she thought I had no mind.
> Now, what she thought I did not care;
> I knowed I was jest as smart as her.

So ther's no use to cry and snub
While I'm a-eatin' old Cundiff's grub;
Though very much better I could do,
If Cundiff would furnish me tobacker to chew.

Although I'm healthy, young and stout,
If I cain't git tobacker, I kin do without.
Well, Mr. Cundiff, ef you'll open your door,
I won't put my britches back on no more.

The old hymn book is layin' on the shelf;
Ef you want any more, you kin sing it yourself.

Well, sir, before I was through with that jail sentence, I'd got a dozen plugs o' Greenville and thirty-seven dollars in money, and my grandpaw says, "Molly, I never was so proud of ye since y'was born." And that's how I begin makin' up songs. I reckon I've wrote hundreds since then.

O. Henry: Drugstore Cartoonist

. . . WHEN O. Henry's boyhood friends recall him it is not usually as a pupil in Miss Lina's school; nor is it as the writer in the great city. It is as the clerk in his uncle Clark Porter's drugstore on Elm Street [, Greensboro,] opposite the old Benbow Hotel. Here he was known and loved by old and young, black and white, rich and poor. He was the wag of the town, but so quiet, so unobtrusive, so apparently preoccupied that it was his pencil rather than his tongue that spread his local fame. His youthful devotion to drawing was stimulated in large part by the pictures painted by his mother. Many of these hung in the Porter home. Some were portraits and some landscapes. They were part of the atmosphere in which O. Henry was reared. One of his own earliest sketches was made when Edgeworth was burned. O. Henry was then only ten years old but the picture that he drew of a playmate rescuing an empty churn from the basement of the burning building, with the milk spilled all over him, is remembered for its ludicrous conception and for its striking fidelity to the boy and to the surroundings.

His five years in his uncle's drugstore meant much to him as a cartoonist. His feeling for the ludicrous, for the odd, for the distinctive, in speech, tone, appearance, conduct, or character responded instantly to the appeal made by the drugstore constituency. Not that he was not witty; he was. But his best things were said with the pencil. There was not a man or woman in the town whom he could not reproduce recognizably with a few strokes of a lead pencil. Thus it was a common occurrence, when Clark Porter returned to the store from lunch, for a conversation like this to take place:

From *O. Henry Biography*, by C. Alphonso Smith, pp. 80–81, 83–85, 86, 87. Copyright, 1916, by Doubleday, Page & Company. Garden City, New York.

O. Henry would say: "Uncle Clark, a man called to see you a little while ago to pay a bill." It should be premised that it was not good form in those days to ask a man to stand and deliver either his name or the amount due. "Who was it?" his uncle would ask. "I never saw him before, but he looks like this," and the pencil would zigzag up and down a piece of wrapping paper. "Oh, that's Bill Jenkins out here at Reedy Fork. He owes me $7.25."

*   *   *   *   *

After Miss Lina's school the drugstore was to O. Henry a sort of advance course in human nature and in the cartoonist's art. George Eliot tells in "Romola" of the part played in medieval Florence by the barber shop. A somewhat analogous part was played in Greensboro forty years ago by Clark Porter's drugstore. It was the rendezvous of all classes, though the rear room was reserved for the more elect. The two rooms constituted in fact the social, political, and anecdotal clearing house of the town. The patronage of the grocery stores and drygoods stores was controlled in part by denominational lines, but everybody patronized the drugstore. It was also a sort of physical confessional. The man who would expend only a few words in purchasing a ham or a hat would talk half an hour of his aches and ills or those of his family before buying twenty-five cents' worth of pills or a ten-cent bottle of liniment. When the ham or the hat was paid for and taken away there was usually an end of it. Not so with the pills or the liniment. The patient usually came back to continue his personal or family history and to add a sketch of the character and conduct of the pills or liniment. All this was grist to O. Henry's mill.

No one, I think, without a training similar to O. Henry's, would be likely to write such a story as "Makes the Whole World Kin." It is not so much the knowledge of drugs displayed as the conversational atmosphere of the drugstore in a small Southern town that gives the local flavour. A burglar, you remember, has entered a house at night. "Hold up both your hands," he said. "Can't raise the other one," was the reply. "What's the matter with it?" "Rheumatism in the shoulder." "Inflammatory?" asked the burglar. "Was. The inflammation has gone down." " 'Scuse me," said the burglar, "but it just socked me one, too." "How long have you had it?" inquired the citizen. "Four years." "Ever try rattlesnake oil?" asked the citizen. "Gallons. If all the snakes I've used the oil of was strung out in a row they'd reach eight times as far as Saturn, and the rattles could be heard at Valparaiso, Indiana, and back." In the end the burglar helps the citizen to dress and they go out together, the burglar standing treat.

*   *   *   *   *

. . . O. Henry's distinctive skill, the skill of the story teller that was to be, is seen to better advantage in his pictures of groups than in his pictures of individuals. Into the group pictures, which he soon came to prefer to any others, he put more of himself and more of the life of the community. . . .

*   *   *   *   *

. . . On the right [of one of his group pictures] is the Superintendent of the Presbyterian Sunday School. He was also a deacon and kept a curiosity shop of a store. His specialties were rabbit skins and Mason and Hamlin organs. But he made his most lasting impression on O. Henry as a dispenser of kerosene oil.

It happened in this way: the Pastor of the Presbyterian Church had always carried his empty oil can, supposed to hold a gallon, to be replenished at the Superintendent's font. But one day the Superintendent's emporium was closed and the pastoral can journeyed on to the hardware store of another deacon. "Why," said the latter, after careful measurement, "this can doesn't hold but three quarts." "That's strange," said the minister pensively; "Brother M. has been squeezing four quarts into it for twenty years." The reply went the rounds of the town at once and O. Henry, who no more doubted Brother M.'s good intentions than he did his uncle's or the sign painter's, put him promptly into the picture. . . .

Tom Wolfe Comes Home

. . . THEY brought him home, after the futile operation at Johns Hopkins, to what was, in every aspect, a Tom Wolfe chapter in a Tom Wolfe book. It will not be written.

"Only Tom's hand, reaching from the grave, could adequately chronicle that day," an Asheville woman, who knew him and understood his work, said of the funeral. "And wouldn't he have enjoyed it?"

His body lay in the old boarding-house where he had spent his boyhood. "Dixieland," he named it. The Wolfes were not poor, but his mother was, to say the very least, thrifty. It is now, as Tom said it was then, a rambling, unplanned appearing, old wooden house on a pleasant, sloping, middle-class street, close to the business section. Its back hangs over one of the mountain town's ravines. It is the same house where, Tom wrote, before his mother bought it from an evangelist who had turned to drink, one boarder had hanged himself, a tubercular had stained the floor in hemorrhage, an old man had cut his throat. The boy was ashamed of it. . . .

As pallbearer, I looked at him lying against the crinkly undertaker's satin in that Dixieland tourist home. If they had not told me, I would not have known that after he died a wigmaker had to make a wig for him to be dead in. They did tell me. They told me, also, that there had not been in Baltimore a coffin big enough for the six-foot-six length of him. The oversized one, that had to be assembled in New York, filled half the front room which was hall also of the old boarding-house. Above it there were long cracks in the yellow plaster ceiling. He was home.

"Those melancholy cracks in the yellow plaster looking down at him!"

From *Tar Heels*, A Portrait of North Carolina, by Jonathan Daniels, pp. 229–235. Copyright, 1941, by Jonathan Daniels. New York: Dodd, Mead & Company. 1947.

the woman who was his friend said. "I know he fled from those cracks, and there he lay helpless while they triumphed over him."

I am not sure. I am not even sure I know what triumph is. But in little cities in North Carolina you can see a tribe. The matriarch stood beside the coffin of the man. She was both the mother Tom put in the book and the living woman who seemed to have walked out of it. Tearless and strong, she stayed through the morning and talked, as one to whom the realities of living and dying are alike unterrifying, about the operation on Tom's brain. (It was tuberculosis, they found, which had developed in a killing rush inside his skull after what they thought on the West Coast was pneumonia.) The brothers were there, in the house where the brother Ben had died. The sister Tom loved most of all, who had nursed him across the continent on those roaring trains he loved too, was there—vigorous and talkative and overwhelmed together. She did not go to the funeral.

"I went out with a bang," she told me.

All of them were not only Wolfes, tremendously alive, native North Carolina mountain people; they were also Gants out of the book, utterly true. Tom had come home to them. Man-Dead and Man-Creating did not seem very far apart. The distinction between art and life was scarcely perceptible.

A great many flowers came from far away, but not many people. Professor Frederick H. Koch was there. Tom was one of his boys. Tom had taken his playwriting course at Chapel Hill the first two years Koch was there. . . .

* * * * *

. . . Tom liked him and at Tom's funeral he was almost desperately determined in dramatics that he must find violets to send to the funeral from the Carolina Playmakers, because Tom had mentioned violets in his first Playmakers play. Elizabeth and Paul Green tried, in vain, to help him find them.

Not many others of Tom's literary friends were there. Clifford Odets had been, I think, in Tennessee and came over the mountains. Hamilton Basso, little, able, dark Louisiana creole who lives at Brevard, was there as another pallbearer. Olive Tilford Dargan, North Carolina novelist and poet, was at home in her Asheville. Phillips Russell, biographer and Tom's friend, too, had come up from Chapel Hill. Maxwell Perkins, who had been Tom's first and great editor, stood on the edge of the funeral party like a man hurt and as lonely as the saddest spirit in Tom's books.

The rest of us were a part of Tom's native land. Three of us were pallbearers who had been with Tom on a party at my house not many months before. In my closet there's still a quarter-bottle of an American absinthe Tom had picked up in New Orleans. There were Asheville people—a few bewildered and uncertain ones, some boarders in the house, people of the big Gant-Wolfe tribe; and there were thousands who stayed away and hardly knew he was dead. But there were enough to fill the Presbyterian Church and to make it look like the funeral of a prominent local insurance man. I remember there was a smooth young preacher. We sang lusty hymns. And then there was the old preacher who knew Tom was saved because he had always come to call on him when he was in Asheville.

The coffin was heavy. There was a steep terrace up to the lot in the cemetery, and we cut the turf on it with our shoes. I remembered while we moved toward the long hole in the yellow clay that O. Henry was buried somewhere in the same cemetery and that he had looked at the mountains around us without getting an idea into his head. But Tom had been a mountain man who could see city streets as well and people in cities and in the mountains also. Perhaps he was home in both. It was a magnificent day. In the later afternoon sun there was mist on the mountains, or perhaps it was smoke from the noisy trains which run down the valley of the French Broad. Their whistles had been forever in Tom's head.

* * * * *

Afterward Paul and Elizabeth Green and Olive Tilford Dargan and I went to a restaurant and sought the biggest steak we could find.

"The size Tom would have liked," I said.

Mrs. Dargan does not eat meat, but that night she did. The steak was not big enough. We told Mrs. Dargan good-by afterward. Paul had his car and we drove all night long down the mountains, across the Piedmont to Chapel Hill. It did not seem long since Tom was there, a big popular campus philosopher and campus politician, too. He was on his way from home then. But I don't think he ever got away. Sometimes hill people cuss each other as Man-Creating or Man-Alive, but in their hearts they never hate the hills. They are home.

PART THREE

SOUTHERN STORY-TELLERS

It is a fancy of mine—although a fancy based on a considerable amount of first-hand observation— that there is a story-telling belt in this country. It starts at high-water mark on the shores of Eastern Virginia and it stretches westward through Tennessee and Kentucky, broadening out to include southern Indiana and parts of North Carolina and Georgia and Alabama, and then it bridges the Mississippi and crosses Missouri and Arkansas and invades Northern Texas, and after that it jumps the Rocky Mountains, and the glittering buckle on its other end is the city of San Francisco.

—Irvin S. Cobb

Theorizers about Southern humor have forgotten that they ever sat on creek banks, around hunters' fires, on crossroads store fronts, or on plantation-house verandahs, and listened to the "natives" yarn. In my opinion, the reason why Longstreet, Baldwin, and the lesser fry from the lower South originated something new in writing was that they had the wit to realize that something old in talking might look new in writing. For the kind of stories they told are, with due allowances for "literary" finish, exactly the kinds of stories one can hear to-day on the "front galleries" of farmhouses all over the South.

—Arthur Palmer Hudson

[Fay Ingalls:] "I don't see why they called you as a witness, [Ed]; I've always heard you are the biggest liar in Bath County."
[Ed Porter:] " 'Tain't so, Fay. Not so long as Howard McClintic lives. While he's around I'm only the second greatest."

—Fay Ingalls

It is only when our old songs and old tales are passing from one human being to another, by word-of-mouth, that they can attain their full fascination. No printed page can create this spell. It is the living word—the sung ballad and the told tale—that holds our attention and reaches our hearts.

—Richard Chase

I. YARNS AND TALL TALES

"Well, Zora, did we lie enough for you las' night?"
"You lied good but not enough," I answered.—ZORA NEALE HURSTON

1. TRAVELERS IN EDEN-LAND

As a storied region, celebrated in history and romance, the South has never lacked inspiration or material for story-telling. Ever since the first voyagers touched on its shores, the eden-land of the South has been an eden-land of the imagination, rich not only in heroic saga and memorabilia but in folk tale and anecdote. Those who came seeking wonders—explorers, colonists, and travelers—found even more than they had dreamed of, and what they did not discover they invented. As Captain John Smith wrote of Virginia, "heaven and earth never agreed better to frame a place for mans habitation." [1] And not the least among the wonders he chronicles (thus earning a place among "unnatural" natural historians) are a small fish "so like the picture of *S. George* his Dragon, as possible can be, except his legs and wings: and the To[a]defish which will swell till it be like to brust, when it commeth into the aire." [2]

As the back country was opened up and the settlers pushed west, the wonders and beauties of Virginia, the Carolinas, Florida, etc., were eclipsed by those of the "new Eldorado and Paradise for hunters." Captain Imlay, who, in early times, visited Kentucky in the spring, described it in the hyperbole that was to become the stock-in-trade of guide books and promotional literature, rivaling the tall talk and expansive eloquence of the backwoods.

Everything here assumes a dignity and splendor I have never seen in any other part of the world. Here an eternal verdure reigns and the brilliant sun piercing through the azure heavens produces in this prolific soil an early maturity truly astonishing. . . . Soft zephyrs gently breathe on sweets and the inhaled air gives a voluptuous glow of health and vigor that seems to ravish the intoxicated senses. . . . Everything here gives delight, and we feel a glow of gratitude for what an all-bountiful Creator has bestowed upon us." [3]

"So prodigal of sweetness" were the edens of the old Southwest that, according to the author of *Miami County Traditions*, "In the spring and summer months, a drove of hogs could be scented at a considerable distance from the flavor of the annis [anise] root." [4] And, speaking of animals,

---

[1] *A Map of Virginia . . .* (1612), *Travels and Works of Captain John Smith*, edited by Edward Arber and A. G. Bradley (Edinburgh, 1910), Part I, p. 48.

[2] *Ibid.*, p. 61.

[3] Charles McKnight, *Our Western Border* (Philadelphia, 1876), pp. 254–255.

[4] *Ibid.*, p. 256.

"it was while viewing the vast herds of buffalo from a spur of the Cumberland mountains, that he [Boone] exclaimed: 'I am richer than the one mentioned in Scripture who owned the cattle of a thousand hills, for I own the wild beasts of more than a thousand valleys.' " [5]

This virgin "land of Canaan, flowing with milk and honey," was also the "dark and bloody ground" of a race of giants and supermen, led by Boone, Crockett, and Mike Fink. Their combats, stratagems, and death-defying stunts (e.g., the famous leap of Major Samuel McColloch astride his horse over a three-hundred foot precipice down Wheeling hill), their wild sports and sprees, " 'scapes and scrapes," brags and hoaxes were the subjects or models of endless yarns and tall tales.

2. Raconteurs in Homespun

As the South has never lacked story materials, so it has never lacked story-tellers, audiences, and occasions for story-telling. On farmhouse, plantation house, and country-store porches, in the parlor and the nursery, at religious and political gatherings, on courthouse steps and benches, at picnics and barbecues, around the campfire, on the job—wherever people came together for sociability and entertaining or persuasive talk, there have been tongues to tell and ears to hear the inherited repertoire.

In addition to the universal themes and motifs of yarns and tall tales and historical and local traditions the South has a rich source of anecdote and story in the characters and doings of kinfolk, friends, and neighbors, who are all the more readily assimilated to folk tradition by reason of the Southern code of personal ethics, which regards them first of all as human beings and individuals.

Besides the inherited themes there are the inherited techniques; and the art of casual narrative flourishes where life is casual, leisurely, and informal, paced to the relaxed tempo of Southern living. In an environment where people "do not like books so well, but . . . like to remember and memorize many things that [they] do love," according to Bascom Lamar Lunsford, book-say is close to folk-say; and literate and non-literate raconteurs alike are caught up in the same stream of oral memory and "torrential recollectiveness."

In the 1830's, '40's, and '50's, some of the best and tallest tale-tellers who ever got into print were recruited from the ranks of Southern lawyers, judges, ministers, editors, and sportsmen. This was the "Georgia Scenes" and "Big Bear of Arkansas" school of sketches and yarns, which made the names of A. B. Longstreet, Joseph G. Baldwin, Johnson H. Hooper, George W. Harris, William T. Thompson, Thomas B. Thorpe, C. F. M. Noland, Henry T. Lewis, and H. T. Taliaferro, and their characters—especially Simon Suggs, Sut Lovingood, and Major Jones—household words among readers of Southern newspapers and William T. Porter's New York *Spirit of the Times*, the "most popular humorous journal of this period." With the newspaper as an important link in the story-telling chain, folklore and local color were the soil from which sprang the broad humor, the racy idiom, the anecdotal verve, and the gorgeous yarn-spinning of later humor-

[5] *Ibid.*, p. 254.

ists—Charles Henry Smith ("Bill Arp"), Joel Chandler Harris, Mark Twain, and (in our own day) Irvin S. Cobb and Roark Bradford.

3. Big Liars and Big Lies

Although only incidentally raconteurs and fablers, travelers and naturalists like William Bartram and John James Audubon testify to the thin line that separates nature lore from folklore. For, like the early chroniclers, they deal in a truth that is stranger than fiction or "fiction in excellent disguise," especially as the marvels of natural and "unnatural" history strain both credibility and credulity.

Similarly the narrator of yarns and tall tales has "seen a heap of strange things" in his time; and they grow "curiouser and curiouser" with the telling, as facts are stretched into invented and exaggerated instances.

Of Oaty, who "would rather climb a tree and tell a lie than stay on the ground and tell the truth," his wife said indulgently: "He only lies enough to enjoy hisself." [6] In the same way, the champion liar is always an amateur, who lies for the fun of it.

"Artistic liars" may be divided into two classes: those who boast of their own prowess and exploits; and those who elaborate on rumors and the erroneous perceptions of another person, preferably "a person who is not known directly to the narrator, but who is well known to a close friend" —thus disarming skepticism.

As the type and symbol of the "unnatural" natural history tall tale beloved by the liar of the second class, one may take the joint "snake." This is not a snake but a degenerate, legless lizard, which can escape its enemies with the loss of its tail and later acquire another by regeneration. "A careless or excitable observer, having killed a joint 'snake' with a stick and, of course, having broken off the tail in doing so, goes back and sees the dismembered tail wriggling in the grass, whereupon he rushes off to tell that he saw the severed tail making an effort to find the body." [7] Hence, stories dealing with the frantic attempts of disjointed snakes to put themselves together again and to find substitutes for missing parts.

From Tennessee comes the story of the woman who saw a joint snake while killing her lone rooster for the inevitable preacher's visit. She hacked the snake to pieces and threw them into the pig pen. While the family and the preacher were eating the noonday meal, a rooster started crowing. On investigation she found that the joint snake had tried to gather itself together again and, not finding its own head, had put on the rooster's head and was crowing fit to kill. [8]

B. A. B

---

[6] Alberta Pierson Hannum, in *The Great Smokies and the Blue Ridge,* edited by Roderick Peattie (New York, 1943), p. 107.

[7] Chapman J. Milling, "Is the Serpent Tale an Indian Survival?", *Southern Folklore Quarterly,* Vol. I (March, 1934), No. 1, pp. 47–48.

[8] As told by Mrs. George Emert Townsend, Tennessee, to Mildred Burns, in "Tennessee Tall Tales," by Geneva Anderson, Maryville, Tennessee, *The Tennessee Folklore Society Bulletin,* Vol. V (October, 1939), No. 3, p. 63.

STRETCHING FACTS

A Deal in Pork

FOR pure sagacity no "Yankee trick" can surpass a certain deal in pork which once took place in Old Virginia, and . . . shows the character of some of the business relations between southerners and northerners which gained for the latter the intense enmity of the former. A Yankee skipper had unloaded his cargo of Hingham woodenware at a Virginia river port and determined to invest his money in a livestock sale then being advertised. On the day named the sale began with an offering of hogs which were divided into three lots of seven hogs each. The terms were cash down for live weight, sinking the offal. Part of the drove were fine and fat; many of the others were so far under par that they couldn't "raise a squeal or grunt without laying down or leaning against the wall." The first lot averaged near two hundred pounds, the next one hundred, and the remainder, say, fifty. The captain purchased one lot at seven dollars per hundred; the mate took another at one dollar per hundred, and a sailor took the leavings at fifty cents per hundred.

When delivery was made the captain, to the amazement of all, chose the seven lean kine. A surprised buckskin blurted out:

"My, Captain, what a d——d fool you are; don't you know you've got the choice?"

"Yes, I do," was the reply, "and I chose these nice little roasters." The mate made choice of the next in size and the "leavings" fell to the sailor at fifty cents per hundredweight. And the Yankees sailed away. Had the choice been made according to ordinary methods the twenty-one hogs would have netted $50.75; as it was they brought but $24.50.

*　　*　　*　　*　　*

The matter of speed in hogs was not . . . a thing to be prized, as a pork dealer in Georgetown, D. C., once had forcefully impressed on his mind. He had bargained with a drover on Buck Creek, Ohio, "who had not been long from Yankee land," for a certain number of hogs. The drover brought the hogs across the mountains and down the Potomac. The buyer was to take half the lot; accordingly the westerner stood in the middle of the Georgetown bridge (where the division was to be made) and had the hogs driven rapidly across. When exactly one half had passed on a hog gallop the Ohioan leaped down and headed off the remainder and went his way with them and the money. He was afterwards wont to say

From *The Ohio River*, A Course of Empire, by Archer Butler Hulbert, pp. 316–318. Copyright, 1906, by G. P. Putnam's Sons. New York and London: The Knickerbocker Press.

that a man in Georgetown, D. C., owned what was probably the swiftest lot of hogs in the United States, but as for him he had "rather have heft."

Shooting Frogs without Powder

AFTER all, buffalo hump is a very fair thing, but a frog's hind legs are just about as good. They cook 'em right in New Orleans and I don't know anything suits me much better. When I was a boy, thar was nothing I liked so well. The d——l of it was, I hadn't always money to buy powder with to shoot the creeturs, and so I tried spearing 'em, hooking 'em with red flannel bait; setting traps for 'em, teaching a little spaniel dog of mine to catch 'em; but somehow I never could get enough at a time.

One day I was traveling around the pond, trying to invent some way of laying hold of a lot for supper, when an idea jumped through my head, and afore it could get out I grabbed it. Cutting a long elder stick, as straight a one as I could find, I split it in two, lengthwise, dug out the pith, and so made a long narrow trough. Going up to the house, I filled my pockets with No. 7 shot, and coming back to the pond, snaked round till I saw a thundering big "Bull-paddy" sunning himself right under a clump of weeds; he was rolling his eyes round like a stage-actor, and opening his mouth as if he was going to swallow the pond. There he sat! Slowly and gradually I crept up behind him, till I got near enough to run the elder trough out, so that its eend was about two feet 'bove his nose. Taking a handful of shot, I put one into the eend of the trough and let it run down; it fell in the water—plunk! about an inch in front of him; he jumped at it, missed it, and then squatted quietly down again, with his mouth wide open. I let another lot of lead slide, and he caught it, and another, and another, till he had swallowed 'em all, and I hadn't a shot left in my pocket. There he sot, and when I stepped out from the grass, may be he didn't try to jump: his legs flew up and down like drumsticks, but the rest of him wouldn't work —he had too big a load on! So I picked him up, held my hat under him, gave him a squeeze, and the shot run out in a stream, like they would from a pouch. Fact! and I tell you what, after that I always *shot frogs without powder!*"

Fiddling for His Life

. . . As WE drew nigh to the Washita, the silence was broken alone by our own talk and the clattering of our horse's hoofs, and we imagined our-

By Henry P. Leland. From *The Spirit of the Times*, Vol. 25 (May 26, 1855), p. 170.

From *Life of David Crockett*, the Original Humorist and Irrepressible Backwoodsman . . . , pp. 280–282. Philadelphia: John E. Potter and Company. 1860.

selves pretty much the only travelers, when we were suddenly somewhat startled by the sound of music. We checked our horses, and listened, and the music continued. "What can all that mean?" says I. "Blast my old shoes if I know, Colonel," says one of the party. We listened again, and we now heard, "Hail, Columbia, happy land!" played in first rate style. "That's fine," says I. "Fine as silk, Colonel, and a leetle finer," says the other; "but hark, the tune's changed." We took another spell of listening, and now the musician struck up in a brisk and lively manner, "Over the water to Charley." "That's mighty mysterious," says one. "Can't cipher it out no how," says another. "A notch beyant my measure," says a third. "Then let us go ahead," says I, and off we dashed at a pretty rapid gait, I tell you—by no means slow.

As we approached the river, we saw to the right of the road a new clearing on a hill, where several men were at work, and they running down the hill like wild Indians, or rather, like the office-holders in pursuit of the deposits. There appeared to be no time to be lost, so they ran, and we cut ahead for the crossing. The music continued in all this time stronger and stronger, and the very notes appeared to speak distinctly, "Over the water to Charley."

When we reached the crossing, we were struck all of a heap at beholding a man seated in a sulky in the middle of the river and playing for life on a fiddle. The horse was up to his middle in the water, and it seemed as if the flimsy vehicle was ready to be swept away by the current. Still the fiddler fiddled on composedly, as if his life had been insured, and he was nothing more than a passenger. We thought he was mad, and shouted to him. He heard us, and stopped his music. "You have missed the crossing," shouted one of the men from the clearing. "I know I have," returned the fiddler. "If you go ten feet farther you will be drowned." "I know I shall," returned the fiddler. "Turn back," said the man. "I can't," said the other. "Then how the devil will you get out?" "I'm sure I don't know: come you and help me."

The men from the clearing, who understood the river, took our horses and rode up to the sulky, and after some difficulty succeeded in bringing the traveler safe to shore, when we recognized the worthy parson who had fiddled for us at the puppet show at Little Rock. They told him that he had had a narrow escape, and he replied that he had found that out an hour ago. He said he had been fiddling to the fishes for a full hour, and had exhausted all the tunes that he could play without notes. We then asked him what could have induced him to think of fiddling at a time of such peril; and he replied that he had remarked in his progress through life that there was nothing in univarsal natur so well calculated to draw people together as the sound of a fiddle; and he knew that he might bawl until he was hoarse for assistance, and no one would stir a peg; but they would no sooner hear the scraping of his catgut than they would quit all other business and come to the spot in flocks. We laughed heartily at the knowledge the parson showed of human natur. And he was right.

Sloped for Texas

THIS is an answer given in some of the States of America when a gentleman has decamped from his wife, from his creditors, or from any other responsibility which he finds it troublesome to meet or to support. Among the curious instances of the application of this phrase is an adventure which happened to myself.

It is the boast of the bloods of the town of Rackinsack, in Arkansas, that they are born with skins like alligators, and with strength like bears. They work hard, and they *play* hard. Gaming is the recreation most indulged in, and the gaming-houses of the western part of Arkansas have branded it with an unenviable notoriety.

One dark summer night, I lounged, as a mere spectator, the different rooms, watching the various games of hazard that were being played. Some of the players seemed to have set their very souls upon the stakes; their eyes were bloodshot and fixed, from beneath their wrinkled brows, on the table, as if their everlasting weal or woe depended there upon the turning of the dice; while others—the finished blacklegs—assumed an indifferent and careless look, though a kind of sardonic smile playing round their lips but too plainly revealed a sort of habitual desperation. Three of the players looked the very counterparts of each other, not only in face, but expression; both the physical and moral likeness was indeed striking. The other player was a young man, a stranger, whom they call a "green one," in this and many other parts of the world. His eyes, his nose, his whole physiognomy, seemed to project and to be capable of growing even still longer.

"Fifty dollars more," he exclaimed, with a deep-drawn breath, as he threw down the stake.

Each of his opponents turned up his cards coolly and confidently; but the long-visaged hero laid his stake before them, and, to the astonishment of the three professionals, won.

"Hurrah! the luck has turned, and I crow?" he cried out in an ecstasy, and pocketed the cash.

The worthy trio smiled at this, and recommenced play. The *green* young man displayed a broad but silent grin at his good fortune, and often took out his money to count it over, and see if each piece was good.

"Here are a hundred dollars more," cried the sylvan youth, "and I crow."

"I take them," said one of the trio. The youth won again, and "crowed" louder this time than he did the first.

On went the game; stakes were lost and won. Gradually the rouleaus of the "crower" dwindled down to a three or four dollars, or so. It was clear

From *Harper's New Monthly Magazine*, Vol. II (January, 1851), No. VIII, pp. 187–188.

that the gentlemen in black had been luring him on by that best of decoys, success at first.

"Let me see something for my money. Here's a stake of two dollars, and I crow!" But he spoke now in a very faint treble indeed and looked penitently at the cards.

Again the cards were shuffled, cut, and dealt, and the "plucked pigeon" staked his last dollar upon them.

"The last button on gabe's coat, and I cr—cr—; no, I'll be hamstrung if I do!"

He lost this too, and, with a deep a curse as I ever heard, he rose from the green board.

The apartment was very spacious, and on the ground floor. There was only this one gaming table in it, and not many lookers-on besides myself. Thinking the gaming was over, I turned to go out, but found the door locked, and the key gone. There was evidently something in the wind. At all events, I reflected, in case of need, the windows are not very far to the ground. I returned, and saw the winners dividing the spoil, and the poor shorn "greenhorn," leaning over the back of their chairs, staring intently at the money.

The notes were deliberately spread out one after another. Those which the loser had staked were new, fresh from the press, he said, and they were sorted into a heap distinct from the rest. They were two-dollar, three-dollar, and five-dollar notes, from the Indiana Bank and the Bank of Columbus, in Ohio.

"I say, Ned, I don't think these notes are good," said one of the winners, and examined them.

"I wish they weren't, and I'd crow," cried out the loser, very chop-fallen, at his elbow.

This simple speech lulled the suspicions of the counter, and he resumed his counting. At last, as he took up the last note, and eying it keenly, he exclaimed, in a most emphatic manner, "I'll be hanged if they *are* genuine! They are forged!"

"No, they ain't!" replied the loser, quite as emphatically.

A very opprobrious epithet was now hurled at the latter. He, without more ado, knocked down the speaker at a blow, capsized the table, which put out the lights, and, in the next instant, darted out of the window, while a bullet, fired from a pistol, cracked the pane of glass over his head. He had leaped into the small court-yard, with a wooden paling round it. The winners dashed toward the door, but found that the "green one" had secured it.

When the three worthies were convinced that the door would not yield to their efforts, and when they heard their "victim" galloping away, they gave a laugh at the trick played them, and returned to the table.

"Strike a light, Bill, and let's pick up what notes have fallen. I have nearly the whole lot in my pocket."

The light soon made its appearance.

"What! None on the floor? Capital; I think I must have them all in my pocket, then." Saying which, he drew out the notes, and laid them on the table.

"Fire and Furies! These are the forged notes! The rascal has whipped up the other heap!"

While all this was going on, I stepped toward the window, but had not stood there long before I heard the clanking hoofs of a horse beyond the paling, and a shout wafted into the room—"Sloped for Texas!"

The worst part of the story remains to be told; it was *my* horse on which the rogue was now galloping off.

A Gambler's Tricks

I. THE BIG CATFISH

MY OLD partner (Bush) and I had been up all night in New Orleans playing faro, and were several hundred dollars winners, and thought we would walk down to the French market and get a cup of coffee before we went to bed. We saw a catfish that would weigh about 125 pounds; its mouth was so large that I could put my head into it. We got stuck on the big cat, and while we were looking at it an old man came up to me and said: "That is the largest catfish I ever saw." Bush was a little way off from me just at the time, and knowing I would have some fun (if not a bet) with the old man, he kept out of the way. I said to the old gent: "You are the worst judge of a fish I ever saw; that is not a cat, it is a pike, and the largest one ever brought to this market." He looked at me and then at the fish, and then said: "Look here, my boy, where in the d——l were you raised?" I told him I was born and raised in Indiana. "Well, I thought you were from some hoop-pole State."

We got to arguing about it; and I appeared to be mad, and offered to bet him $100 that the fish was a pike. Says he, "Do you mean it?" I pulled out a roll, threw down $100 and told him to cover it. He lammed her up, and I said: "Who will we leave it to?" We looked around and saw Bush, with a memorandum book in his hand and a pen behind his ear, talking to a woman who sold vegetables, and he was acting as if he was collector of the market. I said: "May be that man with the book in his hand might know." The old fellow called Bush, and said to him, "Do you belong about here?" "Oh, yes; I have belonged about here for a good many years," says

From *Forty Years a Gambler on the Mississippi*, A Cabin Boy in 1839; Could Steal Cards and Cheat the Boys at Eleven; Stock a Deck at Fourteen; Bested Soldiers on the Rio Grande during the Mexican War; Won Hundreds of Thousands from Paymasters, Cotton Buyers, Defaulters, and Thieves; Fought More Rough-and-Tumble Fights than Any Man in America, and was the Most Daring Gambler in the World, by George H. Devol, pp. 39–40, 139–140, 132–133. Second Edition. Entered . . . , 1887, by George H. Devol. . . . New York: George H. Devol. 1892.

Bush. "Well, sir, you are just the man we want to decide our bet," says the old gent. "Well, gentlemen, I am somewhat in a hurry; but if you do not detain me too long, I will be glad to serve you to the best of my ability," said Bush. "We want you to tell us what kind of a fish this is." "Well, gentlemen, that can be done easily." "Out with it," said the old gent. Bush braced himself up, and said: "I have been market-master here for twenty years, and that is the largest *pike* I ever saw in this market." "Well! Well! Well!" says the old man; "I have lived on the Tombigbee River for forty-five years, and I never saw two bigger fools than you two."

I invited the old man and the "market-master" to join me in a cup of coffee. Bush accepted, but the old one from the Tombigbee declined, saying "he did not drink with men that did not know a catfish from a pike." We bid him good morning and went home, and we were both sound asleep in a short time; for we felt we had done an honest night's and morning's work.

II. THE JACK-FISH

My old partner Bush and I would play the trains on the Jackson Road out about forty miles above New Orleans, and then get off and wait for a down train. Some times we would be compelled to get off before we had gone that far; but, as a general thing, it would be about that distance before we would get our work in on suckers. We would go up in the morning to a place called Manshak and fish until the train would come down in the evening. One day we were fishing, and had got some distance apart, when I saw a school of large jack-fish coming down like lightning. I jumped up and grabbed a pike pole that was lying near, slipped the noose over my hand and let fly at them. I struck a big fellow, but he did not stop; he kept right on and pulled me after him. I yelled to Bush, and he came running to assist me; he reached me a long pole, and then pulled me out. The rope was still on my hand, and the fish was on the pike pole, so we pulled him out, and he weighed about sixty pounds. We took him down on the evening train, and had a part of him broiled for our supper. Bush said it was the largest fish he ever caught. I told him I caught it, when he said: "Why, George, I caught you both."

III. SIGNAL SERVICE

Before the war they had an old steamer fitted up as a wharf-boat and lodging-house at Baton Rouge, to accommodate people that landed late at night, or would be waiting for a boat. This old boat was headquarters for the gamblers that ran the river. Many a night we have played cards in the old cabin until morning, or until our boat would arrive. When thorough-bred gamblers meet around the table at a game of cards, then comes the tug of war. We would have some very hard games at times, and we found it pretty hard to hold our own. My partner proposed that we fix up some plan to down the gamblers that played with us on the old boat, so we finally hit upon a scheme. We bored a hole under one of the tables, and another under one of the beds in a state-room opposite. Then we fixed a nail into a spring, and fastened the spring on the under side of the floor, so that the nail would come up through the floor under the table. Next we attached a fine wire to the spring, and ran it up into the state-room. Then we bored a hole in the bulkhead of the state-room, just over the top berth, so that a person could lie in the berth and look out into the cabin. Now we were ready for the thoroughbreds. When we would get one of our smart friends, we would seat him at our table in his chair, which was always on the side of our state-room. We called it ours, for we had fitted it up to suit us; and for fear some one would use it when we were out traveling for our health, we paid for it all the time. We had a good boy that liked to lie down and make money, so we would put him in the upper berth while the game was in progress. He would look through the peep-hole, and if our friend had one pair he would pull the wire once; if two pair, twice; if threes, three times; if fours, four times, etc. We would kick off one boot and put our foot over the nail, and then we would be able to tell what hand our friend held. One day I was playing a friend at our table, and he was seated in his chair. I got the signals all right for some time, and then the under-current seemed to be broken. I waited for the signals until I could not wait any longer, for I was a little behind (time), so I picked up a spittoon and let fly at our room. That restored communications, and I received the signals all right. My friend wanted to know what I threw the spittoon for. I told him the cards were running so bad that I got mad; and that an old Negro had told me once it was a good sign to kick over a spittoon when playing cards; so I thought I would not only kick it over, but would break the d——d thing all to pieces. He replied, "I noticed that your luck changed just after you threw her, and I will try it the next time I play in bad luck."

A Kentucky Shooting Match

. . . MANY years ago, when ——ville, Ky., was a small and handsome country village, a Virginia gambler, by name R——, under the disguise of a thrifty farmer, settled near the place. Old S——, one of his neighbors, a shrewd and thriving farmer, but quite fond of cards, some time afterwards being seduced by him into a quiet game, arose loser of about $2000. The conversation had previously turned upon rifle shooting, and R. rather prided himself upon being a good shot. Said S., "I'll shoot with you for $500 a shot all day, if you wish, at forty yards; you go take a rest and I will shoot offhand; both to use my rifle, and you can stand by and see it fairly loaded every time." No quicker said than closed, and S. started for his rifle, whilst some of his neighbors prepared the mark, measured dis-

By "XX." From *The Spirit of the Times,* Vol. 25 (October 6, 1855), p. 399.

tance, etc., wondering whether S. was not insane, as he was notoriously the poorest shot in the neighborhood.

S. appeared, loaded his gun, and R., after deliberate aim, fired and missed the tree, against which the mark was made. S. fired and chipped the bark upon the right edge of the tree, winning the first $500, and cursing himself for making so mean a shot. R., having seen the bullet unquestionably put in the gun, fired again with the same result, and S. chipped the bark on the left edge, and still abused himself for not doing better. The third round was won by S., hitting some two feet above the mark, R. missing the tree, and the fourth round R. missed again, and S. struck within the black. "I'll be d——d if I know what to make of your cursed gun," said R., after refusing to shoot again. "I have held plump on the mark, and would have bet my life upon hitting the black every time." "I'll tell you what was the matter," replied S., "you stocked the cards on me, and to get even I had to stock the bullets on you," pulling out at the same time a bullet and handing it to R., who, upon examination found it had been almost cut in two, barely sticking together, and the cut neatly closed up, so that it was not perceptible. Upon leaving the gun, one half whirled one way and the other in an opposite direction. R. never undertook to make another shooting match.

Piloting a Flatboat

THIS was the way of it. . . . There was a man and his family come from above somewhar, in a flat bound for Arkansaw. He was pretty well loaded with farm-stock, women, children, and truck; and having heard tell of the Narrows, he was afeared to go through by himself, but wanted a pilot. So, after considerin' a while, I agreed to put him through for two dollars. . . .

* * * * *

I never had been through there, but I had heard people talk about the Skillet, and the Sleek, and the Bilin' Pot, and all that; and I thought I could shoot her through, and if I sunk her I'd lose my money—that's all. So we tuck a few drinks and put off, and I takes the steerin'-oar, and put her head down, and let her rip. Night come on pretty soon, but that was all the same to me; so we tuck a few more drinks, and let her slide. And we went over some rough places, and, after while, come to a pretty smart current runnin' smooth. "Now she goes it slick as goose-grease!" says he to me. So, by-and-by, we see lights on the shore, and passed by a house where a feller was playin' "Old Zip Coon" like a sawmill, and people

From "A Winter in the South," by David Hunter Strother ("Porte Crayon"), *Harper's New Monthly Magazine*, Vol. XVII (August, 1858), No. 99, pp. 302–303. New York: Harper & Brothers, Publishers.

dancin'. "Here's good fun to you!" says he, and we tuck another dig. So we went on pretty sprightly; and, by jingo! before we got well out of sight and hearin' of that house we went past another, whar they were dancin' to the same tune. "Success to 'em!" says I. "Hand us that bottle; while fun is goin', we might as well have our share!" So we drank a mouthful, and before we were done talkin' about it we went past another place, fiddlin' and dancin' like the rest.

"Mister," says he to me, "this here's the jolliest settlement ever I traveled through—all a-goin' it to the same tune." " 'Pears to me," says I, "I hear another fiddle and fellers a-laffin' '"; and presently sure enough, we streaked past another house whar they were goin' it a leetle more extravagant than the others—tune about the same. "Mister," says the boss to me, "this rather beats my time. Do the people along this river mostly spend their nights fiddlin' and dancin'?" "Certain," says I; "that's their reg'lar business." But now, I tell you, I was beginnin' to get bewildered and oneasy myself. So, pretty soon we passed another house, and another, and another, all dancin' and fiddlin' like blazes. The boss he set quiet, and didn't say a word for a while, but tuck a swig now and then. Next house we passed they were goin' it on "Old Zip Coon" with a will. Then the boss spoke up. "Pilot," says he, "there's one of two things—either we're drunk, or there's hell's doin's goin' on along this river to-night." "What time o' night is it?" says I. "About two o'clock in the mornin' by the stars," says he. "How many houses have we passed?" "I've counted nine," says he, and his voice began to shake a little. "Now," says he, "it might be that the hellish thing is a-follerin' of us!" "Nine," says I, "is the devil's number," says I, pretty badly skeered; "if the thing appears agin, go call your wife, and if she can't see it, we're drunk, certain." "Listen!" says he; "don't you hear 'em? That's the lights! ten times! we're drunk, sure. Katy! Katy! sweetheart, wake up!"

This time I headed the flat a little in nearer shore, and we could hear 'em plain, cussin' and swearin'.

"Katy," says boss, "do you see or hear anything over there on shore?"

"I see lights," says she, "and hear a passel of drunken boatmen dancin' 'Old Zip Coon'."

I wanted to put in, but boss says, "No; but sure's I'm a man, if they're carryin' on at the next house we pass we'll tie up and make out the night with 'em!"

In about half an hour, as I expected, we come upon another spree.

"Head her in!" says he. So we tied up at the landing, and went in the house.

Now, stranger, how do you think it was? Why, this was old Jack Cogles' house, down thar fornense the Bilin' Pot, whar some fellers and some gals were dancin' all night; and we went bilin' around and around, passin' by the same place over and over agin! Now at fust it come to me like a sort of a dream; then it was all clare; and without waitin' to be cussed or laughed at, I streaked it. But it's all true, jist as I tell ye.

A Steamboat Race

. . . I WAS once coming up the Mississippi River on one of the Southern steamers when another boat came in sight, evidently bent upon passing us, with immense volumes of black smoke rolling from the tops of her chimneys, and her whistle blazing defiance to our boat in particular and all creation in general. The captain of our boat, on looking back, as he heard the defiant whistle and seeing the unusual quantity of smoke rolling from her chimney tops, saw what was out; he knew that our boat was pretty fast, and determined, as was soon evident from his actions, that he would not be beat if he could avoid it. He went to the pilot-house, and after a few words passing between them, the pilot put his mouth to the mouth of the speaking-trumpet, by which he could communicate with the engineer. The other boat all this time was gradually creeping up behind us. Soon our craft began moving ahead faster through the water, the black smoke rolling, the steam hissing, and the escape pipes belching forth the steam faster and faster, the boat shaking, creaking, and groaning from stem to stern. The passengers were all collected on the roof, the guards, and every place that they could get a sight of the coming boat. All aboard was excitement, but still on she came, nearer and nearer, the faster we went the faster did she; soon she had come so close behind us that we could throw from one to the other; still she was coming nearer and nearer, now our stern was even with her bow as she had turned one side to pass us. The captain became more excited, as well as the passengers, and all on board of our boat. Now we were going slower, and dropping back faster. For the last half hour I had been below watching the firemen pitching in the wood, tar, pitch, and everything else that could be raked up to make an extra quantity of steam. Upstairs I went to the captain. I ran and exclaimed, "Captain, the reason that we are going so much slower all of a sudden is that the firemen are perfectly exhausted, and not able to fire up any longer; may I go down and fire up—I can pitch in the timber pretty fast."

My confidential tone caused the captain to think perhaps I could do some good, and as matters were getting desperate, and it seemed as if we were to be beat anyhow, he told me to do my best. I went below again in a hurry; both boats were now side and side. There are persons who talk of making "the fur fly," but I made the wood "fly" into the furnace, and ten men could not have counted the sticks as they went into it; stick after stick disappeared into the "fiery furnace," and it was soon heated "nine times hotter" than it ever was before. As soon as I had commenced firing, we shot ahead of the other boat; but she was soon alongside again, and gaining on us fast. I looked at the fire, at the wood pile (it was reduced to about two cords), at the river, at the shore, and at the other boat; she was still

From *The Spirit of the Times,* Vol. 25 (December 22, 1855), p. 534.

I give the following as I heard it, with some alterations and additions. It has been attributed to a gentleman by the name of H——. living not many miles below the city of Louisville.—Author.

going ahead of us. The thought struck me that probably our furnace did not have a good draft; I stepped forward to the bow to see, and behold the draft was so good that the sticks of wood were coming out of the tops of the chimneys, and the boat running from under them. The captain had discovered it about the same time that I did, and beckoned to me to come up, rang the bell to wood, and to a wood-pile we went.

The Bull Trial

JUSTICE is sometimes slanted in a peculiar manner in the backhills. Things move from the sublime to the ridiculous in a singular way. Take the "bull trial" of the eighties. Old-timers continue to talk and shake their heads over this famous trial held more than fifty years ago in the Boston Mountains of Arkansas. It is not a tall tale from the windy hilltops but can be verified by persons still living.

A mountain farmer owned a bull that was no respecter of fences or persons. He was monarch of his domain, and the best stake and rider fence in the country was no barrier to his invasions. Even the most modern fence on the more up-to-date farms was only a slight inconvenience to his migrations. He was the terror of the community and even his own despaired of controlling him. Finally, the bull invaded one too many cornfields. The enraged farmer, whose crop had been destroyed, swore out a warrant and had the animal arrested. The law brought his bellowing majesty to the shade of a large oak tree where the trial was held. The case against the bull was plain enough but the proceedings lasted almost all day. Lawyers threw aside their coats and pleaded for or against the aggressor. Witnesses swore, natives cursed, and the bull bellowed his displeasure. After careful deliberation, the jury found the animal guilty in a degree deserving punishment. The verdict rendered, the justice of the peace assessed fine and costs. Then came the puzzling question of payment. After considering the problem from all angles, the judge decided to butcher the animal and use the meat as payment. A barbecue followed with judge, jury, lawyers, witnesses, and the general public taking part. It was a festive occasion and long remembered by those present, but the old-timers to this day shake their heads and say it was not a fair trial. They point out that the judge neglected to appoint an interpreter for the bull.

The Mule-Killer

DR. NEWELL G. RIGGINS, the Burlington physician, today was chuckling and telling about three friends of his bird hunting over near Dover, in

From *Bert Vincent's Strolling*, Being Sort of a Sideglance at the Little Odds and Ends

Stewart County. Said the three drove out to a farmer they knew. One got [out] from the car and went inside to get the farmer's permission to hunt.

"Sure," agreed the farmer. "That's all right, kill all the birds you want."

Then, as the man turned toward the door the farmer added:

"Do me a favor, though."

"Yes, sir. What kind of favor you want me to do?"

"I want," said the farmer, "for you to kill the old mule I have out there in the field. He's sick. Can't get well. I don't have the heart to kill him."

The fellow left the house, and went on with his two companions hunting. He didn't tell either of them about the mule.

And, after they'd shot several birds they came upon this mule. This one hunter who had talked with the farmer just blurted out:

"Wonder how it would feel to kill a mule?"

The other two didn't pay much attention. This fellow was always making fool remarks, anyway. They mosied on through the sedge grass.

This chap got in front of the old mule, and close up. He blazed away. The mule dropped. The other two turned. Saw what he'd done.

"You blasted idiot," one yelled. . . . "Now we'll all go to jail. . . . You ought to rot there. . . . Don't you have any sense. . . . And, after that man gave us permission to hunt, too. . . ."

This mule-killer started grinning sort of silly like. Then, he said, still grinning silly like:

"Wonder how it would feel to shoot a man. . . ."

Dr. Riggins tells that when this man came to he was a patient in a Dover hospital, and a lot of folks, after hearing the story, were surprised he wasn't a corpse in an undertaker's place.

Fox Hunters and Their Dogs

I. Dick Wilson

I FOUND out about that fox them Buzzardtown fellers has been losin' nigh the top of French Mountain where there is nary a hole or a cliff in half a mile. I taken that old speckled bitch o' mine over thar about four o'clock and put her in the pack. They soon jumped it and they all lit out straight for the top in the purtiest race I've heerd in many a day. I finecivilly told them dadblasted Morgans my dog would run that fox in a hole quicker'n hell could scorch a feather, and she would be found a-pintin' her nose in that hole after him, re-gard-less of where that hole was.

of Life in These Parts. (Unpaged.) Copyright, 1940, by Bert Vincent. Knoxville, Tennessee: W. L. Warters Co.

A South Carolina variant, as told by Chapman J. Milling, Columbia, was recorded by B. A. Botkin, January 25, 1949.

As told by Dick Webb, Forest City, North Carolina, and Lee Morris, Marion, North Carolina, to Dudley W. Crawford. Manuscripts of the Federal Writers' Project of the Works Progress Administration for the State of North Carolina.

Jest like common they quit when they struck the top, and we soon met all the dogs but mine comin' back. When we got closeter I could hear her a-barkin' low and a-whinin'. I said, "Boys, she's got him in a hole, jest like I said." You orta heerd them fellers a-ridiculin' me. "Hole hell," one o' them said, "how come our dogs come back?" I said, "Jest 'cause they ain't no fox dogs, that's what." We'd let our lights go out when we got up there and it was darker'n a stack of black cats and we couldn't find her in spite o' hell, after she quit whinin'. It come day purty soon and I seen her in one o' them leanin' sourwoods that sticks out over the bluff. I knowed dad-blamed well they wa'n't no fox in that sourwood, but I clomb up thar and found her pintin' her nose down the bluff at a purty stiff angle. I leaned over where I could see the way she was a-lookin', and what do you reckon I seen?

You've seen these big tall poplars that sometimes die high up and gits broken off? Well, they was one o' them more'n a hundred yards down the bluff, and it had rotted off on the top end. That bastard of a fox was a-layin' up thar with his head on his paws, givin' that dawg o' mine jest a mere indifferent glance once in a while. Now what do you know about that?

II. Lee Hogan

Did I ever tell you about that fine bitch my Grandpap over in Vein Mountain had that time I stayed with him when I was a kid? He'd got him one of them redbones and crossed her up with a beagle expectin' to raise somethin' extra. 'Long in the spring she was purty heavy with pups and got out and jined a pack the Marlow boys had a-runnin' one o' them old red she-foxes that can't never be caught and seldom run in a hole. Grandpap knowed sure as hell she'd die, so he just cussed some and then forgot about her.

'Bout three months after that me and him was goin' up to his mountain field to salt his cattle. Just as we got to the gap o' Bill's Mountain we heerd the most ungodly noise comin' round the north side. It sounded sorter like a dog a-whinin' and sorter like a kid half-mad fixin' to cry. While we was a-tryin' to figger it out there come a-tumblin' out of the ivy bushes, into the trail, the longest, leanest red she-fox I ever did see, and Grandpap's fine bitch dog right on top of her. By the time we got our senses back three little young foxes about three months old scooted down the bank with three of that old dog's pups right after 'em.

III. Don Saunders

You talk about dogs. I had one once that I thought a heap of. Something got wrong with him and I sent for the Vet up at Asheville. The Vet said he was already dead but I thought so much of him I just reckon I couldn't believe it. You see I'd never talked to him much—wasn't necessary, he was so smart. I told Doc I could soon tell if he was dead. So I got my gun and walked up right close and pulled the hammer back, knowing good and well that would rouse him, but it didn't. Then I happened to think I had my new gun, and I'd never hunted him with it. I got the old gun, and when the hammer clicked that hound opened one eye about half and slapped his tail against the ground twice. Then I knowed doggone well that dog wasn't dead.

The Two Ducks

DERE was er ole man, you know, he had a daughter, and he tell he daughter he had invited a preacher to he house, and he say, "Daughter, I guine down to de train to meet de Reverend, and bake two ducks and leave 'em dere for him, don't tech 'em." And she said, "No, I ain't guh tech 'em." And he go to de train to meet de Reverend, and de gal taste de ducks, and dey taste good, and she taste 'em till she taste 'em all up.

And atter de ole man come, he never look in de place wey he had he ducks, and he went in de other room to sharpen he knife on the oil stove, and de preacher was settin' in de room wid de gal. She knewed her papa was guine to whip her, and she started to snifflin' 'bout it, and de preacher say, "What is de matter, daughter?" And she say, "Dat's all de fault I find wid papa,—papa go invite preachers to he house and go and sharpen he knife to cut off both dey years." And de Reverend say, "What is dat, daughter?" And de gal say, "Yes, papa invite preachers here all de time and cut off both dey years." And he say, "Daughter, han' me my hat quick." And de gal guin him he hat and he run out. And she call her papa and say, "Papa, de preacher got both de ducks and gone." And he run to de door and holler to him and say, "Hey, hey, wey you guine? Come back here!" And de preacher answer him and say, "Damned ef you'll git either one of dese."

And he raise a dust de way he flewed down de road. And de ole tales tell you dat womens has always been sharper dan mens.

Huey Long's LeJeune Story

. . . "A TRAVELING man used to make that territory out of New Orleans. He was the kind of a man that sold goods to the stores, bought their cotton,

From *Congaree Sketches,* Scenes from Negro Life in the Swamps of the Congaree and Tales by Tad and Scip of Heaven and Hell, with Other Miscellany, by Edward C. L. Adams, pp. 96–97. Copyright, 1927, by the University of North Carolina Press. Chapel Hill.

From *Every Man a King,* the Autobiography of Huey P. Long, pp. 172–179. Copyright, 1933, by Huey P. Long. New Orleans: National Book Co., Inc.

As Huey Long tells the story, State Senator Hugo Doré called to see him one day, made up their accounts, advanced them money and collected at the end of the year. This drummer reached Opelousas on his route every Thursday.

"In the middle of December he left Opelousas and drove out to cross Niggerfoot Bayou. It was a cold day. There had been a great deal of rain.

"When he reached the bayou he found that it had overflowed. Icicles were hanging on the logs and limbs in the woods. So the drummer said to his driver, 'George, drive up about one mile from here and there is a bridge where you can cross. Then drive down on the other side and I will be at that house over yonder. I'll walk the foot-log across the bayou.' The driver departed.

"When he had gone, the drummer started to cross the bayou on the foot-log. It was partly covered with ice and when he reached the middle of the bayou he slipped and fell.

" 'Help! Help!' he yelled.

"The man in the house on the other side heard him. He ran to the bank, reached the drummer a rail and pulled him to the shore. Then he took the drummer to his home, pulled off his clothes, put him to bed while he dried them; and when they were dried, the drummer dressed and the man's wife sat him in front of a table prepared with good fried ham, biscuits and hot coffee. The drummer ate heartily. When he had finished, the driver having returned with the buggy, he made ready to continue his journey.

"The man of the house was named LeJeune. The drummer turned to him and said: 'Mr. LeJeune, you have saved my life. I would have drowned but for your help. Your kind wife and yourself have done more for me than I can ever do for you. I reach Opelousas every Thursday. I would like to meet you there on one of those days to show you my appreciation in a more material way.'

"The drummer took his leave. LeJeune had promised to see him in Opelousas.

"On the following Thursday the drummer reached Opelousas. LeJeune was standing in front of a saloon. The drummer greeted him. He hugged him. Then LeJeune spoke up:

---

in his bedroom in New Orleans, about getting a little road gravelled leading out east of Mamou; and this conversation led up to and into the tale:

"My gracious, Hugo!" I exclaimed. "Won't you ever get through asking for roads for that country? There isn't room to plow there now, we've got so much pavement and gravel in that country."

"Now, Governor," shot back the senator, "don't get too strong now; remember what we've done for you."

Several of our friends seated in the room laughed at his remark.

"Keep your seat, Hugo," I said. "You fifteen bullies are always reminding me of what you did for me. The time has come to tell you of something that happened over in your neck of the woods. Close to where you live is a creek called Bayou Niggerfoot."

"Yes, yes," chirped the senator. "I know the bayou."

"Well, now, Hugo," I continued, "when you were very young . . ."

At the conclusion of the story, Long said to Doré: "If ever again you fifteen round-robineers find me drowing, for Heaven's sake, let me drown!" Senator Doré repeated the story until it became famous.

" 'I am glad to see you, ma fren'. You is ze man what I pull from ze Bayou Niggerfoot. Ah, ma fren', bot for me you would not be alive to-day.'

"The drummer hastily said, 'I know that, Mr. LeJeune. Let's have a drink.'

" 'You could do dat,' said LeJeune.

"While the two stood at the bar sipping their drink, LeJeune began to speak again. 'Ah, ma fren', ze log was froze over, you slip, you fall; I hear you holler.'

"The drummer broke in again: 'Mr. LeJeune, can't I do anything else for you?'

"LeJeune felt of his hat and looked at his shoes.

" 'Come with me,' said the drummer. 'Let me buy you a new hat and a pair of shoes.'

" 'You could do dat,' said LeJeune.

"So the two left the saloon for a store, where the drummer bought Le-Jeune a good hat and a good pair of shoes, and bade him goodbye.

"On the next Thursday the drummer returned. LeJeune was standing in front of the saloon where the drummer had met him on the previous week. The drummer approached him again.

" 'Howdy, Mr. LeJeune. How you do today?'

" 'Ah, ma fren', I am all right. It makes me feel good to see you today. You remembah, ma fren', ze cold day when I pull you from ze Bayou Niggerfoot? Ze crawfish would have eat you long ago but for LeJeune.'

" 'Right you are, Mr. LeJeune,' said the drummer. 'Let's have a drink.'

" 'Ah, you could do dat,' said LeJeune.

"So the two entered the saloon, where they sipped a drink.

"Halfway through, LeJeune stopped and began again. 'You recolleck, ma fren', ze Bayou was deep, you holler "Help!" I—'

"The drummer broke in:

" 'I know, Mr. LeJeune,' he said. 'Isn't there something else I can do for you besides a hat and a pair of shoes I bought last Thursday?'

"LeJeune felt of his coat and brushed his trousers a bit.

" 'Come,' said the drummer, 'let me get you a suit of clothes.'

"So they left for the store again, where the drummer presented LeJeune with a new suit of clothes and again bade him the time of day.

"Thursday another week later, the drummer on his usual round again came to Opelousas. LeJeune was standing in front of the same saloon. The drummer, seeing him from afar, crossed to the opposite side of the street, pretending that his attention was engaged on something immediately ahead as he passed on the other side by the saloon. But when he was a few steps beyond the corner, LeJeune shouted:

" 'Oh, ma fren'!'

"The drummer turned. LeJeune, patting himself on the breast, yelled:

" 'You recolleck LeJeune, whot pull' you from ze Bayou Niggerfoot?'

"Immediately the drummer crossed to the saloon.

" 'Yes, Mr. LeJeune; I shall always remember you,' he said.

" 'Ah, ma fren', I was 'fraid you forget LeJeune. You remembah, but for me you would not be alive today.'

" 'Come on,' said the drummer to LeJeune, 'let's have a drink.'

" 'Well, you could do dat,' LeJeune answered.

"The two stood at the bar and sipped a drink. When they had finished, the drummer said:

" 'Well, let's have another one.'

"LeJeune replied: 'Well, you could do dat. But for me, ma fren', ze crabs and crawfish would have pick your bones long ago.'

"When they had finished the second drink, the drummer turned to Le-Jeune. LeJeune met his glance.

" 'Ze bayou was deep, ze log was slick; you slip—'

"The drummer broke in:

" 'I know, Mr. LeJeune, I remember. Mr. LeJeune, have you got anything in which you could take something to the folks back home?'

"LeJeune paused, shrugged his shoulders.

" 'I got ze wagon,' he said.

" 'Pull it around to Haas' store,' said the drummer, 'and let us get a few things to take to the folks back home.'

"LeJeune willingly complied. He backed up the wagon. They loaded in three barrels of flour, a barrel of meal, several slabs of side meat, hams, suits of clothes for the boys, dresses for his girls and his wife. They loaded in new harness for the horses, bolts of calico, gingham and silk; they put everything on the wagon it would hold. The drummer wrote out his check to the store for the full amount. Then he turned to LeJeune.

" 'Mr. LeJeune,' he said, 'would you like to have another drink before you go?'

" 'You could do dat,' replied LeJeune.

"So the two stepped next door to another saloon.

"Halfway through the drink LeJeune turned to the drummer again.

" 'Ma fren',' he said, 'it was a cold day when I pull you from dat Bayou Niggerfoot. . . .'

" 'Yes,' interrupted the drummer. 'Mr. LeJeune, I want to mention that matter to you. You pulled me from Niggerfoot Bayou when I was about to drown. I give you credit for saving my life. I am under obligations to you deeper than I can ever discharge. But I want to make one more request of you, Mr. LeJeune. If ever again you find me drowning in that damn Niggerfoot Bayou, damn it, let me drown!' "

Racing with a Black Cat

ME AN' a bunch o' boys one time went to pick cotton out from Taylor. So we walked and we walked till we got tired, an' we hunted for a place to lie

---

As told to John A. Lomax by Clear Rock. From *Adventures of a Ballad Hunter*, by John A. Lomax, pp. 184-185. Copyright, 1947, by the Macmillan Company. New York.

down and sleep. So we was searchin' and lookin' for a lodgment place where we could lay down, an' we come to a ol' vacant house away from the road an' we laid down on the floor on our cotton sacks. Well, bein' hungry, I was cookin' some eggs and meat in the fireplace when a black cat pop outen the chimney into the skillet an' jump from there over in a corner of the room. His eyes was turnin' over just like some buggy wheels. Some boys went out the winduh an' some went out the door an' all was hollerin'. I wound up in Floridy, an' my feets was so sore I had to lay down by a ol' rotten log. An' that same ol' black cat ask me, "Didn't we have a good race?" An' I say, "Ain't nothin' to de race we gwine have!"

* * * * *

I was cookin' at the fireplace, . . . an' I look over my shoulder an' see a li'l black kitten on a little shelf in de corner of the room, an' dat kitten was turnin' roun' an' roun'. Seem like de mo' I look the bigger he got, ontil it got de size of a yellin' [yearling]. An' he jump down off de shelf an' come over to de fire an' spit it out, "Whoosh!" Dat lef' it all dark in that place, an' one o' de boys, hearin' me stumblin' roun', say, "How you comin' out?" An' I say, "Ain't comin' out, gwine out!" We was all scramblin' roun' in dat place tryin' to get away from that cat an' out de door. So boy holler out, "Where's de door?" An' I say, "I don' know, but jes follow me and I'll find daylight somewhere." Dis time I ran to Africy on my hoss and when he cross de Dead Sea, between here an' Africy, dat hoss wuz goin' so fas' he didn't sink down over his hocks!

Wait till Martin Comes

A BUNCH of Negroes was sitting around a fire talking about hants. Finally, one little shale-head Negro sitting way down on the end of the log said:

"Speakin' ob hants, Uncle were comin' home fum chu'ch one night w'en de clouds begin ter gather. Uncle had on his seersucker suit an' he know dat if de rain fall on it it were gwine ter tighten up on him. So he drapped in an' ol' house by de roadside, which wuz said wuz hanted. Uncle he didn' pay no min' ter hants; he wuz a good man an' he had de

From "Negro Tales from West Virginia," by John Harrington Cox, *The Journal of American Folklore*, Vol. 47 (October–December, 1934), No. 186, p. 354. New York: The American Folklore Society.

Contributed by Mr. W. E. Chilton, Jr., Charleston, Kanawha County, April 16, 1925. He writes, "This is an old story that was told for many years on the stage by Bert Williams, but I believe goes farther back than he. Riley Wilson often tells it with telling effect. During the war the story was parodied by a Pittsburgh cartoonist. Uncle was the Kaiser and Italy, France, and England were the cats. The Kaiser was shaking and trembling. Down the steps an enormous tiger was coming, the U. S. A. The caption was, "We can't do nothing till Martin comes" and subtitled, "With apologies to the old story."—J. H. C.

Bible wid 'im. So he built hisself a fiah, an' stahted in ter read de book. Pretty soon de rain it gin ter fall.

"Uncle he bin readin' in de Bible 'bout five minutes, w'en in walked a cat w'at's blacker'n a coal. Dis cat walk ober ter de fiahplace an' sot down in it. Den he picked up er chunck ob libe coal an' licked it [illustrating], jis' like dat he licked it. Uncle he don' pay no min'; he's got cats ob his own at home an' he knows all 'bout 'em. He read on in de book.

"In 'bout two minutes, in walk anudder cat w'at's bigger'n a bulldog an' blacker'n de fus' one. He sot down in de fiah an' pick up a libe coal like dis an' dus' his cheeks wid it [illustrating], dus' his cheeks wid it, he did. Den he tu'n ter de fus' cat an' say, 'Is we ready?' An' de fus' cat he say, 'Us better wait till Martin comes.' Uncle he jump all de way f'um Exodus ter Isaiah, he's readin' so fas'. He ain't neber heerd no cats talk befo', an' it worry 'im.

"In 'bout two minutes mo', in comes a cat w'at's blacker'n de udder two an' bigger'n a wolf. He walk ober an' sot down in de fiah wid de udder cats an' he pick up a libe coal an' he dus' his eyeballs wid it [illustrating], he dus' his eyeballs wid it, he do. Den he tu'n to de fus' cat w'at been doin' all de talkin' an' he say, 'Shall we do it now?' An' de fus' cat he say, 'Us better wait till Martin comes.'

"Uncle close de book. As he went out der winder he say, 'Goodnight, cats. W'en Martin comes, you tell 'im I *were* here.' "

Daddy Mention

I. DADDY MENTION AND THE COPS

Daddy Mention got a long trip to Raiford once. There was a lot of people working on the Canal near Ocala, and they was making good money.

By Martin Richardson. Manuscripts of the Federal Writers' Project of the Works Progress Administration for the State of Florida. 1938.

Just when, or where, Daddy Mention came into being will require some research; none of the "guests" at the "Blue Jay" [City Prison Farm] seems to know. Only one thing is certain about the wonder-working gentleman: he must have existed since so many people claim to have known him.

Not that any of his former friends can describe Daddy Mention to you, or even tell you very many close details about him. They cannot. They agree, however, that he has been an inmate of various and sundry Florida jails, prison camps, and road farms for years, and from the stories told of him must have enjoyed an almost unbroken stay in these places of incarceration.

In fact, it is this unusual power of omnipresence that gives the listener to the exploits of Daddy Mention his first doubts that he is anything more than a legendary figure. Prisoners will insist that he was in the jail at Bartow with a ninety-day sentence, "straight up," at the same time they were there "doing sixty." Others will insist that it must have been some other time, because that was the period when Daddy Mention was in Marion County, "making a bit in the road gang."

Legendary though Daddy Mention might be, however, the tales of his exploits are

Daddy Mention, he was making better money than they was, though. You see, he wasn't working exactly on the Canal; he was selling a little whisky on the side to them that was. They didn't let the Ocala policemen arrest anybody on the Canal, you know. The County cops didn't bother you much, either. There was some special men who could bother you, but if you didn't raise a ruckus, they wouldn't care.

But Daddy Mention used to have to go to Ocala whenever his liquor would run out. He was smart, though; he used to get one of the white men on the Camp to drive him in and bring him back. That way the policemen in Ocala didn't get a chance to get him. It used to make the cops mad as a stunned gopher to see Daddy Mention come riding right into town with this white feller, then go riding back to the Canal again, and they couldn't get their hands on him.

But one time Daddy Mention had just got his little load of liquor, and they had started back, when the white feller he saw somebody he knew. So he got out of the truck and told Daddy Mention to wait a minute. He didn't have to tell him that; the cop came, and put Daddy Mention where he could wait a long time, real comfortable. The policeman had waited a long time for a chance to lock Daddy Mention up, and thought he would have a little fun with him after he was in jail. So he started pretending to joke with Daddy Mention, and kidding him about always riding into town with that white man. "You must think you are good as white folks," he told Daddy Mention, and laughed.

Daddy Mention thought the cop was really playing with him, and started telling stories. One of the best that he told was one about how the Lord was making men, and put all the dough into the oven. He took out the first dough, Daddy Mention told the cops, and it wasn't nowheres near brown; it was just yellow. So he set it aside, and later it became all them folks that lives in foreign countries, them Turks and all. Then he took out a real brown batch of dough. Daddy Mention told the policemen how this batch looked, well-done and seasoned right. This was the colored folks, Daddy Mention told them. They all laughed; he didn't see them winking at each other.

"What became of the rest of the dough, Boy?" one of them asked Daddy Mention at last.

"Oh! that? That's what was left over; it didn't get into the oven at all. It was left raw. They made all the policemen in the world out of that." Then Daddy Mention laughed hard as he could; the policemen laughed, too.

I don't know if the judge laughed, though; I know he gave Daddy Mention two years the next day.

---

vividly told by the prisoners. All of the imagination, the color and action of the John Henry stories of other sections are duplicated in Daddy's activities. It is peculiar that the exploits, far-fetched though they might seem, seldom fall on unbelieving ears inside the "Blue Jay."—M. R.

II. Daddy Mention's Escape

Daddy Mention liked the Polk County jails all right, all except the little jug outside of Lakeland. He told them when they put him in there that he didn't think he could stay with them too long. They had locked him up for vagrancy, you see. And Daddy Mention didn't think so much of that, because just like he had told them he had been picking oranges, and just had too much money to work for a week or two. He tried to tell them that he would go back to work soon as he got broke, but you know you can't say much in Polk County. So they locked Daddy Mention up; they gave him ninety, straight up. [Ninety days, with no time off for good behavior.] He went on the stump-grubbing gang, soon as he got to the Farm.

It was afternoon when Daddy Mention started to work, and he made the first day all right. He fussed a little, kinda under his breath, when he saw what the prisoners et for supper, but he didn't say much. Then next morning he et breakfast—grits and bacon grease, but without no bacon—with the rest of us, and went out to the woods. Before it was ten o'clock—you know you start at six in Polk County—Cap'n Smith had cussed at Daddy Mention two or three times; he didn't work fast enough to suit 'em down there. When he went in for dinner he was growling at the table. "They aint treatin' me right," he said.

After dinner, when we lined up to go back to the woods, Cap'n Smith walked over to Daddy Mention. "Boy," he 'most hollered, "you gonna work this afternoon, or you want to go in the box?" Daddy Mention didn't say nothing at first, then kinda slow he said, "Whatever you want me to do, Cap'n." Cap'n Smith didn't know what to make of that, and he put Daddy Mention in the box in a hurry. He didn't go back for him that day, neither. He didn't go back till the next day. "You think you want to come out of there and work now, Boy?" he asked Daddy Mention, and Daddy Mention told him again: "Whatever you want me to do, Cap'n."

I didn't see Cap'n Smith then, but they tell me he got so hot you could fry eggs on him. He slammed the box shut, and didn't go back for Daddy Mention for another day. Daddy Mention didn't get out then, though. Every day Cap'n Smith asked him the same thing, and every day Daddy Mention said the same thing. Finally Cap'n Smith figgered that maybe Daddy Mention wasn't trying to be smart, but was just dumb that way. So one day he let Daddy Mention come out, and let him go with another gang, the tree-chopping gang, working just ahead of us.

Daddy Mention was glad to get out, 'cause he had made up his mind to go to Tampa. He told some of his gang about it when his Cap'n wasn't listening. But Daddy Mention knew that he couldn't just run away, though; you can't do that down there. They'd have you back in jail before you get as far as Mulberry. Oh! no! Daddy Mention knew he had to have a better plan. And he made up one, too. None of us knew much about it, 'cause he didn't talk about it much. But we begin seeing him doing more work than anybody else in his gang; he would chop a tree by hisself, and wouldn't take but one more man to help him lift it to the pile. Then one day, when he was sure his Cap'n saw him, he lifted one all by hisself and carried it a long ways before he put it down.

The Cap'n didn't believe any man could grab one of them big pines and lift it by hisself, much less carry it around. He called Daddy Mention and made him do it again, then he made him do it so that some of the other guards could see it. It wasn't long before the Cap'n and his friends was picking up a little side money by betting other people that Daddy Mention could pick up any tree they could cut. And they didn't fuss so much when Daddy Mention made a couple of bumpers [nickels] showing off his lifting hisself.

So it got to be a regular sight to see Daddy Mention walking around the jail yard carrying a big tree in his arms. Everybody was getting used to it by then. That was just what Daddy Mention wanted. One afternoon we came in from the woods, and Daddy Mention was bringing a tree-butt with him. The Cap'n thought one of the other guards musta told him to bring it in, and didn't ask him nothing about it. Daddy Mention took his tree-butt to the dining room and stood it up by the wall, then went on in with the rest of us and et his dinner. He didn't seem in no hurry, or nothing, but he just didn't have much to say.

After dinner he waited till nearly everybody had finished, then got up slow and went back to his log. Most of the Cap'ns and guards was around the yard then, and all of them watched while Daddy Mention picked up that big log. Daddy Mention clowned around in front of the guards for a minute, then started towards the gate with the log on his shoulder. None of the guards didn't bother him, because who ever saw a man escape with a pine butt on his shoulder?

You know you have to pass the guards' quarters before you get to the gate in the Lakeland Blue Jay. But Daddy Mention didn't even turn around when he passed it, and nobody didn't say nothing to him. The guards musta thought the other guards sent him somewhere with the log, or was making a bet, or something. Right on out the gate Daddy Mention went, and onto the road that goes to Hillsborough County. He still had the log on his shoulder. I never saw him again till a long time after, in Tampa.

I never did figure out how he got into Hillsborough County from Polk, with watchers all along the road, after he left the Lakeland Blue Jay. So I asked him.

"I didn't have no trouble," he told me. "I just kept that log on my shoulder, and everybody I passed thought it had fell off a truck, and I was carrying it back. They knew nobody wouldn't have nerve enough to steal a good pine log like that and walk along the highway with it. They didn't even bother me when I got out of Polk County. But soon as I got to Plant City, though, I took my log to a little woodyard and sold it. Then I had enough money to *ride* to Tampa. They aint goin' to catch me in Polk County no more."

My Grandfather

MY GRANDFATHER came to Florida in a covered wagon in the early sixties. He settled in the central section of Florida. However, when he landed here, he found this country flat, like sixty per cent of the state is now. He did not like that. Being born and raised back up in Pennsylvania, he wanted a hilly country, and he got down on his hands and knees and he scraped up the sand and the dirt and built all of the hills that you see in this section of Florida. If you will drive over the state you will see where he got a lot of that sand and dirt. There are a lot of places where he frightened me, and I said, "Grandpa, don't take all that sand and dirt away from these people. You know now there are a lot of sections in Florida where you have to use a ladder to get to the ocean."

He said, "Grandson, I am not going to hurt them. I am going to leave them with good soil so they can produce vegetables. I am simply taking up the overburden."

I remember when my grandpa was building the highest point in the State of Florida—well, I will say in the United States—what difference does it make? I was watching him the day he built this precipice; in fact, I had a golf stick keeping the Indians off of him and about that time a wild buffalo charged my grandpa. He stood still like all Danns will, and when that buffalo got within a half foot of my grandpa with his mouth wide open, my grandpa just ran his hand down that buffalo's throat, grabbed him by the tail and jerked him wrong side out. Naturally, that reversed the buffalo and made him run the other way.

When my grandpa came down to Florida, there were no lakes and no water. He did not like that. Being born and raised up in Wisconsin, he wanted water, because he said it took water to make climate. So he built Lake Apopka, Lake Okeechobee, Lake Eustis, Lake Tildepucksasa, Lake Peaatlecahah, Lake Withlacooche and little Lake Econlochhatchie, and he built the Halifax River and the St. Johns River.

Now, if you will stop to think, friends, that that old gentleman hauled that water all the way from the East Coast with oxen, after dipping the water up with gourds and then spreading it out and "aireating" it, in order to take the salt out, and then pouring it into these great cavities after digging them out, you will know he was a wonderful man, and that is why, before I start talking here tonight, I wanted to just give you an idea of how famous the Danns are.

Extract from speech made by Carl Dann of Orlando to the Jacksonville Junior Chamber of Commerce in 1928. From *Carl Dann's Vicissitudes and Catastrophics,* Volume I, pp. 101–104. Copyright, 1929, by Florida Press, Inc. Orlando.

And yet my grandpa has been criticised. All famous people have been criticised. I have been criticised severely. They say that my grandpa built the St. Johns River wrong; that it runs north instead of south. They claim he came down to this country with that great Yankee pep you hear about that the Southerner does not have, and that he started digging the St. Johns River in Jacksonville, and having that northern ambition, he dug the river deep, but as he came on south, that pep gradually died and he dug less and less and finally way down below Orlando, he just quit and went to sleep.

But I say that people who criticised my grandpa have less brains than he had, and the criticism is unjust, because how in the world could he build the Halifax River that those wonderful cities on the East Coast of Florida might exist, unless he ran the water north in the St. Johns River in order to bring it back south through the Halifax River.

SWAPPING LIES

The Double Rat

I HEARED dat ole red nigger tell some lie 'bout a rat.

He say he been back on Lykes's plantation in de ole field by de river. He say he was walkin' 'long 'tendin' to he business when he see sump'n crawl out from under a pile er straw. He say he stand up an' look at it, an' he ain' know ef he see sump'n or no, or whether he eye jest gone wrong. He say at first sight it look like a rat totin' another rat on he back, but when he look good he see it been two rat, back to back, growed together. All two on 'em been full rat. Each on 'em had he own head an' he own leg an' he own tail.

An' dat nigger say he make up he mind he guh try to ketch 'em for he boss. He say he know ain' nobody see no sech rat as dat. An' he say when he make for him, dat rat start 'cross de field—an' him an' dat rat. He say he ain' never been so outdone. He say when he think he mighty nigh ketch him, lo an' behold! dat rat lay down an' roll over an' de other rat start to runnin'.

An' he say dat wey he quit.

Leander, the Telegraphing Rattlesnake

IT WAS soon after I first went to work for the road with which I am still employed, the Illinois Central, than which there is no finer.

From *Nigger to Nigger,* by E. C. L. Adams, p. 177. Copyright, 1928, by Charles Scribner's Sons. New York and London.

From Paul Flowers' "Greenhouse," in *The Commercial Appeal,* Memphis, Tennes-

I was sent to Way, Mississippi, as night operator. The name was about all there was to the station, except a water tank and day and night telegraph operator. Way is back in the Big Black River Bottoms, where the nights get the blackest, the bullfrogs croak the coarsest and the hoot owls hoot the lonesomest of any spot in creation. It is only about 20 miles from Vaughn, where Casey Jones of song and fable pulled his last throttle some 40 years ago.

My duties at Way consisted of reporting trains promptly and staying awake, or vice versa, and sometimes I dozed, and as a consequence could not truthfully report that a string had gone by.

When I failed to get enough rest during the day and was unusually sleepy when I came to work, I would find out when the next train was due to pass and then go out and pour a handful of cinders on the rails. If the passing train did not awaken me, when I did come to I could go out and see if the cinders were swept off, and if so, I knew the train had gone. This system had its disadvantages in bad weather.

I tried another old one, that of tying one end of a string to the coal scuttle in the office, stretching it across the track and tying the other to a stick. When the train came along, it hit the string and rattled the coal hod. This was not entirely satisfactory either, because a wandering mule or cow was liable to come before the train. But fortune brought a happy solution to my problem.

One night as I sat reading a detective magazine and had just reached the point where the villain was about to push the heroine over the cliff, I happened to glance toward the door and was amazed to see a good-sized rattlesnake crawling in the door. As it lay there on the floor I noticed a marked resemblance to our Porter Leander, who was long and svelte too. Well, I sat there, paralyzed with fright, while the snake coiled, waved his head from side to side like the pendulum on a grandfather clock, his beady, unblinking eyes taking in everything in the office. I had used all my snake medicine the night before, so I was just where Moses was.

All at once a complete calm came over me. I rose, strode boldly to where the snake was, and poured some milk out of my lunch kit into a fruit jar lid, and set it where the rattler could see it. He took the hint and lapped it greedily. After he had finished with the milk, we eyed each other for a moment, and seemed to reach a complete understanding. I had a practice telegraph set in the back of the office, and I went over and began tapping out slowly the alphabet in the Morse code. Leander, as I called my visitor, crawled onto the table and was all attention—finest and most apt student I ever had. Soon as I would make a letter, I'd pause, and he'd raise his tail and try to imitate the dots and dashes and spaces with his rattles.

---

see. Reprinted in *Illinois Central Magazine,* Vol. XXXII (February, 1944), No. 8, pp. 29–30. Chicago: Published monthly by the Illinois Central System.

Here is the tale of the rattlesnake that mastered the Morse code, back when telegraphers and pounding brass was a fine and noble profession. J. M. Bryant sets his hand and seal to this story!—P. F.

In an unusually short time he knew the entire alphabet. He had a little trouble with the letter "P," which consists of five dots. He seemed to lose control of his tail muscles on that one, and I thought he'd never quit making dots. But he finally mastered the "P" and his Morse was a joy to listen to. We spent many otherwise lonely hours, I with brass key and sounder, tobacco can and all, and Leander with his natural sounder. He told me he was one of twenty children, but that his brothers and sisters had been drowned in a flood.

Leander was a handy creature around the office; he could grab up a broom in his tail, hump his back, put his nose to the floor and do as good a sweeping job as you ever saw.

But the biggest lift he gave was in helping me report trains. As you know, a snake's tongue when extended from his mouth is sort of like a radio antenna. Leander would crawl on the telegraph table in the depot's bay window, stick his head out, poke his tongue out some more and get the vibration of a train 35 miles away. Then he would come over to the table where I was sleeping, touch my face tenderly with that sensitive tongue of his, and I knew it was time to rouse up and exchange signals with the train crew and report their passing.

All good things come to an end. I got word that I was to be transferred; so one evening, as Leander and I were having our little chat in Morse, I broke the news to him, gently as I knew how. I told him how much I had enjoyed knowing him and how much he had done to keep me from being lonely, in his cordial ophidian way, and I invited him to go on with me to my next station.

But Leander, after thinking it over for a while, tapped out "no," and explained that Big Black River Bottoms were his home, where all his folks had lived since the Ice Age, and he was considerable of a homebody, and didn't think he'd get adjusted to unfamiliar scenes. He thanked me for teaching him Morse, and we had a parting of the Way. As he slithered out, he paused, looked back, transfixed me with those soulful and unblinking eyes, and tapped out "73," which is the telegrapher's traditional symbol for goodby.

I felt no shame as I stood there alone, with the shades of night falling fast, as tears trickled down my cheeks and Leander disappeared. He was a pal.

The Rattlesnake-Bitten Cypress Club

. . . Last week I had a job to do at the sawmill an' I thought I'd take a short cut through the piney woods. I tuk my old cypress club, jest in

From *Suwannee River*, Strange Green Land, by Cecile Hulse Matschat, pp. 110-111. The Rivers of America. Copyright, 1938, by Cecile Hulse Matschat. New York: Farrar & Rinehart, Inc.

case I met a b'ar or a hant. I hadn't gone fur when, quick like, I felt somethin' strike the stick—so hard hit nigh knocked hit clean outen my hand. Well, I looked down, an' thar was the biggest ole buster of a rattlesnake ever I did see, with his fangs caught fast in the wood. I knocked him loose an' hit him a lick, then I hung him over a big gall-berry bush. He was so long his head an' tail dragged for nigh on a yard on each side. On I went, keerless like, a-singin' an' a-whistlin', but soon I noticed that somethin' ailed my old club, it was so big and heavy like.

"Great catawampus!" says I, "that snake was so powerful pizen hit's effected my club; hit's all swelled like." An' 't was so! Come time I got to the mill, I war a-draggin' the biggest cypress log ever come outen the swamp, so I had it cut up for railroad ties an' sold 'em in Waycross. The man as bought 'em said they'd line near a mile o' track, an' he'd guarentee that I'd get a right smart heap of money. But I bin done outen my lawful rights an' I'm a-goin' to have the law on him. 'Cause this mornin' I got a piece of writin' sayin' as how it come on an' rained on the track; an' the pizen in the ties got so weak they shrunk up, like. So they sold 'em for toothpicks, an' sent me a dime. . . .

Texas Mosquitoes

ALL seaport towns suffer from those marine monsters known as mosquitoes. In inland towns you have to raise them in a cistern, or worry along without them. Both coast towns, Galveston and Houston, have fine natural facili-ties for raising mosquitoes. I have tried both brands of mosquitoes, or rather both of them have tried me; and I cannot tell which is the best to avoid associating with. The mosquito, like the sailor, is bred on the water; but he will not return to you after many days, because he will never leave you. In Galveston they grow to such a large size, that a stranger is apt to mistake them for pelicans. A Galvestonian asked me if I had seen any pelicans.

"Are they big birds, that have long bills?" I inquired.

"Yes; that's the kind of an insect they are."

"Are they always flying about the bars, looking for something to eat?"

"Precisely."

"Then my room is full of them, and they raise a blister every time they bite."

In regard to the merits of the rival brands of mosquitoes, it is with pain I state that both Galveston and the other maritime haven are prone to clothe the naked truth with the flowery garments of fiction. In Houston they showed me affidavits stating that in Galveston the mosquitoes were so

From *On a Mexican Mustang, Through Texas, from the Gulf to the Rio Grande*, by Alex E. Sweet and J. Armoy Knox, pp. 52-53. Copyright, 1883, by Sweet & Knox. Hartford, Connecticut: S. S. Scranton & Company.

large as to be included in the cow ordinance, while in Galveston I was told
that the Houston mosquitoes wore forty-five-inch undershirts. There is
probably a happy medium between the two. I do not know how happy
the medium is; but, if he is not under a mosquito-bar, there is a limit to his
bliss. The truth is, that the coast-town mosquito rarely exceeds in size the
ordinary Texas mocking-bird.

(N. B.—When I left New York, I could not have told a lie to save my
life; and here, after three-days' residence in Texas, this is what I have
come to—and all the time I have been associating with the higher classes.
They say in Houston that I caught the infection in passing through Galveston.)

Let me advise all persons visiting Texas ports of entry to leave their
mosquitoes behind; they can get new ones cheaper.

The Lean and the Fat Buck

THE epitome of all Texas talk is perhaps the story of Captain Chaudoin's
lean and fat buck. The captain went hunting on a chilly, dreary winter
day after a droughty summer. Cattle were so poor that their bones rattled
in the wind. Toward twilight he saw a deer leaning against a tree and cut
down on it. The deer did not move. Since he never missed, the captain
walked closer to see what had happened, and as he did so, with a faint
gasp and a slight quiver of limb the deer died. The ball had passed through
the dry and brittle hide as if it had been a pane of glass. Not a drop of
blood flowed from the wound; not an ounce of flesh was on the carcass.
When the captain tried to lift it, the horns fell off, and a sudden gust of
wind tore the body from his hands and sailed it ten yards away. When he
tried to cut the buck's throat, his knife snapped off at the hilt. In anger
he broke off the head, raised the carcass, and shook it. Bleached bones
fell out. The captain soaked the hide in grease for several days but could
do nothing with it. Finally he broke it into bits which he used as flints for
his gun.

On a bright spring morning, just two months later, Captain Chaudoin
again went hunting. Every living thing was fat and sleek, and he saw
a nice buck. This time the captain's bullet melted in the heat generated
by the fat and spread like a silver leaf against the inner side of one shoulder
blade. So much blood flowed from the wound that the captain was forced
to dig a trench and drain it off into a nearby creek before he could approach
his kill. With the help of four Negroes he loaded the deer on a two-horse
wagon and hauled it home. When he stuck his knife in the carcass, it
popped like a swollen bladder and the hide slipped off like the skin from

From *Big Country: Texas,* by Donald Day, pp. 56–57. American Folkways Series
edited by Erskine Caldwell. Copyright, 1947, by Donald Day. New York: Duell, Sloan
& Pearce, Inc.

a freestone peach. The fat swelled out so fast that, after cutting off slices for two hours, the carcass was twice as large as when it was in the hide. He hung the remains up in a cool place and continued to cut parts from it as needed until his entire family—wife, children, Negroes, dogs, and hogs— got prodigiously fat and all the cooking utensils and dishes and the kitchen got to smelling like the buck. In anger he boiled down the remnants of the fat into ten barrels of soap which he used to wash away the grease that had collected around his premises.

The story of the lean and fat buck, to the early Texans, was symbolical of the harsh and lavish way in which nature dealt with them.

The Rooter-Dog

IN THESE warm latitudes, in the cool of the evening, a group of men is always to be found sitting around in chairs under the hotel awning. The group usually consists of the hotel guests, the landlord, and the married men who come "down town to meet a man at the office after supper." Their occupation at these times consists in carving their initials in the arms of the hotel chairs, and their amusement in competitive lying.

When we came out from supper, some of the men were balancing themselves on the hind-legs of the chairs, their feet on the columns of the awning, and their thoughts straying in the realms of imagination.

One jovial-looking liar, with the wreck of a watermelon on his knee, and an impediment in his speech, had just finished a thrilling narrative of an encounter he once had, down in the old Caney bottom, with a hybrid monster, part *coyote* and part bulldog, where his escape was owing to a special providence, assisted by a brindled steer, on whose back he dropped from the tree up which he had taken refuge.

This reminded the landlord of a story: "When I was keeping restaurant up at Bryan, before the railroad got there, I was trying to raise a pair of young pups,—you know, them little Mexican dogs that have got no hair, except a tuft on the top of their heads. When they were about six weeks old, their mother was run over by a delivery-wagon, and died. I had a sow that at the time had a family of young ones about the size of the dogs. I wanted to save the pups if possible, as I had promised one of them to old man Brown: so I took a fool notion that I'd try if the old sow would raise them. Would you believe it, gentlemen! they just took to her as kindly as if she had been their own mother. And there I had six young pigs and two six-weeks-old pups growing up together in perfect harmony.

"In about a week, along came a skipjack of an Englishman,—one of them 'you know, you know' sort of damn fools; that kind of human outrage

From *On a Mexican Mustang, Through Texas, from the Gulf to the Rio Grande*, by Alex. E. Sweet and J. Armory Knox, pp. 43–47. Copyright, 1883, by Sweet and Knox. Hartford, Connecticut: S. S. Scranton & Company.

that has always 'seen something better than that' in the Old Country, and
tells it with an every-thing-different-there-you-know air of superiority. He
had been blowin' around promiscuous for a day or two, before I thought
of the pups. He had sort o' aggravated me more than common that morning by his talk of the 'dawgs and 'orses' they had in England. I posted some
of the boys, and told them to be handy in the evening. So, just as it might
be now, we were all sitting around on the gallery, as it was beginning to get
dark. Says I to the Englishman, 'Major, talking about them dogs you
mentioned this morning, do you have any rooter dogs in your country?'—
'Any what?' says he. 'Rooter dogs,' says I; 'we use them for hunting ta-
rantulas, and for harvesting goober peas. They're a cross between the wild
Mexican hog and the bulldog. You see, the bite of a tarantula will kill
a common dog in less'n a minute,' says I; 'whereas snakebites and such like
don't fizzle on a hog. Well, the rooter being half hog, half dog,' says I, 'is
just what we want. If it hadn't been for their introduction into the country, the tarantula trade would never have been developed; and as for
gathering goober peas,—they grow under ground, you know,—the rooter
dog is the greatest labor-saving animal known. You see, the hog part of
him roots the goobers out, while the-sagacity-of-the-dog part enables him
to be taught to pile the peas up in little heaps all along the row.' The Englishman seemed halfway to believe it all; but he laughed in a knowing sort
of a way, and he says he, 'Aw, now! tell that to the marines; you know you
cawn't expect a fellow to believe all that.'—'Well,' says I, 'you can believe
it or not. These gentlemen here all know that it's nothing but the truth I'm
telling you. Some of them keep rooter dogs themselves; and besides all
that, if you'll come back to the yard with me, I'll show you two genuwine
rooter pups that I am raising right now. You will see them with their
mother; and I reckon that'll convince you.' The Englishman looked
around; but, as he couldn't detect a smile anywhere,—for the boys were all
as solemn-looking as a row of turkey buzzards holding a *post-mortem*
examination on a dead horse,—he says, 'I don't mind stwolling around to
see the blawsted things anyhow.' So we all got up, and filed into the stable-
yard; and there, sure enough, lay the old sow, and the two pups beside
her. I had had the colored boy carry off all the young shotes before we
came into the yard. Great cracky! you should have seen that Englishman
stare, and screw his glass in his eye, when Jim Johnson put one of the
pups in his hand, that he might, as Jim said, examine and see for himself
that we had some *pro*-ducts that they couldn't raise in England.

"One of the boys showed him where the hog part was developed in the
skin, bristles on the back, and curl in the tail, while another called his attention to the cropping-out of the dog in the head and paws.

"Before we got through with the exhibition of the peculiar and valuable
points of the pup, the Englishman was trembling with eagerness to become
possessed of one of them, that he might carry it back to the Old Country
with him. He offered me twenty dollars for it. I wanted thirty. After some
argument, he authorized me to make a charge on his bill for 'One rooter

dog, twenty-five dollars,' with the understanding that I was to take care of it until it could be safely weaned. He was as proud of his purchase as a schoolboy with a new gumboil; and, till late in the night, the boys sat around, relating interesting reminiscences of tarantula hunts, giving him points in natural history, and furnishing valuable statistics relative to the goober interests.

"But, bless your soul! the fun didn't begin till next morning, when the Englishman got to spoutin' about the dawg down to Schmidt's drug-store, and some derned fool that wasn't in the secret dropped the bung out of the whole business. They devilled the poor fellow almost to death. At first he tried to make believe that he had twigged the racket from the start, and was merely humoring the joke; but that was too weak. Then he swore, and cussed the 'demmed country, you know,' but finally got into good humor, and set 'em up all round. He couldn't stand the endless quizzing, however, and next morning hired a team, and lit out for San Antonio."

(I omit the profanity with which this story was emphasized, as it was not intended for publication, merely given as a guaranty of good faith.)

Dr. Ballowe's Possum

ON OTHER occasions the doctor ranged about the parish with his cronies, occasionally participating in great poker games whose every player might be of a different nationality; sometimes he was to be found at the bars and especially at the "bamboches," gatherings of the men for gay evenings of yarn-spinning. These were meetings about large tables, on which sat pitchers of wine. Women were not wanted; the talk had gusto and, not infrequently, anatomical detail. The songs were long ones, short ones; funny ones, sad ones; about animals, about mothers-in-law, foolish husbands, gay lovers, and wives. Dr. Ballowe, a gallant bachelor then as now, was a leading participant. "I could sing like a nightingale, with a voice rich and clear and true." Somewhere in the program, Dr. Ballowe remembers, when the fumes of the wine had stimulated the imagination, and before drowsiness stilled the tongue, someone suggested the telling of "big lies." These were the Paul Bunyan tales of the Delta. The story-tellers vied to see who could concoct the most grotesque and the most whopping; Dr. Ballowe won considerable repute. One of his best, in dialect, went this way:

"I trap' all day. When I get back to camp, I am blow' out an' hongry. At the camp I ax my wife what he have cook'. 'Not much, vieux,' he say. 'I pick up a few swimp an' crab. With these I have make a gombo.' 'A gombo, chère, is very lil' for a man fatigue' like me. For what you don' kill a chicken?' My wife say 'We have only one lef' an' he lay egg every day. It would be mortal sin to kill a beas' like that.'

From *Deep Delta Country*, by Harnett T. Kane, pp. 247–248. Copyright, 1944, by Harnett T. Kane. New York: Duell, Sloan & Pearce, Inc.

"At the same secon' I hear 'qua-ak! qua-ak!' I run, throw open the door, an' what I see? A big rat-de-bois have grab our las' hen by the neck. 'Yas, ahn?' I holler, an' give him a coup de baton what put his feet in the air. 'Look,' I tell my wife, 'le Bon Dieu est bon, oui. I will skin the possum. Zebe in the nex' camp, he will give me bottle wine for the hide. You will cook the meat. With gombo, wine an' it, an' bread and café, we will eat good.' My wife find two-three potato, an' everything come good.

"Befo' we start to eat, with that wine ope' on the table an' that gombo in the bowl, she ope' the do' of the stove to look how ev'ything is go. Maybe you not believe it, but there was the rat-de-bois stand up in that pan! He have eat the potato an' drink the grease. Now he jomp out the stove, he pass between my wife leg, an' on the table. He turn over the gombo, knock over the wine, then he run out the back door, me behin' 'im. Outside was the poor hen still on the groun', his neck all twis', his eye making comme-ci, comme-ça. That rat grab him as he pass an' run away in the grass. That was not all, no. That night, he go to Zebe's camp an' take his skin from the stretching board an' put it back on. Now that was some*thing*, ahn?"

The Bay Filly's Hide

BIB TARKEY the blacksmith told me very solemnly one day about "a 'sperience" which he and his brother had when they were boys, in the hills south of Durgenville. "We seen a feller in town oncet a-wearin' a coat made out'n a piedy horse-hide, tanned with th' ha'r on," said Bib. "Wal, sir, me an' Pucky shore did have a turrible hankerin' atter coats like that, but whar was we goin' t' git th' horse-hide at? Finally one day we snuck up close t' Pap's bay filly, an' all of a suddint we jumps out a whoopin' an' a-hollerin' so loud hit skeerd th' filly dang nigh t' death. Next day we done it ag'in, an' this time th' pore critter was skeerd so bad she jumped plumb out'n her skin! Wal, sir, soon as Pap seen th' filly a-runnin' round bar' neckid thataway he jest blowed up, an' raised more hell in two minutes than us boys ever seen all our life before. He shore did think a heap o' that 'ar bay filly. . . . Soon as he got done a-whuppin' me an' Pucky he jest booted us right out in our shirt-tail, an' he says we cain't never come in th' house no more 'less'n we fix th' filly up some way or 'nother. We was a-bellerin' an' Maw was a-cryin' an' Pap was a-cussin'—hit shore was a bad night at our place. Yas, sir, hit *shore* was!

"Me an' Pucky didn't have no idy whut we better do, but atter while we kilt two o' old man Gifford's sheep, an' skun em, an' put th' pelts on th' filly th' best we could. . . . Th' skin growed on all right, but thar ain't no use denyin' but whut th' filly allus looked kinder funny atter that. But Pap seen we'd done our level best t' fix things up, so he let us come home an'

From *Ozark Mountain Folks*, by Vance Randolph, pp. 162–163. Copyright, 1932, by the Vanguard Press, Inc. New York.

git our britches atter we'd shivered round in th' timber a couple o' nights.
. . . Th' filly didn't grow much wool th' first season, but th' second year
she had wool four foot long an' p'inted three ways, an' th' hull family
worked seven days a-shearin' her. Jest as we was a-gittin' th' job done she
kicked Pap into th' pile o' wool so deep it tuck me an' Pucky all day an' half
th' night t' find him an' dig him out ag'in. He like t' sultered under that 'ar
wool, too, an' he suffered turrible with th' asthmy all th' rest o' his life!"

A Heap of Strange Things

I've seen a heap of strange things in my days, sure's you borned. I've
seen the sun go down in the east and the moon go down in the west, and
I've seen it snow in June and blossoms growing in January, but one of the
beatingest things I ever saw was a dog getting a tick out of his ear.

The old dog was named Dash and he was a big blue speckled hound. He
was always getting ticks in his ears and the children was always pulling
them out. One week the kids had gone to their grandmother's, though, and
there wa'n't nobody to git the ticks out except me and I ain't that kind of
man. Dash kept his ticks till long about Wednesday and then he must have
decided that he couldn't keep them no longer.

I was setting on the river bank fishing when I saw Dash breaking off
a forked limb from a willer bush. He gnawed and gnawed and after he
got it off he hilt it with his paws and pulled the leaves off with his mouth.
After he got the leaves off he gnawed the twigs off and left just the forked
stick. You know willer twigs bends easy and that dog didn't have a bit of
trouble holding the stick in his mouth and bending the prongs back into
his ear. He went down to the river so's he could see what he was doing and
he used that stick just like a woman does a pair of tweezers. He hilt it in
his mouth and used his paw to clamp the prongs together and dad burned,
if he didn't pull the last one of them ticks out'n his ears.

Some of the other critters uses sticks, too, to do things with. The coon
does when he gits full of fleas, only he uses a alder switch. He cuts his
switch about six inches long, maybe a little longer, and when he gits through
he ain't got a flea left.

One night 'bout twenty-five years ago I was going home from a neighbor's when I saw a coon. The moon was shining bright as day and so I lay
down and watched him. He gnawed him off a little limb and went on down
to the crick holding it in his mouth. He didn't get the leaves off like the
dog done, but just toted it off just like it was. When he got to the crick he
turned back'ards and backed in. First he stuck his tail under the water

As told by Charles King, about 70, Cary, North Carolina, to Mary Hicks. Manuscripts of the Federal Writers' Project of the Works Progress Administration for the
State of North Carolina.

and you could see the fleas hopping up on his back. He let his back go under real slow and as he went under the fleas kept hopping up until they all set on his nose. The old coon took his time and he let them set there and git good 'n scared. Directly he hilt up the little bush and, so help me, the fleas jumped on it before the old coon dived under the water. As he went under he chunked the bush as far as he could send it, the fleas drownded to death, and, believe me or not, that old coon come out laughing.

You might think that that's quare but I seed something that beat that all to pieces one time not so long ago.

I was over in the meadow working my corn and I plowed up a bullfrog. I saw that the plow had cut him and he was bleeding bad. I went on down to the end and when I come back I saw five or six other frogs around him. I plowed on down to the end and then I got to wondering why a whole passel of frogs come to the hurted frog. I tied my mule and creeped back up the row to see.

Well, bless my soul, if I didn't see a sight that time. Them frogs was pulling limbs off of a sassafras bush and tying them together with wire grass. They worked and worked and then they got two long bushes and tied them on the side. When they got it fixed to their notion, dad drat my hide, if they didn't put the sick frog on it and head for the pond. It 'peared like a heap of things got in their way 'cause five of them toted the stretcher and the other one hopped along in front blowing a whistle.

That sounds like seeing enough for one day, but what I had seen wa'n't nothing. When they got him to the pond and laid him on the bank a big fat bullfrog come up out of the water and brought a needle in his hand. He flopped the hurted frog over on his side and sewed him up with a blade of nut grass.

* * * * *

I've seed a lot of things in my time and I ain't never been scared but once but that was enough to make up for all the time. I was walking through the woods one night going home from a 'possum hunt. I hadn't killed no 'possums 'cause like usual I had done seed the human side of the thing. I found the old 'possum, but she was a mammy and she had ten little 'possums in her pocket. She wanted to cross the creek but she couldn't git across with the young ones in her pocket and they couldn't swim. I saw that she looked worried but I thought she'd figure it out so I waited and watched. Way atter awhile she took them out of her pocket, bent down a tree, and hanging her tail around the top limb, she jumped to the other bank. The tail hilt the tree down and made a bridge from one bank to the other and in the due course of time the little 'possums all got across. I wouldn't think about killing a 'possum atter that and so I was walking along the woods when I jumped a bear.

Maybe the bear jumped me, but that's the only time I've ever been scared. I saw that he meant to eat me and I didn't have a thing to defend myself with. I run until I give out and then I climbed a tree to rest. I knowed the critter'd git me so I pulled off my shoes and hung them on a limb so's he could make a quick job of it.

I didn't really want to die though, and even as I seed him coming up the tree I tried to think of something. I couldn't think of but one thing and that looked like a mighty slim hope to me. I watched and when he opened his mouth to growl I dropped my big chaw of terbacker down his throat and while he was gagging and trying to git the terbacker up I drapped both of my shoes in his mouth and choked him to death. That's the only time that I've been plumb scared and if I hadn't of had that chaw of terbacker I might not have lived to tell the tale.

Mountain Hogs

I

. . . THE nose of a mountain hog is so long and so tough one can turn over a log for the crickets underneath, or upturn huge stones along the creek bank in search of craw-dads.

My cousin, Richard Wilson, was born and raised here. He was a high school classmate of Chief Justice Fred M. Vinson of the United States. Cousin Richard's reputation for truth and veracity has never been doubted in this community.

Early in life, he learned the carpenter's trade and roamed through quite a bit of Kentucky, West Virginia and Tennessee in pursuit of it.

My cousin relates that several years ago he happened to be in the mountains of Tennessee where a coal camp was under construction. The operators wanted to build a road up the mountain side to provide passage for the mine mules. The route was so rough they were unable to find a contractor with enough heavy equipment to tackle the job.

My cousin relates that a nearby farmer had 250 head of mountain hogs. The farmer applied for the contract to build the road. Inasmuch as the operators had everything to gain and nothing to lose, they gave it to him.

Well, sir, the farmer first took a crowbar and punched holes 18 inches apart in the side of the mountain along where the operators wanted the road to run. He punched them all the way from level ground to the drift mouth of the mine.

The farmer next got several sacks of shelled corn and carefully filled the holes with it. He saved out enough corn, however, to toll his 250 head of mountain hogs from the barn lot to the lowest level of holes.

The farmer stayed with his hogs just long enough for them to discover that the holes up the side of the mountain were filled with corn. Then he went back home, sat down in a cane-back rocker on his front porch, and watched his rootin' hogs root.

From *Greetings from Old Kentucky*, by Allan M. Trout, pp. 3–4, 9. Copyright, 1947, by Allan M. Trout. Louisville, Kentucky: The Courier-Journal.

My cousin relates that ere the sun set that evening, the hogs had rooted out a nice roadbed from the bottom of the mountain to the drift mouth of the mine. Cousin Richard says the operators were well pleased with the road and paid the farmer a handsome sum of money for the job.[1]

II

I was reminded of some remarkable hogs I saw in 1923 near Manchester, in Clay County. I was an inspector of forest products in those days, and had occasion to work quite a bit in the mountains of East Kentucky.

While strolling through the woods one day with my friend, Bill Curry, a ridge runner from London, in Laurel County, we came upon a large bunch of hogs. I stopped in amazement to make a closer inspection.

The hind legs of these hogs were a foot longer than their front legs. And every one of them had a large hole through each ear. I asked Bill why on earth anybody would want to cut holes in the ears of hogs whose hind legs were a foot longer than their front legs.

He explained the hogs were born that way He told me they were a special breed adapted to the steep mountains. It seems their long hind legs were to keep them on even keel as they fed up the side of the mountain. And since their hind legs were so much longer than their front legs, they could not walk down hill; so they stuck their hind legs through the holes in their ears and slid down.

I was skeptical of Bill's explanation, so I asked my friend, Jack Riley, who lived on Goose Creek. Jack told me Bill had been pulling my leg. He said the real purpose of the holes in their ears was to enable the owner to run a wild grapevine through the ear and tie the hog to keep him from falling out of the mountain field into the road below.[2]

Calling the Dog: Mississippi Tall Tales

ONE time they was a bunch of men settin' round the fire tellin' lies and one of the men had a hound pup which he said he'd give to the feller that told the biggest lie. Well, they all taken their turn and the' was some pretty good uns told, too. The last man in the chimney corner, he sot thar and heard all the lies tell finely hit come his time and he jes rared back and 'lowed, "I ain't never told a lie in my life." With that the man that offered the dog got up and called the hound pup and handed him over to the man in the chimney corner. "That's the biggest lie ever told here-

---

[1] From Senator Ira W. See, of Louisa, Kentucky.
[2] From Joseph Edwards, Sr., of Boston, Kentucky.

By Ruth E. Bass. Hazlehurst, Mississippi, November 30, 1938.

abouts. You gits the dog." So ever since then when a bunch of folks starts tellin' lies they calls that pleasurin' "callin' the dog."

I. Hard Times

There was a fellow lived out on the left fork of Indian Creek, and one day a fruit tree agent drove up in this man's yard and tried to sell him some fruit trees. Well this fellow let out a cuss word or two and a couple er whoops and began to poor mouth 'bout hard times and 'lowed as to how he couldn't even buy a peach seed, let alone a sprout. The agent started to guy the fellow about making out like he was busted and the fellow said, "Well, I'll tell you, stranger, jest how it is. Two year ago I had me a wife and eight or nine chillen. I lost count of the chaps but the old woman said there was nine. Then cotton went down and taxes went up till I had to sen' all the younguns to the Orphan's home. That was bad enough but times kept on a-getting worse till I had to sen' my old lady back to her daddy's."

"That was pretty bad," 'lowed the agent.

"I reckon," said the fellow. "But, stranger, things is going bad again and if they get much worse, blamed if I ain't scared that the next thing happens, I'll have to sell my car."

II. Hot Weather

—I've seen hit so hot tell all the stumps and logs on a ten-acre clearin' crawled off in the shade and cleared up the new ground.

—That there weren't hot. One time I seen it so hot tell a couple of hundred pound cakes of ice fell outer the ice house and went out on the street and fainted.

—One time I knowed a couple of men went down to New Awleens all dressed up in their blue serge Sunday suits and hit was so hot when they got there tell the two suits got offen that train by theirselves, the men had done melted outen them.

—Huh! That was chilly weather. One time me and Buck Turner went a-fishin' and hit was so hot tell before we got to the creek we met all the catfish a-swimmin' up the road in the dust.

—That's a fact. I recollect that day. When we got to the river, I struck a match to light my pipe and set the river on fire. Hit burnt up half the river and taken the rest of the water to put out the fire.

—One summer when hit was so hot, I went and sot me some hooks whilst the river was up and that night the river fell and left the hooks outen the water. Next mornin' a catfish which had jumped outen the water and got caught on one of the hooks was swimmin' aroun' in his sweat, nice as you please.

III. High Winds

—One time Oscar Ork and the Patterson boys and a bunch of them was out on a fishing trip and a cyclone hit their camp. Well, they had along a

Negro boy name of John Henry. Well, this John Henry was out in the creek swimming when the storm come roaring up like a freight train. The rest of the men was on their way back to camp and they stopped in a cotton shed outen the rain and was a-watching the cloud and John Henry.

When that boy seen the cloud a-coming, he jumped outen the water and lit a shuck for camp. Just as he got to the cooking place there was a loud clap of thunder that scared the boy so bad he jumped up and hit the skillet where we'd been frying fish and the grease flew all over him. In lessen a minute he was the slickest nigger I ever seen. Before he could jump up and run that cyclone was on him in a twisting funnel about big as a hogshead at the bottom and 'bout fifty feet high—jest a twister out for a frolic. Well, it seen the nigger and it gave a flirt of its tail, jumped over two or three pines and then settled right down on top of John Henry. The men all shet their eyes to keep from seeing that boy tore to splinters for they all thought a right smart of him.

Then they opened up and seen a funny thing was happening. John Henry was so slick with that grease that the twister couldn't get a grip on him. It would raise him purt' nigh offen the ground and then he would slip right back down again. It worried and worked with that boy for half an hour. First it would squat down over him until it warn't over five feet high, and spin like a humming top. Then it would taper up until it warn't no biggern a auger at the bottom and two or three hundred feet high. But the more it twisted that nigger the slicker he got, what with the grease and the sweat pouring offen him.

Well, sir, that cyclone got so mad that it turned plum pale and was wore clean out. At last it give up and with a snort it jumped up in the air and went off up the creek, a-leaving John Henry lying on the ground. The men started to go get him when they heared the wind a-coming back. This time it was colored brown and making a sort of grating sound like it was a-grinding its teeth together.

Do you know what that wind had done? Well sir, it had done run up the creek to a big sand bed and scooped up about fifty barrels of sand and brought it back. It hit that black boy with a rush and sanded ever' bit of that grease on him in about one second. Then it snatched him up and roared off over the tree tops. No sir, hit don't do to fool with no cyclone.

—But that warn't the cyclone that taken that catfish away from Ed Winston. One day Ed was cleaning a catfish and a cyclone come up and taken the fish away from Ed. It blowed that fish inside out, cleaned it and hung it on a barb wire fence which cut it up in portions. Then it taken the pieces and rubbed them against a salt brick down in Cal Patterson's pasture. Next it dipped them in old lady Vernon's meal barrel. Then a flash of lightning fried that fish nice and brown and at last the wind settled and left the whole mess of fish on a blue platter a-settin' on Bowen Anderson's table down at Springville, jest at supper time. Effen anybody disbelieves this tale, Bowen Anderson's still got that platter and can show it to him.

—Them was pretty fast winds but no faster'n that storm which Old John

Wray's buggy mare outrun back in the old days. This mare was the fastest thing ever hitched to a buggy. Well, one day John Wray was driving back to Pontotoc from Cherry Creek when a black cloud rose up from the northwest and started coming down on him. He put the whip on his mare and started to outrun that storm. It looked like it was going to catch him though for just as he got to the Stephens' place the rain began to fall on the 'hind wheels of the buggy. He laid on the whip again and the mare picked up. For seven miles they raced that storm. When he got home and drove under the shed the back end of the buggy was full of water but the seat was dry as powder. That mare had run so fast that half of the buggy was in the storm and half out.

—That was a nice shower but the curiousest thing I ever seen in these parts was the time the Daniel boys that lived out to Old Robbs trapped the lightning.

It was like this. That was the year we had so many thunder storms. The air got so full of electricity that a man's whiskers would spit and crackle like a cat's back, if they was rubbed the wrong way. They all got scared to shave for fear the steel razor'd electrocute 'em. All the barb wire fences would spit fire ever' night. Well, one night about first dark one of them big thunder heads rose up in the southwest and the thunder begin to roll and the lightning started to flash. We was all a-settin' on the front gallery when a clap come that liked to a-busted our ear drums. We all jumped up but seen nobody was hurt, but we heared a peculiar noise out back of the chimney so we went out to find out what it was. Well sir, the younguns had piled up a big pile of old tires, like chaps will. This here pile had fifteen or twenty old casings that the younguns had been a-playing with and in these here casings was caught two yearling lightning bolts about six feet long. The rubber casings kept them from goin' anywheres and they was a-writhin' and twistin' in that pile like a couple of long cottonmouths and a-sparklin' an' spittin' like these here sparklers the kids get for Christmas. The more they whined and moaned, the more they got twisted and hung up in them casings. It was some sight. Well, we made us a sort of lasso outen some strips of rubber we cut from old inner tubes and looped it over them lightning bolts—they was all forked and jagged so we could git a good holt. Then we pulled them out and hung them on the limb of a tree. After a while they quit twistin' and squirmin' and sort of give up to being tied.

Some of us wanted to take and throw them down in the old well, but the younguns wouldn't hear to that. They wanted to keep them for pets. So we let 'em. They named one Pluto and one Ajax. Well, next day we fixed up two long glass boxes to keep Pluto and Ajax in, so they wouldn't leak out, and before long they got to be so useful around the place till I don't know how we'd ever got along without them.

We'd take them two lightning bolts possum-huntin' and when a possum or coon holed up we'd jest loosen Pluto or Ajax in the hole and it was a sight to see them singed coons and possums come runnin' out. People begin to bring all the run-down storage batteries in that part of the country and get Pluto and Ajax to charge 'em up again. On a cold morning when all the wood was wet, we never needed no kindlin'. We'd jest poke one of them bolts in the fireplace and a blazin' fire'd soon be roarin' up the chimney. I never seen anything so handy about a place. The women folks used 'em about the washin'. They'd take one down to the spring and stick it in the wash pot and the clothes would be a-bilin' before you could say, "Jack Robinson." When hog killin' time come we'd heat the scaldin' water and then singe off the hairs with Pluto and Ajax.

What become of 'em? Well, the chaps got a hold of a glass chisel and cut Ajax up into cigarette and pipe lighters, and after he was gone Pluto begin to pine away till one day he passed out. We was all mighty sad.

—Them things was purt' nigh as handy as the eggs from them hens, that et the lightning bugs, which was this away. One spring the' was some hens owned by Vernon Hipp's wife which taken a hankerin' to eat lightnin' bugs. Well, they didn't pay no attention to the old hen's onnatural appetite tell one night Vernon, he went in the kitchen in the dark and seen some of the eggs a-shinin' like electric light bulbs. They was the eggs from the old hens that et the lightnin' bugs. Well, all that summer Vernon's house was lighted up by them eggs. They tried to market these here eggs to the Mississippi Power and Light Co. but they couldn't find no way to keep 'em from spilin'. Then when frost come and killed the lightnin' bugs the old hens started layin' ordinary eggs again.

IV. BEDBUGS

—"Well, boys," said Joe, looking up from the cedar chain he was whittlin'. "You know Aunt Sarah, she's the fattest woman in this county, weighs nigh on to 400 pounds. Well, she woke up one night when she heard somethin' whisperin' around her bed a-sayin', 'Roll 'er over, boys. Roll 'er over. We'll ketch 'er.' Aunt Sarah roused up and struck a light and she seen two big bedbugs a-tryin' to roll her outen the bed, and down on the floor they was a whole bunch all lined up ready to ketch 'er."

V. BIG SKEETERS

—Up at Saddlebags there was a man got down and hitched his horse one day while he looked for a ford so he could cross the creek and when he come back the skeeters had et up his horse, chawed up his saddle and was a-pitchin' that horse's shoes to see who'd git the bridle.

—"Them was sorter like the skeeters round my place," said Drew Mays, as he stopped whittling long enough to cut him off a chew of tobacco. "You know old Bill Jenkins, he's the biggest man in these parts. Well, he woke up one night and two skeeters had him and was a-flyin' off with him betwixt them. Old Bill let out a yell but them skeeters didn't pay it no mind. Then Bill heared them skeeters a-talkin'. One of 'em said to the othern 'I'm hungry. You reckon we'd better eat him now or hide him in the swamp?' The other skeeter shuck his head and said, 'I speck we better eat him here. If we take him down to that swamp some of them big skeeters is liable to take him away from us.' "

Question and Answer Tall Tales

WHAT de *darkest night* you ever done see?
De darkest night ah ever done see, a raindrop knock to my doorstep an' ast fer a light to see how to hit de groun'.

What de *crookedest road* you see?
Ah seen a road so crooked till a gnat broke his neck goin' aroun' de curb [curve].

What is de *tallest man* you ever see?
De tallest man ah ever seen was gittin' a haircut in Heaven an' a shoe-shine in Hell.

What de *highest hill* you ever seen?
Once upon a time ah saw a hill so high till de lightnin' have to take low gear to git over de hill.

What is de *runningest car* you ever see?
The runningest car ah ever see was my uncle's ole car—it run over Monday, kill Tuesday, sen' Wednesday to de hospital, cripple Thursday, an tol' Friday to tell Saddy to be at de fun'al Sunday at 4 o'clock p.m.

What de *fattest woman* you done see?
De fattest woman ah done see—her husban' have to hug her on de installment plan.

What de *lowest person* you ever saw?
De lowest person ah done ever saw kin sit on a dime wid his feet hangin' down.

What de *strongest mule* you ever saw?
Well, ah saw a ol' mule so strong till you hitched him to midnight an' he break daylight.

As collected by Alfred Isaac from the eighth grade pupils of the Wilkinson High School, Orangeburg County, January 11, 1945.

From *Humorous Folk Tales of the South Carolina Negro,* edited by J. Mason Brewer, pp. 27–30. Publications of the South Carolina Negro Folklore Guild, Number 1. Copyright, 1945, by the South Carolina Negro Folklore Guild. Claflin College: Orangeburg, South Carolina.

What de *poorest lan'* you ever done see?

De lan' in de graveyard whar my uncle buried. De lan' so po' till dey hafter put bakin' powder in de coffin so he kin rise in de jedgment day.

The Quickest Man Wins

IT WAS three mens went to court a girl, Ah told you. Dis was a real pretty girl wid shiny black hair and coal black eyes. And all dese men wanted to marry her, so they all went and ast her pa if they could have her. He looked 'em all over, but he couldn't decide which one of 'em would make de best husband and de girl, she couldn't make up her mind, so one Sunday night when he walked into de parlor where they was all sittin' and said to 'em, "Well, all y'all want to marry my daughter and youse all good men and Ah can't decide which one will make her de best husband. So y'all be here tomorrow mornin' at daybreak and we'll have a contest and de one dat can do de quickest trick kin have de girl."

Nex' mornin' de first one got up seen it wasn't no water in de bucket to cook breakfas' wid. So he tole de girl's mama to give him de water bucket and he would go to the spring and git her some.

He took de bucket in his hand and then he found out dat de spring was ten miles off. But he said he didn't mind dat. He went on and dipped up de water and hurried on back wid it. When he got to de five-mile post he looked down into de bucket and seen dat de bottom had done dropped out. Then he recollected dat he heard somethin' fall when he dipped up de water so he turned round and run back to de spring and clapped in dat bottom before de water had time to spill.

De ole man thought dat was a pretty quick trick, but de second man says, "Wait a minute. Ah want a grubbin' hoe and a axe and a plow and a harrow." So he got everything he ast for. There was ten acres of wood lot right nex' to de house. He went out dere and chopped down all de trees, grubbed up de roots, ploughed de field, harrowed it, planted it in cowpeas, and had green pease for dinner.

De ole man says, "Dat's de quickest trick. Can't nobody beat dat. No use in tryin'. He done won de girl."

De last man said, "You ain't even givin' me a chance to win de girl."

So he took his high-powered rifle and went out into de woods about seben or eight miles until he spied a deer. He took aim and fired. Then he run home, run round behind de house and set his gun down and then run back out in de woods and caught de deer and held 'im till de bullet hit 'im.

So he won de girl.

From *Mules and Men,* by Zora Neale Hurston, pp. 61–62. Copyright, 1945, by Zora Neale Hurston. Philadelphia and London: J. B. Lippincott Company.

How Sharp Snaffles Got His Wife and Capital

WILLIAM GILMORE SIMMS visited the mountains of western North Carolina on many occasions to gather material for his stories. He had a friend up there who would bring in the various characters of the community. One Sharp Snaffles was the biggest liar in the community. Sharp was brought in one day to tell Mr. Simms how he got his wife and capital, and this is how he got it:

"The gal that I was tryin' to marry had an old daddy who was so stubborn he wouldn't let her marry unless the man that wanted to marry her could show some capital. I didn't have no capital, and I was a-wonderin' how I could git it when I saw a flock of geese on a pond. So I got me a long cane and bored all the center out of it. And I put that in my mouth and I took a rope and got down under the water, used the cane so I could breathe. And I got up under the geese and I pulled the first goose's foot down and tied it with the rope and then I pulled the next one and so on until I got them all. Then I tied the rope around my waist and jumped up, but the geese all flew and they took me off with them.

"And they'd been flyin' so long I thought they must be about New York, when they got hitched in a tree. And I tied one end of the rope to a limb in the tree, got myself loose, and started down the tree. But it had a big holler in it and I fell down that holler, and when I got to the bottom of the holler there was a couple of cubs. Wall, after a while the old bar she come. I knowed it was her when I couldn't see the stars up through the holler of the tree. So I took my knife out of my pocket and when she slid down backwards I caught her by the tail and jammed that knife into her. And up the tree she went and she got to the top, a-draggin' me behind her. When she got thar, I pushed her off and she fell and broke her neck. And I clumb down out of the tree and I looked around and I found I wasn't more than a mile away from home.

"So I went home and got a ax, come back, cut that tree down, killed all them geese, killed them two cubs. And I found that it was a bee tree! 'T was full of honey. Well, I tuck them geese and dressed them, dressed them bars, and sold the hides, and put away a lot of meat to last me through the winter. I took the rest of the meat and the geese and the honey to Greenville, Spartanburg, and Asheville—Hendersonville and around thar—and I sold it and I made a thousand dollars. And I went to the old man and I said: 'I've got my capital.' 'Well,' he says, 'you can have Sally.' "

As told by Alexander S. Salley, Jr., Columbia, South Carolina. Recorded by B. A. Botkin, January 28, 1949.

For the original story by William Gilmore Simms, "How Sharp Snaffles Got His Capital and Wife," see *Harper's New Monthly Magazine*, Vol. XLI (October, 1870), No. 245, pp. 667–687.

Luck with Potatoes

MY BROTHER over in Yancey County had some mighty good luck with 'taters oncet. They was planted on a steep hillside and when he dug under the row one of the big ones rolled down the hillside and a great slew o' dirt followed after. The dirt dammed up a good-sized stream and made a fifty-acre lake, bored a hole through a little mountain where the railroad company was fixin' to dig a tunnel, and went on down a half mile further and dammed up a stream where a company was plannin' to build a power plant.

With the money he got for his lake, and what the railroad paid him for the tunnel, and with what he got from the power company for saving them the price of a dam, he was sure settin' on top o' the world.

He didn't always have such good luck. I mind the time he couldn't buy a hen and chickens. He got so down and out he tried to kill hisse'f. He had a old pistol, but he was afraid it wouldn't work, so he went down to the store and bought him a gallon o' kerosene, a piece o' strong rope, and some rat poison. Then he went down to the river and got in a boat and rowed down to where some trees hung way out over the water.

He tied the rope around his neck and to the limb of a tree, soaked hisse'f in kerosene, et the rat poison, and set his clothes afire, figgerin' on shootin' hisse'f just as he kicked the boat from under.

Well, he kicked the boat away and the pistol went off and shot the rope in two, he fell in the water and that put out the fire in his clothes, and he got to chokin' and stranglin' when he went under—and throwed up the poison. He figgered his luck had changed, so he swum over to the bank and announced hisse'f as candidate for the legislater. Got elected, too.

The Rolling Log

"As I recollect," began Hite, "pap's strangest 'sperience happened right over thar in Greasy Holler. Must o' been nigh sixty years ago. He took his ax one day an' went up thar t' cut a morsel o' firewood. Th' trees an' bresh had been cleared off on each side o' th' valley up two or three hunderd feet. Th' banks wus slick as owl grease an' so steep that pap had a hard time gittin' up th' side t' whar they wus some tall trees. He got thar though an' picked out a big hick'ry that stuck up 'way 'bove th' other trees.

As told by Lee Morris, Marion, North Carolina, to Dudley W. Crawford. Manuscripts of the Federal Writers' Project of the Works Progress Administration for the State of North Carolina.

From *Ozark Country*, by Otto Ernest Rayburn, pp. 262–264. American Folkways Series, edited by Erskine Caldwell. Copyright, 1941, by Otto Ernest Rayburn. New York: Duell, Sloan & Pearce, Inc.

Pap wus th' best chopper in th' hills an' bracin' hisself careful, he begin makin' chips fly like that thar Paul Bunyan feller what owned a blue ox. Three-four licks from pap's ax an' th' tree come smashin' down."

P-futt went a stream of tobacco juice at a knot in the pine tree in front of us. Hite adjusted his "chaw" and continued.

"Pap jumped back an' th' tree started rollin' down th' steep hill. Down it went, breakin' off all th' limbs and gainin' speed ever' second. When hit got t' th' bed o' th' valley, it didn't stop atall, but rolled right up th' other bank clean t' th' timber line. Then hit started back like a freight train comin' outa hell. Down it come into th' valley an' right up th' hill t' whar pap stood. Hit struck th' timber an' bounced like a bull calf on a stampede. Back down it went, faster 'an ever.

"Pap jist leaned on his choppin' ax an' watched th' thing roll. Down one side an' up t' other, then a big bounce an' down agin. All th' bark wus wore off by now an' pap said hit looked like a greased pig at a picnic. He watched it roll fer a good two hours an' then give up an' follered th' ridge home."

P-futt! P-flu-futt! I passed the plug and the story teller took a fresh chew.

"Next day pap went back up th' ridge t' see what had happened t' th hick'ry an', snakes alive, th' log wus all still rollin'! Pap come back home 'thout no firewood.

"Right after that my ole man wus drafted into th' Civil War an' took his rifle-gun an' went away. After 'bout a year he come back on one o' them thar furloughs. Th' fust thing he thought of when he got home wus that blamed log in Greasy Holler. Couldn't hardly wait t' git up thar.

"Wal, hit wus still a-rollin'. But it was jist 'bout petered-out. Hit had wore down so much that pap picked it up an' brung it home an' used hit fer a ramrod durin' th' rest o' th' war."

The Tin Whistle on the Bass

. . . WILLIE thereupon told a tale that he knew to be true.
"You know how rapidly a bass grows?"
We did not know.
"You know how a bass will use in the same hole year after year?"
That we did know.
"Well, I caught a yearling once, and I bet a man that he would grow six inches in a year. To test it, I tied a little tin whistle to his tail. A year later we went and fished for him. The second day I caught him." Willie knocked the top-ashes from his pipe and puffed silently.
"Well?" we said.

From *Blue-Grass and Rhododendron*, Out-Doors in old Kentucky, by John Fox, Jr., pp. 170–171. Copyright, 1901, by Charles Scribner's Sons. New York.

Willie edged away out of reach, speaking softly.
"That tin whistle had grown to a fog-horn."

Pilot Tall Tales

DESPITE the modern touches, the pilot follows the tradition of the man of the sea, remembering all of the incredible things that he has seen and telling them with salty detail; and he is an artist in the big joke, the mendacity that recounts a wild yarn with the most guileless of countenances. Whoever visits the headquarters has his recollections of the tales the pilots spun to him, of porpoises that form precise lines to guide the ships into the channel, of twenty-foot snakes that wear down the boardwalks with their movement across them, of strange pelicans whose powers of vision are breathtaking.

The pilot lights his pipe and settles back: "There I was that day, fishing off the pier with a line tied around my wrist, and dozing a little. Not much luck. Then all of a sudden a big, big gar grabbed at the line and jerked me right out into the river. I tried to get loose but I couldn't. It kept pulling me down the pass. So I just kept my nose and eyes above water and let it go ahead. Two miles out in the Gulf I hailed a ship and it picked me up." Observing that he is appreciated, he waves a hand: "See that bare patch of mud over there? We had a lot of rice planted, and it was heading up fine. Then one morning we found our whole rice field moving away. We had made a mistake, put that field on an alligator's back! Yeah, they come big down here."

Big Black and the Her-Girls

BIG BLACK was a Greenville nigger a-rousting on the *Tennessee Belle* . . . . But he got tired of the river and went on one of them ships that goes out of New Orleans to the sea. The weather kept getting hotter and hotter. And the mate seen him looking at the water and said, "Don't you go in swimming, Big Black." He didn't tell him why, though, and one day, when it was terrible hot, Big Black jumped in the ocean. And in a minute, a lot of them Her-girls, that's half women, half fish, grabbed him and pulled him down to the bottom. They sit him up on a big rock, and then they all yelled at him: "Greenville Nigger, do you like fish?"

From *Deep Delta Country*, by Harnett T. Kane, pp. 128–129. Copyright, 1944, by Harnett T. Kane. New York: Duell, Sloan & Pearce, Inc.

From *Big River to Cross*, Mississippi Life Today, by Ben Lucien Burman, pp. 47–48. Copyright, 1938, 1939, 1940, by Ben Lucien Burman. New York: The John Day Company.

Big Black was awful scared, and he didn't know what to answer. But he'd been getting too much catfish at Greenville, so he says mighty quiet: "If it's something to eat you wants to give me, if you'll please 'scuse me, I'd mighty like some pork chops or a nice chicken wing. I jest hates fish." And then all them Her-girls clapped their hands. "If you'd a-said you liked fish, we'd a-throwed you to the sharks," they told him. "You're the prettiest man we sure ever seen. We're going to make you our king." And they swum in with a big gold throne. He was their king for a mighty long time. Twice every year he used to go back to Greenville, and give his mammy and pappy all the gold money they could carry and the finest pearls in the sea. But once he walked in the house, and there was a can of canned salmon laying on the table. He never come back no more.

II. FOLK TALES

Tales having their source in traditions of characters and events once actual, but by primitive superstition and naïve credulity metamorphosed beyond recognition, stories not of things which ever were, but of things which never were, their appeal being not to reason but to unreason.

—JOHN BENNETT

It is thus that in every state of society the imagination of man is eternally at war with reason and truth. . . . It is as much as to say that it [fairy-tale] is essential to our amusement; that, for the time being, we must suspend the exercise of reason, and submit to a voluntary deception.

—JOSEPH DODDRIDGE

To crown all, Provinciality, with an amplitude at once motherly and American, spread her homespun frock over the scene.

—JOEL CHANDLER HARRIS

Why, that feller don't know how to spell! . . . *That tale-teller . . . is jest makin' fun of the mountain people by misspellin' our talk. You educated folks don't spell your own words the way you say them.*

—Quoted by HORACE KEPHART

We-uns that cain't read or write have a heap of time to think, and that's the reason we know more than you-all.

—Quoted by ETHEL DE LONG

1. BACK OF BEYOND

As STORIES with "enough truth in them to make good story material and to incite the imagination to try to improve on actual happenings," yarns and tall tales belong to the borderland between fact and fantasy, shifting now to one side and now to the other. With myth and folk tale, however, both the story-teller and his audience cross over the dividing line into the realm of pure fantasy ("a world other than our own"), where one sees only what one wants to see and believes only what one wants to believe; where erroneous perception gives way to artful deception or naïve self-deception as common sense and logic abdicate their throne.

The myth-making imagination has already been seen at work in the heroic saga and epic of the South, rewriting history according to the ideal of perfection or imperfection. Similarly the myth of the plantation or frontier past is strong in the nostalgic legend of the Old South. The desire to return to a golden age is closely related to the dream of a promised land, a land flowing with milk and honey, whose magnet first drew the colonists to these shores and the pioneers to the West.

The same dream of a paradise on earth is behind the "Diddy-Wah-Diddy" of the Florida Negro and "The Enchanted Island" of the Okefinokee Swamp. A kindred dream that never dies, in the South as elsewhere, is the dream of finding buried treasure—Spanish, pirate, outlaw, Confederate.[1]

As yarn and tall tale are constantly passing into myth, so is legend. The difference between legend and myth is (in John Bennett's distinction) the difference between "traditions of characters and events once actual" and traditions of "things which never were." But behind legend, and shining through it, there is always the light of myth, of which legends are only fragmentary reflections.

The mythical element in legend and folk tale often takes the form of a preternatural and malevolent force in nature, as in "The Belled Buzzard," with its recurrent omen of disaster, and "The Date-Tree of Orleans Street," with its prophetic, avenging curse. Or the mythical element may involve magic, as in "The Flying Africans," where the slaves find escape through the witch's power of flight. (Compare the frequent allusions to flight and travel in the spirituals; e.g., "Swing Low, Sweet Chariot," "All God's Children Got Shoes," "The Gospel Train's a-Coming," and "One of these mornings, bright and fair, Hitch on my wings and try the air.") Here, too, belongs the remarkable folk tale of High John de Conquer's giant crow ("one wing rested on the morning, while the other dusted off the evening star") on which he took the slaves for a ride to Hell and Heaven and back, on wings of song.[2]

Corresponding and related to myths of origin (like "The Walk-Off People") are legends of the origins of places and place names (e.g., Bald Mountain and the Brazos), the origins of customs,[3] and the origins of

---

[1] Cf. J. Frank Dobie, "The Dream That Never Dies, Oklahoma Treasure Legends," *Folk-Say: 1929*, pp. 64–68; *Legends of Texas* (1924); and *Coronado's Children* (1930).

[2] Zora Neale Hurston, "High John de Conquer," *The American Mercury*, Vol. LVII (October, 1943), No. 238, pp. 455–458.

[3] E.g., how the Cherokees obtained tobacco, Charles Lanman, *Adventures in the*

songs and sayings. Thus "Oh, Freedom" and "Swing Low" both originated in the tradition of a Tennessee mother who had been sold from
her baby and was about to throw herself and her child over the steep banks
of the Cumberland River. As she stumbled along the road, muttering,
"Before I'd be a slave, I'd be buried in my grave," an old woman, over-
hearing her, read her intention and dissuaded her with these consoling
words: "Don't you do it, honey; wait, let de chariot of de Lord swing low,
and let me take one of de Lord's scrolls an' read it to you. God's got a great
work for dis baby to do; she's goin' to stand befo' kings and queens." [4] The
prophecy was fulfilled when, years later, the slave woman's daughter
entered Fisk University and became one of the "Original Fisk Jubilee
Singers."

Closer to the truth, if not the facts, of songs used to direct slaves to the
Underground Railroad or to warn them of danger are the story of "Follow
the Drinking Gourd," and Harriet Tubman's account of her experiences
in singing songs like "Go Down, Moses." [5] The latter song (traditionally
supposed to have been written in honor of Harriet Tubman as the Negro
"Moses") is only one of many folk-tale versions of Old Testament stories
and parables which the Negro dramatized in his sermons as well as his
spirituals—part of his Biblical heritage of heroic symbols of freedom and
liberation and of ethical concepts of social and divine justice.

Tales of ghosts, witches, and the devil make up a large class of folk
tales based on superstitions, in which the story has often outlived the practice or belief. One of the best Southern folk tales in this class is "The Bell
'Witch' " of Tennessee and Mississippi, a parallel for which is to be found
in the story of Old Nance, a *poltergeist* who bedeviled the Beaver family
in the Cumberlands.[6]

2. "MOSTLY ABOUT A BOY NAMED JACK"

With ghosts and witches and talking animals folk tales step from the
adults' porch or parlor into the nursery. Although children's folk and fairy
tales are typically told for amusement during leisure hours, one occasionally
hears of their being used, like songs, to accompany the labor of many hands
and, like the hands, "make light work."

One interesting phase of the enjoyment of the [Jack] tales in that [Beech
Mountain] region is a very practical application: that of "keeping the kids
on the job" for such communal tasks as stringing beans for canning, or thread-
ing them up to make the dried pods known as "leather britches." Mrs. R. M.
Ward tells us: "We would all get down around a sheet full of dry beans and
start in to shelling 'em. Mon-roe would tell the kids one of them tales and
they'd work for life!" [7]

These Virginia and North Carolina versions of the Jack tales have still
another practical relation to Southern life. In their portrayal of Jack as a

---

Wilds of the United States and British American Provinces (1856), Vol. I, pp. 429–
430.

[4] For this and the origin of other Negro spirituals, see John Wesley Work, *Folk
Song of the American Negro* (1915), pp. 76–88.

[5] See above, pp. 343–347.

[6] Cf. Emma B. Miles, *The Spirit of the Mountains* (1905), pp. 108–117.

[7] Richard Chase, *The Jack Tales* (1943), p. vii.

typical "easy-going, unpretentious" mountain boy as well as in their use of the mountain vernacular, the Jack tales are excellent examples of the adaptation of Old World folk tales to Southern settings and folkways, akin to the democratization and localization of British ballads.

In the Jack tales, too, knight-errantry and chivalry survive on a democratic and popular level. The persistent appeal of the Jack tales to the Southern folk of today rests not simply on their appeal to children but also on the appeal of the ever-triumphant Jack as a symbol of the bottom rail on top. As a "trickster hero who overcomes through quick wit and cunning rather than by physical force," Jack belongs with Brer Rabbit and Old John. Symbolic of the "dreams, desires, ambitions, and experiences of a whole people," all three have their feet on the ground, though, spiritually, the heads of these "little fellers" may touch the clouds.

3. FOLK TALES AS LITERATURE

Although it is true that the printed page cannot compete with the spoken word in transmitting the spell of the folk tale, it is also true that, in both transcribed and transmuted form, the folk tale has been an important creative force in Southern literature and that, whether oral or written, the folk tale is literature—the people's literature. When Joel Chandler Harris denied that his "poor little stories are in the nature of literature, or that their re-telling touches literary art at any point," he was not so much underestimating their aesthetic and social value as he was disclaiming any great "creative effort" on his own part. But the writing down of the folk tale, especially putting a tale together from fragments of oral tradition, is creative. One must distinguish, however, between authentic re-creations and concoctions. Thus, while Harris gathered many of his stories in the kitchen, from cooks of "the plantation type," he insisted that they were not "cooked."

While remaining faithful to the letter and the spirit of the original the transcription inevitably loses a great deal of its flavor, which the re-created version or "translation" may try, sometimes successfully, to restore. Because "dialect writing" substitutes for the naturally beautiful sounds of folk speech the difficult and grotesque conventions of "eye dialect," the best one can hope to do is to arrive at some sort of compromise or middle ground, remembering always that truth to idiom is more important than truth to pronunciation.

Dialect writing, too, often suffers from the limitation of giving the appearance of humor or grotesqueness where none was originally intended. That is why the imitated or simulated folk tale, where dialect is deliberately used for humorous effect, as in stage dialect, smacks of burlesque and caricature. It has little value as folklore or as literature. Not so, however, with the best folk tale chroniclers—including, for the Negro, Harris, Charles Colcock Jones, Mrs. A. M. H. Christensen, Harry Stillwell Edwards, Ambrose E. Gonzales, John Bennett, Samuel Gaillard Stoney, and, on a more sophisticated level, Zora Neale Hurston and Roark Bradford—who combine folkloristic and literary value.

B. A. B.

FABLES AND MYTHS

Thompson's Colt

HAVING frequently heard the expression when a boy, "He's as big a fool as Thompson's colt," Senator Bradley asked one of his old Pulaski county friends, what was its meaning. Whereupon, he explained:

"There was a man named Thompson, who lived on the Cumberland River, and he had a colt. One day the colt was very dry and wanted a drink, so he went down to the river and swam across, and after he walked out on the bank, come back to the river and tuck a drink. In other words, he swum the river to git a drink of water."

Jesse Holmes, the "Fool-Killer"

LEGENDS concerning a "fool-killer" seem prevalent enough in Texas, but they are not commonly, I believe, identified with a definite individual as is the case with the deeds of Paul Bunyan. There is, however, authority for connecting the deeds of the well-known dolt-destroyer with one Jesse Holmes, who flourished at least as long ago as the Civil War. But how he got his name, and what was the range of his activities we do not know.

In the files of the *Southern Literary Messenger* for 1862, I have found an interesting reference to Jesse Holmes on page 693:

Jesse Holmes is the name of the "Fool Killer," employed by the Milton (N. C.) *Chronicle*. He is supposed to carry a great club, with which he beats out the brains of fools. Since the war broke out, all the fools he has killed have been knaves. As for example:

In Pittsylvania I nabbed a "patriotic" lark who charged soldiers five dollars a piece for taking them packages of clothing. You see he was going to Winchester anyhow, and a parcel of neighbours wishing to send their sons clothing, etc., put them in a big box and paid the freight to Richmond, from which point to Winchester the box, as I was informed, went free, my hero, having little or no trouble with it; arriving there he made each soldier shell out five dollars on the bundle. My indignation was so great, that on collaring him, I walked into him with my club without pausing for explanation or to learn his name, and made

From *Stories and Speeches of William O. Bradley,* with a Biographical Sketch of M. H. Thatcher, p. 63. Copyright, 1916, by Transylvania Printing Company, Inc. Lexington, Kentucky.

By Ernest E. Leisy. From *Man, Bird and Beast,* Publications of the Texas Folk-Lore Society, Volume VIII (1930), edited by J. Frank Dobie, pp. 152–154. Copyright, 1930, by the Texas Folk-Lore Society. Austin.

Cf. Ralph S. Boggs, "Running Down the Fool Killer," *Coyote Wisdom,* Texas Folk-Lore Society Publications, No. XIV (Austin, 1938), pp. 169–173.

him "walk-talk ginger-blue," get over on "tother side of Jordan," where the road is a hard one to travel.

To this the *Messenger* adds: "When Jesse is out of employment, let him come to Richmond. What would he do with a man who would carry on Sunday a barrel of snacks—each snack composed of a slice of meat, between two slices of bread—and sell them to General Lee's soldiers at a dollar a piece? What would he do with a man who would boast that he had made $65 on a barrel of apples, sold to the soldiers? Such a man is said to live in Richmond."

O. Henry was familiar with the Jesse Holmes legends, as he indicates in the opening of his story, "The Fool Killer" (in *The Voice of the City*). "Down South," writes O. Henry, "whenever any one perpetrates some particularly monumental piece of foolishness everybody says: 'Send for Jesse Holmes.'

"Jesse Holmes is the Fool-Killer. Of course he is a myth, like Santa Claus, and Jack Frost and General Prosperity and all those concrete conceptions that are supposed to represent an idea that Nature has failed to embody. The wisest of the Southrons cannot tell you whence comes the Fool-Killer's name; but few and happy are the households from the Roanoke to the Rio Grande in which the name of Jesse Holmes has not been pronounced or invoked. Always with a smile, and often with a tear, he is summoned to his official duty. A busy man is Jesse Holmes."

* * * * *

Since writing the foregoing, the author has had a letter from Mr. R. R. Clark, of Stephenville, N. C., as follows:

Fifty years ago, when I entered a country printing office to learn the printer's trade, the editor, who was easily peeved and disposed to be cynical, often made reference to the Fool Killer and the much work that awaited him in that community. So far as I know the only publication at that time making a feature of the Fool Killer was the one quoted by the *Southern Literary Messenger*—the Milton (N. C.) *Chronicle*. The paper was published at Milton, county seat of Caswell County, North Carolina, on the Virginia line. The period at which I heard talk of the Fool Killer and the Milton *Chronicle* was about eighteen years after the date quoted by the *Southern Literary Messenger*. So the *Chronicle* must have featured the Fool Killer over a long period. I think the same man, whose name was Evans, continued as editor of the paper for many years. When I began in a newspaper office fifty years ago he was then and for some years afterward referred to by other papers as "Father Evans" and was presumably quite an old man. He was very outspoken and independent and his paper, for a small paper in a very small town, attracted attention. He was evidently quite original. His stuff was much copied and when he wrote something that went the rounds he would say that "it had legs." If some one told an unusual story, Father Evans was accustomed to ask, "How much did he have on?" intimating that one who saw unusual things was drunk.

I am under the impression that he ran a wooden cut of a man with a club, which he labeled, "Jesse Holmes, the Fool Killer," and his manner of suggesting work for Jesse was as described in the extract you have. When I became editor of the *Landmark* I used on occasion, remembering Jesse Holmes, the Fool Killer, to mention that there was work for him if he could be revived. I never knew whether Jesse originated with Editor Evans, was a creation of the Milton *Chronicle*, or whether he got the idea from another, as is possible. So far as I know, the Milton *Chronicle* was the only paper in which Jesse Holmes, Fool Killer, had a run and that was under the authorship of Mr. Evans. I have no doubt that he got the idea elsewhere, although I can give no good reason for denying him the idea of original creation. But whether or not he was the original creator, Editor Evans was quite original and it is not impossible that he was the creator of the character that he gave so long a run and that seems to have died with him.

Says Fred A. Olds, of the North Carolina Historical Commission, Raleigh: "The Confederate soldiers talked about this Jesse. He was known prior to the Civil War and continued to be known as late as 1875. He played many imaginary pranks, or practical jokes, some of them very rough."

The Belled Buzzard

BACK of the old fiddle tune, "The Belled Buzzard," is a tradition which had its origin in the Ozark mountains. The story concerns a settlement along a river bottom. One bank of the river was bordered for miles by high unscalable bluffs crowned with scrub timber, the home and breeding place of thousands of buzzards.

Hog raising was the main source of income of the community. Mast from the acorn-bearing trees furnished food for the droves of hogs earmarked and turned into the woods each year, to be rounded up in the fall ready for market.

One summer hog cholera broke out among the porkers. The buzzards, feasting on the dead carcasses, carried the disease from one section of the country to another. There was an unwritten law that these birds should not be killed, but the farmers were aware that, unless some action was taken to check the spread of the disease, their hogs, together with their incomes, would be wiped out entirely.

A meeting was called. It was decided to capture one of the birds and fasten a small sheep bell to it, in the hope that it would cause them to leave. One of the birds was accordingly trapped and belled. His arrival among the others created a great commotion and in a few days the flock of buz-

From *Traditional Music of America*, by Ira W. Ford, pp. 187–188. Copyright, 1940, by E. P. Dutton & Co., Inc. New York.
"The Belled Buzzard is an institution. There must be more than one of them . . . but the country people will have it that there is only one Belled Buzzard—a bird that bears a charmed life and on his neck a never silent bell.—Irvin S. Cobb, "The Belled Buzzard," *The Escape of Mr. Trimm* (1913), pp. 66–67.

zards disappeared, only the belled buzzard remaining. Finally he, too, took flight.

At the end of the summer there was an epidemic of typhoid fever in the community, many dying. About that time the belled buzzard reappeared, the tinkle of his bell being plainly heard as he soared above the houses. He came and went time after time and always following his reappearance some sort of calamity happened. The return of the belled bird aroused apprehension in the minds of the more superstitious and his presence became associated with their misfortunes. They believed the repulsive fowl was possessed of an evil spirit. Many believe he still roams the skies, as he has for more than a hundred years, so that even today any report of the belled buzzard casts a spell of gloom over them.

The tune, "The Belled Buzzard," has been handed down through the years with this tradition, the plucking of the fiddle string in certain places in the music representing the tinkle of his bell.

The King Buzzard

MY PA tell me dat 'way back in slavery time—'way back in Af'ica—dere been a nigger, an' he been a big nigger. He been de chief er he tribe, an' when dem white folks was ketchin' niggers for slavery, dat ole nigger nuse to entice 'em into trap. He'd git 'em on boat wey dem white folks could ketch 'em an' chain 'em. White folks nused to gee him money an' all kind er little thing, an' he'd betray 'em. An' one time atter he betray thousands into bondage, an' de white folks say dey ain' guh come to dat coast no more—dat was dey last trip—so dey knocked dat nigger down an' put chain on him an' brung him to dis country.

An' when he dead, dere were no place in heaven for him an' he were not desired in hell. An' de Great Master decide dat he were lower dan all other

From *Nigger to Nigger*, by E. C. L. Adams, pp. 14–15. Copyright, 1928, by Charles Scribner's Sons. New York.

mens or beasts; he punishment were to wander for eternal time over de face er de earth. Dat as he had kilt de sperrits of mens an' womens as well as dere bodies, he must wander on an' on. Dat his sperrit should always travel in de form of a great buzzard, an' dat carrion must be he food.

An' sometimes he appears to mens, but he doom is settled; an' he ain' would er hurt Tad, kaze one er he punishment is dat he evil beak an' claw shall never tech no livin' thing. An' dey say he are known to all de sperrit world as de King Buzzard, an' dat forever he must travel alone.

Follow the Drinking Gourd

I [1]

THE following story is a compilation of three incidents and an attempt to explain them. A number of years ago while a resident of Alaska I became much interested in folklore and consequently anything of this nature came to attract my attention quickly. I was a resident of Hot Springs, North Carolina, during the year of 1912 and had charge of the agricultural work of a large industrial school. This school owned a considerable herd of cattle, which were kept in the meadows on the tops of the Big Rich Mountains on the boundary between North Carolina and Tennessee. One day while riding through the mountains looking after this stock, I heard the following stanza sung by a little Negro boy, who was picking up dry sticks of wood near a Negro cabin:

> Foller the drinkin' gou'd,
> Foller the drinkin' gou'd;
> No one know, the wise man say,
> "Foller the drinkin' gou'd."

It is very doubtful if this part of the song would have attracted anyone's attention had not the old grandfather, who had been sitting on a block of wood in front of the cabin, slowly got up and, taking his cane, given the boy a sound lick across the back with the admonition not to sing that song again. This excited my curiosity and I asked the old man why he did not want the boy to sing the song. The only answer I could get was that it was bad luck.

About a year later I was in the city of Louisville and, having considerable time to wait for a train, I went walking about the city. My journey brought me to the river front, and while standing there watching the wharf activities I was very much surprised to hear a Negro fisherman, who was seated on the edge of the wharf, singing the same stanza on the same tune. The fisherman sang the same stanza over and over again without any variation. . . . When I asked the fisherman what he knew about the song, he replied that he knew nothing about it; he would not even converse with me. This seemed

---

[1] By H. B. Parks, in *Foller De Drinkin' Gou'd,* Publications of the Texas Folk-Lore Society, No. VII, edited by J. Frank Dobie, pp. 81–84. Copyright, 1928, by the Texas Folk-Lore Society. Austin, Texas.

The "drinkin' gou'd" is the Big Dipper.

to be very peculiar, but because of the story of bad luck told by the grand-father in North Carolina I did not question the Negro further.

In 1918 I was standing on the platform of the depot at Waller, Texas, waiting for a train, when, much to my surprise, I heard the familiar tune being picked on a violin and banjo and two voices singing the following words:

> Foller the Risen Lawd,
> Foller the Risen Lawd;
> The bes' thing the Wise Man say,
> "Foller the Risen Lawd."

The singers proved to be two Negro boys about sixteen years of age. When they were asked as to where they learned the song, they gave the following explanation. They said that they were musicians traveling with a colored revivalist and that he had composed this song and that they played it and used it in their revival meetings. They also said the revivalist wrote new stanzas to fit the meetings.

These three incidents led me to inquire into the subject, and I was very fortunate in meeting an old Negro at College Station, Texas, who had known a great many slaves in his boyhood days. After I had gained his confidence, this man told the following story and gave the . . . verses of the song.

He said that just before the Civil War, somewhere in the South, he was not just sure where, there came a sailor who had lost one leg and had the missing member replaced by a peg-leg. He would appear very suddenly at some plantation and ask for work as a painter or carpenter. This he was able to get at almost every place. He made friends with the slaves and soon all of the young colored men were singing the song that is herein mentioned. The peg-leg sailor would stay for a week or two at a place and then disappear. The following spring nearly all the young men among the slaves disappeared and made their way to the north and finally to Canada by following a trail that had been made by the peg-leg sailor and was held in memory by the Negroes in this peculiar song.

* * * * *

Now my birthplace is in the North and I also belong to a family that took considerable part in the underground railroad movement; so I wrote about this story to the older members of the family in the North. One of my great-uncles, who was connected with the railroad movement, re-membered that in the records of the Anti-Slavery Society there was a story of a peg-legged sailor, known as Peg Leg Joe, who made a number of trips through the South and induced young Negroes to run away and escape through the North to Canada. The main scene of his activities was in the country immediately north of Mobile and the trail described in the song followed northward to the head waters of the Tombigbee River, thence over the divide and down the Tennessee River to the Ohio. It seems that the peg-legged sailor would go through the country north of Mobile and teach this song to the young slaves and show them a mark of his natural left foot and the round spot made by the peg-leg. He would then go ahead of them northward and on every dead tree or other conspicuous object he would leave a print made with charcoal or mud of the outline of a human left foot and a round spot in place of the right foot. As nearly as could be found out the last trip was made in 1859. Nothing more could be found relative to this man.

* * * * *

The revivalist realized the power of this sing-song and made it serve his purpose by changing a few words, and in so doing pointed his followers to a far different liberty than the one the peg-leg sailor advocated.

II [2]

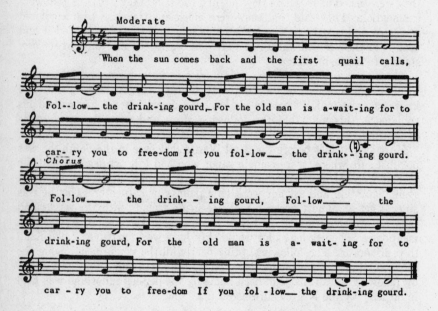

When the sun comes back and the first quail calls,
Fol--low—— the drink-ing gourd,— For the old man is a-wait-ing for to carry you to free-dom If you fol-low—— the drink- - ing gourd.

Chorus
Fol-low—— the drink- - ing gourd, Fol-low—— the drink-ing gourd, For the old man is a- wait- ing for to carry you to free-dom If you fol - low—— the drink-ing gourd.

The river bank will make a very good road,
The dead trees show you the way,
Left foot, peg foot travelling on
    Follow the drinking gourd.

The river ends between two hills
    Follow the drinking gourd.

There's another river on the other side,
    Follow the drinking gourd.

Where the little river meets the great big river,
    Follow the drinking gourd.
The old man is a-waiting for to carry you to freedom,
    If you follow the drinking gourd.

---

[2] From *People's Songs,* Vol. 1 (January, 1947), No. 12, p. 4. Copyright, 1947, by People's Songs, Inc. New York.
    As sung by Lee Hays, who learned it from his nurse "Auntie" Laura.

Mythical Places of the Florida Negro

I. DIDDY-WAH-DIDDY

THIS is the largest and best known of the Negro mythical places. Its geography is that it is "way off somewhere." It is reached by a road that curves so much that a mule pulling a wagon-load of fodder can eat off the back of the wagon as he goes. It is a place of no work and no worry for man and beast. A very restful place where even the curbstones are good sitting-chairs. The food is even already cooked. If a traveller gets hungry all he needs to do is to sit down on the curbstone and wait and soon he will hear something hollering "Eat me! Eat me! Eat me!" and a big baked chicken will come along with a knife and fork stuck in its sides. He can eat all he wants and let the chicken go and it will go on to the next one that needs something to eat. By that time a big deep sweet potato pie is pushing and shoving to get in front of the traveller with a knife all stuck up in the middle of it so he just cuts a piece off of that and so on until he finishes his snack. Nobody can ever eat it all up. No matter how much you eat it grows just that much faster. It is said "Everybody would live in Diddy-Wah-Diddy if it wasn't so hard to find and so hard to get to after you even know the way." Everything is on a large scale there. Even the dogs can stand flat-footed and lick crumbs off heaven's tables. The biggest man there is known as Moon-Regulator because he reaches up and starts and stops it at his convenience. That is why there are some dark nights when the moon does not shine at all. He did not feel like putting it out that night.

II. WEST HELL

West Hell is the hottest and toughest part of that warm territory. The most desperate malefactors are the only ones condemned to West Hell, which is some miles west of Regular Hell. These souls are changed to rubber coffins so that they go bouncing through Regular Hell and on to their destination without having to be carried by attendants as the Devil

---

By Zora Neale Hurston. Manuscripts of the Federal Writers' Project of the Works Progress Administration for the State of Florida, pp. 40–45. 1938.

On Route No. 17 north of Jacksonville the white owner of a large barbecue stand has named his place Diddy-Wah-Diddy. He said he did it because he was always hearing the Negroes around there talking about this mythical place of good things to eat, especially the barbecue.—Z. N. H.

For "Diddy-Wah-Diddy" (familiar to Jack Benny's radio audience), cf. "The Promised Land," *Lay My Burden Down* (1945), p. 10; also Al Capp, *The Life and Times of the Shmoo* (New York, 1948), based on his comic strip, *Li'l Abner*. For an account of the latter and its Kentucky hillbilly setting, see Coulton Waugh, *The Comics* (1947), pp. 200–207.

does not like to send his imps into West Hell oftener than is absolutely necessary. This suburb of Hell is celebrated as the spot where the Devil and Big John de Conqueror had their famous fight. Big John de Conqueror had flown to Hell on the back of an eagle, had met the Devil's daughters and fallen in love with the baby girl child. She agreed to elope with him and they had stolen the Devil's famous pair of horses that went by the name of Hallowed-Be-Thy-Name and Thy-Kingdom-Come. When the Devil found out about it he hitched up his equally famous jumping bull and went in pursuit. He overtook the fleeing lovers in West Hell and they fought all over the place, so good a man, so good a devil! But way after while John tore off one of the Devil's arms and beat him, and married the Devil's daughter. But before he left Hell he passed out ice water to everybody in there. If you don't believe he done it, just go down to Hell and ask anybody there and they will tell you all about it. He even turned the damper down in some parts of Hell so it's a whole lot cooler there now than it used to be. They even have to make a fire in the fireplace in the parlor now on cool nights in the wintertime. John did that because he says him and his wife expect to go home to see her folks some time and he don't like the house kept so hot like the Devil has been keeping it. And if he go back there and find that that damper has been moved up again he means to tear up the whole job and turn West Hell into an ice-house.

Flying Africans

ONCE all Africans could fly like birds; but, owing to their many transgressions, their wings were taken away. There remained, here and there, in the sea islands and out-of-the-way places in the low country, some who had been overlooked, and had retained the power of flight, though they looked like other men.

There was a cruel master on one of the sea islands who worked his people till they died. When they died he brought others to take their places. These also he killed with overwork in the burning summer sun, through the middle hours of the day, although this was against the law.

One day, when all the worn-out Negroes were dead of overwork, he bought, of a broker in the town, a company of native Africans just brought into the country, and put them at once to work in the cottonfield.

From *The Doctor to the Dead,* Grotesque Legends & Folk Tales of Old Charleston, by John Bennett, pp. 139–142. Copyright, 1943, 1946, by John Bennett. New York and Toronto: Rinehart & Company, Inc.

Cf. the short story of the same title by Kenneth Porter, reprinted from *Common Ground* in *Primer for White Folks,* edited by Bucklin Moon (1945), pp. 171–176; also *Drums and Shadows* by the Savannah Unit of the Georgia Writers' Project (1940), where the "Flying African" motif occurs eight times. See also below, p. 497n.

He drove them hard. They went to work at sunrise and did not stop until dark. They were driven with unsparing harshness all day long, men, women and children. There was no pause for rest during the unendurable heat of the midsummer noon, though trees were plenty and near. But through the hardest hours, when fair plantations gave their Negroes rest, this man's driver pushed the work along without a moment's stop for breath, until all grew weak with heat and thirst.

There was among them one young woman who had lately borne a child. It was her first; she had not fully recovered from bearing, and should not have been sent to the field until her strength had come back. She had her child with her, as the other women had, astraddle on her hip, or piggyback.

The baby cried. She spoke to quiet it. The driver could not understand her words. She took her breast with her hand and threw it over her shoulder that the child might suck and be content. Then she went back to chopping knot-grass; but being very weak, and sick with the great heat, she stumbled, slipped, and fell.

The driver struck her with his lash until she rose and staggered on.

She spoke to an old man near her, the oldest man of them all, tall and strong, with a forked beard. He replied; but the driver could not understand what they said; their talk was strange to him.

She returned to work; but in a little while she fell again. Again the driver lashed her until she got to her feet. Again she spoke to the old man. But he said: "Not yet, daughter; not yet." So she went on working, though she was very ill.

Soon she stumbled and fell again. But when the driver came running with his lash to drive her on with her work she turned to the old man and asked: "Is it time yet, daddy?" He answered: "Yes, daughter; the time has come. Go; and peace be with you!" . . . and stretched out his arms toward her . . . so.

With that she leaped straight up into the air and was gone like a bird, flying over field and wood.

The driver and overseer ran after her as far as the edge of the field; but she was gone, high over their heads, over the fence, and over the top of the woods, gone, with her baby astraddle of her hip, sucking at her breast.

Then the driver hurried the rest to make up for her loss; and the sun was very hot indeed. So hot that soon a man fell down. The overseer himself lashed him to his feet. As he got up from where he had fallen the old man called to him in an unknown tongue. My grandfather told me the words that he said; but it was a long time ago, and I have forgotten them. But when he had spoken, the man turned and laughed at the overseer, and leaped up into the air, and was gone, like a gull, flying over field and wood.

Soon another man fell. The driver lashed him. He turned to the old man. The old man cried out to him, and stretched out his arms as he had done for the other two; and he, like them, leaped up, and was gone through the air, flying like a bird over field and wood.

Then the overseer cried to the driver, and the master cried to them both: "Beat the old devil! He is the doer!"

The overseer and the driver ran at the old man with lashes ready; and the master ran too, with a picket pulled from the fence, to beat the life out of the old man who had made those Negroes fly.

But the old man laughed in their faces, and said something loudly to all the Negroes in the field, the new Negroes and the old Negroes.

And as he spoke to them they all remembered what they had forgotten, and recalled the power which had once been theirs. Then all the Negroes, old and new, stood up together; the old man raised his hands; and they all leaped up into the air with a great shout; and in a moment were gone, flying, like a flock of crows, over the field, over the fence, and over the top of the wood; and behind them flew the old man.

The men went clapping their hands; and the women went singing; and those who had children gave them their breasts; and the children laughed and sucked as their mothers flew, and were not afraid.

The master, the overseer, and the driver looked after them as they flew, beyond the wood, beyond the river, miles on miles, until they passed beyond the last rim of the world and disappeared in the sky like a handful of leaves. They were never seen again.

Where they went I do not know; I never was told. Nor what it was that the old man said . . . that I have forgotten. But as he went over the last fence he made a sign in the master's face, and cried "Kuli-ba! Kuli-ba!" I don't know what that means.

But if I could only find the old wood sawyer, he could tell you more; for he was there at the time, and saw the Africans fly away with their women and children. He is an old, old man, over ninety years of age, and remembers a great many strange things.

Why Negroes Are Black

THEN one late afternoon, a woman called Gold, who had come to town from somewhere else, told the why and how of races that pleased me more than what I learned about race derivations later on in Ethnology. This was her explanation:

God did not make folks all at once. He made folks sort of in His spare time. For instance one day He had a little time on his hands, so he got the clay, seasoned it the way He wanted it, then He laid it by and went on to doing something more important. Another day He had some spare moments, so He rolled it all out, and cut out the human shapes, and stood them all up

From *Dust Tracks on a Road*, An Autobiography, by Zora Neale Hurston, pp. 74–77. Copyright, 1942, by Zora Neale Hurston. Philadelphia, London, and New York: J. B. Lippincott Company.

against His long gold fence to dry while He did some important creating. The human shapes all got dry, and when He found time, He blowed the breath of life in them. After that, from time to time, He would call everybody up, and give them spare parts. For instance, one day He called everybody and gave out feet and eyes. Another time He give out toenails that Old Maker figured they could use. Anyhow, they had all that they got up to now. So then one day, He said, "Tomorrow morning, at seven o'clock *sharp,* I aim to give out color. Everybody be here on time. I got plenty of creating to do tomorrow, and I want to give out this color and get it over wid. *Everybody* be round de throne at seven o'clock tomorrow morning!"

So next morning at seven o'clock, God was sitting on His throne with His big crown on His head and seven suns circling around His head. Great multitudes was standing around the throne waiting to get their color. God sat up there and looked east, and He looked west, and He looked north and He looked Australia, and blazing worlds were falling off His teeth. So He looked over to His left and moved His hands over a crowd and said, "You's yellow people!" They all bowed low and said, "Thank you, God," and they went on off. He looked at another crowd, moved His hands over them and said, "You's red folks!" They made their manners and said, "Thank you, Old Maker," and they went on off. He looked towards the center and moved His hand over another crowd and said, "You's white folks!" They bowed low and said, "Much obliged, Jesus," and they went on off. Then God looked way over to the right and said, "Look here, Gabriel, I miss a lot of multitudes from around the throne this morning." Gabriel looked too, and said, "Yessir, there's a heap of multitudes missing from round de throne this morning." So God sat there an hour and a half and waited. Then He called Gabriel and said, "Looka here, Gabriel, I'm sick and tired of this waiting. I got plenty of creating to do this morning. You go find them folks and tell 'em they better hurry on up here [if] they expect to get any color. Fool with me, and I won't give out no more."

So Gabriel run on off and started to hunting around. Way after while, he found the missing multitudes lying around on the grass by the Sea of Life, fast asleep. So Gabriel woke them up and told them, "You better get up from there and come on up to the throne and get your color. Old Maker is might' wore out from waiting. Fool with Him and He won't give out no more color."

So as the multitudes heard that, they all jumped up and went running towards the throne hollering, "Give us our color! We want our color! We got just as much right to color as anybody else." So when the first ones got to the throne, they tried to stop and be polite. But the ones coming on behind got to pushing and shoving so till the first ones got shoved all up against the throne so till the throne was careening all over to one side. So God said, "Here! Here! Git back! Git back!" But they was keeping up such a racket that they misunderstood Him, and thought He said, "Git black!" So they just got black, and kept the thing a-going.

The Walk-Off People

'WAY back yonder in the beginnin' of the world, Old Adam an' Miss Eve was livin' on fawty acres of good bottom land the Lawd had give 'em. They didn't have no boll weevil nor neither high water an' they made a good crop every year. They had 'em two good cows; a heap of shoats an' sheeps, an' they et they own fryin' chickens because it wa'nt no preachers there to eat 'em. They had a fine garden full o' mustard greens an' rosenears an' a house which didn't never leak. Ole Adam had the best mules in the country; two bran'-new Studebaker wagons; an' a pack of fine rabbit dawgs.

Miss Eve, she he'ped Ole Adam make the crop. She done the cookin', washin', an' ironin', an' they got along mighty good. Hit wa'nt but one thing twixt 'em. Ole Adam he was a man that liked to hunt an' fish, and ever-time he could sneak off, there he was chasin' rabbits, or lookin' after his trotlines. But that vexed Miss Eve 'cause when Ole Adam was away she got kin o' lonesome, it not bein' no folks for her to talk to. So one day she say, "Adam, don't you git some folks for me to talk to whilst you 'way, I ain't gwine let you hunt an' fish."

Ole Adam he didn't like that 'cause he loved to hunt an' fish mo' than anything in the world. So he went off down the big road studdin' what could he do 'bout hit, when here come the Lawd. The Lawd he give Adam hi-dy, and Adam he give the Lawd hi-dy.

"Lawd," says Ole Adam, "you sho been good to me. You gi'e me fawty acres of good bottom lan' an' us makes a good crop all the time. You gi'e me Miss Eve and she sho is a good woman. She he'ps make the crop, an' does all the cookin', ironin', an' washin'. But Lawd, you knows I'm a man that'd druther hunt an' fish than anything in this world o' yourn, but Miss Eve say don't I git some folks for her to talk to whilst I'm 'way, she ain't gwine lemme hunt an' fish. Lawd, please suh, can't you make some folks to keep that woman company?"

The Lawd say, "Adam, when does you want them folks made?" and Ole Adam he say, "Please suh, could you make 'em this evenin'?" So the Lawd got out his almanac—the one with the quarterin's of the moon in it—to see did he have anything to do that evenin', and when he see he didn't, he tole Ole Adam to meet him twarge sundown by the creek that got that good clay bank an' he would make the folks.

Well, Ole Adam he was right there when the Lawd come up on his good saddlehorse, got off, and hitched him to a little persimmon tree. Adam handed the Lawd a heap o' clay. He started kneadin' it to make the folks, and Ole Adam he cut some fresh green saplings for the framin' work. The Lawd he made some Hebrew chillun an' some Christian chillun, some white

From *Where I Was Born and Raised,* by David L. Cohn, pp. 226–228. Copyright, 1935, 1947, and 1948, by David L. Cohn. Boston: Houghton Mifflin Company.

chillun an' some colored chillun, some A-rabs an' some Chinermens. Then he put 'em all up by the fence rail an' say, "Now, Adam, you meet me right here soon after sun-up in the mawnin'. I'll be back then to put the brains in these folks."

Ole Adam he was right there at first day. But it wa'nt nothin' there. All them folks had already walked off before the Lawd come back, an' they been multiplyin' an' replenishin' the earth ever since.

The Lord and Noah

"WELL," say de Lawd, "dis ain't gittin' me nowheres. Deseyar mankinds, which I peopled my yearth wid sho ain't much. I got a good mind to wipe 'em off'n de yearth and people my yearth wid angels."

So de Lawd wawked on down de road, tawkin' to hisself and studdyin' 'bout what he gonter do wid de sin.

"Naw," he say, "angels is all right for singin' and playin' and flyin' round, but they ain't much on workin' de crops and buildin' de levees. I guess I won't monkey round wid de angels on my yearth. They jest won't do."

So he wawked along, studdyin' and a-tawkin'. "Mankind," he say, "is jest right for my yearth, ef'n he wa'nt so dad-blame sinful. But I'm sick and tired of his sin. I'd druther have my yearth peopled wid a bunch of channel catfish den mankind and his sin. I jest can't stand sin."

So about dat time de Lawd comed up on old man Noah, wawkin' long de road in a plug hat and a hammer-tail coat.

"Good mawnin', brother," say Noah. "Us missed you at church dis mawnin'."

"I ain't got no time to go to church," say de Lawd. "I got work—"

"Yeah," say Noah, "mighty nigh ev'ybody say they ain't got time to go to church dese days and times. Hit seems like de more I preaches de more people ain't got time to come to church. I ain't hardly got enough members to fill up de choir. I has to do de preachin' and de bassin', too."

"Is dat a fack?" say de Lawd.

"Yeah," say Noah. "Ev'ybody is mighty busy gamblin' and good-timin'

From *Ol' Man Adam an' His Chillun,* Being the Tales They tell about the Time When the Lord Walked the Earth like a Natural Man, by Roark Bradford, pp. 20–25. Copyright, 1928, by Harper & Brothers. New York and London.

Ol' Man Adam an' His Chillun is rip-roaring burlesque, a book of tall tales told by an imaginative humorist in the fine tradition of Mark Twain. A mythical preacher of the old school brings Biblical stories down from heaven to the realistic setting of the delta. . . . For all the truth to idiom, this is obviously not Negro religion. The difference between the personified God in the spirituals, and God with a fedora upon his head and a ten-cent segar in his mouth should be apparent to anyone in the least familiar with Negro believers and their dread of sacrilege.—Sterling Brown, *The Negro in American Fiction* (Washington, D. C., 1937), p. 126.

and sinnin' and goin' on. They ain't got time to come to church. But you jest wait. When old Gabriel blows they hawn they gonter find plenty of time to punch chunks down yonder in hell. They gonter beg to git to come to church, too. But de Lawd ain't gonter pay 'em no mind. They makin' they own fun, now. But when old Gabriel toots, de Lawd gonter be de boss."

"Brother Noah," say de Lawd, "you don't know who I is, does you?"

"Lemme see," say Noah. "Yo' face looks easy. But I jest can't call de name. But I don't keer what yo' name is, you jest come along home wid me. I think de old lady kilt a chicken or so, and den, after us eats and rests up some, you comes wid me to preachin' again tonight."

"I don't keer ef I do," say de Lawd. "Dat chicken sounds mighty good to me. And you say you basses in de singin'?"

"Jest tries hit," say Noah. "I ain't so much on de bass as I is on de leadin'."

"I used to bass purty fair," say de Lawd.

So dey wawked on to Noah's house, and de Lawd didn't let on to Noah dat he wa'n't jest a natchal man like ev'ybody else. So dey r'ared back and et chicken and dumplin's awhile, and all at once de Lawd say, "Brother Noah, I kind of b'lieve hit's gonter rain."

"My cawns is burnin' me, too," say Noah. "Jest slip yo' feet outer yo' shoes and rest yo'self."

"What'd you do, did hit commence to rain, Noah?" say de Lawd.

"Well," say Noah, "I most gen'ally lets hit rain."

"S'posin'," say de Lawd, "hit would haul off and rain fawty days and fawty nights?"

"I ain't worryin'," say Noah. "In de fust place, hit ain't gonter rain dat long onless de Lawd sends hit. And in de second place, I's on de Lawd's side, and de Lawd gonter look after me do he go to monkeyin' wid de weather."

"You b'lieve de Lawd gonter look after you, does you?" say de Lawd.

"Don't b'lieve nothin' 'bout hit," say Noah. "I knows hit. I does de best I kin for de Lawd, and dat's all de Lawd gonter ax any man to do. I don't do much, but hit's de best I got."

So all at once de Lawd reach inside his shirt front and pull out his crown and set it on his haid. Den he start to tawk, and thunder and lightnin' come outer his mouf. So old Noah jest drap down on his knees.

"Yar I is, Lawd," he say. "Yar I is. I ain't much, but I'm de best I got."

"Noah," say de Lawd, "hit's gonter rain fawty days and fawty nights. And hit's gonter drown ev'ybody on de yearth which is a sinner. And dat means about ev'ybody but you and yo' family. Now you jest git out and build me a ark on dry land big enough to hold a pair of mules and a pair of cows and a pair of elephants and a pair of snakes and a pair of ev'ything which creeps or crawls, swims or flies. And you better make hit big enough to pack away a heap of grub, too, 'cause from what I got in mind, hit ain't gonter be no goin' to de commissary and buyin' grub when I starts rainin'."

"And snakes, too, Lawd?" say Noah.

"Snakes," say de Lawd.

"And wid all dat rain and wet weather, too," say Noah.

"I hadn't thought about dat," say de Lawd. "Maybe you better not take no snakes."

"I ain't skeered of snakes," say Noah, "ef'n I got a kag of licker handy," say Noah.

"I ain't so much on de licker," say de Lawd. "But hit do come in handy round snakes."

"And wid all dat rain and wet weather, too," say Noah, "my phthisic is liable to plague me, too, onless I got a little hard licker handy."

"Well, you better put a kag of licker on boa'd, too," say de Lawd.

"Better put two kags," say Noah. "Hit'll help balance de boat. You git a kag on one side, and nothin' on de yuther, and de boat liable to turn over. You got to keep a boat balanced, Lawd."

"One kag," say de Lawd. "You kin set hit in de middle of de deck. One kag of licker is enough for anybody for fawty days and fawty nights. I said one kag, and dat's all you carries."

"Yas, Lawd," say Noah, "one kag."

The Coach Whip Story

PERHAPS the most important of the real myths is the coach whip story. It is distributed over the entire Southeast and has also been reported from the Southwest, particularly Texas. The latter territory was settled mostly by Carolinians and Georgians, who, in successive waves populated Tennessee, Alabama, Mississippi and portions of Louisiana, Arkansas, Oklahoma, and Texas. The coach whip itself (*Zamenis flagelliformis*) or a closely allied species (*Z. taeniatus*) occurs throughout the entire southern half of the United States. In the Southeast the tale, which varies somewhat in form, is found among all three classes. It is usually told in connection with a person who is not known directly to the narrator, but who is well known by a close friend. More rarely it is told of a personal acquaintance or even a relative. A simple version is the following account, obtained from a Marlboro County, South Carolina, Negress:

"Coach whups is long snakes dat kin whup yuh. Dey wuz a man plow' up one in a piece o' new groun' an' dat snake wake up an' fasten he mouf in

From "Is the Serpent Tale an Indian Survival?", by Chapman J. Milling, *Southern Folklore Quarterly*, Vol. 1 (March, 1937), No. 1, pp. 44–46. Gainesville, Florida: The University of Florida, in co-operation with the Southeastern Folklore Society.

Cf. the same author, "A Passel uh Snakes," *Folk-Say: 1931*, pp. 103–112; also Gibbons Poteet, "Joint Snake and Hoop Snake," *Man, Bird, and Beast* (1930), pp. 124–128; and *A Treasury of American Folklore* (1944), pp. 582–584.

de man nose an' wrop roun' he neck an' jus whup him an' whup him an' whup him an' whup him. An' some mens hear de noise an' come runnin'; an' you know dey had to cut dat snake off he haid and de man been all whup down an' out o' bref."

Sometimes it is told of a Negro employee. "Now my nigger Bob had an experience with a coach whip and I always could trust Bob, although, of course, you know how niggers and white people, too, will lie about snakes. . . ." A rather frequent variant is the ox story, generally told somewhat as follows: "Coach whups kin whup yuh! I know they kin 'cause a nigger feller that worked for my Uncle Jake seen one 'most kill an ox." This is the point where some doubting Thomas interrupts with a laugh only to be attacked by several others at once, all rallying to the support of the local Ananias, who, thus encouraged, proceeds:

"Well, anybody that don't believe me kin just ask Uncle Jake; you don't have to take my word." Now as Uncle Jake is often the best man physically in the community, this is usually convincing proof and the skeptics are silenced. The tale continues: "Yes sir, he nearly killed him, he did. Uncle Jake had sent the nigger down to the bottom for the cows and when he got there he didn't see none. They was all scattered and the groun' looked trampled. Well, he listened an' he heard a noise like licks fallin'; heavy licks like somebody had one o' these here rawhide whups, jest a-poppin' an' a-crackin'. An' he run on roun' to the other side o' the briar patch an' if there wan't a great big coach whup, near 'bout six foot long, jes a-frailin' away on the bigges' steer in the lot. He had him down an' the ox was near 'bout gone when the nigger got to him. He had him right by the nose an' he was a-lashin' an' a-flingin' out his tail like forty. Well, the nigger was scared mos' to death, but he taken a stick an' crep' clost enough to hit him a good solid lick an' the snake turnt loose an' come at him but that nigger got him anyway. That snake measured over six feet an' the steer was stove up for nearly a week."

It will be seen that this powerful serpent sometimes castigates a man and sometimes an ox. It may be merely a calf or a dog, but the method is always the same. The snake seizes the victim's nasal septum and twines several superfluous feet of its sinuous length around his neck. Then, securely holding on in this position, the snake deals frightful blows with his tail, which the narrator sometimes avers to be forked. Often the monster heralds his approach by raising his head and neck several feet above the broom-edge and whistling a piercing note. Occasionally he is reinforced by his mate, the one fastening the victim while the other delivers the blows. In connection with the reputed habit of standing on his tail and whistling, there is a belief among Negroes that blacksnakes do this also. A Negro woman from eastern Carolina even quoted her mother as having told her that "in de olden time" all snakes possessed this ability. "My ma say dat long time ago when dey was lot mo' woods dan dey is now de snakes use' to be in de woods ever'where. An' if you'd go out in de woods dey'd come out an' whistle at you an' stan' up on dey tails. Seem lak dey ain't so bol' dese days as dey use' to be." The coach whip story is possessed of great vitality and is often encountered in unexpected places. I know an intelligent professional man who doggedly asserts that when very young he himself witnessed the death of a calf under the snake's cruel flagellation. A graduate of a woman's college of high standard declared that her cousin had been almost "choked to death" by a coach whip when he went to the pasture to bring home the cows.

Of course it is unnecessary to remark that such stories are scientifically untenable. The coach whip is but a feeble species of racer, depending upon his speed rather than upon his prowess, and living chiefly on rats and small birds. Though actually they do attain a length of seven feet or more,[1] I doubt whether a large specimen could conquer an adult rabbit. The body is very slender and the long, yellowish grey tail does resemble a braided rawhide whip, but there is no evidence that it can deliver a blow of any real power. The reptile is, in fact, not even a good constrictor and kills its humble prey by holding its victim in its mouth and beating it about on the ground.

Two-Toe Tom

PAP HAINES lives down between Opp and Florala on the old winding road that they don't keep up any more since the straight clay pike was built. In Model T days people had to drive right careful when the old road went through pond hollows and swamps, and sometimes they had to stop and switch off their lights to let a blinded alligator get out of the way. If he was a baby 'gator he might find himself next day taking it easy in a backyard pond in some town. But if he was big and red-eyed folks mighty well let him take his time. Any alligator will go after anything, take it in water. But a red-eye will go after a man on land and he will more than go after a woman if he catches her off by herself. The farm boys and the lumberjack boys can tell of time after time when an alligator has raped a woman before he ate her. They say old Two-Toe Tom has had more than one.

When Pap Haines bought his forty from the lumber company twenty

---

[1] Ditmars, *The Reptile Book,* New York, 1907, p. 287.

From *Stars Fell on Alabama,* by Carl Carmer, pp. 197–202. Copyright, 1934, by Carl Carmer. New York: Farrar & Rinehart, Inc.

In "Uncle Monday" (*Palmetto Country,* New York, 1942, pp. 131–133) Stetson Kennedy tells the story of the leader of an African crocodile cult who, on escaping from slavery in America, became a medicine man among the Seminoles and their Negro allies, the Maroons. After their defeat by the white men on the shores of Lake Maitland, Uncle Monday retreated to the woods around Blue Sink Lake and changed himself into an alligator. "He still lives in the Blue Sink, but every now and then he changes himself back into a man and walks through the land casting all sorts of good and bad spells on folks."

years ago, folks told him he better not keep any stock on account of old Two-Toe. Two-Toe is a red-eyed 'gator and about fourteen feet long and he can knock a mule into the water with just one flip of his tail. When a farmer sees that track with just two toes on the left forefoot (the rest was cut off by a steel trap long ago), that means he has shore got to pen up his calves and pigs and he can't be too careless with his mules and grown cows either. Got to well-water them for a while instead of letting them wander around just any pond because you can't never tell which one he is in. But well-watering doesn't look out for calves and pigs enough. Any good-sized 'gator will come right up to the lot or cow-pen at night. And Two-Toe Tom is an eating fool. If the farmer's got a dog old Two-Toe just says dog-meat is dessert for a 'gator.

But Pap Haines said he'd run his chances on the forty. Said he would keep some light-wood splinters handy for a light and some big hard-tearing pine knots. A pine knot is better than a gun. Ordinary shots shell off an alligator's back like water. But a good hard lick on the back of the head or the neck with a pine knot will tear in and keel him over—then you can kill him on his tender belly. Of course Pap didn't reckon he could do any good with a steel trap. Ever since Two-Toe left the rest of his foot in one he has known more about steel trap layout than the men who set them. But a good dose of dynamite under that red-eye in some pond would make him feel pretty sick.

Pap Haines says he had right bad luck just at first. He has to go back 'way before his son was married to recollect when Two-Toe Tom threw him back for a cow. The 'gator caught her drinking at a pond and he came two nights later and got the calf out of the cow-pen. Then Two-Toe kind of fell out with this neck of the woods. He didn't bother around for ten years or more. Pap's wife died and his son got married and his wife borned four children, about two years apart. The state began building the clay pike, so they began sleeping four man-boarders in one shed room and Pap had to sleep in the room with his son and his wife and all the children because they used the other shed room to eat in. Boarders made good company, living back country, and their rent helped out when times were bad.

Then after laying-by time Pap Haines and his son lost another mule. They had been keeping all the stock in the lot by the window at night. In the daytime they turned out the mules but they tried to watch them and not let them get off too far. There was no work to do one morning, and the son decided he would like to go over with the old man and take dinner to the boarders and kind of see how they were coming along with the new road. The old lady and the kids wanted to go, too, so they hitched one of the mules to the old buggy and didn't bother about catching up the other mule.

When they got back along towards night they found the mule half eaten down by a pond. A little further along in the mud was that Two-Toe left forefoot track.

One of the boarders said he was acquainted with a man down close to Brewton that could get any 'gator he set out to. He used a blind and a high-powered rifle, and he had a sharp-shooter pin that he got back in the army. The boarder set out in a Model T the next morning and was back with the man by noon. They had stopped at the courthouse in Andalusia and found out that that old ten-year-ago hundred dollar reward for Two-Toe Tom was still in force. Pap Haines said to the man:

"We'll give you twenty-five more and board you even if it takes a week or two."

"It jest takes patience," the man said; "the trouble about a blind, folks generally git too close. A 'gator can smell a man before he gets his head high enough out o' water for the man to see him. I don't like to brag but I most generally git a bad 'gator, give me time enough."

He followed some tracks for a ways and then he said:

"Jedgin' by these tracks he's in one of these three ponds."

Then he climbed high up in a thick-limbed tree with his rifle and his dinner, three hundred yards or more from any one of the ponds. He said the 'gator couldn't see through the limbs that far and he would just naturally come out to the sun in a day or two. It might be a week the man reckoned but he would spot that devil's head somewhere, and one look would be enough.

"It jest takes patience," he said.

So the man was patient in the tree for nigh onto a week, every day, until they heard about Two-Toe Tom's track seven or eight miles down the country where he had killed two calves.

The man went down there but Two-Toe Tom must have had a good nose, or good eyes, one, for he hasn't yet got clipped off with a rifle.

Pap Haines never had any more trouble with that 'gator till last March. He had begun to reckon somebody had got him and then one of his mules didn't come up in the morning. Any mule will get contrary sometimes and not come up, so the old man went down in the brush to look for him, not bothering much, not until he saw that track. It came from a pond up yonder in a clump of water oaks and crab grass and followed along a sluggish branch too shallow for fish, much less a 'gator, and went down the hollow.

"Uh-huh," Pap Haines said. "Hell's up now."

Sure enough, over in the bushes where the spring rains had overflowed the pond he saw the mule lying with his side torn open and a part of the top shoulder and the top ham eaten away. Some of the bushes were bent and torn showing there had been a struggle. And there in the mud was that track. Two-Toe Tom was still alive and he was on the move again.

Pap Haines and his son didn't wait for breakfast. They got some pine knots and they mortally lit out after those tracks. They didn't have any trouble following them past two ponds and on to another one. And there were no tracks leading out anywhere. It was a good piece to another pond in any direction. No two ways about it, Two-Toe Tom was in that pond all right. The son got to where he could see all round the pond and told the old man to hitch the other mule to the buggy and light out to town for some dynamite, some fuses and some caps.

"Make it plenty of dynamite," he said, "and get back quick, and tell my wife to send me some breakfast."

While Pap Haines was gone his son waited for the old red-eye to come out. He was going to let him get some distance and then cut him off from coming back to the pond and whale into him with pine knots.

But Pap got back with the stuff and nothing had happened. They filled about fifteen syrup buckets with dynamite, packed the sticks tight in dirt and cottonseed and cut off some fuses. They lighted three at a time and threw the buckets in the pond. The water shot way up in the air and roots and trees came up from the bottom. Nothing could have been left alive in that pond. Just the same everybody, and there were eight of them by now, went stepping around pretty careful.

After they threw the last bucket Pap Haines said:

"We got him now. He'll be a-floatin' belly up in this pond by mornin'."

They had all started back toward the house when they heard a big splashing down by the first pool Pap had tracked the 'gator through. Then somebody began screaming. Everybody ran as fast as he could and the screams kept up but it was a good ways down there. Pap Haines is over sixty but he got there first, just in time to see two red eyes sinking under the water. Beside the pond was what was left of his twelve-year-old granddaughter. She had heard the blasting and was coming down to see what it was about.

They spent the rest of the day shooting into the water and they set off some more dynamite but nothing happened. Two weeks later a farmer down by Stedman ten miles away lost a couple of shoats and found the two-toed track.

Pap Haines lives alone now. His son and family have moved up north around Tuskegee. They want him to come there for he can hardly scrape a living by himself but he says he has never been above Montgomery and he can't get round to it. Besides, he says he plans to kill that red-eyed hell-demon before he dies. He acts a little queer about it and some folks laugh at him.

They tell him Two-Toe Tom has got tunnels all around from one pond to another and lots of secret ways to get in and out of swamps.

"I know that," he says, "but he won't fool me no more."

They tell him Two-Toe Tom has been heard from down Florida way and he won't be back. He says:

"He might be down there, but he'll be back. And I'll be waitin'." He keeps one old mule and lets him run loose for bait.

PLACE LEGENDS

The Enchanted Island

MANY moons ago there dwelt on an island in the great Okefinokee Swamp a race of Indians, whose women were incomparably beautiful. Neither among the daughters of the brave Creeks, who occupied the lowlands, nor among the dark-eyed maidens of the stalwart Cherokees, whose towns were scattered over the far mountains to the north, could there be found a damsel to match in loveliness of person these angelic beings, who were not formed of common clay, like other mortals, but were born of the great orb of day, from which circumstance, as well as because of the radiant beams of light which they seemed to diffuse, they were called Daughters of the Sun.

The island on which they dwelt in the deep recesses of the swamp was indeed a fragment of the Lost Paradise. It was embowered by the most delightful foliage, which, throughout the whole year, remained perennially green. This was because, on every side, it was well protected by the dense everglades. There were sparkling streams of the most transparent crystal, there were fruits the like of which grew nowhere else, and there were flowers of such an exquisite hue and fragrance that they seemed to have dropped from heaven. But words can give no hint or suggestion of the beauty which belonged to this rare bower. The task must be left to the imagination.

On one occasion, some hunters, in pursuit of game, found themselves hopelessly entangled in the deep labyrinths of the great swamp. They wandered for hours through the bogs and marshes, finding no means of egress, when finally, on the verge of despair, they beheld through an open vista the most inviting of visions—an island, whose soft fringes of emerald, contrasting with the coarse underbrush about them, beckoned the hunters to approach. Revived by the prospect, they pressed eagerly forward. There was no longer any sense of fatigue. They were now invigorated in every limb, whereas a moment ago they were about to faint with exhaustion. Strange it is what a power the mind exercises over the body, thus to give it renewed strength in an instant, simply by an exchange of mental pictures!

As the Indians approached the island, its wealth of attractions became more and more apparent. They espied in the distance, through the green lace-work of foliage, a lake, whose surface glistened like polished steel in the clear sunlight, while bordering it were orange trees whose luscious globes gave it an exquisite fringe of gold. But having so far penetrated with the

From *Georgia's Landmarks, Memorials, and Legends*, by Lucian Lamar Knight, Vol. II, pp. 464–467. Copyright, 1914, by Lucian Lamar Knight. Atlanta, Georgia: Printed for the author by the Byrd Printing Company, State Printers.

For more Okefinokee lore, see Cecile Hulse Matschat, *Suwannee River* (New York, 1938) and Francis Harper, "Tales of the Okefinokee," *American Speech*, Vol. I (May, 1926), No. 8, pp. 407–420.

eye into this strange fairyland, they were destined to approach no further. The very tortures of Tantalus now seized them, for while they continued to move with impulsive haste in the direction of the island, it came, visibly at least, no nearer. At last they were again overcome by fatigue. They also began to feel the sharp pangs of hunger, and once more the Indians were about to sink into the ground, when there arose before them, seemingly out of the very air itself, so ethereal was the dreamlike appearance which they presented, a group of beautiful women, who proved to be none other than the Daughters of the Sun.

If the hunters were bewitched by the scenery of the island, they were transported by the loveliness of the fair inhabitants. But ere the rising raptures within them could be put into articulate expression, they were told to advance no further. The women were exceedingly gracious. They spoke in accents of music and with divine compassion they smiled upon the hunters; but they warned them of the danger in which they stood from irate husbands, who were fierce men and exceedingly cruel to strangers. But the sense of fear produced no disturbance in the presence of such radiant apparitions. The hunters were like men transfixed. They refused to betake themselves to flight.

Finally the women, in tears, besought them to leave at once. The hunters were quite naturally touched by this display of emotion. They were ignorant of the way back to the settlements but agreed to go, first craving a morsel of food to sustain them along the journey home. Without a moment's loss of time they were given abundant supplies, among other things, delicious fruits, marsh eggs, and corn pones, the most delightful they had ever eaten. The hunters were shown a path by which they might return in safety to the settlements. With great reluctance the Indians proceeded to take it, but they mentally resolved to return with re-enforcements to conquer this mysterious region, for they wished to make wives of these beautiful Daughters of the Sun. No sooner were they ready to depart than the women vanished as suddenly as they had come into sight, and the hunters, after encountering manifold difficulties, at last arrived in the settlements. When the adventurous story was told about the camp-fires, there was no lack of volunteers to undertake the hazardous expedition; but every effort to find the enchanted island resulted in utter failure. It was effectually concealed by some subtle power of magic in the bosom of the great swamp.

Bald Mountain

MANY, many generations ago, long before the white man was seen in the land, a large and happy tribe of Indians lived around the base of the mountain in North Carolina now known as Bald Mountain. It was then covered, from base to summit, with gigantic trees, beneath which flourished a dense

From "The Mountain Horror," by W. C. Elam, *The South Atlantic Quarterly*, Vol. I (April, 1878), No. 6, pp. 520–523. Wilmington, North Carolina.

under-growth of vines, bushes and shrubbery. One day, to the terror of the tribe, an immense bird soared above them, over-shadowing them with his outstretched wings. Finally, with terrific cries, he settled upon the very top of the mountain, shaking all the surrounding country as he alighted. That a bird so vast should make his eyry so near them was dreadful enough, even to the warriors of the tribe, who plainly foresaw how ineffectual their weapons must prove against a flying foe of such huge dimensions. But the bird kept quiet, to the great relief of all; and, as day followed day, without his reappearance, his residence over them gradually lost its terrors, except that the boldest hunter among them dared not pursue his game when it fled toward the summit of the mountain.

One night the tribe were wrapped in sleep, when they were suddenly awakened by the shriekings of the bird and the quaking of the earth at his movements. With one fell swoop, he rushed down upon the valley like a storm, crying and roaring with ferocity, and causing the trees and rocks to shake at his coming. Men, women and children fled in tumult, dispersing in all directions, like leaves before a tornado. At length the monster withdrew to his eyry, and the slowly regathered tribe discovered that he had borne off in his cruel talons the beloved child of one of the Chiefs. Every year thereafter the feathered horror repeated his descent upon the tribe, with like hideous sounds and awful commotions, always bearing off a young child as his prey. The afflicted Indians knew not what to do. They shrank in dread from the unequal combat with a bird whose size, strength and ferocity were so prodigious. They invoked the Great Spirit for relief, but He seemed deaf to their invocations. They felt that for some great, unexpiated sins this distressing annual sacrifice was exacted of them, and they submitted as to the inevitable.

At length a Chief arose who could not and would not endure the tyranny and rapacity of the bird of the mountain. Just before the period at which the horrid annual visitation was expected, when the fathers and mothers looked upon their little ones with the fearful certainty that one would be torn from them to be tortured, killed and devoured, this Chief called the tribe together and eloquently exhorted them to make an effort to destroy the bird, even though they should themselves perish in the attempt. Aroused by his example and his appeal, and driven, indeed, to desperation by the repeated sacrifices they had undergone, the warriors unanimously agreed to follow the Chief in his perilous, if not forlorn, enterprise against the mountain horror. The women and children were placed at a distance in secure retreats, and the warriors, armed with all their offensive and defensive weapons, encircled the base of the mountain and resolutely began the ascent. Their progress was slow and difficult up the steep acclivity, their way impeded at every step by the rank growth that clothed the mountain from foot to top. Yet they pressed forward and upward, resolved to do or die, until, at length, they were suddenly and simultaneously arrested all around the mountain by an unexpected spectacle that froze the very blood in their veins with fear. They beheld before them, not merely one monstrous bird, but an innumerable congregation of the same mammoth and savage species, clustering close in rank on rank to the very summit of the mountain, glaring with fierce eyes, and with beaks and wings extended, ready to rush down upon and exterminate the invaders of their heights. Yielding all hope before this appalling apparition, the warriors cast away their weapons and fell upon their faces, to await the destruction so surely impending over them.

At this supreme moment the heart of the Chief did not fail him. He saw as clearly as his followers did how unavailing would be their strength and weapons against this multitudinous brood of monsters: but he was at the same time inspired with a faith that the Great Spirit would not permit the whole tribe to perish before these evil birds, if He were now called on devoutly for succor. Elevating his tall form, therefore, erect above his prostrate people, and raising high his hands and eyes to heaven, he, with a loud voice, earnestly besought the Great Spirit to interpose now in behalf of his helpless and afflicted tribe. The Great Spirit heard.

Before the infuriated birds could rush upon their victims, there flashed forth from every quarter of the cloudless sky vivid and noiseless lightnings, concentering upon the mountain, slaying every bird of the foul brood, riving the trees, and wrapping all the heights in a devouring conflagration. The amazed and awe-stricken Indians arose and gazed in solemn silence as the flames swept furiously up the mountain, destroying everything in their course; but as the last tongue of fire leaped up from the highest peak and expired (its mission of salvation completed), the tribe raised loud and long their song of thanksgiving for their miraculous deliverance.

From that day to this, it is said, no vegetation has grown upon the mountain within the area blasted by the avenging fires of heaven. The anniversary of their great deliverance was duly celebrated by the tribe from year to year, until they wandered westward; and thus the tradition was handed down from generation to generation, till it was narrated by a lingering member of the tribe to white men who are now living at the foot of the mountain. Of late years BALD MOUNTAIN has given forth mysterious rumblings, shocking the adjacent country, and scientists now see in this wondrous legend a veiled account of a pre-historic volcanic eruption, of which BALD MOUNTAIN was the centre.

The Mysterious Music at Pascagoula
(The Sea-Maiden of the Biloxi)

DURING that summer, Governor Périer, leaving New Orleans, visited the first settlements of the French at the Bay of St. Louis, at Biloxi, Pas-

From *Louisiana: Its Colonial History and Romance*, by Charles Gayarré, pp. 389–392. Entered, according to Act of Congress, in the year 1850, by Harper & Brothers, in the Clerk's Office of the District Court of the Southern District of New York. 1851.

cagoula, and Mobile. While among the Pascagoulas, or *bread eaters*, he was invited to go to the mouth of the river of that name, to listen to the mysterious music which floats on the waters, particularly on a calm, moonlight night, and which, to this day, excites the wonder of visitors. It seems to issue from caverns or grottoes in the bed of the river, and sometimes oozes up through the water under the very keel of the boat which contains the inquisitive traveler, whose ear it strikes as the distant concert of a thousand Eolian harps. On the banks of the river, close by the spot where the music is heard, tradition says that there existed a tribe different

---

The story of mass-suicide by the entire Biloxi tribe . . . is obviously impossible, since enough Biloxi were left in Avoyelles Parish, Louisiana in 1886 and near Lecompte, Rapides Parish in 1892, to enable investigators to identify them for the first time as members of the Siouan linguistic family. But it is at least possible that nearly all, or a large part, of some particular band did at some time drown themselves in a river, as asserted.

There are several versions of such a mass-drowning in print, all mentioning Pascagoula Bay, Mississippi, and either the Biloxi tribe, or the Pascagoula, who were closely associated with, and perhaps absorbed by, the former. Probably the earliest version, said to have been current in 1727, states that shortly after De Soto's expedition, a Catholic priest appeared among the peaceful Pascagoula and weaned them away from their earlier mermaid-worship to the religion of the Cross; the mermaid, however, presently appeared and by her singing lured the entire tribe to march, also singing, into the bay, whence their voices can still sometimes be heard. (Charles Gayarré, *History of Louisiana*, New Orleans, 1903, I: 383–386.)

Another version, already an old tradition in the 1850's, is considerably closer to the story I heard in Brackettville [Texas] and Nacimiento [Coahuila], though easily distinguishable therefrom. "According to a local tradition," an English traveler records, ". . . the Biloxi . . . after an unsuccessful battle with a more powerful tribe, marched into the sea and perished as a nation." (Charles Lanman, *Adventures in the Wilds of the United States*, Philadelphia, 1856, 2:200.) A collector of legends repeats the same story, drawn from this or another source, with the sole addition of identifying the "more powerful tribe" as the Choctaw. (Charles M. Skinner, *Myths and Legends of Our Own Land*, Philadelphia, 1896, 2:90–92.) A much more romantic version makes the Pascagoula the victims of aggression and the participants in mass-suicide, and the Biloxi the aggressors; the cause of the war is the traditional emotional attachment between a prince of one of the rival tribes and a princess of the other. (Minnie Walter Myers, *Romance and Realism of the Southern Gulf Coast*, quoted in Dunbar Rowland's *History of Mississippi*, Chicago, 1925, 1:90–91.)

It will be noted that in the oral version the Biloxi drown themselves to avoid expatriation by the Whites, while in all the printed versions the Indians (Biloxi or Pascagoula) commit suicide either at the inducement of an Indian goddess or to escape domination by a rival Indian tribe (Choctaw, Biloxi, or unnamed). There is, indeed, a story of mass-suicide by drowning to escape White domination; the participants, however, are not Indians, whether Biloxi or Pascagoula, but Ibo Negroes fresh from Africa, who, under the leadership of their chief, are said to have marched singing into Dunbar Creek, on St. Simons, one of the Sea Islands off Georgia, to escape slavery. (Georgia Writers Project, *Drums and Shadows*, Athens, Georgia, 1940, 150, 185.) In view of the fact that I encountered the Biloxi story among Seminole *Negroes*, many of whose ancestors were, no doubt, runaway slaves from Georgia and South Carolina, the possibility of an influence from Ibo tradition cannot be immediately and entirely set aside. (Kenneth Porter, "A Legend of the Biloxi," *Journal of American Folklore*, Vol. 59 (April–June, 1946), No. 232, pp. 169–170.)

in color and in other peculiarities from the rest of the Indians. Their ancestors had originally emerged from the sea, where they were born, and were of a light complexion. They were a gentle, gay, inoffensive race, living chiefly on oysters and fish, and they passed their time in festivals and rejoicings. They had a temple in which they adored a mermaid. Every night when the moon was visible, they gathered round the beautifully carved figure of the mermaid, and with instruments of strange shape, worshipped that idol with such soul-stirring music, as had never before blessed human ears.

One day, a short time after the destruction of Mauvila, or Mobile, in 1539, by Soto and his companions, there appeared among them a white man, with a long gray beard, flowing garments, and a large cross in his right hand. He drew from his bosom a book, which he kissed reverentially and he began to explain to them what was contained in that *sacred little casket*. Tradition does not say how he came suddenly to acquire the language of those people, when he attempted to communicate to them the solemn truths of the gospel. It must have been by the operation of that faith which, we are authoritatively told, will remove mountains. Be it as it may, the holy man, in the course of a few months, was proceeding with much success in his pious undertaking, and the work of conversion was going on bravely, when his purposes were defeated by an awful prodigy.

One night, when the moon at her zenith poured on heaven and earth, with more profusion than usual, a flood of light angelic, at the solemn hour of twelve, when all in nature was repose and silence, there came, on a sudden, a rushing on the surface of the river, as if the still air had been flapped into a whirlwind by myriads of invisible wings sweeping onward. The water seemed to be seized with convulsive fury; uttering a deep groan, it rolled several times from one bank to the other with rapid oscillations, and then gathered itself up into a towering column of foaming waves, on the top of which stood a mermaid, looking with magnetic eyes that could draw almost every thing to her, and singing with a voice which fascinated into madness. The Indians and the priest, their new guest, rushed to the bank of the river to contemplate this supernatural spectacle. When she saw them, the mermaid tuned her tones into still more bewitching melody, and kept chanting a sort of mystic song, with this often repeated ditty:—

> "Come to me, come to me, children of the sea,
> Neither bell, book, nor cross shall win ye from
> your queen."

The Indians listened with growing ecstasy, and one of them plunged into the river to rise no more. The rest, men, women, and children, followed in quick succession, moved as it were, with the same irresistible impulse. When the last of the race disappeared, a wild laugh of exultation was heard; down returned the river to its bed with the roar of a cataract, and the whole scene seemed to have been but a dream. Ever since that time, is occasionally heard the distant music which has excited so much attention and investigation. The other Indian tribes of the neighborhood have always thought that it was their musical brethren, who still keep up their revels at the bottom of the river, in the palace of the mermaid. Tradition further relates that the poor priest died in an agony of grief, and that he attributed this awful event and victory of the powers of darkness to his not having been in a perfect state of grace, when he attempted the conversion of those infidels. It is believed also that he said on his death-bed, that those deluded pagan souls would be redeemed from their bondage and sent to the kingdom of heaven, if on a Christmas night, at twelve of the clock, when the moon shall happen to be at her meridian, a priest should dare to come alone to that musical spot, in a boat propelled by himself, and should drop a crucifix into the water. But, alas! if this be ever done, neither the holy man nor the boat are to be seen again by mortal eyes. So far, the attempt has not been made; sceptic minds have sneered, but no one has been found bold enough to try the experiment.

The Date-Tree of Orleans Street

SINCE I am dealing in traditionary lore, I may as well close this lecture with another legend, which, when I was a boy, thirty years ago, a man of eighty related to me, as having been handed down to him by his father.

In a lot situated at the corner of Orleans and Dauphine streets, in the city of New Orleans, there is a tree which nobody looks at without curiosity and without wondering how it came there. For a long time, it was the only one of its kind known in the state, and from its isolated position, it has always been cursed with sterility. It reminds one of the warm climes of Africa or Asia, and wears the aspect of a stranger of distinction driven from his native country. Indeed, with its sharp and thin foliage, sighing mournfully under the blast of one of our November northern winds, it looks as sorrowful as an exile. Its enormous trunk is nothing but an agglomeration of knots and bumps, which each passing year seems to have deposited there as a mark of age and as a protection against the blows of time and of the world. Inquire for its origin, and every one will tell you that it has stood there from time immemorial. A sort of vague but impressive mystery is attached to it, and it is as superstitiously respected as one of the old oaks of Dodona. Bold would be the axe that should strike the first blow at that foreign patriarch; and if it were prostrated to the ground by a profane hand, what native of the city would not mourn over its fall, and brand the act as an unnatural and criminal deed? So, long live the *date-tree* of Orleans-street—that time-honored descendant of Asiatic ancestors!

Ibid., pp. 392–395.

Cf. "Père Antoine's Date Palm," Will H. Coleman's *Historical Sketch Book and Guide to New Orleans* (1885), p. 114; also the stories by Thomas Bailey Aldrich and George W. Cable.

In the beginning of 1727, a French vessel of war landed at New Orleans a man of haughty mien, who wore the Turkish dress and whose whole attendance was a single servant. He was received by the governor with the highest distinction, and was conducted by him to a small but comfortable house with a pretty garden, then existing at the corner of Orleans and Dauphine streets, and which, from the circumstance of its being so distant from other dwellings might have been called a rural retreat, although situated in the limits of the city. There, the stranger, who was understood to be a prisoner of state, lived in the greatest seclusion; and although neither he nor his attendant could be guilty of indiscretion, because none understood their language, and although Governor Périer severely rebuked the slightest inquiry, yet it seemed to be the settled conviction in Louisiana, that the mysterious stranger was a brother of the Sultan, or some great personage of the Ottoman empire, who had fled from the anger of the vicegerent of Mohammed, and who had taken refuge in France. The Sultan had peremptorily demanded the fugitive, and the French government, thinking it derogatory to its dignity to comply with that request, but at the same time not wishing to expose its friendly relations with the Moslem monarch, and perhaps desiring, for political purposes, to keep in hostage the important guest it had in its hands, had recourse to the expedient of answering, that he had fled to Louisiana, which was so distant a country that it might be looked upon as the grave, where, as it was suggested, the fugitive might be suffered to wait in peace for actual death, without danger or offense to the Sultan. Whether this story be true or not is now a matter of so little consequence, that it would not repay the trouble of a strict historical investigation.

The year 1727 was drawing to its close, when on a dark, stormy night, the howling and barking of the numerous dogs in the streets of New Orleans were observed to be fiercer than usual, and some of that class of individuals who pretend to know every thing, declared that by the vivid flashes of lightning, they had seen, swiftly and stealthily gliding toward the residence of the *unknown,* a body of men who wore the scowling appearance of malefactors and ministers of blood. There afterward came also a report that a piratical-looking Turkish vessel had been hovering a few days previous in the bay of Barataria. Be it as it may, on the next morning the house of the stranger was deserted. There were no traces of mortal struggle to be seen; but in the garden, the earth had been dug, and *there* was the unmistakable indication of a recent grave. Soon, however, all doubts were removed by an inscription in Arabic characters, which was affixed to a post, and which was sent to France to be deciphered. It ran thus: "The justice of heaven is satisfied, and the date-tree shall grow on the traitor's tomb. The sublime Emperor of the faithful, the supporter of the faith, the omnipotent master and Sultan of the world, has redeemed his vow. God is great, and Mohammed is his prophet. Allah!" Some time after this event, a foreign-looking tree was seen to peep out of the spot where a corpse must have been deposited in that stormy night, when the rage of the elements yielded to the pitiless fury of man, and it thus explained in some degree this part of the inscription, "the date-tree shall grow on the traitor's grave."

Who was *he* or what had *he* done, who had provoked such relentless and far-seeking revenge? Ask Nemesis, or—at that hour when evil spirits are allowed to 10am over the earth, and magical invocations are made—go, and interrogate *the tree of the dead.*

Two Legends of the Brazos

I. THE MIRACULOUS ESCAPE [1]

THE name of the river is Los Brazos de Dios, which is to say, The Arms of God.

The bed of it is very deep; and the color of the water—when it creeps sluggishly along between its banks, so shallow in places that the blue heron may wade it without wetting his knees—is the color of tarnished brass. But when it comes roaring down from the far-away Redlands, a solid foam-crested wall, leaping upward a foot a minute, and spreading death and destruction into the outlying lowlands, then it is as red as spilled blood.

On its banks, more than a century and a half ago, a handful of barefoot Franciscan friars, who had prayed and fought their way across the country from Mexico, founded the Presidio of St. Jago, and corralled within the boundary walls a flock of *Yndios reducidos.*

There were the stately church, cloistered and towered and rose-windowed —a curious flower of architecture abloom in the savage wilderness—and the blockhouse with its narrow loopholes, and the hut into which the Indian women were thrust at night under lock and key.

The mighty forest and open prairies around teemed with Yndios bravos, who hated the burly, cassocked, fighting monks, and their own Christianized tribesmen.

These came, in number like the leaves of the live oak, to hurl themselves against the Presidio. And, after many days of hard fighting, the single friar who remained alive turned his eyes away from the demolished church, and, under cover of smoke from the burning blockhouse, led the remnant of Yndios reducidos (who because they had learned to pray had not forgotten how to fight) out of the enclosure by a little postern-gate, and down the steep bank to the yellow thread of the river below.

Midway of the stream—thridding the ankle-deep water—they were, before the red devils above discovered their flight. The demoniac yell from a

[1] From *Under the Man-Fig,* by (Mrs.) M. E. M. Davis, pp. 1–3. Boston: Houghton, Mifflin & Co. 1895. Reprinted in *Legends of Texas,* edited by J. Frank Dobie, pp. 212–213. Publications of the Texas Folk-Lore Society, No. III. Copyright, 1924, by J. Frank Dobie, Secretary of the Texas Folk-Lore Society. Austin.

thousand throats pushed them like a battering ram up the opposite bank, whence, looking back, they saw the bed of the River Tockonhono swarming with their foes. Then the Yndios reducidos opened their lips and began to chant the death-song of the Nainis; and the friar, lifting his hand, commended their souls and his own to the God who gives and who takes away.

But, lo, a miracle!

Even as the waves of the Red Sea—opened by the rod of Moses for the passage of his people—closed upon Pharaoh and his host, so, with the hoarse roar of a wild beast springing upon his prey, the foam-crested wall of water fell upon the Yndios bravos, and not a warrior of them all came forth from the river bed but as a bruised and beaten corpse.

So the friar, falling on his knees, gave thanks. And the river, which was the Tockonhono, became from that day Los Brazos de Dios, which is to say, The Arms of God.

Such is the legend of the river.

II. The Great Drouth and the Waters at Waco [2]

It was a time of terrible drouth. The drouth had lasted two years and the little colony of Spaniards at San Saba had gone on mining with their captive Indians and their peons until the Indians had deserted, the peons had died, and there was absolutely no water left in the river or springs. Each month the band of Spaniards hoped that the next new moon would bring rain, but no rain came, and they knew that in the nearly always dry region towards Mexico, the drouth must be even worse. So, instead of going south towards San Antonio as they would normally have gone, the Spaniards set out eastward toward the village of the Waco Indians. They had often heard of a great river flowing by the Waco's camp, and there they hoped to find water. They left not a soul or a hoof behind, but packed on the burros their little store of provisions and what bullion they had accumulated, well knowing that they could not return until the drouth was broken.

At Las Chanas (the Llano), they found a dry bed; the Colorado was as

---

[2] By J. Frank Dobie. From *Legends of Texas,* edited by J. Frank Dobie, pp. 214–215. Publications of the Texas Folk-Lore Society, No. III. Copyright, 1924, by J. Frank Dobie, Secretary of the Texas Folk-Lore Society. Austin.

The [second] legend is connected with the famous "Bowie," or Los Almagres, Mine on the San Saba. Like many other legends, it came to me from West Burton of Austin. He got it from an old man named White, now living out in the Big Bend country, but formerly of Mason or thereabouts. According to Burton, White got the account, written on a parchment, from a grateful old Mexican whom he had befriended in a spell of sickness. The Mexican claimed to have secured the parchment from his grandfather, the date it bore being over one hundred and fifty years old. When the aged Mexican took sick on Mr. White's place in Mason County, he was traveling through the country with a crude Mexican cart and two burros, looking for two dugouts somewhere between the old San Saba Mission or mines and the site of the Waco Indian village, which was located at about the present site of Waco. As the parchment reads, thirty-six (or it may be forty-six, Burton says) jack loads of silver bullion were buried in these two dugouts.—J. F. D.

dry as the top of a rock. Arrived at the Lampassas Springs, they found a little water, a great deal of mud, and dead buffaloes covering the ground. They pulled some of the dead buffaloes out of the bog, got a little stinking water, and slowly moved on. But the burros were poor from want of grass and starved from want of water. To carry the heavy bullion much farther was impossible. The provisions had to be taken at any price. So two small dugouts were made in the side of a hill, the bullion was buried therein, and after the captain of the band had called on all to witness the marks of the place, the cavalcade moved on.

The trail on eastward was marked by dead beasts and dead men, but at last, depleted in numbers and wasted in fortune, the travelers arrived at the village of the Wacos. There they found a great river flowing clear and fresh, and when they had drunk and had seen their beasts drink, they knelt down to give God thanks, and the padre with them blessed the stream and called it Los Brazos de Dios—the Arms of God.

The Spanish built a kind of rude fort and waited. The drouth kept on for three more years. Los Brazos still flowed clear and sweet, and memories of the rich mines and the rich bullion left behind began to grow dim. But at last the drouth broke and the grass and weeds sprang from the earth with a great rush. The grass grew so quickly that a powerful and fierce tribe of Indians was down upon the Spaniards before they could leave. Their little settlement was annihilated. Only one man lived to get back to Mexico, and that years later when he was old and feeble; he was so broken that he had no desire ever again to come into the region of the terrible drouth. But a while before he died he wrote out on a piece of parchment the history of that search across the desert for water, the directions as well as he could give them, to the buried bullion, and this account of the settlement and disaster on the river called Los Brazos de Dios. The hidden dugouts with their wealth have never been found, and history has forgot to record that tragic episode of the first Spanish settlement on the Brazos.

ANIMAL AND NURSERY TALES

How the Deer Obtained His Horns

IN THE old days the animals were fond of amusement, and were constantly getting up grand meetings and contests of various kinds, with prizes for the winner. On one occasion a prize was offered to the animal with the finest

From "Myths of the Cherokees" by James Mooney, *Journal of American Folk-Lore*, Vol. I, July–September, 1888, No. II, pp. 106–108. Copyright, 1888, by the American Folklore Society. Boston and New York: Houghton, Mifflin and Company.

coat, and although the otter deserved to win it, the rabbit stole his coat, and nearly got the prize for himself. After a while the animals got together again, and made a large pair of horns, to be given to the best runner. The race was to be through a thicket, and the one who made the best time, with the horns on his head, was to get them. Everybody knew from the first that either the deer or the rabbit would be the winner, but bets were high on the rabbit, who was a great runner and a general favorite. But the rabbit had no tail, and always went by jumps, and his friends were afraid that the horns would make him fall over in the bushes unless he had something to balance them, so they fixed up a tail for him with a stick and some bird's down.

"Now," says the rabbit, "let me look over the ground where I am to run."

So he went into the thicket, and was gone so long that at last one of the animals went to see what had become of him, and there he found the rabbit hard at work gnawing down bushes and cutting off the hanging limbs of the trees, and making a road for himself clear through to the other side of the swamp. The messenger did not let the rabbit see him, but came back quietly and told his story to the others. Pretty soon the rabbit came out again, ready to put on the horns and begin the race, but several of the animals said that he had been gone so long that it looked as if he must have been cutting a road through the bushes. The rabbit denied it up and down, but they all went into the thicket, and there was the open road, sure enough. Then the chief got very angry, and said to the rabbit, "Since you are so fond of the business, you may spend the rest of your life gnawing twigs and bushes," and so the rabbit does to this day. The other animals would not allow the rabbit to run at all now, so they put the horns on the deer, who plunged into the worse part of the thicket, and made his way out to the other side, then turned round and came back again on a different track, in such fine style that every one said he had won the horns. But the rabbit felt sore about it, and resolved to get even with him.

One day, soon after the contest for the horns, the rabbit stretched a large grape-vine across the trail, and gnawed it nearly in two in the middle. Then he went back a piece, took a good run, and jumped up at the vine. He kept on running and jumping up at the vine, until the deer came along and asked him what he was doing.

"Don't you see?" says the rabbit. "I'm so strong that I can bite through that grape-vine at one jump."

The deer could hardly believe this, and wanted to see it done. So the rabbit ran back, made a tremendous spring, and bit through the vine where he had gnawed it before. The deer, when he saw that, said, "Well, I can do it if you can." So the rabbit stretched a larger grape-vine across the trail, but without gnawing it in the middle. Then the deer ran back as he had seen the rabbit do, made a powerful spring, and struck the grape-vine right in the centre; but it only flew back, and threw him over on his head. He tried again and again, until he was all bruised and bleeding.

"Let me see your teeth," at last said the rabbit. So the deer showed him his teeth, which were long and sharp, like a wolf's teeth.

"No wonder you can't do it," says the rabbit; "your teeth are too blunt to bite anything. Let me sharpen them for you, like mine. My teeth are so sharp that I can cut through a stick just like a knife." And he showed him a black-locust twig, of which rabbits gnaw the young shoots, which he had shaved off as well as a knife could do it, just in rabbit fashion.

The deer thought that was just the thing. So the rabbit got a hard stone, with rough edges, and filed and filed away at the deer's teeth, until they were filed down almost to the gums.

"Now try it," says the rabbit. So the deer tried again, but this time he couldn't bite at all.

"Now you've paid for your horns," said the rabbit, as he laughed and started home through the bushes. Ever since then the deer's teeth are so blunt that he cannot chew anything but grass and leaves.

The Terrapin and the Deer

ONCE, in the olden times, when the animals of the earth had the power of speech, a red deer and a terrapin met on the Black Mountain. The deer ridiculed the terrapin, boasted of his own fleetness, and proposed that the twain should run a race. The creeping animal assented to the proposition. The race was to extend from the Black Mountain to the summit of the third pinnacle extending to the eastward. The day was then fixed, and the animals separated. During the intervening time the cunning terrapin secured the services of three of its fellows resembling itself in appearance, and having given them particular directions, stationed them upon the several peaks over which the race was to take place. The appointed day arrived, and the deer, as well as the first mentioned terrapin, were faithfully on the ground. All things being ready, the word was given, and away started the deer at a break-neck speed. Just as he reached the summit of the first hill he heard the shout of a terrapin, and as he supposed it to be his antagonist, he was greatly perplexed, but continued on his course. On reaching the top of the second hill, he heard another shout of defiance, and was more astonished than ever, but onward still did he continue. Just before reaching the summit of the third hill, the deer heard what he supposed to be the same shout, and he gave up the race in despair. On returning to the starting-place, he found his antagonist in a calm and collected mood, and, when he demanded an explanation, the terrapin solved the mystery, and then begged the deer to remember that mind could sometimes accomplish what was often beyond the reach of the swiftest legs.

From *Adventures in the Wilds of the United States and British American Provinces,* by Charles Lanman, Vol. I, p. 443. Philadelphia: John W. Moore. 1856.

How Brer Rabbit Lost His Tail

BRER RABBIT wa'n't al'a's de prankin' tricky fellow he is now; not him, he was rankin' wid de biggoty onct. He didn't wear no short tail round-'bout dem days. Not him, he was buttoned up befo' and swingin' round de behime same as any long-tail broadcloth nigger preacher is now. He was a good un to rise and foller den. He special lay down de law to his family and his folks.

One night Miss Rabbit she done stepped crost Quarters to beg. Miss Goat fer a pail er fresh milk. Mist' Rabbit he had all his chillun settin' in a row befo' him tellin' 'em how dey bes' do to live long and get wise besides.

He stan' wid his back to de fire, he done made 'em chillun cut a big back log and put in de light 'ood chunks a-top dat back log. He wa'n't no worker even den. He stan' frontin' dem little rabbits tellin' 'em de gotter live to thrive. He say: "Chillun, al'a's you do dis, think twict befo' yuh speak onct. Lil' rabbits all settin' wid de gooseflesh risin' on 'em foh lack er de heat dey pa keep off 'em standin' befo' 'em."

He say: "Dar was Sis Mole; she speak fust 'fo' she think, an' she say she too proud to walk on de groun', she was put under de groun'." He say: "Dar was Mist' Mockin' Bird, he speak onct 'fo' he think twict, and he up and sing de birds' notes—he keepin' up de interest on dem notes twell yit." He say: "Dar was Mist' Robin say he choose a red breast, 'fo' he know what choice was de best."

All dem lil' rabbits set des as solumn thinkin' twict, 'bout what dey pa say. Miss Rabbit she come er runnin' home crost de Quarters, she say: "I see smoke! I smell fire!" She burst into de do'. Old Brer Rabbit he yit standin' 'fo' de fire. Brer Rabbit coat tail was burnt off clean round de crock, er rim er fire, still creepin' up an' round. Miss Rabbit, she says: "Chillun, didn't yuh smell smoke? Chillun, why didn't yuh spoke?"

Lil' rabbits say: "Us thinkin' 'case Dad tells us to think twict 'fo' us spoke onct."

Brer Rabbit been wearin' a round-'bout ever sence. Chillun, it's might' bad when yo' own advice turn agin you.

Brer Rabbit and the Little Girl

"ONE time, after Brer Rabbit done bin trompin' roun' huntin' up some sallid fer ter make out he dinner wid, he fine hisse'f in de neighborhoods

From *Stars Fell on Alabama*, by Carl Carmer, pp. 180–181. Copyright, 1934, by Carl Carmer. New York: Farrar & Rinehart, Inc.

For the "tail-fisher" version, see Joel Chandler Harris, "How Mr. Rabbit Lost His Fine Bushy Tail," in *Uncle Remus, His Songs and His Sayings.*

From *Nights with Uncle Remus,* Myths and Legends of the Old Plantation, by Joel er Mr. Man house, en he pass 'long twel he come ter de gyardin-gate, en nigh de gyardin-gate he see Little Gal playin' roun' in de san'. W'en Brer Rabbit look 'twix' de gyardin-palin's en see de colluds, en de sparrer-grass, en de yuther gyardin truck growin' dar, hit make he mouf water. Den he take en walk up ter de Little Gal, Brer Rabbit did, en pull he roach,[1] en bow, en scrape he foot, en talk mighty nice en slick.

" 'Howdy, Little Gal,' sez Brer Rabbit, sezee; 'how you come on?' sezee.

"Den de Little Gal, she 'spon' howdy, she did, en she ax Brer Rabbit how he come on, en Brer Rabbit, he 'low he mighty po'ly, en den he ax ef dis de Little Gal w'at 'er pa live up dar in de big w'ite house, w'ich de Little Gal, she up'n say 'twer'. Brer Rabbit, he say he mighty glad, kaze he des bin up dar fer to see 'er pa, en he say dat 'er pa, he sont 'im out dar fer ter tell de Little Gal dat she mus' open de gyardin-gate so Brer Rabbit kin go in en git some truck. Den de Little Gal, she jump roun', she did, en she open de gate, en wid dat, Brer Rabbit, he hop in, he did, en got 'im a mess er greens, en hop out ag'in, en w'en he gwine off he make a bow, he did, en tell de Little Gal dat he much 'blije', en den he put out fer home.

"Nex' day, Brer Rabbit, he hide out, he did, twel he see de Little Gal come out ter play, en den he put up de same tale, en walk off wid a n'er mess er truck, en hit keep on dis a-way, twel bimeby Mr. Man, he 'gun ter miss his greens, en he keep on a-missin' un um, twel he got ter excusin' eve'ybody on de place er 'stroyin' un um, en w'en dat come ter pass, de Little Gal, she up'n say:

" 'My goodness, pa!' sez she, 'you done tole Mr. Rabbit fer ter come and make me let 'im in de gyardin atter some greens, en aint he done come en ax me, en aint I done gone en let 'im in?' sez she.

"Mr. Man aint hatter study long 'fo' he see how de lan' lay, en den he laff, en tell de Little Gal dat he done gone en disremember all 'bout Mr. Rabbit, en den he up'n say, sezee:

" 'Nex' time Mr. Rabbit come, you tak'n tu'n 'im in, en den you run des ez fas' ez you kin en come en tell me, kase I got some bizness wid dat young chap dat's bleedze ter be 'ten' ter,' sezee.

"Sho' nuff, nex' mawnin' dar wuz de Little Gal playin' roun', en yer come Brer Rabbit atter he 'lowance er greens. He wuz ready wid de same tale, en den de Little Gal, she tu'n 'im in, she did, en den she run up ter de house en holler:

" 'O pa! pa! O pa! Yer Brer Rabbit in de gyardin now! Yer he is, pa!'

"Den Mr. Man, he rush out, en grab up a fishin'-line w'at bin hangin' in de back po'ch, en mak fer de gyardin, en w'en he git dar, dar wuz Brer Rabbit tromplin' roun' on de strawbe'y-bed en mashin' down de termartusses. W'en Brer Rabbit see Mr. Man, he squot behime a collud leaf, but 't wa'n't

[1] Topknot, foretop.—J. C. H

no use. Mr. Man done seed him, en 'fo' you kin count 'lev'm, he done got ole Brer Rabbit tie hard en fas' wid de fishin'-line. Atter he got him tie good, Mr. Man step back, he did, en say, sezee:

"'You done bin fool me lots er time, but dis time you er mine. I'm gwine ter take you en gin you a larrupin',' sezee, 'en den I'm gwine ter skin you en nail yo' hide on de stable do',' sezee; 'en den ter make sho dat you git de right kinder larrupin', I'll des step up ter de house,' sezee, 'en fetch de little red cowhide, en den I'll take en gin you brinjer,' sezee.

"Den Mr. Man call to der Little Gal ter watch Brer Rabbit w'iles he gone.

"Brer Rabbit aint sayin' nothin', but Mr. Man aint mo'n out de gate 'fo' he 'gun ter sing; en in dem days Brer Rabbit wuz a singer, mon," continued Uncle Remus, with unusual emphasis, "en w'en he chuned up fer ter sing he make dem yuther creeturs hol' der bref."

"What did he sing, Uncle Remus?" asked the little boy.

"Ef I aint fergit dat song off'n my min'," said Uncle Remus, looking over his spectacles at the fire, with a curious air of attempting to remember something, "hit run sorter dish yer way:

> "'De jay-bird hunt de sparrer-nes',
> De bee-martin sail all roun';
> De squer'l, he holler from de top er de tree,
> Mr. Mole, he stay in de groun';
> He hide en he stay twel de dark drap down—
> Mr. Mole, he hide in de groun'.'

"W'en de Little Gal year dat, she laugh, she did, and she up'n ax Brer Rabbit fer ter sing some mo', but Brer Rabbit, he sorter cough, he did, en 'low dat he got a mighty bad ho'seness down inter he win'pipe some'rs. De Little Gal, she swade,[2] en swade, en bimeby Brer Rabbit, he up'n 'low dat he kin dance mo' samer dan w'at he kin sing. Den de Little Gal, she ax' im won't he dance, en Brer Rabbit, he 'spon' how in de name er goodness kin a man dance w'iles he all tie up dis a-way, en den de Little Gal, she say she kin ontie 'im, en Brer Rabbit, he say he aint keerin' ef she do. Wid dat de Little Gal, she retch down en onloose de fish-line, en Brer Rabbit, he sorter stretch hisse'f en look roun'."

Here Uncle Remus paused and sighed, as though he had relieved his mind of a great burden. The little boy waited a few minutes for the old man to resume, and finally he asked:

"Did the Rabbit dance, Uncle Remus?"

"Who? Him?" exclaimed the old man, with a queer affectation of elation. "Bless yo' soul, honey! Brer Rabbit gedder up his foots und' 'im, en he dance outer dat gyardin, en he dance home. He did dat! Sho'ly you don't 'speck dat a ole-timer w'at done had 'spe'unce like Brer Rabbit gwine ter stay dar en let dat ar Mr. Man sackyfice 'im? *Shoo!* Brer Rabbit dance, but he dance home. You year me!"

---

[2] Persuaded.—J. C. H.

Why the Fox's Mouth Is Sharp, Why the Possum Has No Hair on His Tail, and Why the Rabbit Has a Short Tail and a White Spot on His Forehead

ONE day de fox, de 'possum and Brer Rabbit was gwine down in Sister Dimpsey' corn field. Dere was a grave-yard in de corn field dat had a hant in it. Brer Possum ask Brer Fox, was he 'fraid o' hants. Brer Fox say dat if de odder gentermens will stan' dey base, he will hang on till de las' corn was off de stalk. "All right, den," say Brer Possum, "I'se got my bag an' I'se gwine to make corn fly tonight." Brer Rabbit he lay low, 'kase he knowed how Brer Possum was 'fraid o' hant.

Atter a while, Brer Rabbit 'lowed dat dey better start, Brer Fox he led de way. Dey all went thoo de grave-yard an' got ober de fence in de corn field. Brer Fox, he start to fill his bag fust. When he begin to pull de corn de hant say "Macaroni, macaroni, pull down you wine." De Fox look up an' say, "I ain't pullin' wine; I pullin' corn." Bimeby de hant come jumpin' up an' down de row atter Brer Fox. Brer Fox he got skeered, he did, and took out for de fence. When he got dere he stick he mouf thoo de wrong hole in de fence an' mash he mouf right sharp.

Den Brer Possum thought he would try, dat he wasn't afraid. But no sooner dan he begin to pull de corn de hant say, "Macaroni, macaroni, pull down you wine." Brer Possum say, "I ain't pull wine, I pull corn." When Brer Possum got his bag half full, de hant jumped down in front of him. Brer Possum drop de bag an' run for de fence. When he went to jump ober de fence de hant cotch him by de tail an' skinned all de hair off, but he got away.

Now Brer Rabbit say he gwine to try, an' dat he gwine to get de corn, fedder or no. So when Brer Rabbit got his bag mos' full, de hant say, "Macaroni, macaroni, pull down you wine." Brer Rabbit say, "I ain't pullin' wine, I pullin' corn," an' dat he was gwine to get his bag full or bus' dat hant wide open. De hant went off an' come back lookin' like a man wid a long knife in his han'. When Brer Rabbit seed dat, he grab he bag up on he shoulders an' laid out for de fence. When he got dar he dash de bag o' corn ober de fence "ka-blim" an' when he went to go ober, he skin he head agains' de fence, and when he got all ober but de tail, de hant chopped at him and cut de tail right off short.

From *Southern Workman and Hampton School Record,* Vol. 25 (May, 1896), p. 102. Hampton, Virginia: Hampton Normal & Agricultural Institute.

Cf. Samuel Gaillard Stoney and Gertrude Mathews Shelby, "Adam an' Ebe in de Garden," in *Black Genesis* (New York, 1930), pp. 25–35.

You Talk Too Much

A CULLUD man cum to the white folk's house in the country en sed to the man:

"Boss, I'se hongry; gimme sumpin t'eat."

The man sed: "All right, go round to the back do' en tell the cook to feed you."

The cullud man sed: "Boss, I'se neer 'bout starved, I ain't et fur a whole week."

The man sed: "All right, all right, go round to the kitchen."

The cullud man sed: "Boss, if yu gimme sumpin t'eat I'll split up all that stove wood you got in yo' back yard."

The man sed: "All right, all right, go en git that grub like I tole yer."

So he went. After 'bout three hours the man went to his back yard en saw the cullud man, who wuz jest settin'. So he sed:

"Has you et?"

En he sed: "Yassir."

En he sed: "Has you chopped up that wood-pile?"

En he sed: "Boss man, if you jest let me res' round till dinner time, after dinner I'll go en chop out that patch of cotton fur you."

So the man sed: "All right, but don't you fool me no more."

After the cullud man had et him a big dinner he started out to the cotton patch en he met him a cooter [a mud-turtle] en the cooter sed to him:

"Nigger, you talks too much."

The nigger goes tearin' back to the big house en when he gits there the man cums out en sez:

"Nigger, has you chopped out that cotton?"

En the nigger sez:

"Lawd, boss, I wuz on my way, fo' God I wuz, en I met a cooter en he started talkin' to me en I lit out from there en here I is."

The boss man was plenty riled and he sez:

"Nigger, take me to that cooter en if he don't start talkin', I'se goin' to cut your thoat frum year to year."

So they bof uvvem started fur the cotton patch en there in the middle of the big road set that cooter. En he never opened his mouth, he ain't sed nuthin'. So the man hopped on the nigger en whupped him sumpin scand'lous en left fur the big house mighty sore at niggers en cooters. Well, the cullud man wuz neer 'bout through breshing hisself off en jest fo' moseying on off when the cooter poked his head out en looks at him en sez:

"Nigger, I tole you you talks too much."

From *Lanterns on the Levee,* Recollections of a Planter's Son, by William Alexander Percy, pp. 294–296. Copyright, 1941, by Alfred A. Knopf, Inc. New York.

Barnyard Talk

I[1]

PETE once had a cabin in the clearing, he useta tell, and a old turkey gobbler, a guinea, a rooster, and a hen that all scratched around in the dirt.

One day the gobbler flew up to the top of the cabin to have a look around. All of a sudden he straightened up and gobbled, "Preacher comin, preacher comin, preacher comin!"

All the other fowls look down the highway and sho nuff there was the preacher's buggy and old gray mule. They all knew what that meant— one of em would be popped in the boilin pot. So they all run for the woods with the hen a-cacklin, "Cut-cut-cut-cut your head off, cut your head off, cut your head off!"

They all hid in the woods till it was near-bout dinner time, and then the turkey gobbler and the guinea flew up in a tree to have a look at the cabin. The rooster looked up at em and crowed, "Has-e-gaw-n-n-yet?"

"Not yet—not yet—not yet!" clacked the guinea. Then suddenly the gobbler gobbled, "Lord-a-mighty! There's a couple-of-em, couple-of-em, couple-of-em!"

So they all ran deeper into the woods and stayed there till they heard the buggy drive away. The preachers had to eat fat pork and grits instead of a nice fowl like they expected.

II[2]

One time I went to town huntin' a job, up in a little old town they call Rogers. And so I went to a lady's house there and asked her for some work. She says, "Can you cut yards?" an' I says, "Yes, ma'am." She says, "Go roun', go roun' to de back and look under de house, you'll find a lawn-mower there, and then begin cuttin'." I told her, "Yes, ma'am," and I went roun' and got de lawn-mower and started on de back cuttin' grass.

And so—she had some geese out into a vacant park there, she had. And so—under a tree laid a goat. And this old geese in de heat of de day raised up and said, "We's havin' a *hard* time!" Goat says, "Ungh-Ungh." So de geese kep' a-pickin', and they raised up agin and says, 'We's havin' a *ha-ard* time." Goat say, "Ungh-ungh!" And so de geese raised up agin and says, "We're havin' a *ha-a-ard* time." And de goat says, "Ba-a-d managin'!"

---

[1] From *Palmetto Country*, by Stetson Kennedy, pp. 143–144. Copyright, 1942, by Stetson Kennedy. In *American Folkways Series*, edited by Erskine Caldwell. New York: Duell, Sloan & Pearce, Inc.

[2] As told by Clear Rock, age 71, Taylortown, Texas.

From *Adventures of a Ballad Hunter*, by John A. Lomax, pp. 185–186. Copyright, 1947, by the Macmillan Company. New York.

Foolish John

I. JEAN SOTTE [1]

THERE was an old woman who had two sons,—one so simple that he received the name of Jean Sotte, and the other so bright and intelligent that he was known as Jean Esprit.

One day the old woman said to Jean Sotte, "My son, I am old and stiff, but you are young and active and can go on my errands; so go into the storeroom and bring me a bottle of wine you will find there." Jean Sotte went to the storeroom, and, having found the bottle, he thought he would take out the cork and make sure it was wine; and when he had smelled it, he thought he would taste it to be sure it was all right; but the wine was so good and old, he soon felt very merry, and continued to drink until the bottle was quite empty. Now, in a corner of the room an old duck had made her nest in some straw; and when Jean Sotte began capering around, she cried out, "Quack, quack!" and flapped her wings, which so frightened him that he caught her by the neck, and wrung her head off, and seated himself on her eggs. The old woman, having waited some time for Jean Sotte's return, determined to see what was keeping him. What was her surprise, on hobbling to the storeroom, to find her old duck dead and Jean Sotte sitting on her nest. "Silly boy!" she said, "why have you killed my duck, why are you sitting on the nest, and where is the bottle of wine you were to bring me?"—"Mother," said Jean Sotte, rolling his head and looking very sleepy, "I drank the wine; and when the old duck saw me, she cried out, and I knew she would tell you, so I killed her to keep her from telling; and, now she is dead, you will never know!"

The old mother was in despair over the stupidity of her boy, but thought she would try him again, hoping he would do better. So calling him, and giving him some money, she said, "My son, I want a paper of needles, and you must go down the road to the village and buy me one, but do not lose it on the way." Jean Sotte promised to be careful and went off in high glee, for he liked to go on errands to the village. He knew just where to go; and, having counted out the money to the old dame who gave him the needles, he started down the lane which led to his home. He had not gone far when he met a number of cows, who, when they saw him, lifted their heads and cried, "A-moo, a-moo!" and turned into a barnyard. Jean Sotte, thinking they were calling him, followed; and when they continued to cry "A-moo!" he said, "Well, if it is the needles you want, here they are!" and he sprinkled them all over the straw they were eating. Then he went home;

---

[1] As told by Marie Ray, Avery's Island, Louisiana. From *The Journal of American Folk-Lore*, Vol. XXI (October–December, 1908), No. LXXXII, pp. 364–365. Copyright, 1908, by The American Folk-Lore Society. Boston and New York: Houghton, Mifflin Company.

and when the old woman asked where the needles were she had sent him for, he said, "Mother, I obeyed you: I did not lose them, but, when the cows cried so for them, I was obliged to give them to them on their hay."

II. The Cowhide [2]

Foolish John and his mother lived by the bayou in Louisiana and they spoke French. He was such a foolish lad he misunderstood everything he was told.

"Foolish John, go get the cow by the bayou and drive her into the lot," said his mother.

In the French they spoke, "to drive" can also mean "to push." So Foolish John went to fetch the wheelbarrow and rolled it out to where the cow was pasturing. He placed her into the wheelbarrow and rolled her home. When he reached home, he was panting and sweating like a horse.

"What in the world are you doing, Foolish John?" questioned his mother.

"Well, Mama, you told me to push the cow here, and that's what I'm doing."

"Fool! will you ever learn anything!" exclaimed the exasperated woman. "Now take that cow out of there and go milk her."

As with many words that have double meanings, "to milk" also meant "to shoot."

While his mother was busy inside, Foolish John went to get the gun and shot the cow. When he appeared inside without the milk, his mother became worried.

"Foolish John, where is the milk for supper?" she asked.

"Why, Mama, I thought you meant for me to shoot the cow with a gun. . . . That's what I did," replied the lad.

"Ah, foolish son!" she cried, "killing our only cow. . . . Now you must go skin her and sell the hide so we can buy food, because we don't have milk. . . . Hurry now!"

Foolish John fetched the big butcher knife, strung the cow up to a tree by her hind legs and skinned her—head, feet and everything. He put the hide over his head and set out for town. As he walked under the hide, he looked like a strange beast.

---

[2] From "Louisiana Tales of Jean Sot and Bouqui and Lapin," by Calvin Claudel, *Southern Folklore Quarterly*, Vol. VIII (December, 1944), No. 4, pp. 297–298. Gainesville, Florida: The Southeastern Folklore Society.

Told by Jack Vidrine, Eunice, La. See also Charles Roussey, *Contes populaires, recueillis à Bournois* (Paris, 1894), Nos. 8, 22.—C. C.

. . . The fool *Jean Sot*, or Foolish John, . . . always does things perversely and stupidly, to the woe and despair of his people. Sometimes, as if by chance, he displays a flicker of wisdom which ordinary persons do not possess. One feels that the narrator, having made Jean Sot the repository for all human doltishness, makes an about face on rare occasions and shows that there may be a round-about common sense in his mad folly, implying that one may not be so stupid after all. *Jean Sot* is found in folklore under some name or other in almost every cultural tradition.—C. C., *ibid.*, p. 287.

It was getting dark and growing cold, for it was almost winter. He reached a tree that was losing its leaves. The tree groaned and shivered as the cold wind whistled through its limbs.

"That poor tree must be cold," remarked Foolish John to himself. "I'll cover it with this hide to keep it warm."

He began climbing the tree with the cowhide still on his head. When he was up in the top ready to place the hide over the tree, a band of seven men suddenly came and sat down in a circle under the tree. They were robbers with a huge sack of money. The chief began to divide the money.

"This is for me. . . . That's for you," counted the chief as he placed each robber's share before him.

Every time he said this, Foolish John would pluck a hair from his cowhide and cry, "And one hair for me—eee!"

"Listen, listen, the Old Devil!" would exclaim one of the robbers, and the chief would start to divide again. The dividing and counting continued far into the night, and each time the chief would say, "This is for me. . . . That's for you," Foolish John would add while plucking out hair, "And one hair for me—eee!"

Finally when they had all the money spread out, and Foolish John had picked his cowhide clean, he suddenly lost his grip on the limb he was holding and crashed to the ground right into the middle of the circle of thieves. When they beheld this strange apparition with horns, they all took to their heels and fled. Foolish John gathered up the money, placed the hide over the tree and went back home.

"Well, how much did you get for the hide?" inquired his mother.

"I collected a dollar for every hair on the hide," answered Foolish John, laying down the heavy sack load of money.

"Foolish John!" exclaimed the mother with joy, "sometimes I think you are not so foolish!"

III. FOOLISH JOHN AND THE RAIN [3]

Foolish John had just put on a nice, clean suit of clothes and was ready to go somewhere for his mother.

"Foolish John," warned his mother, "be careful not to get caught in the rain with your nice, clean clothes. It looks like bad weather. Don't forget to duck out of the rain if it begins to fall."

"All right, Mother," answered Foolish John, as he set out on his way. However, he had hardly reached the bayou bridge when a great peal of thunder brought down a shower of rain. Foolish John realized he was in the rain and wanted to get out of it, remembering what his mother had told him. He saw no shelter nearby, as he stood on the bayou bridge. So he thought and thought. Finally he jumped from the bridge into the bayou, in order to get out of the shower. As he stood in the muddy bayou water, his

---

[3] *Ibid.,* p. 299. Told by Tony Lelong, New Orleans, La.—C. C.

hat remained over the water on his head that stuck out of the bayou. He took off his hat and held it under the water.

When Foolish John reached home, his mother saw him all wet and covered with mud from head to feet.

"Foolish John!" she exclaimed, "didn't I warn you to keep out of the rain? You are not only wet but all covered with mud."

"Well, Mother," explained Foolish John, "you told me to duck out of the rain if it came. When it did, I ducked into the bayou. I even held my hat under the bayou out of the rain."

IV. The Dollars and the Frogs [4]

Foolish John's mother and father were very poor people. Foolish John, who was the eldest, was their sorrow instead of their solace. The more they tried to correct him, the more he showed himself to be stupid and no account. What I am going to relate will give you a good idea of what his parents had to tolerate and forgive in him. My goodness, what they went through!

One day Foolish John's mother sent him to his uncle's to borrow ten dollars. She warned him to take good care of the money, because there would be ten one-dollar bills, not to lose a single one. Foolish John assured his mother that he understood the errand very well, leaving on the run.

While returning from his uncle's house, Foolish John passed near a pond, where the frogs, springfrogs and bullfrogs, were carrying on a racket, like nobody's business. Foolish John stopped to listen. He heard the tiny voices of the small springfrogs, saying: "You have eight! You have eight! You have eight!" The silly lad believed the creatures were making fun of him, meaning that he didn't know how to count the money he had in his pocket. He became furious and replied: "You lie! Mama says I have ten,

[4] From "The Legend of Foolish John," by Marie Thériot and Marie Lahaye, *Southern Folklore Quarterly*, Vol. VII (September, 1943), No. 3, pp. 154–155. Gainesville, Florida: The Southeastern Folklore Society.

The following tales of Foolish John, which were originally taken down in French from the French-speaking peoples of Louisiana, have been translated by Mr. Calvin Claudel. The folk tales dealing with the character Foolish John, or Jean Sot, are widespread in the folklore of many nations. Foolish John appears as Juan Bobo in Spanish-speaking countries. In Joseph M. Carrière's *Tales from the French Folklore of Missouri* he appears in the tale "Bon Mangeur" ("Good Eater"), p. 304, also in the story "John Bête pis John Sage" ("John the Stupid and John the Wise") and "Jacques Pataud" ("Jack Slew-Foot"). He appears as "Jean Sotte" in Alcée Fortier's collection, *Louisiana Folk-Tales*. In F. H. Lee's *Little Stories to Tell* he appears in "Jack and his Mother"; in R. H. Busk's *The Folk-Lore of Rome,* as "The Booby"; in F. H. Lee's *Folk Tales of All Nations,* as "Silly Matt"; in J. Jacobs' *Celtic Fairy Tales,* as "Jack and his Master"; in Dr. E. H. Campbell's *Santal Folk-Tales,* as "The Story of a Simpleton"; in Joel Chandler Harris' *Evening Tales,* done into English from the French of Frederic Ortoli, as "Loony John."—M. T. and M. L., *ibid.,* p. 153.

The above tale has appeared in the original French in *Cyprière,* I, 1.—M. T. and M. L.

do you hear!" The springfrogs continued more loudly: "You have eight! You have eight! You have eight!" Beside himself, Foolish John cried out to them: "If you know so much about it, here, look!" and he threw the bills out upon the water to the frogs. "Count them for yourselves, if you wish," continued he. "There you are—one, two, three, four, five, six, seven, *eight*, nine and ten! Well now, is that not right? You see that you were wrong. Now return them all to me. I must be off. Mama is waiting for me."

Naturally the springfrogs paid no attention at all to him, and the pretty dollar bills went floating off upon the water like so many leaves in the breeze. Foolish John, poor thing, did not know what to do. He stepped into the water of the pond, while saying: "I'll get them in a little while. Mama needs that money more than those springfrogs and bullfrogs." But just then a huge bullfrog, seated by a cypress knee, began to go: "No bottom! No bottom!" Foolish John, who did not know how to swim and was afraid to get drowned in a deep pond, was frozen with fear. He stopped instantly and began to back up toward the bank of the pond. As soon as he felt the good, firm ground under his feet, he hastened homeward to relate his adventure to his mother. The poor woman! One can imagine what her sorrow was on learning what had happened to her money—borrowed money at that, which had to be returned without having spent it!

"Now don't tell me, my little children, that in such a fool there was not something to make an angel lose patience." *

The Hairy Toe

ONCE there was a woman went out to pick beans, and she found a Hairy Toe. She took the Hairy Toe home with her, and that night, when she went to bed, the wind began to moan and groan. Away off in the distance she seemed to hear a voice crying, "Who's got my Hair-r-ry To-o-oe? Who's got my Hair-r-ry To-o-oe?"

The wind rose and began to screech around the house, and the woman covered her head with the quilts. The voice seemed to come nearer: "Who's got my Hair-r-ry To-o-oe?"

---

* [A] variant has been recorded from New Orleans by Calvin Claudel and appears in his "Some Creole Folk Tales," *Iconograph*, I, 2 (March, 1941). . . .—M. T. and M. L.

By Walter McCanless. As told by Dupris Knight, Negro, age about 25, to Mrs. Walter McCanless, at Cedar Hill, near Ansonville, Anson County, North Carolina, during her childhood, about 1882. Manuscripts of the Federal Writers' Project of the Works Progress Administration for the State of North Carolina.

The final words were always accompanied by the narrator's grabbing someone in the audience very suddenly, when the weird effect had sufficiently been worked up.— W. M.

A variant, as told by Bascom Lamar Lunsford, South Turkey Creek, North Carolina, was recorded by B. A. Botkin, January 19, 1949.

The woman scrooched down, 'way down under the covers, and 'bout that time the wind 'peared to hit the house, swoosh, and the old house creaked and cracked like somethin' was tryin' to get in. The voice had come nearer, almost at the door now, and it said, "Where's my Hair-r-ry To-o-oe? Who's got my Hair-r-ry To-o-oe?"

The woman scrooched further down under the covers and pulled them tight around her head. The wind growled around the house like some big animal, and r-r-um-m-bled over the chimbley. All at once she heard the door cr-r-a-ack open and Somethin' slipped in and began to creep over the floor. The floor would cre-e-eak, cre-e-eak at every step that Thing took toward her bed. The woman could almost feel it bending over her bed. Then in a awful voice it said: "Where's my Hair-r-ry To-o-oe? Who's got my Hair-r-ry To-o-oe? *You've got it!*"

Chicky-Licky-Chow-Chow-Chow

ONCE there was a man and a boy who went out to buy a beef. As they were going home they decided to cook some of the meat. When they came to a little creek they decided that this would be a good place, but they didn't have any fire and the little boy looked up in a tree and saw what looked to him to be a fire in the top of the tree. He went up to get it and the THING said, "What do you want with me?" The little boy replied, "Pop said to come down and get you a piece of beef." The THING answered, "I'll come down afterwhile." So when it came down the man gave it the skin and the head of the animal and it swallowed them and said, "Is this all you allow me?" Then the man gave it more until the meat was all gone. This time the man said, "This is all we have, you will have to wait until we go and get another one." The THING said, "Well, let your little boy stay with me until you come back." The man said the boy would have to go and drive the animal back. So the man and the boy started off. Darkness covered the earth and they came to a house and asked if they might spend the night there and the people told them they could. In a little while they heard something coming and saying, "Bum, bum, Sally Lum, tearing down trees and throwing them as I come." The owner of the house asked, "What is that?" The man replied that it was something after him and his boy and the host told him he would have to get out of the house because they couldn't let them spend the night. They left. In a little while the THING came to the house and asked, "Have you seen ary man and a boy pass this way?" The man replied that he had; that they had passed a little while ago. The THING went on. The man and boy stopped several places but the same noise followed them and no one would take them in. They went

As told by Rosella Rudd. From "Tennessee Tall Tales," by Geneva Anderson, Maryville, Tennessee, *The Tennessee Folklore Society Bulletin,* Vol. V (October, 1939), No. 3, pp. 55–57.

on and came to a rabbit sitting by the side of the road. The rabbit told them to go to his house and he would protect them. The man and the boy crawled into a brush pile and the rabbit remained sitting outside. In a little while they heard the THING coming, "Bum, bum, Sally Lum, tearing down trees and throwing them as I come." The rabbit asked what it was. The man said it was something after him. The rabbit replied, "Stay where you are and I'll protect you." So the THING came up and asked the rabbit, "Have you seen ary man and boy pass this way?" The rabbit replied, "Chicky-licky-chow-chow-chow." The THING said, "Have you seen ary man and boy pass this way?" The rabbit repeated, "Chicky-licky-chow-chow-chow." The THING said if the rabbit didn't tell him he would swallow it. The rabbit got up on the THING's head dancing and singing "Once I had a summer house, now I've got a winter house." The THING said he would butt his brains out against a tree, but the rabbit would not quit. So the THING butted against a tree and busted his head open and the rabbit ran off saying, "Chicky-licky-chow-chow-chow."

The Poopampareno

A MAN who was a great hunter got to thinking he could do without the faithful dogs that had always helped him. Their names were Sambo and Ringo, and one day he left them shut up behind a high picket fence and went off into the woods alone. Before he left, he put a pan of milk in the pen for the dogs, but they felt so bad about being left behind they didn't go near it for a long time. When they did try to drink the milk, they found that it had turned to blood.

Now, the hunter was walking boldly through the woods when suddenly he found himself face to face with the Poopampareno! There was only one place it could be hurt, and that was right under the chin. Anywhere else a bullet would bounce off from its skin like a rubber ball. So it's no wonder the hunter threw down his gun and ran for his life.

Just in time he reached a tall pine tree, the tallest in that section of the woods. He didn't stop climbing until he was at the tip-top. When he looked down, his blood ran cold. The Poopampareno's lips were drawn back from his terrible saw teeth and he was grinning at the hunter like this. (Register exultant malice.) Then he began to saw with his teeth. (Imitate sound of saw.) Through the bark he sawed, and into the wood. Then the hunter called to his dogs as loud as he could:

By Julia Beazley. From *Coyote Wisdom,* edited by J. Frank Dobie, Mody C. Boatright, and Harry H. Ransom, Texas Folk-Lore Society Publications, Number XIV, pp. 252–254. Copyright, 1938, by Texas Folk-Lore Society. Austin.

The story of the terrible and wonderful poopampareno I heard from the Reverend Mr. Werlein, rector of Eastwood Community Church in Houston, who told it at a children's story hour. As he told the story, with action finely suited, he gave the line, "Here Sambo! And Ringo!" a kind of "Old Black Joe" tune.—J. B.

Here, Sambo! And Ringo!
Your master's almost gone!
And a poo-pam and a poo,
And a poo-pam and a po-o-o!

The dogs were far away. They thought they heard something but couldn't be sure. The milk in their bowl was blood. They feared their master was in danger. They looked at the high fence and wished they could jump over it.

When the hunter called, the Poopampareno looked up at the hunter and grinned like this. (Repeat exultant grin.) Then he began to saw harder than ever. (Repeat sawing sounds, turning head from side to side.) The tree began to tremble. Again the hunter called, louder than before:

H-e-r-e, Sambo! A-n-d Ringo!
Your master's almost gone!
And a poo-pam and a poo,
And a poo-pam and a po-o-o!

This time the dogs barely heard him. They looked at the fence. It was too high to jump, and there was no hole anywhere. Far out in the woods the Poopampareno was taking his time, but the tree was now more than half cut through. It would soon fall. So the hunter called louder than ever:

H-e-r-e, Sambo! A-n-d Ringo!
Your master's almost gone!
And a poo-pam and a poo,
And a poo-pam and a po-o-o!

This time the dogs heard their master plainly. They backed off as far as they could, and together they jumped. They cleared those high pickets by a scratch. Then neck and neck they raced into the woods. Just as the tree was about to fall, they tore up to the Poopampareno, and they had him by the throat before he could take his teeth out of the trunk.

Jack and the Calf Hide

ONCE upon a time there was a man who had three boys, Jack, Will, and Tom. Will and Tom were the two oldest sons. Jack was just a little bit of a fellow, not hardly able to take care of himself—the old father thought.

As told to Artus Moser, Swannanoa, North Carolina, by Mrs. Maude Long, Hot Springs, North Carolina.

I recorded this tale in 1941 and have transcribed it from the records. Mrs. Long is the daughter of Jane Gentry of Hot Springs, who furnished the great English folk-song collector, Cecil Sharp, with no less than sixty-four of the traditional English and Scottish folk songs and ballads.—A. M.

So the old man just divided all of his land, cattle, sheep, and horses between these two older boys, and they promised that they would take good care of little old Jack. But no sooner was the father gone than these two older brothers just began to see how bad and mean they could be to that little fellow. They made him do all of the housework, all of the cooking—just everything—and wait on them, hand and foot. And then even at that they were not kind to the little old fellow.

One day when they came in from the field to their dinner, Will said, "Jack, when you finish up with the dinner dishes, I guess you'd better go down to the edge of the woods and get that little old calf of yours and skin it. I've already cut a tree down on it and killed it."

"Well, bedast, I will," said Jack.

So after he finished the dinner dishes, he went down to the edge of the woods, and sure enough there lay his little old calf, the only thing he had in this world. There he skinned it, brought the skin home, tacked it up on the back of the barn, and let it dry good and hard. When it was just bone dry, he took that hide down to moisten it. Then he got him an old piece of shoe leather, made him a thong, and took an awl, and sewed that hide up, stuffed it with chips and straw. Then he took it by the tail and went dragging it up the path to the house, bumpty-bump, bumpty-bump, right up the path to the house. When he got to the porch, Will said:

"Jack, what in the world are you going to do with that thing?"

"Bedad, I'm going out into the world and make my fortune, that's what I'm going to do with it. When I come back to this house, I'm going to come with gold."

"Humph!" Will said, "I guess you'll come with gold. You'll be back here by supper time, good and hungry."

Jack said, "You'll see about that!"

He took his calf hide by the tail, bumpty-bump, bumpty-bump, right down the road in a cloud of dust. As far as they could see Jack, he was just a-traveling with the calf skin a-dragging along behind him.

He walked all day, and late that evening he began to think about a place to spend the night. And looking along the road on this side and that side, he finally saw a nice-looking house.

He thought, "I believe I'll go up there and ask that lady at that house if she just won't let me spend the night."

When he knocked at the door, the woman came. "Please, kind lady, could I spend the night with you here?"

"Why, no, son, you can't. My husband isn't at home. I'm just here by myself. No, you just go on down the road. You'll find a place on further down."

"Oh," he said, "Lady, but I am so tired. Please—I won't be a mite o' trouble, just let me have a bed."

"Oh, well, come on upstairs. What's your name?"

"Jack."

"All right, Jack, come on! Go on upstairs to the top of the steps, and go right into that door to your right. You can sleep there I reckon for the night."

Jack went into the room and closed the door; and while it was just beginning to get dark enough for a light to show, he could see very well where his bed was. He didn't light any lamp or anything. But he saw a knot hole right there in the middle of the floor.

He went over and put his eye down to that knot hole to see what he could see down in the world below. There sat a dining room table and the lady that had let him come into the room, with a traveler sitting on the other side of the table. They were eating and laughing and drinking, having the best time you have ever seen. And, oh, there were the best things to eat on the table. There was chicken and cake and pie and jam and honey—just everything anybody would want.

Oh, Jack was so hungry! He wanted some of that food so bad he didn't know what to do. But those people didn't pay any attention to him.

But about that time he heard somebody yell out, "Wo! Wo! there!"

"Oh," the woman says, "Quick! Quick! That's my husband! coming home! Jump right quick over there in that big old chest. Don't sit there!" And the traveler took one leap and went right into the big cedar chest, and the old woman closed the lid down over him and sat back down as if nothing had happened.

About that time somebody began knocking on the door, and exclaiming, "Old woman, old woman, let me in." She began cleaning those things off the table just as fast as she could and brushed the table cloth clean. Then she went running over to the door, her arms reaching out toward the door as if in great haste.

The old man said, "What on earth is the matter with you? Why can't you get here and let me in?"

"Oh," she says, "my rheumatiz is just a-hurting me so!"

"Well," he says, "rheumatiz or no rheumatiz, I want some supper. I'm just about starved to death."

"Why, old man, there's not a thing in this world in this house to eat but just corn bread and milk."

"Well, bedads, corn bread and milk is just good enough for anybody. Set it out here on the table!"

She went to the kitchen and brought back a great big plate of corn bread, a great pitcher of the best-looking milk, and a big old spoon and a bowl. The old man just began crumbling in the bread and pouring in milk, and, oh, he was having a good time eating!

Jack, all the time, had his eye right down to that knot hole. He stood that just as long as he could, and he didn't stay idle a minute. He took that old calf hide by the tail, gave it a shake or two over the floor, and ooh, it was the strangest sounding noise. The old man looked up and says,

"Old woman, what is that?"

"Oh," she says, "it's just the poorest looking little shab of a boy you've ever seen in your life that I let go upstairs to sleep."

"I'll bet you didn't give him a bite of supper."

"Why, law no, I supposed he had had his supper long ago."

"What was the boy's name, old woman?"

"Jack is all he told me."

The old man walked out into the hall and said,

"Jack, Jack, son, don't you want to come down here and get you a bite of something to eat?"

"Well bedads, I don't care if I do," said Jack.

So he took his old calf hide by the tail and down the steps he came, thumpty-bump, bumpty-thump, right up to the dining room table, threw his old calf hide by him, and sat down.

The old man said, "Old woman, bring Jack now a bowl and a spoon, and bring some more milk and bread here!"

And Jack just crumbled in bowls of milk and bread, and, oh, it was tasting so good, and he was having such a good time. After he had eaten two or three of them, he looked at the old calf, gave him a shake or two right loud, and—

"Ah," he says, "hush, hush! don't you be saying that. No, hush up! This milk and bread is just as good as anybody would want. Now, hush your mouth. I don't want to hear another word out of you!

The old man said, "Jack, what did he say to you?"

"Oh, no sir," said Jack, "I can't tell you—I just can't. I might hurt the good lady's feelings. No sir, I can't tell you, and I don't want to hear another word out of him. I'll just have me a little more of that milk and bread, please."

After he had eaten another bowl of the milk and bread, he reached down and got the old calf hide by the tail and gave him another shake.

"Didn't I tell you before to shut that mouth of yours? Now, listen, don't mention that again. If you do I'm going to give you the thrashing of your life when I get you upstairs. No! hush!"

"But, my dear Jack, listen, what did he say to you? Now tell me, son."

"No, sir, I'm tellin' you, I'm afraid it would make the lady of the house mad."

"Now, old woman, it's not going to make you mad, is it?" said the old man.

"Why, no, I reckon not," said the old woman.

"Well, now," Jack said, "if the kind lady won't get mad, I'll tell you. He said to me that over there in that corner cupboard there's cake and pie and chicken, there's ham, there's honey, there's jelly, there's preserves, there's everything good you can think of to eat—right over there in that chest."

"Old woman, is that the truth?"

"Oh, well, it's just a little something there I've got for me and my poor kinfolks."

"Well, me and Jack's your poor kinfolks. Just bring them out here!"

And the old woman set on the table just all the good things Jack had ever dreamed of. And he just ate and ate all he could hold. Then the old man said,

"Listen, Jack, what will you take for that?"

"Oh," said Jack, "I can't sell you that, mister? Oh, no, I just can't— that's my fortune."

"Well, listen, Jack, surely you can sell it. I'll give you anything you want. Just mention anything and I'll give it to you."

"Oh, no, no," said Jack, "I just couldn't part with that. I just couldn't part with it!"

"Well, now, listen here," the old man said, "will that talk to me just like it talks to you?"

"Yes, sir," Jack said, "it'll talk to you just like it talks to me."

The old man said then, "Jack, I've just got to have it. Now, you name your price, for you've got to let me buy that."

Well, Jack looked all around the room, and he says,

"I'll tell you what I'll do. I'll take that old cedar chest over there for it."

"Oh, all right," the man said, "Jack, just help yourself!"

Jack just threw that old cedar chest up on his shoulder and walked out of the door.

He walked down the road a long way in the moonlight. After a while he said, "Phew! Now I've done it. Here I am gettin' as tired as can be with this old chest on my shoulder. I've a mind to throw this thing in the next well I come to—the next one I come to right down there."

Oh, but inside the old chest the traveler began to beat, beat, beat with all his might.

"Oh, Jack, Jack, listen here. Don't throw me in the well, I'm in here."

"Oh," Jack said, "bedads, you are in there, aren't you? Well, what'll you give me if I don't throw you in the well?"

"Oh," he said, "now listen, Jack, I'll give you all the gold you want."

"All right, bejabbers, I'll just set you down here by the side of the road, and I'll ease open that lid a little bit, and you can begin to put me out the gold."

He opened the lid a little bit, so the man could get his hands out, and he just laid out handfuls of gold and still more gold. Jack filled his pockets, he put gold down his pants legs. He just had every bit he could walk with.

When Jack had got all the gold he could carry, he turned around and started back home. Late the next evening he got in. Will and Tom were sitting there at the supper table just a-fussing and growling about which one should wash the dishes when Jack walked in.

"Well," they said, "and bedad, and where's your calf skin?"

"Why," Jack said, "I sold it. What do you think I done with it?"

"Sold it! What would you get for that calf hide?"

"Well, bedads," Jack said, "I'll just show you." And he began laying out handfuls of gold on the table and laid out handfuls after handfuls.

Well, they waited to see a little of it. Will jumped up and says, "Tom, Tom, come on, let's go quick and kill the finest horse we've got. Why, if Jack could get that for one little old measily calf hide, what'll we get for one of our fine horse hides?"

Away they went. They didn't even wait till morning. They killed the finest horse each one of them had. They couldn't be bothered to wait for the sun to dry out those hides. They sewed them right up green, stuffed them with chips and straw, took them by the tails, and hauled them off to town.

When they got to town, they walked up and down the streets, hollering, "Horse hides for sale, horse hides for sale!" Just up and down the streets day after day. People came out and looked at them as if they thought they were crazy.

Well, they kept at this for three or four days right in the summer time. Those old horse hides were green and began to smell bad. They soon found that the people just weren't going to stand for it. They soon came out with sticks and stones and said,

"Looky here, you two crazy men, get out of this town or we're to show you how to get out," and they just ran them out of the town.

Will and Tom were so mad they didn't know what to do. They came home just a-puffing. They said, "Jack, you plain lied to us. You didn't sell that calf hide for any of that gold, and we're going to throw you in the river. Young man, just come along with us." And they took him and led him right down to the river bridge. All they had in their hands was a sheet. They forgot to bring the rope, to tie him up with. They fussed and fussed about which one should go back and get the rope. Will said, "Tom, you go get it," and Tom said, "No, Will, you go get it." Tom said, "Now, Will, you are the oldest, you go on and get that rope, and I'll stay here with Jack."

Well, finally they made up their minds, and they told Jack to stay right there by himself while they went back to the house to get the rope to tie up the sheet with. They rolled Jack up in the sheet and said,

"Now, listen, there'd better be something right in this sheet when we get back!" And so the two old scruffs went running back to the house to get the rope.

When they got out of hearing, Jack crawled out to the edge of that big old sheet and lay there with his head sticking out somewhat like a terrapin. He heard someone coming on the other end of the bridge and calling out, "Sheep! Sheep! Here!" and he looked and there came a little old gray, fat man driving the prettiest flock of sheep you have ever seen. When he came alongside Jack, he said, "Jack what in the world are you doing there under that sheet?"

"Oh," he said, "Mister, I'm going to heaven."

"Oh, please, Jack, let me get in there and go to heaven. I always wanted to go to heaven. Now, listen, Jack, you are young, and you can have every one of these sheep. They are every one yours if you'll just get out of there and let me get under that sheet so I can go to heaven."

Jack said, "Well, my father always did tell me to be kind to old people. So I'll just let you get right in here."

He rolled the man up in the sheet and said, "Now, just stay right still and after a while there will be somebody here that will send you right off."

Jack called to the sheep, "Sheep! Sheep! and backed them off the end of the bridge opposite home. He quickly drove them around a bend in the road before the two brothers got back. He watched around the bend and saw all that was happening. He saw them come and tie the man up and hastily heave him into the river. He saw them turn and go back to the house. He knew they were arguing about something. He waited until they had had good time to get settled back there, and he started the sheep back across the bridge toward home. Finally he drove them up, and when he stopped outside the gate, he called out, "Will, Tom, I wish you all would come out here and help me get these sheep in."

Will and Tom came running off the porch.

They couldn't believe their eyes. They said,

"Jack, where in the world did you get those sheep?"

"Why," he said, "I gathered them out of the river. Where do you think I got them?"

"Oh, Jack, Jack, will you take us and put us in the river?"

"Well, bedad, I reckon I will, but you shore got to get your own sheet and rope. I'm not going to do that for you!"

Both ran and got a big sheet and a piece of rope as soon as they could and went running just as hard as they could go to the river bridge. Jack went running along with them, but they fussed all the way down about which one wanted to get thrown in first. They finally decided that Tom ought to get to go first since he was usually with the goats.

And so Jack tied Tom up good and tight with a piece of big, strong rope, and gave him a great sling right out into the middle of the river. He went kicking around. Will said, "What's he doin', Jack, what's he doin'?"

"I know he's gathering sheep."

"Quick! Hurry, Jack, before he has time to get them every one! Put me in there!"

Jack tied him up right quick and gave him a great big sling, and over the bridge right out into the middle of the river he went. And you know when I left there, Jack was just as rich and as happy a man as I ever knew.

The Skoonkin Hunting

TRAVELED this world all over: house to the barn, upstairs, downstairs, out the front door plumb to the gate—and then me and Paw started gettin'

From *Grandfather Tales,* American-English Folk Tales Selected and Edited by fixed to go on that larrapin' rarrapin' tarrapin' skoonkin huntin'. So Paw went out to round up all the dogs, all but Old Shorty. And I went and shucked and shelled the pigs a bucket of slop, but when I got down there the punkins was all in the pig-patch, so I picked up a pig and knocked them punkins out of there. Took my bridle out to the chicken-house, slung it on the barn, led the old stump up 'side the horse, throwed the saddle across the fence, jumped a-straddle with both legs on one side, rode down a long straight road that wound all around the mountains, came to a house made of corn bread shingled with flap-jacks, knocked on the woman and a door came out, asked her for a crust of beer and a glass of light-bread, told her no-thank-you-ma'am-please-I-don't-care-for-some-I-just-had-any. Bark came along and dogged at me, so I ran on till I came to a little valley-town sittin' way up on a hill—little roast pigs runnin' up and down the streets with knives and forks stuck in their backs squealin' "Who'll eat me? Who'll eat me?"—Went on to my brother's place. Easy to find it —little brick house made out of logs standin' all by itself in the middle of forty-four others just like it My old mare stumbled and throwed me over her head and tail right face foremost flat on my back and tore my hide and bruised my shirt; so I went on down to see my gal Sal. She was awful glad to see me—had both doors nailed down and both windows nailed up, so I went on in and throwed my hat on the fire and stirred up the bed and we sat down right close together, she in one corner and me in the other and talked about love and politics and dog-ticks and bed-ticks and straw-ticks and beggar-ticks and we played cards and she drawed a heart and I drawed a diamond and about that time her old man came home and he drawed a club and I says, "Good-bye, honey, and if I never see ye no more the old gray mare is yours." So Paw he had all the dogs rounded up by then—all but Old Shorty, and then he rounded him up too; and the dogs all trailed—all but Old Shorty, and then he trailed too; and directly they all treed—all but Old Shorty, then he treed too; so I cloomb up that siceyebuckymore tree 'way out on a chestnut limb sittin' on a pine knot and I shook and I shook, and directly somethin' hit the ground and I looked around—and it was me; and every blame one of them dogs jumped on me—all but Old Shorty, then he jumped too; so I knocked 'em all off— all but Old Shorty and I grabbed him by the tail and cut his tail off right up close behind his ears. So we got back in home from that larrapin', rarrapin', tarrapin', skoonkin huntin', had two 'possum tails, two black eyes, four skinned-up shank bones, no horse, and all the dogs—all but Old Shorty.

Richard Chase, pp. 137–139. Copyright, 1948 by Richard Chase. Boston: Houghton Mifflin Company.

From John Mason, Ray Higgins (16) of Salyersville, Kentucky. George Miniard, William Hardin Greer, John Greer, Jeanette Lewis. Remarks: This is the doctor's long speech in the English Mummers' Play. . . . It is quite common in our oral tradition. There is a parallel in Uncle Remus—"Gwine 'long one day, met Johnny Huby, axed him to grind nine yards of steel for me. . . ," etc. This version is entirely my own compilation from these sources, and from reciting it many times myself.—R. C., *ibid.*, p. 237.

GHOST, WITCH, AND DEVIL TALES

The Bell "Witch"

I. TWO MISSISSIPPI ACCOUNTS [1]

"To PANOLA COUNTY, about a half century ago," Miss Lewellen begins, "there moved with the Bell family a 'witch' that tormented one of the Bell girls and caused a great deal of suspicion to arise among the other members of the family and the community."

Mr. Fonnie Black Ladd, from recollections of the story as he heard it in his childhood at Oakland, adds some details about the circumstances in which the family moved to Mississippi. The Bells were living at Bell, Tennessee. Becoming dissatisfied, the father of the family expressed his desire to sell his farm and go somewhere else. The mother was opposed to going. One of the daughters agreed with her father and argued in favor of going to Mississippi. One night the *lar familiaris* of the family spoke to her and warned her against going. The daughter nevertheless persisted in her arguments and finally persuaded her father to sell out and move to Mississippi. Before the family left, the *lar* addressed her again and threatened to pursue her with its vengeance.

---

[1] From *Specimens of Mississippi Folk-Lore,* collected with the assistance of Students and Citizens of Mississippi and edited by Arthur Palmer Hudson, pp. 158–160. Copyright, 1928, by Arthur Palmer Hudson. Published under the auspices of the Mississippi Folk-Lore Society.

For some time I have known of the existence of the story of the Bell "witch." Miss Lois Womble, of Water Valley, first told me about it. She knew only of its general outlines—a family by the name of Bell pursued from Illinois (as she heard the story) to Mississippi by a sort of *lar familiaris* which its members called a witch, and which exerted its malign powers in various ways, from rough practical jokes terrifying in their effects to serious harm.

Last summer I asked Miss Ethel Lewellen, who was then living in Panola County, the home of one branch of the Bell family, whether she had ever heard of the Bell "witch." She replied that she had, but beyond mentioning that she had heard of a book on the subject she was able to contribute little to what I had heard from Miss Womble. She promised, however, to make inquiries and to transmit to me whatever she discovered. To her I owe most of the facts, presented in her own language below.

One other informant, Mr. Fonnie Black Ladd, who formerly resided at Oakland, Mississippi, and who is now a student in the University, added a few details of the story which Miss Lewellen's account lacked.

The details from both accounts do not, I am sure, tell the whole story of the Bell "witch." It is probable that not even the book referred to tells it all, for the story, like all stories that become the property of the folk, apparently has many mutations, and has undoubtedly been growing since the book was published (as the testimony indicates to be a fact). Lacking the book, which I hope eventually to see, I set down the details in the order which they seem to sustain to one another.—A. P. H.

Cf. the same author, "The Bell Witch of Tennessee and Mississippi," *A Treasury of American Folklore* (1944), pp. 696–707; also James R. Aswell, "The Hag of Red River," *God Bless the Devil!* (1940), pp. 136–149.

When they got to Mississippi, Miss Lewellen's account proceeds, "the members of the family talked of sending this girl away so that they might be free from the 'Witch's' awful presence. They also hoped that the girl might rid herself of the unspeakable torture which the 'Witch' visited upon her. 'There's no use for you to do this,' said a Voice, 'for no matter where she goes I will follow.'

"No one was ever able to see the 'Witch'; but often some member of the family would see food disappear as the 'Witch' carried it from the cupboard to 'his' mouth. 'His' favorite food was cream, and 'he' took it from every jar of milk. The Bells were never able to get any butter from the milk they churned.

"An old Negro woman once hid under a bed and tried to see the 'Witch.' But ere she had long been there, something began to bite, scratch, and pinch her; and she was almost killed before she could get out.

"Although the 'Witch' treated the girl very cruelly, 'he' was not entirely inimical to other members of the family; on the contrary, 'he' proved very helpful on several occasions.

"One day Mr. Bell was talking of visiting a family in which every one was ill. 'I have just come from there,' said a Voice from nowhere, and proceeded to describe the physical condition of every member of the family, and also to tell what every member of the family was doing on that particular day. Investigation showed that the report of illness was false and proved the accuracy of every detail of the Voice's account of the state and activities of the family.

"On another occasion Mr. Bell was preparing to go for a doctor to attend one of his sick children. The Voice said, 'There's no need for you to go; I can get the doctor.' No one else went, but in due time the doctor came.

"One day the 'Witch' caused the wagon in which the Bells were going to church to stop on level ground. After vain efforts to get their horses to start the wagon again, the unseen hand of the 'Witch' lifted the wagon and horses off the road, transported it through the air a short distance, and set it down again without harming any one."

Mr. Ladd tells another story of the wagon which may be merely a variant of the foregoing, but which has some circumstances indicating that it is independent. To understand its proper connection beyond Miss Lewellen's remark that the "Witch's" attentions to other members of the family were not always malignant but were sometimes benevolent, the reader will remember that Mrs. Bell, according to Mr. Ladd's account of the circumstances attending the removal of the family to Mississippi, opposed leaving the Tennessee home. Thus, according to Mr. Ladd, the "Witch" was always kind to the mother. Mr. Ladd's story runs like this:

One day the whole family was invited to attend a quilting bee. Mrs. Bell was ill; there was therefore some discussion about the propriety of leaving Mammy at home sick. As Daddy was invited too, the children all insisted on his going. There was a family row, the upshot of which was that everybody piled into the wagon and started, leaving Mammy at home sick. But before the happy party had proceeded far, the "Witch," champion of Mammy's rights, asserted himself. One of the wheels of the wagon flew off and let the axle down into the road with a bump. Not much disturbed by what seemed to be a mere accident, the boys and the old man piled out and replaced wheel and "tap." They had gone but a short distance when another wheel mysteriously flew off. Again they replaced the wheel and proceeded, somewhat sobered. Then one of the children saw a spectral hand pull another wheel off. When they had put it back in place, they held council, turned the team around, and drove back home, going softly. On the way back not another wheel came off.

Another story by Mr. Ladd illustrates the puckish character which the Bell "Witch" sometimes assumed. On several occasions when the old man and the boys went out to catch the mules and horses in preparation for a day's work or a trip to town, the animals would resist bridling like mustangs, plunging around in the stable as if stung by invisible hornets or possessed of evil spirits. When finally harnessed or saddled, they would buck like broncos. These antics were always explained as the work of the Bell "Witch."

Miss Lewellen's account continues, showing that Mr. Bell had something of the scientific spirit:

"Mr. Bell was very curious about the 'Witch,' and finally persuaded 'him' to permit the familiarity of a handshake. He promised not to squeeze the hand. The hand that Mr. Bell shook was as small, soft, and chubby as a baby's. One day Mr. Bell raised a discussion of how the 'Witch' entered the house. 'I raise a certain corner of the house and come in,' said a Voice outside. 'Watch.' The house top was raised several inches and then let down.

"Other people of the community reported that they often met what appeared to be a riderless horse; but the horse would stop, and some one on his back would carry on a conversation with the person met."

To return to the girl, the devoted object of the "Witch's" vengeance. Mr. Ladd was unable to recall concrete details of the general statement that the "Witch" tormented her and tortured her. Miss Lewellen gives only one instance:

"One time the girl whom the 'Witch' tortured was getting ready to go to a party. As she was combing her hair, it suddenly became full of cockle-burs. The 'Witch' explained, 'I put these in your hair; you have no business going to the party.' The men-folks came in and fired shots in the direction from which the Voice came; but every shot was met by one from the invisible hand of the 'Witch,' and the engagement proved a draw."

Miss Lewellen concludes her account of the Bell "Witch" with the statement; "The girl grieved her life away; and after her death the 'Witch' never returned either to torment or to comfort the Bells."

Mr. Fonnie Black Ladd supplies the final detail describing the funeral of the unhappy girl. The coffin containing the body was conveyed to the country graveyard in a farm wagon. As the little procession drove out of the yard of the homestead, some one looked up and saw a great black bird, something like a buzzard or the bird which the Negroes call a "Good God," with a bell around its neck slowly ringing. This great bird flew with miraculous slowness above and just ahead of the lumbering wagon all the way to the graveyard, and poised in air over the grave while the funeral service was being held. Then it flew away, the bell still slowly ringing. And the Bell "Witch" never visited the family again.

II. ANDREW JACKSON AND THE BELL "WITCH" [2]

. , . Grandfather Fort also told me the story of Gen. Jackson's visit to the witch, which was quite amusing to me. The crowds that gathered at Bell's, many coming a long distance, were so large that the house would not accommodate the company. Mr. Bell would not accept any pay for entertaining, and the imposition on the family, being a constant thing, was so apparent, that parties were made up and went prepared for camping out. So Gen. Jackson's party came from Nashville with a wagon loaded with a tent, provisions, etc., bent on a good time and much fun investigating the witch. The men were riding on horseback and were following along in the rear of the wagon as they approached near the place, discussing the matter and planning how they were going to do up the witch, if it made an exhibition of such pranks as they had heard of. Just then, within a short distance of the house, traveling over a smooth level piece of road, the wagon halted and stuck fast. The driver popped his whip, whooped and shouted to the team, and the horses pulled with all of their might, but could not move the wagon an inch. It was dead stuck as if welded to the earth.

Gen. Jackson commanded all men to dismount and put their shoulders to the wheels and give the wagon a push. The order was promptly obeyed. The driver laid on the lash and the horses and men did their best, making repeated efforts, but all in vain; it was no go. The wheels were then taken off, one at a time, and examined and found to be all right, revolving easily on the axles. Another trial was made to get away, the driver whipping up the team while the men pushed at the wheels, and still it was no go. All stood off looking at the wagon in serious meditation, for they were "stuck." Gen. Jackson after a few moments' thought, realizing that

---

[2] From *An Authenticated History of the Famous Bell Witch,* by M. V. Ingram, pp. 231–235. The Wonder of the 19th Century, and Unexplained Phenomenon of the Christian Era. The Mysterious Talking Goblin That Terrorized the West End of Robertson County, Tennessee, Tormenting John Bell to His Death. The Story of Betsy Bell, Her Lover, and the Haunting Sphinx. Copyright, 1894, by M. V. Ingram. Clarksville, Tennessee.

Col. Thomas L. Yancey, a prominent lawyer of the Clarksville, Tenn., bar, who is closely related to the Fort family, was raised in the Bell settlement, and has been familiar with the stories of the witch as told by different witnesses from his youth up, contributes the following interesting sketch from notes taken with a view to writing the history.—M. V. I.

they were in a fix, threw up his hands exclaiming, "By the eternal, boys, it is the witch." Then came the sound of a sharp metallic voice from the bushes saying, "All right, General, let the wagon move on, I will see you again to-night." The men in bewildered astonishment looked in every direction to see if they could discover from whence came the strange voice, but could find no explanation to the mystery. Gen. Jackson exclaimed again, "By the eternal, boys, this is worse than fighting the British." The horses then started unexpectedly of their own accord, and the wagon rolled along as light and smoothly as ever. Jackson's party was in no good frame of mind for camping out that night, notwithstanding one of the party was a professional "witch layer," and boasted much of his power over evil spirits, and was taken along purposely to deal with Kate, as they called the witch.

The whole party went to the house for quarters and comfort, and Mr. Bell, recognizing the distinguished character of the leader of the party, was lavishing in courtesies and entertainment. But Gen. Jackson was out with the boys for fun—"witch hunting"—and was one of them for the time. They were expecting Kate to put in an appearance according to promise, and they chose to set in a room by the light of a tallow candle waiting for the witch. The witch layer had a big flint lock army or horse pistol, loaded with a silver bullet, which he held steady in hand, keeping a close lookout for Kate. He was a brawny man, with long hair, high cheek-bones, hawk-bill nose and fiery eyes. He talked much, entertaining the company with details of his adventures, and exhibitions of undaunted courage and success in overcoming witches. He exhibited the tip of a black cat's tail, about two inches, telling how he shot the cat with a silver bullet while sitting on a bewitched woman's coffin, and by stroking that cat's tail on his nose it would flash a light on a witch the darkest night that ever come; the light, however, was not visible to any one but a magician. The party was highly entertained by the vain stories of this dolt. They flattered his vanity and encouraged his conceit, laughed at his stories, and called him sage, Apollo, oracle, wiseacre, etc. Yet there was an expectancy in the minds of all left from the wagon experience, which made the mage's stories go well, and all kept wide awake till a late hour, when they became weary and drowsy, and rather tired of hearing the warlock detail his exploits.

Old Hickory was the first one to let off tension. He commenced yawning and twisting in his chair. Leaning over he whispered to the man nearest him, "Sam, I'll bet that fellow is an arrant coward. By the eternal, I do wish the thing would come, I want to see him run." The General did not have long to wait. Presently perfect quiet reigned, and then was heard a noise like dainty footsteps prancing over the floor, and quickly following, the same metallic voice heard in the bushes rang out from one corner of the room, exclaiming, "All right, General, I am on hand ready for business." And then addressing the witch layer, "Now, Mr. Smarty, here I am, shoot." The seer stroked his nose with the cat's tail, leveled his pistol, and pulled the trigger, but it failed to fire. "Try again," exclaimed the witch, which he did with the same result. "Now it's my turn; look out, you old coward, hypocrite, fraud. I'll teach you a lesson." The next thing a sound was heard like that of boxing with the open hand, whack, whack, and the oracle tumbled over like lightning had struck him, but he quickly recovered his feet and went capering around the room like a frightened steer, running over every one in his way, yelling, "Oh my nose, my nose, the devil has got me. Oh Lordy, he's got me by the nose." Suddenly, as if by its own accord, the door flew open and the witch layer dashed out, and made a bee line for the lane at full speed, yelling every jump. Everybody rushed out under the excitement, expecting the man would be killed, but as far as they could hear up the lane, he was still running and yelling, "Oh Lordy." Jackson, they say, dropped down on the ground and rolled over and over, laughing. "By the eternal, boys, I never saw so much fun in all my life. This beats fighting the British." Presently the witch was on hand and joined in the laugh. "Lord Jesus," it exclaimed, "how the old devil did run and beg; I'll bet he won't come here again with his old horse pistol to shoot me. I guess that's fun enough for to-night, General, and you can go to bed now. I will come to-morrow night and show you another rascal in this crowd." Old Hickory was anxious to stay a week, but his party had enough of that thing. No one knew who's turn would come next, and no inducements could keep them. They spent the next night in Springfield, and returned to Nashville the following day.

Hold Him, Tabb

BEFORE railroads were built in Virginia, goods were carried from one inland town to another on wagons. There were a great many men who did this kind of work from one end of the year to the other. One of them, "Uncle Jeter," tells the following story:—

"A number of wagons were travelling together one afternoon in December. It was extremely cold, and about the middle of the afternoon began to snow. They soon came to an abandoned settlement by the roadside, and decided it would be a good place to camp out of the storm, as there were stalls for their horses and an old dwelling-house in which they themselves, could stay. When they had nearly finished unhooking their horses a man came along and said that he was the owner of the place, and that the men were welcome to stay there as long as they wanted to, but that the house was haunted, and not a single person had stayed in it alive for twenty-five years. On hearing this the men immediately moved their camp to a body of woods about one half mile further up the road. One of them, whose name was Tabb, and who was braver than the rest, said that he was not

From *Southern Workman and Hampton School Record,* Vol. 26 (June, 1897), No. 6, pp. 122–123. Hampton, Virginia: Hampton Normal & Agricultural Institute.

afraid of haunts, and that he did not mean to take himself and horses into the woods to perish in the snow, but that he'd stay where he was.

"So Tabb stayed in the house. He built a big fire, cooked and ate his supper, and rested well through the night without being disturbed. About daybreak he awoke and said: 'What fools those other fellows are to have stayed in the woods when they might have stayed in here, and have been as warm as I am!' Just as he had finished speaking he looked up to the ceiling, and there was a large man dressed in white clothes just stretched out under the ceiling and sticking up to it. Before he could get from under the man, the man fell right down upon him, and then commenced a great tussle between Tabb and the man. They made so much noise that the men in the woods heard it and ran to see what was going on. When they looked in at the window and saw the struggle, first Tabb was on top and then the other man. One of them cried, 'Hold him, Tabb, hold him!' 'You can bet your soul I got him!' said Tabb. Soon the man got Tabb out of the window. 'Hold him, Tabb, hold him!' one of the men shouted. 'You can bet your life I got him!' came from Tabb. Soon the man got Tabb upon the roof of the house. 'Hold him, Tabb, hold him!' said one of the men. 'You can bet your boots I got him!' answered Tabb. Finally the man got Tabb up off the roof into the air. 'Hold him, Tabb, hold him!' shouted one of the men. 'I got him and he got me, too!' said Tabb. The man, which was a ghost, carried Tabb straight up into the air until they were both out of sight. Nothing was ever seen of him again."

The Headless Hant

A MAN and his wife was going along the big road. It was cold and the road was muddy and sticky red, and their feet was mighty nigh froze off, and they was hungry, and it got pitch dark before they got where they was going.

'Twan't long before they came to a big fine house with smoke coming outen the chimley and a fire shining through the winder. It was the kind of a house rich folks lives in, so they went round to the back door and knocked on the back porch. Somebody say, "Come in!" They went in, but they didn't see nobody.

They looked all up and down and all round, but still they didn't see nobody. They saw the fire on the hearth with the skillets setting in it all ready for supper to be cooked in 'em. They saw there was meat and flour

From *Bundle of Troubles and Other Tarheel Tales,* by Workers of the Writers' Program of the Work Projects Administration in the State of North Carolina, edited by W. C. Hendricks, pp. 97–99. Copyright, 1943, by the Duke University Press. Durham, North Carolina.

This tale by Nancy Watkins was one of the ghost stories told by Dez Foy, a bound Negro boy, to the Watkins children before the kitchen fire in their home at Madison, N. C.—W. C. H.

and lard and salsody and a pot of beans smoking and a rabbit a-biling in a covered pot.

Still they didn't see nobody, but they saw everything was ready for somebody. The woman took off her wet shoes and stockings to warm her feet at the fire, and the man took the bucket and lit out for the springhouse to get fresh water for the coffee. They 'lowed they was going to have them brown beans and that molly cottontail and that cornbread and hot coffee in three shakes.

The woman was toasting her feet when right through the shut door in walks a man and he don't have no head. He had on his britches and his shoes and his galluses and his vest and his coat and his shirt and his collar, but he don't have no head. Jes raw neck and bloody stump.

And he started to tell the woman, without no mouth to tell her with, how come he happened to come in there that a-way. She mighty nigh jumped outen her skin, but she said, "What in the name of the Lord do you want?" So he said he's in awful misery, being dead and buried in two pieces. He said somebody kilt him for his money and took him to the cellar and buried him in two pieces, his head in one place and his corpse in 'nother. He said them robbers dug all round trying to find his money, and when they didn't find it they went off and left him in two pieces, so now he hankers to be put back together so's to get rid of his misery.

Then the hant said some other folks had been there and asked him what he wanted but they didn't say in the name of the Lord, and 'cause she did is how come he could tell her 'bout his misery.

'Bout that time the woman's husband came back from the springhouse with the bucket of water to make the coffee with and set the bucket on the shelf before he saw the hant. Then he saw the hant with the bloody joint of his neck sticking up and he come nigh jumping outen his skin.

Then the wife told the hant who her husband is, and the hant begun at the start and told it all over agin 'bout how come he is the way he is. He told 'em if they'd come down into the cellar and find his head and bury him all in one grave he'd make 'em rich.

They said they would and that they'd get a torch.

The hant said, "Don't need no torch." And he went up to the fire and stuck his front finger in it and it blazed up like a lightwood knot and he led the way down to the cellar by the light.

They went a long way down steps before they came to the cellar. Then the hant say, "Here's where my head's buried and over here's where the rest of me's buried. Now yo' all dig right over yonder where I throw this spot of light and dig till you touch my barrels of gold and silver money."

So they dug and dug and sure 'nough they found the barrels of money he'd covered up with the thick cellar floor. Then they dug up the hant's head and histed the thing on the spade. The hant jes reached over and picked the head offen the spade and put it on his neck. Then he took off his burning finger and stuck it in a candlestick on a box, and still holding on his head, he crawled back into the hole that he had come out of.

And from under the ground they heard him a-saying, "Yo' all can have my land, can have my house, can have all my money and be as rich as I was, 'cause you buried me in one piece together, head and corpse."

Then they took the candlestick blazing with the hant's finger and went back upstairs and washed themselves with lye soap. Then the woman made up the cornbread with the spring water and greased the skillet with hogmeat and put in the hoecake and lifted the lid on with the tongs and put coals of fire on top of the lid and round the edges of the skillet, and cooked the hoecake done. Her man put the coffee and water in the pot and set it on the trivet to boil. Then they et that supper of them beans and that rabbit and that hoecake and hot coffee. And they lived there all their lives and had barrels of money to buy vittels and clothes with. And they never heard no more 'bout the man that came upstairs without no head where his head ought to be.

Ghost Dinner

PERHAPS the most famous of romantic Mardi Gras stories that Orleanians tell is that one concerning the "ghost dinners" served each Shrove Tuesday night by a restaurant in Royal Street, when all the most delicious dishes for which the restaurant's cuisine is noted are served to empty places.

It began a long time ago, when Mardi Gras balls were held in the French Opera House. One night at Comus a young man from an Eastern city paid no attention at all to the tableaux being enacted but, instead, stared the whole time at a lovely Creole girl seated on the opposite side of the balcony. At last she looked his way, and it seemed that once their gaze met she was as powerless to look away as was he. The young man smiled and a flicker of a smile was returned. Then he rose, made some excuses to the friends he was with and strolled out into the lobby.

Later he confessed that he did not know how he was so positive, but somehow he knew the girl would join him, and in a few minutes she walked quickly through the crimson portieres, and then stood just beyond them, her face very red, for it was a period when girls still blushed.

The young man went swiftly to her side and said words he could never recall, except that among them was a suggestion that they leave together at once. The girl went with him obediently, without saying a word.

But outside she said, "You have done a very wicked thing. You made me come against my will."

"No," he said. "It was your fault."

"I was with my fiancé," she said. "You have ruined my reputation."

"If I've done that," he replied, "then I'll have to marry you, won't I? However, it might be an idea if we had supper first."

From *Mardi Gras,* by Robert Tallant, pp. 209–211. Copyright, 1947, 1948, by Robert Tallant. Garden City, New York: Doubleday & Company, Inc.

So they went into the Royal Street restaurant, and the young man told the waiter that love made him hungry and that they would have anything and everything that the waiter might suggest. And while the food piled up upon the table the couple told each other their names, all about the past of each, and what their future would be like. They sat there all night, talking and eating and drinking wine. In the morning they went together to the Ash Wednesday mass at the St. Louis Cathedral, and then they were married quietly by one of the priests, and the young woman took her husband home to her frantic family, who had searched for her all night.

A few days later the young man took his bride North, and neither of them ever saw Mardi Gras again, for before summer was over, as always happens in such romantic tales, the girl died.

Then came the most startling development of the story. A few days before the next Mardi Gras the proprietor of the restaurant where the couple had spent the morning hours after that day a year ago received a check and a strange request through the mail. The widower asked that the same table be decorated with flowers and that the same food be served in the same way it had been when the couple had sat there. This was done. The next year came another letter and another check, and they continued to come for more than twenty years after that each Mardi Gras time, and every year the owner of the restaurant complied with the request. Finally, one year, came a letter from an attorney. The man who had been buying the ghost dinners had died, but he had left a bequest in his will of a large sum of money, which was to pay for this annual commemoration of his love affair for as long as the restaurant remained in business.

Many people believe this is only a fable, but it is the story they tell, and something of the kind must have occurred, for every Mardi Gras night, if you go to this restaurant, you'll see a waiter setting places for two. There are always flowers on the table and decorations in carnival colors. Then, silently and seriously, a waiter slowly serves the fine foods and wines of an elaborate dinner for two. No one even seems to remember the name of the couple, or they won't tell you if they do, but the ritual continues year after year. It has become one of the traditions of Mardi Gras.

Ghosts of the Cedar Creek (Virginia) Battlefield

I was a young feller at the time that Sheridan battle was fought, and was livin' on my master's farm on the edge of Middletown out beyond the 'Pis-

From *Battleground Adventures*, The Stories of Dwellers on the Scenes of Conflict in Some of the Most Notable Battles of the Civil War, collected in personal interviews by Clifton Johnson, pp. 416–422. Copyright, 1915, by Clifton Johnson. Boston and New York: Houghton Mifflin Company.

I spent a portion of a Sunday afternoon with him. He was a beak-nosed old man copal church. That church was a hospital durin' the battle, and the army band used to practise in it while the troops were camped near hyar. A good many of the wounded died in thar and was buried in the churchyard.

But the bodies had n't been in the ground a great while when they was dug up to be carried away. They was put in coffins—jus' long pine boxes— and the boxes was piled up against the back wall of the church and stayed thar near a month. I pried open a number of 'em and looked in. Some of the dead men was very natural and others was n't fit to look at. One man with a blanket wrapped about him was petrified, and his appearance had n't changed any since he was buried, only his hair had growed way down and his beard had growed long.

Thar was one night while those boxes was in the churchyard that a light come out of the church and went to whar they was piled as if some one was searchin' aroun' with a can'le.

Another night something like a calf come out of the church and walked all aroun'.

The boxes was taken away presently, but the ghos'es stayed at the church or come thar often at night, and we'd hear 'em walkin', groanin', and carryin' on. Other times we'd hear the army band playin' in the church, and one night all of us who lived near was called out of our houses to listen at it.

"Don't you hear the band?" we'd say one to the other.

We heard it all right, and that's the truth. Thar's no story about that. The music sounded way off, but we could hear the lead horn start and the drums tap. The kittle drum would rattle it off, and the bass drum would go bum, bum, bum! You can hear somethin' knockin' thar at the 'Piscopal church now on a dark night.

Right after the war we used to hear the soldiers ghos'es shootin' hyar all aroun' on the battlefield, and we'd hear horses in the back lane comin' klopity, klopity, klopity. The horses would ride right up to you, but you could n't see a thing.

I know one man who lived out on a farm and he come in to the town one night to pra'r meetin'. As he was goin' home 'bout ten o'clock he heard the bugle and the rap of the kittle drum. While he was listenin' he seen a officer a-walkin' ahead of a squad of soldiers. The officer hollered "Halt!" to 'em, and they stopped. But the bugle kep' a-blowin', and pretty soon they marched off.

Thar was another man who used to come to town pretty nigh every night, and some of the nights was tolerable dark. He was co'tin' hyar, I allow. Many a night he'd hear horses comin' 'cross the fields, and canteens and swords hittin' the sides of saddles, blangity, blangity, blangity!

Down near Cedar Crick thar's a ghos' in a barn. The ghos' is supposed

---

who related his spook stories with great vivacity and an unfathomable mixture of solemnity and hilariousness.—C. J.

For the fiddle episode, cf. Chapman J. Milling, "Balaam Foster's Fiddle," *A Treasury of American Folklore* (New York, 1944), pp. 727–731.

to be a soldier that was killed tharabouts. He has Yankee clothes on and wears cavalry boots that come way up to his knees. Some say he has no head, and others say he has a head and wears a plug hat. People see him after night, jus' about dusk, and he only comes at that time of the evening. He walks out of the haymow and part way down the haymow steps, and thar he'll stan'. For one while the railroad ran excursion trains so people could come and see the ghos'. I went thar to see him once, but I was 'fraid to go in the barn.

The first person who ever seen the ghos' was a farmer by the name of Holt Hottel who had rented the place. He went to feed his horses jus' after sundown and was goin' to throw some hay down the hole to the feeding-room when he noticed the ghos'. But he thought it was a tramp, and he says, "Git out of hyar. I don't allow tramps in the barn on account of fire."

The ghos' did n't say anything and jus' stood thar. Holt got mad then and tried to gouge the ghos' with his pitchfork, and the fork went right through the ghos' into the weather-boarding. That was evidence it was n't no tramp, and Holt jumped right down the hole into the feeding-room. His horses did n't git no hay that night, and for a good while afterward he fed 'em tolerable early.

Holt's father used to laugh at him 'bout that ghos', but one evenin' Holt met the ol' man comin' from the barn as hard as he could run. Oh! he was comin' from thar skatin'. He did n't laugh at Holt no mo'.

Another time a black man who'd gone to the barn a little late to feed the stock came out of there a-hustlin', and he was whoopin' as if he was goin' to be killed.

But the ghos' did nobody no harm, and Holt got so he'd go in thar any time of night. He become accustomed to seeing this thing and paid no attention to it. Once when he threshed his wheat the grain was too damp to put in sacks, and he left it on the barn floor a few days to dry. Thar was some danger that it would be stolen, and he stayed in the barn nights to guard it and slept on an ol' lounge he carried out from the house. He said that night after night he went to sleep with that feller standin' on the haymow steps. He seen him perfectly plain even to the straps on his boots what he hooked his fingers in to pull 'em on.

Thar's people who have tried all sorts of ways to see that ghos' and never could, and thar's plenty of others who have seen it. I know this— that Holt Hottel was as reliable a man as thar was in the state. His word was as good as his bond.

Down at Belle Grove House they used to hear a buggy drive up thar of a night, and a bell would tap for a waiter to come and take the team. Another queer thing at that house was a door that would n't keep shut. The good ol' Christian woman who lived thar said she'd shut it and go sit down and the door would swing open.

I used to be told that the way to learn to play the fiddle was to go to a graveyard with it and start practisin'. You had to go at night, and you could n't have any one with you. If you could stand it thar you could learn to play any thing. I've heard ol' people say that often. I bought a fiddle tereckly after the war, and started in to play by ear. That's the best way but I was n't makin' much progress, and I decided to see if it was true that you could learn to play in a graveyard in one night. I was afraid to go to the regular graveyard. So I went to the 'Piscopal churchyard. We called that a graveyard, though nobody had ever been buried thar but soldiers, and they had been taken up.

I got a little ol' box to sit on, and I goes thar and sets myself down. The time was nine o'clock as near as I can git at it now. I set thar and chuned up my fiddle. Then I struck into "Ol' Dan Tucker." That's the devil's chune, you know, and it's the first thing the devil will learn you to play. Well, sir, I set thar and learned to play that real good.

Afterwards I tried "Dixie" and kep' at it till I could play that tolerable good, too, but I'd miss some notes. Then I heard a noise, and I begun to feel kind o' jubous. However, I paid no attention to it. I played away harder than ever—tweeny, tweeny, twang!—so as not to git skeered, and I says to myself, "I won't let no ghos'es bother me."

But pretty soon I heard something over back of the church—bangity, bang! It was a sound jus' like you make when you hit a table leaf and the leaf goes flap, flap! I was listenin' with both ears and still a-playin' my fiddle when some hot steam come about me, and that steam was so warm and fainty it almost made me sick. I thought: "This ain't natural. Thar mus' be ghos'es hyar somewhar."

And yet I could n't see 'em. If I had I'd been like a hog that sees the wind. You know how hogs run and squeal and pick up straws sometimes. That's when they see the wind. If you take a little matter from the corner of a hog's eye and rub it in your eye *you* can see the wind, and it's jus' as red as blood. You would n't want to see it but once. It would skeer you to death.

I used to hear ol'-time people say that thar could n't every one see a ghos', and that the ghos'es took the form of steam when they appeared to a person who could n't see 'em. The mo' I studied 'bout it the mo' skeered I was. I put my hand up to see whether my hat was on my head, and I found my hair was standin' straight up and had carried my hat with it.

Jus' then some steam came aroun' me so hot it scorched my face, and I throwed my fiddle down and ran. If I could have stood it to stay in the churchyard an hour or two longer I could have played anything. Yes, indeedy! But if I'd kep' on very likely I'd have died of fright.

The closer I got to home the mo' skeered I was and the faster I ran. I made the last rod in 'bout two jumps, and as soon as I was in the house I slammed the door behind me.

Nex' mornin' I went and got my fiddle, and I did n't go thar no mo'. The night had been dewy, and the fiddle was pretty near ruined. It was n't no account much afterward. The glue that fastened the pieces together had softened, and the strings had all got wet and had busted off.

What little I learned later in fiddlin' I learned at home. Finally I throwed

the ol' fiddle away. If any ghos'es wanted it they could have it and practise on it all they wanted.

We don't have many ghos'es now like they used to have long ago. Thar
was a time when the ol' people did n't die at all. They lived to be one hundred and twenty years ol' and then turned into monkeys, apes and owls.
They'd jus' go off and be wild animals awhile and afterwards turn into
ghos'es. Those ol'-time ghos'es used to travel, but now there's so much
preachin' they generally keep very quiet.

Aroun' hyar it was only a few years back that we'd see plenty of strange
sights and hear plenty of strange noises. We don't see and hear them
things so much now because the battlefield has been so stirred up by
ploughin' and raisin' crops. That's drivin' nearly all the battlefield ghos'es
away, but thar's some left yet, and thar's other ghos'es, too. Last year a
colored man died quite sudden up at the Junction, and he's jus' keepin'
things warm up thar. The people in the house whar he lived don't git no
comfort at all. But if I was in their place he would n't trouble me. I'd say,
"You go 'way from hyar. *I* done bought this house now."

Then I'd turn the doors and windows upside down so the fastenings
would be on the other side. A ghos' can't git in if you do that.

Yes, sir, thar's still ghos'es. I can take you out with me tonight, and if
you'll look across my left shoulder I'll show you something.

The Black Cat's Message

ONE never knows when the most sociable of cats may turn out to be a
witch or "ha'nt," or to have evil concourse with the occult world. Elmira
tells of an old couple with whom a big old yellow cat "took up." They
were glad to have her, and treated her kindly. All went well until one
day—

"The ole man was a wood-cutter. One evenin' as he was comin' home
from his work, he saw a passel o' black cats out in the road. He looked
to see what they was doin', an' theah was nine black cats totin' a little dead
cat on a stretcher. He thought, 'Well, I never heard o' sich a thing as this:
nine black cats totin' a little dead cat on a stretcher.'

"Jes then one o' them cats called out to the ole man an' says, 'Say,
Mistuh, please tell Aunt Kan that Polly Grundy's daid.'

"The old man nevah answered 'em; he jes' walked on a little peahtah;
but he thought, 'Um-m-m! If this ain't the beatin'est thing, them cats

From "Cats and the Occult," by Martha Emmons, in *Spur-of-the-Cock*, Publications
of the Texas Folk-Lore Society, Number XI, edited by J. Frank Dobie, pp. 99–100.
Copyright, 1933, by the Texas Folk-Lore Society. Austin, Texas.

a-tellin' me to tell Aunt Kan that Polly Grundy's daid. Who is Aunt Kan, I wonder; an' who is Polly Grundy?'

"Well, he jes walked on, an' presen'y one of 'em hollered ag'in, an' say, 'Say, ole man, please tell Aunt Kan Polly Grundy's daid.'

"He jes walked on ag'in, gittin' a little faster all the time; an' presen'y all of 'em squall out: 'Hey there, old man, please suh, tell Aunt Kan Polly Grundy's daid.'

"Then the ole man he broke into a run, an' he nevah stopped till he got to his house. He thought he wouldn' tell his ole 'oman nothin' about it. But that night he was settin' befo' de fiah eatin' his suppah—ole folks lots o' times eats dey suppah befor' de fiah—an' while his wife was a-settin' it foh 'im, he say. 'Well, Ole 'Oman, I guess I'll tell you some'n' dat I didn' think I would tell you.'

"When he say that, the ole yellow cat got up f'om de corner wheres she'uz a-layin', an' come ovah an' set down right by his chaiah, a-lookin' up at 'im.

"His ole 'oman say, 'Well, what is it, Ole Man? I knowed they'uz some'n' on yo' min' when you come in at dat do'.'

"He say, 'Well, when I 'uz comin' in from de woods dis evenin', walkin' down de road, right theah in de road I seen a whole passel o' black cats. When I went ovah an' looked, theah was nine black cats a-totin' a little daid cat on a stretcher; an' them cats squall out to me three diffunt times an' tell me to tell Aunt Kan that Polly Grundy's daid.'

"When he say that, ole yellow cat jumped up an' say, 'Is she? B'God, I mus' go to the buryin'!' An' out that do' she flew, an' she ain' nevah come back yit."

The Red Rag under the Churn

ONE day a man went over to his neighbor's to see him about trading hogs. When he got there the old woman come to the door an' told him her man's off somewheres in the field, but would he come in an' wait a spell till he'd git back. He done so, and when he got hisse'f set down he took notice that she's doin' her churnin'. Hit come to him how quick she's gittin' her butter, too, a heap faster'n his old woman ever got hern. He asked her could he have a drink, an' quick 's she got out the door after him one he lifted up the churn and looked under it, and thar were a little bitty red rag, like off'n a flannel petticoat. He got out his knife and cut him off a piece, and put the rag back under the churn, against she got back with his drink. Then he told her he 'lowed he'd not wait longer, but go out an' see if he could find her man in the field.

By Alice Childs, Columbia, Missouri. From *American Speech,* Vol. V (December, 1929), No. 2, pp. 142–144. Copyright, 1929, by The Williams & Wilkins Company, Baltimore, Md.
A folk-tale of the Kentucky Mountains.—A. C.

But he never went ary a step after that man. He went home to his wife fast's he could ever git there. He says to her, "Sary, git up what cream you have, an' do some churnin' fer me."

She looked at him wonderin'-like, an' says, "What fer ye wantin' me to churn? I ain't got but a dab o' cream, an' they's heaps o' butter, down to the spring-house."

He just says to her, "Sary, you git out what cream they is, an' do a churnin' fer me right off!"

Well, when a man spoke to his old woman thataway, she done what he said. Leastways, in them days she did. She brought out her churn, an' her dab o' cream, an' was just fixin' to begin her churnin' when he says, "Here, Sary, let me hitch up your churn an' put this here little bitty red rag under it."

She looked at him funny-like, but she never said nothing. So he put his rag under the churn an' she begun. Well, will ye believe what I'm tellin' ye? They wasn't scarcely enough cream in that churn to make a splash, but right off she could tell hit was gittin' fuller'n fuller. Hit wasn't no time till the butter was comin' so fast hit scared her. She jumped up and grab up her churn an' started out the door, sayin' she didn't aim to git mixed up in no bewitchment. Her old man picked up the red rag an' stuffed it in his pocket.

That evenin', when he'd done finished up his chores, he was just startin' from his milkin'-shed back to the house when all to onct they was a huge-big figger standin' square in front of him. The sun-ball was settin', and this figger looked plumb queer, with the red glare from the sun-ball lightin' up all the sky behind him.

Hit come up, a-bowin' and smilin', and helt out his hand with a little book in it to the man. He says to the man, "Sign your name right here, if you please."

The man was feelin' mighty queer by this time, but he pulled hisse'f up the best he could an' says, "If you're aimin' fer me to sign your book, bring it over here to me your se'f!"

The feller looked at him surprised an' says, "Why, I can't come over to you."

Then he saw as how they was a circle plumb round him, an' hit come up clost to where the figger was standin', but not quite. So he reached over and took the book and opened it. They was writin' at the top of the page an' hit said, "WE, AND ALL THAT WE POSSESS, BELONG TO THE DEVIL." Below hit was the names of all his neighbors, an' the name of the woman what had the red rag under the churn headed the list!

Well, he looked acrost at the figger, an' hits eyes were glarin' at him like coals of fire, but he says, "I ain't goin' to sign nothing like that! I don't belong to the devil!"

The figger glared at him worse'n ever, an' says, "Hit's strange if ye don't belong to the devil. Ye have took part in witchcraft! What about that there red rag under your churn?"

Right then the man he felt somethin' movin' in his pocket, an' fore he could bat his eyes twict, out come the purtiest little bitty red bird, an' hopped up on his wrist. Hit cocked one eye up at him an' then flew acrost an' lit plumb on the shoulder of that awful-lookin' figger. An' all the time hit were lettin' out the horridest loud chuckles, like a demon laughin' at him.

The man he turned to the book real quick an' writ somethin' down on the other side of the page, an' signed his name. He writ "WE AND ALL THAT WE POSSESS BELONGS TO THE LORD." Then he reached the book back to the figger. He give just one look at it, an' then he—he—, well, I 'low he jist went up in smoke! Leastways they was a flash, like a fire, an' a smell of brimstone, an' the man fell to the ground in a sort o' fit.

Soon's he come to hisse'f he got up an' run in to his wife. He told her what had happened to him, an' said they was aimin' to pack up an' leave thar the very next mornin'. He wasn't aimin' to stay where all his neighbors belonged to the Devil!

I reckon they moved right off. Leastways they hain't no one lived there up on the side of the hill since I can recollec'. An' will ye believe what I'm tellin' ye? Right thar where the figger stood, they hain't nothin but sage-grass growed from that day to this. I reckon that's the reason they've allers named that thar patch of sage-grass

THE DEVIL'S GARDEN

The Witch Bridle

OLD BRAHAM lived in a one-room log house close to the Cheat River, somewhere above Albrightsville, Preston County. In one corner of the house was a big old-fashioned open fireplace, and in the opposite corner was his bed.

Once upon a time just about midnight, he awoke from his first dream to hear men talking in his room. He knew that they thought he was asleep, and in order to find out what was going on, he concluded not to let them know that he was awake. By this means he soon found out their errand. He caught every word they said, although they talked in a low voice, and by the dim light that flickered from the charred embers of the fireplace, he saw everything they did out of one corner of his eye.

The intruders were six out of a band of seven witch-men of that com-

From "The Witch Bridle," by John Harrington Cox, *Southern Folklore Quarterly,* Vol. VII (December, 1943), No. 4, pp. 204–209. Gainesville, Florida: The Southeastern Folklore Society.

The following tale, collected under the auspices of the West Virginia Folklore Society, was taken down from the telling of Miss Sarah Alice Barnes, Bruceton Mills, Preston County, on April 10, 1916. Miss Barnes learned it from hearing it told in the community.—J. H. C.

For the identification of the folktale motifs in this story, see the same, pp. 203–204.

munity, who kept their witch-bridles and their bowl of magic ointment under old Braham's hearthstone. He inferred from their conversation that any one who could put one of the witch-bridles on an animal or a person was able to turn that animal or person into a horse and subject it entirely to his will. Furthermore, any one who rubbed some of the ointment three times on his forehead between the eyes and also on his throat, and then made a cross three times with it over his heart, could fly like a bird. Old Braham also gathered from the men's talk their business there that evening was to ride off his calves, as they had frequently done before, to a witches' meeting somewhere up on Scraggly Mountain several miles away.

As the seventh witch-man had not come, the other six got ready for their trip without him. They rolled back the big hearthstone and each took one of the bridles for himself and laid it aside. Then they all anointed themselves with the ointment out of the bowl and replaced the hearthstone. Taking up their bridles again, the first witch-man waved his arms and flew up the chimney; another man waved his arms and flew up the chimney; a third waved his arms and flew up the chimney; a fourth waved his arms and flew up the chimney; and the other two did likewise.

Out of the chimney all the witch-men flew, down over the yard and into the calf lot. The head witch-man bridled the big spotted calf and jumped on its back; down the calf lot it went, jumped the fence, and ran down the road. The second man bridled the big red calf and mounted it; down the lot it went, jumped the fence and ran down the road. The third man bridled the big black calf and swung himself upon its back; down the lot it went, jumped the fence and ran down the road. The fourth witch-man bridled the big brown calf and mounted its back; down the lot it went, jumped the fence, and ran down the road. The fifth witch-man bridled up the big roan calf, leaped upon its back, and prodded it with his spur; down the lot it went, jumped the fence, and ran down the road. Not much choice was left for the sixth man, only the little white calf and the little red calf. The white being the prettier, he chose that, bridled it and jumped upon its back; down the lot it went, jumped the fence and ran down the road as the others had done, all bound for Scraggly Mountain.

In the meantime old Braham no longer pretended to be asleep, but had arisen and was making some investigations on his own account. He resolved that he, too, would turn witch, take advantage of his newly-acquired knowledge, and ride to Scraggly Mountain that night. The hearthstone was heavy, but he was strong and succeeded in dislodging it. He drew out the remaining witch-bridle, anointed himself with the ointment in the bowl, and replaced the stone. Then as he had seen the witch-men do, he flapped his arms, flew up the chimney, over the yard, and down into the calf lot. He bridled the little red calf, the only one left, and jumped on its back; down the lot it went, jumped the fence, and ran down the road at a death pace, determined to overtake the other calves, all bound for Scraggly Mountain.

So fast the little red calf ran with old Braham on its back, that by the time the others had left the road and run across a piece of fallow land to Nixon's Ford, it was in sight of them. Old Braham watched his other calves with the witch-men on their backs leap the stream. The big spotted calf cleared it with apparent ease. The big red calf, the big black calf, the big brown calf, did the same. The big roan calf, being a little smaller, barely cleared the stream, one of her hind feet coming down in the sand and water. The little white calf made a great bound, jumped nearly across, waded out, and climbed the steep bank on the other side.

By this time old Braham on the little red calf was at the ford. He had seen how the smaller ones of the other calves had barely made the leap across, but his calf, the smallest of all, had certainly out-run all the rest and he determined to make the effort. So he bumped the little red calf in the sides with both the heels of his boots and it made a tremendous spring forward. But the great effort it made caused it to leap sidewise and it came down in the middle of the stream on a fallen tree that served as a foot-log. When the calf with old Braham on its back struck the log, it burst and rolled over into the water. Old Braham managed to hold on to the witch-bridle with one hand and grasp the foot-log with the other. The bridle pulled out of the mouth of the calf, which turned into a red lizard and sank into the stream.

With the bridle still in his hand, old Braham managed to pull himself up on to the fallen tree. But no sooner did he find himself safely anchored on the log, than down from above out of a tree, jumped a big blue cat, right on to his back. Its weight was so heavy that old Braham was considerably stunned when it struck him; and before he had time to realize what had crashed down upon his unprotected back, the cat had seized the witch-bridle, slipped it into his mouth, and mounted him. "Ho!" said the big blue cat. "I'll get to ride to the witch meeting yet. Old man, if you wanted to burst your little red calf so that I could not ride him, well and good. I'll just ride you in his stead. I knew that one of the seven witch-men was not along with the rest. Now for Scraggly Mountain. Ho! come up!"

The cat gave the witch-bridle a big twitch and slapped old Braham smartly on one side of the face with one big blue paw, and then on the other side of the face with the other paw. There was nothing that old Braham could do except to crawl off on his hands and feet as the big blue cat's horse. He scrambled off the log, up the steep stony bank, and climbed the high, tiresome mountain, the big blue cat jumping up and down on his back, jerking the bridle, clucking to him to go faster and striking him with his claws and the end of the bridle rein. When they came near the place where the witches' meeting was to be held, the big blue cat rode his horse up to a tree and tied him so as to be in readiness when the frolic was over and he wanted to ride back.

The revel lasted a long time, but at last the big blue cat returned, very weary. He found old Braham still tied up securely to the tree, just where he had left him. The old cat, being tired and sleepy, concluded to lie down and rest awhile before he rode down the mountain. Accordingly, he stretched himself out under a neighboring tree and went to sleep.

While the big blue cat was asleep, old Braham began to think some on his own account. If he could only get the witch-bridle out of his own mouth and slip it into the cat's! He concluded to try it and after a great effort succeeded in slipping the bit. Then he stepped over stealthily to where the big cat slept. Cautiously he slipped the bit into his mouth, gave the rein a great jerk, and shook him awake. The big blue cat awoke in a fit of temper at such rough treatment and began to growl and to strike with his paws.

"Oh, no," said old Braham softly. "I was your horse up the mountain, now I guess you'll be mine down. Turn about is only fair play. Since I carried you up, it is only right that you carry me down. And since it is much easier to carry a load down hill than it is to carry it up, I shall have to ask you to carry me the rest of the way home in order to even up with you."

No amount of pleading on the part of the cat availed, and so they set off down the mountain, the old blue cat carrying old Braham. The old man was heavy and the cat lost all his courage and bravado when he found he was conquered. His paws gave out and began to bleed, so that old Braham had to stop at a blacksmith shop and have him shod. Then they went on again, the old blue cat bending and groaning under his great load.

When old Braham was nearly home, the old blue cat drew up before a dilapidated hut and wanted to turn in there. Since he had carried the old man so well, Braham's heart was considerably eased and his hatred of the cat a great deal lessened. It was not very much farther to his house and he concluded to let the old blue cat go and walk the rest of the way home. He dismounted, but kept the witch-bridle firmly in the cat's mouth, which, with old Braham at his side, made straight for the door of the hut. As soon as he stepped upon the door sill, he was transformed into an old witch-woman. The old witch had quickly turned on Braham with a smile of triumph on her evil face and said, "Um huh! you see who I am! I am an old witch. I'll bewitch you and you'll die."

"Um huh! and you see who I am," replied old Braham. "I'm your master; I've still got the witch-bridle in your mouth. It's a good plan not to crow until you're out of the woods. I am going to chain you up to that staple in the wall in there, then go home and make a silver bullet, and come back and shoot you."

The old witch lamented and pleaded and pleaded for her freedom and her life, but old Braham was obstinate. He tied her with a chain to the staple and went home to mould the silver bullet.

Soon after old Braham left, the sun came up and it was full day. Then there came a man to the old witch to plead with her to unwitch his son, "Shonny," whom she had bewitched the evening before. The child was in the first throes of the pains of witchcraft, but as he had been bewitched less than twenty-four hours, the old witch did not as yet suffer any pains, not seeing him. When the man looked in and saw the old witch chained to a staple in the wall, he was at first much gratified. However, she soon began to blarney and to try to make terms of peace with him. In her slyest way she told him she would unwitch "Shonny" and never work any of her spells on his family again if he would release her. In proof of her good faith, she drew a silver ring from the index finger of her left hand and gave it to the man. Thereupon, he went out, but returned in a short time with a sharp stone. With this he cut a link in the chain that bound the old witch and she was free. Then the man departed for home.

No sooner was he gone than the old woman hobbled across to an old wooden cupboard that stood in one corner of the hut. She reached up and from above the cupboard took down a brightly scoured shining tin pan, her witch pan, by means of which she worked her spells. With a leer, she sat down on her door sill in the bright sunshine. The rays that glanced off the bright tin pan were too dazzling for the ordinary eye to behold, but the old witch, whose eyes had been hardened to it by the devil, looked steadily at the bright tin in order to weave her spell. She tapped the pan with her ring finger, saying as she tapped, "One, two, three." Then she began to mutter her incantations: "I, here on this brightly scoured tin pan consecrate myself anew to the devil and put my soul in thralldom to him on condition that old Ebenezer Braham shall die as surely as the sun shall set this evening and rise tomorrow morning, and that he shall be in pain, unendurable pain, henceforth till he die, so help me dev—."

But while the old witch was working her spell on old Braham, old Braham himself was not idle. He had run home to make the silver bullet with which to shoot the old witch as he told her he would do. A good deal of time passed before he got his bullet done and put it into his gun. He had also drawn a crude picture of the old witch on a piece of paper. While she was muttering her incantations, old Braham felt the spell coming over him. Quickly seizing his gun and the paper picture, he ran out through the open door, hung the picture on a tree, and running back a short distance, took aim and fired. The silver bullet pierced the heart of the picture of the old witch and sunk into the bark of the tree.

Just as the bullet struck the heart of the picture of the old witch, she was sitting in her doorway over the bright tin pan, saying her last word, "devil." Suddenly, she clapped her hand to her heart and cried out, "O my God! I'm shot! I'm killed!" and fell back dead.

The Devil's Mansion

ONCE, not inappropriately, the Devil lived in New Orleans. He had at the time taken a French mistress and set her up in a stately mansion in St. Charles Avenue.

From *Gumbo Ya-Ya*, A Collection of Louisiana Folk Tales, compiled by Lyle Saxon, State Director, Edward Dreyer, Assistant State Director, Robert Tallant.

The Devil was very fond of his girl friend, and very jealous. Nevertheless, while he was away six days of the week, attending to other duties, the coquette took another lover, a dashing young Creole of the city. Satan returned one night and, leaning against a post outside, waited for the youth to emerge from the house. When he encountered him, Satan told him frankly that he was the lover of the Frenchwoman, but said that now he did not want her any more, and that the boy was to take her and a million pounds of gold and go away. There was one condition, however; they must always be known as Monsieur and Madame L.

The youth agreed, and next night told his sweetheart about the condition at dinner. The French girl was both terrified and furious, for she realized that the "L" stood for Lucifer. In a rage she rushed at her lover with a napkin, whipped it around his throat and strangled him to death. At that moment the Devil appeared, killed her and carried both the bodies to the roof, where he devoured them, all but the skins. These he gave to cats wandering on the housetop.

From that time on the Devil's head was fixed in the gable of that roof, bound there by the sticky flesh of the mortals he had eaten. For years afterward Orleanians used to pass and stop to stare up at the living head of Lucifer set right there in the front of the house. You see, he had forgotten, in his jealous anger, that he must not work in the full of the moon, and was thus punished for his folly.

But the drama in the dining-room continued. Night after night, the great dining table and the magnificent crystal chandeliers materialized. Always a young man and a girl sat down to eat. Then the girl would rise, her face contorted with fury, and strangle her companion with a napkin. Then the girl would find her hands drenched with blood, and try frantically to wipe them clean, but of course she never could. Weeping and wailing, she would gradually fade from view. Night after night the whole sordid crime was re-enacted, again and again.

Many families tried to live in the Devil's Mansion, but no one could endure the nightly drama. Only one family stayed for any length of time, that of Charles B. Larendon, husband of the daughter of General P. G. T. Beauregard. Mrs. Larendon died with the birth of a child, but her husband stayed on in the house until his death. Later, a Mrs. Jacques moved in, but she reported that she could not bear the ghastly manifestations which took place in the dining-room. Her family had to cease using the room entirely and at last moved.

For a number of years the Devil's Mansion remained unoccupied. In 1930 it was demolished. No one would live in a residence where the shades of Lucifer's mistress and her lover returned, and where the living head of the Devil was set in the gable above the roof.

Special Writer, pp. 280–281. Material Gathered by Workers of the Works Progress Administration, Louisiana Writers' Project. Copyright, 1945, by the Louisiana Library Commission, Essae M. Culver, Executive Secretary. Boston: Houghton Mifflin Company.

PART FOUR

SOUTHERN FOLKWAYS

Little Sorrowful Swamp lies like a forty-mile blot on the map of the Low Country and even people in a hurry shy away from its edges as though the blot still reeked. There is no hurrying through Sorrowful. All the fretful people who have exchanged the great god, Patience, for the minor god, Progress, scratch away at their maps with gum rubber and old razor blades, but the stain of Sorrowful still shows through.

Hunters in new boots follow the track of a master buck or the scratchings of a turkey drove until the sun is lost in the trees and compasses only point from one morass to another. Fox horns wail through the night, shots follow each other like clods upon a coffin, and bloodhounds are hurried from the nearest prison camp. Sometimes the fevered, insect-tortured men stumble out to safety. Sometimes, not.

Dinnertime in Little Sorrowful is when the Big eat the Little. Where else is it any different?

Still, there is peace in the swamp and a strange, compelling silence that no riverman can live without. . . . Young men do leave the river but come quickly back or, ultimately, are brought back. The "Outside" is too crowded, too noisy and, above all, too demanding. Sorrowful makes few demands. There is meat in the woods, fish in the river, and the mulch of centuries is guinea-rich along the banks.

Play in the swamp is rough and tempers flare quickly. There is birth and death and sickness in between. Accidents are born of stupidity and sorrow stems from ignorance. The "catch women," as the midwives are called, and the "root doctors" attend the desperations of mankind and of their cattle.

The riverfolk believe in a living God who takes notes of every misstep, who promises a land of milk and honey for those whose books are balanced. They believe that every bush harbors Satan, or one of his imps like the plat-eyes or the boogermen. . . . One thing that never affrights a man of Little Sorrowful is the ghost of a long-dead neighbor. He is truly satisfied that, in time, milk and honey and streets of pure gold would pall upon a man from Big River.

—MARIA HERIOT ALLAN

I. PLEASURES OF THE PALATE

She . . . reminded me . . . that I was in a land of reckless pro-
fusion, where I could almost have loaf-bread, biscuit, rolls, butter-
milk bread, Sally Lunn, batterbread, flannel-cakes, or waffles, any
or all of them, at breakfast, as I pleased—and afterwards be
regaled with buckwheat cakes and syrup, or honey besides. Vir-
ginians, she said, scarcely realized, she was sure, what a mon-
strously unreasonable petition they sent up when they prayed
for their daily bread.—WILLIAM CABELL BRUCE

1. BACKWOODS ECONOMY AND GASTRONOMY

BELOW the "dividing line between cold bread and hot biscuit," in Governor Bob Taylor's phrase, the land of promise was a land of plenty, which in dream or in reality was a paradise for gourmet and glutton. Taylor himself tells the story of "one of these old gluttonous dreamers," ("I think he was the champion eater of the world"), who one day "unfortunately undertook too large a contract for the retirement of an immense slice of ham [which] scraped its way down his rebellious esophagus for about two inches, and lodged as tightly as a bullet in a rusty gun." Getting down on all-fours to receive a powerful blow with a plank about three feet long, the glutton swallowed as it hit, and "shot into the corner of the room like a shell from a mortar; but in a moment he was seated at his place at the table again, with a broad grin on his face," saying: "The durned thing's gone—please pass the ham."[1] For gargantuan appetite, the infant Crockett, who "at eleven o'clock . . . always took a sandwich, which was composed of half a bear's ham, two spare ribs, a loaf of bread, and a quart of whisky"[2] contended with young Eugene Gant, who got his start as a wallower in sensations and food when, feasting from a high chair by his father's side, he "filled his distending belly until it was drum-tight, and was permitted to stop eating by his watchful sire only when his stomach was impregnable to the heavy prod of Gant's big finger."[3]

Big eating (rather than good cooking, which went with the plantation tradition of good manners and "many servants") was part of the backwoods legend, where, according to "Skitt," of Fisher's River, North Carolina, "You may expect, in a healthy country like that, there would be big eaters. Their food was plain and simple . . . bacon and cabbage, chicken soup and pot pies, Irish potatoes and hominy, and their buckwheat pancakes, tarts, and puddings by way of dessert"; and all they required was plenty of it. Prodigious feeding was one of the chief pastimes at social gatherings (reapings, corn-shuckings, ground-clearings) where Long Jimmy

---

[1] *Echoes, Centennial and Other Notable Speeches, Lectures, and Stories* (Nashville, 1899), pp. 179–180.

[2] Richard M. Dorson, *Davy Crockett* (New York, 1939), p. 6.

[3] Thomas Wolfe, *Look Homeward, Angel* (New York, 1929, Modern Library Edition), p. 69.

Thompson, eating hog's feet, could "hull out bones faster nur a cotting-gin can shell out cotting seed"; and Mose Cackerham, eating hog backbones and jowls, kept dropping the bones on the floor as hard as "ears o' corn on the floor of a empty corn-crib at a corn shuckin', and nearly as fast." [4]

A favorite theme in Southern folk tales, like "Diddy-Wah-Diddy," is the mythical place where baked chickens and roast pigs with knives and forks stuck in their sides run around crying, "Eat Me!" or "Who'll eat me?" Similarly, an ex-slave tells of Negroes lured from Alabama to Arkansas by "two Yankee mens" with promises of "hogs just laying around already baked with the knives and forks sticking in them ready to be et" and of "fritter ponds everywhere with the fritters a-frying in them ponds of grease." [5] Such dreams of plenty, like boasting, inevitably proceed from having too little rather than too much, in the feast-or-famine pattern that followed the frontier.

As the game was killed off, the backwoodsman came to depend on the docile, hardy, and prolific hog for meat, while corn was the staple grain, since its cultivation was suited to hillside farming by women, with a yield per acre four times greater than wheat. Accordingly, the "three M" diet —meat (fatback), meal, and molasses—became the standard and traditional diet of the frontier, persisting through slavery times, when the weekly allowance per slave was "three pounds of pork, a peck of corn, a pint of salt, and molasses in proportion." [6]

If the transition from frontier to plantation established the "minimum frontier regimen" (whose cheapness fixed it in the vicious circle of poverty and poor agricultural practice, with their low standard of living and "human inadequacy"), it also resulted in the "South's tradition of good cooking" (which, as it belonged originally to the "big house" rather than to the "quarters" and the cabin, is still limited largely to the better-class homes and eating-places). Even the Southern institution of hot bread had a frontier origin, since, when wheat flour came in, "its most obvious use was in the preparation of hot biscuits" as the successor to hot hoe cakes.

Part and parcel of the hog-and-hominy complex (which belongs to the Middle-Western as well as the Southern frontier) are the traditional Southern delicacies and staples—cracklin' bread, shortenin' bread, cush, pot-likker and cornpone, grits—and the hog in all its parts and forms—ham, bacon, jowls, backbones, liver, sausage, chitlins, headcheese.

To illustrate the mountain subsistence pattern, Henry Harvey Fuson tells the story of a Kentucky mountain boy who went to Texas, where the one crop was cotton, and returned after three years saying: " 'I'm tired living out of a poke [paper bag]'. . . . What he meant was this, that he was tired of living on a farm where he could not raise a diversified crop for his own use." [7]

---

[4] *Fisher's River (North Carolina) Scenes and Characters* (Eona, Virginia, Second Edition, n.d.), pp. 135–137.

[5] As told by Henry Green, Barton, Arkansas, *Lay My Burden Down* (Chicago, 1945), p. 10.

[6] Rupert B. Vance, *Human Geography of the South* (Chapel Hill, 1932), pp. 416–417. To his excellent treatment of Southern "Climate, Diet, and Human Adequacy," pp. 411–441, the present discussion is greatly indebted.

[7] *History of Bell County, Kentucky* (New York, 1947), Vol. II, pp. 337–338.

2. Food Customs and Rituals

In the folkways of Southern gastronomy, eating and drinking have played a part not only in general hospitality and sociability but also in community gatherings where the needs of work, religion, and politics as well as gregariousness are satisfied. Such was the case in harvest suppers, corn shuckings, butchering-day dinners, all-day singing and dinner on the grounds, church picnics, barbecues, and fish muddles. And when the eating was light, as at frolics and dances, the drinking was apt to be heavy.

The jug and the bottle were already firmly established in the backwoods pattern where poor roads made the jug (without benefit of government excise tax) the easiest way to get corn out of corn-patches (especially in the mountains). Where money was scarce, whisky also was used for barter. And where malaria and chills and fever were common, alcohol served as a tonic and a cure-all, being a favorite ingredient in bitters and a morning dose even for children "jest to keep healthy."

Around the regional dishes of the South—fried chicken, barbecue, burgoo, Virginia and Kentucky ham, possum—have grown up family recipes, local traditions, and controversies, and national legends. New Orleans, according to Ralph McGill, is the "only city in America where street quarrels may be heard over the respective merits of certain restaurants and dishes." Marylanders grow lyrical over Brunswick stew, diamond-back terrapin, canvas-back duck, and oysters in many forms; South Carolinians, over rice, calibash, and pilaus (pronounced pé-los, púr-loos); Floridians, over mangoes, turtle, cooter, and hush-puppies; and Louisianians, over the superiorities of the Cajun and Creole cuisine—gombo, jambalaya, bouillabaisse, crayfish bisque.

In finesse and perfection the connoisseurship of concocting dishes and drinks is matched by the connoisseurship of eating and drinking, as in the ritual of rice known only to proper Charlestonians.[8]

The final touch of connoisseurship was displayed by the "two Southern Senators who met at the bar in the Senate cloakroom one afternoon to supervise the broaching of a new cask of bourbon whisky." One detected the faintest trace of a metal taste, the other a taste of leather. They argued, and "The argument became more heated and almost ended in a duel. It turned into a Senate controversy during the month required to empty the cask of liquor." And when the cask was finally emptied and, in the presence of almost all the Senate, the bartender smashed it with a bung-starter, among the broken staves was found a tiny upholsterer's tack, with a metal stem and a head made of leather.[9]

B. A. B.

---

[8] Samuel Gaillard Stoney, *Charleston: Azaleas and Old Bricks* (Boston, 1937), p. 12.
[9] Charles Hurd, *Washington Cavalcade* (New York, 1948), p. 284.

Corn Liquor

I [1]

THE piney woods ridges of Mississippi, the fourth of its four kingdoms, are "po' folks' lan'." It is as different as another world from the Delta, the prairie country, and the swamp region. While folks in "de rich folks' lan'" drink juleps, and Delta folks drink toddies, natives of the "po' folks' lan'" drink corn liquor.

Corn liquor is the most maligned stimulant in America. It is the purest whisky in the world. The only different between bourbon and corn is that bourbon is the parlor name for corn. The idea that only hill folks of Tennessee and Kentucky know how to make real corn whisky is an error. The best corn is made in the swamps because swamp folks have enough time to make it right. The corn should be allowed to sprout before the mash is made. The way to drink it is hold a tin cup of spring water in the right hand and a tin cup of corn in the left. A dipper will do, but a cup is better. Take a sip of water to cool the throat, then a slug of corn. Quickly now, pour down a large swallow of water. That puts out the blaze in your throat but doesn't less that glow in the belly. Don't take but two drinks before breakfast unless you want to get so wild you'll "spit in a wildcat's eye."

A Kentuckian once made some good corn and buried it in barrels under his barn. Lightning destroyed the barn. Many years later he decided to rebuild and in digging his base he discovered the barrels. The lightning by some crazy twist had charred the kegs but hadn't damaged them. The owner tasted the amber liquor and whooped. The neighbors tasted it and they all set to whooping.

They named the fine whisky bourbon after the county in which they lived.

II [2]

At its most romantic, the praise of native corn liquor always belonged to the school of the fox who lost his tail pointing to taillessness as perfection. At its best, aged in home-sized kegs, which could be purchased at most of the chain stores, corn liquor was a potable drink full of the mule's heels. Gentlemen exchanged private systems for reducing the shock to the palate, which extended all the way from the introduction of dried fruits into the liquor to advanced chemical procedures. Sometimes they succeeded. But at their worst, corn liquor and monkey rum (which in North Carolina was the distilled syrup of sorghum cane) were concoctions taken stoically, with retching and running eyes, for the effect beyond the first fusel oil belch.

---

[1] From *Look Away!* A Dixie Notebook, by James H. Street, pp. 53–54. Copyright, 1936, by James H. Street. New York: The Viking Press.

[2] From *Tar Heels*, A Portrait of North Carolina, by Jonathan Daniels, p. 255. Copyright, 1941, by Jonathan Daniels. New York: Dodd, Mead & Company. 1947.

There was certainly a democracy in drinking then. Rich and poor drank with the same gasping. Indeed, when a death by gunshot wound resulted in the relation of the details of a party in one of the State's richest houses, it came out that, before the gun went off, they had been drinking corn whisky and chasing it down with near beer.

III [3]

White Mule, Cawn Likker, Shine, Moon, et al.—Regardless of alias this sequence simply means the raw, new, colorless, distilled product of fermented corn mash, sugar and water. If well made, of decent materials, in a proper still, with the fusel oil rectified out, and aged in wood it starts to be bourbon whisky after not less than four years in the wood of charred oak casks.

None of the manufacturers of bourbons should have any right to call any corn whisky "bourbon" until it has aged at least four or five years, but the demand so exceeded supply that all rules were off.

As far as corn likker goes we have drunk it from a fellow quail and turkey shooter's still in the Big Swamp country of Central Florida—made in a copper wash boiler, run through an old shotgun barrel, and a length of iron pipe into a galvanized washtub covered with a cotton blanket; drunk it in the "dry" mountain sections of Nawth C'hlina last summer. We have drunk it straight, with water, with juices, and disguises. We have drunk it scalding hot on chill October evenings, with cloves, brown sugar, and lemon peel. We've drunk it cold.

In spite of hades and elevated water that old cawn bouquet comes shearing through like a rusty can opener to smite us between the eyes. Hot with cloves, and so on is best; drowned in grapefruit juice is about the only cold method possible. No matter what, that cawn has a scent of decaying vegetation blended with the fluid men used to put in old ship lanterns; and taken neat it burns with all the restless fires of hell.

As you may gather we don't recommend cawn—mentally, morally; or for general wear and tear and declined insurance risk, physically. We certainly don't—until after at least five years in charred oak casks.

Moonshining in the Ozarks

ROUNDER talks freely about all the peculiar problems associated with the making of moonshine. He is, as he says, a retired moonshiner. And how

[3] From *The Gentleman's Companion*, Volume II, Being an Exotic Drinking Book, or, Around the World with Jigger, Beaker and Flask, by Charles H. Baker, Jr., pp. 190–191. Copyright, 1939, by the Derrydale Press, Inc.; 1946, by Crown Publishers. New York: Crown Publishers.

From *Fresh from the Hills,* by Marguerite Lyon, pp. 41–45. Copyright, 1945, by the Bobbs-Merrill Company. Indianapolis and New York.

far back that retirement extends is strictly nobody's business but his own. A long time perhaps, but Rounder is gifted with a fine memory for detail and he can tell many an amusing incident about a profession few of us have ever studied.

* * * * *

"Yes, that's what I always say! It hain't the makin' o' moonshine that's the hard work. It's the cookin' off. That's the hardest day's work you ever done!"

"Oh, you Ozark men hate cooking," I said.

"It's more'n cookin'," said Rounder seriously. "There you are, lookin' after the f'ar, keepin' cold water in the barrel, seein' that the whisky's runnin', and all the time you got to keep watchin' f'r the Law.

"Now take that time," Rounder continued reminiscently, "when me and another feller was cookin' off over in the holler 'longside o' Jack's Fork. Durned if the prosecutin' attorney hisself didn't walk right up on us. Yep, that shows what can happen. He was drivin' through the county election-eerin'. Drove past my pardner's house. Pardner's wife seen him and knowed him 'cause he come from the place where she was raised. So she run out of the house and peered down the road to see that he kept on a-goin'. Then she high-tailed it to the woods to tell us the Law was in the neighborhood. Well, the Law happened to look up in the mirror and see her lookin' after him. He 'spected somethin' was up. So he jis parked his car over the hill and snuck back through the woods. When she run down to warn us, he jis followed her down! Ketched us right there with the moonshine pourin' out in them quart jars purty as a pitchur!"

"Did he arrest you?"

"Oh, shore!" Rounder tossed off casually. "Fifty-dollar fine and ninety days in jail."

"If cooking off is the danger time," I began reasoning, "isn't there some way it might be avoided?"

"Where you been raised, woman?" asked Rounder. "Git yore pencil and I'll give you a recipe f'r making moonshine, then you won't be makin' fool speeches like that!" He waited until paper was found. "Reckon you ought to start with rye whisky. That's the kind they most generally make around here. Corn whisky is jis as good but it takes longer to make. And the Law has that much more chance o' ketchin' you. Now put this down jis as I say:

"Put one peck o' rye in hot water—jis enough to cover it. Let it set three days. Then put it in a fifty-gallon barrel. Put the barrel about two-thirds full o' water. Then you take a tub and heat some water in it and you pour fifty pounds o' sugar in the tub. Stir it up good until all the sugar 'solves. Then you take the warm water with the sugar in it and put it in the barrel. Then you put in nine packages o' yeast—the old-fashioned kind is best. Then in four days it will ferment and finally settle down to jis a blubber. Then you want to commence cookin' it off."

"Would I let the barrel stand right in the kitchen?" I asked.

"Geemuneee! No!" shouted Rounder. "What if the Law would come! Any little old constable right in the neighborhood could make you a lot o' trouble. Git that barrel hid some place. Sometimes I'd dig a hole out in the woods and put the barrel in it. Then I'd put boards and leaves over the hole and a feller'd walk right over it and never know the's anything there. Or a good way is to chop down a tree and let the top fall over on the barrel. In summertime, with all the leaves on, hain't nobody a-goin' to see that barrel. But that cookin' off—" he groaned at the memory— "that's when you've got to look out. Ever'thing's in plain sight!"

"Now what would I need for cooking off?" I wanted that recipe for my files. "Just supposing I were making some moonshine."

"Well, right off you'd need a fifteen-gallon cooker. A copper wash boiler is the best thing. Put the mash in it and build a fire under it. A little fire. A big fire would blow it up. Then you take a copper pipe thirty feet long and coil it around a keg. That makes the 'urm [worm]. Don't be like a feller that coiled his 'urm around a tree. Danged fool had to cut the tree down to git his 'urm loose. You put that 'urm into a bigger barrel and fill the barrel with cold water. Then you've got to have a lead line from the 'urm to the copper wash boiler. That ort to be copper too. But I've used an elder branch with the pith dug out. The whisky drips out o' the end o' the 'urm that's stickin' out of the barrel. You put a fruit jar under that to ketch it!"

"All ready to drink?" I'm a tasting cook.

"Well, purt' nigh! Only one more thing. You've got to fill a funnel full o' wood or charcoal and let the whisky run through it. That takes the fusel oil out. Fusel oil'll kill you," he said, matter-of-factly, then went on in his recipe-giving tone. "A batch like this will give you five gallons o' whisky. This is the sing' wun [single run]. If you run the sing' wun through the cooker again, you get 100-proof whisky. And if you run it through a third time, you get 180-proof alkyhol."

"Corn whisky's made the same way, isn't it?" asked the Jedge.

"Now, Jedge," said Rounder, "you hain't a-figgerin' on doin' a little moonshinin', I hope. If you've got any sugar to spare, Marge, you'd better give it to someone that knows how!"

"He isn't and I haven't," I said firmly.

Rounder sighed. "This sugar shortage has shore raised hell with moonshinin'. Fellers that's got a lot of kids is the lucky ones. But most gen'r'ly the old woman won't turn loose o' the coupons. Gittin' back to this corn whisky now—that's a lot o' trouble. You have to let the corn lay som'ers until it has sprouts a quarter of a inch long or a little better. Then you take it out and dry it in the sunshine or a warm room and when it's dry you grind it into meal, sprouts and all. Then you go ahead like rye, only it takes eight days before it's a mash."

"I thought whisky had to be aged." I read advertisements.

"Shore," said Rounder heartily. "But I do that most gen'r'ly—I mean I did—right while I was cookin' it off. It's got more shake to it then. Jis git you some white-oak chips and put 'em in the cookstove oven until they're all charred. Then you put a handful o' these chips in a barrel o' new whisky, and you can age it purty as you please. Colors it right off, jis like boughten whisky, and I figger it'll taste four years old in a day and a half. It'll taste like eight years old in three days." He sighed.

Rounder sat for a long moment, wrapped in nostalgic memories.

"Dang shame the gov'ment is so sot agin moonshinin'. With stuff like corn and rye growin' right here and with all the springs here in the hills, handy f'r cookin' off, moonshinin' jist sort o' comes natch'ral to folks."

Rounder lifted his feet out of the way while the Jedge put more wood on the fire. I plugged in the percolator and drew him another cup of coffee. He drank it with the lip-drawn derision with which Judy accepts milk of magnesia. I felt downright apologetic that I had nothing stronger to offer.

Suddenly our guest chuckled and his blue eyes twinkled.

"Funny thing about the Law! They git all excited about moonshine, when a feller could be makin' whisky right under their noses unbeknownst to them. You ort to put this down, too, Marge.

"Jis take a punkin, yep, one o' these big ol' cow punkins that you see growin' big and yaller in ever' cornfield. Cut out the top, kinda slonchin' around so there's a good edge on the top and on the punkin too. Clean the punkin out good. Then you fill it full o' sugar. Pack it in good, all it will hold. Then you put the lid o' the punkin back on and fit it down tight. Seal the crack between the lid and the punkin with sealin' wax, so no air can git in. Then you put the punkin under your bed and let it set four days. When you open it up, you've got a quart o' good honest-to-gosh whisky jis as white and clear as if it had been run. The's jis enough moisture in the punkin to make it work."

Rounder laughed loudly and slapped his knee. "Think o' the Law runnin' all around, huntin' stills up and down the crick and 'longside all the springs, jis a-wearin' theirselves out—when a feller could be makin' whisky right under his bed!"

Mint Juleps

I [1]

A TRAVELER in Louisiana in the days before the War between the States tells of a visit to Burnside Plantation where he was awakened in the morning by a slave with a mint julep. Presently the slave disappeared and returned

---

[1] From *Louisiana*, A Guide to the State, compiled by Workers of the Writers' Program of the Work Projects Administration in the State of Louisiana, pp. 229–230. American Guide Series. Copyright, 1941, by the Louisiana Library Commission at Baton Rouge. New York: Hastings House, Publishers.

with a second julep, explaining that the dew was heavy that morning and the drink was good for warding off fever. When the third julep arrived the guest was told that he had better take it because it was "the last drink that will be served before breakfast."

II [2]

Marse Henry Watterson, the great Louisville editor and famous host, had his own method for making the ambrosial beverage. His recipe, according to legend, went like this: "Pluck the mint gently from its bed, just as the dew of evening is about to form upon it. Select the choicer sprigs only, but do not rinse them. Prepare the simple syrup and measure out a half-tumbler of whisky. Pour the whisky into a well-frosted silver cup and throw the other ingredients away and drink the whisky."

III [3]

Right from the meaning of the word Juleps have been a spill-and-pelt of contradiction and disagreement. The very name itself never was mid-wifed on any honeysuckle-bowered southern balcony, but comes from the Persian *gulab,* or Arab *julab,* meaning rose water.

No sane Kentucky planter, in full possession of his faculties, will yield an inch to any Marylander when it comes to admitting rye is superior to bourbon in a Julep, when actually, a Julep is international and has been international for years—just as the matters of radio and flying are international. It is a drink composed of whisky or brandy and, of late, rum; sweetened, iced, and flavored with aromatic leaves of the *mentha* family.

So before the shooting starts let's explain right here and now that there's no more chance of getting the various Julep schools to agree on fabrication of this most delectable of drinks than we have of getting a proud Atlanta great-grandmother to concede General Sherman a nice, gentle, well-meaning, big boy.

First of all there is the silver cup versus the glass school; the chilled glass versus room-temperature school; the slightly bruised mint versus the all-bruised school; the rye versus the bourbon school; the fruit garnish versus the plain school.

Feuds have begun because someone breathed the possibility that city water would make a Julep as well as water dipped from a fern-draped Blue Grass Country spring. Men have been shot at for heaping fruit juices,

2 From *Louisville,* The Gateway City, by Isabel McLennan McMeekin, p. 155. Copyright, 1946, by Isabel McLennan McMeekin. New York: Julian Messner, Inc.

3 From *The Gentleman's Companion,* Volume II, Being an Exotic Drinking Book, or, Around the World with Jigger, Beaker and Flask, by Charles H. Baker, Jr., pp. 61–64. Copyright, 1939, by the Derrydale Press, Inc.; 1946, by Crown Publishers. New York: Crown Publishers.

slices of citrus, and maraschino cherries on a Julep completed. Families have faced divorcement about the slight-appearing concern of red-stemmed mint.

A gentleman who discards the slightly bruised mint from his drink views another who permits the bruised leaves to remain in glass as one who did not have quite the proper forbearance on the distaff side. And so tell they the tale—

* * * * *

But let us inject a word of caution to seekers after this miracle of frosted perfection. No man can rough and tumble his Julep-making and expect that luck must always be on his side, that a lovely arctic frosted thing shall always reward his careless ignorance.

Especially on yachts or boats, for instance, no Julep glass can frost when stood in any considerable wind. Frosting depends solely upon condensed moisture being converted to minor ice through the excessive chill of melting cracked ice and liquids within that glass. Therefore if the breeze whisks it away there can be nothing left to frost. Paradoxically, when the outside of any Julep glass is moist from careless rinsing, handling, or standing about only partially iced in humid weather, frost will be in total lack due to *excess* moisture.

Likewise no Julep can ever frost when caressed by the warm, *bare* palm of an impatient host or guest—not any more than decent frosting can ever result from wet, half-melted cracked ice that is more liquid than solid. Just obey the rules, few but important, and success will crown every amateur effort.

* * * * *

Use red-stemmed mint, simply because red-stemmed mint is more pleasantly aromatic. Use fresh mint, and cut stems short just before putting in as final garnish—to make them bleed.

Don't bruise that first installment of tender mint leaves more than very slightly. The inner leaf juices are bitter and cannot have profitable flavor. Bruise one between the teeth, then chew it up to find out.

* * * * *

Don't over-garnish with sliced orange and random fruits. With Juleps, and in fact any drink of delicate quality in its own right, don't add anything with a different strong scent—and orange, lemon, and certain other fruits have a very potent aroma. The aroma of a bourbon Julep should be bourbon and mint—not bourbon, mint, and a fruit store. Garnish simply without trying to gild the lily. A Julep is more than a mere chilled liquid; it is a tradition which is to be respected. The mint itself is a delight to eye, just as we admire parsley against a fine red snapper, or permit feminine associates the use of red nail polish, or grace a mother's table with flowers. So let the Julep feast the eye and nostril properly—not supply unending, edible diversions from the main theme. We don't need to eat all the trimmings, after all—but *we* always do! That is why ripe pineapple is so beneficial—and eaten after the Julep is gone, the marinated fruit is delicious.

Take care that all sugar is worked into syrup before ice and liquor are put in. Reason: If sugar is left in granular form, when chilled the dissolving process is radically slowed down. Especially when sipping through a straw you will suddenly find yourself inhaling a furiously saccharine slug which will ruin the memory of the lovely drink just preceding this disastrous end. This is why we personally use *gomme,* or bar, syrup for all Juleps. Mint leaves muddle as well in it as they do on sugar; the muddled bits of mint stick to the glass's inner walls even better than with the sugar-water mix. One final stir before garnish goes in distributes this quickly dissolved syrup evenly through the entire drink.

The Sazerac

I [1]

. . . THE most celebrated of New Orleans cocktails—the Sazerac—is a mixture of whisky, bitters, and sugar, served in a glass rinsed with absinthe. Here is a dialogue which appeared in the newspapers in the eighties:

> When you get to New Orleans, my son, drink a Sazerac cocktail for me and one for yourself.
> And a third one?
> For the devil, my son, for no living mortal can accomplish that.

II [2]

It is a sad and shocking fact that more people who should know more know less about this truly remarkable drink than is reasonable—heaven alone knows why. The Sazerac Bar-Chief, who has been building 'em up for 40 years, showed us his way. As did the mixers at several clubs, the old St. Charles; to say nothing about places like our friend Roy Aciatore's, Antoine's Restaurant, Arnaud's, Gabriel Galatoire's, Broussard, and others. The best drinks produced in New Orleans stick to the ancient, simple formula—and please, please, never try to vary it; for if you do you'll not be

---

[1] From *Louisiana,* A Guide to the State, compiled by Workers of the Writers' Program of the Work Projects Administration in the State of Louisiana, p. 230. Copyright, 1941, by the Louisiana Library Commission at Baton Rouge. New York: Hasting House, Publishers.

[2] From *The Gentleman's Companion,* Volume II, Being an Exotic Drinking Book, or, Around the World with Jigger, Beaker and Flask, by Charles H. Baker, Jr., pp. 121–122. Copyright, 1939, by the Derrydale Press, Inc.; 1946, by Crown Publishers. New York: Crown Publishers.

drinking a true Sazerac—just some liquid abortion fit only to pour down drains.

First thing is to get a Sazerac glass: a great big thick-bottomed thing which is nothing more nor less than an Old Fashioned glass blown up to twice normal size! Reason: thick bottom and thick walls keep the strong mixed liquor cold; and *warm* strong mixed liquor is like a chemical in the nostrils and throat, of course. These big crystal affairs are buyable at first-class glass stores; but may take time to order in. If none at hand, use your brandy sniffers as substitute.

Routine is simple and inviolate: Frappe (pre-chill) glass and liquor. For each drink pour 2 ounces of the best rye whisky you can find in a shaker, lash it with 3 or 4 good squirts of Peychaud's bitters. Shake hard and long with big ice. Then strain into your glass, which must be previously coated inside with 3 or 4 good squirts (use a barman's quill top bottle stopper for this) of asbinthe or 120-proof Pernod; and turned or spun between the palms to make this said coating even and thorough. Strain drink in glass, and twist a long curl of thin-cut yellow lemon peel on top, for oil and aroma. Hold under nose, inhale the fragrant blend of scents, sip and relax. This, then, my dear children, is just how little Sazeracs are born! Mark well.

Scuppernong Wine

WHEN Zelma and I were taking the census, we came on an old man far off in the piney-woods who gave us cups of white Scuppernong wine so dry, so fine, that I could not believe my palate. He gave us the recipe, and I took it down as he dictated:

"Now don't look to this not to fail you if you don't do like I tell you. And when I've done told you all I know, then you still got to have a sort o' feelin' about it, and if you ain't got that feelin', you just as good go buy your wine some'eres, for you cain't make it.

"Now you mash your Scuppernongs the very same day you pick 'em. Don't you go pickin' 'em of an evenin' when the sun's low and the day's coolin', and then you go traipsin' off some'eres, sayin', 'I'll start my wine come mornin'.' You pick 'em fust off in the mornin', with the dew on 'em, and you mash 'em with a bread roller. Put 'em in a deep crock. A keg? Well, yes, I've used a keg, but a crock's better. Now you sprinkle sugar or honey over 'em. How much? Now I cain't no more tell you that than why a bird sings. Just sort of kiver 'em light-like, and honey's the best. I'd say flat-woods honey. Palmeeter honey is a mite too dark. Now you let 'em stand three to seven days. I cain't tell you which, nor what day in betweenst. They git a certain look.

From *Cross Creek*, by Marjorie Kinnan Rawlings, pp. 222–224. Copyright, 1942, by Marjorie Kinnan Rawlings. New York: Charles Scribner's Sons.

"Now some folks, when that time comes, skim off the pummies. That ain't my way, and you kin do as you please. When that time comes, I put 'em in a flour sack and I squeezes hell outen 'em. Then I put the juice back in the crock and I add sugar slow, powerful slow, stirrin' all the time. How much sugar? Now if you like your wine sweet, you put the sugar to the juice until a egg'll float. I don't fancy it that sweet. I like wine to lay cool and not sickly on my tongue. I put in sugar to where a egg don't quite float, to where it sort o' bobbles around, and mebbe just raises itself oncet almost to the top.

"Now some folks leaves it lay in the crock. I don't. I put it right now in the bottles, without no tops on. I keep some back in the crock. I kiver the bottles with a cloth. The wine'll work and it'll shrink down, and ever' mornin' come sun-up I'll add some from what I've helt back in the crock. I do this until it quits workin'. Then I cork it tight and lay it down on its side in a dark place. Now that ain't the way of a heap o' folks, but it's my way."

Thankful for These

AT OUR breakfast table we would sit on benches with our stern grand-father at the head of the long table, and we would bow our heads while in one descending breath he would mutter the grace. We had a set blessing that we used in all of our houses: "Lord, make us thankful for these and all Thy blessings." I never heard this invocation varied except once when one of our cousins, who did not care for cowpeas and fatback, bowed his head and said: "Good God, look at this." We had quantities of food on our table; no matter how hard the times were, we always had more than we needed to eat, and even when cotton was down to five cents, there was an air of happiness about our boards. . . .

*   *   *   *   *

At breakfast we had a big bowl of water-ground hominy grits that had simmered for an hour over a slow fire; we never missed having hominy and we never tired of it, we could eat it and we did eat it, every morning of every year, and we were never able to understand why people in the Middle West, in the corn country, did not eat hominy too. Hominy was such a good food, eaten with butter or with sliced tomatoes or with red gravy, and it was so cheap. We do not know what we would do in the South, white folks or black folks, if there were no hominy grits. We had red gravy in bowls and wide platters filled with thick slices of ham, smoked

From *Red Hills and Cotton*, An Upcountry Memory, by Ben Robertson, pp. 65–67, 68–70, 71. Copyright, 1942, by Ben Robertson. New York: Alfred A. Knopf.

For the pros and cons of Southern cooking, cf. Ralph McGill, "What's Wrong with Southern Cooking," *The Saturday Evening Post*, Vol. 221 (March 26, 1949), No. 39, pp. 38–39, 102–103, 105.

and cured and fried, and we had fried eggs right from the nests. We had pitcherfuls of rich milk that had been chilled overnight in the spring branch, and we had blackberry jam for the hot biscuits, and preserves made from the little clingstone peaches that grew wild on the terraces in the cotton patches and were sweeter than anything we ever cultivated in the orchards. We liked everything that was wild.

* * * * *

At my grandfather's house at noontime we had soup and two or three kinds of meat, fried chicken, fried ham, or spareribs or liver pudding; and we had four or five vegetables and a dessert or so and fruit. We all were fond of fried chicken, but the chicken had to be very young and small—we did not fry old roosters, we fricasseed roosters. We threatened to send to the cotton patch cooks who fried tough chickens. To fry chickens, to boil coffee, to boil rice, and to make good biscuits were the four requirements we demanded of cooks. I don't think I ever had all the fried chicken I could eat until I was twenty-one years of age. I never got enough because I liked the thigh and the gizzard, and half the others also preferred those pieces. We never expected ever even to taste the liver—the older men were served the liver. My Aunt Bettie always declared she liked the back, and my grandmother took the wing, but I did not believe they liked those scrawny pieces of the chicken. They ate those bits because they loved us and did not want to take what we liked best—that was their charity. We liked ducks next to chicken and we sometimes ate a goose or a turkey, but it never occurred to us to eat guinea fowl. We kept guineas at our houses because they were decorative and because we liked the way they cackled. It astonished us once to read in the newspaper that in New York the President of the United States had been served a guinea for dinner. We kept peacocks, too; we were fascinated by their pride.

We were fond of red-pepper sauce, fiery hot, of sage in sausage, of cloves in peach pickles, of nutmegs on clabber; we liked turnip greens, collards, possum and sweet potatoes, roasting ear corn stewed and thickened with flour, cornbread with chitterlings, ambrosia, stuffed eggs, pound cake. We were required to eat something of everything on the table at our grandfather's house, for our grandfather said it was nonsense to pick and choose, to like this and not to like that. He said we would get to like anything if we tried hard enough and kept trying long enough. Eventually I got so I could eat everything under the sun but it did require discipline and persistence to relish parsnips.

When the cooks among our kinfolks did not fry, they boiled. They believed in long cooking over slow fires, and in all of our kitchens the open fireplaces had cranes to swing iron pots from. Beans to be eaten at noon had to be on the fire by eight o'clock in the morning. So did cabbage. My grandmother said cabbage boiled less than four hours would kill you. We boiled beans, potatoes, cabbage, turnip greens, with a chunk of fatback. Our folks have boiled vegetables like that clear across the United States, from South Carolina to Texas, and up the Texas trail right into southern

Montana. Either we boil vegetables or we eat them raw—we have never put any stock in the scalding school of vegetable-cooking.

* * * * *

My grandparents never forgot Lee's surrender and the days of starvation in the South, and neither of them ever allowed any of us at their house to waste rations. "You can eat whatever you like and as much as you like," my grandmother told us, "but what you take on your plate you must finish." My grandmother did not mind if we cleaned our plates with a piece of biscuit. "Don't be dainty," was her motto.

Supper with us was simple. We sat down to it at dusk, tired out from the long greatness of the summer day, and often all we would have would be milk, cool from the springhouse buckets; cornbread, sliced thin and almost sizzling hot; soft salted fresh butter; and sorghum molasses. Soon after supper we washed our feet and went to bed. We believed we slept better if at our last meal we had eaten but little. . . .

Sowins and Gopher

. . . The person who acted as our coachman from Alligator to the Suwannee river was quite intelligent, and some of his conversation proved him to be well acquainted with men and things in Florida. He congratulated us upon our escape from Eastern Florida, the land of "hog and hominy," and upon our speedy entrance into Middle Florida, which he denominated the land of "sowins and chickens." The term *sowins* we found to be an abbreviation of *sourings*, which is a dish of pounded corn made sour by baking in the sun, and usually served up with a *gophar-steak*, than which nothing but India-rubber can be more tough and elastic. By way of illustrating the sometime effect of this food upon strangers, he mentioned the following circumstance: A solitary horseman, as Mr. James would say, was on his way through the pine country of this region. Having spent a night in a cabin, where he could procure nothing for his horse but corn husks, and been himself regaled at breakfast by some sourings and gophar-steak, the former dish turned his stomach and made him sick, while the latter resisted all his masticating efforts to the very last, and so he continued his journey. He travelled some thirty miles further, and at night-fall pulled up before another cabin. He asked if he could get a night's lodging and something to eat; to which the good woman replied, "Yes if you can put up with 'sich as it is.'" Sowins and gophar were again placed before him; but he slept soundly and was off before day-light the next morning. As night

---

From the *Adventures in the Wilds of the United States and British American Provinces*, by Charles Lanman, Vol. II, pp. 136–137. Philadelphia: John W. Moore. 1856.

The Gophar is a species of hard-shell turtle, considered, by those accustomed to them, good eating; they are said to live wholly on the land, feeding on grass in the night-time and chewing the cud like the cow.—C. L.

came on again, he made another appeal for food, and "sich as it is" rang again in his ear; upon which he frantically mounted his half-famished steed, exclaiming, "It won't do; I tried 'sich as it is' at the last house and couldn't eat it no how." And thus, by the dim light of a new moon, and looking the picture of famine, he changed his course of travel to the nearest boundary line of the State, and was never more seen in these parts. . . .

When the Collard Greens Talked

. . . T' OTHER day . . . our new minister preached a sermon for us, and you know it's the custom for any man who thinks anything of himself to go up to the preacher and express his opinion of the sermon. I went up to him, and the first thing I knew I didn't know what I was talking about, and very slyly he stole the opportunity to say, "I'll catch you out some day, and I'll measure you on the ground for what you said to me." I tried to say something, but no word would come. I went out wondering at myself. Then I realized that it was a too-much dinner of collards and so and so that had talked to the preacher. My mind kept me awake that night, and the dawn of day found me cussing myself. I got up with the determination to go to the preacher and have it out with him. He had threatened to whip me and I wanted him to keep his word. He lived in a grove not far away, and as soon as I snatched a quick breakfast I started out to look for him. On the way, I stopped at a creek to wash my hands, for the Lord won't like it if a man hits a preacher when his fist is dirty. I was walking along and somebody yelled out, "Hold on!" I stopped, looked up, and here come the preacher. I had tightened my fist, when he said, "I want to beg your pardon for what I said the other day about stretching you on the ground. In fact, it wasn't my mind that was talking to you when I said that I would stretch you on the ground. It was an overindulgence in collard greens." I grabbed him by the arm and said: "Thank God, brother. That was the matter with me. It was collard greens talking."

Grease

THE diet of the mountaineers is enough to kill them even after they've survived the rough handling of the midwives, the "stretchin' hives," the strength-sucking hookworm, and all the gamut of diseases. Of course it varies somewhat with the seasons and economic circumstances, but corn

From *Opie Read,* by Maurice Elfer, pp. 220–221. Copyright, 1940, by Maurice Elfer. Detroit, Michigan: Boyten Miller Press.

From *Bloody Ground,* by John F. Day, pp. 281–282. Copyright, 1941, by John F. Day. Garden City, New York: Doubleday, Doran and Company, Inc.

bread and pork are to the highlanders what rice is to the Chinese. Green vegetables and fruit are all too rare, and even when vegetables are served they're so greasy as to be well-nigh indigestible. Everything is fried, and not well fried at that. For some reason the highlanders put great store by grease. I heard a story once about a mountaineer who went down to Mt. Sterling to visit a relative who had prospered in the comparatively level land. Upon his return his report was this: "You know, Maw, I don't think Tom and them is so well off as we thought they was. They got a nice house and a lot o' nice stock, but they didn't have hardly no grease on the table a-tall." The mountaineers aren't immune to the ills of their diet even though they've developed a tolerance. Those "risin's" they're always talking about are largely due to the grease they consume, and I have an idea a good many shootings stem indirectly from rebellious bellies.

Chitlins

THERE were still more curious foods, which I never saw on the home folks' tables, but which were widely eaten—'possum, tripe, chitterlings, as the English call them but which in our South have been pared down to chitlins. The dictionary tells me that the chitterling is the "frill-like small intestine of the hog." It is available only at hog-killing time in early winter, when it is cleaned, soaked several days in water, parboiled, then fried like an oyster.

There was a chitlin party at Cave City in 1935, and one of the diners described the eating of them as a "chawin' symphony." A Congressman who was present became lyric:

Served with kraut, sour pickles, corn bread, coffee, and taters [said he] chitlin is a dish fit for king or commoner. Even a stuffed chitlin is good if the pepper is red hot. They are delicious, hot or cold, wrapped around a stick and eaten spaghetti style, and contrary to all expressed opinion, it is not necessary to have a drink to fully enjoy the meal. The larger the chitlin, the better, and the more you eat, the more you want. . . . If you find a tough one or another that is slick, swallow it whole. If you encounter anything else, swallow that, too. The real great pleasure is in getting these things down. . . .

If by this time the reader's stomach is getting a bit queasy, may an innocent bystander who has never tasted a chitterling or chitlin in his life and doesn't expect to, be privileged to ask whether there is any great difference in principle between eating the intestine of a barnyard animal and the pancreas, even though the latter be glorified with the name of sweetbread?

From *"Weep No More, My Lady,"* by Alvin F. Harlow, pp. 287–288. Copyright, 1942, by Alvin F. Harlow. Whittlesey House, McGraw-Hill Book Company, Inc. New York.

Cush

THE word *cush* for us Southerners of an earlier generation stirs fond recollections of a dish which in my boyhood was regarded as the ne plus ultra of the culinary art. . . . In the Old South it was the word used for what in these far more degenerate days is known as *dressing*, that is, the breaded preparation placed inside and about a chicken when baked. . . .

. . . The word has not been well treated in the dictionaries. Webster has it, with no indication of its source, and with very little indication that the authorities who compiled that work knew what the word means. The definition given is "Bread or crackers boiled and seasoned, as in water in which meat has been cooked." I should think that one dose of such a lugubrious preparation as this would be the end, and a most horrible end at that, of anyone forced to swallow it. *Cush* as I knew it was prepared from the meal of Indian corn, worked into a thick dough into which chopped-up onions, pepper and salt, and perhaps other enticing ingredients that I was not aware of, were suitably interspersed. And in all cases this preparation was baked thoroughly in immediate or quite close contact with a chicken. . . .

It affords me great pleasure to be the first individual, so far as I know, ever to trace out, briefly, the path by which this word entered the speech of Southerners.

In the earliest, 1770, evidence we have of the word in use in this country, it occurs in the form *cushie*, meaning a kind of pancake made of Indian meal. This first example of the word comes from Maryland, in a region not a great ways from Annapolis. The ending, *-ie*, justifies the suspicion that the immediate source of *cushie* might have been Dutch. Certainly the word *cush* passed into Dutch, where it is spelled *koeskoes*. Fortunately there is an etymological dictionary of the Dutch language, and by reference to that scholarly work we find that *koeskoes* is a Dutch borrowing from the French *couscous*.

There are, again fortunately, excellent etymological dictionaries of the French language, and when we turn to one of these we are informed that the French word *couscous* is not a native French word but has been taken into that language from the language of the Arabs. A fair sprinkling of Arabian words has passed into French, and this term happens to be one of them. As it was used by the Arabs, it meant flour slightly aspersed with water which by force of being stirred forms itself into little grains about like the head of a pin. It was prepared with meat and butter somewhat like rice. It is surprising, therefore, that the definition given in the Dutch dictionary of *koeskoes* is "A mixture of different kinds of meat, greens, etc."

* * * * *

From *Some Sources of Southernisms*, by M. M. Mathews, pp. 120–124. Copyright, 1948, by the University of Alabama Press. University, Alabama.

. . . Turner records that in Gullah the term *cush*, and also the fuller form *cushcush*, occur in the sense of cornmeal dough sweetened and fried. This meaning of the term reminds us strongly of that meaning of *cushie* we have already noticed prevailing in Maryland about 1770, namely a kind of pancake made of Indian corn.

The evidence submitted by Dr. Turner makes it conclusive that the Gullahs have preserved over here a word which their ancestors brought out of Africa with them, for in northern Nigeria and in Angola as well this term *kushkush* prevails. In some of the dialects it is used of a thin cake made of ground-nuts, but in others it means a wheaten food, or parched meal.

With the information supplied by Dr. Turner the whole story of *cush* stands revealed. The word was not native with the Africans. It was one of the many words that have at one time or another passed from the Arabian language into one or another of the African dialects. From Africa the word was transmitted widely. In this country the slaves were not only hewers of wood and drawers of waters; they were cookers of food as well. It is not to be wondered at that this perfectly good Arabian word, *cush* or *kushkush*, was made use of by the old slave mammies nor is it anything other than likely that they fed what they called *cush* to the great men of the South about as soon as they arrived on this earth and had sufficiently oriented themselves to be able to sit up and demand nourishment. Along with the food these children probably imbibed the name for it, and thus *cush* found early and satisfactory use both in nourishing the "white folks" and in enriching their vocabulary. It is a great pity that the word is not in more widespread use.

Hoe Cake and Corn Pone

"BREAD" to the Floridian is cornbread. This is as it should be, for corn is plentiful, it may be bought cheaply when not raised on the place, and may be bought "water-ground" or taken to some local mill for grinding. Until recently, no Florida farm or clearing was complete without its own stone for corn grinding, and on the clearing in the Florida Scrub that I used in my mind as the site of Baxter's Island in *The Yearling*, there still stands the upper and nether millstone turned by a hand crank for making the sweet, fresh cornmeal that makes of cornbread a delectable staple.

There are infinite gradations of cornbread, from the hoe cake of slavery and Civil War times, when the Negroes baked it on hoes before an open flame and the soldiers baked it on their bayonets before the bivouac fires, up to the melting softness of spoonbread. Here are the gradations, from low to high, all good according to the moment's need.

From *Cross Creek Cookery*, by Marjorie Kinnan Rawlings, pp. 22-24. Copyright, 1942, by Marjorie Kinnan Rawlings. New York: Charles Scribner's Sons.

I do not know whether other Southern cooks would agree with me, but I draw a line between hoe cake and corn pone.

1 cup white cornmeal	Boiling water
preferably water-ground	Serves 3 to 4
½ teaspoon salt	

Mix salt and cornmeal. Pour into it, stirring constantly, enough boiling water to make a batter that just holds together, without spreading when placed on the griddle. Have iron griddle or skillet hot but not smoking, grease with bacon rind or bacon fat. Spread batter in one large cake or in smaller cakes three to four inches in diameter, to a thickness of one-half inch. Cook very slowly, turning when well-browned and brown on the other side. This is very much a primitive and fundamental "bread," but the flavor is sweet and nutty, the texture rather ingratiating. The batter may be made thinner, spread on the griddle to a thickness of only one-quarter inch, and in very small cakes, two inches in diameter. These make a good crisp bread for a country or a camp breakfast, served with sausage, ham or bacon. It is good served with butter and Southern cane syrup, for those with a sweet tooth.

Corn pone is hoe cake dressed up a little. One-half cup of flour is used for every cup of cornmeal, a little more salt, milk, or part milk and water used instead of water, two teaspoons of baking powder added for every one and one-half cups of the dry mixture, if sweet milk is used, or one-half teaspoon soda if sour milk or buttermilk. The milk or milk and water is not heated for corn pone. Two tablespoons of melted shortening are added after mixing the other ingredients. Country folk use the fat from white bacon (salt pork), but I prefer a vegetable shortening such as Crisco. The pone is cooked in a deep iron skillet over a slow flame, the batter, just thick enough to hold together, is spread to a depth of one to one and one-half inches, the pone flipped over when well browned on one side, and browned very slowly on the other. It is cut in triangular pieces like pie.

Grits

GRITS are the Deep South member of the hominy family. What the North knows as hominy, we call "big hominy." This is the whole grains of white corn treated, amazingly, with lye, and boiled. Grits are hominy dried and ground fine. They are a staple food in Florida, backwoodsmen eating them three times a day and considering a day without grits, a day wasted. A taste for grits must be cultivated by outsiders, and in any Southern eating place, Yankee tourists may be recognized by their reaction to grits, especially at breakfast. We use them in place of potatoes. Never as a cereal. For the benefit of Northern cooks, they may be found in many grocery

Ibid., pp. 72–73

stores, packaged, and labeled "Hominy Grits." These are coarser than Southern grits.

1 cup grits, washed	1 teaspoon salt
4 cups boiling water	Serves 3 to 4

Stir the grits slowly into the boiling water. Cover and let cook slowly, about thirty to forty minutes, stirring often. There are addicts of "soft grits" for whom more hot water must be added to the cooking mixture. Most of us prefer them of the consistency of mush.

Florida country folk use grits as a base for "gravy." The gravy, unhappily, consists only of the grease from any fat meat, usually that of white bacon (fat salt pork). Rural gravy is one spot where I part company with my neighbors. Grits with butter are a necessity with fried fish. The combination is "a natural." Grits are good served with scrambled eggs, or with a poached egg on top of each serving. A Cross Creek friend horrified me by calling for grits to which he added chopped raw onion and sardines. I tasted dubiously, and remained to gorge.

Hush-Puppies

I DO not know where, among the cornbreads, to place hush-puppies. There are elevated Floridians who turn up their noses at hush-puppies, but any huntsman would not exchange a plate of them for crêpes suzettes. They are made and served only in camp, or when one is frying fresh-caught fish informally at home, with the returned fishermen clustered comfortably in the kitchen while the cook works. Hush-puppies have a background, which is more than many fancy breads can claim. Back of them is the hunt, the fishing trip, the camaraderie, the grease in the Dutch oven aromatic to hungry sportsmen. First, you fry your pristine fish, boned and filleted, rolled in fine cornmeal and salt and dropped into sizzling fat. You lift out the fish, gold-brown, and lay them on pie plates close to the camp fire. While they have been frying, you have stirred up your mixture: fine white cornmeal, salt, a little soda or baking powder, an egg or two or three if the camp be affluent, and, if you want hush-puppies de resistance, finely chipped raw onion. You make the mixture dry and firm. You pat it into little cakes or croquettes between your hands and drop the patties into the smoking deep fat in which the fish have been fried. They brown quickly to the color of winter oak leaves, and you must be sure to have your coffee and any other trifles ready, for when the hush-puppies are brown, your meal is ready.

They must be eaten so hot that they burn the fingers that lift them, for

From *Cross Creek,* by Marjorie Kinnan Rawlings, pp. 209–210. Copyright, 1942, by Marjorie Kinnan Rawlings. New York: Charles Scribner's Sons.

the licking of fingers, as with the Chinese genius who discovered roast pig, is the very best of it. Do they sound impossible? I assure you that under the open sky they are so succulent that you do not care whether you have the rest of your dinner or not. The name? It came, old-timers say, from hunting trips of long ago, when the hunters sat or stood around the camp fire and the Negro cooks and helpers sweat over their cooking and the hunters ate lustily. And although the hunting dogs tethered to nearby trees had been fed their evening meal, they smelled the good smells of man's victuals, and tugged at their leashes, and whined for a tid-bit extra. Then cook or helper or huntsman would toss the left-over little corn patties to the dogs, calling, "Hush, puppies!" And the dogs bolted the toothsome morsels and hushed, in their great content.

Turtle and Cooter

ED AND JEAN HOPKINS introduced me to turtle and cooter and I have blessed them ever since. We have five varieties of turtle in Florida—the rather scarce sea turtle, the hard-shell inland turtle, the alligator cooter, or turtle, the soft-shell cooter, and the so-called "gopher," actually a dusty land turtle. The alligator turtle is close kin to the hard-shell turtle, and perhaps the whitest and sweetest of any of the turtle meats. The alligator turtle takes its name from the ridged shell. It is a vicious creature with an evil beak that can make mince-meat of the hands of the unwary.

Preparing any of the hard-shelled turtles for cooking is the most difficult part of the process. The hard shell must be cut away from the meat, a job calling sometimes for an axe and always for a strong hand. The entrails are discarded, the liver and eggs, if any, being retained. The clawed feet are scalded in boiling water until the tough skin and claws can be slipped off from the meat. The meat is then cut in pieces two to four inches in size and parboiled until thoroughly tender. Add three-quarters teaspoon salt when partly done. Drain. Dip each piece separately in egg batter.

*   *   *   *   *

Drop batter-covered turtle in deep, very hot fat, or in very hot fat to cover in a deep iron skillet.

Soft-shell cooter is prepared in the same way, except that the gelatinous outer edge of the soft shell is scalded until the thin skin can be rubbed off, then cut in two- to four-inch pieces and parboiled with the meat. It is dipped also in the egg batter and deep fried. It has an utterly delicious texture and flavor, but is somehow so rich that no more than two portions should be eaten, under penalty of indigestion. I prefer turtle to fried chicken.

The turtle eggs of all varieties, including the sea turtle, are a great

From *Cross Creek Cookery*, by Marjorie Kinnan Rawlings, pp. 126–129. Copyright, 1942, by Marjorie Kinnan Rawlings. New York: Charles Scribner's Sons.

delicacy. Here and there a Floridian turns up his nose at them, foolishly. Old colored Martha shares my passion for turtle and turtle eggs. I often stop by the road to capture a passing turtle for her, my price for my trouble being always a share of the eggs. They are about the size of golf balls. They are boiled in heavily salted water twenty minutes. The white never solidifies, but the hard-boiled yolk is rich, rather grainy, with a fine and distinct flavor. They are eaten "out of hand," from the shell, breaking off the top of the shell, dotting the egg with salt and pepper and butter, and popping the contents of the shell directly into the mouth. A dozen turtle eggs, with plain bread and butter and a glass of ale, make all I ask of a light luncheon or supper.

The deep-sea turtles lay in summer at the foot of the sand dunes along our coast, so cleverly that only the expert can find the eggs. I have watched a three-hundred-pound turtle lumber in from the sea on a moonlit July night, crawl slowly to the foot of a dune, leaving a track that looks as though a small tractor had passed, dig her nest with her flippers, lay her eggs over a period of a couple of hours, cover the nest and pack down the sand with her hind flippers—and still been hard put to it to find the eggs. Perhaps two feet under the main cavity dug for the nest, she has hollowed a narrow passage at a sharp angle, and here lie the eggs. I have counted as many as one hundred and thirty-five. Conservationists make a habit of leaving at least half of the eggs in the nest. The selfish and greedy take them all, and the criminal have been known to kill the turtle and take out the eggs, rather than discommode themselves by waiting for her to lay. There is now a hundred-dollar fine for this ruthless practice, but the perpetrators are hard to catch.

Hoppin John

SOUTH CAROLINIANS, like my husband, who have been away from home a long time, if they feel a culinary homesickness, always long for something called Hoppin John, with the accent on the John. This substantial dish is as characteristic of South Carolina as are baked beans of Massachusetts. Indeed, it is a dish which performs the same functions. It is made with what are known in the South as cow peas. It may be impossible to secure these in the North, but black beans might be substituted for the cow peas.

Lettie Gay says of this dish: "We were able to get the cow peas (which look to us far more like beans than peas!) and Hoppin John was made. For our tastes the dish seemed a bit flavorless and rather starchy, but

By Mrs. T. J. Woodward. From *200 Years of Charleston Cooking*, Recipes Gathered by Blanche S. Rhett, edited by Lettie Gay, Introduction and Explanatory Matter by Helen Woodward, pp. 58–59. Copyright, 1930, by Jonathan Cape and Harrison Smith, Inc. New York. By permission of Random House, New York.

seasonings may be added and it should be served accompanied with a green salad."

3 tablespoons bacon drippings	2 cups cow peas
Salt to taste	1 cup uncooked rice
3 cups water in which peas were cooked	

Boil the peas until they are tender. Add the rice and bacon drippings and enough of the water in which the peas were boiled to steam the rice (about three cups). Cook over a slow fire for one hour. This serves six.

Pot Liquor

A MUCH sought for dish upon such occasions [as harvests] was "pot liquor," a product of the times of great abundance. "Laws a mussy, chile, whar has yo' bin all dis time widout knowin' w'at pot liquor is," said an old Negro mammy to an inquisitive one who was a stranger to the customs of old time Virginia harvests.

"Ef yo' war to drink a gourd full uv ol' Missus' pot liquor yo' jes' hanker fo' mo'. Dat yo' would!"

"Pot liquor" was not of as humble origin as its name implies. During occasions which demanded "big dinners," a whole ham, or possibly two, were placed in a big pot of water and suspended from the chimney crane over the fire. When the meat was partly cooked, cabbages were added, and later peeled potatoes were placed in the pot, and when these vegetables were partly cooked, corn meal dumplings were added, and after all were sufficiently cooked together, they were taken out and a handful of corn meal was sprinkled over the pot liquor and allowed to cook a few minutes. The pot liquor was thus seasoned with juicy, fat ham, scraps of the cabbages, potatoes, and corn meal dumplings, and thickened with corn meal. It needed no other seasoning, and was superior in flavor and strength of nourishment to the many soups of the present day cooking.

Kentucky Ham

THE preparation of ham in Kentucky is a ritual. It begins with the feeding of the hog, preferably on nuts; chestnuts used to be a requisite, but alas! the chestnut is gone. After killing, the ham must be smoked with the smudge

---

From *Life in Old Virginia*, A Description of Virginia, More Particularly the Tidewater Section . . . , by James J. McDonald, edited by J. A. C. Chandler, p. 235. Copyright, 1907, by the Old Virginia Publishing Company, Inc. Norfolk, Virginia.

From *"Weep No More, My Lady,"* by Alvin F. Harlow, pp. 283–284, 285–287. Copyright, 1942, by Alvin F. Harlow. Whittlesey House, McGraw-Hill Book Company, Inc. New York.

from a smoldering fire of sugar or hickory chips, hickory bark or corn cobs, the sweet juices in those fuels theoretically contributing to the flavor. (Did you know that you can make excellent imitation maple syrup from corn-cobs or the bark of shagbark hickory? My mother, an ardent experimenter in cookery, did it more than once.) Sassafras is used by some for smoking, but frowned upon by others.

Next, the ham is hung up in a ventilated room, sometimes an attic, to season from one to three years or more. No Kentuckian considers a ham worth eating that is under a year old. By the time it is ready, it is covered thickly with mold, and the uninitiated would shudder at the thought of eating it. But the expert knows better. He thrusts an icepick in along the bone, examines the pick and passes it thoughtfully under his nose. Like the famous testers of wine and coffee, he cannot be fooled.

Aging brings out the valued white flecks which appear in hams of super-lative quality. The hostess who serves such a ham is proud of it, but the ignorant outlander shies from it in apprehension. A favorite story in Ken-tucky is that of the family who sent one of these hams to a Northern friend as a Christmas gift. They heard nothing from it for weeks, and finally ventured to ask whether it had been received. Back came an apologetic letter. The recipients had been so embarrassed that they just didn't know what to write. They appreciated the loving thoughtfulness that prompted the gift, but the painful fact was that when they cut into the ham, they found that it was spoiled; it had white spots in it—and so they had to con-sign it to the incinerator!

Now the ham having passed its entrance exams, the next thing is to scrub it with mild soapsuds and brush to eliminate the mold, then rinse it again and again. Incidentally, when you peel off the skin, you do not throw it away. Pieces of it are fine for flavoring beans, greens, and cabbage, for there are many Southerners who still insist that those vegetables are prac-tically inedible unless cooked with pork in some form.

"Let's go over to Hardin's," suggested an acquaintance in Frankfort, "and have some old-fashioned Kentucky food for lunch." So we went over, and there was Hardin himself in full view through the big serving window, carving and dishing up the meats, which are his special care; a good-looking, clear-skinned man, made roly-poly by devotion to the art of cookery.

*   *   *   *   *

"The packing houses don't put out hams like that," said Hardin. "I don't mean to say the biggest hams are necessarily the best. Sometimes they're coarse-grained, especially if they weigh thirty-five to forty pounds. I buy all my hams myself, and I inspect every one. The icepick will tell you whether a ham's sound or got bugs in it, if you know your business. I examine 'em for fine grain and tenderness, too.

"I think a year and a quarter to two years is the right age for a ham. Hog-killin' time here comes with the first cold snap in early winter, you know, and a ham smoked, say, in November, 1940, I'd be willing to begin using in the spring of 1942. By summer, it would be still better. After two years, the meat begins to get strong and firm up too much for my taste."

From experience, I agree with him; but there are many Kentuckians who like their ham well aged and potent. Old Sarah, the colored cook at the John Brown mansion in Frankfort, told me, "We got hams upstairs now dat's three yeahs old; I 'spect some of 'em fo'! Hang right up in de top of de house, wid open places where de wind can blow thoo—no, suh, dey don't spoil, only des one once in a long while. . . ."

But it is in the cooking of the ham that Kentucky splits into factions, some of them consisting of only one family.

"The kind I pick need to be soaked only overnight," maintains Hardin. "I have a huge covered roaster for these big ones. I like to have water enough in the roaster to cover them at first, but with a thirty-two-pounder, that's impossible. In the water I put a half a cup of sugar, half a cup of vinegar, half a cup of pineapple juice, one apple, an onion, a handful of cloves, and some bay leaves. It takes maybe half an hour to bring the water to a boil, and I boil it for an hour longer. Then opening the roaster, I snatch it out of the oven, wrap it tight in blankets, and set it away for twenty-four hours. That fireless cooking is what makes the perfect job."

"In Bourbon County, where they have the best food in the world," said an elderly lady next day when I told her of this, "they have a somewhat similar technic, only they bake the ham in an open pan. At the proper time, the cook takes the pan out and sets it on the floor, covers the ham thickly with brown paper, and then with rugs and blankets, and lets it stand twenty-four to thirty-hours."

As for the liquor in which it is cooked, you will probably find more than as many recipes as there are counties in Kentucky. A doctor in Barren County told me that in his neighborhood there must be, among other things in the cooking water, two ears of hickory cane corn—a slender, long-eared variety now little known.

But disquieting heresy has appeared in far-western Trigg County, where they smoke hams for the market. Here the formula for the baking liquor is one quart of water, one quart of (of all things!) ginger ale, and a pint of sorghum molasses. Here is flat modernism, maybe even communism. What did our grandfathers know about ginger ale? Trigg County goes on to direct that after the ham is tender, the skin be peeled off, being careful not to bring the fat with it. Then you mark off little squares in the fat with a knife, stick a clove in the middle of each, smear mustard over the surface, pat on a cup and a half of brown sugar, and return the ham to the oven until the sugar melts.

That great culinary expert, George Rector, would say that all this is just window dressing. He heard a man offer to bet that a ham boiled in ink would be just as good as one boiled in champagne. The wager was taken, the two hams were so cooked, and nobody could tell the difference! The layer of fat, says Mr. Rector, prevents the surrounding liquid from reaching the lean meat, and only a slice or two of the lard end of the ham is affected by it. But try telling that to anyone in Kentucky!

Creole Cookery

CREOLE cooking to-day is found at its best in the vicinity of New Orleans and in the Teche country; but its excellencies may be enjoyed throughout southern Louisiana and in all other parts of the State where the French influence has penetrated.

Nature has been exceptionally kind to the Louisiana cook. Vegetables in great variety are available throughout the year. Among those usually unfamiliar to visitors are: the *mirliton* (vegetable pear), which is prepared in the same way as squash or egg plant, and frequently stuffed with crabmeat or shrimp; okra, used as an alternative for *filé* in gumbo; and cushaw (neck pumpkin), usually cut in squares and baked in the skin, or mashed and baked in a casserole. Fresh- and salt-water fish, shrimp, oysters, crabs, crayfish, turtles, and frogs are plentiful and cheap. Formerly, when game was sold at markets, snipe, quail, grouse, wild turkey, deer, raccoon, opossum, and a wide variety of wildfowl were important items in the Creole menu. Now, only rabbits, raccoon, and opossum may be sold, and the housewife's supply of game depends upon her husband's hunting.

Well stocked as the larder may be, it is the seasoning that makes Creole food distinctive. Onions, garlic, bay leaf, celery, red, green, black and cayenne pepper, parsley, thyme, shallots, basil, cloves, nutmeg, and allspice are used in different combinations. Several of the most important of these items are often bundled in a "seasoning bunch" and sold at vegetable markets for five or ten cents. The various seasonings are mixed in a *roux,* the basis of many Creole dishes, which is made by the careful browning of flour in melted butter or lard. With patient simmering, the ingredients blend in a composite seasoning. A condiment much in use, and one contributed by the "German Creoles," is "Creole mustard," a preparation made locally of distilled vinegar, salt, and mustard seed imported from Austria and Holland. It has a distinct horseradish flavor.

Gravies and sauces abound. Besides the bottled preparations, the manufacture of which is an important Louisiana industry, there are tomato, wine, tartar, barbecue, cocktail, and numerous other piquant mixtures. The tendency is towards hot condiments, and the visitor early learns to respect what in local restaurant parlance is termed "hot stuff," a pepper sauce manufactured in Louisiana from cayenne or tabasco pepper. The peppers are grown principally in the parishes of St. Martin, Iberia, and Lafayette. One of the earliest of the hot sauces was named after Maunsel White, a planter who was very fond of the raw oysters served at the old Gem Restaurant in New Orleans and who carried with him a small bottle of sauce made by his slaves.

From *Louisiana,* A Guide to the State, compiled by Workers of the Writers' Program of the Work Projects Administration in the State of Louisiana, pp. 225–228. American Guide Series. Copyright, 1941, by the Louisiana Library Commission at Baton Rouge. New York: Hastings House, Publishers.

In the preparation of sea food Creole cuisine is at its best. Mark Twain spoke of the pompano cooked in Louisiana as being "delicious as the less criminal forms of sin," and Thackeray and Irvin S. Cobb found New Orleans *bouillabaisse* unexcelled. The latter is a fish chowder made of two kinds of fish, usually redfish and red snapper, cooked with crabs, crayfish, shrimp, wine, and appropriate seasoning. Redfish prepared as a *court-bouillon* is a similar but simpler dish. Crayfish bisque is a soup full of crayfish heads stuffed with the meat of the tails. Boiled crayfish are also popular. In season, Negroes line the highways to sell their catch to passing motorists. Oysters are eaten on the half shell, in cocktails, fried, baked, stewed, stuffed, in soup, in dressings, and à la Rockefeller. With crabs and shrimp, they are cooked in gumbo, the most distinctive Creole dish. Chicken, veal, or ham are often substituted for shellfish in gumbo, but the basic recipe remains the same, a thick soup prepared with okra or *filé*. The Creole, it has been said, puts everything into gumbo except the Creole. Gombo Zhèbes, a herb gumbo made with seven greens and salt meat or ham, is considered a lucky dish to eat on Holy Thursday. Shrimp (river and lake) and crabs are served in many ways. The latter are considered more of a delicacy in the soft-shell state. "Soft-shells" and "busters" (shedding crabs from which the old shell is pried off) are coated with cracker meal and fried in deep fat. They are then devoured, shell and all. Soft-shell turtle is another delicacy. Frog legs are fried a golden brown and served on crisp lettuce with tartar sauce and lemon.

In addition to sea food, game, and domestic fowl, there are a variety of roasts, and such elaborate dishes as *daube glacée,* jellied veal made with pig's and calf's feet. The French trait of economy is often called upon to balance an over-drawn budget, in which case *soup-en-famille* is cooked. This is a vegetable soup cooked with *bouilli,* a beef brisket, which is served hot or cold, garnished with the vegetables of the soup.

Rice is used by Louisianians as Irish potatoes are used elsewhere. Every Creole dinner includes rice, whether it be served with red beans (a good-luck dish on Monday) or gumbo, as *riz au lait* (a dessert made of rice boiled in milk), in *jambalaya* (rice cooked with ham, sausage, shrimp, or oysters), or simply with gravy. A degree of skill is required to bring out the full tastiness of rice. The best results are obtained by boiling it rapidly without stirring in salted water until tender, rinsing with cold water, and steaming in a colander over boiling water until the grains stand apart. *Calas tout chaud,* an old favorite, are hot rice cakes fried in deep fat and sprinkled with powdered sugar. They were once sold by Negro street hawkers along with *batons amandes* (almond sticks), and *estomacs mulâtres* (mulatto stomachs), a kind of gingerbread made with flour and cane syrup. *Pain-patate,* a kind of cake made of sweet potatoes was also sold on the streets. To-day a popular dish in New Orleans restaurants is *pommes soufflées,* puffed Irish potatoes.

Grits (hominy) is to breakfast what rice is to dinner. There are two varieties—yellow and white—and two grades—coarse and fine. Coarse white grits is considered best, but whatever kind is used, it is broiled as a mush and served with eggs, bacon, sausage, liver, or *grillades* (cooked veal squares). Leftover grits is sliced and fried. Stale bread is made into *pain perdu* (lost bread). A favorite breakfast dish of the Acadians is *coush-coush caillé* (cornbread and clabber). Another popular dairy product is cream cheese, made of clabber drained in perforated molds.

The perfect complement to a Creole meal is Creole dripped coffee. It is brewed to perfection in New Orleans; but though good coffee can be had in most homes in Louisiana, it is not always at its best in restaurants and cafes, connoisseurs being able to reckon their distance from New Orleans by the quality of the coffee they drink in the hinterland. Many natives will not travel without a supply of coffee and their own coffee pot. There is an old Creole saying that "good coffee and the Protestant religion can seldom if ever be found together." Creole coffee differs from "Northern" coffee in that it is a darker roast, is ground finer for dripping, and contains 10 to 20 per cent chicory, from which it derives body. It is best described by an old adage:

Noir comme le Diable,	Black as the devil,
Fort comme la mort,	Strong as death,
Doux comme l'amour,	Sweet as love,
Chaud comme l'enfer!	Hot as Hell!

A taste for it has to be acquired, as does the art of making it. For each cup of coffee a tablespoon of coffee is placed in the strainer of a drip pot. A spoonful of boiling water at a time is slowly, very slowly, dripped through the grounds. Once dripped, the coffee must never be allowed to boil. To be good, the *café noir* thus made should be strong enough to stain a cup. *Café au lait* (coffee with milk) is coffee to which hot milk, not cream, is added, the proportion being about half and half. *Brioche,* a local coffee cake, is an excellent accompaniment. At formal dinners, and during the holiday season, *café brûlot* is served, a mixture of coffee, spices, citrus peel, and burning brandy; it creates an effective scene when the lights are turned out and the shadows play on the faces of the guests.

Burgoo

BURGOO is another story peculiarly Kentuckian. That word was originally the sailor's name for oatmeal porridge as we youngsters used to eat it, with sugar and milk. But trust Kentucky to give it distinction! In that wilful climate, it came to mean something that was neither liquid nor solid, neither soup, hash, nor goulash, but partook of the nature of all of them.

How it originated is lost in mystery. Gus Jaubert, a Lexington chef, com-

From *"Weep No More, My Lady,"* by Alvin F. Harlow, pp. 289–292. Copyright, 1942, by Alvin F. Harlow. Whittlesey House, McGraw-Hill Book Company, Inc. New York.

pounded a mess of it for General Morgan and his hungry cavalrymen at one time during the Civil War; just grabbed up what this and that soldier brought in from his foraging—chickens, ducks, corn, potatoes, wild greens, peppers, et cetera. Some have claimed that this was the birth of burgoo, but not so; one finds mention of it in print thirty years before that. There are almost as many ways of making it as there are Kentuckians. The idea of most burgoo makers is to put in everything but the kitchen stove. One old-timer specifies that it must have squirrel, quail, pa't'idge, pheasant, wild turkey, field corn, barley, tomatoes, flour, celery, turnips, butter, cream, and—well, a little dash of Bourbon wouldn't do it any harm. But the really top-ranking burgoo artists say firmly, only three meats.

Everything is mixed together with plenty of water and cooked and cooked until the meat has all disintegrated and the whole has been reduced to a sort of paste, still nearly enough liquid to be inhaled out of a tin cup, though for those who shrink from making sounds like a pump emptying the last pint of water from an excavation, spoons are nearly always served with the cups. It is far better to eat than it sounds, and when it is served at a big public speaking or other occasion, it's just as free as branch water. The neighbors even used to send boys over with buckets to bring some home for family use. As a persuader in Kentucky politics and civics, burgoo has been well-nigh as widely used as barbecue. Major Gordon of the western Kentucky coal region tells us that he took a whole trunkful of it, kept red hot in thermos jars, all the way to Washington once.

"What for?" we wonder.

"To bribe the National Coal Commission," he confesses, frankly. But when further questioned, he admits gloomily that it didn't work. When Colonel Bennett H. Young and others were promoting the Louisville Southern Railroad in 1886, they strove to induce counties through which the line was projected to buy bonds. For two solid weeks Colonel Young, Judge Hoke, and others stumped well-to-do Anderson County, orating daily from 10 A.M. until nigh supper-time, with burgoo served to the crowd at noon. But those Anderson folk were Kentuckians and stubborn; though stuffed to the gills with burgoo, they didn't vote the bonds. A year later, just to show that they were not susceptible to cajolery, but would do things at their own time and in their own way, they changed their attitude, and the road was eventually built.

Gus Jaubert, a skinny Lexington Frenchman—to Kentucky he was never Zho-behr' as his father would have pronounced it, but just plain Gus Jawbert —was the State's chief burgoo maker in the latter nineteenth century and even into the twentieth. He officiated at political rallies, picnics, religious encampments, and big Bluegrass farm and stock sales. If we are to believe those who knew him, he had one colossal kettle that held 700 gallons, another 300. He undertook what is claimed to have been the greatest barbecue in history, during the Grand Army of the Republic encampment at Louisville in 1895, when he prepared to serve 100,000 people. To this end, he brewed 6,000 gallons of burgoo and barbecued enough steers, sheep, and pigs to stock a county. The attendance was disappointing and there were hundreds of gallons of burgoo untasted.

Gus's meats were lean beef, chicken, and rabbit. When he died, Jim Looney, also of Lexington, succeeded him as No. 1 burgoo maker to the State. Into a little 1,200-gallon mess of burgoo for an ordinary Democratic political rally Jim puts 600 pounds of beef, 200 pounds of chickens, a ton, no less, of potatoes, 840 pounds of canned tomatoes, and smaller but still colossal quantities of onions, cabbage, carrots, and corn. "In season," he adds twelve dozen squirrels. Red pepper, salt, and a dash of a mysterious condiment which he himself prepares complete the heavenly brew, and it is cooked fifteen or twenty hours.

Loony prepared burgoo for Colonel E. R. Bradley's charity race day at his Idle Hour Farm some years ago. It was cool that evening and every drop of the stuff was licked up. "Jim, you're the burgoo King," exclaimed Colonel Bradley, "that's the greatest eating in the world. I'm going to name a colt after you," and so he did in a back-handed way. Instead of Jim Looney, the colt was christened Burgoo King, and it won the Derby in 1932.

Looney has gone as far away as Vermont to show the Yankees the savoriness of a product which has been so peculiarly Kentucky's that when a delegation of Philadelphians came over in 1892 to help celebrate the State's centenary anniversary and were told at Lexington that they were to be given "a burgoo," they hadn't the faintest notion what it meant. In the small hours of the night, as they lay in the old Phoenix Hotel, a peacock, which for some reason was being kept in a rear courtyard, screamed raucously, and one guest, awakened by it, nudged his bedfellow and said, "That must be that burgoo."

Hardin, the Frankfort chef, has a houseboat on the Kentucky River, and confesses to an interest in cockfighting. Once, he and about fifteen of his friends, most of them owners of birds, attended a cocking main near Lexington, and when it was over, ten or twelve of their champions had died a Spartan's death. Having the chicken ingredient already on hand, Hardin suggested preparing a mess of burgoo on his boat. "We calculated," says he, "that that was the most expensive burgoo ever made. The chicken alone, counting the value of the birds and the bets we lost on them, figured up to more than $500."

Barbecue and Fish Muddle

I [1]

MAJOR MAURICE K. GORDON, the historian of Hopkins County, tells how, on the very earliest monthly court days out there, when the court sat in the log home of Robert McGary, barbecue pits had been dug in advance, and on green poles over them, Negroes were roasting venison, mutton, and wild

---

[1] *Ibid.*, pp. 288–289.

turkey and compounding gravy, all of which Mrs. McGary kept hot on the wide kitchen hearth, where she baked quantities of hoe cakes and sweet potatoes as accompaniment. There would always be a barrel of persimmon beer and two tubs of cider, one hard, the other with fermentation checked by mustard seed, all drunk from gourd dippers. An all-day shooting match staged near by entertained those not at the moment engaged in court, and some who had come for no other purpose.

You couldn't call it a really Grade A political rally in Kentucky in other days unless there was a barbecue or a mess of burgoo. But the days of the barbecue as our fathers knew it are over. Somehow or other—and how it happened in a Kentucky Legislature passes understanding—a law was passed a few years ago forbidding the cooking of meat by wholesale in the open air, on the flimsy ground that such procedure isn't sanit'ry. Tears started to the eyes of old Kentuckians the other day when they saw in the rotogravure section a picture of Governor W. Lee (Pass the Biscuits, Pappy) O'Daniel of Texas gloating over the barbecue pits at a public function down there. "To think," they moaned, "that Texas should ever be freer than Kentucky!"

II [2]

Barbecue and fish muddle put the eating customs and the drinking customs of the people together. Both are dishes which have no direct relationship to drinking. Both go with coleslaw and corn pone. Barbecue, which in North Carolina contends with the hamburger and the hot dog at roadside eating stands, is pig roasted, preferably over a pit full of coals, and basted with a peppery sauce while it roasts. Fish muddle is a name for fish stew, the ingredients of which vary with what you have got. Brunswick stew is a thick vegetable stew, which in the old days used to depend upon squirrels for protein content. Both the meat and vegetable content may be altered without departing from the name. All of these are the dishes of congregation, of the political rally, the country get-together, the big entertainment of customers and friends. Each dish may be served on the table at home. Each of them may be, along with fried chicken, pies and cakes and boiled eggs, at the church supper. But the barbecues and the fish muddles (both are the names for the gatherings as well as the dishes), in the eastern part of the State, where they are most often held, are occasions for both eating and drinking—and sometimes a little too much of both. But when men gather at the plank tables under the big trees near the smell of the pigs roasting in the pits, North Carolina is probably present in the truest and most native fashion ever to be found in the State. Barbecue is a dish which binds together the taste of both the people of the big house and the poorest occupants of the back end of the broken-down barn.

------

[2] From *Tar Heels, A Portrait of North Carolina*, by Jonathan Daniels, pp. 257–258. Sovereign States Series. Copyright, 1941, by Jonathan Daniels. New York: Dodd, Mead & Company.

II. SOUTHERN LIGHTS AND SHADOWS

The fiddle, the rifle, the ax and the Bible, the palladium of American liberty, symbolizing music, prowess, labor, and free religion, the four grand forces of our civilization, were the trusty friends and faithful allies of our pioneer ancestry in subduing the wilderness and erecting the great commonwealths of the Republic.
—ROBERT LOVE TAYLOR

The men mostly, I grieve to say, enjoyed, among other things, a horse-race more than the weekly prayer-meeting, and a set-to of thoroughbred game chickens more than a lecture on foreign missions.—ZEBULON BAIRD VANCE

1. IDYLLS AND ORGIES

JOHN BERNARD's story of the old-time Southern planter, who, by an ingenious invention, managed to combine the "four staple enjoyments of bathing, drinking, shooting, and fishing," only to be transformed into a "human alligator" by his hunger for companionship, is a *reductio ad absurdum* of the Southern dualism of hedonism and violence. In our "land of extremes" the South traditionally represents the extremes of content and unrest, of languor and hot blood. A case in point is Sheriff Jeff McCurtain in Erskine Caldwell's *Trouble in July*, who always went fishing when trouble (like a lynching) threatened because "going fishing" was the "only means he had of escaping from a controversial matter."

Clarence Cason makes much of this Southern trait of "going fishing" as a symbol of the Southerner's emancipation "from the everlasting inner demand that he improve his earthly position."[1] This is the "hedonism" which W. J. Cash explains as a corollary of the freedom from labor or the necessity of toil that characterized frontier Southern life in its upper and lower brackets: in other words, if you were a planter aristocrat, you didn't have to work; and if you were a poor white, you didn't have any work, or assiduously avoided it.[2]

The Southerner's "tendency to build up legends about [himself]" goes hand in hand with his tendency "to translate these legends into explosive action." For if one spends one's unlimited leisure in hell-raising and thinking (and making other people think) what a hell of a fellow one is (with one's hard drinking, hard loving, hard fighting—everything except hard work), the ego is bound to assert itself in the "chip-on-shoulder swagger and brag of a boy . . . of which the essence was the boast, voiced or not, on the part of every Southerner, that he would knock hell out of whoever dared to cross him.[3]

The norm of Southern sports and pastimes lies somewhere between the

---

[1] *90° in the Shade* (Chapel Hill, 1935), p. 6.
[2] *The Mind of the South* (New York, 1941), p. 47.
[3] *Ibid.*, pp. 50–51, 42–43.

stickily sentimental pastoral of Governor Bob Taylor's "Candy-Pulling" and the sweaty, orgiastic fights, wrestling-matches, gander-pullings, camp-meetings, and frolics that made up the stock-in-trade of Southern humorists of the mid-nineteenth century.

> In the bright, bright hereafter [writes Taylor], when all the joys of all the ages are gathered up and condensed into globules of transcendent ecstasy, I doubt whether there will be anything half so sweet as were the candy-smeared, ruby lips of the country maidens to the jeans-jacketed swains who tasted them at the candy-pulling in the happy long ago.[4]

One is on just such a middle ground in Washington Irving's rough notes on "Polly Holman's Wedding," a "buxom" account of a wedding frolic in the Green River country of Kentucky, which parallels his description of the frolic in "The Early Experiences of Ralph Ringwood" but with an unbowdlerized "robustness and lustiness [according to J. Frank Dobie] that must have been inherent in the . . . language" of Governor William Duval, of Florida, from whom Irving seems to have heard the tale.[5]

> He [John] drew her [Ruby] on floor, called Coy come Coy play Old sinner lick the ladle—& Ill have another dance come off one—I was sitting on a chest by a stout girl she laughed till her breath was gone then striking me between the shoulders, exclaimed—O L^d—that John is so comical Coy having taken a little more whiskey—ran his tunes into one another. . . . An hour after night the couple retired. company went in the men —— —— with the girls until the groom threw the stocking. Then returned sat round fire. Sparked —every man his lass on his knee—told stories—sang songs—till broad day light.[6]

Of all Southern sports and pastimes, not even excepting coon and possum hunting, the one that seems to be most peculiarly Southern in its combination of ease and excitement is the "auditory" hunting of the fox chase, described by Charles Morrow Wilson as "based upon a sort of gentlemen's agreement between hound and fox to provide a night's entertainment for both, with man as a reclining spectator." [7] The poor man's fox hunt, the fox chase combines the excitement of the hunt with love of talk and story-telling, as the masters of the hounds sit around the fire, swapping yarns and comments while listening to and identifying the hounds and following the progress of the chase with expert knowledge of the ways of dogs and foxes.

Amidst the shifting lights and shadows of Southern hunting folkways, the merry fox chase (imitated by many a fiddler and mouth-harp virtuoso) burns brightly with the love of dogs and men, making one forget, for the moment, that man is the hunted as well as the hunter.

---

[4] Cited by Vachel Lindsay, in "Preface to 'Bob Taylor's Birthday,'" *Collected Poems* (New York, 1925), p. 408.

[5] "John C. Duval: First Texas Man of Letters," *Southwest Review*, Vol. XXIV (April, 1939), No. 3, p. 258n.

[6] Stanley T. Williams and Ernest E. Leisy, editors, "Polly Holman's Wedding, Notes by Washington Irving," *Southwest Review*, Vol. XIX (July, 1934), No. 4, pp. 449–454.

[7] *Backwoods America* (Chapel Hill, 1935), pp. 102–113.

2. Darker Phases of the South

Discussing with Marie Campbell the "dark side" of mountain life— "liquor, feuding, politics, and sex"—one old Kentucky mountaineer put his finger on their dark mystery and tragedy as follows: "Whenever folks goes a mite too fur in them things, what they git conjured off inter doing air a sorry tale to tell." [8]

This fatalistic philosophy of violence is of a piece with the "stern and selfish conception of justice" that Maude Minish Sutton encountered in a Blue Ridge patriarch with whom she discussed the "consequences of sin." Here the notion of "private justice" is supplemented and transcended by divine and poetic justice, in which a man's crime is "mighty apt to come out on him," vengeance is obtained by prayer, miracles bring the guilty to justice, and the murdered man cannot rest in peace until he is avenged.

On January 12, 1948, "Fiddlin' Bill" Hensley, seventy-five-year-old champion fiddler of Avery's Creek township, in western North Carolina, walked to the home of Paul Alexander, about half a mile away, and said: "Get somebody to call the ambulance, Paul. I had a little trouble up at the house and I reckon I killed a man."

On the last day of his trial, before the jury brought in a verdict of guilty of second-degree murder, "The Old Gray Eagle" (as he is known from his favorite fiddle tune) took the stand and testified that—

. . . He was alone in his cabin January 12 when Harwood "showed up at 2 o'clock and said he wanted some whisky." He said he told the younger man he did not sell whisky but would give him some, and that he and Harwood, "who, if I ever saw before, I don't recall it," sat and drank for about four hours.

Describing the fight that led to the slaying, Hensley said:

"He said he was goin' to kill me and grabbed me, and we went to the floor. He was on top of me and beatin' me about the head and face. As we scuffled around and got closer to the gunrack this man pulled my pistol out of the holster and began shootin' around my head. I kept dodgin', fust one way and then t'other, and every time he shot, I thought the next one would kill me shore. I kept strugglin' and I was bad scared. Finally, I managed to get out from under him enough to reach up and grab my shotgun, which was on the same rack about the holster, and I pushed him away toward the chair, and when he saw me pullin' the gun from the rack he lunged at me and I fired the gun about level, afore I got it up to my shoulder, and he fell back in the chair.

"I shot in self-defense. . . . I'm sorry. . . ." [9]

B. A. B.

[8] Marie Campbell, "Liquor Ballads from the Kentucky Mountains," *Southern Folklore Quarterly*, Vol. 2 (September, 1938), No. 3, p. 157.

[9] The Asheville *Citizen*, February 19, 1948, p. 5.

Peculiar Ways

How the Old-Time Planter Captured a Guest

DURING summer he used to rise about nine, when he exerted himself to walk as far as his stables to look at the stud which he kept for the races; at ten he breakfasted on coffee, eggs, and hoe-cake, concluding it with the commencement of his diurnal potations—a stiff glass of mint-sling—a taking disorder peculiar to the South. He then sought the coolest room and stretched himself on a pallet in his shirt and trousers, with a Negress at his head and another at his feet to keep off the flies and promote reflection. Between twelve and one his throat would require another emulsion, and he would sip half a pint of some mystery termed bumbo, apple-toddy, or pumpkin flip. He then mounted a pony, and, with an umbrella over his head, rode gently round his estate to converse with his overseers. At three he dined, and drank everything—brandy, claret, cider, Madeira, punch, and sangaree, then resumed his pallet, with his Negresses, and meditated until tea-time—though he was not particular about tea, unless friends with womenkind dropped in. The inflammation in his throat returned about dusk, and he prescribed for himself cooling washes until bedtime. From this detail the reader will surmise that a planter was a reptile only to be preserved in spirits; but I must guard against the error that he was by choice a solitary toper. On the contrary, he strained every nerve to pick up companions, and it was only when in utter despair of obtaining this pleasure that he gave himself up to bumbo, Dinah, a mattress, and meditation. Many humorous instances were related to me of the plans he adopted to draw guests to his convivial roof in the untracked woods of the interior. One of the most striking was the following:

On the morning of "a clear day"—a decided scorcher—he would order a wagon to be packed with a tub containing bottles of every compound in his closets—sling, nog, flip, and toddy, together with their elements, spirits, lemons, sugar, etc.; a pair of rifles, shot, and powder; a fishing-rod and tackle; soap, towels, clean linen and nankeens; and a canvas awning with poles and cords to support it. He then took his seat in the vehicle, and, attended by a train of blacks, was driven slowly to the nearest highway, along which he proceeded till he came to a clear, clay-bottomed pond. The wagon was then backed into the water where the depth was breast-high, the poles were firmly driven into the bottom, the awning stretched over

From *Retrospections of America, 1797–1811*, by John Bernard, edited from the Manuscript by Mrs. Bayle Bernard, with an Introduction, Notes, and Index by Laurence Hutton and Brander Matthews, pp. 150–153. Copyright, 1886, by Harper & Brothers. New York. 1887.

them, and the horses being turned into the woods, the proprietor disarrayed himself and descended into this local bath. After amusing himself with a few minutes' splashing, a board was slid down from the wagon to support him in a recumbent position, and the tub, like a richly freighted West-Indiaman, was committed to the deep and moored beside him.

Arrangements were now made for the business of the day: while one ebony was placed in charge of the cattle, another carried out a line from his floating fishing-rod, standing ready to give him notice of a bite; a third placed his rifles on the tub, that he might pop at the first bird that offered; and two others were despatched in opposite directions to watch if travellers were approaching. Thus combining the four staple enjoyments of bathing, drinking, shooting, and fishing, this Western Sardanapalus marked the furnace in the skies burn away, but not with a contented heart. He sighed for a victim; his toils were spread and he hungered for his prey. In the deep solitude that reigned around, his ear was triply alive to human sounds; the creak of a cartwheel had more music for him than the finest notes of a thrush, and the sight of any person, not a Negro, more beauty than the loveliest landscape. If at length the form of a stranger appeared, he sprang from his plank and shouted an invitation to alight and take a drop of something sociable. If the traveller refused, up went the rifle to his shoulder, and compliance was demanded in the tone of a European footpad. The stranger now saw that pleasure was policy, however urgent might be his business; but if he were so unguarded as to yield to his next request to "strip and take a swim," he speedily found himself irretrievably in the clutches of this human alligator. The planter fixed in him all the claws of nog, flip, sling, and toddy, until the brain of the victim became so confused that the grinning Negroes had no difficulty in stowing him into the wagon, whereupon the poles were struck, the horses buckled in, and the delighted planter returned home with his prize, whom he probably cooped up in a back-room with a *chevaux-de-frise* of bottles, until, by some desperate effort, the captive made his escape.

Another and more civilized plan was to send the Negroes round at nightfall to the nearest inns (here very properly termed "ordinaries"), with a note to any lady or gentleman who might be putting up there, stating that if they did not like their accommodation, Mr. —— would be happy to see them at his house close by, to which a black with a lantern would conduct them. This system was often successful; for, in the old times, all you could obtain at these places were eggs and bacon, hoe-cake, and peach brandy; a bed stuffed with shavings, on a frame that rocked like a cradle, and in a room so well ventilated that a traveller had some difficulty in keeping his umbrella erect, if endeavoring, under this convenience, to find shelter from the rain while in bed. But as the planter's hospitality proved such an antagonist to the landlord's interests, the latter always had it made up to him in presents, so that all parties were well content; and, probably, the only sufferer in the end was the cerebellum of the guest. Whether the decline of such a spirit may be deplored or not, it is not to be wondered at. As emigrants began to pour into the woods a planter had seldom occasion to lift his rifle to his shoulder in demanding their society, but, on the contrary, he probably soon obtained those who required some such gesticulation to be got rid of.

I was much amused by a story I once heard of a proprietor sending to an inn one evening, when he was in unusually good spirits, to desire the company of any stray gentleman who would so far favor him; and his sable Mercury returning with a New England preacher who was journeying on a crusade against slavery, and who immediately commenced tracing a comparison between the planter and Beelzebub, which lasted until daylight.

Plantation Ways

I. Bells and Horns [1]

I CAN see Old Master setting out under a big tree, smoking one of his long cheroots his tobacco nigger made by hand, and fanning hisself with his big wide hat another nigger platted outen young inside corn shucks for him, and I can hear him holler at a big bunch of white geeses what's gitting in his flower beds and see 'em string off behind the old gander toward the big road.

When the day began to crack, the whole plantation break out with all kinds of noises, and you could tell what going on by the kind of noise you hear.

Come the daybreak you hear the guinea fowls start potracking down at the edge of the woods lot, and then the roosters all start up round the barn, and the ducks finally wake up and jine in. You can smell the sowbelly frying down at the cabins in the Row, to go with the hoecake and the buttermilk.

Then pretty soon the wind rise a little, and you can hear a old bell donging way on some plantation a mile or two off, and then more bells at other places and maybe a horn, and pretty soon yonder go Old Master's old ram horn with a long toot and then some short toots, and here come the overseer down the row of cabins, hollering right and left, and picking the ham outen his teeth with a long shiny goose-quill pick.

Bells and horns! Bells for this and horns for that! All we knowed was go and come by the bells and horns!

Old ram horn blow to send us all to the field. We all line up, about

---

[1] As told by Charley Williams, age 94, Tulsa, Oklahoma; born January 11, 1843, near Monroe Ouachita Parish, Louisiana; slave in Louisiana. From *Lay My Burden Down*, A Folk History of Slavery, edited by B. A. Botkin, pp. 112–113. Copyright, 1945, by the University of Chicago. Chicago: University of Chicago Press.

seventy-five field niggers, and go by the tool shed and git our hoes, or maybe go hitch up the mules to the plows and lay the plows out on the side so the overseer can see iffen the points is sharp. Any plow gits broke or the point gits bungled up on the rocks it goes to the blacksmith nigger, then we all git on down in the field.

Then the anvil start dangling in the blacksmith shop: "Tank! Deling-ding! Tank! Deling-ding!" and that old bull tongue gitting straightened out!

Course you can't hear the shoemaker awling and pegging, and the card spinners, and the old mammy sewing by hand, but maybe you can hear the old loom going "frump, frump," and you know it all right iffen your clothes do be wearing out, 'cause you gwine git new britches pretty soon!

We had about a hundred niggers on that place, young and old, and about twenty on the little place down below. We could make about every kind of thing but coffee and gunpowder that our white folks and us needed.

When we needs a hat we gits inside corn shucks and weave one out, and makes horse collars the same way. Just tie two little soft shucks together and begin plaiting.

All the cloth 'cepting the mistress' Sunday dresses come from the sheep to the carders and the spinners and the weaver, then we dye it with butter-nut and hickory bark and indigo and other things and set it with copperas. Leather tanned on the place made the shoes, and I never see a store-boughten wagon wheel 'cepting among the stages and the freighters along the big road.

We made pretty, long back-combs outen cow horn, and knitting needles outen second hickory. Split a young hickory and put in a big wedge to prize it open, then cut it down and let it season, and you got good bent grain for wagon hames and chair rockers and such.

II. FANNING THE FLIES [2]

When I got big enough for to step around, from the very first, my maw took me into the big house. It still there, 'cept it done 'bout fell down now, to what it was then. But some of Marse's folks, they lives down there still. Then, you see, they is like these white folks up round here now. They ain't got no big money like they had when I was a-running up. Time I got big enough for to run around in my shirttail, my maw, she 'lowed one night to my paw, when he was setting by the fire, "That black little nigger over there, he got to git hisself some pants 'cause I's gwine to put him up over the white folks's table." In them times the doors and windows, they never had no screen wire up to them like they is now. Folks didn't know nothing 'bout no such as that then. My master and all the other big white folks, they raised peafowls. Is you ever seed any? Well, every spring us

---

[2] As told to Caldwell Sims by Henry Coleman, Carlisle, South Carolina. *Ibid.*, pp. 141–142.

little niggers, we cotch them wild things at night. They could fly like a buzzard. They roosted up in the pine trees, right up in the tip top. So the missus, she have us young-uns clamb up there and git 'em when they first took roost. Us would clamb down, and my maw, she would pull the long feathers outen the tails. For weeks the cocks, they wouldn't let nobody see 'em if they could help it. Them birds is sure proud. When they is got the feathers, they just struts on the fences, and the fences was rail in them days. Iffen they could see theirself in a puddle of water after a rain, they would stay there all day a-strutting and carrying on like nobody's business. Yes, sir, them was pretty birds.

After us got the feathers, the missus, she'd 'low that all the nigger gals gwine to come down in the washhouse and make fly brushes. Sometime the missus'd give some of the gals some short feathers to put in their Sunday hats. When them gals got them hats on, I used to git so disgusted with 'em I'd leave 'em at church and walk home by myself. Anyway, by that time all the new fly brushes was made, and the missus, she have fans made from the short feathers for the white folks to fan the air with on hot days. Lordy, I's strayed far from what I had started out for to tell you. But I knowed that you young folks didn't know nothing 'bout all that. In them days the dining-room was big and had the windows open all the summer long, and all the doors stayed stretched, too. Quick as the mess of victuals began to come on the table, a little nigger boy was put up in the swing, I calls it, over the table, to fan the flies and gnats offen the missus' victuals. This swing was just offen the end of the long table. Some of the white folks had steps a-leading up to it. Some of 'em just had the little boys' maws to fetch the young-uns up there till they got through; then they was fetched down again.

Well, when I got my pants, my maw fetched me in and I clumb up the steps that Marse Johnson had, to git up in his swing with. At first, they had to show me just how to hold the brush, 'cause them peacock feathers was so long iffen you didn't mind your business, the ends of them feathers would splash in the gravy or something 'nother, and then the missus' table be all spattered up. Some of the masters would whup the nigger childrens for that carelessness, but Marse Johnson, he always good to his niggers. Most the white folks good to the niggers round'bout where I comes from.

It wa'n't long 'fore I got used to it, and I never did splash the feathers in no ration. But after I got used to it, I took to a-going to sleep up there. Marse Johnson he would just git up and wake me up. All the white folks at the table joke me so 'bout being so lazy I soon stop that foolishness. My maw, she roll her eyes at me when I come down after the master had to wake me up.

That change like everything else. When I got bigger, I got to be houseboy. They took down the swing and got a little gal to stand just 'hind the missus' chair and fan them flies. The missus 'low to Marse Johnson that the style done change, when he want to know how come she took the swing down. So that is the way it is now with the women; they changes the whole house with the style. But I tells my childrens, ain't no days like the old days when I was a shaver.

Kinsmen

You have but to spend a week idling along in the district between New Iberia and Lake Charles and inevitably you reach the conclusion that the population practically is made up of Broussards with a few thousand Trehons thrown in for good measure. The difference is this: The Trehons are a family, one of the most extensive families in the world, yet, when all is said and done, a family. But the Broussards are more than a family; they're a species. They're a highly attractive species, it might be added; kindly, generous, lovable folk, and their women run to good looks and their men run to brains and their offspring run to numbers. Gosh, how they do run to numbers!

One pitchy black night in the hunting season, five years ago, we were feeling our way along the bayou below Abbeville on our way to the ducking grounds. In a sharp turn our launch went hard aground. The prospects seemed to be that we would stay right where we were until morning or even later than that. There were no signs of life in the stretchs of swampy waste that encompassed us—no lamp-lights gleaming, no nothing.

There were four of us in the party—three outlanders and one native—and inevitably the native was a Broussard. He went aft and leaned over the rail and, speaking in French, he sent his voice forth across those apparently empty spaces in a call for assistance. Promptly from out the void came first one answering hail and then another and yet a third. A little later four husky chaps in pirogues ranged up alongside us and after a brief palaver with our friend, overboard they went, armpit deep in the water; and they pulled and pushed and pried until our hull was afloat once more. Then, declining all offers of a cash reward, these dripping good Samaritans climbed back into their boats and paddled away.

When navigation had been resumed I put a question to the resident: "How did you know those chaps were living out here in this wilderness?"

"I didn't," he said. "It was so dark I couldn't tell exactly where we were. So I took a chance. I just yelled out that there was a Broussard in trouble here on a mud bank and that if he had any cousins in this vicinity he'd like for them to rally around. So they rallied round and rescued us."

"Were they all four cousins of yours?" I inquired with reverence. I usually am reverent in the presence of any great established institution.

"No," he said modestly, "only three of them were. The fourth was some sort of foreigner, I guess."

From *Some United States*, A Series of Stops in Various Parts of This Nation with One Excursion across the Line, by Irvin S. Cobb, pp. 263–265. Copyright, 1926, by George H. Doran Company. New York.

Cajun Connections

A COUSIN (coo-zan) is a close relative in the Acadian scale. More than that, one whom you like, any special friend—he can be called a cousin, too. (The politician's great desire is to be known to his constituents as Cousin Jean, Cousin Theo, and so forth.) A godmother (nainaine) and a godfather (parrain) are warm connections. Each may remember the little one for whom they have stood at baptism until he is fifty and they are seventy, or as long beyond that as they all survive. A parrain will give his godchild money, advice, a job on his boat, or his life. The nainaine and parrain are expected, at the least, to send a birthday present every year until the child is grown, a first-communion present, and other tokens at appropriate times. I met one parrain who made a seventy-five mile trip by boat from his new home to his old one, with all his family, to be present for the birthday of a goddaughter. If a mother or father dies and the home must be broken, the parrain may assert a strong claim for the care of the child. A nonc and tante, to be sure, seem far closer than the usual American uncle and aunt, and they may ask for the child as their right. Between the affection of a good tante and a good nainaine, it would be hard to gauge a difference. After some years the voisin (neighbor), too, becomes almost like a relative and is so treated. To be a neighbor on Lafourche, it is no small thing, I can tell you.

A Spitting World

THE men chewed, the finicky and toothless slicing the quid from the plug with a pocket knife—no male was complete without his knife—the rest biting or gnawing it off with such teeth as they had. Of the biters there were two kinds: the clean, whose teeth went through the plug with the click of a precision instrument and left a pattern of perfect occlusion, and the ragged, whose eroded plugs were stringy evidence of missing teeth. While the chewer was talking, his quid, now a spongy and swollen wad, rested between upper jaw and cheek, making a bulge like a small boy's aching

From *The Bayous of Louisiana*, by Harnett T. Kane, p. 166. Copyright, 1943, by Harnett T. Kane. New York: The Hampton Publishing Co., and William Morrow & Company. 1944.

From *I Came Out of the Eighteenth Century*, by John Andrew Rice, pp. 63–65. Copyright, 1942, by Harper & Brothers. New York and London.
For the story of a "champeen terbaccer chawer" and a tobacco-spitting contest, see "Hillbilly Champeen," *Bundle of Troubles and Other Tarheel Tales* (1943), pp. 149–155.

tooth and slightly impeding speech. Dead quids were picked up by Negroes and given a second chewing or stuffed for smoking into corncob pipes. When white men smoked pipes, they shredded the tobacco from the plugs with their knives, for prepared pipe tobacco was unknown. Cigars were smoked mostly for convenience, when spitting must be restrained, or for relaxation; cigarettes were left to dudes.

The woman dipped. Snuff box and dipping stick were that day's equivalent of cigarette case and lighter. The snuff stick was a peeled twig, preferably from the sweet gum tree, shredded at one end to make a brush; the method of use was to wet the stick with spit, dip it into the box, and rub well the gums. One good dip made the dipper's spit reddish brown for hours afterwards. Women, except Negroes and the very old, seldom smoked pipes in public. Cigarettes for women were not banned; they were not even thought of. I never saw a woman smoke a cigarette until I was over twenty-one—twenty-three, to be exact, and in Germany.

Boys learned to chew at an early age, but long before chewing time we had begun to collect tobacco tags, tokens of plain or colored tin stuck on the plugs. While in other parts of this country boys of the same age were learning geography through collecting postage stamps, we were learning and debating the virtues of the various brands of chewing tobacco. Every boy knew which one he would some day chew, his choice being determined, as was fitting, largely by tradition. My family's favorite brand was "Brown Mule"; other families chewed "Jay Bird" or "Snaps." Meanwhile we practiced spitting, sometimes chewing coffee grounds in the cause of realism.

I was born into a spitting world. Everybody, except ladies and aspirants to that title, spat. No public place was without its receptacle. In hotels and local trains one still sees survivals of those days in the cuspidors—"spittoons" to us—squat and dumpy in the trains, tall and shining brass in hotel lobbies and legislative halls. (They cost the state two hundred and fifty dollars apiece during Reconstruction.) Most homes had them also—"bring paw his spittoon" was a familiar command—and in any case it was a wise precaution to have one handy, for the use of a spitting guest. Out of doors there was greater freedom for the sport and it was here that spitters liked to prove themselves expert in placing shots, and the traditional target was a knothole in a fence. To recall the distance and accuracy of the skill of legendary heroes would put a strain upon credulity.

To the clean spitter there was more to spitting than getting rid of spittle; he pressed two fingers at right angles to his lips and ejected an amber pellet of the size and force of a twenty-two, and left no trace on beard or chin. But the sloven was more common, with wedges of deep brown at the corners of the mouth that looked, on the very old, like permanent scars, or with flares thinning to a lighter brown in white beards. Spitting was no indication of social status; only the elegance with which it was done marked the gentleman, who wiped his mouth with a handkerchief instead of the back of his hand.

The Grapevine Telegraph

THIS story illustrates the life among the mountaineers in Western North Carolina, at no great distance in the past:

A doctor in the little town of Saluda was called about four o'clock in the morning to go about fifteen miles out into the mountains to see a sick woman. About a third of the way, his old mare that he was driving suddenly stopped still and refused to budge. He looked and saw that there was something in the road but couldn't make it out. He took a lantern; got out of the buggy; walked along by the old mare holding the reins until he got to the bridle. There he saw a dead possum in the road. He had feared up to that time it was a rattlesnake. It had a bullet hole through its head and considerable blood came from the possum. He knew that all of that blood couldn't come from a wound in the head so he turned the possum over and examined it and found that it had five bullet holes entirely through it. He threw the possum out of the road, got back in the buggy and drove on.

Not far off he came to a settlement of mountaineers. They were all standing around in groups, evidently excited about something but saying very little above whispers or low conversation. Knowing that he could find nothing from them, he drove on. He came to a second settlement a mile or so away. The same condition existed there. The people were standing around listlessly. Women with milk pails had put their pails down and were hanging on the fences having very little to say and only in low tones of voice. When he reached the third settlement he had to go through a field. It had bars to the fence. As he was about to get out of the buggy and lower the bars, a mountaineer stepped forward and said, "Wait a minute, Doc. I'll take down them bars for you and put 'em back up when you get through." As he passed through, the mountaineer said, "Just a minute, Doc," and coming up to the side of the buggy, he inquired in a low tone of voice, "Is you heerd about any shooting?"

"No! Why?"

"Well, one of our fellers was in Rowan's Gap when he seed a light in front of him in the road and he hailed it and he didn't get no answer, so he shot. He emptied his pistol and didn't hear nothing running off, so he was afraid that he killed somebody."

The doctor replied, "He did. It was a possum and he put all five of those bullets through that possum's body."

An hour later he came back after his visit to the sick woman and at all of the three settlements everything was normal and stirring and busy. The grapevine telegraph had worked both ways.

As told by Alexander S. Salley, Jr., Columbia, South Carolina, January 28, 1949. Recorded by B. A. Botkin.

PRIVATE JUSTICE

Guinea Jim

THE first thing I 'members 'bout slavery time, I wa'n't nothing but a boy, 'bout fifteen, I reckon. That's what Marse Johnnie Horn say. Us belong to Marse Ike Horn, Marse Johnnie's pa, right here on this place where us is now. But this here didn't belong to me then. This here was all Marse Ike's place. Marse Ike's gin got outa fix and we couldn't git it fixed. Colonel Lee had two gins, and one of 'em was just below old Turner house. Recollect a big old hickory tree? Well, there's where it was.

I was plenty big 'nough to drive the mules to the gin. Set on the lever and drive 'em, just like a 'lasses mill. So that night Marse Ike told us he want everybody to go with him to Colonel Lee's gin next morning, and didn't want nobody to git out and go ahead of him. That held up the ginning; made us not to go to the ginhouse till sunup.

Us got the mules and just waited. 'Twixt daylight and sunup, us all standing there at the gate, and we heared a little fine horn up the road. Us didn't know what it meant coming to the house. And bimeby Mr. Beesley, what live not far from Marse Ike, he rode up and had five dogs— five nigger dogs, what they call 'em—and soon as he come, Marse Ike's hoss was saddled up, and Marse Ike and him rode off down the road and the dogs with 'em 'head of us. Us followed 'long behind 'em, stay close as they 'low us, to see what they was up to. When they got close to the gin-house—ginhouse right 'side de road—they stop us, and Mr. Beesley told Old Brown to go ahead. Old Brown was the lead dog and had a bell on him, and they was fasten together with a rod, just like steers. He turn 'em loose, and then he popped the whip and hollered at Old Brown and told him, "Nigger." Old Brown hollered like he hit. He want to go. And they was a fence on both sides made it a lane, so he put Old Brown over the fence on the ginhouse side and told Brown to "go ahead." He went ahead and run all around the ginhouse, and they let him in the ginroom, and he grabbled in the cottonseed in a hole.

Then somebody holler, "Guinea Jim."

I looks and I didn't see him. Didn't nobody see him, but they know that's where he been hiding. Mr. Beesley told Old Brown he just fooling him, and Old Brown holler again, like he killing him, and Mr. Beesley say, "Go git that nigger," and Old Brown started 'way from there like he hadn't been hunting nothing, but he went around and around that gin, and Mr. Beesley told him he had to do better than that or he'd kill him, 'cause he hadn't come there for nothing.

As told to Ruby Pickens Tartt by Josh Horn, age 90, Livingston, Alabama. From *Lay My Burden Down*, A Folk History of Slavery, edited by B. A. Botkin, pp. 180-182. Copyright, 1945, by the University of Chicago. Chicago: University of Chicago Press.

Brown made a circle around that gin 'way down to the fence that time, and he was so fat he couldn't git through the fence. You know what sort of fence, a rail fence it was. Then he stop and bark for help. Now I seed this with my own eyes. They put Brown on top the fence, and he jump 'way out in the road, didn't stay on the fence. He jump and run up and down in the road and couldn't find no scent of Jim. You knows how they used to make them rail fences?

Well, Brown come back there, and this is the truth, so help me God. He bark, look like, for them to lift him back up on the fence, and, bless God, if that dog didn't walk that rail fence like he walking a log, as far as from here to that gate yonder, and track Jim just like he was on the ground. He fell off once, and they had to put him back, and he run his track right on to where Jim jumped off the fence, 'way out in the road. Old Brown run right across the road to the other fence and treed again on t'other side the road toward Konkabia. Old Brown walk the fence on that side the road a good piece, just like he done on the other side, and them other dogs, he hadn't never turned them loose.

When Brown he jump off that fence, he jump just as far as he can on the field side, like he gwine catch Jim like a gnat or something, and he never stop barking no more, just like he jumping a rabbit. Then Mr. Beesley turn them other dogs loose that he hadn't never turned loose, 'cause he say Old Brown done got the thing straight. And he had it straight. Them dogs run that track right on down to Konkabia and crossed it to the Blacksher side. They was a big old straw field there then, and they cross it and come on through that field, all them dogs barking just like they looking at Jim. 'Reckly, they come on Jim running with a pine brush tied behind him to drag his scent away, but it didn't bother Old Brown.

When them dogs 'gin to push him, Jim drap the brush and run back toward Konkabia. Now on Konkabia there used to be beavers worse than on Sucarnatchee now. They was a big beaver dam 'twixt the bridge and the Hale place, and Jim run to that beaver dam. You know when beavers build they dam, they cut down trees and let 'em fall in the creek, and pull in trash and brush same as folks, to dam the water up there till it's knee-deep. The dogs seen him, Old Brown looking at him, just 'fore he jump in 'bove the dam right 'mongst the trash and things they'd drug in there. Brown seed him, and he jump in right behind him. Jim just dive down under the raff and let he nose stick outa the water. Every once in a while Jim he put he head down under, he holding to a pole down there, and once Mr. Beesley seed him, he just let him stay there.

Brown would swim 'bout 'mongst the brush, backwards and forwards, and directly Mr. Beesley told Old Brown, "Go git him." Then all the men got poles and dug 'bout in the raff hunting him. They knowed he was there, and Marse Ike had a pole gigging around trying to find him too. Then he told Mr. Beesley to give him the hatchet and let him fix the pole. He sharpen the pole right sharp, then Marse Ike start to gig around with the pole and he kinda laugh to hisself, 'cause he knowed he done found Jim.

'Bout that time Jim poke he head up and say: "This here me," and every-body holler. Then he ax 'em please, for God's sake, don't let them dogs git him. They told him come on out.

You see, Jim belong to Miss Mary Lee, Mr. John Lee's ma, and his pa was kilt in the war, so Mr. Beesley was looking out for her. Well, they took Jim outa there, and Mr. Beesley whipped him a little and told him: "Jim, you put up a pretty good fight, and I's gwine to give you a start for a run with the dogs."

Jim took out towards Miss Mary's, and Mr. Beesley held Old Brown as long as he could. They caught Jim and bit him right smart. You see they had to let 'em bite him a little to satisfy the dogs. Jim could have made it, 'cept he was all hot and wore out.

The Feud Ambush

A FEUD leader who had about exterminated the opposing faction, and had made a good fortune for a mountaineer while doing it, for he kept his men busy getting out the timber when they weren't fighting, said to me, in all seriousness:

"I have triumphed agin my enemies time and time agin. The Lord's on my side, and I gits a better and better Christian ever' year."

A preacher, riding down a ravine, came upon an old mountaineer hiding in the bushes with his rifle.

"What are you doing, my friend?"

"Ride on, stranger," was the easy answer. "I'm a-waitin' fer Jim John-son, and with the help of the Lawd I'm goin' to blow his damn head off."

Even the ambush, the hideous feature of the feud, took root in the days of the Revolution, and was borrowed, maybe, from the Indians. Milfort, the Frenchman, who hated the backwoodsmen, says Mr. Roosevelt, de-scribes with horror their extreme malevolence and their murderous disposi-tion toward one another. He says that whether a wrong had been done to a man personally, or to his family, he would, if necessary, travel a hundred miles and lurk around the forest indefinitely to get a chance to shoot his enemy.

But the Civil War was the chief cause of bloodshed; for there is evi-dence, indeed, that though feeling between families was strong, bloodshed was rare and the English sense of fairness prevailed, in certain communi-ties at least. Often you shall hear an old mountaineer say: "Folks usen to talk about how fer they could kill a deer. Now hit's how fer they can kill a man. Why, I have knowed the time when a man would hev been druv outen the country fer drawin' a knife or a pistol, an' if a man was ever killed, hit wus kinder accidental by a Barlow. I reckon folks got

From *Blue Grass and Rhododendron*, by John Fox, Jr., pp. 42–46. Copyright, 1901, by Charles Scribner's Sons. New York.

used to weapons an' killin' an' shootin' from the bresh endurin' the war.
But hit's been gettin' wuss ever sence, and now hit's dirk an' Winchester
all the time." Even for the ambush there is an explanation.

"Oh, I know all the excuses folks make. Hit's fair for one as 'tis fer
t'other. You can't fight a man fa'r and squar in the courts. A pore man
can't fight money in the courts. Thar hain't no witnesses in the lorrel but
leaves, an' dead men don't hev much to say. I know hit all. Looks like
lots o' decent young folks hev got usen to the idee; thar's so much of it
goin' on and thar's so much talk about shootin' from the bresh. I do
reckon hit's wuss'n stealin' to take a feller critter's life that way."

It is also a fact that most of the men who have been engaged in these
fights were born or were children during the war, and were, in consequence,
accustomed to bloodshed and bushwhacking from infancy. Still, even
among the fighters there is often a strong prejudice against the ambush, and
in most feuds one or the other side discountenances it, and that is the
faction usually defeated. I know of one family that was one by one exterminated because they refused to take to the "bresh."

A Miracle of Mountain Justice

. . . A VERY picturesque old man much like the mountaineer of song and
story . . . told it as we rode in his "kivered wagin" around the Yonah-
lossee. A party of five of us were on a hike through the Blue Ridge. I had
sprained my ankle climbing the Bynum Bluff trail out of Linville gorge and
I made this injury an excuse to accept his invitation to ride. He and his
son were hauling a load of some kind from Jonas' ridge to Carey's Flats.

* * * * *

I climbed in his wagon and seated myself by him on the box of provisions.
He was a magnificent specimen of a Blue Ridge patriarch. Tall, lean,
slightly stooped, he bore his 70 odd years lightly. He had a long gray beard
and heavy gray hair, keen, quizzical blue eyes, and there were many laughter wrinkles in their corners. His son, a red-headed giant, strode by the
front yoke of oxen and called to them. "Whoa, come up in hyar, Buck,
Gee, Haw back, Berry," or some similar unintelligible remark. This was
his sole contribution to the conversation.

I thought of the slow progress civilization had made through the ages.
An ox wagon much like this one had doubtless brought the ancestors of
this interesting pair down from the plains northeast of the Elbe into the
Roman empire, from whence they had gone over into Britain, and centuries
later to America. They had kept through the ages the racial characteristics
that inspired Gregory when he said of the English slaves in the market

---

From "The Feud Spirit," by Maude Minish Sutton, *Greensboro* (N. C.) *Daily News,*
April 24, 1927. Clipping File, Library of the Woman's College of the University of
North Carolina, Greensboro, North Carolina.

place, "Not Angles but angels." Both father and son were of a type that
made the hackneyed phrase, "purest Anglo-Saxon blood in America" seem
to be something other than a myth kept alive by demagogues and politicians. The old man's phraseology was Elizabethan. The "karols" and
"ballits" he gave me were old English and might have been sung by the
Canterbury Pilgrims, and the story that he told was much like the one the
"gentil nun" told on that famous journey.

"Where air you from?" he asked me, and when I told him, Lenoir, he
said, "I've been down thar to court a few times. I'm a-movin' back down
into Caldwell now. Reckon I'll have to go to doin' my lawin' in Lenoir
agin. I've been a-livin' back on Jonas' ridge fur the last ten year, but
Sheriff Green has got so he totes papers fur half the citizens in the county
and I'm a-movin' back down into Carey's Flats. Thar hain't no use of no
sheriff a-keepin' a'ter me and my folks. I'm a Dunkard preacher and I
shore live right. But hit's got so here lately they mighty nigh send a man
off jest on guesswork anyhow. They don't have to prove nothin' on him."

I preserved a discreet silence.

"Don't you believe ef a man does a crime hit's mighty apt to come out
on him?" he asked.

One peculiarity of these old philosophers of the coves is that the ideas
and theories in which they are interested are usually those of our great
thinkers through the ages. Petty problems and small talk do not concern
them. I led him into a discussion of the consequences of sin and found a
stern and selfish conception of justice.

"Vengeance is mine, I will repay, says the Lord God of Hosts," he quoted
with the exultant satisfaction in the harsher attributes of Jehovah that is
often a characteristic of more learned ministers. "I have seen the guilty
brought to punishment. I have beheld the forces of the Almighty at work.
Ef something mistreats you or one of your kin, jest pray and your enemy
will be delivered up into your hands. I have saw a miracle worked to bring
the guilty to jestice."

Here he paused and I was afraid I was not going to get my story.

"Please tell me about the miracle," I begged.

"Ef you live as long as I have, you'll see hit more'n once," he said. "I've
seed a sight of fightin' and shootin' in my day. I've buried a sight of folks
that had got shot, but I hain't never put any murdered man away and had
him to rest good, till the man who shot him was reckoned with. Blood calls
fur blood you know."

Yes, I know. There have been times when the shadow of the beautiful
Blue Ridge has seemed to cast a menacing darkness over even the lonely
little county seat that nestles so peacefully at its foot. The call of a clans-
man's blood for revenge has disturbed the folk of Caldwell less often than
it has many of the mountain counties but a real mountaineer understands
the feeling. The old story-teller sensed my understanding, and found the
telling of his tale less difficult than he had anticipated.

"One time I was sent fur to bury a feller who had been found dead by a still house over yon side the Roan. Hit's been some odd year ago. 'Twa'n't long after I was called to preach. Nobody knowed anything about how he got killed. As fur back as anybody had knowed him they wa'n't a peaceabler feller on that side. His daddy talked to me before we went to the meetin' house.

"'I want him to have a decent buryin',' the old man told me. 'Course he hain't a-goin' to see no rest till I git the hound that done hit.' He'd been shot in the back and hadn't never knowed what hit him. The old man said he had cleaned up his gun. I preached a strong sermon over that thar boy. And I prayed a powerful prayer. I was mighty in prayer in them days. I told the Lord about how some scamp had stoled up to that still house under cover of the night and shot that thar pore boy in his back. I told how he was snatched off right in a second without no time to make his peace. Let the murderer suffer fur the sins he hadn't give the pore boy time to beg forgiveness fur, I asked him. Let the boy's pappy find out who done hit. 'You promised us that you'd let us take an eye fur an eye and a tooth fur a tooth.' I says, 'Let this boy's pappy put a hole between that murderer's shoulders right whar his pore boy was shot. Pint him out to us, oh Lord.' I says. 'Help us to do thy vengeance.' You could hear the amens fur a mile. After that thar prayer we opened up the coffin and let the crowd pass by one at a time and look at him. His pappy stood right by the head of the coffin all the time, and watched the folks pass. His mammy was snubbin' down on the front seat. His sweetheart was a-settin' by her. I'll never forgit how that gal looked. She was as white as a sheet and her face was so black around her eyes they looked like she'd been hit with somebody's fists right plum in both eyes. She wasn't a-cryin', though. She had set thar all the time like a dead woman. I don't think she had batted ary eye all the time I was a-talkin' and a-prayin'.

"Towards the back of the meetin' house had set a big feller from over 'cross State Line hill. He got up and started up to look at the corpse. The crowd was sorter a-shovin' and a-pushin' and he had to stop right by whar the gal was a-settin'. I seed a sort of a shiver run over her. She never looked at him. 'Peared like she somehow jest felt him a-standin' thar an' never seed him. When he got up by the corpse and looked at hit, he made a sort of a moanin' noise and says, 'I done hit.' The gal slipped out of the seat and laid on the floor in a fit. The old man said, 'I knowed hit,' and drawed his gun. I jumped over the stand and cotched his hand, so he couldn't kill in the meetin' house. He got him next day though, and the hole was in the same place in his back that the one in the boy's was. While all this was a-goin' on I hadn't looked at the corpse. When I did I came near a-drappin' in a fit too. He had on a snow white bleachin' shirt and they was a big spot of blood big as a sasser on hit right over his heart. His pappy told me that the spot come right where that thar killer looked at him. The Lord jest plain showed the sign so's the old man could kill him. The gal was raley to blame though. She'd been a-sparkin' em both. Wimmen's got a heap to answer fur in this world, hain't they?"

"Mountain Romeo and Juliet"

THE great romance of the feud is in the history of Rosanna McCoy and Jonce Hatfield. Jonce Hatfield was a married man when he fell in love with Rosanna McCoy. . . . Jonce Hatfield is a handsome fellow—tall, broad shouldered, with a dark complexion set off by a black mustache and a slight beard. His features are irregular. He has a dare-devil look. He is one of the most courageous of the Hatfield crowd. He is not inclined to be quarrelsome, but he is the last one to leave a fight.

He first met Rosanna McCoy at an election gathering in Pike County. Rosanna was then a fresh-faced, regular-featured girl of eighteen. This was in 1882, before the killing of Ellison Hatfield. She came down to the election meeting riding pillion-fashion behind one of her brothers. The women in these communities, where they are not outcasts, have very little to say. They are mere passive spectators at most of the gatherings in the mountains, and in the household circle they have very little to do beyond attending to their domestic affairs. They occupy much the same position as the squaws in the Indian tribes of the West. Rosanna McCoy pleased Jonce Hatfield very much. He became engaged in conversation with her, and found that she was very much interested in him because he was one of the most active of the Hatfields, and for some weeks a quarrel had been brewing between the two families. He met her before any of the killing, however, had begun. Becoming inflamed with liquor drank at this election gathering, he was perfectly infatuated with Rosanna McCoy, and proposed to her to elope with him and go back to the Kentucky side. She objected, but he was so furious and vindictive that she did not dare to resist him.

Towards the close of the night he was seen by the McCoys crossing the river, with Rosanna seated comfortably behind him on his strong black horse. Jonce Hatfield took her to his home and told his wife that he had brought home Rosanna McCoy, and forced her to acknowledge her as the head of the house. He lived with Rosanna for over a year, the McCoys making frequent attempts to cross the river and rescue the girl. She undoubtedly must have been satisfied with her bondage, because when it was broken off it was renewed through her consent. Towards the end of the year the McCoys made such a demonstration that Rosanna concluded to return, particularly as her father threatened that if she did not she would

---

From *An American Vendetta,* by T. C. Crawford, pp. 42–47. Copyright, 1889, by Belford, Clarke & Co. New York, Chicago, and San Francisco.

Rosanna met Jonce in the spring of 1880. After the capture (in 1882) of Jonce [Jonse, Johnse] Rosanna [Rose Anne] returned to her father's cabin to await the birth of her child. According to Virgil Carrington Jones (*The Hatfields and the McCoys,* Chapel Hill, 1948, pp. 38–274), the evidence shows, not that "Rose Anne gave birth to Johnse's child and that it died at an early age," but that "measles caused the girl to have a miscarriage."

have none of his property when it came to a division after his death. But although she returned to the Kentucky side Jonce Hatfield constantly visited her, and it was upon one of the occasions of his visiting her that he himself was captured by the McCoy crowd.

He was taken at 1 o'clock in the morning.

Rosanna McCoy believed that he was being carried out to his death, and the McCoys as much as said that they were going to kill him. She crawled out of her bed after this arrest, unfastened a horse from her father's stables, and started off in the blackest of the black night to warn the Hatfields. The roads between the McCoy household and the Hatfield place are simply a succession of gulches, rocks, bogs, creeks, and madly flowing rivers. How the girl was able to pick her way over these tremendous obstacles can probably be explained only by the intelligence of the horse, who, being familiar with the region, was able to pick a footing over what is difficult enough to pass over in the day-time. Surely that night ride and her alarm of this household would make a subject for a dramatic poem. The girl was the heroine of an illicit love, yet she was as faithful and devoted to her lover as if he were the most worthy. She risked her life over and over again that night to bring the rescue party to him.

The rising of the Hatfields, who followed the girl back, was the work of but a few moments, and the subsequent capture of their kidnapped son was a sharp piece of dramatic action. It is one of the mysteries to-day of the whole feud that the shooting did not begin then and there, as Ance Hatfield was exasperated into a white heat of fury over the capture of his son and the possibilities involved in the midnight arrest. That love affair has been the basis of the feud. The wrong done to Rosanna McCoy was bitterly felt by the McCoy family, and it explains much of their irrational hatred of the Hatfields.

Connie Franklin and the Greenway Boys

SHANTY-BOAT land stretches along the Mississippi from Memphis to Vicksburg and back up the White River to Clarendon, Arkansas.

About one hundred miles north of Clarendon, the foothills of the Ozarks begin rising in gentle swells. That's the home of the hillbillies. Some folks call 'em "stump-jumpers." The hill land of Arkansas is as raw as "de po' folks' lan' " of Mississippi. The farms are rocky and grubby.

The natives say:

"The land is so hilly you can look up the chimney and see the cows come home."

The strange story of Connie Franklin is a saga of the hillbilly folks. Connie was a shanty-boat boy. He got into a little trouble down in southeastern Arkansas and left in a hurry. He appeared one day at Mountain

From *Look Away!* A Dixie Notebook, by James H. Street, pp. 87–91. Copyright, 1936, by James H. Street. New York: The Viking Press.

Home. The stump-jumpers didn't like Connie. He talked a heap. But little Tiller Ruminer thought Connie was the "honey in a bee tree."

Connie ran around with Tiller quite a bit. He used to tell her stories of strange paths he had traveled and faraway cities he had visited, gigantic cities like Memphis and Little Rock, where folks rode in streetcars and elevators. He was an artist with a harmonica—French harp, they call it in the South.

Connie wooed Tiller with his French harp, playing the ballads of the shanty-boat folks and the songs of the hills. One day Connie disappeared. No one thought much about it except Tiller, and she cried a lot. Stories that Connie had met with a little grievous trouble began going the rounds of the community. A young district attorney began investigating. And, on a peaceful Sunday afternoon, I was startled at a message from Mountain Home that the five Greenway brothers had been indicted for burning Connie alive.

The story began when a deaf mute wrote the district attorney that he was an eyewitness for the appalling murder of the shanty-boat boy and French-harp player.

The speechless lad testified in writing that he was walking through the woods one moonless night and saw six men drinking around a fire. A white mule was hitched near by. One of the men was Connie Franklin and the others were the Greenway boys. Connie was playing his harp and all the revelers seemed to be having a pretty good time. Suddenly one of the group started ripping off Connie's clothes. Then the five brothers tied him on the back of the mule and whipped him with heavy brush. The testimony contended the men pulled Connie from the beast and threw him into the fire. The deaf mute wrote that he had not revealed the story before for fear of his life.

The ambitious young district attorney went to the scene and found a bunch of bones which was identified as Connie Franklin. Two bits of tin from Connie's French harp were found near by. The Greenway boys went to trial in the middle of winter. It gets cold in those hills.

The reporters took Mountain Home by storm. There was no hotel in the village and only one telephone. The thermometer was below zero when the Greenway boys went before their hillbilly peers. Feeling was pretty high. Most of the stump-jumpers didn't like the idea of some of their boys being tried for the murder of a shanty-boat boy.

The attorney for the Greenway boys was a brother of the district attorney. The trial went along just so-so until the state closed its case. We all were hovering around a pot-bellied stove when the defense opened. The young lawyer stood before the bar and in a very clear voice said:

"We call Connie Franklin as our first witness."

And down the aisle walked Connie, or his ghost.

I dropped my pencil.

Tiller Ruminer screamed.

The district attorney yelled, "What the hell is this?"

The judge pounded for order.

Never have I experienced such a minute as the one Connie used to walk to the witness stand. His story was simple: Connie Franklin the dead was Connie Franklin the resurrected. He testified that the Greenway boys thrashed him that night in the hills, and he decided to leave town and save his hide. He went to Morrilton, Arkansas, and there a reporter from the *Arkansas Gazette* found him. Connie, if it was Connie, didn't know all the commotion his disappearance had caused, so he came back to testify that the report of his death was "grossly exaggerated."

The district attorney raised quite a howl and insisted the corpus delicti had been established. The town was divided over identity of the man. Some said it was Connie. Others said it was a man who looked like Connie, but who was a faker.

Friends of the Greenway clan insisted the whole case was a frame-up and that the deaf mute had given his evidence because he hated the Greenways. They made no attempt to explain the human bones found in the ashes of the fire, but human bones are not so rare in the hillbilly country.

The case simmered to identification of Connie, whose only testimony was:

"I am Connie Franklin. I am not dead."

The state refused flatly to accept Connie's identity, so the defense attorney asked his brother:

"Will you take the word of Tiller Ruminer?"

The district attorney said he would, realizing the little mountain girl did not like the Greenway boys.

It got so cold in the courthouse that afternoon that the judge adjourned court to the town's only barber shop, which was warm. There they took Connie and there they took Tiller. Connie sat in a hide-bottom chair over by the stove. Tiller wore a faded green coat, woolen stockings, and a toboggan cap.

The district attorney asked her:

"Tiller, is this Connie Franklin?"

Tiller looked at the man a long time, and heard him vow he was her beau. The hillbilly folks crowded close to the stove to watch the drama.

Slowly Tiller spoke:

"He looks like Connie and he talks like Connie, but I don't believe he's Connie."

The man answered her:

"Sure, Tiller, you know I am Connie."

"If you be Connie," the girl spoke again, "then play for me."

The man reached into his windbreaker, pulled out a French harp, and began playing "Arkansas Traveler," and then "Natchez under the Hill."

The girl listened intently and said finally:

"You play like Connie, but if you be Connie, play the song I always liked best."

The musician blew softly into the harp and the wailing strains echoed softly through that jammed, stinking barber shop:

> In the Blue Ridge Mountains of Virginia,
> On the trail of the lonesome pine.

The girl screamed:
"That's Connie!"

There Ain't Nothing to Killin'

Boze: Talkin' bout killin' people, there ain't nothin' to it. I don't see what a man worry his self bout a trial for. If I has enough gainst a man, I'd set on de roadside at night an' pick him off jes like I would a bird. There ain't nothin' to it. If they ketch you an' you use your head a little bit an' know what lawyer to git, you'll come clear.

Pede: It seems to me you'd have to fret some about the trial.

Hate: Well, there oughtn to be nothin' to it. If a man do you dirt, there ain't no use to wait for de courts, cause they ain't goin' to do nothin'. The best way is to trust in God an' your gun.

Pede: Well, how does a lawyer work it in the courts?

Boze: Well, there's several little things that must not be neglected. Sometime you has to have more than one lawyer, an' you got to know how to pick 'em. Then you must have a little money, an' you can almost mighty nigh git enough by rakin' an' scrapin' to clear your conscience an' satisfy the lawyer; then you know your vote counts an' your influence at votin' time.

Hate: You're right bout what you said, but there's more to it.

Boze: I ain't finished yet tellin' you how to work it. First thing, you got to pick a lawyer that stands in with the Governor and the judges. You got to pick one that ain't afraid to have the judge round to his house for dinner and supper an' ain't scared to give him all the liquor he can drink. That's one thing you got to remember. Then you got to have a lawyer that is sharp enough to know what judge to invite to a meal, an' there's plenty of them, an' after you do that, it's well to look over the whole business an' see if you can't find a lawyer that's a member of the Legislature to jine your first lawyer. That's very important. You know Legislature makes judges, an' you can always get a case put off. If the Legislator has duties

From "The Carolina Wilderness," by E. C. L. Adams, *Scribner's Magazine*, Vol. 89 (June, 1931), No. 6, pp. 615–616.

to perform, the judge is only too glad to accommodate him. Another thing, it is always a good thing to have a lawyer who ain't got too good er health. The right kind of judge will always put your case off. In fact, if you use good judgment, you could git your case put off, an' put off, until all the witnesses is either dead or forgot, an' if they ain't dead they memories has become feeble with old age. There ain't nothin' to a trial. The main thing is knowin' how to pick your lawyer.

Pede: How about the jury?

Hate: Most times the jury ain't goin' to be gainst you, an' if they is, they is ways of fixin' that, too. That is, if you got a first-class lawyer.

Pede: How can you fix that when you got enemies on the jury?

Boze: You can mighty nigh always find one friend on the jury, but even without one friend there is a way of fixin' it. The main thing, however, is to pick the right lawyer an' be friends with the courthouse rats.

Pede: What is a courthouse rat?

Boze: Ain't no use for me to go into details bout that, but all I tell you is pick the right lawyer an' stand in with the courthouse rats.

Pede: Well, I ain't exactly understand what a courthouse rat is.

Boze: Well, I'll go this far with you. A courthouse rat hates niggers an' he don't wear no stiff collar, except—but I better keep my mouth shut on that.

Pede: To go back where we left off, you was tellin' us that the main thing was to pick the right lawyer, but you never did explain what you'd do when you had enemies on the jury.

Boze: In a case like that, if you got the right kind of judge with the right kind of lawyer, you can sometimes in very bad cases git the judge to bring a directed verdict of not guilty. There ain't nothin' else for the jury to do but come in an' say: "Not guilty."

Pede: I have heard of that bein' done, an' I heard some lawyers discussin' it an' they said it was unconstitutional; that the judge had no right to come in an' take on himself the freein' of a prisoner that the jury was liable to convict.

Boze: Them ain't no lawyers, an' ain't nobody give a damn bout the Constitution. I'm jes tellin' you how to git loose when you killed a white man, an' the way as I tell you is the way to do it, an' it has been done. You know a judge ain't nothin' but a man, an' most men are lookin' out for they own advantage. There ain't nothin' to the law, an' all this rippin' an' rearin' in the courthouse, this whoopin' an' hollerin', ain't nothin' but a lot of bluff. They got to do that to satisfy a few people who believes in the Ten Commandments, or wants to make an impression that they does.

Pede: Well, I'm larnin' every day.

Hate: Son, you jes listen to you' elders an' you'll grow in wisdom. There ain't nothin' wrong wid you. You jes need a little experience.

Boze: No, there ain't nothin' to no trial ef you know how to work it.

SPORTS, PASTIMES, AND FESTIVALS

The Log Rolling

WHEN the first white men came to Arkansas money was scarce, comparatively few owned slaves, and in many settlements the pioneers depended largely upon each other by "swapping" work. Probably no better illustration of this interdependence can be seen than in the "log rolling." After the settler had built his cabin, the next step was to clear a piece of ground for a crop. The trees were felled, cut, or burned into lengths so that they could be handled, and then the neighbors were invited to the "rolling."

Almost every pioneer had a "hand-spike"—a stick of hard, tough wood, five or six feet in length, from which the bark had been removed, and the ends slightly tapered with the draw-knife. When all had assembled at the appointed time and place, the men were divided into teams. Two of the physically strongest men in each team were selected to make "daylight"; that is, to thrust a hand-spike under one end of the log and lift it high enough for the others to get their spikes under it. Then, two by two, the others followed the "daylight" makers until often ten or twelve could be seen carrying the heaviest logs and piling them in heaps. Smaller logs, carried by four to six men, were added to the heap, so that the whole could be burned. In some localities enough valuable timber was thus destroyed to pay for the land on which it grew, even at present prices, if it could be replaced. But then a crop was of more importance to the settler than the timber.

While the men were "rolling" the logs, the women folks would get together and prepare dinner, each bringing from her own store some delicacy that she thought the others might not be able to supply. Venison, bear meat and corn pone were the chief articles of food on the menu. "Log rolling" was a good appetizer, and when the men arose from the table it looked as if a "cyclone had struck it"; but in "swapping" work each man had his turn, and in the end no one was placed at a disadvantage in the amount of provisions consumed.

The term "log rolling" found its way into the legislative halls, where its meaning is very much the same as in pioneer days. Bills are often passed by members "swapping" votes, just as the early settlers cleared their ground by "swapping" work.

From *Centennial History of Arkansas*, by Dallas T. Herndon, Vol. I, pp. 209–210. Chicago and Little Rock: The S. J. Clarke Publishing Co. 1922.

Imitating Bird and Animal Cries

ONE important pastime of our boys was that of imitating the noise of every bird and beast in the woods. This faculty was not merely a pastime, but a very necessary part of education, on account of its utility in certain circumstances. The imitations of the gobbling and other sounds of wild turkeys often brought those keen eyed and ever watchful tenants of the forest within the reach of the rifle. The bleating of the fawn brought her dam to her death in the same way. The hunter often collected a company of mopish owls to the trees about his camp, and amused himself with their hoarse screaming; his howl would raise and obtain responses from a pack of wolves, so as to inform him of their neighborhood, as well as guard him against their depradations.

This imitative faculty was sometimes requisite as a measure of precaution in war. The Indians, when scattered about in a neighborhood, often collected together by imitating turkeys by day and wolves or owls by night. In similar situations our people did the same. I have often witnessed the consternation of a whole neighborhood in consequence of a few screeches of owls. An early and correct use of this imitative faculty was considered as an indication that its possessor would become in due time a good hunter and a valiant warrior.

Feats with the Rifle

WE HAVE individuals in Kentucky, kind reader, that even there are considered wonderful adepts in the management of the rifle. To *drive a nail* is a common feat, not more thought of by the Kentuckians than to cut off a wild turkey's head, at a distance of a hundred yards. Others will *bark* off squirrels one after another, until satisfied with the number procured. Some, less intent on destroying game, may be seen under night *snuffing a candle* at the distance of fifty yards, off-hand, without extinguishing it. I have been told that some have proved so expert and cool as to make choice of the eye of a foe at a wonderful distance, boasting beforehand of the sureness of their piece, which has afterwards been fully proved when the enemy's head has been examined!

From *Notes on the Settlement and Indian Wars of the Western Parts of Virginia and Pennsylvania from 1763 to 1783 inclusive, together with a Review of the State of Society and Manners of the First Settlers of the Western Country*, by Joseph Doddridge, pp. 123–124. Copyright, 1912, by John S. Ritenour and William T. Lindsey. Pittsburgh, Pennsylvania.

From "Kentucky Sports," in *Audubon and His Journals,* by Maria R. Audubon, with Zoological and Other Notes by Elliott Coues, Vol. II, pp. 459–462. Copyright, 1897, by Charles Scribner's Sons. New York.

Having resided some years in Kentucky, and having more than once been witness of rifle sport, I shall present you with the results of my observation, leaving you to judge how far rifle-shooting is understood in that State.

Several individuals who conceive themselves expert in the management of the gun, are often seen to meet for the purpose of displaying their skill, and betting a trifling sum, put up a target, in the centre of which a common-sized nail is hammered for about two-thirds of its length. The marksmen make choice of what they consider a proper distance, which may be forty paces. Each man cleans the interior of his tube, which is called *wiping* it, places a ball in the palm of his hand, pouring as much powder from his horn upon it as will cover it. This quantity is supposed to be sufficient for any distance within a hundred yards. A shot which comes very close to the nail is considered as that of an indifferent marksman; the bending of the nail is, of course, somewhat better; but nothing less than hitting it right on the head is satisfactory. Well, kind reader, one out of three shots generally hits the nail, and should the shooters amount to half a dozen, two nails are frequently needed before each can have a shot. Those who drive the nails have a further trial amongst themselves, and the two best shots out of these generally settle the affair, when all the sportsmen adjourn to some house, and spend an hour or two in friendly intercourse, appointing, before they part, a day for another trial. This is technically termed *driving the nail*.

Barking off Squirrels is delightful sport, and in my opinion requires a greater degree of accuracy than any other. I first witnessed this manner of procuring Squirrels whilst near the town of Frankfort. The performer was the celebrated Daniel Boone. We walked out together, and followed the rocky margins of the Kentucky River, until we reached a piece of flat land thickly covered with black walnuts, oaks and hickories. As the general mast was a good one that year, Squirrels were seen gamboling on every tree around us. My companion, a stout, hale, and athletic man, dressed in a homespun hunting-shirt, bare-legged and moccasined, carried a long and heavy rifle, which, as he was loading it, he said had proved efficient in all his former undertakings, and which he hoped would not fail on this occasion, as he felt proud to show me his skill. The gun was wiped, the powder measured, the ball patched with six-hundred-thread linen, and the charge sent home with a hickory rod. We moved not a step from the place, for the Squirrels were so numerous that it was unnecessary to go after them. Boone pointed to one of these animals which had observed us, and was crouched on a branch about fifty paces distant, and bade me mark well the spot where the ball should hit. He raised his piece gradually, until the *bead* (that being the name given by the Kentuckians to the *sight*) of the barrel was brought to a line with the spot which he intended to hit. The whip-like report resounded through the woods and along the hills, in repeated echoes. Judge of my surprise when I perceived that the ball had hit the piece of the bark immediately beneath the Squirrel, and shivered it into splinters, the concussion produced by which had killed the animal, and sent it whirling through the air, as if it had been blown up by the explosion of a powder magazine. Boone kept up his firing, and before many hours had elapsed, we had procured as many Squirrels as we wished; for you must know, kind reader, that to load a rifle requires only a moment, and that if it is wiped once after each shot, it will do duty for hours. Since that first interview with our veteran Boone, I have seen many other individuals perform the same feat.

The *snuffing of a candle* with a ball, I first had an opportunity of seeing near the banks of Green River, not far from a large Pigeon-roost, to which I had previously made a visit. I heard many reports of guns during the early part of a dark night, and knowing them to be those of rifles, I went towards the spot to ascertain the cause. On reaching the place, I was welcomed by a dozen of tall stout men, who told me they were exercising, for the purpose of enabling them to shoot under night at the reflected light from the eyes of a Deer or Wolf, by torch-light, of which I shall give you an account somewhere else. A fire was blazing near, the smoke of which rose curling among the thick foliage of the trees. At a distance which rendered it scarcely distinguishable, stood a burning candle, as if intended for an offering to the goddess of night, but which in reality was only fifty yards from the spot on which we all stood. One man was within a few yards of it, to watch the effects of the shots, as well as to light the candle should it chance to go out, or to replace it should the shot cut it across. Each marksman shot in his turn. Some never hit either the snuff or the candle, and were congratulated with a loud laugh; while others actually snuffed the candle without putting it out, and were recompensed for their dexerity by numerous hurrahs. One of them, who was particularly expert, was very fortunate, and snuffed the candle three times out of seven, whilst all the other shots either put out the candle or cut it immediately under the light.

Of the feats performed by the Kentuckians with the rifle, I could say more than might be expedient on the present occasion. In every thinly peopled portion of the state, it is rare to meet one without a gun of that description, as well as a tomahawk. By way of recreation, they often cut off a piece of the bark of a tree, make a target of it, using a little powder wetted with water or saliva for the bull's eye, and shoot into the mark all the balls they have about them, picking them out of the wood again.

After what I have said, you may easily imagine with what ease a Kentuckian procures game, or despatches an enemy, more especially when I tell you that every one in the State is accustomed to handle the rifle from the time when he is first able to shoulder it until near the close of his career. That murderous weapon is the means of procuring them subsistence during all their wild and extensive rambles and is the source of their principal sports and pleasures.

Shooting for Beef

As THIS is a novelty to most of my readers, I will endeavor to give a description of this western amusement.

In the latter part of summer our cattle get very fat, as the range is remarkably fine; and some one, desirous of raising money on one of his cattle, advertises that on a particular day, and at a given place, a first-rate beef will be shot for.

When the day comes, every marksman in the neighborhood will meet at the appointed place, with his gun. After the company has assembled, a subscription paper is handed round, with the following heading:

"A. B. offers a beef worth twenty dollars, to be shot for, at twenty-five cents a shot." Then the names are put down by each person, thus:

> D. C. puts in four shots, ... $1.00
> E. F. puts in eight shots, ... 2.00
> G. H. puts in two shots, ... 0.50

And thus it goes round, until the price is made up.

Two persons are then selected, who have not entered for shots, to act as judges of the match. Every shooter gets a board, and makes a cross in the centre of his target. The shot that drives the centre, or comes nearest to it, gets the *hide and tallow*, which is considered the first choice. The next nearest gets his choice of the hind quarters; the third gets the other hind quarter; the fourth takes choice of the fore quarters; the fifth the remaining quarter; and the sixth gets the lead in the tree against which we shoot.

The judges stand near the tree, and when a man fires they cry out, "Who shot?" and the shooter gives in his name; and so on, till all have shot. The judges then take all the boards, and go off by themselves, and decide what quarter each man has won. Sometimes one will get nearly all.

This is one of our homely amusements—enjoyed as much by us, and perhaps more, than most of your refined entertainments. Here each man takes a part, if he pleases, and no one is excluded, unless his improper conduct renders him unfit as an associate.

Fox-Hunting Fever

Now it is not to be supposed that fox hunting is not attended with its evils. It is followed at the season of the year when the ripening cotton is in perfection. A troop of madcaps in full tilt across a cultivated "hundred-acre

From *Life of Colonel Davy Crockett*, The Original Humorist and Irrepressible Woodsman . . . , pp. 237–238. Philadelphia: John E. Potter and Company. 1860.

From "Cotton and Its Cultivation," by T. B. Thorpe, of Louisiana, *Harper's New Monthly Magazine*, Vol. VIII (March, 1854), No. XLVI, p. 458. New York: Harper & Brothers, Publishers.

field" is at an expense of "a bale" at least; and there are certain unpoetical people who hear the ringing notes of the hound approaching from a distance with any other feelings than those of pleasure. Still resistance would be useless, for public opinion rather claims it as a right than a favor to pursue the fox wherever he may run.

We knew an old gentleman, however, who from his admitted and often demonstrated courage, and his patriarchal character, could enforce laws regarding *his* property upon "the boys" that were dead letters if invoked by younger men. Now this "fine old gentleman" determined to give all due notice of consequences to "trespassers," and so he posted, at favorable places along his fields, a printed exposition of the pains and penalties attending the breaking down of *his* fences and destroying *his* property, more particularly by "the misdemeanor of running foxes and hounds" through the "said plantations."

Now it so happened that on a fine morning of the hunt we have briefly alluded to that our fox-hunters, pushing pell-mell over brake and sward, were brought to a stand by these "official advertisements." The inconsiderate, either by youthful thoughtlessness or the excitement of the chase, leaped the frail barriers of the fence, when the more reflecting of the party called a halt, urged the deference due the feelings of the old gentleman, and at what little cost it would be to reach the hounds by turning the proscribed boundaries in their way; and with a hearty response, in another instant away swept the foaming steeds, down the road hard by. Now our old planter had heard the ominous cry of the hounds, and had gone out among his acres for the especial purpose of defending them from invasion. While riding about, the deep, shrill cry of the approaching pack, unconsciously to himself, struck chords that half a century before had so keenly vibrated in his own bosom. He leaned back upon his horse, his eyes flashed with unwonted fire, his nostrils dilated, and, as if by magic, he was young again; and, waving his hat aloft, he gave forth a wild note of encouragement to the pack, which, at the moment, like fleeing spirits swept his path. Then noticing the hunters, apparently at fault *by taking the road*, he galloped toward them, and, to their astonishment, pointed at the course of the chase with the handle of his riding-whip; and as the sportsmen leaped into his fields, again and again the notes of encouragement burst from the old man's heart, and thus exulting, away he went with the crowd, that knocked the cotton from the stalks until it wastefully covered the earth; and flew in the air, enveloping horse and rider like a driving storm of snow.

Fox Heroes

THE chief sport, however, was fox-hunting. It was, in season, almost universal. Who that lived in that time does not remember the fox-hunts—the

From *Social Life in Old Virginia before the War*, by Thomas Nelson Page, pp. 69–70. Copyright, 1897, by Charles Scribner's Sons. New York.

eager chase after "grays" or "old reds!" The grays furnished more fun, the reds more excitement. The grays did not run so far, but usually kept near home, going in a circuit of six or eight miles. "An old red," generally so called irrespective of age, as a tribute to his prowess, might lead the dogs all day, and end by losing them as evening fell, after taking them a dead stretch for thirty miles. The capture of a gray was what men boasted of; a chase after "an old red" was what they "yarned" about. Some old reds became historical characters, and were as well known and as much discussed in the counties as the leaders of the bar or the crack speakers of the circuit. The wiles and guiles of each veteran were the pride of his neighbors and hunters. Many of them had names. Gentlemen discussed them at their club dinners; lawyers told stories about them in the "Lawyers' Rooms" at the court-houses; young men, while they waited for the preacher to get well into the service before going into church, bragged about them in the churchyards on Sundays. There was one such that I remember; he was known as "Nat Turner," after the notorious leader of "Nat Turner's Rebellion," who remained in hiding for weeks after all his followers were taken.

Coon Dogs and Coon Hunting

TIDEWATER VIRGINIA has ever been famous as a hunting ground. There are wild ducks and geese on the rivers and creeks during the spring and fall months, and partridges, wild turkeys, raccoons, opossums, rabbits ("old hares") and squirrels in the forests, and game birds in the fields and marshes, and in some few sections there are deer and foxes. Dogs are specially trained for these several hunts. The Negroes usually trained the dogs for "night varmints," such as coons and possums. A good coon dog is considered a valuable asset by the Negro who is fond of hunting.

A Negro who was noted for his good coon dogs was asked how many he had, to which he replied: "I hain't got but foh jist now. I hev sich bad luck wid my pups dat it looks laik I nevah kin git a sta't on dogs agin. Boss, has yo' any pups yo' wants to part wid to trade for a 'muley cow'?"

The whites usually trained the dogs for birds, and for running deer and chasing foxes. Each pack had its "leader" dog which could be depended upon to keep the "scent" and the "trail"; he was known as the "harker." The hound dogs were not usually overfed during the hunting season and for that reason were great thieves in stealing food from the kitchen. Hungry, thievish hounds have been known to grab a ham or shoulder of meat from

From *Life in Old Virginia*, A Description of Virginia, More Particularly the Tidewater Section, Narrating Many Incidents relating to the Manners and Customs of Old Virginia So Fast Disappearing as a Result of the War between the States, together with Many Humorous Stories, by James J. McDonald, edited by J. C. Chandler, pp. 282–288. Copyright, 1907, by the Old Virginia Publishing Company, Inc. Norfolk, Virginia.

the scalding hot water in which it was being cooked in the open fireplace.

Every farmer kept several dogs, and the more remote their dwelling house was from the main public highway, the greater the number of dogs. When a stranger approached such dwelling, his coming was announced through the deep baying tones of some watchful hound, whose warning notes were sure to awaken from their slumbers a howling pack of young pups and older dogs to join this sentinel of the homestead in bidding defiance to the newcomer.

* * * * *

Since the Civil War there are few large packs kept as the foxes and deer have in many places become entirely extinct, and the people have become too industrious to spend much time as formerly in hunting.

In years gone by it was the desire of every youngster in Tidewater Virginia to own a whole coon dog or a "right smart share" in one. The dog of a youngster was a fortunate animal, as he was sure to share in all the "good eatings" of his owner.

A good coon dog is of medium size. He is either a "yaller dog" or a mud-brown color. He has no pedigree to speak of. He is best described as a "no account lazy dog." When he's lazy "he's jes restin'," for he knows not what to-morrow's night will bring forth. When he starts "out with the boys" he sheds his laziness in his kennel. A big dog is not fit for a coon hunt because he is too clumsy. A good coon dog must be lively when the occasion arises.

The coon fights lying flat upon his back. When shaken down from a tree, upon which he has taken refuge, and lands upon the ground, he determines at once whether to run or fight. He has sharp claws upon every foot which he works with precision and lightning-like rapidity. These weapons of defense, aided by sharp teeth within snappy jaws, will make a lazy dog lively and keep him busy to save his hide. An old Negro remarked that "de coon suttinly mus' larned his boxin' tricks sparrin' wid light'in'." A good hunter never shoots a coon up a tree; he is always shaken down from the limb upon which he has taken refuge, and if he should fortunately land upon the back of a big dog he would have all the fun to himself.

A coon hunt is not complete without a spry young Negro accompanying the party to climb the tree and shake down the coon. The start for a coon hunt is made by getting together two or three dogs along about bed time. The hunting ground may be reached within a mile or two or more of the starting point, in the dense timbered woods, on the edge of a swamp or marshy place. When this is reached the hunter lets the dogs loose, and "whoops" and whistles in low, long tones to encourage the dogs and shouts "look 'em up," at the same time calling the name of the favorite dog ("Liza"). When the scent is struck, the dogs "give mouth," and the hunter listens and waits to learn which direction the coon will finally decide upon. The voice of the dogs will indicate to the hunter whether they have the coon "on the run" or whether they have "struck a cold scent."

An old man, or a city-bred man with starched clothes and patent leather shoes, had better not engage in a coon hunt. The old man would wear out his bodily strength in following the coon. The city-bred man would wear out his "store clothes" and look like a corn field scarecrow, and before the hunt is ended the coon's claws may reach his face, and then he will look like an Apache Indian at a war dance. A Tidewater Virginia coon will lead the dogs and the hunters through the thickest of laurel bushes and swamp briars, through marshes and deep dark gulleys and into mudholes knee deep, and may select a tree for refuge in a spot that would mire a mule.

When the dogs are "on the run," their baying is open-mouthed and prolonged. When they get close upon the coon, the baying is short, sharp, and eager, and when the coon is treed the dogs will raise their heads and bay slowly, as if listening between each breath for the hunter. If the hunter is within hearing, they are encouraged by him with a "whoop" and "Hold him, Liza." The hunter can distinguish the voice of each dog in the pack. Only one dog gives voice at a time after the coon is treed. The others whine or lie down and wait quietly. When the hunter reaches the tree, a good coon dog will endeavor to point out the coon by going around the tree, and moving backward and forward, his nose pointed upward, and eagerly barking. The hunter scans the tree by walking around it and getting in range of the sky line. If the sky is cloudy, a fire of dry leaves and light limbs is made to burn brightly, the flames from which expose the whole tree to view.

"Ef Mistuh Coon is up dar I'se gwine shake him down," and up climbs the sprightly Negro to his duty. . . . [Coons] are not all alike, either in disposition or courage. Some will fight upon the ground only, others will fight up a tree. A well trained coon dog will stand a few feet from the body of a tree ready to pounce upon anything that first comes down to the ground from that tree, whether it be the coon or the Negro youngster. It is a matter of "first come first served," and the dogs will do it in a hurry. Many trees are matted with wild grape and "Virginia trumpet" vines and dry forest leaves which during the fall months accumulate amongst these vines. Should a coon seek refuge in such a tree and the hunters lose control of the fire, and it should take to the mass of combustibles up that tree while the Negro is shaking down a "sassy coon," then matters take a serious turn. If the Negro remains up the tree, the fire will burn him and the coon will scratch him. If he comes down, the dogs will get him before the hunters can control him.

"Fo' de Lawd's sake, Mass' Jack, hol' Liza, fur I'm a-comin'," and down comes the Negro. "It's too hot up dar fo' me." If he escapes the dog, it is because of the frantic and successful effort of his young master in luckily grabbing the tail of "Liza" when she heard something coming down that tree.

The most exciting time of a young coon hunter's experience is when the coon drops upon the ground and the bright flames of fire, which formerly made all things plain, is suddenly extinguished by the dogs in their scuffle and efforts to reach the coon. Then all is blacker than the famed darkness of "Egypt's midnight," and amid the barking of the dogs, and the screeches of the coon, and the scattering of the fire coals and partly burned limbs and leaves, and the sudden and unexpected bumping of each hunter, one against the other, in their wild and sightless endeavors to avoid being bitten by the dogs, or scratched by the coon, business becomes so brisk under the tree that until the fight is finished no one can tell how many coons were shaken out of it.

If the coon is an old one, he may have learned the trick of fooling the dogs by jumping to the limb of another tree; in that event he leaves the dogs "barking up the wrong tree" to be chided by the hunters as good-for-nothing, worthless curs. Sometimes a coon will seek a hollow tree; in that event he is "smoked out" by a fire of dry leaves, or the tree is cut down and he is reached.

A coon is hunted for the sake of his hide, and a possum for his meat. The hide of a coon is tanned with the hair and tail upon it. In former years, a coonskin cap, with the tail hanging behind, and a calfskin vest were the envied apparel of a dandy.

The possum is the favorite with the Negro. After capture, the possum is usually put in a box or barrel to cleanse and fatten, then it is roasted and served in its own rich gravy with Tidewater Virginia sweet yams.

The possum makes no fight when hunted. He usually runs for his hole in some hollow tree. When captured he "plays possum" by shutting his eyes as if he were asleep, or dead, all the while he is watching out of one corner of his apparently close-shut eyes for an opportunity to escape. While "playing possum" he disguises his breathing as much as possible.

Razorbacks and Piney-Woods Rooters

I [1]

. . . LIKE all true folk-myths, the razorback stories have an unknown origin. Assume that someone commented on a temporary scarcity of acorns and the consequent thinness of his hogs. A second man would agree, saying that his sows were able for the first time to squeeze through the garden gate. A third would testify that he could now hang his hat on the hips of his hogs. The next would aver that his swine had to stand up twice in order to cast a shadow. One man was almost bound to swear that *his* hogs were so desperately starved he could clasp one like a straight razor and shave with the bony ridge of its back.

Outside the imagination, a true razorback probably does not exist. There is no flesh-and-blood counterpart of the little bristle-backed emblem of the

[1] From *Arkansas, A Guide to the State*, compiled by Workers of the Writers' Program of the Work Projects Administration in the State of Arkansas, p. 99. American Guide Series. Copyright, 1941, by C. G. Hall, Secretary of State, Arkansas. New York: Hastings House, Publishers.

University of Arkansas football team, and a State official once vainly offered a reward for a genuine razorback, dead or alive. It has been said by some historians that De Soto's men brought hogs with them when they crossed the Mississippi into Arkansas. Some of these animals strayed into the woods and became gaunt, savage beasts living on mast. That was a long time ago, however, and the truly wild breed, if there ever was one, has forever disappeared. Though many farmers let their hogs forage in the forest for a good part of the year, the swine resemble those to be found in all parts of the United States.

II [2]

Piney-woods rooters live in "de po' folks' lan'." They are hogs, wild hogs. There is a difference between a rooter and a razorback. The razorback is almost extinct, but the rooters roam the ridges and dig a living from among acorns and pine knots. They have outlived the razorbacks because their haunts are not as settled as hills where the razorbacks roamed. Their hams and bacon are the best ever cured.

They should be hunted with "hawg dawgs," a gun, and an ax. The dogs are bred for just such dangerous work. It takes three men to hunt rooters. The dogs trail them. Cornered, the wild hogs will turn on their tormentors. I've seen a tusked rooter rip a hound to pieces. And I've seen a hunter jump into a snarling pack of dogs and beat a hog to death to save his hounds.

The men should walk about ten feet apart in single file. When the hog is "treed"—that is, cornered—he will charge. The first man must drop to his knees and fire. A skilled hunter will aim for the beast's head. If he misses, the next man begins firing. If both miss, they had better run to the nearest stump while the mad brute charges the third man, armed with only a two-edged ax. The coup de grâce is simple. The axman merely waits until the hog drops his head for the attack, then smashes him above the ear.

The catch must be dressed quickly. Waste goes to the dogs. Lard is made from the fat and cracklings from the parched bits of fat. Cracklings are used to make crackling bread. The hams are cured over a hickory-chip fire.

The Chesapeake Bay Dog

A VALUABLE asset to every big ducking club on the Chesapeake is the famous "Chesapeake Bay dog." When some lover of animals undertakes in the future to write "The Complete History of Dogdom," he will not do full

[2] From Look Away! A Dixie Notebook, by James H. Street, pp. 61–62. Copyright, 1936, by James H. Street. New York: The Viking Press.

From The Chesapeake Bay Country, by Swepson Earle, pp. 264–266. Second edition, revised 1924. Copyright, 1923, 1924, by Swepson Earle. Baltimore: Thomsen-Ellis Company, Publishers.

justice unless he devotes one of the principal chapters to the Chesapeake Bay breed. This dog is not only typically American, but for more than a century has been confined to the Chesapeake. With the increase of wild fowl more attention is being given to the perpetuation of this breed.

Several traditions supposed to explain the origin of the Chesapeake Bay dog are extant, three of which have widest attention. The first is that the species resulted from a cross between a retrieving dog and an otter. This probably arose from the fact that "in olden times they were known as otter water dogs from their resemblance to the otter in their form, color, and habits."

Another story is to the effect that in 1807 the ship *Canton*, of Baltimore, fell in at sea with an English brig that was on its way from Newfoundland to a home port. The brig had met with disaster and was sinking. Its crew was taken on board the *Canton*, together with two puppies, a male and a female. The dogs were purchased by the captain of the *Canton* and landed in Baltimore. "Here," states the narrator, "the dogs obtained a great reputation as duck retrievers. No one has ever been able to produce positive evidence that there was ever any progeny from these two, but the natural supposition is that such was the case and that they were the foundation of the stock of the Chesapeake Bay dog."

The third tradition has been given by Joseph A. Graham, of Salisbury, Maryland, in his book, *The Sporting Dog*. He had it from the late Gen. Ferdinand C. Latrobe, who for years had supervision of the dogs of the Carroll Island Club. According to this, "many years ago a vessel from Newfoundland ran ashore near an estate called Walnut Grove, on the banks of the Chesapeake. On board the ship were two Newfoundland dogs which were given by the captain to Mr. Law, owner of the estate, in return for kindness shown the stranded men. The beginning of the Chesapeake Bay dog was from a cross between these Newfoundlands and the common yellow and tan coonhounds of that part of the country."

Which of these traditions is true is not known, but it is probable that the last mentioned is nearer correct history. Whatever his origin, the Chesapeake Bay dog has a lineage running back more than a century. With the exception of color, there is no trace of a similar breed in Ireland, where, it is maintained by some persons, his ancestors originated.

In color the dogs range from a deep seal-brown through the varying shades of brown to a very light sedge, or faded buffalo color, and in coat from the smooth, wavy and short to the heavy and thick, resembling the sheep pelt. This difference in color and coat seems to occur in almost every lot of puppies; just why it is so is a mystery. Frequently on the breast of the Chesapeake Bay dog a small white star is found.

The animals are said to be absolutely fearless and hardy to a degree. They are never known to quit under the most trying circumstances. Deep mud, tangle rushes and extreme cold have no terrors for them. They have been known to break ice over an inch thick in going after a duck and repeat the trick as often as called upon.

Their strength of limb, power of endurance, dense coat and general intelligence fit them especially for winter work in the waters of the Chesapeake, which is frequently covered with floating ice, when much duck shooting is done. Some of these dogs have been known to swim miles through rough water covered with broken ice after a wounded duck. The late Julian F. Bailey told me that he once saw a dog swim over a mile toward the middle of Chester River after a swan that had been killed with a rifle shot. The bird was too large and heavy to be brought ashore in the mouth, as ducks are, but the intelligent animal seized the swan by the neck, swung the body over her shoulders and came ashore with it.

This same dog took the greatest delight in duck hunting and was content to remain in a blind all day with an expert gunner. She had little patience with poor shots, however. She would observe the coming of a flock of ducks as soon as the gunner and would watch carefully over the blind, keeping her body in hiding in order not to alarm the winging and suspicious fowl. If the gunner brought down a duck the dog was out of the blind and into the water almost before the fowl struck the water; if there was a miss, she would give a snort of disgust and lie down to await another chance.

Tournament Day

THE most picturesque fiestas in Maryland are the tournaments. Formerly held in all parts of the state, they are now pretty well restricted to Southern Maryland, though I hear occasionally of one in Harford and there have been sporadic attempts to revive the custom on the Eastern Shore. When a smart society is in the ascendant, tournaments are quickly abandoned; it is only in the unfashionable parts that they flourish. I have asked many of the old men how they started and the answer is always the same; they didn't start, they have come down uninterruptedly from medieval times. I am inclined to suspect that this is a myth; nevertheless the rite is an ancient and a gallant one.

Each little community holds its tournaments once a year, generally in the month of August. The proceeds are devoted to the local church. A flat pasture field is chosen and measured off and three wooden arches erected in line. From the middle of each arch depends an iron rod with a claw in the end which holds an iron ring of the sort you snatch at from the

From *Maryland Main and the Eastern Shore*, by Hulbert Footner, pp. 284–287. Copyright, 1942, by D. Appleton-Century Company, Inc. New York and London.
Cf. G. Harrison Orians, "The Origin of the Ring Tournament in the United States," *Maryland Historical Magazine*, Vol. 36 (September, 1941), No. 3, pp. 263–277.

hobby-horse of a merry-go-round. Meanwhile every boy has been practising assiduously on his own farm. Nowadays they do not tilt at each
other but at the rings. The boy who spears the most rings on the point
of his lance is privileged to crown the Queen of Love and Beauty; the
runners-up crown her Maids of Honor.

The tournament I saw at Mutual last week differed little from the first
one I saw more than thirty years ago. True, the slick automobiles, all so
much alike, were a poor substitute for the quaint family chariots, some of
which dated from the Civil War. They have all disappeared; they ought
to have been preserved in Museums. The Marshal and the Herald, fearful of appearing ridiculous, no longer stick the wife's willow plume in their
old felt hats, or hang the parlor lambrequin over a shoulder. On the other
hand, the riders are beginning to dress up again. They wear striped silk
jockey caps and gay scarfs across their breasts; most of them have achieved
riding breeches and boots. It is remarkable how many of these plain farmer
boys still contrive to keep a good riding horse.

Mutual is not even a village, but only a scattered community. Their
tournament is always the best because they put their hearts in it. The
people of Prince Frederick are becoming too worldly wise. How the women
of Mutual work to prepare and serve the supper! And what a supper!
Country-cured ham, fried chicken, deviled crabs, and fixings. They have
adopted the cafeteria style of serving which I deplore, because it deprives
you of the opportunity to exchange a bit of persiflage with the charming
waitresses, but, of course, it is a great saving of labor. Tom MacKall runs
the soft-drink stand both afternoon and evening, the hottest and the most
thankless job of all; Dr. Everard Briscoe manages the whole show and is
everywhere at once.

The scene on the field is an animated one. The long straight course is
roped off and the automobiles are lined up two or three deep. The modern
steel body permits those in the rear to sit on top of their cars. On a very
small scale, it is like the famous painting of "Derby Day." Midway a little
judge's stand has been built with a few dignitaries down in front and a
band of five or six pieces behind. Up at the start the horses are held by
colored boys while the knights await their turn. Up at this end the real
sports are always to be found kneeling in a row with bills between their
fingers watching the track and offering odds in low voices, for fear the
parson might overhear. The Marshal and the Herald patrol the course on
horseback. Of late years it has been customary to furnish the Herald with
two of the prettiest girls as pages, an innovation I endorse.

To equalize their chances, the contestants are divided into novices, amateurs, and professionals. There are crowns for novices and amateurs and
usually cash prizes for the professionals. Each knight adopts a pseudonym
for the riding, the name of his home place, such as Knight of Preston,
Knight of Parrot's Cage; Knight of Tulip Hill; or a fanciful appellation,
as Knight of Nowhere, Knight of Last Night, Knight of Failure. In choosing such names the lads, without knowing it, are upholding a tradition of

their earliest forbears, who were fond of calling their plantations "Dear-Bought," "Happy-be-Lucky," "Penny Come Quick" and so on.

The band plays a few bars and the Herald bawls out his first command: "Knight of Rousby Hall on deck!" Somebody lately pointed out the absurdity of this order, so now he has changed it to: "Knight of Rousby Hall, get ready!" The next order follows shortly: "Knight of Rousby Hall, prepare to charge!" Then: "Charge, Sir Knight!" and he comes thundering down the track. He leans far over his horse's neck with his eye trained along the lance and the true knight's expression of derring-do. If he takes the rings the band blares a few more triumphant notes; Marshal, Herald, and pages gallop to meet him and escort him back to the judge's stand. If he misses, there is silence, and he generally makes a detour back of the spectators to the starting point.

So it goes throughout the long, sunny afternoon. The star riders of other years bring their wives and babies to the field; each year there is a new crop of skinny youngsters to take their places. Each knight takes three tilts at the rings. At the end there are always ties to be ridden off, and this furnishes the most excitement. I have seen it take an hour to settle a tie between two tight-lipped boys. They put up smaller rings and when that fails, rings only a half-inch in diameter. This provides a marvelous exhibition of skill.

When the riding is over, there is a free-for-all back to the Mutual Hall for supper. It used to be served out-of-doors, but the meal was so often interrupted by a thunderstorm that now the tables are set in the hall. But you can still carry your food outside if you like it that way. Following this delectable meal, after an interval to give the girls time to change their dresses, comes the ball. The tables have been whisked out; the brass band transforms itself into an orchestra. Calvert County is famous for its pretty girls, and each year, I swear, they grow prettier.

There is a deal of oratory spilled on these occasions. Political aspirants are always to be had; one is invited to address the assembled knights in the afternoon, another (of the opposite party) to open the ball. The speeches bear a strong family resemblance with frequent reference to "our brave knights and fair ladies; the ancient chivalry of Maryland" and so on. It is a pretty sight to see the successful knights and their crowned ladies lined up in front of the platform. The crowns are fillets of wax orange blossoms, becoming to every feminine head. Everybody heaves a sigh of relief when the orator finishes his peroration. The first dance, "the royal set," is reserved to the knights and ladies.

"Tou'nament Day" provides Calvert County with its grand opportunity of the year to get together. All the sons and daughters who have gone out into the world try to get home for that day. In the afternoon there is continual visiting from car to car; in the evening the older ladies sit around the stifling hall, fanning themselves, and, of course, you must speak to them all. It is wonderful for anybody like me, brought up in an unfeeling city, to have a community where I belong.

The New Year's Shoot

FROM about the middle of the eighteenth century the Piedmont section of North Carolina centering in the counties of Forsyth, Rowan, and Cabarrus, and lying in the basins of the Yadkin and the Catawba Rivers, received a considerable infusion of Moravians, Rhinelanders, and other German-speaking stock. A few of these settlers came directly from Europe; most of them came down the valleys from Pennsylvania, Maryland, and Virginia in families or settlements. Some of their folklore has been recorded in Miss Adelaide Fries' numerous studies of Moravian church and cultural history and in Dr. Carl Hammer's *Rhinelanders on the Yadkin* (Salisbury, N. C., 1943). A few special features, chiefly the beautiful Easter morning sunrise service at Winston-Salem, have attracted nation-wide attention and drawn numerous pilgrims to the region. But except for fragments preserved in the memories of very old people, it would appear that this folklore has not survived in verbal forms.

One custom, however, is still traditionally current in a picturesque form and is accompanied by something like a folksong in English. This is "The New Year's Shoot," with its rimed greeting and good wish delivered by "The Speech Crier." Though apparently very old, it would appear to be still vigorous, in Cleveland and Gaston Counties at least. . . .

* * * * *

The following account of "The New Year's Shoot" as it is still practised in Gaston and Cleveland Counties suggests that, of the original motivating ideas behind it,—scaring witches, invoking fertility, and well-wishing,— only the last has survived in the consciousness of its practitioners. The accompanying "Speech" of the "Speech Crier" is an especially interesting feature of the North Carolina custom. Such is not mentioned in accounts of the Bohemian, the German, and the Pennsylvania German practices. . . . The "Speech" itself would seem to be a genuine specimen of folk poetry. Curiously enough, it imparts to the custom as it is described a religious tone, of which both the participants and the reporter were conscious, and this is not entirely antithetical to the primitive idea of driving away evil spirits and, perhaps, of invoking fertility for orchards and fields.

The report is from W. Kays Gary, in the *Greensboro* (N. C.) *Daily News*, January 6, 1946, section 2, p. 1.

"Over in Cherryville, Cleveland County, they have a method of celebrating the arrival of the new year that is probably the oldest and certainly the most unique in the country. They call it 'The New Year's Shoot,' when all the descendants of this German settlement's oldest families get

---

From "The New Year's Shoot," by Arthur Palmer Hudson, *Southern Folklore Quarterly*, Vol. XI (December, 1947), No. 4, pp. 235, 237–239, 243. Gainesville, Florida: The Southeastern Folklore Society.

together with 'muzzle-loaders' over 100 years old and and for 18 continuous hours blast out explosive greetings to the new year.

"This tradition is known to be 150 years old and perhaps older. No one knows. It was going on when the grandfathers of Cherryville's oldest citizens were in knee pants. For a very particular reason it has never been highly publicized. That was because a radio engineer was heard to remark, 'Who in hell wants to hear an old gun over the radio?' when the shooters were all set for a broadcast. They wouldn't fire a shot after that and the radio station was left in the lurch.

"When this reporter first heard of the celebration on New Year's Eve he clattered over to Cherryville just before midnight and found some 25 or 30 field-clad men leaning against Civil War muskets, squirting tobacco juice, smoking cigars, and waiting for their 'H' hour. When the reporter's mission was made known, 'Uncle' A. Sidney Beam came over and introduced himself as 'The Speech Crier.' When asked about his part in the celebration, Uncle Sidney said he had chanted the 'New Year's Speech' for 57 years hand-running and that the reporter would hear it later.

"Came the stroke of midnight, and a blast that must rival that of a bomb lifted the reporter's hat and plopped it in the mud. Everybody howled, and the 'shoot' was on. Piling into cars, carrying the reporter in the rush, the crowd headed for the country, stopping several minutes later at a home on a wooded hill known as 'the Carpenter place.' It was then that Uncle Sid called out the names of the house's occupants and launched into his New Year's chant. It sounded weird and great and beautiful—like something out of old England. . . ."

Mr. Gary quotes a part of the "Speech." The following is a complete version supplied to me by Mr. Beam himself, adding, in a postscript, "I am having a record made and I will send you one. The speech is mean[ing]less unless you hear it."

"Good morning to you, Sir.
We wish you a happy New Year,
Great health, long life,
Which God may bestowe
So long as you stay here below.
May he bestowe the house you are in
Where you go out and you go in.
Time by moments steals away
First the hour and then the day.
Small the lost days may appear
But yet the[y] soon amount up to a year.
This another year is gone
And now it is no more of our own
But if it brings our promises good
As the year before the flood.
But let none of us forget
It has left us much in debt,
A favor from the Lord received
Since which our spirits hath been grieved.
Marked by the unerring hand

Thus in his book our records stands.
Who can tell the vast amount
Placed to each of our accounts
But while you owe the debt is large
You may pleade a full discharge.
But poor and selfish sinners, say
What can you to justice pay?
Trembling last for life is past
And into prison you may be cast.
Happy is the believing soul.
Christ for you has paid the whole.
We have this New Year's morning
    call[ed] you by your name
And disturbed you from your rest.
But we hope no harm by the same.
As we ask come tell us your desire
And if it be your desire
Our guns and pistols they shall fire.
Since we hear of no defiance
You shall hear the art of science.

When we pull triggers and powder burns
You shall hear the roaring of guns.
Oh, daughters of righteous[ness], we will
    rise

And warm our eyes and bless our hearts,
For the old year's gone and the New
    Year's come
And for good luck we'll fire our guns."

Mr. Gary's account continues:

"Then once more came the booming of the guns, followed by a moment of silence. There was something religious about it, one 'shooter' said, and the reporter could agree. With the firing of the last gun, one stood stock-still there on the wooded hill at 3 o'clock in the morning and saw the rising of the mists from the bottom lands—heard the rumbling echoes rolling over the hills and swamplands and dying away unchallenged in the distance. Hal Stroupe, tall and rugged, leaned in silence against his old blunderbuss and stared after the rumblings, his bony, powerful face silhouetted in the half-moonlight, reminding an old-timer of 'Uncle Eph,' Hal's grandfather, who had years ago been an ardent follower of the shoot.

"That was the way it went all night—the speech, the guns, the silence, then the food—over swampland and mud-gummed roads—until 6 p.m. on New Year's Day, when, tired and happy with a job well done, the townspeople crowded into the 'Square' and boomed out their last salute to the New Year."

*   *   *   *   *

Thus, "The New Year's Shoot," which, according to the January 8, 1948, number of *The Eagle,* of Cherryville, N. C., was celebrated with great éclat in Gaston County on January 1, 1948, is rooted in customs already old when the Rhinelanders and Moravians left their homelands in the eighteenth century. It has been continuously observed by descendants of these people in North Carolina for at least 175 years. It has picked up, somewhere along the line, possibly from hints in the old English mummers' plays, "The New Year's Speech," which seems to have been reported elsewhere only from Missouri. And according to Mr. Beam, custom and "Speech" have a healthy chance for survival in North Carolina "for many more years to come."

Mardi Gras

IT WAS on the last Monday of the carnival, Lundi Gras, 1699, you remember, that Iberville made his way through the formidable palisades and superstitious terrors that guarded the mouth of the Mississippi. . . . The next morning, on Mardi Gras, he formally took possession of the country, and the first name he gave on the Mississippi was in honour of the day, to a little stream—Bayou Mardi Gras, as it still is printed on the last, as on the first, map of the region. After such a beginning, and with such a co-

From *New Orleans, The Place and the People,* by Grace King, pp. 391–396. Copyright, 1895, by The Macmillan Company. New York and London.

incidence of festivals, it is not surprising to find traces of Mardi Gras celebrations throughout all the early Louisiana chronicles. The boisterous buffooneries of the gay little garrison at Mobile generally made Ash Wednesday a day for military as well as clerical discipline, and the same record was maintained in New Orleans. As for New Orleans, it is safe to say that her streets saw not the sober qualities of life any earlier than the travesty of it, and that since their alignment by Pauger, they have never missed their yearly affluence of Mardi Gras masks and dominoes; nor from the earliest records, have the masks and dominoes missed their yearly balls.

Critical European travellers aver that they recognize by a thousand shades in the colouring of the New Orleans carnival, the Spanish, rather than the French influence, citing as evidence the innocent and respectful fooleries of street maskers, the dignity of the great street parades, the stately etiquette of the large public mask balls, the refined intrigue of the private ones. These characteristics naturally escape the habituated eyes of the natives. The old French and Spanish spirit of the carnival has in their eyes been completely destroyed by the innovation of American ideas, as they are still called. For it was an American idea to organize the carnival, to substitute regular parades for the old impromptu mummery in the streets, and to unite into two or three social assemblages the smaller public mask balls that were scattered through the season, from Twelfth Night to Mardi Gras. The modification was a necessary one in a place where society had so rapidly outgrown the limiting surveillance of a resident governor and of an autocratic court circle; and if much seems to have been lost of the old individual exuberance of wit and fun, specimens of which have come to us in so many fascinating episodes from the always socially enviable past, the gain in preserving at least the forms of the old society through the social upheaval and chaos of revolution and civil war has been real and important.

*   *   *   *   *

There is a theory, usually bruited by the journals on Ash Wednesday morning, that Mardi Gras is a utilitarian festival; that it pays. But this deceives no one in the city. It is assumed, as the sacramental ashes are by many, perfunctorily, or merely for moral effect upon others, upon those who are committed, by birth or conviction, against pleasure for pleasure's sake. . . .

There is a tradition that the royalties of the carnival show a no more satisfactory divine right to their thrones than other royalties; that the kings are the heavy contributors to the organization, and that a queen's claims upon the council boards of the realm of beauty are not entirely by reason of her personal charm. There is such a tradition, but it is never recognized at carnival time, and seldom believed by the ones most interested; never, never, by the society neophyte of the season. Ah, no! Comus, Momus, Proteus, the Lord of Misrule, Rex, find ever in New Orleans the hearty loyalty of the most unquestioned Jacobinism; and the real mask of life never portrays more satisfactorily the fictitious superiority of consecrated individualism in European monarchies than, in the Crescent City, do these sham faces, the eternal youth and beauty of the carnival royalties.

* * * * *

Utilitarian! Alas, no! Look at the children! But they nevertheless have always furnished the sweetest delight of Mardi Gras, as Rex himself must acknowledge from his throne chariot. It is the first note of the day, the twittering of the children in the street, the jingling of the bells on their cambric costumes. What a flight of masquerading butterflies they are! And what fun! what endless fun for them, too, to mystify, to change their chubby little personalities, to hide their cherub faces under a pasteboard mask, and run from house to house of friends and relations, making people guess who they are, and frightening the good-natured servants in the kitchen into such convulsions of terror! And they are all going to be Rex some day, as in other cities the little children are all going to be President.

Profitable! Ah, yes! Ask the crowd in the street; the human olla podrida of carelessness, joviality, and colour; more red, blue, and yellow gowns to the block than can be met in a mile in any other city of the United States. Ask the larking bands of maskers; the strolling minstrels and monkeys; the coloured torchbearers and grooms; Bedouin princes in their scarlet tunics and turbans (no travesty this, but the rightful costume, as the unmasked, black face testifies). Even the mules that draw the cars recognize the true profit of the Saturnalian spirit of the carnival, and in their gold-stamped caparisons, step out like noble steeds of chivalry, despite their ears.

The day is so beautiful, so beautiful that it is a local saying that it never rains on Mardi Gras. It were a better saying that it never should rain on Mardi Gras.

Fais-Dodo

A COUNTRY dance is generally known today among the Cajuns as a *fais-dodo* (literally, go to sleep) ; possibly because the dancers stay up all night and sometimes fall asleep while still dancing; possibly because the mothers sing *fais-dodos* (lullabies) to put the younger children to sleep so that they themselves can leave the *parc aux petits* for the dance floor:

Fais dodo, Minette,	Go to sleep, Kitten,
Trois piti coohon dulaite;	Three little suckling-pigs;
Fais dodo, mon piti babe,	Go to sleep, my little baby,
Jiska l'age de quinze ans.	Until the age of fifteen years.
Quan quinze ans aura passe,	When fifteen years have passed,
Minette va so marier.	Kitten will marry.

From *Louisiana*, A Guide to the State, compiled by Workers of the Writers' Program of the Work Projects Administration in the State of Louisiana, pp. 92–93. American Guide Series. Copyright, 1941, by the Louisiana Library Commission at Baton Rouge. New York: Hastings House, Publishers.

Swing bands, radios, and automatic phonographs have penetrated the Cajun country, but at the genuine *fais-dodo* the music of the fiddle, the accordion, and the triangle (sometimes called the "ting-a-ling") is always featured; for the Acadian retains his love for these instruments and often possesses rare skill in playing them. A full orchestra includes also the guitar and harmonica.

WAYS THAT ARE DARK

Southern Folk Beliefs

I. THE LANGUAGE OF SIGNS

. . . THE superstitious state of mind . . . sees a sign in everything, and believes that "signs wuz putchere fer man t' read." ("De Bible say," one often hears, and "There's signs in the Bible. It says so.") Since a sign is always a sign of the unusual, the unusual is always a sign. *"Ef hit ain't nachal, hit's a sign!"* And "ef you cain' do de readin', de nex' bes' thing t' do is t' ast somebody whut kin, en den, do whut dey tells you. Hit's a whole lot mo' safer t' do wrong tryin' t' do right dan hit is t' do wrong not tryin' t' do nothin' a-tall. . . ." The respect for age is as notable as the respect for tradition. "Ast de ole folks, dey knows."

In general, signs are of two kinds—warning signs, the unnatural signs referred to above, which indicate effects to follow, on the basis that coming events cast their shadows before them (omens, portents) and luck signs, good or bad, which indicate observances (charms, cures, sometimes in the form of countercharms to break another charm or avert a bad omen) or avoidances (taboos). "Warnin's" may be a "good sign" or a "bad sign" or just a "sign" or "mean" something; charms and taboos are described in some such terms as "hit's good luck" to do this or "hit's bad luck" to do that; while a cure is "good for" or a "sure cure for." A person "has a warnin' " or "knows of" a cure; he "can feel" a change in weather coming on, but animals "know" it; signs "come true," "work out," or "work out true." The reading of a weather sign may take the form of "looks like" or something "looks like . . . from the way"; the report of a sign may begin, "I know you don't believe much in signs," or "I don't believe in all signs, but"; the favorite expressions of faith and approval are "I've always heerd that," "I've heerd it that way all my life," "I've never knowed it to fail yet," and of doubt and disapproval, "I never did pay no mind to," "I never knowed it to happen out that way," or "You can't tell."

From "Folk and Folklore," by B. A. Botkin, in *Culture in the South*, edited by W. T. Couch, pp. 580–590. 591–592. Copyright, 1934, by the University of North Carolina Press. Chapel Hill.

II. Birth Lore

. . . Because things increase and decrease with the moon, the days just before or after the new moon are, to quote one Mississippi Negro prophetess, the "bes' time fer birthin' chillun, 'ca'se de moon's gedderin' strengt' t' come new, en de baby is gittin' strengt' t' come wid it. En ef it comes jes atter de new moon, dat's jes ez good, 'ca'se de Bible say 'ez de moon wax strong in de heb'm, so will de young on de ye'th' . . . tell her not t' be skeered 'ca'se d' ain' nothin' t' be skeered uv—jes take kyere uv hers'f, en eve'y day bathe her lines [loins] wid dishwatter, en don' let nothin'—no cat er dawg er rat er snake ner nothin' skeer 'er, 'ca'se dat'll mark de baby. En tell 'er, Ole Mis', she ought t' drink milkweed tea reg'lar, t' make de breas' milk strong, en ef she put some mullein in it, dat'll he'p. (Great Gawd! But dar's a heap dat chile don' know, ain' dey?) En anudder t'ing, Ole Mis', tell 'er t' be *sho* t' tie a red flannin straing roun' 'er wais' fer strengt'."

According to the same laws of similarity and contact, selecting a "name-tree" for the child is "techous" business. It must be a "soon budder," but hackberry, which buds first, has a rough bark, which makes for mean temper; whereas the oak, which is for strength, is a late budder and a slow grower. But a straight elm sapling—" 'Dat's de one,' she said, 'quick budder, grows fas', en, Lawd, how tough a ellum is!' "[1]

So the principle of "like cures like" follows the child every step of the way: a sharp ax (or plowshare) placed under the bed cuts the mother's "birthin'" pains quick. "but hit let's em bleed too much"; watering the name-tree with the baby's first bathing water would make them blood kin; chicken gizzard-linin' tea will cure the colic (also nausea, as chewing dried linings relieves indigestion), on account of the notorious hardness of the chicken's gizzard); a hog-teeth necklace helps the cutting of teeth because a hog's teeth are strong and sharp; so does a field mouse, if you run a needle and white thread through one eye and out the other and while it is still kicking hang it around the baby's neck, and as the life leaves the mouse it goes into the baby and "peartens up" both teeth and baby; and as the boy grows older he has to swallow a fish-bladder before he can learn to swim.[2]

III. Taboos and Social Control

Because of the passive and conservative role of woman, luck signs, omens, and taboos are her special prerogative, especially the "dassents," which suggest the utility of superstition for social control, as in the discipline of children, etiquette, industry. (In the Ozarks a wart, boil, or sty on the posterior is said to be caused by urinating in or fouling a path, though one

---

[1] John B. Sale, *The Tree Named John* (Chapel Hill, 1929), pp. 6–7, 10–11.
[2] *Ibid.*, pp. 10, 18, 69–72.

may escape the consequences by shouting, "I got a sty, it's a lie!"; children are also told that if they foul a path or road their sisters will die; and to eat in a toilet is described as "feedin' th' devil an' starvin' Gawd.") [3]

Taboos surround virtually every daily activity of the household—sleeping, rising, wearing of stockings and garments, care of the hair and nails, signs at sunrise or before breakfast, eating, drinking; treatment of beds, chairs, tables, sinks, stoves, fires, lamps, clocks, mirrors; baking, washing, sewing, carpentry; carrying edged tools, water ashes into, through, or out of the house; turning back, walking backwards, clasping the hands behind, planting of trees, killing of animals, etc. And equally numerous and familiar are the omens in things dropped, spilled, or found, sneezing, itching, twitching, burning sensations, features, furniture, apparel, birds, animals, the moon, the elements.

. . . [Similarly] The Negro cotton farmer's beliefs concerning cotton . . . have their obvious use for social control.

"If one starts picking cotton in a row and leaves it uncompleted to pick another row, one is in danger of being bitten by a snake." "If one starts picking cotton before all the bolls are open, he is in danger of being fired before the end of the day." "If you pick cotton out of the boll and let it fall on the ground, you will not have a successful cotton-picking season."

> "Pick five hundred pounds a day
> Or the Devil will come and carry you away."

"If cotton be left in the boll for a year, there will be a death in the family of the owner of the cotton." "If one takes cotton to a gin without covering all portions of it, the owner will be robbed of his returns." "If cotton falls from the wagon on the way to the gin, the cotton will decrease in value." "Cotton seeds that are to be planted should never be handled by children under two years of age, or the seeds will not grow."

Other cotton signs are more in the nature of rationalizations or adjustments. "If a baby is carried to a cotton field, it will grow up to be a cotton-picker, and that person's children will be cotton-pickers also." "Any one who dreams of a cotton field will be compelled to pick cotton soon."

Still others are simply *a priori* reasonings, including a large number of good and bad luck signs, omens, charms, cures, etc., of which the following are typical: "If a young cotton-picker finds a cotton boll that is being destroyed by a boll weevil, he will have a short and tragic life." "If cotton is seen blowing across a field, a snow storm will follow shortly." "Good luck will come to anybody who makes love while picking cotton." "If a girl is in a cotton field at night and sees cotton blowing towards her, that is the sign of a wedding." "If a devil's horse is found on a boll of cotton, the finder will be pursued by the devil." [4]

---

[3] For these and other Ozark beliefs see Vance Randolph, *The Ozarks: An American Survival of Primitive Society* (New York, 1931); also Charles Morrow Wilson, "Folk Beliefs in the Ozark Hills," *Folk-Say: A Regional Miscellany, 1930* (Norman, Oklahoma), pp. 157–172.

[4] Mary Daggett Lake, "Superstitions about Cotton," *Southwestern Lore, Publications*

IV. The Moon and the Signs of the Zodiac

. . . "The moon had more to do with running the country than the sun did," avers one old-timer of the days of his youth. Root crops and tubers, plants of darkness, are planted in the dark of the moon; above-ground crops in the light of the moon. The dark of the moon is also the time for deadening trees, killing weeds, riving shingles, splitting rails, laying rail fences, taking medicine, charming warts and sties, and (in the last quarter) avoiding venereal disease. The light of the moon is the time when fruit can not be killed, when fruit trees should be pruned and cut for good growth, potatoes dug and pork meat slaughtered. The signs of the zodiac also control planting and disease. Plant cabbage when the sign is in the head; cucumbers, melons, and fruit when it is in the twins; and corn in Scorpio; and castrate pigs "when th' sign leaves th' privates an' is a-startin' down." One is most suspectible to stomach trouble in Cancer, throat diseases in Taurus, venereal disease in Scorpio. Thus the almanac occupies a place beside the Bible, and, if one can make out the text as well as the signs, "not more for the weather prophecies," according to one informant, "than for the witty jokes and sayings together with a good deal of world history."

V. Weather Lore

But for the farmer weather overshadows world history and makes local history, as it makes crops, conversation, and mythology. In Texas and Oklahoma drouth is a menace, especially to the cotton farmer; to cotton delayed by drouth, as always in the Piedmont near the mountains, the first killing frost is another hazard, and, in general, wet springs are a boon to the boll weevil and wet falls the bane of the cotton buyer. In so far as he watches his smoking tobacco for dampness and observes the sweating of pumps and water pipes, the falling of smoke and soot, heavy dews and a gray sky at sunset, the farmer detects rain scientifically. When he bathes a cat in sulphur water, burns driftwood along the creeks or builds a fire in a stump on a cloudy day, hangs a snake on a fence or a bush "belly side up," sweeps down the cobwebs in the house, sprinkles salt on two crossed matches, or is led by the minister in prayer, he is "making" rain. And when he looks for snake tracks leading to higher ground, chickens oiling their feathers, or ants and prairie dogs banking up earth about the entrance to their hills, counts the stars within the circle around the moon to tell the number of days before a storm, measures the severity of the coming winter by the thickness of corn shucks. a hog's milt, or a goose's breastbone, and an extra heavy layer of fat, fur, or feathers in animals and birds, or takes warning of cold weather from a hog with a stick in its mouth, he is only guessing.

of the Texas Folk-Lore Society, Number IX, edited by J. Frank Dobie (Austin and Dallas, 1931), pp. 145–152.

VI. Cures

If the weather, on the whole, is outside of man's control, not so with love and health—his two chief fields for charms and cures. Folk medicine shows some division of labor—in so far as the men minister to the farm animals and stock or serve as "wart takers," "yerb" doctors, and "chills an' fever" doctors—and some scientific foundation, in the empiric *materia medica* (developed by trial and error) of herbs, leaves, barks, roots, seeds, fat meat, etc., used for teas, poultices, and unguents. But the women, especially the "granny woman" or midwife, the herb woman, and the old woman who has raised a large family to healthy maturity, are the chief practitioners; and mysticism and the doctrines of the scapegoat and of "like cures like" (signatures and "the hair of the dog that bit one") predominate.

Thus the poison of tobacco kills poison in the system; smoking makes the corpulent "spit their fat away"; grease rendered from red earthworms mixed with turpentine, asafoetida, and red-onion juice makes a good liniment because all these substances draw their strength from the earth; snake oil cures snake bite; onions are used to take up "yaller jaundice," the cut halves of the onion turning yellow as they take up the disease from the air; a child may be cured of fits by giving it a small dog to play and sleep with so that the dog "takes" the fits from the child and dies; a sty or venereal disease may be cured by passing it on to another; warts may be "bought," or "charmed off" by tying an equal number of knots in a horse-hair or string and burying, burning, or losing it. On the whole, charm cures lend themselves to the treatment of ailments characterized by sudden appearance and disappearance, seizure, or unpredictability, such as fits, insanity, rheumatism, bleeding, chills, and fever, etc., or to panaceas (spitting on a stone to relieve pain) or preventives (wearing asafoetida, a buckeye, beads, red flannel, a copper ring, wrist or ankle band, a coin).

Folk medicine naturally attaches more importance to the "spell" than to the "simple," and there is a good deal of hocus-pocus in "healing," especially in the treatment of affections due to heat and cold, which seem to require the casting out of demons. E.g., old women can cool fevers by the laying on of hands; chills can be driven away by boring a deep hole in the sunny side of an oak tree, blowing your breath into it, and plugging up the hole, with the result that the tree dies; fire can be driven out of burns and scalds by blowing or spitting upon the inflammation, holding it close to a hot fire or stove, or applying a moistened finger-tip and muttering some mystic "sayin'," such as a verse from the Bible, passed on from a person of the opposite sex and shrouded in secrecy, lest the charm be broken. Similar magic formulae are used to heal warts, ulcers, "risin's," sties, etc., and to stop bleeding; a posthumous child can cure croup or "thrash" by blowing into the patient's mouth; seventh sons of seventh sons and persons born with a caul are "double-sighted" and make good doctors. Yet in spite of all this there is rarely a suspicion of charlatanism, positive deception, or insincerity, since most of the healing is done and taken in good faith.

At the same time there is an artistic and even humorous relish of the mystery surrounding secret or "original" cures, and of the even more original conjectures that they give rise to, as in the Oklahoma instance of *hypopalorum* and *lopopahyrum,* two secret teas which were said to be made from the same bark—the former a powerful cathartic which could unlock locked bowels and the latter a strong emetic. "While never defi-nitely admitted by the maker, it was pretty generally believed that the bark. for making hypopalorum was shaved downward, while that for making lopopahyrum was shaved upward from the base of the tree toward the top!" [5] Good-natured "spoofing" also leads to the invention of mock cures and the perpetrating of practical jokes; e.g., the recommendation of non-existent hawk gizzards for eye trouble and goat butter (which can't be made) for croup.

VII. Negro Conjure

Although most Southern charms have European parallels, the fact that they have taken strongest hold on the Negro imagination suggests a cor-relation with voodoo and hoodoo. Thus the small number of charm cures found in northwestern Oklahoma has been partly accounted for by the small Negro population. Voodoo, however (originally a snake cult of the Ewes introduced into this country through Haiti and New Orleans), is generally reputed to have disappeared as a formal organization with the death of Marie Laveau, the last voodoo queen of New Orleans, and to survive only in fragments of hoodoo and conjuration, whose spells, charms, tricks, hands, jacks, tobies, mojos, grigris, wangas, luck balls, conjure bottles, and conjure, tricken, or goofer bags are the special province of the Negro "root doctor" or "hoodoo man." [6]

The persistence of African fetishism among Southern Negroes has been traced to its use for covert revenge by the slaves, who were guarded as strictly against overt violence as against disease, and to its extension into general medical and aleatory practice after emancipation. Because of his more limited opportunities for contact with European beliefs in the fields and because of his desire for more spectacular and awe-inspiring forms, the male clung to the old African beliefs more than the women (who, on the other hand, were more exposed to and influenced by European beliefs in the household), with the result that although women are not excluded, men predominate among Negro conjurers. And the very dissimilarity of these complex and bizarre beliefs kept them from mixing with white beliefs

[5] Walter R. Smith, "Northwestern Oklahoma Folk Cures," *Man, Bird, and Beast, Publications of the Texas Folk-Lore Society,* Volume VIII, edited by J. Frank Dobie (Austin, 1930), pp. 79–80. For weather lore, see the same author, "You Can't Tell about the Weather," *Folk-Say,* as cited, pp. 173–185.

[6] For a full discussion of voodoo and conjuration, on which this summary is based, see Newbell Niles Puckett, *Folk Beliefs of the Southern Negro* (Chapel Hill, 1926).

as the fact that only those who believe in conjuring can be conjured kept them from taking root among the less susceptible whites.

The use of Negro conjuration extends to all the practical affairs of life involving control over persons—injuring or destroying enemies, getting rid of rivals or undesirables, softening hearts, winning or holding love, "shaming yo' fairer," breaking up homes, calling the absent, getting jobs, dodging the law, protecting property, detecting criminals, gambling, collecting debts, disciplining servants, stopping trains and steamboats, producing fertility or barrenness in women, promoting crops, controlling weather, foretelling the future, and locating lost and stolen goods, water, and buried treasure (the use of the divining rod being of European origin and being widely practised by white "water-wigglers," "witch-wigglers," and "water-witchers," even for the purpose of locating oil).

Since conjuration (like all magic) depends upon resemblance and contact for producing its effects, its charms make use of all things connected with the body, "nails, teeth, hair, saliva, perspiration, dandruff, scabs of sores even, and garments worn next to the person,"—even to dirt from a person's track—"one eye-winker or the peeling of one freckle" being enough to save or ruin. These are mixed with a wide variety of symbolic substances, including plants (sampson snakeroot, devil's shoestring, Jimson weed, asafoetida, clover, tobacco); the poisonous powder of a dried puff-ball known as devil's snuff; spices and condiments (saffron, red pepper, sugar, salt, mustard seed); minerals (copperas or bluestone, lodestone, sulphur, alum); pins, needles, rusty nails, and other sharp objects; lizards, toads, scorpions, snakes, alive or dried, or powdered; camel's hair, buzzard feathers, fur from a graveyard rabbit's back, a rabbit's tail or foot, a snake skin, a snail shell, a fish eye; ashes, powdered brick dust or blue glass, anvil dust, graveyard dust, gunpowder.

Wrapped in wool, fur, silk, red flannel, these charms are bad tricks, and made into luck balls and jacks, they are good tricks. To bring the victim in contact with a charm, sprinkle it in his path or in his house, place it on his doorstep or under his bed or pillow, introduce it into his garments, hats, shoes, food, or drink, rub him or strike him with it, etc. Or, barring these bodily contacts with the victim, he may be conjured by burning "goofer dust," by the use of an image (cut out of newspaper, baked in dough, made of rags, or modeled of wax, clay, mud, butter, named after the person, and stuck full of pins or burned), or by turning a photograph upside down. Conjuration can be prevented by the use of a counter-charm, worn on the person (neck, finger, wrist, waist, ankle), tied or sewed to garments, carried in the pockets, shoes, hat, or distributed about the house or under or around the doorstep, placed under the bed or pillow, on gatesill or doorsill, or over the door. Since counter-charms are intended to ward off evil, they make use of the color red, chiefly in the form of red flannel (representing the sacrificial blood offered to the fetish, or perhaps connected with fire, which has been used to drive away spirits), and strong-smelling and strong-tasting substances, also effective in driving away evil (garlic, asafoetida, Jimson weed, mustard seed, sulphur, while red pepper and red onion juice combine both color and odor), and are often wet with camphor or whisky (also used in curing the conjured).

VIII. LOVE CHARMS

In the use of love charms (which have European parallels) the whites do not lag behind the Negroes. Thus, whereas the large drug store sale of sassafras, lodestone, brimstone, asafoetida, resin, and bluestone to the colored trade attests the vitality of Negro conjuring, drug stores in the Ozarks as well as among the Negroes of New Orleans display love powders prominently. And in the Ozarks they are taken so seriously that "the victim of a love charm or philtre is not held morally responsible for his actions, and many a deserted wife is comforted by the reflection that her man did not leave of his own free will, but was 'conjured off.' " [7]

The signature of plants (the doctrine that the color, shape, name, or other symbolic suggestion of a plant is a "sign" of a charm or cure for which it is effective) . . . is no more strikingly demonstrated than in the field of love charms. One of the most general of signatures is the ten-finger plant, a leaf of which, measured by the middle finger of the left hand, rolled up, and kept in the pocket, gives one control over people. Heart-leaves and sampson snakeroot are chewed to soften hearts. (The latter will also make a person brave, give him the best of a bargain, give him some control of the person in whose presence it is chewed, and prevent snakes from biting him, while, boiled into a strong tonic, it will bring back lost manhood.) Devil's shoestring, chewed and rubbed on the hands, will give a man control over a woman when he shakes hands with her. Vervain (sometimes called herb-of-the-cross because it is said to have grown on Mount Calvary and so has miraculous power), grown around doorsteps, will attract lovers. Shameweed or the sensitive plant will shame a recalcitrant woman; sprinkle the powdered dry root in the woman's path and she will close up like a sensitive plant; mix it with snail dust and snail water and she will leave like a snail going into its shell.

The principle of similarity and contact also operates in the liberal use of hair, nails, blood, and tracks in love charms. A woman may win a man by laying hands secretly on the back of his head, by putting a drop of her menstrual fluid into his liquor, by giving him whisky in which her finger-nail trimmings have been soaked, by putting his tracks under the bed or into an ant bed (to make it hot for him), by sprinkling his coat with alcohol into which has been squeezed juice from a piece of beef worn under her arm for two days. A man may win a woman by putting some of his blood on candy and giving it to her to eat, by putting her tracks in his sock or

---

[7] For love charms, see Puckett, *op. cit.*; Randolph, *op. cit.*, Sale, *op. cit.*, Ruth Bass, "Fern Seed—for Peace," *Folk-Say: A Regional Miscellany, 1930*, edited by B. A. Botkin (Norman), pp. 145–156; Charles Morrow Wilson, "Folk Beliefs in the Ozark Hills," *ibid.*, pp. 157–172.

wearing some of her hair in his shoe, and then burying it under his door-step, by mixing red onion juice with tracks (previously worn in his shoe) of her foot and his, and wearing the mixture, wrapped in red flannel, in his left breast pocket (in Oklahoma a wasp nest in the breast pocket will "make the girls fall").

To hold your wife's love make a toby of one of her old menstrual band-ages, then wear it sewed into the waistband of your trousers. To bring a man and a woman together put some of the hair of each into a split made with an ax in the fork of a young sapling, and when the wood grows back over the hairs the two will be eternally united. To break up a home roll the damp tracks of a man and his wife with cat and dog whiskers in a brown paper sack, tie up the sack and let it stand until the earth is dry, then throw it into the fire; or simply put the dog's hair in the man's tracks and the cat's hair in the woman's. To make running men—to drive a person away or make him crazy—throw his tracks into running water, put his hair in the gill of a fish and return it to the stream, spit in the river if the current is running opposite to the direction in which he lives, or tie one of his socks to a freight train. And by a variety of charms involving a person's tracks you may make him stagger or paralyze him, make him follow you or leave.

IX. EVIL SPIRITS

Conjuration is effective not only in the material but also in the spirit world. The Devil is a master of the black art and there are charms for summoning him as well as for seeing and talking with ghosts. But the con-juring of spirits takes the form chiefly of charms to ward off or avoid evil spirits and to keep them from interfering in human affairs. This fact has special interest in view of the absence of benevolent fairies among these supernatural creatures in America. In one Ozark tale (which seems more European than American) the poor, hard-worked old mother of a big, no-'count brat has a dream in which "tiltin on the bed-foot some little folk whinnied with each other and she heard them makin talk 'bout that no-'count whelp she owned" and by "taking their yarnin for truth—she was that near wooden they say"—she managed to cure her son of laziness by means of a magical horseshoe. With hammer for toe and a thousand pins in each calk, it was sewed on his back while he was asleep, and every time "he went to set down or thought on doin aught else but toil that ham-mer beat him and them pins pricked him till he thought not on idle fare more." But such beliefs in the "wee folk" are only "idle fare" and, far from being active, are rare even as survivals in Southern folk tales. Ghosts and the Devil are very much alive, however, and witches only a little less so, for, though charges of witchcraft are heard occasionally, most of the bewitching takes the form of conjuring, and the old broom-riding variety of hag lives only in "the old ones' yarns" and in tales to scare children.

As in all counter-charms, evil smells are effective in driving away spirits, but mustard seed planted under the doorstep, or fern seed in the hollow, a sprinkling of salt, pepper, sulphur, or collard seed, a Bible or a sharp object under the pillow will keep away both "hants" and witches, who can be killed only with a silver (sometimes brass) bullet. Used against witches, a broom or hair brush across the door or a Bible or sifter under the pillow are effective because the witch has to stop to count whatever comes before her. And sharp things (forks, knives, scissors, needles, around the bed, or under the pillow) catch in her skin, which she has to shed before she can ride you, and keep her from getting back into it when she is through.

With the Devil, who when not attired as a silk-hatted gentleman with an "ambrosial curl" to hide his horn, assumes the forms of black cat, rabbit, terrapin, serpent, house fly, grasshopper, toad, bat, yellow dog, black billy goat; with witches, who take the form of old women, black cats, ghouls, vampires, and nightmares, and ride people till they can't sleep and horses till they are all tired out, leaving them with tangled hair or knotted manes; with ghosts of the wicked, who take the form of headless black men, black cats, dogs, hogs, or cows, and good spirits who appear as white doves, men, and children or look like mist or clouds, we enter the world of demons and bestial shapes. These include not only diabolic and spectral transformations but animals with uncanny powers. This is the realm of erroneous nature beliefs, akin to the "unnatural natural history" that preceded the science of zoology. Here the aleatory element is submerged by fantasy; superstition gives way to mythology.

Dr. Ballowe and the Remède-Man

. . . NOT the least of his friends were the remède-men. They and their art had always interested him. He read everything he could find on strange worships, magic, and cults; and meanwhile he set out to find out about survivals of old beliefs in Louisiana. He always got along with the remède people, he observes.

"I'm not narrowminded. I told 'em to do their work, I'd do mine; and let the best man win." Finding a voodoo bag under a pillow, he did not harangue. "Let's try my stuff, too," he suggested. The workers with prayers and strings appreciated his viewpoint. One healer told me with feeling. "The docteur, he is a good docteur. But I think he also makes a good remède." If you know him well, the doctor today will open his pockets and display a nutmeg in each. "They are supposed to take the pain out of my ancient knees," he smiles. "My favorite remède-woman recommended them. I'm passing up no chances, me."

Sometimes it has been a race between Dr. Ballowe and the remède-man;

From *Deep Delta Country*, by Harnett T. Kane, pp. 245–246. Copyright, 1944, by Harnett T. Kane. New York: Duell, Sloan & Pearce.

he admits that a victim has now and then been saved by the quick arrival of the latter. "There are plenty of things I can't understand," he says. "One is the power of these people. I've seen them bring about what looked like cures in cases I thought doomed. According to test-tube analysis, the patients couldn't live. But they did." The healers, he thinks, are at their best in stopping loss of blood. Once during a ball game near Buras, the bat crashed heavily against the catcher's head. Blood spurted thickly from the cut. By the time Dr. Ballowe arrived he found a remède-man there. Wetting his thumbs with his tongue, the healer placed one on each side of the wound, murmured a few words, "and I can swear that the bleeding stopped in a minute or two." Dr. Ballowe complimented him on his skill, but pointed out that the saliva might cause an infection. The remède-man shook his head. "Non, Monsieur Ti' Docteur, no infection." None developed.

Dr. Ballowe received a supreme compliment when a remède-worker called him to assist with his son. As Dr. Ballowe entered, the father, without leaving his patient, called out, "Bon jour. Please, Docteur, to do your best. Docteur, I take the top half. You take the bottom, if you please." Dr. Ballowe found the youth in high fever, suffering from a complication of ailments. If he were to prevent death, he must act quickly to cut down the fever. He used ice and sponges upon the stomach and feet, while the father worked at the head and chest, with appeals to the skies and the making of many signs. The two labored without letup.

Ultimately the father asked in a tired voice, "Docteur, how your end gets along?" "Bien, bien." The father sighed. "My end not so bien. Ah, his poor brain', they look like they want to get cook'. Docteur, please to swap with me?" Dr. Ballowe proceeded with sponge and ice upon the upper body. Before long the father reached out to feel the boy's brow. He smiled: "Docteur, please to take whole boy and make your best if you please."

Voodoo

THE Aradas, St. Méry tell us, introduced [the orgies of the Voodoos]. They brought them from their homes beyond the Slave Coast, one of the most dreadfully benighted regions of all Africa. He makes the word Vaudaux. In Louisiana it is written Voudou and Voodoo, and is often changed on the Negro's lips to Hoodoo. It is the name of an imaginary being of vast supernatural powers residing in the form of a harmless snake. This spiritual influence or potentate is the recognized antagonist and opposite of Obi, the great African manitou or deity, or him whom the Congoes vaguely

From "Creole Slave Songs," by George W. Cable, *The Century Magazine,* Vol. XXXI (April, 1886), No. 6, pp. 815, 817, 820–821. Copyright, 1886, by the Century Company. New York.

generalize as Zombi. In Louisiana, as I have been told by that learned Creole scholar the late Alexander Dimitry, Voodoo bore as a title of greater solemnity the additional name of Maignan, and that even in the Calinda dance, which he had witnessed innumerable times, was sometimes heard, at the height of its frenzy, the invocation—

> "Aïe! Aïe!
> Voodoo Magnan!"

The worship of Voodoo is paid to a snake kept in a box. The worshipers are not merely a sect, but in some rude, savage way also an order. A man and woman chosen from their own number to be the oracles of the serpent deity are called the king and queen. The queen is the more important of the two, and even in the present dilapidated state of the worship in Louisiana, where the king's office has almost or quite disappeared, the queen is still a person of great note.

She reigns as long as she continues to live. She comes to power not by inheritance, but by election or its barbarous equivalent. Chosen for such qualities as would give her a natural supremacy, personal attractions among the rest, and ruling over superstitious fears and desires of every fierce and ignoble sort, she wields no trivial influence. . . .

*   *   *   *   *

To what extent the Voodoo worship still obtains here would be difficult to say with certainty. The affair of June, 1884, as described by Messrs. Augustin and Whitney, eye-witnesses, was an orgy already grown horrid enough when they turned their backs upon it. It took place at a wild and lonely spot where the dismal cypress swamp behind New Orleans meets the waters of Lake Pontchartrain in a wilderness of cypress stumps and rushes. It would be hard to find in nature a more painfully desolate region. Here in a fisherman's cabin sat the Voodoo worshippers cross-legged on the floor about an Indian basket of herbs and some beans, some bits of bone, some oddly wrought bunches of feathers, and some saucers of small cakes. The queen presided, sitting on the only chair in the room. There was no king, no snake—at least none visible to the onlookers. Two drummers beat with their thumbs on gourds covered with sheepskin, and a white-wooled old man scraped that hideous combination of banjo and violin, whose head is covered with rattlesnake skin, and of which the Chinese are the makers and masters. There was singing—"*M'allé couri dans déser*" ("I am going into the wilderness"), a chant and refrain not worth the room they would take—and there was frenzy and a circling march, wild shouts, delirious gesticulations and posturings, drinking, and amongst other frightful nonsense the old trick of making fire blaze from the mouth by spraying alcohol from it upon the flame of a candle.[1]

But whatever may be the quantity of the Voodoo *worship* left in

---

[1] Cf. *Historical Sketchbook and Guide to New Orleans* (New York, 1885), pp. 229–231.

Louisiana, its superstitions are many and are everywhere. Its charms are resorted to by the malicious, the jealous, the revengeful, or the avaricious, or held in terror, not by the timorous only, but by the strong, the courageous, the desperate. To find under his mattress an acorn hollowed out, stuffed with the hair of some dead person, pierced with four holes on four sides, and two small chicken feathers drawn through them so as to cross inside the acorn; or to discover on his door-sill at daybreak a little box containing a dough or waxen heart stuck full of pins; or to hear that his avowed foe or rival has been pouring cheap champagne in the four corners of Congo Square, at midnight, when there was no moon, will strike more abject fear into the heart of many a stalwart Negro or melancholy quadroon than to face a leveled revolver. And it is not only the colored man that holds to these practices and fears. Many a white Creole gives them full credence. What wonder, when African Creoles were the nurses of so nearly all of them? Many shrewd men and women, generally colored persons, drive a trade in these charms and in oracular directions for their use or evasion; many a Creole—white as well as other tints—female, too, as well as male—will pay a Voodoo *"monteure"* to "make a work," *i.e.*, to weave a spell, for the prospering of some scheme or wish too ignoble to be prayed for at any shrine inside the church. These milder incantations are performed within the witch's or wizard's own house, and are made up, for the most part, of a little pound cake, some lighted candle ends, a little syrup of sugar-cane, pins, knitting-needles and a trifle of anisette. But fear naught; an Obi charm will enable you to smile defiance against all such mischief; or if you will but consent to be a magician, it is they, the Voodoos, one and all, who will hold you in absolute terror. Or, easier, a frizzly chicken! If you have on your premises a frizzly chicken, you can lie down and laugh—it is a checkmate!

A planter once found a Voodoo charm, or *ouanga* (wongah); this time it was a bit of cotton cloth folded about three cow-peas and some breast feathers of a barn-yard fowl, and covered with a tight wrapping of thread. When he proposed to take it to New Orleans his slaves were full of consternation. "Marse Ed, ef yo go on d'boat wid dat-ah, de boat'll sink wi' yer. Fore d'Lord, it will!" For some reason it did not. Here is a genuine Voodoo song, given me by Lafcadio Hearn, though what the words mean none could be more ignorant of than the present writer. They are rendered phonetically in French.

> Héron mandé, Héron mandé,
> Tigui li papa, Héron mandé,
> Tigui li papa, Héron mandé,
> Héron mandé, Héron mandé,
> Do sé dan godo.

And another phrase: "Ah tingouai yé, Ah tingouai yé, Ah ouai ya, Ah ouai ya, Ah tingouai yé, Do sé dan go-do, Ah tingouai yé," etc.

Doodlebug

"The Bible," he began, "is really a wonderful book. In it, the man of the Christian epoch has been able to find almost anything he wants to find— consolation, inspiration, poetry, rules of conduct for himself and for others. Between the warnings against the worship of the Golden Calf, and the glorious story of driving the money changers from the temple, man has been able to discover cryptic phrases that will lead him to the location of great treasures, of hidden wealth, of fabulous stores of despised gold. Consider the Psalms, for instance. I remembered while we were at the witch-doctor's place that I have seen individual Psalms printed on thin tissue paper of different colors, and folded into lockets. They are used as charms sometimes to ward off sickness, sometimes as good-luck pieces.

"Here on my watch-chain I have one of the lockets. You can see how ingenious it is. This thing is far superior to a simple solid charm which serves only one purpose. It has the same advantages for the printer and vender of these protective gadgets—and for the user, too, of course—as the safety razor has for its promoters and users. It's not the original investment that matters so much, but the repeat order. You see the locket is permanent. It is handsome as an ornament, even if it contains nothing. You can always put a photograph in it, or if you have nothing better, at least a pinch of snuff, or some magic powders which Don Mariano might be able to provide.

"Each Psalm has its own special purpose."

The Judge launched into a detailed description of different Psalms, naming them by number, and quoting from them as readily as if he had been a preacher instead of a lawyer. I made notes on some of them. Here they are, without any guarantee as to their effectiveness:

For a childless couple wishing to be blessed, Psalm I, verse three:

> And he shall be like a tree planted by the rivers of water,
> that bringeth forth his fruit in his season;
> his leaf also shall not wither, and whatsoever he doeth
> shall prosper.

For a man embarking on a business venture which will take him far from his home, Psalm XVIII, the entire Psalm.

To protect the wearer's life and limb while traveling aboard any conveyance, Psalm XX.

Psalm XXIII is a good one for general use and can be substituted for any of the Psalms which have specific functions in this code of magic lockets.

For the farmer plagued with drought, Psalm LXV, verses nine to thirteen.

From *Saddle in the Sky*, The Lone Star State, by J. H. Plenn, pp. 117–121. Copyright, 1940, by the Bobbs-Merrill Company. Indianapolis and New York.

This rain-prayer must be read aloud, in the morning upon arising, and at night upon going to bed.

The Judge continued:

"There is part of one of the Psalms that I ran into over and over again when I stayed with my folks up on their farm near Wichita Falls, before they discovered oil up there. What people were hunting then was not oil, but water. There were a dozen or more men around the country who made a living locating water wells, and they always made you a proposition that nobody could turn down, because the man who owned the land thought he had nothing to lose. The water-finder said he would spot the water and tell him where to dig. If water was not found, he would not have to be paid. If it was, he would collect a fee.

"The most familiar names for their divining rods were doodlebugs and wigglesticks. Some of the fellows used to tell the kids that they really had a doodlebug—you know the kind; he crawls down the antholes and gobbles himself a mess of ants for breakfast—and that this doodlebug had a nose that could smell out water. They'd just put the bug down on the ground, they said, and let him crawl along. When he smelled water, why he'd start burrowing on down into the ground, and that would be the place to find a well.

"Then we had the religious well-finders, those who claimed they could get divine guidance in their efforts to find water by concentrating in a strong prayer. They would go into a kind of trance and then head right for the spot, just like a ouija board. Some of them used a Bible, and it was from these I learned about Psalm LXXVIII, and the key and Bible system for finding water. Psalm LXXVIII, you may remember, says:

> He clave the rocks in the wilderness,
> and gave them drink as out of the great depths.
> He brought streams also out of the rock,
> and caused waters to run down like rivers.

"Well, this fellow would slip a string inside the page of the Bible that had the Psalm on it, then tie the string around the book. He'd suspend the book from a door key, a special big key. Then he would poke a forked stick into the ground, and on it he would hang the key, from which the string and Bible were suspended. If there was water on the spot, the stick would bend 'way over in an arc. I saw it work once, and I drank water from the well on the spot. Of course we found out later that there was water almost anywhere under the place. If we had sunk a hole at any spot, we would have had just as good a well as the one we drilled."

The Judge stopped for a moment to let all this soak in.

"Come to think of it," he went on, "maybe the symbol of our state should be the doodlebug instead of the blue-bonnet or the mocker or the pecan nut or the Lone Star. Somebody, somewhere in Texas, is always drilling a hole in the ground looking for buried treasure of one kind or another. Ever since the territory that is now Texas was discovered people have been looking for gold.

"There was Coronado and his men hunting the fabulous Seven Cities of Cibola. Almost anywhere you go in the state you will find old maps and charts and landmarks supposed to hold the secret of buried treasure. But we never really know whether any of these have really yielded anything but a lot of good stories. The men who find treasure keep their mouths shut until they can get it all out, and then they vamoose. Those who don't find it either keep on hunting or else begin making up fables. The best digging we've found so far, though, has been the digging for oil."

Plat-Eyes

. . . FAILURE to give the departed a proper burial will result in disaster for the lonely spirit on its way to a final home. This fear is probably a lineal descendant of the old African belief that without proper rites for its protection a soul may be hindered by other spirits from finding its destination and become a pitiful wanderer on the face of the earth. A proper funeral ceremony is believed to be of great help in enabling a soul to find the right road to heaven and God, or to hell and Satan. Otherwise, it will haunt houses and burial grounds and lonely roads and frighten the very people it loved best on earth.

As a rule spirits resemble the bodies they occupied. The most unfortunate ones become plat-eyes and take on many shapes, changing quickly from one to another. Now a dog, then a horse, a man without a head, a warm cloud or a hot smoke that suffocates all living creatures. Plat-eyes fear nothing and stop at nothing. Wise people and beasts flee from them, for "a coward never totes broke bones."

People with vivid imaginations are often terrified by apparitions that walk at night when the moon is young. The vicinity of cemeteries is carefully avoided after dark and so are places where people have met with fatal misfortune. Animals have "second sight" and can see spirits, but only people born with cauls over their faces have this keen vision.

One Saturday evening a plantation mother who had second sight sent her two small sons on a trustworthy mule to the crossroads store to fetch home the week's supply of groceries. She warned them to hurry home before sundown since a young moon was due to shine and set spirits to walking all over the country. The boys put the paper bags of rice, sugar, white flour and coffee all together in a large crocus sack so that none would be dropped on the way home.

The lonely road ran through thick woods that ever look scary, but the mule walked along quietly until the sun dropped and a young moon showed in the sky. Then he began to back his ears and switch his tail. Just as

From *Roll, Jordan, Roll,* the Text by Julia Peterkin, the Photographic Studies by Doris Ulmann, pp. 206, 209–210. Copyright, 1933, by Doris Ulmann and Julia Peterkin. New York: Robert O. Ballou.

they came in sight of the spot where a man had been mysteriously killed years ago, the mule stopped short in his tracks and would not budge. At first they boys thought he was contrary, so the older one got a stick and frailed his sides, then beat him on the head, but the beast only rolled his eyes and snorted like he smelt something dangerous. They did not know what to make of such carrying on, until a warm gust of air passed over their faces and a small white cloud floated across the road right in front of their eyes. The hair on their heads stood up and pushed off their hats, for the cloud smelled like smoke from burning sulphur. The mule shivered and leaped backward with hoarse hee-haws, and tried his best to talk. The boys fell off his back and the groceries tumbled into the road. They did not tarry to pick up the groceries or hats but scrambled onto the mule's back just as he struck out for home. He had always been too lame and broken-winded to go faster than a walk, but he galloped like a colt until he reached home, then he fell down flat in the yard where he laid all night gasping for breath. The mother did what she could to comfort him, then she thanked God on her knees that the poor beast had sense like people and brought her sons home safe instead of letting them be smothered to death by the evil-smelling cloud. It was undoubtedly the spirit of the man who had been secretly killed years ago. His strange end was due to turn him into the most dangerous of all ghostly things, a plat-eye.

The groceries and hats stayed where they fell until the sun shone next morning, for spirits of all kinds, even plat-eyes and hags, dread sunlight and hide in dark places until first dark comes. The incident furnished the preacher with a subject for his sermon the next Sunday. He explained that if the dead man had been given a proper burial, instead of being hurried into the ground with not even a church deacon to pray over his body, he might have been a harmless "ha'nt" instead of a plat-eye which changes from one ugly thing to another as it strives to harm innocent people.

Delta Terrors

To THE Delta the Negroes have brought their superstitions, largely from Africa, and to them the whites, for the most part the French, have joined their own. A lush mixture has resulted, with members of both races and all shadings enjoying a rich spirit world all about them.

Commonest among the spirits are the revenants, simple ghosts—harmless creatures most of the time, with nowhere to go, roaming about a graveyard, fiddling among the orange trees, or trying, poor things, to sample a few oysters on a reef that they once dredged. A zombi is worse, a ghost with something on his mind. When you paddle through a swamp and see a zombi staring at you from a moss-hung branch, get out of that place, just to

From *Deep Delta Country*, by Harnett T. Kane, pp. 220–222. Copyright, 1944, by Harnett T. Kane. New York: Duell, Sloan & Pearce.

be on the safe side. How will you know a plain revenant from a zombi? My Delta friends say that it is simply a matter of personal perception; it cannot be clarified to one who has never beheld either. They can only explain, "When you first get a good look, you'll know the difference, all right!" Many of the poor revenants are only creeping about, trying to find a person who will do a little thing for them, a harmless act that will permit them to go back to their coffins and rest. Usually they want only a handful of salt. But, human nature being what it is, very few people will be inclined to do this for even the most angelic looking of revenants. He might turn out to be a zombi in disguise!

Many places in the Delta are to be avoided because strange things lurk there. For instance, there is Devil's Flat at the river edge, to which the French first gave the title Batture du Diable. Its haunting genius is a soldier lacking a head, a fellow halfway between revenant and zombi. Usually he behaves like a fatherly old man, talking nice as anything. But because he has been good humored, some are supposed to have taken liberties. He will tolerate only a certain amount of familiarity, and then he will explode at you. One drunk offered him a drink, and the old soldier hauled off and slapped him so hard that you could see the marks on his face in the middle of the afternoon the following Thursday.

Loups-garous (loogaroos) are not so plentiful as they used to be, but old people still warn against them. Every once in a while a man or woman is missed. His friends look and look, and always there is a certain animal nearby—a hog that they had never seen before, an odd black bird, a big dog. Eventually they will realize the truth—that thing is poor Emile! Some spirit caught him in its spell, and now Emile is trying to find a way to get back to himself. Or perhaps Emile has been a malevolent being all alone, hopping back and forth into animal shape and up to all kinds of devilment that his friends never realized. At any rate, everybody in the neighborhood had better watch carefully now!

Sooner or later, no matter to whom you talk about the loups-garous, you will hear the classic story of the man and wife. Madame A. wondered when her husband stayed away for a week or more in the marsh, but like an obedient housewife she raised no questions. Occasionally she noticed a curiously spotted tomcat slinking around the levee. It peered and peered at the house, as if it wanted to make sure that it missed nothing. Madame A. grew annoyed, and tossed a bit of mud at it. The cat slipped away. The next day it was back, and she threw a stick. Crying, it moved off. The third morning, truly angry when it made its appearance, she advanced with a kitchen knife. It snarled; she tossed the knife, and it cut deeply into the left hind leg. The cat vanished at once. In an hour or so, Monsieur A. came from the marsh, limping, his left foot heavily bandaged. "I drop' my ax on it," he said, and avoided her eye. "Oui," she nodded, and went back to her housework. That cat didn't come back any more, let me tell you!

Things always to be avoided are the feu follets, the French equivalent of will-o'-the-wisps. Actually, they are bits of marsh gas, forming balls of flame, bouncing about the wet edges, in cemetries, and along the swamps; but do not, I suggest, attempt to impress any superior knowledge of the subject upon a Deltan. (When I did, one fixed me with his eye: Had I ever found it coming after me? When I admitted that I had not, he pointed his finger: *He* had. And that settled me.) Some of the natives are sure these are, alas, the spirits of the poor bébés that died without being christened. Others believe they are merely free-lance villains, on the lookout for any available victim. All of the elderly and middle-aged people have seen them, and they have one bit of advice: If they move after you, you run like crazy.

Men, passing a graveyard at night, have spied little circles of light darting around the headstones, and then run home to creep shaking into bed. Others, catching sight of them at a distance, have stopped only long enough to fix a nail or their knife in a tree, before darting back to safety. A feu follet is fascinated by metal. When one comes at you, your best hope is to sidetrack him in this fashion. A man and his son, rowing together after dark, anxious to get home, suddenly halted at the same time. The father said to his boy, in trembling voice, "Al-*fred,* please to look what back of you!" Alfred was silent a moment, and then he muttered: "Papa, look wha's in back of you!" Each jerked his head about, saw a feu follet balanced on the edge of the skiff, bumping up and down as if anxious to leap upon him; and each jumped into the water and swam home. Just what happens when a feu follet gets you, I have never been able to find out. Come to think of it, I have never talked with one whom the feu follet succeeded in reaching. And it is this uncertainty that makes the feu follet the poor man's terror that it is.

III. RHYTHMS, RITUALS, AND FOLK-SAY

It is only the "Cracker," the mountaineer, the Negro, that we dare to make talk naturally in our books; and the question is in how far our writers do make these classes talk naturally? We are getting to have abundance of literature of this kind. Indeed, these classes, with the Creoles, are filling pretty much the whole field just now.

What is the cause of this change of feeling? Is it because Southern ante-bellum novels describing the old-time life were so poor, as compared with the new Southern literature; or is it because even Southerners have gotten tired of hearing of the grand life of a few people of the olden days? Is it because the aristocratic spirit has gone, and the democratic has come? Is it a sign that our hearts are more open to the world, our sympathies more enlarged?

—CHARLES FORSTER SMITH

1. Homely as Sin

WITH the fascination that good talk and story-telling hold for Southerners, it is natural that Southern writers should long have felt and obeyed the impulse to record the folk talk and stories they hear all about them. Literary interest in making the unlettered "talk naturally" in Southern books goes back before Cable, Harris, and Craddock to mid-nineteenth-century humorists like George W. Harris. Napier Wilt calls *Sut Lovingood's Yarns* the "nearest thing to the undiluted oral humor . . . that has found its way into print." [1] A large part of the humor, of course, lies in the language, which gives (according to Charles Forster Smith) the "dialect in the main correctly." [2]

"Jim Clark has gone to the woods for fat pine, and Peggy Willet is along to take a lite for him—they've been gone a coon's age. Oh, here comes the lost 'babes in the wood,' and no *lite!*" "Whar's that lite! whar's that torch! I say, Peggy, whar *is* that bundle of lite wood?" "Why, I fell over a log and lost it, and we hunted clar to the foot of the holler for it, and never found it. It's no account, no how—nuthin but a little pine—who cares?" "Hello, thar, gin us 'Forked Deer,' old fiddle-teazer, or I'll give you forked litnin! *Ar* you a goin to tumtum all nite on that pot-gutted old pine box of a fiddle, *say?*" "Give him a sock at the crock and a lick at the patent beehive—it'll *ile* his elbows." "Misses Spraggins you're a hoss! cook on, don't mind me—I dident aim to slap *you;* it was Suze Winters I *wanted* to hit; but you stooped so fair—" "Yes, and it's well for your good looks that you didn't hit to hurt me, old feller!" "Turn over them rashers of bacon, they're a burnin!" "Mind your own business, Bob Proffit, I've cooked for frolicks afore you shed your petticotes—so jist hush an talk to Marth Giffin! See! she is beckonin to you!" "That's a lie, marm! If he comes a near me I'll unjint his dratted neck! No sech fool that when a gall puts hir arm round his neck will break and run, shall look at *me*, that's flat! Go an try Bet Holden!" "Thankee, marm, I don't take your leavins," says Bet, hir face lookin like a full cross between a gridiron and a steel-trap. [3]

Language like this, based on the speech of Tennessee "knob-squatters," untouched and unspoiled by "book larnin'," suggests what Charles Forster Smith says of "certain grammatical inaccuracies, especially double negatives"; namely, that "The inclination to go back into it is something like the tendency to lapse into sin." [4]

2. Out of Their Mouths

"Strictly speaking," writes Charles Forster Smith, "there is no Southern dialect, as indeed there is no dialect anywhere in America." "If one will

---

[1] Cited by Walter Blair, *Native American Humor (1800–1900)*, (New York, 1937), p. 96.

[2] "Southern Dialect in Life and Literature," *The Southern Bivouac*, New Series, Vol. I (November, 1885), No. 6, p. 349.

[3] "The Knob Dance," cited by Blair, *op. cit.*, pp. 370–371.

[4] *Op. cit.*, p. 345.

be accurate," he goes on to say, "one must speak of peculiarities in Southern speech that would strike an Englishman or a Northerner, rather than of a dialect." [5] In other words, rather than a dialect the South has dialectal variations in pronunciation, vocabulary, syntax, etc. For the general reader the question is an academic one. What is much more important is the fact that even educated Southerners "speak the speech," as Barrett H. Clark once urged all Americans to do, with full respect for the local pronunciation, the local word, and the local idiom, thus enriching cultural diversity in America.

At its best such speech is full of the homely poetry, pungent wit, and simple wisdom of folk idiom, metaphor, and aphorism, as illustrated by these specimens from interviews with former slaves by field workers of the Federal Writers' Project:

"Mean a man as God every wattled a gut in."—"He done ever'thing he could 'cept eat us."—"I nussed babies till I got against nussing babies."—"Right smart spends it foolish."—"The snakes commenced to rattle like dry butterbeans."—"White folks do as they pleases, and the colored folks do as they can."—"I didn't quite make slavery. Me and freedom come here together."—"She said they didn't know what to do with freedom. She said it was like weaning a child what never learned to eat yet."—"People raised children in them days. Folks just feeds 'em now and lets them grow up."—"You says, why did I run? These feets was made to take care of this body, and I used 'em is all." [6]

Such natural eloquence and unstudied expressiveness are the product of what Percy MacKaye calls the "immediate moment of consciousness," responsive to the demands of "Not what has just been said, or what is about to be said, but *what is now saying*." [7] Here, too, is the accumulated mother wit of generations of handed-down images and idioms, which gives the quality of ritual to improvisation.

The same dualism of improvisation and ritual inheres in the names of Tidewater Maryland plantations—Long Looked for Come at Last, Dear Bought, Come by Chance, Second Choice, None so Good in Finland, Neighbor's Grudge, The Ending of Controversie; [8] the "bizarre and original place names" of the Appalachians—Jerk 'em Tight, Stretch Yer Neck, Shake a Rag, Broke Jug Creek, Tear Breeches Ridge, Rip Shin Thicket; [9] the street names of New Orleans—Love, Desire, Madman's, Mystery, Piety, Craps, Bagatelle"; [10] Cajun nicknames—Jean Patte-Noire, Jean Patte-Rouge, Patate (potato), Coton (towhead); [11] and odd Negro given names—Roosevelt National, Georgia Bacon, Florida Sweets, Coca Cola

[5] *Ibid.*, p. 343.

[6] B. A. Botkin, editor, *Lay My Burden Down* (Chicago, 1945), pp. 1–2.

[7] *This Fine-Pretty World* (New York, 1923), pp. 193–194.

[8] Paul Wilstach, *Tidewater Maryland*, (Indianapolis, 1931), pp. 57–60.

[9] *A Treasury of American Folklore*, (New York, 1944), pp. 326–327.

[10] Will H. Coleman's *Historical Sketch Book and Guide to New Orleans and Environs* (New York, 1885), pp. 43–44, 45.

[11] Harnett T. Kane, *The Bayous of Louisiana* (New York, 1944), pp. 173–174.

Gamble Baggett, Virginia Ham—and nicknames—Po' Chance, Yo-Yo, Bad News, Reach-an-Git-It.[12]

On the Mississippi River barges today, from the timberhead (stanchion) that the men squat on, "relaxing on the tow between jobs," their talk is known as "timberhead talk." [13] Besides such talk—"the unwritten newspaper, the spoken feature story"—every folk group has its rhythms and rituals: of work—the tobacco auctioneer's chant, soundings, hollers, calls; [14] of social intercourse—slave courtship formulae and riddles; of play—children's rhymes, formulae, game songs; [15] of religion—sermons and prayers.

In his dramatic Easter Day sermon, "The Man of Calvary," "Sin-Killer" Griffin, Negro prison chaplain at Darrington State Farm, Sandy Point, Texas, combines rhythm, ritual, and folk-say with poetry of a high order, recalling that all the arts of sound—music, poetry, drama, and oratory—once had their origin in rhythm and ritual.

> I seen while He was hanging,
> The mounting began to tremble on which Jesus was hanging on.
> The blood was dropping on the mounting,
> Holy blood, dropping on the mounting.
> My dear friends, corrupting the mounting,
> I seen about that time, while the blood was drop-ping down,
> One—drop—after—another,
> I seen the sun that Jesus made in creation;
> The sun rose, my dear friends,
> And it recognized Jesus hanging on the cross.
> Just as soon as the sun recognized its Maker,
> Why, it clothed itself in sack cloth-ing and went down,
> *Oh-h, went down in mournin'.*
> "Look at my Maker dying on the cross."
> And when the sun went down,
> We seen the moon, that was his Maker, too,
> *Oh-h, he made the moo-oon,*
> My dear friends, yes, both time and seasons.
> We seen, my dear friends,
> When the moon recognized Jesus dying on the cross,
> I seen the moon, yes, took with a judgment hemorrhage
>   and bled away. . . .[16]

> > > > B. A. B.

---

[12] Marie Campbell, *Folks Do Get Born* (New York, 1946), pp. 49–50; Ruby Terril Lomax, "Negro Nicknames," *Backwoods to Border* (1943), pp. 163–171.

[13] Edwin and Louise Rosskam, *Towboat River* (New York, 1948), pp. 234–235.

[14] Cf. *Folk Music of the United States*, Album 8, "Negro Work Songs and Calls," Washington, D. C., 1943.

[15] Cf. Thomas W. Talley, *Negro Folk Rhymes* (1922); Ray Wood, *The American Mother Goose* (1940).

[16] *Folk Music of the United States*, Album 10, "Negro Religious Songs and Services," Record No. AAFS 48–A, Washington, D. C., 1943.

Plantation Courtship Formulae and Riddles

I [1]

AMONG the slaves there were regular forms of "courtship," and almost every large plantation had an experienced old slave who instructed young gallants in the way in which they should go in the delicate matter of winning the girls of their choice.

*   *   *   *   *

"Uncle Gilbert" was the shoemaker on a plantation where there were a hundred slaves, whose good young master, "Pete," allowed them to receive company Sundays and some evenings in the week from all the surrounding neighborhood.

*   *   *   *   *

"Uncle Gilbert" was very learned in the art of "courtship," and it was to his shop the slave lads went for instruction in "courtship's words and ways." The old man had served a half dozen masters, had won and buried as many wives, and had travelled much. It was therefore conceded by the people of all the neighborhood that nobody thereabouts was a greater authority on wooing than he. "Uncle Gilbert" held the very generally accepted opinion that "courtin' is a mighty ticklish bizness," and that he who would "git a gal wuth havin', mus' know how to talk fur her."

*   *   *   *   *

[1] By Frank D. Banks and Portia Smiley. From *Southern Workman and Hampton School Record,* Vol. 24 (January, 1895), No. 1, pp. 14–15. Hampton, Virginia: Hampton Normal & Agricultural Institute.

We give complete in this issue Mr. Banks' paper read before the Hampton Folk-Lore Society in April, and subsequently printed in the Journal of American Folk-Lore.— Editor, *Southern Workman and Hampton School Record.*

That the Negro wooer should put riddles to the girl makes the usage a curious parallel to the folk-tales and folk-songs which treat of the use of riddles in European courtship. In the first volume of his great work, *The English and Scottish Popular Ballads,* Professor F. J. Child has brought together examples of the class of songs in which a man is described as winning a wife, or a lady a husband, by guessing riddles. To the latter class belongs the ballad of "The Elfin Knight," of which an American version has been printed in this Journal (Vol. vii, p. 228). By comparative examination, Professor Child is led to the conclusion that the ballad in question depends on an ancient and simple tale, having originally some historical sequence (see Vol. vii, p. 231). But the Negro parallel suggests the possibility that the use of riddles in courtship, described in European folk-lore, may refer to a primitive custom; similarly, the obligation of the wooer to justify his suit by the performance of tasks, a trait familiar in folk-tales, seems to depend on an actual usage, in which the bridegroom was obliged to prove his ability by such accomplishment. At all events, the practice is worthy of attention.—William Wells Newell, *Journal of American Folk-Lore,* Vol. VIII (January–March, 1895), No. 28, p. 106.

The American slave courtship words and forms are the result of his attempt at imitating the gushingly elegant manners and speech of his master.

Uncle Gilbert's rule of courtship was that a "young man mus' tes' an' prove a gal befo' offerin' her his han'. Ef er gal gives a man as good anser as he gives her question, den she is all right in min'. Ef she can look him squar in de face when she talks to him, den she kin be trusted; and ef her patches is on straight, an' her close clean, den she is gwine ter keep de house straight and yer britches mended. Sich er ooman is wuth havin'."

Sample of a "Courtship" Conversation

He. My dear kin' miss, has you any objections to me drawin' my cher to yer side, and revolvin' de wheel of my conversation around de axle of your understandin'?

She. I has no objection to a gentleman addressin' me in a proper manner, kin' sir.

He. My dear miss, de worl' is a howlin' wilderness full of devourin' animals, and you has got to walk through hit. Has you made up yer min' to walk through hit by yersef, or wid some bol' wahyer?

She. Yer 'terrigation, kin' sir, shall be answered in a ladylike manner, ef you will prove to me dat it is not for er form and er fashion dat you put de question.

He. Dear miss, I would not so impose on a lady like you as to as' her a question for a form an' a fashion. B'-lieve me, kin' miss, dat I has a pertickler object in ingagin' yer in conversation dis afternoon.

She. Dear kin' sir, I has knowed many a gentleman to talk wid wise words and flatterin' looks, and at de same time he may have a deceivin' heart. May I as' yer, kin' gentleman, ef you has de full right to address a lady in a pertickler manner?

He. I has, kin' miss. I has seen many sweet ladies, but I has never up to dis day an' time lef' de highway of a single gentleman to foller dese beacon lights. But now, kin' miss, as I look in yer dark eyes, and sees yer hones' face, and hears yer kind words, I mus' confess, dear lady, dat I would be joyous to come to yer beck and call in any time of danger.

She. Den, kin' sir, I will reply in answer to your 'terrigation in de fus place, sence I think you is a hones' gentleman dat I feels dat a lady needs de pertection of a bol' wahyer in dis worl' where dere's many wil' animals and plenty of danger.

He. Den, kin' honored miss, will you condescen' to encourage me to hope dat I might, some glorious day in de future, walk by yer side as a perteckter?

She. Kin' sir, ef you thinks you is a bol' wahyer I will condescend to let you pass under my observation from dis day on, an' ef you proves wuthy

of a confidin' lady's trus', some lady might be glad to axcept yer pertection
—and dat lady might be me.

II [2]

1. "Dear lady, I come down on justice an' qualification to advocate de
law condemnin' de lady dat was never condemn befo'—not dat I's gwine
to condemn you, but I can condemn many odders."

2. Kin' lady, I went up on high gum an' came down on Little Peedee,
whar many goes but few knows.

3. Kin' lady, are yo' a standin' dove or a flyin' lark? Would you decide
to trot in double harness and will you give de most excrutish pleasure of
rollin' de wheels of de axil, accordin' to your understandin'? If not my
tracks will be col' an' my voice will not be heard aroun' your do'! I would
bury my tomihawks an' dwell upon de subtell of mos' any T.

4. Kin' lady, ef I was to go up between de heavens and de yarth an'
drop down a grain of wheat over ten acres of land an' plow it up wid a
rooster fedder, would you marry me?

5. Good, miss, ef dere was a beautiful bloom, how could you get it
widout reachin', sendin', walkin', or goin' at it? (Answer—Get it by love.)

6. Kin' lady, s'pose you was to go 'long de road an' meet a pet rabbit,
would you take it home an' call it a pet o' yourn?

7. Good lady, ef you was to come down de riber an' you saw a red
stran' o' thread, black o' white, which one would you choose to walk on?
(In the answer, the color of the thread given is the color of the man she
would accept.)

8. Oh, good kin' lady, kin you go up twix heaven an' de yarth an'
bring me a blue morena wid a needle an thread in it?

9. Kin' lady, since I have been trav'lin' up hill, valley and mountain, I
nebber seed a lady dat suit my fancy mo' so dan you does. Now is you a
towel dat had been spun, or a towel dat had been woven. (Answer—If
spun, single.)

10. Good lady, I was in a garden in my dream an' I saw de lovelies'
table an on de table was a fine cake an' a glass of wine, an' a beautiful lady
was walkin' in de garden, and you were de lady. Ef you saw a peas hull
in de garden which one would you choose,—one wid one pea in it or a hull
full of peas. (Answer—The hull with one pea is a single man, the hull full
of peas is a widower with children.)

11. Good lady ef I was to give you a handkerchief to wash an'
iron how would you do it widout water or iron? (Answer—Iron it with
love.)

Of a kind similar to No 9 in Miss Smiley's collection, the Folk-Lore
Society has contributed the following:

---

[2] To Miss Portia Smiley, of Calhoun, Alabama, we are indebted for the following
delicious bits of sentiment.

Are you a rag on the bush or a rag off the bush? (Answer—If a rag on the bush, free, if off, engaged.)

I saw three ships on the water, one full rigged, one half-rigged, and one with no rigging at all. Which would you rather be? (Full rigged, married; half-rigged, engaged; no rigging, single.)

Sometimes the girl wishes to find out her friend's intentions. If so it may be done without loss of dignity through the following circumlocution:

"Suppose you was walkin' by de side o' de river and dere was three ladies in a boat, an' dat boat was overturned, which lady would you save, a tall lady or a short lady or a middle-sized lady?"

If the young man declares his desire to save a lady corresponding in height to his questioner she may rest assured that his intentions are serious. He may perhaps add the following tender avowal:

"Dear miss, ef I was starvin' an' had jes one ginger-cake, I would give you half, an' dat would be de bigges' half."

Should a girl find herself unable to understand the figurative speech of her lover she may say "Sir, you are a huckleberry beyond my persimmon," and may thus retire in good form from a conversation in which her readiness in repartee has not been equal to her suitor's skill in putting sentimental questions.

Jumping the Broomstick

"JUMPING over the broomstick" is another way in which a man and woman have inaugurated an informal connection. The two stand together; "witnesses" hold the stick a foot or so above the floor, and the pair hop over together. In one case, dating back some years, an English-speaking neighbor was invited to such a ceremony; one man, directing it, went through a kind of service in which he asked the partners whether they were willing to stay with each other. There followed cakes, drinks, and kissing of the bride.

More recently, a French welfare worker happened to arrive in an outlying area at the time of a rite combining "contract" and "broomstick." The neighbors had gathered. The bride had a white dress and long veil, tucked in her belt for convenience, and her paper flowers; and she also wore tennis shoes. The groom was attired more simply, in tan shirt, tan trousers, and tieless collar. After the broomstick was jumped, an "official" wrote out a brief statement in French, to which the others attached their marks. Then the bride, groom, and older men took penknives and fixed their marks on the door of the nuptial chamber.

From *The Bayous of Louisiana,* by Harnett T. Kane, p. 304. Copyright, 1943, by Harnett T. Kane. New York: The Hampton Publishing Co. and William Morrow & Company. 1944.

Tobacco Auctioneer

THE buyers are lined up across the baskets of tobacco, pulling out sample hands, turning to get a truer light, feeling, smelling. There's Carroll, Jones, and Mallory for the Big Three, Imperial's buyer, the new buyer for Export, buyers from the four large independents who are on this market, and seven or eight pinhookers. "Let's go," says Al. "Nine dollars."

You pick it up. Nine dollahs nine dollah bid nine nine nine—(You really make it more "nigh nigh nigh"; no man can sell tobacco fast and get in every syllable. Some of the old boys, old when you were starting in thirty years ago, sort of talked bids. But that was the way they had started, some as courthouse or backwoods auctioneers, talking bids as if they were selling a piece of land. When the sales began speeding up they either dropped into a chant or dropped out of tobacco; a man can't be expected to sell three or four hundred piles of tobacco an hour and say "Nine dollars, nine dollars, nine dollars and a quarter, nine dollars and a half, nine dollars and three quarters," and so on, selling a pile every eight or ten seconds. You have to do just what you're doing now—"nigh nigh nigh anna wahta wahta wahta anna hoff hoff hoff an three ree ree"—which translates into nine dollars, nine dollars and a quarter, nine dollars and a half, nine dollars and three-quarters—the starting bid being nine dollars a hundred-weight or nine cents a pound.)

"Three ree ree." Your eyes are going up and down the line, watching every pair of eyes, every pair of hands. You're holding that three-quarters, hunting the ten-dollar bid. Eight seconds ago Keeney, one of the speculators, had given a little nod that meant he would take the nine-dollar price that Al North had set on the pile as an opener. You'd taken Keeney's bid up the line, back down, and then had caught a wink from Carroll that upped it a notch to nine and a quarter. Then Al had kicked your ankle close to the basket where nobody could see, and you had taken it up another notch, nine and a half. You had gone back to Carroll, got his wink again, had gone to nine and three-quarters, had looked at Keeney, nothing there, no more kicks from Al, up the line once and down, all done, and sold at nine and three-quarters to Carroll.

That had taken ten seconds, a second or two more than most piles. You'd started moving at the first bid, a kind of sideways, backward shuffle, shifting your weight from one foot to another in rhythm with the chant; the steps take you just one basket-length each sale. Ahead, a boy is pulling hands out at random from the basket of tobacco and spreading them on top; but the buyers like to draw their own samples, so the neat piles are in pretty much of a mess after the line gets by. Just ahead of you and on the same side of the baskets is Al North, the starter, who is one of the partners in the warehouse. Now Al gets the starting bid on the second pile. "Twenty—Twenty dollars, gentlemen, for this good lemon leaf;

By Leonard Rapport. Manuscript of the Writers' Program of the Work Projects Administration for the State of North Carolina.

dandy tobacco, gentlemen, dandy tobacco." You slap your hands together like a pistol shot, a trick picked up years ago to keep the sale alive. "Twenny dollah bid twenny wenny wenny wenny" up the line, back down, catch Jones's eye inquiringly, he was buying this type yesterday, Jones shakes his head a fraction of an inch, still no bid, so drop it down to nineteen and a half, no bid, nineteen, no bid, eighteen and a half, eighteen, seventeen and a half, you look at the pile a fraction of a second and see it's good tobacco but poorly graded, seventeen and Al nudges you and the house takes it at seventeen. They'll regrade it and maybe squeeze it in and get it resold on this same sale. Out of the corner of your eye you see the farmer whose pile you just sold and you recognize him; he brings a lot of business to this house and you figure Al started the bid high because he wanted to show him he was trying to do what he could but they just weren't paying that much today.

The next pile belongs to the same man, about two hundred pounds of trashy lugs with a few scattered hands of better tobacco. Four dollars and a quarter, half, three, five dollars, and one of the speculators takes it at five and a quarter. "Sold to the pinhooker," you kid. He grins but you know he doesn't like that name any more than the rest of them do; "speculator," "rehandler," "remodeller," anything but the name everybody calls them. He'll dress that pile up and make a few dollars on the resale.

This pile looks like fair smoking leaf; Al starts it at fifteen, Carroll touches himself and takes the bid; Jones looks at you and from fifteen years of facing each other across millions of pounds of tobacco you know that look and carry the bid to fifteen and a half. (Bids from one to fifteen go by quarters; from fifteen to twenty-five by halves; and from twenty-five up by dollars. You couldn't—or wouldn't—cry a fifteen and a quarter bid any more than you would say "I are.") You look at Mallory, the third of the Big Three buyers, and he crooks a finger toward himself and now they're all bidding. Sixteen, and a half, seventeen, and a half, eighteen, and a half, nineteen—that's Jones's bid. You've got a little problem. Jones, you're sure, is through. Mallory seems to have a twenty-cent top on this type, but Carroll has been going higher; therefore you want to throw Mallory in the twenty-cent hold. So you dodge Mallory for the half bid, catch Carroll's eye, he nods, and then you go to Mallory, and as you figured he crooks his finger and you've got him in the twenty-cent hold, then back to Jones, but, again as you figured, he's through; so back to Carroll, and sure enough he nods and you've got a twenty and a half bid. You go back to Mallory but he's through. For a split second you consider catching a bid off the ceiling and piking Carroll, who is the youngest and greenest of the company buyers, but he might not bite so you decide against it. But you're pleased with the finesse of that particular sale; thirty years of hunting buyers' weak spots and having them hunt yours have taught you a few things.

*   *   *   *   *

Al starts another pile. "Twelve-dollar bid," you begin. "This is good tobacco, gentlemen," rattles on Al. "Good Pitt County bright, nobody in

Pitt raises prettier tobacco or girls than does Dan Jamerson, and this is some of Dan's leaf. And here's one of Dan's little girls who's going to take him home the money, so bid up." Across the basket, behind the buyers, a seventeen-year-old girl smiles and blushes. You remember bolder girls who stood on their tobacco and gave the successful buyer a kiss. That didn't look good to outsiders and you're glad it's about done away with. Some of the buyers turn to smile at the girl. You pop your hands, lean toward the sweating buyers (if you didn't know them personally you could still tell the Big Three by the Camel, Chesterfield, and Lucky packs show-ing through the pockets of their wet shirts), and reach your right hand toward each man as you turn toward him so that it looks like you almost pull that opening bid out of Imperial.

Twelve dollah bid tweh tweh tweh anna wahta (one of the pinhookers raises Imperial) wahta wahta wahta anna hoff (Mallory touches himself) hoff hoff, back to a wahta (Mallory has shaken his head; he was only hitching up his pants) wahta wahta again a hoff (Imperial comes back) hoff hoff ("Good tobacco, gentlemen," says Al, "let's help the little girl.") three ree (the pinhooker comes again) ree ree ree thirteen dollah bid (both Imperial and Jones look up; you nod toward Jones and chant inquiringly at Imperial; he closes his eyes as if tired and you've got another bid) anna wahta wahta wahta (up the line, try Jones, but he is already reaching into the next pile, down the line, all done), sold Imperial. You glance toward the girl and see that she's excited by the whole business, but you know that, like most of those whose tobacco you sell, although she has heard every sound you have made and has followed your every gesture, to her, as to the rest, it's all gibberish. She won't know until she reads it on her tag that her two hundred and thirty-two pounds of lemon-colored primings sold at thirteen and one-quarter cents a pound.

It's now one minute after eleven o'clock. In this minute you have sold six piles of tobacco. You'll have to sell a little faster if you're to finish this three-sixty and still have a couple minutes for another Coca-Cola.

Soundings

WHEN it is necessary to know the depth of the water at any point in the river, the test or sounding is made by dropping a 33-foot rope, to the end of which is fastened a pipe filled with lead. The pipe is about one and a half inches in diameter and twelve inches in length. A few inches of heavy chain are put into the pipe, and around this melted lead is poured. The weight of a lead is between six and ten pounds. The rope is fastened to a link of the chain that is allowed to extend past the length of the pipe. The length of

From *Steamboatin' Days*, Folk Songs of the River Packet Era, by Mary Wheeler, pp. 59–62. Copyright, 1944, by Louisiana State University Press. Baton Rouge.

For other phases of steamboating and steamboat songs, see (in addition to the rest of Mary Wheeler's book), Garnett Laidlaw Eskew, *The Pageant of the Packets* (1929) and Herbert and Edward Quick, *Mississippi Steamboatin'* (1926).

the lead line is marked at four feet by a piece of white flannel woven into the rope, at six feet, by a piece of leather, at nine feet by a piece of red cloth; at Mark Twain there is a piece of leather split into two thongs, at Mark Three a piece of leather in three thongs, and at Mark Four there is a single leather strip with a round hole. These signals are recognized by the leadsman as the rope slips through his hands in the darkness.

The soundings are called out as the line drops. A depth less than Quarter Less Twain is given in feet. After Mark Four is reached the measurement is usually given as No Bottom.

There are two methods of taking soundings. If the length of the pipe at the end of the rope rests in a horizontal position on the ground of the river bed, the measurement is known as Laying Lead. If only the end of the pipe is allowed to touch the bottom the measurement is Standing Lead.

The report of the leadsman must reach the pilot quite a distance away. On large boats the messages are sometimes relayed by a man stationed between the leadsman and the pilothouse. The Negroes call this "passin' the word." In order to make themselves understood, often through wind and rain, the measurements are sung in a sustained chant, and each leadsman evolves his own tune and rhythm that he associates with the various depths.

One old Negro who used to take soundings or "heave the lead" on the Ohio gave this explanation of the prolonged tones, "You hold it out so the man who is passin' the word kin hear it mo' bettuh than if you cuts it off short."

The leadsmen realize the importance of their task. They enjoy the knowledge that their reports can cause such concern to the captain and the pilot. A Negro leadsman once said to the captain, "I laks you better than I do the pilot. I always gives you mo' watuh than I do him."

No darkie would ever confess to the crime of "Dry Leadin'," or reporting a depth not carefully measured. But it was probably on a night in winter that this song was first sung—a night so cold that it was not pleasant to draw up the line dripping with icy water:

> Captain, captain, don't you think I'm sly,
> Goin' to do my leadin' an' keep my lead line dry.

When a pilot "calls for the lead" he gives the command with a signal from the whistle or bell. Soundings are taken from either side of the boat, and when necessary from both sides. One signal from the pilothouse sends a leadsman to the starboard side, two signals to the larboard. The same signals from the pilothouse recall the leadsman from his post. The darkies say, "He blows you on, an' you has to stay out there till he blows you off."

Soundings are taken at the discretion of the pilot, when making a crossing, going through seldom used chutes, or at any time when there is doubt regarding the depth of the water. When a leadsman is at work the pilot expects to be informed of the depth of the channel about every hundred feet.

Throughout the leadsman's chanting, pilots listen hopefully for "No

Bottom." To them this is the leadsman's sweetest song. When a boat can be kept in deep water the danger of going aground is avoided.

Quarter Less Twain	ten and one-half feet
Mark Twain	twelve feet (two fathoms)
Quarter Twain	thirteen and one-half feet
Half Twain	fifteen feet
Quarter Less Ta-ree (three)	sixteen and one-half feet
Mark Ta-ree	eighteen feet (three fathoms)
Quarter Ta-ree	nineteen and one-half feet
Half Ta-ree	twenty-one feet
Quarter Less Fo'	twenty-two and one-half feet
Mark Fo' or Deep Fo' [1]	twenty-four feet (four fathoms)
No Bottom	over twenty-four feet

It was on the Mississippi that I heard Soundings for the first time. That summer afternoon I was on the wharf at Memphis with a former officer of the third *Kate Adams*. He had arranged for an old leadsman to meet us there. We went out in a small boat and as the lead line dropped into the water the old Negro called out the measurements.

Later as he drew up the rope from the sparkling sunlit ripples his strong brown hands coiled it expertly, handling it with the care that should be given to something valuable and useful. Then he courteously repeated his chant more softly while I wrote down the melody given here.

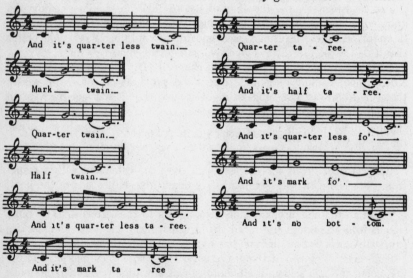

And it's quar-ter less twain.— / Quar-ter ta - ree.

Mark twain.— / And it's half ta - ree.

Quar-ter twain.— / And it's quar-ter less fo'.—

Half twain.— / And it's mark fo'.—

And it's quar-ter less ta - ree. / And it's no bot - tom.

And it's mark ta - ree

---

[1] Some leadsmen use the measurement Deep Four instead of Mark Four. Deep Four indicates a depth slightly greater than four fathoms, or about twenty-five and a half feet instead of twenty-four or Mark Four.—M. W.

The Shout

QUITE as varied in form as the spiritual, and frequently accompanying it, was the "shout" or religious dance. . . . Not all spirituals were shouted. But whenever spirituals were sung they demanded a certain rhythmic movement of the body. This might be confined on formal occasions to a mere swaying backward and forward; it might on other occasions include a tapping of the feet or a patting of the hands; if opportunity offered, it might extend to real shouting. Just where keeping time left off and shouting began is hard to decide. A singer might while seated throw into rhythmic movement every portion of the body as in shouting. To shout properly, however, seems to have demanded that the singers be standing if not actually taking steps.

To define with complete accuracy the meaning of the word "shout" is impossible. The word means many things, or, rather, there are many different forms of shouting. The favorite form in one community differs from that used a few miles away. Even in the same congregation different members shout differently. No attempt, so far as I am aware, has yet been made to collect and to study the various types.

One of the simplest forms, known as the "ring shout," is apparently widespread. In this, the shouters form a circle and proceed around and around in a sort of slow processional, facing always in one direction. The speed is determined by the particular song they are singing, but the advance is always slow and dignified. Hands are held in front, palms together—sometimes vertically at the height of the breast, sometimes horizontally and a little lower—and clapped with a single or double beat. The body sways at the hips, and dips as the knees bend. The feet shuffle, each step advancing the body but slightly.

Even in this simple type of shout, several different steps may be used. In two cases of ring shout, both collected in one locality, I found a marked difference between the ways in which the verses and the chorus were shouted. The ring was formed as usual but the singers walked slowly while they sang the verse:

> Oh we'll walk around the fountain,
> Oh we'll walk around the fountain,
> Yes we'll walk around the fountain—
> Oh religion so sweet.

From "The Negro Spiritual," by Robert W. Gordon, in *The Carolina Low-Country*, by Augustine T. Smythe, Herbert Ravenel Sass, Alfred Huger, Beatrice Ravenel, Thomas R. Waring, Archibald Rutledge, Josephine Pinckney, Caroline Pinckney Rutledge, Dubose Heyward, Katharine C. Hutson, and Robert W. Gordon, pp. 198–203. Copyright, 1931, by the Macmillan Company. New York. 1932.

For a Louisiana ring shout, cf. the recording of "Run, Old Jeremiah," by John A. and Alan Lomax, *Folk Music of the United States*, Album 3, AAFS 12B (Library of Congress, 1942).

The shuffling steps in much quicker rhythm began only when they came to what we should normally call the chorus:

> Oh religion, oh religion, oh religion so sweet!
> Oh religion, oh religion, oh religion so sweet!

These lines were repeated again and again without pause for perhaps ten minutes; then once more the singers dropped back for a single verse to the walk; then shuffled again to the same many times repeated chorus. On asking more about this peculiar type, I was informed that it was known as a "walk around." The words themselves may have been responsible for the introduction of the walk. One wonders if this religious walk around might possibly be the relic of a very old type, and perhaps the ancestor of a later walk around as performed by the blackface minstrels on the stage.

Shouting took many other forms. One might shout acceptably while standing in one place, the feet either shuffling, or rocking backward and forward, tapping alternately with heel and toe, the knees bending, the body swaying, and the hands clapping. Or the singer could alternately advance and retreat. Not infrequently two singers would shout facing one another in a sort of competition of skill or endurance. Sometimes this was done with great dignity and grace, but not infrequently one of the singers, in an attempt to outdo the other, would introduce body motions that seemed to have very little to do with religion. Occasionally one of the women would throw her hands high above her head and pivot slowly, or would indulge in steps that seemed to carry with them a reminiscence of more formal dancing seen at one of the balls at the big house.

The line between shouting and dancing was strictly held. Shouting could be indulged in only while singing a spiritual. Under no circumstances might the feet be crossed. These two rules were universal and inflexible. In addition, the older and stricter church members held that the foot should never be entirely lifted from the floor. Beyond this it was a matter of discretion. It was universally agreed that shouting was dignified, that it was a worship of the Lord, that certain motions were not fitting. For example, whenever, in my own experience, one of the younger women—perhaps while singing the spiritual "Rock, Daniel, rock! Rock I tell you, rock!" where the body rocked from side to side—placed her hands on her hips, elbows out and "danced kimbo," or when she showed the slightest tendency to move her feet too far apart, or to cross them, one of the older sisters would reprimand her sharply, often quoting the words of the spiritual—"Watch out, sister, how you walk on de cross! Yer foot might slip an' yer soul got los'."

In social life, quite apart from the church, the shout also played an important part. While the unregenerate could indulge freely in all forms of dancing, the church member was forbidden to do so. He satisfied his natural craving by the use and development of the form permitted. When work was over, shouting was a favorite form of diversion at the cabins. On holidays, celebrations, or weddings, and particularly on Watch Night, it was a regular custom.

In some forms, it even showed tendencies toward becoming a game. Acting out the story was not infrequent. "Rock, Daniel," shows a trace of this. A better example might be chosen in "Where is Adam?" In this song the heavy sonorous call of God is answered by the higher pitched quicker reply of Eve, while at the proper places the shouters stoop to the ground to pick up the leaves or go through the motions of pinning them on. It begins:

Oh, Eve, where is Adam?	*Oh, Eve, where is Adam?*
Oh, Eve!	*Oh, Eve!*
Adam in de gyarden	Adam in de gyarden
Pickin' up leave'.	Pinnin' up leave'.
Adam in de gyarden	Adam in de gyarden
Pickin' up leave'.	Pinnin' up leave'.
Adam in de gyarden	Adam in de gyarden
Pickin' up leave'.	Pinnin' up leave'.
My Lord call yo'	Adam don' answer,
Pickin' up leave'.	Pinnin' up leave'.
My Lord call yo'	Adam don' answer,
Pickin' up leave'.	Pinnin' up leave'.

Oh, Eve, where is Adam?, etc.

Still more of a game or stunt is the "going down to the mire," in which one sister, surrounded by a group of singers, lowers herself inch by inch to her knees and then still "lowerer and lowerer" till her head touches the ground while the group sings:

Oh, my sister, you shall go down to de mire,
Oh, my sister, you mus' go down to de mire,
Lowerer an' lowerer,
Lowerer an' lowerer, etc.,

and then rises slowly to her feet again as they bid her "rise from de mire, higherer." Then another tries, and another. The one who succeeds in performing the feat mostly slowly and steadily takes great pride, apparently, not only in outdoing her companions but in having definitely established her status as a good church member. I have been told that this is very ancient. If so, it is not impossible that it may be a relic of a primitive test based on the sound psychological principle that fear or a guilty conscience affects the perfect correlation of nerve and muscle.

Service of the Sanctified Saints of God

THE congregation straggles in with languid informality, women with small children depositing them on chairs reserved for the male members, up front near the altar, where they may sleep undisturbed throughout the service.

From *More Mellows*, by R. Emmet Kennedy, pp. 8–21. Copyright, 1931, by R. Emmet Kennedy. New York: Dodd, Mead & Company.

The comfort of their charges seen to, the women then take their seats on narrow wooden benches further back, and commerce to "moan" in melancholy undertones while they commune with the "sperret." The elder, with bowed head, is standing at the rostrum, scanning the pages of a large Bible, gathering texts for his discourse. On either side of the altar, leaning forward on his chair in comfortable ease, with arms resting on his thighs, a deacon sits reading a small Bible. There appears to be no fixed order or church discipline. The women and children sing, hum, and move about from place to place as the inclination prompts.

Members continue to come in, and before long the church is well filled. The mournful humming rises and falls in strange, weird cadences, quickening with the fervor pulsating from seat to seat. Impelled by the ever-increasing surge of seductive harmony, their relaxed forms begin to sway like an undulating wave. Suddenly an ecstatic exclamation, "So glad!" comes from a woman sitting near the front row; and closing her eyes, with head thrown back, she waves her arms in the air. Sympathetic shouts of "Glory!" "A-men!" "Sweet Jesus!" are heard in different parts of the house. After a few sinuous writhings and rhythmic swayings from side to side, the woman springs up and begins to tell with a thrill what religion has done for her. The murmuring chorus, slightly diminished, continues chanting throughout her recital. The testimony is delivered with fluent ease, somewhat in the manner of a half-spoken long meter chant, with peculiar stress given to the vowels of certain words.

After one or two vehement ejaculations of "So glad!", she tells that she wants to give "glory an' praise to Gawd's blessed name, that I'm able to be here tonight to thank Him for the gladness that's workin' in my heart, an' to tell about the peace that come to my soul, w'en Jesus took me from my sinful ways, an' called me to stand with His Christian saints. . . . A-men! Glory to His name!"

She sits down, continuing to sway to and fro, accompanying the movement with ejaculations of "Amen!", "So glad!"

Another woman gets up and begins to talk in very much the same manner. With growing ecstasy she tells how glad she is "to come before Gawd's saints an' give thanks that I saw the light leadin' my feet to the righteous path before it was too late. . . . Yes, so glad! Glory to his name! . . . Two years ago the only thing that held my mind was wickedness an' condemnation. But the sperret spoke through His only son, an' Jesus stooped down low an' sanctified my soul. . . . A-men! So glad!"

One ofter another, men, women, and half grown children, get up and testify; some briefly and unimpressively, some repeating the commonplace formula, accentuated at times with hand clapping and boisterous stamping of feet; others ranting incoherently, "speaking with the gift of tongues" an unintelligible gibberish, and twitching as though bewitched. The wave of hysteria gradually subsides and the congregation lapses into a mood of meditative calm. The low, plaintive humming continues, its soothing influence indispensable to their visionary wanderings.

The elder leaves his Bible and walks to the edge of the platform to say a few words of appreciation on the splendid show of religious feeling. Punctuating his speech with a profusion of "a-men's" and "bless Gawd," he tells how glad he is "to see so many Christians come together, puttin' aside the fun an' frolic of the world to turn your mind on the kind of pleasure recommended by Gawd himself. . . . A-men! Blessed be His name. . . . None of these people outside the church know what the feelin' of gladness is till they done laid aside they worldly ways an' commence to feel religion workin' in they heart. . . . Ain't that true?"

Responsive amens come from all parts of the house. He gives his head a shake of approval, and with a dramatic wave of the right arm, goes on talking:

" 'Course it's true. Religion is a mighty breastplate for to help you to overcome. An' all that Gawd's askin' for is a little bit of the genuine, true feelin' . . . the kind of ole-time religion He was tryin' to get his chosen people to practice over yonder in the land of Babylon, before He come down on 'um in His wrath an' wrecked the city with death an' destruction."

The word Babylon, to their literal minds the symbol of sin and wrongdoing to be shunned by all good Christians, reminds them that the moment for rejoicing is now at hand, and with sudden energy a triumphant burst of harmony rolls through the building. It falls on their inflammable souls like sparks on withered summer grass. Exulting bosoms heave and throb as the lighted embers of faith break into full flame, and expectant eyes glow as if beholding the glory of the everlasting dawn.

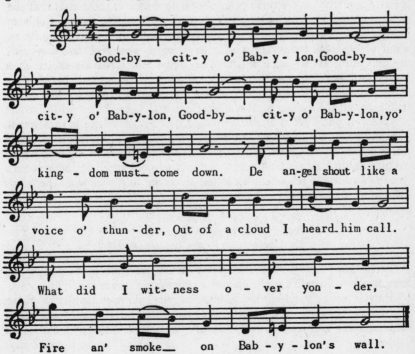

Good-by___ cit-y o' Bab-y-lon, Good-by___
cit-y o' Bab-y-lon, Good-by___ cit-y o' Bab-y-lon, yo'
king-dom must___ come down. De an-gel shout like a
voice o' thun-der, Out of a cloud I heard_him call.
What did I wit-ness o-ver yon-der,
Fire an' smoke___ on Bab-y-lon's wall.

The tempo quickens perceptibly as the ardor grows, and very soon the infectious rhythm becomes an invitation to the dance which is disregarded only by the aged and the infirm. Men, women, and children rise from their seats and begin dancing where they stand, very soon coming out into the aisles and advancing slowly towards the altar platform, where they continue to express themselves with joyful abandon. The deacons lay their Bibles aside and join in the celebration, doing fantastic steps and contortions on either side of the rostrum, while the elder walks back and forth, encouraging the harmonious tumult with loud hand clapping and vociferous singing. As verse follows verse, with a certain monotonous variation of thought, the song wells up like a paean of wild exuberance, with cymbals clanging and the building rocking to the rhythmic vibration of untiring feet. No two dancers appear to be doing the same step; the result being a most amazing exhibition of terpsichorean technique combined with religious emotionalism.

After a prolonged demonstration the singing comes to an end and the half-exhausted dancers quietly return to their seats. A colored man brings a lady's work basket from the back of the altar and begins taking up the collection. For the benefit of any visitors present, the elder explains the spectacular feature of the ritual.

"People from the outside, an' Christians of another faith might think it strange to see dancin' in a church, an' they might want to say that we carryin' on hyuh the same way sinner folks do wen you find 'um yonder to them balls an' cheap picnics wen they takin' they enjoyment; but the kind of gladness that makes these people want to dance in the house of Gawd, ain't the same kind of feelin' *a-tall* them pleasure-seekin' people has when you see 'um get up an' strut in the common dance-hall. . . . It's a different kind of gladness *altogether* what these people here feel, an' they ain't nothin' sinful an' wrong about it. They only doin' what Moses' daughter Mary did, way long ago in the ancient Hebrew days. . . . Because the fifteen chapter of Exodus tells you how Aaron sister took a cymbal in her hand, an' all the women went out after her with cymbals an' with dancin'. . . . An' if you look at Psalm number 33, you'll see where it tells you to praise the Lawd with a harp, an' sing unto him with a psalter an' a instrument of ten strings; an' it tells you again to sing unto him a new song an' to play skillful with a *loud* noise. . . . So we only tryin' to follow what's wrote down in the testament scripture, an' tryin' to realize what the words of that good ole gospel jubilee hymn say,—

> Wid a clappin' o' de hands
> An' a pattin' o' de feet,
> De love o' Gawd does run so sweet."

Exclamations of "A-men!", "Blessed be the holy word," intoned by the congregation, intrude like the lines of an answering chorus.

Having made the rounds of the building, the collection man stops in the front aisle before a white visitor who had dropped a crumpled dollar bill in the basket, and leaning over, respectfully inquires how much change he wanted back; it being the custom for members to ask for change for dimes, quarters and half dollars presented. Going over to a table placed in full view of the congregation, he empties the contents of the basket and proceeds to count the money, arranging the silver in stacks of one dollar each. He announces that he finds the offering twenty cents short of making an even four dollars, and asks if the "members can't do a little better an' come up an' show that the love of Gawd an' the blessin' of religion represents more than the four little nickels that go to make up twenty cents."

After several unsuccessful requests, the elder then reminds them that "the Lawd loveth a cheerful giver," and that "the best way to keep your mind feelin' cheerful, is to ask the sperret to give you that OLE TIME RELIGION!"

The catch-word of the hymn being given, they burst forth singing with loud voice.

Gim-me that ole time re-li-gion, Gim-me that ole time re-li-gion, Gim-me that ole time re-li-gion, It's good e-nough for me.

During the rejoicing contributors walk up to the table, singing, and deposit the required twenty cents. The song finishes after nine or ten verses, then the money is put back in the basket and a blessing called down upon it, after which it is placed on the altar. The elder then announces that he will talk a little while "on what the book's got to say about the word o' Gawd." He scans the Bible thoughtfully for a few moments, then turning to one of the deacons, asks him to "tell something from the gospel of Matthew, twelfth chapter, verse 38 an' 39."

Intoning the text in a high-pitched voice, the deacon reads:

"Then certain of the scribes and of the Pharisees answered, saying, Master, we would see a sign from thee. But he answered and said unto them, An evil and adulterous generation asketh after a sign. . . ."

Without waiting for him to finish, the elder plunges into his discourse, exclaiming: "Yes! an evil generation got to have a *sign* before they come to understand anything about the love o' Gawd an' all the comforts He done put here on this earth to better they condition an' make 'um happy. . . . Yes! they say they got to have a *sign*. . . . They ain't satisfied to look around an' see they ain't livin' like they was twenty-five an' thirty years ago, when they had to plod up an' down on the mud streets, where

today they able to go back an' forth on brick walks an' pavement. . . . An'
they done got so used to turnin' on the 'lectric light, they done forgot all
about the time they had to go 'round totin' candles an' coal oil lamps to
git along in the dark. . . . Yes! all these benefits an' comforts ain't sufficient to show 'um the lovin' power an' greatness o' the heavenly father.
. . . A-men! Blessed be His name! . . . they say they got to have a *sign*.
. . . Yes, leave us see again what they got to say about it in second Corinthians, twelfth chapter an' twelfth verse."

The second deacon calls out the text with stentorian voice:

"Truly the signs of an apostle were wrought among you in all patience,
in signs, and wonders, and mighty deeds."

Accompanied by the low-murmured humming of the members, with occasional exclamations and snatches of song, the elder resumes his expound-
ing of the Holy Writ. He chants monotonously for a while on two or three
resonant notes of a light baritone quality, then jumps with ease to a
strident falsetto, dropping down suddenly to deep ringing tones, displaying a range of voice truly phenomenal.

"Yes! He wrought in patience all around everywhere, signs an' wonders
an' mighty deeds. . . . Everything got a sign, 'cause Gawd say He was
goin' to give His people a sign, an' by these signs ye shall know 'um. . . .
A-men! Praise the Lawd. . . . Coca-cola got a sign; Camel cigarette got
a sign; police patrol wagon got a sign; weather man at the Custom House
got a flag he h'ist up for a sign. Yes! any place you walk you can look
up an' read some kind o' sign. . . . But how many people ever think about
seekin' for a sign that'll show 'um how they walkin' in corruption an' only
got a little while to get they mind in order before death stop 'um in the
road an' cut 'um down? . . . A-men! Blessed be the name o' the
Lawd. . . . All these wonders an' mighty deeds ain't goin' to count for
nothin' when the last day comes an' sinner man goes away from here without *religion* in his heart. . . . Heaven is a place for the upright an' the
worthy, an' all these bootleggin' people an' cigarette-smokin' women sho
got to make a *struggle* before they can get in. 'Cause Gawd don't need no
tobacco smoke an' no liquor up yonder. *Prayer* is the only pass word
that'll open the door to let 'um in. So they better put off they evil habits an'
commence practicin' a little Christian behavior if they expect to find salvation for they soul. . . . The Lawd done showed 'um signs an' wonders,
but they look like they don't want to understand. . . . All them people
what study hist'ry done found out that it only take *one* gram of nicquitine
to kill a dog in lesser than some minutes; but that don't keep 'um from
smokin' they cigarettes an' pipes an' cigars, do it? . . ."

Fervid amens and loud groans of contrition ring out from the chorus
of murmuring voices.

"No!" he shouts with righteous disapproval. "Body enjoyment an' every
other kind o' frolic is so engagin' to they mind they ain't got *time* to think
about studyin' Gawd's secret commands. . . . Blessed be His name. . . .
But whatsomever sinner folks present in this gatherin' here tonight, I want

'um to take time an' come up an' pray *right now!* . . . An' me an' these two deacons goin' to ask the Lawd to grant mercy an' give you faith. 'Cause they only got *one* meditator between Gawd an' man, an' that's Jesus. . . . Blessed be His holy name. . . . So come on up here an' get down on your knees. With these prayers we goin' to say over you, we want to see Him raise you out the darkness an' put you in the light. . . . An' if they got any devil hidin' 'round in here, we goin' to pull his kingdom down. . . . *A*-men!"

During this exhortation the deacons have placed in front of the platform a row of "repentance chairs," six or eight in number. As soon as the elder pronounces the closing amen and takes his seat at the side of the altar, the congregation begins singing a plaintive, appealing melody, beseeching the penitents to come forward.

Repeated again and again, with ever increasing fervor and bewitching

harmonizations, the pleading canticle continues to resound until the last penitent has taken a seat. The deacons standing at either end of the row give a signal and they all kneel before their chairs, with heads bowed down on the seats.

The elder walks to the edge of the platform, where he stands with arms extended over the heads of the kneeling figures, and the three men lift their voices in moving prayer, invoking the heavenly father to aid and protect His weak and helpless servants. The majestic chorus meanwhile grows fainter and fainter, changing to a soft undertone of wistful lamenting, like the far-away sound of November night winds wailing in the branches of leafless trees. Its mournful, haunting quality, together with the affecting simplicity of language and humble sincerity of appeal voiced by the praying trio, exert an influence which makes the dramatic scene intensely impressive; not only to the susceptible, religious-minded participants, but to the heretic onlooker as well, who, despite his positive unbelief, cannot fail to experience an elemental thrill or unaccountable emotional reaction of some kind.

The prayers are soon over, and the penitents rise and go back to their

places. Once more the welcome interval is given to loud rejoicing. Irrespective of the mirthless minor cadence of the melody, it is sung with a spirit of happy declamation; partly from a feeling of gladness for the regenerated backsliders and partly from a sense of personal exemption and a selfish exultation in their own worthiness.

After doubting Thomas "weepin' Mary" is called on to "weep no mo'," then "mournin' Marthy" is requested to "mourn no mo'," and one after another the company of the incredulous is invoked to listen to the wonder of the incarnation and the presence of the angel at the tomb. The remaining hours are devoted to singing, with brief intervals of humming between the ending of one song and the "lining out" of the verses of another by some inspired member. "Ballets," "long meter himes," and "shoutin' praise" follow in turn, with little diminution of ardor until the approach of midnight when the ranks begin to thin. . . .

Street Cries of Charleston

THE streets of this quaint, old Southern City are teeming with sights and sounds of interest to those in whom Familiarity has not "bred contempt." To a stranger nothing is so amusing or unintelligible as the various cries of the hucksters as they ply their street trade, endeavoring to inform the "world and his wife" concerning their wares. To an inhabitant of this enchanted old "City by the Sea," numerous members of this "Brotherhood of the streets" become well-known friends; their several cries, familiar music.

When asked about themselves these hucksters tell you that they come "From up de road" or "Across from Jeems Island, Mam" and some from "Ober de new bridge" and still others again are town Negroes who secure their wares "Down at Cantini Wharf and Tradd Street Breakwater, my missis."

They congregate there to receive the boat loads of fresh "Vegetubble" and "Swimpy, raw raw." Long before even these enterprising denizens of the sleepy town are up and doing, the "Mosquito Fleet" has put to sea while the still, grey dawn is breaking and you hear them sending back in calm weather the long, faint cadence of a rowing song:

> "Rosy am a handsome gal!
> Haul away Rosy—Haul away gal!
> Fancy slippers and fancy shawl!
> Haul away Rosy, Haul—away!
> Rosy gwine ter de fancy ball!
> Haul away Rosy—haul away gal!"

From *Street Cries of an Old Southern City,* by Harriette Kershaw Leiding, pp. 1–12. Charleston: Press of the Daggett Printing Co. 1910.

Even in wet or windy weather when the wind is fresh and strong, sails are hoisted and silently the fishing fleet flits out like a flock of ghostly birds across the harbor, across the bar, and out to the fishing banks, forty miles away. For these fishing boats are manned by intrepid sailors known far and wide for skill and daring.

All of the folk songs have a queer minor catch in them and even the street cries have an echo of sadness in their closing cadence. Early one morning the usual shrimp "Fiend's" cry of

Raw!   Raw!   Raw   swimp!

was superseded by a strange, unfamiliar, and piercing sweet cry in a boy's faint, clear soprano. Like a little lark this "Jean DeReszke" of the small, black world, gave his name and advertised his wares, in a voice that made you think of the freshness of dawn across dewy fields. He stood under the window and sung:

An   a   Daw-try Daw! an a   swim-py raw!

an   a Daw- try,   Daw - try, Daw-try Raw   swimp. __

The shrimp are sold early in the morning. When the "Mosquito Fleet" puts back into port, the fish are hawked about the streets and the lusty lunged fishermen cry then

Whit- — ing

with an ominous voice, that seems to hold in its queer, breaking sound a reminder of the days and nights of danger which falls to the daily lot of these toilers of the deep who still must put out to sea in calm or storm alike, regardless of the death which threatens when "the harbor bar be moaning."

All is not sadness, for here and there a quaint bit of human nature or glint of humor, shows. For instance, even in the street cry parlance, "The Sex" holds its wonted superiority and you will find that "She Crabs," called through the nose of the vendor, "She Craib, She Craib" bring more money than just ordinary "Raw Crabs"—by which distinguished title is meant the less desirable male crab.

"Old Joe Cole, good old soul," who does a thriving business in lower
King Street under the quaint sign of "Joe Cole & Wife" is the bright, particular, though fast-waning, star of our galaxy of street artists. He sets the
fashion, so to speak, in "hucksterdom." Joe has many imitators but no
equals, for he looks like an Indian Chief, walks with a limp that would "do
a general proud," and uses his walking stick as a baton, while bellowing
like the "Bull of Bashan." It is a never-to-be-forgotten occasion when Joe
lustily yells:

> "Old Joe Cole—Good Old Soul
> Porgy in the Summer-time
> An e Whiting in the Spring
> 8 upon a string.
> Don't be late I'm waitin at de gate
> Don't be mad—Heres your shad
> Old Joe Cole—Good Old Soul."

Porgy, it may be remarked in passing, is a much prized variety of chub,
and is much esteemed among the colored brethren, "embracin of the
sisterin," as one old, colored preacher said.

When asked to sing so that his remarkable cry might be correctly reproduced, Joe gravely informed the awe-struck crowd surrounding him,
"Yunna niggers gwan from here now cos little Miss done ax me to sing in
de megafone so as she can write *Me* down in de white folks' book and she
aint ax *none* ob yunna niggers to do dat ting, jest *Me*." And sure enough
I did.

The "Vegetubble" Maumas are wonderful, wide-chested, big-hipped
specimens of womanhood that balance a fifty pound basket of vegetables
on their heads and ever and anon cry their goods with as much ease and
grace as a society lady wears her "Merry Widow" hat and carries on a
conversation. As these splendid, black Hebes come along with a firm,
swinging stride you may hear:

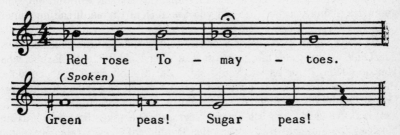

Perhaps it will vary in season to "Strawberry." While the masculine rendition of "Strawberry" is put in the following enticing form

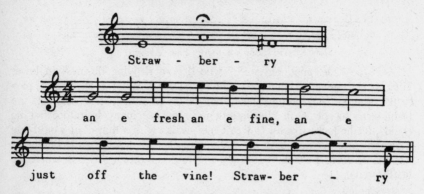

Straw - ber - ry

an e fresh an e fine, an e

just   off   the   vine! Straw- ber - ry

Or may be that yet again you will be informed that "Sweet Pete ate her."
Which being interpreted means that they are selling sweet potatoes to the
tune of Red Rose Tomatoes, only it sounds quite cannibalistic sung thus-
wise.

Amongst all this babble of femininity the masculine call of "Little John,"
as he styles himself, comes as a relief to the ear. He sings as he wends his
way: "Here's your 'Little John' Mam. I got Hoppen John Peas Mam! I
got cabbage—I got yaller turnips Mam, Oh yes Mam"—and so he comes
and you buy what you want and on he goes still singing what he's "got"
to sell. "I got sweet petater—I got beets; I got spinach"; and so on like
the brook, forever, "Little John" sings, his approach marked by the
musical sign "Crescendo" his retreat by "Diminuendo."

When I hear "Little John," I think of an old street crier, long since dead
and gone, whose cry was used to advertise his load of water-melons, thusly:

> Load my Gun
> Wid Sweet Sugar Plum
> An Shoot dem nung gal
> One by one
> Barder lingo
> Water-millon.

Now—a "nung gal" is "Darkese" for young girl, as you will find out when
you get a plantation darky to tell you the ancient rhyme of the love affair
of the old Oyster Opener and the Young Girl.

His tragic affair of the heart is briefly told in the dialogue which follows:
The Old Oyster Opener taking the part of "Ber Rabbit." "Ber Rabbit what
you de do day?" or as we would say "Ber Rabbit what are you doing
there?" and "Ber Rabbit" sadly answers—"I open de oyster for nung gal.
Oyster he bite off ma finger an nung gal he tek me for laugh at."

It is a curious fact that the Island Negroes make no distinction in talking,
between "he and she" and when "Ber Rabbit" of the above says "Young
gal he take me to laugh at," the old man gives a good illustration of that
peculiar trait of their language.

There is a gentle looking old woman who gives vent to the most ferocious and nasal howl of—"come on chilluns and get yer monkey meat."

Mon - key   meat

Should you hear it, do not be alarmed for it heralds nothing worse than a harmless, old body selling the children's favorite cocoanut and molasses candy.

This performance is only equalled by the one of the mild, antediluvian "Daddy" who gravely thrusts his woolly head into your back-gate and emits in an eminently respectful tone of voice the following jargon:

"Enny Yad aigs terday my Miss" which being interpreted means—Do you wish any eggs which my hens have laid in my yard and which therefore are fresh eggs Q. E. D. Fresh Yard Eggs.

In Charleston, even the chimney-sweeps are musical, and as their tiny faces appear at the top of the chimney they are sweeping, you hear "Roo roo" sung out over the sounds of the street below. Also to this tribe the charcoal boy belongs. He drives into town a tiny donkey hitched to a tiny, two-wheeled cart. The cart and load are black, the donkey is black, the boy is black, and the only other color that you can see in the whole outfit is the whites of the boy's eyes as he rolls them around and calls the eerie, long-drawn-out "Char———coal." He sounds weird, melancholy, and even doomed, with his mournful cry of "char-coal." You wonder which is the saddest and blackest; the driver, the driven, cart or contents, as they wend their solitary and spooky way onward, crying ever that sad, minor wail of

Char   -   coal.

All these interesting things and more too are here, jostling your elbows, passing your window, begging your custom and offering rich and picturesque effects to those who have "Eyes to see," and furnishing a queer, original but fast fading, street symphony to those who have "Ears to hear."

Street Cries of New Orleans

AMONG the many quaint old customs which still prevail there, perhaps the most characteristic is the going about of the Negro street vendors with

From *Mellows*, A Chronicle of Unknown Singers, by R. Emmet Kennedy, pp. 19–23. Copyright, 1925, by Albert & Charles Boni, Inc. New York.

their plaintive, melodious cries by which they announce their wares. Many of the old families still adhere to the time-honored custom of having the weekly washing done in the back yards, thereby enabling the clothes-pole man to continue plying his simple trade, making his periodical visits to town with a bundle of long white ash clothes-poles on his shoulder. His cry is a sort of spasmodic ejaculation given in loud, deep tones:

Several times a week the buttermilk man comes around with his large can of buttermilk, walking all the way from his little dairy out on Tele-machus Street, across the Basin, in the "back-of-town" section of the city. His cry is one of chromatic pleading, enticing you to buy in spite of your-self:

The selling of hot potato-cakes seems to be the exclusive prerogative of women. These cakes are made of sweet potatoes, though occasionally they are made of Irish potatoes, and they are sold hot. Whether from tradition or because of a better musical effect, the cry is always given in "gombo" French, the patois spoken by the Creole Negroes. These vendors are heard mostly down in the French Quarter around nightfall. And it is very sooth-ing to your mental condition on a hot August night when you are sitting in your room sizzling, . . . to hear the potato-cake woman go by in the street below singing:

Then along in the early part of the month of May, the blackberry woman comes to town with her belated spring-song. Her call is full of melancholy poetry which seems to tell you that she has been up since the "crackin' o' day," picking blackberries in the woods and along the bayou banks, and that she has walked miles and miles over dew-wet, dusty, country roads in order to get to town to sell her berries before noon. You are assured of this when you see her with her basket of berries on her head, the dew and the berry juice dripping from the basket and running down her back in purple rillets. The basket is covered with sprays of elder and syca-more leaves to protect the berries from the heat of the sun. On her head, serving as a cushion under the basket, she has a "tosh," formed of an old garment of some kind which has been twisted and coiled, resembling a sort of thick mat. Her skirt is tucked up gypsy-fashion all around her waist, and her dusty shoes and bare legs show every trace of long travel. Per-haps it is due to her weariness of body that her cry has a suggestion of melancholy:

Black- ber-ries, __ fresh an' fine, I got
black __ ber-ries, la-dy, Fresh from de vine', I got
black- ber-ries, la- dy, Three glass__ fo' a dime, I got
black- berries, I got black-berries, black-berries.

Then in the autumn, when the crows come back from the fields of the North, the chimney-sweeper comes around to remind people that their chimneys need cleaning before the coming of winter. His dress is tra-ditional, in strict accordance with the chimney-sweeper's idea of correct convention. He wears a top hat, a long linen duster, and over his shoulder he carries a bundle of sacks and ropes and long brushes made from the frayed leaves of the palmetto. He calls himself "Rom-ma-nay," which is "gombo" French for the word "ramoneur," meaning chimney-sweeper. He comes along singing in a loud voice:

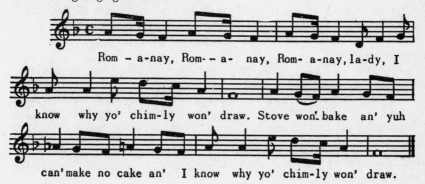

Rom - a-nay, Rom- - a- nay, Rom- a-nay, la-dy, I
know why yo' chim-ly won' draw. Stove won'. bake an' yuh
can' make no cake an' I know why yo' chim-ly won' draw.

The charcoal man has no special season. His visits are usually twice a week, as charcoal is in constant demand by the washerwomen who do "de w'ite-folks washin' an' i'nin' on de primisis."

There was a man who used to go around with an old white mule and a rickety springwagon, and his cry was like this:

Mah mule is white, mah chah-coal is black, I sells mah chah-coal_ two-bits_ a sack_____ Chah - coal_____ Chah - coal.__

Mississippi Folksay

THE first category [of Mississippi proverbs] comprises sayings which pertain to the moods, appearance, or characteristics of persons. In a part of central Mississippi it is said of one who is angry, "The pigs are runnin' through the 'tater patch." In a nearby area a person with a deceitful appearance is said to have a "skim milk eye." If he has faulty vision, he may be described as "too blind to see through a wire fence." "She's beef to the heels" is the proverbial description of a particularly stout woman. More conventionally than these, a seasoned reprobate is characterized as "old as the hills and crooked as a ram's horn." The inexperienced person is hailed as "so green that when it rains he'll sprout."

In northeast Mississippi a person who is debilitated through illness or fatigue is sometimes said to be "so weak he can't pull a hen off the roost," or he may reply to a greeting by saying, "I'm not fit to drive a hen from the door." If his joints or muscles are stiff, he may insist that he is "as stiff as a good road mule."

From the Vicksburg area comes this manner of describing an emaciated person: "He looks like a coon-hide stretched over some barrel hoops." "His hide wouldn't hold shucks" appears to be in somewhat general use as a picture of a victim of violence. In the Delta it is sometimes said of a bow-legged person: "He couldn't hem a pig in a one-foot ditch."

From "Rustic Imagery in Mississippi Proverbs," by Ernest Cox, *Southern Folklore Quarterly*, Vol. XI (December, 1947), No. 4, pp. 263–267. Gainesville, Florida: The Southeastern Folklore Society.

According to the conventions of northeast Mississippi, if a person is hot, he may be "as hot as a blistered man in a pepper patch," "as a country boy's pistol on the Fourth of July," or "as a hen in a wool basket trying to lay a goose-egg."

In south Mississippi we learn that "a stingy man gives an egg to get a chicken"; in north Mississippi that "he'd skin an ant for his tallow"; and in the central part of the state that "he'd skin a louse for his hide and tallow."

Man's voluntary inertia is recognized in the well-known "If the corn's not shelled, drive on." . . . In northeast Mississippi it is customary to say of the afflicted person, "He was born tired and raised lazy"; and in south Mississippi, "He was born lazy and had a relapse." The inspired epithet, however, comes from Vicksburg, where the Negro description of the shiftless person is "He's got the hook-worm hustle." Along with this, one may place "He has the sharecropper stance."

Proverbial remarks disparaging to a person's character [include] . . . this pronunciamento from central Mississippi: "He ought to have been hung when a potato vine would hang him." An untruthful man is described as "such a liar he has to get somebody else to call his hogs."

This search for proverbial expressions has revealed that an ugly person may not be merely "as ugly as home-made soap," or "as ugly as a mud fence," but that he may be even "as ugly as a mud fence daubed with tadpoles." At the same time, he may be "as smart as forty crickets"; "as rough as a cob and twice as corny"; or "as busy as a blue-tailed fly." For the last of these is sometimes used the expression "like a fly in a molasses jug," or "like a bee in a honey bucket."

The second category comprises sayings which pertain to the actions of persons or things. A politician, for example, may—and sometimes does— tell his listeners that voting for his opponent is "like wintering a dry cow." One's aggressiveness in pursuit may be described in "He was after it like the stink after onion," or "like a duck on a June bug," or "like a pet coon into the churn." . . . Versatility and force are expressed in the widely used phrase, "more ways than a country man can whip a mule." . . . If an idle person is quizzed, he may insist that he's "helping Joe pile brush." If he considers a task trivial, he may brush it off by saying, "I'm not going to take the time and trouble to shuck a nubbin." One of the most vivid of these images is one which describes a person's squirming "like a country mule hitched beside the railroad track." Other similarly effective images are in the expressions, "work like maulin' rails," "talkin' like a cotton gin in pickin' time," "gruntin' like a fat sow when you scratch her back with a corn-cob," and "He slunk across the yard like a suck-egg hound." The final image in this group involves a variation of a well-known challenge: "I'll see him as deep in hell as a pigeon can fly in a fortnight." This and the last half-dozen other sayings come from the Vicksburg area.

The third group of sayings deals with the characteristics of objects. Something sour, for example, may be . . . "sour enough to make a pig squeal." If it is noisy, it may make as much noise "as a new saddle," or "as hogs under the house." Objects that are thick may be "thicker than fishing poles in a cane-brake," "than boll-weevils," or "than fleas on a fat pup," or "as thick as cuckleburs in a colt's tail." . . .

The fourth group of expressions is concerned with situations or circumstances, rather than with persons or objects. If a project turns out disappointingly for some woman, a friend may observe, "She will have to lick her calf over again." The expression belongs to northeast Mississippi. If a person charges another mistakenly, it is said of him, "He has the wrong sow by the ear." The futility of an undertaking is vividly set forth in the expression, "Just as well try to make a worm walk on his tail." Vocational misdirection is forcefully put in "You ain't done nothin' 'cept spile a mighty good field hand." When there is occasion to add something for good measure, the act may be accompanied by the words, "Let the tail go with the hide." Of a field of high weeds, it is sometimes said, "If you don't cut 'em soon, you'll have to ring 'em." The Negroes of central Mississippi have a vivid image for the act of silencing a person: "He poured me back in the jug." In northeast Mississippi, a man occasionally makes the facetious remark, "When I married, all I promised my wife was wood and water— wood on her back and water in her eyes."

Some of the most interesting of this group of images relate to meals. When the guests arrive, the host may issue this modest invitation to the table: "Let's go rattle the dishes and fool the cats." Sometimes the complaint is heard that there is a "lot of shiftin' of the dishes for the fewness of the *vittles*." And from central Mississippi we have this characterization of a slouchy woman: "She wipes the plate with the cat's tail." Then, too, sometimes the guests explain early, "We've just come after a chunk of fire"—that is, for a short visit.

The final category consists of shrewd observations about both persons and things. Generally, they incorporate much provincial philosophy. "No telling which way luck, or a half-broke steer, is going to run," and "To see how folks will miss you, stick your finger in the pond, then pull it out and look at the hole" are fair examples. The second of these is a Negro proverb, as is also another, which has been used on occasion when a Negro has been inconsiderately treated by a railway station agent: "The littler the station, the bigger the agent." . . . From central Mississippi we get this Negro observation: "Cows can't catch no rabbits." . . . "A lean horse for a long race" and "Horse-sense is just stable thinking" come from central Mississippi. It is observed in north Mississippi that "It rains on the just and on the unjust. It rains on the unjust at fodder-pulling time." . . .

The behavior of creatures . . . is described by the . . . proverbs . . . from northeast Mississippi . . .: "A worm is about the only thing that does not fall down," "You can't make a hog squeal by hitting him with an ear of corn." . . .

Gullah Proverbs

BETTER belly bus' dan good bittle spile. [It is better for your belly to burst than for you to let good food spoil uneaten.] A repentant gourmand, who had taken this too literally, is reported to have said: "De nex' time peas spile, dey gwine spile outside o' me."

If you play wid puppy, 'ee lick yo' face, or lick you in de mout'. [Familiarity breeds contempt.]

Cut finger 'f'aid axe. [A burnt child dreads the fire.]

A still calf git de mores' milk.

Yaas, bubbuh, uh haa'kee, but uh yent yeddy. [I hear what you are saying, but I am not paying any attention to it.]

T'ief is bad, but t'ief en' ketch is de debble. [To steal is bad, but to steal and get caught is the devil.]

Little axe cut down big tree.

Ef you ent hab hoss to ride, ride cow. [Half a loaf is better than no bread.]

'E yent matter 'bout de road so long as 'e kah you to de right place.

A good dog fuh evryt'ing is good fuh nutt'n. [Jack of all trades, master of none.]

Po' buckra an' dog walk one paat. [The poor white man and a dog walk the same path.]

'Mos' kill bud don't mek soup. [Almost killed bird doesn't make soup.]

A man ain't eny mo' dan a man. [There's a limit to all things.]

Fisherman never say 'e fish spoil. [That is, when he wants to sell. Also: One does not decry himself or his things.]

If you knock de nose, de eye cry. [If you hurt one of the family, you hurt all.]

You muss nebber eat cooter an' de shell too. [This was the reply of an old man when he was told that the girl he had married was too young for him, and he ought to have taken her mother.]

You better not fool wid 'oman and fire.

Dog hab four feet, but him trabble only one paat. [One cannot do more than one thing at a time, or go different roads at the same time.]

Prayer nebber git grass out de field. [If one wants to do any work, etc., he must pull off his coat and go to work, and not rely upon prayer alone.]

Ef you call man "boy" 'e ain't mine, but call boy "boy" an' 'e bex. [One whose position or manhood is assured does not mind what he is

From "South Carolina Proverbs," by F. W. Bradley, *Southern Folklore Quarterly*, Vol. I (March, 1937), No. 1, pp. 99–101 *passim*. Gainesville, Florida: The University of Florida in co-operation with the Southeastern Folklore Society.

The Gullah proverbs listed below are principally from two sources—namely Reed Smith's *Gullah* (Bulletin of the University of South Carolina, No. 190, Columbia, South Carolina, 1926), and the *Charleston Museum Quarterly* ("Down State Negro Proverbs," collected and annotated by the late David Doar of Santee).—F. W. B.

called, it is only the boy and the upstart who is hurt by being told what he is.]

Pot can't bile widout fire.

You can't expect nuttin' from a hog but a grunt.

Dutty han' can't wash nuttin' clean.

Plantation Proverbs

BIG 'possum clime little tree.

Dem w'at eats kin say grace.

Ole man Know-All died las' year.

Better de gravy dan no grease 'tall.

Lazy fokes' stummucks don't git tired.

Mole don't see w'at his naber doin'.

Don't rain eve'y time de pig squeal.

Crow en corn can't grow in de same fiel'.

Tattlin' 'oman can't make de bread rise.

Rails split 'fo' bre'kfus' 'll season de dinner.

Hog dunner w'ich part un 'im'll season de turnip salad.

Mighty po' bee dat don't make mo' honey dan he want.

Kwishins on mule's foots done gone out er fashun.

Pigs dunno w'at a pen's fer.

Possum's tail good as a paw.

Dogs don't bite at de front gate.

Colt in de barley-patch kick high.

Jay-bird don't rob his own nes'.

Pullet can't roost too high for de owl.

De howlin' dog know w'at he sees.

Bline hoss don't fall w'en he follers de bit.

Hongry nigger won't w'ar his maul out.

Don't fling away de empty wallet.

Settin' hens don't hanker arter fresh aigs.

Tater-vine growin' w'ile you sleep.

Hit take two birds fer to make a nes'.

Ef you bleedzd ter eat dirt, eat clean dirt.

Tarrypin walk fast 'nuff fer to go visitin'.

Empty smoke-house makes de pullet holler.

W'en coon take water he fixin' fer ter fight.

Corn makes mo' at de mill dan it does in de crib.

Good luck say: "Op'n yo' mouf en shet yo' eyes."

Rooster makes mo' racket dan de hin w'at lay de aig.

From *Uncle Remus, His Songs and His Sayings,* by Joel Chandler Harris, pp. 173–177. New and Revised Edition. Copyright, 1880, 1895, by D. Appleton and Company, and 1908, 1921, by Esther La Rose Harris. New York and London: D. Appleton-Century Company. 1934.

Meller mush-million hollers at you fum over de fence.
Nigger wid a pocket-han'kcher better be looked atter.
Rain-crow don't sing no chune, but youk'n 'pen' on 'im.
One-eyed mule can't be handled on de bline side.
Moon may shine, but a lightered knot's mighty handy.
Licker talks mighty loud w'en it git loose fum de jug.
De proudness un a man don't count w'en his head's cold.
Hongry rooster don't cackle w'en he fine a wum.
Youk'n hide de fier, but w'at you gwine do wid de smoke?
Ter-morrow may be de carridge-driver's day for ploughin'.
Hit's a mighty deaf nigger dat don't year de dinner-ho'n.
Hit takes a bee fer ter git de sweetness out'n de hoar-houn' blossom.
You'd see mo' er de mink ef he know'd whar de yard dog sleeps.
Watch out w'en you'er gittin all you want. Fattenin' hogs ain't in luck.

Creole Animal Proverbs

BOUKI fait gombo, lapin mangé li.
Le bouc fait le gombo, lapin le mangé.
"He-goat makes the gombo; but Rabbit eats it."

From *"Gombo Zhèbes,"* Little Dictionary of Creole Proverbs, Selected from Six Creole Dialects, Translated into French and into English, with Notes, Complete Index to Subjects and Some Brief Remarks upon the Creole Idioms of Louisiana, by Lafcadio Hearn, pp. 11–32 *passim.* New York: Will H. Coleman, Publisher, 1885.

Any one who has ever paid a flying visit to New Orleans probably knows something about those various culinary preparations whose generic name is "Gombo"—compounded of many odds and ends, with the okra-plant, or true gombo for a basis, but also comprising occasionally "losé, zepinard, laitie," and the other vegetables sold in bunches in the French market. At all events any person who has remained in the city for a season must have become familiar with the nature of "gombo filé," "gombo févi," and "gombo aux herbes," or as our colored cook calls it, "gombo zhèbes"—for she belongs to the older generation of Creole *cuisinières,* and speaks the patois in its primitive purity, without using a single "r." Her daughter, who has been to school, would pronounce it *gombo zhairbes:*—the modern patois is becoming more and more Frenchified, and will soon be altogether forgotten, not only throughout Louisiana, but even in the Antilles. It still, however, retains originality enough to be understood with difficulty by persons thoroughly familiar with French; and even those who know nothing of any language but English readily recognize it by the peculiarly rapid syllabification and musical intonation. Such English-speaking residents of New Orleans seldom speak of it as "Creole"; they call it *gombo,* for some mysterious reason which I have never been able to explain satisfactorily. The colored Creoles of the city have themselves begun to use the term to characterize the patois spoken by the survivors of slavery days. Turiault tells us that in the towns of Martinique, where the Creole is gradually changing into French, the *Bitacos,* or country Negroes who still speak the patois nearly pure, are much ridiculed by their municipal brethren:—*Ça ou ka palé là, chè, c'est nèg:—Ça pas Créole! "What you talk is 'nigger,' my dear: —that isn't Creole!"* In like manner a young Creole Negro or Negress of New Orleans might tell an aged member of his race: *"Ça qui to parlé ça pas Créole: ça c'est gombo!"* I have sometimes heard the pure and primitive Creole also called "Congo" by colored folks of the new generation.—L. H., *ibid.,* p. 3.

This proverb is founded upon one of the many amusing Creole animal-fables, all bearing the title: *Compè Bouki épis Compè Lapin* ("Daddy Goat and Daddy Rabbit"). The rabbit always comes out victorious, as in the stories of Uncle Remus.

Cochon conné sir qui bois l'apé frotté.
(Le cochon sait bien sur quel arbre [bois] il va se frotter.)
"The hog knows well what sort of tree to rub himself against."

In most of the Creole dialects several different versions of a popular proverb are current. A friend gives me this one of [this] proverb . . . : *Cochon-marron conné enhaut qui bois li frotté.* ("The wild hog knows what tree to rub himself upon.") *Marron* is applied in all forms of the Creole patois to *wild* things: *zhèbes marrons* signifies "wild plants." The term, *couri-marron,* or *nègue-marron* formerly designated a runaway slave in Louisiana as it did in the Antilles. There is an old New Orleans saying:

> Après yé tiré canon
> Nègue sans passe c'est nègue-marron.

This referred to the old custom in New Orleans of firing a cannon at eight p.m. in winter, and nine p.m. in summer, as a warning to all slaves to retire. It was a species of modern curfew-signal. Any slave found abroad after those hours, without a pass, was liable to arrest and a whipping of twenty-five lashes. *Marron,* from which the English word "Maroon" is derived, has a Spanish origin. "It is," says Skeats, "a clipt form of the Spanish *cimarron,* wild, unruly: literally, "living in the mountain-tops." *Cimarron,* from Span. *Cina,* a mountain-summit. The original term for "Maroon" was *negro-cimarrón,* as it still is in some parts of Cuba.

Compé Torti va doucement; mais li rivé coté bîte pendant Compé Chivreil apé dormi.
(Compère Tortue va doucement; mais il arrive au bût pendant que Compère Chevreuil dort.)
"Daddy Tortoise goes slow; but he gets to the goal while Daddy Deer is asleep."

Based upon the Creole fable of *Compère Tortue* and *Compère Chevreuil,* rather different from the primitive story of the Hare and the Tortoise.

Coupé zoré milet fait pas choual.
(Couper les oreilles au mulet, n'en fait pas un cheval.)
"Cutting off a mule's ears won't make him a horse."

This seems to me much wittier than our old proverb: "You can't make a silk purse out of a sow's ear."

Faut pas marré tayau avec saucisse.

(Il ne faut pas attacher le chien-courant [taïant] avec des saucisses.)

"Mustn't tie up the hound with a string of sausages."

Adopted from old French *"taïaut"* (tally-ho!) the cry of the hunts-man to his hounds. The Creoles have thus curiously, but forcibly, named the hound itself.

Macaque dan calebasse.

(Le macaque dans la calebasse.)

"Monkey in the calabash."

Allusion to the old fable about the monkey, who after putting his hand easily into the orifice of a gourd, could not withdraw it without let-ting go what he sought to steal from within, and so got caught. In the figurative Creole speech one who allows his passions to ruin or disgrace him, is a *macaque dans calebasse.*

Macaque dit si so croupion plimé ças pas gàdé lezautt.

(Le macaque dit que si son croupion est plumé, ça ne régarde pas les autres.)

"Monkey says if his rump is bare, it's nobody's business."

Allusion to the callosities of the monkey. Plimé literally means "plucked"; but the Creole Negroes use it to signify "bare" from any cause. A Negro in rags might use the above proverb as a hint to those who wish to joke him about his personal appearance.

Maringouin perdi so temps quand li piqué caïman.

(Le maringoin perd son temps quand il pique le caïman.)

"The mosquito loses his time when he tries to sting the alligator."

Ripost to a threat—as we would say: "All that has as little effect on me as water on a duck's back!"

Où y'en a charogne, y'en a carencro.

(Où il a charogne, il y a des busards.)

"Wherever there's carrion, there are buzzards."

This is one of several instances of the Creole adoption of English words. The name "carrion-crow" has been applied to the buzzard in Louisiana from an early period of its American history.

Quand bois tombé, cabri monté.

(Quand l'arbre tombe, le cabri monte.)

"When the tree falls, the kid can climb it."

This saying has quite a variety of curious applications. The last time I heard it, a Creole Negress was informing me that the master of the house in which she worked was lying at the point of death: *"pauve diabe!"* I asked after the health of her mistress. *"Ah! Madame se porte bien; mais . . . quand bois tombé cabri monté,"* she replied, half in French, half in her own patois; signifying that after the husband's death, wife and children would find themselves reduced to destitution.

Ratte mangé canne, zanzoli mouri innocent.
(Le rat mange la canne-(à-sucre) le lézard en meurt.)
" 'Tis the rat eats the cane; but the lizard dies for it."

This proverb is certainly of West Indian origin, though I first obtained it from a Louisianian. In consequence of the depredations committed by rats in the West-Indian cane-fields, it is customary, after the crop has been taken off, to fire the dry cane tops and leaves. The blaze, spreading over the fields, destroys many rats, but also a variety of harmless lizards and other creatures.

The Mountain Dialect

ONE day I handed a volume of John Fox's stories to a neighbor and asked him to read it, being curious to learn how those vivid pictures of mountain life would impress one who was born and bred in the same atmosphere. He scanned a few lines of the dialogue, then suddenly stared at me in amazement.

"What's the matter with it?" I asked, wondering what he could have found to startle him at the very beginning of a story.

"Why, that feller *don't know how to spell*!"

Gravely I explained that dialect must be spelled as it is pronounced, so far as possible, or the life and savor of it would be lost. But it was of no use. My friend was outraged. "That taleteller then is jest makin' fun of the mountain people by misspellin' our talk. You educated folks don't spell your own words the way you say them."

A most palpable hit; and it gave me a new point of view.

To the mountaineers themselves their speech is natural and proper, of course, and when they see it bared to the spotlight, all eyes drawn toward it by an orthography that is as odd to them as it is to us, they are stirred to wrath, just as we would be if our conversation were reported by some Josh Billings or Artemus Ward.

The curse of dialect writing is elision. Still, no one can write it without using the apostrophe more than he likes to; for our highland speech is excessively clipped. "I'm comin' d'reck'ly" has a quaintness that should not be lost. We cannot visualize the shambling but eager mountaineer with a sample of ore in his hand unless the writer reports him faithfully: "Wisht

From *Our Southern Highlanders,* by Horace Kephart, pp. 276–299. Copyright, 1913, by Outing Publishing Company. New York.

Cf. B. A. Botkin, "Folk Speech in the Kentucky Mountain Cycle of Percy MacKaye," *American Speech,* Vol. VI (April, 1931), No. 4, pp. 264–276.

you'd 'zamine this rock fer me—I heern tell you was one o' them 'sperts."

Although the hillsman save some breath in this way, they waste a good deal by inserting sounds where they do not belong. Sometimes it is only an added consonant: gyarden, acrost, corkus (caucus); sometimes a syllable: loaferer, musicianer, suddenty. Occasionally a word is both added to and clipped from, as cyarn (carrion). They are fond of grace syllables: "I gotta me a deck o' cyards." "There ain't nary bitty sense in it."

More interesting are substitutions of one sound for another. In mountain dialect all vowels may be interchanged with others. Various sounds of *a* are confused with *e*, as hed (had), kem (came), keerful; or with *i*, grit (grate), rifle (raffle); with *o*, pomper, toper (taper), wrop; or with *u*, fur, ruther. So any other vowel may serve in place of *e*: sarve, chist, upsot, turrible. Any other may displace *i*: arn (iron), eetch, hender, whope or whup. The *o* sounds are more stable, but we have crap (crop), yan, clus, and many similar variants. Any other vowel may do for *u*: braysh or bresh (brush), shet, sich, shore (sure).

Mountaineers have peculiar difficulty with diphthongs: haar (hair), cheer (chair), brile, and a host of others. The word coil is variously pronounced quile, querl or quorl.

Substitution of consonants is not so common as of vowels, but most hillsmen say nabel (navel), ballet (ballad), Babtis', rench or rinch, brickle (brittle), and many say atter or arter, jue (due), tejus, vascinator (fascinator—a woman's scarf). They never drop *h*, nor substitute anything for it.

The word woman has suffered some strange sea-changes. Most mountaineers pronounce it correctly, but some drop the *w* ('oman), others add an *r* (womern and wimmern), while in Mitchell County, North Carolina, we hear the extraordinary forms ummern and dummern ("La, look at all the dummerunses a-comin'!")

On the other hand, some words that most Americans mispronounce are always sounded correctly in the southern highlands, as dew and new (never doo, noo). Creek is always given its true *ee* sound, never crick. Nare (as we spell it in dialect stories) is simply the right pronunciation of ne'er, and nary is ne'er a, with the *a* turned into a short *i* sound.

It should be understood that the dialect varies a good deal from place to place, and, even in the same neighborhood, we rarely hear all families speaking it alike. Outlanders who essay to write it are prone to err by making their characters speak it too consistently. It is only in the backwoods, or among old people and the penned-at-home women, that the dialect is used with any integrity. In railroad towns we hear little of it, and farmers who trade in those towns adapt their speech somewhat to the company they may be in. The same man, at different times, may say can't and cain't, set and sot, jest and jes' and jist, atter and arter or after, seed and seen, here and hyur and hyar, heerd and heern or heard, sich and sech, took and tuk—there is no uniformity about it. An unconscious sense of euphony seems to govern the choice of hit or it, there or thar.

Since the Appalachian people have a marked Scotch-Irish strain, we would expect their speech to show a strong Scotch influence. So far as vocabulary is concerned, there is really little of it. A few words, caigy (cadgy), coggled, fernent, gin for if, needcessity, trollop, almost exhaust the list of distinct Scotticisms. The Scotch-Irish, as we call them, were mainly Ulstermen, and the Ulster dialect of to-day bears little analogy to that of Appalachia.

Scotch influence does appear, however, in one vital characteristic of the pronunciation: with few exceptions our highlanders sound *r* distinctly wherever it occurs, though they never trill it. In the British Isles this constant sounding of *r* in all positions is peculiar, I think, to Scotland, Ireland, and a few small districts in the northern border counties of England. With us it is general practice outside of New England and those parts of the southern lowlands that had no flood of Celtic immigration in the eighteenth century. I have never heard a Carolina mountaineer say niggah or No'th Ca'lina, though in the last word the syllable *ro* is often elided.

In some mountain districts we hear do' (door), flo', mo', yo', co'te, sca'ce (long *a*), pusson; but such skipping of the *r* is common only where lowland influence has crept in. Much oftener the *r* is dropped from dare, first, girl, horse, nurse, parcel, worth (dast, fust, gal, hoss, nuss, passel, wuth). By way of compensation the hillsmen sometimes insert a euphonic *r* where it has no business; just as many New Englanders say, "The idear of it!"

Throughout Appalachia such words as last, past, advantage, are pronounced with the same vowel sound as is heard in man. This helps to delimit the people, classifying them with Pennsylvanians and Westerners: a linguistic grouping that will prove significant when we come to study the origin and history of this isolated race.

An editor who had made one or two short trips into the mountains once wrote me that he thought the average mountaineer's vocabulary did not exceed three hundred words. This may be a natural inference if one spends but a few weeks among these people and sees them only under the prosaic conditions of workaday life. But gain their intimacy and you shall find that even the illiterates among them have a range of expression that is truly remarkable. I have myself taken down from the lips of Carolina mountaineers some eight hundred dialectical or obsolete words, to say nothing of the much greater number of standard English terms that they command.

Seldom is a "hill-billy" at a lose for a word. Lacking other means of expression, there will come "spang" from his mouth a coinage of his own. Instantly he will create (always from English roots, of course) new words by combination, or by turning nouns into verbs or otherwise interchanging the parts of speech.

Crudity or deficiency of the verb characterizes the speech of all primitive peoples. In mountain vernacular many words that serve as verbs are only nouns of action, or adjectives, or even adverbs. "That bear 'll meat me a month." "They churched Pitt for tale-bearin'." "Granny kept faultin' us all day." "Are ye fixin' to go squirrelin'?" "Sis blouses her waist a-purpose to carry a pistol." "My boy Jesse book-kept for the camp." "I disgust bad liquor." "This poke salat eats good." "I ain't goin' to bed it no longer" (lie abed). "We can muscle this log up." "I wouldn't pleasure them enough to say it." "Josh ain't much on sweet-heartin'." "I don't confidence them dogs much." "The creek away up thar turkey-tails out into numerous leetle forks."

A verb will be coined from an adverb: "We better git some wood, bettern we?" Or from an adjective: "Much that dog and see won't he come along" (pet him, make much of him). "I didn't do nary thing to contrary her." "Baby, that onion 'll strong ye!" "Little Jimmy fell down and benastied himself to beat the devil."

Conversely, nouns are created from verbs. "Hit don't make no differ." "I didn't hear no give-out at meetin'" (announcement). "You can git ye one more gittin' o' wood up thar." "That Nantahala is a master shut-in, jest a plumb gorge." Or from an adjective: "Them bugs—the little old hatefuls!" "If anybody wanted a history of this county for fifty years he'd git a lavish of it by reading that mine-suit testimony." Or from an adverb: "Nance tuk the biggest through at meetin'!" (shouting spell). An old lady quoted to me in a plaintive quaver:

> "It matters not, so I've been told,
> Where the body goes when the heart grows cold;

"But," she added, "a person has a rather about where he'd be put."

In mountain vernacular the Old English strong past tense still lives in begun, drunk, holped, rung, shrunk, sprung, stunk, sung, sunk, swum. Holp is used both as preterite and as infinitive: the *o* is long, and the *l* distinctly sounded by most of the people, but elided by such as drop it from almost, already, self (the *l* is elided from help by many who use that form of the verb).

Examples of a strong preterite with dialectical change of the vowel are bruk, brung, drap or drapped, drug, friz, roke or ruck (raked), saunt (sent), shet, shuck (shook), whoped (long *o*). The variant whupped is a Scotticism. Whope is sometimes used in the present tense, but whup is more common. By some the vowel of whup is sounded like *oo* in book (Mr. Fox writes "whoop," which, I presume, he intends for that sound).

In many cases a weak preterite supplants the proper strong one: div, driv, fit, gi'n or give, rid, riv, riz, writ, done, run, seen or sed, blowed, crowed, drawed, growed, knowed, throwed.

There are many corrupt forms of the verb, such as gwine for gone or going, mought (mowt) for might, clim, het, ort or orter, wed (weeded), war (was or were—the *a* as in far), shun (shone), cotch (in all tenses) or cotched, fotch or fotched, borned, hurted, dremp.

Peculiar adjectives are formed from verbs. "Chair-bottoming is easy settin'-down work." "When my youngest was a leetle set-along child" (interpreted as "settin' along the floor"). "That Thunderhead is the torn-downdest place!" "Them's the travellinest hosses ever I seed." "She's the workinest woman!" "Jim is the disablest one o' the fam'ly." "Damn this fotch-on kraut that comes in tin cans!"

A verb may serve as an adverb: "If I'd a-been thoughted enough." An adverb may be used as an adjective: "I hope the folks with you is gaily" (well). An adjective can serve as an adverb: "He laughed master." . . . These are not mere blunders of individual illiterates, but usages common throughout the mountains, and hence real dialect.

The ancient syllabic plural is preserved in beasties (horses), nesties, posties, trousies (these are not diminutives), and in that strange word dummerunses that I cited before.

Pleonasms are abundant. "I done done it" (have done it or did do it). "Durin' the while." "In this day and time." "I thought it would surely, undoubtedly turn cold." "A small, little bitty hole." "Jane's a tol'able big, large, fleshy woman." "I ginerally, usually take a dram mornin's." "These ridges is might' nigh straight up and down, and, as the feller said, per-pendic'lar."

Everywhere in the mountains we hear of biscuit-bread, ham-meat, rifle-gun, rock-clift, ridin'-critter, cow-brute, man-person, women-folks, preacher-man, granny-woman and neighbor-people. In this category belong the famous double-barreled pronouns: we-all and you-all in Kentucky, we-uns and you-uns in Carolina and Tennessee. (I have even heard such locution as this: "Let's we-uns all go over to you-erunses house.") Such usages are regarded generally as mere barbarisms, and so they are in English, but Miss Murfree cites correlatives in the Romance languages: French *nous autres*, Italian *noi altri*, Spanish *nosotros*.

The mountaineers have some queer ways of intensifying expression. "I'd *tell* a man," with the stress as here indicated, is simply a strong affirmative. "We had one more *time*" means a rousing good time. "P'int-blank" is a superlative or an epithet: "We jist p'int-blank got it to do." "Well, p'int-blank, if they ever come back again, I'll move!"

A double negative is so common that it may be crowded into a single word: "I did it the unthoughtless of anything I ever done in my life." Triple negatives are easy: "I ain't got nary none." A mountaineer can accomplish the quadruple: "That boy ain't never done nothin' nohow." Yea, even the quintuple: "I ain't never seen no men-folks of no kind do no washin'."

On the other hand, the veriest illiterates often startle a stranger by glib use of some word that most of us picked up in school or seldom use informally. "I can make a hunderd pound o' pork outen that hog—tutor it jist right." "Them clouds denote rain." "She's so dilitary!" "They stood thar and caviled about it." "That exceeds the measure." "Old Tom is blind, but he can discern when the sun is shinin'." "Jerry proffered to fix the gun for me." I had supposed that the words cuckold and mooncalf had none but literary usage in America, but we often hear them in the mountains, cuckold being employed both as verb and as noun, and moon-calf in its baldly literal sense that would make Prospero's taunt to Caliban a superlative insult.

Our highlander often speaks in Elizabethan or Chaucerian or even pre-Chaucerian terms. His pronoun hit antedates English itself, being the Anglo-Saxon neuter of he. Ey God, a favorite expletive, is the original of egad, and goes back of Chaucer. Ax for ask and kag for keg were the primitive and legitimate forms, which we trace as far as the time of Layamon. When the mountain boy challenges his mate: "I dar ye—I ain't afeared!" his verb and participle are of the same ancient and sterling rank. Afore, atwixt, awar, heap o' folks, peart, up and done it, usen for used, all these everyday expressions of the backwoods were contemporary with the *Canterbury Tales*.

A man said to me of three of our acquaintances: "There's been a fray on the river—I don't know how the fraction begun, but Os feathered into Dan and Phil, feedin' them lead." He meant fray in its original sense of deadly combat, as was fitting where two men were killed. Fraction for rupture is an archaic word, rare in literature, though we find it in *Troilus and Cressida*. "Feathered into them!" Where else can we hear to-day a phrase that passed out of standard English when "villainous saltpetre" supplanted the long-bow? It means to bury an arrow up to the feather, as when the old chronicler Harrison says, "An other arrow should haue beene fethered in his bowels."

Our schoolmaster, composing a form of oath for the new mail-carrier, remarked: "Let me study this thing over; then I can edzact it"—a verb so rare and obsolete that we find it in no American dictionary, but only in Murray.

A remarkable word, common in the Smokies, is dauncy, defined for me as "mincy about eating," which is to say fastidious, over-nice. Dauncy probably is a variant of daunch, of which the Oxford *New English Dictionary* cites but one example, from the *Townley Mysteries* of *circa* 1460.

A queer term used by Carolina mountaineers, without the faintest notion of its origin, is doney (long *o*) or doney-gal, meaning a sweetheart. Its history is unique. British sailors of the olden time brought it to England from Spanish or Italian ports. Doney is simply *doña* or *donna* a trifle anglicized in pronunciation. Odd, though, that it should be preserved in America by none but backwoodsmen whose ancestors for two centuries never saw the tides!

In the vocabulary of the mountaineers I have detected only three words of directly foreign origin. Doney is one. Another is kraut, which is the sole contribution to highland speech of those numerous Germans (mostly Pennsylvania Dutch) who joined the first settlers in this region, and whose descendants, under wondrously anglicized names, form to-day a considerable element of the highland population. The third sashiate (French *chassé*), used in calling figures at the country dances.

There is something intrinsically, stubbornly English in the nature of the mountaineer: he will assimilate nothing foreign. In the Smokies the Eastern Band of Cherokees still holds its ancient capital on the Okona Lufty River, and the whites mingle freely with these redskins, bearing them no such despite as they do Negroes, but eating at the same table and admitting Indians to the white compartment of a Jim Crow car. Yet the mountain dialect contains not one word of Cherokee origin, albeit many of the whites can speak a little Cherokee.

In our county some Indians always appear at each term of court, and an interpreter must be engaged. He never goes by that name, but by the obsolete title linkister or link'ster, by some lin-gis-ter.

Many other old-fashioned terms are preserved in Appalachia that sound delightfully quaint to strangers who never met them outside of books. A married woman is not addressed as Missis by the mountaineers, but as Mistress when they speak formally, and as Mis' or Miz' for a contraction. We will hear an aged man referred to as "Old Grandsir'" So-and-So. "Back this letter for me" is a phrase unchanged from the days before envelopes, when an address had to be written on the back of the letter itself. "Can I borry a race of ginger?" means the unground root—you will find the word in *A Winter's Tale*. "Them sorry fellers" denotes scabby knaves, good-for-nothings. Sorry has no etymological connection with sorrow, but literally means sore-y, covered with sores, and the highlander sticks to its original import.

We have in the mountains many home-born words to fit the circumstances of backwoods life. When maize has passed from the soft and milky stage of roasting-ears, but is not yet hard enough for grinding, the ears are grated into a soft meal and baked into delectable pones called gritted-bread.

* * * * *

When one dines in a cabin back in the hills he will taste some strange dishes that go by still stranger names. Beans dried in the pod, then boiled "hull and all," are called leather-breeches (this is not slang, but the regular name). Green beans in the pod are called snaps; when shelled they are shuck-beans. The old Germans taught their Scotch and English neighbors the merits of scrapple, but here it is known as poor-do. Lath-open bread is made from biscuit dough, with soda and buttermilk, in the usual way, except that the shortening is worked in last. It is then baked in flat cakes, and has the peculiar property of parting readily into thin flakes when broken edgewise. I suppose that poor-do was originally poor-doin's, and lath-open bread denotes that it opens into lath-like strips. But etymology cannot be pushed recklessly in the mountains, and I offer these clews as a mere surmise.

Your hostess, proffering apple sauce, will ask, "Do you love sass?" I had to kick my chum Andy's shin the first time he faced this question. It is well for a traveler to be forewarned that the word love is commonly used here in the sense of like or relish.

If one is especially fond of a certain dish he declares that he is a fool about it. "I'm a plumb fool about pickle-beans." Conversely, "I ain't much of a fool about liver" is rather more than a hint of distaste. "I et me a bait" literally means a mere snack, but jocosely it may admit a hearty meal. If the provender be scant the hostess may say, "That's right at a smidgeon," meaning little more than a mite; but if plenteous, then there are rimptions.

To "grabble 'taters" is to pick from a hill of new potatoes a few of the best, then smooth back the soil without disturbing the immature ones.

If the house be in disorder it is said to be all gormed or gaumed up, or things are just in a mommick.

When a man is tired he likely will call it worried; if in a hurry, he is in a swivvet; if nervous, he has the all-overs; if declining in health, he is on the down-go. If he and his neighbor dislike each other, there is a hardness between them; if they quarrel, it is a ruction, a rippit, a jower, or an up-scuddle—so be it there are no fatalities which would amount to a real fray.

A choleric or fretful person is tetchious. Survigrous (ser-*vi*-grus) is a superlative of vigorous (here pronounced *vi*-grus, with long *i*): as "a survigrous baby," "a most survigrous cusser." Bodaciously means bodily or entirely: "I'm bodaciously ruint" (seriously injured). "Sim greened him out bodaciously" (to green out or sap is to outwit in trade). To disfurnish or discon*fit* means to incommode: "I hope it has not disconfit you very bad."

To shamp means to shingle or trim one's hair. A bastard is a woods-colt or an outsider. Slaunchways denotes slanting, and si-godlin or si-antigodlin is out of plumb or out of square (factitious words, of course—mere nonsense terms, like catawampus).

Critter and beast are usually restricted to horse and mule, and brute to a bovine. A bull or boar is not to be mentioned as such in mixed company, but male-brute and male-hog are used as euphemisms.[1]

A female shoat is called a gilt. A spotted animal is said to be pieded (pied), and a striped one is listed. In the Smokies a toad is called a frog or a toad-frog, and a toadstool is a frog-stool. The woodpecker is turned around into a peckerwood, except that the giant woodpecker (here still a common bird) is known as a woodcock or woodhen.

What the mountaineers call hemlock is the shrub leucothoe. The hemlock tree is named spruce-pine, while spruce is he-balsam, balsam itself is she-balsam, laurel is ivy, and rhododendron is laurel. In some places pine needles are called twinkles, and the locust insect is known as a ferro (Pharaoh?). A treetop left on the ground after logging is called the lap. Sobby wood means soggy or sodden, and the verb is to sob.

Evening, in the mountains, begins at noon instead of at sunset. Spell is used in the sense of while ("a good spell atterward") and soon for early

---

[1] So also in the lowland South. An extraordinary affectation of propriety appeared in a dispatch to the *Atlanta Constitution* of October 29, 1912, which reported that an exhibitor of cattle at the State fair had been seriously horned by a *male cow*.—H. K.

("a soon start in the morning"). The hillsmen say "a year come June," "Thursday 'twas a week ago," and "the year nineteen and eight."

Many common English words are used in peculiar senses by the mountain folk, as call for name or mention or occasion, clever for obliging, mimic or mock for resemble, a power or sight for much, risin' for exceeding (also for inflammation), ruin for injure, scout for elude, stove for jabbed, surround for go around, word for phrase, take off for help yourself. Tale always means an idle or malicious report.

Some highlander usages that sound odd to us are really no more than the original and literal meanings, as budget for bag or parcel, hampered for shackled or jailed. When a mountain swain "carries his gal to meetin' '" he is not performing so great an athletic feat as was reported by Benjamin Franklin, who said, "My father carried his wife with three children to New England" (from Pennsylvania).

A mountaineer does not throw a stone; he "flings a rock." He sharpens tools on a grindin'-rock or whet rock. Tomato, cabbage, molasses and baking powder are always used as plural nouns. "Pass me them molasses." "I'll have a few more of them cabbage." "How many bakin'-powders has you got?"

The speech of the southern highlanders is alive with quaint idioms. "I swapped hosses, and I'll tell you fer why." "Your name ain't much common." "Who got to beat?" "You think me of it in the mornin'." "I 'low to go to town to-morrow." "The woman's aimin' to go to meetin'." "I had in head to plow to-day, but it's come on to rain." "I've laid off and laid off to fix that fence." "Reckon Pete was knowin' to the sarcumstance?" "I'll name it to Newt, if so be he's thar." "I knowed in reason she'd have the mullygrubs over them doin's." "You cain't handily blame her."

"Air ye plumb bereft?" "How come it was this: he done me dirt." "I ain't carin' which nor whether about it." "Sam went to Andrews or to Murphy, one." "I tuk my fut in my hand and lit out." "He lit a rag fer home." "Don't much believe the wagon 'll come to-day." " 'Tain't powerful long to dinner, I don't reckon." "Phil's Ann give it out to each and every that Walt and Layunie 'd orter wed."

"Howdy, Tom: light and hitch."

"Reckon I'd better git on."

"Come in and set."

"Cain't stop long."

"Oh, set down and eat you some supper!"

"I've been."

"Won't ye stay the night? Look like to me we'll have a rainin', windin spell."

"No: I'll haffter go down."

"Well, come agin, and fix to stay a week."

"You-uns come down with me."

"Won't go now, I guess, Tom."

"Giddep! I'll be back by in the mornin'."

"Farwell!"

Rather laconic. Yet, on occasion, when the mountaineer is drawn out of his natural reserve and allows his emotions free rein, there are few educated people who can match his picturesque and pungent diction. His trick of apt phrasing is intuitive. Like an artist striking off a portrait or a caricature with a few swift strokes his characterization is quick and vivid. Whether he use quaint obsolete English or equally delightful perversions, what he says will go straight to the mark with epigrammatic force.

The Speech of the Negro

MORE and more white skeletons are being found in the Negro's woodpile. Superstitions which have often been attributed to African heritage have been found to be respectable white superstitions; folk tales, games, and riddles which were thought to be purely Negro have turned out in many cases to be of European descent; folk songs which have been pictured as rising from the Negro's sufferings in slavery are being traced to white camp meeting songs; and numerous little customs and folkways long considered peculiar to Negroes have turned out to be cast-off or outgrown bits of white culture.

What of Negro dialect? Of course, in a general way every one realizes that Negro dialect is an English dialect, but most people stand ready to accuse the Negro of having corrupted the English language, yea, even of corrupting the speech of Southern white people. Let us look into Negro English and white English for a moment. First, a word on the background of American English.

There is no standard spoken English, even among educated people, in this country. So strong are our dialectical traits and so diverse our ideas as to what constitutes good English that we have no standard pronunciation of English. Among the masses of white people, the variations are still greater, for their speech still follows the lines of the various traditional dialects.

Broadly speaking, we may distinguish three great dialect types in this country: the Southern, the Northern, and the Western. There are sub-dialects within and gradations between these main divisions. For example, the Southern speech of Charleston, S. C., is not the speech of the Southern upcountry folk; the speech of Boston is not the speech of the up-state New Yorker; the speech of the Texan is a sort of hybrid, not quite Southern, not quite Western, but partaking liberally of both. However, this threefold division will do for our purposes.

By Guy B. Johnson. From *Folk-Say, A Regional Miscellany: 1930,* edited by B. A Botkin, pp. 346–358. Copyright, 1930, by B. A. Botkin. Norman: University of Oklahoma Press.

How did these dialect types come about? Does the Southerner talk as he does because of the climate, because of contact with the Negro, or for some other reason? Various reasons have been advanced, but it is lately becoming apparent that our dialect areas represent perpetuations of dialect types brought over from the Mother Country. New England was first settled largely from Southern and Southeastern England, while Virginia and South Carolina were settled from Southern and Southwestern England. Our oldest settlements had certain things in common, then,—such as the broad *a* and the tendency to suppress the *r*, which traits are rather wide-spread over the lower part of England—and enough points of difference to give them distinctive speech atmospheres.

From the Atlantic seaboard these early settlers began pushing the frontier line westward, taking with them their dialect traits. But another factor intervened before the frontier had gone very far. Thousands of Northern English and Scotch-Irish people, with rolling *r's* and other characteristic traits, poured into America, modifying the speech of the North, except for the entrenched aristocratic sections of New England, and dominating the speech of the West. Many of these people came South, but their migration did not affect the old areas along the coast, because they came down the valleys and settled in the mountains and foothills from Pennsylvania on down to the Southwest. Spoken English in the Southern foothills and mountains is a blend of the Scotch-Irish type with the Southern England type which was brought inward from the coast.

From the differences between dialects in England came the differences between dialects in America. What we call Northern speech is a hybrid, a fusion of Southern English with the Scotch-Irish. Fusion, relative predominance of one over another, geographical isolation, and other factors have made for differentiation of sub-types, but the three general types still hold good.

Are there any areas or types of Negro dialect? Yes. All three of the major white dialects are represented to some extent among Negroes, but Negro dialect is predominantly Southern, showing the same regional differentiations as does Southern white speech. The areas are rather hard to define, because they shade almost imperceptibly into one another. However, no one would deny that the low-country or Gullah dialect of South Carolina constitutes a distinct type. The upper South, including North Carolina, seems to represent another dialect area. The lower South, a region of large plantations and absentee landlordism during slavery, contains a type of Negro speech which might be said to be slightly less "advanced" than that of the upper South. Beyond the Appalachians is a fourth type in the making, while in the Southwest there is still another type arising. This latter reflects the heterogeneity of the elements which have gone into the making of Southwestern white speech. We should append a sixth variety, perhaps; namely, the Negro-French dialect of Louisiana. It is doubtful whether we should name still another, the Northern, as a Negro dialect, for Negro speech in the North is not uniform, but a hodgepodge of all possible gradations of American English. This is particularly true after the recent flood of migration to the North.

Now, we who live among Negroes are apt to magnify the differences between their speech and our own, but it is probable that if the Man from Mars could look us over he would conclude that Negro speech in any given area comes pretty near being a copy of white speech in that area. Taking this as a cue, let us attempt to see just how far Negro dialect traits can be attributed to white dialect traits.

The scientific comparison of white and Negro dialects has only begun. Unfortunately, many of the dialect writers have failed to give accurate representations of Negro speech in their works, and it is largely to trained students of folklore that we must look in the future for authentic examples of dialect. The following list of traits is suggested as a working arrangement for classifying data on dialect:

1. *Vocal traits:* timbre of the voice, pitch of voice, pitch inflections, intonations, intensity, speed of speech, rhythmic factors, etc.
2. *Pronunciation:* vowel and consonant sounds, mutilations, corruptions, etc.
3. *Grammar:* nouns, pronouns, verbs, etc.; number, gender, tense, etc.
4. *Vocabulary:* unusual words, archaisms, phrases, idioms, etc.

Certain vocal qualities such as timbre, resonance, pitch of the speaking voice, etc., are largely derived from hereditary factors, and they would of course persist in spite of long contact with a strange language. Other vocal traits, such as pitch inflections, musical intonations, intensity of vocalization, speed, and rhythm, are matters of habit, but in the present state of our knowledge we cannot say to what extent Negro speech differs from white speech with respect to these traits, or whether the differences, if any, represent adherence to African language habits. It seems probable that there are little quirks of Negro speech, such as the intonations used to express surprise, anger, joy, etc., which have an African basis. The whole Gullah dialect of the sea islands, by far our most archaic Negro dialect, is characterized by musical and rhythmic traits which might easily have an African provenience, for it is well known that the languages of West Africa employ pitch inflections to denote meanings of words just as we employ stress accents. There is much yet to be learned about the vocal qualities of both white and Negro dialect speech, and it is to be hoped that collectors in the future will give these matters the attention they deserve.

To go into the phonology of Negro English in detail would require a volume or two, so we may content ourselves here with a few illustrations of typical vowel and consonant sounds. Any one wanting to mimic Negro speech would probably pronounce *head* and *dead* as if they were *haid* and *daid*. This vowel change is probably more common than any other among Negroes, and it is easy to assume that there is some particular racial reason for their failure to say *head, dead,* etc. If it be pointed out that there are illiterate white people who use the same pronunciations, there are those who retort that these people have been affected by Negroes. But, consulting the *English Dialect Grammar*, we find that the *haid* and *daid* pronunciations are widespread, being used, for example, in Yorkshire, Lancashire, Northampton, Norfolk, Suffolk, Kent, Somerset, and Devonshire. It is not accidental, then, that Negro speech took on these pronunciations, for they were the common pronunciations of the ordinary English people from whom the Negro learned English in early slavery days.

No better proof of the borrowed nature of Negro vowel sounds can be found than in the exceptions to the sound just mentioned. Take the following words which have the same vowel as *head* and *dead: get, yellow, instead, deaf.* The prevailing Negro pronunciations are *git, yalluh, instid, deef.* A glance through the *English Dialect Grammar* or through some of the numerous glossaries of English dialect shows at once that these are exactly the pronunciations which were most common in England. For example, *git* for *get* occurs generally in England and in parts of Ireland.

Anyone who wants to take the trouble can go through all of the vowel sounds in English, note the Negro pronunciations, and compare them with the dialect pronunciations of Southern England. In every case he will find that Negro pronunciations can be traced to English dialect. Most of them can also be found among the various isolated white groups in this country, particularly in the Appalachians and Ozarks, and some of them were once the standard pronunciations in England.

Coming next to consonants, we find that the most widespread Negro dialect traits here are the omission of *r* and the substitution of *n* for *ng*. Northerners often attribute the loss of the Southern *r* and the use of *n* for *ng* to contact with the Negro. They forget that in New England there is no more regard for the *r* than there is in the South and that pronunciations like *runnin', singin', goin',* can be heard among illiterate people in every part of the United States, as well as among many educated people in England. Referring to English dialect again, we find that outside of Scotland and Northern England *r* tended to be seen and not heard. Walker's *Critical and Pronouncing Dictionary and Expositor of the English Language* (3rd edition, reprinted in this country in 1823) states: "In England, and particularly in London, the *r* in *lard, bard, card, regard,* etc., is pronounced so much in the throat as to be little more than the middle or Italian *a,* lengthened into *laad, baad, caad, regaad,"* Of the *ng* sound in England, Wright says in the *English Dialect Grammar:* "Final unstressed *ng* has become *n* in all the dialects, *evenin(g), farthin(g), mornin(g), sendin(g),* and similarly in all present participles and verbal nouns in *ing.*" It is evident, then, that the presence of these traits and their distribution in the United States are accounted for by their distribution in England.

The same may be said for all the consonantal peculiarities of Negro dialect, with the possible exception of *th* and intrusive *n.* The average Negro has mastered the *th* sounds of English and says *then, thin,* etc., as the white man does, but in the Gullah dialect and by older Negroes all over the South *th* is almost invariably replaced by *t* or *d. Th* as in *then* becomes *d, den. Th* as in *thin* becomes *t, t'in.* Now it happens that in the West African languages there are no *th* sounds, so it might be argued that in learning English the slaves fell back upon the nearest approach they knew to our *th* sounds. On the other hand, in the Orkney and Shetland Islands, in Pembroke, Kent, and Sussex, the English folk used *th* sounds in the same way our Negroes do. The use of *d* for *th,* and several other Negroisms, might be detected, for example, in the following stanza from the famous Kentish dialect poem, *Dick and Sal:*

> My nable! dair was lots of fun,
> An sich hubbub an hollar;
> De donkeys dey for cheeses run,
> An I grinn'd through a collar.

An intrusive *n* sound, as in *nyoung* for *young, nused* for *used,* etc., is heard occasionally among Negroes all over the South, but is particularly noticeable in the Gullah dialect. N is prefixed to many words in the African languages, as in *nkuruma, ngola,* etc., and this has been suggested as the explanation of its use by our Negroes. However, in the African languages the *n* precedes a consonant, whereas no instance of *n* prefixed to an initial consonant has been shown to exist in American Negro dialect. On the other hand, English dialect contains words like *noration* for *oration, narrow* for *arrow,* etc., these having arisen in nearly every case from the effect of a preceding *an.* Still this does not quite account for *nyoung* and *nused* in Negro dialect, so it is possible that there remains some slight effect of the African *n.*

Perhaps the most striking consonantal trait in all Negro dialect is the interchange of *v* and *w,* which is quite common in the Gullah dialect of the sea islands. *Wine* is pronounced *vine,* and if the speaker means *vine* he says *wine.* Yet this peculiarity is exactly the same as in the Kentish dialect, examples of which some may recall from Dickens' Sam Weller sketches.

The phonology of Negro dialect is affected by the omission of various prefixes and other syllables. It is easy to attribute pronunciations like *'spise (despise), 'cept (except),* and hundreds of others to Negro laziness, but this explanation falls flat when it is discovered that English dialect abounds in exactly the same sort of thing. Furthermore, Negroes are supposed to have corrupted numerous English words, as in *ballet (ballad), gin (given), sparrowgrass (asparagus), watermilyon (watermelon), rubbidge (rubbish), argify (argue),* and many others. Even a hasty examination of the *English Dialect Dictionary* will show that practically every word of this kind should be attributed to our English forbears rather than to Negro vocal economizing. In fact, it is extremely doubtful whether there is a single word of more than individual or local importance which the Negro has coined by corrupting English words.

The grammar of Negro dialect is likewise found to have no characteristics which are not explainable on the basis of English dialect. A statement of the outstanding traits of Negro grammar may be summarized as follows:

1. Errors in use of singular and plural of nouns: "fifty poun' "; "twelve mont' "; "one oxen"; "five ox"; "de mens"; "five-dollahs hat"; etc.; all of which are easily paralleled in English dialect.

2. Omission of sign of the genitive (among old-time speakers): "my wife house"; "Brer Rabbit tail"; "de man in de nex' house cow"; etc. In English dialect one finds such expressions as "my father boots," "the Queen cousin," and a Lancashire magistrate is said to have asked a witness, "Was it your brother dog?"

3. Errors in comparison of adjectives: *worser, worstest, more better, morest, mostest,* etc. These are so patent in English dialect as to need no comment.

4. Confusion in use of pronouns: "him an' me"; "him told me"; "me said to he"; "he (his) coat"; "us house"; "he (her) husband"; etc. Says the *English Dialect Grammar:* "In all the dialects of Scotland and England the objective form of the personal pronoun is used for the nominative . . . the nominative of the personal pronoun is used as the emphatic form of the objective case." In the Gullah dialect and among old-time Negroes elsewhere there is a confusion of masculine and feminine pronouns. In the Gullah it is quite the thing to speak of one's wife, one's ox, one's bull, one's niece, as *he* or *'e.* Even this trait may be attributed to English dialect patterns. In Hampshire, for example, according to Halliwell, it used to be said that "everything is called *he* except a tom-cat which is called *she."*

5. Errors in verb endings and tense, and use of nouns and adjectives as verbs: "he run" may mean that he ran, has run, runs, etc. "I seen," "I done," "I knowed," etc., are of course used freely, as they are among illiterate whites. Even "I is" or "I's" for "I am" is widely used in England by the peasantry. Such usages as "he pleasured himself," "she gonna dead," "dey been foolishin' aroun'," which sound so characteristically Negro, are also found among the white people in the Appalachians and Ozarks, and they represent survivals of an English dialect trait. The use of an enclytic *a* or *uh* with some verbs, as in "he's a-runnin'," "if I had a-hit 'im," survives among both whites and Negroes from a very old and respectable English usage. In the Gullah there is still another survival; namely, *do* or *duh,* as in "de win' duh blow," "my mudder duh call me," from English dialect *do, doth,* etc.

Many other minor points of Negro dialect grammar might be cited, but there is yet to be found one which cannot be shown to be merely the same sort of simplified English grammar as that which was used by the lower classes of English folk.

The vocabulary of the Negro contains quite a few obsolete English words and a handful of African words. These two classes of words are not always easily separated. When a word is unknown to us but is used by Negroes we tend to brand it as an African importation. For example, *tote,* to carry, was laid on the Negro, also on the Indian, and there are still persons who do not recognize a rather obvious English derivation. Likewise *brawtus,* meaning something thrown in for good measure, was recently cited by

Professor Robert A. Law, of the University of Texas, as probably an African word, in spite of the archaic English word *brotts,* fragments, leavings, and the Lancashire word *brotta,* meaning "a few drops, a small quantity, a little in addition."

Words of undisputed African origin in Negro dialect are relatively rare. A few African words like *okra, gumbo, goober, pinder,* are in common use among both whites and Negroes over a large part of the country—are, in fact, so well accepted that many may be surprised to know that they came from Africa. *Buckra,* white man, *cooter,* terrapin, *yam* or *nyam,* to eat, *ki,* an exclamation, are very probably African. They are found especially in the Gullah dialect, but occur occasionally in other parts of the lower South, even being used by the Negroes in the Sabine and Red River valleys in Texas and Louisiana. Here and there, in out-of-the-way places may be found African words used by individuals or families, but there are very few of these left to-day.

The list of archaic English words in use among Negroes is not yet complete, for every study of dialect turns up additional survivals. The best place to look for these words is in the Gullah dialect, although they are plentiful in other sections which have been somewhat isolated from the trends of modern civilization. It is no accident that practically every archaism found among the Negroes of the sea islands is also found among the whites of the Southern mountains. Following are a few of the archaic words found in Negro dialect:

Ax, ask. Not a Negroism, but a usage which was once good English. Chaucer used *ax.*

Brawtus, something in addition. Discussed above.

Find, to supply with provisions, victuals, etc.

Gaum or *gorm,* to smear one's face with grease, etc. Hence *gormy,* sticky, dirty.

Gall, swamp, boggy land.

Hippo, ipecac.

Killick, an anchor made of stone.

Meet, to find, to observe, to experience. "Did you meet a good time?" "Did he meet any fish?"

Peruse, to saunter, to walk leisurely.

Piggin, a small wooden pail with one stave extended to serve as a handle.

Poke, sack, bag.

Pure, fully, absolutely. "He pyore love dat gal."

Quizzett, to quiz, to question sharply.

Remoan, to remove.

Soon, early, quick, alert. "A soon breakfast," "a soon man."

Start-naked, stark-naked. Not a corruption of *stark-naked,* but a descendant of Anglo-Saxon *steort-naked,* literally, *tail-naked.*

Swinge, to singe.

Toad, a young female dog.

Too, very. "I's too sorry you gwine." "Lawd, dat fish too big!"

Tote, to carry.

Use, to frequent or roam over a given area, as of cattle and game. Used by Milton, Shakespeare, and others.

Yowe, ewe.

Many a Negro phrase is rooted in the dialects of England. When a Negro tells his child, on the approach of a white person, "Make yo' manners," he is repeating a command used in England to remind children to curtsy or touch the hat in the presence of superiors. The Negro raises "a right smart" of potatoes, raises "great big" hogs, and tries to "get shet of" his enemies, just as poor white folk have done for hundreds of years. To "tell a story" is to tell a lie, and to "favor" some one is to resemble him. "I'm a good mind to whup you," says a Negro mother to her son, meaning that she has a strong intention to do so. "I like to have got killed" means "I almost got killed." It is surprising how many phrases used by Negroes are exactly the phrases used by English folk. Scratch a Negro idiom and nine times out of ten you will find an English dialect phrase.

Taking into account the paternalistic nature of the slave régime in the Southern States, the variety of African tribal heritages thrust into the slave melting pot, and the planters' deliberate weeding out of pagan customs, it is easy to see that Negro speech could be nothing more than a copy of white speech. In studying Negro dialect the white man is, in a very real sense, studying his own dialectal past.

PART FIVE

THE SINGING SOUTH

In this rude, rough, and remote region, where civilization has been arrested for a hundred years; where illiteracy is still the rule; and where books and papers of all sorts are still rare, the man or boy who "follows" writing ballads is the real journalist, and it is in his crude verse that is enshrined the memory of such events as quicken the pulse of the mountaineer and appeal to his imagination.
—WILLIAM ASPENWALL BRADLEY

The three figures [in the running set], hitherto known only in children's singing games, . . . are one and all derived from ancient pagan ceremonials. The California Show Basket is an adaptation to the dance of a children's singing-game, Draw a pail of water, which is a dramatic representation of several incidents connected with the ceremony of well-worship. The only one of these ritual acts which survives in the dance-figure is the passing first of the women under the arms of the men and then of the men under the arms of the women, in imitation of the creeping of the devotee under the sacred bush, which was frequently found by the side of the holy well.
—CECIL J. SHARP and MAUD KARPELES

Southern Negroes sang about everything. Trains, steamboats, steam whistles, sledge hammers, fast women, mean bosses, stubborn mules—all became subjects for their songs. They accompany themselves on anything from which they can extract a musical sound or rhythmical effect, anything from a harmonica to a washboard. In this way, and from these materials, they set the mood for what we now call blues.
—W. C. HANDY

Bunk [Johnson] never cared to read. When a leader once wrote down some of the music Bunk had played and stuck it up for him to do again, Bunk said: "Do you think I'm a fool? I can't play that."
—WILLIAM RUSSELL and STEPHEN W. SMITH

1. Singing in the Wilderness

THE odyssey of the first organ to be brought into North Carolina, as related in the diaries of the Moravian Church, reveals the pioneer's devotion to music. On April 20, 1762, a band of sixteen settlers prepared to emigrate to Bethabara (House of Passage), sometimes known as Old Town, just outside the present Winston-Salem, in the Moravian colony of Wachovia, founded in 1753. A minister and musician in the group, Brother Johann Michael Graff (later bishop of the province), had in his special charge a box containing a small pipe organ. Carried by wagon to Easton, by riverboat down the Delaware to Philadelphia, by sloop through Delaware Bay, round Cape Hatteras, Cape Lookout, and Cape Fear to Wilmington, by open boat up the Cape Fear River to Spring Hill, and by wagon again to Bethabara, the precious cargo arrived safely at its destination on June 8.

In the first volume of Dr. Adelaide Fries' translations from the records of the Moravians in North Carolina there occurs this modest entry, found in the Diary of Bethabara and Bethania for the year 1762: "July 8. Reaping continued. Br. Graff set up in our Saal the organ he brought from Bethlehem; and during the Singstunde in the evening we heard an organ played for the first time in Carolina and were very happy and thankful that it had reached us safely." [1]

On the folk level a thin and shifting line separates sacred from secular music. When the spiritual was born in the Great Southern and Western revival, and cradled in the camp meeting (first held in Logan County, Kentucky, in July, 1800), the holiday spirit and "singing ecstasy" of this great folk gathering called for jubilant words and lively tunes. Here, as elsewhere in oral tradition, hybridization was the rule, with improvisation building on ritual, making the inherited repertoire spontaneous. Scriptural phrases and "'errant stanzas' of the orthodox hymnody of the eighteenth century" were mingled with ejaculatory phrases, in the favorite folk pattern of repetition and refrain and in the simple, direct, dramatic spirit of backwoods preaching and exhortation.

In the same way tunes were borrowed from the older hymnody and from secular folk music, including dance tunes. Further mingling written and unwritten tradition, the shape-note song books and singing schools of the fasola folk (so called from the practice of sol-faing the notes before singing the words) kept the "spiritual songs" alive and current. [2]

Taking over the basic musical form and concepts of the spirituals as well as individual tunes and stanzas (as George Pullen Jackson has demon-

---

[1] Charles G. Vardell, *Organs in the Wilderness* (Winston-Salem, 1944), pp. 3–6.
[2] For the most authoritative treatment of the subject, cf. George Pullen Jackson, *White Spirituals of the Southern Uplands* (1933); *Spiritual Folk-Songs of Early America* (1937); and *White and Negro Spirituals* (1943).

strated), the Negro has, by a process of assimilation and heightening, made them indubitably his own, especially in the performance, where his highly developed sense of rhythm and polyphony are paramount.[3] In the case of the blues—"earth-born" like the spirituals—the process has been reversed. The Negro folk blues have been widely imitated by Tin Pan Alley, while the "blue note" and the instrumental blues have been the most important influence in popular music since ragtime.

Meanwhile, the sanctified song, the shout, and the holy dance continue to be an important part of the ritual and communal expression of the Negro church; while throughout the South the radio has fostered hillbilly hymns and quartet singing that show the inroads of civilization on singing in the wilderness.

2. "Song-Ballets and Devil's Ditties"

Besides his "jubilee" and "sorrow songs," the Negro has his "sinful" songs, including (in addition to reels and play songs) his distinctive work songs—rowing songs, field songs, railroad construction songs, prison and chain-gang songs, steamboat and roustabout songs, calls and hollers. Not only were these the mold of the blues, but, as Roland Hayes points out, writing of his native Georgia, "So closely contiguous were the sacred and profane worlds in the Flatwoods that their music was nearly identical." In the roustabout song, beginning, "Rock me, Julie," the "melody went like a spiritual. With the substitution of the Holy Name for 'Julie,' you might have had a characteristic religious song."[4] Conversely, Sister Rosetta Tharpe makes an erotic song of her recorded version of the Holiness hymn "Rock Me."

In his autobiography Peter Cartwright throws light on the relationship between the sacred and profane worlds, in the story of his experience at a Saturday night dance held at a house in the Cumberlands where he had taken lodging. As he sat quietly musing in the corner, thinking that he would spend the Sabbath there and preach to these Godless folk—

a beautiful, ruddy young lady walked very gracefully up to me, dropped a handsome courtesy, and pleasantly, with winning smiles, invited me out to take a dance with her. I can hardly describe my thoughts or feelings on that occasion. However, in a moment I resolved on a desperate experiment. I rose as gracefully as I could; I will not say with some emotion, but with many emotions.

After leading her out on the floor, he spoke to the fiddler a moment, adding that for several years he "had not undertaken any matter of importance without first asking the blessing of God upon it, and [he] desired now to ask the blessing of God upon this beautiful young lady and the whole company, that had shown such an act of politeness to a total stranger."

---

[3] Cf. Robert W. Gordon, "The Negro Spiritual," in *The Carolina Low-Country* (New York), pp. 191–192.

[4] McKinley Helm, "Angel Mo' and Her Son, Roland Hayes," reprinted by Edward Wagenknecht in *When I was a Child*, An Anthology (New York, 1946), p. 107.

Here I grasped the young lady's hand tightly, and said, "Let us all kneel down and pray," and then instantly dropped on my knees and commenced praying with all the power of soul and body that I could command. The young lady tried to get loose from me, but I held her tight. Presently she fell on her knees. Some of the company kneeled, some stood, some fled, some sat still, all looked curious. . . . While I prayed some wept, and wept out aloud, and some cried for mercy. I rose from my knees and commenced an exhortation, after which I sang a hymn. The young lady who invited me on the floor lay prostrate, crying earnestly for mercy. I exhorted again, I sang and prayed all night.

Fifteen were converted that night and as many more during the next day and night. He organized a society, took thirty-two into the Church, and sent them a preacher. Thus began a great and glorious revival, which led him to conclude: "I should succeed by taking the devil at surprise, as he had often served me." [5]

When John Wesley asked, "Why should the devil have all the pretty tunes?" he did not anticipate that devotees of the "devil's music box" and "devil's ditties" might ask, "Why should the Church have all the religion?" Certainly one of the judges at the eleventh annual Mountain Dance and Music Festival at Asheville, North Carolina, August 5, 1938, was more than on the defensive against church criticism of dancing when he stated, in announcing the awards:

We say these folk dances, next only to our church meetings and religious songs in this section, God's country, typify our Scottish traditions, our local sufficiency within ourselves, our love for and desire to be with each other in happiness, in exultation; it's the all for each and each for all spirit within us, which is our heritage, our raising, so to speak.

The fervor and pathos of mountain music, the community exuberances of these dances, the full, physical, spirited outpourings of the folks into them: the snap, the zest, the go-git in them, are entirely unhurtful expressions of whole-hearted mountaineerishness. [6]

In the mountains the traditional ballads are dying out, largely through the competition of native ballads and hillbilly songs, though the folk festival has helped to revive them. Meanwhile, folk music is still as vigorous and flourishing as when Bob Taylor's fiddle, rifle, ax, and Bible were the humble penates of the pioneer's cabin. And the modesty of the folk musician is also a part of the tradition. As one North Carolina fiddler and fiddle-maker put it, while explaining and demonstrating the different tunings for different pieces:

I'm a fiddler, you know, not a violinist. What I play is old-time stuff. I don't know a thing about music. Yes, I made that fiddle. It's got my name on it. It's not a very good job; it isn't finished up. I play quite a number of tunes. They're what you call old-fashioned stuff. You may not know them. Scolding Wife, Sandy River, a piece you call Calico, a piece you call Happy Holler, Cluck Old Hen. Old-time stuff. Cumberland Gap, Turkey in the Straw,

---

[5] *Autobiography of Peter Cartwright* (New York and Cincinnati, 1856), pp. 206–209.
[6] The Asheville *Citizen,* August 6. 1938, p. 3.

Tennessee Wagoner, Billy in the Lowgrounds, Cripple Creek, Sourwood Mountain, what I call Booth—you remember Garfield was shot by Booth—that was written for it. The selection fits the key. But there's not one in one thousand that does it. They all tune their violins to the regular key. I don't know a thing about music.[7]

B. A. B.

EXPLANATION OF SIGNS

Small notes indicate occasional variations in succeeding stanzas or an optional pitch variation .

A non-musical pitch, as in speaking, chanting, hand-clapping, wood-chopping, etc.

Glissando, or upward slide of pitch in voice or instrument.

An exhalation, with slight downward slide of pitch, at the end of a phrase.

"Bend" of a note; i.e., slight departure from, and return to, original pitch, varying from a quarter to a half tone.

---

[7] Marcus L. Martin, as told to B. A. Botkin, Swannanoa, North Carolina, August 6, 1938.

LULLABIES AND GAME SONGS

You Shall Have a Horse to Ride

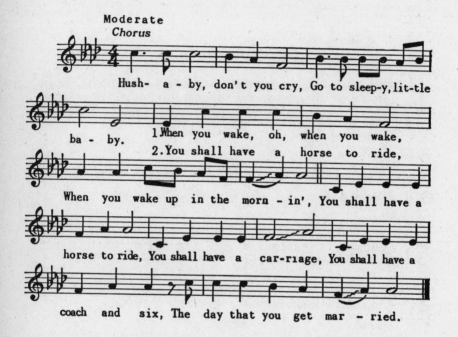

Moderate
Chorus

Hush- a - by, don't you cry, Go to sleep-y, lit-tle ba - by.

1. When you wake, oh, when you wake, When you wake up in the morn - in',

2. You shall have a horse to ride, You shall have a horse to ride, You shall have a car-riage, You shall have a coach and six, The day that you get mar - ried.

Hushaby, don't you cry,
Go to sleepy, little baby.
You shall have a horse to ride
When you wake up in the mornin'.

Sung by Louise Jones DuBose, Columbia, South Carolina, January 26, 1949, as learned from her grandmother. Recorded by B. A. Botkin.

My grandmother lived in Columbus, Georgia. She got it from the Negroes on the place before the Confederate War, and she used to sing us grandchildren to sleep by this song and a good many more.—L. J. D.

Aunt Maria

Moderately fast

Old Aunt Ma-ri-a, Jump in the fi-ah. Fire too hot, Jump in the pot.

Pot too black, Jump in the crack. Crack too high, Jump in the sky.

Sky too blue, Jump in ca-noe. Ca-noe too shallow, Jump in the tal-low.

Tal-low too soft, Jump in the loft. Loft too rot-ten, Jump in the cotton.

Cot-ton so white, She stay there all night.

Old Lady Sittin' in the Dining Room

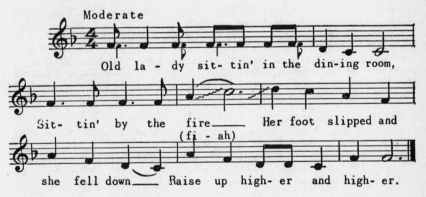

Moderate

Old la - dy sit- tin' in the din-ing room,

Sit- tin' by the fire___ Her foot slipped and
(fi - ah)

she fell down___ Raise up high- er and high- er.

Choose the one the ring go round,
Choose the one the morning,

Choose the one with the coal black hair,
And kiss her and call her honey.
(Repeat.)

By Louise Jones DuBose, Columbia, South Carolina, January 26, 1949. Recorded by B. A. Botkin.

Here's another one of those old patting songs. Remember, the baby's on your lap, now, and you're patting the baby to make the baby go to sleep.—L. J. D.

From *Folk Music of the United States*, Album 9, "Play and Dance Songs and Tunes,"

All around the Maypole

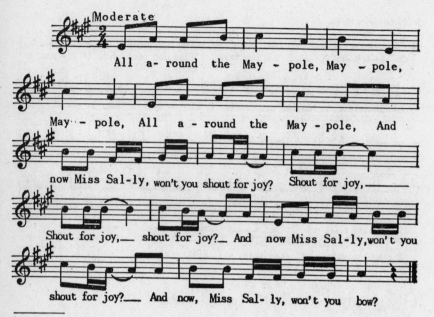

All a-round the May-pole, May-pole, May-pole, All a-round the May-pole, And now Miss Sal-ly, won't you shout for joy? Shout for joy,— Shout for joy,— shout for joy?— And now Miss Sal-ly, won't you shout for joy?— And now, Miss Sal-ly, won't you bow?

edited by B. A. Botkin, Record No. AAFS 45–A2. Washington, D. C.: Archive of American Folk Song, Library of Congress. 1943.

Sung by Eva Grace Boone and group at Brandon, Mississippi, 1939. Recorded by Herbert Halpert.

Directions: The players join hands in a ring and skip about, while the player in the center acts out the words—squatting, falling, rising, choosing and kissing a partner. The game is repeated, with the one chosen taking the center, while the other joins the ring.—B. A. B.

Ibid., Record No. AAFS 45–A4.

Sung by Eva Grace Boone and group at Brandon, Mississippi, 1939. Recorded by Herbert Halpert. Transcribed by Charles Seeger.

Directions: The players join hands in a ring and walk around, stopping and clapping hands while the player skipping in the center bows and chooses a partner to "jump" or dance with.—B. A. B.

Gwan Round, Rabbit

Moderately fast

Solo: My dog treed (a) rab-bit, My dog treed (a) rab-bit.
Chorus: 2. Now gwan roun', Rab-bit, Now gwan roun' Rab-bit.

Now watch that crit-ter sit-tin' on that log, Now watch that crit-ter how he do that dog.——

Solo: Gonna milk my cow, gonna catch her by the tail,
Gonna milk her in the coffee pot, pour it in the pail.

(Refrains 2, 1, and 2.)

Solo: Now watch that critter sittin' on that log, etc.

(Refrains 2 and 1.)

Solo: Gonna catch my cow, gonna catch her by the tail,
Gonna milk her in the coffee pot and throw it in the pail.

(Refrain 2.)

Solo: My rabbit's gittin'—
My rabbit's gittin' my turnip top.

(Refrain 2.)

Ibid., Record No. AAFS 45–B3.
Sung by Anne Williams and group of Dundee, Mississippi, at Moorhead Plantation, Lula, Mississippi, 1942. Recorded by Alan Lomax and Lewis Jones.
["Gwan Round, Rabbit"] is a particularly good example of the "call" and "response" (solo and chorus) structure of Negro folk songs, including work songs and spirituals as well as game songs.—B. A. B.

DANCE, INSTRUMENTAL, AND MINSTREL SONGS

Juba

Juba, Juba,
Juba this 'n' Juba that,
Juba killed the yaller cat.

Juba, Juba,
Juba left 'n' Juba right,
Juba, Juba, gettin' night.

By Louise Jones DuBose, Columbia, South Carolina, January 26, 1949. Recorded by B. A. Botkin.

"Juba" means jubilee. According to Solomon Northup (*Twelve Years a Slave*, 1853, pp. 219–220), patting, "accompanied with one of those unmeaning songs," was used in lieu of the fiddle for square dance music in slavery times. "The patting is performed by striking the hands on the knees, then striking the hands together, then striking the right shoulder with one hand, the left with the other—all the while keeping time with the feet and singing."

Cf. the following note on "patting" as an accompaniment to the "running set" (often in the absence of instrumental music) in Kentucky: "Throughout the dance the onlookers and the performers also, when not actually dancing, should enforce the rhythm of the music by 'patting,' i.e., alternately stamping and clapping. 'Patting' is done in various ways, but the usual method is to stamp with the right foot on the strong accent and clap the hands on the weak one, the executant throwing his head back, inclining his body to the left and emphasizing the movements of feet and hands so that the rhythm may be seen as well as heard. In 6/8 time the hands are usually clapped on the third and sixth quavers, but the 'patter' will often strike his thighs, right hand on right thigh on the second and fifth quavers, and left hand on left thigh on the third and sixth, stamping, of course, on the first and fourth quavers."—*The Country Dance Book, Part V, Containing The Running Set*, collected in Kentucky, U.S.A., and described by Cecil J. Sharp and Maud Karpeles (London and New York, 1918), p. 17.

For "Juba" as a jig or short-step dance tune, see Dorothy Scarborough, *On the Trail of Negro Folk-Songs* (1925), pp. 98–99.

Bow-Legged Rabbit

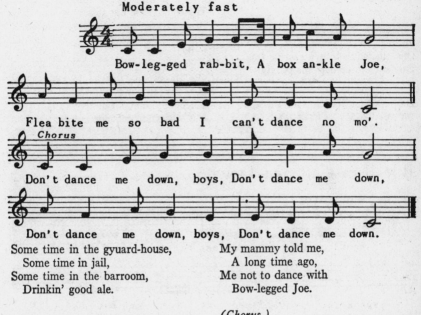

Some time in the gyuard-house,
   Some time in jail,
Some time in the barroom,
   Drinkin' good ale.

My mammy told me,
   A long time ago,
Me not to dance with
   Bow-legged Joe.

(Chorus.)

The Blue-Tail Fly

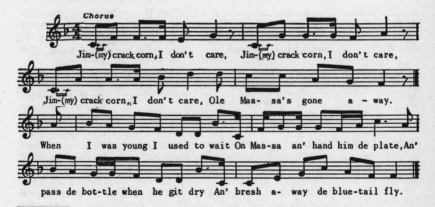

Sung by Louise Jones DuBose, Columbia, South Carolina, January 26, 1949, as learned from her grandmother. Recorded by B. A. Botkin.

From *On the Trail of Negro Folk-Songs,* by Dorothy Scarborough, pp. 201–203.

An' when he ride in de arternoon,
I foller wid a hickory broom;
De pony being berry shy,
When bitten by de blue-tail fly.

One day he ride aroun' de farm;
De flies so numerous dey did swarm;
One chance to bite 'im on de thigh,
De debble take dat blue-tail fly.

De pony run, he jump an' pitch,
An' tumble Massa in de ditch.

He died, an' de jury wondered why;
De verdic' was de blue-tail fly.

Dey laid 'im under a 'simmon tree;
His epitaph am dar to see:
"Beneath dis stone I'm forced to lie,
All by de means ob de blue-tail
    fly."

Ole Massa gone, now let 'im rest;
Dey say all t'ings am for de best.
I nebber forget till de day I die,
Ole Massa an' dat blue-tail fly.

Bile dem Cabbage Down

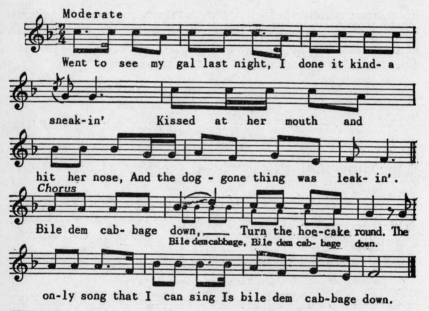

Went to see my gal last night, I done it kind-a sneak-in' Kissed at her mouth and hit her nose, And the dog-gone thing was leak-in'.

Chorus

Bile dem cab-bage down,___ Turn the hoe-cake round. The on-ly song that I can sing Is bile dem cab-bage down.

Bile dem cabbage, Bile dem cab-bage down.

A variant of the minstrel song, "*Jim Crack Corn*," found in *The Negro Melodist*, 1857, and elsewhere.—D. S.

From *Folk Music of the United States*, Album 9, "Play and Dance Songs and Tunes," edited by B. A. Botkin, Record No. AAFS 43–A2. Washington, D. C.: Archive of American Folk Song, Library of Congress. 1943.
Played by E. C. Ball on the guitar and Blair C. Reedy on the mandolin, with singing by E. C. Ball, at Rugby, Virginia, 1941. Recorded by Alan Lomax.
For additional stanzas and the tune of the minstrel song, "Bile Dem Cabbage Down,"

Went up on the mountain and
  I give my horn a blow.
Thought I heard my true love say,
  Yonder comes my beau.

Took my girl to the blacksmith shop
  To have her mouth made small.
She turned around a time or two
  And swallowed shop and all.

Where'd You Get Yo' Whisky?

Where'd you get yo' whis-ky? Where'd you get yo' dram?

Stole it from a boot-leg-ger_ Way down in Boot-leg Town.

CHORUS

Got a lit-tle home to go to, Got a lit-tle home to go to,

Got a lit-tle home to go to, Way down in jail-house now.

---

see *On the Trail of Negro Folk-Songs*, by Dorothy Scarborough (Cambridge, 1925), pp. 124–125, 168, where it is given both as a slavery-time dance song and as a song about animals.—B. A. B.

Ibid., Record No. AAFS 42–A2.

Sung with fiddle by Enos Canoy, with beating of straws by Jim F. Myers, at Magee, Mississippi, 1939. Recorded by Herbert Halpert.

The symbols under the regular notes indicate the beating of two straws on the open strings of the fiddle while the other strings are being fingered.

A version of "Where'd You Git Yo' Whisky?" appears as a stanza of "Cindy," in Bascom Lamar Lunsford's *30 and 1 Folk Songs from the Southern Mountains* (New York, 1929), pp. 42–43.—B. A. B.

Soldier's Joy

Fast

Acadian Waltz

Tuning

Moderately fast - *lively*

Ibid., Record No. AAFS 43–A1.

Played by Nashville Washboard Band (James Kelly on the mandolin, Frank Dalton on the guitar, Tom Carroll on the tin can bull fiddle, and Theopolis Stokes on the washboard), Nashville, Tenn., 1941. Recorded by Alan Lomax and John W. Work.

From *Folk Music of the United States*, Album 5, "Bahaman Songs, French Ballads and Dance Tunes, Spanish Religious Songs and Game Songs," edited by Alan Lomax, Record No. AAFS 23–A1. Washington, D. C.: Archive of American Folk Song, Library of Congress. 1942.

Played on the fiddle by Wayne Perry, Crowley, Louisiana, 1934. Recorded by John A. and Alan Lomax.

Songs of the Confederacy

Dixie

I__ wish I was__ in de land ob cot-ton,__ Old times dar am not for-got-ten, Look a-way! Look a-way! Look a-way! Dix-ie Land. In__ Dix-ie Land__ what I was born in, Ear-ly__ on one frost-y morn-in' Look a-way! Look a-way! Look a-way! Dix-ie Land. Den__ I wish I was in Dix-ie, Hoo-ray! Hoo-ray! In___ Dix-ie Land I'll take my stand, To lib and die in Dix-ie, A-way, A-way, A-way down south in Dix-ie, A-way, A-way, A-way down south in Dix-ie.

First stanza and chorus, from "I Wish I Was in Dixie's Land," written and composed expressly for Bryant's Minstrels, by Dan. D. Emmett. New York: Firth, Pond & Co. 1860. Cf. Hans Nathan, "Dixie," *The Musical Quarterly*, Vol. XXXV (January, 1949), No. 1, pp. 60–84.

Cumberland Gap

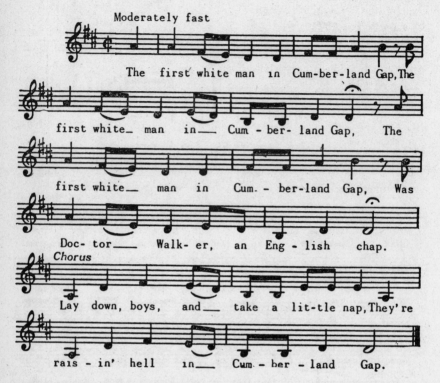

Moderately fast

The first white man in Cum-ber-land Gap, The
first white man in Cum - ber- land Gap, The
first white man in Cum. - ber-land Gap, Was
Doc- tor Walk- er, an Eng - lish chap.

Chorus

Lay down, boys, and take a lit-tle nap, They're
rais - in' hell in Cum. - ber - land Gap.

Daniel Boone on the Pinnacle Rock, *(three times)*
He killed Indians with an old flint lock.

Cumberland Gap is a noted place, *(three times)*
There's three kinds of water to wash your face.

Cumberland Gap with its cliffs and rocks, *(three times)*
The home of the panther, bear, and fox.

Me and my wife and our little chap, *(three times)*
All made a living in Cumberland Gap.

September morn in '62, *(three times)*
Morgan's Yankees all withdrew.

Sung by Artus M. Moser, Wilson's Cove, North Carolina, January 22, 1949.
Recorded by B. A. Botkin.

It's a ballad which came out of the Civil War. It's supposed to have been composed at Cumberland Gap, Kentucky during the conflict. This ballad is published
with music in Jean Thomas's *Devil's Ditties.* But the way I sing it here is somewhat
different from that. I have never seen this in print exactly the way I sing it, either
words or music.—A. M. M.

[Oh] they spiked Long Tom [1] on the mountain top, *(three times)*
And over the cliffs they let him drop.

They burned the hay, the meal, and meat, *(three times)*
And left the Rebels nothing to eat.

Braxton Bragg with his rebel band, *(three times)*
He ran George Morgan to the Bluegrass land.

Now Cumberland Gap is not very far, *(three times)*
It's just a little piece from Middlesbar.

Eating Goober Peas

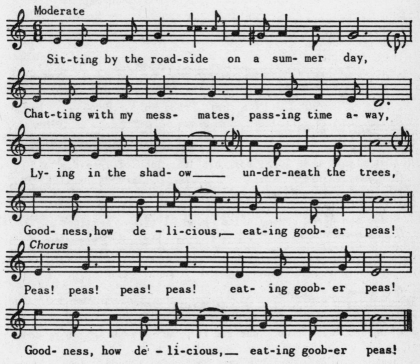

Moderate

Sit-ting by the road-side on a sum-mer day,

Chat-ting with my mess- mates, pass-ing time a-way,

Ly- ing in the shad- ow___ un-der-neath the trees,

Good- ness, how de - li-cious,___ eat-ing goob- er peas!

Chorus

Peas! peas! peas! peas! eat- ing goob- er peas!

Good- ness, how de - li-cious, ___ eat-ing goob-er peas!

When a horseman passes the soldiers have a rule,
To cry out at their loudest, "Mister, here's your mule";

---

[1] An old cannon of the Civil War times. This one changed hands and was located on top of the Cumberland Mountain between Tennessee and Kentucky.—A. M. M.

From *"Sound Off!"* Soldier Songs from the Revolution to World War II, by Edward Arthur Dolph, music arranged by Philip Egner, pp. 302–304. Copyright, 1929, 1942, by Farrar & Rinehart, Inc. New York and Toronto.

"Goober peas" are peanuts; Georgians are sometimes called "goober grabbers."
—E. A. D.

But another pleasure, enchantinger than these,
Is wearing out your grinders, eating goober peas!

Just before the battle the Gen'ral hears a row.
He says, "The Yanks are coming, I hear their rifles now."
He turns around in wonder, and what do you think he sees?
The Georgia Militia, eating goober peas!

I think my song has lasted almost long enough;
The subject's interesting, but rhymes are mighty rough.
I wish this war was over, when free from rags and fleas,
We'd kiss our wives and sweethearts, and gobble goober peas!

I'm a Good Old Rebel

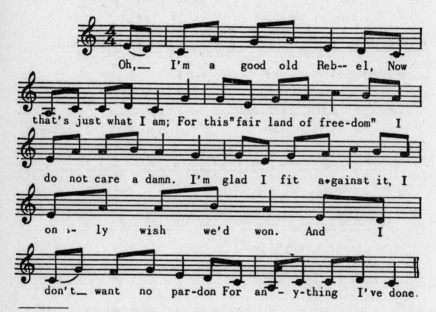

Oh,— I'm a good old Reb--el, Now that's just what I am; For this "fair land of free-dom" I do not care a damn. I'm glad I fit a-gainst it, I on-ly wish we'd won. And I don't— want no par-don For an-y-thing I've done.

From *American Ballads and Folk Songs,* collected and compiled by John A. Lomax and Alan Lomax, pp. 535–540. Copyright, 1934, by The Macmillan Company. New York.

Collier's Weekly, April 4, 1914, devoted a column to this famous song of Reconstruction days. It was written by Major Innes Randolph, a member of the staff of General J. E. B. Stuart, and a native of Virginia. Richard N. Brooke of Washington, D. C., suggests that the song is "a bit of fun not supposed to reflect Major Randolph's own sentiments but to illustrate the irreconcilable spirit of the illiterate element in some sections."

Herbert Quick, who wrote the story for *Collier's,* added that millions sang the song who had never heard of Major Randolph. When the Duchess of Manchester sang it before the Prince of Wales on one occasion, he repeatedly encored "that fine American

I hates the Constitution,
This great Republic too;
I hates the Freedmen's Bureau,
In uniforms of blue.
I hates the nasty eagle,
With all his brag and fuss;
But the lyin', thievin' Yankees,
I hates 'em wuss and wuss.

I hates the Yankee nation,
And everything they do;
I hates the Declaration
Of Independence too.
I hates the glorious Union,
'Tis dripping with our blood;
And I hates the striped banner—
I fit it all I could.

I followed Old Marse Robert
For four years, near about.
Got wounded in three places,
And starved at Point Lookout.

I cotch the roomatism
A-campin' in the snow,
But I killed a chance of Yankees—
And I'd like to kill some mo'.

Three hundred thousand Yankees
Is stiff Southern dust;
We got three hundred thousand
Befo' they conquered us.
They died of Southern fever
And Southern steel and shot;
And I wish it was three million
Instead of what we got.

I can't take up my musket
And fight 'em now no mo',
But I ain't a-goin' to love 'em,
Now that is sartin sho;
And I don't want no pardon
For what I was and am;
And I won't be reconstructed,
And I don't care a damn.

British Songs and Ballads

The Devil's Nine Questions

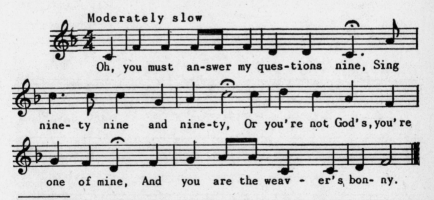

song with the cuss words in it." Laura Lee Davidson of Baltimore says the song was sung "in many a Southern parlor in the bitter days of Reconstruction; and to have heard the author himself sing it is a joy to be remembered." . . .

Tune from Mrs. Harriett Wyckoff, Washington, D. C., niece of the author of the song, and John T. Vance, Law Librarian, Library of Congress.—J. A. L.

From *Folk Music of the United States*, Album 1, "Anglo-American Ballads," edited

"What is whiter than the milk?
  Sing ninety-nine and ninety,
And what is softer then the silk?
  And you are the weaver's bonny."

"Snow is whiter than the milk,
  Sing ninety-nine and ninety,
And down is softer than the silk,
  And I am the weaver's bonny."

"O what is higher than a tree?
And what is deeper than the sea?"

"Heaven's higher than a tree,
And Hell is deeper than the sea."

"What is louder than a horn?
And what is sharper than a thorn?"

"Thunder's louder than a horn,
And death is sharper than a thorn."

"What's more innocent than a lamb?
And what is meaner than woman-
  kind?"

"A babe's more innocent than a lamb,
And the devil is meaner than woman-
  kind."

"O you have answered my questions
  nine,
And you are God's, you're none of
  mine."

by Alan Lomax, Record No. AAFS 4–A1. Washington, D. C.: Archive of American Folk Song, Library of Congress. 1942.

Sung by Mrs. Texas Gladden, Salem, Virginia, 1941. Recorded by Alan and Elizabeth Lomax through the courtesy of Miss Alfreda Peel.

The song (Child No. 1) is an ancient riddling ballad, sung with great purity of style, the text being in a fine state of preservation; it is undoubtedly one of the most ancient ballads in the entire British ballad tradition. It was discovered far back in the Virginia mountains in the possession of a mountain woman whose ideas and language were colored by her heritage from Elizabethan England.

For another Virginia version see Arthur Kyle Davis, Jr., *Traditional Ballads of Virginia* (Cambridge, 1929), pp. 59–60, 549.—A. L.

Young Rogers the Miller

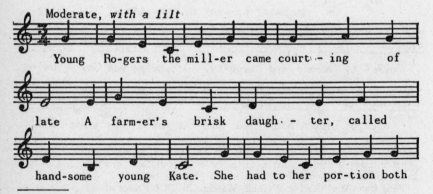

Moderate, *with a lilt*

Young Ro-gers the mill-er came court - ing of late A farm-er's brisk daugh - ter, called hand-some young Kate. She had to her por-tion both

Sung by Dr. Chapman J. Milling, Columbia, South Carolina, January 25, 1949, as learned from his wife's aunt, Mrs. Alva Hembree, Atlanta, Georgia. Recorded by B. A. Botkin.

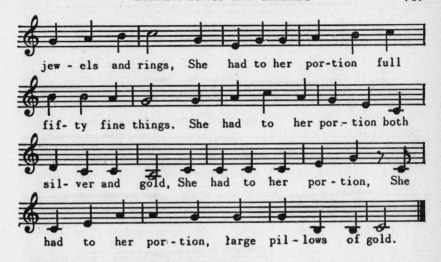

jew - els and rings, She had to her por-tion full

fif- ty fine things. She had to her por.-tion both

sil- ver and gold, She had to her por - tion, She

had to her por-tion, large pil-lows of gold.

The wedding was ordered, the money paid down,
A very fine portion, full five hundred pound.
But Rogers was greedy, you all may declare,
He wanted the nag that was called the Gray Mare.
"Although that your daughter is handsome and fair,
I'll not have your daughter, I'll not have your daughter, without the gray mare."

Up stepped the old farmer, in quite of a speed.
"I thought you'd have married my daughter indeed.
But since it's no better, I'm glad it's no worse.
My money once more I'll put up in my purse.
For she is my daughter, I'll vow and declare
You'll not have my daughter, you'll not have my daughter—no, nor the gray
    mare.

The money was quickly taken out of his sight,
And likewise Miss Katie, his own heart's delight.
And Rogers the rascal kicked out of the door,
And told to be gone and come back no more.
Which caused him to pull down his long yellow hair
And wish that he'd never, and wish that he'd never stood for the gray mare.

About six months later, or a little above,
He chanced for to meet her, Miss Katie, his love,
And bowing, says Roger, "And don't you know me?"
"If I'm not mistaken, I've seen you," says she,
"Or a man of your likeness, wore long yellow hair,
That once came a-courting, that once came a-courting my father's gray mare."

Fair Fanny Moore

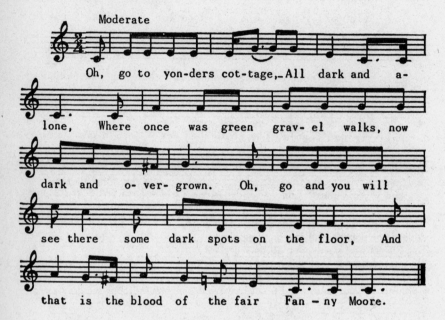

Oh, go to yon-ders cot-tage,—All dark and a-lone, Where once was green grav-el walks, now dark and o-ver-grown. Oh, go and you will see there some dark spots on the floor, And that is the blood of the fair Fan-ny Moore.

As Fanny was blooming, two lovers there came.
They offered her wealth, they offered her fame.
The fame and the riches they failed to allure
The heart and the hand of the fair Fanny Moore.

The first was young Raniel, of high life degree.
He offered her wealth, enraptured was he.
The fame and the riches they failed to allure
The long burning bosom of fair Fanny Moore.

The next was young Edward, of low life degree.
He offered her love, enraptured was he.
Straightway to the altar they both did secure
The heart and the hand of the fair Fanny Moore.

As Fanny was sitting in her cottage one day,
As business had called her fond husband away,
Young Raniel, the hater, strode in by the door
And clasped to his bosom the fair Fanny Moore.

"Oh, spare me, oh, spare me, young Raniel!" she cried.
Oh, spare me, oh, spare me, for mercy's sake!" said she.

Ibid.

"Oh, Fanny, dear Fanny, go home to thy rest!"
And straightway plunged the dagger in her snowy white breast.

As Fanny was blooming, in blood-stain she died.
Young Raniel was arrested and straightway was tried,
And straightway was hanged by a chain near the door
For shedding the blood of the fair Fanny Moore.

Devilish Mary

When I was young and in my prime, I thought I nev-er could mar-ry, I fell in love with a pret-ty lit-tle girl, Sure 'nough we got mar-ried.

Chorus

Rink- tum-dink-tum- tar - ry, Pret-tiest lit-tle girl in all this world, Her name was Dev-'lish Mar - y.

She washed my clothes in live soap
  suds,
  She peeled my back with switches,
She let me know right up to date
  She's gonna wear my britches.

We'd just been married about two
  weeks,
  We thought we'd better be parted,

She bundled her up a little bundle of
  clothes
And down the road she started .

If I ever marry the second time,
  It'll be for love nor [not] riches,
I'll marry one about two feet high,
  So she can't wear my britches.

From *Folk Music of the United States*, Album 14, "Anglo-American Songs and Ballads," edited by Duncan B. M. Emrich, Record No. AAFS 69–B1. Washington, D. C.: Archive of American Folk Song, Library of Congress. 1948.

Sung by Paul Rogers of Paint Lick, Kentucky, at Renfro Valley, Kentucky, 1946. Recorded by Artus M. Moser.

The plight of the young man who marries only to find that his wife is wearing the "britches" in the family is humorously set forth in "Devilish Mary." It is a mountain song and typical of the tongue-in-cheek "feuding" between the men and women folk.

Frog Went A-Courting

Frog went a-court-in', he did ride,
Rink-tum bod-y mit cha cam-bo, Sword and pis-tol
by his side, Rink-tum bod-y mit cha cam-bo.

Chorus

Key-me-ni-ro down to Cai-ro, Key-me-ni-ro Cai-ro,
Strad-dle-ad-dle-ad-dle, bob-a-lad-da, bob-a-link-tum,
Rink-tum bod-y mit cha cam-bo.

He rode up to Mousie's door,
Seemed like he'd been there before.

Mister Rat done come along,
"Who that been here while I's gone."

"A very fine gentleman, he was by,
Gwine to take me for his bride."

Now Mister Rat he laughed and
laughed,
Then he says, "I'll cut that boy in half.

"Where that weddin' supper be?"
"Way down yonder by the holler tree."

"That's one feast I'll sure be at,
I'm gonna eat and eat till I git fat.

"Gwine to fill myself with brandywine
Whet that knife down mighty fine."

Frog and the Mouse come in that night,
Mousie dressed in her weddin' white.

Sung by Ben West, of New Canaan, Connecticut, formerly of Lexington, Virginia, at Croton-on-Hudson, New York, May 15, 1949, as learned from Tom White, Pierce Stable, Arlington, Virginia. Recorded by B. A. Botkin.

For the history of the song, see note by G. L. Kittredge, "Traditional Texts and Tunes," by Albert H. Tolman and Mary O. Eddy, *The Journal of American Folklore*, Vol. 35 (October–December, 1922), No. 138, pp. 394–399. For a Kentucky version sung to the same tune, see Loraine Wyman and Howard Brockway, *Lonesome Tunes* (New York, 1916), pp. 25–29. Cf. "The Frog in the Spring," *A Treasury of New England Folklore* (New York, 1947), pp. 881–882.

Frog all dressed in silk and green,
The mostest sight you ever seen.

The guests they come and they all sat
down,
And passed that whisky round and
round.

Fiddler he was a bumblebee,
He kept that fiddle on his knee.

When all of a sudden the cat come in
And wiped the grease right off his chin.

He 'lowed this was his party call,
And swallowed them up one and all.

Set out across the lake,
Got swallowed up by a big black snake.

Gentlemen and Ladies fine,
'Member this next time you dine.

TOPICAL SONGS AND BALLADS

The Ship Titanic

Moderate

Oh, they built the ship Ti - tan - ic, and when they had got through, They__ said that's a ship that the wa - ter would nev - er leak through. But the Lord with His might - y hand, Said "that ship would nev - er stand." It was sad____ when that great____ ship went down.

Sung by Augustus D. Graydon, Columbia, South Carolina, January 25, 1949. Recorded by B. A. Botkin.

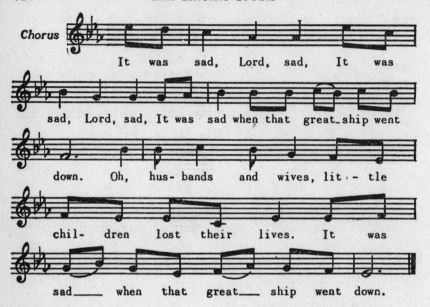

Chorus

It was sad, Lord, sad, It was sad, Lord, sad, It was sad when that great ship went down. Oh, hus-bands and wives, lit-tle chil-dren lost their lives. It was sad___ when that great___ ship went down.

They were a-headed for Eng-e-land,
  And a-headed for the shore,
And the rich they refused
  To associate with the poor.
So they put them down below,
And they were the first to go.
  It was sad when that great ship went
  down.

Now the ship began to settle,
  And they all tried to flee,
And the band it struck up
  With "Nearer my God to thee."

Oh, the captain tried to wire,
  But the wires they were on fire.
    It was sad when that great ship went
    down.

Now the ship began to sink,
  And the sides began to bust,
And the captain he shouted,
  "Women and children fust!"
So they passed the belts around,
And they all prepared to drown.
    It was sad when that great ship went
    down.

The Wreck on the C. & O.

Moderate

A-long came the F. F.V., The fast-est on the line, A-
run-ning o'er the C. & O. Road, twen-ty
min-utes be-hind the time; A-
run-ning in-to Sew-ell yard, was quar-tered on the line, A-
wait-ing for strict or-ders and in the cab to ride.

Chorus

Man-y a man's been mur-dered by the
rail-road, Rail-road, rail-road;
Man-y a man's been mur-dered by the
rail-road, And laid in his lone-some grave.

From *Folk-Songs of the South,* Collected under the Auspices of the West Virginia Folk-Lore Society and edited by John Harrington Cox, pp. 226–227, 525–526. Copyright, 1925, by Harvard University Press. Cambridge.

Original title: "George Alley." Communicated by Professor Walter Barnes, Fairmont, Marion County, May, 1916; obtained from George W. Gregg, Durbin, Pocahontas County, who learned it from Addison Collins.

And when she blew for Hinton, her engineer was there.
George Alley was his name, with bright and wavery hair;
His fireman, Jack Dixon, was standing by his side,
Awaiting for strict orders and in the cab to ride.

George Alley's mother came to him with a basket on her arm,
She handed him a letter, saying, "Be careful how you run;
And if you run your engine right, you'll get there just on time,
For many a man has lost his life in trying to make lost time."

George Alley said, "Dear mother, your letter I'll take heed.
I know my engine is all right and I know that she will speed;

... The facts out of which the song grew were obtained from Miss Margaret Alley and Mr. Ernest N. Alley, Alderson, West Virginia, sister and brother of George Alley, the man killed in the wreck, and from Mr. R. E. Noel, Hinton, formerly an engineer on the Chesapeake & Ohio Railroad.

George Alley was born in Richmond, Virginia, July 10, 1860, was married November 10, 1881, and had four children. The wreck on the C. & O. in which he was killed occurred at 5:40 A.M., October 23, 1890. He was running train No. 4, the F. F. V (Fast Flying Vestibule), engine No. 134. He lived five hours after being hurt. The wreck occurred three miles east of Hinton, and was caused by a landslide. Lewis Withrow, the regular fireman, was firing the engine. He had been "laying off," but, on the morning of the wreck, took his run back at Hinton. Jack Dickinson was not on the engine, but Robert Foster was. He had been working in Withrow's place, and his run being out of Clifton Forge, he was deadheading back home that morning. Neither he nor Withrow jumped into the New River: he went out of the window on the left side of the engine, that being the side away from the river, and Withrow went out of the gangway on the same side. The engine turned over on the opposite side from which they jumped, that is, toward the river. Withrow was badly hurt, and for a long time it was thought he would not live. Hinton is an important town on the C. & O. in Summers County. Sewell is forty miles west of Hinton; the Big Bend Tunnel is eight miles east of Hinton; Stock Yards, then, is now Pence's Spring, fourteen miles east of Hinton; and Clifton Forge, a terminal, or division point, where train crews change, is eighty miles east of Hinton.

George Alley was six feet tall, weighed about one hundred seventy pounds, had a dark complexion, black eyes, and straight black hair. At the time of the wreck, his home was at Clifton Forge. His father and his stepmother lived at Alderson, West Virginia, his own mother having died many years before, when the family was living at White Sulphur Springs, in the same state. Mr. Ernest N. Alley thinks the ballad was first started on its way by a Negro engine-wiper, who worked in the roundhouse at Hinton. Mr. H. S. Walker, a former student in West Virginia University told the Editor that the ballad was composed by a Negro who worked in the roundhouse at Hinton.

The ballad and the facts agree as follows: (1) The F. F. V., train No. 4, running east on the C. & O. Railroad, was wrecked near Hinton by a landslide. (2) The regular engineer, George Alley, was killed. (3) The fireman saved his life by jumping from the engine. As in "John Hardy" ["John Henry"], certain fundamental facts are retained in an atmosphere of verisimilitude, but the details are entirely untrustworthy.
—J. H. C., *ibid.*, p. 221.

So o'er this road I mean to run with a speed unknown to all,
And when I blow for Clifton Forge, they'll surely hear my call."

George Alley said to his fireman, "Jack, a little extra steam;
I intend to run old No. 4 the fastest ever seen;
So o'er this road I mean to fly like angels' wings unfold,
And when I blow for the Big Bend Tunnel, they'll surely hear my call."

George Alley said to his fireman, "Jack, a rock ahead I see,
And I know that death is lurking there for to grab both you and me;
So from this cab, dear Jack, you leap, your darling life to save,
For I want you to be an engineer while I'm sleeping in my grave."

"Oh no, dear George! that will not do, I want to die with you."
"Oh no, no dear Jack! that will not be, I'll die for you and me."
So from the cab dear Jack did leap, old New River was running high,
And he kissed the hand of darling George as No. 4 flew by.

So in the cab dear George did leap, the throttle he did pull;
Old No. 4 just started off, like a mad and angry bull.

. . . .

. . . .

So up the road she dashed; against the rock she crashed;
The engine turning over and the coaches they came last;
George Alley's head in the firebox lay, while the burning flames rolled o'er:
"I'm glad I was born an engineer, to die on the C. & O. Road."

George Alley's mother came to him and in sorrow she did sigh,
When she looked upon her darling boy and saw that he must die.
"Too late, too late, dear mother! my doom is almost o'er,
And I know that God will let me in when I reach that golden shore."

The doctor said, "Dear George, O darling boy, keep still;
Your life may yet be spared, if it be God's precious will."
"O no, dear Doc, that can not be, I want to die so free,
I want to die on the engine I love, 143."

The people came from miles around this engineer to see.
George Alley said, "God bless you, friends, I am sure you will find me here."
His head and face all covered with blood, his eyes you could not see,
And as he died he cried aloud, "O near, my God, to Thee!"

Wasn't That a Mighty Storm!

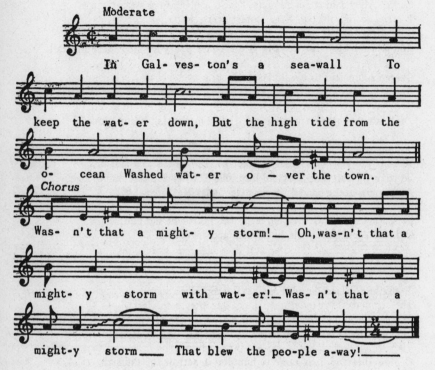

In Gal-ves-ton's a sea-wall To keep the wat-er down, But the high tide from the o-cean Washed wat-er o-ver the town.

Chorus

Was-n't that a might-y storm!__ Oh, was-n't that a might-y storm with wat-er!__ Was-n't that a might-y storm__ That blew the peo-ple a-way!__

Their trumpets give them warning,
  "You'd better leave this place."
They never thought of leaving
  Till death looked them in the face.

The trains they were loaded
  With people leaving town.
The tracks give away from the ocean.
  The trains they went on down.

Death like a cruel master,
  As the wind began to blow,
Rode out on a train of horses.
  Said, "Death, let me go."

Now, Death, in 1900—
  That was fifteen years ago—
You throwed a stone at my mother.
  With you she had to go.

From *Folk Music of the United States*, Album 10, "Negro Religious Songs and Services," edited by B. A. Botkin, Record No. AAFS 48–B. Washington, D. C.: Archive of American Folk Song, Library of Congress. 1943.

Sung by Sin-Killer Griffin and congregation, Darrington State Farm, Sandy Point, Texas, 1934. Recorded by John A. Lomax.

In structure and style this song about the Galveston tidal wave is in the tradition of ballads about disasters, such as the more familiar "Sinking of the Titanic." At the same time it has the religious setting and flavor of a song sermon on death, as Sin-Killer Griffin and his congregation point up the awfulness of physical destruction, with implied spiritual symbolism.—B. A. B.

Now, Death, your hands is icy,
  You've got them on my knees.
You done carried away my mother,
  Now come back after me.

The trees fell on the island,
  The houses give away.
Some people strived and drownded,
  Some died 'most every way.

The lightning played [around them],
  The thunder began to roar,
The wind it began blowing,
  The rain began to fall.

The sea it began rolling,
  The ships could not land.
I heard the captain crying,
  "Please save a drownding man."

Dark as a Dungeon

Come and lis-ten you fel-lers— so young and so fine And seek not your for-tune in the dark, drear-y mine,— It will form as a hab-it— and seep in your soul Till the stream of your blood is as black as the coal.—

Chorus
[Where] It's dark as a dun-geon and damp as the dew— For dan-ger is dou-ble and pleas-ures are few— Where the rain nev-er falls and the sun nev-er shines, It's dark as a dun-geon way down in the mine.—

From *Folk Songs of the Hills,* sung with guitar by Merle Travis. Capitol Americana Album AD–50, Record No. 48001. Copyright, 1947, by American Music, Inc. Hollywood, California. Used by special permission.

(Spoken:) I never will forget one time when I was on a little visit down home in Ebenezer, Kentucky. I was a-talkin' to an old man that had known me ever since the day I was born—and an old friend of the family. He says, "Son, you don't know how lucky you are to have a nice job like you've got and don't have to dig out a livin' from under these old hills and hollers like me and your pappy used to." When I asked him why he never had left and tried some other kind of work, he said, "Nawsir, you just

It's a many a man I've seen in my day
Who lived just to labor his whole life away.
Like a fiend with his dope and a drunkard his wine,
A man will have lust for the lure of the mine.

I hope when I'm gone and the ages shall roll
My body will blacken and turn into coal.
Then I'll look from the door of my heavenly home
And pity the miner a-digging my bones.

Miner's Lifeguard

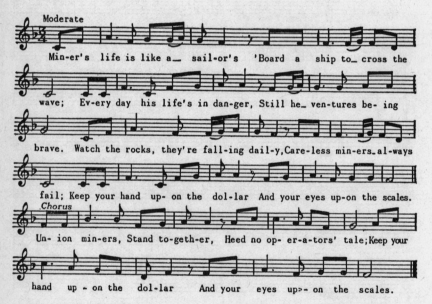

Moderate

Min-er's life is like a— sail-or's 'Board a ship to— cross the wave; Ev-ery day his life's in dan-ger, Still he— ven-tures be- ing brave. Watch the rocks, they're fall-ing dail-y, Care-less min-ers— al-ways fail; Keep your hand up-on the dol-lar And your eyes up-on the scales.

Chorus

Un- ion min-ers, Stand to-geth-er, Heed no op- er-a-tors' tale; Keep your hand up - on the dol-lar And your eyes up— on the scales.

Soon this trouble will be ended,
  Union men will have their rights,
After many years of bondage,
  Digging days and digging nights.

Then by honest weight we labor,
  Union workers never fail;
Keep your hand upon the dollar
And your eyes upon the scales.

won't do that. If ever you get this old coal dust in your blood, you're just gonna be a plain old coal miner as long as you live. He went on to say, "It's a habit—sorta like chewin' tobaccer."—M. T.

From *Coal Dust on the Fiddle,* Songs and Stories of the Bituminous Industry, by George Korson, pp. 413–415. Copyright, 1943, by University of Pennsylvania Press. Philadelphia.
  Sung by Mrs. Luigi Gugliotta, Mt. Hope, West Virginia, March 27, 1940. Recorded by George Korson. Transcribed by Ruth Crawford Seeger.

Let no union man be weakened
  By newspapers' false reports;
Be like sailors on the ocean,
  Trusting in their safe lifeboats.
Let your lifeboat be Jehovah
  Those who trust Him never fail.
Keep your hand upon the dollar
  And your eyes upon the scales.

You've been docked and docked, my
    boys,
  You've been loading two for one;
What have you to show for working
Since this mining has begun?

Overalls, and cans for rockers,
  In your shanties sleep on rails.
Keep your hand upon the dollar
  And your eyes upon the scales.

In conclusion, bear in memory,
  Keep the password in your mind;
God provides for every nation,
  When in union they combine.
Stand like men and linked together,
  Victory for you will prevail,
Keep your hand upon the dollar
  And your eyes upon the scales.

Cotton-Mill Colic

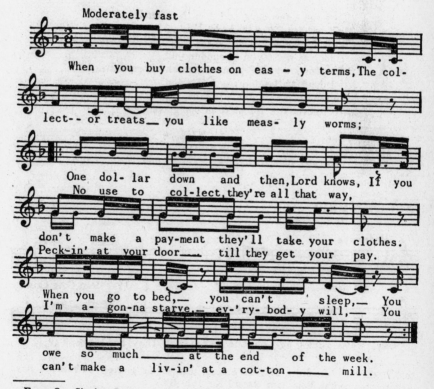

Moderately fast

When you buy clothes on eas-y terms, The col-
lect-- or treats— you like meas-ly worms;
One dol-lar down and then, Lord knows, If you
No use to col-lect, they're all that way,
don't make a pay-ment they'll take your clothes.
Peck-in' at your door— till they get your pay.
When you go to bed,— you can't sleep,— You
I'm a-gon-na starve,— ev-'ry-bod-y will,— You
owe so much— at the end of the week.
can't make a liv-in' at a cot-ton— mill.

From *Our Singing Country*, A Second Volume of American Ballads and Folk Songs, collected and compiled by John A. Lomax and Alan Lomax; Ruth Crawford Seeger, Music Editor, pp. 291–292. Copyright, 1941, by John A. Lomax. New York: The Macmillan Company.

Sung with guitar by Joe Sharp, of Skyline Farms, Scottsboro, Alabama, in Washing-

When you go to work, you work like the devil,
At the end of the week you're not on the level.
Pay day comes, you pay your rent,
When you get through, you've not got a cent
To buy fat-back n.eat, pinto beans;
Now and then you get a turnip green.
No use to collect, they're all that way,
You can't get the money to move away.

Twelve dollars a week is all I get—
How in the heck can I live on that?
I got a wife and fourteen kids,
We all have to sleep on two bedsteads.
Patches on my breeches, holes in my hat,
Ain't had a shave since my wife got fat.
No use to collect, ever' day at noon—
Kids get to cryin' in a different tune.

They run a few days, and then they stand,
Just to keep down the workin' man.
We'll never make it, we never will,
As long as we stay in a roundin' mill.
The poor are gettin' poorer, the rich are gettin' ric'
If I don't starve, I'm a son of a gun.
No use to collect, no use to rave,
We'll never rest till we're in our grave.

Chorus 2:
    If I don't starve, nobody will,
    You can't make a livin' at a cotton mill.

T.V.A. Song

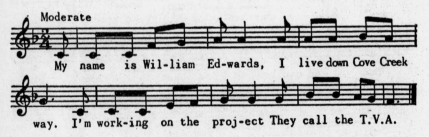

Moderate

My name is Wil-liam Ed-wards, I live down Cove Creek way. I'm work-ing on the proj-ect They call the T.V.A.

ton, D. C., 1939. Recorded by Alan Lomax, through the courtesy of Nicholas Ray. Archive of American Folk Song Record No. 1629–B2.

The story of what happens to the cotton farmer when he becomes a cotton-mill worker, with the "collection man" as the villain of the piece. See also "Cotton Mill Blues," Decca Record No. 5559.—J. A. L. and A. L.

From *Ballad Makin' in the Mountains of Kentucky*, by Jean Thomas, The Traipsin'

The Government begun it
  When I was but a child;
But now they are in earnest,
  And Tennessee's gone wild.

Just see them boys a-comin'
  Their tool kits on their arm;
They come from Clinch and Holston
  And many a valley farm.

From villages and cities,
  A French Broad man I see;
For things are up and doing
  In sunny Tennessee.

All up and down the valley
  They heard the glad alarm,
"The Government means business!"
  It's working like a charm.

Oh, see them boys a-comin',
  Their Government they trust;
Just hear their hammers ringing,
  They'll build that dam or bust.

I meant to marry Sally
  But work I could not find;
The T.V.A. was started
  And surely eased my mind.

I'm writing her a letter,
  These words I'll surely say;
"The Government has surely saved us,
  Just name our wedding day."

We'll build a little cabin
  On Cove Creek near her home;
We'll settle down forever
  And never care to roam.

Oh, things looked blue and lonely
  Until this come along;
Now hear the crew a-singin'
  And listen to their song.

"The Government employs us,
  Short hours and certain pay;
Oh things are up and comin',
  God Bless the T.V.A.

Woman, with music arranged by Walter Kolb, pp. 232–235. Copyright, 1939, by Henry Holt and Company, Inc. New York.

Many times I have heard this ballad sung in various sections of the Kentucky mountains, though it was composed and set to tune by a Preston of the Big Sandy country. Mountain singers are apt in substituting the names of their own vicinity for those of the villages and creeks and coves of their sister State—Tennessee.

With our permission it was used by the Federal Music Project in its presentation of *Power,* a musical portrayal of the power of electricity. The T.V.A. ballad, however, was first sung at the American Folk Song Festival with a kinsman of the composer giving the explanation of its origin.—J. T.

Mountain Songs and Ballads

Darling Cory

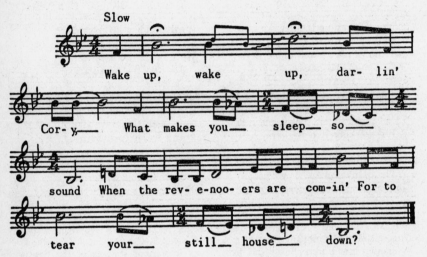

Slow

Wake up, wake up, dar- lin'

Cor- y,— What makes you— sleep— so—

sound When the rev- e-noo- ers are com-in' For to

tear your— still— house— down?

Go away, go away, darlin' Cory,
   Stop hangin' around my bed.
Bad liquor destroyed my body,
   Pretty women's gone to my head.

Don't you hear those bluebirds a-singin'?
Don't you hear their mournful sound?

They are preachin' Cory's funeral
   In some lonesome graveyard ground.

The last time I saw darlin' Cory
   She was sittin' on the bank of the sea,
With a jug of liquor in her arm
   And a .45 across her knee.

From *Folk Music of the United States*, Album 14, "Anglo-American Songs and Ballads," edited by Duncan B. M. Emrich, Record No. AAFS 69–B2. Washington, D. C.: Archive of American Folk Song, Library of Congress. 1948.

Sung with guitar by Pleaz Mobley of Manchester, Kentucky, at Renfro Valley, Kentucky, 1946. Recorded by Artus M. Moser.

Considerable study remains to be done on the white "blues" of the hills, of which "Darling Cory" is an excellent example. Mobley, prefacing the song, gives a good account of the setting for the song, the natural conditions under which it is sung, and a general guess at its origin.

"All right, Prof, here we go. Now this song is as mountain as hog and hominy or po'k and possum. Might have been inspired by a boy ridin' down the creek on a mule after he'd been up to the still house on Hell for Sartin or Goose Creek or Red Bird or Wild Cat—they're all names of creeks over in eastern Kentucky. The title is Darlin' Cory. Not Cora, its Cory."—D. B. M. E.

Zeb Turney's [Turner's] Girl

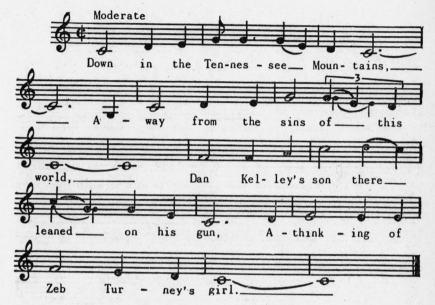

Down in the Ten-nes - see— Moun-tains,— A - way from the sins of— this world,— Dan Kel- ley's son there— leaned— on his gun, A - think - ing of Zeb Tur - ney's girl.—

Dan was a hot-headed youngster,
    His pap raised him steady and right,
And he had him sworn, from the day
        he was born,
    To shoot every Turney on sight.

"Powder and shot for the Turneys,
    Don't save a hair on their heads,"
Dan Kelley cried as he lay down and
        died,
    With young Danny there by his bed.

Dan took the oath with his pappy,
    And swore he would kill every one,
With his heart in a whirl with his love
        for the girl,
    He loaded his double-barreled gun.

Moon shining down on the mountain,
    Moon shining down on the hill,
Young Dan took the tip, swung the gun
        to his hip,

And started out to slaughter and
    kill.

Over the mountains he wandered,
    This son of a Tennessee man,
With fire in his eye and his gun at his
        thigh,
    A-looking for Zeb Turney's clan.

Shots ring out on the mountain,
    Shots ring out in the breeze,
Dan Kelley's son there with smoke on
        his gun,
    The Turney's all down on their
        knees.

The story of the Kelleys and Turneys
    Rang far and wide o'er the world,
How Dan killed a clan, shot 'em down
        to a man,
    And brought back old Zeb Turney's
        girl.

Sung by Artus M. Moser, Wilson's Cove, North Carolina, January 22, 1949.
Recorded by B. A. Botkin.

Good Old Mountain Dew

My Uncle Nort is sawed off and short,
He measures about four foot two;
But he thinks he's a gi'nt when you give him a pint
Of that good old mountain dew.

Ibid.

A native Western North Carolina song. This song was originally composed by
Bascom Lamar Lunsford, of Leicester, North Carolina. It has been taken over by the
folk singers and it has spread all over the United States. About twenty years ago Lunsford had some records made of this song, and the song was quite different from what it
is now. Many stanzas have been added, and even the tune has been changed. The
words were from the singing of Grandpaw Jones on a King Record.

Well, my old Aunt June bought some brand new perfume
   Which had a most wonderful fume [phew];
But to her surprise, when she got it in her eyes,
   It was nothing but that good old mountain dew.

Well, the preacher rode by with his head histed high,
   Said his wife had been down with the flu,
And he thought that I ort just to sell him a quart
   Of that good old mountain dew.

My brother Bill has a still on the hill,
   Where he runs me off a gallon or two,
And the buzzards in the sky get so drunk they can't fly,
   From smelling that good old mountain dew.

The Knoxville Girl

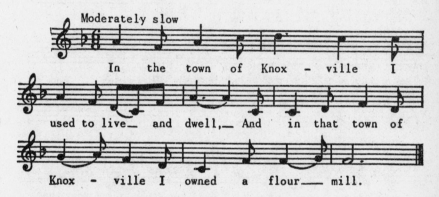

Moderately slow

In the town of Knox - ville I used to live__ and dwell,__ And in that town of Knox - ville I owned a flour__ mill.

I fell in love with a Knoxville girl, with dark and rolling eyes,
I promised her I'd marry her if me she'd ne'er deny.

I called her at her sister's house, about nine o'clock at night,
And little did that fair girl think I owned her in a fright.

I said to her, "Let's take a walk and view the meadows gay,
That we might have a little talk and plan our wedding day."

We walked along, we talked along, till we came to level ground.
There I picked up an edgewood stick and I knocked that fair girl down.

Ibid.

   A Southern version of the British broadside ballad, "Berkshire Tragedy," or "The
Wittam Miller," *circa* 1700, the scene of which was laid at Wittam, near Oxford, or
near Wexford. Cf. John Harrington Cox, *Folk-Songs of the South* (1925), pp. 311–
313.

She fell upon her bended knee. "Oh Lord, have mercy!" she cried.
"Oh, Willie, dear, don't murder me here. I'm not prepared to die."

Not minding one word she said, I beat her more and more.
I beat her till the ground around stood in a bloody gore.

I took her by her long yellow hair, I dragged her round and round.
I dragged her to still waters deep that flows through Knoxville town.

I called at my mother's house about twelve o'clock that night,
And Mother, being worried, got up all in a fright,

Saying, "Son, oh son, what have you done to bloody your hands and clothes?"
I answered to my mother's request, "Been bleeding at the nose."

I called for a candle to light myself to bed,
And also for a handkerchief to bind my aching head.

I rolled and tumbled the livelong night. Nothing could I see,
Nothing but the flames of hell a-sweeping over me.

About six weeks or later that Knoxville girl was found,
A-floating down still waters that flows through Knoxville town.

Her sister swore my life away, she swore without a doubt
That I must be the very lad that took her sister out.

And now they're going to hang me, a death I hate to die,
They're going to hang me up so high between the earth and sky.

Old Blue

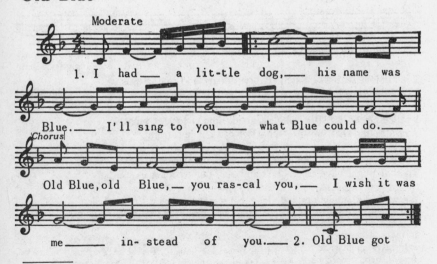

Sung with guitar by Ruby Lovingood Lunsford, South Turkey Creek, North Carolina, January 19, 1949. Recorded by B. A. Botkin.

Old Blue got sick, so very sick.
I sent for the doctor mighty quick.

Old Blue he died, he died so hard.
He dug dirt holes all in the yard.

The doctor came, he came on a run.
He says: "Old Blue, what have you
done?"

Dogget's Gap

Chest-nut— tree full of chest- nut sap,
Snow knee— deep in— Dog - get's Gap.

Sheepskin collar and a coonskin cap,
I don't mind the weather in Dogget's
Gap.

I got a girl in Dogget's Gap,
She don't mind a-sittin' in her sweetheart's lap.

The old man's a-cussin' but I don't
give a rap,
The women wear the britches in
Dogget's Gap.

It's walnut bark and walnut sap
Colors all the stockings in Dogget's
Gap.

Oh, they went to my buggy and they
raised up the flap,
And they stole all my liquor in Dogget's
Gap.

Run home, boys, and tell your pap,
I'm agonna start trouble in Dogget's
Gap.

I shot about twice and I raised a little
yell,
And the boys all ran like a bat out o'
hell.

Sung by Artus M. Moser, Wilson's Cove, North Carolina, January 22, 1949. Recorded by B. A. Botkin.
  Now this old ballad of Cumberland Gap was taken over by the people in various
parts of the mountains and was readapted to local conditions, you might say. For
instance, Dogget's Gap in Western North Carolina has a very similar song which is
evidently indebted to "Cumberland Gap." This follows the melody of the first two
lines. There is no chorus.—A. M. M.
  Cf. "Dogget Gap," Bascom Lamar Lunsford and Lamar Stringfield, *30 and 1 Folk-
songs from the Southern Mountains* (New York, 1929), p. 52.

On Top of Old Smoky

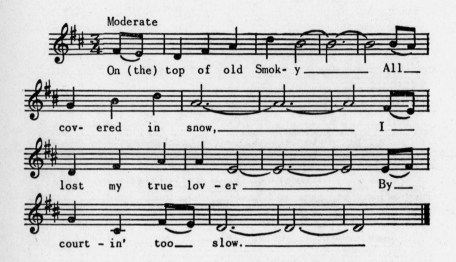

Moderate

On (the) top of old Smok- y _____ All ___
cov- ered in snow, _____ I ___
lost my true lov - er _____ By ___
court - in' too ___ slow. _____

Come all you young ladies,
    Take warning by me.
Don't place your affection
    In a green willow tree.

For the leaves they will wither
    And the roots they will die,
And you'll be forgotten
    And never know why.

Additional stanzas:[1]
A-courtin's a pleasure,
    A-partin's a grief,
For a false-hearted lover
    Is worse than a thief.

A thief he will rob you
    Of all that you save,
But a false-hearted lover
    Will send you to your grave.

On top of Mount Smoky
    I went there to weep,
For a false-hearted lover
    Is worse than a thief.

He'll hug you and kiss you
    And tell you more lies
Than cross-ties in a railroad
    Or stars in the sky.

On (the) top of old Smoky, etc.

From *The Martins and the Coys,* A Mountain Ballad Opera, written by Elizabeth Lomax, arranged by Alan Lomax, produced by the British Broadcasting Corporation, New York, April 4, 1944. Sung by Lily Mae Pearson.
[1] As sung by Esmereldy, Musicraft Record No. 289–B.

Cumberland Mountain Bear Chase

A- way, a- way, we're bound for the mount- ain,

Bound for the moun- tain, bound for the moun- tain,

O - ver the moun- tain the hounds are sound-in', A-

way for the chase a- way, a-way.

1.Now we're set just
2.Ro- ver, Ro- ver,

right for the race, The old hound dogs are
see 'im, see 'im, Ro- ver, Ro- ver,

read-y for the chase, The bear is a-bound-in', the
catch 'im, catch 'im.

hounds are a-sound - in' Right on the trail that

leads to the moun - tain.

O- ver the moun-tain, the
O- ver the moun-tain, the

hills and the foun- tains, A-
hills and the foun- tains, A-

way for the chase, a - way, a - way.
way to the woods, a - way, a - way.

Ibid. Sung by Burl Ives.

NEGRO WORK SONGS AND BALLADS

Poor Little Johnny

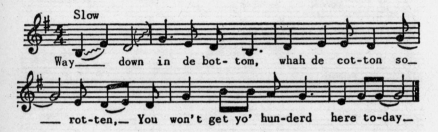

Way___ down in de bot-tom, whah de cot-ton so___
___ rot-ten,___ You won't get yo' hun-derd here to-day___

Po' little Johnny,
He's a po' little feller,
He won't get his hunderd here today.

From *Folk Music of the United States*, Album 4, "Afro-American Blues and Game Songs," edited by Alan Lomax, Record AAFS 20–B1. Washington, D. C.: Archive of American Folk Song, Library of Congress. 1942.

Sung by Harriet McClintock, Livingston, Alabama, 1940. Recorded by John A. and Ruby T. Lomax and Ruby P. Tartt.

Aunt Harriet McClintock (McClention?) is now well over eighty years old. She was born a slave on an Alabama plantation. . . . Aunt Harriet said that "Poor Little Johnny" was sung as a cotton picking song.

Little Johnny is picking in the wet river bottom field where the cotton has been rotted by exposure to damp. Therefore he won't be able to pick a hundred pounds of cotton in a day. One hundred and fifty to one hundred and seventy pounds a day is considered good picking for a strong woman, two hundred up to five hundred for a man.

The following dialogue between John Lomax and Aunt Hattie is heard on the record.

Q: Aunt Hattie, how did you . . . where did you get this song? A: My mamma learnt it to me. Q: How long ago? A: Woo! I don't know. She been dead 'bout near thirty year. Q: Did you ever pick any cotton? A: Me? Yassuh! Q: How much did you pick a day? A: I pick about a hundred and fifty, an' a hundred and twenty-five. —A. L.

Come on, Boys, and Let's Go to Hunting

Moderately fast
Chorus

Come on, girls, ('n')let's go to hunt-in'. (boys)

Come on girls, ('n')let's go to hunt-- in'. (boys)

Dog in the woods, and he done treed sum-p'n.

Dog in the woods, and he done treed sum-p'n.

Yo' dog bark, he don't see___ noth-in'.

Yo' dog bark, he don't see___ noth-in'. When

my dog bark,___ he done treed sum-p'n.

Chorus 2:
Come on, boys, let's go to huntin'.
Dog in the woods, and he done treed sump'n.

From *Folk Music of the United States*, Album 8, "Negro Work Songs and Calls," edited by B. A. Botkin, Record No. AAFS 37–B2. Washington, D. C.: Archive of American Folk Song. Library of Congress. 1943.

Sung by Henry Truvillion, Burkeville, Texas, 1940. Recorded by John A. and Ruby T. Lomax.

. . . One must visualize the setting in the cotton fields, where children have been picking cotton and are thinking of a feast of fat possum baked with sweet potatoes. "Along toward sundown," says Henry Truvillion, "we'd all leave and go on home, and you can hear sometimes twenty-five boys and twenty-five girls all going home through the woods and across the fields, and they're all singing the same song back at one another."—B. A. B.

The woods is wet, the roads is muddy.
I'm so drunk till I can't stand steady.

Chorus 3:
    Come on, boys, let's go to huntin',
    Dog in the woods, and he done treed sump'n.
    Come on boys, let's go to huntin',
    Dog in the woods, and he done treed sump'n.

Possum up a gum stump, coon in the holler.
Rabbit give a backtrack, and stole a half a dollar.

(Chorus 3).

(Repeat last stanza and chorus 1.)
    Dog in the woods, and he done treed sump'n.

Quitting Time Song

Ibid., Record No. AAFS. Sung by Thomas J. Marshall, Edwards, Mississippi, 1939. Recorded by Herbert Halpert.
    According to Mr. Marshall, the "original name" of the cornfield holler is "arwhoolie"

Go Down, Old Hannah

Slow

Go down, old Hannah,

Won't you rise no more? Go down, old

Han-nah, Won't you rise no more?

Lawd, if you rise,
  Bring Judgment on.
Lawd, if you rise,
  Bring Judgment on.

Oh, did you hear
  What the captain said?
Oh, did you hear
  What the captain said?

That if you work
  He'll treat you well,
And if you don't
  He'll give you hell.

Oh, go down, old Hannah,
  Won't you rise no more?
Won't you go down, old Hannah,
  Won't you rise no more?

Oh, long-time man,
  Hold up your head.
Well, you may get a pardon
  And you may drop dead.

Lawdy, nobody feels sorry
  For the life-time man.
Nobody feels sorry
  For the life-time man.

---

or "hoolie." Mr. Brooks, who sang a similar quitting-time song, says: "They sing it late in the evening. About the time they quit, they generally feel good and they like to sing this kind of thing. . . . They usually sing it on a plantation. . . . If one man starts, well, across maybe another field close by, why, they sing that same tune back to him. . . . Then maybe another man may answer him another tune."

For a discussion of "call" and "response" in field calls, see Thomas W. Talley, *Negro Folk Rhymes* (1922), pp. 264 ff.—B. A. B.

Ibid., Record No. AAFS 38–B.

Sung by James (Iron Head) Baker, Will Crosby, R. D. Allen, and Moses (Clear Rock) Platt, Central State Farm, Sugarland, Texas, 1933. Recorded by John A. and Alan Lomax.

This is one of the best-known of the slow-drag work songs sung by Negro prisoners in South Texas. James (Iron Head) Baker says that he first sang it in 1908, on long hot summer days when, about three o'clock in the afternoon, the sun (Old Hannah) seemed to stop and "just hang" in the sky.

For another version, sung to a similar tune, see *Our Singing Country*, collected and compiled by John A. Lomax and Alan Lomax; Ruth Crawford Seeger, Music Editor (New York, 1941), pp. 356–358.—B. A. B.

Can't You Line It?

Moderately fast

When I get— in Il- li- nois,— I'm gon- na

spread the news— a-bout the Flo- ri-da boys.—

Chorus

Shove it o - ver!— Hey! hey!— Can't you line— it?— Ah,

Shack-a lack-a, lack-a, lack-a, lack-a, lack-a, Unh! Can't you

move— it?— Hey! hey!— Can't you try?

Me and my buddy goin across the field.
I heard that train when it left Mobile.

I heard a mighty noise around the river
bend.
Must be the Southern crossin' the L.
& N.

A nickel's worth o' bacon, a dime's
worth o' lard.
I would buy more but the times so
hard.

Jack the rabbit, jack the bear.
Two fat buzzards on the run from
there.

Cap'n got a burner I'd like to have,
A .32–20 with a shiny barrel.

There comes a woman walkin' across
the field,
Her mouth exhaustin' like an automobile.

From Archive of American Folk Song, Records No. 362–A and 363–A. Washington, D. C.: Library of Congress.

Sung by A. B. Hicks, Eatonville, Florida, 1935. Recorded by Alan Lomax, Zora Neale Hurston, and Mary Elizabeth Barnicle. Transcribed by Alan Lomax.

This song is common in the railroad camps. It is suited to the "lining" rhythm. That is, it fits the straining of the men at the lining bars as the rail is placed in position to be spiked down.

On the chorus: All men strain at rail in concert; then shake rail; then grunt as they move rail.—Zora Neale Hurston, *Mules and Men* (Philadelphia and London, 1935), pp. 322–323.

For a variant of the tune and additional stanzas, see *Mules and Men, loc. cit.*

Rock About, My Saro Jane

Biler's busted an' the whistle done blowed,
The head cap'n's done fell overboa'd.
O Saro Jane.

From *Listen to Our Story*, A Panorama of American Ballads, American Folk Music Series, edited by Alan Lomax, Brunswick Album, No. B-1024, Record No. 80091-B. Originally Vocalion No. 5152. Recorded April, 1927. *Sing-Along-Book*, copyright, 1947, by Brunswick Radio Corporation. New York.
Sung with his Fruit Jar Drinkers by Uncle Dave Macon.

Here is a story from the great period of river-boats on the Mississippi, the Ohio and the Tennessee. There have been collections of the songs of the Negro roustabouts who

Engine give a crack and the whistle give a squall,
The engineer gone to the Hole-in-the-Wall,
   O Saro Jane.

Yankee build boats for to shoot dem Rebels,
My musket's loaded and I'm gonna hold her level.
   O Saro Jane.

The Death of John Henry

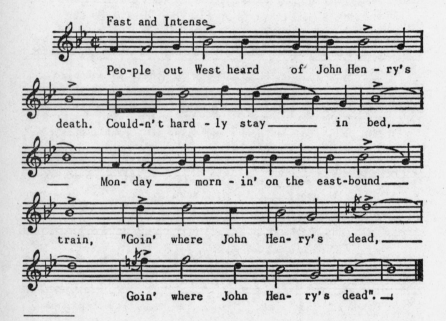

Fast and Intense

Peo-ple out West heard of John Hen-ry's death. Could-n't hard-ly stay in bed, Mon-day mornin' on the east-bound train, "Goin' where John Hen-ry's dead, Goin' where John Hen-ry's dead".

toted the freight and fed the boilers of these queens of the western rivers, but in "Rock About" I believe we have the best preserved specimen of a river-boat song yet discovered.

The whole picture is here: the reason the hand decides to ship out on the "Big MacMillan"; the chorus pointing out with great irony that "You don' have nothin' to do, man, but jes set around and sing all day"; the description of the frequent accidents of the river when the engineers required more pressure from their boilers than they could take; and the final stanza which stamps the song as Civil War in vintage, perhaps as even a recruiting song for the Federal gun-boats that wrested control of the Southern rivers from the Confederacy.

It is curious and interesting that this old Negro song has been preserved by Uncle Dave Macon, banjo, king of "The Grand Old Opry," backwoods minstrel for the so-called "poor whites" throughout the South.—A. L.

Ibid., Record No. 80091–A. Originally Vocalion No. 5096.
Sung with 5-string banjo by Dave Macon.
What happened? What are the facts? About 1870, probably, on the Big Bend

(Spoken:)

Listen,
In every heart their burns a flame
For the love of glory or the dread of
shame;
But, oh, how happy we would be if we
understood
There's no safety but in doing good.

Carried John Henry to the graveyard,
They looked at him good and long;
Very last words his wife said to him:
"My husband he is dead an' gone,
My husband he is dead an' gone."

John Henry's wife wore a brand new
dress;
It was all trimmed in blue.
Very last words she said to him:

"Honey, I've been good to you,
Honey, I've been good to you."

John Henry told the shaker,
"Lord-a, shake while I sing.
Pullin' the hammer from my shoulder;
I'm bound to hear her when she ring,
Bound to hear her when she ring."

John Henry told his captain,
"I am a Tennessee man;
Before I would see that steam drill
beat me down,
Die with the hammer in my han',
Die with the hammer in my han'."

John Henry hammered in the mountain
Till the hammer caught on fire.
Very last words I heard him say:
"Cool drink of water 'fore I die,
Cool drink of water 'fore I die."

Swannanoa Tunnel

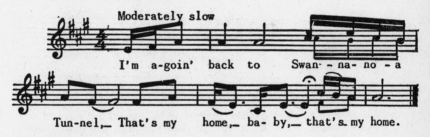

Tunnel on the C. & O. road in West Virginia, a steel driver named John Henry was
matched against the first machine—hand-labor against machine-work.

John Henry was a steel-driving man. Steel drivers had to be made of steel. Swinging their ten pound mauls across their shoulders, whipping them down on the drills,
driving those drills into the face of the living rock, these men were the steely-muscled
heroes of the early days of tunnel building in the mountains. John Henry was the
king of the steel drivers, so the story goes. Nobody knows for sure whether he was
white or Negro, whether he was dark or light, big or small. I have met all kinds of
men who said they knew him or had a third cousin by marriage who knew him. For
John Henry has become a legend for brave men. Everybody from West Virginia to
Texas agrees on this much, however—John Henry proved that a man with a brave
heart was better than a machine.—A. L.

Sung with guitar by Bascom Lamar Lunsford, South Turkey Creek, North Carolina,
January 19, 1949. Recorded by B. A. Botkin.

For a slightly different version see Bascom Lamar Lunsford and Lamar Stringfield,
30 and 1 Folksongs from the Southern Mountains (New York, 1929), pp. 34–35.

Asheville Junction, Swannanoa Tunnel,
All caved in, baby, all caved in.

Last December, I remember
The wind blow cold, baby, the wind blow cold.

When you hear my watch-dog a-howlin',
Somebody dyin', baby, somebody dyin'.

When you hear the hoot-owl squallin',
Somebody dyin', baby, somebody dyin'.

This old hammer killed John Henry.
Didn't kill me, baby, didn't kill me.

This old hammer rings like silver,
It shines like gold, baby, it shines like gold.

Take this hammer, throw it in the river,
It shines right on, baby, it rings right on.

Reilley Gardner, he killed my partner.
Couldn't kill me, baby, couldn't kill me.

Some of these days I'll see 'at woman,
That's no dream, baby, that's no dream.

An old labor song, sung by the section hands while building the Swannanoa Tunnel, 1880–1884. Starting to sing on the fourth beat of each measure, the worker began to raise his pick and continued until just after the second beat of the next measure. On the third beat is a heavy grunt when he strikes.—B. L. L., *ibid.*, p. iii.

Boll Weevil

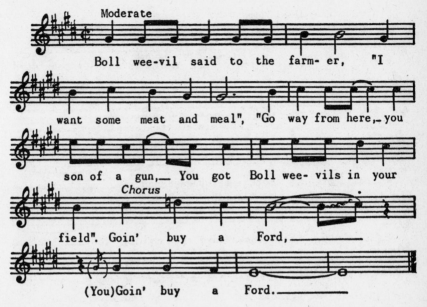

Moderate

Boll wee-vil said to the farm-er, "I want some meat and meal", "Go way from here,_ you son of a gun,_ You got Boll wee-vils in your field". Goin' buy a Ford,_____

Chorus

(You)Goin' buy a Ford._____

Farmer said to the merchant,
  "I'm goin' right on your gate.
When I get through with your cotton,
  You'll sell that Cadillac Eight."

The boll weevil said to the farmer,
  "I wish all you well.
All you farmin' mens ought've been
  Killed and dead in hell."

The farmer said to the boll weevil,
  "I wish you well.
When I get through burnin' you,
  I'm goin' burn every one in hell."

The boll weevil said to the farmer,
  "I want some meat and meal."
"Go way from here, you son of a gun,
  You got boll weevil in your field."

Farmer said to the boll weevil,
  "I'm goin' bury you in the sand."
The boll weevil said to the farmer,
  "I'm goin' stand it like a man."

Farmer said to the boll weevil,
  "I'm goin' put you on some ice."
Boll weevil said to the farmer,
  "It'll sure be cool and nice."

Sung by Lee Myer, Columbia, South Carolina, January 28, 1949. Recorded by B. A. Botkin and Chapman J. Milling.

Dupree

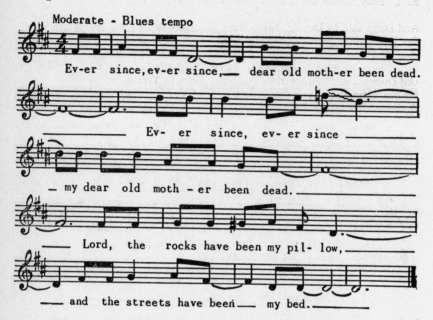

Ev-er since, ev-er since,— dear old moth-er been dead.

————— Ev- er since, ev- er since —————

—— my dear old moth - er been dead. ———

—— Lord, the rocks have been my pil- low,

—— and the streets have been — my bed. ———

"Babe, I'm goin away, Mamma, just to wear you off my mind.
Babe, I'm goin away from here. Please don't make me stay.
He said, "The more you try, Mamma, the further you drive me away."

Betty told Dupree, said, "I want a diamond ring."
Betty told Dupree, said, "I want you to buy me a diamond ring.
Said, "Your darlin' little old baby ain't wanted too much from you."

And Dupree said to Betty, "A woman like you, I'll buy you 'most anything.
A little woman like you, baby, I'll buy you 'most anything."
And old Dupree went on down, down to the jewelry store. (*Oh, my Lord.*)

And he said to the jewelry man, "I want to look at some of your diamond rings."
He said to the jewelry man, "Let me see some of your diamond rings."
The man had a four-thousand-dollar diamond ring on the counter, and old
    Dupree picked it up and started away.

The plain-clothes detective tried to turn old Dupree around.
The plain-clothes detective tried to turn old Dupree around.
And old Dupree turned around, and he blowed that detective down. (*Oh, my
    Lord.*)

———

Sung with guitar by James White, Asheville, North Carolina, January 20, 1949.
Recorded by B. A. Botkin and E. Y. Harburg.

Old Dupree went home to his Betty, said, "Betty, here's that diamond ring."
Dupree went on back home to his Betty, said, "Baby, here's that diamond ring."
Said, "Baby, I done killed me a man. I gotta make my getaway."

And Betty said to Dupree, "Just don't get in trouble on account of me."
Betty said to Dupree, "Don't get in trouble on account of me."
And old Dupree hired him a taxi to run him down in Tennessee.

Old Dupree hired him a taxi to carry him down to Tennessee.
He hired him a taxi to run him down in Tennessee.
And that's the last that I heard, heard from old Dupree.

RELIGIOUS SONGS

Holy Babe

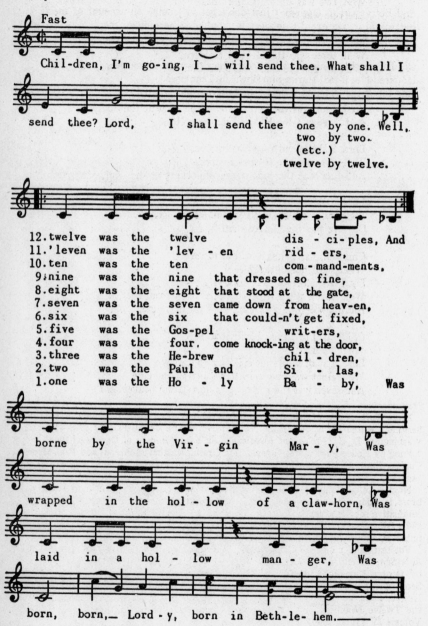

Chil-dren, I'm go-ing, I__ will send thee. What shall I send thee? Lord, I shall send thee one by one. Well, two by two. (etc.) twelve by twelve.

12. twelve was the twelve   dis - ci - ples, And
11. 'leven was the 'lev - en   rid - ers,
10. ten was the ten   com - mand-ments,
9. nine was the nine that dressed so fine,
8. eight was the eight that stood at the gate,
7. seven was the seven came down from heav-en,
6. six was the six that could-n't get fixed,
5. five was the Gos-pel   writ-ers,
4. four was the four come knock-ing at the door,
3. three was the He-brew   chil - dren,
2. two was the Paul and Si - las,
1. one was the Ho - ly Ba - by, Was

borne by the Vir - gin Mar - y, Was

wrapped in the hol - low of a claw-horn, Was

laid in a hol - low man - ger, Was

born, born,__ Lord - y, born in Beth-le- hem.__

Children, I'm going, I will send [sing] thee.
What shall I send thee?
Lord, I shall send thee two by two.
Well, two was the Paul and Silas,
And one was the Holy Baby, etc.

Lord, I shall send thee three by three.
Well, three was the Hebrew children,
And two was the Paul and Silas, etc.

Lord, I shall send thee four by four.
Well, four was the four come a-knocking at the door,
And three was the Hebrew children, etc.

Lord, I shall send thee five by five.
Well, five was the Gospel writers,
And four was the four come a-knocking at the door, etc.

Lord, I shall send thee six by six.
Well, six was the six that couldn't get fixed.
Oh, five was the Gospel writers, etc.

Children, I'm going, I will send thee.
What shall I send thee?
Lord, I shall send thee seven by seven.
Well, seven was the seven came down from heaven,
And six was the six that couldn't get fixed, etc.

Children, I'm going, I will send thee.
What shall I send thee?
Lord, I shall send thee eight by eight.
Well, eight was the eight that stood at the gate,
And seven was the seven came down from heaven, etc.

From *Folk Music of the United States,* Album 10, "Negro Religious Songs and Services," edited by B. A. Botkin, Record No. AAFS 49-A—Part I, 49-B—Part II. Washington, D. C.: Archive of American Folk Song, Library of Congress. 1943.

Sung by Kelley Pace, Aaron Brown, Joe Green, Matthew Johnson, and Paul Hayes, Cumins State Farm, Gould, Arkansas, 1942. Recorded by John A. and Ruby T. Lomax.

Number songs, counting either forward or backward, are common in most languages. Most familiar are the counting and counting-out rhymes of children. The present cumulative song is a version of "The Carol of the Twelve Numbers" (often known as "The Dilly Song"). There is a good deal of variation in the symbolism of the twelve numbers, and in the present song their significance has often been lost.

For texts and notes, see "The Twelve Apostles," by Phillips Barry, *Bulletin of the Folk-Song Society of the Northeast,* Number 9 (1935), pp. 3–4; "Ballads and Songs," by George Lyman Kittredge, *Journal of American Folklore,* Volume XXX (July–September, 1917), pp. 335–337; "The Carol of the Twelve Numbers," by William Wells Newell, *ibid.,* Volume IV (July–September, 1891), pp. 215–220; and "The Carol of the Twelve Numbers," by Leah Rachel Clara Yoffie, *Southern Folklore Quarterly,* Volume IV (June, 1940), pp. 73–75.—B. A. B.

Children, I'm going, I will send thee.
What shall I send thee?
Lord, I shall send thee nine by nine.
Well, nine was the nine that dressed so fine.
Oh, eight was the eight that stood at the gate, etc.

Children, I'm going, I will send thee.
What shall I send thee?
Lord, I shall send thee ten by ten.
Well, ten was the Ten Commandments,
And nine was the nine that dressed so fine, etc.

Children, I'm going, I will send thee.
What shall I send thee?
Lord, I shall send thee eleven by eleven.
Well, 'leven was the 'leven riders,
And ten was the Ten Commandments, etc.

Children, I'm going, I will send thee.
What shall I send thee?
Lord, I shall send thee twelve by twelve.
Well, twelve was the twelve disciples,
And eleven was the eleven riders,
And ten was the Ten Commandments,
And nine was the nine that dressed so fine,
And eight was the eight that stood at the gate,
And seven was the seven came down from heaven,
And six was the six that couldn't get fixed,
And five was the Gospel writers,
Well, four was the four come knocking at the door,
And three was the Hebrew children,
And two was the Paul and Silas,
And one was the Holy Baby,
Was borne by the Virgin Mary,
Was wrapped in the hollow of a clawhorn,
Was laid in a hollow manger,
Was born, born, Lordy, born in Bethlehem.

THE BABE OF BETHLEHEM. 8, 7

Wm. Walker

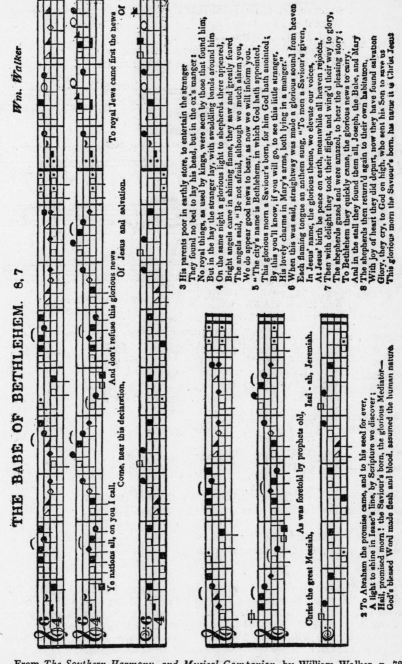

Ye nations all, on you I call,
Come, near this declaration,
And don't refuse this glorious news
Of Jesus and salvation.
To royal Jews came first the news,
Of

2 To Abraham the promise came, and to his seed for ever,
A light to shine in Isaac's line, by Scripture we discover;
Hail, promised morn! the Saviour's born, the glorious Mediator—
God's blessed Word made flesh and blood, assumed the human nature.

As was foretold by prophets old, Isai - ah, Jeremiah,
Christ the great Messiah.

3 His parents poor in earthly store, to entertain the stranger
They found no bed to lay his head, but in the ox's manger?
No royal things, as used by kings, were seen by those that found him,
But in the hay the stranger lay, with swaddling bands around him.

4 On the same night a glorious light to shepherds there appeared,
Bright angels came in shining flame, they saw and greatly feared
The angels said, "Be not afraid, although we much alarm you,
We do appear good news to bear, as now we will inform you.

5 "The city's name is Bethlehem, in which God hath appointed,
This glorious morn a Saviour's born, for him God hath anointed;
By this you'll know, if you will go, to see this little stranger,
His lovely charms in Mary's arms, both lying in a manger."

6 When this was said, straightway was made a glorious sound from heaven
Each flaming tongue an anthem sung, "To men a Saviour's given,
In Jesus' name, the glorious theme, we elevate our voices,
At Jesus' birth be peace on earth, meanwhile all heaven rejoices.'

7 Then with delight they took their flight, and wing'd their way to glory,
The shepherds gazed and were amazed, to hear the pleasing story;
To Bethlehem they quickly came, the glorious news to carry,
And in the stall they found them all, Joseph, the Babe, and Mary

8 The shepherds then return'd again to their own habitation,
With joy of heart they did depart, now they have found salvation
Glory, they cry, to God on high, who sent his Son to save us
This glorious morn the Saviour's born, his name it is Christ Jesus

From *The Southern Harmony, and Musical Companion*, by William Walker, p. 78.
Philadelphia: E. W. Miller and J. B. Lippincott & Co. 1847.

The Cherry Tree Carol

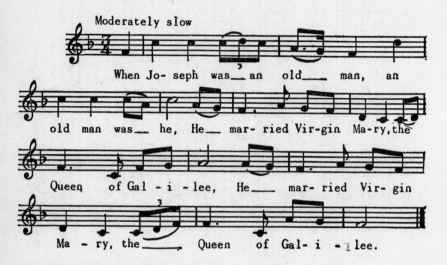

As Joseph and Mary were walking one day,
Here are apples, here are cherries enough to behold.* *(twice)*

Then Mary spoke to Joseph so meek and so mild,
"Joseph gather me some cherries, for I am with child." *(twice)*

Then Joseph flew in anger, in anger flew he,
"Let the father of the baby gather cherries for thee." *(twice)*

Then Jesus spoke a few words, a few words spoke He,
"Let my mother have some cherries, bow low down Cherry Tree." *(twice)*

The cherry tree bowed low down, bowed low down to the ground,
And Mary gathered cherries while Joseph stood around. *(twice)*

Then Joseph took Mary all on his right knee:
"What have I done? Lord, have mercy on me!" *(twice)*

From *Folk-Songs of the Kentucky Mountains,* Twenty Traditional Ballads and
Other English Folk-Songs, Notated from the Singing of the Kentucky Mountain
People and arranged with Piano Accompaniment, by Josephine McGill, introductory
note by H. E. Krehbiel, pp. 59–64. Copyright, 1917, by Boosey & Co. New York.
   * The Cambridge Edition of Child's *English and Scottish Popular Ballads* gives
two versions of this carol. In version A the above stanza appears thus:
   Joseph and Mary walked through an orchard green
   Where was berries and cherries as thick as might be seen.—J. M.

Then Joseph took Mary all on his left knee:
"O tell me little baby when Thy birthday will be?" *(twice)*

"On the sixth day of January my birthday will be,
When the stars in the elements shall tremble with glee." *(twice)*

He Never Said a Mumbalin' Word

Well, they pierced them in the side,
   He never said a mumbalin' word
They pierced him in the side,
   He never said a mumbalin' word.
God knows, they pierced him in the side,
   He never said a mumbalin' word,
   Not a word, not a word.

Sung by Leo Leggette, South Carolina State Hospital, Columbia, South Carolina, January 20, 1949. Recorded by B. A. Botkin and Chapman J. Milling.

He hung his head and died, etc. *(twice)*
You know, he hung his head and died, etc.

You see how they done my Lord, etc. *(twice)* [1]
You know, you see how they done my Lord, etc.

The Blood Done Signed My Name

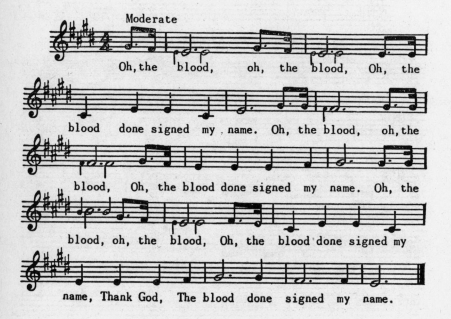

Oh, the blood, oh, the blood, Oh, the blood done signed my name. Oh, the blood, oh, the blood, Oh, the blood done signed my name. Oh, the blood, oh, the blood, Oh, the blood done signed my name, Thank God, The blood done signed my name.

I know it, I know it,
    Oh, the blood done signed my name.
I know it, I know it,
    Oh, the blood done signed my name.
I know it, I know it,
    Oh, the blood done signed my name,
Thank God,
    The blood done signed my name.

[1] These lines are hummed.

Sung by a chorus of men and women patients of the South Carolina State Hospital, Columbia, South Carolina, January 26, 1949. Recorded by B. A. Botkin and Chapman J. Milling.

Jesus told me, etc.

God's a witness, etc.

Going to heaven, etc.

Motherless Children Sees a Hard Time

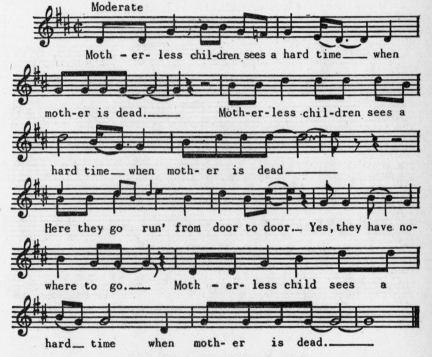

Some people say your father will do when mother is dead.
Some people say father will do when mother is dead.
  Some people say father will do.
  Soon as he get married, turn his back on you.
Nobody treat you like mother will when mother is dead.

Some people say your older sister gonna do when mother is dead.
Some people say your older sister will do when mother is dead.
  Some people say your sister will do.
  Soon as she get married, she turn her back on you.
Nobody treat you like mother will when mother is dead.

Sung by Lee Myer, Columbia, South Carolina, January 28, 1949. Recorded by B. A. Botkin and Chapman J. Milling.

I said, motherless children sees a hard time when mother is dead. *(Lord, Lord.)*
Motherless children sees a hard time when mother is dead.
  Father will do the best he can,
  But, you know, father can't understand.
Nobody treat you like your mother will when mother is dead.

I said, motherless child sees a hard time when mother is gone. *(Lord, Lord.)*
Motherless children sees a hard time when mother is gone.
  Here they go run' from door to door,
  But they have nowhere to go.
Motherless child sees a hard time when mother is dead.

Lonesome Valley

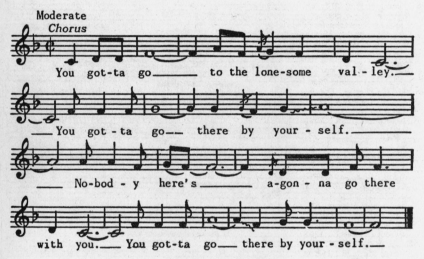

I'm gonna go down to that valley.
  I'm gonna go there by myself.
Nobody here's a-gonna go there with me.
  I'm gonna go there by myself.

Some folks say that John was a Baptist.
  Others say he was a Jew.
But the Holy Bible tells us
  That he was a preacher too.

(Chorus.)

Sung with violin by Ruby Lovingood Lunsford, accompanied on the banjo by
Millard Revis, South Turkey Creek, North Carolina, January 19, 1949. Recorded by
B. A. Botkin.

INDEX OF AUTHORS,* TITLES, AND
FIRST LINES OF SONGS

* Including names of singers and other informants and persons who recorded them.

763

INDEX OF AUTHORS, TITLES, AND FIRST LINES OF SONGS

INDEX OF SUBJECTS, NAMES, AND PLACES

INDEX OF SUBJECTS, NAMES, AND PLACES